Homelessness and Alloc

CW01475555

13th Edition

Homelessness and Allocations

Thirteenth Edition

Andrew Arden KC
Barrister

Justin Bates KC
Barrister, Landmark Chambers

Bloomsbury Professional

LONDON • DUBLIN • EDINBURGH • NEW YORK • NEW DELHI • SYDNEY

BLOOMSBURY PROFESSIONAL

Bloomsbury Publishing Plc

50 Bedford Square, London, WC1B 3DP, UK
1385 Broadway, New York, NY 10018, USA
29 Earlsfort Terrace, Dublin 2, Ireland

BLOOMSBURY and the Diana logo are trademarks of Bloomsbury Publishing Plc

British Library Cataloguing-in-Publication Data

A catalogue record for this book is available from the British Library.

ISBN:	PB:	978 1 52652 831 5
	Epdf	978 1 52652 833 9
	Epub	978 1 52652 832 2

Typeset by Evolution Design and Digital (Kent)
Printed and bound by CPI Group (UK) Ltd, Croydon, CR0 4YY

To find out more about our authors and books visit www.bloomsburyprofessional.com. Here
you will find extracts, author information, details of forthcoming events and the option to
sign up for our newsletters

Dedication

This edition of Homelessness and Allocations is dedicated with gratitude to Esther Pilger, the long-time publisher of several earlier editions, for all she did on behalf of the book and of us as its authors.

Preface

The chapter files for this book were delivered on 4 December 2023; we were able to add new developments during the first stage of the publishing process, until 23 February 2024, and briefly to note further changes during the final stage, until 31 March 2024; the law is therefore stated as at 31 March although the treatment of post-4 December material is somewhat less full than that which was available beforehand, and the treatment of post-23 February material is necessarily limited.

This is the first edition of *Homelessness and Allocations* not to have been published by the Legal Action Group, for whom I have been producing the book – initially under the title The Homeless Persons Act – since 1982. As some readers may wonder why the publisher has changed, I should stress that the move does not reflect any change in emphasis or approach on my and Justin's part: rather, LAG was changing its own approach to book publishing and it was that change which was the main reason for ours.

We have dedicated this edition to Esther Pilger, LAG's long-standing publisher who has also left LAG, to reflect our gratitude and respect for the work she did on all those editions, much of which continues to inform – and enhance – the present edition. That said, we regard ourselves as exceptionally fortunate to have – as it were – landed with such ease and speed at Bloomsbury Professional, to find a first-rate team to take the book over and with whom we look forward to working over future editions.

For the first time, the homelessness and allocations codes of guidance and other non-statutory materials are not reproduced in the book: these materials are easily accessible online and are so frequently altered that there is not merely a risk but a likelihood that whatever we would print would be swiftly out of date, carrying with it the risk to readers of error by way of using the wrong version.

Andrew Arden KC
31 March 2024

Contents

Table of Cases

K

L

Q

R

Table of Statutes

[All references are to paragraph numbers.]

Table of Statutory Instruments

[All references are to paragraph numbers.]

Table of European Legislation

Table of International Conventions

CHAPTER 1

The history and policy of the provisions

INTRODUCTION

1.1   This chapter outlines the history of the law on homelessness and allocations, from before the Housing (Homeless Persons) Act (H(HP)A) 1977 through Housing Act (HA) 1996, Parts 6 and 7 – the present, principal Acts in England – and Homelessness Act 2002 to changes in England under the Localism Act (LA) 2011 followed by major changes to assist the homeless in Wales under Housing (Wales) Act (H(W)A) 2014, Part 2 and the adoption of some of these in England by the Homeless Reduction Act (HRA) 2017. The history of the law reflects policy; as such, it is primarily a history of legislation rather than law as developed by the courts, although on occasion the two sources of law have if not clashed then at least interacted.

1.2   Although HA 1996, Parts 6 and 7 comprise free-standing legislation – in the sense that they are neither consolidation nor amendment – and it is unnecessary always to approach them by reference to their evolution, both Parts are nonetheless best understood historically not least because of the adoption by Part 7 of the well-litigated, critical definitions introduced by H(HP)A 1977 which had subsequently been consolidated into Housing Act (HA) 1985, Part 3.

1.3   Thus, the then Minister for Local Government, Housing and Urban Regeneration (Mr Curry) said of the changes to homelessness law to be made by the HA 1996:

> 'We shall not go back to pre-1977 days. We shall keep the 1977 Act concepts of entitlement, homelessness, priority need, intentionality and local connection. Essentially, what we are changing is the way in which the duty is to be discharged.'[1]

1.4   That discharge was closely interwoven with the allocation of local authority housing – Part 6 was the first major conceptual change in allocations law since the Housing Act 1935, when the concept of 'reasonable preference' for certain categories of housing need was introduced: in practice, however, allocations policy (and certainly its practice) had been dominated by the homeless since H(HP)A 1977.

1.5   Since HA 1996, the Homelessness Act 2002 again changed the shape of the law, introducing a new 'strategic' duty to formulate a response to homelessness and reshaping HA 1996, Part 6 to seek to include 'choice-based letting' within allocations law. Further changes have been made by regulations. Subsequently, LA 2011 reversed some of the effects of the Homelessness Act 2002 both by placing more emphasis on the use of private sector accommodation, and by introducing much greater freedom for authorities in England to determine their own criteria as to whom they will house in their own accommodation (although, as will be seen in Chapter 11, the case-law has rather limited this apparent freedom, see paras **9.49–9.53**).

---

1   *Hansard*, Standing Committee G, 12 March 1996, col 587.

1.6 Wales subsequently led the way for further change in H(W)A 2014, including: extension of the period during which a person is threatened with homelessness from 28 to 56 days; assessment of those who need help to retain or obtain accommodation and help to prevent them becoming homeless; and, a power for authorities in conjunction with Welsh ministers to jettison intentional homelessness (historically the most controversial of all of the homelessness provisions although perhaps supplanted as such in recent years by issues around the quality of accommodation). The first two of these reforms were then adopted in England through what appropriately started life as a Private Member's Bill,[2] the HRA 2017.

1.7 In this chapter, homelessness and allocations policy as embodied in law are approached as follows:

a) National Assistance Act (NAA) 1948, Part 3;

b) H(HP)A 1977; HA 1985, Part 3;

c) *Re Puhlhofer*;[3]

d) Housing and Planning Act (HPA) 1986;

e) Asylum and Immigration Appeals Act (AIAA) 1993;

f) *ex p Awua*;[4]

g) HA 1996, Parts 6 and 7;

h) between the 1996 and 2002 Acts;

i) Homelessness Act 2002;

j) changes following the Homelessness Act 2002;

k) LA 2011;

l) H(W)A 2014;

m) HRA 2017; and

n) Brexit.

NATIONAL ASSISTANCE ACT 1948

1.8 The provisions of NAA 1948, s 21(1) placed local authorities under a duty to provide:

---

2 H(HP)A 1977 was itself a Private Member's Bill.
3 *R v Hillingdon LBC ex p Puhlhofer* [1986] AC 484, (1986) 18 HLR 158, HL.
4 *R v Brent LBC ex p Awua* [1996] AC 55, (1995) 27 HLR 453, HL.

'. . . residential accommodation for persons who by reason of age, infirmity or any other circumstances are in need of care and attention which is not otherwise available to them, [and] temporary accommodation for persons who are in urgent need thereof, being need arising in circumstances which could not reasonably have been foreseen or in such other circumstances as the authority may in any particular case determine'.

1.9   Homelessness law – starting with H(HP)A 1977 – replaces only the second limb of that duty, ie, the duty to provide temporary accommodation in urgent need.[5] (The first limb was replaced in England by the Care Act 2014, and in Wales by the Social Services and Well-being (Wales) Act 2014.)

1.10   The NAA 1948 duty extended to people ordinarily resident in a local authority's area.[6] Where satisfied that such a person was in urgent need of accommodation, the National Assistance Board (NAB) (later the Supplementary Benefits Commission) had power to require an authority to provide it. The local authority was under a further duty to protect the property of a person to whom it provided assistance under these provisions.[7]

1.11   Local authority duties under NAA 1948 were exercised under the general guidance of the minister: for these purposes at the time, the Minister of Health.[8]

1.12   This legal structure fell far short of imposing a duty on local authorities to protect all homeless people, let alone to provide permanent accommodation. Rather, it provided for emergencies, especially unforeseeable emergencies.[9] The duration of accommodation was a matter for the authority. It probably meant no more than for so long as the authority considered appropriate or necessary;[10] urgent need for temporary accommodation was not to be equated with a vital but continuing need for permanent accommodation.[11]

1.13   The discretionary and temporary nature of this provision was the principal problem. Another problem was that of deciding 'ordinary residence' in an area. Reminiscent of the Poor Laws which the NAA 1948 had repealed and replaced, authorities 'shuttled' homeless people between areas, asserting that they were ordinarily resident in the area of another authority, which should therefore take responsibility for them.

5   H(HP)A 1977, s 20 and Schedule, repealing this part of NAA 1948, s 21.
6   NAA 1948, s 24.
7   NAA 1948, s 24.
8   NAA 1948, s 33, subsequently Local Authority Social Services Act 1970, s 7.
9   *Southwark LBC v Williams* [1971] Ch 734, CA; see also Ministry of Health Circular 87/48 illustrating 'urgent and unforeseen need' as homelessness arising as a result of 'fire, flood or eviction'.
10   *Bristol Corporation v Stockford* (1973), reported in Carnwath, *A guide to the Housing (Homeless Persons) Act 1977*, Knight's Annotated Acts, 1978.
11   *Roberts v Dorset CC* (1976) 75 LGR 462.

1.14   Even more problematic was the division of responsibilities between different authorities within a single geographical area: homelessness provision was to be found in NAA 1948 and was regarded as a social services problem; the duty to provide housing in any area lay, however, with the authority having responsibility under the Housing Acts.[12]

1.15   This problem was exacerbated by the re-organisation undertaken by the Local Government Act (LGA) 1972 with effect from 1 April 1974. From that date, social services outside London, and in non-metropolitan areas, became the responsibility of county councils, while housing was the responsibility of the district council.[13] Even in London and the metropolitan areas, where social services and housing remained the responsibility of the same authority, different departments would usually handle the different responsibilities. In either event, this brought with it a different kind of shuttling, not in this case between different geographical areas, but between different authorities or different departments carrying out different functions in the same locality.

1.16   This was an unsatisfactory division. Popular perception was changing – homelessness was no longer readily regarded as a symptom of personal or social inadequacy, but had come to be recognised as part of the continuing severe housing problem (whether a crude shortage of housing or a shortage of adequate housing where it was needed).[14]

1.17   The fact that children were commonly taken into care for no reason other than their parents' want of accommodation was itself a significant factor in the changing attitudes which produced the climate for H(HP)A 1977.

1.18   There are two other points to make concerning the pre-H(HP)A 1977 position, both of them occurring in 1974. The first is largely technical. The LGA 1972 contained an amendment to the NAA 1948, additional to the redistribution of responsibilities in non-metropolitan areas. The amendment reduced to a mere power what had previously been a duty.[15] The Secretary of State, however, was empowered to re-impose the duty by directive, and, following an outcry by voluntary and welfare workers, lawyers and others concerned with the homeless,[16] did so in February 1974 before the 1972 Act came into effect.

---

12   Formerly HA 1957, Part 5, now HA 1985, Part 2.
13   Formerly HA 1957, s 1, as amended by LGA 1972, s 193 and Sch 22, now HA 1985, s 1.
14   Significant contributions to this rise in awareness included those of J Sandford and K Loach, *Cathy come home*, 'The Wednesday Play', 1966 television film; J Greve et al, *Homelessness in London* (Scottish Academic Press, 1971); Bryan Glastonbury, *Homeless near a thousand homes* (Allen & Unwin, 1971); F Berry, *Housing – the great British failure* (Charles Knight, 1974). Of less populist, but greater official, influence was the Cullingworth Report, *Council housing – purposes, procedures and priorities*, 9th report of Housing Management Sub-committee of the Central Housing Advisory Committee, 1969.
15   LGA 1972, s 195, Sch 23.
16   See Partington, *Housing (Homeless Persons) Act 1977* (Sweet & Maxwell, 1978), introductory notes.

1.19   Second, and of more significance, was the circular issued in February 1974, which came to be known as the 'Joint Circular',[17] directed both to social services departments and authorities, and to housing departments and authorities.

1.20   The Joint Circular had two main aims: first, it urged the transfer to housing authorities or departments of such stock as was held by social services authorities and social services departments for the purpose of discharging their responsibilities towards the homeless; second, it identified what it described as 'priority groups' who were intended to enjoy a claim on local authority stock.

1.21   The definition of 'priority groups' in the Joint Circular closely resembled the definition of 'priority need' that came to be adopted in H(HP)A 1977, s 2, subsequently in HA 1985, s 59 and now to be found in HA 1996, s 189 and H(W) A 2014, s 70:

> 'The Priority Groups comprise families with dependent children living with them or in care; and adult families or people living alone who either become homeless in an emergency such as fire or flooding or are vulnerable because of old age, disability, pregnancy or other special reasons. For these priority groups, the issue is not whether, but by what means, local authorities should provide accommodation themselves or help those concerned to obtain accommodation in the private sector...
>
> Where a family has children there is no acceptable alternative to accommodation in which the family can be together as a family. The social cost, personal hardship, the long-term damage to children, as well as the expense involved in receiving a child into care rules this out as an acceptable course, other than in the exceptional case when professional social work advice is that there are compelling reasons apart from homelessness for separating children from their family. The provision of shelter from which the husband is excluded is also not acceptable unless there are sound social reasons, as, for example, where a wife is seeking temporary refuge following matrimonial dispute and it is undesirable that she should be under pressure to return home.'[18]

1.22   Notwithstanding this advice, many authorities failed to transfer responsibility from social services to housing, or to give the priority groups preference over their own, local priorities.[19] Accordingly, when a Liberal MP, Stephen Ross, was successful in the ballot for Private Members' Bills, the government of the day supported him in introducing a Homeless Persons Bill and the opposition announced that it, too, would broadly support the measure. The Bill was introduced and became law as the H(HP)A 1977.

---

17   Department of Environment (DoE) Circular 18/74; Department of Health and Social Security (DHSS) Circular 4/74.

18   DoE Circular 18/74 paras 10–12.

19   *Hansard* HC Debs, 15 December 1975, Vol 902 cols 473–475.

HOUSING (HOMELESS PERSONS) ACT 1977; HOUSING ACT 1985, PART 3

Overview

1.23   These two Acts are taken together, as the HA 1985 was an exercise of consolidation of housing law – as such, save so far as there were recommendations of the Law Commission (Cmnd 9515) to effect explicit changes (of which there were none relevant to the policy of the legislation), no substantive change in homelessness law was intended or achieved.

1.24   One clear aim of H(HP)A 1977 was to place responsibility for the homeless on district councils and London borough councils,[20] ie, on housing authorities. Provision was made to transfer staff and stock from social services to housing: the Secretary of State for the Environment enjoyed power to compel the transfer of property and staff from one authority to another, not merely between London borough councils and district councils, but as between all 'relevant authorities', defined to include social service authorities.[21]

1.25   Another aim was to provide a uniform and national definition of, or criteria for, the circumstances in which one authority could shift on to another responsibility for a homeless person, so as to end shuttling. These 'local connection' provisions included a positive link between employment and housing.[22]

1.26   The local connection provisions operated not so much to permit an authority to shift the burden of assisting a homeless person on to another authority, as to prevent it from doing so once the applicant was shown to have a local connection with the area of the authority to which they had applied. Thus, the authority for the area in which an applicant had only an employment connection had to assist the applicant, even though the applicant might have had no other connections with that area, for example, family or residence.

1.27   The most important provision of H(HP)A 1977, however, was the establishment of a national criterion which required local authorities to accommodate, or to secure accommodation for, those who:

a)   were homeless;

b)   were in priority need of accommodation; and

c)   did not become homeless intentionally.

---

20   H(HP)A 1977, s 19.
21   H(HP)A 1977, s 14; Housing (Consequential Provisions) Act 1985, s 5 and Sch 4 para 8.
22   H(HP)A 1977, s 18; HA 1985, s 61.

1.28 Leaving aside the resolution of responsibility embodied in the local connection provisions, the three key questions, therefore, became:

a) what was homelessness?

b) who was in priority need? and

c) when was homelessness intentional?

Homelessness

1.29 Defining homelessness is not easy, either as a matter of law or as a matter of policy.[23] The most literal approach is to deal with those without a roof over their heads. This is not only difficult to estimate, but is likely to exclude those with children as, commonly, some form of accommodation, however inadequate, is found for them.

1.30 The most radical approach, advocated by Shelter, the National Campaign for the Homeless, was that a person was homeless if the person lived 'in conditions so bad that a civilised family life is impossible': this was homelessness 'in the true sense of the word'.[24]

1.31 Another approach is to consider those families who have no home where they can live together. This excludes both single people and childless couples, but it was at the core of the definition which was adopted.

1.32 Under H(HP)A 1977, Parliament started with legal rights of occupation: a person was homeless if there was no accommodation which they could occupy by virtue of an interest or estate, or contract, together with anyone else who usually resided with them either as a member of the family, or in circumstances in which it was reasonable for that person to do so.[25]

1.33 A person was not to be regarded as homeless, however, if they were in occupation in circumstances in which a court order was required for eviction – for example, tenants whose tenancies had been determined. A person was nonetheless homeless if they had been locked out of accommodation, had to leave accommodation because of domestic violence or, in the case of mobile homes and houseboats, if there was nowhere to park/moor accommodation and to live in it.[26]

---

23 This and the next paragraph are based largely on Partington, *Housing (Homeless Persons) Act 1977* (Sweet & Maxwell, 1978), introductory notes, subheading 'Definitions of homelessness and extent of homelessness'.

24 *The grief report*, Shelter, 1972.

25 H(HP)A 1977, s 1; HA 1985, s 58.

26 H(HP)A 1977, s 1; HA 1985, s 58.

Priority need

1.34   The definition of homelessness did not create any substantive rights on its own. It had to be read together with the definition of 'priority need'.

1.35   Only homeless people with a priority need for accommodation received housing assistance under H(HP)A 1977 and HA 1985:

a)   those with children who were residing, or who might reasonably be expected to reside, with either the applicant or with anyone with whom the applicant might be expected to reside;

b)   those who were residing, or who might reasonably be expected to reside, with someone who had become homeless as a result of an emergency;

c)   those who were residing, or who might reasonably be expected to reside, with someone who was vulnerable on account of age, handicap or other special reason; and

d)   a person who was residing, or who might reasonably be expected to reside, with someone who was a pregnant woman.[27]

1.36   The important point to note was this: in determining whether or not there was a priority need, not only the applicant but anyone who might reasonably be expected to reside with the applicant had to be taken into account, regardless of whether they had hitherto lived together.

Intentional homelessness

1.37   Homeless people in priority need thus acquired a prima facie right to accommodation assistance. To have become homeless, however, did not necessarily mean that someone had been evicted: the person might have quit of their own accord.

1.38   This provoked a hostile local authority reaction to H(HP)A 1977 as a Bill and, in turn, led to the inclusion of 'intentional homelessness' provisions which had not been in the original Bill.

1.39   Infamously, the Bill was described as a charter for 'scroungers and scrimshankers'.[28]

1.40   Mr G Cunningham acquired a notoriety that in earlier editions of this book was described as 'unenviable' when he suggested that women would become pregnant in order to acquire a priority need and then terminate their pregnancies

---

27   H(HP)A 1977, s 2; HA 1985, s 59; cf para **1.21**.
28   Per Mr W R Rees-Davies, *Hansard* HC Debs, 18 February 1977, Vol 926 col 905.

once housing had been secured.[29] 'Families who have hesitated in the past to make themselves homeless [as opposed to finding themselves homeless] need have no such reluctance now . . .' 'It will mean chaos.' 'Fifty per cent of alleged claims of homelessness are "try-ons".'[30]

1.41   Mr Cunningham's observation was nonetheless later to be given a degree of judicial sanction by the House of Lords decision in *R v Brent LBC ex p Awua*,[31] in which Lord Hoffmann, delivering the only substantive speech, suggested that local authorities could decide to provide only temporary accommodation to a pregnant woman and 'wait and see' whether or not the child is placed for adoption.

1.42   Parliament did not wholly give in to these fears. Under H(HP)A 1977, and then HA 1985, not everyone who voluntarily quit accommodation was considered to be homeless intentionally, from which it followed that some could quit and yet be entitled to assistance from a local authority. It is when this class is considered – those who could quit of their own accord yet not be deemed homeless intentionally – that the remit of H(HP)A 1977 and HA 1985 is finally defined.

1.43   For an authority to find that someone had become homeless intentionally – and, thus, had forfeited their right to assistance – required satisfaction by the authority as to four conditions:

a)   the applicant had to have ceased to occupy accommodation – so that those who had never had accommodation or last had it so long ago that it could not properly be taken into account, could not be homeless intentionally;

b)   the applicant had to have ceased to occupy accommodation in consequence of a deliberate act or omission – an act or omission in good faith, in ignorance of a material fact (for example, ignorance of security of tenure or financial assistance towards housing costs), was not to be considered deliberate;

c)   the accommodation had to have been such that it was reasonable to continue to occupy it, although those who left bad physical conditions were faced with the qualification that, in determining whether or not it was reasonable to remain in occupation, a housing authority could take into account housing conditions in its area generally; and

d)   the accommodation which had been quit had to have been 'available for the occupation' of the applicant.[32] Accommodation was only 'available for occupation' if it was available both for the homeless person and for anyone who might reasonably be expected to reside with them.[33] In determining

---

29   *Hansard* HC Debs, 8 July 1977, Vol 934 col 1689.
30   Quotes to be found in Widdowson, *Intentional homelessness*, Shelter, 1981, p6.
31   [1996] AC 55, (1995) 27 HLR 453, HL.
32   H(HP)A 1977, s 17; HA 1985, s 60.
33   H(HP)A 1977, s 16; HA 1985, s 75.

who might reasonably be expected to live together, no account was to be taken of want of accommodation.[34]

1.44 It followed that people who had never been able to live together but who were reasonably to be expected to do so – for example, the young couple who had to live apart for want of accommodation – and who acquired a priority need (for example, through pregnancy), could not be found to be intentionally homeless should one or other or both of them leave the separate accommodations in which they had hitherto been living. Only those who had quit accommodation which was available both for themselves and for those with whom they might reasonably be expected to live could be deemed homeless intentionally.

Discharge

1.45 Homeless people, then, for whom it was the policy of H(HP)A 1977 to ensure that any authority with which there was a local connection provided substantive assistance, were those: a) who had no accommodation as defined; b) who were in priority need of accommodation, which most commonly meant that they had children; and, c) who did not quit accommodation which was available for themselves and for the whole of their family unit.

1.46 The right which such applicants acquired was not, however, the legal right to council housing itself. Rather, the authority's duty was to ensure that accommodation was made available for the applicant (and for those who might reasonably be expected to reside with them). The authority might discharge this duty in any of the following ways:

a) by making available accommodation held by it under what is now HA 1985, Part 2 (ie, the principal part of that Act under which council housing is held)[35] or under any other enactment (for example, housing acquired in the exercise of other functions, such as education, highways, etc); or

b) by securing that the applicant obtained accommodation from some other person; or

c) by giving such advice and assistance as would secure that accommodation was obtained from some other person.[36]

1.47 The principal burden was in practice, however, bound to be placed on the local authority's own stock. Since 1935,[37] local authorities had been under an obligation to 'secure that in the selection of their tenants a reasonable preference is given to persons who were occupying insanitary or overcrowded houses, had

---

34 *Re Islam* [1983] 1 AC 688, (1981) 1 HLR 107, HL.
35 Formerly HA 1957, Part 5.
36 H(HP)A 1977, s 6(1); HA 1985, s 69(1).
37 HA 1935, s 51.

large families or were living under unsatisfactory housing conditions';[38] subject to this somewhat loose 'reasonable preference' obligation, they were free to determine their own priorities. To this there was now added a new group: those to whom authorities owed a duty under the homeless legislation.[39]

1.48 In principle, this did no more than require authorities to treat the homeless on the same footing as others, which in law was largely a matter of local choice. In practice, however, provision for the homeless was bound to make a significant impact – especially as no added money was made available to authorities under the H(HP)A 1977.[40] Exacerbating the problem, public spending powers were severely restricted from 1980 onwards.[41] In addition, the introduction of security of tenure and the right to buy under the HA 1980, Part 1[42] meant that the stock of new housing available to local authorities was in decline. Inevitably, therefore, an increasing proportion of available allocations went to homeless people.

Re Puhlhofer

1.49 With so much at stake for individuals, and with authorities unable – and in some cases unwilling – to fulfil the hope that H(HP)A 1977 appeared to hold out, it was inevitable that the courts would come to broker the interests of these two main parties. Because of the structure of the rights and duties created by the legislation[43] – and following a period during which it had been considered that challenges to authorities' decisions might be mounted by way of an ordinary civil claim (in the county court or the High Court)[44] – it was held that this was a role which could only be fulfilled by way of judicial review in the High Court,[45] a process with which many practitioners were unfamiliar and which was – to put it mildly – a process which most of the homeless found opaque.

1.50 In time, practitioners adjusted and a very substantial number of cases in what has subsequently become the Administrative Court[46] came to be heard as

---

38   As consolidated in HA 1936, s 85(2).
39   H(HP)A 1977, s 6(2), amending HA 1957, s 113(2), subsequently HA 1985, s 22.
40   A point made by Lord Brightman in *R v Hillingdon LBC ex p Puhlhofer* [1986] AC 484, (1986) 18 HLR 158, HL.
41   Local Government, Planning and Land Act 1980; subsequently, see Local Government and
   ⋅ Housing Act 1989. See now, the somewhat more liberal regime of Local Government Act 2003, Part 1. The financial crisis of 1976 had, in any event, led to stringent controls effectively imposed by the International Monetary Fund.
42   See now HA 1985, Parts 4, 5.
43   Duties arose when the authority was of the opinion, had reason to believe or was satisfied that a particular state of affairs existed as distinct from whether that state of affairs does exist as a matter of fact for a court to determine: this structure remains to the present day.
44   But see, now, Chapter 12, for appeal to the county court on a point of law under HA 1996, s 204.
45   Under RSC Order 53, now CPR 54; *Cocks v Thanet DC* [1983] 2 AC 286, (1983) 6 HLR 15, HL.
46   Formerly, the Crown Office List of the High Court.

judicial review applications at first instance.[47] Any analysis runs the risk of being subjective, but there was a popular perception that the High Court (and, on appeal, the Court of Appeal), far from maintaining a bias against the homeless, were not uncommonly helpful in their interpretation of the legislation – a perception which derives much support from many of the earlier decisions referred to in the body of this book.

1.51   One body of this judge-made law developed the obviously sensible notion that if a person was occupying accommodation so poor that it could be quit without a finding of intentionality, they ought to be treated as if already homeless. This in effect wrote into the definition of homelessness itself – with its reliance on rights of occupation – a minimum standard below which any accommodation should be entirely disregarded, even if there was a right to occupy it.[48]

1.52   Another, related, body of judge-made law introduced the concept of 'settled accommodation'.[49] Only departure from settled accommodation could constitute intentionality, whether because of its condition, terms of occupation or temporary quality. Conversely, only acquisition of settled accommodation would, in normal circumstances, break a period of intentional homelessness and entitle an applicant to re-apply.

1.53   Sympathy – while on occasion expressed – was rarely to be seen in action, however, at the highest level, the House of Lords. Of the nine cases under the 1977/1985 legislation which reached the House of Lords,[50] the homeless were successful in only two of them.[51]

1.54   One of those nine cases was *Re Puhlhofer*,[52] in which the equiparation of homelessness and want of intentionality was firmly rejected. No words such as

---

47   By 1991, almost 20% of all cases in the Crown Office list were homelessness cases, second only to immigration: Bridges, Meszaros and Sunkin, *Judicial review in perspective*, Public Law Project, 1995.

48   See *R v South Herefordshire DC ex p Miles* (1985) 17 HLR 82, QBD; *City of Gloucester v Miles* (1985) 17 HLR 292, CA; *R v Dinefwr BC ex p Marshall* (1985) 17 HLR 310, QBD; see also the judgment of Ackner LJ in *Re Puhlhofer* at the Court of Appeal (1985) 17 HLR 558.

49   The phrase was coined by Ackner LJ in *Din v Wandsworth LBC* at the Court of Appeal: [1983] 1 AC 657, (1983) 1 HLR 73, HL; see also *Dyson v Kerrier DC* [1980] 1 WLR 1205, CA. See Chapter 6.

50   *Re Islam* [1983] 1 AC 688, (1981) 1 HLR 107, HL; *Din v Wandsworth LBC* [1983] 1 AC 657, (1983) 1 HLR 73; *Re Betts* [1983] 2 AC 613, (1983) 10 HLR 97; *Cocks v Thanet DC* [1983] 2 AC 286, (1983) 6 HLR 15, HL; *Eastleigh BC v Walsh* [1985] 1 WLR 525, (1985) 17 HLR 392; *R v Hillingdon LBC ex p Puhlhofer* [1986] AC 484, (1986) 18 HLR 158, HL; *R v Oldham BC ex p G, R v Bexley LBC ex p Bentum, R v Tower Hamlets LBC ex p Begum* [1993] AC 509, (1993) 25 HLR 319; *R v Northavon DC ex p Smith* [1994] 2 AC 402, (1994) 26 HLR 659; *R v Brent LBC ex p Awua* [1996] AC 55, (1995) 27 HLR 453, HL.

51   *Re Islam and Eastleigh BC v Walsh*, above. Of these, *Walsh* was part of a wider issue – the distinction between tenancy and licence – which was contemporaneously being reviewed (and recast more favourably towards residential occupiers) by the House of Lords: see *Street v Mountford* [1985] AC 809, (1985) 17 HLR 402.

52   *R v Hillingdon LBC ex p Puhlhofer* [1986] AC 484, (1986) 18 HLR 158, HL.

'appropriate' or 'reasonable' were to be imported into the term 'accommodation' in H(HP)A 1977, s 1 / HA 1985, s 58 (definition of homelessness), as Parliament had 'plainly and wisely' determined. The only example of what would not comprise accommodation was that of Diogenes' tub.

1.55   The House of Lords also took the opportunity forcefully to express its concern about the 'prolific' use of judicial review in this area: great restraint should be exercised when giving leave to proceed by way of judicial review; the courts should be used to monitor the actions of local authorities under the legislation only in exceptional cases. The speech of Lord Brightman, in particular, expressed the hope that there would be a lessening in the number of challenges under the legislation.[53]

> 'My Lords, I am troubled at the prolific use of judicial review for the purpose of challenging the performance by local authorities of their functions under the Act of 1977. Parliament intended the local authority to be the judge of fact. The Act abounds with the formula when, or if the housing authority are satisfied as to this, or that, or have reason to believe this, or that. Although the action or inaction of a local authority is clearly susceptible to judicial review where they have misconstrued the Act, or abused their powers or otherwise acted perversely, I think that great restraint should be exercised in giving leave to proceed by judicial review. The plight of the homeless is a desperate one, and the plight of the applicants in the present case commands the deepest sympathy. But it is not, in my opinion, appropriate that the remedy of judicial review, which is a discretionary remedy, should be made use of to monitor the actions of local authorities under the Act save in the exceptional case. The ground upon which the courts will review the exercise of an administrative discretion is abuse of power – eg bad faith, a mistake in construing the limits of the power, a procedural irregularity, or unreasonableness in the *Wednesbury* sense – unreasonableness verging on an absurdity: see the speech of Lord Scarman in *R v Secretary of State for the Environment, ex p Nottinghamshire CC*.[54] Where the existence or non-existence of a fact is left to the judgment and discretion of a public body and that fact involves a broad spectrum ranging from the obvious to the debatable to the just conceivable, it is the duty of the court to leave the decision of that fact to the public body to whom Parliament has entrusted the decision-making power save in a case where it is obvious that the public body, consciously or unconsciously, are acting perversely.
>
> ... I express the hope that there will be a lessening in the number of challenges which are mounted against local authorities who are endeavouring, in extremely difficult circumstances, to perform their duties under the Homeless Persons Act with due regard for all their other housing problems.'

53   [1986] AC 484 at 518.
54   [1986] AC 240, 247–248 – see para **10.25**.

1.56 Save for a relatively brief period, however, there was no appearance of any such reduction, or indeed of a lower rate of success on the part of the homeless.

HOUSING AND PLANNING ACT 1986

1.57 In 1986, in direct response to *Puhlhofer*,[55] Parliament reacted to the judgment that it had been 'wise' not to qualify the accommodation the absence of which rendered a person homeless by amending the principal definition of 'homelessness' to do precisely that, in substance to harmonise the criteria of homelessness and intentionality: the homeless were now those who, even if enjoying one of the qualifying rights of occupation, occupied accommodation of which it would not be reasonable to remain in occupation (having regard to the general housing circumstances of their area).[56]

1.58 This, in substance, preferred the High Court approach to that of the House of Lords, although it did not go quite so far because the amendment did not require that the accommodation of which the person was in occupation was also available for their occupation in the statutory sense, ie, available for themselves together with anyone who might reasonably be expected to reside with them. Nonetheless, in practical or applied terms it tended towards treating as homeless a person without settled accommodation.

1.59 The HPA 1986 also amended HA 1985 to ensure that accommodation provided under Part 3 met broadly the same minimum criterion, likewise rejecting critical observations by Lord Brightman in *Re Puhlhofer* in relation to what had not otherwise proved to be controversial.[57] In practice, it was now accepted that the accommodation to be provided also had to be settled.

1.60 It may be said that at this point homelessness law had reached its greatest coherence or cohesiveness – the lower courts had taken the parliamentary framework and, reinforced by HPA 1986, fleshed it out to identify a level of accommodation to which all those in priority need were entitled, below which they could quit without being intentionally homeless or in occupation of which they were already homeless; and, they were entitled to the benefit of accommodation assistance under the Act, including priority in the allocation of local authority stock, to the same level.

---

55 Above.
56 HPA 1986, s 14(2), amending HA 1985, s 58.
57 In two cases, without drawing the same link that had been drawn between homelessness and non-intentionality, it had been held that accommodation to be provided had to be appropriate or suitable or habitable (having regard to the applicant and those to reside with them): *Parr v Wyre BC* (1982) 2 HLR 71, CA (disapproved in *Re Puhlhofer*); and *R v Ryedale DC ex p Smith* (1984) 16 HLR 64.

ASYLUM AND IMMIGRATION APPEALS ACT 1993

1.61   For a period, homelessness and allocations law enjoyed a period of statutory stability. Complaints of unfairness towards others awaiting public sector accommodation, or of an unduly liberal approach to intentionality, were met with revisions to the Code of Guidance issued by the Secretary of State for the Environment,[58] but neither achieved – nor sought to achieve – any substantive differences in effect.

1.62   During the 1990s, however, there was growing antagonism towards asylum-seekers, many of whom remained in the UK for years before a final decision on a claim was reached. As persons lawfully in the country pending that decision, they had at all times fallen within the protection of the legislation.[59] Under the AIAA 1993, however, they were now placed on a different footing from other homeless people. Until the final determination of a claim for asylum, when authorities were bound to reach a new decision,[60] there would be no duty towards any asylum-seeker who had the benefit of some accommodation, however temporary. Likewise, the accommodation to be provided did not have to be more than temporary.[61] In effect, therefore, for the duration of their period as such, asylum-seekers did not have a right to settled accommodation.

Ex p Awua

1.63   Leaving aside the policy of the AIAA 1993, as a matter of legal structure, that Act acknowledged what the courts, and the HPA 1986, had achieved in terms of quality of accommodation; that was what asylum-seekers were to be deprived of, not rights under the legislation altogether.

1.64   This did not stop the House of Lords taking another crack at minimum standards, in *R v Brent LBC ex p Awua*,[62] rejecting the idea that 'accommodation' in both HA 1985, s 58(1) (definition of homelessness) and s 60(1) (definition of intentionality) had to be 'settled', still less 'permanent': notwithstanding the HPA 1986 amendments, the provisions meant no more than a place which could fairly be described as accommodation which it would be reasonable, having regard to general housing conditions in the local housing authority's district, for the person in question to continue to occupy.

1.65   The same was held to be true of the accommodation which a local housing authority had to make available to an unintentionally homeless person

---

58   Under HA 1985, s 71; see now HA 1996, s 182 and H(W)A 2014, s 98.
59   *R v Hillingdon LBC ex p Streeting (No 2)* [1980] 1 WLR 1425, CA; *R v Westminster City Council ex p Castelli, Same ex p Tristram-Garcia* (1996) 28 HLR 616, CA.
60   AIAA 1993, s 4(4).
61   AIAA 1993, s 4(4).
62   [1996] AC 55, (1995) 27 HLR 453, HL.

under HA 1985, s 65(2); the accommodation had to be 'suitable', but there was no requirement of permanence.

1.66   Temporary accommodation was accordingly not, per se, unsuitable. If the tenure was so precarious that the person was likely to have to leave within 28 days without any alternative accommodation being available, then they remained threatened with homelessness[63] and the authority would not have discharged its duty. Otherwise, the period for which the accommodation was provided was a matter for the authority to decide.

1.67   The decision abandoned the concept of settled accommodation save for the purpose of defining what class of accommodation an intentionally homeless applicant would need to have secured for themselves before being entitled to re-apply. It was no longer to be used to identify accommodation which a person could quit without being found intentionally homeless or as the class of accommodation to which a qualifying applicant was entitled.

1.68   The committee was not referred to – and did not refer to – the AIAA 1993, although it is unlikely that this would have rendered the decision per incuriam, as it is unlikely that it would have led the committee to a different result. Given the forceful thrust of the decision, it seems more likely that the committee would have brushed it aside as an error into which the lower courts had led Parliament.

HOUSING ACT 1996, PARTS 6 AND 7

Policy

1.69   The decision in *Awua*:

> '... caught most people in the housing world somewhat by surprise. It said that a housing authority's duty could be discharged in as little as 28 days. The legal landscape ... has, therefore, changed.'

This was how the Minister for Local Government, Housing and Urban Regeneration described the decision, noting that HA 1996 was neither introduced because of the *Awua* case nor was a response to it.[64]

1.70   Indeed, the minister suggested that it went further than the government intended, by removing the safety net of immediate help that it was its new policy

---

63   HA 1985, s 58(4); see now HA 1996, s 175(4).
64   *Hansard*, Standing Committee G, 19 March 1996, col 691.

to provide,[65] in order to reduce the (increasing) proportion of (decreasing) local authority accommodation that was then being allocated to the homeless.

1.71   HA 1996 was foreshadowed by a consultation paper –, which described:

> '... two main methods of acquiring a local authority or housing association tenancy – by making a direct application to the landlord concerned (and usually going on the relevant waiting list until a suitable property becomes available), or by being accepted as statutorily 'homeless' by a local authority ...'[66]

1.72   Government research[67] published contemporaneously:

> '... shows that people rehoused from the waiting list are in many important respects (such as income, employment status and previous tenure) similar to households through the homelessness route ... But statutorily homeless households receive automatic priority over others ... As a result, in some areas – particularly in parts of London – it is almost impossible for any applicant ever to be rehoused from the waiting list ... Of those who did manage to get rehoused, people using the waiting list route had to wait nearly twice as long ... as people housed under the homelessness legislation...[68]

> By giving the local authority a greater responsibility towards those who can demonstrate 'homelessness' than towards anyone else in housing need, the current legislation creates a perverse incentive for people to have themselves accepted by a local authority as homeless ... In the great majority of cases, someone accepted as homeless is in fact occupying accommodation of some sort at the time they approached the authority. Indeed, the largest single category of households accepted as statutorily homeless are people living as licensees of parents, relatives or friends who are no longer willing or able to accommodate them ... There is a growing belief that the homelessness provisions are frequently used as a quick route into a separate home...[69]

> Against this background, the government is proposing measures to ensure fairer access to all parts of the rented housing sector. These include measures to prevent homelessness, to remove the distorting effect that the present provisions have on the allocation of housing, and to ensure that subsidised housing is equally available to all who genuinely need it,

---

65   *Hansard*, Standing Committee G, 21 March 1996, col 776. The minister was aware of the implications of *Pepper v Hart* [1993] AC 593, HL, even if none too accurately, when he remarked, at col 769: 'The Hon Gentleman should also know that what Ministers say during the passage of a Bill is taken into consideration in legal proceedings'.

66   January 1994 Consultation Paper, para 2.5.

67   *Routes into local authority housing*, DoE Housing Research Summary No 16, 1994.

68   January 1994 Consultation Paper, para 2.6.

69   January 1994 Consultation Paper, para 2.8.

particularly couples seeking to establish a good home in which to start and raise a family.'[70]

1.73   The proposals were threefold:

a)   to limit the extent of an authority's duties to the homeless;

b)   to limit local authority housing allocation to the homeless; and

c)   to encourage more advisory activity to help people find other accommodation.[71]

1.74   The idea was to provide an immediate safety net, while longer-term allocation to homeless people would be considered alongside others seeking council housing.[72] This would be achieved by new constraints on allocation, subject to 'broad principles' to be laid down by central government.[73]

1.75   The white paper on which HA 1996 was based,[74] pursued the theme that homelessness was:

> '. . . usually a short term crisis . . . We are committed to maintaining an immediate safety net, but this should be separate from a fair system of allocating long-term accommodation in a house or flat owned by a local authority or housing association...[75]

> Local authorities will continue to have an immediate duty to secure accommodation for families and vulnerable individuals who have nowhere to go. Where such people are found to have no alternative available accommodation, the local housing authority will have to secure suitable accommodation for not less than twelve months.[76] The authority may continue to secure accommodation for longer than that, although after two years it must check that the household's housing circumstances have not changed . . . These arrangements are intended to tide people over the immediate crisis of homelessness, and to give them time to find longer-term accommodation ...'[77]

1.76   The white paper was followed in January 1996 by a linked consultation paper, *Allocation of housing accommodation by local authorities*. This introduced

70   January 1994 Consultation Paper, para 3.1.
71   January 1994 Consultation Paper, para 3.2.
72   January 1994 Consultation Paper, para 3.4.
73   January 1994 Consultation Paper, paras 20.2, 22.1.
74   Cm 2901, HMSO, June 1995.
75   *Our future homes* (see para **1.75**), p36, claiming that over 40% of local authority new tenancies
       – over 80% in some London authorities – and over 25% of allocations of housing association
       tenancies were going to those accepted under the homelessness legislation.
76   Later changed to two years: see HA 1996, s 193(2). See also *Hansard*, Standing Committee
       G, 21 March 1996, col 776 – reflecting a concern that, even if renewable, one year would not
       provide sufficient security.
77   White paper, *Our future homes*, p37.

the ideas that were to become Part 6 of HA 1996, governing the waiting list. It identified changes proposed to HA 1985, s 22, designed to 'create a single route into social housing',[78] in accordance with the policy[79] of putting '*all* those with long-term housing needs on the same footing, while providing a safety net for emergency and pressing needs' (emphasis in original). It will be 'the only route into social housing allocated by local authorities; it will be dynamic, and will focus on basic underlying need rather than immediate emergency'.[80]

1.77   The consultation paper proposed to retain the long-established categories of those occupying insanitary or overcrowded housing, or living in unsatisfactory housing conditions, to which it would add:

a)   those living in conditions of temporary or insecure tenure (including those at risk of losing accommodation, for example, tied accommodation);

b)   families with dependent children or who are expecting a child ('recognising the importance of a stable home environment to children's development');

c)   households containing a person with an identified need for settled accommodation (for example, those who give or need to receive care or other personal circumstances); and

d)   those households with limited opportunities to secure settled accommodation (for example, low income), bearing in mind longer-term prospects.[81]

1.78   The principal policy change – to minimise the priority call of homeless people on local authority stock – may be addressed under its two heads:

a) principal homelessness changes; and

b) allocation changes.

In addition, there was a number of other discrete changes.

Principal homelessness changes

1.79   The principal homelessness changes were:

a)   persons subject to immigration control under the Asylum and Immigration Act (AIA) 1996, unless of a class prescribed by the Secretary of State, were no longer eligible under HA 1996, Part 7;[82] nor were others within

78   *Hansard* (HC), Standing Committee G, 16th Sitting, 12 March 1996, Minister for Local Government, Housing and Urban Regeneration (Mr Curry), col 614.
79   White paper, *Our future homes*, Chapter 6.
80   *Hansard* (HC), Standing Committee G, 15th Sitting, 12 March 1996, Minister for Local Government, Housing and Urban Regeneration (Mr Curry), col 588.
81   January 1996 Consultation Paper (see para **1.76**), paras 26, 27, 28–31, 33.
82   HA 1996, s 185.

any class prescribed by the Secretary of State; nor were such persons to be taken into consideration when determining whether someone else was homeless, threatened with homelessness or had a priority need for accommodation;[83]

b) where the authority was satisfied that there was other suitable accommodation available in its area, the duty was limited to giving 'such advice and assistance as the authority consider is reasonably required to enable' the applicant to secure such accommodation;[84] however, 'So far as reasonably practicable', the authority had to secure accommodation in its own area;[85]

c) in cases where such suitable accommodation was not available, the duty to secure that accommodation was made available to the applicant was limited to two years (although could be continued in defined circumstances following a review, and – in default – a new application could otherwise be made);[86]

d) unless and until the authority could make an offer from its waiting list, the authority was prohibited from providing its own accommodation in discharge of functions under HA 1996, Part 7 for more than two years out of any three (whether continuously or in aggregate), unless it was hostel accommodation or accommodation privately leased by the authority from a private landlord.[87]

Allocations

1.80   Meanwhile, HA 1996, Part 6 provided that:

a) local authorities were bound to comply with Part 6 when making any allocation decision, including the selection of their own tenants and nominations to a registered social landlord,[88] but not including, among others, transfers;[89]

b) allocation could also only be to persons qualified on the housing register which they were bound to maintain,[90] which could not include a person subject to immigration control under the AIA 1996, unless of a class prescribed by the Secretary of State, nor could it include others within

---

83   HA 1996, s 185(4).
84   HA 1996, s 197.
85   HA 1996, s 208(1).
86   HA 1996, ss 193, 194.
87   HA 1996, s 207; private landlord included housing associations or, as they and other similar bodies were known by HA 1996, Part 1, registered social landlords.
88   HA 1996, s 159.
89   HA 1996, s 159(9).
90   HA 1996, s 162.

any class prescribed by the secretary of state; qualification was otherwise within the discretion of the authority;[91]

c) authorities had to adopt an allocation scheme for determining priority between applicants, including by whom decisions could be taken.

1.81   Subject to this, the scheme had to be framed to secure a reasonable preference not for the homeless to whom duties were owed per se,[92] but for:

a) those occupying insanitary or overcrowded housing, or otherwise living in insanitary conditions;

b) those living in temporary accommodation or on insecure terms;

c) families with dependent children;

d) households consisting of or including someone who was expecting a child;

e) households consisting of or including someone with a particular need for settled accommodation on medical or welfare grounds, with added preference under this heading to those who could not reasonably be expected to find their own settled accommodation in the near future; and

f) households whose social or economic circumstances were such that they had difficulty in securing settled accommodation.[93]

Other changes

1.82   HA 1996, Part 6 included a number of ancillary provisions, including notification of entry on and removal from the register, review of entries and review of decisions. Part 7 also effected a number of other changes to homelessness law, of which the most significant were the introduction of a right to internal review and subsequent appeal to the county court.[94]

BETWEEN 1996 AND 2002 ACTS

Restoration of priority to homeless people

1.83   HA 1996, Parts 6 and 7 had been in force for only a relatively short period of time when the general election of 1997 brought in a new government.

---

91 HA 1996, s 161.
92 Though plainly many of the homeless would qualify within the classes to be given a reasonable preference.
93 HA 1996, s 167(2).
94 HA 1996, ss 202, 204.

One of its first acts was to restore priority to homeless people under HA 1996, Part 6. Using a power[95] to specify further descriptions of people to whom a preference should be given, the Allocation of Housing (Reasonable and Additional Preference) Regulations 1997[96] re-instated a reasonable preference for the unintentionally homeless towards whom a duty was owed under HA 1996, Part 7 or its predecessor provisions in the HA 1985.

Asylum-seekers

1.84   The Immigration and Asylum Act 1999 set up an entirely separate national service – the National Asylum Support Service (NASS) – to deal with destitute asylum-seekers. As a result, all asylum-seekers whose claims were made on or after 3 April 2000 were taken out of HA 1996, Part 7.

A decent home for all

1.85   These changes were followed, in April 2000, by 'the first comprehensive review of housing policy for 23 years' – the green paper, *Quality and choice: a decent home for all*,[97] which set out aims for reform in relation to both homelessness and allocations. The changes to the allocations provisions were subject to an overall aim of encouraging 'social landlords to see themselves more as providers of a lettings service which is responsive to the needs and wishes of individuals rather than purely as housing "allocators"'.[98]

1.86   The aims were to ensure that lettings and transfer services:

a)   meet the long-term housing requirements of those who need social housing most, in a way which is sustainable both for individuals and the community;

b)   adopt a simple and customer-centred approach, empowering first-time applicants and existing tenants to make decisions in choosing housing which meets their requirements;

c)   make better use of the national housing stock, by widening the scope for lettings and transfers across local authority boundaries, and between local authorities and registered social landlords; and

d)   give local authorities more flexibility to build sustainable communities within the national context of extreme variations in local housing markets.[99]

---

95   HA 1996, s 167(3).
96   Allocation of Housing (Reasonable and Additional Preference) Regulations 1997, SI 1997/1902.
97   Department of the Environment, Transport and the Regions (DETR), 2000.
98   *Quality and choice: a decent home for all*, para 9.3.
99   *Quality and choice: a decent home for all*, para 9.4.

1.87   The green paper's proposals for the reform of homelessness policy were intended to:

a)   ensure that unintentionally homeless people in priority need were provided with temporary accommodation until they obtained settled accommodation (in either the public or private sector);

b)   broaden the definition of priority need to ensure that the most vulnerable citizens were protected by the homelessness safety net;

c)   enable local authorities to use their own housing stock to provide temporary accommodation, without the restriction that it could only be provided for two years in any three;

d)   give those housed in temporary accommodation a reasonable period in which they could exercise the same degree of customer choice of settled accommodation as available to other people with urgent housing needs waiting on the housing register;

e)   allow local authorities greater flexibility to assist non-priority homeless households, particularly in areas of low demand; and

f)   encourage a more strategic approach to the prevention of homelessness and the rehousing of homeless households.[100]

1.88   Following consultation, the government published *Quality and choice: a decent home for all – The way forward*.[101] 'The principle of choice in lettings was broadly welcomed.'[102] In relation to the homelessness proposals, 'there was almost unanimous support, from those who responded'.[103] Legislation was promised.

1.89   This legislation originally formed part of the Homes Bill 2001, which also included provisions to improve the process of buying and selling homes through a requirement for a 'home-buyers pack'. The Bill fell at committee stage in the House of Lords, as a result of the general election in May 2001. Following re-election, the government decided not to proceed immediately with the provisions relating to home-buying, but re-introduced those relating to homelessness and allocation, in the Homelessness Bill.

Priority need categories

1.90   Not all the elements of the green paper proposals required primary legislation, however. In particular, the paper had proposed extending the

---

100   *Quality and choice: a decent home for all*, para 9.42.
101   DETR, December 2000.
102   *The way forward*, para 6.2.
103   *The way forward*, para 7.3.

categories of priority need[104] to those leaving an institutional or care background, those fleeing domestic violence, and 16- and 17-year-olds. This could be achieved by statutory instrument, under HA 1996, s 189(2).

1.91 An amendment to this effect was made by the National Assembly for Wales on 1 March 2001.[105] In England, there was consultation on a draft statutory instrument during 2001, and it was not until 2002 that the changes were made, to coincide with the coming into force of most of the homelessness provisions in the Homelessness Act 2002.[106]

1.92 The Welsh and English provisions are not worded identically, illustrating an increasing divergence in housing policy following devolution. In particular, while the Welsh identified certain applicants as being in priority need,[107] the English provisions identified certain applicants as being in priority need but only if vulnerable,[108] leaving a measure of room for manoeuvre for recalcitrant authorities.

HOMELESSNESS ACT 2002

Strategies

1.93 The green paper had emphasised the need for authorities to develop a more strategic approach to the prevention and redress of homelessness. This was embodied in Homelessness Act 2002, ss 1–4, by a duty requiring each local housing authority to undertake a review of homelessness and to formulate an effective strategy to deal with it, in consultation with both social services (whether of the same authority or another) and other organisations.

Duties

1.94 One of the main changes of HA 1996 had been to limit the initial duty to house homeless people to a period of two years. This limit was repealed by the Homelessness Act 2002, along with the prohibition on use of an authority's stock to house the homeless.[109] Also repealed was the provision of HA 1996, s 197 which allowed the main duties to be avoided if other suitable accommodation was available.[110]

---

104 *Quality and choice: a decent home for all*, paras 9.55, 9.56.
105 Homeless Persons (Priority Need) (Wales) Order 2001, SI 2001/607.
106 See the Homelessness (Priority Need for Accommodation) (England) Order 2002, SI 2002/2051.
107 See now H(W)A 2014, s 70.
108 Homelessness (Priority Need for Accommodation) (England) Order 2002, SI 2002/2051.
109 Homelessness Act 2002, s 6.
110 Homelessness Act 2002, s 9.

1.95 Nonetheless, the duty was not intended to last indefinitely, and the circumstances which bring an authority's duty to an end under HA 1996, s 193 were accordingly widened to allow more reliance on assured tenancies, and – in certain circumstances – even assured shorthold tenancies.[111]

Non-priority need applicants

1.96 Homelessness Act 2002, s 5 also gave local authorities power to house the unintentionally homeless under HA 1996, Part 7, even where not in priority need.

Other changes

1.97 Further changes were made to the definitions of 'homelessness' and 'intentionality', to ensure that any kind of violence – not only domestic violence – would mean that it is not reasonable to continue to occupy accommodation.[112] This helps, for example, those fleeing racial harassment or intimidation.

1.98 In addition, there was an extension to the jurisdiction of the county court to allow an applicant who appeals against an authority's decision also to appeal to that court against a refusal by the authority to provide the applicant with interim accommodation pending the outcome of the appeal process.[113]

1.99 The Homelessness Act 2002 made two other amendments to the review process: applicants were allowed both to accept an offer of accommodation and to challenge its suitability by way of review;[114] and, the county court could itself extend the 21-day time limit for appealing.[115]

Allocations

1.100 The amendments to HA 1996, Part 6 almost all reflected the government's aim of bringing greater choice to the allocation process by local authorities.

1.101 One change was to bring transfer applications (whether within the stock of a single landlord or between the stocks of more than one landlord) into the ambit of HA 1996, Part 6.[116] This ensured both that existing tenants are dealt with

---

111 Homelessness Act 2002, s 7.
112 Homelessness Act 2002, s 10.
113 Homelessness Act 2002, s 11.
114 Homelessness Act 2002, s 8(2).
115 Homelessness Act 2002, Sch 1 para 17.
116 Homelessness Act 2002, s 13.

on the same basis as new applicants and that their qualification for rehousing is not limited.[117]

1.102   The HA 1996 requirement to keep a housing register was abolished:

'Removing the requirement to have a register is an important step in facilitating the development by local authorities of choice-based letting schemes that put the applicant at the centre of the decision-making process. We want to encourage authorities to move away from the rigid formulas of an often artificial points-based system, which typically becomes associated with allocation schemes based on the housing register.'[118]

1.103   The government retained the ineligibility of persons from abroad for an allocation. In addition, the Homelessness Act 2002 (as had the green paper) reflected a widespread concern about anti-social behaviour, and the Act therefore contained provisions allowing those guilty of 'unacceptable behaviour serious enough to make them unsuitable to be a tenant' to be excluded from social housing.[119]

1.104   The requirement that allocation schemes reflect housing need in some way was not abandoned and the Homelessness Act 2002 retained the concept of the 'reasonable preference' to be given to certain groups, albeit subject to some changes.[120] Authorities' schemes were explicitly allowed to take into account financial resources, behaviour and local connection when determining preference and, even where those guilty of seriously unacceptable behaviour were not excluded from the allocation scheme altogether, they could be accorded no preference.

1.105   Changes were made to the ancillary provisions on notification and internal review to allow an applicant to seek an internal review in relation to any decision about the facts of the applicant's case, including a decision that the applicant is to be excluded or given no preference because of unacceptable behaviour.[121]

1.106   The Homelessness Act 2002 provisions still did not comprise a tightly-prescriptive framework and there remained considerable room for local variation.

'We believe the right way forward is for local authorities and registered social landlords to decide in the light of local circumstances, and drawing

---

117 See *Quality and choice: a decent home for all*, DETR, 2000, para 9.8.
118 Standing Committee A, 12 July 2001, col 81, per Dr Alan Whitehead, Parliamentary Under-Secretary for Transport, Local Government and the Regions.
119 Homelessness Act 2002, s 16.
120 Including giving preference to all homeless people, whether in priority need or not, and whether or not intentionally homeless: HA 1996, s 167(2)(a) as amended by Homelessness Act 2002, s 16(3).
121 Homelessness Act 2002, s 14.

on the experiences of the pilot studies, the ways in which they should amend or develop their existing arrangements.'[122]

BETWEEN 2002 AND 2011 ACTS

1.107 Devolution is an issue that goes well beyond this book. It may be said, however, that by the transfer of powers[123] it has brought benefits (in terms of this book) not only to the people of Wales but also to those of England, by introducing new approaches and otherwise leading the way towards a markedly less harsh approach, albeit at the cost of some added length to any description of the subject which sets out to cover both, increasingly divergent systems.

1.108 Leaving this aside, the focus of Westminster government policy following the Homelessness Act 2002 and prior to the change of administration in 2010 was primarily on implementation. One particular area of attack was on use of bed and breakfast accommodation: in 2003, secondary legislation made it unlawful in England for local authorities to place families in bed and breakfast accommodation for more than six weeks.[124]

1.109 Other key changes governed immigration and asylum. While it has already been noted that asylum-seekers were taken outside the existing statutory provisions in April 2000 by the establishment of NASS, the question arose whether accommodation provided by NASS gave rise to a local connection under HA 1996, Part 7 if and when asylum-seekers achieved refugee status and were thus able to apply under Part 7. The House of Lords initially answered this question in the negative.[125] The government, concerned that refugees would

---

122 *The way forward*, para 6.4.
123 In Wales, ministerial functions in many areas of activity (including housing) were transferred to the National Assembly for Wales by Government of Wales Act 1998, s 22, Sch 2 para 9; National Assembly for Wales (Transfer of Functions) Order 1999, SI 1999, SI 1999/672. The Government of Wales Act 2006 then transferred those functions from the Assembly to the Welsh Ministers (ss 58, 161, Sch 11 para 30). The National Assembly for Wales was not granted legislative competence over housing matters but, by Government of Wales Act 2006, s 95, could be given such competence by Order in Council. Under that regime, two relevant Orders were made: the National Assembly for Wales (Legislative Competence) (Housing) (Fire Safety) Order 2010, SI 20101210 and the National Assembly for Wales (Legislative Competence) (Housing and Local Government) Order 2010, SI 2010/1838. The Wales Act 2017 changed the position again, so that, rather than identifying an order which devolved legislative competence to the Welsh Assembly/Senedd Cymru, the position is now that Acts of the Assembly/Senedd are "not law" only insofar as they purport to apply outside of Wales or relate to reserved matters (Government of Wales Act 2006, s 108A). The reserved matters are found in Government of Wales Act 2006, Schs 7A and 7B and do not include housing or homelessness.
124 Homelessness (Suitability of Accommodation) (England) Order 2003, SI 2003, SI 2003/3326. Similar (although not identical) limitations were introduced in Wales in 2006.
125 *Al-ameri v Kensington and Chelsea RLBC; Osmani v Harrow LBC* [2004] UKHL 4, [2004] HLR 20.

overwhelmingly apply to areas of greatest housing stress in London and the south-east, reversed this decision by amendments to HA 1996, s 199 contained in Asylum and Immigration (Treatment of Claimants, etc) Act 2004, s 11.

1.110 Another immigration-related statutory change followed from the exclusion of ineligible persons when considering whether an applicant for HA 1996, Part 7 assistance was homeless, threatened with homelessness or in priority need. This was held to be incompatible with the family life provisions of Article 8 of the European Convention on Human Rights (ECHR).[126] As a result, the Housing and Regeneration Act (H&RA) 2008 amended HA 1996, s 185(4) so as to take such persons into account, except in those cases where, although eligible, the applicant[127] is subject to immigration control;[128] such an application would, however, be known as a 'restricted case' to whom the authority owes a – somewhat lesser – duty by way of making a 'private accommodation offer',[129] and by exclusion from the reasonable preference afforded to the homeless under HA 1996, Part 6.[130]

1.111 The H&RA 2008 also made changes to the local connection provisions, so as to include employment in the armed forces and residence during such service as grounds for a local connection, where they had formerly been excluded.[131]

1.112 No case-law,[132] however, had the seminal effect of a *Puhlhofer* or *Awua*, with the possible exception of the HA 1996, Part 6 decision in *R (Ahmad) v Newham LBC*,[133] in which shades of Lord Brightman's speech in *Puhlhofer*[134] are to be found in the speech of Lord Neuberger,[135] albeit on a reasoned basis.

> '[A]s a general proposition, it is undesirable for the courts to get involved in questions of how priorities are accorded in housing allocation policies. Of course, there will be cases where the court has a duty to interfere, for instance if a policy does not comply with statutory requirements, or if it is

---

126 *R (Morris) v Westminster City Council (No 3)* [2005] EWCA Civ 1184, [2006] 1 WLR 505, [2006] HLR 8. In *Bah v UK* App No 56328/07, [2012] HLR 2, however, the European Court of Human Rights held that it was not in contravention.

127 Not being a European Economic Area (EEA) or Swiss national, who were fully eligible: see paras **A.127–A.133**.

128 Ie, asylum-seekers, those with indefinite leave to remain: see paras **A.136–A.167**.

129 H&RA 2008, s 314 and Sch 15, Part 1; now called a 'private rented sector offer'. The details of what this duty entails may be seen at paras **5.8–5.11**.

130 HA 1996, s 167(2ZA), inserted by H&RA 2008, s 314 and Sch 15, Part 1.

131 See para **7.36**.

132 Other important decisions include *Holmes-Moorhouse v Richmond upon Thames LBC* [2009] UKHL 7, [2009] HLR 34 (see para **3.30**) rejecting the proposition that if a court in family proceedings makes a shared residence order, both parents are in priority need, and *Birmingham City Council v Ali, Moran v Manchester City Council* [2009] UKHL 36, [2009] 1 WLR 1506 (see paras **2.16** and **2.72**) opening the way to the practice of treating people as 'homeless at home', ie, without loss of preference. The first of these has also been much relied on by authorities for its relatively relaxed approach to the wording of decision-letters (see para **10.105**).

133 [2009] UKHL 14, [2009] HLR 31.

134 See para **1.55**.

135 At [46]–[47].

plainly irrational. It seems unlikely, however, that the legislature can have intended that Judges should embark on the exercise of telling authorities how to decide on priorities as between applicants in need of rehousing, save in relatively rare and extreme circumstances. Housing allocation policy is a difficult exercise which requires not only social and political sensitivity and judgment, but also local expertise and knowledge.

In relation to the provision of accommodation under the National Assistance Act 1948, my noble and learned friend, Baroness Hale of Richmond, then Hale LJ, said in *R (Wahid) v Tower Hamlets LBC*,[136] para 33, '[n]eed is a relative concept, which trained and experienced social workers are much better equipped to assess than are lawyers and courts, provided that they act rationally'. Precisely the same is true of relative housing needs under Part 6 of the 1996 Act, and trained and experienced local authority housing officers.'

LOCALISM ACT 2011

1.113   The 'coalition government' which followed the general election in 2010 made a number of changes to housing, including changes to both the homelessness and allocation provisions of HA 1996, Part 6 (as amended by the Homelessness Act 2002).

1.114   The consultation paper which preceded the Act – *Local decisions: a fairer future for social housing*[137] – was reminiscent of the policy which preceded the HA 1996.

1.115   Thus, on homelessness:

> '6.7 Under the current legislation, although local authorities have considerable flexibility in how to meet the immediate housing needs of people owed the main homelessness duty, they are very restricted in the way they can bring the duty to an end. Suitable accommodation in the private rented sector can be offered as a settled home that ends the duty, but applicants can refuse such offers without good reason, and the duty continues to be owed ...

> 6.8 People owed the main homelessness duty can therefore effectively insist on being provided with temporary accommodation until offered social housing (and under housing allocation legislation, they must be given reasonable preference for social housing). We believe this encourages some households to apply as homeless in order to secure reasonable preference and an effective guarantee of being offered social housing ...

---

136 [2002] EWCA Civ 287, [2003] HLR 13.
137 Consultation paper, Department for Communities and Local Government (DCLG), November 2010, para 6.8. See ww.gov.uk/government/consultations/a-fairer-future-for-social-housing.

...

6.12 We intend to give authorities the discretion to decide in any particular case whether a person owed the homelessness duty needs social housing or whether their needs could be met with suitable accommodation in the private rented sector...'.

1.116 Likewise, on allocations:

'4.6 The requirement to maintain open waiting lists, coupled with the introduction of choice-based lettings, may also have encouraged a commonly held – but mistaken – perception that anyone will be able to get into social housing if they wait long enough. Open waiting lists may be acceptable – should even perhaps be encouraged – where there is low demand for social housing. Where there is not enough housing, even for those who really need it, continuing to operate an open waiting list raises false expectations and is likely to fuel the belief that the allocation system is unfair.

...

4.9 We take the view that it should be for local authorities to put in place arrangements which suit the particular needs of their local area. Some local authorities might restrict social housing to those in housing need (e.g. homeless households and overcrowded families). Other local authorities might impose residency criteria or exclude applicants with a poor tenancy record or those with sufficient financial resources to rent or buy privately. Others may decide to continue with open waiting lists. If, having taken into account the views of their local community, local authorities decide that there are benefits in maintaining open waiting lists (for example, to stimulate demand for social housing), we believe they should be able to do so.'

1.117 In relation to homelessness, the principal change was designed to allow authorities more use of the private sector, so that even the offer of an assured shorthold tenancy – without the consent of the applicant – could be used to discharge the full duty, subject to a right to a further offer within two years (even if not by then in priority need).[138] In substance, even if not in form, this reinstated the original HA 1996, s 197 power to bypass Part 7 where there was other suitable accommodation available in the authority's area, which had been repealed by the Homelessness Act 2002.

1.118 In relation to allocations, the principal change – applicable only in England – was to allow authorities, subject to any overriding regulations, to define classes of 'qualifying' applicant,[139] ie, to abandon 'open' waiting lists in

138 HA 1996, s 195A.
139 HA 1996, s 160ZA.

favour of an authority's own criteria, no longer confined to the exclusion of the anti-social. In addition, transfer applicants were removed from the allocation provisions, likewise effectively reinstating the HA 1996 as unamended,[140] otherwise than where (in effect) the tenant has applied for a transfer and qualifies for a reasonable preference.[141]

1.119 The purpose was to restore authorities' historical discretion over to whom they allocate housing from what was something closer to a national code of preferences. This apparent freedom was, however, significantly undermined by the Court of Appeal in *Jakimaviciute*[142] (see para **9.50**), in which it was held that the qualification criteria adopted by an authority are subject to the reasonable preference duty, so that an authority is not able to adopt qualification criteria which exclude a person entitled to a reasonable preference. This was a conclusion that, however welcome to the homeless, plainly conflicted with the policy intention.

HOUSING (WALES) ACT 2014

1.120 In 2009, the Welsh Assembly Government published a 'Ten Year Homelessness Plan for Wales: 2009 to 2019'. It expressed concern that there were inconsistencies around decision-making, interpretation and implementation of the legislation, with too little attention being paid to the needs of the vulnerable. There was an undertaking to 'review . . . key areas of homelessness legislation and the duties placed on Local Authorities, especially around the areas of priority need, intentionality, local connection and the discharge of duty into the private rented sector'.[143]

1.121 As part of this process, a review was commissioned[144] 'of homelessness legislation in Wales in order to explore whether and how the existing legislative framework might be changed to minimise homelessness'.[145] The review concluded that the priority need categories were 'used to ration limited housing resources'[146] and that applicants found it painful and upsetting to have to 'prove' that they were vulnerable.[147] While homelessness prevention techniques were generally thought to be successful, both in terms of assisting a wide range of households and in exploring a broader range of solutions, there was concern that

---

140 HA 1996, s 159(5).
141 HA 1996, s 159(4A), (4B).
142 *R (Jakimaviciute) v Hammersmith and Fulham LBC* [2014] EWCA Civ 1438, [2015] HLR 5.
143 'Ten Year Homelessness Plan for Wales', p26.
144 Dr Peter Mackie, Ian Thomas, Kate Hodgson, *Impact analysis of existing homelessness legislation in Wales*, January 2012.
145 *Impact analysis of existing homelessness legislation in Wales*, p3.
146 *Impact analysis of existing homelessness legislation in Wales*, para 7.2.2.
147 *Impact analysis of existing homelessness legislation in Wales*, para 7.2.14.

such prevention techniques sat uncomfortably with statutory duties.[148] Moreover, there was only limited support provided for those who became homeless after leaving care or other institutional accommodation.[149]

1.122 That report was followed, in May 2012, by the Welsh Government's white paper *Homes for Wales*. Chapter 8 noted that, as a result of economic decline and welfare reform, homelessness was rising in Wales. The priority of the Welsh Government was to prevent homelessness and, in the long term, eliminate it completely.

1.123 The white paper promised a 'radical shift from existing legislation' with greater focus on duties designed to prevent homelessness.[150] The period of time in which a person was considered to be 'threatened with homelessness' would be increased from 28 to 56 days, but the intention of the new legislative model would be that people should approach authorities for assistance as early as possible once they experienced a housing problem.[151] A new duty would be introduced which would require authorities to take 'all reasonable steps to achieve a suitable housing solution for all [eligible] households which are homeless or threatened with homelessness'.[152]

1.124 Although the existing law on intentional homelessness would be re-enacted, authorities would be given a power to disapply the intentionality test altogether; in time, the Welsh Government planned to prevent any consideration of intentionality where the household included children,[153] a policy it partially implemented from December 2019.[154] The Welsh Government also intended to 'gradually phase out' the priority need test.[155]

148 *Impact analysis of existing homelessness legislation in Wales*, p44, second bullet point.
149 *Impact analysis of existing homelessness legislation in Wales*, para 7.3.6.
150 *Homes for Wales*, para 8.40.
151 *Homes for Wales*, para 8.43.
152 *Homes for Wales*, para 8.44.
153 *Homes for Wales*, para 8.53.
154 The full housing duty is now owed in Wales, even if there has been a finding of intentional homelessness, if the applicant is: a) a pregnant woman or a person with whom she resides or might reasonably be expected to reside; b) a person with whom a dependent child resides or might reasonably be expected to reside; c) a person who had not attained the age of 21 when the application was made or a person with whom such a person resides or might reasonably be expected to reside; or d) a person who had attained the age of 21, but not the age of 25, when the application was made and who was looked after, accommodated or fostered at any time while under the age of 18, or a person with whom such a person resides or might reasonably be expected to reside – see H(W)A 2014, s 75(3); Housing (Wales) Act 2014 (Commencement No 10) Order 2019, SI 2019/1479 (W263). However, s 75(3)(f)(i) limits this provision so that where someone has been found intentionally homeless twice in a five-year period, they would not be owed the full housing duty. See para **4.4**.
155 *Homes for Wales*, paras 8.55–8.56; see also *Life on the streets: preventing and tackling rough sleeping in Wales*, Welsh Assembly, April 2018. In Scotland, see Homelessness (Abolition of Priority Need Test) (Scotland) Order 2012, SI 2012/330.

1.125   Save for the last of these, the proposals were introduced in the H(W) A 2014, Part 2. The majority of that Part re-enacted provisions already found in HA 1996, Part 7 and subordinate legislation, but new provisions included:

   a)   extending the time within which a person may be threatened with homelessness to 56 days;[156]

   b)   a requirement to ensure that information and advice about prevention, securing accommodation and other help is provided, in particular, to people leaving prison, youth detention, hospital after treatment for a mental disorder and young people leaving care;[157]

   c)   a new requirement to assess the needs of those who need help in retaining or obtaining accommodation[158] and to help to prevent an applicant from becoming homeless;[159] and,

   d)   power for the authorities, in conjunction with the Welsh ministers, to resolve not to apply the intentionality test to specified categories of applicant.[160]

HOMELESSNESS REDUCTION ACT 2017

1.126   The period from 2008 was one of significant reduction of public funding, particularly for local authorities.[161] One consequence of this of which practitioners were acutely aware was an increase in efforts by some local authorities to minimise their HA 1996, Part 7 duties, by way of tactics generically referred to as 'gate-keeping', including measures to divert applicants to other sources of accommodation without ever getting a foot on the Part 7 ladder. In addition, homelessness was statistically and visibly on the rise.[162]

1.127   In December 2015, the Communities and Local Government (CLG) Select Committee launched an inquiry into homelessness in England. The Committee was concerned both that homelessness, particularly rough sleeping, was increasing and that government data was not robust enough to provide an

---

156 H(W)A 2014, s 55(4).
157 See paras **12.11, 12.21** and H(W)A 2014, s 60.
158 H(W)A 2014, s 62.
159 H(W)A 2014, s 66.
160 H(W)A 2014, s 78; para **4.3**.
161 Figures vary wildly, but no one doubts that they have been very significant indeed.
162 In Autumn 2017, there were 4,751 people sleeping rough in England (a 15% rise from 2016 and up from a low of 1,768 people in 2010); in the third quarter of 2017, 79,190 households were in temporary accommodation, of which 61,090 were households with children, giving a total of 121,360 children in temporary accommodation, the highest figures since 2007: *Live tables on homelessness*, February 2018 (www.gov.uk/government/statistical-data-sets/live-tables-on-homelessness).

accurate picture.[163] The final report praised the 'prevention' elements of the H(W) A 2014, particularly the duty to help to prevent an applicant from becoming homeless and the extension of time within which a person is threatened with homelessness to 56 days.[164]

1.128 During the inquiry, a member of the Committee (Bob Blackman MP) drew second place in the private members' Bill ballot and announced that he would introduce a Homelessness Reduction Bill. The government subsequently announced that it would support the Bill. The general election in June 2017 affected the timetable, but it came into force on 3 April 2018.[165]

1.129 The key provisions of the HRA 2017 are as follows.

a) Section 1 extended the period of time within which a person is threatened with homelessness from 28 to 56 days. It also provides that a person is threatened with homelessness if they have been served with a valid notice under HA 1988, s 21 expiring within 56 days in respect of their only home.[166]

b) Section 3 created a new HA 1996, s 189A, introducing an assessment duty in England. Where an applicant is homeless (or threatened with homelessness) and eligible for assistance, the authority must assess the applicant's housing needs and consider what support it can provide to ensure that the applicant has or retains suitable accommodation. The authority and applicant must try to agree a written list of the actions that each will take: if they cannot agree, the authority must produce a record of the reasons for the disagreement and specify what steps the authority will take and those that it expects of the applicant.

c) Section 4 amended HA 1996, s 195 so that, where an applicant is threatened with homelessness and eligible for assistance, the authority will have to take reasonable steps to help the applicant secure that accommodation does not cease to be available for their occupation, having regard to the assessment under HA 1996, s 189A.

---

163 A National Audit Office (NAO) report, *Homelessness* (September 2017; www.nao.org.uk/ report/homelessness/) was also critical: it concluded that the DCLG did not achieve value for money in the administration of homelessness policy, noting that it costs the public sector in excess of £1bn per annum and concluding that the rise in the number of homeless people and households had been driven, at least in part, by restrictions and caps on welfare benefit payments, the effect of which changes the government had taken no steps to evaluate; the DCLG had provided only a 'light touch' approach to working with local authorities with which the report found it 'difficult to understand why the Department' had 'persisted . . . in the face of such a visibly growing problem'.

164 CLG Select Committee, Homelessness, HC40, August 2016.

165 Homelessness Reduction Act 2017 (Commencement and Transitional and Savings Provisions) Regulations 2018, SI 2018/167 reg 3, only applicable to applications made and reviews sought on or after that date – see reg 4.

166 Ie, notice of seeking possession in respect of an assured shorthold tenancy.

d) Section 5 introduced new HA 1996, s 189B, requiring the authority to take reasonable steps for 56 days to help the applicant try to secure suitable accommodation for a minimum period of six months, regardless of whether the applicant is in priority need or intentionally homeless, known as the relief duty.

1.130 The government initially indicated that it would make £35.4 million available in 2017/18 and £12.1 million in 2018/19 to assist with the likely costs authorities will incur in respect of the new Act, but that no funding would be provided beyond that.[167] This was subsequently increased to £61 million over the same period.[168] None of these figures takes into account any increase in legal costs[169] flowing from additional judicial review claims or HA 1996, s 204 appeals. There was much concern as to whether this would be sufficient.[170]

1.131 As to how effectively the Act would be implemented, while well-intentioned, there was room– bearing in mind the tension recognised in the Welsh review between prevention techniques and statutory housing duties – to fear that the Act would institutionalise gate-keeping.[171]

1.132 Indeed, a report in 2020 by the Local Government and Social Care Ombudsman[172] (LGO) based on the first 50 investigations into complaints about the operation of the Act identified that:

a) some councils took too long to accept that the relief duty had arisen, and there were delays in producing a personal housing plan, meaning that opportunities to prevent or relieve homelessness were missed; in some cases, authorities were not producing plans at all or keeping them under review and updated;

---

167 House of Commons Written Statement 17 January 2017 (HCWS418). There was also the possibility of the government making 'available a small amount of further funding for local authorities in high-pressure areas to manage the transition to the new duties'.
168 House of Commons Written Statement, 15 March 2017 (HCWS538).
169 Whether to authorities or to the legal aid fund.
170 In submissions to the CLG Select Committee, Bedford BC suggested that the new duties would add c£1m pa to its homelessness costs; Kensington and Chelsea RLBC put its figure at closer to £3.5m and Redbridge BC considered that its costs (including additional staffing) could eventually reach £4.3m. The Association of Housing Advice Services put the costs in London alone at £161m. On 12 December 2017, Clive Betts MP, Chair of the Communities and Local Government Committee, wrote to the government to express concern that, in London alone, there was a funding gap of £67m pa.
171 *Evaluation of the homelessness prevention trailblazers*, Ministry of Housing, Communities and Local Government (MHCLG), November 2018 (www.gov.uk/government/publications/homelessness-prevention-trailblazers-evaluation), across 30 'trailblazer' local authorities in connection with the HRA 2017 concludes that the added emphasis on prevention of homelessness requires 'a more flexible, helping mindset than that of a conventional Housing Officer' (Executive Summary, p3); prevention was found to work best when authorities proactively seek to identify families at risk of homelessness, and it was considered that authorities should develop better links with, in particular, charitable organisations.
172 *Home truths: how well are councils implementing the Homelessness Reduction Act?*, LGO, July 2020 (www.lgo.org.uk/assets/attach/5853/FR-Home-Truths-July-2020.pdf).

b) authorities were telling people that they were owed the wrong duty; authorities were sometimes failing to notify applicants when a duty had ended; and

c) the LGO still 'regularly see problems with councils "gatekeeping" access to homelessness services'.[173]

BREXIT AND BEYOND

Brexit

1.133 Immigration as a policy element in homelessness law has been described in a number of places, above. Throughout, however, the UK was a member of what became the European Union (EU). It led to an influx of workers from numerous EU countries, many of them – particularly from the countries which joined in 2004[174] – in low-paying work which not uncommonly meant recourse to social housing, from which, exercising EU rights, they were not excluded. As, over the period of homelessness law, there have been long periods of what may be called 'housing austerity',[175] this ultimately translated into one of the features which are commonly identified with the success of the Brexit campaign in 2016, ie, that these workers were taking social housing away from the indigenous population.

1.134 It was, however, highly unlikely that departure from the EU would mean any noticeable increase in the amount and the availability of social housing, at least in the near future, as:

a) all those EU nationals who were lawfully present in the UK before 1 January 2021 and who had been lawfully present for at least five years were entitled to 'settled status' under Appendix EU of the Immigration Rules and thus entitled to access homelessness support and social housing allocations on the same basis as a UK national;

b) those EU nationals who were lawfully present in the UK on 1 January 2021 but who had not yet been so present for at least five years were entitled to 'pre-settled status' (which could be upgraded to settled status once the five-year qualification period had been met); while pre-settled status did not, of itself, entitle someone to homelessness support or to an allocation of social housing, a person with pre-settled status who was exercising a relevant EU treaty right before 1 January 2021 (eg, a worker)

---

173 *Home truths* p20. See below, paras **7.171–7.175**.
174 Including Poland, Estonia, Latvia, Czech Republic, Hungary, Lithuania, Slovakia and Slovenia.
175 Ie, a paucity of social housing, see conclusion below.

remained eligible for both homelessness support and an allocation of social housing;[176] and

c)   Brexit did not provide a legal basis for terminating a tenancy which had previously been granted, nor for terminating an ongoing application under the homelessness legislation, with the result that an EU national who held existing accrued rights (eg, a secure tenancy, with the right to buy, succession rights etc, or an accepted homelessness duty) retained those rights in the same way as a UK national.

1.135   Put briefly, Brexit was unlikely to prove to be any kind of panacea to continuing high levels of homelessness and, thus far, has not done so.

Beyond

1.136   There has been a number of developments which have impacted on homelessness law, although none so direct as the 2017 Act; nonetheless, three statutory provisions are sufficiently significant to merit a mention.

(i)   The Armed Forces Act 2021 added sections (343AA – England, 343AB – Wales) to the Armed Forces Act 2006, imposing a requirement that authorities under Parts 6 and 7 must have regard to the obligations of, and sacrifices made by, the armed forces, the desirability of removing disadvantages arising for service people from membership, or former membership, of the armed forces, and that special provision for service people may be justified by the effects on them of membership, or former membership, of the armed forces.

(ii)   The Domestic Abuse Act 2021, with its extensive definition of abuse, imposed obligations under homelessness law and otherwise aimed at behaviour which has played a significant role in the generation of homelessness and much homelessness caselaw focused on it.

(iii) The Homelessness (Priority Need and Intentionality) (Wales) Regulations 2022, SI 2022/1069, reg 2 added a category of the 'street' homeless to those in priority need in Wales.

RENTERS (REFORM) BILL

The Renters (Reform) Bill was introduced into Parliament in May 2023 and is currently proceeding through it. It will abolish the assured shorthold tenancy, and fixed term assured tenancies, replacing both with periodic assured tenancies, subject to an enlarged set of grounds for possession, one of

---

176 As at 30 November 2020, some 4.28m people had obtained settled or pre-settled status; of these, 2.3m had been granted settled status ('EU Settlement Scheme statistics', Home Office; www.gov.uk/government/collections/eu-settlement-scheme-statistics).

which will be applicable if the tenancy was granted in pursuance of a housing authority's duty under Housing Act 1996, s 193 but is no longer required for that purpose. The Bill does not make significant changes to homelessness law itself, but – leaving aside minor consequential amendments – has its primary impact on the way duties are discharged. As usual in homelessness law, it is likely that the current law will need to be considered alongside any changes once the Bill becomes an Act and comes into force, for some considerable time to come. Nor is it not known as the time of writing either when the abolition will apply to new tenancies or – under the Bill's provisions for an 'extended application date' – to those in existence at the date the Bill becomes law. So far as affects homelessness and allocations, the Bill is fully addressed in its current form (see Preface, p vii) throughout the text, in grey 'boxes' (like this), in order to distinguish its provisions and their meaning from the current position. Reference is not made at this stage to clause numbers of the Bill, as these are usually highly susceptible to change. Presently, the government intends to provide 'at least six months' notice prior of the new tenancy system taking effect,' during which time it will amend the Code of Guidance accordingly (see 'Consequential changes to the homelessness legislation: government response to consultation' DLUHC, May 2023).

1.137 As for caselaw, the approach of the courts in the last few years has – until recently – not been unsympathetic to the homeless, save in cases where the merits might be thought to have been weak. It is often difficult to assess the full implications of a case until it has been tested over time, although there are exceptions when the 'message' is unequivocal. The Supreme Court decision in *Imam*,[177] handed down on the eve of submission of this edition to its publishers, does not *quite* fall into the 'unequivocal' category, not least – indeed primarily – because the facts and the points of law conceded and argued before the Court did not allow anything more, but offers local authorities a blueprint for avoiding mandatory orders when in breach of their s193(2) duties,[178] and invites lower courts to reconsider what was widely thought to be a settled proposition that the duty itself is immediate, non-deferrable and unqualified.[179]

1.138 One major event to impact on homelessness was the coronavirus pandemic which led to the 'Everyone In' initiative to bring rough sleepers off the streets, raising many to ask why, if rough sleeping could be ended during such an emergency, it could not be achieved at other times. Both the English and the Welsh governments continue to seek to end rough sleeping:[180] neither has yet

177 *R (Imam) v Croydon LBC* [2023] UKSC 45; [2024] HLR 6.
178 See paras **10.192–10.196**.
179 See para **8.145**.
180 In England, see *Ending Rough Sleeping for Good* DLUHC September 2022; in Wales, *Ending homelessness: a high level action plan* Welsh Government October 2021.

made a serious dent in the problem.[181] Notwithstanding the failure of the Law Commission in *Hate Crime Laws: Final Report*, to recommend that homelessness be added as a status akin to protected classes,[182] and notwithstanding views and evidence which made a 'strong case in principle' in favour, there is, however, some movement at least to abolish the archaic and discriminatory vagrancy laws.[183]

CONCLUSION

1.139 Homelessness law requires local authorities to secure housing for qualifying applicants, but it does not require them to provide that housing: beyond their general duty to consider the housing conditions and needs of their areas,[184] and the power to provide housing,[185] no one is obliged to do so, leaving homelessness legislation buffeted by the vagaries of housing supply and demand, public and private. It is this fundamental mismatch between the objective of eliminating homelessness and the lack of resources with which to do so that accounts for the chronic failure of the legislation to achieve its aims.

1.140 In particular, there has been a substantial decline in the provision of social housing. In 1977, just over 5 million properties were rented from local authorities in England. This has dropped every year since 1980 and, in 2022 stood

---

181 The principal conclusion of the DLUCH report *Flow of Rough Sleeping – Final Report*, January 2024, that the primary causes of rough sleeping are 'Crisis Events' such as loss of employment, relationship breakdown and mental or physical health problems is hardly surprising; it does also conclude that there is low awareness of local authority housing support services and that many rough sleepers are distrustful of the local authority but, again, this is not news and does not take the matter forward.

182 Law Com No.402. With the passage of time, this increasingly looks like a missed opportunity. In December 2023, the Office for National Statistics published an analysis of the characteristics of the homeless population in England and Wales and concluded that both non-white and disabled persons were significantly over-represented in the homeless population as against the proportion of the general public (*People experiencing homelessness, England and Wales: Census 2021*, ONS, 2023; https://www.ons.gov.uk/peoplepopulationandcommunity/housing/articles/peopleexperiencinghomelessnessenglandandwales/census2021).

183 Abolition is provided for by Police, Crime, Sentencing and Courts Act 2022, s 81. That provision has not yet been brought into force and government policy is not to do so until 'appropriate replacement legislation' is in place. See *Repeal of the Vagrancy Act 1824: Police, Crime, Sentencing and Courts Act 2022*, Home Office, August 2022 and *Review of the Vagrancy Act: consultation on effective replacement* MoJ, Home Office, DLUHC April 2022. Instead, Levelling Up and Regeneration Act 2023, s 242 will, when it is brought into force, require the Secretary of State to report to Parliament on the impact of the enforcement of the 1824 Act; the duty arises only once, and ceases to apply once the 1824 Act is repealed.

184 Housing Act 1985, s 8.

185 Housing Act 1985, s 9.

at a low of 1.576 million.[186] Housing associations have filled some of this gap: during the same period, the number of properties rented from private registered providers of social housing (PRPs) has risen from 300,000 to 2.542 million,[187] a very long way from all of which has been let on tenancies at a social rent, and which in any event still means there has been a reduction of almost 1 million properties available to rent from social landlords since 1977, notwithstanding a growth in England's population from 46.64 million in 1977 to 56.54 million in 2021.[188]

1.141   The consequences can be seen in the data on households in temporary accommodation (TA). In the fourth quarter of 1988 (the earliest recorded data point), there were 53,790 households in TA in England.[189] That steadily increased to a peak of 101,020 in the third quarter of 2005 before dropping to 48,920 by the fourth quarter of 2011, a decline of less than 5,000 over 23 years of operation of the legislation. Subsequently, however, the figure has risen again and stood at 109,000 in the third quarter of 2023,[190] which means that (against 53,790) it has risen by 55,210 during the last 35 years of operation of the legislation, ie it has more than doubled in that period.

1.142   The same trend can be seen in the rough sleeping statistics. These are available for the period 2010/22. They show 1,768 rough sleepers in 2010 (in England), rising year-on-year to a high of 4,751 in 2017, before dropping to 2,688 in 2020 during the pandemic when the Everyone In programme took effect, rising again to 3,898 in 2023.[191] Nonetheless, when the National Audit Office (NAO) carried out a provisional analysis of 'Everyone In',[192] it concluded that 33,139 people had been helped to find accommodation as at the end of November

---

186 Live Table 104 ('Statistical data set: Live tables on dwelling stock (including vacants)', DLUHC; www.gov.uk/government/statistical-data-sets/live-tables-on-dwelling-stock-including-vacants). There has been a year-on-year decline since 1980.

187 Live Table 104, DLUHC.

188 https://www.ons.gov.uk/peoplepopulationandcommunity/populationandmigration/populationestimates/timeseries/enpop/pop accessed 29 July 2023.

189 Separate statistics for Wales did not start until April 2014 with commencement of the H(W) A 2014; the statistics in this and the following two paragraphs are accordingly confined to England. On 30 September 2023, there were 11,273 people in temporary accommodation, 3,403 of whom were children, in Wales, while on 31 October 2023, there were an estimated 160 rough sleepers in Wales: Homelessness Statistics, Welsh government, January 2024.

190 Live Table TA1 ('Statistical data set: Live tables on homelessness', DLUHC; www.gov.uk/government/statistical-data-sets/live-tables-on-homelessness).

191 'Official Statistics: Rough sleeping snapshot in England: autumn 2023', DLUHC, February 2024 (https://www.gov.uk/government/statistics/rough-sleeping-snapshot-in-england-autumn-2023/rough-sleeping-snapshot-in-england-autumn-2023), but note para 6.2 of the statistical release on the limitations to the data. The absence of statistics for Wales is as a result of the decision to suspend the national rough sleeper count from 2020-23 due to the pandemic; as at February 2024, the Welsh Government is considering whether to reintroduce the national count (see https://www.gov.wales/homelessness-accommodation-provision-and-rough-sleeping-december-2023).

192 *Investigation into the housing of rough sleepers during the COVID-19 pandemic*, NAO and MHCLG, January 2021 (www.nao.org.uk/report/the-housing-of-rough-sleepers-during-the-covid19-pandemic/).

2020, ie, in less than a full year – the figures are impossible to reconcile, but it is also hard to think that the latter could be an illusory exaggeration.[193]

1.143 Since December 2020, the Office for National Statistics (ONS) has been publishing experimental statistical analysis of the number of deaths of homeless people in England and Wales, defining the homeless as 'mainly [to] include people sleeping rough or using emergency accommodation such as homeless shelters and direct access hostels'.[194] In 2021, there were an estimated 741 deaths of homeless people in England and Wales against a rough sleeper population of 2,443.[195] This represented a 7.7% increase on 2020 which was itself a 7.2% increase on 2019.[196]

1.144 If homelessness as statutorily defined (to include those in inadequate accommodation) is to be ended, indeed if rough sleeping alone is to be ended, there is a long way to go.[197] Without an increase in the amount of social housing,[198] neither will be achieved in numbers sufficient for the legislation to rest on its laurels.

---

193 While still not accounting for the difference, in November 2023, the DLUHC published a new assessment of rough sleeping, based on a new methodology. That assessment suggested that there were 8,442 rough sleepers in England in September 2023 *(Ending Rough Sleeping Data Framework*, September 2023; https://www.gov.uk/government/publications/ending-rough-sleeping-data-framework-september-2023/ending-rough-sleeping-data-framework-september-2023),

194 'Deaths of homeless people in England and Wales: Statistical bulletins', https://www.ons.gov.uk/peoplepopulationandcommunity/birthsdeathsandmarriages/deaths/bulletins/deathsofhomelesspeopleinenglandandwales/2021registrations).

195 https://www.gov.uk/government/statistics/rough-sleeping-snapshot-in-england-autumn-2022/rough-sleeping-snapshot-in-england-autumn-2022

196 See previous edition of this book.

197 A point recognised by the Welsh government in the October 2023 consultation paper *"Ending Homelessness"*. The Welsh government proposes abolishing both the priority need test and the intentional homelessness test and imposing a new duty on the public sector to refer persons at risk of homelessness to the local authority. As welcome as such reforms would be, they will only be effective if accompanied by a corresponding increase in the supply of social housing.

198 Some attention appears to be being paid to ways of reducing the number of people eligible for social housing under Part 6, Housing Act 1996 (see Chapter 9): see *Consultation on reforms to social housing allocation*, DLUHC, January 2024, proposing a ten-year UK minimum residence qualification for all applicants except those in resettlement schemes, which would exclude those qualifying under refugee categories (see paras **A.184-A.194**) for that period, a two-year connection with an authority, subject to exceptions, eg victims of domestic abuse, a maximum income (unspecified) test, disqualification for those with an unspent conviction for anti-social behaviour or terrorism offences, along with those subject to certain civil sanctions, eg ASBIs, and a mandatory period of exclusion for those who knowingly or recklessly made a false statement when applying for social housing. The principal effect of these proposals if implemented, however, would seem to be an increase in the number of people who are homeless and, as such, entitled to assistance under Part 7, 1996 Act, with a self-evident cost consequence.

CHAPTER 2

Homelessness

- Location
- Permanence
- Physical conditions
- Overcrowding
- Legal conditions
- Employment
- Type of accommodation
- Other considerations
- Financial considerations
- Affordability

2.147 Threatened with homelessness

INTRODUCTION

2.1 This chapter addresses the statutory definitions of 'homelessness' and of being 'threatened with homelessness'; unless an applicant for accommodation qualifies under one or other definition, a local authority will owe no duties to them under Part 7, Housing Act (HA) 1996; they may, however, be able to apply for an allocation under Part 6, HA 1996 (Chapter 9) and duties may be owed under other legislation – see Chapter 11.

2.2 If a person does appear to qualify under Part 7, their rights will be determined by whether or not they are eligible for assistance (see Annex: Immigration Eligibility), whether they have a priority need for accommodation (Chapter 3), and whether or not they have become homeless or threatened with homelessness intentionally (Chapter 4); if there is a question over which local authority has responsibility for them, it will be resolved under the local connection provisions (Chapter 5). Protection of an applicant's property is considered in Chapter 6. The process of decision-making under Part 7 is discussed in Chapter 7; all Part 7 duties are considered in Chapter 8. Legal challenge to an authority's decisions is considered in Chapter 10.

2.3 'Homelessness' is defined by Housing Act (HA) 1996, s 175 and Housing (Wales) Act (H(W)A) 2014, s 55 as:

a) accommodation, which is

b) available for the applicant's occupation, to which

c) there are rights of occupation (subsection (1)),

d) entry to or use of which is not restricted (subsection (2)), and which

e) it is reasonable for the applicant to continue to occupy (subsection (3)).[1]

---

1 See *Nipa Begum v Tower Hamlets LBC* (1999) 32 HLR 445, CA, for a discussion of the interaction of these different subsections.

2.4   It is important to stress from the outset that there is no requirement that the accommodation be suitable, but there is an obvious practical relationship between whether it is reasonable to occupy accommodation and whether that accommodation is suitable: that relationship is recognised in law and is discussed at paras **2.72–2.76**.

2.5   The same terms defining homelessness (para **2.3**) also apply to:

f)   what is meant by being threatened with homelessness (subsection (4)).

2.6   When determining whether someone is homeless, eg, whether it is reasonable for an applicant to continue to occupy accommodation, a local authority must have regard to:

> '(a)   the unique obligations of, and sacrifices made by, the armed forces,
>
> (b)   the principle that it is desirable to remove disadvantages arising for service people from membership, or former membership, of the armed forces, and
>
> (c)   the principle that special provision for service people may be justified by the effects on such people of membership, or former membership, of the armed forces'.[2]

ACCOMMODATION

Location

2.7   Under HA 1985, only accommodation in England, Wales or Scotland was to be taken into account. This had not been stated explicitly in the original legislation – the Housing (Homeless Persons) Act 1977 – but had been accepted, albeit obiter, in *Streeting*[3] and was expressly enacted in HA 1985.

2.8   As departure from accommodation abroad can, however, qualify as intentional homelessness,[4] this does not mean that accommodation abroad is irrelevant: HA 1996, s 175(1) and H(W)A 2014, s 55(1) now refer to accommodation in the UK 'or elsewhere'.[5]

---

2   Armed Forces Act 2006, ss 343AA (England) and 343AB (Wales), added by Armed Forces Act 2021, s 8(3).
3   *R v Hillingdon LBC ex p Streeting* [1980] 1 WLR 1425, CA.
4   See *de Falco, Silvestri v Crawley BC* [1980] QB 460, CA, and other cases considered at paras **4.148–4.150**.
5   See, eg, *Nipa Begum v Tower Hamlets LBC* (1999) 32 HLR 445, CA, where the accommodation in question was situated in Bangladesh.

Nature

2.9   The term 'accommodation' has proved one of the most controversial under the homelessness legislation, not so much as between applicant and authority, but between, on the one hand, the lower courts and the House of Lords, and, on the other, the House of Lords and Parliament.

Settled accommodation

2.10   Between 1977 and 1986, there was a growing tendency on the part of the courts – High Court and Court of Appeal – to equiparate a want of accommodation with accommodation of such poor quality that it could be quit without a finding of intentionality. In this context, a distinction was drawn for both purposes (and arguably for the purpose of defining the duties owed by authorities) between 'settled' and 'unsettled' accommodation.

2.11   Both applications of this approach were firmly rejected by the House of Lords, first in *Puhlhofer*,[6] and, later, in *Awua*.[7] The first of these led to further legislation in the Housing and Planning Act 1986 reversing the view of the House of Lords, and, to an extent, also under HA 1996, Part 7 itself.

2.12   In the second of these cases,[8] the House of Lords held that the only gloss on the word 'accommodation' which can properly be imported, other than pursuant to the statute itself (ie, availability and reasonableness to continue in occupation),[9] is that it must mean 'a place which can fairly be described as accommodation'.[10]

Non-qualifying accommodation

2.13   As an example of shelter which would have failed this test, Lord Brightman in *Puhlhofer* instanced Diogenes' tub.

2.14   In *Awua*, the modern equivalent was said to be the night shelter in *R v Waveney DC ex p Bowers*,[11] in which the applicant could have a bed if one was available but where he could not remain by day so that he had to walk the streets.[12]

---

6   *R v Hillingdon LBC ex p Puhlhofer* [1986] AC 484, (1986) 18 HLR 158, HL.
7   *R v Brent LBC ex p Awua* [1996] AC 55, (1995) 27 HLR 453, HL.
8   *Awua*, above.
9   See paras **2.19–2.41** and **2.72–2.146**.
10 *R v Brent LBC ex p Awua*, above, per Lord Hoffmann at 461.
11 (1982) *Times* 25 May, QBD. Not cross-appealed on this point – see further [1983] QB 238, (1983) 4 HLR 118, CA.
12 *R v Brent LBC ex p Awua*, above, at 459.

2.15 In *Sidhu*,[13] it was held that a women's refuge was not accommodation: a woman who left her violent partner and found temporary shelter in a refuge was still homeless while residing there.[14]

2.16 In *Ali* and *Moran*,[15] however, the House of Lords concluded that *Sidhu* could probably not survive the decisions in *Puhlhofer*[16] and *Awua*[17] as a theoretical proposition, although the effect of the decision was preserved by reference to HA 1996, ss 175(3) and 177, ie, it would not normally be reasonable to continue to occupy accommodation in a women's refuge.[18] (The House of Lords declined to comment on whether a prison cell or a hospital ward could amount to accommodation).[19]

2.17 An applicant who occupies interim accommodation provided to them pending enquiries, review or appeal under HA 1996, ss 188 or 204(4) is nevertheless homeless for the purpose of s 175(1), because to find otherwise would create the absurd result that a homeless person who is temporarily accommodated would not be entitled to benefit from Part 7.[20]

2.18 Reference may also be made to *Miles*,[21] in which it was held that accommodation within the definition of homelessness means 'habitable'. This decision was followed by the majority in the Court of Appeal in *Puhlhofer*,[22] which was upheld by the House of Lords without reference to *Miles*; nor was the case mentioned in *Awua*.

13 *R v Ealing LBC ex p Sidhu* (1982) 2 HLR 45, QBD.
14 *Sidhu* followed a county court decision, *Williams v Cynon Valley Council*, January 1980 *LAG Bulletin* 16, CC. In addition to *Bowers* (see para **2.14**), other cases to consider the meaning of accommodation within the definition of homelessness before *Puhlhofer* and *Awua* were: *Parr v Wyre BC* (1982) 2 HLR 71, CA; *R v South Herefordshire DC ex p Miles* (1985) 17 HLR 82; *R v Preseli DC ex p Fisher* (1985) 17 HLR 147, QBD; and *R v Dinefwr BC ex p Marshall* (1985) 17 HLR 310, QBD.
15 *Birmingham City Council v Ali; Moran v Manchester City Council (Secretary of State for Communities and Local Government and another intervening)* [2009] UKHL 36, [2009] 1 WLR 1506 at [56].
16 *R v Hillingdon LBC ex p Puhlhofer* [1986] AC 484, (1986) 18 HLR 158, HL.
17 *R v Brent LBC ex p Awua* [1996] AC 55, (1995) 27 HLR 453, HL.
18 See para **2.77**.
19 *Stewart v Lambeth LBC* [2002] HLR 747; *R (B) v Southwark LBC* [2004] HLR 40.
20 *R (Alam) v Tower Hamlets LBC* [2009] EWHC 44 (Admin), [2009] JHL D47. Approved by the House of Lords in *Ali* at [54]. See, to like effect, H(W)A 2014, ss 68(1), 69(11) and 88(5). Likewise, where an authority has concluded that a person is owed the full housing duty under HA 1996, s 193(2), but has not identified any specific property in which they could live, there is therefore no accommodation available for their occupation: *Johnston v Westminster City Council* [2015] EWCA Civ 554, [2015] HLR 35.
21 *City of Gloucester v Miles* (1985) 17 HLR 292, CA.
22 See (1985) 17 HLR 588.

ACCOMMODATION AVAILABLE FOR OCCUPATION

Preconditions

2.19   The requirement that accommodation is 'available for occupation' requires consideration of a number of elements:

   a)   whether accommodation allows occupation 'together with' others;

   b)   practical accessibility; and

   c)   for whom the accommodation must be available.

2.20   The requirement of availability means that the accommodation must be available to occupy 'together with' other members of the applicant's household: HA 1996, s 176 and H(W)A 2014, s 56. This can be satisfied by a single unit of accommodation in which a family can live together, but may also be satisfied by two units of accommodation if they are so located as to enable the family to live 'together' in practical terms; it does not require shared living space.[23]

2.21   To be practically accessible and accordingly available to an applicant, it must be possible for the applicant physically to access the accommodation, a question which includes whether an applicant can afford to return to accommodation overseas which is otherwise available.[24]

2.22   Accommodation will not be available if the applicant is not legally entitled to live in the country in which the accommodation is situated.

Accommodation for whom?

2.23   By HA 1996, s 176 and H(W)A 2014, s 56, accommodation is only 'available' if it is available for the applicant together[25] with:

   a)   any person who usually resides with the applicant as a member of his or her family; or

   b)   any other person who might reasonably be expected to do so.

---

23   *Sharif v Camden LBC* [2013] UKSC 10, [2013] HLR 16.
24   See *Nipa Begum v Tower Hamlets LBC* (1999) 32 HLR 445, CA. Although the authority had failed to consider this issue in the case, the Court of Appeal refused to quash the decision since the applicant had not raised the issue, and the authority was accordingly not required to investigate the matter (see para **7.131**).
25   Cf para **2.20**.

Immigration

2.24   HA 1996, s 185(4) formerly[26] required local housing authorities in England and Wales to disregard household members (including dependent children) who were ineligible[27] for housing assistance when considering whether an eligible housing applicant was homeless. This provision was amended[28] so that it applies only to an eligible applicant who is themselves a person subject to immigration control[29] – for example, those granted refugee status,[30] indefinite leave to remain[31] or humanitarian protection.[32] It was further amended with effect from 1 January 2021 to reflect the changes arising out of Brexit.[33] Accordingly, when deciding whether an applicant who is a person subject to immigration control (excluding for this purpose a European Economic Area (EEA) or Swiss national)[34] and who is eligible for assistance, is homeless, a local authority must continue to disregard any dependants or other household members who are ineligible for assistance.

2.25   The effect is that HA 1996, s 185(4) no longer applies to eligible[35] applicants who are not subject to immigration control[36] – for example, a British citizen,[37] a Commonwealth citizen with a right of abode in the UK[38] or an EEA or Swiss national with a right to reside in the UK where the EEA or Swiss national was resident in the UK before 1 January 2021.[39] This group of eligible applicants will be able to rely on ineligible household members, known as 'restricted persons', to establish homelessness.[40]

2.26   If, however, the authority can be satisfied that the applicant is homeless only by taking into account the restricted person, the application is known as a 'restricted case'.[41] In these circumstances, the authority must, so far as reasonably

---

26   In respect of all applications for accommodation or assistance in obtaining accommodation within the meaning of HA 1996, s 183, made before 2 March 2009.
27   See Annex: Immigration Eligibility.
28   By Housing and Regeneration Act 2008, s 314 and Sch 15, Part 1, in respect of all applications for accommodation or assistance in obtaining accommodation within the meaning of HA 1996, s 183, made on or after 2 March 2009.
29   See para **A.14**.
30   See paras **A.136–A.143**.
31   See paras **A.144–A.146**.
32   See paras **A.151–A.154**.
33   Immigration and Social Security Co-ordination (EU Withdrawal) Act 2020 (Consequential, Saving, Transitional and Transitory Provisions) (EU Exit) Regulations 2020, SI 2020/1309.
34   See para **2.25**.
35   See Annex: Immigration Eligibility.
36   See paras **A.15–A.18**.
37   See para **A.21**.
38   See para **A.22**.
39   *Homelessness code of guidance for local authorities*, para 7.32 (Ministry of Housing, Communities and Local Government (MHCLG), February 2018, updated April 2021; www.gov.uk/guidance/homelessness-code-of-guidance-for-local-authorities).
40   HA 1996, s 184(7): someone who is not eligible for assistance under Part 7, who is subject to immigration control and who either does not have leave to enter or remain in the UK or who has leave subject to a condition of no recourse to public funds.
41   HA 1996, s 193(3B).

practical, bring any HA 1996, s 193(2) duty to an end by arranging for an offer of an assured shorthold tenancy to be made to the applicant by a private landlord.[42] This is known as a 'private rented sector offer'.[43]

RENTERS (REFORM) BILL

Once the Bill becomes law and is brought into full relevant force and subject to any transitional provisions, the offer will be of an assured, rather than assured shorthold, tenancy.

2.27 In Wales, the substantive position is the same, as the provisions of HA 1996, ss 185 and 186 are deemed to apply to the H(W)A 2014.[44] It follows that, as in England, a duty owed to a restricted person must, so far as is reasonably practicable, be brought to an end by securing an offer of accommodation from a private sector landlord.[45]

Family

2.28 'Member of the family' is not defined. Both the English and Welsh Codes of Guidance say that the expression will 'include those with close blood or marital relationships and cohabiting partners'.[46]

2.29 Both Codes also suggest that 'any other person' (who normally resides with the applicant as a member of the family) might cover a companion for an elderly or disabled person, or children being fostered by the applicant or by a member of their family.[47]

2.30 The English and Welsh Codes conclude:

'Persons who would normally live with the applicant but who are unable to do so because there is no accommodation in which they can all live together should be included in the assessment.'[48]

---

42 HA 1996, s 193(7AD). See further paras **8.272–8.281**.
43 HA 1996, s 193(7AC). From 9 November 2012, when Localism Act (LA) 2011, s 148 came into force in England, a new offer by an English authority has been known as a 'private rented sector offer': Localism Act 2011 (Commencement No 2 and Transitional Provisions) (England) Order 2012, SI 2012/2599 art 2.
44 H(W)A 2014, Sch 2 para 2.
45 H(W)A 2014, s 76.
46 English Homelessness Code para 6.7; Welsh Code paras 8.6–8.8; the Welsh Code goes on to say that the expression will include 'same sex partners, adopted or foster children and legal guardianship'.
47 English Homelessness Code para 6.8; Welsh Code paras 8.6–8.8.
48 English Homelessness Code para 6.9; Welsh Code para 8.8.

2.31   This approach echoes the decision of the House of Lords in *Islam*,[49] where the applicant lost his right to a shared room as a result of the arrival of his wife and four children from Bangladesh. A finding of intentionality was quashed by the House of Lords on the basis that what had been lost was not accommodation 'available for his occupation', meaning that of the applicant *and* his family.[50]

2.32   Accordingly, a family which has never enjoyed accommodation in which there were rights of occupation for all of its members will at all times have been homeless. For example, a couple without a home of their own, each still living with their parents, will be able to assert an effective right to assistance under Part 7 or Part 2 as soon as a priority need is acquired. An authority wishing to resist the claim cannot resort to intentional homelessness based on the pregnancy itself, as this is precluded by *Islam*.[51]

2.33   Note, however, that an unborn child will not be a person with whom the applicant would be expected to reside. Accordingly, the future housing needs of the unborn child need not be considered by the authority when determining homelessness,[52] save to the extent to which it had otherwise rendered the mother's accommodation unavailable in her own right.

2.34   That does not make the pregnancy irrelevant. In *Rouf*,[53] it was held that an authority could not jump to the conclusion that accommodation would continue to be available to an applicant with an increasing family. See also *Ali*,[54] in which the court found the proposition that a single, small room was 'available' for a large family (applicant, wife and five children) 'quite extraordinary'.

2.35   In other cases, hopelessly inadequate accommodation has been held not to be accommodation which it was reasonable to continue to occupy.[55]

2.36   A member of the family who usually resides with the applicant need not also be shown to do so reasonably.[56] On the other hand, where children who were not reasonably to be expected to reside with the applicant came to live with him in a single room, he was (to that point) occupying accommodation that was

---

49   *Re Islam* [1983] 1 AC 688, (1981) 1 HLR 107, HL.
50   The argument in the Court of Appeal that Mr Islam had made the accommodation unavailable by bringing his family over was dismissed as 'circular . . . because that lack is the very circumstance which section 16 [of the Housing (Homeless Persons) Act 1977, subsequently HA 1985, s 75, now HA 1996, s 176] and the Act are designed to relieve'.
51   In *R v Eastleigh BC ex p Beattie (No 1)* (1983) 10 HLR 134, QBD, the court rejected out of hand a suggestion that pregnancy causing accommodation to cease to be reasonable to occupy could amount to intentionality.
52   See *R v Newham LBC ex p Dada* (1995) 27 HLR 502, CA.
53   *R v Tower Hamlets LBC ex p Rouf* (1989) 21 HLR 294, QBD.
54   *R v Westminster City Council ex p Ali* (1984) 11 HLR 83, QBD.
55   See paras **2.104–2.110**.
56   Compare *R v Hillingdon Homeless Persons Panel ex p Islam* (1980) *Times*, February 10, QBD, not cross-appealed on the proposition, as it relates to priority need.

available for him, so that he could be held intentionally homeless for allowing them to come and live with him (which made the accommodation unavailable).[57]

Others

2.37 The question of who is reasonably to be expected to reside with an applicant is a matter for the authority, challengeable on conventional grounds of public law,[58] rather than a question of fact which a court can decide for itself: see *Ly*.[59] Cases turn quite largely on their own facts.

2.38 In *Carr*,[60] it was held that the authority had erred in law in failing to consider whether the applicant's boyfriend – the father of her child – was a person with whom she might reasonably be expected to reside. The authority had wrongly reached its decision solely on the basis that they had not lived together at the applicant's last settled accommodation.

2.39 In *Okuneye*,[61] however, the fact that two people were intending or expecting to reside together did not mean that – when each departed from their separate accommodation – they were necessarily reasonably to be expected to reside together at that time. The authority was accordingly entitled to conclude that each had become homeless intentionally for ceasing to occupy available accommodation.

2.40 In *Ryder*,[62] the authority approached the question of whether a carer could reasonably be expected to reside with a disabled applicant by reference to whether the applicant was eligible for Disability Living Allowance. As the test for such an allowance was more stringent – and different – from what is now HA 1996, s 176 (H(W)A 2014, s 56), the decision was quashed. Similarly, the authority in *Tonnicodi*[63] was wrong to apply the test whether the applicant needed a live-in carer rather than whether the carer was a person who might reasonably be expected to reside with the applicant.

2.41 In *Curtis*,[64] the applicant was occupying her former matrimonial home under a separation agreement which contained a cohabitation clause to the effect that if she cohabited or remarried the property would be sold. The applicant started to cohabit and her husband enforced the power of sale. The authority found the applicant to be homeless intentionally, a decision that was quashed

57 *Oxford City Council v Bull* [2011] EWCA Civ 609, [2011] HLR 35.
58 See Chapter 10.
59 *R v Lambeth LBC ex p Ly* (1987) 19 HLR 51, QBD. Compare *R v Newham LBC ex p Khan and Hussain* (2001) 33 HLR 29, QBD, where a decision that a grandmother, her two daughters and their respective husbands and children did not usually reside together was quashed as *Wednesbury* unreasonable (as to which, see paras **10.23–24, 10.63**).
60 *R v Peterborough City Council ex p Carr* (1990) 22 HLR 206, CA.
61 *R v Barking and Dagenham LBC ex p Okuneye* (1995) 28 HLR 174, QBD.
62 *R v Southwark LBC ex p Ryder* (1996) 28 HLR 56, QBD.
63 *R v Hackney LBC ex p Tonnicodi* (1998) 30 HLR 916, QBD.
64 *R v Wimborne DC ex p Curtis* (1986) 18 HLR 79, QBD.

because it had not considered availability in the statutory sense, ie, whether, if it was reasonable for her and her cohabitant to live together, the property was available to both of them (which it was not).

RIGHTS OF OCCUPATION

2.42   It is only accommodation occupied under one of three categories of right which will prevent a finding of homelessness (HA 1996, s 175(1); H(W)A 2014, s 55(1)):

a)   occupation under interest or order;

b)   occupation under express or implied licence; or

c)   occupation by enactment or restriction.

2.43   It has been held that accommodation in a prison does not fall within any of these rights of occupation, as the prisoner has no enforceable right to occupy the cell;[65] this question was, however, reserved by the House of Lords.[66]

Occupation under interest or order

2.44   The right of occupation may be by virtue of an 'interest' in the accommodation: this would seem to mean a legal or equitable interest.

2.45   Those with a legal interest will include both owner-occupiers and tenants, whether under long leases or on short, periodic tenancies, and whether under an initially agreed contractual period or under the contract as statutorily extended by HA 1985 and HA 1988 (secure tenants and assured tenants). If one of a pair of joint tenants unilaterally terminates the joint tenancy, regardless of the concurrence or knowledge of the other, the remaining joint tenant no longer has an interest in the property and therefore cannot be said to have a right of occupation as a tenant.[67]

2.46   Those with an equitable interest commonly include the spouse of an owner-occupier. Spouses and civil partners, whether of owner-occupiers or of tenants, also have rights of occupation under Part 4, Family Law Act 1996, enforceable if needs be by court order.[68]

---

65   *R (B) v Southwark LBC* [2003] EWHC 1678 (Admin), [2004] HLR 3.
66   *Birmingham City Council v Ali; Moran v Manchester City Council (Secretary of State for Communities and Local Government and another intervening)* [2009] UKHL 36, [2009] 1 WLR 1506; see para **2.16**.
67   *Fletcher v Brent LBC* [2006] EWCA Civ 960, [2007] HLR 12; see further para **2.48**.
68   See, in particular, Family Law Act 1996, Part 4. The powers can also be applied to former spouses, civil partners, cohabitants and former cohabitants.

Occupation under express or implied licence

2.47　Where spouses or other partners are living together, and only one has a right of occupation (such as ownership or tenancy) the other is technically their licensee,[69] though as noted above they may well have rights of occupation under Family Law Act 1996. Lodgers will usually be licensees rather than tenants; flat-sharers may be only licensees rather than joint tenants; a child in the home of their parents will be a licensee rather than a tenant or sub-tenant,[70] except in the most exceptional circumstances.[71]

2.48　Where the authority claims that an applicant has a licence to occupy accommodation, it must determine its precise nature. In *Fletcher*,[72] the applicant's wife terminated their joint tenancy by service of a notice to quit. The local authority nonetheless concluded that the applicant was not homeless. On appeal to the county court, the judge held that the applicant had some form of licence to occupy the property – the nature of which she decided that it was unnecessary for her to determine – and was therefore not homeless. The Court of Appeal, allowing a further appeal, remitted the case to the authority to determine whether a licence existed and, if so, on what terms.

Tied accommodation

2.49　Where the applicant's licence is as a service occupier and contingent on the contract of employment, there cannot be said to be a licence to occupy once the contract of employment has been terminated, although there may be a restriction on any eviction (see below).

2.50　Even where the employer of a live-in housekeeper, having terminated the contract of employment, said that the applicant could return to occupy her room, the local authority was in error in concluding that she had a licence to occupy. The licence was dependent on a contract for employment which no longer existed.[73]

69　*Hemans & Hemans v Windsor and Maidenhead BC* [2011] EWCA Civ 374, [2011] HLR 25.

70　On the distinction between tenant and licensee, see the decisions in *Street v Mountford* [1985] AC 809, (1985) 17 HLR 402, HL; and *AG Securities v Vaughan; Antoniades v Villiers* [1990] 1 AC 417, (1988) 21 HLR 79, HL. See also English Homelessness Code of Guidance paras 6.12–6.16 and Welsh Code paras 8.11–8.12 on applicants asked to leave accommodation by family or friends.

71　For example, where the house has been subdivided into two flats (self-contained or not), for one of which the parents are charging rent and there are no other criteria which lean against tenancy (such as sharing utilities).

72　*Fletcher v Brent LBC* [2006] EWCA Civ 960, [2007] HLR 12.

73　See *R v Kensington and Chelsea RLBC ex p Minton* (1988) 20 HLR 648, QBD and *Norris v Checksfield* (1991) 23 HLR 425, CA.

Occupation by enactment or restriction

2.51   The final category of 'right of occupation' is occupation as a residence by virtue of any enactment or rule of law giving the applicant the right to remain in occupation, or restricting the right of any other person to recover possession of it.

Actual occupation v right to occupy

2.52   This category predicates actual occupation, as distinct from a right to occupy, so that a person who walks out of accommodation occupied on this basis will be homeless, albeit at risk of a finding of intentionality.[74] In contrast, a person who walks out of a house in which they have an interest will, presuming it is available for their occupation,[75] not be homeless until such time as they divest themselves of that interest, for example, by release or sale, at which point the question of intentionality may arise.

Rent Act protection

2.53   A tenant within the protection of the Rent Act (RA) 1977 will occupy by virtue of an interest until the determination of the tenancy; thereafter, the person is a statutory tenant. A statutory tenancy is not an interest in land.[76] It is, however, a right of occupation by virtue of an enactment or rule of law, as well as one which gives the tenant the right to remain in occupation and which restricts the right of another to recover possession.

Secure/assured protection

2.54   The same approach was not taken for secure and assured tenants under HA 1985 and HA 1988. Rather, there is a restriction on the landlord's right to determine the tenancy itself save by order of the court. Accordingly, the tenancy continues and, as such, occupation is under that interest.

Tied accommodation

2.55   An agricultural worker in tied accommodation, enjoying the benefit of the Rent (Agriculture) Act (R(A)A) 1976,[77] will usually occupy by virtue of a licence before its determination, and thereafter in the same way as a Rent

---

74   But see further 'Reasonable to continue to occupy' at para **2.72** onwards.
75   See paras **2.19–2.41**.
76   *Keeves v Dean* [1924] 1 KB 685, CA.
77   There are conditions which apply before the protection is available.

Act statutory tenant. Those whose rights were granted after commencement of HA 1988, Part 1 may have assured agricultural occupancies[78] which – as with assured tenancies[79] – can only be terminated by an order of the court. Those in tied accommodation who do not enjoy the benefit of R(A)A 1976 or HA 1988 derive some temporary benefits under Protection from Eviction Act (PEA) 1977.[80]

Former long leaseholders

2.56   Long leaseholders usually continue to occupy beyond what would otherwise contractually be the termination of their interests by virtue of a statutorily extended tenancy, which is thus still an interest. They will subsequently become either statutory tenants under RA 1977 or assured tenants under HA 1988.[81]

Other tenants and licensees

2.57   PEA 1977, s 3 prohibits the eviction – otherwise than by court proceedings – of former unprotected tenants and licensees,[82] those who had licences granted on or after 28 November 1980 which qualify as restricted contracts within RA 1977, s 19, as well as certain service occupiers. All these people will occupy either by virtue of an interest or a licence until determination, and subsequently by virtue of an enactment restricting the right of another to recover possession.[83]

Spouses, civil partners and cohabitants

2.58   Even where the applicant is not the tenant, Family Law Act 1996, Part 4[84] protects spouses, civil partners and some cohabitants (including those living together as civil partners) by giving them a right to remain in occupation, or restricting the right of another to recover possession.[85]

---

78   Ibid.
79   See para **2.54**.
80   See PEA 1977, s 8(2) applying provisions of that Act to 'a person who, under the terms of his employment, had exclusive possession of any premises other than as a tenant'.
81   Landlord and Tenant Act 1954, Part 1; Local Government and Housing Act 1989, Sch 10.
82   Other than excluded tenants and licensees: see PEA 1977, s 3(2B). Note that, by judicial extension, temporary accommodation provided under a licence pursuant to what is now HA 1996, ss 188(1), (3), 190(2), 200(1) and 204(4) is incapable of qualifying under PEA 1977, s 3: see *R (ZH and CN) v Newham LBC and Lewisham LBC* [2014] UKSC 62, [2015] HLR 6. See also *Mohamed v Manek* (1995) 27 HLR 439, CA and *Desnousse v Newham LBC* [2006] EWCA Civ 547, [2006] HLR 38. It is, however, unclear whether this proposition applies (as it was said in *Manek* to apply) to both tenancies and licences so provided, or only to licences (a difference expressly raised and left open by the court in *Desnousse*).
83   PEA 1977, ss 2, 3, as amended by HA 1980, s 69(1) and HA 1988, s 30.
84   As amended by the Civil Partnership Act 2004.
85   *Abdullah v Westminster City Council* [2011] EWCA Civ 1171, [2012] HLR 5.

Non-qualifying persons

2.59   Those who are left outside the definition altogether are:

a)   those who have been trespassers from the outset and remain so; and

b)   those who have excluded tenancies and licences which have been brought to an end;[86] or who are otherwise excluded from PEA 1977.[87]

2.60   It follows that 'squatters' properly so-called, as distinct from those to whom a licence to occupy has been granted,[88] are statutorily homeless even though no possession order may yet have been made against them – for, even though they may have the benefit of a roof over their heads, they have no accommodation within any of the classes specified.

2.61   As noted above,[89] an applicant who occupies interim accommodation provided to them pending enquiries, review or appeal under HA 1996, ss 188 or 204(4) is nevertheless homeless for the purpose of s 175(1).

Timing

2.62   The right not to be evicted otherwise than by court proceedings in PEA 1977, s 3 confers protection until execution of a possession order by the court bailiff in accordance with the relevant court rules.[90]

2.63   In *Sacupima*,[91] it was held that the same applied under the Civil Procedure Rules (CPR) 1998 and, therefore, under HA 1996, s 175(1)(c).[92] Accordingly, an assured tenant[93] does not become homeless for the purposes of s 175(1)(c) until the warrant for possession against them is executed.[94] Note, however, that

---

86   *R v Blankley* [1979] Crim LR 166 and see PEA 1977, s 3(2B).
87   Cf para **2.57**.
88   Ie, a short-life occupation agreement, usually pending redevelopment.
89   Para **2.17**.
90   *Hanniff v Robinson* [1993] QB 419, CA. The relevant county court rules are found in CPR Part 83. Special provision was also made during the Covid–19 pandemic: see Public Health (Coronavirus) (Protection from Eviction and Taking Control of Goods) (England) Regulations 2020, SI 2020/1290; Public Health (Coronavirus) (Protection from Eviction) (England) (No 2) Regulations 2021/164; Public Health (Coronavirus) (Protection from Eviction) (England) Regulations 2021, SI 2021/15; and in Wales, Public Health (Protection from Eviction) (Wales) (Coronavirus) Regulations 2020, SI 2020/1490; Public Health (Protection from Eviction) (Wales) (Coronavirus) Regulations 2021, SI 2021/12.
91   *R v Newham LBC ex p Sacupima* (2001) 33 HLR 1, QBD. See also *R v Newham LBC ex p Khan* (2001) 33 HLR 29, QBD.
92   HA 1996, s 230 defines 'enactment' as including subordinate legislation.
93   Entitled to remain in occupation under HA 1988, s 5 until a court order is made. The same argument will apply to secure tenancies: see HA 1985, s 82.
94   In these circumstances, however, the applicant will be threatened with homelessness: see para **2.147** onwards.

from 9 November 2012 when Localism Act (LA) 2011, s 149 came into force,[95] an applicant who makes a fresh application to an English authority within two years of a previous application which had resulted in the offer and acceptance of an assured shorthold tenancy, in respect of which notice has been given under HA 1988, s 21, is entitled to be treated as homeless from the expiry of that notice, so that they need not await proceedings for eviction.[96] This does not apply where the application was made before – and the duty to secure accommodation was still in existence at – that date.[97]

RENTERS (REFORM) BILL

Once in full relevant force and subject to any transitional provisions, s 195A will be repealed and the amendment made by Localism Act 2011 will therefore cease to have effect so that the additional category of homelessness will not exist.

RESTRICTION ON ENTRY OR USE

Entry prevented

2.64   A person is also homeless if they 'cannot secure entry to' their accommodation.[98]

2.65   This provision is primarily intended to benefit the illegally evicted tenant or occupier, but covers anyone else who for some reason cannot immediately be restored to occupation of a home to which they have a legal entitlement – for example, because of occupation by squatters.[99]

2.66   This provision has not proved to be of as much practical use as was intended, because authorities have tended to consider that unless the applicant uses available legal remedies to re-enter, they will be considered intentionally homeless, albeit possibly provided with temporary assistance until an order from the court is obtained.

---

95   Localism Act 2011 (Commencement No 2 and Transitional Provisions) (England) Order 2012, SI 2012/2599, art 2.
96   HA 1996, s 195A(2). This right only arises on one re-application: HA 1996, s 195A(6).
97   Localism Act 2011 (Commencement No 2 and Transitional Provisions) (England) Order 2012, SI 2012/2599, art 3.
98   HA 1996, s 175(2)(a); H(W)A 2014, s 55(2)(a).
99   English Homelessness Code paras 6.20–6.21; Welsh Code para 8.16. It does not include where an applicant cannot travel to accommodation (which is otherwise available): *Nipa Begum v Tower Hamlets LBC* (1999) 32 HLR 445, CA.

2.67   Authorities should, however, have no rigid policy to this effect:[100] there may be circumstances in which, even though legal redress exists, both the benefits to be gained from using it and the circumstances generally suggest that it would be inappropriate, for example, illegal eviction by a resident landlord who will shortly recover possession in any event, where tensions are such that it is impracticable for the tenant to remain in the property.[101]

Moveable structures

2.68   A person is also homeless if their accommodation consists of a moveable structure, vehicle or vessel designed or adapted for human habitation, and there is no place where the applicant is entitled or permitted[102] both to place it and to reside in it – for example, a mobile home, caravan or house-boat.[103]

2.69   In *Roberts*,[104] travelling showmen were considered to be neither homeless nor threatened with homelessness while moving between fairgrounds during the fairground season, residing at each ground in caravans on a temporary basis. 'Reside' does not require permanence: it means 'live' or 'occupy'.

2.70   In *Smith v Wokingham DC*,[105] a county court held that a caravan parked on land belonging to a county council, without express permission but in which the applicant and his family had lived for two-and-a-half years, had been the subject of acquiescence sufficient to constitute permission for the purpose of what is now HA 1996, s 175(2)(b).

REASONABLE TO CONTINUE TO OCCUPY

2.71   A person is homeless if their accommodation is such that it is not reasonable to continue to occupy it.[106] Subject to the provisions of HA 1996, s 177(2) and H(W)A 2014, s 57(3), allowing the authority to have regard to the

---

100 See, eg, *British Oxygen Co Ltd v Minister of Technology* [1971] AC 610, HL; *Re Betts* [1983] 2 AC 613, 10 HLR 97, HL; *Attorney-General ex rel Tilley v Wandsworth LBC* [1981] 1 WLR 854, CA; *R v Warwickshire CC ex p Williams* [1995] COD 182, QBD; *R v North Yorkshire CC ex p Hargreaves* (1997) 96 LGR 39, QBD.

101 This could in any event mean that it was not reasonable to continue to occupy the accommodation: see paras **2.72–2.146.**

102 In *Higgs v Brighton and Hove City Council* [2003] EWCA Civ 895, [2004] HLR 2, the loss of the applicant's caravan was an emergency but it had not caused his homelessness; he was already homeless – prior to the loss – because the caravan was illegally sited, ie, he was not 'entitled or permitted'.

103 HA 1996, s 175(2)(b); H(W)A 2014, s 55(2)(b).

104 *R v Chiltern DC ex p Roberts et al* (1990) 23 HLR 387, QBD.

105 April 1980 *LAG Bulletin* 92, CC. See also *Higgs v Brighton and Hove City Council* [2003] EWCA Civ 895, [2004] HLR 2.

106 HA 1996, s 175(3); H(W)A 2014, s 55(3).

general housing circumstances of the area,[107] the question whether it is reasonable to continue to occupy has been described as subjective, and not susceptible to a generalised or objective standard: *McManus*.[108] This does not mean wholly subjective in the view of the applicant, however, but rather that the issue has to be determined on all the facts of the case – not, on the one hand, determined simply by reference to local conditions or the local authority's policy, nor, on the other, looked at from the perspective of the applicant alone, so that the role of other persons or factors is ignored.[109]

Reasonableness to occupy and suitability

2.72   As noted above (para.**2.4**), there is a relationship between reasonableness to continue to occupy and suitability of accommodation.[110] Case-law on one of these issues may therefore be relevant to the other.[111] This is implicit in *Birmingham City Council v Ali; Moran v Manchester City Council (Secretary of State for Communities and Local Government)*[112] where the House of Lords came close to eliding the two concepts: accommodation which is not reasonable for an applicant to continue to occupy may nevertheless be suitable for the time being; there are degrees of suitability and what is suitable for occupation in the short term may not be suitable in the longer term.[113]

> 'It may be that, in some, or conceivably all, of the Birmingham cases, a critical examination of the facts would establish that the council were at some point in breach of their duty under Part VII of the1996 Act. Thus the time it has taken to find Mr Ali suitable accommodation may well be beyond what is defensible. While the council were entitled in principle to leave the families in their current accommodation for a period notwithstanding that it was accepted that that accommodation "would [not] be reasonable for [them and their families] to continue to occupy" (section 175(3)), it must be a question, which turns on the particular facts, whether, in any particular case, the period was simply too long. ...' (Baroness Hale at [49]).

2.73   This is most relevant when it comes to consideration of the financial constraints on authorities and the shortage of accommodation:

> '50. It is right to face up to the practical implications of this conclusion. First, there is the approach to be adopted by a court, when considering the question whether a local housing authority have left an applicant who occupies "accommodation which it would [not] be reasonable for him to continue to occupy" in that accommodation for too long a period. The question is of course primarily one for the authority,

---

107 See paras **2.72–2.146**.
108 *R v Brent LBC ex p McManus* (1993) 25 HLR 643, QBD.
109 *Denton v Southwark LBC* [2007] EWCA Civ 623, [2008] HLR 11, at [13], [30] and [31]. .
110 See further paras **8.183–8.234**.
111 *Harouki v Kensington and Chelsea RLBC* [2007] EWCA Civ 1000, [2008] HLR 16.
112 [2009] UKHL 36, [2009] 1 WLR 1506; [2009] HLR 41.
113 *Ali* and *Moran* at [47]. See para **8.139**.

and a court should normally be slow to accept that the authority have left an applicant in his unsatisfactory accommodation too long. In a place such as Birmingham, there are many families in unsatisfactory accommodation, severe constraints on budgets and personnel, and a very limited number of satisfactory properties for large families and those with disabilities. It would be wrong to ignore those pressures when deciding whether, in a particular case, an authority had left an applicant in her present accommodation for an unacceptably long period".'[114]

2.74   The point was taken up in *Elkundi*[115] at [136].

'It is also correct that Baroness Hale referred in *Ali* to the general situation in relation to housing in a particular area, severe constraints on budgets and a limited number of satisfactory properties for very large families and those with disabilities. She considered that those factors were relevant to the question of whether a housing authority had left an applicant in his present accommodation for too long. She referred to the situation of a particular applicant in his current accommodation being so bad or having continued for so long that "enough is enough". ... Such considerations may also be relevant to whether his current accommodation is suitable.'[116]

2.75   There is no presumption that an applicant's current accommodation is unsuitable, such as to impose a burden on the authority to rebut it: *McCarthy*.[117]

2.76   So far as the question of whether it is reasonable for an applicant to continue to occupy accommodation relies on the constraints on the resources available to the authority, it may be argued that a general assertion about demand and shortage will not be sufficient in the event of a legal challenge,[118] and that the authority may need to provide specific evidence as to, eg, numbers of relevant properties and demand:[119] if this is necessary when the issue is whether to make a mandatory order,[120] there is no reason for a lesser standard when the issue is whether the authority owes a duty at all.

114 *Ali* and *Moran* at [50]. Baroness Hale continued: 'None the less, there will be cases where the court ought to step in and require an authority to offer alternative accommodation, or at least to declare that they are in breach of their duty so long as they fail to do so. While one must take into account the practical realities of the situation in which authorities find themselves, one cannot overlook the fact that Parliament has imposed on them clear duties to the homeless, including those occupying unsuitable accommodation. In some cases, the situation of a particular applicant in her present accommodation may be so bad, or her occupation may have continued for so long, that the court will conclude that enough is enough.' (At [51]).
115 *R (Elkundi and others) v Birmingham City Council; R (Imam) v Croydon LBC* [2022] EWCA Civ 601; [2022] QB 604; [2022] HLR 31.
116 The omitted words are: 'Those words however, were used in the context of whether the duty was owed (that, is whether the person was homeless because he was in accommodation that it was not reasonable for him to continue to occupy).'
117 *R v Sedgemoor DC ex p McCarthy* (1996) 28 HLR 608, QBD.
118 See para **10.195**.
119 *Elkundi* at [135].
120 See para **10.195**.

Generally

2.77   The test is satisfied only if it is reasonable for the applicant to occupy the accommodation indefinitely, or at least for as long as the applicant otherwise would do so if the authority did not intervene to rehouse them: *Ali* and *Moran*.[121] Thus, an applicant may be homeless long before the situation becomes so bad that it is not reasonable for them to occupy the accommodation for another night; what this recognises is that accommodation which it may be unreasonable for a person to occupy for a long period, may nonetheless be reasonable to occupy for a short period.[122] A woman who has left her home because of abuse or violence[123] normally remains homeless even if she has found a temporary haven in a women's refuge[124] because it would usually not be reasonable for her to continue to occupy her place in the refuge indefinitely,[125] ie, for as long as she would have to occupy it if the authority did not intervene to rehouse her.[126]

2.78   Indefinitely does not mean 'forever': it may be reasonable to continue to occupy temporary accommodation;[127] the question is not whether the accommodation is *available* indefinitely but whether it is accommodation which an applicant is expected to put up with indefinitely – it does not mean that the applicant has to be able to stay in the accommodation indefinitely or even for a particular period of time;[128] nor even does it mean 'put up with it for ever' so much as for the foreseeable future, for a long period, for so long as it would be occupied if the authority did not intervene or a relatively long-term basis.[129]

2.79   The Court of Appeal in *Kyle* summarised the position as follows.[130]

> '(i) There is no need for accommodation to be so bad that a person could not be expected to stay there another night for there to be homelessness for the purposes of the 1996 Act. On the other hand, a person does not have to be entitled to remain in accommodation indefinitely, or for any particular period of time, for it to be 'reasonable for him to continue to occupy' it, and neither need he have accommodation which it would be 'reasonable … to

---

121 *Ali* and *Moran* at [34]. This has to be decided on the basis of the position as at the date of the decision: in *Safi v Sandwell BC* [2018] EWCA Civ 2876; [2019] HLR 16, the authority had misapplied *Ali* and *Moran* because it had considered whether it was reasonable to continue to occupy on the basis of the family composition as at the date of application (applicant, husband and one child in one-bedroom flat) without taking into account the impending birth of a second child.

122 *Ali* and *Moran* at [42].

123 See paras **2.83–2.90**.

124 *Ali* and *Moran* at [65].

125 *Ali* and *Moran* at [52].

126 *Ali* and *Moran* at [46].

127 *R v Brent London Borough Council, ex p. Awua* [1996] AC 55; (1995) 27 HLR 453 at [67]–[68].

128 *(Ahamed) v Haringey London Borough Council* [2023] EWCA Civ 975; [2024] HLR 43 at [47]; *Kyle v Coventry CC* [2023] EWCA Civ 1360; [2024] HLR 7 at [34].

129 *Kyle* at [39] citing *Moran* at [9], [34], [42].

130 At [42].

continue to occupy' for ever. In general at least, section 175(3) of the 1996 Act will be satisfied, and a person will not be 'homeless', if there is accommodation which it would be 'reasonable for him to continue to occupy' over the period which would elapse before the local housing authority re-housed him;

(ii) The physical characteristics of accommodation will often be of central importance in determining whether it is 'reasonable ... to continue to occupy' it. Restrictions affecting the person's life in, and use of, the accommodation may also be relevant.[131] Possibly, the length of time that a person has the right to remain in accommodation may sometimes be of significance, but that is much less likely to matter. Without attempting to be exhaustive, other factors that might be material, depending on the particular facts, include affordability, violence, abuse and threats'.

2.80   The test of reasonableness to continue to occupy does not apply only to accommodation which is actually occupied: continuation refers to the entitlement rather than the occupation; the words 'accommodation which it would be reasonable for him to continue to occupy' in s 175(3) mean 'accommodation which it would be reasonable for that person to occupy for a continuing period', whether or not he is in occupation of it when he applies for assistance or when the authority determine his application for assistance.[132]

2.81   The question is not, however, whether it is reasonable to leave accommodation, but whether or not it is reasonable to continue to occupy it.[133] The distinction is significant: it will commonly be reasonable (ie, not unreasonable) to leave somewhere; what has to be sustained is the proposition that it is positively not reasonable to stay. Whether or not it is reasonable to continue to occupy accommodation relates not only to the applicant but also to any other person who might reasonably be expected to reside with them: *Bishop*.[134] This must be as true of a person residing with the applicant as a member of the family.

Statutory definition

2.82   The term 'reasonable to continue to occupy' is governed by HA 1996, s 177 or H(W)A 2014, s 57, as to both:

a)   violence (HA 1996, s 177(1), (1A)) or abuse (H(W)A 2014, s 57(1)); and

---

131 'I find it hard to see how the 'no visitors' and 'no smoking' rules (whatever their scope, which is not clear) or 79 St Margaret Road's role as 'as a half-way house whilst other accommodation was secured could have detracted from the reasonableness of continued occupation' – *Kyle v Coventry CC* [2023] EWCA Civ 1360; [2024] HLR 7 at [49].

132 *Waltham Forest LBC v Maloba* [2007] EWCA Civ 1281, [2008] HLR 26, rejecting the majority *obiter* conclusion to the conclusion in *Nipa Begum Nipa Begum v Tower Hamlets LBC* (1999) 32 HLR 445, CA.

133 See *R v Kensington and Chelsea RLBC ex p Bayani* (1990) 22 HLR 406, CA; see also *R v Gravesham BC ex p Winchester* (1986) 18 HLR 208, QBD.

134 *R v Westminster City Council ex p Bishop* (1993) 25 HLR 459, CA.

b) the general housing circumstances of the area (HA 1996, s 177(2); H(W) A 2014, s 57(3)).

Violence and abuse

2.83 It is not reasonable to continue to occupy accommodation if, even though there may be a legal entitlement to do so, it is 'probable' that occupation of it will lead to violence or domestic abuse, or (in Wales) other abuse:[135]

a) against the applicant; or

b) against any person who normally resides with the applicant, or against any person who might reasonably be expected to reside with the applicant.[136]

England

2.84 Violence means violence from another person or threats of violence from another person which are likely to be carried out.[137] Abuse is domestic abuse if one person aged 16 or over is abusive towards another person[138] aged 16 or over, with whom they are personally connected, meaning physical or sexual abuse, violent or threatening behaviour; controlling or coercive behaviour; economic abuse[139] or psychological, emotional or other abuse, whether comprised of a single act of a course of conduct.[140]

2.85 People are personally connected if:[141]

(a) they are, or have been, married to each other;

(b) they are, or have been, civil partners of each other;

(c) they have agreed to marry one another (whether or not the agreement has been terminated);

(d) they have entered into a civil partnership agreement[142] (whether or not the agreement has been terminated);

---

135 In Wales, 'abuse' means physical violence, threatening or intimidating behaviour and any other form of abuse which, directly or indirectly, may give rise to the risk of harm: H(W)A 2014, s 58(1).

136 HA 1996, s 177(1), (1A) as amended by Domestic Abuse Act (DAA) 2021, s 78, with effect from 5 July 2021 (Domestic Abuse Act 2021 (Commencement No. 1 and Saving Provisions) Regulations 2021, SI 2021/797; H(W)A 2014, s 57(1).

137 HA 1996, s 177(1), (1A) as amended by Domestic Abuse Act (DAA) 2021, s 78.

138 Behaviour may be towards another person, even though it consists of conduct directed at another *e.g.* the other person's child: DAA 2021, 1(5).

139 Any behaviour that has a substantial adverse effect on the other person's ability to acquire, use or maintain money or other property, or obtain goods or services: Domestic Abuse Act 2021, s 1(4).

140 DAA 2021, s 1.

141 DAA 2021, s 2(1).

142 Within Civil Partnership Act 2004, s 73: DAA 2021, s 2(3).

(e) they are, or have been, in an intimate personal relationship with each other;

(f) they each have, or there has been a time when they each have had, a parental relationship in relation to the same child[143];[144]

(g) they are relatives.[145]

2.86   Children[146] may be victims of domestic abuse if they are related to[147] either the person committing, or the person subject to, the domestic abuse, and they see or hear, or experience the effects of, the abuse.[148]

Wales

2.87   It is not reasonable for a person to continue to occupy accommodation if it is probable that it will lead to the person, or a member of their household,[149] being subjected to abuse.[150] For this purpose, abuse means 'physical violence, threatening or intimidating behaviour and any other form of abuse which, directly or indirectly, may give rise to the risk of harm'; the abuse is domestic abuse if the victim is associated with[151] the abuser.[152]

---

143 Child means a person under the age of 18 years: DAA 2021, s 2(3).
144 A person has a parental relationship in relation to a child either if they are a parent of the child, or they parental responsibility for the child within the meaning of the Children Act 1989, s 3, ie, someone with 'all the rights, duties, powers, responsibilities and authority which by law a parent of a child has in relation to the child and his property" including "the rights, powers and duties which a guardian of the child's estate…would have had in relation to the child and his property': DAA 2021, s 2(3).
145 Within Family Law Act 1996, s 63(1), ie, parent, step-parent, child, step-child, grandparent, grandchild, sibling, uncle, aunt, niece. Nephew. First cousin (whether full or half blood or by marriage or civil partnership) of a person or of their spouse, former spouse, civil partner, or civil partner, including where people are cohabiting or who have cohabited anyone who would fall within this description if they were married to or civil partners of each other: DAA 2021, s 2(3).
146 A person under the age of 18: DAA 2021, s 3(4).
147 Either of the persons involved is a parent or has parental responsibility for the child, or is their relative: DAA 2021, s 3(3).
148 DAA 2021, s 3(2).
149 A person who normally resides with them as member of their family or any other person who might reasonably be expected to reside with them: H(W)A 2014, s 57(2).
150 H(W)A 2014, s 57(1).
151 They are or have been married to each other or civil partners, live or have lived together in an enduring family relationship or in the same household, are relatives (parent, grandparent, child, grandchild, sibling or half-sibling, uncle, aunt, nephew, niece, including by marriage, civil partnership or an enduring family relationship – H(W)A 2014, s 58(5)), have agreed to marry or enter into a civil partnership agreement (whether or not that agreement has been terminated), have or have had an intimate personal relationship with each other which is or was of significant duration or, in relation to a child, each of them is a parent of the child or has, or has had, parental responsibility (within Children Act 1989, s 3) for the child: H(W)A 2014, s 58(2) (5). There is an extended definition of person associated governing a child who has been adopted or who falls within a number of specified adoption provisions: H(W)A 2014, s 58(3)-(5).
152 H(W)A 2014, s 58(1).

Violence

2.88   These provisions overtake the case-law on abuse and violence,[153] in particular rejecting the narrow definition of 'violence' adopted in *Danesh*,[154] meaning actual physical violence, not including threats of violence or acts or gestures which lead a person to fear physical violence, in favour of – and extending beyond – the broader approach of the Supreme Court in *Yemshaw*,[155] including physical violence, threats, intimidating behaviour and any other form of abuse which, directly or indirectly, may give rise to a risk of harm.[156]

2.89   It is not necessary to show an actual history of violence. While the lower standard, ie, threats by someone likely to carry them out, is only incorporated into the statutory language in England (contrast paras **2.84** and **2.86**), the Welsh test – threats – is if anything higher than threats by a person likely to carry them out; it is unlikely that there is a real difference in practice. Many authorities fail to observe this important distinction, and require a high standard of proof of actual past violence as evidence of both probability and likelihood. As the provisions draw a distinction, so also must authorities.

2.90   The position is not on all fours with failure to use legal redress in connection with 'entry prevented'.[157] Authorities are not to concern themselves with what steps to prevent the violence applicants should (in the authority's view) take or could have taken: *Bond*.[158] Whether a victim of violence had failed to take measures to prevent the violence (such as contacting the police or taking out an injunction) is irrelevant: if, however, the victim does take preventative measures which it is considered will probably prove effective in preventing actual or threatened violence, the level of risk may factually be reduced below likelihood, although it is difficult to see that they have ceased to be threats for the purpose of the Welsh provisions.

---

153 Prior to Homelessness Act 2002, non-domestic violence was only relevant to the question of reasonableness 'at large': *R v Hillingdon LBC, ex p H* (1988) 20 HLR 554, QBD.
154 *Danesh v Kensington and Chelsea RLBC* [2006] EWCA Civ 1404, [2007] HLR 17.
155 *Yemshaw v Hounslow LBC* [2011] UKSC 3, [2011] HLR 16; see also H(W)A 2014, s 58.
156 The wider view was also adopted in the 2006 edition of the English Code of Guidance para 8.21 which *Danesh* had criticised. In in *Waltham Forest LBC v Hussein* [2015] EWCA Civ 14, [2015] HLR 16 it was held that, although *Danesh* had not been expressly overruled by *Yemshaw*, it was clear that much of the reasoning was disapproved; the wider approach in *Yemshaw* should therefore be followed.
157 See para **2.66**.
158 *Bond v Leicester City Council* [2001] EWCA Civ 1544, [2002] HLR 6. The earlier decision in *R v Wandsworth LBC ex p Nimako-Boateng* (1984) 11 HLR 95, QBD, in which it had been held that an authority could conclude that it would be reasonable for a woman to continue to occupy accommodation – notwithstanding domestic violence – by reference to the remedies otherwise available to her for her protection, was decided under HA 1985, s 58, now HA 1996, s 175(3), at a time when the question of reasonableness was at large, rather than statutorily defined. *Nimako-Boateng* was accordingly distinguished in *Bond*, as was the decision to like effect in *R v Purbeck DC ex p Cadney* (1985) 17 HLR 534. See also the pre-*Bond* decicion in *R v Eastleigh BC ex p Evans* (19845 17 HLR 515, QBD.

General housing circumstances of area

2.91   The comparison between: a) accommodation occupied; and b) the general circumstances prevailing in relation to housing accommodation in the district of the authority to which an application has been made,[159] is one of the central concepts of homelessness law, albeit that most of it was developed in relation to intentionality.

2.92   Initially, it bore not at all on the definition of homelessness, although it was in practice being applied by the courts at the point in the evolution of the law[160] at which an there was an equiparation between being homeless and occupation of accommodation so poor that it could be left without a finding of intentionality.

2.93   *Awua*[161] notwithstanding, it is plain that Parliament intended the importation of an identical criterion when it adopted the exact same phraseology for use in the definition (HA 1985, s 58) of homelessness as had long existed in relation to intentionality (HA 1985, s 60), ie, whether or not it was reasonable to continue to occupy, subject to the general housing conditions of the area.[162]

2.94   The comparison is between: a) current accommodation, wherever situated, and b) conditions in the area of the authority to which application is made.[163]

2.95   HA 1996, s 177(2) requires the authority to carry out a balancing act between the housing conditions in the authority's area and the accommodation quit, although whether or not it is reasonable to continue to occupy accommodation involves other questions, such as the pattern of life followed by the applicant: *Monaf*.[164] Such comparisons should only be made, however, where relevant to an application.[165]

2.96   The decision in *Tickner v Mole Valley DC*,[166] in which the applicants were evicted from a caravan site because they refused to pay increased rents

---

159 HA 1996, s 177(2); H(W)A 2014, s 57(3).
160 See para **2.10** in relation to accommodation.
161 *R v Brent LBC ex p Awua* [1996] AC 55, (1995) 27 HLR 453, HL.
162 Housing and Planning Act 1986, s 14(2). See also *R v Wandsworth LBC ex p Wingrove*, and *R v Wandsworth LBC ex p Mansoor* [1996] 3 All ER 913, (1997) 29 HLR 801, CA. See also *Nipa Begum v Tower Hamlets LBC* (1999) 32 HLR 445, CA, at p319/H ('[T]he plain intention of Parliament was to enable a local authority to determine the question of homelessness . . . without having to go on to the corresponding question in the test of intentional homelessness') and at p326/A–B.
163 *R v Tower Hamlets LBC ex p Monaf* (1988) 20 HLR 529, CA.
164 See paras **2.125–2.132**. See also *R v Newham LBC ex p Ajayi* (1996) 28 HLR 25, QBD, referring to matters 'of social history and national status', such as where children were born and how long a person has lived somewhere.
165 *R v Newham LBC ex p Tower Hamlets LBC* (1990) 23 HLR 62, CA.
166 August 1980 *LAG Bulletin* 187, CA.

which they thought excessive in view of the conditions on the site, turned on what is now HA 1996, s 177(2), albeit in the context of intentionality:

> 'That is what influenced this authority here. They had long waiting lists for housing. On those lists there were young couples waiting to be married: or young married couples sometimes staying with their in-laws: or people in poor accommodation. All those people were on the housing waiting lists – people who had been waiting for housing for years. The council thought it would be extremely unfair to all those on the waiting lists if these caravan dwellers – by coming in in this way – jumped the queue, when they were well able to pay the rent for the caravans and stay on. Those were perfectly legitimate considerations for the local authority to consider.'[167]

2.97   In order to rely on this provision, the authority need not consider in great detail all the information on housing conditions in its area, but may have regard to 'the generally prevailing standard of accommodation in their area, with which people have to be satisfied'.[168]

2.98   In *Puhlhofer* at the Court of Appeal,[169] Ackner LJ's view as to whether or not the applicants had any accommodation (within the meaning of the legislation) at all[170] was based in part on the question whether or not it would have been reasonable to continue to occupy it. He considered that accommodation for the applicant, his wife and two children in one room in a guesthouse, with no cooking or laundry facilities, could have been reasonable to continue to occupy in the light of the authority's evidence that there were at least 44 families on the council's waiting list for two-bedroomed accommodation considered to be of higher priority.

Other Considerations

2.99   The statutory considerations are not exhaustive of matters to be taken into account in determining whether or not it is reasonable to continue in occupation: *Duro-Rama*.[171] Nor is the question limited to consideration of size, structural quality and amenities of accommodation.[172] It follows that, in addition to violence and the general housing circumstances of the area and any other considerations that may be specified, there is a wide range of other matters which may affect the issue.[173]

---

167 *Per* Lord Denning MR. In *de Falco, Silvestri v Crawley BC* [1980] QB 460, CA, he described the provision as a 'ray of hope', allowing the authority to say: 'You ought to have stayed where you were before. You ought not to have landed yourself on us when it would have been reasonable for you to stay where you were.'
168 *Tickner*, para **2.96**.
169 (1985) 17 HLR 588, CA.
170 See para **2.11**.
171 *R v Hammersmith and Fulham LBC ex p Duro-Rama* (1983) 9 HLR 71, QBD.
172 *Waltham Forest LBC v Maloba* [2007] EWCA Civ 1281, [2008] HLR 26.
173 See also above, para **2.79(ii)**.

Disability

2.100   If reliance is placed on a disability as a reason why an applicant cannot continue to occupy accommodation,[174] Equality Act 2010, s 149 – the public sector equality duty[175] – may oblige the authority to treat them more favourably than a person who is not disabled:[176] an appeal against a finding that an applicant was not homeless was upheld on the basis that there had been no 'sharp focus' on the applicant's disabilities and the consequences for her of remaining in her current accommodation and the particular reasons why continuing to occupy that accommodation would damage her mental health; a generalised reference to the situation of people on the authority's waiting list, who may or may not have disabilities, let alone disabilities as severe as those of the appellant, was not sufficient.[177]

2.101   If the applicant has a disability, there can be no reliance on the general housing conditions in the area without considering how many of those said also to be living in unsatisfactory conditions have disabilities;[178] it is otherwise not comparing like with like.

Location

2.102   The question is not confined to the accommodation in itself, but can extend to its location: *Homes*.[179]

Permanence

2.103   The fact that the accommodation is not permanent is not, however, relevant to whether or not it is reasonable to continue the occupation: *Nipa Begum*.[180]

---

174 In *Wilson v Birmingham City Council* [2016] EWCA Civ 1137, [2017] HLR 4, it was held that a review officer was entitled to expect the appellant to bring forward any information which might be relevant to show that her children had a disability.

175 In the exercise of functions, to have due regard to the need to eliminate unlawful discrimination, harassment and victimisation and to advance equality of opportunity and foster good relations between persons with 'protected characteristics' (age; disability; gender reassignment; marriage and civil partnership; pregnancy and maternity; race; religion or belief; sex; sexual orientation) and other persons.

176 The duty is a duty to have regard to the specified matters, not to achieve a particular result: *Baker v Secretary of State for Communities and Local Government* [2008] EWCA Civ 141; [2009] PTSR 809; *Bracking v Secretary of State for Work and Pensions* [2013] EWCA Civ 1345; *Hotak v Southwark LBC; Kanu v Southwark LBC; Johnson v Solihull MBC* [2015] UKSC 30, [2015] HLR 23. See generally paras **7.93–7.101**.

177 *Lomax v Gosport BC* [2018] EWCA Civ 1846; [2019] PTSR 167; [2018] HLR 40.

178 *Kannan v Newham LBC* [2019] EWCA Civ 57; [2019] HLR 22.

179 *R v Wycombe DC ex p Homes* (1990) 22 HLR 150, QBD.

180 *Nipa Begum v Tower Hamlets LBC* (1999) 32 HLR 445, CA.

Physical conditions

2.104   Physical conditions may produce circumstances in which it is not reasonable to continue to occupy accommodation.

2.105   Accommodation will have to be very poor indeed before an applicant can claim with confidence that it would not be reasonable to continue to occupy it on the ground of its physical condition, although in some cases (for example, a wheelchair user) the physical characteristics of the accommodation may make it per se unsuitable for the particular applicant.[181]

2.106   In *Miles*,[182] a hut approximately 20 feet by 10 feet, with two rooms, infested by rats, and with no mains services (although services were available in a nearby caravan occupied by relatives), was held to constitute accommodation of which an authority could consider it reasonable for the applicant to continue in occupation, at a time when there were two adults and two children living in it, albeit that it was on the 'borderline' of what was reasonable and would cross the borderline into what no authority could consider reasonable on the birth of a third child.

2.107   In *Fisher*,[183] the applicant and her children had been living in temporary accommodation. For a period they lived in a caravan. Immediately before her application, they lived on a boat, without bath, shower, WC, electricity, hot water system or kitchen with a sink. There was one cabin, which was kitchen, living room and bedroom combined, and the applicant occupied it with her children and two friends. It was held that this was not accommodation of which it was reasonable to continue in occupation.

2.108   In *Winchester*,[184] the applicant and his family had left accommodation in Alderney. Among the reasons for leaving was that the accommodation was in an appalling state of disrepair, suffering from damp and a dangerous outside staircase and balcony. The family was found to be intentionally homeless. The decision of the local authority that it would have been reasonable to remain was not considered to be unreasonable or perverse.

2.109   In *Dee*,[185] a decision that it would have been reasonable for a young woman and her new baby to occupy a pre-fabricated beach bungalow which suffered severe damp problems was quashed because the authority had given too much weight to the fact that the property was not considered to be unfit for

181 English Homelessness Code para 6.39; Welsh Code para 8.27.
182 *R v South Herefordshire DC ex p Miles* (1985) 17 HLR 82, QBD.
183 *R v Preseli DC ex p Fisher* (1985) 17 HLR 147, QBD.
184 *R v Gravesham BC ex p Winchester* (1986) 18 HLR 208, QBD.
185 *R v Medina BC ex p Dee* (1992) 24 HLR 562, QBD.

human habitation and too little to the medical advice which had been given to the applicant.[186]

2.110   In *Ben-El-Mabrouk*,[187] the want of adequate means of escape from fire did not necessarily mean that it was not reasonable for a couple with a small baby to stay in occupation of a fifth-floor flat in a house in multiple occupation (HMO), although a delay in rehousing the family under the provisions of the Land Compensation Act 1973[188] might itself (in the absence of an explanation from the authority) have been challengeable.

Overcrowding

2.111   Overcrowding is a relevant consideration: *Beattie (No 1)*.[189] An authority cannot refuse to consider an application simply because the accommodation is not statutorily overcrowded: *Alouat*.[190] The authority is, however, entitled to take into account the fact that the property is not statutorily overcrowded: *Beattie (No 2)*.[191] Even if it is, this does not prevent it being reasonable for an applicant to continue to occupy the accommodation.[192]

2.112   In *Ali*,[193] even if accommodation had been 'available', it was said:

> '... that anyone should regard it as reasonable that a family of that size should live in one room 10ft × 12ft in size, or thereabouts, is something which I find astonishing. However, the matter has to be seen in the light of s 17(4) [now HA 1996, s 177(2)] which requires that reasonableness must take account of the general circumstances prevailing in relation to housing in the area. No evidence has been placed before me that accommodation in the area of the Westminster City Council is so desperately short that it is reasonable to accept overcrowding of this degree. In the absence of such

---

186 See also the discussion of *Shala v Birmingham City Council* [2007] EWCA Civ 624, [2008] HLR 8 at paras **3.53–3.54**, the principle of which must apply in the same way to issues of suitability having regard to medical conditions.

187 *R v Kensington and Chelsea RLBC ex p Youssef Ben-El-Mabrouk* (1995) 27 HLR 564, CA.

188 Land Compensation Act 1973, s 39 requires an authority to re-house residential occupiers displaced from their accommodation as a result of specified enforcement action taken by the authority under (now) HA 2004, Part 1, previously under HA 1985, Part 10.

189 *R v Eastleigh BC ex p Beattie (No 1)* (1983) 10 HLR 134, QBD.

190 *R v Westminster City Council ex p Alouat* (1989) 21 HLR 477, QBD. See also English Homelessness Code para 6.27. The Welsh Code para 8.27 says that: 'Although statutory overcrowding, by itself, is not sufficient to determine whether it is unreasonable for the applicant to continue to live in accommodation, it can be a key factor which suggests unreasonableness.'

191 *R v Eastleigh BC ex p Beattie (No 2)* (1985) 17 HLR 168, QBD. See also, on overcrowding, *Krishnan v Hillingdon LBC* January 1981 *LAG Bulletin* 137, QBD; *R v Tower Hamlets LBC ex p Ojo* (1991) 23 HLR 488, QBD; and *R v Tower Hamlets LBC ex p Bibi* (1991) 23 HLR 500, QBD.

192 *Harouki v Kensington and Chelsea RLBC* [2007] EWCA Civ 1000, [2008] HLR 16.

193 *R v Westminster City Council ex p Ali* (1984) 11 HLR 83, QBD.

evidence I am driven to the conclusion that this question could not properly have been determined against the applicant.'[194]

2.113   In *Osei*,[195] it was held that, even if the applicant's flat in Madrid had been overcrowded when he surrendered his tenancy, it was open to the authority to conclude that it was reasonable for him and his family to continue to occupy it until he had secured alternative accommodation for his family in London.

Legal conditions

2.114   The fact that accommodation had been obtained by deception meant that it would not have been reasonable to remain in occupation of it: *Gliddon*.[196]

2.115   In *Knight*,[197] and in *Li*,[198] once service occupancies had been ended and there could be no defence to an action for possession, the authorities were not able to consider that occupiers should reasonably have remained in occupation pending proceedings.

2.116   These decisions can be difficult to reconcile with the definition of rights of occupation (including the right to remain in occupation under an enactment),[199] although it is not hard to see the common sense in discouraging authorities from requiring possession orders where there would be no defence. The Codes of Guidance have long made clear that authorities should not require tenants to fight possession proceedings where the landlord has a strong prospect of success.[200] In *Ugbo*,[201] the authority's failure to consider such guidance (and the implications of the fact that that applicant was only an assured shorthold tenant rather than fully assured) invalidated its decision on this issue.

194   The applicant had left a shared single room to return to Bangladesh; he returned with his wife and four children. The observations were made both in relation to the shared single room, which put it on a par with *Re Islam* [1983] 1 AC 688, (1981) 1 HLR 107, HL, para **2.31**, and to a notional single room for the family.
195   *Osei v Southwark LBC* [2007] EWCA Civ 787, [2008] HLR 15.
196   *R v Exeter City Council ex p Gliddon* (1984) 14 HLR 103, QBD; *Chishimba v Kensington and Chelsea RLBC* [2013] EWCA Civ 786, [2013] HLR 34.
197   *R v Portsmouth City Council ex p Knight* (1983) 10 HLR 115, QBD.
198   *R v Surrey Heath BC ex p Li* (1984) 16 HLR 79, QBD.
199   See paras **2.42–2.63**.
200   See English Homelessness Code para 6.35; Welsh Code paras 8.14, 8.31. The concept appears to have first been stated in para A1.3 of the 2nd edn of the Code, although has been strengthened and developed in subsequent editions.
201   *R v Newham LBC ex p Ugbo* (1994) 26 HLR 263, QBD, a case on para 10.12 of the 3rd edn of the Code: 'Local authorities should not require tenants to fight a possession action where the landlord has a certain prospect of success, such as an action for recovery of property let on an assured shorthold tenant, on the ground that the fixed term of the tenancy has ended. Authorities need only be satisfied that proper notice had been served with the intention to proceed.'

2.117   The current Codes[202] suggest that where the applicant is an assured shorthold tenant who has received proper notice (under HA 1988, s 21) that the tenancy is to be terminated and the landlord intends to seek possession, that further efforts from the housing authority to resolve the situation and persuade the landlord to allow the tenant to remain in the property are unlikely to be successful, and that there is no defence to the possession proceedings, it is unlikely to be reasonable for the applicant to occupy the accommodation beyond the date given in the section 21 notice, unless they are taking steps to persuade the landlord to withdraw the notice.

RENTERS (REFORM) BILL

Once the Bill is in full relevant force and subject to any transitional provisions, there will be no further notices under s 21; it remains to be seen in relation to what analogous provisions, if any, the Code will offer the same guidance, eg, possession proceedings under the new Ground 5G (tenancy granted pursuant to s 193 duty, for which it is no longer required) or other new mandatory grounds.

2.118   *Ugbo* must be compared with *Jarvis*,[203] where the authority had considered the Code but was held still to be entitled to reach the conclusion that it was reasonable to continue to occupy pending a court order following termination of an assured shorthold tenancy.[204]

2.119   In *Minnett*,[205] the authority should have disregarded departure one day before the date specified in a consent order for possession. Given the decision in *Khan and Hussain*[206] that a tenant who is subject to a possession order only becomes homeless when that order is executed, authorities should also consider cases where the applicant leaves between the possession order and physical eviction by the court bailiffs, even though – on that analysis – the applicant will not yet be homeless.[207]

---

202 English Homelessness Code para 6.35; Welsh Code para 8.31. See also the letter from the secretary of state to English Local Authority CEOs (Department for Communities and Local Government, June 2016) reminding authorities that they 'should not adopt a general policy of accepting – or refusing to accept – applicants as homeless or threatened with homelessness when they are threatened with eviction but a court has not yet made an order for possession or issued a warrant of execution'; see, to the same effect, English Code paras 6.33, 6.36–6.37.
203 *R v Croydon LBC ex p Jarvis* (1994) 26 HLR 194, QBD; see also *R v Bradford City Council ex p Parveen* (1996) 28 HLR 681, QBD.
204 The 2nd edn of the Code at para 1.3 read: 'Where it is clear from the facts that tenants have no defence . . . to an application for possession, authorities should not insist that an order is obtained, and a date for eviction set, before agreeing to help the tenant.'
205 *R v Mole Valley DC ex p Minnett* (1984) 12 HLR 48, QBD.
206 *R v Newham LBC ex p Khan and Hussain* (2001) 33 HLR 29, QBD.
207 *R v Newham LBC ex p Sacupima* (2001) 33 HLR 1, QBD.

2.120 Since commencement of the Homelessness Reduction Act (HRA) 2017,[208] authorities have been under a set of new duties to assess applications and provide help to postpone homelessness or to secure accommodation for a period of time.[209] In certain circumstances,[210] an authority may end its duty to help postpone homelessness for those threatened with homelessness,[211] one of which[212] is that it has taken reasonable steps to secure that accommodation does not cease to be available, that the applicant has suitable accommodation, and that a period of 56 days has elapsed since it was first satisfied that the applicant was threatened with homelessness and eligible for assistance. No such notice may, however, be given if the applicant has been given a valid notice under HA 1988, s 21 to terminate an assured shorthold tenancy, in respect of the only accommodation available to the applicant and which has expired or will expire within 56 days.[213] This provides support for the proposition that it is not reasonable to continue to occupy accommodation in the face of court proceedings to which there will be no defence.

RENTERS (REFORM) BILL

Once in full relevant force and subject to any transitional provisions, the prohibition on notice under s 195(5), where applicable, will cease to apply.

Employment

2.121 In *Duro-Rama*,[214] employment was said to be a relevant considerations which the authority had ignored. This reflects the comment of Lord Lowry in *Islam*,[215] that:

> 'There will, of course, and in the interests of mobility of labour ought to be, cases where the housing authority will . . . accept that it would not have been reasonable in the circumstances for the applicant to continue to occupy the accommodation which he has left.'

2.122 In *Ashton*,[216] to the same effect, it was held that no reasonable authority would have allowed the provisions of what is now HA 1996, s 177(2) to have

---

208 3 April 2018: see Homelessness Reduction Act 2017 (Commencement and Transitional and Savings Provisions) Regulations 2018, SI 2018/167, reg 3.
209 See, generally, Chapter 8.
210 HA 1996, s 195(8).
211 HA 1996, s 195(5); see paras **2.147–2.154**.
212 HA 1996, s 195(8)(b).
213 HA 1996, s 195(6). See also para **2.148** as to the definition of threatened with homelessness when a section 21 notice has been served.
214 *R v Hammersmith and Fulham LBC ex p Duro-Rama* (1983) 9 HLR 71, QBD.
215 *Re Islam* [1983] 1 AC 688, (1981) 1 HLR 107, HL.
216 *R v Winchester City Council ex p Ashton* (1992) 24 HLR 520, CA.

led to a decision on intentionality where a middle-aged woman who had been unemployed for six years, and who had chronic active hepatitis, left settled accommodation to take up work in another area.

Type of accommodation

2.123 It has been held that accommodation in a prison cell is not accommodation which it is reasonable for the applicant to continue to occupy (where the applicant has the opportunity to obtain early release under a tagging scheme): *B.*[217]

2.124 Both the English and Welsh Codes[218] suggest that some types of accommodation – for example, women's refuges; direct access hostels; and night shelters intended to provide very short-term temporary accommodation in a crisis – should not be regarded as reasonable for someone to continue to occupy in the medium and longer term.[219]

Other considerations

2.125 There are potentially as many reasons why people may not wish to remain in accommodation as there are applicants; accordingly, there is no simple test of reasonableness.[220]

2.126 In *Rowe*,[221] it was conceded by the authority that, in deciding that it was reasonable for the applicant to continue to reside in an HMO, it ought to have considered whether the house had an HMO licence under Pt 2, Housing Act 2004. But for that concession, the appeal would have been dismissed: the absence of a tenancy agreement was not something so important that no reasonable authority would have failed to consider it; the authority had drawn a reasonable distinction between feeling uncomfortable and feeling at risk while living in a shared house – the applicant was able to carry out all her day-to-day activities; the authority had considered the size of the accommodation available and concluded that it did not have a significant effect on the applicant or her children; and there was no evidence that communal facilities were inadequate.

---

217 *R (B) v Southwark LBC* [2003] EWHC 1678 (Admin), [2004] HLR 3. But see *Birmingham City Council v Ali; Moran v Manchester City Council (Secretary of State for Communities and Local Government and another intervening)* [2009] UKHL 36, [2009] 1 WLR 1506, and para **2.16**, where the House of Lords expressly reserved the issue of whether prison could comprise accommodation at all.

218 English Homelessness Code para 6.39; Welsh Code para 8.27.

219 See also para **2.16**, where in *Birmingham CC v. Ali, Moran v. Manchester CC*, it was said that accommodation in a women's refuge was not accommodation it which it was reasonable to continue in occupation.

220 See English Homelessness Code paras 6.39–6.40; Welsh Code para 8.20.

221 *Rowe v Haringey LBC* [2022] EWCA Civ 1370; [2023] HLR 5.

2.127 In *Bassett*,[222] the court held that a woman who had followed her husband to Canada, notwithstanding the uncertainties of their prospects there, could not reasonably have remained in occupation of their secure council accommodation, when going to join him was her only chance of saving their marriage.

2.128 It would be wrong, however, to view this as anything more than an illustration of the proposition that it is the particular circumstances of applicant and household which are relevant.[223]

2.129 In *Hearn*,[224] the applicant's sense of isolation was held to be a factor relevant to deciding whether it was reasonable for her to continue to occupy premises.

2.130 In *Healiss*,[225] the authority failed to consider the applicant's reasons for leaving accommodation of which she was a secure tenant, including repeated break-ins to empty flats in her block, two burglaries of her own flat, harassment involving strangers knocking at the door, stones thrown at windows, and shouting up to her windows at all hours of the day and night; in addition, gangs of youths congregated on the stairway smoking what was assumed to be drugs, the first-floor landing was used as a latrine and smelled as such, and the applicant was too frightened to allow her child to play in the block and gardens.

2.131 In *Nimako-Boateng*,[226] however, the court upheld the decision of the authority that a woman could reasonably have remained in occupation of the matrimonial home in Ghana, even though her relationship with her husband had broken down. (The court noted that it had been given no information about Ghanaian family law, and assumed that the woman's rights would have been the same as under English law. There was no complaint of domestic violence.)[227] *Nimako-Boateng* was followed in *Evans*.[228]

2.132 In *Moncada*,[229] the applicant was divorced from his wife and had custody of his two sons. The court refused to interfere with a finding that, given the shortage of accommodation in London, it was reasonable for him to continue to live in the four-bedroomed matrimonial home, even though his ex-wife and daughter were also still living in it.

---

222 *R v Basingstoke and Deane BC ex p Bassett* (1983) 10 HLR 125, QBD.
223 Cf, above, *R v Brent LBC ex p McManus* (1993) 25 HLR 643, QBD; and *R v Shrewsbury BC ex p Griffiths* (1993) 25 HLR 613, QBD.
224 *R v Swansea City Council ex p Hearn* (1991) 23 HLR 372, QBD.
225 *R v Sefton MBC ex p Healiss* (1995) 27 HLR 34, QBD.
226 *R v Wandsworth LBC ex p Nimako-Boateng* (1983) 11 HLR 95, QBD.
227 On the issue of domestic violence, as distinct from matrimonial breakdown, see now, however, *Bond*, para **2.90**.
228 *R v Eastleigh BC ex p Evans* (1985) 17 HLR 515, QBD.
229 *R v Kensington and Chelsea RLBC ex p Moncada* (1997) 29 HLR 289, QBD.

2.133　All violence and threats of violence, whatever their source, will now fall to be considered under HA 1996, s 177[230] rather than – as previously – under s 175(2).[231]

Financial Considerations

2.134　Financial considerations raise the question of 'affordability': see *Hawthorne*,[232] in which the authority had to consider whether the applicant's failure to pay rent had been caused by the inadequacy of her financial resources. This is now governed by the suitability Order, below.

Affordability

2.135　The Secretary of State and the Welsh ministers have power to specify other circumstances in which it is or is not to be regarded as reasonable to continue to occupy accommodation, and matters (other than the general housing circumstances of the area) which are to be taken into account when determining whether or not it is reasonable to continue in occupation (HA 1996, s 177(3); H(W)A 2014, s 57(4)).

2.136　Authorities in England are required to take affordability into account when determining whether or not it is reasonable to continue to occupy accommodation: Homelessness (Suitability of Accommodation) Order 1996.[233] This requires the authority to consider:

a)　the financial resources available to the person;

b)　the costs of the accommodation;

c)　payments being made under a court order to a spouse, or former spouse;

d)　any payments made to support children, whether under a court order or under the Child Support Act 1991; and

e)　the applicant's other reasonable living expenses.[234]

2.137　In reaching this decision, the authority must consider the financial resources available to a person, including, but not limited to: the costs of the accommodation; payments being made under a court order to a spouse or former spouse; any payments made to support children; whether under a court order or

---

230　See paras **2.83–2.90**.

231　See, for example, *R v Hillingdon LBC ex p H* (1988) 20 HLR 559, QBD; *R v Northampton BC ex p Clarkson* (1992) 24 HLR 529, QBD; *R v Croydon LBC ex p Toth* (1988) 20 HLR 576, CA; and *R v Newham LBC ex p McIlroy and McIlroy* (1991) 23 HLR 570, QBD.

232　*R v Wandsworth LBC ex p Hawthorne* (1995) 27 HLR 59, CA.

233　Homelessness (Suitability of Accommodation) Order 1996/3204 (see appendix B). In Wales, see H(W)A 2014, s 59(2), to the same effect.

234　See also English Code of Guidance paras 17.46.

under the Child Support Act 1991; and the applicant's other reasonable living expenses.[235]

2.138 The Order also contains a detailed list of deductible accommodation costs,[236] although authorities are not limited to consideration of these.[237]

2.139 In determining the amount that an applicant requires for residual living costs, the English code of Guidance[238] suggests that authorities may be guided by universal credit standard allowances when assessing the income that an applicant will require to meet essential needs aside from housing costs, but should ensure that the wishes, needs and circumstances of the applicant and their household are taken into account.[239] Both the English and Welsh Codes[240] make it clear that affordability is always an issue which must be considered.[241]

2.140 This is consistent with prior case-law. In *Duro-Rama*,[242] the availability of benefits was held to be a relevant consideration which the authority had ignored[243] by confining itself to the matters set out in HA 1985, s 60(4) (now HA 1996, s 177(2)).

2.141 In *Griffiths*,[244] it was said that it cannot be assumed that income support is sufficient to meet housing costs. In *Tinn*,[245] Kennedy J expressed the view that, as a matter of common sense, it cannot be reasonable for someone to continue to occupy accommodation when they can no longer discharge the financial obligations in relation to it without so straining their resources as to deprive

---

235 1996 Order art 2(a).
236 1996 Order art 2(b).
237 Unlike under the 1996 Order in England, in Wales H(W)A 2014, s 59(2) provides no further details. The Welsh Code requires consideration of the 'financial resources available to the applicant; the costs in respect of the accommodation; maintenance payments (in respect of ex-family members); and the applicant's other reasonable living expenses': see para 8.29; see also para 19.26.
238 English Homelessness Code para 17.47.
239 This does not mean that the authority is bound to use those figures or that officers are advised or recommended to do so or that an authority must treat the amount of benefits received as a benchmark for how much an applicant can reasonably spend on living expenses: *Baptie v Kingston upon Thames RBC* [2022] EWCA Civ 888; [2022] HLR 35.
240 English Homelessness Code para 6.28; Welsh Code para 8.29.
241 Welsh Code para 19.28 is more prescriptive: accommodation is not to be considered affordable if the applicant 'would be left with a residual income which would be significantly less than the level of income support or income-based Jobseekers allowance or Universal Credit that is applicable in respect of the applicant, or would be applicable if he or she was entitled to claim such benefit . . . Local authorities will need to consider whether the applicant can afford the housing costs without being deprived of basic essentials such as food, clothing, heating, transport and other essentials'.
242 *R v Hammersmith and Fulham LBC ex p Duro-Rama* (1983) 9 HLR 71, QBD.
243 When considering the applicants' reasons for departing their previous accommodation.
244 *R v Shrewsbury BC ex p Griffiths* (1993) 25 HLR 613, QBD. See further *R v Hillingdon LBC ex p Tinn* (1988) 20 HLR 305, QBD; and *R v Camden LBC ex p Aranda* (1996) 28 HLR 672, QBD. Cf *R v Westminster City Council ex p Moklis Ali* (1996) 29 HLR 580, QBD.
245 *R v Hillingdon LBC ex p Tinn* (1988) 20 HLR 305, QBD.

themselves of the ordinary necessities of life. This was followed in *Bibi*,[246] where it was likewise said that inadequacy of financial resources goes not merely to ability to pay the rent, but also to funding the necessities of life, including food, following *Tinn*.[247]

2.142 On the other hand, in *Khan*,[248] the authority was entitled to reach the view that the applicants had not been forced to sell their previous home by reason of financial pressure; and in *Baruwa*[249] it was said that deciding what are the necessities of life for any particular family affords a substantial 'margin of appreciation' to authorities, although this must now be read subject to *Samuels* at [34]:[250] the authority was entitled to be satisfied that the applicant had sufficient income, given that – although no longer in work – she was spending £954 on a university course for herself and over £50 per week on nursery education for her child.

2.143 In *Samuels*,[251] the argument that only housing benefit should be taken into account when deciding whether a property was affordable for the applicant was rejected; all household income should be taken into account; the question is not, however, whether there is sufficient flexibility to enable the applicant to cope, but what the other (non-rent) reasonable living expenses of the household are, having regard to the needs of the applicant(s) and any children, including promotion of the welfare of the latter,[252] which 'requires an objective assessment; it cannot depend simply on the subjective view of the case officer'.[253] In the absence of any other source of objective guidance on this issue,[254] benefit levels – which 'are not generally designed to provide a surplus above subsistence needs for the family' – are themselves a material consideration when assessing reasonable living expenses.[255] It is only once that assessment has taken place that the question arises whether the amount left after taking all income into account and deducting those (objectively assessed) reasonable living expenses is sufficient to cover the shortfall between housing benefit (or the housing element of universal credit) and the rent payable that the accommodation could be considered affordable.

246 *R v Islington LBC ex p Bibi* (1997) 29 HLR 498, QBD.
247 *R v Hillingdon LBC ex p Tinn* (1988) 20 HLR 206, QBD.
248 *R v Westminster City Council ex p Khan* (1991) 23 HLR 230, QBD. See also *R v Leeds City Council ex p Adamiec* (1992) 24 HLR 138, QBD; and *R v Westminster City Council ex p Moklis Ali* (1997) 29 HLR 580, QBD.
249 *R v Brent LBC ex p Baruwa* (1997) 29 HLR 915, CA.
250 *Samuels v Birmingham City Council* [2019] UKSC 28, [2019] PTSR 1229, [2019] HLR 32.
251 *Samuels v Birmingham City Council*, above.
252 Children Act 2004, s 11; and see *Samuels v Birmingham City Council*, above, at [36].
253 *Samuels v Birmingham City Council*, above, at [34].
254 *Samuels v Birmingham City Council*, above, at [36]. In *Baptie v Kingston upon Thames RBC* [2022] EWCA 888; [2022] HLR 35, the *Evidence base for cost of living and guidance for caseworkers* published by the Association of Housing Advice Services (AHAS) was considered both objective and reliable so that the authority could rely on it when determining the applicant's reasonable living expenses.
255 *Samuels v Birmingham City Council*, above, at [35]. It has been held that this conclusion followed from the language of the Code of Guidance, coupled with the review officer's failure in *Samuels* to take account of any other objective source of guidance but does not reflect any wider legal principle: *Baptie v Kingston upon Thames RBC* [2022] EWCA 888; [2022] HLR 35.

2.144 More recently, it has been said that the requirement to consider an applicant's reasonable living expenses directs an inquiry into the needs of the applicant and their family and imposes an objective standard for determining whether any expenditure relied on to prove that accommodation was unaffordable should be taken into account; the Order requires the authority to decide what in a particular case constitutes a reasonable level of expenditure and the Code suggests that this should be measured by what the applicant requires in order to provide as a minimum standard the basic essentials of life; an authority should conduct its own calculations, which must be evidence-based[256] and have regard to points raised by the applicant; provided that the officer making the assessment has paid due regard to the relevant guidance and has reached a conclusion open to them on the material available, there are no grounds for interfering with the decision; it is not for the court to review the multifactorial assessment which the authority has carried out; unless it can be shown that the authority materially misdirected itself or failed to take relevant matters into account, there is no error of law.[257]

2.145 In that case, an officer of the authority calculated the appellant's weekly income to be £565.42 and his weekly expenditure to be £539.70, including £32 per week for replacement white goods. She decided that the appellant could have afforded to pay the rent for the flat. An officer conducting a review of the decision re-calculated the applicant's weekly income as £548.97 and weekly expenditure as £545.62, not including any amount for replacement white goods which the officer did not consider to be an essential expense; in a subsequent letter, he said that there was sufficient flexibility to cater for such an eventuality. This recognised that such expenditure might be both necessary and reasonable but that it would be occasional; the review officer's assessment that there was sufficient flexibility in the family budget to cater for occasional expenditure on replacement white goods was a conclusion which was properly open to him on the information available.

2.146 Conversely, in *Paley*,[258] the applicant completed an Accommodation Needs Form, which included details of her weekly income and expenditure, including £29.50 for bus fares, £8 for taxis, and two judgment debts being paid off at the rate of £35 and £20 respectively. She was offered accommodation in Stoke-on-Trent, 161 miles from Waltham Forest, which she challenged, among other matters, on the ground of affordability. The authority assessed her income as £395.31 and expenditure as £384.61 with no specific allowance for the costs of public transport or repaying her judgment debts but including a figure of £50

---

256 See also para **2.143** on the use of the *Evidence base for cost of living and guidance for caseworkers* published by the Association of Housing Advice Services (AHAS) upheld in, In *Baptie v Kingston upon Thames RBC* [2022] EWCA 888; [2022] HLR 35.
257 *Patel v.Hackney LBC* [2021] EWCA Civ 897; [2021] HLR 39. See also *R v Brent LBC ex p Grossett* (1996) 28 HLR 9, CA; *R v Brent LBC ex p Baruwa* (1997) 29 HLR 915, CA; and. *Bernard v Enfield LBC* [2001] EWCA Civ 1831, CA.
258 *Paley v Waltham Forest LBC* [2022] EWCA Civ 112; [2022] HLR 24,

per week for 'other' expenses. On review, in its minded-to letter,[259] the authority noted that there was a bus stop near the flat and that shops and other facilities were not far by public transport. The Court of Appeal held that the authority had failed to consider the appellant's particular needs; its assessment of expenditure made no allowance for routine and frugal use of local public transport nor did it allow for the cost of occasional visits to her family in London; nor did the authority's figure of £50 per week to cover other expenditure begin to cover the applicant's reasonable expenses; on an objective assessment of the appellant's income and expenditure, no reasonable authority could have concluded that it was affordable.

THREATENED WITH HOMELESSNESS

2.147   A person is 'threatened with homelessness' for the purposes of HA 1996, Part 7 if it is likely that they will become homeless within 56 days.[260]

2.148   Since 9 November 2012, when LA 2011, s 149 came fully into force in England,[261] an applicant who makes a fresh application to an English authority within two years of a previous application which had resulted in the offer and acceptance of an assured shorthold tenancy, in respect of which notice has been given under HA 1988, s 21, is entitled to be treated as threatened with homelessness from when the notice is given.[262] This does not apply where the application was made before – and the duty to secure accommodation was still in existence at – that date.[263]

> RENTERS (REFORM) BILL
>
> Once in full relevant force and subject to any transitional provisions, s 195A will be repealed and the amendment made by Localism Act 2011 will therefore cease to have effect so that this additional category of threatened with homelessness will not exist.

259 Para **7.227**.
260 HA 1996, s 175(4), H(W)A 2014, s 55(4).
261 Localism Act 2011 (Commencement No 2 and Transitional Provisions) (England) Order 2012, SI 2012/2599 art 2.
262 HA 1996, s 195A(4). This right only arises on one re-application: HA 1996, s 195A(6). See also the letter in June 2016, from the secretary of state to all local authority chief executives reminding them that authorities 'should not adopt a general policy of accepting – or refusing to accept – applicants as homeless or threatened with homelessness when they are threatened with eviction but a court has not yet made an order for possession or issued a warrant of execution'.
263 Localism Act 2011 (Commencement No 2 and Transitional Provisions) (England) Order 2012, SI 2012/2599 art 3.

2.149   Since 3 April 2018 when the HRA 2017 came into force,[264] an assured shorthold tenant served with a valid notice under HA 1988, s 21, in respect of the only accommodation which that person has[265] which is available for their occupation,[266] and which will expire within 56 days, is also threatened with homelessness.[267]

> RENTERS (REFORM) BILL
>
> Once in full relevant force and subject to any transitional provisions, s 175(5) will be repealed so that this additional category of threatened with homelessness will not exist.

2.150   Until the HRA 2017 in England, and H(W)A 2014 in Wales, the period was 28 days; it was originally referable to the 'normal' period granted by a court before a possession order would take effect. Since 3 October 1980, however, courts have been obliged to make orders to take effect within 14 days, save where exceptional hardship would be caused: see HA 1980, s 89, although this is applicable only where the court has no other discretion to suspend, for example, under the RA 1977, HA 1985 or HA 1988.

2.151   Even once the date for possession has passed, the applicant will not be homeless until the warrant for possession is executed.[268] During this period, the applicant will, however, be threatened with homelessness.

2.152   There is no reason to draw any distinction of principle between the definitions of 'homelessness' and 'threatened with homelessness', other than the 56-day criterion: *Dyson*.[269] This seems to be based on a concession by counsel, but must surely be correct.

2.153   Once faced with an applicant who is threatened with homelessness, the authority must start making appropriate enquiries under HA 1996, s 184 or H(W) A 2014, s 60.[270] The duty cannot be postponed until the applicant is actually homeless: *Khan and Hussain*.[271]

2.154   If enquiries are made before the 56 days, they will be non-statutory: *Hunt*.[272]

---

264 Homelessness Reduction Act 2017 (Commencement and Transitional and Savings Provisions) Regulations 2018, SI 2018/167 reg 3, only applicable to applications made and reviews sought on or after that date – see reg.4.
265 For a tenancy to be assured – including assured shorthold – it must be occupied as an only or principal home; accordingly, a tenant could have a principal home with a second home elsewhere, eg used for weekends or holidays; such a tenant will therefore not benefit from this extension.
266 This will be interpreted in the usual way: paras **2.19–2.41**.
267 HA 1996, s 175(5).
268 See *R v Newham LBC ex p Sacupima* (2001) 33 HLR 1, QBD.
269 *Dyson v Kerrier DC* [1980] 1 WLR 1205, CA, at p1212.
270 See Chapter 7.
271 *R v Newham LBC ex p Khan and Hussain* (2001) 33 HLR 29, QBD.
272 *R v Rugby BC ex p Hunt* (1994) 26 HLR 1, QBD.

CHAPTER 3

Priority need

INTRODUCTION

Overview

3.1   There are – normally[1] – no substantive, long-term housing rights or duties under either Housing Act (HA) 1996, Part 7 or Housing (Wales) Act (H(W) A) 2014, Part 2[2] unless the applicant has a 'priority need for accommodation'. There are, however, more limited rights, considered in Chapter 8; a homeless person not in priority need may nonetheless be able to apply for an allocation – see Chapter 9; an authority may be willing to take steps to protect the property of a person with no priority need – see Chapter 6. Chapter 5 governs which authority will be responsible for an applicant with connections with more than one area. An applicant in priority need may, however, lose the principal benefits of HA 1996 and H(W)A 2014 if they are intentionally homeless – see Chapter 4. Chapter 7 discusses the authority's process towards a decision.

3.2   Additionally, since the Localism Act (LA) 2011, s 149 came into force in England,[3] an applicant who makes a fresh application to an English authority within two years of a previous application which resulted in an assured shorthold tenancy, will – if still eligible (see Annex; Immigration Eligibility) and not homeless intentionally (see Chapter 4) – be entitled to assistance if homeless (defined as arising when the notice expires) or threatened with homelessness (defined as arising when the notice is given) regardless of whether or not the applicant is still in priority need.[4] This right only arises on one re-application.[5] It only arises where the new duty to secure accommodation has arisen and had not ceased before the 9 November 2012.[6]

---

1   See para **3.2**.
2   But see paras **8.61–8.78**.
3   9 November 2012: see Localism Act 2011 (Commencement No 2 and Transitional Provisions) (England) Order 2012, SI 2012/2599 art 2.
4   HA 1996, s 195A(1), (3).
5   HA 1996, s 195A(6).
6   Localism Act 2011 (Commencement No 2 and Transitional Provisions) (England) Order 2012, SI 2012/2599 art 3.

RENTERS (REFORM) BILL

Subject to any transitional provisions, this provision will cease to apply once the Bill has been brought into full relevant force as s 195A will have been repealed and the additional category of homelessness will not exist.

3.3 In England, a homeless person or a person threatened with homelessness has a priority need for accommodation if the person is within one of the following categories:[7]

a) she is a pregnant woman, or a person with whom a pregnant woman resides or might reasonably be expected to reside;

b) they are a person with whom dependent children reside or might reasonably be expected to reside;

c) they are vulnerable as a result of old age, mental illness or handicap or physical disability or other special reason, or is someone with whom such a person resides or might reasonably be expected to reside;

d) they are homeless or threatened with homelessness as a result of an emergency such as flood, fire or other disaster;

e) they have become homeless as a result of being a victim of domestic abuse.[8]

3.4 The first four of these categories closely follow those formerly described in Department of the Environment (DoE) Circular 18/74 as the 'priority groups' who were to have the first claim on resources available:

'The Priority Groups comprise families with dependent children living with them, or in care; and adult families or people living alone who either become homeless in an emergency such as fire or flooding or are vulnerable because of old age, disability, pregnancy or other special reasons.'[9]

3.5 In England, the Secretary of State[10] may add to these categories, which power has been exercised in the Homelessness (Priority Need for Accommodation) (England) Order 2002[11] and is discussed below.[12] In Wales, the position is similar but not identical. The English priority need categories in HA 1996, s 189 and the 2002 Order are largely mirrored in H(W)A 2014, s 70. Differences are discussed in the relevant subheadings below. As in England, there is a power in Wales to

---

7   HA 1996, s 189(1).
8   HA 1996, s 189(1) as amended by DAA 2021, s 78(5); H(W)A 2014, s 70(1)(a)–(d).
9   DoE Circular 18/74 para 10; see above, para **1.21**.
10   HA 1996, s 189(2).
11   Homelessness (Priority Need for Accommodation) (England) Order 2002, SI 2002/2051.
12   See further paras **3.78–3.101**.

add to these categories[13] this has been exercised to add the 'street homeless' to the categories of priority need in Wales: para **3.102**.

3.6   Whether in England or Wales, a local authority cannot fetter its discretion by pre-determining that people within specified groups – for example, the single or childless homeless – should never be considered 'vulnerable' within category c) or d) in para **3.2**.[14]

Time of priority need

3.7   Authorities must, when reaching decisions, take into account all material factors up to the date of the decision and, if there is a review, up to the date of the review: *Mohamed v Hammersmith and Fulham LBC*.[15] Accordingly, a priority need can be acquired after application but before decision, or after decision but before review, eg, pregnancy; thus, where children were accommodated with an applicant pending the authority's enquiries, who would not otherwise have been able to live with him, the applicant was still in priority need.[16]

IMMIGRATION

3.8   HA 1996, s 185(4) formerly[17] required local housing authorities in England and Wales to disregard household members (including dependent children) who were ineligible[18] for housing assistance, when considering

---

13   H(W)A 2014, s 72. Unlike in England, there is an additional power for the Welsh Ministers to remove any condition that a local housing authority must have reason to believe or be satisfied that an applicant is in priority need for accommodation before any power or duty to secure accommodation arises, which would allow a court to decide that issue for itself, instead of being confined to principles of public law intervention. It is, accordingly, a power of great potential significance. No plans to exercise this power have yet been announced. See generally, the research paper *Review of priority need in Wales*, Mackie et al, Welsh Government, October 2020.

14   See also paras **10.54–10.55**.

15   [2001] UKHL 57, [2002] HLR 7.

16   *Oxford City Council v Bull* [2011] EWCA Civ 609, [2011] HLR 35.

17   In respect of all applications for accommodation or assistance in obtaining accommodation within the meaning of HA 1996, s 183, made before 2 March 2009.

18   See para **A.128**. For example, in *Ehiabor v Kensington and Chelsea RLBC* [2008] EWCA Civ 1074, the applicant could not rely on the dependent child to establish a priority need because the child, although born in the UK, was not a British citizen and therefore required leave to remain under the Immigration Act 1971, s 1(2) and was subject to immigration control. The restriction was declared incompatible with Article 14 when read with Article 8 of the European Convention on Human Rights (ECHR) in *R (Morris) v Westminster City Council (No 3)* [2005] EWCA Civ 1184, [2006] HLR 8. Cf the different approach taken by the European Court of Human Rights (ECtHR) in *Bah v UK*, App No 56328/07, [2012] HLR 2.

whether any eligible housing applicant was in priority need. This provision was amended[19] so that:

a)   it only applies on its face in England (but see para **3.11**); and

b)   it applies only to an eligible applicant who is themselves a person subject to immigration control,[20] other than a European Economic Area (EEA) or Swiss national (where the EEA or Swiss national was resident in the UK before 1 January 2021),[21] for example, those granted refugee status,[22] indefinite leave to remain[23] or one of the other categories of humanitarian protection.[24]

Thus, the ineligible dependants or other household members of those who are not subject to immigration control, or who – though subject to immigration control – are EEA or Swiss nationals (and who were resident In the UK before 1 January 2021), are to be taken into account when deciding whether the applicant is in priority need; while those who are still subject to the requirement are to be disregarded when deciding that question if they are themselves ineligible for assistance.

3.9   These ineligible household members on whom – since the amendment – reliance can be placed when deciding whether or not the applicant is in priority need are known as 'restricted persons':[25] they are persons who are not themselves eligible for assistance under HA 1996, Part 7, who are subject to immigration control, and who either do not have leave to enter or remain in the UK or who have leave subject to a condition of no recourse to public funds.[26]

3.10   If the authority is only satisfied that the applicant is in priority need by taking into account the restricted person, the application is known as a 'restricted case'.[27] In these circumstances, the authority must, so far as reasonably practical, bring any HA 1996, s 193(2) duty to an end by arranging for an offer of an assured shorthold tenancy to be made to the applicant by a private landlord.[28] This is known as a 'private rented sector offer'.[29]

---

19   By Housing and Regeneration Act 2008, s 314 and Sch 15, Part 1, in respect of all applications for accommodation or assistance in obtaining accommodation within the meaning of HA 1996, s 183, made on or after 2 March 2009. It was further amended with effect from 1 January 2021 to reflect the changes arising out of Brexit by the Immigration and Social Security Co-ordination (EU Withdrawal) Act 2020 (Consequential, Saving, Transitional and Transitory Provisions) (EU Exit) Regulations 2020, SI 2020/1309.
20   See para **A.14**.
21   See para **A.19** onwards. For the Brexit changes, see *Homelessness Code of Guidance for local authorities*, para 7.31-7.344.
22   See paras **A.136–A.143**.
23   See paras **A.144–A.146**.
24   See paras **A.147–A.167**.
25   HA 1996, s 184(7).
26   See *Lekpo-Bozua v Hackney LBC* [2010] EWCA Civ 909, [2010] HLR 46.
27   HA 1996, s 193(3B). See also paras **A.127–A.133**.
28   HA 1996, s 193(7AD). See further paras **8.272–8.281**.
29   HA 1996, s 193.

RENTERS (REFORM) BILL

Once the Bill becomes law and is brought into full relevant force and subject to any transitional provisions, the offer will be of an assured, rather than assured shorthold, tenancy.

3.11   In Wales, the substantive position is the same: the provisions of HA 1996, ss 185 and 186 are deemed to apply to the H(W)A 2014.[30] It follows that, as in England, a duty owed to a restricted person must, so far as is reasonably practicable, be brought to an end by securing an offer of accommodation from a private sector landlord.[31]

PREGNANCY

3.12   Pregnancy:[32] Any stage of pregnancy qualifies as priority need. One of the objects of the Housing (Homeless Persons) Act 1977 was to eliminate the practice of some authorities, who refused to consider a woman's pregnancy as a factor until a given stage of pregnancy. Once the pregnancy is established, there is priority need.[33]

DEPENDENT CHILDREN[34]
Generally

3.13   Dependent children do not qualify in priority need in their own right; nor will they qualify as vulnerable either because of their youth or because of any disability: *ex p G*.[35] Dependent children are expected to be provided for (with assistance where appropriate, including under HA 1996, Part 7 or H(W)A 2014, Part 2) by those on whom they are dependent.

---

30   H(W)A 2014, Sch 2 para 2.
31   H(W)A 2014, s 76.
32   HA 1996, s 189(1)(a); H(W)A 2014, s 70(1)(a).
33   See also below, para **3.7**. Both the English and the Welsh Codes consider that the 'normal letter of confirmation of pregnancy from the medical services issued to pregnant women or a midwife's letter' should be adequate evidence of pregnancy (English Code para 8.5; Welsh Code para 16.5). They note that, if the woman suffers a miscarriage, the authority may need to consider whether she nonetheless remains in priority need because she is vulnerable for another special reason (English Code para 8.5; Welsh Code para 16.5).
34   HA 1996, s 189(1)(b); H(W)A 2014, s 70(1)(b).
35   *R v Oldham BC ex p G; R v Bexley LBC ex p B; R v Tower Hamlets LBC ex p Begum* [1993] AC 509, (1993) 25 HLR 319, HL; and see para **7.21**.

3.14   The notion of a dependent child connotes a relationship akin to that of parent–child:[36] an applicant with a 17-year-old wife could not claim to be in priority need under this category on the basis of her dependency on him.[37] The same is likely to be held in relation to siblings, eg, an 18-year-old applicant with a 17-year-old sibling. A greater age difference between siblings, however, giving rise to a truly dependent relationship more akin to that of parent–child, could still give rise to a priority need.[38]

3.15   Children must be 'residing' with an applicant, not merely 'staying' – that is to say that some degree of permanence or regularity must exist.[39]

Alternative tests

3.16   The tests are alternative. In *Islam*,[40] not cross-appealed on this point,[41] the authority unsuccessfully contended that, where reliance is placed by an applicant on dependent children living with the applicant, it is also necessary to show that such children might reasonably be expected to reside with the applicant. This is not correct: if there are dependent children actually residing with the applicant at the date of the authority's decision (not the date of application),[42] it is not relevant to consider whether or not they are reasonably expected to do so.

3.17   In *Sidhu*,[43] the applicant and her children were living in a women's refuge.[44] The applicant had obtained an interim custody order from the county court, but the authority contended that it was entitled not to consider her to be in priority need until a full custody order was granted. The court rejected this argument: the full order was irrelevant (nor could the authority defer its decision in order to have time to assure itself that no change would take place in the future[45] – in that case, the prospective change was the remote prospect of the applicant losing custody at full hearing). The same may now be said of child arrangement orders.[46]

3.18   An order of a court will, however, be relevant where an applicant's children are not currently residing with the applicant, but reliance is placed on a

---

36   See English Code of Guidance para 8.8; Welsh Code para 16.6.
37   *Hackney LBC v Ekinci* [2001] EWCA Civ 776, [2002] HLR 2.
38   *R (Lusamba) v Islington LBC* [2008] EWHC 1149 (Admin), [2008] JHL D89.
39   See also *R v Lewisham LBC ex p Creppy* (1992) 24 HLR 121, CA and *R v Lambeth LBC ex p Bodunrin* (1992) 24 HLR 647, QBD. This may, however, have started while in interim accommodation provided by the authority pending enquiries, ie it need not pre-date the application; this is consistent with the normal approach to time of priority need: para **3.7**.
40   *R v Hillingdon Homeless Persons Panel ex p Islam* (1980) *Times* 10 February, QBD.
41   *Re Islam* [1983] 1 AC 688, (1981) 1 HLR 107, HL.
42   See para **7.176**.
43   *R v Ealing LBC ex p Sidhu* (1982) 2 HLR 45, QBD.
44   See paras **2.15–2.16**.
45   A proposition approved in *Robinson v Hammersmith and Fulham LBC* [2006] EWCA Civ 1122, [2006] 1 WLR 3295, [2006] HLR 7.
46   Under Children Act (CA) 1989, s 8.

claim that they are reasonably to be expected to do so – for example, where the applicant has won custody but cannot in practice take care of the children for want of accommodation.

Dependence

3.19   There must be dependence on the applicant: an applicant is not in priority need where children who reside with them are dependent on someone else.[47]

3.20   'Dependent' is not defined in HA 1996, Part 7 or in H(W)A 2014, Part 2. In *Amarfio*,[48] the Court of Appeal considered the Code of Guidance under HA 1985, Part 3 (reproduced so far as relevant in the current Codes),[49] which referred to children under the age of 16 as dependent, together with those under the age of 19 either receiving full-time education or training or otherwise unable to support themselves. It was held that once a child has gone into full-time employment, the child could not be dependant: a young person on a youth training scheme was considered to be in gainful employment by way of training and therefore to be regarded as being in full-time employment.

3.21   The court did, however, recognise that there may be circumstances where a 16- or 17-year-old, even though not financially dependent on their parents, is sufficiently dependent on them in other respects to fall within the subsection.[50]

3.22   In *Miah v Newham LBC*,[51] the authority had treated the Code of Guidance as limited to children up to their 18th birthday. The Court of Appeal held that the Code addressed children under 19 years old (who are in full-time education or training or otherwise unable to support themselves): the Code had therefore been misinterpreted by the authority.

Separated parents

3.23   Where parents are separated, a child may divide their time between parents or others.[52] Three separate issues arise:

---

47   See *R v Westminster City Council ex p Bishop* (1997) 29 HLR 546, QBD. See also *R v Camden LBC ex p Hersi* (2001) 33 HLR 52, QBD.
48   *R v Kensington and Chelsea RLBC ex p Amarfio* (1995) 27 HLR 543, CA.
49   English Code of Guidance para 8.7; Welsh Code para 16.6.
50   This accords with the conclusion in *Shortt v Secretary of State for Communities and Local Government and Tewkesbury BC* [2015] EWCA Civ 1192, [2016] 1 P&CR 15 in which the differing views expressed in the non-homelessness decision of *Fawcett Properties Ltd v Buckingham CC* [1961] AC 636, HL were considered in relation to a planning condition imposed by a local authority, the effect of which was to limit occupation of a property to persons employed in agricultural activities and their dependants: it was held that dependency was not confined to financial dependency; 'dependant' was an ordinary word, capable of referring to relationships involving non-financial dependency.
51   [2001] EWCA Civ 487.
52   See English Code of Guidance paras 8.6–8.12; Welsh Code para 16.8.

a) whether the child is dependent on the applicant;

b) whether the child resides with the applicant; and

c) if the child is not currently residing with the applicant, whether the child may reasonably be expected to do so.

Dependence on applicant

3.24   In *Vagliviello*,[53] the authority erred by applying a 'wholly and exclusively dependent' test. For the purposes of HA 1985, s 59, now HA 1996, s 189, it is possible for a child to reside with and be dependent on more than one person, only one of whom may be applying for assistance.[54]

3.25   In *Bishop*,[55] parents had agreed that the children should split their time between each of them; the authority was nonetheless entitled to conclude that the children were not dependent on one of them, the father. In reaching this decision, it took into account that the children were adequately housed with the mother; that she received income support and child benefit for them; and that the applicant, who was unemployed, did not have the financial means of supporting them.

Residing with applicant

3.26   In *Smith-Morse*,[56] the authority erred because it applied a 'main' residence test; it also failed to consider the future as well as present arrangements for the child. On the other hand, in *McCarthy*,[57] the parents were divorced and, though there was a joint custody order, care and control had been given to the mother. Although it had been agreed that the children should spend three days per week with their father, this sort of 'staying access' did not equate to residence. It would only be in very exceptional circumstances that a child might reside with both parents living apart: this type of arrangement has become much more common since the Children Act (CA) 1989 came into force.[58]

3.27   The question is to be determined at the date of the decision.[59] Where the decision is made while the applicant is still only threatened with

---

53   *R v Lambeth LBC ex p Vagliviello* (1990) 22 HLR 392, CA.
54   But see *Holmes-Moorhouse v Richmond upon Thames LBC* [2009] UKHL 7, [2009] HLR 34, para **3.30**.
55   *R v Westminster City Council ex p Bishop* (1997) 29 HLR 546, QBD.
56   *R v Kingswood BC ex p Smith-Morse* (1994) *Times*, December 8, QBD.
57   *R v Port Talbot BC ex p McCarthy* (1991) 23 HLR 207, CA.
58   See also *Holmes-Moorhouse v Richmond upon Thames LBC* [2009] UKHL 7, [2009] HLR 34. It was recognised that shared residence orders (now 'child arrangement orders') are much more common now. The policy reasons for a local authority not providing a family that previously lived under one roof with a second home were, however, considered to be overwhelming.
59   See para **3.7**.

homelessness,[60] at which point the applicant may still be residing with children, for example, before leaving the family home, the applicant will only be in priority need if the children will be residing with the applicant once they are actually homeless, which may not be the case if the authority provides no accommodation.[61]

Reasonably expected to reside

3.28   *McCarthy*[62] also held that, while not bound to do so, the authority could conclude that children are usually reasonably to be expected to reside with the parent who has care and control.

3.29   A child arrangement order[63] does not, however, mean that the children are reasonably to be expected to reside with both parents. In *Doyle*,[64] four children were to spend half the week with each parent under such an order. The father applied to the authority as homeless. The authority took the joint residence order into account but could still decide that the children were not reasonably expected to reside with the applicant. In reaching this decision, the authority was entitled to take into account the shortage of housing stock in its area and the under-occupation for part of each week that would result.

3.30   In *Holmes-Moorhouse v Richmond upon Thames LBC*,[65] the separated parents of four children agreed to a shared residence order pursuant to which the three youngest children would spend alternate weeks and half of each school holiday with the father. The father then applied to the local authority relying on the order to demonstrate priority need. The House of Lords held that, although such an order is part of the material to which an authority should have regard when making its decision, whether children are reasonably expected to reside with an applicant is a matter for the local authority to decide and cannot be dictated by a residence order.[66]

3.31   The question that the local authority should ask is whether it is reasonably to be expected, *in the context of a scheme for housing the homeless*, that children who already have a home with their mother should be able also to reside with their father, ie, asking that question in the context of a scheme for the allocation

---

60   See paras **2.147–2.154**.
61   *Holmes-Moorhouse v Richmond upon Thames LBC*, above, at [20].
62   See para **3.26**.
63   Under CA 1989, s 8, known as a 'residence order' or 'shared/joint residence order' prior to 22 April 2014.
64   *R v Oxford City Council ex p Doyle* (1998) 30 HLR 506, QBD.
65   [2009] UKHL 7, [2009] HLR 34.
66   [2009] UKHL 7, [2009] HLR 34 at [17].

of a scarce resource.[67] Only in exceptional circumstances[68] will it be reasonable to expect a child who has a home with one parent to be provided under HA 1996, Part 7[69] with another so that the child can reside with both parents.

3.32   The reference to exceptional circumstances is not a gloss on the statutory scheme, but an observation as to the probable result in the majority of cases involving separated parents.[70] The policy reasons referred to in *Holmes-Moorhouse*[71] are far from illusory: if it had been held that both parents were entitled to be treated as being in priority need, this could mean not only that families in social housing would commonly require the provision of two homes in place of one but also many in the private rented sector and also in owner-occupation, where many, particularly those with a mortgage, would not be able to afford to purchase a second home.

Children in social services care

3.33   The alternative limbs – 'are residing, or might reasonably be expected to reside' – avoid the difficulties which might otherwise arise where children are in temporary accommodation.

3.34   Where children are being looked after by the local social services authority, they may still be dependent on their parents and liaison with social services will be essential. 'Joint consideration with social services will ensure that the best interests of the applicant and the children are served.'[72] In the context of an assessment,[73] it has been held that it was "obvious' that some or all children in care under an interim order who were the subject of contested proceedings 'might well return' to live with the applicant[74] and, as such, were to be regarded as persons who were reasonably to be expected to reside with the applicant;[75] the wording of the judgment suggests that this would be true of all children the subject of contested care proceedings but it may be obvious that some will not

---

67   [2009] UKHL 7, [2009] HLR 34 at [9] and [14]–[16].
68   [2009] UKHL 7, [2009] HLR 34 at [21]: 'It seems to me that the likely needs of the children will have to be exceptional before a housing authority will decide that it is reasonable to expect an applicant to be provided with accommodation for them which will stand empty for at least half the time. I do not say that there may not be such a case; for example, if there is a child suffering from a disability which makes it imperative for care to be shared between separated parents. But such cases, in which that child (but not necessarily any sibling) might reasonably be expected to reside with both parents, will be unusual.'
69   Or H(W)A 2014, Part 2.
70   *El Goure v Kensington and Chelsea RLBC* [2012] EWCA Civ 670, [2012] HLR 36, in which it was stressed that the question of reasonableness is primarily one for the authority.
71   See para **3.26**.
72   English Code of Guidance para 8.12; Welsh Code para 16.10.
73   See paras 8.61-8.78.
74   And accordingly should have been taken into account on the assessment: see para 8.61.
75   *R (SK) v Royal Borough of Windsor and Maidenhead* [2024] EWHC 158 (Admin); [2024] HLR forthcoming.

be returning and, as such, they would not be persons likely to reside with the applicant – it will turn on the facts.

VULNERABILITY[76]

Generally

Armed Forces

3.35   When determining whether someone is vulnerable, as in all matters under Part 7, a local authority must have regard to:

> '(a) the unique obligations of, and sacrifices made by, the armed forces,
>
> (b) the principle that it is desirable to remove disadvantages arising for service people from membership, or former membership, of the armed forces, and
>
> (c) the principle that special provision for service people may be justified by the effects on such people of membership, or former membership, of the armed forces'.[77]

3.36   It is not hard to see that some effects of service may generate a vulnerability when homeless that might not otherwise be recognised.

England

3.37   The question in England is whether a person is vulnerable as a result of old age, mental illness or handicap or physical disability or other special reason. Much of the litigation in this area has focused on the meaning of 'vulnerable'. The 2015 Supreme Court decision in *Hotak v Southwark LBC and other appeals*[78] represented a change in approach, but it is easiest and best understood in light of the law as it stood previously.

3.38   It had formerly been held that vulnerability meant that someone was 'less able to fend for himself than an ordinary homeless person so that injury

---

76   HA 1996, s 189(1)(c); H(W)A 2014, s 70(1)(c).

77   Armed Forces Act 2006, ss 343AA (England) and 343AB (Wales) added by Armed Forces Act 2021, s 8(3).

78   *Hotak v Southwark LBC; Kanu v Southwark LBC; Johnson v Solihull MBC* [2015] UKSC 30, [2015] HLR 23.

or detriment to him will result where a less vulnerable man will be able to cope without harmful effects': *Pereira*.[79]

3.39   Detriment could include a significantly increased risk of suicide or of developing a serious ailment, but it did not have to be measured in percentage terms.[80] The authority was not obliged to identify precisely the attributes of the ordinary homeless person against whom the applicant was being compared;[81] it made no difference whether the authority expressed its conclusions in terms of the applicant being at no greater risk of injury or detriment than the ordinary homeless person, or in terms of the applicant being no less able to fend for themselves than the ordinary homeless person: they were considered to be no more than two ways of saying the same thing.[82]

3.40   The *Periera* test was considered and approved in *Osmani*,[83] although it was stressed that it was a judicial guide, not a statutory formulation. It was said to involve a necessarily imprecise exercise in comparison between the applicant and the 'ordinary homeless person'.

> 'Given that each authority is charged with local application of a national scheme of priorities but against its own burden of homeless persons and

79   *R v Camden LBC ex p Pereira* (1999) 31 HLR 317, CA at 330, applying *Bowers* (above), overruling *R v Reigate and Banstead BC ex p Di Domenico* (1988) 20 HLR 153, QBD and *Ortiz v Westminster City Council* (1995) 27 HLR 364, CA. These cases had added the gloss – amounting to a two-part test – that in addition to being less able to fend when homeless, there had to be a lessened ability to find and keep accommodation. In *R v Kensington and Chelsea RLBC, Hammersmith and Fulham LBC, Westminster City Council, and Islington LBC ex p Kihara and others* (1997) 29 HLR 147, CA, however, Simon Brown LJ doubted his own proposition to this effect in *Ortiz* (although not the outcome on the facts), which he had not intended to comprise a new statement of principle, and *Pereira* disposed of it. The issue at this stage of the law's development was whether the applicant was less able to fend with the consequences of homelessness than a less vulnerable person, without a risk of injury or detriment. The cases of *R v Bath City Council ex p Sangermano* (1985) 17 HLR 94, QBD (approved in *R v Wandsworth LBC ex p Banbury* (1987) 19 HLR 76) and *R v Lambeth LBC ex p Carroll* (1988) 20 HLR 142, QBD, which had referred to vulnerability as being 'loosely in housing terms or the context of housing', while not overruled, were not to be taken to suggest anything other than assessment of ability to cope without the risk of injury or detriment: *Pereira* at 330. See also *Osmani v Camden LBC* [2004] EWCA Civ 1706, [2005] HLR 22.
80   *Griffin v Westminster City Council* [2004] EWCA Civ 108, [2004] HLR 32. In *Ajilore v Hackney LBC* [2014] EWCA Civ 1273, [2014] HLR 46, the applicant's depression and suicidal ideation did not make him vulnerable as statistics showed that significant numbers of homeless people had similar conditions; an appeal was unsuccessful: even though the reviewing officer had misunderstood the statistics, it did not undermine the thrust of the decision. The decision was overtaken by *Hotak* and other appeals.
81   *Tetteh v Kingston upon Thames RLBC* [2004] EWCA Civ 1775, [2005] HLR 21. Cf *Hall v Wandsworth LBC; Carter v Wandsworth LBC* [2004] EWCA Civ 1740, [2005] HLR 23, where the authority posed the wrong question.
82   *Bellouti v Wandsworth LBC* [2005] EWCA Civ 602, [2005] HLR 46.
83   *Osmani v Camden LBC* [2004] EWCA Civ 1706, [2005] HLR 22. The judgment of Auld LJ in *Osmani* was described by Jonathon Parker LJ in *Bellouti v Wandsworth LBC* [2005] EWCA Civ 602, [2005] HLR 46 at [57] as saying 'all that (at least for present purposes) need be said or can be said on the matter' of deciding whether an applicant is vulnerable.

finite resources, such decisions are often likely to be highly judgmental. In the context of balancing the priorities of such persons a local housing authority is likely to be better placed in most instances for making such a judgment.'[84]

3.41 The authority was required to be careful to assess and apply the test on the assumption that an applicant had become or would become street homeless, not on the applicant's ability to fend for themselves while still housed.[85]

3.42 This was the context in which *Hotak and other appeals* settled a new approach,[86] more clearly focused on the individual applicant: when assessing whether an applicant is vulnerable, an authority must pay close attention to their particular circumstances rather than to a statistical analysis of the homeless population; expressions such as 'street homeless' and 'fend for oneself' are not found in HA 1996 and should be avoided; whether a person is considered to be 'vulnerable' requires comparison between the ordinary person who is homeless, not the ordinary homeless person; '"vulnerable" ... connotes "significantly more vulnerable than ordinarily vulnerable" as a result [of being rendered homeless'[87].[88]

3.43 An applicant who would otherwise be vulnerable might not be so, however, if – when homeless – they would be provided with support and care by a third party; whether a particular applicant will in fact receive support and, if so, what support, is a case-specific question, to which the answer must be based on evidence; even if very substantial support is provided, it does not necessarily mean that an applicant is not vulnerable.[89]

---

84 Per Auld LJ at [38].
85 *Osmani*, above, per Auld LJ at [38].
86 In *Hemley v Croydon LBC* [2018] HLR 1, the Court of Appeal considered that *Hotak* had so substantially modified the previous test that where the review officer had applied the *Pereira* test, it could not be certain that he would have reached the same conclusion had he applied the *Hotak* test; his decision was therefore quashed.
87 Lord Neuberger in *Hotak* at [53]; see also English Code of Guidance para 8.15.
88 In *Panayiotou v Waltham Forest LBC; Smith v Haringey LBC* [2017] EWCA Civ 1624, [2018] QB 1232, [2017] HLR 48, it was held that this gave rise to a qualitative test rather than setting a quantitative threshold: 'In other words, the question to be asked is whether, when compared to an ordinary person if made homeless, the applicant, in consequence of a characteristic within section 189(1)(c), would suffer or be at risk of suffering harm or detriment which the ordinary person would not suffer or be at risk of suffering such that the harm or detriment would make a noticeable difference to his ability to deal with the consequences of homelessness': at [64]. The authority does not need explicitly to spell out the comparison, provided that it can be discerned that it has approached the issue correctly: see *Rother DC v Freeman-Roach* [2018] EWCA Civ 368, [2019] PTSR 61, [2018] HLR 22, where it was sufficient for the review officer to have correctly set out the *Hotak* test and given reasons why he did not consider the applicant's health conditions (osteoarthritis and two strokes) made him more vulnerable than an ordinary person who was homeless.
89 English Code of Guidance para 8.16.

3.44 Moreover,[90] Equality Act (EqA) 2010, s 149 (public sector equality duty) is complementary to the authority's duties under HA 1996, Part 7, and requires the authority to focus on: i) whether the applicant is under a disability (or has another relevant 'protected characteristic' under the EqA 2010); ii) the extent of such disability; iii) the likely effect of the disability, when taken together with any other features, on the applicant if and when homeless; and iv) whether the applicant is, as a result, vulnerable.[91] The 'weight and extent of the duty are highly fact-sensitive and dependant on individual judgment'.[92]

3.45 *Hotak* does not, however, lay down a rigid four-stage test which has to be adopted as a 'formulaic and high-minded mantra': the public sector equality duty is not a free-standing duty, nor is it a duty to achieve a particular result; the duty applies to the way in which an authority exercises its functions.[93] It is not necessary to address the specific questions set out in *Hotak*;[94] a failure to mention the public sector equality duty or to recite each feature of it will not necessarily vitiate an assessment although, conversely, mere recitation of the elements of the duty will not save an assessment if the decision has failed in substance to address the relevant questions; what has to be considered is whether the applicant's disability affects their ability to deal with the consequences of being homeless; what matters is the substance of the assessment not the form provided that the decision-maker has appreciated the mental or physical problems from which the applicant suffers.[95]

3.46 Before *Hotak*, there had also been some discussion about the relationship between vulnerability and the statutory causes:[96] it had been held to be a composite question, rather than two separate stages,[97] ie, not asking separately whether there is vulnerability at all and, discretely, whether it was attributable to any of the factors.[98]

---

90 *Hotak* at [78].
91 This was considered and expanded in *Hackney LBC v Haque* [2017] EWCA Civ 4, [2017] HLR 14: see below, para **7.94**. See also English Code of Guidance para 8.17.
92 *Hotak* at [74].
93 *McMahon v Watford BC; Kiefer v Hertsmere BC* [2020] EWCA Civ 497, [2020] PTSR 1217, [2020] HLR 29.
94 Authorities are, however, well-advised to do so.
95 Nor is it necessary for a reviewing officer to make an express finding as to whether an applicant is disabled, provided that the reviewer has considered whether their problems (both individually and cumulatively) impacted on the applicant's ability to carry out normal day-to-day activities and, more particularly whether they rendered them vulnerable.
96 Old age, mental illness or handicap or physical disability or other special reason.
97 *R v Kensington and Chelsea RLBC, Hammersmith and Fulham LBC, Westminster City Council, and Islington LBC ex p Kihara and others* (1997) 29 HLR 147, CA.
98 As the court had suggested in *R v Waveney DC ex p Bowers* [1983] QB 238, (1982) 4 HLR 118, CA. *Bowers* was not overruled by *Kihara*, but it was thought that the two-stage test was capable of causing confusion, which the composite approach would not. The composite approach was approved in *Osmani v Camden LBC* [2004] EWCA Civ 1706, [2005] HLR 22 and said to have been correctly applied in *Bellouti v Wandsworth LBC* [2005] EWCA Civ 602, [2005] HLR 46. See also *Crossley v Westminster City Council* [2006] EWCA Civ 140, [2006] HLR 26.

3.47   On this aspect, *Hotak* largely disagreed as a matter of theory, although it may be thought to have ended up making not much difference.[99]

> '[T]he cases reveal a disagreement as to whether section 189(1)(c) gives rise to a two-stage test – (i) whether the applicant is "vulnerable", and (ii) whether it is as a result of "old age, mental illness or handicap or physical disability or other special reason" – or whether there is a single, composite test. This is a somewhat arid argument, and I am unconvinced that it is sensible to force housing authorities and reviewing officers into a straitjacket on this sort of issue. In any event, the correct answer may depend on the facts of the particular case. However, given the reference to "other special reason", and given the fact that in many cases there will be a mixture of reasons as to why an applicant is said to be vulnerable, I suspect that the one-stage test will probably be more practical in most cases.'

Wales

3.48   The position is slightly different in Wales. The sole question is whether a person is vulnerable as a result of some special reason.[100] The H(W)A 2014 then illustrates special reason in terms of 'old age, physical or mental illness or physical or mental disability'. The H(W)A 2014 preceded *Hotak*; it defines someone as 'vulnerable' if, having regard to all the circumstances, they are less able to fend for themselves if they were to become street homeless[101] than would an ordinary homeless person who became street homeless, and this would lead to the person suffering more harm than would be suffered by the ordinary homeless person.[102] Although this was plainly a codification of the *Pereira* test[103] effectively rejected by *Hotak*, the Welsh Code of Guidance[104] nonetheless recommends that authorities adopt *Hotak*.

3.49   Those who are already street homeless are, however, already in priority need whether they are vulnerable or not.[105]

---

99   At [46].

100 H(W)A 2014, s 70(1)(c).

101 'Street homelessness' meaning that the applicant has no accommodation available for their occupation in the UK or elsewhere, which they are entitled to occupy by virtue of an interest in it or by virtue of an order of a court, has an express or implied licence to occupy, or occupies as a residence by virtue of any enactment or rule of law giving the person the right to remain in occupation or restricting the right of another person to recover possession (see paras **2.42–2.63**): H(W)A 2014, s 71(2).

102 H(W)A 2014, s 71.

103 See *Panayiotou v Waltham Forest LBC; Smith v Haringey LBC* [2017] EWCA Civ 1624, [2018] QB 1232, [2017] HLR 48: 'The *Pereira* test has been given statutory force in Wales (Housing (Wales) Act 2014, section 71)': at [4]. See also *Hemley v Croydon LBC* [2018] HLR 1: 'in Wales the test laid down by *Pereira* has been given statutory force by s 71 of the Housing (Wales) Act 2014': at [9].

104 Para 16.71 and following.

105 See para **3.102**.

Old age[106]

3.50   The English Code suggests that authorities should consider whether old age makes the applicant significantly more vulnerable than an ordinary person would be if homeless; the Welsh Code refers to it as a factor which may make it harder for an applicant to fend for themselves; both Codes stress the need to consider each case on its individual circumstances.[107]

Mental illness or handicap[108] or physical disability[109]

3.51   In considering vulnerability due to mental or physical illness or disability, both the English and Welsh Codes[110] suggest that authorities should have regard to medical advice and – where appropriate – seek social services advice. It is for the local authority to decide whether to obtain its own advice in respect of medical reports relied on by a homeless applicant; there is no absolute requirement to refer an applicant's medical reports for evaluation by a medical adviser in every case; it depends on the facts.[111] Local authorities are not, however, expected to make their own critical evaluation of an applicant's medical evidence and should have access to specialist advice where necessary.[112]

3.52   Where the authority does decide to refer the applicant's medical reports to an adviser for specialist advice, it must take care not to appear to be using the opinion of the medical adviser to provide or support the authority's reasons for not finding a priority on medical grounds.

3.53   In *Shala v Birmingham City Council*,[113] the applicants – a husband and wife – applied as homeless and asserted that the wife had mental health issues which meant that she had a priority need. Information was provided from a GP setting out the diagnosis and treatment of post-traumatic stress disorder and depression. The authority concluded that the wife was not in priority need. The couple asked for a review and obtained medical evidence from a psychiatrist stating that the wife was 'very depressed'. The local authority referred this to a medical adviser – who did not have psychiatric qualifications – who provided an opinion that 'there was no particular assertion of severity' and no suggestion

---

106 HA 1996, s 189(1)(c); H(W)A 2014, s 70(1)(c).

107 English Code of Guidance para 8.24; Welsh Code para 16.20. English Code of Guidance para 8.45 suggests that for patients affected by Covid-19 with a history of rough sleeping, authorities should carefully consider whether age and health make them vulnerable.

108 This may raise questions about the capacity of an applicant to conduct proceedings to challenge a decision: see, *e.g.*, *R (BL) v Islington LBC* [2021] EWHC 3044 (Admin); [2022] ACD 14, where, after hearing from the claimant and considering her written submissions and medical evidence, the court was satisfied that she did have capacity to conduct the proceedings: she understood the purpose of her claim and the nature of her challenge and was able to engage with questions from the court: see paras **10.28–10.31.**

109 HA 1996, s 189(1)(c); H(W)A 2014, s 70(1)(c).

110 English Code of Guidance paras 8.26–8.28; Welsh Code para 16.21.

111 *Simms v Islington LBC* [2008] EWCA Civ 1083, [2009] HLR 20.

112 *Shala v Birmingham City Council* [2007] EWCA Civ 624, [2008] HLR 8.

113 *Shala v Birmingham City Council* [2007] EWCA Civ 624, [2008] HLR 8.

of admission to a psychiatric hospital or of other significant treatment being necessary. The medical adviser did not, however, carry out any examination of the wife. Further information was subsequently provided as to the wife's vulnerability from the psychiatrist and the GP. None of that information was referred to the medical adviser. The authority upheld the original decision that there was no priority need.

3.54   On appeal, quashing the authority's decision, it was said that:

a)   where an authority's medical expert lacks parity of qualification with the appellant's expert (as here the authority's medical adviser did not have the qualifications of the psychiatrist), the authority – while the not doing anything wrong in obtaining medical advice – 'must not fall into the trap of thinking that it is comparing like with like';[114] and

b)   the function of the medical adviser was to assist the authority in understanding the medical issues and to evaluate the applicant's expert evidence; if one medical expert advises on the implications of another expert's report without examining the patient, 'his advice cannot itself ordinarily constitute expert evidence of the applicant's condition'; and, if they do advise without examination, 'the decision-maker needs to take the absence of an examination into account'.[115]

3.55   In *Guiste*,[116] where likewise the authority had preferred the opinion of its own adviser who had not seen the applicant, over that of the applicants who had done so, it was held that the decision-letter must explain why the authority differed from the report of the applicant's medical adviser and, in particular, to provide a rational explanation of why the authority had decided to prefer its own expert given that they had not met with or interviewed the applicant, although it is not an error of law to fail to mention each and every occasion where it disagreed with what the applicant's adviser's assessment of what the applicant had told it.[117]

3.56   The local authority should also consider the nature and extent of the illness or disability; the relationship between the illness or disability and the individual's housing difficulties; and the relationship between the illness or disability and other factors such as drug/alcohol misuse, offending behaviour, challenging behaviours, age and personality disorder.[118] In *Osmani*,[119] Auld LJ

---

114   *Shala* at [22].
115   *Shala* at [22]–[23].
116   *Guiste v Lambeth LBC*, [2019] EWCA Civ 1758, [2020] HLR 12.
117   Applied in *R (Islam) v Haringey LBC* [2022] EWHC 3933 (Admin) [HLR 14.
118   English Code of Guidance para 8.26; Welsh Code para 14.16.
119   *Osmani v Camden LBC,* above, at [38] referring to the observations of Brooke LJ in *R v Newham LBC ex p Lumley* (2001) 33 HLR 111, QBD at [63]. Cf *R (Yeter) v Enfield LBC* [2002] EWHC 2185 (Admin), [2003] JHL D19, where a decision that an applicant suffering from depression was not vulnerable – on the basis that an ordinary homeless person can be expected to suffer from depression so that the applicant was no more vulnerable than an ordinary homeless person – was upheld; this would not now survive the approach in *Hotak* and other cases (paras **3.37–3.47**).

said that authorities should have regard to the particular debilitating effects of depressive disorders and the fragility of those suffering from them if suddenly deprived of the prop of their own home.

3.57 Particular reference is made in both the English and Welsh Codes[120] to those with mental health problems who have been discharged from psychiatric hospitals. The need for effective liaison between housing, social services and health authorities is stressed. Authorities should also be sensitive to direct approaches from homeless discharged patients.

3.58 Cases of vulnerability due solely to the problems of drink will not usually be attributable to one of the specified causes,[121] although an extreme case may amount to a mental or physical handicap or disability. While in some cases vulnerability may be a medical question only, it may also be a question of housing and social welfare.[122] In all cases, the question must be determined by the local authority; it cannot merely 'rubber stamp' a decision of its medical experts.[123]

3.59 In *Banbury*,[124] whether epilepsy amounted to vulnerability was said to be a question of fact and degree, which would be established if attacks occurred with intense regularity. In *Leek*,[125] a decision on the vulnerability of an epileptic – comprising refusal to reconsider an earlier decision – was quashed on the ground that the position of any particular sufferer may need to be re-assessed from time to time.

3.60 A delusional condition which rendered the applicant unable to manage his own financial affairs made him vulnerable in *Dukic*.[126]

3.61 In *Sangermano*,[127] the court distinguished between mental illness that is psychotic and mental handicap. The latter is not concerned with illness, but with subnormality or severe subnormality, although not all subnormality will necessarily amount to vulnerability; where medical evidence of subnormality is

---

120 English Code of Guidance para 8.27; Welsh Code para 16.26.
121 *R v Waveney DC ex p Bowers* [1983] QB 238, (1982) 4 HLR 118, CA.
122 *R v Lambeth LBC ex p Carroll* (1988) 20 HLR 142, QBD.
123 *R v Wandsworth LBC ex p Banbury* (1987) 19 HLR 76, QBD and *Osmani v Camden LBC* [2004] EWCA Civ 1706, [2005] HLR 22. Note, however, the comments of Auld LJ at [38] in *Osmani* stressing the need to look for and pay close regard to medical evidence submitted in support of applicants' claims of vulnerability on account of mental illness or handicap. Compare *Hall v Wandsworth LBC; Carter v Wandsworth LBC* [2004] EWCA Civ 1740, [2005] HLR 23, where the medical officer was entitled to advise that no further enquiries or specialist advice was required and *R v Newham LBC ex p Lumley* (2001) 33 HLR 11, QBD, where the medical officer failed to carry out adequate enquiries (see para **7.135**).
124 *R v Wandsworth LBC ex p Banbury*, above.
125 *R v Sheffield City Council ex p Leek* (1994) 26 HLR 669, CA.
126 *R v Greenwich LBC ex p Dukic* (1997) 29 HLR 87, QBD.
127 *R v Bath City Council ex p Sangermano* (1985) 17 HLR 94.

put before an authority, the authority ought either to accept it or make its own further enquiries.[128]

3.62   The Welsh Code also refers to those who are chronically sick.[129] It suggests that while some chronically sick people may have progressed to the point of physical or mental disability, they may also be vulnerable 'because the manifestations or effects of their illness, or common attitudes to it, make it very difficult for them to find stable or suitable accommodation'.

3.63   Referable to the coronavirus pandemic, local authorities in England were advised to 'carefully consider the vulnerability of applicants' arising from coronavirus.[130] Applicants whose GP or specialist had identified as clinically extremely vulnerable were likely to be in priority need; authorities should also have carefully considered whether an applicant with a history of rough sleeping is vulnerable, having regard to their age and health conditions.[131]

3.64   In Wales, the guidance said that it was 'almost inevitable that a person who is either street homeless or faced with street homelessness is less able than an ordinary homeless person to fend for himself or herself and would suffer more harm than an ordinary homeless person would suffer'. If an authority decided that such a person was not vulnerable then that decision had to be documented and have a robust evidential basis which would withstand 'rigorous scrutiny and legal challenge'.[132]

Other special reason[133]

3.65   In *Kihara*,[134] the court rejected an approach to 'other special reason' which would mean that it had to be of the same order as the specific causes so that it would be limited to the mental or physical characteristics of an applicant: rather, the category is free-standing, untrammelled by any notion of physical or

---

128 Furthermore, when determining priority need, the applicant's earlier rent arrears had been a wholly irrelevant consideration.
129 Welsh Code para 16.27.
130 English Code of Guidance paras 8.45–8.46.
131 English Code of Guidance paras 8.45–8.46. See also *Guidance for local authorities in supporting people sleeping rough: Covid-19 outbreak*, Welsh Government, 28 April 2020. Paragraph 8.45 of the Homelessness Code of Guidance was amended in October 2021 to draw attention to the guidance from the Joint Committee on Vaccinations concerning people whose underlying health conditions make them more vulnerable to the effect of Covid-19.
132 *Guidance for local authorities in supporting people sleeping rough: Covid-19 outbreak*, Welsh Government, 28 April 2020.
133 HA 1996, s 189(1)(c); H(W)A 2014, s 70(1)(c); see English Code of Guidance paras 8.38–8.42 and chapters 21, 25 for suggestions as to groups who might fall within this category; Welsh Code paras 16.28–16.33.
134 *R v Kensington and Chelsea RLBC, Hammersmith and Fulham LBC, Westminster City Council, and Islington LBC ex p Kihara and others* (1997) 29 HLR 147, CA.

mental weakness other than is inherent in the word 'vulnerable'. It can comprise a combination of circumstances.[135]

3.66   The word 'special' imports the requirement that the housing difficulties faced by an applicant are to an unusual degree of gravity, enough to differentiate the applicant from others. This does not include impecuniosity by itself, because an absence of means alone does not mark out one case from the generality of cases to a sufficient degree to render it 'special', but, eg, would include someone peculiarly in need of housing because of the risk of physical harm from continuing homelessness.[136]

3.67   The expression 'other special reason' requires examination of all the personal circumstances of an applicant, including physical or mental characteristics or disabilities, but is not limited to those. Accordingly, impecuniosity may still be relevant as will be opportunities to raise money (for example, whether or not a person[137] is prohibited from employment), or whether or not an applicant has family and friends and familiarity with the language, or – put another way – is subject to 'utter poverty and resourcelessness'.[138]

3.68   In *Sangermano*,[139] the court considered that language difficulties on their own would not amount to a 'special reason' within what is now HA 1996, s 189(1)(c). Drug addiction alone does not amount to a 'special reason', but a likelihood of relapse into such addiction may do so.[140]

3.69   The English Code also draws attention to the position of young homeless people, noting that they may be vulnerable and have a priority need for a variety of reasons. It also draws attention to the plight of applicants who are the victims of harassment and people trafficking/modern slavery.[141] Those who are reasonably expected to die within six months, or who are otherwise receiving palliative care, will 'almost certainly' have a priority need.[142] In Wales, guidance suggested that the 'Covid-19 pandemic and the actions required to be taken in response to it, for example the need to self-isolate and to socially distance' may suggest priority need 'as a result of some special reason'.[143]

3.70   In *Bankole-Jones*,[144] it was held that the English guidance[145] did not support a proposition that all rough sleepers should be considered to be vulnerable

---

135   *R v Waveney DC ex p Bowers* [1983] QB 238, (1982) 4 HLR 118, CA.
136   *R v Kensington and Chelsea RLBC, Hammersmith and Fulham LBC, Westminster City Council, and Islington LBC ex p Kihara and others,* above.
137   By reason of immigration status.
138   *Kihara,* above.
139   *R v Bath City Council ex p Sangermano,* above.
140   *Crossley v Westminster City Council* [2006] EWCA Civ 140, [2006] HLR 26.
141   English Code of Guidance paras 8.44 and Chapter 25.
142   English Code of Guidance para 8.41.
143   *Guidance for local authorities in supporting people sleeping rough: Covid-19 outbreak*, Welsh Government, 28 April 2020.
144   *Bankole-Jones v Watford BC* [2020] EWHC 3100 (Admin); [2021] H.L.R. 33.
145   English Code of Guidance paras 8.45–8.46, above, para **3.63.**

during the pandemic as a result of a special reason in the absence of evidence of a particular health issue meaning that the applicant was more vulnerable to harm than an ordinary person as a result of being homeless, whether generally or as a result of the Covid-19 pandemic; the authority had been entitled to conclude that he was not significantly more at risk, when homeless, than an ordinary person would be.

Multiple causes

3.71   In *Crossley*,[146] the applicant, as well as being a drug addict at risk of relapse and accordingly – it was contended – vulnerable for a 'special reason', had also been in care between the ages of three and 17. It was while in care that he had become a drug addict. The authority had failed to consider whether his vulnerability had arisen from the period in care. The court stated:[147]

> 'This appeal has not needed to address the question of how the decision-maker should deal with a case involving two of the prescribed causes of vulnerability – here, if the claimant is right, having been in care and some other special reason. We would nevertheless observe that where two such causes have produced a single set of effects, it would not seem consistent with Parliament's intention that the effects should be artificially distributed between the causes in arriving at a decision on the critical question of vulnerability.'[148]

EMERGENCY[149]

3.72   This covers homelessness caused by an emergency such as flood, fire or other disaster. HA 1996, Part 7 and H(W)A 2014, Part 2 are in the same form: each requires that the event which causes the homelessness and the priority need must be both an emergency and a disaster.[150]

3.73   Fire and flood are not the only qualifying disasters. In *Noble v South Herefordshire DC*,[151] the words 'or any other disaster' (in Housing (Homeless Persons) Act 1977, s 2(1)(b)) were held to mean another disaster similar to flood or fire. The omission of the word 'any' in HA 1996, s 189(1)(d) would not seem to affect this.

---

146 *Crossley v Westminster City Council*, above.
147 At [31].
148 This is consistent with *Hotak* and other cases, at [46], see paras **3.42–3.45**.
149 HA 1996, s 189(1)(d); H(W)A 2014, s 70(1)(d).
150 The need for the emergency to have caused the homelessness was illustrated in *Higgs v Brighton and Hove City Council* [2003] EWCA Civ 895, [2004] HLR 2 – see para **2.68**.
151 *Noble v South Herefordshire DC* (1985) 17 HLR 80, CA.

3.74 *Noble* was concerned with a demolition order under what is now HA 1985, Part 9. This was not considered to comprise a disaster similar to flood or fire, although the facts were unhelpful to the argument insofar as the occupiers had moved in after the demolition order had been made and it is therefore distinguishable in the case of a dangerous structure notice under Building Act 1984, s 77, or analogous urgency powers, imposed without any real forewarning.[152] Where a demolition order under HA 1985 was imposed, however, its procedural provisions suggested that it would not qualify as an emergency, and an occupier will in any event usually be entitled to rehousing under Land Compensation Act 1973, s 39;[153] the modern equivalents[154] are to be found in HA 2004, Part 1.

3.75 The words 'other disaster' are of the same order as fire or floor.[155] Accordingly, a person who has been unlawfully evicted from their home is not in priority need within the subsection: it is not an emergency similar to flood or fire – *Bradic*. The subsection is not confined to emergencies amounting to force majeure, however, but embraces all emergencies consisting of physical damage: *Bradic*.

3.76 Where the applicant occupies a moving structure, such as a caravan, as their home, the disappearance of that structure is an emergency within the subsection because it involves the sudden and unexpected loss of the applicant's home in circumstances outside their control: *Higgs*.[156]

3.77 The following are statutorily deemed to have become homeless or threatened with homelessness as a result of emergency such as flood, fire or other disaster:[157]

a) a person who resides in a building in outer London in respect of which an order has been made by a magistrates' court under the Greater London Council (General Powers) Act 1984, s 37 that the occupants are to be removed because of its dangerous state;

---

152 But compare the provisions of Greater London Council (General Powers) Act 1984, s 39, para **3.77**. If these were considered both to need, and to justify, deeming emergencies, it might be implied by the courts (on a common principle of statutory interpretation that if one thing is explicitly included, other similar things are impliedly excluded) that other provisions of a like quality do not have the same effect; this is an argument that, it is submitted, does not hold water: the 1984 Act has no effect outside Greater London, therefore the same could not be argued outside Greater London so as to ignore some such similar event; and if such cannot be argued outside Greater London, it is difficult to suggest that it can do so within.

153 See also *R v Kensington and Chelsea RLBC ex p Ben-El-Mabrouk* (1995) 27 HLR 564, CA (para **2.110**), in which accommodation subject to action for want of means of escape from fire could reasonably continue to be occupied pending rehousing under the Land Compensation Act 1973.

154 Prohibition and demolition orders.

155 *R v Bristol City Council ex p Bradic* (1995) 27 HLR 584, CA (following *Noble v South Herefordshire DC*, above).

156 *Higgs v Brighton and Hove City Council* [2003] EWCA Civ 895, [2004] HLR 2.

157 Greater London Council (General Powers) Act 1984, s 39, as amended by HA 1996, Sch 17.

b) a person who resides in a building in inner or outer London whose occupants are in danger by reason of its proximity to a dangerous structure or building, within Greater London Council (General Powers) Act 1984, s 38(1), in respect of which an order has been made by the magistrates' court under s 38(2).

OTHER CATEGORIES

Introduction

3.78 The Secretary of State and, in Wales, the Welsh Ministers[158] can add further categories of priority need, or alter or remove existing categories,[159] after consultation with such associations representing authorities and such other persons as the secretary of state considers or Welsh Ministers consider appropriate.[160]

3.79 In England, the categories have been supplemented so as to reflect concerns about homelessness among young people, those leaving care, those leaving institutional settings, such as prison and the armed forces, and those fleeing (non-domestic) violence. These additional categories have largely been mirrored in Wales, where they are incorporated in H(W)A 2014, s 70.

3.80 In England, the Homelessness (Priority Need for Accommodation) (England) Order 2002[161] came into force on 31 July 2002. It has six additional categories of priority need.[162] See also English Code of Guidance paras 8.19–8.23 and 8.28–8.37. These six categories are also relevant in Wales as they are largely adopted into H(W)A 2014, s 70, although there are differences, noted in the text and footnotes. These six categories are:

a) 16- and 17-year-olds;

b) 18- to 20-year-old care leavers;

c) vulnerable care leavers;

d) former members of the armed forces;

e) vulnerable former prisoners;

f) persons fleeing non-domestic[163] violence.

---

158 HA 1996, s 189(2); H(W)A 2014, s 72.
159 HA 1996, s 189(2); H(W)A 2014, s 72.
160 HA 1996, s 189(3); H(W)A 2014, s 72(3).
161 Homelessness (Priority Need for Accommodation) (England) Order 2002, SI 2002/2051.
162 Homelessness (Priority Need for Accommodation) (England) Order 2002, SI 2002/2051 art 3.
163 As amended by DAA 2021, s 78(8).

3.81 Wales has two additional category:

g) young persons at risk of exploitation;

h) those who are street homeless.

16- and 17-year-olds

England

3.82 All 16- and 17-year-olds are in priority need provided they are not classified as a relevant child[164] or its Welsh equivalent[165] (who will therefore remain the responsibility of the social services authority) nor are owed a duty by a local authority under CA 1989, s 20[166] or its Welsh equivalent.[167]

3.83 Whether a 16- or 17-year-old is a child in need for the purposes of CA 1989, and accordingly owed a duty under section 20, is a mixed question of law and fact for the local authority to decide: *M*.[168]

3.84 When considering whether to house a 16- or 17-year-old applicant under HA 1996, s 188 pending enquiries,[169] a housing officer is not required to assess whether the applicant is a child in need, but – if the young person is eligible and is (or may be) homeless – the authority should provide interim accommodation while an assessment is carried out by social services,[170] to whom the child should be referred.[171] It is unlawful for a social services department to sidestep its responsibilities under section 20 by assuming that a child in need can be suitably accommodated as a homeless person.[172]

---

164 See para **11.108.**
165 A 'category 2' young person, see Social Services and Well-being (Wales) Act (SSWB(W)A) 2014, s 104(2).
166 *R (S) v Sutton LBC* [2007] EWCA Civ 790. See further paras **11.71–11.82.**
167 See para **11.122.**
168 *R (M) v Hammersmith and Fulham LBC* [2008] UKHL 14, [2008] 1 WLR 535, (2008) 4 All ER 271, HL, per Baroness Hale at [29].
169 See Chapter 8.
170 *Prevention of homelessness and provision of accommodation for 16 and 17 year old young people who may be homeless and/or require accommodation*, MHCLG / Department for Education, April 2018, para 4.5.
171 See also *R (M) v Hammersmith and Fulham LBC*, above, at [33], [36] and [42].
172 *R (S) v Sutton LBC* [2007] EWCA Civ 790. See also *R (M) v Hammersmith and Fulham LBC*, above, HL, per Baroness Hale at [33] and [42]. Although there was no evidence of a deliberate policy in that case, to seek 'to avoid its responsibilities under the 1989 Act by shifting them on to the housing department ... would be unlawful'. The observation was made in connection with *any* duty under the CA 1989, not section 20 alone. Social services authorities may, however, enter into an arrangement with another authority for assistance in discharge of the section 20 duty: *R (G) v Southwark LBC* [2009] UKHL 26, [2009] 1 WLR 1299.

3.85   If an authority's normal enquiry time would mean that an applicant will have turned 18 by the time of the decision, the authority cannot take the view that the applicant will not be in priority need and refuse all assistance, or simply provide accommodation until the birthday, even though, if enquiries in fact happen to take the applicant to 18, the applicant will not be in priority need at the time of the decision.[173]

3.86   Nor may the authority postpone its decision to that date.[174] Nor can an authority take the benefit of an invalid decision which forces the applicant into a review, by which time the applicant has turned 18: the principle in *Mohamed v Hammersmith and Fulham LBC*,[175] that the reviewer takes into account all facts to the date of the review,[176] cannot apply in this way, for:

> 'If the original decision was unlawful ... the review decision maker should have so held and made a decision that would have restored to the appellant the rights she would have had if the decision had been lawful.'[177]

3.87   The April 2018 guidance[178] suggests that for some young homeless applicants the most appropriate solution may be reconciliation with their families so that they can return home. It recognises that in some cases, however, relationships may have broken down irretrievably, and in others that it may not be safe for a young person to return to the family home. Accordingly, any mediation or reconciliation will need careful brokering, and social services should be involved.[179] Temporary accommodation may need to be provided while the process takes place.[180]

3.88   If mediation would take an applicant beyond their 18th birthday, however, the authority is bound to reach its decision without awaiting the outcome, as – if unsuccessful – the effect would otherwise be to deprive the applicant of their right to a full duty.[181] Mediation and enquiries are separate processes:

---

173   *Robinson v Hammersmith and Fulham LBC* [2006] EWCA Civ 1122, [2006] 1 WLR 3295, [2007] HLR 7.
174   *Robinson v Hammersmith and Fulham LBC*, above, even for a short period.
175   [2001] UKHL 57, [2002] HLR 7.
176   See para **3.7**.
177   *Robinson v Hammersmith and Fulham LBC*, above, per Waller LJ at [32].
178   *Prevention and homelessness and provision of accommodation for 16 and 17 year old young people who may be homeless and/or require accommodation*, MHCLG / Department for Education, April 2018, chapter 2; Welsh Code para 14.39 simply suggests that this should be considered for 16- and 17-year-olds.
179   See also the comments of Baroness Hale who approved the 'wisdom of this guidance' in *R (M) v Hammersmith and Fulham LBC* [2008] UKHL 14, [2008] 1 WLR 535, [2008] 4 All ER 271, HL at [27].
180   Such matters may form part of a joint protocol between the housing and children's services departments: *Prevention and homelessness and provision of accommodation for 16 and 17 year old young people who may be homeless and/or require accommodation*, MHCLG / Department for Education, April 2018, para.6.10. Temporary accommodation should not be provided in an 'all-ages night shelter provision, even in an emergency' (para 3.12).
181   *Robinson v Hammersmith and Fulham LBC*, above.

'The two processes may of course proceed in parallel; and if mediation is successful while the section 184 inquiry process is still on foot, then of course there will be no need for the latter process to continue any further. On the other hand, a local housing authority has … no power to defer making inquiries pursuant to section 184 on the ground that there is a pending mediation.'[182]

Wales

3.89   Any child who is aged 16 or 17 when they apply to a local housing authority for accommodation or help in obtaining or retaining accommodation is in priority need.[183]

18- to 20-year-old care leavers

England

3.90   Any person who is aged 18 to 20 (other than a relevant student)[184] who at any time after reaching the age of 16, but while under 18, was, but is no longer, looked after, accommodated or fostered[185] is in priority need.

Wales

3.91   Any person who is aged 18 to 20 who was looked after, accommodated or fostered at any time while under the age of 18 is in priority need.[186]

---

182 *Robinson*, above, at [42], per Jonathan Parker LJ. See also per Jacob LJ at [45], who additionally relied on the HA 1996, s 179 duty (para **12.20**) to provide advice and information: 'A near-18-year-old who came to the authority could obviously not be properly be advised to mediate if the effect of mediation would be to delay the actual s 184 decision past the 18th birthday.'

183 H(W)A 2014, s 70(1)(f). The Welsh Code similarly stresses that it is in the best interests of most 16- and 17-year-olds to live in the family home unless this is unsafe or it is unsuitable for them because of risk of violence or abuse; in recognition of this, authorities are encouraged to consider the possibility of reconciliation through mediation: para 16.44.

184 'Relevant student' is defined by the CA 1989 as a care leaver under 24 to whom CA 1989, s 24B(3) applies, who is in full-time further or higher education and whose term time accommodation is not available to them during a vacation. Relevant students remain the responsibility of social services authorities.

185 As defined by CA 1989, s 22, ie, looked after by a local authority (ie, has been subject to a care order or voluntarily accommodated); accommodated by or on behalf of a voluntary organisation; accommodated in a private children's home; accommodated for a consecutive period of at least three months by a health authority, special health authority, primary care trust or local education authority or in any care home or independent hospital or in any accommodation provided by the National Health Service Trust; or, privately fostered.

186 H(W)A 2014, s 70(1)(h). 'Looked after' within the meaning of SSWB(W)A 2014, s 74 or CA 1989, s 22, accommodated by or on behalf of a voluntary organisation; accommodated in a private children's home; accommodated for a continuous period of at least three months by a local health board, special health authority, primary care trust or local education authority, or in any care home or independent hospital or in any accommodation provided by the National Health Service Trust; or, privately fostered: Welsh Code para 16.49. See also *Provision of accommodation for 16 and 17 year old young people who may be homeless* (Welsh Assembly Government, September 2010) and Welsh Code paras 16.41–16.43.

Vulnerable care leavers

England

3.92   Where a person has previously been looked after, accommodated or fostered,[187] the person will be in priority need no matter what their age, if this has resulted in the person being vulnerable.[188]

Wales

3.93   There is no equivalent in Wales. The Welsh Code does, however, stress that care leavers who are over 20 are 'likely to be vulnerable as a result of being in care' and so in priority need in their own right.[189]

Former members of the armed forces[190]

England

3.94   Those who have been members of Her Majesty's regular armed forces[191] are in priority need, but only if they are vulnerable[192] as a result of that service.

Wales

3.95   A person who has served in the regular armed forces of the Crown who has been homeless since leaving those forces is in priority need (ie, there is no need for the applicant also to be vulnerable).[193]

Vulnerable former prisoners

England

3.96   A person who is vulnerable[194] as a result of having served a custodial sentence,[195] having been committed for contempt of court or having been remanded in custody[196] is also in priority need.

---

187 See para **3.91**.
188 As to whether someone is vulnerable, see paras **3.35–3.76**. See also *Crossley v Westminster City Council* [2006] EWCA Civ 140, [2006] HLR 26.
189 Welsh Code para 16.52.
190 See also para **3.35**, for the special consideration to be given to present and former members of the armed forces.
191 See HA 1996, s 199(4); para **5.36**.
192 As to whether someone is vulnerable, see paras **3.35–3.76**.
193 H(W)A 2014, s 70(1)(i).
194 It is not to be assumed that a person released from prison will always be vulnerable: *Johnson v Solihull MBC* [2013] EWCA Civ 752, [2013] HLR 39 (not considered on appeal: [2015] UKSC 30, [2015] HLR 23).
195 Within the meaning of Powers of Criminal Courts (Sentencing) Act 2000, s 76.
196 Within the meaning of Criminal Justice Act 2003, s 242(2).

Wales

3.97   The position is the same, save that the prisoner must also have a local connection with the area of the local authority.[197]

Persons fleeing violence

England

3.98   If an applicant has had to cease to occupy accommodation because of violence[198] or threats of violence which are likely to be carried out, the applicant will be in priority need if they are vulnerable[199] as a result.

Domestic abuse

3.99   In Wales, if an applicant is homeless as a result of being subject to domestic abuse, they will be in priority need, ie, there is no need that they also be vulnerable.[200] In England, since the provisions of the Domestic Abuse Act 2021 came into force,[201] it is also the case that a person who is homeless as a result of being a victim of domestic abuse is in priority need.[202]

3.100   Domestic abuse is defined in the same terms as considered in relation to whether it is reasonable to continue to occupy accommodation.[203]

Young person at risk of exploitation

Wales

3.101   A person aged between 18 and 21 who requires help in obtaining or retaining accommodation and who is at particular risk of sexual or financial exploitation, is in priority need.[204]

Street homelessness

Wales

3.102   A person who is street homeless[205] or someone with whom a person who is street homeless might reasonably be expected to reside is in priority need.[206]

---

197 H(W)A 2014, s 70(1)(j); as to local connection, see chapter 5.
198 See the definition of violence in HA 1996, s 177(1), para **2.84**.
199 As to whether someone is vulnerable, see paras **3.35–3.76**.
200 H(W)A 2014, s 70(1)(e).
201 5 July 2021: Domestic Abuse Act 2021 (Commencement No. 1 and Saving Provisions) Regulations 2021, SI 20201/797.
202 HA 1996, s 189(1), as amended by DAA 2021, s 78. English Code of Guidance para 8.13.
203 Para **2.84.**
204 H(W)A 2014, s 70(1)(g); Welsh Code para 16.48. If a person turns 21 while still being assessed, this category of vulnerability remains applicable: Welsh Code para 16.46.
205 'For the definition of street homelessness' see **para 3.48**.
206 H(W)Act s 70(1)(k), added by Homelessness (Priority Need and Intentionality) (Wales) Regulations 2022, SI 2022/1069, reg.2.

CHAPTER 4

Intentional homelessness

INTRODUCTION

4.1   This chapter concerns the provision which at one time attracted most attention and controversy in homelessness law, intentional homelessness – although with so many issues related to it fairly well settled in law, more recent attention passed to the definition of vulnerability in relation to priority need,[1] to the suitability of accommodation,[2] and otherwise to discharge of duties.[3] The issue nonetheless remains of considerable importance as, where a person is homeless intentionally, the authority's principal housing duty[4] is limited to temporary accommodation only for as long as it thinks is reasonable for the applicant to get their own accommodation.[5]

4.2   The principal definition of intentionality is the same under both the Housing Act (HA) 1996 and the Housing (Wales) Act (H(W)A) 2014 as it was under HA 1985. It was extended by HA 1996 to include collusive arrangements under which an applicant is required to cease to occupy accommodation which it would have been reasonable for the applicant to continue to occupy, being an arrangement entered into so as to entitle the applicant to assistance under HA 1996, Part 7, where there is no other good reason for the applicant to be homeless.[6] The same extension is to be found in the H(W)A 2014.[7] This extension is considered at the end of this chapter.[8]

4.3   In Wales there is, however, this critical distinction: local housing authorities must decide whether to apply the intentionality test at all in their

---

1   See paras **3.35–3.76**.
2   See paras **8.128–8.234**.
3   See Chapter 8.
4   There are other duties which apply, including assessment, relief and advice and assistance: see Chapter 8.
5   See Chapter 8.
6   HA 1996, s 191(3). A further extension – to include persons to whom advice and assistance had been given under HA 1996, s 197 (where the authority was satisfied that other suitable accommodation was available for the applicant's occupation in its area) but who failed to secure accommodation in circumstances where it was reasonable to be expected to do so (s 191(4)) – was repealed by the Homelessness Act 2002.
7   H(W)A 2014, s 77(4).
8   Paras **4.166–4.170**.

areas;[9] and it can only be applied once the authority has notified the Welsh Government that the test will apply and has published a notice to this effect.[10]

4.4 Moreover, the test may only be applied to categories of applicant specified by the Welsh Ministers, although currently all the priority need categories are specified.[11] An authority may choose to adopt none, some, or all of the specified categories.[12] The Welsh Government does not appear to publish a centralised list of decisions made by authorities, and it is accordingly necessary to check the website of each.

4.5 That said, the full housing duty is now owed in Wales, even if there has been a finding of intentional homelessness, if the applicant is:

a) a pregnant woman or a person with whom she resides or might reasonably be expected to reside;

b) a person with whom a dependent child resides or might reasonably be expected to reside;

c) a person who had not attained the age of 21 when the application was made or a person with whom such a person resides or might reasonably be expected to reside; or

d) a person who had attained the age of 21, but not the age of 25, when the application was made and who was looked after, accommodated or fostered at any time while under the age of 18, or a person with whom such a person resides or might reasonably be expected to reside.[13]

---

9   H(W)A 2014, s 78.
10 H(W)A 2014, s 78(3).
11 Homelessness (Intentionality) (Specified Categories) (Wales) Regulations 2015, SI 2015/1265 as amended by Homelessness (Priority Need and Intentionality) (Wales) Regulations 2022, SI 2022/1069, reg 3. The full housing duty is now owed in Wales, even if there has been a finding of intentional homelessness, if the applicant is: a) a pregnant woman or a person with whom she resides or might reasonably be expected to reside; b) a person with whom a dependent child resides or might reasonably be expected to reside; c) a person who had not attained the age of 21 when the application was made or a person with whom such a person resides or might reasonably be expected to reside; or d) a person who had attained the age of 21, but not the age of 25, when the application was made and who was looked after, accommodated or fostered at any time while under the age of 18, or a person with whom such a person resides or might reasonably be expected to reside – see H(W)A 2014, s 75(3), brought into force on 2 December 2019: Housing (Wales) Act 2014 (Commencement No 10) Order 2019, SI 2019/1479. See also *Additional provisions under section 75(3)*, Welsh Government, 2019; H(W)A 2014, s 75(3)(f)(i) limits this provision so that where someone has been found intentionally homeless twice in a five year period, they would not be owed the full housing duty.
12 Welsh Code paras 17.6–17.11.
13 H(W)A 2014, s 75(3), brought into force on 2 December 2019: Housing (Wales) Act 2014 (Commencement No 10) Order 2019, SI 2019/1479. See also *Additional provisions under section 75(3)*, Welsh Government, 2019.

4.6   While this may well be thought to take the sting out of intentionality for many applicants in Wales, it is not rendered obsolete, even for them: where someone within the above categories has been found intentionally homeless twice in a five year period, they would not be owed the full housing duty.[14]

PRINCIPAL DEFINITION

Overview

4.7   A person is 'homeless intentionally' if they have deliberately done or failed to do something, in consequence of which they cease to occupy accommodation which is available for their occupation, and which it would have been reasonable for them to continue to occupy.[15]

4.8   A person is 'threatened with' homelessness intentionally if the person has deliberately done or failed to do something, the likely result of which is that the person will be forced to leave accommodation, which is available for their occupation, and which it would have been reasonable for them to continue to occupy.[16] There is no reason for drawing any distinction of principle between the operation of the two definitions.[17]

4.9   In addition, the Supported Housing (Regulatory Oversight) Act 2023 makes discrete provision to prevent a finding of intentional homelessness against anyone who ceases to occupy 'supported exempt accommodation',[18] where the reason for leaving it relates to the standard of the accommodation or the standard of care, support or supervision provided in it, and that accommodation,

---

14   H(W)A 2014, s 75(3)(f)(i).
15   HA 1996, s 191(1); H(W)A 2014, s 77(2).
16   HA 1996, s 196(1); there is no direct equivalent in Wales, but see H(W)A 2014, s 55 which defines 'threatened with homelessness'.
17   *Dyson v Kerrier DC* [1980] 1 WLR 1205, CA, at 1212. This seems to be based on a concession by counsel, but must surely be correct.
18   Defined in Supported Housing (Regulatory Oversight) Act 2023, s 12: see Appendix A. The Act requires local authorities to carry out a review of the supported exempt accommodation in their districts, and, in light of that review, publish a supported housing strategy for the provision of supported exempt (as defined in s 12) accommodation in their districts; it also allows the Secretary of State to publish National Supported Housing Standards, setting minimum standards in respect of the type or condition of premises used for the provision of supported exempt accommodation, or the provision of care, support or supervision at supported exempt accommodation (s 3). Providers may be required to obtain and comply with a local authority licence (s 4). Section 12 contains a wide definition of supported exempt accommodation, the principal (but not the only) category of which is accommodation provided by non-metropolitan county councils, housing associations, registered charities and voluntary organisations, where the body (or a person acting on its behalf) also provides a person resident in the accommodation with care, support or supervision.

or the care, support or supervision, did not meet National Supported Housing Standards.[19]

4.10   Before an applicant can be considered homeless intentionally, the authority must satisfy itself that *all* the elements of the definition apply: for example, if the applicant left accommodation that was not available for the applicant's occupation, there can be no finding of intentionality.[20]

4.11   As with all matters under Part 7, when reaching a decision on the issues raised by the definition, a local authority must have regard to:

> '(a) the unique obligations of, and sacrifices made by, the armed forces,
>
> (b)   the principle that it is desirable to remove disadvantages arising for service people from membership, or former membership, of the armed forces, and
>
> (c)   the principle that special provision for service people may be justified by the effects on such people of membership, or former membership, of the armed forces'.[21]

Elements of principal definition

4.12   The elements of the principal definition are:

a)   the applicant must deliberately have done something or failed to do something;

b)   the loss of accommodation must be in consequence of the act or omission;

c)   there must be a cessation of occupation, as distinct from a failure to take up accommodation;

d)   the accommodation must have been available for the occupation of the homeless person; and

e)   it must have been reasonable for the homeless person to continue to occupy the accommodation.

4.13   Before turning to these questions, there is one preliminary issue which requires discussion: that is, when an application is by or on behalf of more than one person, whose conduct is to be taken into account.

---

19   1996 Act, s 191(1A), added by Supported Housing (Regulatory Oversight) Act 2023, s 9.

20   *Re Islam* [1983] 1 AC 688, (1981) 1 HLR 107, HL; see also, eg, *R v Eastleigh BC ex p Beattie (No 1)* (1983) 10 HLR 134, QBD.

21   Armed Forces Act 2006, ss 343AA (England) and 343AB (Wales), added by Armed Forces Act 2021, s 8(3). This may be particularly relevant when determining whether it was reasonable to continue to occupy accommodation.

Whose conduct?

Generally

4.14   A number of cases have considered how an authority should treat an application where one of the applicants, or a member of the applicant's household, has either already been adjudged homeless intentionally, or is susceptible to a finding of intentionality. The point tends to arouse strong views for, as will be seen below,[22] the duty to a homeless person is also owed to anyone who might reasonably be expected to reside with them, which may well include the putatively intentionally homeless member of the household.[23]

4.15   The question was first considered in *Lewis*,[24] where a man quit his employment and lost his tied accommodation. He applied to the authority, which held that he had become homeless intentionally.[25] Thereupon, the woman with whom he lived applied in her own name. The court rejected the authority's argument that it need only consider one application for the family unit as a whole: each applicant was entitled to individual consideration.[26]

4.16   The court nonetheless upheld the authority's argument that, in considering whether or not the women had become homeless intentionally, it could take into account conduct to which she had been a party or in which she had acquiesced:

> 'In my view, the fact that the Act requires consideration of the family unit as a whole indicates that it would be perfectly proper in the ordinary case for the housing authority to look at the family as a whole and assume, in the absence of material which indicates to the contrary, where the conduct of one member of the family was such that he should be regarded as having become homeless intentionally, that was conduct to which the other members of the family were a party . . .
>
> If, however, at the end of the day because of material put before the housing authority by the wife, the housing authority are not satisfied that she was a party to the decision, they would have to regard her as not having become homeless intentionally. In argument the housing authority drew my attention to the difficulties which could arise in cases where the husband spent the rent on drink. If the wife acquiesced to his doing this then it seems to me it would be proper to regard her, as well as him, as having become homeless intentionally. If, on the other hand, she had done what she could to prevent the husband spending his money on drink instead of rent then she had not failed to do anything (the likely result of which would be that

---

22   See para **8.28**.
23   See also the English *Homelessness code of guidance for local authorities* para 9.5; Welsh Code para 17.3.
24   *R v North Devon DC ex p Lewis* [1981] 1 WLR 328, QBD.
25   See further paras **4.81–4.90**.
26   See paras **7.47–7.48**.

she would be forced to leave the accommodation) and it would not be right to regard her as having become homeless intentionally.'

4.17   See also *Caine*,[27] in which the Court of Appeal held that the authority was entitled to look at the family as a whole, to infer that the applicant was aware that her partner had been withholding rent, and – even though there was no direct evidence that they had done so – to infer that the couple would have discussed the matter. The authority could not be criticised for proceeding on the basis that what it was considering was a normal family/couple in which such information would be shared.

Burden

4.18   If correct beyond its own facts, this creates a shift in the normal burden lying on an authority to make enquiries, because it imposes on an applicant who wants to avail themselves of the principle of non-acquiescence something of a positive obligation to show why acquiescence should not be presumed.[28] It is difficult to see, however, why an authority should be excused even minimal enquiry.

Non-acquiescent applicants

4.19   *Lewis* was applied to the benefit of the applicant in *Sidhu*,[29] where the authority additionally[30] sought to rely on an earlier finding of intentionality relating to rent arrears which had occurred while the applicant was still living with her husband, even though the couple had since separated.

4.20   *Lewis* was also applied to the applicant's benefit in *Beattie (No 2)*,[31] a case of non-payment of mortgage arrears,[32] even though the applicants were still living together as a couple; and in *Phillips*,[33] a case of rent arrears caused by the husband's drinking, likewise even though the applicants were still living together as a couple.

4.21   In *Trevena*,[34] a wife – the sole tenant of a flat – surrendered the tenancy in order to move in with another man in another town, leaving her husband in (unlawful) occupation. Possession proceedings had to be taken for his eviction. Subsequently, the couple were reconciled and he was able to rely on his lack of acquiescence in (indeed, opposition to) the surrender.

---

27   *R v Nottingham City Council ex p Caine* (1996) 28 HLR 373, CA. See too *R v Hillingdon LBC ex p Thomas* (1987) 19 HLR 196, QBD.
28   See Chapter 7.
29   *R v Ealing LBC ex p Sidhu* (1982) 2 HLR 45, QBD.
30   See paras **2.15** and **3.17**.
31   *R v Eastleigh BC ex p Beattie (No 2)* (1985) 17 HLR 168, QBD.
32   See further, paras **4.68–4.73**.
33   *R v West Dorset DC ex p Phillips* (1985) 17 HLR 336, QBD.
34   *R v Penwith DC ex p Trevena* (1985) 17 HLR 526, QBD.

4.22   An attempt to raise a finding of intentionality against a wife for her husband's conduct, dating from before she even met him, was (unsurprisingly) rejected by the court in *Puhlhofer*.[35]

Findings of acquiescence

4.23   In *Thomas*,[36] however, Woolf J (who had decided *Lewis*), while restating the principle, upheld 'acquiescence' on the part of a male joint tenant whose cohabitant had caused the loss of their council tenancy by nuisance and annoyance, even though he had been in prison both at the time of the conduct and at the time of the proceedings for possession.

4.24   The factors which influenced the court were:

a)   that the man had been offered, but had declined, an opportunity to attend the hearing; and

b)   that there was no evidence of attempts by him to persuade the woman to desist in the conduct, which had persisted up until the hearing.

4.25   In *Khatun*,[37] it was unsuccessfully argued on behalf of a Bangladeshi wife that she had not acquiesced in her husband's conduct in leaving accommodation which it would have been reasonable to continue to occupy, on the basis that – as a matter of culture and practice – she had no choice but to abide by her husband's decision. Dismissing her appeal, the court held that, as she had been content to leave decisions to her spouse and to co-operate in implementing those decisions, she could properly be regarded as having acquiesced.

Rent arrears

4.26   It may be the case, particularly in arrears cases, that the spouse has found out too late to be able to do anything about rent arrears. So, for example, arrears may be so substantial when the spouse discovers them that simple awareness of the debt before homelessness cannot be said to amount to acquiescence: see *Spruce*.[38]

4.27   On the other hand, in *O'Connor*[39] the authority was entitled to conclude that there had been acquiescence, and in *Salmons*[40] the authority had addressed

---

35   *R v Hillingdon LBC ex p Puhlhofer* (1985) 17 HLR 278, QBD, not appealed on this point; cf [1986] AC 484, CA and HL, (1985) 17 HLR 588, CA, (1986) 18 HLR 158, HL.
36   *R v Swansea City Council ex p Thomas* (1983) 9 HLR 64, QBD.
37   *R v Tower Hamlets LBC ex p Khatun* (1995) 27 HLR 344, CA.
38   *R v East Northamptonshire DC ex p Spruce* (1988) 20 HLR 508, QBD.
39   *R v Barnet LBC ex p O'Connor* (1990) 22 HLR 486, QBD.
40   *R v Ealing LBC ex p Salmons* (1991) 23 HLR 272, QBD.

the critical question of whether it was entitled to conclude that the applicant must have known about, or at least turned a blind eye to, the arrears, and was accordingly entitled to reach the view that the applicant had either not been honest about his knowledge of the arrears, or that he had at the least been reckless about the true situation.

Non-cohabitants

4.28   The acquiescence point is not confined to married and unmarried cohabitants. In *Smith v Bristol City Council*,[41] a woman was held responsible for acts of nuisance caused by her son and lodgers, which resulted in her eviction. Similarly, the basis for the order for possession which resulted[42] in a finding of intentionality in *Devenport*[43] was conduct by the children of the family; conduct by children was included in the reasons for the finding of intentionality in *Ward*.[44]

4.29   In *Bannon*,[45] acquiescence was upheld in relation to nuisance by the family as a whole, to which the applicant had either been a party or else which she had done nothing to prevent. In *John*,[46] nuisance and annoyance by a lodger caused the eviction of the tenant even though it occurred only when she was out of the flat, and the lodger was both younger and considerably stronger than she, so that she was unable to control his behaviour. Her 'acquiescence' was the failure to evict him.[47]

4.30   An attempt to use the principle of non-acquiescence on behalf of child applicants failed on the basis that the children were not in priority need in their own right: *ex p G*.[48]

---

41   See discussion at December 1981 *LAG Bulletin* 287.
42   But see para **4.31**.
43   *Devenport v Salford City Council* (1983) 8 HLR 54, CA.
44   *R v Southampton City Council ex p Ward* (1984) 14 HLR 114, QBD.
45   *R v East Hertfordshire DC ex p Bannon* (1986) 18 HLR 515, QBD.
46   *R v Swansea City Council ex p John* (1983) 9 HLR 55, QBD.
47   In *Darlington BC v Sterling* (1997) 29 HLR 309, CA, it was taken for granted that eviction on the grounds of nuisance and annoyance by – in that case – the tenant's son was capable of giving rise to a finding of intentionality (which should not, it was held, have prevented an order for possession being made against the tenant).
48   *R v Oldham MBC ex p G; R v Bexley LBC ex p B* (1993) 25 HLR 319, HL, see para **3.13**. See also *R v Camden LBC ex p Hersi* (2001) 33 HLR 52, CA. On the applicability of the Children Act 1989 in such cases, see paras **11.61–11.70**. Children Act 2004, s 11 (duty on authorities to have regard to the need to safeguard and promote the welfare of children when discharging any functions) adds nothing to the assessment of whether someone is intentionally homeless: *Huzrat v Hounslow LBC* [2013] EWCA Civ 1865, [2014] HLR 17. The correct forum for deploying arguments about section 11 is at the application and/or review stage: *Mohamoud v Kensington and Chelsea RLBC; Saleem v Wandsworth LBC* [2015] EWCA Civ 780, [2015] HLR 38.

DELIBERATE ACT OR OMISSION

General principles

4.31   The issue is not whether a person deliberately became homeless, but whether they deliberately did (or failed to do) something as a result of which they became homeless: the word 'deliberate' only governs the act or omission – *Devenport*.[49] The link between the act and the homelessness must be judged objectively: *Robinson v Torbay BC*.[50]

4.32   Under the provisions of an allocation scheme, it has been held that 'deliberate' implies that the applicant had a choice between two or more viable options and voluntarily elected to do the act in question: thus, in that case, it could not be said that the applicant's occupation of overcrowded accommodation[51] resulted from his own deliberate act because the choices open to him[52] were both unaffordable.[53] It is hard to see that a different decision should follow under these intentionality provisions.

Good faith

4.33   That said, 'an act or omission in good faith on the part of a person who was unaware of any relevant fact shall not be treated as deliberate' for the purposes of establishing intentional homelessness.[54] This statutory qualification introduces a subjective element into the issue.[55] Subsections HA 1996, 191(1) and (2) pose 'serial questions': whether an act is in good faith *and* in ignorance of relevant facts must be considered separately – *O'Connor*,[56] in which the authority had wrongly merged the two subsections and obscured the critical, good faith question.

4.34   If it is established that the applicant was unaware of a relevant fact, the question is not whether the ignorance was reasonable, but whether it was in good faith.[57] Good faith can include cases where the applicant's ignorance of a relevant

---

49   *Devenport v Salford City Council,* above. Cf the obiter comments of the Master of the Rolls in *R v Slough BC ex p Ealing LBC* [1981] QB 801, CA.
50   *Robinson v Torbay BC* [1982] 1 All ER 726, QBD.
51   Which would otherwise have increased his priority for an allocation.
52   Leaving his wife and family in Ecuador was unaffordable because his wife could not find work there and he could not afford to pay for accommodation both in England and Ecuador; and, when he had moved into the overcrowded accommodation after they arrived, he was not able to find anything affordable.
53   *R. (Roman) v Southwark LBC* [2022] EWHC 1232 (Admin); [2023] HLR. 4.
54   HA 1996, ss 191(2) and 196(2); H(W)A 2014, s 77(3).
55   *R v Exeter City Council ex p Tranckle* (1994) 26 HLR 244, CA. See the examples in the English Code of Guidance para 9.26; Welsh Code para 17.26.
56   *O'Connor v Kensington and Chelsea RLBC* [2004] EWCA Civ 394, [2004] HLR 37.
57   *F v Birmingham City Council* [2006] EWCA Civ 1427, [2007] HLR 18 at [17].

fact was due to their own unreasonable conduct[58] and where the applicant could be said to have been foolish or imprudent.[59] The good faith requirement will not, however, be satisfied where an applicant has shut their eyes to the obvious, or has acted with wilful ignorance or on little more than a wing and a prayer.[60]

4.35   Want of 'good faith' carries the connotation of some kind of impropriety, or an element of misuse or abuse of the legislation.[61] Dishonesty will not constitute good faith.[62] Whether or not an act is laudable or done for good motives has no bearing on whether it is in good faith.[63]

Ignorance of facts

4.36   An applicant's failure properly to appreciate their prospects (or lack of prospects) of future housing can be treated as lack of 'awareness of a relevant fact' for the purposes of HA 1996, s 191(2),[64] provided that it is sufficiently specific and based on a degree of genuine investigation, not mere aspiration.[65] If the prospect of future housing rests on next to nothing but hope, not applying section 191(2) in the applicant's favour is not an error of law;[66] in such a case, the subsection is a non-starter and no specific reference to it is needed.[67]

4.37   In *Ugiagbe*,[68] the applicant was unaware of a relevant fact because she did not know that she could not be required to leave without a court order.[69] It is, however, ignorance of a relevant fact which must not have been deliberate, not ignorance of the legal consequences.[70]

58   *F*, above, at [17].
59   *Ugiagbe v Southwark LBC* [2009] EWCA Civ 31, [2009] HLR 35 at [26].
60   *F*, above, at [17].
61   *Ugiagbe*, above, at [27].
62   *Ugiagbe*, above, at [27].
63   In *Alfonso-da-Trindade v Hackney LBC* [2017] EWCA Civ 942, [2017] HLR 37, the appellant had come to the UK in order to seek better medical provision for her disabled child; whilst that was laudable, good faith did not turn on motivation; the applicant had left her settled accommodation with a reckless disregard for her housing prospects in the UK.
64   *F v Birmingham City Council,* above, at [17].
65   *R v Westminster City Council ex p Obeid* (1997) 29 HLR 389, QBD at 398; *Aw-Aden v Birmingham City Council* [2005] EWCA Civ 1834 at [10] and [11].
66   *Aw-Aden*, above, at [11].
67   *Aw-Aden*, above, at [12].
68   *Ugiagbe v Southwark LBC* [2009] EWCA Civ 31, [2009] HLR 35 at [8].
69   For the facts, see further para **4.49**.
70   *R v Eastleigh BC ex p Beattie (No 2)* (1985) 17 HLR 168, QBD; *R v Croydon LBC ex p Toth* (1988) 20 HLR 576, CA; cf *R v Mole Valley DC ex p Burton* (1988) 20 HLR 479, QBD, where the applicant's belief in assurances by her husband that they would be rehoused under a union agreement was held to be a belief of fact, not of law. See also *Alfonso-da-Trinade v Hackney LBC* [2017] EWCA Civ 942, [2017] HLR 37, in which the authority had been entitled to find that the appellant's ignorance of the possibility that her sister could be evicted was not ignorance of a relevant fact but of a possible future event.

4.38   Where an applicant temporarily went to live with her mother while at college but was warned by her father that she would not be allowed to return, the authority misdirected itself in disregarding her genuine belief that he did not mean it, ie, that she would be able to go back. The father's state of mind was a relevant fact and so his daughter's action – taken in genuine ignorance of her father's true intent – could not be classified as deliberate: *Wincentzen v Monklands DC.*[71]

4.39   It was a relevant fact of which the applicant was ignorant where a person was misled as to business prospects, which caused him to move abroad: *Lusi.*[72]

4.40   In *Sukhija,*[73] a distinction was drawn between a mistake of fact (which could be within the good faith defence) and a mere unfulfilled hope (which was not). The decision that the applicant – who had come to England in the mistaken belief that she would be able to find employment and a home – was intentionally homeless was accordingly upheld.

4.41   See also *Khatun,*[74] in which the applicant was described as having no more than an expectation of being able to live temporarily with her parents-in-law on her return to the UK: it was not a fact to which the good faith defence could be applied.

4.42   Again, in *Ciftci,*[75] a disabled woman and her son left her flat in Switzerland after a friend of her sister said that there was a job available for her and that she could stay with her, sleeping on a bed sofa; she could not keep the job because of her disability and after nine months the friend asked her to leave. The authority's decision decided that she was intentionally homeless: she had made no sufficient plan to obtain settled accommodation in England, had made insufficient enquiries about the job and had moved into accommodation which she knew would be temporary – in short, in giving up her flat in Switzerland, she had acted "on a wing and a prayer". Her challenge that further enquiries[76] would have led to a finding that she had been ignorant of relevant facts failed and the authority's decision upheld: there was no evidence that the appellant had made any inquiry into the nature of the job available to her in England before she had left her accommodation in Switzerland; it was obvious that she would only be able to stay with the family friend on a temporary basis and she simply had not turned her mind to how she would live or support herself in the UK.

---

71   *Wincentzen v Monklands DC* (1988) SLT (Court of Session) 259, September 1988 *LAG Bulletin* 13.
72   *R v Hammersmith and Fulham RLBC ex p Lusi* (1991) 23 HLR 460, QBD.
73   *R v Ealing LBC ex p Sukhija* (1994) 26 HLR 726, QBD.
74   *R v Tower Hamlets LBC ex p Khatun* (1994) 27 HLR 465, CA.
75   *Ciftci v Haringey LBC* [2021] EWCA 1772; [2022] HLR 9.
76   Paras **7.91–7.92.**

4.43   In *Ashton*,[77] a middle-aged woman moved from her home in Tunbridge Wells to take up a temporary job in Winchester, where the authority provided her with a one-year tenancy subject to the exception in HA 1985, Sch 1 para 5.[78] After a year, the authority obtained possession of the premises. A finding that the applicant was intentionally homeless was quashed on the basis, inter alia, that, in leaving Tunbridge Wells, the applicant had acted in good faith because she was unaware that she would be unable to find either housing or employment after the initial year. Accordingly, her action in surrendering the tenancy at Tunbridge Wells should not have been treated as deliberate.

4.44   In *Conway*,[79] a woman erroneously but genuinely believed that she had a further period of a year in which to decide whether or not to extend her existing shorthold tenancy. This was ignorance of a material fact, ie, the time remaining in which to make her decision.

4.45   In *Rose*,[80] the applicant had been born in the UK but when her parents separated, she had gone to live with her mother in Jamaica. Subsequently, her siblings came to England, to live with their father, who paid their fares and accommodated them; when the applicant asked her father if she, and her daughter, could also come to England, her father was unable to pay her fare but otherwise confirmed that she could come to England, which the applicant understood to mean that he would have adequate accommodation for them, though she made no specific inquiries about long they would be able to stay with him. There was no accommodation for them and her father asked them to leave after a week. The authority's decision that she had become homeless intentionally was quashed: it had failed to take into account a material consideration, ie, her unawareness of the lack of accommodation with her father; it was not entitled to assume without further inquiry that because she had made no specific inquiries, she had acted other than in good faith in ignorance of a relevant fact.

4.46   In *Obeid*,[81] the applicant had taken private-sector accommodation in the belief that her rent would be covered by housing benefit, in ignorance of (and without making enquiries about) the provisions of the then regulations which could limit her benefit to a proportion of her rent. This was capable of

---

77   *R v Winchester City Council ex p Ashton* (1991) 24 HLR 48, QBD. The decision of Kennedy J was upheld by the Court of Appeal (see (1992) 24 HLR 520) on the additional basis that, although the authority had stated that it had had regard to the general circumstances prevailing in relation to housing in its area (H(HP)A 1977, s 60, now HA 1996, s 177), it had failed to balance that against the 'quite exceptional circumstances' of the applicant (ie, that she had left her previous accommodation in Tunbridge Wells in order to take up employment in Winchester after six years of involuntary unemployment): see para **2.122**.
78   Temporary accommodation for people taking up employment.
79   *R v Christchurch BC ex p Conway* (1987) 19 HLR 238, QBD.
80   *R v Wandsworth LBC ex p Rose* (1984) 11 HLR 105, QBD.
81   *R v Westminster City Council ex p Obeid* (1997) 29 HLR 389, QBD.

constituting ignorance of a relevant fact. Carnwath J, considering, among other things, the decisions in *Lusi*[82] and *Sukhija*,[83] said that:

> 'The effect of those judgments, as I understand them, is that an applicant's appreciation of the prospects of future housing or future employment can be treated as "awareness of a relevant fact" for the purposes of this subsection, provided it is sufficiently specific (that is related to specific employment or specific housing opportunities) and provided it is based on some genuine investigation and not mere "aspiration".'[84]

4.47   Leaving settled accommodation to move into unsettled accommodation may form part of the circumstances amounting to intentional homelessness, under the HA 1996 extended definition of intentionality governing 'collusive arrangements' – see further below.[85] Ignorance of the unsettled quality of intended accommodation would, however, amount to ignorance of a relevant fact and as such should mean that a move is not caught, because 'the purpose of the arrangement' implies an element of intention ('to enable [the applicant] to become entitled to assistance').[86]

Carelessness v deliberate conduct

4.48   In deciding whether the ignorance is in good faith, an authority must distinguish between honest blundering or carelessness on the one hand, which can amount to good faith conduct;[87] and dishonesty, where there can be no question of good faith: *Lusi*;[88] *Ali and Bibi*.[89] The question is whether the action is taken in good faith, not whether it was reasonable.

4.49   In *Ugiagbe*,[90] the applicant was asked by her landlord to leave; she went to her local authority's 'One-Stop Shop' and was told to go to the Homeless Persons' Unit (HPU) to get temporary accommodation; as she did not want to be treated as homeless, she returned to the property. Eventually, her landlord again asked her to leave, which she did, and she applied for homelessness assistance. Her omission to follow the advice to go to the HPU could be described as foolish or imprudent, yet it was the opposite of bad faith because her subjective

---

82   *R v Hammersmith and Fulham LBC ex p Lusi*, above; see para **4.39**.
83   *R v Ealing LBC ex p Sukhija*, para **4.40**.
84   This statement was approved in *Aw-Aden v Birmingham City Council* [2005] EWCA Civ 1834, where the applicant's unfulfilled hope of finding employment in this country was insufficiently specific; rather, it was a mere aspiration.
85   See paras **4.166–4.170**.
86   HA 1996, s 191(4)(b).
87   The line between good faith carelessness and the sort of circumstances which can give rise to a finding of intentional homelessness – cf paras **4.39–4.32**, mere unfulfilled hope, mere expectation, moving on a wing and a prayer – is far from fixed or, perhaps, even clear. Indeed, it would at times seem to border on the subjective.
88   *R v Hammersmith and Fulham LBC ex p Lusi* (1991) 23 HLR 460, QBD.
89   *R v Westminster City Council ex p Ali and Bibi* (1993) 25 HLR 109, QBD.
90   *Ugiagbe v Southwark LBC* [2009] EWCA Civ 31, [2009] HLR 35 at [3].

motivation in not doing so was because she had been led to believe that she would be treated as homeless, which was the last thing she wanted.[91]

4.50   In *F*,[92] the applicant surrendered a secure tenancy of a two-bedroom flat, ignoring advice from her social worker that she risked being found intentionally homeless, and took a tenancy of a three-bedroom house, from which she was evicted for arrears which accrued because she did not receive housing benefit. She was found, at best, to have proceeded on a wing and a prayer; her conduct was described as wilful ignorance or shutting her eyes to the obvious which could not satisfy the good faith test; HA 1996, s 191(2) did not arise for consideration.[93] See also *Ciftci*, above.[94]

4.51   In *Rouf*,[95] a finding of intentionality against an applicant who returned to a flat that had been repossessed after an absence of three years, but who nonetheless had believed it would still be available to him, was quashed. The authority had failed to consider whether the belief was genuine, wrongly approaching the question as one of the reasonableness of his conduct.

4.52   In *Onwudiwe*,[96] however, an unemployed applicant's conduct in taking on large mortgage commitments in order to fund a business for which there had been no market-testing took the case beyond the stage of honest incompetence and provided material on which it could be said that he was deliberately putting his house at risk.

4.53   In *Beattie (No 2)*,[97] persistent failure to pay mortgage arrears was deliberate, notwithstanding that the applicant had been advised by his solicitors that it would not be.

4.54   On the other hand, in *White*,[98] the applicant believed that the then Department of Health and Social Security (DHSS) was, or ought to be, paying the whole of the interest element on the mortgage instalments by direct deduction from his benefit. In fact, his supplementary benefit entitlement was so low that it did not cover the full amount of the interest, so that arrears continued to mount. The court held that – for most of the period in question – the applicant was under a genuine misapprehension as to a relevant fact,[99] and that he had acted in good faith in failing to make the payments himself. There was, accordingly, no deliberate omission and, in consequence, no intentional homelessness.

---

91   *Ugiagbe*, above, at [25], [26] and [28].
92   *F v Birmingham City Council* [2006] EWCA Civ 1427, [2007] HLR 18 at [9].
93   *F*, above, at [19].
94   Para **4.42**.
95   *R v Tower Hamlets LBC ex p Rouf* (1991) 23 HLR 460, QBD.
96   *R v Wandsworth LBC ex p Onwudiwe* (1994) 26 HLR 302, CA.
97   *R v Eastleigh BC ex p Beattie (No 2)* (1985) 17 HLR 168, QBD.
98   *White v Exeter City Council*, December 1981 *LAG Bulletin* 287, QBD.
99   Whether or not the DHSS was paying the whole of the interest payments.

4.55   In *O'Connor v Kensington and Chelsea RLBC*,[100] the applicant husband and wife believed that a friend, who was staying at their flat while they were visiting Ireland for a funeral and while the husband recovered from depression, was paying the rent. He was not in fact doing so; a suspended possession order was obtained in their absence and subsequently enforced after their return. The Court of Appeal held that it is not necessary for the ignorance of the relevant fact to be reasonable before an omission qualifies as non-deliberate; a person's ignorance may well be due to unreasonable behaviour, yet what the person does in consequence may still be in good faith. The dividing line is not at the point where an applicant's ignorance of a relevant fact is due to the applicant's own unreasonable conduct but at the point where, by shutting their eyes to the obvious, the applicant cannot be said to have acted in good faith.

Act causing loss of accommodation

4.56   The act of good faith referred to in HA 1996, s 191(2) is the act or omission causing homelessness; this is the act which must be considered under s 191(1).[101]

4.57   In *Stewart*,[102] the authority found that the deliberate act which caused the homelessness was the commission of a criminal act by the applicant, following which he was imprisoned and a warrant executed (without notice) on the basis of an earlier possession order for arrears. The authority accepted that, after his imprisonment, the applicant had made an arrangement with his sister to maintain the tenancy, but no rent was in fact paid under it. He argued that the deliberate act or omission was the failure to pay the rent, which was an act in good faith because he had been unaware of a relevant fact, ie, his sister's failure to keep to the arrangement. The Court of Appeal held that, given a proper finding that the deliberate act which caused the homelessness was the offence, the subsequent acts in good faith were irrelevant and the authority was not obliged to investigate them.

4.58   Where the cause of homelessness was an applicant's inability to meet mortgage repayments as a result of a severe downturn in business, the homelessness was intentional because the mortgage itself had been obtained as a result of the applicant's fraudulent misrepresentation of her income: *Rughooputh*.[103]

4.59   In *Chishimba v Kensington and Chelsea RLBC*,[104] however, the appellant used a counterfeit passport to secure assistance under HA 1996, Part 7; she was granted a tenancy by the authority but, when it was discovered that she had not

---

100 *O'Connor v Kensington and Chelsea RLBC* [2004] EWCA Civ 394, [2004] HLR 37.

101 Which is why it is important correctly to identify the date when the (putatively intentional) homelessness began – cf *O'Connor v Kensington and Chelsea RLBC*, above. See also *Ugiagbe v Southwark LBC*, above at [6].

102 *Stewart v Lambeth LBC* [2002] EWCA Civ 753, [2002] HLR 40.

103 *R v Barnet LBC ex p Rughooputh* (1993) 25 HLR 607, CA.

104 [2013] EWCA Civ 786, [2013] HLR 34.

been eligible for assistance, the authority sought possession. After being granted leave to remain, the appellant re-applied, following which she was evicted from the flat. The authority held that she was homeless intentionally, as the cause of her homelessness was her use of the counterfeit passport.

4.60 The Court of Appeal accepted that the immediate cause of the appellant's homelessness was the discovery that she had obtained her tenancy by deception; proceeding back in time from that immediate cause, however, the effective cause of her homelessness was that she had been ineligible for assistance, so that she was not intentionally homeless as it could not have been reasonable for her to continue to occupy accommodation to which she never had any lawful right.

4.61 In *Tranckle*,[105] the applicant entered into an imprudent financial arrangement in good faith, unaware of the (un)reality of the prospects of success for the public house which she was purchasing, which had been concealed from her by the brewery; her decision to purchase the pub in good faith was the act causing her homelessness.

4.62 In *Watchman*,[106] the applicant was a secure tenant who exercised the right to buy with the aid of a mortgage on which the repayments were significantly higher than the rent she had previously been paying in respect of which there was a history of arrears. Her husband subsequently lost his job but, although he found another at a lower salary, mortgage arrears built up and the mortgagee repossessed the property. The authority decided that the applicant was intentionally homeless by taking on the mortgage when it was inevitable that she would get into severe financial difficulties within a short time; her husband's employment problems had not caused the repossession but merely accelerated the inevitable eviction.[107]

4.63 Upholding that decision, it was held that – when deciding whether an applicant is intentionally homeless where there are several potential causes of the homelessness – the authority must make a careful judgment on the particular facts in order to decide whether the homelessness is a likely consequence of a deliberate act on the part of the applicant, bearing in mind that it is the applicant's responsibility for the homelessness that is in question.[108] While the authority has to consider the time when the applicant in fact became homeless,[109] it is entitled to take account of events prior to that date.[110]

4.64 Ironically, in some cases a person who takes the trouble to find out relevant facts, and reaches a decision on them, will be more vulnerable to a

---

105 *R v Exeter City Council ex p Tranckle* (1994) 26 HLR 244, CA.
106 *Watchman v Ipswich BC* [2007] EWCA Civ 348, [2007] HLR 33 at [6].
107 *Watchman*, above, at [9].
108 *Watchman*, above, at [22]; see also *Carthew v Exeter City Council* [2012] EWCA Civ 1913, [2013] HLR 19, in which the authority failed to consider why the appellant had transferred her interest in a property to her former partner.
109 *Din v Wandsworth LBC* [1983] 1 AC 657, HL.
110 *Watchman* at [23].

finding of intentionality than a person who has omitted to make any enquiries at all.[111]

Bad faith

4.65 Where bad faith is suspected, it has been suggested that it may not invariably be necessary to put the matter to the applicant (*Hobbs v Sutton LBC*)[112] – but see *Moozary-Oraky*,[113] in which good faith relative to awareness of housing benefit was considered to be a question of jurisdictional fact, without which no reasonable authority could reach a conclusion on intentionality, into which the authority was accordingly required to make explicit enquiry of the applicant.[114]

4.66 In *Joyce*,[115] the authority did not even ask the applicant why mortgage arrears had arisen. This failure was fatal to its decision, as it had omitted to take something relevant into account,[116] ie, the applicant's explanation or answer.

Illustrations

4.67 There is much guidance and a large number of cases on intentionality, which can conveniently be approached under a series of headings – but it is essential to remember that the cases are all illustrative of the operation of the provisions rather than precedents on their facts, and that guidance is not binding.[117]

Rent/mortgage arrears

4.68 The English Code gives as an example of homelessness which should not be treated as deliberate:

'An applicant's actions would not amount to intentional homelessness where they have lost their home, or were obliged to sell it, because of rent or mortgage arrears resulting from significant financial difficulties, and the applicant was genuinely unable to keep up the rent or mortgage payments even after claiming benefits, and no further financial help was available. Housing authorities should be alert to the impact of economic abuse and

111 *R v Westminster City Council ex p Obeid* (1997) 29 HLR 389, QBD.
112 (1994) 26 HLR 132, CA.
113 *R v Westminste City Council ex p Moozary-Oraky* (1994) 26 HLR 213, QBD.
114 As to whether or not the applicant had seen a letter informing her that her benefit had been stopped.
115 *R v Wyre BC ex p Joyce* (1984) 11 HLR 72, QBD.
116 See para **10.48**.
117 As to departing from guidance, see *De Falco v Crawley BC* [1980] QB 460, CA, at 478; see also the recent summary of authorities in relation to departing from statutory guidance in *R (X) v Tower Hamlets LBC* [2013] EWHC 480 (Admin), at [27]–[35]: see generally paras **10.49–10.50**.

control and coercion on a victim of domestic abuse's ability to meet rent or mortgage payments.'[118]

4.69   This is to be contrasted with cases where an applicant:

a)   chooses to sell their home in circumstances where is the applicant is under no risk of losing it;

b)   has lost their home because of wilful and persistent refusal to pay rent or mortgage payments.[119]

4.70   The Code issued under HA 1985, Part 3 was in similar terms. In *Hawthorne*,[120] it was considered not to misstate the law. In *Bryant*,[121] it was said that the Code drew a distinction 'between those who can, or could reasonably be expected to, pay mortgage payments or rent but do not do so, and those who in reality cannot pay because of real financial difficulties'. It was a question of fact for the authority to decide into which category an applicant fell, open only to challenge on usual public law principles.[122]

4.71   The English Code also considers that authorities should not find an applicant to be intentionally homeless where the non-payment of rent or mortgage costs arose from financial difficulties which were beyond the applicant's control or which were the result of housing benefit or universal credit delays.[123]

4.72   By way of example of circumstances where, notwithstanding financial difficulty, intentionality may still be found, in *Noel v Hillingdon LBC*,[124] the applicant had taken a tenancy which he could not afford; his partner and child then moved in and he failed to apply for an increase in his housing benefit. Both the decision to take an unaffordable tenancy and the failure to apply for an increase in housing benefit were held to amount to intentional homelessness. In *Oduneye v Brent LBC*,[125] the applicant did not respond to the authority's requests for financial and employment information in relation to her housing benefit which led to its suspension and consequential arrears; she was held homeless intentionally.

---

118 English Code of Guidance para 9.18; note that the last sentence was added in July 2021 in light of the Domestic Abuse Act 2021 coming info force; see Welsh Code para 17.18 to like effect, but without anything equivalent to the last sentence of the English code.

119 English Code of Guidance para 9.20; Welsh Code para 17.23.

120 *R v Wandsworth LBC ex p Hawthorne* (1995) 27 HLR 59, CA. See also *Ekwuru v Westminster City Council* [2003] EWCA Civ 1293, [2004] HLR 14, where arrears arose because of a housing benefit cap.

121 *R v Warrington BC ex p Bryant* (2001) JHL D5, QBD.

122 As to which, see Chapter 10. See also *William v Wandsworth LBC; Bellamy v Hounslow LBC* [2006] EWCA Civ 535, on failure to make mortgage payments after taking out a further loan.

123 English Code para 9.17(a).

124 [2013] EWCA Civ 1602, [2014] HLR 10.

125 [2018] EWCA Civ 1595, [2018] HLR 45.

4.73   In *Viackiene v Tower Hamlets LBC*,[126] a failure to seek a joint tenant who could have assisted with paying the rent – as suggested by the landlord – was held to amount to intentional homelessness.

Nuisance and annoyance

4.74   Nuisance and annoyance can clearly be considered 'deliberate' for this purpose.[127] In *ex p P*,[128] a finding of intentionality was upheld in relation to alleged criminal and anti-social behaviour[129] (confirmed by the authority's own enquiries) which had led to threats from the IRA that the applicants would be killed if they did not leave their accommodation.

4.75   In *Bell*,[130] a possession order was obtained against the applicant on the grounds of nuisance and annoyance. She was accepted by Wirral MBC as having a priority need because of the state of her mental health. Applying a test to be found in the Code of Guidance under HA 1985, Part 3 – which referred to capacity to manage affairs[131] – the authority nonetheless found that she had become homeless intentionally. Her application for judicial review was dismissed. It was said to be one thing to be less able to fend for oneself (for the purpose of establishing vulnerability),[132] and another to be incapable of managing one's own affairs (for the purpose of intentionality); the two findings were accordingly not inconsistent.

4.76   In *Denton*,[133] the applicant's mother asked him to leave the family home because of his behaviour. The authority found that he had become homeless intentionally, a decision upheld by the Court of Appeal: when people live together, they must show appropriate respect for each other's needs and follow reasonable requests; there had been nothing inappropriate about the rules the mother had laid down.[134] It was relevant that what the applicant had lost was a family home rather than rented accommodation, because a child has no enforceable right to remain in

---

126 [2013] EWCA Civ 1764, [2014] HLR 13.
127 *Devenport v Salford City Council* (1983) 8 HLR 54, CA; *R v Swansea City Council ex p John* (1983) 9 HLR 55, QBD; and *R v East Hertfordshire DC ex p Bannon* (1986) 18 HLR 515, QBD. See also English Code of Guidance para 9.20; Welsh Code para 17.23.
128 *R v Hammersmith and Fulham LBC ex p P* (1990) 22 HLR 21, QBD.
129 In *Bristol City Council v Mousah* (1998) 30 HLR 32, CA, allowing premises to be used in connection with the sale of drugs, even though the tenant was himself absent and was not charged, appears to have been presumed to be capable of giving rise to a finding of intentionality (which it was held should not have prevented the making of an order for possession on the basis of 'reasonableness'; compare also the details of *Darlington BC v Sterling* (1997) 29 HLR 309, CA, summarised at para **4.29**).
130 *R v Wirral MBC ex p Bell* (1995) 27 HLR 234, QBD.
131 The English Code refers to persons who are 'incapable of managing their affairs, for example, by reason of age, mental Illness or disability' and those with 'limited mental capacity; or a temporary aberration or aberrations caused by mental illness, frailty, or an assessed substance misuse problem': paras 9.17(b), (c). There is no equivalent in the Welsh Code.
132 See paras **3.35–3.76**.
133 *Denton v Southwark LBC* [2007] EWCA Civ 623, [2008] HLR 11 at [1].
134 *Denton*, above, at [21].

their family home and therefore has to obey the house rules.[135] Accordingly, when deciding the issue of intentionality, the reasonableness of those rules should be considered.

Pregnancy

4.77 A person does not become homeless intentionally by becoming pregnant,[136] for example, because accommodation is lost (on account of size or for other reasons, such as terms of accommodation), or because it is the family home and the family reject the pregnant woman.

Failure to use other remedies

4.78 Two common examples of omission alleged to amount to intentional homelessness are:

a) failure by an evicted private tenant to take civil proceedings to secure re-entry; and

b) failure by a cohabitant or spouse to use domestic remedies.

Each of these examples merits closer consideration.

4.79 Under HA 1996, s 175(2), 'a person is also homeless if he has accommodation but . . . he cannot secure entry to it'.[137] This defines as homeless a person who has been locked out of their home, and is generally taken to refer to the illegally evicted occupier.[138] While it is open to an authority to treat an occupier who does not use their civil remedies as intentionally homeless, it would be unlawful to adopt a blanket policy that all such occupiers must do so.[139]

4.80 Detailed provision is now made for cases of violence and domestic abuse,[140] and – since the decision in *Bond*[141] – it is clear that authorities cannot require an applicant to use civil remedies. A person who knows what can be done to prevent violence but deliberately fails to do it has not caused the probability of the abuse or violence which makes the continued occupation of that accommodation unreasonable.[142] The probability of abuse or violence is to be assessed objectively, by the person carrying out the assessment.[143]

---

135 *Denton*, above, at [14].
136 *R v Eastleigh BC ex p Beattie (No 1)* (1983) 10 HLR 134, QBD.
137 In Wales, H(W)A 2014, s 55(2); see paras **2.64–2.70**.
138 English Code of Guidance paras 6.20-6.21; Welsh Code para 8.16.
139 See para **2.67**; see also paras **10.54–10.55**.
140 See paras **2.84–2.90**.
141 *Bond v Leicester City Council* [2001] EWCA Civ 1544, (2002) HLR 6. On domestic abuse, see also English Code chapter 12.
142 *Bond*, above, at [33].
143 *Danesh v Kensington and Chelsea RLBC* [2006] EWCA Civ 1404, [2007] HLR 17.

Loss of tied accommodation

4.81   Another common example is loss of tied accommodation.[144] It was not merely accepted in the High Court in *Lewis*[145] that the man's departure from his job, and consequent loss of accommodation, qualified as intentional, but an earlier challenge[146] to that decision had been, albeit reluctantly, dismissed. Loss of tied accommodation also amounted to intentionality in *Goddard*[147] and *Jennings*,[148] but the cases were determined on the meaning of 'in consequence' and are, as such, considered below.

4.82   Detailed consideration was given to this problem in *Williams*.[149] The manager of a public house was dismissed for stock and profit irregularities, which he denied. In the course of an appeals procedure, which he pursued with the assistance of his union representative, his employers offered him the choice of resigning or dismissal. He resigned and, while threatened with homelessness, applied to the local authority for accommodation.

4.83   The authority made enquiries of the former employers and concluded:

> 'My understanding of the circumstances of your resignation lead me to the conclusion that, had you not resigned, the end result would be the same, ie, that events leading up to your appeal against dismissal would be regarded as something "the likely result of which is that you will be forced to leave accommodation which is available for your occupation and which it would have been reasonable for you to continue to occupy".'

4.84   The court interpreted this as:

> '. . . saying it was intentional because he resigned. It also seems to go on to say that in any event "even if you had not resigned you would have been dismissed because of your own faults." In either event, it would have been an intentional homelessness.'

4.85   During the course of the judgment, the court likened the position of the applicant to that of a person who had been constructively dismissed for the purposes of employment law:

> 'Had he gone to an industrial tribunal and complained that he had been unfairly dismissed, it would not have been open to the employers to say by

---

144 See English Code of Guidance para 9.20(g); Welsh Code para 17.23. Note, however, English Code of Guidance para 24.11, which states that the Secretary of State considers that service personnel required to vacate service quarters as a result of taking up an option to give notice to leave the service should not be considered to have become homeless intentionally. There is no direct equivalent in the Welsh Code.
145 See para **4.15**.
146 Unreported.
147 *Goddard v Torridge DC* January 1982 *LAG Bulletin* 9, QBD.
148 *Jennings v Northavon DC* January 1982 *LAG Bulletin* 9, QBD.
149 *R v Thurrock DC ex p Williams* (1981) 1 HLR 128, QBD.

way of answer . . . you resigned, because he would have been able to reply that he resigned only because he had been told that if he did not do so, he would be dismissed.'

4.86   This may be a basis for distinguishing a resignation from dismissal, but what the authority was seeking to do was to say: either the applicant resigned (intentional homelessness) or he was dismissed (intentional homelessness), and it ignored the 'grey area' of dispute, which had led to the compromise.

4.87   The court analysed the case in stages. It asked:

a)   why the applicant was homeless (because there had been a possession order against him);

b)   why a possession order was made (because his contract of employment came to an end);

c)   why did it end (because he resigned);

d)   why did he resign (because if he did not do so, he would be dismissed);

e)   why would he have been dismissed, was it his fault (this was in dispute).

The authority was therefore bound to reach a view as to fault, however hard it was for it to do so.

4.88   The court approved the authority's initial approach to 'job loss cases'. An act the consequences of which can be construed as a deliberate departure can qualify within the provisions; but someone who loses their job for incompetence, which will usually comprise a course of conduct spread over a period of time, cannot be said to be carrying out a deliberate act. The person would lack the necessary intention, or state of mind, in the absence of clear proof that a course of incompetent conduct had been adopted in order to provoke dismissal.

4.89   *Reeve*[150] was also a case on loss of tied accommodation, although it was as much on the meaning of 'in consequence' as 'deliberate'. A woman worked as a receptionist for a car hire firm and lived above the office. She was living with a man. She told her employers that he was not disqualified from driving, although he was. When the employers found out, they dismissed her. The authority found that she lost her accommodation because of the misconduct leading to loss of employment, which misconduct was the statement made to the employers.

4.90   This allegation was, at the time of dismissal and indeed at the time of the local authority's decision and of the hearing at the High Court, disputed. Nonetheless, the authority had investigated, and it had concluded that the dismissal was 'for that deliberate act of misconduct'. This was the crucial point of distinction from *Williams* (above):

---

150   *R v Thanet DC ex p Reeve* (1983) 6 HLR 31, QBD.

'Some acts which a person does will lead indirectly to their becoming homeless . . . Other acts will be sufficiently proximate to render the person within the category of those who become homeless intentionally . . . [T] his case probably comes close to the border-line. For it to fall on the right side so far as the local authority are concerned it seems to me that the termination of the employment . . . must be lawful. It must be some conduct on the part of the applicant which justifies the employer treating the contract as at an end . . .'

Sale of jointly owned home

4.91   In *Bellamy*,[151] the applicant was the joint owner of a property with her mother. She applied as homeless when the property was sold, having waived all rights to any of the proceeds of sale in favour of her mother. The authority found her intentionally homeless. On review, the authority rejected the applicant's assertion that she had intended her mother to be the sole owner of the property and concluded that the she had been aware that she had the right to object to the sale and had also been aware that – as a beneficial owner – she had a right to an interest in the property: her failure to object to the sale constituted a deliberate act which caused her to become homeless.

4.92   The decision was quashed at first instance, but restored by the Court of Appeal: the authority had been entitled, on the basis of the evidence before it, to conclude that the appellant was a joint legal owner of the property with rights over it, including the right to object to the sale under Trusts of Land and Appointment of Trustees Act 1996, ss 14 and 15. The question for the judge had not been what the appellant and the mother intended when jointly purchasing the property, but whether the authority had been obviously wrong in its understanding of that intention.

Overlap with 'reasonable to continue to occupy'

4.93   The question whether there has been a deliberate act or omission has a relationship with the question whether it was reasonable for the applicant to continue to occupy the accommodation: this has been considered in chapter 2 so far as it concerns affordability[152] and is considered further below, under its own heading.[153] Whether accommodation is accommodation which it would have been reasonable for an applicant to continue to occupy must be determined at a time before – and without regard to – the deliberate acts or omissions which led to the loss of that accommodation.[154]

---

151 *William v Wandsworth LBC; Bellamy v Hounslow LBC* [2006] EWCA Civ 535, [2006] HLR 42.
152 See paras **2.135–2.146**, and, in particular, now the Homelessness (Suitability of Accommodation) Order 1996, SI 1996/3204: see paras **4.135–1.138**.
153 Paras **4.158–4.164**.
154 *Denton v Southwark LBC* [2007] EWCA Civ 623, [2008] HLR 11 at [2], [25].

IN CONSEQUENCE

Overview

4.94   The homelessness must be 'in consequence of' the deliberate act or omission. This is a question of 'cause and effect'.[155] The principal issue which has arisen is the attribution of present homelessness to past act or omission. That is to say, there is commonly an act which has or could have been the subject of a finding of intentionality, and the argument becomes whether or not that act or omission is the cause of the current homelessness.

4.95   See also *Bashir Hassan*,[156] where the authority wrongly sought to rely on events which post-dated the onset of homelessness. See also, generally, above, under the heading 'Act causing loss of accommodation'.[157]

Cause and effect

4.96   A causal link may continue to subsist following the act of intentionality even though the applicant ceases to be homeless in the interim – for example, because they find some temporary accommodation which is subsequently lost: *Awua*.[158]

4.97   The authority must look back to the original cause of the homelessness and determine whether it was intentional.[159] This follows from the wording of the provisions and the distinction between tenses within what is now HA 1996, s 191(1) – 'is' homeless, but 'became' homeless intentionally; see also HA 1996, s 189(2) – 'has' a priority need', and s 191 'is homeless . . . and has a priority need, but did not become homeless intentionally'.

4.98   Thus, in *Bull*,[160] the applicant allowed his children to come to live with him in a single room (rather than continuing to live with their mother in a property with sufficient rooms for them), from which they were then evicted: the authority having provided accommodation for them all pending enquiries, he was in priority need (at the date of decision), regardless of whether the children were reasonably to be expected to reside with him,[161] but because the accommodation

---

155 *Dyson v Kerrier DC* [1980] 1 WLR 1205, CA; *Din v Wandsworth LBC* [1983] 1 AC 657, (1981) 1 HLR 73, HL.

156 *R v Islington LBC ex p Bashir Hassan* (1995) 27 HLR 485, although compare *R v Newham LBC ex p Campbell* (1994) 26 HLR 183, QBD.

157 Paras **4.56–4.64**.

158 *R v Brent LBC ex p Awua* [1996] AC 55, (1995) 27 HLR 453, HL. See also *Bratton v Croydon LBC* [2002] EWCA Civ 1494, [2002] All ER (D) 404.

159 *Din v Wandsworth LBC*, above.

160 *Oxford City Council v Bull* [2011] EWCA Civ 609, [2011] HLR 35.

161 See para **3.7**.

had been available for him when he allowed them to join him,[162] he was homeless intentionally for allowing them to reside with him when they were not reasonably to be expected to do so – allowing them to come to live with him had caused his homelessness.

4.99   In *Reeve*,[163] Woolf J said:

> 'It seems to me that the answer to the question of whether or not the council were entitled to take the view which they did of the applicant's conduct depends on the proper interpretation of s 17(1) [now HA 1996, s 191(1)]. It appears to me that the use of the words 'in consequence' in that subsection does raise problems of causation. Really, what is involved in deciding whether or not the applicant is right is a decision as to remoteness . . .'

4.100   In *ex p P*,[164] Schiemann J commented that causation was a notorious minefield in jurisprudence and philosophy. The authority was entitled to conclude that the misbehaviour of the applicants – resulting in threats from the IRA causing them to have to leave their home – was something 'in consequence of which' the applicants had ceased to occupy accommodation.

4.101   In *Hinds*,[165] the applicant undertook to leave the matrimonial home to avoid an ouster order; this led to termination of the secure tenancy. The authority's conclusion that his violence towards his wife had caused the loss of accommodation was upheld.

4.102   In *Aranda*,[166] the judge applied a 'but for' test.[167] The applicant and her husband received a grant of £20,000 from the authority to give up a secure tenancy. That money was used to partially fund the purchase of a family home in Colombia. Shortly after the family arrived in Colombia, the marriage failed. The house was transferred to a relative and the applicant and her children returned to the UK, where she applied as homeless. The authority concluded that she was intentionally homeless. The matters relied on by the authority, including the grant, were matters 'but for' which she might never have gone to Colombia at all, rather than matters but for which the applicant would have continued in occupation of the property in Colombia. Accordingly, they could not be considered deliberate acts which had caused the applicant's loss of (the Colombian) accommodation.

162 See para **2.36**.
163 *R v Thanet DC ex p Reeve* (1983) 6 HLR 31, QBD.
164 *R v Hammersmith and Fulham LBC ex p P* (19890 22 HLR 21, QBD.
165 *R v Islington LBC ex p Hinds* (1996) 28 HLR 302, CA.
166 *R v Camden LBC ex p Aranda* (1996) 28 HLR 672, QBD.
167 See now *Haile v Waltham Forest LBC* [2015] UKSC 34, [2015] AC 1471, [2015] HLR 24 at paras **4.145–4.147**.

4.103   In *Robinson v Torbay BC*,[168] it was said that the loss of the home must be the 'reasonable result' of the deliberate act. This approach was adopted in *Reid*.[169]

4.104   In *R v Hounslow LBC ex p R*,[170] the applicant had terminated his tenancy when he was sentenced to seven years' imprisonment for indecent assault, as he could no longer pay his rent. In considering whether he was intentionally homeless, the test correctly applied was whether ceasing to occupy the accommodation would reasonably have been regarded at the time as a likely consequence of the deliberate conduct.[171]

4.105   *Ex p R* was approved in *Stewart v Lambeth LBC*,[172] where the applicant lost his home after being convicted of drug dealing. In *Goodger v Ealing LBC*,[173] the Court of Appeal described the decision of a review panel that an applicant had become homeless intentionally by breaching a prohibition in his tenancy agreement against drug dealing from the property – which had led to a term of six years' imprisonment – as being the only decision possible in the circumstances, so much so that what might otherwise have been the procedural unfairness[174] of failing to disclose his housing file until a few days before the review hearing was irrelevant.

4.106   The decision in *City of Gloucester v Miles*[175] may also be considered to turn on cause and effect. The applicant had left her home for a period of time, but had not clearly or certainly quit it. During her absence, her estranged husband returned and caused damage which rendered the property entirely uninhabitable. As she was not a party to the vandalism, she had done nothing that could be classed as intentional, even though she might subsequently have lost the property either through failing to resume residence or because arrears had accrued and there was a threat of proceedings.

4.107   The authority must act reasonably in regarding present homelessness as being caused by a departure from earlier accommodation. In *Krishnan*,[176] Birmingham City Council was putting pressure on owner-occupiers to reduce overcrowding in their premises. A family of relatives sharing the home were offered accommodation by another relative in Uxbridge until such time as they could afford to buy their own house. At the same time, there was a possibility of promotion if the family moved to London. Subsequently, the Uxbridge relative

168 [1982] 1 All ER 726, QBD.
169 *R v Westminster City Council ex p Reid* (1994) 26 HLR 690, QBD.
170 (1997) 29 HLR 939, QBD.
171 Which, on the facts, it was.
172 *Stewart v Lambeth LBC* [2002] EWCA Civ 753, [2002] HLR 40.
173 [2002] EWCA Civ 751, [2003] HLR 6.
174 See paras **10.66–10.70**.
175 (1985) 17 HLR 292, CA, referred to in the Court of Appeal in *Puhlhofer* (1985) 17 HLR 558, CA, but not criticised either in that case at the House of Lords ([1986] AC 484, 18 HLR 158) or in *R v Brent LBC ex p Awua* [1996] AC 55, (1995) 27 HLR 453, HL.
176 *Krishnan v Hillingdon LBC* January 1981 *LAG Bulletin* 137, QBD.

decided to sell his house and move to Canada, at which point the family became homeless.

4.108   The authority wrongly considered that the family could reasonably have gone on occupying the Birmingham property and wrongly took the view that the Uxbridge arrangement was only temporary:[177]

> 'I also hold that the Council's officers made insufficient enquiry as to the state of knowledge and expectations of the Plaintiff with regard to the availability of his accommodation at Uxbridge at the time when he moved here. Mrs Bates states in her note . . . that the Plaintiff did not deny that his accommodation at [Uxbridge] was temporary. That, however, was not the point. The word 'temporary' can aptly cover a considerable period. Thus, accommodation held on a tenancy for a year or more can rightly be described as temporary.
>
> As I have already indicated, the Plaintiff's expectation at the time when he moved . . . was that the accommodation there would be available for him for at least a year. It follows as it seems to me that if the Council's officers had been aware of that fact they might well have taken the view that the Plaintiff became homeless not because he moved to [Uxbridge] from . . . Birmingham, but because the Plaintiff's cousin changed his mind about the length of time for which he was willing to accommodate the Plaintiff and his family . . .'

4.109   Similarly, in *Rose*,[178] although decided on the meaning of 'deliberate',[179] the point may as easily be made that an earlier departure had not caused the homelessness: what had caused the homelessness was the loss of the intervening, temporary accommodation, which the applicant had not appreciated was – or was likely to be – temporary.

4.110   In *Gliddon*,[180] the applicants quit private-sector accommodation. Initially, they had been granted a tenancy. The landlord alleged that they had obtained it by deception and compelled them to enter into a licence agreement in substitution. It was the loss of accommodation under licence which was the immediate cause of the homelessness.

4.111   At first, the authority advised the applicants to await court proceedings for determination of their status; the court held that this was a valid approach.[181] On the applicants' failure to follow this advice, however, the authority reached a new decision, based on the deception pursuant to which the accommodation had been obtained, and concluded that it had therefore been lost by the applicants'

---

177 Ie, unsettled; cf para **4.114**.
178 *R v Wandsworth LBC ex p Rose* (1984) 11 HLR 105, QBD.
179 Para **4.45**.
180 *R v Exeter City Council ex p Gliddon* (1984) 14 HLR 103, QBD.
181 See para **4.159**.

own fault. In the light of this finding of fact by the authority, however, the authority could no longer conclude that the applicants could reasonably have remained in occupation. Accordingly, the accommodation obtained by deception ought to have been ignored and the authority was obliged to look back instead to the loss of the applicants' previous accommodation.

4.112   *R (Flores) v Southwark LBC*[182] is a case which arose under HA 1996, Part 6 (see para **9.147**), but might be thought to apply equally in cases on intentionality. In that case, the authority's scheme provided a priority for those who were statutorily overcrowded, unless caused by a 'deliberate act'. A family comprising parents and two children who moved into privately rented one-bedroom accommodation which became statutorily overcrowded[183] when the elder child turned 10 could not be considered to have caused the overcrowding by a deliberate act; the act that caused the overcrowding was the growth in age of the children which could not sensibly be considered a deliberate act.[184]

Breaking the chain of causation

4.113   The question, then, becomes one of how the chain of causation between an act causing homelessness and current homelessness may be broken.

4.114   Where the applicant has enjoyed a period of 'settled accommodation'[185] or 'other than temporary accommodation',[186] this will break the chain.[187] There is no reverse corollary: acquisition and loss of settled accommodation is not the only means of breaking the chain; the fact that what has been lost is unsettled does not mean that the applicant is still homeless intentionally.[188]

---

182 [2020] EWCA Civ 1697; [2021] HLR 16. See also *R. (Roman) v Southwark LBC* [2022] EWHC 1232 (Admin); [2023] HLR 4 at para 9.148, likewise under HA 1996, Part 6, to the effect that 'deliberate' requires that there must have been a real choice between two or more viable options.

183 Housing Act 1985, Part 10.

184 The reasoning lends itself well to the same issues in relation to intentionality: 'the council's approach leads to some odd, or even perverse, consequences. It means that an applicant who acts reasonably in taking the most suitable accommodation for his family that he can afford disqualifies himself from priority once his children grow to an age which renders that accommodation statutorily overcrowded. An interpretation of the Scheme which has that consequence, or which incentivises an applicant to refuse accommodation which is suitable for his current needs because of the consequences which will ensue when his children reach the age of 10, is to say the least counter-intuitive and requires careful scrutiny' (*R (Flores)*, above, at [49]).

185 *Din v Wandsworth LBC* [1983] 1 AC 657, (1981) 1 HLR 73, HL, per Lord Wilberforce, adopting Ackner LJ in the Court of Appeal.

186 *Din*, above, per Lord Lowry.

187 *R v Brent LBC ex p Awua*, above. See also *Mohammed v Westminster City Council* [2005] EWCA Civ 796, [2005] HLR 47.

188 See paras **4.133–4.147**.

Settled accommodation

4.115   The concept of settled accommodation was developed by the judiciary – under the Housing (Homeless Persons) Act 1977 and under HA 1985, Part 3 – and was used in a number of different contexts:

a)   HA 1985, s 58(1) – definition of homelessness;

b)   HA 1985, s 60(1) – intentionality: whether what was quit could give rise to a finding of intentionality/whether there had been a break in a period of intentionality;

c)   HA 1985, s 65(2) – discharge of duty in relation to unintentionally homeless.

Following the decision in *Awua*,[189] however, the distinction between settled and unsettled accommodation is now only relevant to the question of whether the chain of causation has been broken.[190]

4.116   In *Din*, in which the concept of settled accommodation first emerged, what it comprised was said to be a question of 'fact and degree'. Whether accommodation is settled must be assessed by reference to all relevant factors, including: the nature of the occupation (lease or licence); the parties' expectations as to the period of occupation; whether the arrangement was on a commercial basis or with friends/family; the affordability of the property and any overcrowding – not to any one of them alone (*Bullale*),[191] although, obviously, one or more circumstance may be such as to tend to dominate the outcome.

4.117   It needs to be remembered that cases have to be read on their facts and how they were argued, which in turn reflects how the law was understood at the date of a hearing: the cases below are helpful illustrations of the features which will be likely to determine whether or not accommodation is likely to be considered settled but might, in the light of *Bullale*,[192] be decided differently now.

Physical conditions

4.118   If physical conditions are so poor as to be unfit for human habitation,[193] or otherwise in such a condition that no reasonable person could consider it to

---

189   *R v Brent LBC ex p Awua*, above.
190   As *Awua* preserved this use of the concept of settled accommodation, albeit only for the purpose of determining whether the chain of causation has been broken, it remains appropriate to consider pre-*Awua* cases alongside subsequent decisions.
191   *Bullale v Westminster City Council* [2020] EWCA Civ 1587, [2021] HLR 21.
192   *Bullale*, above.
193   As it was put in *R v South Herefordshire DC ex p Miles* (1983) 17 HLR 82, QBD. *City of Gloucester v Miles* (1985) 17 HLR 292, CA, to the same effect, ask whether the property was 'uninhabitable'. It is doubtful, however, that this is synonymous with the *statutory* definition of unfitness (Landlord and Tenant Act 1985, s 8 (Wales), s 9A (England)) or with whether the causes of the unfitness are such as to qualify as hazards which the local authority could require to be remedied under HA 2004, Part 1, as distinct from a common sense view of it.

be capable of amounting to accommodation,[194] the accommodation is highly likely not to be treated as settled.[195] In *Mohammed*,[196] one of the reasons why accommodation occupied by the applicant was not settled was because it was severely overcrowded.[197]

Security/temporal conditions

4.119 Most of the cases have turned on security.

4.120 *Ruffle*[198] concerned a family who had earlier applied to the authority and been found intentionally homeless. That decision was not contested. The applicants subsequently moved into the flat of a council tenant under an arrangement which was intended to be permanent but which broke down after a few months through no fault of their own. The family returned to the authority, which decided that they were still intentionally homeless because the intervening period had not 'been one in settled occupation which would give rise to a new cause of homelessness'.

4.121 The applicants argued that the authority had asked the wrong question: it should have asked not whether the intervening accommodation was settled, but whether it was obviously temporary. There was a spectrum of accommodation of which 'settled' and 'obviously temporary' were only the extremes. The applicants contended that they needed only to have secured something more than the least secure type of accommodation in order to have ended homelessness and broken the chain, not the most secure.

4.122 The judge disagreed:[199]

'I think that one or the other term encompasses all states of accommodation. Thus, it is correct to contrast, as the various cases do, settled or permanent accommodation on the one hand with less than secure accommodation, variously described as precarious or temporary or transient on the other . . . [For] the authority to ask themselves . . . has the intervening period been one of settled accommodation occupation, involves asking the same question as whether the accommodation was only temporary. These questions are merely the opposite sides of the same coin.'[200]

---

194 (1983) 17 HLR 82, QBD.
195 See the early cases of *R v South Herefordshire DC ex p Miles* (1985) 17 HLR 82, QBD; *City of Gloucester v Miles* (1985) 17 HLR 292, CA; *R v Dinefwr BC ex p Marshall* (1985) 17 HLR 310, which – notwithstanding their disapproval in *R v Hillingdon LBC ex p Puhlhofer* [1986] AC 484, HL, on the question of whether the accommodation was so physically poor that the applicant was already homeless – remain illustrative of when the physical condition of a property is so bad that it is unlikely to be considered settled.
196 *Mohammed v Westminster City Council*, above.
197 Para **4.131**.
198 *R v Merton LBC ex p Ruffle* (1989) 21 HLR 361, QBD.
199 *Ruffle*, above.
200 Simon Brown J contemplated an alternative analysis, which he considered contains possible tensions, of three possible types of accommodation: one so tenuous that it is discounted altogether; one which is sufficient to preclude homelessness; and a further type, 'settled' accommodation, which is required to break the chain of intentionality.

4.123 In *Evans*,[201] a couple left a secure tenancy for larger premises in the private sector, purportedly on a bed and breakfast basis. There was, however, a strong argument that they had full protection under the Rent Act 1977. Following threats of – and actual – violence from their landlord, the couple left the new accommodation. The authority's decision that they were intentionally homeless was quashed because the authority had failed to consider whether the new accommodation, with security, had been settled.

4.124 Authorities are not bound to accept the applicant's view as to whether accommodation was settled. In *Cadney*,[202] a woman sought to rely on a period of three months during which she had moved out of the matrimonial home and into the home of another man. Their relationship was not successful and she left. She sought to rely on this as a period of intervening accommodation, because she had intended to stay with him permanently. The court considered this too subjective an approach. The authority had been entitled to take the view that it was a transient or precarious arrangement, ie, that an objective test could be applied:[203] this is, however, a good example of a case that may need to be reconsidered in the light of *Bullale*.[204]

4.125 In *Ashton*,[205] the authority's decision that occupation of premises under a tenancy falling within the exception in HA 1985, Sch 1 para 5[206] was not occupation of settled accommodation was upheld, allowing the authority to look back to the previous accommodation: again, this may be reconsidered in the light of *Bullale*.[207] Length of time will be important in establishing whether accommodation is settled: see *Easom*,[208] in which it was held to be open to the authority to conclude that accommodation was not settled – over several years – because the applicants had at all times been illegal immigrants to Australia who might have been deported at any moment: there was, however, no reason to apply an artificial limit on the facts that could be taken into account, of which time was a very relevant factor.[209]

4.126 In *Ajayi*,[210] Dyson J reiterated that whether accommodation was settled is a question of fact and degree. The applicant had lived with family friends (in the first instance for a period of 20 months, and in the second for some nine months) since leaving her family home in Nigeria. The authority concluded that neither arrangement had been settled. The term 'settled accommodation' was

201 *R v Swansea City Council ex p Evans* (1990) 22 HLR 467, CA.
202 *R v Purbeck DC ex p Cadney* (1985) 17 HLR 534, QBD.
203 See also *R v Merton LBC ex p Ruffle*, above.
204 *Bullale*, para **4.116**.
205 *R v Winchester City Council ex p Ashton* (1991) 24 HLR 48, QBD, (1992) 24 HLR 520, CA.
206 Temporary accommodation for persons taking up employment.
207 *Bullale*, para **4.116**.
208 *R v Croydon LBC ex p Easom* (1993) 25 HLR 262, QBD.
209 There is no substantive inconsistency between this and *Bullale*, para **4.116**, at most a difference in emphasis.
210 *R v Hackney LBC ex p Ajayi* (1998) 30 HLR 473, QBD.

an ordinary English expression, not a term of art. Although when the applicant moved in with her friends the duration of the accommodation had been uncertain, the authority was entitled – having regard to the circumstances – to conclude that it had been precarious.

4.127 The fact and degree test was re-stated in *Knight*,[211] where the question was whether occupation of a property under a six-month assured shorthold tenancy could amount to settled accommodation for the purpose of breaking the chain of causation. Although the Court of Appeal accepted that such occupation was capable of constituting settled accommodation, indeed was normally a significant pointer to it being settled,[212] it did not as a matter of law always do so.[213] The question remained one of fact and degree to be determined by the authority. In the circumstances of the particular case, it was open to the authority to find that the accommodation was not settled, because the applicant had known from the outset that the tenancy was only for six months and would not be renewed.

4.128 The issue was raised recently in *Hodge v Folkstone and Hythe DC*,[214] where the applicant was living as a licensee in a hostel run by a charity; she argued that the hostel room could not amount to accommodation at all because of the want of any security of tenure; and, if it could, it was not settled accommodation. The Court of Appeal rejected both arguments: whether the room in the hostel comprised accommodation was a matter of fact for the authority to decide and the authority had been entitled to conclude that it did; it had not been necessary to determine whether it comprised settled accommodation but it had in any event likewise been open to the authority to conclude that it was – the authority had only been required to consider whether the room had been accommodation and whether it had been reasonable to continue to occupy it, which the authority had done.

RENTERS (REFORM) BILL

Although once in full relevant force and subject to any transitional provisions, there will be no more assured shorthold tenancies or six-month fixed term tenancies, while there is no reason to doubt the 'fact and degree' test, *Knight* will nonetheless cease to be of much relevance.

---

211 *Knight v Vale Royal BC* [2003] EWCA Civ 1258, [2004] HLR 9.
212 At [25].
213 Given that this is one of the ways in which an authority can discharge a duty to house under HA 1996, s 193 (see paras **8.155, 8.260–8.271**), even when it is not a restricted case (see paras **8.272–8.281**), it is suggested that there would seem to need to be some discrete factor to suggest that it is not settled and that in the ordinary case it will be.
214 [2023] EWCA Civ 896, [2023] HLR 46.

4.129 In *Huda*[215] the applicant had been provided with temporary accommodation by the authority under a licence agreement with a third party. He was subsequently found to be intentionally homeless but, due to an administrative oversight, no steps were taken to evict him. After four years he re-applied for assistance, contending that his lengthy occupation of the temporary accommodation amounted to settled accommodation. The authority decided that it was not settled accommodation as it had been due to administrative error and was of a precarious nature with no security of tenure; the Court of Appeal repeated that settled accommodation was a matter of fact and degree and held that the decision was one the authority were entitled to reach: it might be that this would be decided differently following *Bullale*.[216]

4.130 In *Doka*[217] the applicant was evicted for rent arrears. For the following two years, he rented a room in the house of his former employer, but had to vacate the room for short periods from time to time when the son of the former employer came home from university. The authority was entitled to conclude that this was not settled accommodation as it had been too precarious; what was required was a real prospect of the accommodation continuing for a significant or indefinite period of time. Again, this might be decided differently following *Bullale*.[218]

Combination of factors

4.131 This may now be considered the only proper approach,[219] although on a detailed study of most of the cases it is one that was commonly being applied. The applicant in *Mohammed*[220] also took an assured shorthold tenancy. She was evicted after 12 months because of a shortfall in housing benefit leading to arrears of rent. The authority on review considered that the accommodation was not settled for three reasons:

a) the applicant had obtained the accommodation with a view to making a second application to the authority as homeless;[221]

b) she could not afford the rent for the accommodation; and

c) the accommodation was overcrowded.

The Court of Appeal held that the reviewing officer was entitled to have regard to all these matters in reaching his decision.

---

215 *Huda v Redbridge LBC* [2016] EWCA Civ 709, [2016] HLR 30.
216 *Bullale*, para **4.116**.
217 *Doka v Southwark LBC* [2017] EWCA Civ 1532; [2017] HLR 786.
218 *Bullale*, para **4.116**.
219 *Bullale*, para **4.116**.
220 *Mohammed v Westminster City Council* [2005] EWCA Civ 796, [2005] HLR 47.
221 See now paras **4.166–4.170**.

Prison

4.132 An argument that a period of imprisonment could amount to settled accommodation was rejected in *Stewart*.[222] In the leading decision of *Ali* and *Moran*,[223] however, the Supreme Court noted as follows.

> 'We have heard some interesting debate upon whether a prison cell, or a hospital ward, could amount to accommodation under the Act: see *Stewart v Lambeth LBC; R (B) v Southwark LBC*. If the answer to the *Ex p Sidhu*[224] question can now generally be found in section 175(3), we would be inclined to accept that its approach to the question of "accommodation" cannot survive the decisions of this House in *Ex p Puhlhofer*[225] and *Ex p Awua*.[226] It does not need to do so and the concerns so clearly expressed by Hodgson J can be addressed in another way. But we would not be inclined to enter into any further discussion of whether a prison cell or a hospital bed amounts to 'accommodation' within the meaning of the Act until the need arises.'[227]

Breaking the chain by other means

4.133 Whether acquisition of settled accommodation is the only means of breaking the causal link was expressly reserved in *Awua*.[228] The question was considered by the Court of Appeal in *Fahia*.[229] The applicant had been found intentionally homeless by the authority and housed temporarily in a guest house. She remained in the guest house for over a year, her rent paid by housing benefit. A subsequent review of her housing benefit led to payments being cut and she was, in consequence, evicted from the guest house.

4.134 The authority decided that it had no new duty towards the applicant because the accommodation at the guest house did not constitute intervening settled accommodation such as to break the causal link with the applicant's original intentional homelessness.

4.135 The Court of Appeal rejected this approach and decided that events other than securing settled accommodation could break the chain; it remitted the case to the authority to decide whether the change in housing benefit had constituted such an event.

---

222 *Stewart v Lambeth LBC* [2002] EWCA Civ 753, [2002] HLR 40. See also *R (B) v. Southwark LBC* [2004] HLR 3.
223 *Birmingham City Council v Ali; Moran v Manchester City Council (Secretary of State for Communities and Local Government)* [2009] UKHL 36, [2009] 1 WLR 1506.
224 *R v Ealing LBC ex p Sidhu* (1982) 2 HLR 45, QBD, para **2.15**.
225 *R v Hillingdon LBC ex p Puhlhofer* [1986] AC 484, HL (1985) 17 HLR 588, CA, (1986) 18 HLR 158, HL.
226 *R v Brent LBC ex p Awua* [1996] AC 55, (1995) 27 HLR 453, HL.
227 Baroness Hale of Richmond at [56].
228 *Stewart v Lambeth LBC*, above.
229 *R v Harrow LBC ex p Fahia* (1997) 29 HLR 974, CA (not overruled by the House of Lords on this point, see [1998] 1 WLR 1396, (1998) 30 HLR 1124).

4.136   The court expressly approved the earlier decision in *Bassett*[230] as an example of a break in the chain of causation otherwise than by settled accommodation. In that case, temporary accommodation was lost not because of its temporary quality but because the applicant had been staying with her sister-in-law and had to leave when she separated from her husband.

4.137   Although *Fahia* went to the House of Lords, the authority abandoned its appeal on this aspect.[231]

4.138   In subsequent cases, following *Fahia* at the Court of Appeal (and its approval of *Bassett*), it has been held that the subsequent event must be unconnected to the temporary nature of the accommodation.

4.139   Thus, in *Harvey*,[232] the applicant was evicted from his home for noise nuisance and he moved in with a friend. After four months, the friend was taken into hospital and the applicant had to move out. The loss of the friend's accommodation did not break the chain of causation because it could not be said to be unconnected with the temporary or unsettled nature of the accommodation the applicant had been occupying.[233]

4.140   Likewise, in *Ajayi*,[234] the applicant left accommodation in Nigeria and moved to London, where she stayed with various friends and acquaintances. She moved in with one friend in January 1996, at the same time as she discovered she was pregnant and, on the birth of the baby, was asked to leave. The chain of causation had not been broken. The real and effective cause of her homelessness was not the pregnancy but leaving her accommodation in Nigeria.

4.141   A term of imprisonment cannot amount to a supervening event which breaks the chain of causation.[235]

4.142   A slightly different question was posed in *Din*[236] – whether an act which at its inception was one causing intentional homelessness can cease to qualify as such merely through the passage of time, ie, whether it can become 'spent'?

4.143   In that case, a family were living in accommodation under extremely trying circumstances, and would ultimately have had to leave, but they were advised by the authority to remain in occupation until a court order was made.[237]

---

230 *R v Basingstoke and Deane BC ex p Bassett* (1983) 10 HLR 125, QBD; see para **2.127**.
231 *R v Harrow LBC ex p Fahia*, above, at p1130.
232 *R v Brighton BC ex p Harvey* (1998) 30 HLR 670, QBD.
233 For instance, because the hospitalisation was no different from being asked to leave, which could have happened at any time due to the temporary nature of the accommodation: *Harvey*, above.
234 *R v Hackney LBC ex p Ajayi* (1998) 30 HLR 473, QBD.
235 *Stewart v Lambeth LBC*, above. In *Birmingham City Council v Ali; Moran v Manchester City Council (Secretary of State for Communities and Local Government and another intervening)* [2009] UKHL 36, [2009] 1 WLR 1506, the House of Lords expressly reserved the issue of whether prison could comprise accommodation at all – para **4.132**.
236 *Din v Wandsworth LBC* [1983] 1 AC 657, (1981) 1 HLR 73, HL.
237 Para **4.159**.

It was common ground, at least on appeal, that if an application had been made immediately after the departure, the authority could have found the family to be homeless intentionally, because at that date it would have been reasonable to remain in occupation (see further below), whereas, on application at a later date, it was conceded by the authority that the family would by then have become homeless in any event, and not intentionally so.[238]

4.144 During the interim period, the family had stayed with relatives and it was not argued that there had, on that account, been a break in the homelessness. Rather, it was argued that the original cause of homelessness had ceased to be effective because the family would have become homeless unintentionally by the time of application, ie, whether the homelessness would have happened anyway, so that it could not be said that but for the early departure the family would not have been homeless. This 'but for' argument was upheld in the county court, but dismissed on appeal. The question was whether the present period of homelessness had, at its inception, been intentional. The fact that the applicants would have become homeless unintentionally by the date of application was held to be irrelevant.[239]

4.145 *Din* was re-considered in *Haile*.[240] While stating that *Din* remained good law, the Supreme Court held that, when considering whether an applicant is intentionally homeless, the authority must look at the conduct which caused the present homelessness unless a later event (which is not itself an act of voluntary homelessness) supersedes the earlier conduct, so that it cannot reasonably be said that 'but for' that earlier conduct, the applicant would not have become homeless, in which case the causal connection between current homelessness and earlier conduct will have been interrupted.

4.146 In the absence of any such event, the question is whether the proximate cause of the homelessness is an event which is unconnected to the earlier conduct. The question may be approached in two stages: first, was the homelessness intentional at its inception; second, has it been superseded by a later (unconnected) event which means that the authority must ignore the origins of the homelessness because the applicant would have been homeless in any event. The connection between the initial event and the immediate cause is therefore a critical element in the analysis.

4.147 It is not easy to square this decision with *Din*:[241] in particular, it is extremely difficult – if even possible – to distinguish the reasoning adopted in *Haile* from the homeless person's submissions which were rejected in *Din*.[242]

---

238 There was no defence to the landlord's proposed proceedings for possession and the order would have already taken effect.

239 See also *R v Brent LBC ex p Yusuf* (1997) 29 HLR 48, QBD.

240 *Haile v Waltham Forest LBC* [2015] UKSC 34, [2015] AC 1471, [2015] HLR 24.

241 Lord Carnwath in the minority commented that the majority had engaged in a re-analysis of *Din* that had not been contended for by the appellant. Moreover, it is extremely difficult – if even possible – to distinguish the reasoning adopted in *Haile* from the homeless person's argument which was rejected in *Din*.

242 See, in particular, pp658/F-661/B, and, at 660/A and 661/A: the reliance in *Din* is on precisely the 'but for' approach that is at the heart of the majority decision in *Haile*.

CESSATION OF OCCUPATION

Accommodation abroad

4.148   The accommodation which has been lost can be accommodation abroad and the act causing its loss can be an act abroad.

4.149   In *de Falco*,[243] the reason given by the authority for finding intentional homelessness was that the family in question had come to the UK without arranging permanent accommodation.

4.150   That reason was patently bad on its face. It was upheld by the Court of Appeal, however, by expanding it – against the factual background – to refer to a departure from accommodation in Italy. That this approach had been devised by the Court of Appeal was made clear in *Paris*,[244] where the authority used the same wording as in *de Falco* but had erred because it had failed actually to consider the accommodation which had been quit and the circumstances of departure from it.

Short-term accommodation

4.151   Where the authority is providing temporary housing pending a permanent allocation, its loss may lead to a finding of intentionality: *Hunt*.[245]

4.152   In *Conway*,[246] the applicant failed to renew a protected shorthold tenancy. It was held that this could amount to a deliberate omission[247] (although on the facts, it had not been).

Notional occupation

4.153   In *Islam*,[248] at the Court of Appeal, it was argued that the accommodation lost had not been available for the occupation of the applicant and his family (who had recently arrived from Bangladesh).[249] One of the grounds advanced for upholding the decision in the Court of Appeal was that the applicant – while living in a shared single room in Uxbridge – had at all material times nonetheless been in 'notional occupation' of the family home in Bangladesh, through his wife

---

243 *De Falco, Silvestri v Crawley BC* [1980] QB 460, CA.
244 *R v Reigate and Banstead BC ex p Paris* (1985) 17 HLR 103, QBD.
245 *R v East Hertfordshire DC ex p Hunt* (1985) 18 HLR 51, QBD. The basis for the decision was politely criticised (described as 'heroic') in *Awua*, but the outcome remains correct. In any event, in such circumstances the authority will now be considered to have discharged its duty to the applicant: see HA 1996, s 193(6)(b).
246 *R v Christchurch BC ex p Conway* (1987) 19 HLR 238, QBD.
247 See para **4.31**.
248 *Re Islam* [1983] 1 AC 688, (1981) 1 HLR 107, HL.
249 See para **2.31**.

and children. Another suggestion was that the accommodation available for, and occupied by, the family was made up of the family home in Bangladesh and the room in Uxbridge.

4.154   The House of Lords rejected both of these approaches:

'The Master of the Rolls was . . . using the word occupation in an artificial sense, which . . . is quite inconsistent with its ordinary meaning and with the probably narrower sense in which it is used in the Act. When it speaks of occupying accommodation, the Act has in contemplation people who are residing in that accommodation . . .'

4.155   It has been held, however, that an applicant may be occupying accommodation even though not physically residing in it. Thus, in *Khan*,[250] the applicants represented to immigration authorities that they would be living in a house which the first applicant subsequently sold. The applicants never occupied the house, although the first applicant's family had done so. This was held to be sufficient occupation for the purposes of intentionality so that, on sale of the house, the applicants could be considered to have ceased to occupy it.

4.156   In *Lee-Lawrence*,[251] the applicant had to leave his home because it became uninhabitable following an arson attack. He accepted the offer of a tenancy elsewhere, on which he claimed housing benefit, but, when he subsequently applied as homeless, he asserted that he had never in fact occupied the new property. The Court of Appeal held that the fact that a person had a legal right to possession or held the keys was not, of itself, sufficient to establish occupation; nonetheless, those factors combined with the claim for housing benefit and other representations by the applicant that he had been resident in the premises, were sufficient to support a finding of occupancy.

AVAILABLE FOR OCCUPATION

4.157   This has been considered in Chapter 2.[252]

REASONABLE TO CONTINUE TO OCCUPY

4.158   It must have been reasonable to continue to occupy the accommodation which has been lost: the authority must consider this – see, eg, *Griffiths*,[253]

250 *R v Westminster City Council ex p Khan* (1991) 23 HLR 230, QBD.
251 *Lee-Lawrence v Penwith DC* [2006] EWCA Civ 1672.
252 See paras **2.19–2.41**.
253 *R v Shrewsbury and Atcham BC ex p Griffiths* (1993) 25 HLR 613, QBD.

in which the authority was held to have failed to have regard to the family's particular circumstances, and *Bibi*,[254] where the authority had failed to make a finding whether the applicant could reasonably have continued to occupy accommodation, in the light of her stated financial inability to feed her family. Likewise, in *Hawthorne*,[255] the authority's omission to consider whether the applicant's failure to pay rent was caused by the inadequacy of her financial resources allowed her to succeed in her application to quash a finding of intentionality: it was a question the authority was bound to address.

4.159 The question whether it is reasonable to continue to occupy accommodation was extensively considered in Chapter 2,[256] to which full reference should be made, including on the issues of what is meant by reasonableness to continue to occupy[257] and by affordability.[258] There are, however, other circumstances which are particular to findings of intentionality which merit mention. This is particularly so where advice has been given to the applicant by the authority prior to departure from the accommodation.[259]

4.160 In *Hughes*,[260] it appeared that an alleged winter letting might not fall within the provisions of Rent Act 1977, Sch 15 case 13, so that there would be no mandatory ground for possession available to the landlord. The occupier was accordingly advised to await the outcome of proceedings but did not do so:

> 'The important point which this application raises . . . is the question as to what extent an authority exercising its powers under [the] Act is entitled to say to a person . . . 'You should remain in accommodation which you at present occupy and not leave that accommodation until there is a court order made against you requiring you to vacate . . .'
>
> [W]here there is a situation which is doubtful or difficult, it is reasonable for the authority to give advice to a person who is a prospective candidate for assistance under the . . . Act . . . that they should not vacate the accommodation which they are at present occupying without the order of the court because otherwise they may be regarded as persons intentionally homeless.'

4.161 In *Adamiec*,[261] the failure of an applicant to heed advice not to sell his home resulted in a finding of intentionality which was upheld as, although he

---

254 *R v Islington LBC ex p Bibi* (1997) 29 HLR 498, QBD.
255 *R v Wandsworth LBC ex p Hawthorne* (1995) 27 HLR 59, CA.
256 See paras **2.71–2.146**.
257 See paras **2.177–2.179**.
258 Paras **2.135–2.146**.
259 See also *F v Birmingham City Council* [2006] EWCA Civ 1427, [2007] HLR 18; and *Ugiagbe v Southwark LBC* [2009] EWCA Civ 31, [2009] HLR 35.
260 *R v Penwith DC ex p Hughes* August 1980 *LAG Bulletin* 187, QBD.
261 *R v Leeds City Council ex p Adamiec* (1992) 24 HLR 138, QBD. See also *R v Westminster City Council ex p Moklis Ali* (1997) 29 HLR 580, QBD.

might ultimately have been forced to sell because of his financial circumstances, that was a stage he had not yet reached.

4.162 Whether it was reasonable for an applicant to continue to occupy accommodation is to be judged at the time that the conduct in consequence of which the accommodation was lost took place, not at some later date when the applicant actually left: *ex p P*.[262] In answering this question, an authority must ignore the act or omission itself, looking instead to the position beforehand: *Denton*.[263] The assessment of whether or not it was reasonable to continue to occupy accommodation may, however, take into account subsequent events, up to the time of decision (initial or on review), as in *LB v Tower Hamlets LBC*,[264] where the authority's decision was upheld that the applicant had lost accommodation because of arrears rather than the probability of domestic violence, which relied, inter alia, on events after her eviction.

4.163 Whether it is reasonable to continue to occupy may be affected by whether alternative accommodation will be available if the applicants remain in their present accommodation in the short term.[265] See also *McIlory*,[266] in which Catholic applicants left accommodation in Northern Ireland after being subjected to several years of harassment by Protestant factions, culminating in a shooting incident. A finding of intentionality was upheld on the ground that they had failed to wait and see whether they would be rehoused by the Northern Ireland Housing Executive.

4.164 This may be contrasted with *McManus*,[267] where the applicant lived in a house in Belfast just off a road which was the dividing line between the two main religious groups and the scene of much sectarian violence. The applicant left her home and went to London where she applied for homelessness assistance; the authority found her to have become homeless intentionally. Her challenge was successful: the authority should have examined the effect of the situation in Belfast on the applicant and her daughter and focused on the particular area of Belfast where they lived, which the evidence suggested was particularly prone to the worst sectarian violence in the city.[268]

4.165 In *Wilson*,[269] the court, albeit with some hesitation, held that it had not been reasonable for a woman to remain in accommodation in Australia because: a) she had no legal permission to remain; and b) she was pregnant and would

---

262 *R v Hammersmith and Fulham LBC ex p P* (1990) 22 HLR 21, QBD. See also *Denton v Southwark LBC* [2007] EWCA Civ 623, [2008] HLR 11.
263 *Denton v Southwark LBC*, above.
264 [2020] EWCA Civ 439; [2021] HLR 3 at [32]–[33].
265 *R v Hammersmith and Fulham LBC ex p P* (1990) 22 HLR 21, QBD.
266 *R v Newham LBC ex p McIlroy* (1991) 23 HLR 570, QBD.
267 *R v Brent LBC ex p McManus* (1993) 25 HLR 643, QBD at 645, 646.
268 *McManus*, above, at 648.
269 *R v Hillingdon LBC ex p Wilson* (1984) 12 HLR 61, QBD.

shortly have reached the stage of pregnancy when she would not have been able to fly back to the UK.

4.166 While a person will remain homeless in accommodation provided under s 188 pending inquiries[270] so that its loss cannot give rise to a finding of intentionality relative to the provision of accommodation under s 193,[271] temporary accommodation provided under s 193(2) pending a permanent offer is accommodation which it may be reasonable to continue to occupy, so that its loss can give rise to such a finding of intentionality.[272]

EXTENDED DEFINITION – COLLUSIVE ARRANGEMENTS

4.167 HA 1996, s 191(3) and H(W)A 2014, s 77(4) contain extended definitions of intentionality under which a person is to be treated as intentionally homeless if they enter into an arrangement pursuant to which they have to cease to occupy accommodation, which it would have been reasonable to continue to occupy,[273] and the purpose of the arrangement is to enable them to become entitled to assistance under HA 1996, Part 7 or H(W)A 2014, Part 2, and there is no other good reason why the applicant is homeless.

4.168 This provision is aimed at arrangements designed to give the impression of being obliged to leave accommodation[274] which would have been reasonable to continue to occupy, so as to create an apparent right to assistance under HA 1996, Part 7 or H(W)A 2014, Part 2. If it would not have been accommodation which it was reasonable to continue to occupy in any event, the arrangement may be disregarded, although this would not prevent the authority looking back to the loss of any previous accommodation which may properly be considered to be the cause of the present homelessness.

4.169 The English Code[275] suggests that collusion is not confined to those staying with friends or relatives, but can also arise between landlords and tenants:

---

270 See paras **8.12-8.14.** Consider also *R (Ahamed) v Haringey LBC* [2023] EWCA Civ 975; [2023] HLR 43 – see para **8.96.**

271 But it may be that if s 188 accommodation is lost by the applicant's own fault, the authority does not have to provide further s 188 accommodation: see *R (Brooks) v. Islington LBC* [2015] EWHC 2657 Admin; [2016] HLR 2 (refusal of alternative s 188 accommodation) at [41], and *Kyle v. Coventry CC* [2023] EWCA Cv 1360; [2024] HLR 7 at [43].

272 See paras **2.77–2.79.**

273 See paras **2.71–2.146, 4.158–4.164.**

274 Note that it does not also have to have been 'available for . . . occupation'.

275 English Code of Guidance para 9.28; Welsh Code para 17.30 is in similar terms.

'Housing authorities, while relying on experience, nonetheless need to be satisfied that collusion exists, and must not rely on hearsay or unfounded suspicions . . .'[276]

4.170   Even if the subsection is prima facie applicable, there must also be no other 'good reason' for the homelessness. Examples of 'other good reasons' include overcrowding, or an obvious breakdown in relationship between the applicant and the 'host' household or landlord.[277]

4.171   Authorities do not frequently find collusive arrangements. A rare example is to be found in *Lomotey v Enfield LBC*,[278] where the claimant surrendered her joint interest in a property to her brother, who then evicted her.

---

276 This is true for all decision-making (see Chapter 7) but may be a particular problem in reaching decisions on collusion given the connotation of discreditable conduct.
277 English Code of Guidance para 9.29; Welsh Code para 17.30.
278 [2004] EWCA Civ 627, [2004] HLR 45.

CHAPTER 5

Local connection

INTRODUCTION

5.1 The local connection provisions of Housing Act (HA) 1996, Part 7 and Housing (Wales) Act (H(W)A) 2014, Part 2 allow one authority to pass on to another the burden of providing the relief duty and of securing permanent accommodation for an applicant.

5.2 This chapter represents something of a turning-point in this book. The previous three chapters have been purely definitional; save in passing, nothing about the duties to which the definitions relate is discussed – it has been all about what the terms mean. The local connections provisions cannot, however, properly be understood in the abstract: they represent a mixture of substance and procedure, and of binding law and voluntary agreement. Accordingly, this chapter describes not only the concept of local connection but also its operation. The chapter is therefore both the last to describe key concepts and the first in a series of chapters describing duties.

5.3 The local connection provisions operate only in specified circumstances. It was one of the principal aims of the Housing (Homeless Persons) Act (H(HP) A) 1977 to end 'shuttling' homeless people between different local authorities, each alleging there was a 'greater' connection with the other.[1] The original provisions were described[2] as 'curiously reminiscent of one of the features of the old Poor Law 1601, whereby paupers could be sent back to the parishes where they had a settlement'.

5.4 Reference will be made in this chapter not only to HA 1996, Part 7 and H(W)A 2014, Part 2, and the Codes of Guidance; but also to the agreement reached by the Association of London Government, the Convention of Scottish Local Authorities (CoSLA), the Local Government Association (LGA) and the Welsh Local Government Association (WLGA) in 2006 known as the Local Authorities Agreement;[3] and to the statutory instrument governing arbitration of disputes between authorities;[4] as well as operation of the review regime.

5.5 At the core of the provisions are the local connection 'conditions for referral': if they apply, an authority to which application has been made (the 'notifying' authority') may be exempt both from the relief duty under HA 1996, s 189B(2),[5] and/or the duty to secure that accommodation is made available

---

1 See Chapter 1.
2 *R v Slough BC ex p Ealing LBC* [1981] QB 801, CA, per Lord Denning MR.
3 *Procedures for referrals of homeless applicants to another local authority: guidelines for local authorities on procedures for referral*, agreed by Local Government Association (LGA), Convention of Scottish Local Authorities (CoSLA), Welsh Local Government Association (WLGA) ('the local authority associations' – https://www.local.gov.uk/sites/default/files/documents/PROCEDURES%20FOR%20REFERRALS%20OF%20HOMELESS%20 APPLICANTS%20TO%20ANOTHER%20LOCAL%20AUTHORITY_1.pdf).
4 Homelessness (Decisions on Referrals) Order 1998, SI 1981/1578.
5 HA 1996, 199A(1); H(W)A 2014, s 73.

under HA 1996, s 193[6] or H(W)A 2014, ss 68 and 73.[7] These duties will pass to the 'notified authority'.[8]

5.6   At a number of stages, there are obligations to notify applicants; there are also rights to review; there is provision for accommodation pending resolution of which authority has final responsibility for an applicant; and for protection of their property. The position governing cross-boundary referrals – ie, between England, Wales and Scotland – also needs consideration. While overlapping with the content of later chapters, these topics are all considered in this chapter.

5.7   The matters which must be considered are:

a)   what are the conditions for referral?

b)   what is a local connection?

c)   when are the local connection provisions applicable?

d)   relief duty;

e)   duty to secure housing;

f)   resolution of disputes;

g)   cross-border referrals;

h)   notification duties;

i)   rights to review;

j)   accommodation pending resolution and protection of property.

CONDITIONS FOR REFERRAL

Generally

5.8   The conditions for referral are that:

a)   neither the applicant nor any person who might reasonably be expected to reside with them, has a local connection with the area of the authority to which application is made; and

b)   the applicant or a person who might reasonably be expected to reside with the applicant, does have a local connection with the area of another housing authority; and

---

6   HA 1996, s 200(1); H(W)A 2014, s 83(1).
7   H(W)A 2014, s 82(1).
8   HA 1996, ss 199A(5), 200(4); H(W)A 2014, ss 82(4), 83(2). See also *Johnston v City of Westminster* [2015] EWCA Civ 554, [2015] HLR 35.

c) neither the applicant nor any person who might reasonably be expected to reside with the applicant, will run the risk of domestic abuse in that other authority's area.[9]

5.9 All three conditions must usually be fulfilled before the local connection provisions can be relied on. The procedure is unavailable if there is a local connection with the area to which application has been made, but the authority is of the opinion that the applicant has a greater or closer local connection elsewhere.[10]

Abuse and violence

5.10 The referral conditions are not met, however, if the applicant or any person who might reasonably be expected to reside with the applicant has suffered non-domestic violence[11] (in Wales, non-domestic abuse) in the area of another authority, and it is probable that return to the area will lead to further violence (or abuse) of a similar kind against the victim.[12]

5.11 The circumstances in which a person runs the risk of either domestic abuse or non-domestic violence are the same as those considered in relation to whether or not it would have been reasonable – on this ground – to continue to occupy accommodation, pursuant to HA 1996, s 177.[13] The authority is under a positive duty to enquire whether the applicant is subject to such a risk.[14]

5.12 One point which may be made here relates to the interaction with intentional homelessness. It is not uncommon for someone not merely to leave home on account of domestic abuse, but to want to leave the area. Some authorities who find that a person is not homeless intentionally on account of domestic abuse will nonetheless seek to refer them back. While there is no necessary or theoretical conflict between finding that someone is homeless (perhaps on account of the domestic abuse) and finding that they will not run the risk of domestic abuse in the area from which they have fled, this represents a relatively fine distinction, for which there needs to be a material basis.[15]

9   HA 1996, s 198(2); H(W)A 2014, s 80(3). On the meaning of 'domestic abuse', see paras **2.84–2.87**.
10   See *Re Betts* [1983] 2 AC 613, (1983) 10 HLR 97, HL; the House of Lords did not overrule the Court of Appeal on this point. See also Welsh Code para 18.10.
11   Violence means violence from another person; or threats of violence from another person which are likely to be carried out: HA 1996, s 198(2A), (3), as amended by DAA 2021, s 78(5).
12   HA 1996, s 198(2A); H(W)A 2014, s 80(4).
13   HA 1996, s 198(3); H(W)A 2014, s 57; see paras **2.84–2.90**.
14   *Patterson v Greenwich LBC* (1994) 26 HLR 159, CA.
15   Ie, that although the applicant left because of violence, the risk no longer subsists.

5.13   In *Browne*,[16] which for these purposes and on this issue may be treated as if a local connection case, the authority had not found intentional homelessness, but appeared to have addressed itself expressly to the point made in the last paragraph.[17] In *Adigun*,[18] it was stressed that the task of determining whether or not there was a risk of domestic violence[19] is one for the local authority: so long as there was material on which it could base its decision, the court would not intervene.

No connections

5.14   If a person has no local connection with *any* housing authority in England, Wales or Scotland, they will be entitled to help and housing from the authority to which the application has been made.[20]

Time for determining connection

5.15   When seeking to establish whether an applicant has a local connection with a particular area, the authority must look at the facts at the time of the decision. If there is a review of the decision,[21] it is the facts at the date of the review which must be considered.[22] An applicant may not have a local connection with an authority at the date of application, but may acquire one subsequently, either prior to a decision or between decision and review – for example, by obtaining permanent employment or through normal residence in the area.[23]

England: additional application of provisions

Placement by another authority

5.16   By HA 1996, s 198(4), the conditions for referral are deemed to be fulfilled – regardless, therefore, of local connection with the authority to which the application was made (on any of the foregoing grounds), and regardless of risk of domestic or other violence – if:

---

16   *R v Bristol City Council ex p Browne* [1979] 1 WLR 1437, DC.
17   See para **8.158**.
18   *R v Islington LBC ex p Adigun* (1988) 20 HLR 600, QBD. See also *R v Newham LBC ex p Smith* (1997) 29 HLR 213, QBD.
19   Now, abuse.
20   *R v Hillingdon LBC ex p Streeting (No 2)* [1980] 1 WLR 1425, CA. Although note the limitations in relation to former asylum-seekers at paras **5.21–5.24**.
21   See paras **7.190–7.260**.
22   *Mohamed v Hammersmith and Fulham LBC* [2001] UKHL 57, [2002] HLR 7.
23   See further para **7.176**.

a) the applicant was placed by another authority[24] in accommodation in the area of the authority to which the application has been made;

b) in discharge of its functions under HA 1996, Part 7 or H(W)A 2014, Part 2;

c) within such period as may be prescribed.

5.17 The current prescribed period is five years from the date of the placement, plus the time between the date the application was initially made to the time of the first placement in the area of the authority to which the application has now been made.[25]

5.18 From 9 November 2012, when Localism Act (LA) 2011, s 149(6) came into force in England,[26] the conditions for referral were also met (in England) if the applicant had accepted a private sector offer of accommodation[27] from another authority, in the area of the authority to which the application was subsequently made, within the previous two years, and neither the applicant nor anyone who might reasonably be expected to reside with the applicant ran the risk of domestic abuse in the district of that other authority.[28]

5.19 This only applies, however, where the private sector offer had been made before – and the duty to secure accommodation was still in existence at – that date;[29] accordingly, it can now only apply to an application made before 9 November 2014 which is still undetermined.

Former asylum-seekers

5.20 In *Al-ameri*,[30] the House of Lords held that a former asylum-seeker who subsequently applied as homeless did not have a local connection with the area in which he had been provided with accommodation by the National Asylum Support Service (NASS),[31] because residence in that accommodation was not 'of choice'.[32] HA 1996, Part 7 was amended by Asylum and Immigration (Treatment

---

24 Including a Welsh authority, see HA 1996, s 198(4A).
25 Allocation of Housing and Homelessness (Miscellaneous Provisions) (England) Regulations 2006, SI 2006/2527.
26 Localism Act 2011 (Commencement No 2 and Transitional Provisions) (England) Order 2012, SI 2012/2599, art 2.
27 See paras **8.260–8.271**.
28 HA 1996, s 198(2ZA) as amended by DAA 2021, s 78.
29 Localism Act 2011 (Commencement No 2 and Transitional Provisions) (England) Order 2012, SI 2012/2599, art 3.
30 *Al-ameri v Kensington and Chelsea RLBC; Osmani v Harrow LBC* [2004] UKHL 4, [2004] HLR 20.
31 Now UK Visas and Immigration (UKVI), as it has been since 2013. Between 2008 and 2013, the UK Border Agency (UKBA) dealt with such matters. Asylum support was previously administered by the NASS which was part of the Home Office.
32 See paras **5.35–5.36**.

of Claimants, etc) Act 2004, s 11 to reverse this.[33] The H(W)A 2014 adopted the same approach.[34]

5.21 Accordingly, by HA 1996, s 199(6), (7) and H(W)A 2014, s 81(5), (6), a person has a local connection with an authority's district if they were at any time provided with accommodation in that district under Immigration and Asylum Act 1999, s 95[35] unless:

a) the applicant was subsequently provided with accommodation under section 95 in another authority's district; or

b) the accommodation was provided in an accommodation centre under Nationality, Immigration and Asylum Act 2002, s 22.[36]

5.22 This only applies where the accommodation is provided by UK Visas and Immigration (UKVI) in England or Wales.[37]

5.23 Therefore, a former asylum-seeker who has been housed by UKVI in Scotland will not have a local connection in the district where the accommodation was provided.

5.24 Where a former asylum-seeker who has been housed by UKVI in Scotland[38] applies to an authority in England,[39] and has no local connection with the authority to which they have applied nor any with an authority in Scotland, the principal housing duty under HA 1996, s 193[40] is, however, disapplied.[41] Instead, the local authority has a discretion to secure accommodation for a reasonable period and may provide advice and assistance.[42]

---

33 Given the statutory amendment, the absence of support from family and friends in the area in which an asylum-seeker has been housed by UKVI does not provide sufficient reason for an authority to decide against making a referral which it is otherwise entitled to make: *Ozbek v Ispwich BC* [2006] EWCA Civ 534, [2006] HLR 41.

34 H(W)A 2014, s 81(5), (6), in the same terms as HA 1996, s 199(6), (7); Welsh Code paras 18.16–18.18.

35 See further paras **11.42–11.59**, on the provision of accommodation by UKVI under this section.

36 This provision has not yet been brought into force.

37 See paras **11.42–11.59**.

38 Other than in an accommodation centre under Nationality, Immigration and Asylum Act 2002, s 22. This provision has not yet been brought into force.

39 The position appears to be different in Wales. The Asylum and Immigration (Treatment of Claimants, etc) Act 2004, s 11 has not been amended in the light of the H(W)A 2014, so that the disapplication provisions do not apply to Wales, with the effect that a former asylum-seeker who was housed in Scotland is potentially entitled to the full range of services and support if they apply to a Welsh local housing authority.

40 See paras **8.132–8.234**.

41 Asylum and Immigration (Treatment of Claimants, etc) Act 2004, s 11(2), (3)(a).

42 Asylum and Immigration (Treatment of Claimants, etc) Act 2004, s 11(3)(b). This discretion is framed in the same terms as the duty towards the intentionally homeless; see paras **8.108–8.123**.

Children Act 1989 cases

5.25   From 3 April 2018, when Homelessness Reduction Act (HRA) 2017 came into force,[43] there are additional provisions governing those towards whom a social services authority[44] in England has a duty under Children Act (CA) 1989, s 23C,[45] as a former relevant child.[46] So long as an authority in England has such a duty, then, if the authority is a local housing authority as well as a social services authority,[47] the former relevant child is deemed to have a local connection with its area; if the authority is not a local housing authority,[48] the former relevant child is deemed to have a local connection with every district in the area of the social services authority.

5.26   Furthermore, where accommodation for a child in care has been provided under CA 1989, s 22A,[49] so that the child is normally resident in the district of a local housing authority for a continuous period of at all least two years, some or all of which falls before they turn 16, they are likewise deemed to have a local connection with that district,[50] although ceases to do so once they turn 21 unless a local connection can be established on any of the other grounds for it.[51]

WHAT IS A LOCAL CONNECTION?

Overview

5.27   The term 'local connection' is defined in HA 1996, s 199 and H(W) A 2014, s 81.[52] A person may have a local connection with the district of a local housing authority[53] based on one of four grounds:

    a)   because the person is, or in the past was, normally resident in it, and the person's residence is or was of their own choice;

---

43   Homelessness Reduction Act 2017 (Commencement and Transitional and Savings Provisions) Regulations 2018, SI 2018/167, reg 3. This does not apply to applications made or sought before 3 April 2018: reg 4. For the position before this date, see the 10th edition of this work.

44   See para **11.7**.

45   See para **11.110**.

46   HA 1996, s 199(8).

47   Which will mean all London Boroughs and the Common Council of the City of London, all unitary authorities and all district councils in metropolitan areas.

48   Ie, county council in non-metropolitan areas.

49   See para **11.85**.

50   HA 1996, s 199(9).

51   HA 1996, s 199(10).

52   It may be noted that the provisions do not apply in relation to the Isles of Scilly, where there is a requirement of residence of two years and six months during the previous three years: Homelessness (Isles of Scilly) Order 1997, SI 1997/797.

53   For these purposes, this includes a local authority within the meaning of the Housing (Scotland) Act 1988: HA 1996, ss 201, 217.

b)   because the person is employed in it;

c)   because of family associations; and

d)   because of any special circumstances.[54]

As noted above, special provisions apply to applicants who have previously been housed by UKVI,[55] as well as to a small number of additional categories.[56]

5.28   It is important not to pay so much attention to the four grounds that insufficient regard is had to the governing phrase 'local connection' itself: see *Re Betts*.[57] In that case, the applicant was living with his family in the area of Blaby DC between 1978 and 1980. In August 1980, he got a job in Southampton, and moved into a houseboat in the area, where he was joined by his family. In October 1980, he was given a house by Eastleigh BC. Soon after, he lost his job through no fault of his own, fell into arrears with his rent and was evicted. In February 1981, shortly before the order for possession expired, he applied under H(HP)A 1977. Eastleigh BC referred the application to Blaby DC on the basis that the family had lived in Eastleigh BC's district for less than six months, and, accordingly, was not normally resident in its area.[58] The applicant challenged this decision.

5.29   The Court of Appeal allowed the challenge.[59] The only reason for the finding that the family was not normally resident in the area was that the family had lived in the area for less than six months, which decision had been reached by rigid application of the Local Authorities Agreement.[60] Normal residence was where a person intended to settle, not necessarily permanently or indefinitely, and a person may have more than one normal residence at different times. It requires consideration of many features, not merely the application of a six-month, or any other arbitrary, period.

5.30   Allowing the authority's appeal, however, the House of Lords held that the fundamental question was whether or not the applicant had a local connection with the area. This meant more than 'normal residence'. Normal residence, and the other specified grounds of local connection, are subsidiary components of the

---

54   HA 1996, s 199(1); H(W)A 2014, s 81(1).It is possible for a person to have no local connection with any authority (eg, if they have just arrived in the country), in which case these provisions will not be applicable and the applicant will be the responsibility of the authority to whom they applied: see English Code para 10.35; Welsh Code para 18.19.
55   As it has been since 2013. Between 2008 and 2013, the UKBA dealt with such matters. Asylum support was previously administered by the National Asylum Support Service (NASS) which was part of the Home Office. See paras **5.21–5.24**.
56   Paras **5.16–5.19**. There are no equivalent provisions in Wales.
57   *Re Betts* [1983] 2 AC 613, (1983) 10 HLR 97, HL.
58   This is the time used in the Local Authorities Agreement – see below, paras **5.31, 5.32** and **5.76–5.82**.
59   *Betts v Eastleigh BC* [1983] 1 WLR 774, (1983) 8 HLR 28, CA.
60   See paras **5.76–5.82**. See also Welsh Code para 18.8.

formula to be applied. The formula is governed by the proposition that residence of any sort will be irrelevant unless and until it is such as to establish a local connection.[61]

5.31   The House of Lords did not dissent from the Court of Appeal's analysis of 'residence'.[62] Nor did it dissent from the proposition that rigid application of the Local Authorities Agreement would constitute a fetter on the authority's discretion.[63] The Agreement could certainly be taken into account and applied as a guideline, provided an authority does not shut out the particular facts of the individual case, ie, provided its application is given individual consideration.[64] The House of Lords found that the authority had not misdirected itself in this respect.

Residence

5.32   The Local Authorities Agreement suggests a working (or extended) definition of 'normal residence' as six months in an area during the previous 12 months, or not less than three years during the previous five-year period.[65] In *Re Betts*, this was described as 'eminently sensible and proper to have been included in the agreement'.

5.33   In *Smith and Hay*,[66] a period of a few months, some ten years before application, during which one of the spouses had been employed – and therefore resident – in an area, was considered too short necessarily to have established a local connection.

5.34   Compare, however, *Hughes*,[67] where the applicant had moved into the area to set up a permanent home with the man by whom she became pregnant. The relationship broke down owing to domestic violence after only two months, and the applicant applied as homeless. A decision made some months later – during which the applicant had resided in a local women's aid refuge – that the applicant did not have a local connection with the area, was quashed as one to which no reasonable authority could have come.

---

61   This approach was taken in *R v Islington LBC ex p Adigun* (1988) 20 HLR 600, QBD and *R v Westminster City Council ex p Benniche* (1997) 29 HLR 230, CA.
62   It was based on *R v Barnet LBC ex p Shah* [1983] 2 AC 309, HL under the Education Act 1962.
63   See paras **10.54–10.54**.
64   In *Ozbek v Ispwich BC* [2006] EWCA Civ 534, [2006] HLR 41, at [39], Chadwick LJ stated that the need for a common basis of decision-making meant that there was an 'imperative for all authorities to apply the guidelines generally to all applications which come before them'. This must be read in the light of *Betts*.
65   Local Authorities Agreement para 4.3(i).
66   *R v Vale of White Horse DC ex p Smith and Hay* (1985) 17 HLR 160, QBD.
67   *R v Southwark LBC ex p Hughes* (1998) 30 HLR 1082, QBD.

5.35   Residence must be 'of choice'.[68] There is no residence of choice if the applicant, or a person who might reasonably be expected to reside with the applicant, is detained under the authority of any Act of Parliament.[69] Thus, prisoners (whether or not convicted) and those detained under the Mental Health Act 1983 will not acquire a local connection with the area in which the prison or hospital is situated. The Secretary of State has power to specify further circumstances in which residence is not to be considered 'of choice',[70] although this power has not been exercised. In Wales, the Welsh Ministers have the same power, which has likewise not been exercised.[71]

5.36   Prior to 1 December 2008, residence resulting from service in the armed forces did not constitute residence 'of choice' for serving members of the armed forces.[72] This still applies to applications made before 1 December 2008.[73] For applications made on or after that date, residence resulting from service in the armed forces is to be treated as 'of choice' for the purposes of HA 1996, s 199 or H(W)A 2014, s 82.[74]

5.37   In *Mohamed*,[75] the House of Lords concluded that occupation of interim accommodation provided[76] by a local authority during enquiries and pending review could amount to normal residence:

---

68   HA 1996, s 199(1)(a); H(W)A 2014, s 81(2)(a). See *Wandsworth LBC v NJ* [2013] EWCA Civ 1373, [2014] HLR 6 as to whether accommodation in a refuge is 'of choice'.
69   HA 1996, s 199(3); H(W)A 2014, s 81(3) and Welsh Code para 18.14.
70   HA 1996, s 199(5).
71   H(W)A 2014, s 81(4)(b).
72   The armed forces were defined as the Royal Navy, the regular armed forces as defined by Army Act 1955, s 225, and the regular air forces as defined by Air Force Act 1955, s 223: HA 1996, s 199(4). From 31 October 2009, the armed forces are defined as Royal Navy, the Royal Marines, the regular army or the Royal Air Force: Armed Forces Act 2006, s 374. The repealed provision was addressed in *R v Vale of White Horse DC ex p Smith and Hay* (1985) 17 HLR 160, QBD, two cases heard together which considered the usual practice of the armed forces to allow a period of time after the termination of service before recovering possession of married quarters. It was held that the exclusion of residence as a result of service in the armed forces referred to the time residence commenced; a fresh residence after leaving the armed forces could be established, even in the same premises, but would not usually be established merely by holding over after the right to occupy married quarters had come to an end.
73   While now long ago, someone may have remained in housing provided under HA 1996, Part 7, without cessation of the duty under HA 1996, s 193, whether by a final offer of accommodation or otherwise.
74   HA 1996, s 199(2) repealed with effect from 1 December 2008. See also Circular 04/2009 *Housing allocations – members of the armed forces* from the DCLG; and English Code para 10.21 and Chapter 24. No such restriction was included in H(W)A 2014; see Welsh Code para 18.11.
75   *Mohamed v Hammersmith and Fulham LBC*, above. Cf *Al-ameri v Kensington and Chelsea RLBC; Osmani v Harrow LBC* [2004] UKHL 4, [2004] HLR 20 where accommodation provided by NASS to asylum-seekers was not residence of choice. The effect of this latter decision has now been statutorily overturned: see para **5.22**.
76   Usually under HA 1996, s 188(1) but also potentially under s 200(1) or s 188(3) or s 200(5) pending the review.

'. . . the prima facie meaning of normal residence is a place where at the relevant time the person in fact resides. That therefore is the question to be asked . . . So long as that place where he eats and sleeps is voluntarily accepted by him, the reason why he is there rather than somewhere else does not prevent that place from being his normal residence. He may not like it, he may prefer some other place, but that place is for the relevant time the place where he normally resides . . . Where he is given interim accommodation by a local housing authority even more clearly is that the place where for the time being he is normally resident. The fact that it is provided subject to statutory duty does not . . . prevent it from being such.'

5.38   In *Minott*,[77] On 26 March 2019, the claimant applied for assistance and was provided with accommodation pending inquiries; on 8 August 2019, the authority decided that he was homeless and eligible for assistance but that he did not have a local connection with Cambridge but did have one with Sandwell, to which his application was referred; that referral was accepted but the applicant sought a review of the decision to refer him to Sandwell MBC. The authority gave notice for him to quit the interim accommodation but the applicant refused to leave and evaded attempts to evict him, knowing that if was still in occupation on 26 September, it might mean that he had acquired a local connection with Cambridge because of the working definition of normal residence in the Local Authorities Agreement. On 25 September, the review officer decided that the applicant did not have a local connection, a decision the applicant did not appeal. Instead, on 17 October 2019, he again applied to the authority for assistance, contending that there had been a change of facts[78] as he had been by then been living in Cambridge for over six months. The authority refused to accept the application, of which decision the applicant sought judicial review.

5.39   The High Court dismissed the claim[79] on the basis that nothing other than the passage of time had changed between the applications; the authority had terminated his right to occupy his interim accommodation; thereafter he had deliberately frustrated the authority's attempts to evict him and his unlawful occupation of that accommodation could not provide him with a local connection with the authority's district. The Court of Appeal disagreed:[80] mere lapse of time between two applications is normally of no consequence, but the applicant was here relying on the possibility that his residence meant that he had acquired a local connection, which was a different factual basis to the previous application. The authority could therefore not suggest that his second application was based on exactly the same facts as the earlier one. Moreover, whether or not a local connection had been established was not an issue to be determined when deciding whether or not to accept the second application, but on consideration of that application itself.

---

77   *R (Minott) v. Cambridge City Council* [2022] EWCA Civ 159; [2022] HLR 27.
78   Paras **7.31–7.46**.
79   [2021] EWHC 211 (Admin); [2021] HLR 29.
80   *R (Minott) v Cambridge City Council* [2022] EWCA Civ 159; [2022] HLR 27.

Employment

5.40   The Local Authorities Agreement suggests that an authority should seek confirmation from an employer both of the employment and that it is not of a casual nature.[81] This implies that 'employment' is to be given a restrictive meaning, ie, one in the employ of another – but neither HA 1996, Part 7 nor H(W)A 2014 suggests that self-employed people should be excluded, or that employment need be full-time.

5.41   Given that employment is a subsidiary consideration, and merely one of the grounds for establishing a local connection,[82] while it may be open to an authority to exclude a relatively short period of casual work, it would not, it is submitted, permit the exclusion of self-employment. In *Smith and Hay* (above), the same few months' employment, some ten years before the application, was described as limited and of short duration and the authority did not err in finding that it did not give rise to a local connection, but – especially in this day and age when employment relationships are markedly more diverse than traditional – to suggest, say, that someone who has been a self-employed trader (eg a local builder) for a period of time long enough to be considered a connection is not employed in an area would not only be a gloss on the legislation but would fly in its face.

5.42   A person was not formerly regarded as employed in an area either if they were serving in the regular armed forces,[83] or in such other circumstance as the Secretary of State or Welsh Ministers[84] may by order specify.[85] (This power has not been exercised.) For applications made on or after 1 December 2008, a person serving as a member of the regular armed forces is regarded as employed so as to give rise to a local connection.[86]

Family associations

5.43   There is no statutory definition of the phrase 'family associations'. The English Code of Guidance[87] suggests that, in addition to partners, parents, adult children or siblings, it may include associations with family members such as step-parents, grandparents, grandchildren, aunts or uncles 'provided

81   Local Authorities Agreement para 4.3(ii).
82   See also paras **5.27–5.31**.
83   HA 1996, s 199(2). This subsection was repealed with effect from 1 December 2008: Housing and Regeneration Act 2008, ss 315(a), 321(1) and Sch 16, and Housing and Regeneration Act 2008 (Commencement No 2 and Transitional, Saving and Transitory Provisions) Order 2008, SI 2008/3068.
84   See H(W)A 2014, s 81(4)(a).
85   HA 1996, s 199(5).
86   Housing and Regeneration Act 2008, ss 315(a), 321(1) and Sch 16 and Housing and Regeneration Act 2008 (Commencement No 2 and Transitional, Saving and Transitory Provisions) Order 2008/3068. See Welsh Code para 18.11.
87   English Code para 10.9. The Welsh Code does not comment on this matter.

there are sufficiently close links in the form of frequent contact, commitment or dependency'. This goes further than the Local Authorities Agreement, which suggests that it arises where an applicant or a member of the applicant's household has parents, adult children, brothers or sisters currently residing in the area in question.[88]

5.44   In *Avdic*,[89] a claim based on a first-cousin-once-removed was insufficient. The decision is not, however, to be interpreted as limiting family associations to those mentioned in the Agreement: see *Ozbek*,[90] where it was said that the character of the family association was at least as relevant – if not more so – than the degree of consanguinity.[91]

5.45   In that case, the applicants sought to establish their local connection with the borough to which they had applied through brothers who had lived in the area for only 18 months, and cousins and other extended family members who had lived there for over five years. The relevant question for the authority in these circumstance was 'whether, in the particular circumstances of the individual case, the bond between the applicant and one or more members of the extended family was of such a nature that it would be appropriate to regard those members of the extended family as "near relatives" in the sense in which that concept is recognised in [the Local Authorities Agreement]'.[92] The authority had correctly asked itself this question in reaching its conclusion that there was no local connection.

5.46   The Local Authorities Agreement suggests that relatives must have been resident for a period of at least five years and that the applicant must indicate a wish to be near the:[93] again, this cannot be applied rigidly and needs to be considered in each case on its own facts. It also says that an applicant who objects to being referred to an area on account of family associations should not be so referred.[94]

---

88   Local Authorities Agreement para 4.3(iii). It continues that '[o]nly in exceptional circumstances would the residence of relatives other than those listed above be taken to establish a local connection'.

89   *R v Hammersmith and Fulham LBC ex p Avdic* (1996) 28 HLR 897, QBD; (1998) 30 HLR 1, CA.

90   *Ozbek v Ispwich BC* [2006] EWCA Civ 534, [2006] HLR 41. This is now reflected in the English Code of Guidance, see previous paragraph. See also the first instance decision of *Munting v Hammersmith and Fulham LBC* [1998] JHL D91, where the authority had wrongly concluded that a step-father could not be a close relative.

91   At [64].

92   At [49].

93   Local Authorities Agreement para 4.3(iii).

94   Local Authorities Agreement para 4.1(ii), but compare, *R v McCall and others ex p Eastbourne BC*, (1981) *LAG Bulletin* 210, referred to at (1981) 8 HLR 48, QBD, in which it was observed that though the applicant's wishes are relevant, where other factors are equally balanced, they cannot override the words of the statute.

5.47   Once family association has been raised by the applicant, the authority should address the issue. A decision letter which failed to do so after the issue had been raised was held to be defective in *Khan*,[95] as it appeared from the letter that only residence had been addressed.

Other special circumstances

5.48   'Other special circumstances' is a phrase likewise left undefined in HA 1996, Part 7 and H(W)A 2014, Part 2. The English Code[96] suggests, by way of example, the need to be near medical or support services which are only available in a particular district. The Welsh Code suggests that young adults leaving the care system should be considered to have a local connection either to their original area of residence or to the area where they were placed.[97]

5.49   The Local Authorities Agreement mentions[98] those who have been in prison or in hospital or who wish to return to an area where they were brought up or had lived for a considerable length of time in the past. It stresses that an authority must exercise its discretion when considering whether special circumstances apply.

5.50   In *Smith and Hay*,[99] one of the families sought to place some reliance on membership of an evangelical church, around which their lives revolved. Following *Betts* (see para **5.28**) – which held that the fundamental test is whether or not there is a local connection – the authority had not erred in concluding as a matter of fact that this did not amount to a special circumstance giving rise to a local connection in their case. Nor does a mere desire not to return to an area with which the applicant has a local connection amount to a special circumstance giving rise to a local connection with a different area: *Adigun*.[100]

5.51   It has been suggested that family associations too weak to qualify under HA 1996, s 199(1)(c) cannot amount to a special circumstance under this subsection: see *Khan* and *Avdic*.[101] This also seems too rigid. If a connection of importance exists, which could be based on what might also be described as a weak family association, it cannot automatically rule out qualification as a special circumstance.

95   *R v Slough BC ex p Khan* (1995) 27 HLR 492, QBD.
96   English Code of Guidance para 10.11; the Welsh Code does not comment on this.
97   Welsh Code para 18.9, perhaps akin to the position in England, see above, paras **5.25–5.26**.
98   Local Authorities Agreement para 4.3(iv).
99   *R v Vale of White Horse DC ex p Smith and Hay* (1985) 17 HLR 160, QBD. See also *R v Westminster City Council ex p Benniche* (1997) 29 HLR 230, CA.
100 *R v Islington LBC ex p Adigun* (1988) 20 HLR 600, QBD.
101 *R v Slough BC ex p Khan* (1995) 27 HLR 492, QBD; *R v Hammersmith and Fulham LBC ex p Avdic* (1996) 28 HLR 897, QBD; (1998) 30 HLR 1, CA.

WHEN ARE THE LOCAL CONNECTION PROVISIONS APPLICABLE?

Generally

5.52 The principal application of the local connection provisions is when the conditions for referral – actual or deemed[102] – exist so that the authority to which application has been made may be exempt from the relief duty under HA 1996, ss 189B(2),[103] and/or the duty to secure that accommodation is made available under HA 1996, s 193[104] or H(W)A 2014, ss 68 and 73,[105] and these duties will pass instead to the 'notified' authority.[106]

Threatened with homelessness

5.53 It has been held that the local connection provisions are not applicable when the authority's duty arises because of threatened homelessness under HA 1996, s 195(2).[107] In *Williams v Exeter City Council*,[108] a woman was occupying army property let to her husband, a serviceman, in the Exeter area. As such, she had[109] no connection with Exeter on the basis of residence of choice,[110] nor on any other ground. The Ministry of Defence secured an order for possession against her and, before it was executed, she applied to the authority which agreed that she was threatened with homelessness, but referred her case to East Devon DC. The applicant challenged this decision: it was held that the local connection provisions applied only once the duty arose under HA 1985, s 65(2) (now HA 1996, s 193), not under s 195(2), ie, once she was actually homeless.

Discretion

5.54 The decision to make enquiries into local connection, and, therefore, whether or not to refer, is discretionary and, as such, may be vulnerable to challenge if exercised unreasonably.[111] Given the discretionary nature of the exercise, however, authorities are under no obligation to investigate local connection, even where the applicant indicates that they wish to live in another area.[112]

---

102 See paras **5.8–5.9, 5.16**.
103 HA 1996 199A(1); H(W)A 2014, s 73.
104 HA 1996, s 200(1); H(W)A 2014, s 83(1).
105 H(W)A 2014, s 82(1).
106 HA 1996, s 199A(5); H(W)A 2014, ss 82(4), 83(2). See also *Johnston v City of Westminster* [2015] EWCA Civ 554, [2015] HLR 35.
107 As enacted.
108 *Williams v Exeter City Council* September 1981 *LAG Bulletin* 211.
109 At that time: see now para **5.43**.
110 Under the provisions at that time: see now para **5.36**.
111 HA 1996, s 184(2). *R v Newham LBC ex p Tower Hamlets LBC* (1990) 23 HLR 62, CA; *Ozbek v Ispwich BC* [2006] EWCA Civ 534, [2006] HLR 41. See also *R v East Devon DC ex p Robb* (1998) 30 HLR 922, QBD, where the authority failed to consider whether it had a discretion to refer the applicant.
112 *Hackney LBC v Sareen* [2003] EWCA Civ 351, [2003] HLR 54.

5.55   In *Tower Hamlets*,[113] a decision by Newham LBC to refer an applicant to Tower Hamlets LBC was quashed. The referral concerned a Bangladeshi man who had originally applied to Tower Hamlets LBC for housing but was found to be intentionally homeless. He subsequently applied to Newham LBC, who found him not to be intentionally homeless. In reaching its decision, Newham LBC wrongly made a comparison between the housing conditions in Bangladesh and housing conditions in its own area, rather than to the general circumstances prevailing in relation to housing in Tower Hamlets LBC.[114] Tower Hamlets challenged the referral.

5.56   While the decision on intentionality was for the notifying authority,[115] the Court of Appeal held that: 'Whilst its decision cannot be appealed, that decision cannot found a referral if it is flawed to an extent and in respects which, in appropriate judicial review proceedings, would lead to its being quashed'.[116] In effect, Newham's exercise of its discretion was flawed and could be treated as such.[117] It has been held that the decision does not allow the notified authority to disregard the decision to refer without taking judicial review proceedings,[118] although the language used does suggest that it could be.[119]

5.57   Although it is lawful for an authority to have a policy about how it proposes to exercise its discretion, it cannot decide in advance that every applicant who qualifies for referral should be referred: *Carter*.[120]

5.58   Independently of the specific provisions governing the armed forces,[121] the obligation applicable to all decisions under Part 7, HA 1996, to have regard to:

> '(a) the unique obligations of, and sacrifices made by, the armed forces,
>
> (b)   the principle that it is desirable to remove disadvantages arising for service people from membership, or former membership, of the armed forces, and

---

113 *R v Newham LBC ex p Tower Hamlets LBC*, above, CA. See also Local Authorities Agreement para 3.7, advising on this decision.
114 See paras **2.91–2.98**.
115 Para **5.59**.
116 At paras **10.20–10.22**.
117 The decision was also flawed in that it failed to take account of the applicant's prospects of obtaining employment in the UK and to ascertain and consider Tower Hamlets' reasons for holding that Mr. Ullah had become homeless intentionally.
118 *R (Bantamagbari) v Westminster City Council* [2003] EWHC 1350 (Admin), [2003] JHL D70, transcript at [21].
119 Whether and when a decision can be treated as void without being quashed is a difficult area of law: see paras **10.20–10.22** where it is touched on briefly. In the homelessness context, it will invariably be best practice to obtain an order; it is unattractive for one public authority simply to treat the decision of another as void; in *Bantamagbari*, above, the court adopted counsel's submission that 'it would lead to anarchy'.
120 *R v Harrow LBC ex p Carter* (1994) 26 HLR 32, QBD.
121 Paras **5.36, 5.42**.

(c) the principle that special provision for service people may be justified by the effects on such people of membership, or former membership, of the armed forces'[122]

is clearly relevant here, where discretion may be exercised: the specific provisions governing the armed forces do not prevent the 2006 Act as amended having effect in this context.

Enquiries

5.59 The duty to make all preliminary enquiries initially lies on the authority to which application is made, culminating in a duty to notify the applicant what, if any, duty is owed them under HA 1996, Part 7.[123] The latter obligation may be fulfilled even if, as it is entitled to do,[124] the authority elects at some point during its enquiries – or contemporaneously with its conclusion – to make a local connection referral without determining all the key issues, provided it is satisfied that the applicant is eligible for assistance and homeless.[125] If it takes this course, and the referral is successful in the sense of transferring the duty, then it is the notified authority which will need to determine the questions of priority need and intentionality.[126]

5.60 In England, if the notifying authority does not refer the case before its initial duty has arisen, it may not do so until the initial duty has come to an end.[127] This may be on a number of grounds, including that it has complied with the duty for 56 days.[128] This means that an authority cannot accept the relief duty and then change its mind, eg, because it finds it more difficult than it had anticipated to secure accommodation for at least six months.[129]

5.61 It follows that in such a case, where the notifying authority has not referred the case before its initial duty has arisen, it will have discharged the relief duty and there is no such duty on the notified authority when the reference is made later. Such a later reference can, however, only be made provided not only that the notifying authority is satisfied that the applicant is eligible for assistance and homeless, but also that they are in priority need and not homeless

---

122 Armed Forces Act 2006, ss 343AA (England) and 343AB (Wales), added by Armed Forces Act 2021, s 8(3).
123 HA 1996, s 184(1); H(W)A 2014, s 82(1); Welsh Code para 18.3.
124 HA 1996, ss 189B(1), 198(A1); H(W)A 2014, s 73(2).
125 HA 1996, ss 189B(1), 198(1A); H(W)A 2014, s 80(1)(b).
126 But see paras **5.62–5.63** where the notifying authority *has* determined the issue of intentionality.
127 HA 1996, s 200(1A). There is no statutory equivalent in Wales. The Welsh Code of Guidance envisages the referral taking place before the initial duty has arisen (para 18.3). If the referral is accepted, then the notified authority will be subject to the relief duty (H(W)A 2014, s 82(4)); if the referral is rejected, then the relief duty is imposed on the notifying authority (H(W)A 2014, s 82(3)).
128 HA 1996, s 189B(7)(b). For the position in Wales, see ibid.
129 HA 1996, s 189B(2)(a). For the position in Wales, see para **5.60**.

intentionally.[130] If the reference is successful – in the sense that it is agreed or decided that the conditions for referral are present – the obligation to secure housing passes to the notified authority.[131] Otherwise, lesser duties remain with the first authority (ie, what would be the notifying authority if a referral was permissible in such circumstances).

5.62   Assuming a successful reference, however, the notified authority is bound by the decisions of the notifying authority on the issues of eligibility, homelessness, priority need and intentionality, unless the decision on those issues is so flawed that it can be quashed in judicial review proceedings:[132] there is no statutory power[133] permitting the notified authority to reach its own decisions on these questions; nor is there a deemed new application.[134]

5.63   This leads to what has been described as a 'merry-go-round',[135] in which a person may apply to authority A, be found homeless intentionally, move across to the area of authority B, make a new application, be found homeless unintentionally and then be referred back for permanent housing to authority A.[136] This is less likely to occur since the HRA 2017 came into force,[137] as authority B may well refer the applicant back before the initial duty arises, in which case the decision on intentionality will be for authority A.[138]

RELIEF DUTY

Overview

5.64   From 3 April 2018, when the HRA 2017 came into force in England,[139] a new relief duty was introduced for the homeless who are eligible for assistance

---

130 HA 1996, s 193(1) and s 198(1). For the position in Wales, see para **5.60**.
131 Which may include a Welsh local authority – see HA 1996, s 201A and H(W)A 2015, s 83 – or a Scottish local authority: under Housing (Scotland) Act 1987: HA 1996, ss 201, 217.
132 See para **5.56**.
133 Cf HA 1996, s 199A(5)(c), where the reference is before the initial duty has arisen: see para **5.67**. There is no equivalent provision in H(W)A 2014.
134 Again, cf HA 1996, s 199A(5)(a) where the reference is before the initial duty arises: see para **5.68**. There is no equivalent provision in H(W)A 2014.
135 *R v Slough BC ex p Ealing LBC*, above.
136 *R v Slough BC ex p Ealing LBC*, above. See also *R (Sambotin) v Brent LBC* [2018] EWCA Civ 1826, [2019] PTSR 371, [2019] HLR 5: once an authority has decided that an applicant is eligible for assistance, homeless, in priority need and not intentionally homeless, its duty under HA 1996, s 193(2) crystallises; if the authority decides to refer the applicant to another authority under the local connection provisions, the only issue is which authority is responsible for discharging the duty.
137 3 April 2018: see Homelessness Reduction Act 2017 (Commencement and Transitional and Savings Provisions) Regulations 2018, SI 2018/167, reg 3.
138 See para **5.66**.
139 Homelessness Reduction Act 2017 (Commencement and Transitional and Savings Provisions) Regulations 2018/167, reg 3, only applicable to applications made and reviews sought on or after that date – see reg 4. For the position before this date, see the 10th edition of this work.

(regardless of priority need or intentionality).[140] The provisions are similar to those which were already in force in Wales in the H(W)A 2014.[141]

5.65   If the authority to which application is made would be subject to the relief duty, but considers that the conditions for referral are met, it will not be subject to the relief duty,[142] but may instead notify the other authority of its opinion. If it does so, it ceases to be under any HA 1996, s 188 preliminary duty[143] for applicants whom the authority has reason to believe may be in priority need,[144] but is instead subject to an identical duty under HA 1996, s 199A(2) to secure that accommodation is available until the applicant is notified[145] of the decision whether the conditions for referral are met;[146] that duty ends even if there is a request for a review, although the authority has a discretion to continue it pending the decision on review.[147]

RENTERS (REFORM) BILL

At Committee Stage in the House of Commons, the government moved an amendment the effect of which will be that the general exclusion from assured tenancy status in s 209 will apply to private sector accommodation provided under s.199A. This was said to be a necessary consequential change arising from the Homelessness Reduction Act 2017 rather than an amendment necessitated by the Renters (Reform) Bill.

5.66   If it is decided that the conditions for referral are not met, the notifying authority is subject to the relief duty[148] and, if it has reason to believe that the applicant has a priority need, it must continue to secure that accommodation is available for occupation by the applicant until the later of when the HA 1996, s 189B duty itself comes to an end[149] or when the authority decides what (if any) other duty it owes the applicant under HA 1996, Part 7 following the duty under s 189B;[150] the duty ends even if there is a request for a review, although the authority has a discretion to continue it pending the decision on review.[151]

---

140 See paras **8.88–8.92**.
141 H(W)A 2014, s 73, and see paras **8.104–8.105**.
142 HA 1996, ss 189B(2), 199A(1); in Wales, H(W)A 2014, s 73.
143 See paras **8.12–8.14**.
144 HA 1996, s 198(A1); in Wales, H(W)A 2014, s 73(2).
145 Paras **5.100–5.103**.
146 HA 1996, s 199A(2); in Wales, H(W)A 2014, s 82(1).
147 HA 1996, s 199A(6); in Wales, H(W)A 2014, s 82(6).
148 HA 1996, s 199A(4). The references in HA 1996, s 189B(4) and (7) – in the context of the duty being brought to an end – to dates when the authority is first satisfied as to the s 189B criteria (paras **8.88–8.96**) are to be read as references to the day on which notice is given under HA 1996, s 199A(3). In Wales, see H(W)A 2014, s 82(3).
149 Paras **8.97–8.103**.
150 HA 1996, s 199A(4); H(W)A 2014, s 82(3). For the position in Wales, see para 8.98 for the circumstances in which the relief duty may be brought to an end.
151 HA 1996, s 199A(6).

5.67   If it is decided that the conditions for referral are met, then the applicant is treated as having made an application to the notified authority on the date on which they are given notice of the decision,[152] thus imposing on it the relief duty (among others).[153] From that date, the notifying authority owes no duties under HA 1996, Part 7.[154] The notifying authority must give the notified authority copies of any notifications that it gave the applicant as to its assessment of their case.[155]

Relief duty or housing duty

5.68   As the relief duty arises once the authority is satisfied that an applicant is eligible for assistance and homeless,[156] without necessarily deciding the issues of priority need and intentionality or issuing a decision under HA 2006, s 184,[157] these provisions allow the authority to avoid the relief duty altogether. If, however, the authority does start to discharge the relief duty, then – as noted[158] – it will not be able to invoke the local connection provisions until it has brought the relief duty to an end.[159]

Decision on intentional homelessness

5.69   It may be, however, that the notifying authority has also reached a decision on intentionality: if so, then under these new, statutory provisions, and contrary to the usual position,[160] the notified authority is now allowed to come to a different decision but only if it is satisfied that the applicant's circumstances have changed, or that further information has come to light, since the notifying authority came to that decision, and that the change in circumstances or further information justifies coming to a different decision.[161]

Decision on priority need

5.70   There is no equivalent statutory provision governing priority need: if the notifying authority has also reached a decision on priority need, the previous position applies, that the notified authority is normally bound by the decision of the notifying authority.[162]

---

152 Paras **5.100–5.103**.
153 Including the duty to secure interim housing under HA 1996, s 188.
154 HA 1996, s 199A(5)(a), (b); H(W)A 2014, s 82(4).
155 See paras **8.61-8.65**. HA 1996, s 199A(5); there is no equivalent in Wales.
156 HA 1996, s 189B(1).
157 See para **7.183**.
158 Para **5.60**.
159 HA 1996, s 200(1A).
160 Paras **5.62–5.63**.
161 HA 1996, s 199A(5)(c).
162 See the discussion at paras **5.62–5.63**.

DUTY TO SECURE HOUSING

5.71 If the referral takes place after the relief duty has been discharged, it will be under HA 1996, s 198 or H(W)A 2014, s 80. Such a referral gives rise to a new HA 1996, s 193 or H(W)A 2014, s 73 housing duty, so that if an applicant applies to authority A, is not found homeless intentionally but rejects its offer of accommodation, and then applies to authority B which refers the applicant back to authority A, authority A cannot rely on its earlier offer.[163]

5.72 An authority which finds an applicant homeless intentionally but wrongly refers the applicant to another authority, is not bound by its error; the erroneous reference may simply be ignored: merely because the local connection provisions do not apply to the duty to secure housing if there is intentionality, it does not follow that the erroneous referral in some way nullifies the intentionality decision.[164]

RESOLUTION OF DISPUTES

Overview

5.73 Especially in times of constraints on public expenditure, which has effectively been the case for most of the time since the 1977 Act, the local connection provisions are a breeding ground for disputes between authorities. In the event of such a dispute, between two (or more) authorities, the first stage in both England and Wales will be to try to resolve it by reference to the Local Authorities Agreement.[165] In default of agreement, the matter must be referred to arbitration.[166] Pending the resolution of the dispute, principal responsibility[167] for the homeless person or family continues to rest with the authority to which application was initially made, ie, the notifying authority.[168]

---

163 *R v Tower Hamlets LBC ex p Ali; R v Tower Hamlets LBC ex p Bibi* (1993) 25 HLR 158, CA (overruling *R v Hammersmith and Fulham LBC ex p O'Brian* (1985) 17 HLR 471, QBD on this point).

164 This is consistent with the approach and decision in *Crawley BC v B* (2000) 32 HLR 636, CA: see para **7.160**.

165 HA 1996, s 198(5); H(W)A 2014, s 80(5). See also *Procedures for referrals of homeless applicants to another local authority: consultation*, Local Government Association, February 2018.

166 HA 1996, s 198(5); H(W)A 2014, s 80(5).

167 Including protection of property: HA 1996, s 211(2): see Chapter 6.

168 HA 1996, s 200(1); H(W)A 2014, s 82(1). See, eg, *R (Tanushi) v (1) Westminster City Council (2) Hillingdon LBC* [2016] EWHC 3874 (Admin), in which Westminster sought to refer the application to Hillingdon, who had not accepted it; Ms Tanushi was granted interim relief requiring Westminster to continue to provide her with accommodation.

5.74   The question whether the conditions for referral of an application[169] are satisfied is to be determined by agreement between the notifying authority and the notified authority or, in default of agreement, in accordance with such arrangements as the Secretary of State or Welsh Ministers may order by statutory instrument.[170] 'Arrangements' are those agreed by the authorities, or by associations of authorities, or in default of agreement such as appears to the Secretary of State and/or Welsh Ministers to be suitable, after consultation with the local authority associations and such other persons as they think appropriate.[171]

5.75   The current arrangements are to be found in the Homelessness (Decisions on Referrals) Order 1998[172] and the Local Authorities Agreement.

Local Authorities Agreement

5.76   Some of the substantive provisions of the Local Authorities Agreement in relation to the four grounds for local connections have been noted above.

5.77   The authority to which application has been made is urged to investigate all circumstances with the same thoroughness that it would use if it did not have it in mind to refer the application to another authority. These enquiries may be of another authority, one to which it may be making a referral, and such enquiries should be made as soon as possible.[173]

5.78   Where an applicant has a local connection with a number of authorities, the English Code of Guidance[174] suggests that the preference of the applicant should be taken into account in deciding which authority to notify.

5.79   In *McCall*,[175] it was held that, although an arbitrator[176] will not – without the consent of the authorities – usually be entitled to apply the criteria set out in the Local Authorities Agreement, it is proper for them to have regard to the wishes of the applicant if issues are evenly balanced. Indeed, where all other considerations give no indication one way or another, the court described it as 'perfectly reasonable and perfectly sensible, and within the spirit of the statutory provisions', to have regard to the wishes of the family.

---

169 See para **5.8**.
170 HA 1996, s 198(5), (5A); H(W)A 2014, s 80(5). This applies only to disputes about whether the applicant has a local connection. If an authority wishes to challenge a referral, eg, because it believes the applicant should have been found intentionally homeless, it should do so by judicial review: see the discussion at paras **5.55–5.56**.
171 HA 1996, s 198(6); H(W)A 2014, s 80(6).
172 Homelessness (Decisions on Referrals) Order 1998/1578.
173 Local Authorities Agreement para 5.1.
174 English Code of Guidance para 10.34.
175 *R v McCall and others ex p Eastbourne BC* (1981) *LAG Bulletin* 210, referred to at (1981) 8 HLR 48, QBD, in which it was observed that though the applicant's wishes are relevant, where other factors are equally balanced, they cannot override the words of the statute.
176 See paras **5.83–5.89**.

5.80   Under the terms of the Local Authorities Agreement, each authority should nominate one person to receive notifications of referral from other authorities.[177] Unless it has clear evidence to the contrary, the notified authority should accept all statements of the facts of the case as stated by the notifying authority.[178]

5.81   If the notified authority provides new information which causes the notifying authority to want to reconsider questions of homelessness, priority need or intentionality, the position will be the same as in other reconsideration cases.[179] The Local Authorities Agreement stresses that the disputes procedures should be used only where there is a disagreement over the existence of a local connection, not for resolving disagreement on any other matter; and that – once enquiries have been completed – a challenge to the notifying authority's decision that the applicant is eligible, homeless, in priority need and not intentionally homeless can only be made by judicial review.[180]

5.82   If the issue is resolved through the Local Authorities Agreement, then the notified authority should, if it has accepted responsibility, provide accommodation for the applicant and the applicant's family immediately. Once the notified authority has accepted responsibility, it is liable to repay the notifying authority for expenses incurred in the provision of temporary accommodation, although if the notifying authority has delayed unduly[181] the notified authority need only reimburse it for expenses incurred since notification of the referral was received.[182]

Arbitration

5.83   Where a notified authority disputes the referral, it should set out its reasons in full within ten days.[183] If there is still no agreement, the authorities must seek, within 21 days of receipt of the referral, to agree on an arbitrator who will make the decision.[184] The LGA maintains an independent panel of persons – generally known as referees – for this purpose.[185] In default of agreement as to the referee, the authorities must jointly request the chair of the LGA or their nominee (the proper officer) to appoint a person from the panel.[186] If an arbitrator

177 Local Authorities Agreement para 6.2.
178 Local Authorities Agreement para 6.3.
179 See paras **7.156–7.165**.
180 Local Authorities Agreement paras 5.4, 5.6. See above, paras **5.55–5.56** and **5.62**.
181 Usually a period of more than 30 working days from the date of initial application: Local Authorities Agreement para 7.4.
182 Local Authorities Agreement para 7.4.
183 Local Authorities Agreement para 10.1.
184 Homelessness (Decisions on Referrals) Order ('Homelessness Order') 1998, SI 1998/1578, Schedule paras 1 and 2; Local Authorities Agreement para 10.3.
185 Homelessness Order 1998, Schedule para 3; Local Authorities Agreement para 10.3.
186 Homelessness Order 1998, Schedule para 4(1); Local Authorities Agreement para 10.5.

has not been appointed within six weeks of the date of notification, the notifying authority must request the proper officer to appoint a referee from the panel.[187]

5.84   The referee must invite written representations from both the notifying and the notified authority.[188] The referee may also invite further written representations from the authorities, written representations from any other person[189] and oral representations from any person.[190] The Local Authorities Agreement suggests[191] that, where an oral hearing is necessary or more convenient (for example, where the applicant is illiterate, where English is not the applicant's first language or where further information is necessary to resolve the dispute), the notifying authority should be invited to present its case first, followed by the notified authority and any other persons whom the referee wishes to hear.

5.85   It is for the referee to arrange the venue, although it is suggested that the offices of the notifying authority will often be the most convenient location.[192] Where a person has made oral representations, the referee may direct that reasonable travelling expenses are paid by either or both authorities.[193]

5.86   It is no part of the referee's duties to enquire into matters preceding a local connection reference: homelessness, eligibility, priority need or intentional homelessness.[194]

5.87   The referee must notify both authorities of their decision and the reasons for it.[195] The Local Authorities Agreement[196] suggests a target of one month for the decision, from receipt of the authorities' written submissions. There is no obligation on the referee to notify the applicant of their decision – that is the notifying authority's duty.[197]

5.88   The previous regulations[198] provided that the decision of the referee was final and binding on the authorities. No such provision is included in the current regulations, but the Local Authorities Agreement states[199] that the decision is binding on the participating authorities, subject to the applicant's right to review.[200]

---

187 Homelessness Order 1998, Schedule para 4(2); Local Authorities Agreement para 10.6.
188 Homelessness Order 1998, Schedule para 5(2); Local Authorities Agreement para 14.2.
189 Most obviously the applicant, who the Local Authorities Agreement suggests (paras 14.3–14.4), should be supplied with copies of the authorities' submissions. Representations may be made by someone, whether or not legally qualified, acting on behalf of the person invited to submit them: Homelessness Order 1998, Schedule para 5(4).
190 Homelessness Order 1998, Schedule para 5(3).
191 Local Authorities Agreement para 15.1.
192 Local Authorities Agreement para 15.2.
193 Homelessness Order 1998, Schedule para 7(2); Local Authorities Agreement para 15.3.
194 *R v Slough BC ex p Ealing LBC* [1981] QB 801, CA.
195 Homelessness Order 1998, Schedule para 6.
196 Local Authorities Agreement para 14.5.
197 HA 1996, s 200(2); H(W)A 2014, s 82(2).
198 Housing (Homeless Persons) (Appropriate Arrangements) Order 1978, SI 1978/69.
199 Local Authorities Agreement para 16.1.
200 See paras **7.190–7.204**.

Once a referee has made the determination, the referee should not reopen the case, even though facts may be presented to them, unless it is to rectify an error arising from a mistake or omission.[201] The proviso that the decision is final and binding on the authority does not, however, prevent challenge on the grounds that the decision is wrong in law.[202]

5.89   The notifying and notified authorities pay their own costs of the determination.[203] Unlike the 1978 Order,[204] there is no explicit discretion for the referee to make a costs order against either party. The Local Authorities Agreement suggests,[205] however, that the referee's fees and expenses, and any third party costs, would usually be recovered from the unsuccessful party to the dispute, although the referee may choose to apportion expenses between the authorities if the referee considers it warranted.

Post-resolution procedure

5.90   If the burden of providing housing does not shift to the notified authority, it will remain with the notifying authority[206] and the principal housing duty under HA 1996, s 193[207] will apply.[208]

5.91   The mere fact that an authority has unsuccessfully sought to shift the burden on to another authority is not a basis on which to alter the original decision that the applicant has not become homeless intentionally. If the duty does pass to the notified authority, it will (in the case of an English authority) be a HA 1996, s 193 duty and (in Wales) be a duty under either H(W)A 2014, s 68 or s 73.[209]

CROSS-BORDER REFERRALS

Wales

5.92   The local connection provisions governing referral are largely the same in Wales as in England.[210] Duties are, however, different: see Chapter 8.

---

201 Local Authorities Agreement para 20.1.
202 See Chapter 10.
203 Homelessness Order 1998, Schedule para 7(1).
204 Housing (Homeless Persons) (Appropriate Arrangements) Order 1978, SI 1978/69.
205 Local Authorities Agreement para 19.3.
206 HA 1996, s 200(3); H(W)A 2014, s 82(3).
207 In Wales, H(W)A 2014, s 73.
208 See Chapter 8.
209 Where an English authority refers to another English authority, see HA 1996, s 200(4); where an English authority refers to a Welsh authority, see H(W)A 2014, s 83; where a Welsh authority refers to an English authority, see HA 1996, s 201A; and, where a Welsh authority refers to another Welsh authority, see H(W)A 2014, s 82(4).
210 And sources have been provided accordingly.

5.93   When a reference is made by an authority in Wales to an English authority, and the final duty lies with the English authority, the English authority will owe a duty to house[211] under HA 1996, s 193;[212] otherwise, the application continues to be dealt with under the Welsh legislation.[213] Where the reference is by an English authority to one in Wales, with which the final duty is agreed or held to lie, it is the Welsh provisions which will apply;[214] otherwise, the application remains with the English authority.[215]

5.94   Although an English authority can normally seek to transfer the relief duty to another authority,[216] this is not so if the other authority is in Wales.[217] Accordingly, it is only the duty to secure housing, ie, the final duty, which is transferable. Nonetheless, even though the English authority will have been under, and will have brought to an end, its relief duty, the Welsh authority will also still be subject to that duty, albeit in its Welsh[218] form.[219]

5.95   In the reverse case, ie, where a Welsh authority seeks to refer the application to an English authority, a Welsh authority is under no relief duty if it refers the application to another authority,[220] including an English authority, but it can only refer an application where the applicant is in priority need and unintentionally homeless.[221] It would seem, therefore, that where the Welsh authority considers that there is the prospect of a referral, it will proceed to reach a full decision on all the key elements and[222] such an applicant will at no time benefit from the relief duty but will proceed directly to the full duty imposed by HA 1996, s 193.

Scotland

5.96   Scottish authorities may refer an applicant to an English or Welsh authority in the circumstances set out in Housing (Scotland) Act 1987, s 33.[223] Where such a reference is made, and agreed or upheld, the provisions which relate to England are applicable.[224]

---

211 Para **5.108**.
212 HA 1996, s 201A.
213 HA 1996, s 201A; H(W)A 2014, s 80.
214 H(W)A 2014, s 83.
215 HA 1996, s 200; H(W)A 2014, s 83.
216 Paras **5.64–5.67**.
217 HA 1996, s 198(A1).
218 Paras **8.104–8.105**.
219 H(W)A 2014, s 83(2).
220 H(W)A 2014, s 73(2).
221 H(W)A 2014, s 80(1)(a).
222 Premising that the referral is agreed or upheld.
223 Scottish law is beyond the scope of this book, but it may be said that the circumstances are very similar indeed to those in England and Wales.
224 HA 1996, s 201.

5.97 There is no corresponding provision in the Welsh legislation governing referrals between Scotland and Wales; it remains open for consideration, therefore, whether HA 1996, s 201 – which was originally applicable to Wales before the homelessness provisions of HA 1996, Part 7 were replaced by those of H(W)A 2014, Part 2 – continues to apply in such a case, ie, whether s 201 can be construed as filling the gap.

Resolution of disputes

5.98 It has been noted that the CoSLA and the WLGA were parties to the Local Authorities Agreement in 2006.[225]

5.99 Disputes between an English and a Welsh authority may be decided by agreement between them.[226] In default, the Homelessness (Decisions on Referrals) Order 1998[227] applied to Wales and, as it has not been repealed or replaced by any legislation made by the Welsh Ministers, continues to apply in Wales,[228] although there is power for the English Secretary of State and the Welsh Ministers to make a joint order in its place.[229] There is no order that directly deals with referrals to Scotland.[230]

NOTIFICATION DUTIES

5.100 The power to refer an application to another authority begins, in relation both to a referral designed to transfer the relief duty and a referral after that duty has come to an end which is designed to transfer the duty to secure housing, with notification to the applicant.[231] The notification must inform the applicant of the referral and of the authority's reasons.[232] The notification must inform the applicant of their right to seek a review, and the time within which the request must be made.[233]

5.101 Only a decision to notify in relation to the duty to secure housing is – apparently – subject to review.[234]

225 Para **5.4**.
226 HA 1996, s 198(5A).
227 Homelessness (Decisions on Referrals) Order 1998, SI 1998/1578.
228 Welsh Code para 18.30.
229 HA 1996, s 198(5A).
230 See the Homelessness (Decisions on Referrals) (Scotland) Order 1998, SI 1998/1603, made under Housing (Scotland) Act 1987, s 33, for the provisions applicable there.
231 HA 1996, s 198(A1), (1).
232 HA 1996, s 184(4); H(W)A 2014, s 84.
233 HA 1996, s 184(5); H(W)A 2014, s 84(1).
234 HA 1996, s 202(1)(c). This appears to be an oversight: see further para **5.106** for discussion of whether it is nonetheless possible to seek a review of a decision to seek to transfer the relief duty. H(W)A 2014, s 85(1)(c).

5.102 Once it has been agreed or decided[235] whether the conditions for referral are met, likewise in relation to either duty, the notifying authority must give the applicant notice of the decision and of the reasons for it, and must inform the applicant of their right to request a review of the decision and of the time within which such a request must be made.[236]

5.103 Notices must be in writing and, if not received by the applicant, are treated as given if made available at the authority's office for a reasonable period for collection by the applicant or on their behalf.[237]

REVIEWS

5.104 The detailed provisions governing reviews generally are considered in Chapter 7.[238] As noted, review may be sought of a decision to refer to another authority, at least when it is sought to transfer the duty to secure housing,[239] and when it is decided which authority has responsibility for securing housing under these provisions. It seems clear that a review can encompass the 'decision' of the arbitrator.[240] Thus, an applicant has two opportunities to challenge a referral: a) on the decision to refer; and b) on the outcome of the referral. There is, however, no review of a decision not to make a local connection referral.[241]

5.105 A decision that the conditions of referral are met may be reached either as a result of an agreement between the authorities, or as the result of an arbitration between them. It may at first glance seem somewhat surprising to find provision for review of a decision that the conditions for referral are met when it is statutorily provided that this is to be a matter for agreement or approved arbitration arrangements.[242] It needs to be remembered, however, that the applicant is themselves party to neither agreement nor arbitration: this is accordingly the applicant's opportunity to dispute the outcome.

235 Ie, by arbitration: paras **5.83–5.89**.
236 HA 1996, ss 199A(3), 200(2); in Wales, H(W)A 2014, ss 82(2) and 84.
237 HA 1996, ss 184(6), 199A(7), 200(6); H(W)A 2014, s 84(3), (4).
238 Paras **7.190–7.260**.
239 Para **5.71**.
240 HA 1996, s 202(1)(d) explicitly conferring such a right in relation to a decision under s 189(5) whether the conditions are met *not* involving a referral to a Welsh authority, not limited to a decision by an authority (cf other provisions in s 202(1)). It is not so clear that it is available where the referral is by an English authority to a Welsh authority: there is no reference in s 202(1) to a decision under s 189(5A); on the other hand, there can be a review of a decision under s 200(3), (4) – where it is decided that the conditions for referral are met so that the duty passes to the notified authority – which explicitly includes referrals to a Welsh authority.
241 *Hackney LBC v Sareen* [2003] EWCA Civ 351, [2003] HLR 54.
242 See paras **5.83–5.89**.

5.106   Notwithstanding the references to reviews in HA 1996, s 199A(6) (referral of relief duty) which explicitly applies to s 199A(2)[243] and (4)(c),[244] HA 1996, s 202(1)[245] as amended by HRA 2017 does not specify a decision that no further duty is owed under s 199A as one of those of which a review may be sought.[246] This appears to be an oversight and the courts may decide that the express references to review in s 199A(6) are sufficient to conclude that there is a right.

5.107   Decisions on how the duty is to be discharged may themselves also be reviewed. This includes discharge both where the local connection referral conditions are met[247] and where they are not.[248]

ACCOMMODATION PENDING RESOLUTION AND PROTECTION OF PROPERTY

5.108   Until it is decided whether or not the conditions for referral mean that a duty[249] will transfer, it is the duty of the notifying authority to secure that accommodation is available for an applicant in priority need until they are notified of the outcome of the referral.[250] It will continue to be under such a duty if it is decided that the conditions for referral are not met.[251] The duty ends even if there is a request for a review, although the authority has a discretion to continue it pending the decision on review.[252]

5.109   So long as it remains under a duty towards the applicant, whether to accommodate pending enquiries or pending resolution of a local connection referral, the notifying authority also has duties in relation to the protection of the applicant's property.[253]

5.110   The law applicable to the provision of temporary accommodation under other provisions of HA 1996, Part 7 is considered in chapter 8, and will be applicable to interim accommodation for those potentially or actually to be

---

243 Interim duty to housing pending outcome of referral: para **5.108**.
244 Duty on notifying authority if conditions not met: para **5.66**.
245 Which specifies when a review lies: see paras **5.104–5.107**.
246 In contrast, it does so when the local connection referral is under HA 1996, s 198(1): see s 202(1)(e).
247 HA 1996, s 200(4).
248 HA 1996, s 200(3).
249 Whether relief or to secure housing.
250 HA 1996, s 199A(2); H(WA) 2014, s 82(1). It is not wholly clear that in Wales this is confined to applicants in priority need, as s 82(1) does not include this requirement; on the other hand, s 82(1) is directed to what follows interim accommodation under s 68, which is so confined. The Welsh Code assumes that the applicant must be in priority need: paras 18.2–18.3.
251 HA 1996, s 199A(4); H(W)A 2014, s 82(3).
252 HA 1996, s 199A(6); H(W)A 2014, s 82(5), (6).
253 HA 1996, s 211(2); H(W)A 2014, s 93; see chapter 6.

referred to another authority: see the observations on quality[254] and termination made in relation to interim accommodation,[255] those on availability,[256] payment[257] and security,[258] exclusion from Protection from Eviction Act 1977[259] and defences on eviction.[260]

5.111   How accommodation may be provided,[261] suitability[262] and the constraints on out-of-area placements,[263] which are all considered in chapter 8 in relation to the principal housing duty under HA 1996, s 193 and H(W)A 2014, s 75, also apply to discharge under this section.

254 Paras **8.38–8.41**.
255 Paras **8.43–8.47**.
256 Para **8.28**.
257 Paras **8.32–8.33**.
258 Paras **8.34–8.37**.
259 Para **8.48**.
260 Para **8.49**.
261 See paras **8.148-150**.
262 See paras **8.183–8.234**.
263 See para **8.160–8.182**.

Protection of property

INTRODUCTION

6.1   Both Housing Act (HA) 1996, Part 7 and Housing (Wales) Act (H(W)A) 2014, Part 2 make provision for local housing authorities to take steps to protect the property of homeless people. These provisions – which appeared in the Housing (Homeless Persons) Act 1977 and the HA 1985 – are of considerable practical importance. Failure to take steps to protect the belongings of those who are homeless or threatened with homelessness can only have the effect of prolonging or worsening their economic position.

6.2   HA 1996, Part 7 and H(W)A 2014, Part 2 each contain:

a)   a duty to protect property in some circumstances; and

b)   a power to do so in others.

The discharge of this duty and the power[1] are not co-extensive with the discharge of housing duties and it is necessary, therefore, to consider these property provisions in their own right. Authorities do not necessarily have to discharge duties themselves, but can contract them out – this is discussed at the start of Chapter 7.

TO WHOM IS A DUTY OWED?

6.3   In England, the duty is owed[2] to an applicant towards whom the authority has become subject to a duty under one of the following provisions of the HA 1996:

---

1   Both of which may be contracted out; see paras **7.6–7.8**.
2   HA 1996, s 211(2).

a)   section 188 – interim accommodation;

b)   section 190 – temporary accommodation for the intentionally homeless in priority need;

c)   section 193 – full duty;

d)   section 195 – accommodation for those threatened with homelessness, in priority need and not so threatened intentionally; and

e)   section 200 – accommodation for those who are or have been the subject of a local connection issue.

In addition, the duty is owed to someone who is reasonably to be expected to reside with the applicant, ie, for whom housing must also be provided.[3] Since the Homelessness Reduction Act (HRA) 2017 came into force on 3 April 2018,[4] the property duty is also owed where the authority has become subject to the initial duty to help under HA 1996, s 189B (paras **8.79–8.83**).[5]

6.4   In Wales, the duty is owed[6] to an applicant towards whom the authority has become subject to a duty under one of the following provisions of the H(W)A 2014:

a)   section 66 – duty to prevent an applicant who is in priority need from becoming homeless;

b)   section 68 – interim accommodation;

c)   section 75 – full duty; and

d)   section 82 – accommodation for those who are or have been the subject of a local connection issue.

In addition, the duty is owed to someone who might reasonably be expected to reside with the applicant.[7]

WHEN IS THE DUTY OWED?

6.5   The duty is owed when the authority has reason to believe that:

a)   by reason of the applicant's inability to protect or deal with it, there is a danger of loss of, or damage to, any personal property of the applicant or other person to whom the duty is owed; and

b)   no other suitable arrangements have been or are being made.[8]

---

3   HA 1996, s 211(5).
4   Homelessness Reduction Act 2017 (Commencement and Transitional and Savings Provisions) Regulations 2018, SI 2018/167, reg 3, only applicable to applications made and reviews sought on or after that date – see reg 4.
5   HA 1996, s 211(2).
6   H(W)A 2014, s 93(2).
7   H(W)A 2014, s 93(6).
8   HA 1996, s 211(1); H(W)A 2014, s 93(1).

'Danger' of loss or damage means a likelihood of harm, not merely a possibility.[9]

6.6   The duty continues until the authority is of the opinion that there is no longer any reason to believe that there is a danger of loss of, or damage to, that property by reason of the applicant's inability to protect or deal with it, or that of someone else to whom the duty is owed.[10]

6.7   The duty is owed not only when the authority is subject to one of the prescribed duties, but also when it has been.[11] For example, a person may be evicted from accommodation and subsequently be held to be homeless intentionally. The former landlord may have been willing to hold on to the person's property for a period of time. That period may be no longer than the period for which accommodation has been provided under HA 1996, s 190(2) (a). If, after the expiry of s 190(2)(a) accommodation, the property duty has not expired, application may yet be made for assistance under s 211 and, if the relevant conditions are fulfilled, the authority will be obliged to provide it.

6.8   Even when the property duty has expired, because the authority has formed the view that there is no further danger of loss of or damage to the property, or that the applicant is no longer unable to protect or deal with it, the authority has power to continue to protect that property.[12] Property may be kept in store; the conditions on which it was taken into store will continue to have effect, with any necessary modifications.[13]

6.9   Both the English and Welsh Codes of Guidance illustrate inability to protect property with the example of a person who is ill or who cannot afford to have their property placed in store.[14] The English Code also suggests that a person could be deemed capable of taking back responsibility if they are no longer ill, or have obtained accommodation, or are able to afford the cost of storage.[15]

WHAT IS THE DUTY?

6.10   The duty is to take reasonable steps to prevent loss or prevent or mitigate damage to the property.[16] In order to discharge the duty, the authority has power of

---

9   *Deadman v Southwark LBC* (2001) 33 HLR 75, CA.
10   HA 1996, s 212(3); H(W)A 2014, s 94(6).
11   HA 1996, s 211(2); H(W)A 2014, s 93(3).
12   HA 1996, s 212(3); H(W)A 2014, s 94(7).
13   HA 1996, s 212(3); H(W)A 2014, s 94(7).
14   English *Homelessness code of guidance for local authorities*, para 20.6); Welsh Code para 11.16.
15   English Code of Guidance para 20.11; there is no equivalent example in the Welsh Code.
16   HA 1996, s 211(2); H(W)A 2014, s 93(1).

entry on to private property.[17] At all reasonable times, it may enter any premises which are 'the usual place of residence of the applicant or which were his last usual place of residence', and deal with the applicant's property in any way that is reasonably necessary, including by storing or arranging to store the property.[18]

6.11   The duty is owed in respect of 'personal property'. In *Roberts*,[19] there are dicta that suggest that this would not extend to equipment used by an applicant in their business, at any rate where the business is conducted other than at the accommodation.

6.12   The authority generally has responsibility for arranging storage. It may, however, refuse to exercise the duty except on appropriate conditions.[20] This means such conditions as it considers appropriate in a particular case, and can include conditions empowering it:

a)   to charge for discharge of the duty; and

b)   to dispose of the property in respect of which it discharged the duty, in such circumstances as may be specified.[21]

6.13   Both the English and the Welsh Codes suggest[22] that the authority might dispose of the property if it loses touch with the person concerned and is unable to trace them after a specified period. Whether or not a charge is made or a duty to store exists, the authority must, as bailee of the property, take reasonable care of it, and deliver it up when reasonably requested to do so. Failure to do this will render the authority liable to damages, even if the failure to deliver up is accidental, albeit a negligent accident.[23] The standard of care is high; the burden of disproving negligence when damage has resulted from an accident lies on the authority, as bailee.[24]

6.14   The position set out in the above paragraphs may, however, need to be considered in the light of Local Government (Miscellaneous Provisions) Act (LG(MP)A) 1982, s 41. That section applies wherever property comes into the possession of a local authority, after being found on premises owned or managed

---

17   HA 1996, s 212(1); H(W)A 2014, s 94(1). Such provisions were also to be found in the National Assistance Act 1948, s 48.

18   HA 1996, s 212(1); H(W)A 2014, s 94(1).Under H(W)A 2014, s 94(2), where the authority proposes to exercise a power of entry, the officer it authorises to do so must, on request, produce valid documentation setting out the authorisation. A person who without reasonable excuse obstructs the exercise of the power of entry commits an offence and, on summary conviction, is liable for a fine not exceeding level 4 on the standard scale (currently £2,500) (H(W)A 2014, s 94(3)). There is no equivalent to either of these provisions in England.

19   *R v Chiltern DC ex p Roberts* (1990) 23 HLR 387, QBD.

20   HA 1996, s 211(4); H(W)A 2014, s 93(4).

21   HA 1996, s 211(4); H(W)A 2014, s 93(4).

22   English Code of Guidance para 20.10; Welsh Code para 11.19.

23   *Mitchell v Ealing LBC* [1979] QB 1.

24   *Port Swettenham Authority v TW Wu & Co* [1979] AC 580, PC (Malaysia).

by it, or property has been deposited with the local authority and is not collected from it in accordance with the terms on which it was deposited.

6.15   LG(MP)A 1982, s 41 entitles the authority to give the owner or depositor of the property notice in writing that it requires them to collect the property by a date specified in the notice, and that if they do not do so the property will vest in the authority as from that date. If the person notified then fails to comply with the notice, the property vests in the authority on that date.

6.16   The date to be specified has to be not less than one month from the date of the notice. When an authority finds property, as distinct from when property is deposited with it, and it appears to it that it is impossible to serve a notice, the property vests in it one month from the date when it found the property. In any other case, including deposit, if the authority is satisfied after reasonable enquiry that it is impossible to serve notice, the property vests in it six months after the property was deposited with it or six months from the date when the period from which the property was deposited with it expired, whichever is the later.

6.17   Perishable property, and property which would involve the authority in unreasonable expense or inconvenience storing, may, in any event, be sold or otherwise disposed of by the authority as it thinks fit. In such a case, the proceeds of sale vest in the authority on the same date as the property itself would have done were it not perishable or too inconvenient or expensive to store. If property is claimed by its owner prior to the date when it vests in the authority, the owner can collect it on payment to the authority of its costs in storing the property, and in making enquiries or carrying out any of the other steps referred to in this section.

6.18   There is no express reference in the LG(MP)A 1982 to the provisions of the Housing (Homeless Persons) Act 1977, nor (by way of amendment) to the HA 1985 nor HA 1996, Part 7 nor H(W)A 2014, Part 2. The courts may therefore take the view that references to the LG(MP)A 1982 to 'property deposited' with the authority do not include property taken into safe-keeping under HA 1996, s 211 or H(W)A 2014, s 93. If so, the HA 1996, Part 7 (or H(W)A 2014, Part 2) provisions only will apply. Otherwise, the LG(MP)A 1982 makes it somewhat easier for authorities to limit the impact of their HA 1996, s 211 or H(W)A 2014, s 93 duties.

THE POWER TO PROTECT PROPERTY

6.19   The authority has power to take the identical steps to prevent loss of property, or to prevent or mitigate damage to it, as it is obliged to take under the duty described above, in any case where there is no duty to do so.[25] This power

---

25   HA 1996, s 211(3); H(W)A 2014, s 93(5).

might benefit those not in priority need of accommodation or those who, though in priority need, are only threatened with homelessness, and in respect of whom no decision on intentionality has yet been taken. It might also benefit current or former members of the armed forces who may, eg, have previously had many decisions, including as to their property, taken for them,[26] once the amendments made by the Armed Forces Act 2021 are considered.[27]

6.20   Where the authority exercises this power, it has the same ancillary powers as in relation to the duty – ie, entry into premises, imposing conditions, etc.

NOTIFICATION OF CESSATION OF RESPONSIBILITY

6.21   When the authority considers that it no longer has a duty or a power to protect property, it is obliged to notify the person towards whom it was subject to the duty, or in relation to whose property it has exercised the power:

a) that it has ceased to be subject to the duty, or to enjoy the power; and

b) why it is of the opinion that the duty or power has come to an end.[28]

The notification must be by personal delivery to the person to be notified or by leaving it or sending it by post to their last known address.[29]

26 Ie, may be suffering from a degree of institutionalisation.
27 When exercising any function under Parts 6 or 7, HA 1996, a local authority must have regard to: the unique obligations of, and sacrifices made by, the armed forces, the principle that it is desirable to remove disadvantages arising for service people from membership, or former membership, of the armed forces, and the principle that special provision for service people may be justified by the effects on such people of membership, or former membership, of the armed forces: Armed Forces Act 2006, ss 343AA (England) and 343AB (Wales), added by Armed Forces Act 2021, s 8(3).
28 HA 1996, s 212(4); H(W)A 2014, s 94(8).
29 HA 1996, s 212(5); H(W)A 2014, s 94(9).

CHAPTER 7

Homelessness decisions

INTRODUCTION

Overview

7.1   The previous chapters have addressed the elements of entitlement as homeless. This and the following chapters are concerned with:

a) the procedure by which an applicant applies as homeless;

b) the procedures to be followed by an authority on receipt of the application;

c) the formal requirements concerning the authority's decision-making process;

d) the right to request an internal review of an adverse decision; and

e) the method by which the duty (if any) is discharged.

7.2   The next chapter is concerned with the discharge of duty – this chapter is therefore concerned with the steps from application to decision and (if any) to review. This process involves a number of steps:

a) application;

b) enquiry into the application;

c) initial decision;

d) request for a review;

e) further enquiries on review;

f) 'minded to find' letter where necessary;

g) review decision.

Preliminary points

Changes in law and attitude

7.3   A number of points may be made at the outset. First, it is to be remembered that the body of homelessness law is organic and develops over time, whether court-led, by the introduction of new legislation and/or through the relationship between housing and other areas of public law,[1] so that reliance on previous court decisions may not always be possible.

7.4   It may also be thought that attitudes have changed over the – now – half century of homelessness law, from a then (1977) novel acceptance that homelessness was a societal rather than personal problem (as discussed in Chapter 1) which may have led to some somewhat anachronistic attitudes on the part of the judiciary (not to say hesitant) to a much greater recognition of the part national policies – housing, welfare benefits, immigration – have played, accompanied by a greater recognition of, or respect for, the independent position of individual members of family units, eg, for the position of women. Older cases, while still available to inform the operation of the law, may therefore need to be treated with some caution.

Decision-making

7.5   The second point of general significance is the question of who may discharge the various duties under Housing Act (HA) 1996, Part 7 or Housing (Wales) Act (H(W)A) 2014. It is common for decision-making in relation to homelessness to be delegated to an individual officer; the reviewing function – which in England[2] must in any event be conducted by a person senior to the

---

1   Including the impact of immigration law and European law on the issue of eligibility (Annex: Immigration Eligibility) and of human rights law on the extent of housing duties. See generally Chapter 10.

2   But not in Wales, where regulations only require that the reviewing officer be someone who was not involved in the original decision, see Homelessness (Review Procedure) (Wales) Regulations 2015, SI 2015/1266 reg 3; see also Welsh Code para 20.9.

person carrying out the initial decision – is sometimes reserved to a panel rather than an individual, whether a panel of members, officers or both.

7.6   Under the Local Authorities (Contracting Out of Allocation of Housing and Homelessness Functions) Order 1996,[3] an authority may 'contract out' all or part[4] of its homelessness functions (including enquiries or reviews),[5] save for functions relating to:[6] the provision of advisory services;[7] assistance for voluntary organisations;[8] and the duty to co-operate with relevant housing authorities and bodies.[9]

7.7   A contract may be for a period of up to 10 years, but 'may be revoked at any time' by the authority.[10] A challenge to the legality of a particular contracting out arrangement is a point of law which may be raised on an appeal[11] to the county court; the county court is not confined to considering errors that are intrinsic to the making of the decision or to the events during the period between the request for a review and the review decision; but a decision reached without authority on the ground that it did not fall within the parameters of the agreement, eg, because it had expired, can be ratified retrospectively, at least if the defect in the decision has 'nothing to do with the merits of the matter' and deprives the applicant of 'no genuine legal right'.[12]

7.8   The 1996 Order continues to apply in Wales, even after the commencement of the H(W)A 2014.[13]

Relationship between decision and review

7.9   A third preliminary point should be made in relation to enquiries. Authorities are under obligations to conduct all relevant enquiries when an

---

3   Contracting Out of Allocation of Housing and Homelessness Functions) Order 1996, SI 1996/3205. See further para **10.57**.
4   Deregulation and Contracting Out Act 1994, ss 70(4) and 69(5).
5   The 'public sector equality duty' imposed on authorities by Equality Act (EqA) 2010, s 149 does not prevent contracting out: first, the decisions of the contractor are treated as the decision of the authority by Deregulation and Contracting Out Act 1994, s 72; in any event, the contractor is performing a public function and, as such, is bound by the same duty under section 149(2) – see *Panayiotou v Waltham Forest LBC; Smith v Haringey LBC* [2017] EWCA Civ 1624, [2017] HLR 48.
6   Allocation of Housing and Homelessness Functions) Order 1996, SI 1996/3205, art 3 and Sch 2.
7   See para **12.20**.
8   See para **12.29**.
9   See para **7.73**.
10   Local Authorities (Contracting Out of Allocation of Housing and Homelessness Functions) Order 1996, SI 1996/3205, art 3 and Sch 2.
11   See para **10.3**.
12   *James v Hertsmere BC* [2020] EWCA Civ 489, [2020] WLR 3606, [2020] HLR 28 at [45].
13   See Housing (Wales) Act 2014 (Consequential Amendments) Regulations 2015/752, amending the 1996 Order.

application is received – it would nonetheless be wrong to proceed on the basis that a failure to do so (or that there is a defect in the enquiries process) is sufficient immediately to vitiate the decision-making process.

7.10 The availability of a review of a decision affords an applicant an opportunity to remedy any perceived failure to conduct enquiries; it goes further than this, because it can be said positively to require the applicant to draw to the authority's attention all matters that the applicant wishes to be considered or in relation to which they believe there to be a need for enquiries.[14] In this sense, the review process serves to remedy any failures in the initial enquiry process, without necessarily vitiating it.

7.11 Otherwise, although the substance of the duties on enquiries is discussed below in relation to the application itself,[15] the same principles apply both to the initial enquiries and on review.

Decision and discretion

7.12 A further preliminary point may be made in relation to the nature of decisions. While there are some elements of discretion in the provisions, decisions on the key issues – eg, homelessness, priority need, intentionality and whether there is a local connection – involve consideration and determination of the facts and the correct application to them of the law: this is not 'discretionary decision-making' in the way that term is otherwise used and understood.[16]

Armed Forces

7.13 The final preliminary point is to note that the provisions of the Armed Forces Act 2006, ss 343AA (England) and 343AB (Wales),[17] must be kept in mind when reaching any decision under Part 7, that the authority must have regard to:

'(a) the unique obligations of, and sacrifices made by, the armed forces,

(b) the principle that it is desirable to remove disadvantages arising for service people from membership, or former membership, of the armed forces, and

(c) the principle that special provision for service people may be justified by the effects on such people of membership, or former membership, of the armed forces.'

---

14 See, eg, *Bellouti v Wandsworth LBC* [2005] EWCA Civ 602, [2005] HLR 46 and *Ciftci v Haringey LBC* [2021] EWCA 1772; [2022] HLR 9.

15 Under HA 1996, s 184(1).

16 *Tachie v Welwyn Hatfield BC* [2013] EWHC 3972 (QB), [26]–[27], approved in *Panayiotou v Waltham Forest LBC; Smith v Haringey LBC* [2017] EWCA Civ 1624, [2017] HLR 48, [81]–[84].

17 Added by s 8(3), Armed Forces Act 2021.

APPLICATIONS

Who can apply?

Generally

7.14   Applications as homeless may in principle be made by any person who is lawfully in the country. 'Lawfully' in this context means 'not unlawfully', ie, someone who is not an offender under Immigration Act 1971, s 14 – see *Castelli and Tristran-Garcia, Tower Hamlets* and *Streeting*.[18] Accordingly, 'applicant' under HA 1996, Part 7 means any person who applies to a local housing authority for accommodation, or for assistance in obtaining accommodation, whom the authority has reason to believe is or may be homeless, or threatened with homelessness.[19]

7.15   In Wales, 'applicant' means any person who applies to a local housing authority for accommodation or help in retaining or obtaining accommodation, and whom it appears to the authority may be homeless or threatened with homelessness.[20] If the person has previously been assessed for assistance under H(W)A 2014, Part 2, then there must have been a material change in circumstances since the previous assessment or new information which materially affects the assessment must have come to light, before they will be considered an applicant again.[21]

7.16   Subject to these qualifications, it follows that anyone – regardless of whether they have a local connection with the authority (or any other authority in the UK)[22] – is entitled to make an application, and refusal to permit them to do so is a breach of duty. This bald proposition does, however, merit a number of qualifications.

Qualifications

Immigrants

7.17   As noted,[23] a person unlawfully in the UK will not be permitted to make an application. An authority is entitled to reach its own decision as to whether or not an applicant for assistance is disqualified as such an illegal immigrant, albeit:

a)   only for its own purposes; and

b)   subject to a contrary decision by the Home Secretary.[24]

---

18   *R v Westminster City Council ex p Castelli and Tristran-Garcia* (1996) 28 HLR 617, CA; *R v Secretary of State for the Environment ex p Tower Hamlets LBC* [1993] QB 632, 25 HLR 524, CA; *R v Hillingdon LBC ex p Streeting (No 2)* [1980] 1 WLR 1425, CA. A person is lawfully here even where the person has only been given temporary permission to enter, eg, as an asylum-seeker: *Szoma v Secretary of State for Work and Pensions* [2005] UKHL 64, [2006] 1 All ER 1.

19   HA 1996, s 183(1), (2); See *R (Edwards and others) v Birmingham City Council* [2016] EWHC 173 (Admin), [2016] HLR 11.

20   H(W)A 2014, s 62(1).

21   H(W)A 2014, s 62(2).

22   *R v Hillingdon LBC ex p Streeting (No 2)*, above.

23   See para **7.14**.

24   See *Castelli and Tristran-Garcia* and *ex p Tower Hamlets LBC*, above.

7.18   If, after the housing authority has decided the issue against an applicant, the immigration authorities later determine the issue of legality in the applicant's favour, or else decide not to take immigration action against the applicant, they will cease to be an illegal immigrant for the purposes of HA 1996, Part 7 (or H(W)A 2014, Part 2), and will be entitled to apply. The question of more detailed immigration status will then govern the question of eligibility.[25]

7.19   If a person has already been granted accommodation by the authority, questions of status do not deprive the person of their rights under the accommodation agreement: see *Akinbolu v Hackney LBC*.[26]

7.20   In *Tower Hamlets*,[27] it was held – by concession – that, in addition to making enquiries of the immigration authorities and providing them with information, the authority was under a positive duty to report suspected illegal immigrants to the immigration authorities.

Dependent children

7.21   A dependent child cannot apply in their own right: see *Garlick* and *Bentum*.[28] Children are expected to be provided for by those on whom they are dependent (with – where appropriate and qualifying – assistance under HA 1996, Part 7 or H(W)A 2014, Part 2).

7.22   The emphasis here is on 'dependent' children. The statutory scheme itself envisages the possibility of minors – 16- or 17-year-olds – applying as homeless.[29] It may be that subsequent enquiries disclose a family home to which the minor can return, but the absence of such at the date of the application is sufficient to require an application to be received and considered.

Capacity

7.23   A person must be capable of accepting or rejecting an offer of accommodation or assistance in order to qualify as an applicant: see *Begum*.[30]

---

25   See Annex: Immigration Eligibility.
26   (1996) 29 HLR 259, CA.
27   *R v Secretary of State for the Environment ex p Tower Hamlets LBC*, above.
28   *R v Oldham MBC ex p Garlick; R v Bexley LBC ex p Bentum; R v Tower Hamlets LBC ex p Begum* [1993] AC 509, (1993) 25 HLR 319, HL.
29   See Homelessness (Priority Need for Accommodation) (England) Order 2002, SI 2002/2051 arts 3, 4; and H(W)A 2014, s 70(1)(f); see paras **3.82–3.89**.
30   *R v Tower Hamlets LBC ex p Begum* [1993] AC 509, (1993) 25 HLR 319, HL. This remains good law notwithstanding Article 14 of the European Convention on Human Rights (which has been applied to disability, even though not specifically mentioned in it: see *AM (Somalia) v Entry Clearance Officer* [2009] EWCA Civ 634, [2009] UKHRR 1073): see *R (MT, by his father as litigation friend) v Oxford City Council* [2015] EWHC 795 (Admin). Where a deputy is appointed under the Mental Capacity Act 2005, who has been given power to make decisions about where a person should live or whether they should acquire property, they may apply on the person's behalf for homelessness assistance: *WB (by her litigation friend, the Official Solicitor) v W District Council* [2018] EWCA Civ 982, [2019] QB 625, [2018] HLR 30.

Persons so disabled that they have neither the capacity themselves to apply nor to authorise an agent on their behalf do not qualify unless a deputy is appointed to make decisions under the Mental Capacity Act 2005. There must otherwise be the capacity to understand and respond to the offer, and to undertake its responsibilities; whether or not a person so qualifies is a matter for the authority.

Transfers

7.24   In *Pattinson*,[31] it was suggested that an application for housing by an existing tenant of the authority is usually to be presumed to be an application for transfer, rather than for assistance under HA 1996, Part 7. That approach was, however, rejected in *ex p B*,[32] in which it was noted than an application for a transfer could overlap with what may on its facts require to be treated as an application as a homeless person. Although the point was not taken in it, the latter approach may be considered to have been put beyond doubt by the decision (and its factual basis) in *Ali*.[33]

7.25   This does not mean that every application for a transfer is an application under Part 7: rather, the authority must consider the facts disclosed in the application and decide whether it amounts to reason to believe that the applicant may be homeless or threatened with homeless. The question in each case is whether the conditions are satisfied. Even if an existing tenant is accepted as homeless, an authority must nonetheless continue to consider their transfer application and it may be possible to resolve the homelessness by that means.[34]

Renewed applications

7.26   From 9 November 2012 when Localism Act (LA) 2011, s 149 came fully into force in England,[35] an applicant who makes a fresh application[36] within two years of a previous application to an English authority, which resulted in discharge by means of an assured shorthold tenancy, in respect of which tenancy notice has been given under HA 1988, s 21, is:

   a)   homeless from the expiry of that notice;[37]

31   *R v Lambeth LBC ex p Pattinson* (1996) 28 HLR 214, QBD.
32   *R v Islington LBC ex p B* (1998) 30 HLR 706, QBD.
33   *Birmingham City Council v Ali; Moran v Manchester City Council (Secretary of State for Communities and Local Government and another intervening)* [2009] UKHL 36, [2009] HLR 41 at [56].
34   *R (Bilverstone) v Oxford CC* [2003] EWHC 2434 (Admin), [2004] JHL D12.
35   Localism Act 2011 (Commencement No 2 and Transitional Provisions) (England) Order 2012, SI 2012/2599, art 2.
36   Provided that the authority's duty to secure accommodation had not ceased before that date: Localism Act 2011 (Commencement No 2 and Transitional Provisions) (England) Order 2012, art 3.
37   HA 1996, s 195A(2), cf the normal position (which usually means when actual eviction occurs) at paras **2.62–2.63**.

b) entitled to further assistance by way of accommodation provided that the applicant is still eligible and did not become homeless intentionally, even if no longer in priority need;[38] and

c) entitled to interim accommodation if there is reason to believe that the applicant may qualify under this provision.[39]

RENTERS (REFORM) BILL

Once in full relevant force and subject to any transitional provisions, ss 188(1A) and 195A will be repealed and these provisions will therefore cease to have effect so that the additional category of homelessness and its corresponding rights will not exist.

Repeat applications

7.27 This is an area which has attracted much litigation. Where an applicant who was refused assistance in the past, or in respect of whom a duty has been discharged because the applicant abandoned accommodation offered by the authority following a previous application, applies again to the authority for assistance, there is a conflict between:

a) the absolute right of a person to make an application as homeless and the fact that the HA 1996 'does not place any express limitation on who can make an application or as to how many applications can be made';[40] and

b) the need to prevent repetitive applications on the same grounds which serve only to waste the authority's resources, which entitle the applicant to temporary accommodation[41] pending the authority's enquiries,[42] and which may have arisen as a result of the applicant's own actions – for example, because the applicant refused accommodation previously offered to them by the authority.[43]

7.28 In many cases, an authority will have to accept a repeat application. A number of separate questions arise:

a) Who may make a repeat application?

38 HA 1996, s 195A(1).
39 HA 1996, s 188(1A). This right only arises on one re-application: HA 1996, s 195A(6).
40 *R v North Devon DC ex p Lewis* [1981] 1 WLR 328, QBD, under HA 1985, Part 3.
41 See para **8.12** onwards.
42 *Delahaye v Oswestry BC* (1980) *Times* 29 July, QBD.
43 *R v Westminster City Council ex p Chambers* (1983) 6 HLR 24, QBD. In *R (Minott) v. Cambridge City Council* [2022] EWCA Civ 159; [2022] HLR 27, para **7.43**, the applicant deliberately avoided eviction in order to acquire six.months' residence and, as such, the possibility of a local connection – para **5.32**.

b) What needs to have occurred before an applicant can re-apply?

c) Where one member of a household has, or may be treated as having, become homeless intentionally, but another member seeks 'separate treatment',[44] do they have to make a separate application, or does a duty to consider this issue arise whoever makes the application?

d) What is the position when there are applications to different authorities?

Who may make a repeat application?

7.29 In England, a person who has become homeless intentionally[45] from accommodation provided under HA 1996, s 193 or who loses its benefits for some other reason, has a statutory right to re-apply.[46] Other applicants, including those in respect of whom the authority has previously refused assistance and those who have previously refused assistance offered by the authority under HA 1996, Part 7, are not governed by statutory provisions and must therefore be considered in the light of the case-law.

7.30 The position is, on the face of it, different in Wales: a person has a right to apply for assistance (and the authority must carry out an assessment).[47] The duty to assess does not arise, however, if a person has previously been assessed and there has been no material change in their circumstances and no new material information.[48] This is something of a codification of the case-law, and it may be thought that the cases still serve to illustrate what this provision means.

What needs to have occurred before an applicant can re-apply?

7.31 Until the decision of the House of Lords in *Fahia*,[49] it had been held that what was needed before an applicant could make a repeat application was a material change of circumstances.[50]

7.32 In *Fahia*, the applicant, who had one year previously been found intentionally homeless, made a new application for assistance, after being evicted from the bed and breakfast accommodation in which she had initially been placed by the authority and in which she had remained. There had been no intervening settled accommodation.[51] The application was refused by the authority.

---

44   See para **4.14** onwards.
45   See Chapter 4.
46   HA 1996, s 193(9).
47   H(W)A 2014, s 62(1).
48   H(W)A 2014, s 62(2).
49   *R v Harrow LBC ex p Fahia* [1998] 1 WLR 1396, (1998) 30 HLR 1124, HL.
50   See *R v Westminster City Council ex p Chambers* (1983) 6 HLR 24, QBD; *R v Ealing LBC ex p McBain* [1985] 1 WLR 1351, (1986) 18 HLR 59, CA; *R v Southwark LBC ex p Campisi* (1999) 31 HLR 560, CA.
51   See paras **4.115–4.132**.

7.33   In the House of Lords it was decided that, if it has reason to believe that an applicant is homeless, the authority is bound to accept the application and make necessary enquiries.

> '[W]hen an applicant has been given temporary accommodation . . . and is then found to be intentionally homeless, he cannot then make a further application based on exactly the same facts as his earlier application . . . But those are very special cases when it is possible to say that there is no application before the local authority and therefore the mandatory duty under [HA 1996, s 184] has not arisen. But in the present case there is no doubt that when Mrs Fahia made her further application for accommodation she was threatened with homelessness. Moreover in my judgment her application could not be treated as identical with the earlier 1994 application. She was relying on her eviction from the guesthouse which, for one year, she had been occupying as the direct licensee of the guesthouse proprietor, paying the rent for that accommodation . . . It is impossible to say that there has been no relevant change in circumstances at all.'[52]

This introduced a test of whether the application is 'identical', but begged the question of how that was to be approached – change of circumstances or change of facts.

7.34   In the post-*Fahia* case of *J*,[53] the applicant was living with a friend who had asked her to leave. She was found not to be threatened with homelessness. More than a year later, when possession proceedings were issued against the friend, she re-applied. The authority refused to conduct any enquiries, contending that there had been no material change in circumstances. The decision was quashed. *Fahia* was authority for the proposition that an authority is not under a duty to make enquiries in relation to an application based on exactly the same facts as an earlier application but it did not entitle an authority to refuse to make enquiries where there had been a material change of circumstances. There had clearly been a material change in circumstances: possession proceedings against the friend were imminent.

7.35   In *Rikha Begum*,[54] the applicant, who had been living with her parents when she initially applied as homeless, refused an offer of accommodation made under HA 1996, s 193 and the authority decided that it had discharged its duty towards her. She returned to live with her family. Nearly two years later, she re-applied. She claimed there had been a change in circumstances since her first

---

52   At WLR 1402/D–E, HLR 1130. *Delahaye v Oswestry BC* (1980) *Times,* July 29, QBD, which appeared to have decided to the contrary was distinguished on the basis of the requirement for a change in the facts.
53   *R (J) v Waltham Forest LBC* [2002] EWHC 487 (Admin), [2002] JHL D38.
54   *Rikha Begum v Tower Hamlets LBC* [2005] EWCA Civ 340, [2005] HLR 34.

application, because she had given birth to a second child[55] and other family members had come to live at her parents' home so that it was now overcrowded. The authority decided there had been no material change of circumstances and refused to accept an application. It was held that this was the wrong test: the authority ought to have asked whether the application was based on exactly the same facts as the previous application, not whether there had been a material change in circumstances.

7.36   These decisions raise as many questions as they resolve – for example, what constitutes a change of fact and when must the change have occurred. Most importantly, they could have re-opened the flood-gates to repeat applications, which could not be summarily dismissed, regardless of how insignificant the factual change was.

7.37   To address those concerns, the Court of Appeal in *Rikha Begum* offered guidance in identifying when an application may be refused on the ground that it is not on exactly the same facts:

a)   while it is for the applicant to identify in any subsequent application the facts which they contend render the application different from prior applications, it is for the authority to assess whether the circumstances of the two applications are exactly the same;

b)   if a subsequent application for assistance purports to reveal new facts but those facts are, to the authority's knowledge (and without the need for further enquiry), not new, or else they are fanciful or trivial, the authority may reject the application as 'incompetent'; and

c)   if a subsequent application reveals new facts which, in the light of the information then available to the authority, are neither fanciful nor trivial, the authority must accept the application; it is not open to the authority to investigate the accuracy of the alleged new facts before deciding whether to treat the application as valid, even if it suspects (but does not know) that the new facts are inaccurate.

7.38   While there plainly is a difference, at least in theory and occasionally in practice, between a change of circumstances and new facts, the reality is that the distinction will rarely be one on which an authority can rely with any confidence as a basis for refusing to entertain a new application, unless it falls within the second limb of this guidance.

7.39   Thus, in *Gardiner v Haringey LBC*,[56] the applicant was a British national living in Colombia, where she had a house. Her daughter suffered from autism and needed care and support – including educational support – that was not available in Colombia. She came to the UK and applied to the authority as homeless. That

---

55   The child had been born between the previous application and the refusal of an offer, and the decision by the authority that it had discharged its duty.
56   *R (Gardiner) v Haringey LBC* [2009] EWHC 2699 (Admin).

authority refused the application because it was considered reasonable for the applicant to continue to occupy the house in Colombia, and she was accordingly not homeless.

7.40 Almost a year later, the applicant made another application to the authority and provided new information about her daughter's special needs and an updated medical report in support of the application. The new information included a statement that since the daughter had been in the UK she had demonstrated 'considerable and dramatic improvements'. The authority sought to rely on *Rikha Begum* and refused to accept the application on the ground that there had been no change in the facts since the previous application. The claimant successfully applied for judicial review: the new information amounted to new facts which rendered it different from the earlier application.

7.41 In *Bukartyk*,[57] a woman whom the authority had concluded was not in priority need re-applied, providing, for the first time, medical evidence from a psychiatrist that she was 'struggling to cope' and that she was on anti-depressants; there was nothing to show that the authority had taken these concerns into account and the authority's decision that this did not comprise new evidence was quashed and it was ordered to treat the second application as an effective application.

7.42 See also *R (Hoyte) v Southwark LBC*[58] in which the applicant had attempted suicide between the first and second applications. See also *R (Abdulrahman) v Hillingdon LBC*[59] in which the new facts were that the applicant's husband had left her and three of her nine children no longer lived with her.

7.43 See further *Minott*,[60] where the applicant deliberately resisted attempts to evict him from the interim accommodation provided by the authority pending enquiries on his first application[61] in order to acquire six months' residence[62] and re-apply. The authority rejected the second application as being on the same facts as the first, a decision overturned by the Court of Appeal which held that while mere residence is not normally of consequence, the application could not be said to be on the same facts as reliance was now place on a definition of local connection which was not previously applicable – moreover, the question of whether he did now have a local connection was not something to be considered when deciding whether or not he was entitled to make a new application but on its determination.

7.44 To determine whether a subsequent application is based on exactly the same facts as an earlier application, the comparison is not between the facts as they existed at the time of the original application, and those existing at the time

---

57   *R (Bukartyk) v Welwyn Hatfield BC* [2019] EWHC 3480 (Admin), [2020] HLR 19.
58   [2016] EWHC 1665 (Admin), [2016] HLR 35.
59   [2016] EWHC 2647 (Admin), [2017] HLR 1.
60   *R (Minott) v. Cambridge City Council* [2022] EWCA Civ 159; [2022] HLR 27.
61   Which led to a local connection referral which he did not want and therefore did not take up.
62   See para **5.32**.

of the second application. Rather, it is between the facts as they were understood[63] at the time of the authority's original decision (or review if there was one) on the earlier application, and the facts revealed by the subsequent application.[64]

7.45   There is a mild discrepancy within *Rikha Begum*: although reference is made to 'the date of the authority's *decision*'[65] as the appropriate date for comparison, there is also reference to 'the circumstances as they were known to be when the earlier application was *disposed of*' as the appropriate date for comparison;[66] and, when disposing of the appeal,[67] there is reference to the facts at the date of *discharge* of the original decision.

7.46   This might seem to suggest that – where the original application was determined by way of discharge by the authority of its duty by means of an offer that was not accepted – the time for comparison is the date of discharge rather than that of the authority's decision. That theory draws some support from *Griffin*,[68] in which a new application was properly held to have been based on the same facts: the change – relationship breakdown – had been known to the authority and taken into account at the time when the earlier offer of accommodation had been made, but had occurred subsequent to the decision on the original application.

Applications by other family members

7.47   There is no bar to a family member of an unsuccessful applicant making a fresh application in their own name. This not uncommonly occurs where an applicant is found intentionally homeless and a member of the applicant's family claims not to have acquiesced in the act which gave rise to the intentionality.[69]

7.48   An application by another member of the family cannot, however, be used to circumvent a decision that the authority has discharged its duty towards the family: it has been held to be irrelevant that the member of the family making the new application did not acquiesce in or agree to the refusal of accommodation which led to the decision that the duty had been discharged.[70] Given the reasoning applicable to the intentionality cases, it is hard to see why a non-acquiescent, non-applicant family member should be fixed with the decision of the (previous)

---

63   The facts need not *post*-date the first application: see *R. (Ibrahim) v Westminster CC* [2021] EWHC 2616 (Admin); [2022] HLR 13 where a new psychiatrist's report, differing from previous such reports, explained why it has not been reasonable for the applicant to remain in her previous accommodation by reference to her personal history, whereas the authority's previous decision had focused exclusively on whether she was at risk of violence if she remained in it – this entitled her to make a new application.

64   *Rikha Begum* at [43].

65   *Rikha Begum* at [43].

66   *Rikha Begum* at [44].

67   *Rikha Begum* at [54].

68   *R (Griffin) v Southwark LBC* [2004] EWHC 2463 (Admin), [2005] HLR 12.

69   *R v North Devon DC ex p Lewis* [1981] 1 WLR 328, QBD. See also paras **4.14–4.30**.

70   *R v Camden LBC ex p Hersi* (2001) 33 HLR 52, CA.

applicant, even if, in many cases, acquiescence will be found as a matter of fact or even strong inference.[71]

Applications to other authorities

7.49   In *R v Slough BC ex p Ealing LBC*,[72] two applicants were found homeless intentionally in Slough. One moved and applied to Ealing, the other to Hillingdon; both authorities concluded that the applicants were not homeless intentionally. In each case, however, the local connection provisions entitled them to refer the applicants back to Slough. It was held that Slough BC was bound by the unintentionally decisions of Ealing and Hillingdon.

7.50   There is therefore nothing in principle to stop an applicant moving around until they find an authority which concludes that they are not homeless intentionally, and – unless the second authority's decision can be vitiated as a matter of public law[73] – there is no way in which the authority fixed with final responsibility for the applicant can defeat the decision, even though it conflicts with its own finding.[74]

7.51   *Ex p Ealing LBC* was applied in *ex p Camden LBC*,[75] which was on like facts. In its discretion, however, the court refused judicial review to quash the original authority's refusal to accept the referral, because the referring authority had failed to make adequate enquiries either of the applicant or of the other authority to resolve certain factual discrepancies between the applicant's statements to the two authorities. Authorities should therefore examine with care applications by people who have been declared homeless intentionally elsewhere. They should afford the first authority to which application was made (and which will bear the burden if a second application is successful) an opportunity to comment on any discrepancies between the applications.

7.52   The Court of Appeal went somewhat further in *ex p Tower Hamlets LBC*:[76] where an application is made to a second authority, that authority's enquiries should extend to examination of the reasons for the first authority's

---

71   See para **4.23–4.25**, although the cases cited are – in homelessness law terms – somewhat old and it may be thought that modern thinking accords much more respect for the independent position of family members: see para **7.4**.

72   *R v Slough BC ex p Ealing LBC* [1981] QB 801, CA.

73   See paras **10.20** onwards. See the discussion of *R v Newham LBC ex p Tower Hamlets LBC* (1990) 23 HLR 62, CA and *R (Bantamagbari) v Westminster City Council* [2003] EWHC 1350 (Admin), [2003] JHL D70 as to whether this means that the new decision has to be quashed by proceedings for judicial review.

74   See also *R (Sambotin) v Brent LBC* [2018] EWCA Civ 1826, [2019] PTSR 371, [2019] HLR 5: once an authority has decided that an applicant is eligible for assistance, homeless, in priority need and not intentionally homeless, its duty under HA 1996, s 193(2) crystallises; if the authority decides to refer the applicant to another authority under the local connection provisions, the only issue is which authority is responsible for discharging the duty.

75   *R v Tower Hamlets LBC ex p Camden LBC* (1989) 21 HLR 197, QBD.

76   *R v Newham LBC ex p Tower Hamlets LBC* (1990) 23 HLR 62, QBD.

refusal to assist, and should take into account the general housing circumstances prevailing in the first authority's district, just as it may take into account the housing circumstances in its own.[77]

7.53   In *Ali and Bibi*,[78] it was held that, when the duty to house an applicant on a first application was discharged by reference to another authority under what is now HA 1996, s 198, there was no discharge of duty (by the first authority) under what is now s 193. Accordingly, assuming there had been no take-up of an accommodation offer from the other authority, the acquisition of a local connection with the area of the first authority entitled an applicant to re-apply. This was consistent with the early decision in *Wyness v Poole BC*,[79] in which the family declined to accept a reference to another authority, but 'made do' until one of its members had acquired employment and – thence – a local connection.

7.54   It has recently been explicitly determined that the principle derived from *ex p Ealing LBC*[80] applies where the application to the second authority is made even when the first authority had accepted a duty and made an offer.[81]

7.55   In practice, both *Ali and Bibi* and *Wyness* are overtaken by – and absorbed into – the post-*Fahia* position:[82] *Wyness* was decided on the basis of 'change of circumstance' but it was also a change of facts and *Ali and Bibi*, while on a somewhat different point (whether there had been any previous discharge such as to prevent a new application), becomes somewhat redundant.

How to apply

7.56   Authorities have a duty to hear and adjudicate on applications[83] made by people who are potentially homeless, and they must therefore make provision to

---

77   See para **2.91**.
78   *R v Tower Hamlets LBC ex p Ali; R v Tower Hamlets LBC ex p Bibi* (1993) 25 HLR 158, CA, overruling *R v Hammersmith and Fulham LBC ex p O'Brian* (1985) 17 HLR 471, QBD.
79   *Wyness v Poole DC* July 1979 *LAG Bulletin* 166, CC.
80   See para **7.49**.
81   *R (Kensington and Chelsea RLBC) v Ealing LBC* [2017] EWHC 24 (Admin), [2017] HLR 13.
82   Paras **7.31–7.46**.
83   The English Code of Guidance (para 18.5) suggests that applications can be made 'to any department of the local authority', but it is submitted that this in wrong. It is inconsistent with paras 18.2–18.4, all of which envisage (leaving aside out-of-hours provision) a dedicated and expert service with sole responsibility for accepting and processing applications; taken literally, it would also mean that applications could be made at a library or a school, the leisure department or even the waste collection department. Such departments are manifestly unsuitable for dealing with such an application, could not arrange interim accommodation where necessary and may not even recognise that an application is being made at all, for which failure an authority should surely not be held to be legally in default. It is submitted that the correct position is that an application is not made until there is an approach to a suitable or appropriate department or service which a homeless person could reasonably think might be able to help: this does not necessarily mean a *housing* department or service, but would include, eg, a general help-line or an out-of-hours emergency service for all the functions of the authority

receive applications. In heavily populated areas, reasonable provision would be expected to comprise some form of 24-hour cover.[84]

7.57 There is no requirement that applications be in writing or in any particular form, and an authority is therefore not at liberty to refuse an application on that basis.[85] Once a person has applied to the authority for accommodation or assistance in obtaining accommodation,[86] and the authority has enough information to comprise reason to believe[87] that the applicant may be homeless or threatened with homelessness, an application under HA 1996, Part 7 has been made,[88] although circumstances – including action taken by the authority – may mean that the applicant is no longer homeless or threatened with homelessness by the time a decision is taken on the application.[89]

7.58 The key is whether the authority has reason to believe that a person who has sought accommodation or assistance in obtaining accommodation may be homeless or threatened with homelessness, not whether something which might discretely be characterised as an application as homeless has been made: thus, an application for an allocation under Part 6 may give rise to a duty under Part 7 if the information provided suggests that the applicant may be homeless or threatened with homelessness[90] – again, so that a Part 7 application has[91] been made or received.

---

84   *R v Camden LBC ex p Gillan* (1989) 21 HLR 114, QBD.
85   *R v Chiltern DC ex p Roberts* (1990) 23 HLR 387, QBD. See also *R (Aweys) v Birmingham City Council* [2007] EWHC 52 (Admin), [2007] HLR 27 (point not taken in Court of Appeal or House of Lords – see *Birmingham City Council v Aweys and others* [2008] EWCA Civ 48, [2008] HLR 32 and *Birmingham City Council v Ali and others; Moran v Manchester City Council* [2009] UKHL 36, [2009] HLR 41).
86   HA 1996, s 183(1).
87   Whether this standard is met is a matter for the authority, subject to challenge on conventional *Wednesbury* grounds: see *R (Edwards and others) v Birmingham City Council* [2016] EWHC 173 (Admin), [2016] HLR 11 and paras **10.23–10.24**.
88   Thus, in *Bury MBC v Gibbons* [2010] EWCA Civ 327, [2010] HLR 33, an approach to the authority asking for assistance when the applicant had been given notice meant that he was threatened with homelessness, and the authority should at that stage have treated the approach as an application under HA 1996, Part 7. See also *R (Edwards and others) v Birmingham City Council* [2016] EWHC 173 (Admin), [2016] HLR 11: an authority is entitled to question an applicant to clarify whether, in fact, there is reason to believe that any accommodation presently occupied is such that it may not be reasonable to continue to occupy it; it is not the case that every complaint about conditions is sufficient to meet the 'reason to believe' threshold. In the highly idiosyncratic case of *R. (EL) v Kensington and Chelsea R.L.B.C.* [2022] EWHC 3185 (Admin); [2023] HLR 24, it was not irrational to treat the application under Part 6: being treated as homeless was the opposite of what the applicant wanted.
89   See paras **7.171–7.175**.
90   See, eg, *R (McDonagh) v Enfield LBC* [2018] EWHC 1287, [2018] HLR 43, where a combination of application under HA 1996, Part 6 and an occupational therapist's report sufficed to give rise to the duty.
91   If one will, de facto.

Provision of accommodation on application

7.59   Once a HA 1996, Part 7 application has been made or received,[92] the preliminary consideration for any local authority is whether it must provide accommodation pending the decision on the application, because the applicant appears to it to be eligible for assistance and in priority need.[93] This is considered in Chapter 8.[94] (Priority need is not, however, a precondition in the case of a first renewed application (ie, within two years of acceptance of a private sector offer on a previous application).[95]

RENTERS (REFORM) BILL

Subject to any transitional provisions, the qualification in parentheses that priority need is not a precondition in the case of a first renewed application will no longer exist once the Bill becomes law and comes into full relevant effect, as s 195A will be repealed.

ENQUIRIES

7.60   Once an application has been made, in England, the next stage in the application process is for the authority to make enquiries into the application to determine what (if any) duty is owed: the duty arises when the authority considers that an applicant is or may be homeless or threatened with homelessness.

7.61   In Wales, this first-stage duty has been replaced by a duty to make an assessment of the applicant's housing needs,[96] a duty which does not apply in England[97] until a later stage, when the authority is satisfied that the applicant is homeless or threatened with homelessness and eligible for assistance, albeit that the authority may not yet have reached a determination on priority need, intentionality or local connection.

7.62   Assessment duties are considered in Chapter 8,[98] although there is a considerable overlap with the enquiry duty and frequent references are

---

92   Whether formally as such, or because the conditions which amount to such an application are present: throughout the text, references to an application having been made or received includes application which, because of the information known to the authority, must be considered to have been made or received: see paras **7.56–7.58**.
93   HA 1996, s 188(1); H(W)A 2014, s 68, see HA 1996, s 195A(6)): see para **7.26**.
94   Paras **8.12–8.14**.
95   HA 1996, s 195A(6)): see para **7.26**.
96   H(W)A 2014, s 62.
97   HA 1996, s 189A with effect from 3 April 2018: see Homelessness Reduction Act (HRA) 2017 (Commencement and Transitional and Savings Provisions) Regulations 2018, SI 2018/167 reg 3, but only applicable to applications made and reviews sought on or after that date – see reg 4.
98   Paras **8.61–8.75**.

accordingly made to the assessment duty in this chapter: how far the court treats the assessment duty as impacting on the enquiry duty is discussed at paras **8.66–8.74**.

The duty to make enquiries

7.63   The duty to make enquiries arises in England where a person applies to a local authority for accommodation or for assistance in obtaining accommodation and the authority has reason to believe that the applicant may be homeless or threatened with homelessness.[99] These conditions arise relatively easily: the wording is important – the authority need only 'have reason to believe'[100] that the applicant 'may' be homeless or threatened with homelessness.[101]

7.64   Note that an assured shorthold applicant in England may be threatened with homelessness as a result of service of a valid HA 1988, s 21 notice which will expire within 56 days.[102] Note, too, the different dates when the application is a first renewed application,[103] ie, following an earlier application which resulted in a private sector letting; if an assured shorthold, homelessness arises once notice under HA 1988, s 21 has expired.[104]

RENTERS (REFORM) BILL

The effects of ss 175(5) and 195A(6) will, once the Bill becomes law and comes into full relevant effect and subject to any transitional provisions, cease to apply as ss 175(5) and 195A will be repealed so that the additional category of threatened with homelessness will not exist.

7.65   Since commencement of the HRA 2017,[105] certain specified English public authorities[106] have notification duties under HA 1996, s 213B: these arise

---

99   HA 1996, s 183(1).
100   HA 1996, s 184(1). See also *R (Edwards and others) v Birmingham City Council* [2016] EWHC 173 (Admin), [2016] HLR 11: the authority is entitled to question an applicant to clarify whether, in fact, there is reason to believe that any accommodation presently occupied is such that it may be reasonable to continue to occupy it; it is not the case that every complaint about the condition is sufficient to meet the 'reason to believe' threshold.
101   HA 1996, s 184(1).
102   HA 1996, s 175(5) with effect from 3 April 2018, commencement of HRA 2017: see Homelessness Reduction Act 2017 (Commencement and Transitional and Savings Provisions) Regulations 2018, SI 2018/167 reg 3, only applicable to applications made and reviews sought on or after that date – see reg 4.
103   HA 1996, s 195A(6).
104   HA 1996, s 195A(2): see para **7.26**.
105   3 April 2018: see Homelessness Reduction Act 2017 (Commencement and Transitional and Savings Provisions) Regulations 2018, SI 2018/167 reg 3.
106   See para **11.94–11.102**.

when the authority considers that a person in relation to whom it exercises any functions is or may be homeless or threatened with homelessness. The duty only exists if the person agrees to the notification and identifies a local housing authority in England which they would like to be notified of the public authority's opinion.[107]

7.66 It is arguable that if the notification asserts, in whatever terms, that the individual is applying to the housing authority for accommodation or assistance in obtaining it, this will activate the housing authority's enquiry duty.[108] Indeed, if any other public authority, or anyone whom the housing authority considers a credible source of information, provides the appropriate information, that condition would appear to be fulfilled regardless of whether they are under any duty to do so.

7.67 In neither case, however, is the first condition on its face fulfilled by a notification – statutory or voluntary – unless it also asserts, in whatever terms, that the individual is applying to the housing authority for accommodation or assistance in obtaining it, although this could, depending on the circumstances, be implied. In the case of a statutory notification under HA 1996, s 213B, however, it is strongly arguable that this is the intention of s 213B and that s 184 should be construed commensurately with it; it is difficult to see what other purpose s 213B could have sought to achieve.

7.68 Failure to undertake the necessary enquiries does not, however, give rise to an action in damages: *Palmer*.[109]

7.69 Where there is no reason to believe that an applicant is yet threatened with homelessness, the duty to make enquiries has not been triggered and the authority cannot make a decision whether or not an applicant is threatened with homelessness intentionally: *Hunt*.[110] Thus, in *Jarvis*,[111] notice that possession would be required of premises let on an assured shorthold tenancy was not of itself sufficient to trigger a duty under HA 1996, s 184. (This would not be the case now, as a person is threatened with homelessness if given a valid notice seeking possession under HA 1988, s 21 in respect of the only accommodation the person has that is available for their occupation and the notice will expire within 56 days).[112]

---

107 HA 1996, s 213B; contact details must also be notified.
108 The English Code of Guidance puts it this way (paras 4.19–4.21): 'A referral made by a public authority to the housing authority under section 213B will not in itself constitute an application for assistance under Part 7, but housing authorities should always respond to any referral received . . . If the housing authority's subsequent contact with the individual following receipt of the referral reveals details that provide the housing authority with reason to believe that they might be homeless or threatened with homelessness and the individual indicates they would like assistance it will trigger an application for assistance under Part 7.'
109 *R v Northavon DC ex p Palmer* (1995) 27 HLR 576, CA.
110 *R v Rugby BC ex p Hunt* (1994) 26 HLR 1, QBD.
111 *R v Croydon LBC ex p Jarvis* (1994) 26 HLR 194, QBD.
112 HA 1996, s 175(5).

RENTERS (REFORM) BILL

The effect of s 175(5), described in parentheses in the above paragraph, will, once the Bill becomes law and comes into full relevant effect and subject to any transitional provisions, cease to exist as s 175(5) will be repealed so that the additional category of threatened with homelessness will not exist.

7.70 The enquiries must be sufficient to satisfy the authority whether the applicant is eligible for assistance and if so what (if any) duty is owed to the applicant under HA 1996, Part 7 or H(W)A 2014, Part 2.

7.71 The subject of enquiries into local connection has been considered in Chapter 5.[113] The authority can start local connection enquiries without awaiting the conclusion of its other enquiries, but the issue has to be determined as at the date of the decision,[114] and it may therefore become necessary to reconsider a decision to refer on local connection grounds if other enquiries are prolonged,[115] as the connection itself may be based on factors arising during the enquiries.[116]

Who must make the enquiries?

7.72 The burden of making enquiries rests with the authority to whom the application was made. In the absence of a contracting out agreement,[117] the duty to enquire may not be delegated to another organisation although the authority may ask another housing authority or relevant body,[118] or a social services authority,[119] to assist in discharging the enquiry duty, which body is obliged to co-operate in the discharge of the function to which the request relates, to the extent that is reasonable in the circumstances.[120]

7.73 In *Gerrard*,[121] before the contracting out power (paras **7.6–7.8**) came into play, the authority had transferred all of its housing stock to a registered housing

---

113 Paras **5.59–5.63**.
114 *Mohamed v Hammersmith and Fulham LBC* [2001] UKHL 57, [2002] HLR 7.
115 *R v Newham LBC ex p Smith* (1997) 29 HLR 213, QBD.
116 See *Mohamed*, above.
117 See paras **7.6–7.8**.
118 Registered provider (in Wales, registered social landlord) or housing action trust, or in Scotland a local authority, development corporation, registered housing association or Scottish Homes: HA 1996, s 213(2); H(W)A 2014, s 95(5).
119 In the case of 16- and 17-year-olds, the English Code of Guidance (para 18.8) recognises that such a child may apply under HA 1996, Part 7 but requires an assessment under Children Act 1989 to be completed (Welsh Code para 11.10). See also *R (M) v Hammersmith and Fulham LBC* [2008] UKHL 14, [2008] 1 WLR 535, [2008] 4 All ER 271.
120 HA 1996, s 213; H(W)A 2014, s 95. In Wales, there are additional provisions with which the other body must comply: see paras **11.103–11.105**.
121 *R v West Dorset DC, West Dorset HA ex p Gerrard* (1995) 27 HLR 150, QBD.

association,[122] and had reached an agreement pursuant to which the association was to carry out the enquiries under what is now HA 1996, s 184, on the basis of which enquiries the authority would make its decisions. Quashing the authority's decision that the applicant was not homeless, it was held that, although entitled under what is now HA 1996, s 213 to enlist assistance from it in making its enquiries, the authority nonetheless had to take an active and dominant role in the investigative process.

7.74   On the other hand, in *Woolgar*,[123] likewise before the contracting out power was enacted (para **7.6–7.8**), it was held that it is only the decision-making function which is exclusive to the authority, so that the investigative function involved in making enquiries could properly be delegated to an outside body (at least, one recognised by statute, such as what is now a private registered provider or, in Wales, registered social landlord).[124]

7.75   The cases remain relevant where the contracting out power has not been used, or has not been not properly used, eg, if the agreement had expired. The two cases are not irreconcilable: as a matter of law, authorities are not bound to carry out all their functions through employees but may retain outside contractors; if it can be said, however, that the contractor has determined what enquiries need to be made, and takes them to such a point that the decision is 'all but' made before the authority exercises its decision-making function, the authority will improperly have delegated rather than properly used an outside service in order to lay the ground for its decision.

Conduct of enquiries

7.76   It is for the authority, not the courts, to determine how the necessary enquiries are made, including who should conduct interviews and what questions should be asked.[125] Enquiries should nonetheless be carried out in a sympathetic way:[126] *Phillips*.[127]

---

122 Now, private registered providers of social housing (PRP).
123 *R v Hertsmere BC ex p Woolgar* (1995) 27 HLR 703, QBD.
124 HA 1996, s 213(2)(a).
125 Subject to *Wednesbury* review: see *R (IA) v Westminster City Council* [2013] EWHC 1273 (QB) where a short interview with the applicant was considered insufficient, leading to 'irrational and, indeed, perverse' conclusions.
126 See English Code para 11.9, which, although in the context of the new assessment duty (HA 1996, s 189A), must be of relevance more generally: 'Applicants should be encouraged to share information without fear that this will reduce their chances of receiving support, and questions should be asked in a sensitive way and with an awareness that the applicant may be reluctant to disclose personal details if they lack confidence that their circumstances will be understood and considered sympathetically. Housing authorities should ensure staff have sufficient skills and training to conduct assessments of applicants who may find it difficult to disclose their circumstances, including people at risk of domestic abuse, violence or hate crime.' See also the English Code chapters 21, 22, 23, 24 and 25 for advice on how to deal with applications by victims of domestic abuse; care leavers; people with an offending history; former members of the armed forces; and victims of modern slavery and people trafficking.
127 *R v West Dorset DC ex p Phillips* (1985) 17 HLR 336, QBD. See also comments in the decision in *R v Camden LBC ex p Gillan* (1989) 21 HLR 114, QBD.

7.77   Whether an interview is necessary is likewise primarily for the authority to decide,[128] although the new assessment duty now makes it all but inevitable.[129] In *Tetteh*,[130] the applicant had set out his position in correspondence and there was nothing which required the authority to interview him; failure to do so could therefore not be seen to be a breach of the principles of natural justice.[131]

7.78   A number of authorities – and/or contractors – carry out interviews by telephone, and it may be thought that some will seek to carry out assessments the same way.[132] While this may be proper where all that is involved is to establish or check facts, it is submitted that this will nonetheless not be sufficient where the matter under consideration calls for a face-to-face interview,[133] for example, vulnerability.[134]

7.79   Thus, many people find it difficult to express themselves on the telephone, whether because of language difficulties or mental ability or through unease at being asked to talk about potentially sensitive issues without forewarning, as is often the case on receipt of a telephone call.

7.80   Likewise, the interviewer is deprived of the ability to assess 'body language', a concept that may be difficult to describe but that is well-recognised and that is essential to the overall evaluative exercise in which the interviewer is engaged. It may be observed that the interviewee, too, is deprived of the element of 'reading' the interviewer that is likewise central to comprehension (and to assessing reactions).[135]

7.81   Furthermore, the interviewee may, without the knowledge of the interviewer, be distracted by other people or events;[136] indeed, the interviewee may be temporarily impaired, for example, through drink or drugs.[137] Nor is it

128 If an interview is needed, the interviewer must speak fluent English: see Immigration Act 2016, s 77(1) and the Code of Practice (English Language Requirements for Public Sector Workers) Regulations 2016, SI 2016/1157.
129 See paras **8.61–8.75**.
130 *Tetteh v Kingston upon Thames RLBC* [2004] EWCA Civ 1775, [2005] HLR 21.
131 See paras **10.65–10.69**.
132 There is nothing in HA 1996, s 189A which prohibits this, though it may be thought to be far from consonant with the spirit of the exercise.
133 In *R v Camden LBC ex p Gillan* (1989) 21 HLR 114, QBD, the Divisional Court referred to the expectation of a 'face-to-face' opportunity to explain an applicant's situation, in contrast to a telephone-based system, and criticised the authority's 'cavalier treatment' of applicants who were required to explain their circumstances by telephone. See also the position on review, para **7.243**.
134 An authority must approach vulnerability with 'great care' – see *Crossley v Westminster City Council* [2006] EWCA Civ 140, [2006] HLR 26, at [30].
135 An interviewee may – is likely to – wish to appear co-operative, and/or may be more suggestible, at least to a point.
136 Particularly if the interview is with someone in a hostel, taking the call on a telephone in the common parts.
137 It is not impossible, including in cases such as those referred to in the previous footnotes, for there to be a mistake in identity, whether by misunderstanding or even deliberate conduct by a third party.

impossible for someone else to be answering questions, eg in a hostel or house in multiple occupation (HMO), whether maliciously or through mistake: such conversations are ripe for misunderstanding.

7.82 Even in person, inconsistencies will frequently be found when someone's native language is not English: *Li*.[138] Previous editions of the Code recommended that authorities secure access to competent interpreters for the community languages of their area, but that recommendation is not found in either the current English Code or the Welsh Code.[139]

7.83 Where there is doubt about the competence of an interpreter, the test is whether it has been shown that the interpreter is not – to the knowledge of the authority – competent to conduct the interview: *Jalika Begum*.[140] In *Khatun*,[141] interviews with an applicant (without the applicant's own independent adviser or counsellor) were not inherently flawed on the basis that they had been conducted by an employee of the council who would be inclined to protect the employer's limited resources.[142]

Ambit of enquiries

Generally

7.84 The burden of making enquiries is squarely on the authority.[143] Even without the duty to assess the applicant's case, which carries with it a number of specific matters which need to be included,[144] inquiries have to cover all the relevant factors – for example, priority need,[145] or risk of domestic violence in another area.[146]

---

138 *R v Surrey Heath BC ex p Li* (1984) 16 HLR 79, QBD.
139 The English Code does, however, suggest that 'translated information and interpreting services should be made available to applicants for who[m] English is not a first language, and the availability of these services publicised to residents and community organisations': para 18.4. The Welsh Code also recommends that consideration be given to producing Information in minority languages: see Welsh Code para 7.17.
140 *R v Tower Hamlets LBC ex p Begum* (1992) 24 HLR 188, QBD.
141 *R v Tower Hamlets LBC ex p Khatun* (1995) 27 HLR 465, CA.
142 Cf the 'fairness' discussions in *Runa Begum v Tower Hamlets LBC* [2003] UKHL 5, [2003] 2 AC 430, [2003] HLR 32; compare *Feld v Barnet LBC* [2004] EWCA Civ 1307, [2005] HLR 9; *De-Winter Heald and others v Brent LBC* [2009] EWCA Civ 930, [2010] HLR 8. See paras **10.73–10.74** and see generally paras **7.143–7.154**.
143 *R v Woodspring DC ex p Walters* (1984) 16 HLR 73, QBD; *R v Reigate and Banstead DC ex p Paris* (1985) 17 HLR 103, QBD; *R v Barnet LBC ex p Babalola* (1996) 28 HLR 196, QBD; *R v Wandsworth LBC ex p Dodia* (1998) 30 HLR 562, QBD.
144 HA 1996, s 189A(2); see paras **8.61–8.75**.
145 *R v Ryedale DC ex p Smith* (1984) 16 HLR 66, QBD.
146 *Patterson v Greenwich LBC* (1994) 26 HLR 159, CA.

7.85   Enquiries need not, however, amount to 'CID-type' enquiries.[147] The approach is summarised in *Winchester*:[148]

'The burden lies upon the local authority to make appropriate enquiries . . . in a caring and sympathetic way . . . These enquiries should be pursued rigorously and fairly albeit the authority are not under a duty to conduct detailed CID-type enquiries . . . The applicant must be given an opportunity to explain matters which the local authority is minded to regard as weighing substantially against him . . .'

7.86   It follows that there may be some limited circumstances where a local housing authority need not make enquiries into some matters, although the new assessment duty requires the authority to consider 'the circumstances that caused the applicant to become homeless or threatened with homelessness',[149] which will certainly affect the ambit of the enquiries. Nonetheless, there are some limits.

7.87   For example, in *Green v Croydon LBC*[150] the applicant had been evicted from a privately rented property for rent arrears; when she applied as homeless, the authority decided that she was intentionally homeless. She contended that the possession order was wrongly made as they had proceeded on the basis of a monthly rent of £700, whereas the true rent was only £650 per month. It was held that the authority did not have to make enquiries of the landlord, applicant or district judge but was entitled to rely on the possession order which was only consistent with a rent of £700 per month. It is unlikely that this would be different today, notwithstanding the assessment duty.

7.88   In most cases where accommodation has been lost as a result of rent (or mortgage) arrears, the authority will need to make enquiries about the applicant's financial affairs, if only to be satisfied whether the accommodation that was lost was affordable,[151] although it has been held that when considering whether an applicant has been occupying what was asserted by her to be settled accommodation, an authority does not necessarily have to determine

147 *Lally v Kensington and Chelsea RLBC* (1980) *Times,* March 27, QBD. They must, however, address obviously relevant factors, see *Wandsworth LBC v NJ* [2013] EWCA Civ 1373, [2014] HLR 6, in which the authority failed to make any enquiries into the possibility that a violent man would be able to locate his ex-partner (the applicant), despite clear evidence that he was attempting to do so.
148 *R v Gravesham BC ex p Winchester* (1986) 18 HLR 208, QBD, at 214–215. The case is still relied on: see *R (Saint Sepulchre) v Kensington & Chelsea RLBC* [2023] EWHC 2913 (Admin); [2024] HLR 12.
149 HA 1996, s 189A(2)(a); see paras **8.61–8.75**.
150 [2007] EWCA Civ 1367, [2008] HLR 28.
151 As to which, see the Homelessness (Suitability of Accommodation) Order 1996, SI 1996/3204 and H(W)A 2014, s 59(2), above, paras **2.134–2.146**. See further, English Cove, para.17.46, 17.47; Welsh Code, 8.29, 8.30, 17.19.

its legal character,[152] which again might remain the position even subject to the assessment duty.

7.89 In *Gilby v Westminster City Council*,[153] the applicant occupied accommodation either as an unlawful subtenant or as a bare licensee. The question was whether the occupation constituted settled accommodation, for which purpose the relevant question was whether the applicant had the basis for a reasonable expectation of continued occupation: the difference between bare license and unlawful sub-tenancy was irrelevant to that question; the authority had been entitled to determine that the accommodation was not settled either way.

7.90 Enquiries may extend to other departments within the authority – for example, the housing department (referable to an earlier tenancy): *Adair*.[154] Where an application is made by an occupier of property owned by the authority, the duty to make enquiries does not, however, fetter any decision to recover possession, nor is it likely to be fettered by the assessment duty: in *Grumbridge*,[155] a trespasser sought judicial review of the authority's decision to evict him before determining his application for housing: it was held that there was no requirement or statutory obligation on the authority to determine whether a person is either homeless or in priority need or, indeed, as to any of the other matters under (then) HA 1985, Part 3 (now HA 1996, Part 7), before deciding whether to obtain possession of property.

7.91 Where the facts relating to an application are fairly placed before the applicant for the applicant to agree, dispute or supplement, and the applicant agrees them, it is not unfair for the decision-maker or the reviewing officer to proceed on the basis that the agreed facts are accurate,[156] bearing particularly in

---

152 *Gilby v Westminster City Council* [2007] EWCA Civ 604, [2008] HLR 7. see next para. In general, however, whether accommodation is settled is a question which must be assessed by reference to all relevant factors, including the nature of the occupation (lease or licence), the parties' expectations as to the period of occupation, whether the arrangement was on a commercial basis or with friends/family, the affordability of the property and any overcrowding, not to any one of them alone: *Bullale v Westminster City Council* [2020] EWCA Civ 1587; [2021] HLR 21 – see paras **4.115–4.130**.

153 [2007] EWCA Civ 604, [2008] HLR 7.

154 *R v Camden LBC ex p Adair* (1997) 29 HLR 236, QBD.

155 *R v Barnet LBC ex p Grumbridge* (1992) 24 HLR 433, QBD.

156 *Rowley v Rugby BC* [2007] EWCA Civ 483, [2007] HLR 40. See also *R (Lynch) v Lambeth LBC* [2007] HLR 15 at [32]: 'All the medical evidence was accepted, and the housing authority did not consider, either before the s 184 or the review, that any further inquiries were necessary. No suggestion was made by the claimant or her advisers that further information should be sought, nor was any more offered. No response was made to the minded to find letter of the reviewing officer. In line with the decision of the *Cramp* case, . . . the Housing Authority were not unreasonable in failing to make further inquiries. It is difficult to envisage what other inquiries needed to be made, given the wealth of information with the original application.'

mind that the burden is normally on the applicant to put forward the matters and evidence which they wish to be taken into account:[157] see *Cramp*.[158]

7.92 In *Paley*,[159] the applicant was offered accommodation in Stoke-on-Trent, 161 miles from the authority's area. The principal issue was one of affordability, including travel.[160] In the course of the appeal to the county court, the applicant contended that the authority had not made sufficient enquiries – if they had done so, it was claimed, they would have discovered that her children had a close relationship with their father, whom they visited in London on a weekly basis. This part of her appeal was dismissed: despite having been sent a 'minded to' letter,[161] the appellant had only raised the issue of her children needing to have regular contact with their father when she appealed to the county court; the authority could not be criticised for failing to make further inquiries on that matter.

7.93 Note, however, that if reliance is placed on a disability,[162] EqA 2010, s 149 – the public sector equality duty[163] – may[164] oblige the authority to carry out further inquiries if some feature of the evidence presents a real possibility that an applicant is within it. The duty is a duty to have regard to the specified matters,

---

157 In *Ciftci v Haringey LBC* [2021] EWCA 1772; [2022] HLR 9, above, para **4.42**, the applicant had been given ample opportunity to make representations on her application and the authority's review officer could not be criticised for failing to make further enquiries.

158 *Cramp v Hastings BC; Phillips v Camden LBC* [2005] EWCA Civ 1005, [2005] HLR 48, see para **7.122**. See also *Mohamoud v Kensington and Chelsea RLBC; Saleem v Wandsworth LBC* [2015] EWCA Civ 780, [2015] HLR 38: where an applicant seeks to rely on Children Act 2004, s 11 (duty on authorities to safeguard and promote the welfare of children when discharging any functions), they must notify the authority of any relevant matters relating to the child on which they wish to rely.

159 *Paley v Waltham Forest LBC* [2022] EWCA Civ 112; [2022] HLR 24.

160 Described at para **2.146**.

161 Para **7.227**.

162 In *Wilson v Birmingham City Council* [2016] EWCA Civ 1137, [2017] HLR 4, it was held that a review officer was entitled to expect the appellant to bring forward any information which might be relevant to show that her children had a disability; the absence of any response from the appellant to invitations to submit information meant that the officer had been entitled to conclude that any problems experienced by the children were not such as to engage the EqA 2010.

163 In the exercise of functions, to have due regard to the need to eliminate unlawful discrimination, harassment and victimisation and to advance equality of opportunity and foster good relations between persons with protected characteristics (age, disability, gender reassignment, pregnancy or maternity, race, sex, sexual orientation, religion or belief) and other persons.

164 *Pieretti v Enfield LBC* [2010] EWCA Civ 1104, [2011] HLR 3, rejecting arguments: a) that the predecessor provisions of Disability Discrimination Act 1995, s 49A had no application to homelessness applications, but only to the formulation of policy; b) that HA 1996, Part 7 was a complete code that comprehensively addressed the rights and needs of disabled people so that s 49A added nothing; c) that a determination under Part 7 was not a 'function' within the meaning of s 49A; and d) that neither the original decision-maker nor the review officer had been asked to consider s 49A.

not to achieve a particular result.[165] In *Webb-Harnden*,[166] reliance was sought to be placed on the s 149 duty to contend that the authority ought not to have taken the benefits cap into account in reaching a decision that accommodation in or nearer to their area would be unaffordable and, as such, not suitable, in offering out-of-area accommodation at some considerable distance;[167] it was also suggested that the authority could have offered their own temporary accommodation, which would not attract a cap, in order to provide in-area or closer accommodation: both arguments comprised an attempt to use s 149 to compel the authority to perform its duty differently, and achieve a different result, which is not the purpose of s 149.

7.94   In *Hackney LBC v Haque*,[168] it was held, in the context of a suitability review, that EqA 2010, s 149 required the authority:

a)   to recognise that the appellant had a disability;

b)   to focus on specific aspects of his impairments to the extent that they were relevant to the suitability of the accommodation;

c)   to focus on the disadvantages he might suffer when compared to a person without those impairments;

d)   to focus on his accommodation needs arising from those impairments and the extent to which the accommodation met those needs;

e)   to recognise that the appellant's particular needs might require him to be treated more favourably than a person without a disability; and

f)   to review the suitability of the accommodation, paying due regard to those matters.[169]

---

165 *Baker v Secretary of State for Communities and Local Government* [2008] EWCA Civ 141; [2009] PTSR 809; *Bracking v Secretary of State for Work and Pensions* [2013] EWCA Civ 1345; *Hotak v Southwark LBC; Kanu v Southwark LBC; Johnson v Solihull MBC* [2015] UKSC 30, [2015] HLR 23. Of *Pieretti* (see last footnote), it was said in *Wilson v Birmingham City Council* [2016] EWCA Civ 1137, [2017] HLR that the provision was intended 'to introduce a culture of greater awareness of the existence and legal consequences of disability' – the provision in question in *Pieretti* was the predecessor to s 149, s 49A Disability Discrimination Act 1995.

166 *Webb-Harnden v. Waltham Forest LBC* [2023] EWCA Civ 992; [2023] HLR 45.

167 Below, paras **8.160–8.182**.

168 [2017] EWCA Civ 4, [2017] HLR 14. See also *R (Ahamed) v. Haringey LBC* [2023] EWCA Civ 975; [2023] HLR 43, where *Haque* was cited (at [56]) and the authority was considered to have applied a sharp focus to the applicant's disabilities 'with rigour, and with an open mind' in determining that accommodation was suitable, an outcome unsurprising in light of the facts (as recited in the judgment): the review officer specifically recorded that he considered the applicant to be disabled, that he had regard to the 2010 Act, he identified her medical conditions and addressed their implications in relation to the accommodation in detail, including her dietary needs and need for frequent access to a lavatory, and had considered NHS advice and spoken, as suggested on behalf of the applicant, to her GP practice.

169 There is no need to refer in terms to EqA 2010, s 149, what matters is whether the substance has been complied with: *Haque*, above, *Poshteh v Kensington and Chelsea RLBC* [2015] EWCA Civ 711, [2015] HLR 36, *Poshteh* went on appeal to the Supreme Court ([2017] UKSC 36, [2017] HLR 28) where there was no substantive discussion of the nature of the duty under EqA 2010, s 149 and the argument that it had not been considered by the review officer was dismissed as an example of the 'over-zealous linguistic analysis' deprecated in *Holmes-Moorhouse v Richmond-upon-Thames LBC* [2009] UKHL 7, [2009] HLR 34.

7.95   Thus, In *Lomax v Gosport BC*,[170] an appeal against a finding that an applicant was not homeless was upheld on the basis that there had been no 'sharp focus' on the applicant's disabilities and the consequences for her of remaining in her current accommodation and the particular reasons why continuing to occupy that accommodation would damage her mental health; a generalised reference to the situation of people on the authority's waiting list, who might or might not have disabilities, let alone disabilities as severe as those of the appellant, was not sufficient. EqA 2010, s 149 may involve treating a disabled person more favourably than a person who is not disabled – the reviewing officer had not complied with this duty and had failed to ask himself whether the appellant's situation was out of the ordinary; had he properly applied the public sector equality duty, he would probably have reached a different conclusion.

7.96   By way of example, in *Kannan v Newham LBC*,[171] the applicant suffered from a medical condition which necessitated extensive reconstructive surgery which seriously affected his mobility. He applied to Newham LBC which decided that he was owed the full housing duty and provided him with temporary accommodation in a flat on the first floor of a building. The flat was only accessible via an external staircase which was difficult for the applicant to use. The bathroom had no shower, only a bath, which the applicant could not use. The authority's medical adviser considered that he needed a ground floor property or one he could reach by lift. The authority nonetheless decided that the property was suitable.

7.97   The Court of Appeal allowed an appeal: EqA 2010, s 149 required a 'sharp focus' on the nature of the applicant's disability and how it affected the suitability of the property; the starting-point should have been the medical officer's conclusion that the property was not suitable;[172] the medical evidence showed that it was extremely difficult for Mr Kannan to access and that he was in 'severe' pain as a result of the use of the external staircase, which the authority had downgraded to 'uncomfortable and inconvenient' without explanation; nor had there been any consideration by the authority of the problems caused by the absence of a shower. Nor could reliance be placed on the general housing conditions in the area, without considering how many of those also living in unsatisfactory conditions suffered from a disability.

7.98   In *Biden*,[173] however, the applicant was a transgender woman who suffered from mobility difficulties; the issue was the suitability of the authority's offer, in the course of which the applicant relied on discrimination and incidents which had left her frightened and concerned to be in remote unfamiliar areas; she contended that the authority had not complied with its duties under the Equality

---

170 [2018] EWCA Civ 1846, [2019] PTSR 167, [2018] HLR 40.
171 [2019] EWCA Civ 57, [2019] HLR 22.
172 The property might have been suitable for a period of time, but by the time of the review the applicant had been in it for more than a year, which the reviewing officer had failed to take into account.
173 *Biden v Waverley BC* [2022] EWCA 442; [2022] HLR 32.

Act 2010. The review officer made inquiries of a Police Community Support Officer about the area in which the offer was located and recorded that crime in the area was low and that violent crime and threats of violence were almost non-existent, including that the PCSO had told her there was no evidence of LGBT+ hate crime in the area and had advised that it would be safe for a transgender woman and that he would have no concerns for her safety in the surrounding area.

7.99   The review officer's decision letter recorded the applicant's concern about remote or unfamiliar areas and that there had been incidents which had left her feeling suicidal; that she suffered from depression for which she took medication; and, it recognised that, if she was subsequently the victim of harassment, it would worsen her depression. Also, in event of a distressing incident, it would be more difficult for her to extricate herself from it because of her mobility issues. The officer noted that the authority had decided to offer a flat owned by a housing association specifically because social landlords were more understanding of transgender issues than many private sector landlords.

7.100   On appeal, it was contended that, in making her inquiries of the police, the review officer should have consulted a lesbian, gay, bisexual, transgender (LGBT) liaison officer rather than a PCSO, and that failure to do so was in breach of the public sector equality duty under s 149, Equality Act 2010. The appeal was dismissed: it was absurd to suggest that the review officer's failure to expand the scope of her inquiries to involve a lesbian, gay, bisexual and transgender (LGBT) liaison officer reflected a failure to have due regard to the protected characteristic of gender reassignment, whether considered alone or in conjunction with the appellant's disability; the officer had recognised the nature of the applicant's protected characteristics and the difference between her and a transgender person without a disability; she had due regard to the possibility of victimisation; the decision to offer a housing association property because private sector landlords were more likely to discriminate against transgender persons could be regarded as more favourable treatment of the application; the authority had accordingly complied with the public sector equality duty.

7.101   A detailed analysis of a claim by a wheelchair user suffering from paranoid schizophrenia who was held by Kensington and Chelsea RLBC not to be homeless referable to rented accommodation in Cornwall is – as most cases – largely particular to its facts[174] Nonetheless, its conclusions illustrate how the duty to make inquiries operates when s 149 is in play. The challenge to the authority's refusal to accommodate pending review was successful on the basis of the following defects in its decision:[175]

---

174 *R (Saint Sepulchre) v. Kensington & Chelsea RLBC* [2023] EWHC 2913 (Admin); [2024] HLR 12.

175 At [60]. At [61], the court also referred to a failure to consider the complexities of the applicant's mental and physical conditions beyond a description of them, and that, while the public sector equality duty is recognised 'it is not obviously applied through the inquiry process'. Nor did the authority explore with its Care Act assessor what the effect on the applicant's mental health would be if he was referred back to Cornwall (at [59]).

'(i) the safety of the address beyond communication with the landlord in Cornwall,[176]

(ii) combined with the lack of consideration of the complaints of assault from the perspective of Mr. Saint Sepulchre, with his particular mental illness (at minimum, he believed they happened);[177]

(iii) the Defendant's Care Act assessment in the Decision and lack of consideration of its findings in the Review Letter;

(iv) personal circumstances and consequences of not providing accommodation, there is a lack of inquiry of the Care Act assessment assessor and of Mr. Saint Sepulchre's social worker as to the effect of not providing accommodation in light of his hospital admissions in June 2023; there is some challenge in the Review Letter to the wheelchair dependency without further inquiries of [the applicant's Occupational Therapist]

(v) the basis for the assertion in the both the Decision and Review Letter that Mr. Saint Sepulchre will receive the same care in Cornwall'.[178]

Whose circumstances?

7.102 HA 1996, s 183(2) – governing applications – refers to 'a person making . . . an application', and enquiries under s 184[179] are whether 'he is' eligible for assistance, or whether 'he has a local connection' with another authority. The wording might therefore be said to suggest that it is only the applicant who is to be considered.[180] On the other hand, enquiries into the local connection of the applicant alone would not suffice, for the local connections of a person reasonably to be expected to reside with the applicant are not merely relevant but as central to whether or not an application may be referred as the local connections of the applicant,[181] and priority need will commonly arise by reference to non-applicants.[182] The circumstances of a person reasonably to be expected to reside

---

176 The authority did not communicate with the applicant's solicitor who had been acting for him in Cornwall. This meant that the applicant had a strong case because reliance on information about his circumstances in Cornwall had not been balanced (at [61]).

177 The authority relied on lack of corroboration by the applicant's landlord as to violence he had suffered, and feared, in and around his Cornwall flat: the court applied the Code, para 26.15, addressing lack of corroboration by police, that people can be fearful of making complaints because of the risk that it increases violence. The court also noted that the authority failed to consider that the applicant might have a mistrust of the police (at [54]).

178 The authority in Cornwall had concluded that the applicant had no eligible social care needs (see para **11.22**) whereas their own Adult Social Care department did so: see also para **8.56.**

179 See para **7.57.**

180 In Wales, the H(W)A 2014 speaks of an assessment of 'a person's case': s 62. Likewise, the assessment duty in HA 1996, s 189A talks of 'an assessment of the applicant's case'.

181 See para **5.8.**

182 See para **3.3.**

with the applicant may also affect the issue of intentionality – for example, if those circumstances meant that the accommodation which has been quit was not available or reasonable to continue to be occupied;[183] likewise, that person is explicitly relevant to an assessment of the applicant's housing needs.[184] The suitability of accommodation offered will also require regard to be had to those reasonably to be expected to reside with the applicant.[185]

7.103 It would introduce a surprising – and inconsistent – degree of legality or formality into HA 1996, Part 7 and H(W)A 2014, Part 2 if anything turned on who actually approaches the authority or signs an application form. It seems clear, therefore, that any person whose circumstances will, under HA 1996, Part 7 (or H(W)A 2014, Part 2), necessarily be taken into consideration in determining either eligibility for assistance or the level of that assistance, should be considered within the ambit of an application and its enquiries.[186]

Burden of proof

7.104 It is not for the applicant to 'prove' their homelessness. In *Walters*,[187] the applicant's solicitor gave the authority information which, if confirmed, would have led to a finding that the applicant was homeless; the authority said that she had not established that she was homeless. This wrongly treated the burden as being on the applicant to prove homelessness. The assessment duty in HA 1996, s 189A is, in any event, inquisitorial in nature.[188]

Relevant matters

7.105 It is a trite proposition that enquiries must cover all relevant matters; this means more than merely 'touching on' relevant matters: an authority must engage with the issues that are germane to the application.[189]

---

183 See paras **2.19–2.41, 4.158–4.164**.
184 HA 1996, s 189A(2)(b); para **8.61**.
185 See paras **8.160–8.234**.
186 In turn, this could lead to a finding that there had not been intentional homelessness – where one member is or could be held to have become homeless intentionally but another is or could not be. At that point, assuming that there is at least a minimal degree of knowledge that the 'second' person is asking the authority for housing assistance, there is in substance an 'application', and that person is entitled to their separate consideration: see paras **7.102–7.103**.
187 *R v Woodspring DC ex p Walters* (1984) 16 HLR 73, QBD.
188 HA 1996, s 189A(1) – 'The authority must make an assessment of the applicant's case'.
189 See *Islington LBC v Mohammed* [2013] EWCA Civ 739, [2013] HLR 41 (not engaged with whether applicant would be vulnerable because fainting attacks more likely if street homeless). See also *Farah v Hillingdon LBC* [2014] EWCA Civ 359, [2014] HLR 24 (intentional homelessness because of arrears which could have been avoided by unnecessary expenditure, including taxis: the authority had not engaged with whether the applicant's argument that some of the fares were necessary expenditure because of her mobility difficulties). See generally paras **10.10, 10.48–10.51**.

7.106 A relevant matter may evolve from the factual background provided by the applicant or of the authority's own motion. In *Paris*,[190] it was held that enquiries into matters relevant to a finding of intentionality have to be made whether or not the applicant provides information which suggests that there may be something to follow up – eg, whether or not the last accommodation occupied was available and whether it was reasonable to continue in occupation of it.

7.107 Thus, in *Silchenstedt*,[191] the applicant was asked to leave accommodation consisting of two bedrooms on the basis of rent arrears, but was offered alternative accommodation by the same landlord, which the applicant refused on the ground that it was not suitable. The authority found the applicant intentionally homeless and that the alternative accommodation was available for him and reasonable for him to occupy.[192] The applicant successfully challenged the decision because the authority had not conducted sufficient enquiries into the size and nature of the accommodation which the applicant had refused.

7.108 By way of contrast, in *de Falco*[193] the applicants gave their reason for leaving Italy as unemployment and did not put forward any material from which it might have been inferred that the accommodation that they had left was not accommodation which had been reasonable to continue to occupy.[194] The authority was held not to have erred in drawing the inference that what they had left had been suitable,[195] even though it had made no express enquiry to this effect. *De Falco* was, however, an interlocutory application and was treated as such in *Paris*.[196] On this aspect, it is somewhat out of harmony with subsequent decisions.

7.109 In *Fisher*,[197] it was held that intentionality enquiries may have to go back over several years, to the last accommodation occupied by the applicant (if any) which was available and reasonable. See also *Iqbal*,[198] where insufficient enquiries were made into the applicant's claim that he was a political refugee.

Adequacy of enquiries

7.110 The requirement to enquire into all relevant matters does not, however, mean that a failure to enquire into every matter raised will necessarily make

---

190 *R v Reigate and Banstead BC ex p Paris* (1985) 17 HLR 103, QBD.
191 *R v Kensington and Chelsea RLBC ex p Silchenstedt* (1997) 29 HLR 728, QBD.
192 For reasons that are not apparent on the face of the report, the argument (described as 'legalistic, although it may be a perfectly proper, approach') that the applicant could not be homeless intentionally as a result of a failure to take up accommodation 'has not been pressed in this application before me': *Silchenstedt*, at 731.
193 *De Falco, Silvestri v Crawley BC* [1980] QB 460, CA.
194 Although Bridge LJ considered the reason for leaving Italy to be 'not their lack of suitable accommodation, but their lack of employment' (at 482F; a phrase then picked up by the headnote writer), the correct test was reasonable to continue to occupy, as is recognised later in the same paragraph.
195 Ie, reasonable for them to continue to occupy, see last footnote.
196 *R v Reigate and Banstead BC ex p Paris* (1985) 17 HLR 103, QBD.
197 *R v Preseli DC ex p Fisher* (1985) 17 HLR 147, QBD.
198 *R v Westminster City Council ex p Iqbal* (1990) 22 HLR 215, QBD.

the enquiry (or assessment) process flawed. What is relevant will be different in every case. The duty to make enquiries means enquiries appropriate to the facts known to the authority, or of which it ought reasonably to have been aware;[199] the applicant should normally put forward the matters and evidence which they wish to be taken into account.[200] In *Zaman v Waltham Forest LBC; Uduezue v Bexley LBC*,[201] the applicant in Bexley contended that a final offer of three-bedroom accommodation in Chatham, Kent, was not suitable in part because, having raised the issue of disruption to one of her daughter's education, the authority had made no enquiries of her current school as to the impact of a move, and in part because the authority had not considered placing her in closer two-bedroom accommodation (which there was evidence could be available): it was held that merely raising possible disruption did not call for further enquiries of the school; and, the applicant had never told the authority she wished to be considered for a two-bedroom property.[202]

7.111   Enquiries can only be attacked as inadequate if they are enquiries that no reasonable authority could have failed to make; the court should not intervene merely because further enquiries would have been sensible or desirable, only if they were such that no reasonable authority could be satisfied had been sufficient – see *Costello*,[203] *Bayani*[204] and *Kassam*.[205] These older examples will need to be reconsidered in light of the assessment duty in HA 1996, s 189A,[206] but it is likely that many of them would be decided the same way nonetheless and the same approach was adopted in *Cifci* and *Ahamet*.[207]

Examples – unsuccessful challenge

7.112   In *Adamiec*,[208] where the applicant alleged that he had been constrained to sell his home because of financial circumstances, the court refused to quash the decision that he was intentionally homeless either on the basis that a

---

199 *R v Sedgemoor DC ex p McCarthy* (1996) 28 HLR 608, QBD.

200 *Cramp v Hastings BC; see also, eg, Phillips v Camden LBC* [2005] EWCA Civ 1005, [2005] HLR 48, *Cifci v Haringey LBC* [2021] EWCA 1772; [2022] HLR 9 and *Moge v Ealing LBC* [2023] EWCA Civ 464; [2023] HLR 35; see also paras **7.91–7.92**.

201 [2023] EWCA Civ 322; [2023] HLR 30.

202 The applicant succeeded, however, on the point that the authority's decision-letter had not explained the effect of s 195A(2) (further assistance within two years), so that its duty had not come to an end, following *Norton v Haringey LBC* [2022] EWCA Civ 1340; [2023] HLR 3 – see para **8.268**.

203 *R v Nottingham City Council ex p Costello* (1989) 21 HLR 301, QBD.

204 *R v Kensington and Chelsea RLBC ex p Bayani* (1990) 22 HLR 406, CA.

205 *R v Kensington and Chelsea RLBC ex p Kassam* (1994) 26 HLR 455, QBD. See also *R v Nottingham City Council ex p Edwards* (1999) 31 HLR 33, QBD.

206 Paras **8.61–8.75**.

207 *Cifci v Haringey LBC* [2021] EWCA 1772; [2022] HLR 9 at [34–[35] citing – among other cases – *Bayani* and the non-homelessness case of *R (Balajigari) v Secretary of State for the Home Department* [2019] EWCA Civ 763, [2019] 1 WLR 4674; *R (Ahamed) v Haringey LBC* [2023] EWCA Civ 975; [2023] HLR 43, at [52].

208 *R v Leeds City Council ex p Adamiec* (1992) 24 HLR 138, QBD.

reasonable authority would have further tested the financial material before it or that a reasonable authority would have made further enquiries; this is a decision which, even before the assessment duty came into force, would probably not have survived more modern approaches.

7.113   On the other hand, in *Baruwa*,[209] where the applicant claimed that she could not afford her rent because of other necessary outgoings, the Court of Appeal held that it was not necessary for the authority to investigate every detail and every inconsistency in the income and expenditure figures provided by the applicant before reaching its decision,[210] which is likely to remain an approach which would still be taken.

7.114   In *Bariise*,[211] the applicant complained that insufficient enquiries had been made into her allegations that those she had shared a house with had stolen her food and had scolded her children, making them cry. All the allegations were, however, known to the authority; there were no further enquiries which it could usefully have made. This would probably be decided the same way today.

7.115   In *McDonagh*,[212] a failure to enquire into the applicant's British nationality could not be criticised, as the applicant had informed the authority that his family was a large Irish travelling family just arrived from Dublin, and only claimed to be British after the decision that he was intentionally homeless had been made.

7.116   In *Augustin*,[213] it could not be said – on the material before it – that the authority could not have been satisfied that the applicant was homeless intentionally. In the circumstances, it could not be said that it had not made necessary enquiries.

Examples – successful challenge

7.117   In *Beattie (No 2)*,[214] affidavit evidence in earlier proceedings was considered to be material which the authority ought to have taken into account, even though it had not expressly been referred to during the course of a further application.

7.118   In *Krishnan v Hillingdon LBC*,[215] the authority had made inadequate enquiries when it failed to chase up its letter to another authority, or to follow

209 *R v Brent LBC ex p Baruwa* (1997) 29 HLR 915, CA.
210 Contrast *R v Tower Hamlets LBC ex p Ullah* (1992) 24 HLR 680, QBD, where further enquiries were held to have been necessary on very similar facts to *Baruwa*.
211 *R v Brent LBC ex p Bariise* (1999) 31 HLR 50, CA.
212 *R (McDonagh) v Hounslow LBC* [2004] EWHC 511 (Admin), [2004] JHL D61.
213 *R v Westminster City Council ex p Augustin* (1993) 25 HLR 281, CA.
214 *R v Eastleigh BC ex p Beattie (No 2)* (1985) 17 HLR 168, QBD.
215 *Krishnan v Hillingdon LBC* June 1981 *LAG Bulletin* 137, QBD.

up the applicant's own description of pressure on him to leave his earlier accommodation because of overcrowding.

7.119 In *Phillips*,[216] the applicant burst out at her husband during their interview that she had always told him his drinking would get them into trouble. This was said not to be capable of being construed as acquiescence,[217] even by the most hard-hearted of officers; it was astonishing that the officer had not made further enquiries. If he had, for example, of social services, it would inevitably have led to the conclusion that the applicant could not be blamed.

7.120 In *Ajayi*,[218] the authority had failed to enquire into 'important matters of social history and national status' – such as for how long the applicant had been away from the UK and where her children were born – which failure led the authority to consider that the applicant was an immigrant, whereas she had actually been born in the UK.

7.121 In *Tickner v Mole Valley DC*,[219] Lord Denning MR criticised the enquiries made as to whether or not the applicants were actually homeless. The applicants, while living in mobile homes, had given permanent addresses to the site manager, on which the authority based its conclusion that they were not homeless:

> 'They made that finding because each couple gave their permanent address elsewhere. One gave a mother-in-law's address. Another gave a divorced husband's address. I think that was not sufficient. Enquiries should have been made at the addresses given as permanent addresses. If the mother-in-law was asked – or if the divorced husband was asked – the answer would have been: "We are not going to have that person back." So Mole Council should have found these couples were homeless.'

7.122 As foreshadowed above,[220] the right to review is likely to cure any deficiency or failure to conduct adequate enquiries. In *Cramp*,[221] Brooke LJ said:[222]

> 'Given the full-scale nature of the review, a court whose powers are limited to considering points of law should now be even more hesitant than the High Court was encouraged to be at the time of *ex p Bayani*[223] if the appellant's ground of appeal relates to a matter which the reviewing officer was never

---

216 *R v West Dorset DC ex p Phillips* (1985) 17 HLR 336, QBD.
217 See para **4.20**.
218 *R v Newham LBC ex p Ajayi* (1996) 28 HLR 25, QBD.
219 *Tickner v Mole Valley DC* August 1980 *LAG Bulletin* 187, CA.
220 See para **7.10**.
221 *Cramp v Hastings BC; Phillips v Camden LBC,* above.
222 *Cramp* at [14].
223 *R v Kensington and Chelsea RLBC ex p Bayani* (1990) 22 HLR 406, CA.

invited to consider, and which was not an obvious matter he should have considered.'[224]

7.123   Although *Cramp* undoubtedly raised the bar which an applicant must cross in order to establish illegality on the grounds of the adequacy of enquiries, that is not to say that the issue can no longer be raised. Challenges are frequently pursued on the basis of failure to make enquiries and the obligation to do so remains extant and, if anything, the inquisitorial nature of the assessment duty in HA 1996, s 189A,[225] has made the chance of such a challenge stronger. If a failure to make an enquiry remains uncorrected on review, the right to challenge remains fully available.

7.124   In *Pieretti v Enfield LBC*,[226] it was said that the dictum of Brooke LJ in *Cramp* requires qualification where the applicant is a disabled[227] person; even where a decision-maker (whether under HA 1996, s 184 or s 202) is not expressly invited to consider a putative[228] disability, they must still have due regard to the need to take steps to take account of it; if some feature of the evidence presents a real possibility that an applicant is within provisions of EqA 2010, s 149 – the public sector equality duty – it is likely to oblige the authority to carry out further inquiries.

7.125   The pre-*Cramp* case-law still provides useful guidance as to the matters which will influence the court's decision. It should, however, be read with the limitations of *Cramp* in mind. Advisers should always try to put all relevant matters before an authority; they cannot rely on challenging an omission instead.

---

224 See also *Moge v Ealing LBC* [2023] EWCA Civ 464; [2023] HLR 35 at [150]–[153]: 'Ms Moge was represented from the outset by experienced housing solicitors, who made representations on her behalf before the Council's "minded to letter" dated 28th July and then again before the reviewing officer's decision letter dated 12th August 2021. Nowhere in those representations was there any suggestion that the Council had failed in its duty under section 208(1), either by failing to carry out adequate searches or indeed at all. The only point made in the initial representations was that Ms Moge had not refused the Council's offer of accommodation. That point was then supplemented by a suggestion that the Flat was unsuitable because of its distance from Ms Moge's places of work within the borough – but that is a separate point. ... Moreover, it was no part of Ms Moge's case in the County Court that the Council had failed to comply with the 2018 Guidance or that the 2006 Guidance referred to in the review decision was out of date'.

225 Paras **8.61–8.75**.

226 [2010] EWCA Civ 1104, [2011] HLR 3.

227 *Pieretti* concerned Disability Discrimination Act 1995, s 49A; this has been replaced with the broader 'public sector equality duty' in EqA 2010, s 149 and, as such, the full range of 'protected characteristics' should be considered, ie, age; disability; gender reassignment; marriage and civil partnership; pregnancy and maternity; race; religion or belief; sex; sexual orientation.

228 The decision-maker is, however, entitled to ask for evidence of an alleged disability and, if none is provided, may conclude that there is none: *Birmingham City Council v Wilson* [2016] EWCA Civ 1137, [2017] HLR 4.

Reliance on particular circumstances

7.126   If reliance is sought to be placed on some eventuality which is not to be taken for granted – eg, some idiosyncratic or uncommon circumstance which would alter the decision – of which not even a suspicion has come to the authority's attention, it is very much harder to complain of its failure to ask a relevant question.[229]

7.127   In the same vein, an authority will not be criticised for failing to make enquiries of someone they have no reason to believe will provide relevant information – for example, a doctor or a school where health or education did not appear to be in issue – especially if an experienced adviser has not raised the point.

7.128   In *Holland*,[230] a couple applied as homeless. They had been living at a series of temporary addresses since leaving a caravan site, which the authority was satisfied had been quit in circumstances which amounted to intentional homelessness. At the Court of Appeal, the couple sought to rely on a suggestion that the man had enjoyed an intervening period of what would have been permanent accommodation in a boarding-house (because he and his wife had at that time separated), but which he had lost for reasons beyond his control, so that he could not be treated as being intentionally homeless. This argument was rejected: the authority had been given no reason to suspect that the accommodation might have been permanent or acceptable to the man, whose separation from his wife had never been mentioned.

7.129   In *Henderson*,[231] the applicants contended that they were unaware of material facts when they agreed to an order for possession being made against them. The authority could not, however, be faulted for failing to make appropriate enquiries when, on the facts available to it (including what it had been told by the applicants), it had no reason to be aware of this.

7.130   See also *Mahsood*,[232] in which it was held that the authority had no reason to be aware of the applicant's ignorance of housing benefit entitlement during a period of absence.[233] In *Cunha*,[234] there had been little or no reference to the illness of the applicant's child as a reason for her return from Brazil; in contrast, see *Ajayi*,[235] where the authority had failed to enquire into 'important matters of social history and national status', such as for how long the applicant had been away from the UK and where her children were born, which failure led to an error in the way in which the application was considered

---

229 See *Cramp*. See also *Bellouti v Wandsworth LBC* [2005] EWCA Civ 602, [2005] HLR 46.
230 *R v Harrow LBC ex p Holland* (1982) 4 HLR 108, CA.
231 *R v Wandsworth LBC ex p Henderson* (1986) 18 HLR 522, QBD.
232 *R v Wycombe DC ex p Mahsood* (1988) 20 HLR 683, QBD.
233 This could surely not survive the duty to assess the circumstances that caused the applicant's homelessness in HA 1996, s 189A(2)(a).
234 *R v Kensington and Chelsea RLBC ex p Cunha* (1989) 21 HLR 16, QBD.
235 *R v Newham LBC ex p Ajayi* (1996) 28 HLR 25, QBD.

7.131   In *Nipa Begum*,[236] although it was relevant to consider whether an applicant could afford to travel to accommodation when deciding whether it was available to her,[237] the challenge failed because the applicant had not raised the issue, nor was it evident from any of the information before the authority that it was an issue. The authority was accordingly entitled to conclude without further enquiries that she could return to it.

Medical evidence

7.132   In cases where vulnerability is claimed for medical reasons, it will be both proper and a necessary part of an authority's enquiries to consider a medical opinion. The authority must, however, still decide the question of vulnerability for itself: *Carroll*.[238] It has been suggested that a decision involves three stages: consideration of what is stated in the application and whether it is supported by evidence; consideration of the housing authority's own historic file if any and that of social services if needs be; and, if in doubt, clarification of medical matters with the applicant or third parties.[239] Where the applicant is street homeless, this should be undertaken within hours or a day; if the medical needs are complex and the applicant is living in accommodation which they have occupied for some time, the timescale be longer.[240] If the applicant does not provide current medical evidence and does not respond to reasonable requests for clarification, the timescale may be extended or existence of the duty may even be rejected.[241]

7.133   A medical report obtained in pursuance of enquiries is not necessarily required to be disclosed to an applicant. In *R (Lynch) v Lambeth LBC*,[242] the authority made reference to extracts of its medical officer's report within the 'minded to find' letter sent in compliance with the Allocation of Housing and Homelessness (Review Procedures) Regulations 1999.[243] The applicant had the opportunity to make representations in response to the letter on any matter with which she disagreed, including the references to the medical officer's report. She did not do so. The failure by the authority to provide the applicant with a copy of the medical report was therefore 'not conclusive of any error of public law'.[244]

7.134   In *Sangermano*,[245] the authority ought either to have accepted medical evidence which was submitted by the applicant's advisers, or to have made its

---

236 *Nipa Begum v Tower Hamlets LBC* (1999) 32 HLR 445, CA.
237 See paras **2.19–2.41**.
238 *R v Lambeth LBC ex p Carroll* (1988) 20 HLR 142, QBD; *Osmani v Camden LBC* [2004] EWCA Civ 1706, [2004] HLR 22.
239 *R (Yabari) v Westminster CC* [2023] EWHC 185 (Admin); [2023] HLR 34.
240 *Yabari*, ibid.
241 *Yabari*.
242 [2006] EWHC 2737 (Admin), [2007] HLR 15.
243 Allocation of Housing and Homelessness (Review Procedure) Regulations 1999, SI 1999/71. See paras **7.227–7.235**.
244 *R (Lynch) v Lambeth LBC* [2006] EWHC 2737 (Admin), [2007] HLR 15, at [33].
245 *R v Bath City Council ex p Sangermano* (1985) 17 HLR 94, QBD.

own further enquiries. Once medical evidence has been provided to an authority and properly considered, however, it is open to the authority to reject it.[246] Medical evidence may also be rejected if it does not relate to a relevant time. In *Hijazi*,[247] a psychiatrist's opinion was rejected because it did not relate to the applicant's condition at the material time of his eviction.

7.135   In *Lumley*,[248] the authority was provided with a questionnaire completed by the applicant's GP which confirmed that the applicant suffered from severe depression for which he was on medication. The information was passed to the authority's medical officer, who was not qualified in psychiatric medicine, and who neither saw the applicant nor made any further enquiries. He concluded, without giving any reasons, that the applicant was not vulnerable on medical grounds. The enquiries made by the medical officer were held to be inadequate.

7.136   In *Kacar*,[249] however, the applicant claimed that it was not reasonable for him to continue to live away from London because of his wife's depression and phobia of being alone. His wife was not receiving any medical treatment, nor had she consulted her GP, nor had she spoken to her social worker. There were no further enquiries which a reasonable authority could have been expected to make; it had sufficient information to assess the seriousness of the wife's depression.

7.137   See also the discussion of the role of medical advice and evidence in *Shala v Birmingham City Council*[250] and *Guiste*[251] at paras **3.53–3.55**.

Blanket policies

7.138   A decision reached without proper enquiries will be invalid. A decision reached pursuant to a policy to treat all those evicted for arrears as homeless intentionally will be plainly void as a failure to exercise properly the duty to reach an individual decision:[252] *Williams v Cynon Valley Council*.[253] Nor may an authority automatically or invariably treat as homeless intentionally all those who have been evicted from premises on grounds which reflect tenant default (for example, nuisance and annoyance) – the authority must take the reasons for the eviction into account and look at the circumstances giving rise to the order.[254]

---

246 *Noh v Hammersmith and Fulham LBC* [2001] JHL D54, CA.
247 *Hijazi v Kensington and Chelsea RLBC* [2003] EWCA Civ 692, [2003] HLR 73.
248 *R v Newham LBC ex p Lumley* (2001) 33 HLR 11, QBD.
249 *Kacar v Enfield LBC* (2001) 33 HLR 5, CA.
250 *Shala v Birmingham City Council* [2007] EWCA Civ 624, [2008] HLR 8. See also paras **3.53–3.54**.
251 *Guiste v Lambeth LBC* [2019] EWCA Civ 1758, [2020] HLR 12.
252 See paras **10-54–10.55**.
253 January 1980 *LAG Bulletin* 16, CC.
254 *Devenport v Salford City Council* (1983) 8 HLR 54, CA; *R v Cardiff City Council ex p John* (1982) 9 HLR 56, QBD.

7.139   An authority must also bear in mind that some possession orders are within the discretion of the county court judge, who may have taken into account matters for which the applicant has no responsibility. In *Stubbs v Slough BC*,[255] a county court ordered the authority to reconsider its finding of intentionality because an element in the decision to order possession on the ground of nuisance had been the proximity of landlord and tenant, and their relationship, over which the tenant had no control.

Loss of employment

7.140   If the cause of an application is loss of employment, the authority must enquire why the job was lost: *Williams*.[256] Consider also *Cosmo*,[257] where there was a successful challenge on the ground that the authority had failed to make enquiries into whether the loss of accommodation was due to the failure of the applicant's business.

7.141   In *Cunha*,[258] however, the claimant sought to require the authority to consider the difficulties in sustaining employment in Brazil before deciding that she had become intentionally homeless when she had left employment there to come to the UK; it was held that there was no requirement for the authority to enquire into local employment conditions in Brazil.

7.142   Likewise in *Bayani*,[259] the failure of the local authority to make full enquiries into the applicant's employment situation in the Philippines was not fatal to its finding of intentionality.

Fairness

7.143   It is a trite proposition that fairness calls for all basic issues (that may be decided adversely to the applicant) to be put to an applicant.[260] When conducting enquiries fairly, authorities are not bound to treat the issue as if in a court of law: *Ward*.[261] They act reasonably if they act on responsible material from responsible people who might reasonably be expected to provide a reliable account. An authority can rely on hearsay, in the sense that it is not obliged to confine itself to direct evidence – for example, where an authority relied on evidence from a social worker's supervisor, rather than the social worker themselves.[262]

255 January 1980 *LAG Bulletin* 16, CC.
256 *R v Thurrock DC ex p Williams* (1981) 1 HLR 128, QBD; see para **4.82**.
257 *R v Camden LBC ex p Cosmo* (1998) 30 HLR 817, QBD.
258 *R v Kensington and Chelsea RLBC ex p Cunha* (1989) 21 HLR 16, QBD.
259 *R v Kensington and Chelsea RLBC ex p Bayani* (1990) 22 HLR 406, CA.
260 On the requirements of fairness, see paras **10.65–10.68**.
261 *R v Southampton City Council ex p Ward* (1984) 14 HLR 114, QBD.
262 *Ward*, above. See also *R v Nottingham City Council ex p Costello* (1989) 21 HLR 301, QBD.

7.144 In *Goddard v Torridge DC*,[263] the authority discussed with the applicant's former employers the circumstances in which he had quit his job and, accordingly, had lost his tied accommodation, and went into these matters fully with the applicant on three separate occasions, which was sufficient for these purposes.

7.145 In the Divisional Court hearing in *Islam*,[264] an allegation of want of natural justice failed because – by the time of the decision – the authority had given the applicant the benefit of no fewer than six interviews. The judgment nonetheless takes for granted that a want of natural justice would be fatal to an authority's decision.

7.146 The authority is, however, not obliged to put every detail to an applicant, although the applicant must have an opportunity to deal with at least the generality of material which will adversely affect them; this will usually include matters of factual detail.[265] Where facts are agreed by an applicant, which facts form the basis of the decision, the decision-maker is entitled to take the applicant's acceptance of the facts at face value.[266]

7.147 A failure to ask why the applicant fell into mortgage arrears,[267] or a failure to enquire into the applicant's state of mind when she quit her previous accommodation, ie, what she had believed about the accommodation that she was coming to (which turned out to be less than settled),[268] have both been held to have been errors on the part of an authority and would now fall within the assessment duty in any event.[269]

7.148 Where matters are put, they must be put to the applicant themselves[270] and, if during interview, a record of the interview should be kept: *Brown*.[271]

7.149 All matters that are ultimately decided against the applicant should be put to the applicant,[272] whether related to an admission by the applicant of which they are aware[273] (regardless of whether it was provided on a 'confidential' basis)[274] or where the authority obtains information from a third party on which

---

263 January 1982 *LAG Bulletin* 9, QBD.
264 *R v Hillingdon Homeless Panel ex p Islam* (1980) *Times*, February 10, QBD (not forming part of the subsequent appeals – see [1983] 1 AC 688, CA and HL, (1981) 1 HLR 107, HL).
265 On the requirements of fairness, see paras **10.65–10.68**.
266 *Rowley v Rugby BC* [2007] EWCA Civ 483, [2007] HLR 40.
267 *R v Wyre BC ex p Joyce* (1984) 11 HLR 72, QBD.
268 *R v Wandsworth LBC ex p Rose* (1984) 11 HLR 105, QBD.
269 HA 1996, s 189(12)(a); see paras **8.61–8.75**.
270 *R v Tower Hamlets LBC ex p Saber* (1992) 24 HLR 611, QBD.
271 *R v Dacorum BC ex p Brown* (1989) 21 HLR 405, QBD. If part of the assessment, written records of certain matters need to be kept in any event: see para **8.11**.
272 *R v Tower Hamlets LBC ex p Rouf* (1989) 21 HLR 294, QBD.
273 *Robinson v Brent LBC* (1999) 31 HLR 1015, CA. See also *R v Wandsworth LBC ex p Dodia* (1998) 30 HLR 562, QBD and *R v Camden LBC ex p Mohammed* (1998) 30 HLR 315, QBD on inconsistent statements given by applicants.
274 *R v Poole BC ex p Cooper* (1995) 27 HLR 605, QBD.

it intends to rely, such as a bank,[275] or information from the applicant's GP which is inconsistent with that which has been provided by the applicant themselves.[276]

7.150   The duty is not, however, absolute. A finding of intentionality was upheld in *Reynolds*,[277] even though important but ultimately not decisive issues had not been put directly to the applicant, who had refused both a home visit and an interview and who had requested that all communication be made through her solicitors.

7.151   Nor, in *Jaafer*,[278] was the authority required to put to the applicant its conclusion that her husband and child were illegal immigrants, as it had given her every opportunity to offer her version of events in an interview.

7.152   Where the facts are uncontested, there is no general obligation to inform each and every applicant in advance of any negative decision; this would place an unrealistically heavy burden on authorities: *Tetteh*.[279]

7.153   Nor is there an obligation to give the applicant the last word in every case. Whether or not it is unfair not to do so depends on the facts of the particular case.

7.154   Thus, in *Bellouti*,[280] medical evidence from the applicant's GP was submitted to the authority's medical adviser, who advised that it did not make the applicant vulnerable. Taking into account the evidence and the views of the medical adviser, a decision that the applicant was not vulnerable was upheld on review and appeal. The views of the medical adviser did not have to be put to the applicant because they did not comprise factual material obtained from a third party; all the authority had done was to refer material on which the applicant relied to its own medical adviser for comment. There was no unfairness in the comments not being shown to the applicant.

Doubt

7.155   If enquiries suggest that the applicant may have become homeless intentionally, but any doubt or uncertainty remains, the issue must be resolved in favour of the applicant.[281]

---

275 *R v Shrewsbury and Atcham BC ex p Griffiths* (1993) 25 HLR 613, QBD. See also *R v Brent LBC ex p McManus* (1993) 25 HLR 643, QBD and *R v Hackney LBC ex p Decordova* (1995) 27 HLR 108, QBD.
276 *R (Begum) v Tower Hamlets LBC* [2002] EWHC 633 (Admin), [2003] HLR 8.
277 *R v Sevenoaks DC ex p Reynolds* (1990) 22 HLR 250, CA.
278 *R v Westminster City Council ex p Jaafer* (1998) 30 HLR 698, QBD.
279 *Tetteh v Kingston upon Thames RLBC* [2004] EWCA Civ 1775, [2005] HLR 21.
280 *Bellouti v Wandsworth LBC* [2005] EWCA Civ 602, [2005] HLR 46. See also *Hall v Wandsworth LBC; Carter v Wandsworth LBC* [2004] EWCA Civ 1740, [2005] HLR 23.
281 *R v North Devon DC ex p Lewis* [1981] 1 WLR 328, QBD; see also *R v Thurrock BC ex p Williams* (1982) 1 HLR 71, QBD and *R v Gravesham BC ex p Winchester* (1986) 18 HLR 208, QBD.

Further enquiries and reconsideration

7.156 Once a decision has been made, there is no statutory power to make further enquiries unless an application is made for a review[282] or there is a fresh application.[283] If there is a review, the local authority is entitled to take as its starting point the matters which the applicant has specifically raised on review.[284] If a decision taken has been adverse to an applicant, it seems that the authority can nonetheless re-open its enquiries of its own motion if it receives new information.[285] This will cure any defects in its earlier procedure, for example, failure to consider relevant matters.

7.157 If the authority has power to reopen enquiries of its own motion, then it is hard to see how any reasonable authority could refuse to exercise it, ie, at the request of a disappointed applicant, provided that the new information has some degree of credibility and could (if accepted) affect the decision. If an authority refuses to do so, there are alternatives: a fresh application could be made relying on the hitherto unconsidered information,[286] or it has been held that the applicant could appeal the decision to the county court if still in time to do so (but not seek judicial review)[287] It would be risky to rely on the former course unless and until the authority agrees to entertain a new application; the soundest approach would seem to be to pursue both avenues, offering to withdraw the appeal should a new application be accepted.

7.158 In *Walsh*,[288] further enquiries led the authority to the conclusion that an earlier account of being locked out of accommodation was entirely false: while there was no general right to make a new decision on the same facts, the authority could do so if there was a material change, including new facts or the ascertained falsity of former facts.

7.159 In *Dagou*,[289] however, it was suggested that only fraud and deception would entitle the authority to re-open enquiries once its decision had been reached, although new information might still be relevant to the accommodation which was to be provided.

7.160 In *Crawley BC v B*,[290] the authority decided initially that an applicant was not in priority need and had so notified her (without reaching a decision on intentionality). Subsequently, during an appeal, it changed the priority need

---

282 *Mohamed v Hammersmith and Fulham LBC* [2001] UKHL 57, [2002] HLR 7, HL.
283 *R v Lambeth LBC ex p Miah* (1995) 27 HLR 21, QBD, and see paras **7.31–7.46** as to when a new application may be made.
284 *Williams v Birmingham City Council* [2007] EWCA Civ 691, [2008] HLR 4.
285 Consider *R v Hambleton DC ex p Geoghan* [1985] JPL 394, QBD.
286 See paras **7.41** and **7.44**.
287 *Demetri v Westminster City Council* [2000] 1 WLR 772, (2000) 32 HLR 470, CA. See further para **7.207**.
288 *R v Dacorum BC ex p Walsh* (1992) 24 HLR 401, QBD. Under HA 1985, there was no statutory review process.
289 *R v Southwark LBC ex p Dagou* (1996) 28 HLR 72, QBD.
290 (2000) 32 HLR 636, CA.

decision. It was still entitled to go on to consider whether the applicant had become intentionally homeless. This was, however, not so much a case of revising a decision as completing it. Some dicta in the case do, however, suggest that an authority may revisit a decision whenever, on public law grounds, it would be reasonable to do so.[291]

7.161   *Crawley* was distinguished in *Sadiq*.[292] Once a duty had been accepted under HA 1996, s 193,[293] the section provides a complete code of when an authority ceases to be subject to its requirements, so that, for example, loss of priority need after acceptance of a section 193 duty does not entitle the authority to make a new decision that no further duty is owed.

7.162   Nonetheless, in *Porteous*,[294] the authority was permitted to change its decision even after a duty had been accepted under section 193. Rejecting the proposition in *Dagou*[295] – that decisions could only be re-opened in cases of fraud or deception – it was held that they could also be revisited where the original decision was based on a fundamental mistake of fact.[296]

7.163   Likewise, in *Slaiman*,[297] the return of an applicant to her husband following domestic violence was held to go to the existence or non-existence of the original allegation of domestic violence, rather than comprising a change of circumstances arising after acceptance of a full duty; accordingly, the authority was entitled to reconsider.

7.164   *Porteous* was applied by the Court of Appeal in *Sambotin*:[298] only fraud or deception or a fundamental mistake of fact entitles the authority to re-open the decision. In that case, the applicant was a Romanian national who initially applied to Waltham Forest LBC for assistance under HA 1996, Part 7; the authority decided that he was not eligible for assistance. After moving to Brent, he applied for assistance from Brent LBC, providing the authority with a copy of the earlier decision made by Waltham Forest. Brent decided that he was eligible for assistance and was owed the full housing duty, but that they would refer his application to Waltham Forest under the local connection provisions. Waltham Forest refused

---

291   See per Buxton LJ at 645.
292   *R v Brent LBC ex p Sadiq* (2000) 33 HLR 47, QBD.
293   See paras **8.132–8.137**.
294   *Porteous v West Dorset DC* [2004] EWCA Civ 244, [2004] HLR 30.
295   *R v Southwark LBC ex p Dagou* (1995) 28 HLR 72, QBD; see para **7.159**.
296   Both applicant and authority had operated under a fundamental mistake of fact relating to a tenancy which neither had realised the applicant still held.
297   *R (Slaiman) v Richmond upon Thames LBC* [2006] EWHC 329 (Admin), [2006] HLR 20.
298   *R (Sambotin) v Brent LBC* [2018] EWCA Civ 1826, [2019] PTSR 371, [2019] HLR 5. In *R (Elkundi and others) v Birmingham City Council* [2021] EWHC 1024 (Admin); [2021] 1 WLR 4031; [2021] HLR 45, it was said (at [82]) that If an authority decides that an applicant's accommodation is unsuitable, it can only revisit that decision if it was reached on the basis of a fraudulent misrepresentation by the applicant or on the basis of a fundamental mistake of fact. The Court of Appeal ([2022] EWCA Civ 601; [2022] QB 604; [2022] HLR 31) did not decide this point as it did not arise, but explicitly declined to endorse it, commenting (at [121]–[123]) that the position may be different where the provision of suitable accommodation is in issue, as it is a continuing duty.

to accept the referral, relying on its earlier decision that he was not eligible for assistance. In response, Brent notified Mr Sambotin that it had now determined that he was not eligible for assistance and sought to withdraw their earlier decision.

7.165 It was held that Brent had made a final and concluded decision that Mr Sambotin was eligible for assistance which could only be revisited in the event of fraud or deception, or a fundamental mistake of fact, neither of which was present: once an authority has decided that an applicant is eligible for assistance, homeless, in priority need and not intentionally homeless, its duty under HA 1996, s 193(2) crystallises; if the authority decides to refer the applicant to another authority under the local connection provisions, the only issue is which authority is responsible for discharging the duty.

Time-scales

7.166 There is no statutory requirement that enquiries be carried out within any specific time; in Wales, where the enquiry and assessment duties are fully assimilated,[299] there is a target of ten days, although 'The priority is that the assessment and the decision are correct'.[300]

7.167 An authority may not avoid the enquiry duty on the basis that it will owe no duty to a person whose priority need will be lost by the time they are completed, eg, where a young person with an automatic priority need because they are 16 or 17 years old[301] will turn 18 during that period.[302]

DECISIONS

Postponement

7.168 While the obligation to reach a decision is not spelled out in s 184, HA 1996, it was held to be implicit in *Sidhu*,[303] but in any event it is overtaken by

---

299 See paras **8.76–8.78**.
300 See Welsh Code para 10.54: 'The Welsh Government recommends where the eligibility and housing status has been determined the decision on which duty is owed if any can be relayed to the customer as soon as possible and the remaining elements of the assessment can be concluded within the 10 working days'. There is no equivalent in the English Code, in fairly stark contrast with the previous version of the Code at para 6.16 which said that authorities should deal with enquiries as quickly as possible and suggested that authorities should aim to achieve interview and initial assessment of eligibility on the day of application with enquiries and notification within 33 working days of accepting the duty to make enquiries.
301 See paras **3.82–3.88**.
302 *Robinson v Hammersmith and Fulham LBC* [2006] EWCA Civ 1122, [2006] 1 WLR 3295, [2007] HLR 7 at [35].
303 *R v Ealing LBC ex p Sidhu* (1982) 2 HLR 45, QBD, approved in *Robinson v Hammersmith and Fulham LBC*, above, at [36]. The obligation to reach a decision means that a statement of *intention* to reach a decision is not a decision (see recently *R (Bano) v Waltham Forest LBC* [2024] EWHC 654 (Admin) at [55] and [63]), although communications need to be considered carefully to see whether they represent no more than an intention or whether properly read they do comprise a decision

the assessment duty, both in England, and in Wales. An authority may not defer the obligation in the hope or expectation of a change in circumstances such as might reduce its duties, for example, by loss of priority need.[304]

7.169   Nor can an authority seek to use mediation (eg, to reconcile a 17-year-old with their family) to prolong the decision-making process, so that the child turns 18 and loses their automatic priority need. Where mediation cannot take place without depriving the child of a right they would otherwise have had, the authority must perform its full duty – although it may be able to use mediation in order to fulfil that duty.[305] Mediation and enquiries are entirely independent processes.[306]

7.170   If the issue is eligibility for accommodation,[307] there would in any event be no point in deferring because the authority's housing duty under HA 1996, Part 7 ceases if the applicant's eligibility ends.[308]

Gatekeeping

7.171   An authority's decision on completion of its enquiries is taken on the basis of the information known to it at the time it is reached. It follows that changed circumstances – including those generated by the authority itself – may lead to a different finding than might have been taken had the decision immediately followed the application.

7.172   This, in turn, opens the way for authorities to engage in forms of 'gatekeeping', ie, action which obviates homelessness by ensuring that the applicant finds accommodation otherwise than through HA 1996, Part 7 or H(W) A 2014, Part 2.

7.173   There is a number of reasons why authorities may engage in this, eg: to help to ensure that targets are achieved for the purposes of audit or performance criteria and/or in the interests of returns to central government; for local presentational purposes; and to avoid the need to comply with ancillary provisions, including written decision with reasons, right to review and a reasonable preference in relation to allocations.

---

304 *R v Ealing LBC ex p Sidhu* (1982) 2 HLR 45, QBD. A suggestion in the *Encyclopaedia of housing law and practice* (Sweet & Maxwell) that in an appropriate case, a de minimis deferral, perhaps a few days, may be permissible where there is a substantive basis (as distinct from speculation or a remote chance) for the authority to anticipate a material change was not disapproved, but 'in the case of a 17 year old child, it would not seem to me to be lawful for a local authority to postpone the taking of a decision even for a short period on the basis that by postponing that decision the child will have reached the age of 18 before the decision is taken': per Waller LJ in *Robinson v Hammersmith and Fulham LBC* at [38]. The effect would seem to be that the proposition will not apply if it will cause loss of the priority need (as where priority need will, absent other grounds, be lost on reaching 18, see paras **3.82–3.88**).
305 *Robinson v Hammersmith and Fulham LBC*, above, per Waller LJ at [41].
306 *Robinson v Hammersmith and Fulham LBC*, above, at [42] and [45].
307 See Annex: Immigration Eligibility.
308 HA 1996, s 193(6)(a).

7.174 In *Hanton-Rhouila*,[309] a challenge based on failure to advise the applicant of the implications of accepting private accommodation[310] without completing the HA 1996, Part 7 process failed on the facts, and the review officer had been entitled to conclude that the applicant was no longer homeless.

7.175 The new help duties – towards those threatened with homelessness[311] and towards the homeless[312] – mean that authorities are now bound to take steps to obviate homelessness within HA 1996, Part 7 and H(W)A 2014, Part 2, but it is not certain that this will mean an end to practices outside the legislation.

Material to be taken into account

7.176 An authority must always take into account all that is relevant up to the date of its decision. Thus, in *Safi v Sandwell BC*,[313] the authority erred because it had considered whether it was reasonable to continue to occupy on the basis of the family composition as at the date of application (applicant, husband and one child in one-bedroom flat) without taking into account the impending birth of a second child; the authority should have asked itself two questions: first, taking account of the appellant's current circumstances and the impending birth of her second child, whether it was reasonable, looking to the foreseeable future as well as the present, for her to continue to occupy the flat; and second, how long in the short term was it reasonable for her to continue to occupy the flat and whether she would be able to obtain suitable accommodation in that time through her application under HA 1996, Part 6.[314]

7.177 An applicant cannot, however, complain of a decision which failed to take into account a matter which only came to the knowledge of the authority after it had made its final decision: *Islam*.[315] If material comes to light after the initial decision, but before the review, it must be taken into account on the review.[316] If it comes to light after the review, see the discussion of further reviews, below.[317]

7.178 In *Crossley*,[318] the decision was so at odds with the evidence put before the authority that the authority must have failed to take it into account. As the court put it:[319]

---

309 *Hanton-Rhouila v Westminster City Council* [2010] EWCA Civ 1334, [2011] HLR 12.
310 An assured shorthold tenancy arranged by the authority's Private Sector Housing Initiatives team under its Finders Payment Scheme (a discretionary scheme for helping people find suitable accommodation in the private sector).
311 Paras **8.79–8.87**.
312 Paras **8.88–8.107**.
313 [2018] EWCA Civ 2876, [2019] HLR 16.
314 See para **2.77**.
315 *R v Hillingdon Homeless Panel ex p Islam* (198) *Times*, February 24, QBD (not forming part of the subsequent appeals [1983] 1 AC 688, [1981] 1 HLR 107, HL).
316 See para **7.235**.
317 See paras **7.207–7.208**.
318 *Crossley v Westminster City Council* [2006] EWCA Civ 140, [2006] HLR 26.
319 At [28].

'. . . there were also stark facts, or appraisals of fact, pointing towards vulnerability for a statutorily recognised reason; and these the decision-maker had an obligation to acknowledge, take into account and evaluate along with everything else'.

7.179 An authority must consider those matters which sensibly arise on the facts of a case. In *F*,[320] the applicant took a tenancy of a property that she could not afford and contended that she had made appropriate enquiries with the housing benefit department before doing so. The authority found that she had not acted in good faith when accepting the tenancy.[321] Although it had not explicitly been invited to consider whether the applicant had acted in good faith, the court held that it was a matter that was sensibly capable of arising on the facts and therefore required consideration by the authority – which, however, the authority had undertaken.

7.180 In *Elrify*,[322] the applicant applied as homeless by reason of overcrowding. Both in its original decision and on review, the authority had applied only one part of the statutory test for overcrowding under HA 1985, Part 10. The review decision was accordingly flawed because the authority had failed properly to apply the statutory test and had therefore miscalculated the level of statutory overcrowding in the applicant's flat.

Own decision

7.181 The decision must be the authority's own, meaning that it must be taken by the authority pursuant to its decision-making arrangements, which can include contracting out,[323] not by the adoption of some other body's decision,[324] although the decision of another body may be relevant or the authority may reach the same decision having considered it for itself. Even though other authorities from which an authority requests assistance must co-operate,[325] one authority cannot simply 'rubber-stamp' the decision of another: *Miles*.[326]

7.182 This principle applies even to decisions of a court[327] – thus, while an authority must take into consideration decisions by family courts relating to with whom children are to live, the authority is not bound by them but must reach its own decision in the context of its own duties in the (different) legislative context in which they arise: *Holmes-Moorhouse*.[328]

---

320 *F v Birmingham City Council* [2006] EWCA Civ 1427, [2007] HLR 18.
321 Within the meaning of HA 1996, s 191(2); see paras **4.33–4.35**.
322 *Elrify v Westminster City Council* [2007] EWCA Civ 332, [2007] HLR 36.
323 Paras **7.6–7.8**.
324 See generally para **8.56**.
325 HA 1996, s 213.
326 *R v South Herefordshire DC ex p Miles* (1985) 17 HLR 82, QBD. See also *Eren v Haringey LBC* [2007] EWCA Civ 409.
327 Otherwise than so far as they are decisions of a court directly relating to the decision, ie, appeal against it or on judicial review.
328 *Holmes-Moorhouse v Richmond upon Thames LBC* [2009] UKHL 7, [2009] HLR 34. *See also recently Querino v Cambridge CC* [2024] EWCA Civ 314; HLR forthcoming, in which it was also held – at [25] – that, unless an order of the family court has been made authorising its disclosure, a Cafcass report cannot be disclosed to the authority or, therefore, taken into account by it.

Notification

Reasons

7.183   Once the authority has reached its decision, it must notify the applicant.[329] While there will generally be no reason to distinguish between when the decision is made and notification of reasons, these do not necessarily occur on the same date: ascertaining the date of the decision is essentially a question of fact.[330] If the authority decides an issue – relating either to eligibility or to level of duty – adversely to an applicant, it must also notify the applicant of its reasons.[331]

Local connection

7.184   A decision to refer an application to another authority under the local connection provisions, and the reasons for doing so, must likewise be notified.[332]

Review

7.185   Notifications must inform applicants of the right to request a review of a decision and of the time within which the request must be made.[333]

Relationship of notification duty and substantive duty

7.186   Duties to notify and to give reasons for decisions arise independently of the substantive duties to which they refer: *R v Beverley BC ex p McPhee*.[334] It is not open to an authority to claim that it has no duty under, for example, HA 1996, s 193 or s 200, on the basis that, although its enquiries are complete, it has not yet given notice of its decision; that would be to allow an authority to rely on its own wrong, ie, its failure to provide notice 'on completion' of enquiries.

Written notification

7.187   Notification, and reasons, must be given in writing; if not received by the applicant, notification will be treated as having been given only if made available at the authority's office for a reasonable time for collection by the applicant or on

---

329   HA 1996, s 184(3); H(W)A 2014, s 63.
330   *Robinson v Hammersmith and Fulham LBC* [2006] EWCA Civ 1122, [2006] 1 WLR 3295, [2007] HLR 7, at [25], referring (at [24]) to *R v Beverley BC ex p McPhee* (1978) *Times* 27 October, QBD.
331   *Robinson v Hammersmith and Fulham LBC*, above.
332   HA 1996, s 184(4); H(W)A 2014, s 82(2).
333   HA 1996, s 184(5); H(W)A 2014, s 84.
334   (1978) *Times* 27 October, QBD.

the applicant's behalf.[335] This appears to be so even if a copy of the notice is sent by registered post to one of the authority's own hostels or other property.[336]

Restricted cases[337]

7.188 If the authority decides that a duty is, or[338] after the end of its relief duty under HA 1996, s 189B(2)[339] would be, owed under HA 1996, s 193(2), or H(W) A 2014, s 75,[340] but only because of a restricted person, the notification is subject to additional requirements.[341] It must inform the applicant that the decision was reached on this basis, include the name of the restricted person, explain why the person is a restricted person, and explain the effect of HA 1996, s 193(7AD)[342] or, in Wales, H(W)A 2014, s 76(5).

Oral explanation

7.189 Where the applicant may have difficulty understanding the implications of a decision, authorities may need to arrange for a member of staff to provide and explain the notification in person.[343]

REVIEW

7.190 Neither the Housing (Homeless Persons) Act 1977 nor HA 1985, Part 3 made any provision for an applicant to seek an internal review of the authority's decision. The third edition of the Code of Guidance issued under HA 1985, Part 3 had, however, recommended[344] that authorities 'should have in place arrangements to review decisions on homelessness cases where an applicant

---

335 HA 1996, s 184(6); H(W)A 2014, s 84.
336 There was no express requirement for writing in the Housing (Homeless Persons) Act 1977; it was added to HA 1985 pursuant to Law Commission Recommendations (Cmnd 9515), No 5. On 19 April 2021, new para 18.30 was added to the Homelessness Code of Guidance, to the effect that the notification may be by email or letter, depending on the needs of the applicant.
337 See paras **A.127–A.133**.
338 Since commencement of HRA 2017 on 3 April 2018: see Homelessness Reduction Act 2017 (Commencement and Transitional and Savings Provisions) Regulations 2018, SI 2018/167 reg 3, only applicable to applications made and reviews sought on or after that date – see reg 4.
339 See para **8.93–8.103**.
340 See para **8.128**.
341 HA 1996, s 184(3A); H(W)A 2014, s 63(2).
342 See para **8.274.**
343 Although this is no longer recommended (see previous version of the English Code para 6.23) by the English Code of Guidance, it may be that the authority is required to take such steps if, eg, the applicant has a learning disability which engages the EqA 2010, in order to avoid unlawful discrimination. See also Welsh Code para 15.95.
344 Code of Guidance para 7.6.

wishes to appeal against the decision'.[345] That recommendation is now a statutory requirement.[346] An applicant is statutorily entitled to request a review, provided that the decision complained of falls within those specified in HA 1996, s 202 or H(W)A 2014, s 85.

7.191 It may be that the request for a review should be interpreted generously. In *Nzamy*,[347] the authority informed the applicant that if he did not accept an offer of alternative accommodation, it would treat its duty as discharged: a request for a review of the suitability of the offer, in the course of which the applicant made clear that the family was willing to remain in their current temporary accommodation pending a permanent offer, should also have been treated as a request for a review of the discharge decision.

7.192 Conversely, however, in *Bereket*,[348] the applicant was offered temporary accommodation which she rejected the accommodation as unsuitable. The authority stated that their duties had ended and provided an email address to which she could write if she wanted to request a s 202 review. She wrote to that address and reiterated that the property was not suitable. The authority considered that this did not amount to a request for a review and did not conduct one. Her claim for judicial review was dismissed. Whether the email amounted to a request for a review was determined by the substance of the content. Even on a generous interpretation, it was held, her email was not a request for a review but simply a reiteration of her previous complaints about the suitability of the property. It is, however, very difficult indeed to see how or why writing to the specified address with a statement of the reason for rejecting the offer could in such circumstances be anything other than a request for a review.

7.193 The right to request a review arises in relation to the following decisions.

Eligibility[349]

7.194 A decision on eligibility may be reviewed.[350] This includes whether or not the applicant is a person subject to immigration control.[351]

Duties[352]

7.195 An applicant may also seek review of any decision on what, if any, duty is owed under HA 1996, ss 190, 193 and 195–196 or H(W)A 2014, ss 66, 68, 73

---

345 'Appeal' was used generically not legally: there was no right of appeal under HA 1985 and a legal challenge had therefore to be by way of a claim for judicial review.
346 HA 1996, s 202(4); H(W)A 2014, s 85.
347 *Nzamy v Brent LBC* [2011] EWCA (Civ) 283, [2011] HLR 20.
348 *R (Bereket) v Waltham Forest LBC* [2021] EWHC 3120 (Admin).
349 See generally Annex: Immigration Eligibility.
350 HA 1996, s 202(1)(a); H(W)A 2014, s 85(1).
351 See para **A.14**.
352 See generally Chapter 8.

or 75.[353] This expressly encompasses whether or not the applicant is in priority need,[354] whether intentionally homeless,[355] and whether a duty has ceased under HA 1996, s 193(6) or (7).[356]

7.196 A review may be sought of an authority's decision as to what steps to take to secure accommodation under the relief duty[357] or to secure that accommodation for those threatened with homelessness does not cease to be available,[358] or to bring its duty to those threatened with homelessness or its relief duty to an end,[359] along with the corresponding provisions of HA 1996, ss 193A–193C governing cessation of those new duties by reference to final offers or deliberate and unreasonable refusal to co-operate.[360]

7.197 Whether an authority has complied with the requirement to notify the applicant of the consequences of refusal and the right to request a review under HA 1996, s 193(7) and (7A)[361] is itself also subject to review under this provision.[362]

Local connection

7.198 The review provisions governing local connection referrals have been considered in Chapter 5.[363]

---

353 HA 1996, s 202(1)(b); in Wales, see H(W)A 2014, s 85(1)(b), (c).
354 HA 1996, s 190(3). See also H(W)A 2014, ss 70, 71.
355 HA 1996, s 190(1); H(W)A 2014, s 77.
356 A decision that a duty once owed is no longer owed is a decision within HA 1996, s 193 (and, therefore, susceptible to review): *Warsame v Hounslow LBC* (1999) 32 HLR 335, CA, affirmed notwithstanding intervening legislative changes under Homelessness Act 2002 in *Ravichandran v Lewisham LBC* [2010] EWCA Civ 755, [2010] HLR 42 (discussed below). See also recently *R (Bano) v Waltham Forest LBC* [2024] EWHC 654 (Admin). In Wales, see H(W)A 2014, s 85(1)(c).
357 HA 1996, s 189B(2); H(W)A 2014, s 73(1). The English Code suggests that 'Housing authorities should encourage applicants to raise any concerns they have about their plan and work to resolve disagreements to minimise the occasions on which the applicant will feel the need to request a review': para 11.36, updated 20 June 2018.
358 HA 1996, s 195(2); H(W)A 2014, s 66.
359 HA 1996, ss 189B(6), 195(7); H(W)A 2014, s 67.
360 HA 1996, s 202(1); H(W)A 2014, s 85.
361 See paras **8.247, 8.258**.
362 *Tower Hamlets LBC v Rahanara Begum* [2005] EWCA Civ 116, [2006] HLR 9. The applicant had, however, failed to seek an internal review and the matter could not be raised as a defence to eviction proceedings being brought against her. Cf *R (Zaher) v Westminster City Council* [2003] EWHC 101 (Admin), where the failure of the authority to inform the applicant of his right to review entitled the applicant to challenge the decision on suitability by judicial review. In Wales, the equivalent to HA 1996, s 193(7) and (7A) is now H(W)A 2014, s 76(3)(c) and it is likely that the cases cited in this footnote will apply equally.
363 Paras **5.104–5.107**.

Suitability and availability of offers

7.199   An applicant may seek a review of whether accommodation offered in discharge of duty under HA 1996, s 190, s 193[364] or s 200 is 'suitable'[365] and, where applicable,[366] whether it is reasonable to accept it.

7.200   An applicant may seek a review of a decision of an authority as to the suitability of accommodation offered by way of a private accommodation offer,[367] ie, in a restricted case;[368] from the commencement of LA 2011, s 148,[369] there is likewise a right to seek a review of a decision as to the suitability of a private rented sector offer,[370] in a restricted case or otherwise.[371] There is no need for a formal notification that accommodation is considered suitable before an applicant can seek a review; informal notification or de facto treatment of accommodation as suitable suffices; that said, best practice is for the authority to make clear that it considers accommodation to be suitable, if only so the parties are clear where they stand.[372]

7.201   It had formerly been held that, where an applicant accepted an offer of accommodation, the applicant could not also seek a review as to its suitability: *Alghile*.[373] The result of this was that an applicant to whom an unsatisfactory offer of accommodation had been made had to face 'an unwholesome opportunity to gamble',[374] either to refuse – which gave rise to the risk that, if unsuccessful on the review, the applicant would end up with nowhere to live – or to accept,

---

364 Including expressly HA 1996, s 193(7) (see para **8.247**) to clear up any residual doubt following the decision in *Warsame v Hounslow LBC* (2000) 32 HLR 335, CA, which had the effect of confining application of HA 1996, s 202(1)(f) to the question of the suitability of an offer under s 193(6). In Wales, see H(W)A 2014, s 85(1)(c).

365 HA 1996, s 202(1)(f); H(W)A 2014, s 59.

366 HA 1996, s 193(7F). See, in particular, *Ravichandran v Lewisham LBC* [2010] EWCA Civ 755, [2010] HLR 42, where the authority had considered suitability at a previous review, but at no time had considered whether it was reasonable for the applicant to accept it, for which reason its decision could not stand.

367 HA 1996, s 202(1)(g); H(W)A 2014, s 76(2) requires all private rented sector offers to be suitable, ie the position in Wales is the same as the post-Localism Act (LA) 2011 position in England.

368 See paras **A.127–A.133** and paras **8.272–8.281**.

369 Localism Act 2011 (Commencement No 2 and Transitional Provisions) (England) Order 2012/2599, art 2.

370 Provided that the authority's duty to secure accommodation has not ceased before, SI 2012 that date: Localism Act 2011 (Commencement No 2 and Transitional Provisions) (England) Order 2012/2599, art 3.

371 See paras **8.272–8.281**.

372 *R (AB & CD) v. Westminster CC* [2024] EWHC 226 (Admin) – claimant prepared for judicial review hearing without realising that the authority considered that the property was suitable for the time being, leading ultimately to dismissal of the claim on the basis that s202 review was the appropriate remedy.

373 *Alghile v Westminster City Council* (2001) 33 HLR 57, CA, overruling *R v Kensington and Chelsea RLBC ex p Byfield* (1997) 31 HLR 913, QBD.

374 *Alghile v Westminster City Council* [2001] EWCA Civ 363, (2001) 33 HLR 57 per Tuckey LJ at [28].

which meant putting up with accommodation that the applicant considered unsatisfactory.[375]

7.202   There is now a right to seek an internal review of the suitability of accommodation offered under HA 1996, s 193(5) or (7), whether or not the applicant has accepted the offer of accommodation.[376]

7.203   The date at which suitability of accommodation should be considered on a review will differ depending whether the accommodation was accepted or refused. If an offer of accommodation was accepted, then the authority should consider the facts at the date of review because the accommodation is still available.[377]

7.204   Conversely, where an offer of accommodation has been refused, then the authority has taken the decision that it has fulfilled its duty and the property will no longer be available; in those circumstances, the issue has to be tested by reference to the circumstances as they existed at the date of the decision that the duty had been discharged,[378] or the offer.[379]

Request for review

7.205   A request for a review should be made within 21 days of notification of a decision under HA 1996, s 184.[380] The applicant must be told about the right to request a review in the decision notification;[381] if the notification does not do so, time cannot be considered to have started to run. The authority has power to extend time,[382] but if it does not do so, it has no power to conduct a review which is not sought within time, whether a second review[383] or otherwise.[384] If circumstances have changed, and the authority is unwilling to extend time, it may be possible to make a new application as homeless.[385]

---

375 This contrasts with the outcome in *R v Wycombe DC ex p Hazeltine* (1993) 25 HLR 313, CA; see para **8.231**.
376 HA 1996, s 202(1A); H(W)A 2014, s 85(3).
377 *Omar v Westminster City Council* [2008] EWCA Civ 421, [2008] HLR 36; *Bromley LBC v Broderick* [2020] EWCA Civ 1522; [2021] HLR 20.
378 *Omar*, above, per Waller LJ at [25].
379 *Broderick*, above, per Newey LJ at [46]; *Moge v Ealing LBC* [2023] EWCA Civ 464; [2023] HLR 35 at [148].
380 HA 1996, s 202(3); H(W)A 2014, s 85(5). The wording need not be followed slavishly – thus, saying that the appeal 'must be made within 21 days of the date of this letter' rather than of when the applicant was notified of the decision did not vitiate the letter in *Dharmaraj v Hounslow LBC* [2011] EWCA Civ 312, [2011] HLR 18.
381 HA 1996, s 202(3); H(W)A 2015, s 85(5). Notification to an applicant's solicitor suffices: *Dharmaraj v Hounslow LBC*, above. See also *Dragic v Wandsworth LBC* [2011] JHL D59.
382 HA 1996, s 202(3).
383 *R (B) v Redbridge LB* [2019] EWHC 250 (Admin), [2019] PTSR 1525, [2021] HLR 9, in which the court rejected the parties' agreement that there was power to do so.
384 A refusal to extend time may be judicially reviewable in a clear case of misdirection: *R (C) v Lewisham LBC* [2003] EWCA Civ 927, [2004] HLR 4.
385 *R (B) v Redbridge LBC*, above.

7.206   If the notification does inform the applicant of the right to review, the applicant who fails to exercise it in time will on the face of it lose it. The authority has power to extend time.[386] This discretion must be exercised in furtherance of its statutory purpose, which is to establish procedures and time limits necessary to enable the authority to manage its housing stock in an orderly way, and – where appropriate – to grant an indulgence to an applicant where the merits of the applicant's claim for review are deserving enough to override the failure to request a review in time. Accordingly, the authority is entitled but not bound to take into account the prospect of the review's success.[387]

Further review[388]

7.207   There is no right to request a review of a decision reached on an earlier review[389] but if the authority has failed to consider relevant matters, it may reconsider or review a decision on review; the authority must make clear that they do not regard the original review as remaining in force or having any effect and if they do not do so, an adviser should ask them to do so – if the authority refuses, then there is no appeal to the county court[390] against that decision and the applicant can only pursue an appeal against the original review decision, which they will need to do within the time limit for it, unless the authority clearly agrees to extend it, eg, to 21 days after the new review decision.[391]

7.208   Although HA 1996, s 202(2) does not prevent an authority from further reconsidering a decision if asked and willing to do so, a refusal to exercise the discretion to reconsider has been held not to be judicially reviewable.[392]

Identity of the reviewer

7.209   Both sets of regulations may require that the decision on review be made by a person of appropriate seniority who was not involved in the original decision.[393] The Welsh regulations do not do so; they only require that the review officer be someone who was not involved in the original decision.[394]

---

386 HA 1996, s 202(3); H(W)A 2014, s 85(5).
387 *R (C) v Lewisham LBC* [2003] EWCA Civ 927, [2004] HLR 4. See also *R (Slaiman) v Richmond upon Thames LBC* [2006] EWHC 329 (Admin), [2006] HLR 20.
388 Leaving aside a further review where the decision on a previous review has been quashed on appeal to the county court or in a claim for judicial review, after which the previous decision has no legal existence.
389 HA 1996, s 202(2); H(W)A 2014, s 85(4).
390 See paras **10.203** and **10.211–10.213**.
391 *Demetri v Westminster City Council* [2000] 1 WLR 772, (2000) 32 HLR 470, CA.
392 *R v Westminster City Council ex p Ellioua* (1998) 31 HLR 440, CA. See also *R (C) v Lewisham LBC* [2003] EWCA Civ 927, [2004] HLR 4.
393 HA 1996, s 203(2)(a); H(W)A 2014, s 86(2)(a).
394 Welsh Review Procedure Regs 2015 reg 3; see also Welsh Code para 20.9.

7.210   The English regulations,[395] however, do require that, when the original decision was made by an officer of the authority[396] and the review is also to be carried out by an officer of the authority, the latter must be someone who was not involved in the original decision and who is senior to the original decision-maker:

> 'Seniority for these purposes means seniority in rank within the authority's organisational structure.'[397]

7.211   The officer who is undertaking the review may nonetheless enlist the assistance of a more junior officer, even where that junior officer made the original decision.[398] A view expressed by a more senior officer about the type of allocation for which an applicant qualified under the authority's HA 1996, Part 6 allocation scheme was not a decision for the purposes of the (then) English Review Procedure Regs 1999, reg 2, nor could it be subject to a HA 1996, s 202 review, nor therefore did it disqualify a more junior officer from conducting the review: *Feld*.[399]

7.212   If elected members are involved in the review process,[400] neither the English nor the Welsh regulations set any particular requirements.

7.213   There may be more than one review on a single application, for example, following a successful county court appeal or where – following a finding that an original offer of accommodation was unsuitable – the applicant seeks to challenge a further offer. The fact that a review officer has conducted an earlier review does not prevent them conducting a second review; there is no apparent bias and any actual unfairness can be cured on appeal to the county court: *Feld*.[401]

7.214   There is nothing in HA 1996, Part 7 or H(W)A 2014, Part 2 that requires a decision as to whether or not to secure interim accommodation under HA 1996, s 188(3) or H(W)A 2014, s 85[402] pending a review[403] to be made by an officer who is senior to the officer who made the original decision on the application; nor is there anything necessarily objectionable in the same officer who made the decision under review also making the decision on such interim accommodation.[404]

---

395 English Review Procedure Regs 2018 reg 8.
396 The decision must be made by the authority by its executive (single member, committee, sub-committee or officer) to whom the function is delegated: see Local Government Act 2000, ss 13–15 and Local Authorities (Functions and Responsibilities) (England) Regulations 2000, SI 2000/2853.
397 English Code of Guidance para 19.9; see also Welsh Code para 20.9.
398 *Butler v Fareham BC* May 2001 *Legal Action* 24, CA.
399 *Feld v Barnet LBC; Pour v Westminster City Council* [2004] EWCA Civ 1307, [2005] HLR 9.
400 These will have to be members of the executive: see para **7.210**.
401 *Feld v Barnet LBC; Pour v Westminster City Council*, above.
402 See Welsh Code para 20.29.
403 See paras **8.51–8.60**.
404 *R (Abdi) v Lambeth LBC* [2007] EWHC 1565 (Admin), [2008] HLR 5.

7.215   The review function may be contracted out.[405]

Local connection reviews

7.216   The particular considerations relevant to a local connection have been considered in Chapter 5.[406]

Impact of the Human Rights Act 1998

7.217   The review procedure is not the determination of a civil right for the purposes of Article 6[407] of the ECHR.[408] Even if it was, it was considered in *Runa Begum*[409] that an internal review coupled with the right to an appeal to the county court under HA 1996, s 204 comprised compliance with Article 6, an approach followed in *Ali v Birmingham City Council.*[410]

7.218   In *Ali v UK*,[411] which was the latter case at the European Court of Human Rights, *Runa Begum* was qualified to the extent that it was held that Article 6(1) is engaged once an authority has decided that a duty is owed under HA 1996, s 193 because there is a sufficiently certain right to amount to a 'civil right'; in agreement with *Runa Begum* and *Ali* at the Supreme Court, however, it was also held that there was no violation of Article 6 as the rights to a reasoned decision, review and appeal were adequate safeguards.

7.219   In *Poshteh v Kensington and Chelsea RLBC*,[412] the Supreme Court declined to depart from its decision in *Ali v Birmingham City Council*, notwithstanding *Ali v UK*: the decision in *Ali v UK* did not engage in any detail with the decision in *Ali v Birmingham City Council*; the scope and limit of the concept of a 'civil right' was suitable for consideration by the Grand Chamber of the European Court of Human Rights; without such a decision, it was not appropriate to depart from the fully reasoned decision in *Ali v Birmingham City Council.*

---

405   See paras **7.6–7.8**, above; and English Code of Guidance para 19.9. See Housing (Wales) Act 2014 (Consequential Amendments) Regulations 2015, SI 2015/752, amending the Local Authorities (Contracting Out of Allocation of Housing and Homelessness Functions) Order 1996, SI 1996/3205 so as to apply to H(W)A 2014, Part 2.

406   Paras **5.104–5.107**.

407   'In the determination of his civil rights and obligations . . . everyone is entitled to a fair and public hearing within a reasonable time by an independent and impartial tribunal established by law. . .'

408   See paras **10.117–10.122**.

409   *Runa Begum v Tower Hamlets LBC* [2003] UKHL 5, [2003] 2 AC 430, [2003] HLR 32.

410   [2010] UKSC 8.

411   App No 40378/10, [2015] HLR 46.

412   [2017] UKSC 3, [2017] HLR 28.

REVIEW PROCEDURE

7.220   The Secretary of State has power to make regulations as to the procedure to be followed in connection with a review:[413] see the Homelessness (Review Procedures etc) Regulations ('English Review Procedure Regs') 2018.[414] In Wales, the Welsh Ministers have the same power: see Homelessness (Review Procedure) (Wales) Regulations ('Welsh Review Procedure Regs') 2015.[415]

7.221   Once the applicant has requested a review, the authority must notify the applicant that they – or someone acting on the applicant's behalf – may make representations in writing.[416] If the applicant has not already been informed of the procedure to be followed,[417] then the notification must also set out what it is.[418]

7.222   The purpose of this requirement is to invite the applicant to state their grounds for requesting a review (if the applicant has not already done so) and to elicit any new information that the applicant may have in relation to it.[419]

7.223   A failure to notify the applicant of the procedure on review was one of the grounds on which an appeal was upheld in *Safi v Sandwell BC*.[420] In particular, no date by which representations had to be made had been stated. It was not possible to say that, if such a date had been set, no representations would have been made in time; if representations had been made in time, it was likely that they would have been similar to those made later by the appellant's solicitors, which would have prompted a 'minded to' decision[421] which would have included suggestions made for the first time in the review decision letter as to how the appellant could deal with problems of access and as to the likelihood of her obtaining accommodation through her HA 1996, Part 6 application – the

---

413   HA 1996, s 203(1); in Wales, the Welsh Ministers have the same power, see H(W)A 2014, s 86 and Homelessness (Review Procedure) (Wales) Regulations 2015, SI 2015/1266.

414   Homelessness (Review Procedures etc) Regulations 2018, SI 2018/223. For reviews requested prior to 3 April 2018, see the Allocation of Housing and Homelessness (Review Procedures) Regulations 1999, SI 1999/71 and the 10th edition of this work.

415   See H(W)A 2014, s 86 .

416   English Review Procedure Regs 2018 reg 5(3)(a). Where the review is under HA 1996, s 202(1) (ba)(i), (bc), the representations must be received within two weeks beginning with the day on which the review was requested (or such longer period as may be greed); the same two week period also applies to a review under 202(1)(bb) where the effect of the decision is to bring the s 195(2) duty to an end. Where the case concerns a local connection referral that has been referred to a referee (see paras **5.83–5.89**), it is the referee who must make the notification: reg 5(4)(a). Welsh Review Procedure Regs 2015 reg 2, gives a right to make representations in writing, orally, or both.

417   English Review Procedure Regs 2018 reg 5(3)(c); Welsh Review Procedure Regs 2015 reg 2(2) (b).

418   The suggestion in the 1996 edition of the Code of Guidance that authorities should have an approved document setting out their procedure available to the public is not included in the present Code.

419   English Code of Guidance para 19.13; Welsh Code para 20.11.

420   [2018] EWCA Civ 2876, [2019] HLR 16.

421   Paras **2.227–7.235**.

authority's breach had denied the appellant the opportunity to address these arguments.

7.224 Where the applicant's legal representatives requested information from the authority prior to making representations, and the authority failed to provide the information or await the representations prior to making a review decision, the decision was likewise unlawful.[422]

7.225 The original regulations[423] required the reviewer to consider any representations made by the applicant and to carry out the review on the basis of the facts known to them at its date. The latter requirement is not explicit in the current English Review Procedure Regs 2018.[424] This change notwithstanding, the reviewing officer:

> '. . . is not simply considering whether the initial decision was right on the material before it at the date it was made. He may have regard to information relevant to the period before the decision but only obtained thereafter and to matters occurring after the initial decision.'[425]

7.226 There is nothing in the regulations which prevents a reviewing officer from making a decision which is less favourable to the applicant than the original decision.[426]

7.227 If there is a deficiency or irregularity in the original decision, or in the way it was made, but the reviewer is nonetheless minded to make a decision which is against the interests of the applicant, the reviewer must notify the applicant that they are so minded and of the reasons why, and that the applicant or someone on the applicant's behalf may make representations to them, orally or in writing or both, which representations the reviewer must consider.[427]

---

422 *Aw-Aden v Birmingham City Council* [2005] EWCA Civ 1834 at [21], although as the authority subsequently reconsidered the decision it was in fact upheld by the Court of Appeal.

423 Allocation of Housing and Homelessness (Review Procedures and Amendment) Regulations 1996, SI 1996/3122 reg 8(1).

424 The former is included: English Review Procedure Regs 2018 reg 7(1). Where the review is being conducted by a referee (see paras **5.83–5.89**, above) the referee must send any representations to both authorities involved and seek their comments: reg 5(5). The position is the same in Wales: reg 4.

425 *Mohamed v Hammersmith and Fulham LBC* [2001] UKHL 57, [2002] HLR 7 at [26]. As to reviews of suitability, see paras **7.199–7.204**.

426 *Temur v Hackney LBC* [2014] EWCA Civ 877, [2014] HLR 39.

427 English Review Procedure Regs 2018 reg 7(2). The Court of Appeal has assumed – without argument – that the wording of the previous regulations (Allocation of Housing and Homelessness (Review Procedures) Regulations 1999 reg 8(2)(b)) gave the applicant the right to choose how representations are made – orally, in writing, or orally and in writing: see *Lambeth LBC v Johnston* [2008] EWCA Civ 690, [2009] HLR 10 at [53]; and *Hall v Wandsworth LBC; Carter v Wandsworth LBC* [2004] EWCA Civ 1740, [2005] HLR 23 at [25]–[26]. In Wales, see Welsh Review Procedure Regs 2015 reg 5(2). The authority does not have to spell out the right to a face-to-face meeting as it is evident from the words of the language of the regulation: *Kamara v Southwark LBC and other cases* [2018] EWCA Civ 1616, [2019] PTSR 279, [2018] HLR 37. Decisions to which the minded-to provisions apply include a decision on suitability of offer: see recently *Querino v Cambridge CC* [2024] EWCA Civ 314; HLR forthcoming at [35].

7.228   If the applicant is represented, notification to their solicitor suffices for the purposes of this requirement.[428] This procedure is capable of remedying any defect in the original decision letter and is suitable as a means for challenging the original decision of a local authority, rather than judicial review.[429]

7.229   The duty is two-fold:

a)   first, to consider whether there was a deficiency or irregularity in the original decision or in the manner in which it was made; and

b)   second, if there was – and if the review officer is nonetheless minded to make a decision adverse to the applicant on one or more issues – to serve a 'minded to find' notice on the applicant explaining the reasons for the reviewer's provisional views.[430]

7.230   The review officer is only under a duty to 'consider' the representations, on the face of it not necessarily to give any notification or indication of that consideration.[431] Where consideration of deficiency and/or irregularity has taken place, but no reasons have been given for an adverse conclusion in relation to it,[432] the review procedure could still be susceptible on public law grounds.[433] Accordingly, in practice a local authority is now effectively obliged to state in every review decision letter why there is no deficiency or irregularity in the original decision, and consequently why no 'minded to find' letter has been sent.

7.231   Neither 'deficiency' nor 'irregularity' is defined in either the English or Welsh Review Procedure Regs.[434] 'Deficiency' is not confined to an error of law in the original decision; there is a deficiency if there is 'something lacking' in it which is of sufficient importance to the fairness of the procedure to justify the additional procedural safeguard: *Hall* and *Carter*.[435]

---

428   *Maswaku v Westminster City Council* [2012] EWCA Civ 669; *El Goure v Kensington and Chelsea RLBC* [2012] EWCA Civ 670.

429   *R (Lynch) v Lambeth LBC* [2007] HLR 15.

430   *Lambeth LBC v Johnston*, above.

431   *Johnston*, above, per Rimer LJ at [51].

432   A poorly worded letter which, however, had addressed all the important aspects of the case and which meant that a reasonable reader would have had no doubt about the basis of the decision sufficed in one (*Nagi*) of the three cases heard together in *Makisi v Birmingham City Council; Yosief v Birmingham City Council; Nagi v Birmingham City Council* [2011] EWCA Civ 355, [2011] HLR 27.

433   *Johnston*, per Rimer LJ at [54].

434   See English Code of Guidance para 19.21 which suggests matters which might be included (eg, failure to take into account relevant considerations; failure to base decision on the facts; bad faith or dishonesty; error of law; decisions which are contrary to the purpose of the HA 1996; irrational or unreasonable decisions; procedurally unfair decisions); see also Welsh Code para 20.13, which contains the same list of examples as in the English Code.

435   *Hall v Wandsworth LBC; Carter v Wandsworth LBC*, above. See now English Code of Guidance para 19.22, Welsh Code para 21.9 reflecting this decision. The simple fact that something is not mentioned in an offer letter does not necessarily mean that it was not taken into account, or that it suggests a deficiency – it will depend on proper consideration of the facts and the letter; the facts may include what representations were made by or on behalf of the applicant – see recently *Querino v Cambridge CC* [2024] EWCA Civ 314; HLR forthcoming at [39].

7.232 A reviewing officer should therefore apply English Review Procedure Regs 2018 reg 7(2)[436] whenever the officer considers that an important aspect of the case was either not addressed or was not addressed adequately by the original decision-maker, even if the reason it was not addressed is because the applicant had not raised it with the original decision-maker.

7.233 In *Mitu*,[437] the original decision held both that the applicant was not in priority need and that he had become homeless intentionally; the review concluded that he was not homeless intentionally but upheld the finding on priority need; there was nonetheless a deficiency in the original decision, and what is now reg 7(2) therefore applied.

7.234 This may be contrasted with *Mohamoud v Birmingham City Council*,[438] in which the applicant had rejected a flat and the authority decided that its duty towards her had been discharged; on review, she claimed for the first time that she had misunderstood what she had originally been told by the authority and that she had thought that she would receive up to three offers of accommodation, a confusion that could have arisen as English was not her first language. The review officer rejected these contentions and upheld the original decision. The court held that this should have triggered a 'minded to' letter under what is now reg 7(2).

7.235 If circumstances have changed between the original decision and decision on review,[439] reviewers will need to undertake further enquiries before reaching a decision and may need to serve a 'minded to find' letter,[440] even though strictly there was no deficiency in the original decision at the time it was taken.

7.236 Applicants should be aware that it is not only new circumstances which count in the applicant's favour which are to be taken into account, but also any developments which adversely affect the applicant's entitlement.[441] A change of circumstances may yet lead to the loss of a qualifying element in the previous decision, for example, priority need.[442] The requirement to allow further representations, including an oral hearing,[443] will apply.

---

436 Or Welsh Review Procedure Regs 2015 reg 5(2).
437 *Mitu v Camden LBC* [2011] EWCA Civ 1249, [2012] HLR 10.
438 [2014] EWCA Civ 227, [2014] HLR 22.
439 As in *Mohamed v Hammersmith and Fulham LBC* [2001] UKHL 57, [2002] HLR 7, HL.
440 *Banks v Kingston upon Thames RLBC* [2008] EWCA Civ 1443, [2009] HLR 29. In the original decision, the applicant was found to be not homeless. Between the original decision and the review decision, the applicant was served with notice to quit by his landlord. The reviewer found that the applicant was homeless, and went on to consider the question of priority need without giving the applicant the opportunity to make representations on that issue, before deciding it against the applicant. The applicant successfully appealed to the Court of Appeal that the change in question under consideration invoked his right to receive a 'minded to find' letter in accordance with what is now English Review Procedure Regs 2018 reg 7(2).
441 See further para **7.171**.
442 For example, a dependent child leaving home, death of a vulnerable co-resident.
443 See para **7.727**.

7.237 An adverse change will not, however, cause the loss of an element of the first decision if that decision was itself unlawful. In *Robinson*,[444] the authority unlawfully decided that the applicant was not in priority need, notwithstanding that she was only 17 years old at the time.[445] By the time of the review, she was 18 and no longer in priority need. The authority unsuccessfully sought to uphold its original decision on that basis: it was held that the proper decision on the review should be that an unlawful decision had been made such as to have denied the applicant her rights; she should therefore have been given the rights to which she was entitled had a lawful decision been made, and the reviewer should accordingly have found her to be in priority need.[446]

7.238 The court applied the dictum of Chadwick LJ in *Crawley BC v B*[447] that:

'. . . an applicant ought not to be deprived, by events which had occurred between the date of the original decision and the date of the appeal, of some benefit or advantage to which he would have been entitled if the original decision had been taken in accordance with the law'.

7.239 Points made earlier about enquiries before the first decision are equally relevant here.[448] For example, if the reviewer fails to make sufficient enquiries into a matter, or fails to make those enquiries that a reasonable authority would make, the decision on review is itself susceptible to challenge (by way of appeal).[449] Subject to this, the point of the review is to cure any defects in the original decision and therefore a failure to conduct sufficient enquiries at the first stage can be resolved at this stage by the person conducting the review.

7.240 It is incumbent on the applicant to put forward the matters and evidence which the applicant wishes to be taken into account: see *Cramp*.[450] This is particularly important where a 'minded to' letter has been sent. Thus, in *Bellouti*, 'it was for Mr Bellouti to put forward the material on which he relied in support of his assertion of priority need'.[451] Bearing in mind that a decision can only be based on the information available to the authority, there will be difficulty complaining to the county court on appeal of a failure to make enquiries if a matter has not been raised before the review, at least sufficiently to put the

---

444 *Robinson v Hammersmith and Fulham LBC* [2006] EWCA Civ 1122, [2006] 1 WLR 3295, [2007] HLR 7.
445 See paras **3.82–3.89**.
446 *Robinson v Hammersmith and Fulham LBC*, above, at [32].
447 (2000) 32 HLR 636, CA, at 651.
448 See paras **7.60–7.167**.
449 Para **10.203**.
450 See paras **7.91–7.92**.
451 *Bellouti v Wandsworth LBC* [2005] EWCA Civ 602, [2005] HLR 46, at [59].

reviewer on notice, or to call for them to make such further enquiries as are necessary.[452]

7.241 In *Pieretti v Enfield LBC*,[453] however, it was said that the approach in *Cramp* requires qualification where the applicant is a disabled[454] person: where a decision-maker (whether under HA 1996, s 184 or s 202) is not expressly invited to consider a putative[455] disability, they must still have due regard to the need to take steps to take account of it.

7.242 The review must be carried out fairly. Applicants should be given the opportunity to refute matters on which the authority wishes to rely: *Robinson v Brent LBC*.[456]

7.243 The right to make representations 'orally or in writing or both orally and in writing' is not satisfied by a telephone interview: the right includes a right exercisable at a face-to-face meeting,[457] though amounts to no more than a 'simple and relatively brief opportunity' for the applicant (with or without someone acting on their behalf) to make oral representations to the review officer; it does not authorise the calling of third party witnesses or cross-examination.[458]

---

452 In *Adam v Westminster CC* [2018] EWCA Civ 2742, [2019] HLR 15, the appellant's request for a review did not raise the issue of why the authority had decided to make a private sector offer rather than continue to accommodate her in accommodation under HA 1996, s 193(2); the reviewing officer had therefore not been required to explain why the authority had chosen to make a private sector offer. See also *Alibkhiet v Brent LBC* [2018] EWCA Civ 2742, [2019] HLR 15 at [88]–[89].

453 [2010] EWCA Civ 1104, [2011] HLR 3.

454 *Pieretti* concerned Disability Discrimination Act 1995, s 49A; this has been replaced with the broader 'public sector equality duty' in EqA 2010, s 149 and, as such, the full range of 'protected characteristics' should be considered, ie, age; disability; gender reassignment; marriage and civil partnership; pregnancy and maternity; race; religion or belief; sex; sexual orientation.

455 The decision-maker is entitled to ask for evidence of an alleged disability and, if none is provided, may conclude that there is none: *Birmingham City Council v Wilson* [2016] EWCA Civ 1137, [2017] HLR 4.

456 *Robinson v Brent LBC* (1999) 31 HLR 1015, CA. See further, paras **7.143–7.154**, on the fairness of conducting enquiries by authorities.

457 The authority does not have to spell out the right to a face-to-face meeting: *Kamara v Southwark LBC and other cases* (para **7.227**).

458 *Makisi v Birmingham City Council; Yosief v Birmingham City Council; Nagi v Birmingham City Council* [2011] EWCA Civ 355, [2011] HLR 27 (see also *Kamara*, above). The court does not appear to have been assisted by *Bury MBC v Gibbons* [2010] EWCA Civ 327, [2010] HLR 33, in which it had been said that, while there were some cases (such as that) in which the requirements of what is now English Review Procedure Regs 2018 reg 7(2) could not be satisfied without a face-to-face meeting with the applicant, in other cases it would be sufficient for representations to be made over the telephone. There is no reference in the judgment to *Lomotey v Enfield LBC* [2004] EWCA Civ 627, [2004] HLR 45 in which it had been said that a refusal to hold a face-to-face hearing had not been unfair, but in that case it was not argued that what is now reg 7(2) gave a right to an oral hearing (to the contrary, it was conceded that it did not apply).

7.244 What comprises fairness in carrying out a review has to be determined having regard to the basis of the decision under review. In *Goodger*,[459] the authority's decision-making file was not disclosed to the applicant's advisers until a few days before the review. There was no procedural unfairness, however, as the applicant had known the case against him and the decision of intentional homelessness had been the only one possible in the circumstances.

7.245 Where an applicant deliberately withholds information so as to hinder the authority's enquiries, the authority may be entitled to decide matters against the applicant.[460]

7.246 As at the initial enquiry stage,[461] authorities may obtain expert medical opinion. If this raises new issues or contentious points on which the applicant has not been able to comment, the applicant should normally be given a chance to do so in the interests of fairness.

7.247 If, however, the advice is merely directed to assisting the authority to assess the weight to be given to evidence on matters which are already fully in play, there is no automatic obligation to disclose it to the applicant before the authority reaches its decision.[462]

Time

7.248 The English and Welsh Review Procedure Regs[463] normally require authorities to notify applicants of their decision within eight weeks of the request for the review being made.[464] Where the review is under HA 1996, s 202(1)(ba) (i) or (bc) (steps to be taken under the initial duty for the homeless and those threatened with homelessness, for bringing the duty to an end)[465] or (bb) (decision to give notice to those who deliberately and unreasonably refuse to co-operate, the effect of which is to bring the authority's relief duty to an end),[466] it must be

---

459 *Goodger v Ealing LBC* [2002] EWCA Civ 751, [2003] HLR 6.
460 *R (Abdi) v Lambeth LBC* [2007] EWHC 1565 (Admin), [2008] HLR 5, although a case about accommodation pending review. This issue commonly arises in the context of assessments under the Children Act (CA) 1989, ie, where a parent appears to the authority to be withholding information for the purposes of trying to secure accommodation with a child under CA 1989, s 17(6): see eg *R (MN and KN) v Hackney LBC* [2013] EWHC 1205 (Admin).
461 See para **7.63**.
462 *Hall v Wandsworth LBC; Carter v Wandsworth LBC* [2004] EWCA Civ 1740, [2005] HLR 23. See also *Shala v Birmingham City Council* [2007] EWCA Civ 624, [2008] HLR 8, in particular [19]–[23].
463 See para **7.220**.
464 English Review Procedure Regs 2018 reg 9(1)(b); Welsh Review Procedure Regs 2014, reg 6(1).
465 See para **8.82**.
466 See para **8.83**.

notified within three weeks.[467] There are exceptions for certain local connection reviews: these have been considered in Chapter 5.

7.249   The parties may, however, agree a longer period, which must be in writing.[468] The agreement may be for a general extension of time, even though the precise date may not have been agreed and may be inferred from conduct and correspondence.[469]

7.250   If the decision on the review is not notified within time, as specified or as extended by agreement, the applicant may appeal against the original decision within 21 days of when the notification on review should have been received.[470]

7.251   If the review decision is issued late, the applicant may choose to appeal the HA 1996, s 184 decision (if in time to do so) *or* the review decision, but not both. If the applicant does issue appeals against both, then while they do not waive their right to appeal against the original decision, the later decision renders the appeal academic save in exceptional circumstances.[471] The appeal should be treated as an appeal against the review decision, unless there is a factor which gives rise to a legitimate interest in pursuing the appeal against the original decision.[472]

Notification of review decision

7.252   The authority must notify the applicant of the outcome of the decision.[473] Where the decision is against the interests of the applicant,[474] reasons for the decision must be included.[475]

7.253   The notification of the decision on the review must also inform the applicant of their right of appeal to the county court on a point of law.[476]

---

467   English Review Procedure Regs 2018 reg 9(1)(b); in Wales, reg 6(1)(a).
468   English Review Procedure Regs 2018 reg 9(1); English Code para 19.23; Welsh Code para 20.15.
469   *Stanley v Welwyn Hatfield BC* [2020] EWCA Civ 1458; [2021] HLR 12.
470   HA 1996, s 204(1)(b)).
471   *Ngnoguem v Milton Keynes Council* [2021] EWCA Civ 396; [2021] 1 WLR 5147; [2021] HLR 32.
472   *Stanley v Welwyn Hatfield BC*, above; *Ngnoguem v Milton Keynes Council* [2001] EWCA Civ 396; [2021] 1 WLR 5147; [2021] HLR 32.
473   HA 1996, s 203(4); H(W)A 2014, s 86(3).
474   Identifying decisions to refer to another authority separately out of an abundance of caution, as the applicant may be presumed so to have considered it when they elected to seek a review under HA 1996, s 203.
475   See para **7.183**.
476   See Chapter 10.

Housing pending review

7.254   This is considered in Chapter 8.[477]

Reasons

7.255   Both a) the original decision and b) a decision reached on a review the outcome of which is adverse to the applicant, must contain sufficient reasons.[478]

7.256   In cases where there has been an internal review,[479] it is likely to be the reasons in the review decision which will be the focus of any challenge, although these may well rely on, reflect or be elaborated by, the first decision, which may therefore remain relevant.

7.257   There is no obligation to give reasons for deciding the review in the applicant's favour nor, therefore, any appeal from such a decision (ie, of its reasoning).[480]

7.258   What is imported by the requirement to give reasons is considered in Chapter 10.[481]

---

477 See paras **8.51–8.60**.
478 HA 1996, ss 184(3), 203(4); H(W)A 2014, s 86(4).
479 See para **7.186**.
480 *Akhtar v Birmingham City Council* [2011] EWCA Civ 383, [2011] HLR 28, in which the applicant rejected a second offer on an erroneous assumption as to why an earlier review had been successful; nor had it been unfair to explain the basis of the first review decision. See also *Solihull MBC v Khan* [2014] EWCA Civ 41, [2014] HLR 33.
481 See paras **10.76–10.105**.

CHAPTER 8

Discharge of homelessness duties

INTRODUCTION

Overview

8.1 The Housing Act (HA) 1996, Part 7 and the Housing (Wales) Act (H(W)A) 2014, Part 2 impose duties on local authorities:

a) to make enquiries and carry out assessments;

b) to provide help to those threatened with homelessness and to the homeless;

c) to make and notify decisions;

d) to protect property; and

e) to secure that accommodation is made available.

8.2 Duties on a local connection referral (see Chapter 5) and relating to property (see Chapter 6) have already been considered; so also have the duties to entertain applications, make enquiries and reach decisions (see Chapter 7). Other statutory duties (eg, under children and social care legislation) are considered in Chapter 11.

8.3 This chapter is accordingly concerned with the remaining duties under HA 1996, Part 7 and H(W)A 2014, Part 2. These will be considered under the following headings:

a)   interim accommodation;

b)   accommodation pending review;

c)   assessment and plan;

d)   duties to those threatened with homelessness;

e)   relief duty towards the homeless;

f)   other duties to the intentionally homeless; and

g)   other duties to the unintentionally homeless in priority need.

Armed Forces

8.4   The provisions of the Armed Forces Act 2006, ss 343AA (England) and 343AB (Wales),[1] must be kept in mind when reaching any decision under Part 7, to the effect that the authority must have regard to:

'(a) the unique obligations of, and sacrifices made by, the armed forces,

(b) the principle that it is desirable to remove disadvantages arising for service people from membership, or former membership, of the armed forces, and

(c) the principle that special provision for service people may be justified by the effects on such people of membership, or former membership, of the armed forces.'

Contracting out of functions

8.5   The power of an authority to contract out functions under HA 1996, Part 7 and H(W)A 2014, Part 2 has been discussed at the start of Chapter 7.

Co-operation

England

8.6   An English authority is entitled to ask another local housing or social services authority (in England, Wales or Scotland) to exercise its own functions in relation to a case with which the authority is dealing or, may ask such an authority, a private registered provider of social housing, a registered social landlord or a housing action trust, or a development corporation, registered housing association or Scottish Homes to co-operate in rendering assistance to the authority in the discharge its functions.[2] The other authority (or body)

---

1   Added by Armed Forces Act 2021, s 8(3).
2   HA 1996, s 213(1), (2). A Scottish authority may also ask for co-operation under this provision: HA 1996, s 213(3).

must co-operate with the housing authority by rendering such assistance as is reasonable in the circumstances.[3]

Wales

8.7   In Wales, where all authorities are unitary and therefore have both housing and social services functions, the corresponding provisions require each authority to make arrangements to promote co-operation between those of its officers who exercise its social services functions and those who exercise its functions as the local housing authority, with a view to achieving the following objectives in its area:

a)   the prevention of homelessness;

b)   that suitable accommodation is or will be available for people who are or may become homeless;

c)   that satisfactory support is available for people who are or may become homeless; and

d)   the effective discharge of its functions under H(W)A 2014, Part 2.[4]

8.8   In addition, the authority may request the co-operation in the exercise of its functions of the following persons (whether in Wales or England): a local housing authority; a social services authority; a registered social landlord; a private registered provider of social housing; or a housing action trust.[5] The body is bound to comply with the request unless it considers that doing so would be incompatible with its own duties, or would otherwise have an adverse effect on the exercise of its functions.[6]

8.9   The authority may seek information it requires in order to exercise its functions under H(W)A 2014, Part 2 from the same bodies, in which case that body must comply with the request unless it considers that doing so would be incompatible with its own duties or would otherwise have an adverse effect on the exercise of the body's functions.[7]

8.10   In the case of both a co-operation and an information request, a body which decides not to comply with the request must give the local housing authority which made the request written reasons for its decision.[8]

---

3   HA 1996, s 213(1). As to the effect of this, see *R v Northavon DC ex p Smith* [1994] 2 AC 402, (1994) 26 HLR 659, HL; see para **11.88**.
4   H(W)A 2014, s 95(1).
5   H(W)A 2014, s 95(5). The Welsh Ministers may add or omit persons from this list, other than a Minister of the Crown: H(W)A 2014, s 95(6), (7).
6   H(W)A 2014, s 95(2).
7   H(W)A 2014, s 95(3).
8   H(W)A 2014, s 95(4).

Notifications

8.11   In a number of cases, the legislation requires notification to be made to an applicant, of a decision or other matter, eg, a written record. In all cases, the notice or other matter must be in writing and, if not received by the applicant, is treated as having been given if made available at the authority's office for a reasonable period for collection by the applicant or on their behalf; where there is a right to review, the notice will invariably need to say so and specify the time (21 days or such longer period as may be allowed) with which the review must be sought.[9] In some cases, the secretary of state or Welsh Ministers may make provision by regulations as to the procedure to be followed in connection with notices.[10]

INTERIM ACCOMMODATION

Overview

Generally

8.12   If an authority has reason to believe that an applicant who has a priority need may be eligible for assistance and homeless, it has to secure that accommodation is made available for the applicant's occupation pending any decision that it may make as a result of its enquiries.[11] The test is exhaustive: the authority cannot qualify it by adding any further criteria, for example, that an applicant must be at risk of harm in their current accommodation if not provided with other accommodation pending the decision.[12]

8.13   The threshold test for the provision of accommodation pending decision is very low:[13] it only requires the authority to have 'reason to believe' that an applicant may be homeless, eligible for assistance and have a priority need for

---

9   HA 1996, ss 184(5), (6), 189A(12), 193B(3), (7), (8), 195(7), (9), 199A(3), (7), 200(6), 202(1), (3), 203(8); H(W)A 2014, ss 84(1), (3), (4), 85(5), 86.

10   HA 1996, s 193B(7).

11   HA 1996, s 188(1); H(W)A 2014, s 68. This duty is met by an offer of suitable accommodation. If the applicant does not take up the offer then – absent a material change in circumstances which affects the suitability of the accommodation – they cannot require the authority to make a further offer of interim accommodation: *R (Brooks) v Islington LBC* [2015] EWHC 2657 (Admin), [2016] HLR 2.

12   *R (Kelly and Mehari) v Birmingham City Council* [2009] EWHC 3240 (Admin), [2009] JHL D24.

13   *R (M) v Hammersmith and Fulham LBC* [2006] EWCA Civ 917. The case was appealed to the House of Lords (*R (M) v Hammersmith and Fulham LBC* [2008] UKHL 14, [2008] 1 WLR 535, [2008] 4 All ER 271) but the point on the threshold for HA 1996, s 188(1) was not in issue. A similar point on the threshold was made in the High Court in *R (Aweys) v Birmingham City Council* [2007] EWHC 52 (Admin), [2007] HLR 27, not pursued on appeal; see also para **7.63**.

the duty to secure accommodation to be activated[14] – although the authority itself may take action that obviates the homelessness before a decision is taken.[15]

8.14   A local housing authority may be able to leave an applicant in their current accommodation (where it remains available) in satisfaction of the duty under HA 1996, s 188(1).[16] Even if the application is based on it not being reasonable to continue in occupation, the authority may conclude that the accommodation is suitable in the short term, until its inquiries are complete.[17] Interim accommodation must, however, be suitable.[18]

England

Re-application following private sector offer

8.15   From 9 November 2012, when Localism Act (LA) 2011, s 149(2) came into force in England,[19] the duty also arises if the authority has reason to believe that the new duty in HA 1996, s 195A may apply to the applicant.[20] Consequent on the extended powers of an authority to discharge the full duty in HA 1996, s 193[21] by using private sector accommodation,[22] s 195A provides for the full duty to recur even if there is no priority need,[23] if the applicant becomes homeless[24] again within two years of acceptance of the offer, provided that they are still eligible for assistance, and did not become homeless intentionally.[25] When assessing whether this duty has arisen, the authority must disregard any restricted person.[26]

---

14   HA 1996, s 188(1), H(W)A 2014, s 68.
15   *Hanton-Rhouila v Westminster City Council* [2010] EWCA Civ 1334, [2011] HLR 12.
16   *Birmingham City Council v Ali; Moran v Manchester City Council (Secretary of State for Communities and Local Government and another intervening)* [2009] UKHL 36, [2009] HLR 41. See also paras **2.72**, **8.39**, **8.139**.
17   *R (Yabari) v Westminster CC* [2023] EWHC 185 (Admin); [2022] HLR 34.
18   An applicant's claim that his mental health problems meant that he could not cope in temporary accommodation was a challenge to its suitability (albeit unsuccessful): *R (Islam) v Haringey LBC* [2022] EWHC 3933 (Admin); [2024] HLR forthcoming.
19   Localism Act 2011 (Commencement No 2 and Transitional Provisions) (England) Order 2012, SI 2012/2599, art 2.
20   HA 1996, s 188(1A). This is only applicable where the duty to secure accommodation had arisen but had not ceased before 9 November 2012: Localism Act 2011 (Commencement No 2 and Transitional Provisions) (England) Order 2012, SI 2012/2599, art 3.
21   Paras **8.280–8.281**.
22   LA 2011, s 148, amending HA 1996, s 193.
23   Ie, it has been lost since the original application, eg, if a child leaves home.
24   Defined to mean when valid notice under HA 1988, s 21, expires: there is no need for the applicant to await proceedings for possession or an order – HA 1996, s 195A(2).
25   This duty applies only to the first re-application: HA 1996, s 195A(6).
26   HA 1996, s 195(1), (5). As to restricted person, see paras **A.127–A.133**, and as to duties towards them, see paras **8.272–8.281**.

RENTERS (REFORM) BILL

Once the provisions of the Bill come into full relevant force and subject to any transitional provisions, consequent on the repeal of s 195A (re-application within two years after private rented sector offer – see para **3.2**), this additional interim duty will not apply and s 188(1A) will be repealed.

Ending the duty – without priority need

8.16   Since commencement of the Homelessness Reduction Act (HRA) 2017,[27] in England, the duty to secure interim accommodation ends on different dates depending on what the authority decides. If the authority concludes that the applicant is not in priority need, and the authority also decides that it does not owe them an relief duty under HA 1996, s 189B(2) (paras **8.88–8.107**),[28] the duty ends when the authority notifies the applicant of that decision.[29]

8.17   If the authority decides that there is no priority need but that it does owe the relief duty, the interim accommodation duty ends when the authority notifies the applicant of its decision that, on the coming to an end of its relief duty, it does not owe the applicant any duty under either HA 1996, s 190 (duties to the intentionally homeless: paras **8.108–8.128**) or s 193 (principal duty: paras **8.129–8.283**).[30]

8.18   In either case, it is important that the authority states under which duty or duties it has decided that it does not owe the applicant a duty, ie, whether it is under HA 1996, s 189B(2) or under s 190 or s 193; notification which does not do so will be void – see *R (Mitchell) v Islington LBC*.[31]

Ending the duty – with priority need

8.19   In any other case,[32] the duty comes to an end on the later of either a) when the HA 1996, s 189B(2) duty comes to an end or the authority notifies the applicant that it does not owe them a duty under that section, or b) when the authority notifies the applicant of its decision as to what other duty (if any) it

---

27   3 April 2018: see Homelessness Reduction Act 2017 (Commencement and Transitional and Savings Provisions) Regulations 2018, SI 2018/167, reg 3, only applicable to applications made and reviews sought on or after that date – see reg 4.
28   Ie, is either not eligible for assistance and/or not homeless: HA 1996, s 189B(1).
29   HA 1996, s 188(1ZA).
30   HA 1996, s 188(1ZA).
31   [2020] EWHC 1478 (Admin); [2021] HLR 5.
32   Ie, when it is decided that there is a priority need.

owes to the applicant under HA 1996, Part 7 following the relief duty.[33] These alternatives will also apply to the duty under HA 1996, s 188(1A) (re-application following private sector offer: para **8.15**).[34]

RENTERS (REFORM) BILL

Once the provisions of the Bill come into full relevant force and subject to any transitional provisions, s 188(1A) will be repealed and the final sentence of the last paragraph will be irrelevant.

Wales

8.20   In Wales, the duty ends if the authority notifies the applicant that it has no relief duty because it is not satisfied that the applicant is homeless and eligible.[35] If such a duty is owed, the accommodation duty ends when the authority notifies the applicant that the relief duty has come to an end and that a duty is or is not owed to the applicant under H(W)A 2014, s 75 (paras **8.16–8.17**).[36]

8.21   If the reason for the decision that there is no such principal duty is either on the ground that the applicant became homeless intentionally (in the circumstances which gave rise to the application) or on the ground that it had previously secured accommodation to the applicant following a previous application for help, at any time within the period of five years before the day on which the applicant was notified that a duty was owed to them, the duty does not come to an end.[37]

8.22   In either of these cases, the accommodation duty continues until the authority is satisfied that the period of accommodation has been sufficient to allow the applicant a reasonable opportunity of securing their own accommodation,[38] not being less than 56 days that the relief duty was applicable.[39]

8.23   The duty also ends if the applicant, having been notified of the possible consequences, refused an offer of suitable interim accommodation, or became homeless intentionally from that accommodation, or voluntarily ceased to occupy such accommodation as their only or principal home.[40]

---

33   HA 1996, s 188(1ZB).
34   HA 1996, s 188(1A).
35   H(W)A 2014, s 69(2).
36   H(W)A 2014, s 69(3).
37   H(W)A 2014, s 69(4), (5).
38   H(W)A 2014, s 69(5).
39   H(W)A 2014, s 69(6).
40   H(W)A 2014, s 69(7)–(9).

8.24   The duty also comes to an end if: the authority is no longer satisfied that the applicant is eligible; or the authority is satisfied that a mistake of fact led to the decision that the duty was owed at all; or the authority is satisfied that the applicant has withdrawn their application; or the authority is satisfied that the applicant is unreasonably failing to co-operate with it in connection with the exercise of its homelessness functions which relate to the applicant.[41]

8.25   The duty comes to an end even if a review is sought, but the authority has a discretion to continue to secure suitable accommodation pending a decision on the review.[42]

General considerations

Reason to believe

8.26   The threshold – 'reason to believe'[43] – is designedly low; the authority should provide the accommodation when it is needed and then make further enquiries.[44] Even this threshold was not reached in *Burns*,[45] however, where the authority had no reason to believe that the applicant was eligible. The applicant, who had married a European Union (EU) national, had been refused a residence permit by the Home Office, which refusal the authority was entitled to take at face value so that it was reasonable for it to have refused interim accommodation without making any further enquiries.

8.27   In *R (Edwards) v Birmingham City Council*,[46] it was held that, although the threshold is a low one, the authority is nonetheless entitled to question a person who claims to be homeless at home to clarify whether in fact there is reason to believe that the accommodation occupied by that person is such that it may not be reasonable for them to continue to occupy it; the applicant's assertion to this effect – or one on the applicant's behalf – does not have to be accepted on its face.

Available for occupation

8.28   The requirement to make accommodation available for the applicant's occupation is, by definition, a requirement to make it available for the applicant

---

41   H(W)A 2014, ss 69(12), 79.
42   H(W)A 2014, s 69(10), (11).
43   Whether this threshold is met is primarily a matter for the authority; any review is on conventional *Wednesbury* grounds: *R (Edwards) v Birmingham City Council* [2016] EWHC 173 (Admin), [2016] HLR 11.
44   *R (M) v Hammersmith and Fulham LBC* [2008] UKHL 14, [2008] 1 WLR 535 at [36].
45   *R (Burns) v Southwark LBC* [2004] EWHC 1901 (Admin), [2004] JHL D105; see also, by way of example *R (Omar) v Wandsworth LBC* [2015] EWHC 4110 (Admin).
46   [2016] EWHC 173 (Admin), [2016] HLR 11.

and for any person who might reasonably be expected to reside with them.[47] The meaning of this has been considered in Chapter 2.[48]

Securing accommodation

8.29 An authority may discharge its interim accommodation duties by providing its own accommodation; by arranging for it to be provided by someone else; or by giving advice such as will secure that it is provided by someone else.[49] These provisions are considered below, in relation to the principal housing duty.[50]

8.30 The requirement calls for some action on the part of the authority. In *Sidhu*,[51] a women's refuge, not even in the same area, provided accommodation, but as the authority had not been involved in procuring it, it could not rely on it as a discharge of its duty.

8.31 The fact that the accommodation was in another area was not itself fundamental to the result, but it may not be without relevance. Many such refuges are funded by local authorities. In such circumstances, there are two reasons why accommodation in a refuge in the same area, which is provided voluntarily and other than at the arrangement of the authority may be less susceptible to challenge:

a) as a matter of practice, the refuge is not entirely independent of the authority; and

b) the provision of funds for the refuge may be held to denote a sufficient degree of participation or assistance by the authority,[52] although probably only if the accommodation is provided at the express request of the authority, or it is agreed – or at the lowest 'understood' – that the organisation will accommodate those referred to it by the authority; anything more vague should not qualify.

Payment

8.32 The authority may require a person housed under this provision to pay such reasonable charges[53] as it may determine, or to pay an amount towards

47 HA 1996, s 176; H(W)A 2014, s 68.
48 Paras **2.19–2.41**; and see, in particular, *Sharif v Camden LBC* [2013] UKSC 10, [2013] HLR 16 in which it was held that two flats yards apart in the same building can comprise accommodation in which a household can live together.
49 HA 1996, s 206(1); H(W)A 2014, ss 92, 92A; see further paras **8.148, 8.155–8.158**.
50 Paras **8.129–8.281**.
51 *R v Ealing LBC ex p Sidhu* (1982) 2 HLR 45, QBD.
52 It may depend on the circumstances, including the powers under which assistance was provided and the terms of assistance.
53 Which can be 'nil': *R (Yekini) v Southwark LBC* [2014] EWHC 2096 (Admin).

the payment made by the authority to a third party for accommodation – for example, a contribution towards the cost of private sector accommodation.[54] If the authority provides its own accommodation, it can in any event make a reasonable charge under HA 1985, s 24.

8.33 The provision of assistance under HA 1996, Part 7 or H(W)A 2014, Part 2 is not, however, contingent on ability to pay,[55] although there is no reason why – even if the applicant is unable to make a payment – an authority should not reserve the right to payment, eg, against a future change of fortunes on the part of an applicant.

Security

8.34 In *Miah*,[56] *Buscombe*[57] and *Hayden*,[58] some doubt was cast on whether accommodation provided under the Housing (Homeless Persons) Act (H(HP)A) 1977 amounted to a tenancy or licence within the security provisions of what is now HA 1985, Part 4. In *Walsh*,[59] however, the authority's argument that any temporary accommodation so provided would necessarily be by way of licence was rejected by the House of Lords and the letting was held to amount to a tenancy.[60]

8.35 The importance of this issue is diminished[61] by the exclusion of security of tenure under the HAs 1985[62] and 1988[63] and Renting Homes (Wales) Act 2016 for homeless applicants, although it may still bear on determination of the right of occupation at common law,[64] disrepair claims and whether court proceedings are required to evict an occupier.[65]

54 HA 1996, s 206(2); H(W)A 2014, s 90. If accommodation is provided or secured by the authority but is subsequently found not to be suitable on grounds of costs (paras **8.210, 2.135–2.146**), it is difficult to see how it can have been a 'reasonable charge'; if that is correct, it would provide a basis for the applicant to seek to resist a claim for arrears.

55 *R v Secretary of State for Social Security ex p B and Joint Council for the Welfare of Immigrants* (1997) 29 HLR 129, CA.

56 *Family Housing Association v Miah* (1982) 5 HLR 94, CA.

57 *Restormel DC v Buscombe* (1982) 14 HLR 91, CA.

58 *Kensington and Chelsea RLBC v Hayden* (1985) 17 HLR 114, CA.

59 *Eastleigh DC v Walsh* [1985] 1 WLR 525, (1985) 17 HLR 392, HL.

60 See also *Street v Mountford* [1985] AC 809, (1985) 17 HLR 402, HL.

61 If not eliminated: see next paragraph.

62 HA 1985, Sch 1, para 4 as amended by H(W)A 2014, Sch 3, para 1; such a tenancy will become secure if the authority notifies the tenant that the tenancy is to be regarded as a secure tenancy. In *Tompkins v Wandsworth LBC* [2015] EWCA Civ 846, [2015] HLR 44, use of an incorrect form of tenancy agreement was held not to amount to 'notification' for these purposes. In Wales, post-RH(W)A 2016, the exclusion from security is now to be found in Sch 2, para 11 RH(W)A 2016, as applied by s 92A, H(W)A 2014.

63 HA 1996, s 209; H(W)A 2014, s 92A, incorporating the exclusion in Sch 2, para 11 RH(W) A 2016.

64 A homeless person who has been granted a daily licence to occupy a room with a lock in a local authority hostel is entitled to exclude trespassers: *Thomas v Director of Public Prosecutions* [2009] EWHC 3906 (Admin).

65 Para **8.48**.

8.36   The exclusion from assured protection under the HA 1988 lasts for a period of 12 months beginning on the date on which the applicant is notified of the decision on their application,[66] unless the landlord notifies them to the contrary, either that it is to be a fully assured tenancy or an assured shorthold tenancy.[67]

RENTERS (REFORM) BILL

Once the provisions of the Bill come into full relevant force and subject to any transitional provisions, the corresponding notification will be that the tenancy is to be assured: s 209(2)(b) will be amended to delete the reference to an assured shorthold tenancy.

8.37   For these purposes, a 'private sector landlord' is any landlord who is not within HA 1985, s 80(1);[68] the term therefore includes registered providers of social housing and registered social landlords.[69] It follows that someone initially provided with interim accommodation but left in it for long enough afterwards could become assured through the passage of time; secure protection under the HA 1985 is not, however, likewise limited by time, only by whether or not it is provided under HA 1996, Part 7 or H(W)A 2014, Part 2.

Quality

8.38   Under H(HP)A 1977 and HA 1985, as unamended, there was no statutory standard governing the quality of accommodation provided.[70] Under HA 1985, as amended by Housing and Planning Act 1986,[71] statutory requirements for suitability were introduced, but were not applicable to accommodation pending enquiries. The suitability requirements[72] of HA 1996 and H(W)A 2014 are, however, applicable to every requirement to secure that accommodation is available, including the interim duties. An authority does not have to give reasons

---

66   Or, in the case of a review or appeal to the county court, of the date on which they are notified of the outcome of the review or of when the appeal is finally determined.

67   HA 1996, s 209(2); in Wales, analogous provision is made by H(W)A 2014, s 92A and in Sch 2, para 12(4) RH(W)A 2016.

68   Ie, local authorities, new town corporations, housing action trusts, urban development corporations, or housing co-operatives within the meaning of HA 1985, s 27B.

69   HA 1996, s 217; H(W)A 2014, s 99.

70   *R v Hillingdon LBC ex p Puhlhofer* [1986] AC 484, (1986) 18 HLR 158, HL.

71   Section 14(3).

72   See HA 1996, ss 206(1) and 210(1) and H(W)A 2014, s 59, (paras **8.183–8.226**). See, eg, *R (Lindsay) v (1) Watford BC (2) Hertfordshire CC* High Court (QBD), 13 October 2017, in which it was considered doubtful that bed and breakfast accommodation was suitable for an applicant whose complex medical and mental health issues made it impossible for her to live independently.

why it considers that a property offered under these provisions is suitable.[73] Suitability is considered below in relation to the principal housing duty.[74]

8.39   In *Ali* and *Moran*,[75] it was observed that 'what is regarded as suitable for discharging the interim duty may be rather different from what is regarded as suitable for discharging the more open-ended duty in [HA 1996] section 193(2)'. This accords with two earlier decisions on the quality of temporary accommodation under the H(HP)A 1977, even though there was then no statutory suitability requirement,[76] although both related to temporary accommodation for the intentionally homeless.[77]

8.40   In *Gliddon*,[78] the authority was alleged to have been in breach of its temporary duty because the accommodation provided was in substantial disrepair, requiring works to prevent it becoming statutorily unfit for human habitation. It was held that the authority could have regard to the time for which accommodation was likely to be occupied: while some quality of accommodation would fall below the line of acceptable discharge of even a temporary duty, accommodation needing works to pre-empt statutory unfitness did not necessarily do so; accommodation so unfit that it is not even repairable, however, might well have been inadequate even for a temporary purpose.

8.41   In *Ward*,[79] accommodation on a caravan site described by a social worker as being in appalling condition was nonetheless an adequate discharge of the temporary duty, having regard to the family's wish to live on a site, rather than in a permanent structure.

Area

8.42   There are constraints on out-of-area placements which apply to discharge under this section: these are considered below in relation to the full duty.[80]

Termination of accommodation

8.43   On occasion, in particular when enquiries have taken some time (for example, into accommodation abroad), a local authority will wish to terminate

---

73   *Akhtar v Birmingham City Council* [2011] EWCA Civ 383, [2011] HLR 28; *Solihull MBC v Khan* [2014] EWCA Civ 41, [2014] HLR 33.
74   See paras **8.183–8.226**.
75   *Birmingham City Council v Ali; Moran v Manchester City Council (Secretary of State for Communities and Local Government and another intervening)* [2009] UKHL 36, [2009] 1 WLR 1506 at [18].
76   See paras **8.38–8.41**.
77   See paras **8.109–8.123**.
78   *R v Exeter City Council ex p Gliddon* (1984) 14 HLR 103, QBD.
79   *R v Southampton City Council ex p Ward* (1984) 14 HLR 114, QBD.
80   See paras **8.160–8.182**.

a right of occupation, either because it wants to move the applicant elsewhere or because of some fault on the part of the applicant[81] or it will have to deal with the position which arises if another landlord providing accommodation on its behalf has taken or wants to evict the applicant.

8.44 It is clear that the authority may move the occupier, for example, for reasons of cost, provided the new accommodation is also suitable, and it is otherwise acting reasonably. Where the accommodation is lost because of the applicant's default, it is not open to an authority to conclude that the applicant has thereby become homeless intentionally, as this would not have been the accommodation the loss of which gives rise to the homelessness application requiring a decision: see *Din*.[82] It may, however, be that no further interim duty is owed.[83]

8.45 Where the applicant refuses the accommodation offered (under HA 1996, s 188), the authority may nonetheless be able to conclude that it has discharged its duty under this section, and decline to provide further accommodation pursuant to it,[84] albeit that it will still be bound to consider and discharge the appropriate HA 1996, s 193 duty following its decision under s 184, based on the accommodation lost which led to the homelessness which gave rise to the application.

8.46 In reaching its decision on whether or not that loss amounted to intentionality, the loss of the intervening accommodation will therefore not be relevant,[85] save if and so far as the conduct involved can properly be considered to have some evidential value in reaching a view on the earlier loss of accommodation, for example, analogous conduct.

---

81 Eg, non-payment of charges, nuisance and annoyance, damage to property.
82 *Din v Wandsworth LBC* [1983] 1 AC 657, (1983) 1 HLR 73, HL. Consider, too, that HA 1996, s 193(6)(b) makes explicit provision for an authority to determine that its duty towards a homeless applicant – following a decision that the applicant is homeless, in priority need and not intentionally homeless – has been discharged in the event of becoming intentionally homeless from *that* accommodation; it would be anomalous to reach the same conclusion in relation to temporary accommodation *pending* a decision.
83 In *R v Kensington and Chelsea RLBC ex p Kujtim* (2000) 32 HLR 579, (1999) 2 CCLR 460, CA, the duty to provide accommodation under National Assistance Act 1948, s 21 (see now Chapter 11 for the provisions replacing that section) was held not to be absolute. Where the applicant manifests a persistent and unequivocal refusal to observe the authority's reasonable requirements in relation to occupation of the accommodation, the authority is entitled to treat its duty as discharged and to refuse to provide further accommodation.
84 Consider *R (Brooks) v Islington LBC* [2015] EWHC 2657 (Admin), [2016] HLR 2 where the applicant refused an offer of interim accommodation and the authority did not have to make a further such offer. The same point may be made by parity of reasoning with *R v Westminster City Council ex p Chambers* (1983) 6 HLR 15, QBD on refusal of a final offer (before statutory provision was made to govern such refusals): see para **7.50**.
85 *R v Islington LBC ex p Hassan* (1995) 27 HLR 485, QBD.

8.47 Since commencement of the HRA 2017,[86] if the authority has continued accommodation while discharging the relief duty,[87] there are statutory provisions governing refusal of offers and non co-operation, which are likely to apply[88] which may render it unnecessary to resort to previous case-law.

Eviction

8.48 Accommodation provided under HA 1996, Part 7 or H(W)A 2014, Part 2 is not protected by Protection from Eviction Act (PEA) 1977, s 3, and the applicant may be evicted without a court order;[89] any challenge based on Article 8 of the European Convention on Human Rights (ECHR) can, however, be raised on an appeal to the county court against any decision which means that a full duty is not to be accepted.[90]

8.49 If court proceedings are used, it seems likely that they can be resisted both on the basis that the authority's decision to seek possession is ultra vires in domestic public law,[91] or on the basis of Article 8[92] and/or (where appropriate) that it would amount to unlawful discrimination under the Equality Act (EqA) 2010.[93]

Terminal stage of life

8.50 Authorities should be alert to the need to review the suitability of any accommodation provided to a person who is reasonably expected to die of a progressive illness within six months or who is in receipt of palliative care who will 'almost certainly' have a priority need.[94]

---

86   3 April 2018: see Homelessness Reduction Act 2017 (Commencement and Transitional and Savings Provisions) Regulations 2018, SI 2018/167, reg 3, only applicable to applications made and reviews sought on or after that date – see reg 4.
87   Paras **8.88–8.103**.
88   Paras **8.97–8.103**.
89   In *Ibrahim v Haringey LBC* [2021] EWHC 731 (QB); [2022] HLR 3, it is suggested that temporary accommodation provided outside of Part 7, under the 'Everyone In' scheme during the coronavirus pandemic, may be in a different position, ie, may still be within PEA, s 3.
90   *R (ZH and CN) v Newham LBC and Lewisham LBC* [2014] UKSC 62, [2015] HLR 6.
91   *Barber v Croydon LBC* [2010] EWCA Civ 51, [2010] HLR 26.
92   *Powell v Hounslow LBC; Frisby v Birmingham CC; Hall v Leeds CC* [2011] UKSC 8, [2011] HLR 23.
93   *Akerman-Livingstone v Aster Communities Ltd* [2015] UKSC 15, [2015] HLR 20.
94   English *Homelessness code of guidance for local authorities*, para 17.10. See also Code para 8.41 in relation to priority need; and above, para **3.69**.

ACCOMMODATION PENDING REVIEW

8.51   The duty to provide interim accommodation under HA 1996, s 188 comes to an end even if a review is sought.[95] The duty is, however, replaced with a power to provide accommodation pending the review.[96] The authority is not obliged of its own motion to consider whether to exercise this power, but may await a request from the applicant before deciding whether to do so.[97]

8.52   As a refusal to house pending a review is not a decision that is itself susceptible to the statutory review process, any challenge has to be by way of judicial review.[98]

8.53   As an applicant has an unfettered right to a review,[99] it is not envisaged that the discretion to house pending review will be exercised as a matter of course. An authority may therefore decide to exercise the discretion only in exceptional circumstances: *Mohammed*.[100]

8.54   In exercising its discretion, the authority must balance the objective of maintaining fairness between other homeless persons – in circumstances where it has decided that no duty is owed to the applicant – and proper consideration of the possibility that the applicant may be right.[101] In carrying out this balancing exercise, certain matters will always require consideration, although other matters may also be relevant:[102]

    a)   the merits of the case and the extent to which it can properly be said that the decision was one which was either contrary to the apparent merits or was one which involved a very fine balance of judgment;

    b)   whether consideration is required of new material, information or argument which could have a real effect on the decision under review;

---

95   HA 1996, s 188(3); H(W)A 2014, s 69. See also *R (Faizi) v Brent LBC* [2015] EWHC 2449 (Admin).

96   HA 1996, s 188(3); H(W)A 2014, s 69(11).

97   *R (Ahmed) v Waltham Forest LBC* [2001] EWHC (Admin) 540, [2001] JHL D89.

98   *R v Camden LBC ex p Mohammed* (1998) 30 HLR 315, QBD. This sets a high bar: consider *R (Abdusemed) v Lambeth LBC*, High Court (Administrative Court), 19 February 2016; *HousingView*, 29 February 2016, where interim relief on judicial review was refused to a woman whom the authority had declined to house pending review even though she was walking the streets during the day and spending the night at a local mosque. See para **10.141**.

99   Paras **7.190–7.204**.

100 *R v Camden LBC ex p Mohammed*. See also *R v Hammersmith and Fulham LBC ex p Fleck* (1998) 30 HLR 679, QBD and *R v Newham LBC ex p Bautista* April 2001 *Legal Action* 22. See also, English Code of Guidance paras 15.25–15.27. For a detailed example, applying *Mohammed* and the Code, see *R (Saint Sepulchre) v Kensington & Chelsea RLBC* [2023] EWHC 2913 (Admin); [2024] HLR 12– see para **7.100**.

101 *R v Camden LBC ex p Mohammed* (1998) 30 HLR 315, QBD.

102 *Ie these considerations are not exhaustive: R (Saint Sepulchre) v Kensington & Chelsea RLBC* [2023] EWHC 2913 (Admin); [2024] HLR 12.

   c)   the personal circumstances of the applicant and the consequences to them of a decision not to exercise the discretion.[103]

8.55   In *Lumley*,[104] Brooke LJ explained that the merits of the case meant 'the merits of the applicant's case that the council's original decision was flawed'. In that case, the decision was quashed because the initial decision that the applicant was not in priority need was seriously flawed and the authority had failed to take the flaws into account when considering the exercise of its discretion to house pending review.

8.56   In every case, the principles must be applied to the relevant facts[105] and a properly reasoned decision provided.[106] The authority must be able to show that the balancing exercise has been fully or properly carried out – 'In other words, there should not be lip-service to the considerations'.[107] In *Mohammed*,[108] the judge found that the council had considered the matters set out properly, but he nonetheless quashed its decision not to house the applicant pending review because it had failed to give her an opportunity to explain inconsistencies in her statements and had therefore failed to take into account a relevant and material consideration in exercising its discretion.

8.57   In *Nacion*,[109] the Court of Appeal applied *Mohammed* to a decision under the discretion to house pending an appeal.[110] Housing pending appeal is considered in Chapter 10, as part of the machinery for enforcement of duties.[111]

---

103 *Mohammed, above.*

104 *R v Newham LBC ex p Lumley* (2001) 33 HLR 11, QBD.

105 Most cases turn on their facts, particularly on this issue; those facts are often confused and almost always idiosyncratic from which little by way of principle can be derived. Thus in *R (Laryea) v Ealing LBC* [2019] EWHC 3598 (Admin), [2020] JHL D14, the applicant had a range of physical and mental health problems. The authority conducted an assessment; it subsequently decided that its duty had been discharged. The applicant sought a review of that decision and requested accommodation pending that review, which the authority refused. The applicant sought judicial review and an interim order that accommodation be provided. Interim relief was granted: while the applicant had not taken full advantage of the opportunities presented by his HA 1996, s 189A assessment, that failure had to be judged against his complex physical and mental health difficulties; there was medical evidence that his condition would worsen if he were not housed; the letter containing the decision to refuse to provide interim accommodation contained factual errors and did not engage with the negative consequences if he was not provided with accommodation; the decision to refuse to provide accommodation was therefore deficient and an interim order was appropriate.

106 See *R (Paul-Coker) v Southwark LBC* [2006] EWHC 497 (Admin), [2006] HLR 32.

107 *R (Saint Sepulchre) v Kensington & Chelsea RLBC* [2023] EWHC 2913 (Admin); [2024] HLR 12: in that case, while making enquiries of the applicant's landlord, the authority failed to make enquiries of his solicitors about aspects of his claim, even though they were known to have recently acted for him, which meant that they had not fully and properly engaged with the *Mohammed* considerations; nor had they considered new information, namely that while the previous authority had concluded that the applicant had no eligible social care needs (see para **11.22**), their own Adult Social Care department did so.

108 *R v Camden LBC ex p Mohammed* (1997) 30 HLR 315, QBD.

109 *R v Brighton and Hove Council ex p Nacion* (1999) 31 HLR 1095, CA.

110 HA 1996, s 204(4). But see now s 204A, allowing an appeal from such a refusal to be made to the county court itself – paras **10.254–10.261**.

111 Paras **10.254–10.261**.

8.58   There is, however, a difference between housing pending review and housing pending appeal, as recognised by Brooke LJ in *Lumley*:[112] in *Nacion* there had already been a review, so that 'most of the errors, if any, made on the first consideration of the case should have been put right by the senior officer who conducted the review', while pending review, there will only have been the one decision and consideration. Accordingly, the bar may be a little lower when considering housing pending review than when considering housing pending appeal.

8.59   In deciding when to terminate accommodation provided pending a decision following an unsuccessful review, an authority must give the person reasonable notice so that they can have an opportunity to make alternative arrangements.[113]

8.60   It was previously held that there is no requirement for a local housing authority to take into consideration possible duties owed to the children of an applicant under Children Act (CA) 1989, or the potential break-up of the family, when deciding whether to continue to provide accommodation under HA 1996, s 188(3),[114] although the correctness of this must now be in doubt given the impact of ECHR Article 8, CA 2004, s 11[115] and the trend of homelessness legislation under HRA 2017.

ASSESSMENT AND PLAN

England

8.61   Since the HRA 2017 came into force,[116] there has been a new duty of 'assessment' applicable to all applicants whom an English authority is satisfied are homeless or threatened with homelessness[117] and eligible[118] for assistance.[119] Priority need is therefore not needed. The duty is to 'make an assessment of the

---

112 (2001) 33 HLR 11, QBD.
113 *R v Newham LBC ex p Ojuri (No 5)* (1998) 31 HLR 631, QBD.
114 *R (Hassan) v Croydon LBC* [2009] JHL D56, Administrative Court.
115 Local authorities must have regard 'to the need to safeguard and promote the welfare of children' when discharging their functions: CA 2004, s 11 (England), s 28 (Wales). This includes functions under HA 1996, Part 7: *Huzrat v Hounslow LBC* [2013] EWCA Civ 1865, [2014] HLR 17. See also *Nzolameso v Westminster City Council* [2015] UKSC 22, [2015] HLR 22: when considering whether accommodation is suitable for a family, the authority must identify the principal needs of the children both individually and collectively when making the decision. If there is a review of suitability, those issues must be reconsidered as at the date of the review: *Waltham Forest LBC v Saleh* [2019] EWCA Civ 1944, [2020] PTSR 621, [2020] HLR 15.
116 3 April 2018: see Homelessness Reduction Act 2017 (Commencement and Transitional and Savings Provisions) Regulations 2018, SI 2018/167, reg 3, only applicable to applications made and reviews sought on or after that date – see reg 4.
117 Chapter 2.
118 Annex: Immigration Eligibility.
119 HA 1996, s 189A.

applicant's case',[120] which must include an assessment of the circumstances which resulted in the applicant's homelessness or being threatened with homelessness, the applicant's housing needs,[121] and their needs for support[122] in order to be able to have and retain suitable accommodation.[123] The authority has to notify the applicant in writing of the assessment it makes.[124]

8.62   The next stage is for the authority to try to agree with the applicant what steps they are to be required to take in order to secure that they[125] have and is able to retain suitable accommodation, and what steps the authority is to take under HA 1996, Part 7 for those purposes,[126] commonly referred to as a personal plan.

8.63   If the authority and the applicant reach an agreement, the authority has to record it in writing.[127] If they cannot reach agreement, the authority has to record in writing why it could not agree; what steps it considers it would be reasonable to require the applicant to take; and what steps the authority is to take under HA 1996, Part 7 for those purposes.[128] Either class of record can include any advice the authority considers appropriate, including the steps the authority thinks it would be 'a good idea for the applicant to take', albeit that the applicant is not to be required to take.[129] The authority has to give the applicant a copy of the written record.[130]

8.64   Until the authority decides that it owes the applicant no duty under any of the remaining provisions of Part 7, the authority has to keep the assessment under review, together with the appropriateness of any agreement

---

120 HA 1996, s 189A(1).
121 In particular, what accommodation would be suitable for them and anyone with whom they reside or might reasonably be expected to reside. As to those reasonably to be expected to reside with the applicant, see paras **3.28-3.34** and in particular *R (SK) v Royal Borough of Windsor and Maidenhead* [2024] EWHC 158 (Admin); [2024] HLR forthcoming at para **3.34**.
122 Together with anyone with whom they reside or might reasonably be expected to reside. Again, see also paras **3.34-3.24** and *SK*, above.
123 HA 1996, s 189A(2).
124 HA 1996, s 189A(3).
125 Together with anyone with whom they reside or might reasonably be expected to reside.
126 HA 1996, s 189A(4). This could include the applicant and the authority working together to ensure that the applicant is receiving all welfare benefits to which they might be entitled, whether as of right or pursuant to any discretionary scheme. For example, if the applicant is entitled to housing benefit or universal credit and requires further financial assistance in order to meet their housing costs, then the authority has power to make a discretionary housing payment (DHP): Discretionary Financial Assistance Regulations 2001, SI 2001/1167 and Discretionary Housing Payments (Grants) Order 2001, SI 2001/2340. Such payments can be made in any amount and for any period of time and are a legitimate tool for preventing homelessness: *R (Halvai) v Hammersmith and Fulham LBC* [2017] EWHC 802 (Admin). A refusal to provide such – or other financial – assistance can, however, only be challenged on conventional public law grounds: cf *R (Conville) v Richmond upon Thames LBC* [2005] EWHC 1430 (Admin), [2006] HLR 1, not appealed on this point, see [2006] EWCA Civ 718, [2006] HLR 45.
127 HA 1996, s 189A(5).
128 HA 1996, s 189A(6).
129 HA 1996, s 189A(7).
130 HA 1996, s 189A(8).

reached or steps recorded.[131] If the assessment of the mandatory considerations (circumstances resulting in homelessness or being threatened with homelessness, housing needs and needs for support)[132] changes, the authority must notify the applicant, in writing, of how its assessment has changed (whether by providing a revised written assessment or otherwise);[133] the same is true if the authority's assessment otherwise changes in a way that it considers it appropriate to notify the applicant.[134]

8.65   If the authority considers that any agreement reached or any step recorded under it is no longer appropriate, it must notify the applicant in writing to this effect and that any subsequent failure to take a step that was agreed or recorded is to be disregarded; the provisions governing attempt to reach agreement, or to record a failure to do so, described above (paras **8.62–8.63**) re-apply.[135]

8.66   The duties were considered in some detail in *R. (ZK) v Havering LBC*,[136] the applicant was an asylum seeker, a victim of torture suffering from post-traumatic stress disorder, anxiety and depression. After the grant of refugee status, he applied to the authority for assistance under Pt 7: the authority decided that he was eligible for assistance and threatened with homelessness and issued a personalised housing plan for him. The authority secured temporary accommodation for the family which the applicant considered unsuitable and he wrote requesting a re-assessment of his housing needs, a revised personalised housing plan and a review of the suitability of his accommodation. The authority provided a second personalised housing plan which the applicant also considered inadequate and he issued a claim for judicial review which was withdrawn on the authority agreeing to provide a third plan and to review the suitability of his accommodation. Subsequently, the applicant provided the authority with reports from a clinical psychologist, an occupational therapist and a psychotherapist, all of which emphasised that he was extremely vulnerable and needed suitable, permanent accommodation. The third personalised plan recorded that the applicant had 'advised' the authority of certain matters relating to his health and his family and recorded: 'You stated the assistance which would be helpful would be helping you secure a suitable stability home for your wife and your children. You stated that you would like an extra bedroom to accommodate yourself due to your medical issues.'

8.67   The applicant again contended that the authority had failed to carry out a lawful assessment and to provide a lawful plan and again wrote threatening

---

131 HA 1996, s 189A(9).
132 See para **8.64**.
133 In *R (SK) v Royal Borough of Windsor and Maidenhead* [2024] EWHC 158 (Admin); [2024] HLR forthcoming, a delay of one month in notifying the applicant was unreasonable and as such unlawful.
134 HA 1996, s 189A(10).
135 HA 1996, s 189A(11).
136 [2022] EWHC 1854 (Admin); [2022] HLR 47.

to issue a claim for judicial review, in response to which authority again said that it would revise the plan and review the suitability of the applicant's current accommodation. This led to a visit from a housing officer employed by the authority who concluded that the accommodation was unsuitable because the steps up to the property were a health and safety concern and it was too far from the children's school. After a period in which nothing happened, the claimant issued the claim for judicial review. In response, the authority offered alternative accommodation which the applicant accepted but requested a review of its suitability. By the time the claim was heard, the authority had accepted that the applicant needed long-term accommodation which was easily accessible, close to the children's school and in a relatively quiet area. There was a dispute as to how many bedrooms the family required: the claimant argued that they needed four bedrooms but the authority considered that only three were required.

8.68   The court noted that the assessment duty is important as it will inform any decision later taken on suitability; it was held that although an assessment need not include an exhaustive list of housing needs, it must include the key needs that provide the 'nuts and bolts' for any offer of suitable accommodation. The assessment duty, and the plan duty, are separate but intrinsically linked; while the first must address the nuts and bolts of the applicant's housing needs, it does not need to be in one clearly indexed document; likewise, there is no requirement that the housing needs assessment and the personalised housing plan are produced as two separate documents; that said, the needs assessment and the personal plan must be communicated to the applicant in writing. To decide whether or not the duties have been discharged requires an assessment of the whole of the housing file as it might be viewed by a "reasonable and sensible housing officer".

8.69   The assessment addresses needs not wishes though there may be a crossover between them – 'needs' are what are required whereas 'wishes' are merely desirable; a reasonable and sensible housing officer reading an applicant's file ought to be able to understand what was 'needed' as distinct from what would be 'nice to have' when considering the suitability of current or future accommodation. In *SK*, the distinction was unclear; even though the authority and the applicant were substantially in agreement as to the applicant's needs, the housing file did not contain an adequate assessment of those needs nor were they set out sufficiently in writing, and the duty had accordingly not been fulfilled.

8.70   In *R (UO) v Redbridge LBC*,[137] the applicant stressed that her children needed to remain in their current school; in particular, her eldest child was making excellent progress after missing months of school during consideration of the applicant's refugee claim, and her headteacher subsequently wrote to the authority saying that stable housing was then more important for the eldest child 'than in any other year of her life'. An assessment undertaken a few days after the application made no reference to the Childrens' needs or the disruption to their

137 [2023] EWHC 1355 (Admin); [2023] HLR 39.

education if they were forced to move schools or make a long commute, nor did it contain any evidence to show that the authority had looked for accommodation nearer to the school, and accommodation was provided in a series of hotels, each of which was between one-and-a-half and two-and-a-half hours from the school. It was held that the assessment had been wholly inadequate and unlawful and the accommodation unsuitable. Nor had the authority undertaken a review after receipt of the letter from the headteacher as it ought to have done. A final offer of accommodation in Peterborough was rejected by the applicant because she did not want a change of schools: a review of the suitability of that offer recorded that the children were not at a critical point in their education but, again, made no mention of the eldest child's particular position nor of the letter from the headteacher – it was also unlawful.[138]

8.71   In *R (YR) v Lambeth LBC*,[139] the authority provided temporary accommodation in its area in January 2022 and the applicant's children were enrolled in schools there, although her application under Part 7 was not until 25 July 2022. She was interviewed by a housing adviser employed by the authority in August 2022 but was not asked about her children's needs. The adviser completed a Relief Assessment and Personalised Plan, a document which combined the assessment and the personalised plan. It contained no reference to the welfare needs of the claimant's children, in particular how their education would be disrupted by any out-of-area placement. Under the authority's Placements Policy, Group A was prioritised for accommodation in Lambeth and Group B for accommodation within Lambeth or neighbouring boroughs; Group C were provided with accommodation wherever the authority could procure it. Group B included households with one child (or more) in secondary school in Lambeth in Year 11, in which the child would normally be taking their GCSE examinations. The applicant's eldest child was due to start in Year 11 in September 2022.

8.72   The day after the interview, the authority offered the family interim accommodation in a village in Thurrock; the applicant's solicitors wrote that this was unsuitable because of the disruption to the children's schooling and because the claimant would lose the support from a friend in Lambeth who helped her care for her youngest child. The applicant nonetheless accepted the offer and her children continued to attend school in Lambeth but she issued a claim for judicial review. Subsequently, an officer of the authority conducted a review of the assessment and plan and decided that her circumstances did not bring her within Group B of the Placements Policy. While he accepted that the move would cause disruption to the children's education, he identified a number of schools near the property in Thurrock. In the light of the extreme shortage of affordable

138 It was also held that, while suitability could have been challenged by way of review and appeal, that issue was so closely related to the assessment challenge that there would have been no purpose acceding to the authority's argument that relief should have been refused on that ground.

139 *R. (YR) v Lambeth LBC* [2022] EWHC 2813 (Admin); [2023] HLR 16.

housing in Lambeth, he considered that the accommodation in Thurrock was suitable.

8.73 The claim for judicial review was successful. The duties call for a written assessment and housing plan that are sufficiently reasoned to show that the authority has addressed the requirements of s 189A(2)(a)-(c)[140] The assessment and plan had not referred to the children's needs and the disruption to their education, which the authority was required to consider by virtue of both art 2, Homelessness (Suitability of Accommodation) (England) Order[141] and s 11, Children Act 2004;[142] both assessment and were therefore unlawful. Moreover, no reasonable authority could have failed to make inquiries about the disruption that might be caused to the children's education before concluding that it was not reasonably practical to accommodate them in or near the authority's area; neither the assessment nor plan showed any such inquiries were made, eg, of the authority's social services department or the children's schools, ie, how the schools thought the impact a move to a new school would have on the children's education and welfare; in particular, the authority had not known that the applicant's eldest child was in her GCSE year, which was highly relevant factor given the authority's Placements Policy.[143]

8.74 In most cases, an applicant with children who is to be accommodated in another local authority area can be expected to liaise with that authority to ascertain whether school places are available. The applicant's circumstances, however, were highly unusual; she was not an English speaker; she was single and had a young baby; she had no family or other support where the offer was located; there were six school age children for whom placements had to be made; her eldest child was in her GCSE year. Accordingly, to be able to decide that suitable arrangements would be in place to meet the educational needs of all the children, the authority had to satisfy itself of two matters: first, that school places were in fact available for all the children; secondly, that it would be reasonably practicable for the claimant to ensure that all the children could attend those schools; the authority had failed to make inquiries into these issues.[144]

8.75 The English Code of Guidance leans towards arrangements by the authority.

> 'Before a family that includes a school age child is placed out of district, the housing authority should liaise with the receiving authority and make

---

140 Para **8.61**, ie, the circumstances which resulted in the applicant's homelessness or being threatened with homelessness, the applicant's housing needs and their needs for support
141 Para **8.211**.
142 Arrangements to safeguard and protect welfare: para **11.84.**
143 See further paras **8.192, 8.200, 8.213–8.213**, on the education issue.
144 In any event, the authority's decision that the interim accommodation was suitable was vitiated by the fact that it was based on an unlawful assessment under s 189A. In the absence of a reasoned decision, it was to be inferred that the authority unlawfully failed to apply its placement policy at that time. If there was a good reason why priority should not be given contrary to the policy, that should have been recorded in writing.

every reasonable effort to ensure arrangements are or will be put in place to meet the child's educational needs.'[145]

Wales

8.76   In Wales, the H(W)A 2014 contains similar – but not identical – duties.[146] If it appears to the authority that an applicant may be homeless or threatened with homelessness, it must carry out an assessment of the person's case.[147] The assessment must consider whether the applicant is eligible.[148] If the applicant is eligible, the assessment must then address:

a)   how the applicant has become homeless or threatened with homelessness;

b)   the applicant's housing needs and those of anyone with whom they live or might reasonably be expected to live;

c)   the support required to meet those needs; and

d)   whether or not the authority has any duty under H(W)A 2014, Part 2 to the applicant.[149]

8.77   The assessment must seek to identify what the applicant wishes to achieve with the authority's help; the authority must consider whether the exercise of any of its powers under Part 2 can contribute to that outcome.[150] The assessment must be kept under review.[151] The authority must notify the applicant of the outcome of the assessment (and of any review) and, insofar as any issue is decided against their interests, give reasons for the decision.[152] It must also inform the applicant or their right to request a review.[153]

8.78   Additional notification duties[154] apply where a duty under H(W)A 2014, s 75[155] is owed only because of a restricted person[156] or where the authority has already notified or intends to notify another authority under the local connection provisions.[157]

---

145 At English Code, para 17.54.
146 H(W)A 2014 applies from 27 April 2015: see Housing (Wales) Act 2014 (Commencement No 3 and Transitory, Transitional and Saving Provisions) Order 2015, SI 2015/1272.
147 H(W)A 2014, s 62(1), (4), (5).
148 H(W)A 2014, s 62(3).
149 H(W)A 2014, s 62(5).
150 H(W)A 2014, s 62(6).
151 H(W)A 2014, s 62(8), (9).
152 H(W)A 2014, s 63(1).
153 H(W)A 2014, s 63(4).
154 H(W)A 2014, s 63(2), (3).
155 Ie, the full duty.
156 As to whom, see paras **A.127–A.133**; as to duties towards the, see paras **8.272–8.281**.
157 As to which, see Chapter 5.

DUTIES TO THOSE THREATENED WITH HOMELESSNESS

England

8.79   Since commencement of the HRA 2017,[158] a new duty has been imposed on English authorities – replacing previous provisions to be found in HA 1996, s 195 as enacted – in all cases where the authority is satisfied that an applicant is threatened with homelessness[159] and eligible[160] for assistance.[161] Priority need is again[162] not relevant to whether or not there is a duty.[163]

8.80   The authority is obliged to take reasonable steps to help the applicant to secure that accommodation does not cease to be available for their occupation.[164] The term 'reasonable steps' is not defined; plainly, however, it cannot mean 'no steps'. Authorities cannot refuse as a matter of policy to take any action until physical eviction: each case must be considered on its merits, and where it is obvious that homelessness will ensue steps must be taken to prepare for it.[165]

8.81   In deciding what steps to take, the authority has to have regard to its assessment (paras **8.61–8.78**) of the applicant's case.[166] The obligation is without prejudice to the authority's right to recover possession of any accommodation.[167]

8.82   The authority can give notice bringing this duty to an end when it is satisfied that any one of the following circumstances is applicable:[168]

    a)   the applicant both has suitable accommodation which is available for their occupation[169] and there is a reasonable prospect of the applicant having

---

158 3 April 2018: see Homelessness Reduction Act 2017 (Commencement and Transitional and Savings Provisions) Regulations 2018, SI 2018/167, reg 3, only applicable to applications made and reviews sought on or after that date – see reg 4.

159 See paras **2.147–2.154**.

160 Annex: Immigration Eligibility.

161 HA 1996, s 195(1).

162 Para **8.61**.

163 It is highly relevant, of course, to the rights that the applicant will enjoy: see further paras **8.129–8.281**.

164 HA 1996, s 195(2). The duties apply even although an issue of local connection may apply: see *Williams v Exeter City Council*, September 1981 *LAG Bulletin* 211, CC, under the Housing (Homeless Persons) Act 1977.

165 *R v Newham LBC ex p Khan* (2001) 33 HLR 29, QBD, under the predecessor provisions of HA 1996, s 195 (as enacted).

166 HA 1996, s 195(3).

167 HA 1996, s 195(4). The provision does not make an authority's refusal to withdraw 'stop notices', under planning legislation, perverse, even though it would render the applicants, a group of travelling showmen, homeless: *R v Chiltern DC ex p Dyason* (1991) 23 HLR 387, QBD.

168 HA 1996, s 195(5), (8). The notice must specify which of the circumstances applies and inform the applicant that they have a right to request a review of the decision to bring the duty to an end and of the time within which such a request must be made: HA 1996, s 195(7).

169 See paras **2.19–2.41**.

suitable accommodation[170] available for at least six months[171] from the date of the notice;

b) the authority has complied with the duty to take reasonable steps and the period of 56 days beginning with the day that the authority was first satisfied that the applicant is threatened with homeless and eligible has ended (whether or not they are still threatened with homelessness);[172]

c) the applicant has become homeless;[173]

d) the applicant has refused an offer of suitable accommodation and, on the date of refusal, there was a reasonable prospect that suitable accommodation would be available for occupation by the applicant for at least six months or such longer period[174] as may be prescribed;

e) the applicant has become homeless intentionally[175] from any accommodation that has been made available to them as a result of the authority's exercise of its functions under this duty;[176]

f) the applicant is no longer eligible for assistance; or

g) the applicant has withdrawn the application for accommodation or assistance in obtaining it.

RENTERS (REFORM) BILL

Once the provisions of the Bill come into full relevant force and subject to any transitional provisions, consequent on the repeal of s 195A (re-application within two years after private rented sector offer – see para **3.2**), the prohibition on serving notice in circumstance (b) in the above paragraph referable to s 195(6) will no longer apply.

---

170 It need not be the same accommodation.
171 Or such longer period not exceeding 12 months as may be prescribed.
172 The authority cannot give notice to the applicant in this circumstances if a valid notice has been given to the applicant under HA 1988, s 21 which will expire within 56 days or has expired and is in respect of the only accommodation that is available for their occupation (see para **2.120**): HA 1996, s 195(6).
173 So that the relief duty will apply: see paras **8.88–8.103**.
174 Not exceeding 12 months.
175 Chapter 4.
176 The English Code illustrates the operation of this provision: '[T]he provisions could apply for example, if an applicant had suitable accommodation secured as part of the housing authorities reasonable steps, and had surrendered without good reason or been excluded from that accommodation due to their actions, before the housing authority had served notice that the duty had been brought to an end under section 195(8)(a) or section 189B (suitable accommodation has been secured)' – para 14.31.

8.83   The duty may also be brought to an end under HA 1996, s 193B (deliberate and unreasonable refusal to co-operate: paras **8.100–8.103**),[177] although this does not end a right to accommodation for an applicant who is homeless, eligible, in priority need and not homeless intentionally, under s 193C (para **8.97**).[178]

RENTERS (REFORM) BILL

Once the provisions of the Bill come into full relevant force and subject to any transitional provisions, the accommodation provisions of s193C (subs (3)-(9)) will be repealed, as will be exclusion from s 193 by s 193(1A)(b). Accordingly, where the relief duty in s 189B ends because of deliberate and unreasonable refusal to co-operate, the housing duty in s 193 will be available.

Wales

8.84   In Wales, an authority which is satisfied that an applicant is eligible and threatened with homelessness must 'help to secure' that accommodation does not cease to be available to the applicant.[179] This duty cannot be used to prevent the authority itself obtaining vacant possession of any accommodation; accordingly, it cannot be raised as a defence by a tenant in possession proceedings by the authority.[180]

8.85   The duty to help to secure that accommodation does not cease to be available requires the authority to take reasonable steps to help, having regard to (among other things) the need to make the best use of its resources.[181] It does not require the authority to offer accommodation, whether under H(W)A 2014, Part 6 or otherwise.[182]

8.86   An authority can help to secure that suitable accommodation does not cease to be available either by providing some form of assistance itself or arranging for someone else to provide it.[183] Examples in the H(W)A 2014 of what may be provided or arranged are:

---

177 HA 1996, s 195(10).
178 HA 1996, s 193C(3), (4).
179 H(W)A 2014, s 66(1).
180 H(W)A 2014, s 66(2).
181 H(W)A 2014, s 65(a).
182 H(W)A 2014, ss 65(b)–(c).
183 H(W)A 2014, s 64(1).

a) mediation;

b) grants or loans;

c) guarantees;

d) support in management of debt, mortgage or rent arrears;

e) security measures for applicants at risk of abuse;

f) advocacy or other representation;

g) accommodation;

h) information and advice; and

i) other services, goods or facilities.[184]

8.87 The authority can give notice[185] bringing this duty to and end if the authority is satisfied that:[186]

a) the applicant has become homeless;[187]

b) the applicant is no longer threatened with homelessness and suitable accommodation is likely to remain available for their occupation for at least another six months;[188]

c) the applicant refuses an offer of accommodation – which the authority is satisfied was suitable and was likely to be available for at least the next six months – from any person, having been notified in writing of the possible consequences of refusal or acceptance of the offer;[189]

d) the applicant ceases to be eligible;[190]

e) a mistake of fact led to authority to notify the applicant that it owed them a duty to help to secure accommodation for the applicant;[191]

f) the applicant has withdrawn the application;[192] or

g) the applicant is unreasonably failing to co-operate with the authority.[193]

184 H(W)A 2014, s 64(2).
185 H(W)A 2014, s 84: the authority has to provide reasons why it considers the duty has come to an end, and inform the applicant of the right to a review and of the time within which it must be sought. See also para **8.11**.
186 H(W)A 2014, s 67.
187 H(W)A 2014, s 67(2).
188 H(W)A 2014, s 67(3).
189 H(W)A 2014, s 67(4).
190 H(W)A 2014, s 79(2).
191 H(W)A 2014, s 79(3).
192 H(W)A 2014, s 79(4).
193 H(W)A 2014, s 79(5).

RELIEF DUTY

England

Overview

8.88   Since the HRA 2017 came into force,[194] there has been a new duty[195] applicable where the authority is satisfied that an applicant is homeless[196] and eligible[197] for assistance;[198] the duty does not, however, arise where the authority refers the application to another local housing authority in England under the local connection provisions (see para **5.65**).[199] The duty also[200] arises regardless of priority need.

8.89   The duty is to take reasonable steps[201] to help the applicant to secure that suitable accommodation becomes available for their occupation[202] for at least six months or such longer period[203] as may be prescribed.[204] In deciding what steps to take, the authority must have regard to its assessment of the applicant's case (paras **8.61–8.75**).[205] Suitability is considered below in relation to the principal housing duty.[206]

RENTERS (REFORM) BILL

The government has proposed to amend the Bill so that anyone served with a valid notice of seeking possession under Housing Act 1988, s 8 will be entitled to the same or similar assistance.

8.90   While the authority can fulfil the duty by providing accommodation,[207] it is only a duty to take reasonable steps to help to secure accommodation. It seems highly likely that the courts will take the view that what is reasonable for the authority to do is a matter for the authority, rather than the court.

194 3 April 2018: see Homelessness Reduction Act 2017 (Commencement and Transitional and Savings Provisions) Regulations 2018, SI 2018/167, reg 3, only applicable to applications made and reviews sought on or after that date – see reg 4.
195 Also based on provisions already in force in Wales.
196 Chapter 2.
197 Annex: Immigration Eligibility.
198 HA 1996, s 189B(1).
199 HA 1996, s 189B(2).
200 Para **8.79**.
201 See the observation at para **8.80**: reasonable steps cannot mean no steps.
202 See paras **2.19–2.41**.
203 Not exceeding 12 months.
204 HA 1996, s 189B(2).
205 HA 1996, s 189B(3).
206 See paras **8.183–8.226**.
207 Although this is not explicitly stated, it is not merely implied but supported by other provisions of the HRA 2017, amending HA 1996: see, in particular, HRA 2017, s 6, amending HA 1996, s 205, and s 7(1) adding s 193A.

8.91   It is also currently considered that the duty does not give rise to a duty of care on the part of the authority to ensure that any accommodation towards which the applicant is directed is safe. In *Ephraim v Newham LBC*,[208] the plaintiff had been directed by the authority – by way of advice and assistance[209] – to a guesthouse, a house in multiple occupation (HMO). She took up occupation in a bedsitting room in it. The HMO lacked proper fire precautions. Subsequently, there was a fire in the property and she suffered severe injuries. She sued, unsuccessfully alleging that Newham LBC was under a duty of care to satisfy itself that the premises to which it had referred her were reasonably safe, particularly in relation to fire.

8.92   It was held that the imposition of such a duty would put the authority in the dilemma of having either to inspect a particular property, or else not advise people to seek available accommodation; it was more desirable that the authority should give advice which enables homeless people to obtain accommodation, even though some of the properties where they obtain accommodation might prove not to be properly equipped, than it was to restrict the range of advice and make it more difficult for homeless people to find housing. It is, however, arguable that the relief duty is intended to impose a more active obligation on authorities than the former 'advice and assistance' duty which might in turn be considered to suggest a higher duty of care, reliance being also placed on an authority's HMO duties.[210]

When the duty comes to an end

Generally

No priority need

8.93   Where the applicant is eligible for assistance and homeless, but not in priority need, the authority may give notice that it has complied with its duty under HA 1996, s 189B(2) (paras **8.88–8.103**) and that the period of 56 days has elapsed since it did so.[211] The period begins with the day when the authority is first satisfied that the applicant was owed the relief duty under section 189B (para **8.88**); the notice must specify that this is the ground on which it relies for concluding that it has complied with its duty, and must inform the applicant that they have a right to request a review of the decision to bring the duty to an end and of the time within which such a request must be made.[212]

---

208 *Ephraim v Newham LBC* (1993) 25 HLR 207, CA.
209 Under the predecessor provision to HA 1996, s 192 prior to repeal by HRA 2017, s 5(1), (6).
210 Under HA 2004, Part 2. The question seems ripe for consideration by the Supreme Court, in light of a range of developments as to duty of care by public authorities in other areas of the law.
211 HA 1996, s 189B(5), (7)(b).
212 HA 1996, s 189B(6). See also para **8.11**.

8.94   The authority is not obliged to cease to help simply because an applicant is not in priority need. While there is no explicit power to afford relief to those not in priority need, the section is cast in terms of allowing the authority to serve notice stating that it has complied with its relief duty on a number of grounds, of which this is one.[213] The authority could, accordingly, decide it will continue to comply with the duty until other grounds for termination – those applicable to applicants in priority need (paras **8.95–8.103**) – exist. Financial pressures do, however, mean that this is likely to be the exception rather than the norm.

With priority need

8.95   Where the authority is satisfied that the applicant does have a priority need[214] and is not satisfied that the applicant became homeless intentionally,[215] the duty comes to an end 56 days after the day the authority was first satisfied that the applicant was homeless and eligible.[216] The duty is normally followed by the principal housing duty under HA 1996, s 193.[217]

8.96   The authority may also give notice bringing the duty to an end when it is satisfied that any one of certain circumstances is applicable.[218] The circumstances are as follows:[219]

a)   the applicant both has suitable accommodation which is available for the applicant's occupation and there is a reasonable prospect of them having suitable accommodation[220] available for at least six months[221] from the date of the notice;

b)   the authority has complied with the duty to take reasonable steps and the period of 56 days beginning with the day that the authority is first satisfied

---

213 HA 1996, s 189B(5)–(7).

214 Chapter 3.

215 Chapter 4.

216 HA 1996, s 189B(4), unless disapplied by s 193A (refusal of final accommodation offer or final Part 6 offer): s 193(1A).

217 HA 1996, s 193(1) unless disapplied by s 193A (refusal of final accommodation offer or final Part 6 offer): s 193(1A) (paras **8.98–8.99**).

218 HA 1996, s 189B(5). The notice must specify which of the circumstances applies and inform the applicant of their right to a review and of the time within which a review must be sought: HA 1996, s 189B(6).

219 HA 1996, s 189B(7).

220 It need not be the same accommodation. In theory, an applicant may remain homeless notwithstanding that there is suitable accommodation available and a reasonable prospect of them having it for at least six months on the basis that it is not reasonable to continue in occupation of it, *per Birmingham City Council v Ali; Moran v Manchester City Council (Secretary of State for Communities and Local Government and another intervening)* [2009] UKHL 36, [2009] 1 WLR 1506 (see para **8.39**), in which case a duty under s 193 could subsist, but this it is unlikely as the two conditions will also tend to make it reasonable to continue to occupy the accommodation: *R (Ahamed) v Haringey LBC* [2023] EWCA Civ 975; [2023] HLR 43, at [46] and [49].

221 Or such longer period not exceeding 12 months as may be prescribed.

that the applicant was homeless and eligible has ended (whether or not they have secured accommodation);

c) the applicant has refused an offer of suitable accommodation and, on the date of refusal, there was a reasonable prospect that suitable accommodation would be available for occupation by the applicant for at least six months or such longer period[222] as may be prescribed;

d) the applicant has become homeless intentionally from any accommodation that has been made available to them as a result of the authority's exercise of its functions under this duty;[223]

e) the applicant is no longer eligible for assistance; or

f) the applicant has withdrawn the application for accommodation or assistance in obtaining it.

Additional circumstances

8.97 Additionally, the duty can be brought to an end under:

a) HA 1996, s 193A – refusal of final offer (see paras **8.98–8.99**); or

b) HA 1996, s 193B – deliberate and unreasonable refusal to co-operate (see paras **8.100–8.103**),[224]

although – by HA 1996, s 193C – the latter will not end a right to accommodation for an applicant who is homeless, eligible, in priority need and not homeless intentionally.[225]

RENTERS (REFORM) BILL

Once the provisions of the Bill come into full relevant force and subject to any transitional provisions, the accommodation provisions of s 193C (subs (3)-(9)) will be repealed, as will be exclusion from s 193 by s 193(1A)(b). Accordingly, where the relief duty in s 189B ends because of deliberate and unreasonable refusal to co-operate, the housing duty in s 193 will be available.

---

222 Not exceeding 12 months.
223 The English Code illustrates the operation of this provision: '[T]he provisions could apply for example, if an applicant had suitable accommodation secured as part of' the housing authority's 'reasonable steps, and had surrendered without good reason or been excluded from that accommodation due to their actions, before the housing authority had served notice that the duty had been brought to an end under s 195(8)(a) or s 189B (suitable accommodation has been secured)' – para 14.31, =.
224 HA 1996, s 189B(9). This is also applicable to termination of the duty to those who are threatened with homelessness intentionally (paras **8.79–8.83**): HA 1996, s 195(1).
225 HA 1996, s 193C(3)-(4).

Refusal of final offer

8.98   The first of these additional circumstances in which the relief duty can be brought to an end is if the applicant, having been informed of the consequences of refusal and of their right to request a review of the suitability of the accommodation,[226] refuses either a final accommodation offer, or a final Part 6 offer.[227] A final accommodation offer is an offer of an assured shorthold tenancy made by a private landlord – including a private registered provider of social housing (England) or a registered social landlord (Wales) – in relation to any accommodation which is, or may become, available for the applicant's occupation, made, with the approval of the authority, in pursuance of arrangements made by the authority in discharge of the relief duty, which is a fixed term tenancy for a period of at least six months.[228] A final Part 6 offer is an offer of accommodation under Part 6 made in writing in discharge of the authority's relief duty, which states that it is a final offer for that purpose.[229] If it is brought to an end on this basis, the principal housing duty in HA 1996, s 193 (paras **8.129–8.286**) does not apply.[230]

> ## RENTERS (REFORM) BILL
>
> Once the provisions of the Bill come into full relevant force and subject to any transitional provisions, a final accommodation offer will be of an assured tenancy which is not for a fixed term: s 193A(4) will be amended to delete the reference to an assured shorthold tenancy and to being a fixed term of a least six months.

8.99   The authority cannot approve a final accommodation offer or make a final Part 6 offer unless it is satisfied that it is suitable for the applicant;[231] nor can it approve or make such an offer if the applicant is under contractual or other obligations in respect of their existing accommodation, which they are not able to bring to an end before they would have to take up the offer.[232] The provisions are modelled on, and similar to, those which may determine that a s 193 duty has ceased.[233]

Deliberate and unreasonable refusal to co-operate

8.100   The second of the additional circumstances in which the relief duty can be brought to an end – which can also bring to an end the new duty to

226 Paras **7.199–7.203**.
227 HA 1996, s 193A(1), (2).
228 HA 1996, s 193A(4).
229 HA 1996, s 193A(5).
230 HA 1996, s 193A(3).
231 HA 1996, s 193A(6).
232 HA 1996, s 193A(7).
233 See paras **8.235–8.281**.

those threatened with homelessness (paras **8.79–8.83**) – arises where the authority gives notice to an applicant that it considers that they have deliberately and unreasonably refused to take any step that they agreed to take or that was recorded by the authority under the assessment and plan provisions considered above (paras **8.61–8.75**).[234]

8.101   The refusal must be both deliberate and unreasonable. When deciding whether a refusal is unreasonable, the authority must have regard to the particular circumstances and needs of the applicant (whether identified in its assessment of their case or not).[235]

8.102   The notice must explain why the authority is giving it and its effect, and inform the applicant that they have a right to request a review[236] of the decision to give the notice and of the time within which such a request must be made.[237] No notice may be given without a prior 'relevant warning' notice[238] and a reasonable period[239] has elapsed since it was given.[240] The decision to give the notice must be made by an officer of the authority and authorised by a second officer who was not involved in the decision to give the notice and who is at least as senior as the person who made the decision to serve the notice.[241]

8.103   If either duty[242] is brought to an end on this basis,[243] then while the principal housing duty in HA 1996, s 193 (paras **8.129–8.281**) will not apply,[244] the homeless who are eligible and in priority need but not homeless intentionally will be entitled to accommodation under s 193C (paras **8.287–8.292**).[245] This is considered below, alongside other duties to the unintentionally homeless in priority need.[246] Otherwise, the duty under s 193 is still owed.[247]

234 HA 1996, s 193B(1), (2).
235 HA 1996, s 193B(6).
236 See paras **7.190–7.216**.
237 HA 1996, s 193B(3).
238 This is a notice given by the authority after the refusal to take the agreed or recorded step, which warns the applicant that, if they continue deliberately and unreasonably to refuse to take the step after receiving the notice, the authority intends to give the notice which will bring the duty to an end, and which explains the consequences of that notice: HA 1996, s 193B(5).
239 This is not defined.
240 HA 1996, s 193B(4).
241 Homelessness (Review Procedure etc) Regulations 2018, SI 2018/223, reg 3. The process adopted in connection with notices under HA 1996, s 193B(2) must be in writing, kept under review and comply with the requirements of reg 3: reg 2.
242 HA 1996, ss 189B(2), 195(2).
243 Which will be the effect of a notice which fulfils all its requirements: HA 1996, s 193C(1), (2).
244 HA 1996, s 193C(3).
245 HA 1996, s 193C(4).
246 See paras **8.287–8.292**.
247 HA 1996, s 193(1).

RENTERS (REFORM) BILL

Once the provisions of the Bill come into full relevant force and subject to any transitional provisions, the accommodation provisions of s 193C (subs (3)-(9)) will be repealed, as will be exclusion from s 193 by s 193(1A)(b). Accordingly, where the relief duty in s 189B ends because of deliberate and unreasonable refusal to co-operate, the housing duty in s 193 will be available.

Wales

Overview

8.104   If an authority is satisfied that an applicant is homeless and eligible for assistance, whether or not they have a priority need or may be homeless intentionally, it must help to secure that accommodation is available for them.[248] The duty does not apply if the authority refers the application to another local housing authority[249] in England or Wales.[250]

8.105   The duty requires the authority to take reasonable steps to help, having regard to (among other things) the need to make the best use of its resources.[251] It does not require the authority to offer accommodation, whether under Part 6 or otherwise.[252]

When the duty comes to an end

8.106   This duty lasts for 56 days,[253] although the authority can decide on a shorter period if reasonable steps to secure accommodation for the applicant have been taken.[254] The duty will come to an end before the end of that period if one of the following occurs:

   a)   the authority is satisfied that the applicant has suitable accommodation available for occupation, which accommodation is likely to be available for occupation by the applicant for a period of at least six months;[255]

---

248 H(W)A 2014, s 73(1).
249 H(W)A 2014, s 73(2).
250 H(W)A 2014, s 18(1).
251 H(W)A 2014, s 65(a).
252 H(W)A 2014, s 65(b)–(c).
253 H(W)A 2014, s 74(2).
254 H(W)A 2014, s 74(3).
255 H(W)A 2014, s 74(4).

b) the applicant refuses an offer of accommodation from any person, having been notified in writing of the possible consequences of refusal or acceptance of the offer, provided that the authority is satisfied that the accommodation was suitable for the applicant and was likely to be available for at least the next six months;[256]

c) the applicant ceases to be eligible;[257]

d) a mistake of fact led the authority to notify the applicant that it owed them a duty to help to secure accommodation for the applicant;[258]

e) the applicant has withdrawn the application;[259]

f) the applicant is unreasonably failing to co-operate with the authority.[260]

Unreasonable failure to co-operate

8.107   While HA 1996 as amended by HRA 2017 contains detailed provisions governing the refusal of an applicant in England to co-operate (paras **8.100– 8.103**), H(W)A 2014 has no equivalent. The Welsh Code of Guidance suggests that authorities should satisfy themselves that the applicant is not failing to co-operate because they are vulnerable, have an unmet support need or have difficulty communicating and recommends a 'minded to' letter be sent before discharging any duty.[261]

OTHER DUTIES TO THE INTENTIONALLY HOMELESS

England

Advice and assistance

8.108   Since the HRA 2017 came into force,[262] the long-standing duty to provide advice and assistance formerly applicable where an applicant was either not in priority need, or else in priority need but was homeless intentionally,[263]

---

256 H(W)A 2014, s 74(5).
257 H(W)A 2014, s 79(2).
258 H(W)A 2014, s 79(3).
259 H(W)A 2014, s 79(4).
260 H(W)A 2014, s 79(5).
261 Paras 15.86–15.89. The English Code suggests that an authority 'should take into account any particular difficulties that the applicant may have in managing communications when considering if failure to cooperate is deliberate and unreasonable': para 14.52.
262 3 April 2018: Homelessness Reduction Act 2017 (Commencement and Transitional and Savings Provisions) Regulations 2018, SI 2018/167, reg 3, only applicable to applications made on or after that date – see reg 4.
263 HA 1996, ss 190(2), 192(2).

now only applies to the intentionally homeless in priority need, and then only once the duty under HA 1996, s 189B(2) (relief duty: paras **8.88–8.103**) has come to an end (on whatever ground). When discharging it, an authority must have regard to its assessment under HA 1996, s 189A (paras **8.61–8.75**).[264]

Accommodation

8.109   This class of applicant benefits from the additional duty imposed on an authority to secure that suitable[265] accommodation is made available for the applicant's occupation[266] – together with any person who normally resides, or who might reasonably be expected to reside, with them – 'for such period as' the authority considers 'will give him a reasonable opportunity of himself securing accommodation for his occupation'.[267]

8.110   The observations on quality and termination made in relation to interim accommodation (paras **8.38–8.41**) also apply to accommodation provided under this power, as do those on availability (para **8.28**), payment (para **8.32–8.33**), security (paras **8.34–8.37**), exclusion from PEA 1977 (para **8.48**) and defences on eviction (para **8.49**). How accommodation may be provided,[268] suitability[269] and the constraints on out-of-area placements[270] (which are all considered below in relation to the principal duty) also apply to discharge under this section.

8.111   This duty has given rise to a number of problems. The first question is from when time runs when determining what comprises a reasonable opportunity. Whether or not an applicant seeks internal review does not affect this issue: time runs from the date of the decision regardless of whether an internal review is sought: *Conville*.[271]

8.112   In *Dyson*,[272] the applicant was told on 21 May that she would be provided with one month's accommodation from 25 May (the date when her homelessness would actually occur). This decision appears to have been taken by an official, but appears to have required ratification by a committee. The time was subsequently extended to 6 July, but it was not until 3 July that committee ratification was communicated to the applicant. Time was nonetheless held to run from the notification by the official, of which the letter of 3 July was mere confirmation.

---

264 HA 1996, s 190(4).
265 See HA 1996, ss 205, 206.
266 HA 1996, s 176.
267 HA 1996, s 190(2)(a).
268 See para **8.148**.
269 See paras **8.183–8.187**.
270 See paras **8.160–8.182**.
271 *R (Conville) v Richmond upon Thames LBC* [2005] EWHC 1430 (Admin), [2006] HLR 1, not appealed on this point see [2006] EWCA Civ 718, [2006] HLR 45.
272 *Dyson v Kerrier DC* [1980] 1 WLR 120, CA.

8.113   In *de Falco*,[273] only four days had been allowed between notification of decision and the expiry of what is now HA 1996, s 188 accommodation. The Master of the Rolls thought that this period was probably adequate, having regard to several weeks in accommodation provided by the authority prior to its decision. He was, however, also influenced by the time during which the applicants had been accommodated between the issue of proceedings and the hearing before the Court of Appeal. As *de Falco* was the hearing of an interlocutory appeal for an interlocutory injunction to house until trial, he treated that matter as conclusive as a matter of the court's discretion.

8.114   The same point influenced Bridge LJ, although he was otherwise of the view that time prior to communication of the local authority's decision was irrelevant so that only time since that decision was communicated could count. As the purpose of the provisions is to give the applicant time to find somewhere else to live once it has been decided that the authority need not provide full assistance, this view seems preferable.[274]

8.115   The courts may be less generous towards an applicant who lives with another person who has previously been found homeless intentionally, and who has already enjoyed a period of HA 1996, s 190(2)(a) accommodation, although such a person may indeed reapply and it seems to be an irresistible inference from *Lewis*[275] and the other cases on this point[276] that such a person will then be entitled to a new period of s 190(2)(a) accommodation; it is strongly arguable that they can and should benefit from the reasoning of Bridge LJ in *de Falco*.

8.116   Some reconciliation of merits and principle may be found in the extent of acquiescence or participation in the act which results in the finding of intentionality and therefore the extent to which an adverse finding should have been anticipated.

8.117   In *Smith v Bristol City Council*,[277] a county court judge held that, even where a substantial period of warning had been given to the applicant, the authority was still obliged to give more time:

> 'I cannot accept that 'no time' can in any circumstances be a reasonable period . . . [A] reasonable time must be given to the applicant after she actually becomes homeless . . .'

8.118   When an authority decides for how long it should secure that accommodation is available so as to give an applicant a reasonable opportunity

---

273   *de Falco, Silvestri v Crawley BC* [1980] QB 460, CA.
274   Sir David Cairns thought that the decision was unreviewable, although this proposition does not find any support elsewhere and is wholly out of line with modern public law.
275   *R v North Devon DC ex p Lewis* [1981] 1 WLR 328, QBD.
276   See paras **4.14–4.30**. See also *R (Savage) v Hillingdon LBC* [2010] EWHC 88 (Admin), [2010] JHL D44, where it was held that it was for the authority to determine what period of time afforded a reasonable opportunity of securing accommodation.
277   December 1981 *LAG Bulletin* 287, CC.

of securing accommodation for themselves, pursuant to its duty under HA 1996, s 190(2)(a), it may not have regard to considerations peculiar to itself, eg, the extent of its resources and other demands.[278] While it is for the authority to decide what is a reasonable opportunity, subject to the usual principles of intervention,[279] what is reasonable for these purposes is to be assessed by reference to the particular needs and circumstances of the applicant, including the availability of other accommodation; if the applicant is not making reasonable efforts to pursue other possibilities, however, that will be a strong indication that they should not be given more time; and, even if the applicant makes reasonable efforts, a moment will normally be reached when time will expire if those possibilities have not come to fruition; the opportunity is no more than that – it cannot be converted into a duty to provide long-term accommodation.[280]

8.119   The English Code no longer suggests any particular time frame:[281]

'A few weeks may provide the applicant with a reasonable opportunity to secure accommodation for themselves. However, some applicants might require longer and others, particularly where the housing authority provides pro-active and effective assistance, might require less time.'[282]

8.120   It continues that:

'Housing authorities will need to take into account (a) the particular needs and circumstances of the applicant and the resources available to them to secure accommodation . . . (b) the housing circumstances in the local area, and the length of time it might reasonably take to secure accommodation . . . (c) arrangements that have already been made by the applicant which are likely to be successful within a reasonable timescale.'[283]

8.121   This much is clear: an applicant's circumstances must be individually considered, and if it can be shown that the time allowed has been reached without regard to them or was such a short period that no reasonable authority could have considered that it gave the applicant a reasonable opportunity to find somewhere for themselves, the courts will order sufficient time.[284]

8.122   It would seem from *Monaf*[285] that – at least where the housing authority is also a social services authority – the authority ought to have regard to its duties

278 *R (Conville) v Richmond upon Thames LBC* [2006] EWCA Civ 718, [2006] HLR 45.
279 See Chapter 10.
280 *R (Conville) v Richmond upon Thames LBC*, above.
281 Previous editions of the Code referred to 28 days being adequate in most cases.
282 English Code of Guidance para 15.14; Welsh Code paras 9.27, 17.45–17.46.
283 English Code of Guidance para 15.15; Welsh Code paras 9.27, 17.45–17.46.
284 *Lally v Kensington and Chelsea RLBC* (1980) *Times* 27 March, ChD.
285 *R v Tower Hamlets LBC ex p Monaf* (1988) 20 HLR 529, CA.

under the CA 1989, s 20(1)[286] when determining this period.[287] Prior to this stage, the housing authority should in any event have sought the applicant's consent to refer the case to the social services authority,[288] so that the latter authority can consider exercise of its powers under the CA 1989.[289]

8.123   A further issue is raised by 'policies'. In particular, the frequency with which all kinds of applicant receive identical offers of 28 days' accommodation suggests that many authorities operate a policy under this provision.[290] If an inflexible policy can be proven, it can be set aside.[291] If, however, the 28-day rule is merely a guideline, genuinely reconsidered in each case, it will be valid.

Wales

8.124   In Wales, the position is somewhat different. Where the authority decides that a person is eligible for assistance, homeless and in priority need, it has a duty to secure that accommodation is made available for their occupation (unless it refers the applicant to another authority under the local connection provisions of the legislation).[292]

8.125   When discharging this duty, however, the authority has power to consider whether or not the applicant became homeless intentionally.[293]

8.126   If the authority decides to exercise that power, the principal duty to accommodate under H(W)A 2014, s 75[294] will arise either if the authority is not satisfied that the applicant is homeless intentionally or if the applicant is:

   a)   a pregnant woman or a person with whom she resides or might reasonably
        be expected to reside;

---

286 See paras **11.71–11.82**.
287 Moreover, local authorities must now have regard 'to the need to safeguard and promote the welfare of children' when discharging their functions: CA 2004, s 11 (England); s 28 (Wales). This includes functions under HA 1996, Part 7: *Huzrat v Hounslow LBC* [2013] EWCA Civ 1865, [2014] HLR 17. See also *Nzolameso v Westminster City Council* [2015] UKSC 22, [2015] HLR 22: when considering whether accommodation is suitable for a family, the authority must identify the principal needs of the children both individually and collectively when making the decision. If there is a review of suitability, those issues must be reconsidered as at the date of the review: *Waltham Forest LBC v Saleh* [2019] EWCA Civ 1944, [2020] PTSR 621, [2020] HLR 15.
288 See further HA 1996, s 213A.
289 See further paras **11.61–11.87**.
290 In *Birmingham City Council v Ali; Moran v Manchester City Council (Secretary of State for Communities and Local Government and another intervening)* [2009] UKHL 36, [2009] 1 WLR 1506 at [17], Baroness Hale commented: 'We are told that up to six weeks is usually thought enough for this although there is no statutory limit.'
291 See paras **10.54–10.55**.
292 H(W)A 2014, s 75(1), (2); see Chapter 5.
293 H(W)A 2014, s 78; see para **4.3**.
294 Paras **8.129–8.281**.

b) a person with whom a dependent child resides or might reasonably be expected to reside;

c) a person who had not attained the age of 21 when the application was made or a person with whom such a person resides or might reasonably be expected to reside; or

d) a person who had attained the age of 21, but not the age of 25, when the application was made and who was looked after, accommodated or fostered at any time while under the age of 18, or a person with whom such a person resides or might reasonably be expected to reside.[295]

8.127 In these circumstances, the full duty will arise if:

a) the applicant has no suitable accommodation available for occupation, or suitable accommodation which it is not likely will be available for occupation for at least six months starting on the day on which the applicant is notified[296] that the full duty will not apply;

b) the applicant is eligible for help and has a priority need for accommodation; and

c) the authority has not previously secured an offer of accommodation to the applicant under these provisions following a previous application for help, at any time within the period of five years before the day on which the applicant was notified[297] that a duty was owed to them under them.[298]

8.128 If the full duty does not arise for any of these reasons, or because the applicant is not within the H(W)A 2014, s 75(3) class,[299] then the initial duty to help[300] is limited to 56 days.[301]

OTHER DUTIES TOWARDS THE UNINTENTIONALLY HOMELESS IN PRIORITY NEED

Introduction

8.129 Duties towards those whom the authority is satisfied are eligible, homeless, in priority need and is not satisfied became intentionally homeless,

---

295 H(W)A 2014, s 75(3), brought into force on 2 December 2019: Housing (Wales) Act 2014 (Commencement No 10) Order 2019, SI 2019/1479. See also *Additional provisions under section 75(3)*, Welsh Government, December 2019.
296 Under H(W)A 2014, s 84.
297 The applicant is to be treated as notified on the day the notice is sent or first made available for collection: H(W)A 2014, s 75(4).
298 H(W)A 2014, s 75(3).
299 See 8.118.
300 See paras **8.88–8.103**.
301 H(W)A 2014, s 74(2).

are governed by HA 1996, s 193 and H(W)A 2014, s 75. Since the HRA 2017 came into force in England,[302] the HA 1996, s 193 duty does not arise until the authority's duty under HA 1996, s 189B(2) (relief duty: paras **8.88–8.103**) has come to an end.[303] Likewise, in Wales, the H(W)A 2014, s 75 duty does not arise until the relief duty in H(W)A 2014, s 73 duty has come to an end.[304]

8.130   In England, the HA 1996, s 193 duty does not arise at all, however, if it has been disapplied by HA 1996, s 193A(3) (refusal of final offer: paras **8.98–8.99**) or if the authority has given notice to the applicant under s 193B(2) (deliberate and unreasonable refusal to co-operate: paras **8.100–8.103**),[305] although in the latter case it is replaced by duties under s 193C (paras **8.287–8.292**).

RENTERS (REFORM) BILL

Once the provisions of the Bill come into full relevant force and subject to any transitional provisions, the accommodation provisions of s 193C (subs (3)-(9)) will be repealed, as will be exclusion from s 193 by s 193(1A)(b). Accordingly, where the relief duty in s 189B ends because of deliberate and unreasonable refusal to co-operate, the housing duty in s 193 will be available.

8.131   In Wales, the H(W)A 2014, s 75 duty can only arise where the s 73 duty has come to an end and the applicant is eligible, in priority need, not intentionally homeless[306] and does not have suitable accommodation available for their occupation or, if they do have such accommodation, it is not likely that it will be available for at least six months: accordingly, if the s 73 duty has come to an end because the applicant accepted other accommodation or refused an offer or unreasonably refused to co-operate with the authority, the s 75 duty will not be owed.[307]

Housing Act 1996, s 193 and Housing (Wales) Act 2014, s 75

Overview

8.132   Under HA 1996, s 193, the duty towards the unintentionally homeless is to secure that suitable[308] accommodation is available for occupation by the

---

302 3 April 2018: Homelessness Reduction Act 2017 (Commencement and Transitional and Savings Provisions) Regulations 2018, SI 2018/167, reg 3, only applicable to applications made and reviews sought on or after that date – see reg 4.
303 HA 1996, s 193(1).
304 H(W)A 2014, s 75(1).
305 HA 1996, s 193(1A).
306 Assuming the authority is applying the intentionality provisions: H(W)A 2014, ss 77, 78. See also H(W)A 2014, s 75(3).
307 H(W)A 2014, s 75(1).
308 HA 1996, s 206.

applicant until the duty ceases in accordance with the sections;[309] it is the principal – or 'highest' – duty under the Acts, sometimes referred to as permanent or indefinite, although it will be seen that neither description is wholly accurate; in particular, housing may be provided under HA 1996, s 193(2) pending a final arrangement, which may continue for years.

8.133   The observations on availability (para **8.28**), payment (paras **8.32–8.33**) and security (paras **8.34–8.37**) made in relation to interim accommodation (paras **8.12–8.50**) in principle also apply to accommodation provided under this power, save that there is no exclusion from assured security under HA 1996, s 209 for accommodation so provided, although as it is likely to be provided on a shorthold basis it is not required.

RENTERS (REFORM) BILL

Once the provisions of the Bill come into full relevant force and subject to any transitional provisions, the proposition that no exclusion from security is needed because the accommodation is likely to be provided on a shorthold basis will cease to apply: instead, there will be a new mandatory ground for possession (Housing Act 1988, s 7), Ground 5G, where the grant of the tenancy was in pursuance of a local housing authority's duty to the tenant under s 193 of the Housing Act 1996, the local housing authority has notified the landlord that the tenancy is no longer required for the purposes of that duty, and the date specified in the notice of proceedings for possession is within 12 months following the date on which the authority so notified the landlord.

8.134   Whether exclusion from PEA 1977 (para **8.48**) applies once the principal duty is owed, has been held to be a question of fact in each case.[310] In *Bucknall*, the applicant was provided with temporary accommodation under HA 1996, s 188; when the authority subsequently decided that it owed her the section 193(2) duty, it said that she should continue to occupy the same accommodation pending identification of a suitable property. The authority subsequently offered her a property which she rejected; it served notice to quit which did not comply with the requirements of the PEA 1977.[311] As she had been told that she should occupy the accommodation for an indefinite period, it was held that the PEA 1977 applied and that, as the notice was invalid, her tenancy had not been terminated.

---

309 HA 1996, s 193(2) and (3); s 193(3) was amended by the Homelessness Act 2002 to remove the restriction on the duty to a period of two years. In Wales, see H(W)A 2014, ss 75 and 76; as in England, there is no 'two-year' restriction.
310 *Bucknall v Dacorum BC* [2017] EWHC 2094 (QB), [2017] HLR 40.
311 Section 5, and the Notices to Quit etc (Prescribed Information) Regulations 1988, SI 1988/2201.

8.135   This conclusion is somewhat narrower than might be thought. In *R (ZH and CN) v Lewisham LBC*,[312] Lady Hale referred to the 'generally accepted view that the protection of section 3 of the 1977 Act will apply once the local authority has accepted that it owes the family the "full housing duty"',[313] presumably picking up the local authorities' submission that the 'licences were expressly limited to the period to be taken to provide a decision'[314] and the secretary of state's submission that the premises were 'temporary accommodation while the council made inquiries'.[315]

8.136   Other observations on defences on eviction (para **8.49**) will apply should an authority seek to evict an applicant while they are still being housed under HA 1996, Part 7 or H(W)A 2014, Part 2.

8.137   A number of issues fall to be considered:

a)   postponement of the duty;

b)   means of discharge;

c)   out-of-area placements;

d)   suitability of accommodation;

e)   cessation of duty.

Postponement of the duty

8.138   The question whether discharge of the duty under s 193(2) can be postponed, deferred or delayed, has been the subject of a number of decisions in the courts,[316] expressing conflicting views.[317] The *current* position may be considered by reference to three cases *Elkundi*,[318] *Birmingham CC v Ali; Moran v Manchester CC*.[319] and *R (M) v Newham LBC*,[320] to the effect that the duty may not be deferred. That said, one of the cases[321] heard together with *Elkundi* was recently considered by the Supreme Court.[322] As the authority conceded that it was

---

312 [2014] UKSC 62, [2015] AC 1259, [2015] HLR 6.
313 At [165].
314 At 1287F.
315 At 1288D. See also Lord Hodge at [16] and [45].
316 *R v Tower Hamlets LBC ex p Khalique* (1994) 26 HLR 517, QBD; *R v Southwark LBC ex p Anderson* (2000) 32 HLR 96, QBD; *R v Merton LBC ex p Sembi* (1999) 32 HLR 439, QBD; *R v Newham LBC ex p Begum* (2000) 32 HLR 808, QBD; *Codona v Mid-Bedfordshire DC* [2004] EWCA Civ 925, [2005] HLR 1.
317 Particularly *Begum* and *Codona*.
318 *R (Elkundi and others) v Birmingham City Council; R (Imam) v Croydon BC* [2022] EWCA Civ 601; [2022] QB 604; [2022] HLR 31.
319 [2009] UKHL 36, [2009] 1 WLR 1506, [2009] HLR 41.
320 [2020] EWHC 327 (Admin), [2020] PTSR 1077, [2021] HLR 1.
321 *Imam*.
322 *R (Imam) v Croydon LBC* [2023] UKSC 45; [2024] HLR 6.

in breach of its duty,[323] the argument was therefore confined to the circumstances in which a mandatory order requiring performance is to be made.,[324] The court nonetheless made observations on the nature of the duty which also need to be considered here as they will undoubtedly have an influence on future decisions on this issue: the observations are considered below.[325]

8.139 In *Ali* and *Moran*,[326] Baroness Hale said (at [46]–[50]):

'[I]n our view it is proper for a local authority to decide that it would not be reasonable for a person to continue to occupy the accommodation which is available to him or her, even if it is reasonable for that person to occupy it for a little while longer, if it would not be reasonable for the person to continue to occupy the accommodation for as long as he or she will have to do so unless the authority take action.

47   This does not mean that Birmingham were entitled to leave these families where they were indefinitely. Obviously, there would come a point where they could not continue to occupy for another night and the council would have to act immediately. But there is more to it than that. It does not follow that, because that point has not yet been reached, the accommodation is "suitable" for the family within the meaning of section 206(1). There are degrees of suitability. What is suitable for occupation in the short term may not be suitable for occupation in the medium term, and what is suitable for occupation in the medium term may not be suitable for occupation in the longer term. The council seem to have thought that they could discharge their duty under section 193(2) by putting these families on the waiting list for permanent council accommodation under their Part VI allocation scheme. But the duty to secure that suitable accommodation is available for a homeless family under section 193(2) is quite separate from the allocation of council housing under Part VI. There are many different ways of discharging it, and if a council house is provided, this does not create a secure tenancy unless the council decides that it should. As we have already pointed out, the suitability of a place can be linked to the time that a person is expected to live there. Suitability for the purpose of section 193(2) does not imply permanence or security of tenure. Accommodation under section 193(2) is another kind of staging post, along the way to permanent accommodation in either the public or the private sector.

323 The authority applied for permission to appeal to the Supreme Court on the basis that it was not challenging *Elkundi*, which therefore meant that it was not challenging the *Elkundi* conclusion that the s 193(2) duty was 'an immediate, non-deferrable, unqualified duty to secure that suitable accommodation is available' (at [108]; see also at [77] – see below, para **8.144**.
324 See paras **10.192–196**.
325 See para **8.145**.
326 See also para **2.72**.

48 Hence Birmingham were entitled to decide that these families were homeless even though they could stay where they were for the time being.[327] But they were not entitled to leave them there indefinitely. There was bound to come a time when their accommodation could no longer be described as "suitable" in the discharge of the duty under section 193(2).

49 It may be that, in some, or conceivably all, of the Birmingham cases, a critical examination of the facts would establish that the council were at some point in breach of their duty under Part VII of the1996 Act. Thus the time it has taken to find Mr Ali suitable accommodation may well be beyond what is defensible. While the council were entitled in principle to leave the families in their current accommodation for a period notwithstanding that it was accepted that that accommodation "would [not] be reasonable for [them and their families] to continue to occupy" (section 175(3)), it must be a question, which turns on the particular facts, whether, in any particular case, the period was simply too long. ...'[328]

8.140 In *R(M) v Newham LBC*,[329] the authority accepted a s 193(2) duty towards the claimant in 2005. He and his family were provided with temporary accommodation in a three-bedroomed house. By 2017, one of his children had developed a serious disability and needed easy access to a disabled toilet and walk-in shower/bath which were not available in the temporary accommodation and, in December 2017, the authority moved the family to a different property which, however, had toilet and washing facilities which could not be adapted to meet the needs of the disabled child with the result that, in February 2018, the authority accepted that it was not suitable. Notwithstanding this, by September 2019, no suitable accommodation had been identified and the family remained in the same property. The claimant issued a claim for judicial review contending that the authority had accepted that the property was not suitable and was therefore in breach of the s 193(2) duty.

8.141 The claim was allowed. The authority had accepted that it owed the s 193(2) duty and had accepted that the present accommodation was not suitable. The approach in *ex p Begum*[330] was to be preferred to that in *Anderson*[331] or *Sembi*:[332] this was implicit in *Birmingham CC v Ali; Moran v Manchester CC*[333]

---

327 Accommodation need not be available indefinitely or even for any particular period of time in order for it to be reasonable to continue to occupy it: *R (Ahamed) v Haringey LBC* [2023] EWCA Civ 975; [2023] HLR 43, at [47].

328 However, at [50], Baroness Hale said that a court should normally be slow to accept that the authority has left an applicant in unsatisfactory accommodation for too long: para **2.73**.

329 [2020] EWHC 327 (Admin), [2020] PTSR 1077, [2021] HLR 1.

330 *R v Newham LBC ex p Begum* (2000) 32 HLR 808, QBD – duties could not be deferred though if great difficulties finding suitable accommodation, it could affect relief (see now paras **10.192–10.196**).

331 *R v Southwark LBC ex p Anderson* (2000) 32 HLR 96, QBD – no time limit within which a housing authority is obliged under the statute to comply with a duty to secure available accommodation for those who fall within s 193.

332 *R v Merton LBC ex p Sembi* (1999) 32 HLR 439, QBD – following *Anderson*, see ibid.

333 Ibid.

– had Baroness Hale considered that the duty was merely to make suitable accommodation available within a reasonable time, she would surely have said so; a reasonable delay in finding alternative accommodation is only permissible if the accommodation is regarded as suitable for the time being. It followed that the authority was in breach of its s 193(2) duty.[334]

8.142 In *Elkundi*, the authority operated a Planned Move List, a spreadsheet listing those applicants for assistance under Pt 7, 1996 Act, who wanted to be moved from accommodation secured for them under s 193(2), which recorded the size property needed for an applicant and the date on which they were first entered onto the list. Once a property became available. it was offered to the person who had waited longest for a property of the relevant size, although a property might be offered to another applicant on the list if they had complex needs or medical issues.

8.143 Four cases were heard together, in each of which it was accepted by the authority that the accommodation occupied by the applicants was not suitable; three of them were placed on the Planned Move List. In the fourth, *Al-Shameri*, when the claimant applied to the authority for assistance under Pt 7, his application form answered the question whether he needed temporary accommodation 'No', although he did subsequently seek such accommodation from the authority. During the proceedings for judicial review, the authority contended, among other matters, that the statement that he did not want temporary accommodation in his application form meant that he had chosen to remain in his current accommodation and had therefore waived his right to require the authority to secure temporary accommodation for him under s 193(2).

8.144 The applicants were all successful in their claims and the authority appealed: the appeal was heard together with that in *R. (Imam) v Croydon LBC*,[335] in which relief had been refused, even though the authority had likewise conceded that the claimant's current accommodation was unsuitable for her,[336] a decision from which she appealed. In the Court of Appeal, it was held (at [108]) that

---

334 As the authority had not made any meaningful efforts to identify suitable accommodation and the impression given was that the authority had not taken the claimant's case seriously, the court considered it appropriate to make a mandatory order requiring the provision of suitable accommodation within 12 weeks. As to mandatory orders generally, however, see now paras **10.192–10.196**.

335 [2021] EWHC 736 (Admin) I [2021]; [2021] HLR 43.

336 The claimant was a full-time wheelchair user, and the mother of three children. She applied as homeless in 2014 and the authority accepted that it owed her a duty under s 193. She accepted the offer of a three-bedroom house under s 193(2), but contended that it was not suitable as it lacked a same-level toilet for her to use during the night, a contention that Croydon accepted in June 2015, from which date Croydon accepted that it was in breach of its duty under s 193(2) to provide her with suitable accommodation. The claimant contended that the absence of an upstairs toilet led to incontinence accidents which were humiliating and distressing, that cupboards and windows were too high for her to use and that an internal lift occupied so much of the bedroom and living-room that it impeded her manoeuvrability. Nor could she access her children's bedrooms. Other than in relation to the toilet on the first floor, the authority considered that the property was reasonably suited to meet her needs – it was adapted for wheelchair use, of a size appropriate to her family and suitably located.

'The duty under section 193(2) is a duty to secure that suitable accommodation is available. That duty arises once the criteria in section 193(1) are met. The duty is an immediate, non-deferrable, unqualified duty to secure that suitable accommodation is available. What is "suitable" will depend upon a number of factors. Furthermore, accommodation may be suitable in the short term even if that particular accommodation would not be suitable in the medium or long term. If the duty is owed, and particular accommodation ceases to be suitable, the local housing authority is under a duty to secure that other suitable accommodation is available (whether or not that is also only suitable in the short term) until the duty in section 193(2) comes to an end.'

8.145   As noted above,[337] the Supreme Court considered this issue in *Imam*.[338]

'38. As Lewis LJ observed…the duty owed is immediate, non-deferrable and unqualified. The precise steps to be taken to comply with the duty were not the subject of detailed submissions in the present appeal. The nature of the duty is such that it calls for the authority to go through a process of giving due consideration to the applicant's case and forming a judgment about what should be done to satisfy the obligation which has arisen. …

39. Lewis LJ considered…that suitable accommodation is to be available from the time when the duty is owed. I reserve my opinion whether that way of putting it is exactly right. As I have said, we did not hear submissions on that point. But it is clear that the duty is directed towards achieving an end result (the provision of suitable accommodation) and, even if some time is required for consideration how ultimately to achieve this, it would be implicit that the end result would have to be achieved within a reasonable time. Moreover, since the end result is intended to satisfy an urgent and important need (the provision of suitable living accommodation), a reasonable time to allow for consideration of the appropriate means to secure it would be short. It may be that a local authority has an obligation to proceed in stages, by accommodating someone with an urgent need as best can be achieved at very short notice, while taking somewhat longer to consider how better accommodation which could be regarded as suitable can be secured thereafter. It is not necessary for us to examine this issue. In the present case, Croydon has failed to fulfil its duty over almost six years. It breached its duty at a very early stage. The question, therefore, is what remedy the court should grant in relation to that breach of duty'.[339]

---

337 See para **8.138**.

338 *R (Imam) v Croydon LBC* [2023] UKSC 45; [2024] HLR 6.

339 In practice, this is how most authorities tend to discharge the duty. The observations are only intended to be a paraphrase of what Lewis LJ had said and, while they do not address the point in this connection, they accommodate the proposition in *Ali* and *Moran* [2009] UKHL 36, [2009] 1 WLR 1506, [2009] HLR 41 at [47] that 'What is suitable for occupation in the short term may not be suitable for occupation in the medium term, and what is suitable for occupation in the medium term may not be suitable for occupation in the longer term' – see para **8.139**.

Waiver of rights

8.146 It was therefore not lawful for the authority to put applicants owed a duty whose current accommodation it accepted was unsuitable on a waiting list while taking time to find alternative suitable accommodation; once the authority decided that the current accommodation was unsuitable, it had an immediate duty to secure that suitable accommodation became available (at [112]–[113]).[340]

8.147 In principle, however, an authority may not be in breach of its duty if an applicant indicates that they prefer to stay in their current accommodation rather than in accommodation secured by the authority; that will only be the case if the applicant is in a position to give fully informed consent and the duty remains in existence and must be discharged once they indicate that they no longer wish to remain in their current accommodation. Accordingly, in *Al-Shameri*, the court below had been entitled to find on the evidence that while the applicant had had indicated that he would prefer to stay in his current accommodation pending the outcome of s 188 inquiries, he had never been asked whether he wished to remain there once the authority accepted a duty under s 193(2), nor was he adequately informed about what accommodation he would be provided with once the authority accepted that duty.[341]

Means of discharge

8.148 By HA 1996, s 206 or H(W)A 2014, s 76, a local authority may discharge its duty under s 193 in one of three ways:[342]

a) by securing that suitable accommodation provided by it is available for the applicant;

b) by securing that the applicant obtains suitable accommodation from some other person; or

c) by giving the applicant such advice and assistance as will secure that suitable accommodation is available from some other person.

---

340 The Planned Move List was also unlawful because it failed to distinguish those who were in suitable or unsuitable accommodation. Nor (at [114]) was there any evidence that, in relation to the Planned Move List, the authority had due regard to matters arising out of disability – the authority had failed to comply with its public sector equality duty under s 149, Equality Act 2010 (see para **7.93**).

341 At [117]–[120]. See also *R (Edwards and others) v Birmingham CC* [2016] EWHC 173 (Admin), [2016] HLR 11 in which the authority was entitled to rely on an applicant's 'self-certification' as to the suitability of property they were occupying on a 'homeless at home' application; this was not objectionable so long as the applicant was aware of their right to interim accommodation and knew they could return to request it at a later date. Even where accommodation is unsuitable (disabled applicant unable to escape in case of fire), if the applicant refuses an offer of interim accommodation and chooses to remain in their current accommodation, the authority is not in breach, although if the applicant changes their mind and asks for accommodation, it must then be provided: *R (Yabari) v Westminster CC* [2023] EWHC 185 (Admin); [2023] HLR 34.

342 HA 1996, s 206(1); H(W)A 2014, ss 64, 76.

8.149   As a matter of language and construction, HA 1996, s 206 is exhaustive of the means of providing accommodation, and so cannot be used – even in conjunction with Local Government Act 1972, s 111 – to guarantee the provision of accommodation by another.[343]

8.150   Since the HRA 2017 came into force in England,[344] bringing with it the relief duty (paras **8.88–8.103**) and new duties to those in priority need (para **8.95**), HA 1996, s 206 only applies where the authority decides to discharge those duties by the first means identified, ie, by securing that accommodation is available for an applicant's accommodation.[345]

Resources

8.151   The issue of resources is not irrelevant to how an authority decides to discharge its duty. Thus, if an applicant has a particular and perhaps unusual need, the authority can – in deciding whether to meet it by purchasing a property on the open market – take into account the cost of doing so.[346]

8.152   In *Calgin*,[347] the cost of providing accommodation was likewise held to be a factor that the authority could take into account in deciding how to discharge its duty.

8.153   In *Sheridan v Basildon BC*,[348] the applicants were travellers living at unauthorised sites in Basildon's area; they applied under HA 1996, Part 7; the authority accepted that they were owed the full housing duty under HA 1996, s 193(2). Having decided that there were no suitable traveller sites in their area, Basildon offered them tenancies of conventional properties, which were refused, relying, inter alia, on a regional planning strategy which recommended that the authority should provide further pitches, so that – they contended – Basildon ought to be required to purchase land to be used as a traveller site, an argument that failed: while it might be said that, as a matter of planning policy, Basildon should have provided suitable sites, it was unrealistic to expect a HA 1996, s 202 review to consider such matters; planning policy was outside the expertise of housing officers and Parliament could not have intended such matters to fall

---

343 *Crédit Suisse v Waltham Forest LBC* (1996) 29 HLR 115, CA. Nor would it seem to be available in conjunction with the general power of competence in LA 2011, s 1. See paras **11.125–11.129**.

344 3 April 2018: Homelessness Reduction Act 2017 (Commencement and Transitional and Savings Provisions) Regulations 2018, SI 2018/167, reg 3, only applicable to applications made and reviews sought on or after that date – see reg 4.

345 HA 1996, s 205(3).

346 *R v Lambeth LBC ex p Ekpo-Wedderman* (1999) 31 HLR 498, QBD. See also *R v Lambeth LBC ex p A1* (1998) 30 HLR 933, CA, where the homeless applicant's challenge to a decision of the authority not to exercise its powers under HA 1985, ss 9 and 17 to add to its stock failed.

347 *R (Calgin) v Enfield LBC* [2005] EWHC 1716 (Admin), [2006] HLR 4.

348 [2012] EWCA Civ 335, [2012] HLR 29. See also *Slattery v Basildon BC* [2014] EWCA Civ 30, [2014] HLR 16, following *Sheridan*.

within the scope of a section 202 review; nor was there any basis for requiring Basildon to purchase land; the s 193 duty was to be discharged within the existing resources of the authority.

Advice and assistance

8.154   Advice and assistance such that the applicant secures accommodation from another under HA 1996, s 206(1)(c) or H(W)A 2014, s 64 seems wide enough to cover advice and assistance leading to house purchase by an applicant who is financially able to undertake it.[349] It may also cover the provision of mediation designed to ensure that a 16- or 17-year-old applicant returns to live in their family home.[350]

Discharge through another

8.155   The authority may discharge the duty by securing an assured shorthold tenancy from a private sector landlord or, in Wales, an occupation contract from a private sector landlord.[351]

RENTERS (REFORM) BILL

Once the provisions of the Bill come into full relevant force and subject to any transitional provisions, it will not be possible for an authority to discharge the duty by securing an assured shorthold as s 193(7A)(c) will be repealed: instead, there will be a new mandatory ground for possession (s 7, Housing Act 1988), Ground 5G, where the grant of the tenancy was in pursuance of a local housing authority's duty to the tenant under s 193 of the Housing Act 1996, the local housing authority has notified the landlord that the tenancy is no longer required for the purposes of that duty, and the date specified in the notice of proceedings for possession is within 12 months following the date on which the authority so notified the landlord.

8.156   The provision of successful mediation which enables a 16- or 17-year-old applicant to return to live in the family home may be considered to secure 'accommodation from some other person'.[352]

---

349 See English Code of Guidance para 3.7(k), including through shared equity or similar schemes for low cost home ownership. There is no equivalent in the Welsh Code.
350 See *Robinson v Hammersmith and Fulham LBC* [2006] EWCA Civ 1122, [2007] HLR 7 at [39].
351 HA 1996, s 193(7AC); H(W)A 2014, s 76(2)(aa) and (b).
352 See *Robinson v Hammersmith and Fulham LBC, above.*

8.157   Some other person may be a person or body – or an authority – abroad. In *Browne*,[353] a woman with no local connection with Bristol, and no local connection with the area of any other housing authority in England, Wales or Scotland, was offered assistance to return to her home town of Tralee, Ireland, where the authorities were prepared to ensure that she was housed. In order to sustain its decision, Bristol CC did not need to know the exact details of the accommodation to be made available to her.[354]

8.158   The arrangement was, however, only appropriate once it was established by Bristol CC that, in its opinion, the woman ran no risk of domestic violence in Tralee. It would seem from the report that had there been a risk of domestic violence, the arrangement would not have been acceptable, for otherwise Bristol CC would have managed to circumvent the spirit of the local connection provisions,[355] even though, not being a referral to another authority in the UK, they did not apply.

Discharge by authority

8.159   Although an authority may now use its own stock without limit of time to house an applicant under HA 1996, Part 7 or H(W)A 2014, Part 2,[356] applicants do not become secure tenants or enjoy occupation contracts unless, in England, so notified, or in Wales, until the authority is satisfied that it owes a duty under H(W)A 2014, s 75(1).[357]

Out-of-area placements

8.160   Authorities have not uncommonly sought to discharge duties by placing applicants in the area of another authority. In the early case of *Wyness v Poole BC*,[358] a county court rejected an attempt to house an applicant in the area of another authority when the local connection provisions were inapplicable because of an employment connection, because living in the area of that other authority would have meant that the employment would have to be given up. The court held that no reasonable authority could so discharge the duty.[359]

353 *R v Bristol City Council ex p Browne* [1979] 1 WLR 1437, DC.
354 The decision preceded the introduction of the requirement of suitability. Today, an authority would be bound to take steps to satisfy itself about suitability (see para **8.215**) – this accords with the approach taken in *Browne* to domestic violence, see next paragraph.
355 See Chapter 5.
356 Cf HA 1996, s 207, which was repealed by the Homelessness Act 2002.
357 HA 1985, Sch 1, para 4; RH(W)A 2016, Sch 2, para 11. Notification in England under para 4 is an allocation under HA 1996, Part 6 (see para **9.15**). Where a tenancy is granted pursuant to a Part 7 function, then the property cannot be said to be occupied' by the local authority for the purposes of the Landlord and Tenant Act 1954: *Kensington & Chelsea RLBC v Mellcraft Ltd* [2024] EWHC 539 (Ch). If, however, the local authority grants a licence rather than a tenancy, then the authority may be in occupation for the purposes of the 1954 Act: *Mellcraft*.
358 July 1979 *LAG Bulletin* 166, CC.
359 See also paras **8.160–8.182**, on out-of-area placements.

8.161 The Homelessness (Suitability of Accommodation) (England) Order 2012[360] has introduced detailed provisions governing out-of-area placements, prior to which there was a number of other such cases which remain usefully illustrative of the practice. In *Parr v Wyre BC*,[361] an authority sought to discharge its duty by securing an offer of accommodation in Birmingham, an area with which the applicants had no connection at all. There were no details available of the accommodation to be provided, and the applicants had a limited time in which to accept. While it was common ground that discharge could be in another area, the Court of Appeal, distinguishing *Browne*,[362] did not uphold the offer: the offer had to be of 'appropriate accommodation', in terms both of size of family and of area. In *Puhlhofer*,[363] however, the House of Lords rejected introduction of the qualification 'appropriate'.[364]

8.162 HA 1996, s 208 introduced a new requirement that 'So far as reasonably practicable', the authority must secure accommodation in its own area:[365] this is as applicable to temporary accommodation – and indeed to accommodation secured pursuant to the relief duty[366] – as it is to permanent, and is particularly pertinent where the authority provide accommodation under HA 1996, s 193(2) pending a final offer.

8.163 In *Sacupima*,[367] Latham LJ stated[368] that 'the clear and sensible purpose' of HA 1996, s 208 is 'to ensure that so far as possible that authorities do not simply decant homeless persons into areas for which other authorities are responsible'.[369] A failure to consider section 208 was a significant factor in rendering the decision in *Cafun*[370] unlawful.

8.164 In that case, the authority purported to discharge its duty by referring the applicant to another (neighbouring) authority with which it had a reciprocal agreement. It failed to consider either whether accommodation in the neighbouring

360 Paras **8.209–8.226**.
361 (1982) 2 HLR 71, CA.
362 Paras **8.157–8.158**.
363 *R v Hillingdon LBC ex p Puhlhofer* [1986] AC 484, (1986) 18 HLR 158, HL.
364 See para **2.12**.
365 HA 1996, s 208(1). Note that this requirement is disapplied in England in relation to eligible asylum-seekers, if there is written agreement with another authority that it may place asylum-seekers in its area: HA 1996, s 208(1A). By way of example, an authority was not obliged to investigate whether a housing association was prepared to make a bespoke arrangement to house an applicant, outside the allocation scheme: *Moge v Ealing LBC* [2023] EWCA Civ 464; [2023] HLR 35 at [138].
366 *Moge*, above, at [20].
367 *R v Newham LBC ex p Sacupima* (2001) 33 HLR 2, CA.
368 *R v Newham LBC ex p Sacupima*, above, at [31].
369 A failure by one authority to notify another under HA 1996, s 208 made a significant contribution to the problems that arose in conducting a needs assessment under CA 1989, s 17: see *R (AM) v Havering LBC and Tower Hamlets LBC* [2015] EWHC 1004 (Admin). See para **11.61**.
370 *R (Cafun) v Bromley LBC* 17 October 2000, CO/1481/2000, QBD (unreported); see next paragraph.

area would be suitable for the particular applicant, or the limits on out-of-area placements.[371] The decision was quashed.

8.165   In *Yumsak*,[372] a decision by Enfield LBC, in whose area the applicant had lived for the previous eight years since arriving as an asylum-seeker[373] and where her children were in school, to secure accommodation for an applicant in bed and breakfast accommodation in Birmingham, with which city the applicant had no connection, was held to be irrational and an infringement of the applicant's rights under ECHR Article 8(1).[374]

8.166   In *Calgin*,[375] the authority, a London borough, had a policy of providing accommodation to some homeless households outside its district because of an acute shortage of affordable housing locally. The applicant was offered accommodation in Birmingham and challenged its suitability. On review, the authority decided that the accommodation was suitable and that its policy was not incompatible with HA 1996, s 208 because it was not reasonably practical to provide accommodation locally.

8.167   The decision was upheld: it was for the authority to decide whether or not it was reasonably practical to obtain accommodation within its district, an assessment with which the court would only interfere on *Wednesbury* grounds.[376] The decision to use out-of-district accommodation for a small proportion of those seeking accommodation was not *Wednesbury* unreasonable.

8.168   It was subsequent to these cases that the Homelessness (Suitability of Accommodation) (England) Order 2012 made distance from the authority's area a mandatory consideration.[377] Note, however, that for a period of two years from 1 June 2022,[378] there is a class of recent arrivals for whom bed and breakfast accommodation may be suitable for a period of more than six weeks,[379] to whom the location considerations in the 2012 Order are statutorily inapplicable;[380]

---

371   See paras **8.160–8.182**.
372   *R (Yumsak) v Enfield LBC* [2002] EWHC 280 (Admin), [2002] JHL D38.
373   Acceptance of her refugee status, bringing an end to her assistance from the social services department of the council, prompted her homelessness application.
374   Paras **10.123–10.125**.
375   *R (Calgin) v Enfield LBC* [2005] EWHC 1716 (Admin), [2006] HLR 4.
376   See paras **10.23–10.35, 10.62**.
377   Homelessness (Suitability of Accommodation) (England) Order 2012, SI 2012/260, art 2, in force from 9 November 2012: it was brought into force contemporaneously with the new provisions governing private sector discharge: paras **8.210–8.211**.
378   Homelessness (Suitability of Accommodation) (England) Order 2012, SI 2012/2601 as amended initially for a period of one year from 1 June 2022 by Homelessness (Suitability of Accommodation) (Amendment) (England) Order 2022, SI 2022/521, as amended by the Homelessness (Suitability of Accommodation) (England) (Amendment) Order 2023, SI 2023/509 to extend the period for a further year., as amended by the Homelessness (Suitability of Accommodation) (England) (Amendment) Order 2024, SI 2024/371
379   Para **8.218**.
380   Which is not to say that they cannot be relevant considerations in a particular case in any event: see paras **8.160–8.161, 4.164**.

moreover, for the period of three years from 1 June 2022, the only out-of-area consideration for this class is the significance of any disruption which would be caused by the location of the accommodation to any caring responsibilities of the person or members of the person's household for persons with whom there are (undefined) family associations.[381]

8.169 Location is to be considered from the point of view of members of the household.[382]

'Where accommodation which is otherwise suitable and affordable is available nearer to the authority's district . . . the accommodation which it has secured is not likely to be suitable unless the applicant has specified a preference, or the accommodation has been offered in accordance with a published policy which provides for fair and reasonable allocation of accommodation that is or may become available to applicants.'[383]

8.170 The law was then considered and developed by the Supreme Court in *Nzolameso v Westminster City Council*,[384] in which it was held that if it is not reasonably practicable to accommodate in its own district, an authority must try to place the household as close as possible to where it had previously been living.[385] It was held that authorities should adopt policies[386] relating to the procurement of temporary accommodation, which should be approved by elected members and made available to the public; the policy should explain how accommodation will be allocated and what factors will be taken into account in allocating out-of-borough units; the authority can take into account the resources available to

---

381 Homelessness (Suitability of Accommodation) (England) Order 2012, SI 2012/2601, art 2A, inserted by Homelessness (Suitability of Accommodation) (Amendment) (England) Order 2022, SI 2022/521, art 5, as amended by the Homelessness (Suitability of Accommodation) (England) (Amendment) Order 2023, SI 2023/509 to extend the period for a further year, as amended by the Homelessness (Suitability of Accommodation) (England) (Amendment) Order 2024, SI 2024/371. The class is where the application under Part 7 is made on or after 1 June 2022, within two years beginning with the date on which the applicant arrived in the United Kingdom, by a person who is eligible for assistance under Part 7 who did not have a right to occupy accommodation in the United Kingdom for an uninterrupted period of six months or more in the three years prior to the date on which they arrived in the United Kingdom.
382 English Code para 17.2. Authorities are urged to seek accommodation as close as possible to previous accommodation as 'accommodation for an applicant in a different location can cause difficulties for some applicants. Where possible the authority should seek to retain established links with schools, doctors, social workers and other key services and support': English Code para 17.50.
383 English Code para 17.49.
384 *Nzolameso v Westminster City Council* [2015] UKSC 22, [2015] HLR 22.
385 If there is a review of suitability, then the same applies as at the date of the review so that, in deciding whether an appellant's accommodation is suitable, a reviewing officer must consider all material circumstances at the date of the review, including the availability of suitable accommodation either in, or closer to, the authority's area: *Waltham Forest LBC v Saleh* [2019] EWCA Civ 1944, [2020] PTSR 621, [2020] HLR 15.
386 There is no requirement to have an out-of-area policy applicable to interim accommodation, separate from the policy governing the allocation of such property: *Hajjaj v Westminster CC, Akhter v Waltham Forest LBC* [2021] EWCA 1688; [2022] HLR 12.

it and the difficulty procuring affordable housing in its own area.[387] Where there is more than one suitable property outside the district, the authority should carry out a comparative exercise between them and offer the applicant the closest unless they have expressed a preference for another or the offer complies with the authority's published policy for the allocation of properties between applicants.[388] The issue is not solely about physical distance between the accommodation and the authority's district; means of communication between the accommodation and the authority's district may also be considered when deciding whether an out-of-area offer is suitable.[389]

8.171 There is no obligation to explain why out-of-area accommodation is being offered at the time of an offer,[390] but on a challenge the onus is in practice on the authority to show that it has discharged its duty.[391] Provided that there is no successful challenge to the policy, an allocation to out-of-borough accommodation cannot be challenged on the basis that there is available in-borough accommodation; it is lawful for the authority to reserve these for other applicants who will be entitled to an in-borough allocation pursuant to the policy.[392] The timescale for making an out-of-area offer of accommodation may be relevant: thus, if an authority is aware that a development of affordable housing in its district is nearing completion, it may be relevant to whether they should make an offer of accommodation outside its district or wait until the development has been completed.[393]

8.172 In *Zaman v Waltham Forest LBC; Uduezue v Bexley LBC*,[394] Waltham Forest had an Accommodation Acquisitions Policy setting out its policy for procuring privately owned properties for discharging its duties to the homeless under which properties would if possible be procured in its area; where there were insufficient such properties, then in Greater London and specified neighbouring South-East districts; if still not possible, elsewhere. All properties would be as close to the area as reasonable practicable. The appellant lived in the authority's area but was made a final offer in Stoke-on-Trent. A Law Centre wrote to the authority that there was no evidence it had looked for accommodation nearer to Waltham Forest; subsequently, it emerged that in the two previous years, it had housed 121 homeless households in Stoke-on-Trent. While its policy was lawful, it was held to be incumbent on the authority to demonstrate that it had complied with its policy; as there was no explanation why so many properties had been procured in Stoke-on-Trent when common sense suggested that it should have

---

387 *Nzolameso v Westminster City Council*, above.
388 *Saleh*, above, at [26]; *Moge v Ealing LBC* [2023] EWCA Civ 464; [2023] HLR 35 at [75].
389 *Alibkhiet v Brent LB*, above.
390 *Alibkhiet v Brent LB*, above.
391 *Nzolameso v Westminster City Council*, above, at [37]; *Abdikadir v Ealing LBC*, above, at [37], *Moge v Ealing LBC*, above, at [86].
392 *Adam v Westminster CC; Alibkhiet v Brent LB* [2018] EWCA Civ 2742, [2019] HLR 15; *Abdikadir v Ealing LBC* [2022] EWCA Civ 979, [2022] HLR 36 at [37](ii).
393 *Adam v Westminster CC*, above.
394 [2023] EWCA Civ 322; [2023] HLR 30.

been possible to obtain accommodation closer to London, the authority had not demonstrated that it had done so.

8.173 Policies must thus be properly applied. In *Abdikadir v Ealing LBC*,[395] the authority's Temporary Accommodation Allocation gave some categories of homeless person priority for accommodation in its district or in other boroughs in West London. Households were prioritised for accommodation in Ealing 'where accommodation in Ealing would be suitable in the longer term due to the household's circumstances'. The policy set out a number of factors which meant that a household would have a priority for accommodation in Ealing, including where at least one person was in permanent or settled employment in Ealing. The policy provided, however, that: 'Working household members are expected to commute and consideration of 60 minutes commuting time from home to work is reasonable within London'. The policy also stated that the fact that an applicant fell within such a priority group did not guarantee a placement within Ealing. The authority also had a Temporary Accommodation Acquisitions policy which included working with private sector landlords and which stated that officers would 'check relevant websites on a daily basis for new supply'.

8.174 The applicant was offered property owned by a housing association in Hillingdon but close to Hillingdon's border with Ealing. The applicant refused the offer on the basis of size of rooms and distance from her youngest daughter's school but, in two reviews,[396] the authority upheld the decision. In its second decision letter, it recorded that while the appellant worked in Ealing, the property was only a 40-minute commute from her workplace. The officer also considered that the distance of the property from her youngest daughter's school was suitable in terms of location. The applicant's solicitors wrote to the authority asking about steps had taken to secure accommodation in Ealing; in response. the authority did not mention any steps taken to investigate the availability of private sector accommodation.

8.175 The Court of Appeal interpreted Ealing's policy as meaning that the overarching consideration was whether only accommodation in Ealing would be suitable in the longer term for an applicant; on that issue, working household members were expected to be able to commute up to 60 minutes each way; the review officer had decided that the property was a 40-minute commute from the appellant's work-place and the authority had therefore correctly applied its policy. The policy, however, contemplated the authority making a private rented sector offer; the authority did not mention any investigation of its availability nor was there any evidence that officers had checked websites on a daily basis for new private rented sector properties; the appeal was allowed because there was no evidence that the authority had complied with these aspects of its policy.

8.176 Conversely, however, in *Moge v Ealing LBC*,[397] also a refusal of offer case, the same authority was able to rely on a detailed statement as to how it operated

---

395 [2022] EWCA 979; [2022] HLR 36.
396 The first of which was subject to a successful county court appeal.
397 [2023] EWCA Civ 464; [2023] HLR 35.

its policy, including the daily steps taken by officers to find accommodation, as providing sufficient evidence of efforts to secure accommodation in-area or nearer to the area and a conclusion that the property offered had been the only suitable property available at the time,[398] even though it did not deal with how the applicant's own case had been handled.

8.177   Lord Justice Snowden summarised the position.

> '122.   It is plainly not the law that in every case, a local authority should have to give chapter and verse on each and every internet search and property inquiry that its officers made to find accommodation as close as possible to an applicant's previous home or place of work. That would place an intolerable burden on hard-pressed local authorities dealing with homelessness cases. The question of how detailed and specific the information provided or evidence adduced will depend upon the facts of the particular case.

> '123.   In that regard, I consider that Lady Hale in *Nzolameso* and Lewison LJ in *Abdikadir* both envisaged that a local authority facing a challenge under section 208(1) on review should generally be entitled to meet that challenge by pointing to a relevant published policy and explaining in general terms what is done to apply that policy. That is, I believe, what Lewison LJ indicated should have been done in *Abdikadir* at paragraph [59].

> '124.   That approach will not, of course, be sufficient in every case. There may be cases where more detail is required. The recent decision in *Zaman v London Borough of Waltham Forest*[399] provides an example. The local authority had an acquisitions policy that stated that properties would be procured as close to Waltham Forest in London as was reasonably practicable. The local authority had, however, offered the applicant accommodation in Stoke-on-Trent. As Newey LJ remarked, common sense indicated that it should normally have been possible for the authority to obtain accommodation much closer to London, for example in the major metropolitan locations in the West Midlands. However, in spite of repeated requests from the applicant, the local authority did not produce any evidence explaining how it had applied its policy and yet had still not been able to find any available properties closer to the borough. In allowing the appeal on the basis of a failure by the local authority to demonstrate compliance with section 208(1), Newey LJ concluded, "there is a dearth of evidence to show that [the policy] was followed, and common sense rather suggests that it was not".

---

398 The court rejected as unrealistic an argument that the duty extended to seeing if a housing association property could be made available on a bespoke basis, outside of any Part 6 nomination arrangements.

399 [2023] EWCA Civ 322.

'130. Accordingly, ...I think that with Ms. Grant's evidence there is (just) sufficient evidence before this Court to show that at the relevant time the Council's acquisitions officers did carry out an appropriate search to find suitable private sector properties for Ms. Moge in neighbouring boroughs to Ealing, that there is no evidence that any other more suitable property of this type was available, and hence that the offer of the Flat did not breach the Council's obligations under section 208(1) or the 2018 Guidance in this respect'.

8.178   The Homelessness (Suitability of Accommodation) (England) Order 2012 is considered further below,[400] as it is applicable not only to out-of-area placements but to all placements and also goes to where accommodation is located within an authority's district.

Notification of other authority

8.179   Under HA 1996, s 208(2), if the authority accommodates someone in another area, it must – within 14 days of the accommodation being made available to the applicant[401] – give notice to the local housing authority for the area in which that accommodation is situated.[402] If the applicant refuses the accommodation and the authority decides that its duty has come to an end before the 14-day period has expired, there is no duty to notify the other authority.[403]

8.180   The notice must state:

a)   the name of the applicant;

b)   the number and description of the persons residing with the applicant;

c)   the address of the accommodation;

d)   the date on which it became available; and

e)   the function under which it was made available.[404]

8.181   The notification function is designed to allow the notified authority to refer the applicant back under the local connection provisions,[405] should a later application be made to it for assistance: as such, it is considered in Chapter 5.[406]

---

400   Paras **8.209–8.221**.
401   HA 1996, s 208(4); in Wales, see H(W)A 2014, s 91(2)–(3).
402   The duty is triggered as soon as the applicant can move into the accommodation without delay: *Abdikadir v Ealing LBC* [2022] EWCA 979; [2022] HLR 36.
403   *Abdikadir v Ealing LBC*, above.
404   HA 1996, s 208(3). For example, under HA 1996, ss 193, 200 or 190. In Wales, see H(W)A 2014, s 91(3).
405   See HA 1996, s 198(4); H(W)A 2014, s 75.
406   See paras **5.16–5.19**.

8.182   Since the HRA 2017 came into force in England,[407] bringing with it the relief duty (paras **8.88–8.103**) and new duties to those in priority need (para **8.95**), HA 1996, s 208 only applies where the authority decides to discharge those duties by securing that accommodation is available for an applicant's accommodation:[408] it does not apply where the help proffered suggests that the applicant move to another area to find their own accommodation.

Suitability of accommodation

8.183   The duty to provide suitable accommodation is a continuing one; authorities must consider any changes in circumstances which occur while they are discharging their duty: *Zaher*.[409] Likewise, if there is a review of suitability, circumstances must be considered as at the date of the review.[410] It has been suggested that as suitability is a continuing duty, it is possible to seek a further decision should circumstances change, without a new application as homeless:[411] it is very difficult to see any statutory basis for this proposition and it may not have been more than an alternative way of saying that a new application could be made as homeless on account of the change (ie, accommodation ceasing to be suitable), which plainly is possible in appropriate circumstances.[412]

8.184   While not exhaustive as to the relevant considerations, suitability is statutorily governed by HA 1996, s 210 and H(W)A 2014, s 59, and suitability statutory orders,[413] which identify considerations which must be taken into

---

407 3 April 2018: Homelessness Reduction Act 2017 (Commencement and Transitional and Savings Provisions) Regulations 2018, SI 2018/167, reg 3, only applicable to applications made and reviews sought on or after that date – see reg 4.

408 HA 1996, s 205(3).

409 *R (Zaher) v Westminster City Council* [2003] EWHC 101 (Admin), [2003] JHL D41.

410 *Waltham Forest LBC v Saleh* [2019] EWCA Civ 1994, [2020] PTSR 621, [2020] HLR 15.

411 In *R (B) v Redbridge LBC* [2019] EWHC 250 (Admin), [2019] PTSR 1525, [2021] HLR 9, in which electricity costs proved to be higher than the authority had estimated when determining – on decision and review – that accommodation was suitable, it was held that a second review was only possible if within 21 days of the s 184 decision (or such longer period as the authority in writing allowed).

412 Paras **7.31–7.46**. In *B*, above, it was also suggested that the authority could be asked to make a new determination of whether the property remained suitable, and seek a review of a decision that it was not: HA 1996, s 202(1)(f) does not seem to preclude such an approach. The authority could also be asked to extend time to allow a second review of the decision.

413 In England, the orders are: Homelessness (Suitability of Accommodation) Order 1996, SI 1996/3204, as amended by the Homelessness (Suitability of Accommodation) (Amendment) Order 1997, SI 1997/1741; Homelessness (Suitability of Accommodation) (England) Order 2003, SI 2003/3326 (as amended by Homelessness (Suitability of Accommodation) (Amendment) (England) Order 2022, SI 2022/521) and the Homelessness (Suitability of Accommodation) (England) (Amendment) Order 2023, SI 2023/509; and, Homelessness (Suitability of Accommodation) (England) Order 2012, SI 2012/2601 as amended by SI 2022/521, itself as amended by SI 2023/509. There is also a specific order for accommodation provided for asylum-seekers: Homelessness (Asylum-seekers) (Interim Period) (England) Order 1999, SI 1999/3126. In Wales, Homelessness (Suitability of Accommodation) (Wales) Order 2015, SI 2015/1268, as amended by Renting Homes (Wales) Act 2016 and Homelessness (Suitability of Accommodation) (Wales) Order 2015 (Amendment) Regulations 2023, SI 2023/1277. See below, paras **8.209–8.206**.

account, including the law governing housing conditions, overcrowding and HMOs.[414] The primary obligation is to 'have regard to' these provisions of HA 1985 and HA 2004.[415]

8.185 Even now, and save so far as overtaken by the specific grounds of unsuitability in the secondary legislation, the statutory wording is not strong enough to prevent an authority using overcrowded[416] or property in which there may be hazards,[417] or an HMO which falls below standard, although it will vitiate a decision in relation to which the authority had ignored these considerations; the wording is sufficient, however, to require the authority to justify a decision to use such substandard accommodation.[418] The Code of Guidance was amended on 28 February 2024 to provide that temporary accommodation will not be suitable 'for a household with children under the age of 2 if there is not adequate space for a cot for each child aged under 2' (para **17.12**). If such a household does not have a cot then the authority should 'consider what support is available for the provision of a cot', with particular regard to cases where someone has become homeless as a result of domestic abuse (para **17.13**).

8.186 Older cases fall to be reconsidered in the light of any statutory (primary and secondary) considerations which may have followed them, but will still be relevant where the statutory considerations are not mandatory[419] and the authority disclaims compliance on the ground of insufficient accommodation which meets the standard to which they refer. They may even be of some relevance where the considerations are mandatory, so far as they are illustrative of the matters which Parliament has subsequently addressed (and in some cases, which it may be contended that Parliament has sought to redress). They are accordingly considered first, with statutory considerations addressed below, under the heading 'Suitability Orders' (paras **8.209–8.234**).

8.187 Although there is no explicit statutory duty to enquire into questions of suitability, it is implicit: authorities cannot otherwise reach a decision that accommodation is suitable for the particular applicant. The principles developed

---

414 Additionally, in Wales, regard must be had to H(W)A 2014, Part 1 (landlord licencing).
415 Even if there is a complaint about conditions, it is for the authority to decide whether or not to carry out an inspection under, eg, Part 1, Housing Act 2004: *Firoozmand v Lambeth LBC* [2015] EWCA Civ 952; [2015] HLR 45.
416 See *Harouki v Kensington and Chelsea RLBC* [2007] EWCA Civ 1000, [2008] HLR 16 in which it was said that the wording of HA 1996, s 210 recognises that accommodation is not necessarily unsuitable because it is statutorily overcrowded.
417 The English Code of Guidance para 17.25 recommends that, when determining the suitability of accommodation, authorities should, as a minimum, ensure that all accommodation is free of category 1 hazards under HA 2004, Part 1. See now the Homelessness (Suitability of Accommodation) (England) Order 2012, SI 2012/2601, art 3 – private sector accommodation which the authority is of the view is not in a reasonable physical condition is not suitable.
418 Consider *Padfield v Minister of Agriculture, Fisheries and Food* [1968] AC 997, HL; see para **10.50**.
419 Ibid.

in relation to HA 1996, s 184 enquiries[420] therefore also apply to enquiries as to suitability: *Thomas.*[421] Note the particular position of those expected to die within six months or otherwise in palliative care: para **8.50**.

Physical condition

8.188 In *Campbell,*[422] a cockroach-infested property was not suitable for the applicant, a decision which, on its facts, could still stand. On the other hand, in *Jibril,*[423] an offer of a five-bedroom house with only one toilet – situated in the bathroom – for a family of 12 was held to be within the 'margin of appreciation' of that which an authority could consider suitable. In *Khan,*[424] the authority conceded that a bed and breakfast property with communal kitchen and bathroom facilities – in which the applicant, his wife and their four children occupied two bedrooms on different floors – was unsuitable. Ordering the authority to find alternative accommodation, the judge stressed that bed and breakfast accommodation should only be used in the short term and that authorities should look for alternative ways to discharge their HA 1996, s 193 duty. This has now been embodied in statutory constraints on use of bed and breakfast: see paras **8.218–8.221, 8.225–8.226**.

8.189 In *Flash,*[425] a one-bedroom flat provided to the applicant and her grandson was suitable: the grandson could sleep in the living room. In *El-Dinnaoui,*[426] the complaint was about an offer on the ninth floor of a block of flats; the applicant's wife had a fear of heights; the reviewing officer concluded that the appellant's wife would have settled into the flat over time. That conclusion failed to give proper weight to the medical evidence: she had collapsed during her visit to the flat and had been taken to hospital; the collapse had been caused by a panic attack; the discharging doctor had recorded that she had a lifelong fear of high buildings; her GP had advised that, owing to the severity of her symptoms, she should be offered a flat on a lower floor to avoid further panic attacks. It had therefore not been open to the reviewing officer to conclude that the wife merely had a general dislike of heights rather than a fear which made it impractical for her to live above a certain floor level.

8.190 In *Jaberi,*[427] it was irrational to provide a two-bedroom maisonette with internal stairs where the authority had concluded that what the claimant needed was a three-bedroom property without internal stairs, even only pending

---

420 See paras **7.84–7.101**.
421 *R v Islington LBC ex p Thomas* (1998) 30 HLR 111, QBD. See also *R v South Holland DC ex p Baxter* (1998) 30 HLR 1069, QBD.
422 *R v Lambeth LBC ex p Campbell* (1994) 26 HLR 618, QBD.
423 *R v Camden LBC ex p Jibril* (1997) 29 HLR 785, QBD.
424 *R (Khan) v Newham LBC* [2001] EWHC Admin 589, [2001] JHL D90.
425 *R (Flash) v Southwark LBC* [2004] EWHC 717 (Admin), [2004] JHL D60.
426 *El-Dinnaoui v Westminster City Council* [2013] EWCA Civ 231, [2013] HLR 23.
427 *R (Jaberi) v Westminster CC* [2023] EWHC 1045 (Admin), [2023] HLR 37.

adaptation of another property for longer-term occupation; by the time the claim was issued, three years had passed since the authority had concluded he needed a property without stairs, and 14 months since it had concluded that he needed a three-bedroom property, leaving him virtually confined to the upper floor; meanwhile, his wife was sleeping on the floor of the children's bedroom, as she would not otherwise have been able to hear either the applicant's call for assistance or those of their youngest child – no reasonable authority could conclude that the maisonette comprised suitable accommodation, even if for only a short-term until the alternative accommodation was ready.[428]

Other considerations

8.191   In *Awua*,[429] it was said that suitability is primarily a matter of space and arrangement, but that other matters, such as whether the applicant can afford the rent, may also be material.[430] In *Kaur*,[431] decided before the Homelessness (Suitability of Accommodation) (England) Order 1997 required consideration of affordability (see paras **8.210, 2.135–2.146**), it was held that accommodation secured for the applicant in the private sector was not suitable because the contractual rent exceeded the amount which would be met in housing benefit and the shortfall could not be afforded from the applicant's own resources. In *Maloba*,[432] on the related issue[433] of whether accommodation was reasonable to continue to occupy, it was held that the question was not limited to consideration of the size, structural quality and amenities of accommodation.

Personal circumstances

8.192   In deciding the question of suitability, it was held that the authority must consider the individual needs of the applicant and their family, including needs as to work, education and health,[434] matters now (para **8.211**) statutorily required to be taken into account.

---

428 As the adapted property had been made available by the time of the hearing, there was no continuing breach as any complaints about it could be considered on review or on appeal to the county court, so that only a declaration was made.

429 *R v Brent LBC ex p Awua* [1996] AC 55, (1995) 27 HLR 453, HL.

430 This decision preceded the statutory requirement (see para **8.210**) to take affordability into account.

431 *R v Tower Hamlets LBC ex p Kaur* (1994) 26 HLR 597, QBD.

432 *Waltham Forest LBC v Maloba* [2007] EWCA Civ 1281, [2008] HLR 26 at [59]–[61].

433 In *Rowe v Haringey LBC* [2022] EWCA Civ 1370; [2023] HLR 5, it was said to be more accurate to describe the two concepts as related than to say that the concepts overlap.

434 *R v Newham LBC ex p Sacupima* (2001) 33 HLR 1, QBD and (2001) 33 HLR 2, CA. See also *R v Newham LBC ex p Ojuri (No 3)* (1999) 31 HLR 452, QBD. The decision in *Holmes-Moorhouse v Richmond upon Thames LBC* [2009] UKHL 7, [2009] HLR 34 on separated families (above, para **7.182**) may also come into play determining suitability; see recently *Querino v Cambridge CC* [2024] EWCA Civ 314; HLR forthcoming.

8.193 In *Omar*,[435] a political refugee was offered accommodation in a basement flat in an estate. The condition of the premises and the layout of the estate strongly reminded the applicant of the prisons in which she had been held and abused, to such an extent that she maintained that she would rather commit suicide than live there. The court held that the accommodation must be suitable for the person to whom the duty was owed, in determining which the authority should have regard to the relevant circumstances of the applicant as well as to the statutory requirements.

8.194 *Omar* was considered in *Dolan*,[436] where the authority's decision to offer accommodation was flawed because it had separated out medical and social considerations and had not taken an overall view of the applicant's needs: 'the ultimate decision as to suitability must be the result of a composite assessment'. *Omar* was also considered in *Karaman*,[437] where the applicant's terror of her husband's domestic violence was such that the authority's decision to house her within two miles of where her husband was believed to be living was *Wednesbury* unreasonable. In *Slater*,[438] Ward LJ said of a young single mother who was fleeing domestic violence 'that the particular needs of the applicant, for example, to be protected from domestic violence and to be located near to support networks, are relevant when considering suitability'.

8.195 In *SH*,[439] the applicant had arrived in the UK having fled people traffickers who had raped her, as a result of which she was pregnant, and who were intending to force her into prostitution. She was granted refugee status in 2014 and applied to Waltham Forest LBC who decided that they owed the s 193(2) duty. She was made an offer of a flat in Tottenham, which she accepted. She subsequently discovered that there was a considerable prostitution problem in the communal gardens of the block in which the flat was situated, which she could see from her flat. She produced medical evidence that witnessing such activities was having a detrimental impact on her mental health. The court held that the offer was not suitable for her.

Family

8.196 An authority has a wide discretion to determine who is within an applicant's household.[440] In *Ariemuguvbe*,[441] the claimant was living in a three-bedroom property with her husband, five adult children who had come to the UK from Nigeria in 1998 who had overstayed their visitor's visas, and three

---

435 *R v Brent LBC ex p Omar* (1991) 23 HLR 446, QBD.
436 *R v Lewisham LBC ex p Dolan* (1993) 25 HLR 68, QBD.
437 *R v Haringey LBC ex p Karaman* (1997) 29 HLR 366, QBD. Cf *R v Lambeth LBC ex p Woodburne* (1997) 29 HLR 836, QBD.
438 *Slater v Lewisham LBC* [2006] EWCA Civ 394, [2006] HLR 37 at [30].
439 *R (SH) v Waltham Forest LBC* [2019] EWHC 2618 (Admin), [2021] HLR 10.
440 *R (Ariemuguvbe) v Islington LBC* [2009] EWCA Civ 1308.
441 *R (Ariemuguvbe) v Islington LBC*, above.

grandchildren. The claimant argued that the points allocated to her under the authority's allocation scheme should be increased to take account of the five adult children.[442]

8.197 It was held that the authority was entitled to conclude that it was not appropriate to allocate a larger property to the claimant because her five children were all independent adults, some having their own families, who should have been able to make their own housing arrangements; also, they were subject to immigration control[443] in circumstances where providing accommodation for them would amount to them having recourse to public funds in breach of their conditions of entry to the UK.[444]

Racial harassment

8.198 Issues of racial harassment and violence are also relevant. In *Abdul Subhan*,[445] Tower Hamlets LBC offered a Bangladeshi applicant accommodation in a block of flats in which there was active racial harassment. The authority had itself set up a Racial Incidents Panel, had been provided with details of incidents of racial harassment by the local law centre, and had received reports from a research project set up by the Home Office Crime Prevention Unit. The decision to make the offer was quashed because the authority had failed to take into account the material on harassment which was before it.

Separation

8.199 Accommodation which split a family between two hostels was held not to be suitable in *Surdonja*.[446] In *Camden LBC v Sharif*,[447] however, the accommodation was split between two flats, yards apart in the same building. The decision that the flats were suitable was not challenged. The challenge was confined to whether it was accommodation which was available, which it was held to be: see paras **2.19–2.41**.

Location

8.200 Independently of the requirement, applicable in England, to consider locality under the Homelessness (Suitability of Accommodation) (England)

---

442 *R (Ariemuguvbe) v Islington LBC*, above.
443 See para **A.14**.
444 *R (Ariemuguvbe) v Islington LBC*, above, at [19].
445 *R v Tower Hamlets LBC ex p Abdul Subhan* (1992) 24 HLR 541, QBD; see also *R v Southwark LBC ex p Solomon* (1994) 26 HLR 693, QBD.
446 *R v Ealing LBC ex p Surdonja* (1999) 31 HLR 686, QBD.
447 [2013] UKSC 10, [2013] HLR 16.

Order 2012,[448] location will in any event impact on suitability,[449] and an authority must consider how location will affect employment, education and healthcare for the applicant and their family.[450]

8.201 In *Abdullah*,[451] the review officer had taken into account the appellant's submissions and the medical evidence provided and was entitled to conclude that the medical evidence meant no more than that it would be advantageous for the appellant to live near to her family and friends, rather than meaning that was being necessary for her to do so; it was also open to the reviewer to assume that social services would provide assistance where necessary, regardless of where the appellant lived.[452]

Adaptations

8.202 The suitability of accommodation offered by an authority pursuant to HA 1996, s 193(2) is not to be judged exclusively by reference to the condition of the accommodation at the time of the offer: regard may be had to proposed adaptations or alterations provided that the proposals can fairly be regarded as certain, binding and enforceable; adaptations that are proposed after the date of the offer are, however, irrelevant to the question of suitability.[453]

Furnishings

8.203 In *R (Escott) v Chichester DC*,[454] the claimant had mental health problems and was a substance abuser. He was also suffering from sepsis and pneumonia. He applied for assistance under HA 1996, Part 7 and was provided with temporary accommodation in a shared hostel. In light of the coronavirus pandemic and his health problems, he contended that the accommodation was not suitable and that he required self-contained accommodation so that he could self-isolate. The local authority provided him with a self-contained unfurnished flat

---

448 Homelessness (Suitability of Accommodation) (England) Order 2012, SI 2012/2601, art 2.
449 See also paras **8.160–8.182**, on discharging the duty by securing accommodation outside the authority's area.
450 *R v Newham LBC ex p Sacupima* (2001) 33 HLR 1, QBD and (2001) 33 HLR 2, CA; *R v Newham LBC ex p Ojuri (No 3)* (1999) 31 HLR 452, QBD; *R (Yumsak) v Enfield LBC* [2002] EWHC 280 (Admin), [2002] JHL D38. See above, paras **8.160–8.167**. The English Code of Guidance is somewhat less generous, referring to 'the needs of the applicant and their household' and how any health problems will be met (para 17.59), but the Welsh Code adds 'Authorities should also consider factors such as access to schools and other services and facilities (eg, GPs and informal support networks) with a view to maintaining stability for the household, particularly in respect of children's schooling, wherever possible' (para 19.11).
451 *Abdullah v Westminster City Council* [2007] EWCA Civ 1566, [2007] JHL D89.
452 The decision in *Shala v Birmingham City Council* [2007] EWCA Civ 624, [2008] HLR 8 was not considered: see paras **3.53–3.54**. While this may not have led to a different result, the same principles must surely apply to how the authority approaches the medical evidence.
453 *Boreh v Ealing LBC* [2008] EWCA Civ 1176, [2009] HLR 22 at [31].
454 [2020] EWHC 1687 (Admin), [2020] PTSR 1678; [2021] HLR 4.

which contained a mattress and microwave. He argued that this accommodation was also not suitable: the absence of cooking and food storage facilities meant that he could not isolate himself from others. The High Court dismissed a claim for interim relief. There was no authority for the proposition that accommodation could not be suitable if it was unfurnished. The microwave allowed him to cook food. The authority had offered to provide him with a fridge, but he had rejected that offer because he would have been required to disinfect it. That was a 'wholly unreasonable' attitude for him to take.

Security

8.204   In *Wingrove* and *Mansoor*,[455] Evans LJ thought that the tenure, or time element, of suitability had to be proportionate to the circumstances of the case, including the needs of the applicant – for example, the need for the applicant's children to remain in an area to attend the same school for a number of years. Suitability for the purpose of HA 1996, s 193(2) does not imply permanence or security of tenure;[456] thus, even pre-LA 2011,[457] an assured shorthold tenancy could be suitable: see *Wingrove* and *Mansoor*[458] and *Griffiths*.[459]

RENTERS (REFORM) BILL

Once the provisions of the Bill come into full relevant force and subject to any transitional provisions, assured shorthold tenancies will no longer exist and will therefore no longer be an example of impermanent accommodation which was nonetheless considered suitable in the cases cited in the above paragraph.

Gypsies

8.205   Where the applicant is a gypsy, authorities must give special consideration to securing accommodation that will facilitate their traditional way of life: *Codona*.[460] Nonetheless, in *Codona*, the authority was unable to find any suitable accommodation other than bed and breakfast accommodation in

455 *R v Wandsworth LBC ex p Wingrove; R v Wandsworth LBC ex p Mansoor* [1997] QB 953, CA.
456 *Birmingham City Council v Ali; Moran v Manchester City Council (Secretary of State for Communities and Local Government and another intervening)* [2009] UKHL 36, [2009] 1 WLR 1506 at [47].
457 See paras **8.260–8.266**.
458 *R v Wandsworth LBC ex p Wingrove; R v Wandsworth LBC ex p Mansoor* [1997] QB 953, CA, per Sir Thomas Bingham MR at 923G.
459 *Griffiths v St Helens MBC* [2006] EWCA Civ 160, [2006] 1 WLR 2233, [2006] HLR 29. It was noted that if the assured shorthold came to an end, then – in the absence of other relevant changes, eg, cessation of priority need – the full duty would recur.
460 *Codona v Mid-Bedfordshire DC* [2004] EWCA Civ 925, [2005] HLR 1. See also *R (Price) v Carmarthenshire CC* [2003] EWHC 42 (Admin), [2003] JHL D43.

the short term, and a decision that it was suitable was not unlawful and did not violate the applicant's rights under ECHR Articles 8 and 14.[461]

8.206 A person who has adopted a lifestyle similar to that of a gypsy, but is not a gypsy, is not entitled to the special protection afforded to gypsies under human rights jurisprudence.[462]

Asylum-seekers

8.207 In relation to certain asylum-seekers in England, HA 1996, s 210 was modified for a particular category of asylum-seeker. While the homelessness provisions have not been repealed,[463] the relevant immigration provisions were, in 2014, and it is therefore considered no longer necessary to address this class separately.

Terminal stage of life

8.208 Authorities should be alert to the need to review the suitability of any accommodation provided to a person who is reasonably expected to die of a progressive illness within six months or who is in receipt of palliative care who will 'almost certainly' have a priority need.[464]

Suitability orders

8.209 The secretary of state and Welsh Ministers have power to specify circumstances in which accommodation is (or is not) to be regarded as suitable and to specify other matters to be taken into account or disregarded.[465]

England

8.210 This power has been used in England to require authorities to take affordability into account when determining suitability:[466] see Homelessness

---

461 See also paras **10.123–10.129**.
462 *Steward v Kingston Upon Thames LBC* [2007] EWCA Civ 565, [2007] HLR 42.
463 Homelessness (Asylum-seekers) (Interim Period) (England) Order 1999, SI 1999/3126. HA 1996, s 206(1A).
464 English Code of Guidance para 17.10. See also Code para 8.41 in relation to priority need; and above, para **3.69**.
465 HA 1996, s 210(2); H(W)A 2014, s 59(3).
466 This will include the availability of benefits, and – where applicable – the benefits cap: the fact that this may adversely affect an applicant, by confining their options to more distant accommodation where more local accommodation is unaffordable, is not incompatible with EHCR Art 14 (*R v (SG) v Secretary of State for Work and Pensions* [2015] UKSC 16, [2015] 1 WLR 1449) nor requires the authority to show that it has considered the public sector equality duty in s 149, Equality Act 2010: *Webb-Harnden v. Waltham Forest LBC* [2023] EWCA Civ 992; [2023] HLR 45.

(Suitability of Accommodation) Order 1996.[467] This is the same provision as applies to whether it is reasonable to continue to occupy accommodation and has been considered in Chapter 2.[468]

8.211   The power has also been used in England to require the authority to consider the location of accommodation,[469] including:

a)   the significance of any disruption to employment, caring responsibilities or education;[470]

b)   proximity and accessibility to medical facilities and other support which is currently used by or provided to the applicant or a member of their household and which is essential to that person's wellbeing;[471] and,

c)   proximity and accessibility to local services, amenities and transport.[472]

8.212   Education is a common issue. The passage in the English Code concerning s 11, Children Act 2004,[473] considers that the duty to discharge functions with regard to the need to safeguard and promote the welfare of children suggests that it

> 'would include minimising the disruption to the education of children and young people, particularly (but not solely) at critical points in time such as leading up to taking GCSE (or their equivalent) examinations.'

8.213   In *R (E) v Islington LBC*,[474] no such arrangements were made for a child placed in the area of another authority: it was held that there was a breach of ECHR Protocol 1, Article 2 (right to education);[475] the same could apply within the

---

467   Homelessness (Suitability of Accommodation) Order 1996, SI 1996/3204 (appendix B).
468   Paras **2.135–2.146**.
469   See also paras **8.60–8.182**, where the placement is outside the authority's own area.
470   '[A]ccount should be taken of the type and importance of the care household members provide and the likely impact the withdrawal would cause': English Code para 17.52. 'When securing accommodation for families with children housing authorities should be mindful of their duties under section 11 of the Children Act 2004 to discharge their functions with regard to the need to safeguard and promote the welfare of children': English Code para 17.53.
471   'Housing authorities should consider the potential impact on the health and wellbeing of an applicant or any person reasonably expected to reside with them, were such support to be removed or medical facilities were no longer accessible. They should also consider whether similar facilities are accessible and available near the accommodation being offered and whether there would be any specific difficulties in the applicant or person residing with them using those essential facilities, compared to the support they are currently receiving': English Code para 17.55.
472   'Housing authorities should avoid placing applicants in isolated accommodation away from public transport, shops and other facilities, where possible': English Code para 17.56.
473   At para 17.53.
474   [2017] EWHC 1440 (Admin), [2018] PTSR 349.
475   Interim relief was refused in *R (Fokou) v Southwark LBC* [2022] EWHC 1452 (Admin), where children in interim out-of-area accommodation had to travel 55 minutes each way to school. (The claim was that they had to travel 1 hr and 45 minutes, but it was held that there was a more direct route). If this was unmanageable, they could move school.

authority's area depending on the extent of the disruption. *R (YR) v Lambeth LBC*[476] and *R (UO) v Redbridge LBC*,[477] are more detailed studies of the education issue.[478]

8.214 Additionally, the authority may not consider private rented sector accommodation[479] as suitable if any of the following applies.[480]

a) the authority considers that the accommodation is not in a reasonable physical condition;[481]

b) the authority considers that any electrical equipment supplied with the accommodation does not meet Electrical Equipment (Safety) Regulations 1994, regs 5 and 7;[482]

c) the authority considers that the landlord has not taken reasonable fire safety precautions in respect of the accommodation and furnishings;[483]

d) the authority considers that the landlord has not taken reasonable precautions to prevent carbon monoxide poisoning in the accommodation;[484]

---

476 *R. (YR) v Lambeth LBC* [2022] EWHC 2813 (Admin); [2023] HLR 16.
477 [2023] EWHC 1355 (Admin); [2023] HLR 39.
478 Paras **8.70–8.74**.
479 Since the HRA 2017 came into force on 3 April 2018 (see Homelessness Reduction Act 2017 (Commencement and Transitional and Savings Provisions) Regulations 2018, SI 2018/167, reg 3, only applicable to applications made and reviews sought on or after that date – see reg 4), reg 3 spells out that the requirements apply not only to private sector offers under HA 1996, s 193(7F) but also to the suitability of final such offers under HA 1996, ss 193A and 193C and of accommodation for applicants in priority need by way of arrangements with private landlords under the relief duty in HA 1996, s 189B and the replacement provisions governing threatened with homelessness in HA 1996, s 195: HRA 2017, s 12. The amendments are without prejudice to any power by order to amend or revoke reg 3: HRA 2017, s 12(5).
480 Homelessness (Suitability of Accommodation) (England) Order 2012, SI 2012/2601, art 3, in force from 9 November 2012.
481 '[H]ousing authorities are advised to ensure it is visited by a local authority officer or someone acting on their behalf able to carry out an inspection. Attention should be paid to signs of damp or mould and indications that the property would be cold as well as to a visual check made of electrical installations and equipment (for example; looking for loose wiring, cracked or broken electrical sockets, light switches that do not work and appliances which do not appear to have been safety tested)': English Code para 17.17.
482 Electrical Equipment (Safety) Regulations 1994, SI 1994/3260.
483 Eg, consideration of Regulatory Reform (Fire Safety) Order 2005, SI 2005/1541, which applies to the common or shared parts of multi-occupied residential buildings, and Furniture and Furnishings (Fire) (Safety) Regulations 1988, SI 1988/1324, as amended: 'Housing authorities and fire and rescue authorities should work together to ensure the safety of domestic premises including the provision of fire safety advice to households. Housing authorities will need to satisfy themselves that these regulations have been adhered to': English Code para 17.19.
484 'Housing authorities are asked to satisfy themselves that there are reasonable precautions to prevent the possibility of carbon monoxide poisoning in the accommodation, where such a risk exists. Since 2015, private sector landlords have been required to have at least one smoke alarm installed on every storey of their properties and a carbon monoxide alarm in any room containing a solid fuel burning appliance (for example a coal fire or wood burning stove). After that, the landlord must make sure the alarms are in working order at the start of each new tenancy': English Code para 17.20.

e) the authority considers that the landlord is not a fit and proper person to act as landlord, after considering if they have committed any one of a number of specified categories of offence,[485] or has practised unlawful discrimination in or in connection with carrying on any business,[486] contravened any provision of housing law,[487] or acted otherwise than in accordance with any approved[488] and applicable code of practice for the management of an HMO;

f & g) the accommodation is an unlicensed HMO which ought to be licensed;[489]

h & i) the accommodation is or forms part of residential property which does not have a valid energy performance certificate[490] or a current gas safety record;[491]

j) the landlord has not provided the authority with a written tenancy agreement which they propose to use for the purposes of the private rented sector offer and which the authority considers adequate.[492]

8.215 The authority has to be satisfied that none of the ten criteria applies; it has to be satisfied of that on the basis of evidence rather than assumptions; an authority cannot form a view about the condition of a property unless it investigates before approving an offer either by inspecting or by being supplied with a report from a reliable source.[493] Accordingly, an authority cannot simply assume that a property will comply just because the landlord is established and respectable although evidence about the condition of the property from third parties, such as the manager of the property, may be sufficient for these purposes.[494]

8.216 In *Hajjaj*, the authority assumed that the property was suitable because the landlord was a reputable charity but knew nothing about its physical condition,

---

485 Offences involving fraud or other dishonest, violence or illegal drugs, or offences attracting notification requirements in Sexual Offences Act 2003, Sch 3. When placing households outside of their own district, authorities should check with the authority for the receiving district to see whether it has taken enforcement activity against the landlord and may consult the Rogue Landlord database (Housing and Planning Act 2016): English Code para 17.22.

486 On the grounds of age; disability; gender reassignment; marriage and civil partnership; pregnancy and maternity; race; religion or belief; sex, sexual orientation (EqA 2010).

487 Including landlord and tenant law.

488 Under HA 2004, s 133.

489 Under HA 2004, ss 54 or 55.

490 As required by the Energy Performance of Buildings (England and Wales) Regulations 2012, SI 2012/3118.

491 In accordance with Gas Safety (Installation and Use) Regulations 1998, SI 1988/2451, reg 36.

492 'It is expected that the local authority should review the tenancy agreement to ensure that it sets out, ideally in a clear and comprehensible way, the tenant's obligations, for example a clear statement of the rent and other charges, and the responsibilities of the landlord, but does not contain unfair or unreasonable terms, such as call-out charges for repairs or professional cleaning at the end of the tenancy': English Code para 17.15(e). 'Whilst a local authority will not be able to check that a tenant's deposit has been placed in a tenancy deposit protection scheme prior to them taking the tenancy housing authorities should remind prospective landlords and tenants of their responsibilities in this area': English Code para 17.23.

493 *Norton v Haringey LBC* [2022] EWCA Civ 1340; [2023] HLR 3.7F).

494 *Hajjaj v Westminster CC, Akhter v Waltham Forest LBC* [2021] EWCA 1688; [2022] HLR 12.

fire precautions or whether there was an energy performance certificate; the offer was accordingly not suitable. On the other hand, in *Akhter*, the authority inspected the property and agreed a list of repairs to be carried out by managing agents and its offer letter noted both that it had considered the 2012 Order and that the agents would provide the applicant with copies of energy performance certificate, gas safety certification and electrical safety certificate for the property; this was ample evidence on which to find that the property was in reasonable condition and that safety checks had been carried out.

8.217 While the decision in *Ephraim v Newham LBC*,[495] considered in relation to advice and assistance that helped the applicant to find accommodation where there was no obligation to secure it for her, that the authority was under no duty of care to satisfy itself that the premises to which it had referred her were reasonably safe, particularly in relation to fire, remains correct in law on its face (paras **8.91–8.92**), its reasoning relied on the absence of any duty to inspect; while the 2012 Order does not explicitly require an authority to inspect, the English Code[496] and the caselaw[497] do envisage inspection or, at the lowest, reliance on a reliable source. This does shift the balance of policy interest,[498] and in these cases, therefore, it may well be that *Ephraim* would not apply and that an authority may be held liable for injury, loss or damage if it places an applicant in non-compliant accommodation.

8.218 Bed and breakfast accommodation is not in itself necessarily unsuitable,[499] but the Homelessness (Suitability of Accommodation) (England) Order 2003[500] limits its use: where it is provided to families (including pregnant women), it is not to be regarded as suitable, save where there is no other accommodation available and then only for a period not exceeding six weeks (or periods not exceeding six weeks in total).

8.219 For a period of one year from 1 June 2022,[501] this limitation is, however, inapplicable – so that bed and breakfast accommodation may be suitable – in the same class of case[502] as that to which the principal statutory considerations as so suitability do not apply (for the same period).[503]

---

495 *Ephraim v Newham LBC* (1993) 25 HLR 207, CA.
496 See para **8.214**.
497 See paras **8.215–8.216**.
498 See para **8.92**.
499 See English Code of Guidance para 17.42 suggesting its use in emergencies or as a last resort, but also (at para 17.31) stating that authorities should avoid using it wherever possible.
500 Homelessness (Suitability of Accommodation) (England) Order 2003, SI 2003/3326 (appendix B).
501 Homelessness (Suitability of Accommodation) (Amendment) (England) Order 2022, SI 2022/521, art 2.
502 Para 8.169.
503 Homelessness (Suitability of Accommodation) (England) Order 2003, SI 2003/3326, art 4 as amended by Homelessness (Suitability of Accommodation) (Amendment) (England) Order 2022, SI 2022/521, art 4(2)(b).

8.220 Bed and breakfast accommodation is defined[504] as accommodation (whether or not breakfast is provided) which is not separate and self-contained and in which

a) cooking facilities are not provided, or

b) more than one household share one or more of the following:

   i) a toilet;

   ii) personal washing facilities; or

   iii) cooking facilities.

8.221 Accommodation owned or managed by an authority, a non-profit registered provider of social housing[505] or a voluntary organisation[506] and accommodation in a private dwelling[507] is, however, exempt from the prohibition.

Wales

8.222 There is no need for an affordability statutory instrument in Wales because H(W)A 2014, s 59(2) requires authorities to have regard to whether or not accommodation is affordable.[508]

8.223 The Homelessness (Suitability of Accommodation) (Wales) Order 2015[509] requires Welsh authorities to take into account the following additional matters when considering suitability of accommodation for a person in priority need:

a) the specific health needs of the person;

b) the proximity and accessibility of the support of the family or other support services;

c) any disability of the person;

d) the proximity and accessibility of medical facilities, and other support services which:

   are currently used by or provided to the person; and

   are essential to the wellbeing of the person;

---

504 Suitability Order 2003, art 2 as amended by Homelessness (Suitability of Accommodation) (England) (Amendment) Order 2023, SI 2023/509.

505 As amended by Housing and Regeneration Act 2008 (Consequential Provisions) (No 2) Order 2010, SI 2010/671, Sch 1, para 36.

506 See para **12.29** as to the definition of voluntary organisation.

507 Added by Homelessness (Suitability of Accommodation) (Amendment) (England) Order 2022, SI 2022/521, art 3.

508 See also see Welsh Code para 19.26 on factors to be taken into account when assessing affordability under H(W)A 2014, s 59(2).

509 Homelessness (Suitability of Accommodation) (Wales) Order 2015, SI 2015/1268 (Welsh Suitability Order).

e) where the accommodation is situated outside the area of the authority, the distance of the accommodation from the area of the authority;

f) the significance of any disruption which would be caused to the employment, caring responsibilities or education of the person by the location of the accommodation; and

g) the proximity of alleged perpetrators and victims of domestic abuse.

8.224 Additionally, the authority may not consider private rented sector accommodation as suitable if any of the following applies.[510]

a) the authority is of the view that the accommodation is not in a reasonable physical condition;

b) the authority is of the view that the accommodation does not comply with all statutory requirements (such as, where applicable, requirements relating to fire, gas, electrical, carbon monoxide and other safety; planning; and licences for HMOs);

c) the authority is of the view that the landlord is not a fit and proper person within the meaning of H(W)A 2014, s 20, to act in the capacity of landlord.

8.225 As in England,[511] bed and breakfast accommodation is not in itself necessarily unsuitable,[512] but, since 27 April 2015, there have been restrictions on its use and that of other shared accommodation, both as regards quality and duration.[513] Bed and breakfast or shared accommodation will be unsuitable for a person who is, or who may be, in priority need unless:

a) offered in response to an emergency (eg, fire, flood) and no other accommodation is reasonably available;

b) the applicant has been offered other suitable accommodation but has chosen bed and breakfast; or

c) it is used for less than a fixed period (two weeks, or six weeks if the accommodation meets a 'higher standard', as defined in the Schedule to the Order, taking into account, among other things, room size, heating facilities, storage facilities, toilet and washing facilities).

8.226 'Bed and breakfast accommodation' is defined[514] as accommodation – whether or not breakfast is included – in which a kitchen is either unavailable

---

510 Welsh Suitability Order Part 3.

511 See paras **8.218–8.221**.

512 See Welsh Code paras 5.40, 19.56–19.62.

513 Homelessness (Suitability of Accommodation) (Wales) Order 2015, SI 2015/1268. See also the previous restrictions in the Homelessness (Suitability of Accommodation) (Wales) Order 2006, SI 2006/650.

514 Welsh Suitability Order 2015 reg 2, as substituted by Renting Homes (Wales) Act 2016 and Homelessness (Suitability of Accommodation) (Wales) Order 2015 (Amendment) Regulations 2023, SI 2023/1277, reg 3.

to the occupier, or, although available, is shared by others who are not part of the occupier's household, in which a toilet and personal washing facilities are available but may be shared by others who are not part of the household, which accommodation is not owned or managed by a community landlord within the meaning of s 9 of the Renting Homes (Wales) Act 2016,[515] a registered charity or a voluntary organisation.[516]

Keeping offers open

8.227　In *Khatun*,[517] the Court of Appeal reviewed earlier cases in which it had been held that an offer (under HA 1985, Part 3) should remain open for consideration by the applicant for a reasonable time.[518] It was held that – while an authority may have regard to the applicant's subjective view on suitability – the cases did not support the proposition that the authority is bound to do so.

8.228　It was also held that an applicant does not have a right to view and comment on a property offered by a local authority in discharge of a duty to them before being required to decide whether or not to accept it, although a policy denying an applicant an opportunity to view and comment on the suitability of accommodation offered in discharge of a duty under the HA 1996 would be struck down if no reasonable authority could fail to give them such an opportunity.

8.229　It was said that it was not oppressive, perverse or disproportionate to the fair and efficient administration of the authority's scheme for housing the homeless for the authority to require an applicant who had not viewed accommodation offered in discharge of a duty to decide whether or not to accept it on pain of cancellation of his bed and breakfast accommodation if he did not accept; moreover, while the authority's policy of not allowing applicants a reasonable period to consider whether to accept offers of accommodation represented a departure from the recommendations in the Code of Guidance, it could not be criticised as it pursued the lawful aim of moving families out of bed and breakfast accommodation as quickly as possible.

---

515 A local authority, new town corporation, housing action trust, urban development corporation, or a housing co-operative where the dwelling is comprised in a housing co-operative agreement within s 27B, Housing Act 1985, registered social landlord (see Housing Act 1996, s 1) other than a fully mutual housing association or a co-operative housing association (see Housing Associations Act 1985, s 1(2)), or a private registered provider of social housing (see Housing and Regeneration Act 2008, s 80(3)), Renting Homes (Wales) Act 2016, s 9.

516 A body (other than a public or local authority) whose activities are not carried on for profit: Housing (Wales) Act 2014, s 99.

517 *Khatun v Newham LBC* [2004] EWCA Civ 55, [2004] HLR 29.

518 *R v Wandsworth LBC ex p Lindsay* (1986) 18 HLR 502, QBD. The same had been held in *Parr v Wyre BC* (1982) 2 HLR 71, CA, which was disapproved in *R v Hillingdon LBC ex p Puhlhofer* [1986] AC 484, (1986) 18 HLR 158, HL, so far as it was based on the introduction of the word 'appropriate'. See also *R v Ealing LBC ex p Denny* (1995) 27 HLR 424, CA.

8.230   Given the right to seek a review of suitability after moving in, authorities may therefore insist that an applicant makes a decision whether or not to accept an offer at the time that it is made, without holding it open to afford them an opportunity to view it.

8.231   The position is different where the authority knows that admittedly relevant material, for example, medical evidence, is yet to be produced. In *Hazeltine*,[519] the applicant challenged suitability on medical grounds; the authority agreed to keep the offer open, but only for a limited period, before the end of which it would not have received or evaluated the medical reports that it had requested from her. The authority's proposal was that, if she accepted the offer, she should abandon her challenge to it, but that, if she did not do so, the authority would determine the issue of suitability retrospectively, ie, if considered unsuitable she would get another offer, but if suitable she would not and the authority would take the position that it had discharged its duty to her. The court held that this procedure was not fair.

8.232   Where an authority notifies an applicant that it has ceased to be subject to the duty under HA 1996, s 193(2), because the applicant has refused an offer of suitable accommodation under section 193(5),[520] the authority was not obliged to keep the accommodation available during the period when the applicant has the right to request a review or until the authority has reached its review decision.[521]

8.233   Where there is a challenge to an authority's decision, based on lack of time to decide whether or not to accept an offer, the question whether there was sufficient time before the original decision will be academic if there has been sufficient time before the review decision to make any points the applicant wished to make.[522]

Challenges to suitability

8.234   Challenge to the suitability of an offer is by review under HA 1996, s 202 (H(W)A 2014, s 85),[523] which may be exercised whether or not the applicant has accepted the offer,[524] and appeal under s 204 (H(W)A 2014, s 88).[525] Save in exceptional circumstances, a decision on suitability of offer may not be challenged in a defence to eviction from temporary accommodation.[526]

---

519   *R v Wycombe DC ex p Hazeltine* (1993) 25 HLR 313, CA. See *Khatun v Newham LBC*, above, at [37] where *Hazeltine* was held to be consistent with the decision in that case.
520   Paras **8.240–8.243, 8.247–8.256, 8.259, 8.276, 8.279**.
521   *Osseily v Westminster City Council* [2007] EWCA Civ 1108, [2008] HLR 18 at [11].
522   *Adesotu v Lewisham LBC (Equality and Human Rights Commission intervening)* [2019] EWCA Civ 1405, [2019] 1 WLR 5637, [2019] HLR 48.
523   See paras **7.199–7.204.**
524   HA 1996, s 202(1A); reversing the effect of *Alghile v Westminster City Council* (2001) 33 HLR 57, CA, so as to afford the applicant the option of moving into the property while still contesting its suitability. In Wales, see H(W)A 2014, s 85.
525   See para **10.203**.
526   *Tower Hamlets LBC v Rahnara Begum* [2005] EWCA Civ 116, [2006] HLR 9.

Cessation of the duty

8.235   The duty under HA 1996, s 193 or H(W)A 2014, s 75 will terminate in the following circumstances.[527]

Eligibility

8.236   The duty will cease if the applicant ceases to be eligible for assistance,[528] for example, if their immigration status changes.[529]

Loss of accommodation

8.237   If the applicant becomes homeless intentionally from the accommodation made available, or otherwise voluntarily ceases to occupy it as their only or principal home,[530] the duty will cease.[531]

Offers

8.238   A number of instances terminate the duty through offers of accommodation. Although the LA 2011, which made a number of changes to the provisions governing subsequent applications, came into force on 9 November 2012,[532] the length of time during which applicants may remain in Part 7/Part 2 accommodation before the duty towards them is discharged means that the position before (as well as the position since) the LA 2011 may still be relevant, and the position before (as well as since) the H(W)A 2014 will certainly still be relevant[533] and, somewhat more obviously, so also will the position before and since the HRA 2017 came into force.[534]

8.239   Moreover, the pre-LA 2011 position in England is the same as the pre-H(W)A 2014 position, so that, in practice, there is nothing to be gained

---

527 But see also para **8.49**, on the possibility of a public law defence (whether on domestic grounds or under the ECHR).
528 See Annex: Immigration Eligibility.
529 HA 1996, s 193(6)(a); H(W)A 2014, s 79(2).
530 See *Crawley BC v Sawyer* (1998) 20 HLR 98, CA.
531 HA 1996, s 193(6)(b) and (d); H(W)A 2014, s 76(6).
532 9 November 2012: Localism Act 2011 (Commencement No 2 and Transitional Provisions) (England) Order 2012, SI 2012/2599, art 2.
533 Practitioners confirm that pre-LA 2011 cases continue to arise in more than a negligible number of cases; see also, by way of illustration, *Nikolaeva v Redbridge LBC* [2020] EWCA Civ 1586; [2021] HLR 15, in which acceptance of the duty – final discharge of which in 2017 was in contention – was in 2004.
534 3 April 2018: Homelessness Reduction Act 2017 (Commencement and Transitional and Savings Provisions) Regulations 2018, SI 2018/167, reg 3, only applicable to applications made and reviews sought on or after that date – see reg 4.

by removing consideration of it on the basis of the time that has elapsed since LA 2011 came into for*ce*.

Refusal of suitable offers

England pre-LA 2011 and Wales pre-H(W)A 2014

8.240   By HA 1996, s 193(5), in relation to applications made before commencement of the LA 2011, s 148(3)[535] in respect of which the duty to secure accommodation had arisen but had not ceased by that date,[536] and in Wales for applications made prior to 27 April 2015,[537] the duty ceases if the applicant is made an offer of suitable accommodation which they refuse, having been warned that the authority will regard itself as having discharged its duty if they do does so[538] and having been informed of the right to an internal review.[539] It has been held that the authority needs to prove that it provided the requisite information.[540]

8.241   This provision operates to bring to an end the full housing duty regardless of whether the accommodation offered to the applicant is temporary or permanent.[541]

8.242   Thus, where an authority had placed an applicant in accommodation pursuant to its duty under HA 1996, s 193(2), pending a final offer, which accommodation became unsuitable because of the applicant's change of circumstances so that the applicant had to move, the authority's duty ceased under subs (5) when the applicant refused a new offer of suitable alternative s 193(2) accommodation.[542] Nor had the authority acted unfairly as it had followed the procedural safeguards set out in the subsection and had not led the applicant to believe that she was entitled to any additional procedural protection.

---

535   9 November 2012: Localism Act 2011 (Commencement No 2 and Transitional Provisions) (England) Order 2012, SI 2012/2599, art 2.

536   Localism Act 2011 (Commencement No 2 and Transitional Provisions) (England) Order 2012, SI 2012/2599, art 3.

537   For applications made on or after that date, H(W)A 2014 applies: see Housing (Wales) Act 2014 (Commencement No 3 and Transitory, Transitional and Saving Provisions) Order 2015, SI 2015/1272, art 7.

538   In *Maswaku v Westminster City Council* [2012] EWCA Civ 669, [2012] HLR 37 an offer letter which informed the applicant that, should she refuse it, she would have to find her own accommodation, was a sufficient warning for this purpose.

539   HA 1996, s 193(5).

540   *R (SH) v Waltham Forest LBC* [2019] EWHC 2618 (Admin), [2021] HLR 10. Compare also *Norton v Haringey LBC* [2022] EWCA Civ 1340; [2023] HLR 3, paras **8.268, 8.271**.

541   *Griffiths v St Helens BC* [2006] EWCA Civ 160, [2006] 1 WLR 2233, [2006] HLR 29. At that time, Part 6 and private rented accommodation offers were within s 193(5), but see subsequently the discrete sets of provisions considered below, paras **8.244–8.271**.

542   *Muse v Brent LBC* [2008] EWCA Civ 1447.

8.243 The authority must notify the applicant that it considers the duty to have been discharged.[543] As such notification comprises a decision as to what duty is owed to the applicant, ie, that there is no duty because it has ceased,[544] it must comply with HA 1996, s 184, which means that it must give reasons and inform the applicant of their right to a review and be in writing.[545]

England post-LA 2011 and Wales post-H(W)A 2014

8.244 Since LA 2011, s 148(3) came into force in England,[546] the duty does not cease by reason of HA 1996, s 193(5), in the case either of an offer of accommodation under Part 6 or of private sector accommodation,[547] but is governed instead by discrete provisions which determine when the duties come to an end: these are considered below.[548]

8.245 In substance, therefore, HA 1996, s 193(5) is now limited to a refusal of a suitable offer of further interim accommodation. In Wales, the position remains the same, ie, the refusal of an offer of suitable interim accommodation brings the duty to an end.[549]

Part 6 offer

England pre-LA 2011 and Wales pre-H(W)A 2014

8.246 In relation to applications made before commencement of LA 2011, s 148(3),[550] in respect of which the duty to secure accommodation had arisen but had not ceased by that date,[551] and in Wales for applications made prior to 27 April 2015,[552] the duty will cease if the applicant accepts an offer of accommodation under Part 6.[553]

---

543 HA 1996, s 193(5). Given the applicant's right to challenge the suitability of the offer, the reasons should encompass why the authority considers the accommodation to be suitable for the applicant. Surprisingly there is no express requirement that the notification has to be in writing in Wales, see H(W)A 2014, s 84.
544 HA 1996, s 184(1); H(W)A 2014, s 84.
545 See para **8.11**.
546 9 November 2012: Localism Act 2011 (Commencement No 2 and Transitional Provisions) (England) Order 2012, SI 2012/2599, art 2.
547 Paras **8.240**.
548 Paras **8.57–8.259, 8.267–8.271**.
549 H(W)A 2014, s 76(3)(a).
550 9 November 2012: Localism Act 2011 (Commencement No 2 and Transitional Provisions) (England) Order 2012, SI 2012/2599, art 2.
551 Localism Act 2011 (Commencement No 2 and Transitional Provisions) (England) Order 2012, SI 2012/2599, art 3.
552 For applications made on or after that date, the H(W)A 2014 applies: see Housing (Wales) Act 2014 (Commencement No 3 and Transitory, Transitional and Saving Provisions) Order 2015, SI 2015/1272, art 7.
553 HA 1996, s 193(6)(c); see Chapter 9. Such an offer could have been made by way of nomination to become the assured tenant of a private registered provider of social housing (England) or a registered social landlord (Wales): HA 1996, s 159(1)(c).

8.247   The duty will also cease if the applicant, having been informed of the possible consequences of refusal[554] and of their right to request a review of the suitability of the accommodation, refuses a final offer of accommodation under Part 6.[555] A final offer of accommodation cannot be made unless the authority is satisfied that the accommodation is suitable for the applicant and that it is reasonable for them to accept it.[556]

8.248   The questions of suitability and whether it is reasonable for the applicant to accept the offer have to be considered separately.[557]

8.249   In judging whether it is unreasonable to refuse an offer:

> '. . . the decision-maker must have regard to all the personal characteristics of the applicant, her needs, her hopes and her fears and then taking account of those individual aspects, the subjective factors, ask whether it is reasonable, an objective test, for the applicant to accept. The test is whether a right-thinking local housing authority would conclude that it was reasonable that *this applicant* should have accepted the offer of *this* accommodation.'[558]

8.250   An offer is a final offer for this purpose if it is in writing and states that it is a final offer for the purposes of HA 1996, s 193(7).

8.251   The exact wording of s 193(7) does not need to be followed, provided that the notification contains every matter of substance which the subsection requires; the authority should, however, convey to the applicant that it is satisfied both that the accommodation is suitable for them and that it is reasonable for them to accept it.[559]

8.252   In *Begum*,[560] the notification was inadequate because it merely stated that the accommodation offered was a reasonable and suitable offer of permanent

---

554 HA 1996, s 193(7).
555 HA 1996, s 193(7); in Wales, see H(W)A 2014, s 76(3). A rejection can be inferred from conduct: *Nikolaeva v Redbridge LBC* [2020] EWCA Civ 1586, [2021] 1 HLR 15, where the applicant had declined to sign a tenancy agreement with a housing association because she had concerns about the terms of the tenancy (*eg*, a prohibition on keeping pot plants on the rear communal pathway and growing plants in the communal garden and on keeping pets); the authority had been entitled to conclude that she had rejected the offer of accommodation.
556 HA 1996, s 193(7F)(a).
557 *Slater v Lewisham LBC* [2006] EWCA Civ 394, [2006] HLR 37, where the authority had failed to apply its mind to the element of reasonableness.
558 Ward LJ in *Slater v Lewisham LBC* (emphasis in original).
559 *Tower Hamlets LBC v Rahanara Begum* [2005] EWCA Civ 116, [2006] HLR 9 at [27], though that case concerned HA 1996, s 193(7)(b) prior to its amendment by the Homelessness Act 2002.
560 *Tower Hamlets LBC v Rahanara Begum* [2005] EWCA Civ 116, [2006] HLR 9.

accommodation. The requirements may, however, be fulfilled by information in more than one document, provided that they can properly be read together.[561]

8.253 An applicant's genuine belief that it was not reasonable to accept an offer of accommodation is not conclusive of whether it was reasonable to do so; if the authority has evidence which entitles it to consider that the belief was not objectively reasonable, even if that evidence was not available to the applicant at the time of the refusal, the authority may nonetheless decide that it was reasonable for the applicant to accept the offer: *Ahmed*.[562]

8.254 It had been held that an offer under Part 6 which does not satisfy the requirements of subs (7) may nonetheless serve to discharge the authority's duty if it satisfied the requirements of s 193(5) (para **8.240**): *Omar*.[563] In *Ravichandran*,[564] however, it was said that *Omar* should be confined to its own facts. It is submitted that this is correct: it is difficult to see how compliance with the less stringent requirements of s 193(5) could properly be considered compliance with the detailed requirements of s 193(7).[565]

8.255 The courts will not easily interfere with an authority's allocation scheme,[566] nor, therefore, with its policy in relation to Part 6 offers to homeless persons: thus, once a homeless person housed in temporary accommodation achieved the requisite number of points to qualify to bid on an appropriate property, he was given only two months in which to make a voluntary bid before a successful 'auto-bid' was generated on his behalf,[567] which auto-bid could be treated as a final offer, refusal of which meant that the authority's duty could lawfully be treated as discharged.[568]

8.256 It would seem, however, to have been central to the court's decision that, before the two months began, a housing officer would visit, which would allow any particular personal considerations or difficulties to be taken into account before the bid was placed on the applicant's behalf.

---

561 *Vilvarasa v Harrow LBC* [2010] EWCA Civ 1278, [2010] HLR 11 – the information was spread across two letters, one in July (which did not specify the property in question) and one in August (which did so); the two documents could be read together.

562 *Ahmed v Leicester City Council* [2007] EWCA Civ 843, [2008] HLR 6.

563 *Omar v Birmingham City Council* [2007] EWCA Civ 610, [2007] HLR 43 at [29] and [36]; see also *Tower Hamlets LBC v Rahanara Begum* [2005] EWCA Civ 116, [2006] HLR 9 at [27].

564 *Ravichandran v Lewisham LBC* [2010] EWCA Civ 755, [2010] HLR 42. See recently *R (Bano) v Waltham Forest LBC* [2024] EWHC 654 (Admin).

565 The issue does not arise in relation to the post-LA 2011/H(W)A 2014 applications considered under the next heading, in respect of which HA 1996, s 193(5) is expressed only to apply to an offer which is neither a Part 6 offer nor an offer of private sector accommodation.

566 See *R (Ahmad) v Newham LBC* [2009] UKHL 14, [2009] HLR 31; paras **9.112–9.122**.

567 Ie, a bid by an officer of the authority on his behalf.

568 *R (Tout a Tout) v Haringey LBC; R (Heff) v Haringey LBC* [2012] EWHC 873 (Admin), [2012] JHL D77.

8.257 *Discharge of homelessness duties*

England post-LA 2011 and Wales post-H(W)A 2014

8.257   The law considered in relation to pre-LA 2011/H(W)A 2014 applicants is largely the same for applications in relation to which the duty had not arisen before commencement of LA 2011, s 148(3)[569] and those in Wales made prior to 27 April 2015.

8.258   The duty will cease if the applicant accepts an offer of accommodation under Part 6.[570] The duty will also cease if the applicant, having been informed of the possible consequences of refusal and acceptance[571] and of their right to request a review of the suitability of the accommodation, refuses a final offer of accommodation under Part 6.[572] An offer is a final offer for this purpose if it is in writing and states that it is a final offer for the purposes of HA 1996, s 193(7).[573] Accordingly, the earlier cases considered at paras **8.227–8.233** will remain relevant.

8.259   Apart from the requirement in England to inform the applicant about the possible consequences of acceptance as well as of refusal (para **8.258**), the other difference is that the issue considered at para **8.254**[574] is not relevant to these post-LA 2011/H(W)A 2014 applications, as HA 1996, s 193(5) is now expressed to apply only to an offer which is neither a Part 6 offer nor an offer of private sector accommodation.[575]

Private sector accommodation offers

England pre-LA 2011 and Wales pre-H(W)A 2014

8.260   The following provisions applied until LA 2011, s 148 came into force in England,[576] and continue to apply to applications made before that date, in relation to which the duty to secure accommodation had arisen but had not ceased by it;[577] in Wales they apply to applications made prior to 27 April 2015.[578]

---

569 9 November 2012: Localism Act 2011 (Commencement No 2 and Transitional Provisions) (England) Order 2012, SI 2012/2599, art 2.
570 HA 1996, s 193(6)(c); H(W)A 2014, s 76(2). See Chapter 9.
571 HA 1996, s 193(7) as amended from 9 November 2012. In Wales, see H(W)A 2014, s 76(3).
572 HA 1996, s 193(7); in Wales, see H(W)A 2014, s 76(3). Such an offer may include a nomination to become the assured tenant of a private registered provider of social housing (England) or a registered social landlord (Wales): HA 1996, s 159(1)(c).
573 HA 1996, s 193(7A). There is no such requirement in Wales.
574 Ie, whether an offer under HA 1996, Part 6 which does not satisfy the requirements of HA 1996, s 193(7) may nonetheless serve to discharge the authority's duty if it satisfied the requirements of s 193(5).
575 See also Supplementary Suitability Guidance 2012, para 19.
576 9 November 2012: Localism Act 2011 (Commencement No 2 and Transitional Provisions) (England) Order 2012, SI 2012/2599, art 2.
577 Localism Act 2011 (Commencement No 2 and Transitional Provisions) (England) Order 2012, SI 2012/2599, art 3.
578 For applications made on or after that date, the H(W)A 2014 applies: see Housing (Wales) Act 2014 (Commencement No 3 and Transitory, Transitional and Saving Provisions) Order 2015, SI 2015/1272, art 7.

8.261   The duty will cease if the applicant accepts an offer of an assured (but not an assured shorthold) tenancy from a private landlord.[579] The duty will also cease if the applicant accepts a 'qualifying offer' of an assured shorthold.[580]

8.262   An offer qualifies if:

a)   it is made with the approval of the authority,[581] pursuant to arrangements made between it and the private landlord in order to bring the HA 1996, s 193 duty to an end;

b)   the tenancy is a fixed-term tenancy;[582] and

c)   it is accompanied by a statement in writing,[583] which states the term of the tenancy being offered and explains in ordinary language that there is no obligation to accept the offer, but that if it is accepted the duty under HA 1996, s 193 will cease.[584]

RENTERS (REFORM) BILL

Although they should be few, it remains the case that an applicant in this class (pre-9 November 2012) may still not have been made an offer complying with s 193(5)-(7F). Once the provisions of the Bill come into full relevant force and subject to any transitional provisions, acceptance will be of an assured tenancy and will not for a fixed term; instead, there will be a new mandatory ground for possession (Housing Act 1988, s 7), Ground 5G, where the grant of the tenancy was in pursuance of a local housing authority's duty to the tenant under s 193 of the Housing Act 1996, the local housing authority has notified the landlord that the tenancy is no longer required for the purposes of that duty, and the date specified in the notice of proceedings for possession is within 12 months following the date on which the authority so notified the landlord.

---

579   HA 1996, s 193(6)(cc); as defined by HA 1996, s 217(1). A private landlord is any landlord other than one within HA 1985, s 80 and therefore includes a private registered provider of social housing (England) or a registered social landlord (Wales): HA 1996, s 217 and H(W) A 2014, s 99.

580   HA 1996, s 193(7B), continued in force for this class of application by Localism Act 2011 (Commencement No 2 and Transitional Provisions) (England) Order 2012, SI 2012/2599, art.3.

581   The offer may not be approved unless the authority is satisfied that the accommodation is suitable for the applicant and that it is reasonable for them to accept the offer: HA 1996, s 193(7F)(b). For this purpose, however, an applicant may reasonably be expected to accept an offer even though they are under contractual or other obligations in respect of their existing accommodation, those obligations can be brought to an end before they are required to take up the offer: HA 1996, s 193(8).

582   As defined by HA 1988, s 45(1), ie, any tenancy other than a periodic tenancy.

583   The authority may need to prove that this statement was provided, as it has been held that a court will not presume that it has done so in the absence of evidence, so that there had been no qualifying offer: *R (SH) v Waltham Forest LBC* [2019] EWHC 2618 (Admin), [2021] HLR 10.

584   HA 1996, s 193(7D).

8.263 The authority must be satisfied that the accommodation was suitable for the applicant and that it was reasonable for them to accept the offer.[585]

8.264 An applicant is free to reject a qualifying offer; the duty under HA 1996, s 193 is not discharged,[586] and acceptance is only effective if the applicant signs a statement acknowledging that they have read and understood the statement made with the offer.[587]

8.265 An offer of accommodation let on an assured shorthold tenancy which does not comply with the requirements of HA 1996, s 193(7D) (para **8.262**) cannot be a qualifying offer but, if refused, s 193(5) can nevertheless operate to bring the authority's duty under s 193(2) to an end,[588] provided that the requirements of the later subsection have been fulfilled, as qualified in the case of an assured shorthold.[589]

8.266 If an applicant accepts an offer of an assured shorthold tenancy that is not a qualifying offer, which accommodation subsequently ceases to be available, the authority will continue to owe them a duty under s 193(2) (provided that the applicant's circumstances have not otherwise materially changed).[590]

> RENTERS (REFORM) BILL
>
> Once the provisions of the Bill come into full relevant force and subject to any transitional provisions, the above two paragraphs will not recur as examples of impermanent accommodation which nonetheless discharge the authority's duty.

England post-LA 2011 and Wales post-H(W)A 2014

8.267 An offer of private rented sector accommodation by an authority leads to cessation of the duty even if the tenancy is an assured shorthold or, post-RH(W) A 2016, an occupation contract.[591] A private rented sector accommodation offer is of an assured shorthold tenancy (or occupation contract), from a private landlord[592] to the applicant in respect of any accommodation which is, or may become, available for the applicant's occupation, which is made with the approval of the authority in pursuance of arrangements made between it and the landlord,

---

585 HA 1996, s 193(7F).
586 HA 1996, s 193(7C).
587 HA 1996, s 193(7E).
588 Paras **8.240–8.241**.
589 *Griffiths v St Helens MBC* [2006] EWCA Civ 160, [2006] 1 WLR 2233.
590 *Griffiths v St Helens MBC*, above.
591 HA 1996, s 193(7AA); H(W)A 2014, s 76(2)–(4).
592 Ie, any landlord other than one within HA 1985, s 80 and thus including a private registered provider of social housing (England) or a registered social landlord (Wales): HA 1996, s 217.

with a view to bringing its duty to an end; in England, the tenancy must be for a fixed term of at least 12 months[593] or – otherwise than in a restricted case – such longer period as the secretary of state may by regulations prescribe.[594]

RENTERS (REFORM) BILL

Once the provisions of the Bill come into full relevant force and subject to any transitional provisions, s 193(7AC) is due to be amended to remove the reference to an assured shorthold tenancy and to be for a fixed term of at least 12 months: a private rented offer will therefore be of an assured tenancy, and not for a fixed term, made, with the approval of the authority, in pursuance of arrangements it made with the landlord with a view to bringing the authority's duty to an end; instead, there will be a new mandatory ground for possession (Housing Act 1988, s 7), Ground 5G, where the grant of the tenancy was in pursuance of a local housing authority's duty to the tenant under s 193 of the Housing Act 1996, the local housing authority has notified the landlord that the tenancy is no longer required for the purposes of that duty, and the date specified in the notice of proceedings for possession is within 12 months following the date on which the authority so notified the landlord.

8.268 In England, the offer must comply with specified qualifying conditions:[595] the applicant must be informed in writing of the consequences of refusal or acceptance, that they have the right to a review of the suitability of the accommodation and – otherwise than in a restricted case – that they will be entitled to further assistance from the authority if a new application is made within two years of acceptance,[596] even if they are no longer in priority need, provided that they are not ineligible when that application is made nor had become homeless intentionally.[597] Where the authority failed to explain the effect of s 195A(2) (further assistance within two years), its duty had not come to an end.[598]

---

593 If a Welsh authority arranges for the provision of private rented sector accommodation in England, then the period is six months: see H(W)A 2014, s 76(4)(c).

594 HA 1996, s 193(7AC). There is no equivalent in Wales.

595 The authority may need to prove that this statement was provided, as it has been held that a court will not presume that it has done so in the absence of evidence, so that there was no qualifying offer: *R (SH) v Waltham Forest LBC* [2019] EWHC 2618 (Admin); [2021] HLR 10.

596 Homelessness in this case arises when a valid notice under HA 1988, s 21, expires (HA 1996, s 195A(2)).

597 HA 1996, ss 193(7AA)–(7AD), 195A(1), (5), (6). Similar provision is made for those threatened with homelessness, which is defined as arising once a valid notice under HA 1988, s 21 is served: HA 1996, s 195A(2).

598 *Norton v Haringey LBC* [2022] EWCA Civ 1340; [2023] HLR 3, followed in *Zaman v Waltham Forest LBC; Uduezue v Bexley LBC* [2023] EWCA Civ 322; [2023] HLR 30.

RENTERS (REFORM) BILL

Once the provisions of the Bill come into full relevant force and subject to any transitional provisions, consequent on the repeal of s 195A (re-application within two years after private rented sector offer – see para **3.2**), the requirement to inform the applicant about the effect of s 195A (which will be repealed) to be found in s 193(7AB) will also be repealed.

8.269   In Wales, applicants need only be informed in writing of the consequences of refusal and acceptance and of their right to seek a review.[599]

8.270   While there is (in these cases) still a requirement that the authority considers the accommodation suitable[600] for the applicant, there is no requirement that the authority additionally considers it reasonable[601] for the applicant to accept the offer.[602] The latter is replaced by a prohibition on the offer if the applicant is under contractual or other obligations in respect of their existing accommodation which they cannot bring to an end before being required to take up the offer.[603]

8.271   In *Norton*,[604] On 8 January 2021, the authority's offer stated that the tenancy would be an assured shorthold tenancy for a term of 24 months but did not say when it would start – although the authority knew the terms of the applicant's current accommodation, which it had provided under licence, it needed to be satisfied, at the time it approved the offer, that she could bring the licence to an end before being required to take up the offer; to be satisfied of that, the authority had to know when she would be required to take up the offer, a question the authority had not addressed; the authority could therefore not have been satisfied that she could bring her licence to an end before being required to accept the offer and was prevented from approving it by s 193(7F).

Restricted cases

England pre-LA 2011 and Wales pre-H(W)A 2014

8.272   The following provisions governing restricted cases applied until the LA 2011, s 148 came into force in England,[605] and continue to apply to applications

---

599   H(W)A 2014, ss 76(3), 84.
600   HA 1996, s 193(7F); H(W)A 2014, s 76(2).
601   HA 1996 193(7F) as it read prior to amendment by LA 2011.
602   Para **8.263**.
603   HA 1996, s 193(7F), (8). This does not apply where the authority relies on cessation of duty under s 193(6) – see recently *Querino v Cambridge CC* [2024] EWCA Civ 314; HLR forthcoming at [47], in which it was also held – at [45] – that where the landlord under the existing accommodation is the authority itself, it may be possible for the authority to be satisfied that the existing accommodation can be brought to an end on the basis that it has the power to ensure that the applicant is able to do so, ie notwithstanding the contractual arrangement.
604   *Norton v Haringey LBC* [2022] EWCA Civ 1340; [2023] HLR 3.
605   9 November 2012: Localism Act 2011 (Commencement No 2 and Transitional Provisions) (England) Order 2012, SI 2012/2599, art 2.

made before that date, in relation to which the duty to secure accommodation had arisen but had not ceased by it,[606] and in Wales they apply to applications made prior to 27 April 2015.[607]

8.273   A restricted case[608] is one where the authority is only satisfied that the applicant is homeless, threatened with homelessness or in priority need because of a restricted person.[609]

8.274   If the authority only owes a full housing duty[610] to the applicant because of the restricted person, then, so far as reasonably practicable, it must bring the duty to an end by making a private accommodation offer.[611] Where it is not reasonably practicable to do so, the authority may discharge its duty under the other provisions of HA 1996, s 193, but should continue to try to bring the duty to an end with a private accommodation offer.[612]

8.275   A private accommodation offer is of an assured shorthold tenancy made by a private landlord[613] to the applicant in relation to any accommodation which is, or may become, available for the applicant's occupation, which is made with the approval of the authority in pursuance of arrangements made between it and the landlord with a view to bringing the authority's duty to an end; the tenancy must be for a fixed term of at least 12 months.[614]

RENTERS (REFORM) BILL

Although they should be few, it remains the case that an applicant in this class (pre-9 November 2012) may still not have been made an offer complying with s 193(5)-(7F). Once the provisions of the Bill come into full relevant force and subject to any transitional provisions, assured shorthold tenancies will cease to be available and there will therefore be no requirement that the duty towards a restricted case is (so far as reasonably practicable) to be discharged with such an offer; instead, there will be a new mandatory ground for possession (Housing Act 1988, s 7), Ground 5G, where the grant of the tenancy was in pursuance of a local housing authority's duty to the tenant under section 193 of the Housing Act 1996, the local housing authority has

---

606 Localism Act 2011 (Commencement No 2 and Transitional Provisions) (England) Order 2012, SI 2012/2599, art 3.
607 For applications made on or after that date, the H(W)A 2014 applies: see Housing (Wales) Act 2014 (Commencement No 3 and Transitory, Transitional and Saving Provisions) Order 2015, SI 2015/1272, art 7.
608 HA 1996, s 193(3B). See paras **A.117–A.133**.
609 HA 1996, s 184(7).
610 Under HA 1996, s 193(2).
611 HA 1996, s 193(7AD).
612 Department of Communities and Local Government (DCLG) Guidance Note, 16 February 2009, para 14.
613 Ie, any landlord other than one within HA 1985, s 80 and thus including a private registered provider of social housing (England) or a registered social landlord (Wales): HA 1996, s 217 and H(W)A 2014, s 99.
614 HA 1996, s 193(7AC).

notified the landlord that the tenancy is no longer required for the purposes of that duty, and the date specified in the notice of proceedings for possession is within 12 months following the date on which the authority so notified the landlord.

8.276 When making a private accommodation offer, the authority must inform the applicant[615] in writing of the possible consequences of refusal and of the right to request a review of the suitability of the accommodation.[616] The duty ceases if the applicant either accepts or refuses the private accommodation offer.[617]

England post-LA 2011 and in Wales post-H(W)A 2014

8.277 In a restricted case,[618] the authority must, so far as is reasonably practicable, bring the full housing duty to an end by arranging for a private accommodation offer to be made.[619]

8.278 This means an offer of an assured shorthold tenancy or, in Wales, an occupation contract, made by a private landlord to the applicant, made with the approval of the authority in pursuance of arrangements made by between it and the landlord with a view to bringing the authority's duty to an end; in England, the tenancy must be a fixed tenancy for a period of at least 12 months.[620]

RENTERS (REFORM) BILL

Once the provisions of the Bill come into full relevant force and subject to any transitional provisions, assured shorthold tenancies will cease to be available and there will therefore be no requirement that the duty towards a restricted case is (so far as reasonably practicable) to be discharged with such an offer.

8.279 The full housing duty ends if the applicant, having been informed in writing of the possible consequences of refusal of the offer and the right to

615 The authority may need to prove that this statement was provided, as it has been held (in relation to an offer under s 193(7AA)) that a court will not presume that it has done so in the absence of evidence, for which reason there had been no discharge by private accommodation offer: *R (SH) v Waltham Forest LBC* [2019] EWHC 2618 (Admin); [2021] HLR 10.
616 HA 1996, s 193(7AB).
617 HA 1996, s 193(7AA).
618 See paras **A.127–A.133**.
619 HA 1996, s 193(7AD); H(W)A 2014, s 76(6).
620 HA 1996, s 193(7AC). If a Welsh authority arranges for the provision of private rented sector accommodation in England, then the period is six months: H(W)A 2014, s 76(4)(c).

request a review of the suitability of the accommodation,[621] either accepts or refuses a private accommodation offer.[622]

8.280   The authority must inform the applicant that the basis for the decision was that the duty was only owed because of a restricted person,[623] identify the restricted person by name, and explain both why the person is a restricted person and that it is necessary to bring the duty to an end with a private accommodation offer.[624]

8.281   In Wales, as in England, a duty owed to a restricted person must, so far as is reasonably practicable, be brought to an end by securing an offer of accommodation from a private sector landlord.[625]

Re-application

England

8.282   A person towards whom the authority has been under a duty under HA 1996, s 193 which has ceased, may re-apply.[626] This prevents an authority from simply relying on the previous discharge.[627] Rather, the authority must reconsider the case, so that a new duty will arise unless the authority can properly conclude that the applicant no longer fulfils the preconditions, for example, is not eligible or had become intentionally homeless.[628] This is, however, subject to the discussion in *Fahia,*[629] *Rikha Begum*[630] and other cases of when a further application may be made and when it may be said to be identical with a previous application, such that there is no application before the authority at all.[631]

---

621   HA 1996, s 193(7AB).
622   HA 1996, s 193(7AA).
623   HA 1996, s 184(3A). Since HRA 2017 came into force in England on 3 April 2018 (Homelessness Reduction Act 2017 (Commencement and Transitional and Savings Provisions) Regulations 2018, SI 2018/167, reg 3, only applicable to applications made and reviews sought on or after that date – see reg 4), the duty also arises if the authority decides that a duty would be owed after its duty under HA 1996, s 189B(2) comes to an end: HA 1996, s 184(3A).
624   HA 1996, s 184(3).
625   H(W)A 2014, s 76.
626   HA 1996, s 193(9).
627   Cf paras **7.31–7.46**. The case-law discussed there would suggest that, notwithstanding HA 1996, s 193(9), an authority may refuse to accept a new application from an applicant who has refused a suitable offer of accommodation if the application is based on exactly the same facts.
628   See also para **8.15**, for the right to re-apply within two years even if not in priority need.
629   *R v Harrow LBC ex p Fahia* [1998] 1 WLR 1396, (1998) 30 HLR 1124, HL.
630   *Rikha Begum v Tower Hamlets LBC* [2005] EWCA Civ 340, [2005] HLR 34: HA 1996, s 193(9) is expressly considered at [53]. See also *R Kensington and Chelsea RLBC) v Ealing LBC* [2017] EWHC 24 (Admin), [2017] HLR 13 at [18].
631   See the discussion of repeat applications at paras **7.31–7.44**.

Wales

8.283   There is no measure in H(W)A 2014 equivalent to s 193(9) (see para **8.282**). However, the structure of duties achieves the same effect as an application from a person who the authority has reason to believe may be homeless or threatened with homelessness must be accepted – with duties to follow in the usual way, as discussed throughout this chapter, unless there has been a previous assessment and the authority is satisfied that the applicant's circumstances have not materially changed since the previous assessment, and there is no new information which materially affects it.[632]

ALTERNATIVE PROVISIONS UNDER THE HOMELESSNESS REDUCTION ACT 2017 – ENGLAND

Housing Act 1996, s 193A

8.284   As noted,[633] since the HRA 2017 came into force,[634] the relief duty can be brought to an end if the applicant, having been informed of the consequences of refusal and of their right to request a review of the suitability of the accommodation,[635] refuses either a final accommodation offer,[636] or a final Part 6[637] offer.[638]

8.285   The authority cannot, however, approve a final accommodation offer or make a final Part 6 offer unless it is satisfied that it is suitable for the applicant;[639] nor can it approve or make such an offer if the applicant is under contractual or other obligations in respect of their existing accommodation, which they are not able to bring to an end before they would have to take up the offer.[640]

8.286   If it is brought to an end on this basis, the principal housing duty in section 193 does not apply.[641]

632   H(W)A 2014, s 62(1), (2).
633   See paras **8.97–8.99**.
634   3 April 2018: see Homelessness Reduction Act 2017 (Commencement and Transitional and Savings Provisions) Regulations 2018, SI 2018/167, reg 3, only applicable to applications made and reviews sought on or after that date – see reg 4.
635   See para **7.196**.
636   As to which. see para **8.98**.
637   As to which. see para **8.98**.
638   HA 1996, s 193A(1), (2).
639   HA 1996, s 193A(6).
640   HA 1996, s 193A(7).
641   HA 1996, s 193A(3).

HA 1996, s 193C

8.287 Also since HRA 2017 came into force,[642] HA 1996, s 193 does not apply when either the duty towards those threatened with homelessness (paras **8.79–8.83**) or the relief duty (paras **8.88–8.103**) is brought to an end by reason of the applicant's deliberate and unreasonable refusal to co-operate (paras **8.100–8.103**).[643] In either case, however, an applicant who is homeless, eligible, in priority need and not homeless intentionally will be entitled to accommodation under HA 1996, s 193C instead.[644]

RENTERS (REFORM) BILL

Once the provisions of the Bill come into full relevant force and subject to any transitional provisions, the above paragraph will not be correct. The accommodation provisions of s193C (subs (3)-(9)) will be repealed, as will be exclusion from s 193 by s 193(1A)(b). Accordingly, while the relief duty in s 189B will end, the housing duty in s 193 will be available. The following paragraphs of this chapter will therefore cease to be relevant.

8.288 The authority's duty under HA 1996, s 193C is to secure that accommodation is available for occupation by the applicant.[645] Much of the law considered in relation to s 193 will apply: the observations on availability (para **8.28**); payment (paras **8.32–8.33**); and security (paras **8.34–8.37**), subject to the same qualification applicable to assured security as in paras **8.36–8.37**, and it remains to be seen whether the exclusion from PEA 1977 (para **8.48**) applies to this duty: it is submitted that the close relationship between ss 193 and 193C suggests that it should also not do so.

8.289 Observations on defences on eviction (para **8.49**) will likewise apply should an authority seek to evict an applicant while they are still being housed under this provision. In addition, the following headings in relation to s 193 should also apply save so far as qualified specific statutory qualification: postponement of the duty (paras **8.138–8.145**); means of discharge (paras **8.148–8.159**); out-of-area placements (paras **8.160–8.182**); suitability of accommodation (paras **8.183–8.226**); keeping offers open (paras **8.227–8.233**).

8.290 The duty will cease if the applicant:

a) ceases to be eligible for assistance;

---

642 3 April 2018: Homelessness Reduction Act 2017 (Commencement and Transitional and Savings Provisions) Regulations 2018, SI 2018/167, reg 3, only applicable to applications made and reviews sought on or after that date – see reg 4.
643 HA 1996, ss 195(10), 189B(9).
644 HA 1996, s 193C(3), (4).
645 HA 1996, s 193C(3), (4).

b) becomes homeless intentionally from accommodation made available for their occupation;

c) accepts an offer of an assured tenancy from a private landlord; or

d) otherwise voluntarily ceases to occupy, as their only or principal home, the accommodation made available for their occupation.[646]

8.291 The duty will also cease if the applicant, having been informed of the possible consequences of refusal or acceptance and of their right to request a review[647] of the suitability of the accommodation, refuses or accepts a final accommodation offer, or a final Part 6 offer.[648] A final accommodation offer is an offer of an assured shorthold tenancy made by a private landlord – including a private registered provider of social housing (PRP) (England) or a registered social landlord (RSL) (Wales) – in relation to any accommodation which is, or may become, available for the applicant's occupation, made, with the approval of the authority, in pursuance of arrangements made by the authority in discharge of the HA 1996, s 193C duty, which is a fixed term tenancy for a period of at least six months.[649] A final Part 6 offer is an offer of accommodation under HA 1996, Part 6 made in writing in discharge of the authority's HA 1996, s 193C duty, which states that it is a final offer for that purpose.[650]

8.292 The authority cannot approve a final accommodation offer or make a final Part 6 offer unless it is satisfied that it is suitable for the applicant;[651] nor can it approve or make such an offer if the applicant is under contractual or other obligations in respect of their existing accommodation, which they are not able to bring to an end before they would have to take up the offer.[652]

---

646 HA 1996, s 193C(5).
647 See paras **7.199–7.204**.
648 HA 1996, s 193C(6).
649 HA 1996, s 193C(7).
650 HA 1996, s 193C(8).
651 HA 1996, s 193C(9).
652 HA 1996, s 193C(10).

CHAPTER 9

Allocations

355

INTRODUCTION

9.1   Local authorities hold the bulk of their housing stock under Housing Act (HA) 1985, Part 2.

9.2   Until 1996, the statutory constraints on the allocation of that stock were to be found in HA 1985, s 22, which required that in the selection of tenants, certain groups were to be given a reasonable preference, including (by amendment in 1977) homeless people, a formulation so loose that there was negligible case-law under it.

9.3   Under HA 1985, Part 3, duties towards the homeless could be discharged by allocating housing held by the authority under HA 1985, Part 2 or any other power.[1] The Housing Act (HA) 1996 was intended to reduce the proportion of permanent housing which went directly to homeless people, whether from an authority's own stock or by way of nomination to the stock of registered providers of social housing; accordingly, it repealed and replaced HA 1985, s 22,[2] with, among other provisions regulating allocation, its own categories of reasonable preference.

9.4   Under the 1996 Act, homelessness was not in itself one of the grounds of preference – although the homeless could qualify, along with others, on the grounds of, for example, unsatisfactory housing conditions, temporary or

---

1   HA 1985, s 69(1)(a).
2   See paras **1.100–1.106.**

insecure housing, a particular need for settled accommodation, or social or economic circumstances which made it difficult for an applicant to secure settled accommodation.[3]

9.5   HA 1996 also introduced a statutory requirement to maintain a housing register, which the authority could keep in such form as it thought fit and which it could, if it wished, maintain in common with other landlords, eg, other social housing landlords.[4]

9.6   In 1997, following the general election of that year, a degree of direct priority for homeless people was restored in the allocation of permanent stock by regulations.[5]

9.7   Subsequently, the Homelessness Act 2002 extensively amended HA 1996, Part 6,[6] primarily:

a)   to remove the detailed requirements governing the housing register;

b)   to remove the power of local authorities to impose blanket restrictions on groups of people;[7]

c)   to introduce arrangements to exclude or give a lower priority to those guilty of 'serious unacceptable behaviour'; and

d)   to advance the policy of more applicant choice in the allocation of housing.

9.8   In England, the provisions were changed again by the Localism Act (LA) 2011, primarily by re-introducing a right for local authorities to determine for themselves who qualifies for an allocation, subject to any regulations which require them to include or exclude specified classes of person.

9.9   This chapter addresses allocations under the following headings:

a)   meaning of 'allocation';

b)   qualifying persons;

c)   applications for housing;

---

3   HA 1996, s 167 as enacted.
4   See generally, HA 1996, ss 162–166 as enacted; as to common registers, see HA 1996, s 162(3).
5   Allocation of Housing (Reasonable and Additional Preference) Regulations 1997, SI 1997/1902.
6   The amendments came into force in Wales on 27 January 2003 (Homelessness Act 2002 (Commencement) (Wales) Order 2002, SI 2002/1736) and 31 January 2003 in England (Homelessness Act 2002 (Commencement No 3) (England) Order 2002, SI 2002/3114).
7   A practice facilitated by the wording of the former HA 1996, s 161(4), which provided that authorities could decide what classes of persons were or were not 'qualifying persons' for the purposes of an allocation of housing.

d) the allocation scheme;

e) procedure;

f) internal reviews and challenges; and

g) allocation of housing by registered providers of social housing/registered social landlords.

9.10 Criminal offences which may be committed in relation to housing applications under HA 1996, Part 6 – as under Part 7 – are considered in Chapter 12. The Secretary of State[8] and Welsh Ministers[9] have power – which has been exercised – to issue guidance to local authorities on the exercise of their functions under Part 6.[10]

9.11 The interaction of allocation schemes with other statutory duties, in particular the Care Act 2014 and Children Act (CA) 1989, ss 17 and 20, is considered in chapter 11.

MEANING OF 'ALLOCATION'

9.12 The provisions of HA 1996, Part 6 apply only to the allocation of housing accommodation, as defined by HA 1996, s 159(2).[11]

---

8   HA 1996, s 169.
9   H(W)A 2014, s 98.
10 *Allocation of accommodation: guidance for local housing authorities in England,* Department for Communities and Local Government (DCLG) (now the Ministry of Housing, Communities and Local Government (MHCLG)), 2012, as amended from time to time (most recently October 2023) (www.gov.uk/guidance/allocation-of-accommodation-guidance-for-local-authorities); as with the English *Homelessness code of guidance for local authorities,* (MHCLG,; www.gov.uk/guidance/homelessness-code-of-guidance-for-local-authorities) central government practice is to update the Allocations Guidance online, without re-issuing it: while changes (and when they were made) are identified in a Version Control Sheet, this can pose difficulties in relation to challenges based on a failure to have regard to guidance – hence, authorities and advisers would be well advised to put measures in place to retain previous guidance in a format which allows them to be retrieved if needed. See also para **10.51**. In Wales, see the *Code of guidance for local authorities on the allocation of accommodation and homelessness,* Welsh Government, March 2016 (gov.wales/allocation-accommodation-and-homelessness-guidance-local-authorities). See also the Housing Association Circular RSL 004/15 (replacing circular RSL 003/12, which itself replaced RLS 023/09) which requires all housing associations registered in Wales to take account of the Welsh Allocations Guidance.
11 An authority will not normally owe a duty of care to anyone seeking an allocation under HA 1996, Part 6; the remedy for a person dissatisfied with a decision is to seek internal review or use the ombudsman service: *R (Darby, as administratix of the estate of Lee Rabbetts) v Richmond upon Thames LBC* [2015] EWHC 909 (QB). As to internal review, see paras **9.162–9.165**; and see paras **9.175–9.180** on the Housing Ombudsman Service. Ultimately, judicial review may be available.

Selecting a person to be a secure or introductory tenant (England) or a secure contract holder or introductory standard contract holder (Wales)

9.13   Any selection of a person to be a secure[12] or introductory tenant (or, in Wales, contract holder),[13] whether or not of property held under HA 1985, Part 2, is an allocation.[14] Selection is not synonymous with the grant of a tenancy:[15] the provisions accordingly govern how people are selected to become tenants, but the grant itself is a separate process under HA 1985, Part 2; it follows that a grant that is not in accordance with the HA 1996, Part 6 allocations policy of the authority is not invalid[16] for that reason.[17]

9.14   For this purpose, 'tenancy' includes 'licence'.[18]

9.15   'Selection' includes notifying a tenant or licensee who is not currently secure that they are to become so.[19] The transition from introductory to secure tenant, effected by the passage of time,[20] is not, however, a selection in itself: the allocation process was at the introductory tenancy stage.[21]

Nominations

9.16   Nomination of a person to be the secure or introductory tenant (or licensee) of another, for example, of a housing action trust, is an allocation.[22]

9.17   Likewise, the nomination of a person to become an assured tenant of a private registered provider of social housing (PRP) or registered social landlord (RSL) is an allocation: accordingly, this does not include a nomination to a tenancy that will not be assured under HA 1988, Sch 1, but it does include nomination to an assured shorthold.[23]

---

12   HA 1985, Part 4 (England); Renting Homes (Wales) Act 2016, Part 2 (RH(W)A 2016).
13   Introductory tenancies were brought in by HA 1996, Part 5 Chapter 1. Introductory standard contracts in Wales were brought in by RH(W)A 2016, Sch 3.
14   HA 1996, s 159(2)(a) – England; HA 1996, s 159(2)(d) – Wales.
15   Ie, the disposal of stock by way of the grant of a tenancy, under HA 1985, s 32.
16   Cf para **9.88**.
17   *Birmingham City Council v Qasim* [2009] EWCA Civ 1080, [2010] HLR 19.
18   HA 1996, s 159(3), applicable in both England and Wales; see also HA 1985, s 79(3) (England) and RH(W)A 2016, s 1(1) (Wales).
19   HA 1996, s 159(3). For example, under HA 1985, Sch 1, paras 4 (homeless persons), 5 (temporary accommodation for persons taking up employment) and 10 (student lettings), as amended by HA 1996, Schs 16 and 17.
20   HA 1996, s 125.
21   Ibid.
22   HA 1996, s 159(2)(b) – England; HA 1996, s 159(2)(e) – Wales.
23   HA 1996, s 159(2)(c).

RENTERS (REFORM) BILL

There will be no nominations to assured shorthold tenancies once the provisions of the Bill come into full relevant force.

9.18   Nominations include those made in pursuance of an arrangement (whether or not legally enforceable) to require that accommodation is made available to a person or a number of persons nominated by the authority.[24]

9.19   These provisions reflect long-standing arrangements with housing associations and trusts to which funding has been provided,[25] linked to a right on the part of an authority to nominate a proportion (or even all) of the tenants to a particular property, group of properties (for example, block of flats), or to an association's stock as a whole.

9.20   The wording of HA 1996, s 159(4) is oxymoronic: if the entitlement is to 'require' that accommodation is made available to a person or number of persons, it is 'legally enforceable'. It may be that what was in mind is that a particular nomination is not legally enforceable, because such arrangements commonly work by way of proportions of voids, but the wording does not lend itself to this, because it is the arrangement that must 'require' – even if putatively not 'legally enforceable'. To give the wording some meaning (within the apparent intention of the provision), it would seem that a voluntary nomination arrangement not made by deed and for which there is no consideration will still qualify.

Exemptions

9.21   In England, HA 1996, s 159(4A) and (4B)[26] provide that the allocation provisions do not apply to anyone who is already a secure or introductory tenant, or an assured tenant of a PRP or an RSL, unless the person has applied to the authority for a transfer and the authority decide that the applicant is entitled to a reasonable preference[27] in the allocation.[28]

---

24 HA 1996, s 159(4).
25 Whether under Local Government Act 1988, Part 3 or HA 1996, s 22. (Since 1 April 2010, the latter provision has only been applicable in Wales as a result of amendments by Housing and Regeneration Act 2008.)
26 As amended by the Homelessness Act 2002, s 13 and the LA 2011, s 145.
27 See paras **9.89–9.96**.
28 HA 1996, s 159(4A), (4B), as amended by LA 2011, s 145(2). So far as concerns assured tenants, the wording is difficult: HA 1996, s 159(4B) refers to someone within s 159(4A)(a) or (b), the former referring to local authority tenants, the latter to private registered providers and registered social landlords; it is, however, an unusual use of the word 'transfer' and if s 159(4B) had only referred to s 159(4A), it may have been assumed that it applied only to local authority tenants.

9.22 The position is slightly different in Wales:[29] HA 1996, s 159(5) exempts from these allocation provisions an allocation to anyone who is already a tenant under a secure or introductory standard contract, unless the allocation involves a transfer of housing accommodation for that person which has been made on their application.[30] Those moved at the behest of the landlord – for example, for redevelopment – are exempt from both sets of provisions.

9.23 Also exempt from HA 1996, Part 6 are the categories specified in HA 1996, s 160:

a) succession to secure tenancy (or a secure occupation contract) on death, or devolution of a fixed term in such circumstances that the tenancy remains secure;[31]

b) assignment by way of exchange of secure tenancy (or a secure occupation contract) or to a person who could have succeeded to it;[32]

c) transfers by way of surrender and re-grant where one of the tenancies is a flexible tenancy[33] or an assured shorthold tenancy or a secure occupation contract;[34]

d) transfers of secure or introductory tenancies or secure or introductory occupation contracts under the provisions of matrimonial and related domestic legislation;[35]

e) becoming a secure tenant following an introductory tenancy or a secure contract following either an introductory standard contract or a prohibited conduct standard contract;[36]

f) succession to an introductory tenancy;[37]

g) assignment of an introductory tenancy to a person who could have succeeded to it.[38]

---

29 HA 1996, s 159(5), as amended by the RH(W)A 2016.
30 Before amendment, transfers were also exempt. The re-inclusion within the provisions of transfer applications accords with the practice of many local authorities to deal with transfer applications on the same basis as those of new applicants (see, eg, *R v Islington LBC ex p Reilly and Mannix* (1999) 31 HLR 651, QBD).
31 HA 1985, ss 87–90; RH(W)A 2016, ss 73, 78, 80.
32 HA 1985, s 92; RH(W)A 2016, s 114.
33 See HA 1985, s 107A.
34 LA 2011, s 158; RH(W)A 2016, s 118.
35 Matrimonial Causes Act 1973, s 24; Matrimonial and Family Proceedings Act 1984, s 17; CA 1989, Sch 1 para 1; and Civil Partnership Act 2004, Sch 5, Part 2 or Sch 7 para 9(2) or (3).
36 HA 1996, s 125; RH(W)A 2016, ss 16, 117; a prohibited conduct standard contract is, broadly, analogous to a demoted tenancy in England.
37 HA 1996, s 133.
38 HA 1996, s 134.

RENTERS (REFORM) BILL

There is no amendment in the Bill of Localism Act 2011, s 158 – see (c), above; as, once the provisions of the Bill come into full relevant force, there will be no assured shorthold tenancies to transfer by surrender and regrant, and that exemption from Part 6 will cease to have any application, unless the Secretary of State exercises the power to make consequential provision by regulations, including power to amend, repeal or revoke statutory provisions.

9.24   The Secretary of State and the Welsh Ministers may prescribe other categories of allocation which are to fall outside HA 1996, Part 6, subject to restrictions or conditions, including by reference to a specific category or proportion of housing.[39]

9.25   This power has been exercised to exempt allocation of housing to:[40]

a)   those entitled to rehousing under Land Compensation Act 1973, s 39;[41]

b)   those whose homes are repurchased under HA 1985, ss 554 or 555;[42] and

c)   in England, those to whom accommodation is let on a family intervention tenancy.[43]

ELIGIBILITY AND QUALIFICATION

Ineligible applicants

9.26   The principal class of person to whom a property cannot be allocated is someone who is ineligible because of immigration status.[44] This is considered in the Annex: Immigration Eligibility. The English Allocations Guidance suggests that eligibility be considered both when an initial application is made and when considering making an allocation, especially where a substantial period of time has elapsed since the application.[45]

---

39   HA 1996, s 160(4) and (5).
40   Allocation of Housing (England) Regulations 2002, SI 2002/3264, reg 3 and Allocation of Housing (Wales) Regulations 2003, SI 2003/239, reg 3.
41   Following compulsory purchase or a number of specified actions leading to loss of the home, eg, a demolition order under HA 1985 or a prohibition order under HA 2004.
42   Repurchase of a designated defective dwelling.
43   As to family intervention tenancies, see HA 1985, s 79 and Sch 1 para 4ZA.
44   HA 1996, s 160ZA(1) in England; HA 1996, s 160A(1) in Wales.
45   English Allocations Guidance para 3.3, 'particularly where a substantial amount of time has elapsed since the original application'. There is no similar advice in the Welsh Allocations Guidance.

9.27   If a person is ineligible, then the authority may not allocate a tenancy to the person, even jointly with someone else who is qualified.[46]

9.28   This does not mean that an allocation may not be made to someone who is eligible simply because a member of their household is not, although the fact that a member is ineligible may in some circumstances need to be taken into account when determining an applicant's housing needs under an allocation scheme.[47]

9.29   This is, in any event, unlikely to arise because, under HA 1996, Part 7 or Housing (Wales) Act (H(W)A) 2014, Part 2, such cases (known as 'restricted cases') are, so far as is reasonably practicable, to be dealt with by way of an offer of private sector accommodation.

9.30   Unless a person is ineligible, they may therefore – subject to the following paragraphs – be allocated housing accommodation by an authority.[48]

Transfer applicants

9.31   Where an applicant[49] is an existing secure or introductory tenant, or an assured tenant (or, in Wales, a contract holder of any sort) of housing accommodation allocated[50] to them by a local housing authority, the applicant is not disqualified on the basis of their immigration status.[51]

Ineligibility for unacceptable behaviour in Wales

9.32   Local authorities in Wales may disqualify those who – or whose household members[52] – have been guilty of unacceptable behaviour serious enough to make them unsuitable to be tenants of the authority and who – in the circumstances at the time their application is considered – are unsuitable to be tenants of the authority because of the unacceptable behaviour.[53]

---

46   HA 1996, s 160ZA(1)(b); HA 1996, s 160A(1)(c) in Wales.
47   See paras **A.127–A.132**.
48   HA 1996, s 160A(2).
49   In England only, an applicant whom the authority considers is entitled to a reasonable preference, HA 1996, s 160ZA(5), referring to s 159(4B). See para **9.21**.
50   See para **9.21**.
51   HA 1996, s 160ZA(5) (England) and s 160A(6) (Wales).
52   'Household' is not defined, but is presumably wider than 'family'.
53   HA 1996, s 160A(7). This entitles the authority to take into account criminal convictions which are 'spent' under the Rehabilitation of Offenders Act 1974 and may even allow it to take the conviction itself into account: see the discussion at para **9.66** and *Hussain and others v Waltham Forest LBC* [2020] EWCA Civ 1539, [2021] HLR 14 disapproving *R (YA) v Hammersmith and Fulham LBC* [2016] EWHC 1850 (Admin), [2016] HLR 39.

9.33 'Unacceptable behaviour' is defined as behaviour which would, if the person was a contract holder of the authority, breach s 55 of the Renting Homes (Wales) Act 2016[54].[55]

9.34 Accordingly, a former contract holder evicted on analogous grounds could be treated as disqualified.

9.35 Section 55 covers the following matters.

(a) The contract holder has engaged or threatened to engage in conduct capable of causing nuisance or annoyance to a person with a right (of whatever description) to live in the dwelling subject to the occupation contract, or to live in a dwelling or other accommodation in the locality of the dwelling subject to the occupation contract.[56]

(b) The contract holder has engaged or threatened to engage in conduct capable of causing nuisance or annoyance to a person engaged in lawful activity in the dwelling subject to the occupation contract, or in the locality of that dwelling.[57]

(c) The contract holder has engaged or threatened to engage in conduct capable of causing nuisance or annoyance to the landlord under the occupation contract, or a person (whether or not employed by the landlord) acting in connection with the exercise of the landlord's housing management functions, which is directly or indirectly related to or affects the landlord's housing management functions.[58]

(d) The contract-holder has used or threatened to use the dwelling subject to the occupation contract, including any common parts and any other part of a building comprising the dwelling, for criminal purposes.[59]

9.36 The conduct of the contract holder includes acts or omissions as well as incitement or encouragement of any other person to act in a prohibited manner (s 55(5)).

9.37 Note that s 55 is always incorporated into an occupation contract; a claim for possession is accordingly on the basis of breach of contract which, in turn, imports the requirement that it must be reasonable to make an order for possession.[60] Authorities will therefore need to address this issue of reasonableness for themselves,[61] ie, they will need to reach a public law decision

---

54   Anti-social behaviour and other prohibited conduct.
55   HA 1996, s 160A(8).
56   RH(W)A 2016, s 55(1).
57   RH(W)A 2016, s 55(2).
58   RH(W)A 2016, s 55(3).
59   RH(W)A 2016, s 55(4).
60   RH(W)A 2016, ss 55(6), 157, 209, Sch 10.
61   See Welsh Allocations Guidance para 2.34.

(that in itself is not so unreasonable as to be irrational or perverse)[62] on whether or not a county court would have found it reasonable to make the order.

9.38   There need not have been an eviction on the particular ground relied on, only behaviour which would entitle the landlord to a possession order under one of them.[63]

9.39   Sight must not be lost of the overriding test, whether the authority is satisfied that the applicant or member of the applicant's household has been guilty of behaviour 'serious enough to make [the applicant] unsuitable to be' its tenant, and that – in the circumstances at the time of their application – the applicant is thus unsuitable.[64]

9.40   The latter qualification means that the fact that an order for possession has been made on a relevant ground will not be sufficient on its own,[65] nor will a fixed rule or practice to treat all those evicted on one of the relevant grounds as qualifying under the first limb of the test (ie, past unsuitability) be lawful.[66] The separation in HA 1996, s 160A(7) between past conduct and suitability at time of application is likely to be strictly applied.

9.41   Criminal convictions for drug-related offences can be sufficient.[67] Convictions for sexual offences, including offences against children, were sufficient to render an applicant for a transfer ineligible, even though he had been assessed as having a critical need for ground-floor accommodation and, due to his disabilities, was unable to climb stairs; if he had been allocated the ground-floor flat that he had identified, he would have had easy access to a playground, which posed an obvious risk to children in the area.[68]

9.42   Conduct leading to an outright, a suspended or a postponed order can suffice, because postponement and suspension are under s 211 and Sch 10 RH(W) A 2016, which does not come into play unless an order for possession is available. There is a difficult relationship here. In *Portsmouth City Council v Bryant*,[69] it was said that: 'In deciding whether it is reasonable to make an order under (Housing Act 1985, s 84(2)) the judge can properly take into account his power… to suspend that order.' The burden of the decision was that a court could decide to make an order because it had power to suspend or postpone knowing that it intended to do so, where if there were no such power it might not make an order at all.

---

62 See paras **10.23, 10.47**.
63 See Welsh Allocations Guidance para 2.33. Note that the Guidance has not yet been updated to reflect the changes made by RH(W)A 2016.
64 Still or, eg. if there has been a period of good behaviour, again.
65 See Welsh Allocations Guidance para 2.35.
66 See paras **10.54–10.55**.
67 *R (Dixon) v Wandsworth LBC* [2007] EWHC 3075 (Admin), [2008] JHL D21.
68 *R (M) v Hackney LBC* [2009] EWHC 2255 (Admin), [2010] JHL D1.
69 (2000) 32 HLR 906, CA, per Simon Brown LJ at 916.

9.43 It follows that there is a material difference between an outright order made under RH(W)A 2016, s 210 and one made in contemplation of the exercise of the s 211 power to suspend or postpone. On the face of it, any such order could suffice; on the other hand, if the conduct was such that a court would have been likely to suspend or postpone, it is tantamount to recognising that a court would have been operating from the premise that the conduct had not yet reached the point at which the occupier was – in terms of the overriding issue for the authority – unsuitable to be a tenant.

9.44 In turn, this should impact on the overriding issue (whether or not the conduct was sufficient to make the applicant unsuitable to be a tenant). Accordingly, it is suggested that the authority should ask itself whether it was likely that an outright, suspended or postponed order would have been made: if one of the latter two, while it still has the right to treat the applicant as unsuitable, it should nonetheless be able to justify why.

9.45 The Welsh Allocations Guidance suggests that the authority needs 'to satisfy itself that if a possession order were granted it would have been an outright order'.[70] It may be thought that this is an overstatement of the law; the essential issue is selection of tenants, to which conduct is, on the face of it, not irrelevant; on the other hand, there is much practical merit in this reconciliation.

9.46 Relevant too would seem to be the distinction drawn in some of the anti-social behaviour cases between conduct by the tenant themselves and conduct by a member of the tenant's household which the tenant had failed to control, such that an outright order might be made in the first case but a suspended order in the second, depending on the degree of acquiescence.[71]

9.47 Thus, a transfer applicant against whom a suspended order has been made (which has not subsequently led to eviction) would prima facie still be suitable.

9.48 Likewise, a person against whom a suspended order was made on the ground of, for example, nuisance and annoyance, but put into effect because of arrears,[72] would be in a different class from an applicant whose order was put into effect because of continued nuisance or annoyance.

---

70 Welsh Guidance at para 2.35.
71 See, eg, *Gallagher v Castle Vale HAT* [2001] EWCA Civ 944, (2001) 33 HLR 72; see also *Kensington and Chelsea RLBC v Simmonds* (1997) 29 HLR 507, CA, per Simon Brown LJ at 512; *Newcastle City Council v Morrison* (2000) 32 HLR 891, CA; *Manchester City Council v Higgins* [2005] EWCA Civ 1423, [2006] HLR 14; and *Knowsley Housing Trust v McMullen (by her litigation friend)* [2006] EWCA Civ 539, [2006] HLR 43. Cf *London and Quadrant Housing Trust v Root* [2005] EWCA Civ 43, [2005] HLR 28.
72 See *Sheffield City Council v Hopkins* [2001] EWCA Civ 1023, [2002] HLR 12.

Disqualification in England

Overview

9.49 The previous class of ineligibility based on anti-social behaviour was replaced in England by a power entitling the local authority to decide for itself who does – or does not – qualify for an allocation.[73] Accommodation can only be allocated to someone who qualifies according to those local criteria (or to joint tenants, one of whom so qualifies).[74] The power is, however, subject to the overriding immigration criteria considered in the Annex: Immigration Eligibility, ie, there can be no allocation in contravention of them.[75]

9.50 Although there is power to decide what persons are or are not qualifying persons,[76] it has been held that it may not be used to disqualify persons entitled to a reasonable preference: 'the duty under s 166A(3) to frame the allocation scheme so as to secure that reasonable preference is given to certain classes of people is a fundamental requirement which applies to the arrangements for allocation as a whole, including the setting of any qualification criteria under s 160ZA(7)';[77] 'on the natural interpretation of the statutory provisions the setting of the qualification criteria is subject to the reasonable preference duty'.[78] It follows that an English authority which wants to adopt a restriction similar to that applicable in Wales[79] would need to frame it carefully.

9.51 Thus, in *R (Khayyat and Ibrahim) v Westminster CC*,[80] the authority's scheme did not allow all homeless persons within the meaning of Part 7 to apply for an allocation, only those to whom an assessed housing duty under s 193(2) was owed; the authority contended that some 43.25% of all homeless applicants were accepted into its scheme which was sufficient to comply with s 166A(3)(a). The court disagreed: the authority could exclude applicants within a reasonable preference category on account of a factor of general application to all applicants which is therefore not a redefinition of the statutory scheme but not on account of a factor which is not of general application which will inevitably amount to such a redefinition; the authority's scheme was unlawful because it excluded

---

73 HA 1996, s 160ZA(7), added by LA 2011, s 146 with effect from 18 June 2012.
74 HA 1996, s 160ZA(6), added by LA 2011, s 146 with effect from 18 June 2012.
75 HA 1996, s 160ZA(7), added by LA 2011, s 146; see paras **9.26–9.30.**
76 HA 1996, s 160ZA(7). For an example of the lawful application of an allocation scheme, see *R (Kuznetsov) v Camden LBC* [2019] EWHC 1154 (Admin), [2019] JHL D66, where a challenge to the authority's disqualification of the applicant under its provision excluding persons with a 'high level of household savings or assets' failed.
77 *R (Jakimaviciute) v Hammersmith and Fulham LBC* [2014] EWCA Civ 1438, [2015] PTSR 822, [2015] HLR 5 at [26] setting out the argument for the claimant, which was upheld at [27] – exclusion of those in suitable long-term private rented accommodation. See also *R (Alemi) v Westminster City Council* [2014] EWHC 3858 (Admin) – not able to bid for local authority accommodation for first 12 months; *R (HA) v Ealing LBC* [2015] EWHC 2375 (Admin) – five-year residential qualification.
78 *Jakimaviciute* at [31].
79 Paras **9.32–9.48.**
80 [2023] EWHC 30 (Admin); [2023] HLR 23.

those who were homeless but not owed a duty under s 193(2) which prevented the majority of a reasonable preference class from applying for an allocation.

9.52   On the other hand, in *Montero*,[81] the authority's scheme provided that, subject to exceptions, people without a local connection with its area did not qualify for an allocation, defining local connection as, *inter alia*, having been resident in its area for a period of five years at the time of application. In June 2018, the claimant and her family moved to the authority's area. They lived in a two-bedroom flat let to them by a private landlord. The claimant and her husband shared one bedroom with their daughter, aged seven, while their two sons, aged 16 and 14, shared the other. She contended that, as she was living in overcrowded accommodation,[82] it was unlawful for the authority to decide that she was not a qualifying person.

9.53   The court dismissed her challenge: *Jakimaviciute* distinguished disqualifying a class of person in a way that fundamentally undermined a requirement to accord reasonable preference to a class of persons specified in s 166A(3), Housing Act 1996, and adopting a rule excluding individual applicants by reference to factors of general application, such as lack of local connection or being in rent arrears; the authority had therefore been entitled to disqualify the claimant on the basis of her lack of a local connection with its area notwithstanding that she was living in overcrowded accommodation.

9.54   Authorities are under a statutory duty – the 'public sector equality duty' – to seek to eliminate discrimination:[83] they must be careful not to offend anti-discrimination legislation in relation to those with 'protected characteristics'.[84] In addition, the allocation of housing under Part 6 is itself a provision of a service under Part 3, Equality Act 2010, which imports not only the general prohibition on unlawful discrimination (see next paragraph) but also gives rise to individually enforceable duties to make reasonable adjustments to ensure the disabled can access housing.[85]

---

81   *R. (Montero) v Lewisham LBC* [2021] EWHC 1359 (Admin); [2022] HLR 4.
82   And as such had a reasonable preference – para **9.89.**
83   Equality Act (EqA) 2010, s 149. Authorities should carefully consider what statistical data monitoring needs to be carried out in order to ensure that they have all relevant information about how persons with protected characteristics are affected by the allocation scheme because, without such data, it is likely to be difficult to show how the authority has had due regard to this duty: see the discussion (in the context of the provision of housing to pregnant and new mothers who were asylum seekers/failed asylum seekers) in *R (DXK) v Secretary of State for the Home Department* [2024] EWHC 579 (Admin).
84   EqA 2010, s 4: age; disability; gender reassignment; marriage and civil partnership; pregnancy and maternity; race; religion or belief; sex; and sexual orientation. Some of these (age; marriage and civil partnership) are not protected in relation to the disposal and management of premises, but it may be doubted whether disposal here goes as far as formulating an allocation scheme: see EqA 2010, s 38: '(3) A reference to disposing of premises includes, in the case of premises subject to a tenancy, a reference to– (a) assigning the premises, (b) sub-letting them, or (c) parting with possession of them. (4) A reference to disposing of premises also includes a reference to granting a right to occupy them.'
85   *R (Nur) v Birmingham CC No.2* [2021] EWHC 1138 (Admin); [2021] HLR 41.

9.55   Discrimination may be:

a)   direct discrimination, ie, treating a person less favourably because of a protected characteristic[86] – although treating the disabled more favourably is not discrimination;[87] or

b)   indirect discrimination, as defined:[88] this occurs if the authority applies to an applicant a provision, criterion or practice (PCP) which is discriminatory in relation to a relevant protected characteristic,[89] meaning a provision, criterion or practice which, while applied to others, puts, or would put, persons with that characteristic at a particular disadvantage when compared to persons without it, which provision, criterion or practice cannot be shown to be a 'proportionate means of achieving a legitimate aim'; or[90]

c)   discrimination arising from a disability:[91] this occurs where a person discriminates against a disabled person by treating that person unfavourably because of something arising in consequence of their disability and the discrimination cannot be shown to be a proportionate means of achieving a legitimate aim; it is a defence to show that the alleged discriminator did not know and could not reasonably be expected to have known that the person had the disability.

9.56   These provisions do not prohibit positive action to alleviate disadvantage (eg, positive discrimination);[92] nor do they prevent a charity taking proportionate steps to meet its charitable objectives.[93]

9.57   Authorities are also prohibited from discriminating under Article 14 of the European Convention on Human Rights (ECHR).[94] Thus, in *R (HA) v Ealing LBC*,[95] a requirement that applicants had lived in the borough for five years was held to violate Article 14[96] in respect of female victims of domestic violence; on the other hand, in *R (H) v Ealing LBC*,[97] a majority of the Court of Appeal expressed the provisional view that the provision and allocation of social housing

---

86   EqA 2010, s 13.
87   EqA 2010, s 13(3).
88   EqA 2010, s 19.
89   EqA 2010, s 19(1). Indirect discrimination does not apply to the protected characteristic of pregnancy and maternity: EqA 2010, s 19(3).
90   EqA 2010, s 19(2).
91   EqA 2010, s 15.
92   EqA 2010, s 158.
93   EqA 2010, s 193. See paras **9.64–9.65**.
94   Article 14 provides that the rights protected by the ECHR must be enjoyed by all persons without discrimination on 'any ground such as sex, race, colour, language, religion, political or other opinion, national or social origin, association with a national minority, property, birth or other status'. Although disability discrimination is not expressly mentioned in Article 14, it has been held that it is also prohibited under Article 14: *AM (Somalia) v Entry Clearance Officer* [2009] EWCA Civ 634, [2009] UKHRR 1073.
95   [2015] EWHC 2375 (Admin).
96   It also offended the prohibition on the exclusion of those with a reasonable preference: para **9.50.**
97   [2017] EWCA Civ 1127, [2018] HLR 2.

was a social welfare benefit which did not, without more, fall within the ambit of Article 8, so that no issue under Article 14 would arise.

9.58   In *R (Gullu) v Hillingdon LBC; R (Ward) v Hillingdon LBC*,[98] a requirement of 10 years continuous residence was quashed as discriminatory against both Irish Travellers and refugees who had been granted asylum, both of which groups were likely to have been disadvantaged by the rule. Hillingdon made no attempt to justify the discrimination as there had been no consideration of the particular circumstances of either group. It was, however, held that the public sector equality duty does not require a policy-maker to assess the potential indirect discrimination of every conceivable group that shares a protected characteristic so that if a policy-maker has given adequate thought to deciding which groups ought to be considered, the fact that a particular protected group has not been considered does not of itself necessarily mean that there has been a breach of the public sector equality duty.[99]

9.59   Concluding that there was no evidence to show that other provisions in the authority's scheme eliminated the discrimination but that at least in theory it might be possible to justify the requirement, which Hillingdon had not done, a declaration was made to the effect that the policy amounted to unlawful indirect discrimination and that Hillingdon had not yet shown any basis for justifying that discrimination. Review and reconsideration by Hillingdon led to the conclusion that no change need be made to its scheme: a further challenge again held that the authority had not justified the discrimination – there was no evidence that the authors of the review had sought advice or assistance from external sources, such as the Equality and Human Rights Commission (EHRC), about the circumstances of Irish Travellers seeking accommodation; nor had any inquiries been made of Irish Travellers living in the authority's area; nor did the review give a clear analysis of how the residence requirement impacted on Irish Travellers in practice.[100]

9.60   In *R. (TX) v Adur DC*,[101] the authority's scheme provided that applicants who did not live in its area but who did have a local connection with it could apply but could not qualify for either of its top two bands: these were available to those with the appropriate needs who had been residing in its area for two years and to those employed in its area. The applicant left her partner because of domestic abuse and went to live with her mother in the authority's area, and applied under Part 6. The could held that the policy was indirectly discriminatory against women as they were significantly more likely than men to have to flee domestic abuse and move to another area, and were disadvantaged because they were less likely to get an allocation from the two lower bands. Nor had the authority provided any evidence to show that it had considered the effect of the

---

98   [2019] EWCA Civ 692, [2019] PTSR 1738, [2019] HLR 30.
99   *Gullo and Ward* at [72].
100 *R (TW and others) v Hillingdon LBC (No 2)* [2019] EWHC 157 (Admin), [2019] HLR 23.
101 [2022] EWHC 3340 (Admin); [2023] HLR 17.

reduction in banding on women fleeing domestic abuse so that, while removing the limitation would have a knock-on effect on other applicants, it could not show that the effect was proportionate and, if so, why.[102]

9.61   An allocation scheme which gave priority to people who were working or who volunteered in the local community was held to be indirectly discriminatory against disabled persons,[103] but the discrimination was justified: it was legitimate for the authority to seek to ensure that their tenants included a reasonable proportion of working people and to encourage volunteering.[104] The scheme accorded with the English Allocations Guidance, which encourages authorities to 'consider how they can use their allocation policies to support those households who want to work as well as those who . . . are contributing . . . through voluntary work' (Guidance, para 2.27). There was no alternative measure which could have been applied to achieve these legitimate aims.

9.62   Likewise, an allocation scheme which reserved a proportion of lettings for working households was indirectly discriminatory against women (as persons likely to be caring for children), the elderly and the disabled because they were less likely to be able to secure paid employment but the discrimination was justified as the authority was entitled to reward those who were in work and encourage others to seek work; the policy was a rational means of achieving those legitimate aims.[105]

9.63   See also *R (C) v Islington LBC*,[106] in which it was held that provisions of an allocation scheme which prioritised existing social housing tenants who wanted to move were potentially discriminatory against homeless people, victims of domestic violence and women; any discrimination was, however, justified as it served the legitimate purpose of encouraging existing tenants to move to smaller homes and free up larger units.[107] In *Willott*,[108] a challenge based in part on disability[109] failed both for want of sufficient evidence to make out discrimination and also because the relevant provisions of the scheme were proportionate.

9.64   In *R (Z and another) v (1) Hackney LBC (2) Agudas Israel Housing Association Ltd*,[110] the claimants were awaiting an allocation of social housing from Hackney LBC, which was entitled to make nominations to the defendant

---

102 A further decision had been made before the hearing, reducing the claimant's banding still further, because of a housing-related debt: the authority's contention that this made the judicial review proceedings academic was rejected – the issue affected others and was not limited to the claimant's personal circumstances.
103 Who would be less likely to be able to work or to volunteer.
104 *R (XC) v Southwark LBC* [2017] EWHC 736 (Admin), [2017] HLR 24. See also *R (TW and others) v Hillingdon LBC (No 2)* [2019] EWHC 157 (Admin), [2019] HLR 23.
105 *R (H) v Ealing LBC* [2017] EWCA Civ 1127, [2018] HLR 2.
106 [2017] EWHC 1288 (Admin), [2017] HLR 32.
107 The claim was, however, allowed in part on a different point, see para **9.152**.
108 *R (Willott) v Eastbourne BC* [2024] EWHC 113 (Admin); [2024] HLR forthcoming.
109 See para 9.100.
110 [2020] UKSC 40, [2020] 1 WLR 4327, [2020] HLR 48.

housing association, a charitable housing association whose allocation policy prioritised Orthodox Jews. It averaged only 12–13 lettings a year which, because demand outstripped supply, were all allocated to Orthodox Jews. The claimants contended that this amounted to unlawful discrimination.

9.65 The claim was dismissed: Orthodox Jews faced real and substantial disadvantage in society, suffering from very high levels of poverty and deprivation and low levels of home ownership; there was also widespread anti-Semitism and anti-Semitic crime. A small housing association which existed to provide a safe community for Orthodox Jews was engaging in positive discrimination within EqA 2010, s 158, which permits discrimination by proportionate means to alleviate disadvantage. The exception in EqA 2010, s 193 was also engaged: the policy comprised proportionate steps by a charity to meet its charitable objectives (s 193(2)(a));[111] moreover, there was no requirement for a proportionality assessment under s 193(2)(b).[112]

9.66 It would seem that an authority cannot rely on a criminal conviction which is 'spent' for the purposes of the Rehabilitation of Offenders Act (ROA) 1974 to exclude an otherwise qualified applicant, although it can rely on the facts which gave rise to it;[113] it seems that it can even rely on the conviction itself using the power in ROA 1974, s 7(3), if 'justice cannot be done' without doing so, if the authority is considered a 'judicial authority'[114] within ROA 1974, s 4(6).[115]

Regulations

9.67 The power to decide who qualifies to apply is subject to the power of the Secretary of State by regulations to prescribe classes of persons who are, or are not, to be treated as qualifying persons and to prescribe criteria that may not be used in deciding what classes of persons are not qualifying persons.[116]

---

111 EqA 2010, s 193(1) provides that there is no contravention of the Act 'by restricting the provision of benefits to persons who share a protected characteristic if– (a) the person acts in pursuance of a charitable instrument, and (b) the provision of the benefits is within subsection (2)'. Section 193(2)(a) provides that benefits are within it if their provision is a 'proportionate means of achieving a legitimate aim'.

112 EqA 2010, s 193(2)(b) is an alternative basis for qualification under s 193(1) to that in s 193(2)(a) (see ibid), and applies where the provision is 'for the purpose of preventing or compensating for a disadvantage linked to the protected characteristic'.

113 *Hussain v Waltham Forest LBC* [2020] EWCA Civ 1539; [2021] HLR 14 disapproving *R (YA) v Hammersmith and Fulham LBC* [2016] EWHC 1850 (Admin), [2016] HLR 39 to the contrary effect.

114 Defined to mean 'ordinary courts of law … tribunal, body or person having power … to determine any question affecting the rights, privileges, obligations or liabilities of any person': ROA 1974, s 4(6).

115 In *Hussain v Waltham Forest LBC* [2020] EWCA Civ 1539; [2021] HLR 14, it was held, obiter, that an authority determining licence applications under Housing Act 2004, Parts 2 and 3, does so qualify, so that an authority has power to admit evidence of a spent conviction if it is satisfied that justice cannot be done without admitting that evidence.

116 HA 1996, s 160ZA(8), added by LA 2011, s 146.

Authorities may not disqualify – on the basis that they have no local connection with their areas – the following applicants:

a)   someone who is serving in the regular forces,[117] or who has served in the regular forces within five years of the date of application;

b)   someone who has recently ceased, or will cease, to be entitled to reside in accommodation provided by the Ministry of Defence following the death of that person's spouse or civil partner, which spouse or civil partner had served in the regular forces and whose death was attributable (wholly or partly) to that service;

c)   someone who is serving or has served in the reserve forces[118] and who is suffering from a serious injury, illness or disability which is attributable (wholly or partly) to that service; or[119]

d)   a person with the 'right to move'.[120]

Guidance

9.68   Since before *Jakimaviciute*,[121] guidance has stated that authorities should avoid setting qualifying criteria which disqualify groups of people whose members are likely to qualify for a reasonable preference, but has also recognised that 'authorities may wish to adopt criteria which would disqualify individuals who satisfy the reasonable preference requirements. . . . [F]or example, if applicants are disqualified on a ground of anti-social behaviour'[122], which pursuant to

---

117 The Royal Navy, the Royal Marines, the regular army or the Royal Air Force: see Armed Forces Act 2006, s 374 (applied by Allocation of Housing (Qualification Criteria for Armed Forces) (England) Regulations 2012, SI 2012/1869, reg 2).

118 The Royal Fleet Reserve, the Royal Naval Reserve, the Royal Marines Reserve, the Regular Reserve, the Army Reserve, the Royal Air Force Reserve or the Royal Auxiliary Air Force: see Armed Forces Act 2006, s 374 (applied by Allocation of Housing (Qualification Criteria for Armed Forces) (England) Regulations 2012, SI 2012/1869, reg 2).

119 Allocation of Housing (Qualification Criteria for Armed Forces) (England) Regulations 2012, SI 2012/1869, reg 3. Such persons must be given additional preference (see para **9.96**) – see HA 1996, s 166A, as amended by Housing Act 1996 (Additional Preference for Armed Forces) (England) Regulations 2012, SI 2012/2989; and see English Allocations Guidance para 4.14.

120 Allocation of Housing (Qualification Criteria for Right to Move) (England) Regulations 2015, SI 2015/967. This is a three-stage test. First, the person must be a secure or introductory tenant or an assured tenant of a social landlord (reg 4(a)); second, the person must be entitled to a reasonable preference because they need to move to a particular locality in the authority's district, where failure to meet that need would cause hardship (reg 4(b)); third, the person must have a 'need to move', either because they work in the authority's district or they have been offered work in its district and they have a genuine intention of taking up the offer (regs 4(c) and 5); see also the *Right to move: statutory guidance on social housing allocations for local housing authorities in England*, DCLG, March 2015 and *Allocation of accommodation: guidance for local housing authorities in England*, para 3.27.

121 *R (Jakimaviciute) v Hammersmith and Fulham LBC* [2014] EWCA Civ 1438, [2015] HLR 5, at [40]: see para **9.50**.

122 English Allocations Guidance para 3.27.

Jakimaviciute would appear to be unlawful,[123] although this passage is also one of those which the court considered showed that the guidance was 'unequivocal in its indication that the qualification criteria adopted by an authority form part of an allocation scheme and are subject to the reasonable preference duty.'[124] It is not easy to reconcile *Jakimaviciute* and the guidance: the former is clear that disqualification equals no preference, which is impermissible;[125] the latter – in the passages cited here – clearly envisages that a class which includes people who may well (indeed, are likely to) fall within one of the reasonable preference categories may nonetheless be disqualified.

9.69 Guidance also suggests that authorities should avoid allocating to people who already own their own homes, save in exceptional circumstances, eg, elderly owner occupiers who cannot stay in their own home and need to move into sheltered accommodation.[126] It also notes that there may be reasons for applying different qualification criteria in relation to existing tenants from those which apply to new applicants, eg, to ensure that residency requirements do not restrict existing social tenants moving to take up work or downsizing to a smaller home; and, authorities could apply different qualification criteria in relation to different stock, eg, properties which are hard to let.[127]

9.70 The guidance reminds authorities that there may always be exceptional circumstances when it will be necessary not to apply criteria in the case of an individual applicant, eg, an intimidated witness who needs to move quickly to another area; authorities are encouraged to include provision for dealing with exceptional cases within their qualification rules.[128] As with eligibility,[129] authorities are advised to consider whether an applicant qualifies for an allocation at the time of the initial application and again when considering making an allocation, 'particularly where a long time has elapsed since the original application'.[130]

9.71 Guidance issued in November 2018,[131] strongly encourages authorities which operate a residency requirement to exempt those living in a refuge or

---

123 At its para 2.4 (as published and now), the English Allocations Guidance correspondingly explains that HA 1996, s 160ZA, replacing s 160A in England, gave authorities the power to determine who qualified for an allocation: 'The power for a housing authority to decide that an applicant is to be treated as ineligible by reason of unacceptable behaviour serious enough to make him unsuitable to be a tenant is redundant and has therefore been repealed', a proposition which would seem likewise to be contradicted by *Jakimaviciute*.

124 At [40].

125 At [43]–[47].

126 English Allocations Guidance para 3.29.

127 English Allocations Guidance para 3.30.

128 English Allocations Guidance para 3.31.

129 See paras **9.26–9.30**.

130 English Allocations Guidance para 3.32.

131 *Improving access to social housing for victims of domestic abuse: Statutory guidance for local authorities to improve access to social housing for victims of domestic abuse in refuges or other types of temporary accommodation*, MHCLG, November 2018, updated January 2022 following commencement of the Domestic Abuse Act 2021 (www.gov.uk/government/publications/improving-access-to-social-housing-for-victims-of-domestic-abuse).

other similar temporary accommodation from any such requirement (para 19). In addition, in the Allocations Guidance 'the need to recover from the effects of violence or threats of violence, or physical, emotional or sexual abuse' is considered an illustration of those who need to move on medical or welfare grounds.[132] This category is in practice enhanced by the provisions of the Domestic Abuse Act 2021.[133]

Notification

9.72   If an authority decides that an applicant is ineligible or is not a qualifying person, it must serve the applicant with a written notice of that decision[134] together with the reasons for it.[135] An applicant has the right to a statutory review of that decision.[136]

Re-applications

9.73   In Wales, an applicant who is treated as ineligible due to serious unacceptable behaviour may make a fresh application if they consider that they should no longer be treated as ineligible[137] – for example, because someone who had been guilty of anti-social behaviour is no longer part of their household.[138]

9.74   Likewise, in England, an applicant who is not being treated as a qualifying person by an English authority may (if they consider that they should

---

132 English Allocations Guidance Annex 1. There is concern that victims of domestic abuse are often denied an allocation because they have no sufficient connection to the local authority to which they have applied (even where the person needs to resettle in a new area because they are at risk in the area from which they fled); the government is proposing legislation to prevent residence tests being used: see *Local connection requirements for social housing for victims of domestic abuse*, DLHUC, February 2022.

133 See paras **2.83–2.87**, **3.99**, **5.10** and **12.21**. See also *Improving access to social housing for victims of domestic abuse*, DLUHC January 2022, guidance under HA 1996, s 169, updated to reflect the commencement of DAA 2021, noting, among other matters, that 'Those who are recovering from the impact of domestic abuse are likely to have medical and welfare needs, including physical and mental health issues, which may be complex and long lasting. Children who are victims of abuse may be affected in particular. Authorities are also reminded that a serious and long-lasting mental health condition is likely to come within the definition of a disability under the Equality Act 2010' (at para 31) noting also the provisions of HA 1996, s 81ZA, inserted by DAA 2021, s 79, designed to ensure that victims of domestic abuse who are or were secure or fully assured tenants (sole or joint) and who are rehoused for reasons connected with abuse are granted fully secure tenancies rather than flexible tenancies.

134 If the notification is not received by the applicant, it is to be treated as having been received if it is made available at the authority's office for a reasonable period for collection: HA 1996, s 160ZA(10) (England) and s 160(10) (Wales).

135 HA 1996, s 160ZA(9).

136 HA 1996, s 166A(9)(c); para **9.162**.

137 HA 1996, s 160A(11).

138 Cf the distinction drawn at para **9.46**: see *Gallagher v Castle Vale HAT* [2001] EWCA Civ 944, (2001) 33 HLR 72; *Kensington and Chelsea RLBC v Simmonds* (1997) 29 HLR 507, CA.

now be treated as a qualifying person) make a fresh application to the authority for an allocation.[139]

9.75 Superficially, the entitlement to re-apply might seem to suggest an analogy with the law on re-applications for assistance under HA 1996, Part 7.[140] This would, however, be wrong because, while the test – whether the application is made on exactly the same facts – in relation to a homelessness re-application is in principle a question for the authority to determine,[141] the obligation to reconsider qualification for an allocation arises when the applicant considers that they should no longer be treated as ineligible or that they should be treated as a qualifying person.

9.76 That said, it is unlikely that an authority can be required to reconsider application after application, week in week out, each to be followed by a review,[142] without some basis for suggesting a relevant change. There would seem to be two broad approaches – either:

a) the courts will oblige authorities to engage in consideration (and review), but they will be entitled to do no more than ask whether there has been a change 'in the [applicant's] circumstances'[143] and what that change is, so that if the applicant fails to put forward anything which could justify reconsideration, the authority may reach the same decision on that basis alone; or

b) the courts will impose a somewhat more rigorous test along the lines of whether 'a reasonable applicant' could themselves consider that there had been any material change such as to lead them to consider that they should no longer be treated as ineligible or should not be treated as qualifying.

The latter seems a lot less likely.

9.77 In practice, the issue is only likely to reach court where there has been something that could lead the applicant to re-apply, both because a challenge will have to be by way of judicial review for which permission will be required and in order to procure public funding to make a claim.

9.78 Nonetheless, authorities need to determine a proper response to such applications. The safest course is for authorities to ask the applicant to identify the putative change and ensure that that they consider it along with any other material changes of which they are aware, including, for example, to their own policies and/or in the overall demographics of an area.[144] The Welsh Allocations Guidance suggests that unless there has been a considerable lapse of time, it

---

139 HA 1996, s 160ZA(11), added by LA 2011, s 146.
140 See paras **7.27–7.46**.
141 See *Rikha Begum v Tower Hamlets LBC* [2005] EWCA Civ 340, [2005] HLR 34; see para **7.37**.
142 See para **9.162**.
143 Cf the wording of HA 1996, s 160(7)(b).
144 See, in particular, HA 1996, s 166(3).

will be for the applicant to show that their circumstances or behaviour have changed,[145] ie, the first approach in para **9.76**.

Existing applicants

9.79   The eligibility provisions of HA 1996, s 160A came into force on 27 January 2003 in Wales and 31 January 2003 in England. All applicants who were on a local authority housing register immediately before that date, or who had made an application which had not yet been determined, were to be treated as persons who had applied for an allocation of housing, which had the effect of applying the provisions of HA 1996, s 160A to them.

9.80   Any entitlement to an allocation of housing will largely depend on the allocation scheme of the local housing authority to which the applicant has applied.[146] An authority must take steps to bring to the attention of those likely to be affected by it any alteration to its allocation scheme which reflects a major change of policy.[147] Some applicants may therefore find that, following a change in allocation scheme by the local housing authority, they are no longer to be entitled to an allocation of housing either because they are ineligible or because they do not satisfy the authority's qualification criteria. If an authority decides that an applicant is ineligible or is not a qualifying person, it must serve the applicant with a written notice that decision together with the reasons for it.[148] An applicant has the right to a statutory review of that decision.[149]

APPLICATIONS FOR HOUSING

Housing register

9.81   Prior to amendment by the Homelessness Act 2002, HA 1996, Part 6 required all local authorities to establish and maintain a housing register. That requirement has now been repealed.

Acceptance of applications

9.82   All applications must, if made in accordance with the procedures laid down in an authority's allocation scheme, be considered by that authority.[150] It

---

145 Welsh Allocations Guidance para 2.40.
146 See paras **9.85–9.131**.
147 HA 1996, s 168(3).
148 HA 1996, s 160ZA(9).
149 HA 1996, s 166A(9)(c).
150 HA 1996, s 166(3). Provided proper consideration has been given, a court will not interfere with the authority's findings or how it decides to treat the application: see, eg, *R (Heaney) v Lambeth LBC* [2006] EWHC 3332 (Admin), [2007] JHL D25.

is a matter for the authority how it records that application and the information contained in it.

Advice and information

9.83　All authorities must make available, free of charge, advice and information about the right to make an application for an allocation of housing.[151] They must also provide the necessary assistance in making an application to those who are likely otherwise to have difficulty in doing so.[152] All applicants must be informed of the right to request information about their applications,[153] and about any decisions made in relation to them,[154] and to seek an internal review.[155]

Disclosure of information

9.84　The fact that a person is an applicant for housing must not be disclosed – without the consent of the applicant – to any other member of the public.[156]

THE ALLOCATION SCHEME

Introduction

9.85　Each local housing authority must establish an allocation scheme for determining priorities between qualifying persons[157] and for the procedure to be followed in allocating housing accommodation.[158] Authorities in England must – when preparing or modifying their schemes – have regard to their homelessness strategy,[159] as well as to their 'current tenant strategy';[160] London boroughs will also have to have regard to the London housing strategy,[161] prepared by the Mayor.[162]

151　HA 1996, s 166(1)(a).
152　HA 1996, s 166(1)(b).
153　Under HA 1996, s 166A(9)(a) (England) or s 167(4A)(a) (Wales): see paras **9.151–9.154**.
154　Under HA 1996, s 166A(9)(b) (England) or s 167(4A)(b) (Wales): see para **9.162**.
155　Under HA 1996, s 167(4A)(c); see para **9.162**.
156　HA 1996, s 166(4). This provision does not give rise to the right to an anonymity order in court proceedings: see *XXX v Camden LBC* [2020] EWCA Civ 1468, [2021] HLR 13; see paras **10.199–10.201**.
157　See paras **9.26-9.72**.
158　HA 1996, s 167(1) (from commencement of LA 2011, s 147, in England, s 166A(1)).
159　Under Homelessness Act 2002, s 1: see paras **12.3–12.19**.
160　The strategy under LA 2011, s 150, pursuant to which authorities decide, among other matters, whether and when to grant flexible tenancies, ie, outside of full security.
161　Under LA 2011, s 151.
162　HA 1996, s 166A(12).

Interpretation

9.86   Interpretation of an allocation scheme is a matter for the court[163] – see *R (Flores) v Southwark LBC*:[164]

> '39.   The meaning of a housing allocation scheme, like that of any other comparable policy document, is for the court to determine . . . but the court's approach to its interpretation should be in accordance with the guidance given by this court in *R (Ariemuguvbe) v Islington LBC* [2009] EWCA Civ 1308, [2010] HLR 14. Sullivan LJ said:

> '24.   . . . since this is a local authority housing allocation scheme and not an enactment, it has to be read in a practical, common sense, and not in a legalistic way'.

> 40.   Lord Neuberger MR added:

> '31.   . . . While any document prepared for public consumption should be as clear, short and simple as possible, it is particularly true of housing allocation schemes required to be prepared under [what was then] Section 167, and published under Section 168, of the Housing Act 1996. They are intended to be read by, and administered for, the benefit of people who require public housing and their families, and they are intended to be applied in multifarious different circumstances in which great difficulties can often arise. . . . It is plainly right for the court to apply a common sense and a practical approach to the interpretation of the scheme, and indeed an interpretation which allows a sensible degree of flexibility when it comes to dealing with individual cases. That this approach is appropriate is reinforced by the wide discretion given to local housing authorities . . .'

Choice-based housing

9.87   The scheme must include a statement of the authority's policy on offering applicants a 'choice of housing accommodation' or 'the opportunity to express preferences' about the accommodation to be allocated to them.[165]

---

163   See also *R (Gomes) v Kensington and Chelsea RLBC* [2023] EWHC 778 (Admin), HousingView, 24 April 2023, *R (Montano) v Lambeth LBC* [2024] EWHC 249 (Admin); [2024] HLR forthcoming, below para **9.146** and *R (Nur) v Birmingham CC* [2020] EWHC 3526 (Admin), [2021] HLR 23, below, para **9.122**.
164   [2020] EWCA Civ 1697; [2021] HLR 16.
165   HA 1996, s 166A(2) (England); s 167(1A) (Wales).

Unlawful allocations

9.88 Allocation from the waiting list must be in accordance with the scheme.[166] An allocation which is not in accordance with the scheme will be ultra vires.[167] Notwithstanding what might be thought the obvious purpose of this provision, to constrain lettings that are not in accordance with the scheme, it has been held that a non-compliant tenancy is nonetheless valid.[168]

Categories of reasonable preference

Generally

9.89 When establishing priorities, a reasonable preference must be given to:[169]

a) those who are homeless (within the meaning of HA 1996, Part 7 or in Wales H(W)A 2014, Part 2);[170]

b) those who are owed a duty by any local housing authority under HA 1996, s 190(2),[171] s 193(2)[172] or s 195(2)[173] (or under HA 1985, s 65(2) or s 68(2)),[174] or, in Wales, those who are owed any duty under H(W)A 2014, s 66, s 73 or s 75;[175]

c) those in insanitary or overcrowded housing or otherwise in unsatisfactory housing conditions;

---

166 HA 1996, s 166A(14) (England). See *Sahardid v Camden LBC* [2004] EWCA Civ 1485, [2005] HLR 11; *R (Bibi) v Camden LBC* [2004] EWHC 2527 (Admin), [2005] HLR 18, where failures by the local authority to apply the scheme led to the quashing of its decisions. Cf *R (Osei) v Newham LBC* [2010] EWHC 368 (Admin), [2010] JHL D37.

167 See *R v Macclesfield BC ex p Duddy* [2001] JHL D16, QBD (allocation to a former employee outside the provisions of the scheme).

168 *Birmingham City Council v Qasim* [2009] EWCA Civ 1080, [2010] HLR 19.

169 HA 1996, s 166A(3) (England); s 167(2) (Wales).

170 See Chapter 2. The class is not qualified in any way (cf HA 1996, ss 167(2)(b) and 166A(3)(b)), and therefore encompasses those who are homeless but not in priority need. There is no requirement that an applicant should have applied as homeless before an authority must consider whether or not they qualify under this ground (again, cf HA 1996, s 167(2)(b)/s166A(3)(b)): *R (Alam) v Tower Hamlets LBC* [2009] EWHC 44 (Admin), [2009] JHL D47.

171 This is the duty to those who are in priority need but intentionally homeless. Any exclusion or reduction of preference for this group must be in accordance with HA 1996, s 160ZA(7) or s 166A(5) (England) or s 160A(7) or s 167(2A) or (2B) (Wales) see paras **8.109–8.123**.

172 The duty to those who are eligible, in priority need and not intentionally homeless: see paras **8.129** onwards.

173 The duty to those threatened with homelessness unintentionally: see para **8.80**.

174 The equivalent duties under the HA 1985 to the unintentionally homeless.

175 H(W)A 2014, s 66 – duty to help to secure accommodation for those threatened with homelessness; s 73 – initial duty owed to those who are eligible and homeless; s 75 – full duty equivalent to HA 1996, s 193(2).

d) those who need to move on medical or welfare grounds (including grounds relating to a disability);[176] and

e) those who need to move to a particular locality in the district of the authority, where failure to meet that need would cause hardship (to themselves or others).[177]

9.90 Reasonable preference must not be given to an applicant who only falls within any of the reasonable preference categories because of a restricted person.[178] A 'restricted person' is someone who is ineligible,[179] subject to immigration control,[180] and who either does not have leave to enter or remain in the UK, or whose leave is subject to a condition to maintain and accommodate themselves, and any dependants, without recourse to public funds.[181]

9.91 Additional preference may be given to sub-groups within those specified, being persons with urgent housing needs.[182] This means giving those applicants 'additional weight' or 'an extra head start, but does not require an allocation to be made to applicants entitled to it ahead of all others'.[183]

---

176 The express reference to disability was added by HA 2004, s 223 because of concerns that local authorities were interpreting the need for a move on 'medical' grounds too narrowly. The English Allocations Guidance (at its para 4.10) envisages that this could include care leavers; a person moving on from a drug or alcohol recovery programme; young adults with learning disabilities; and those who provide care or support, eg, foster carers, those approved to adopt, or those being assessed to foster or adopt, special guardians, and family and friend carers who – without fostering or adopting – have taken care of a child because the parents are unable to do so. The extension to disability is not found in H(W)A 2014, but see also Welsh Allocations Guidance paras 3.31–3.33. The 'need to recover from the effects of violence or threats of violence, or physical, emotional or sexual abuse' is an illustration of people who need to move on medical or welfare grounds in the English Allocations Guidance Annex 1 'Indicators of criteria in reasonable preference categories (c) and (d)'.

177 'This would include, for example, a person who needs to move to a different locality in order to give or receive care, to access specialised medical treatment, or to take up a particular employment, education or training opportunity': English Allocations Guidance para 4.11; similar provision is at Welsh Allocations Guidance para 3.35.

178 HA 1996, s 166A(4) (England); s 167(2ZA) (Wales).

179 See paras **A.127–A.133.**

180 See para **A.14**.

181 HA 1996, s 184(7).

182 HA 1996, s 166A(3) (England); s 167(2) (Wales). See also *R (Heaney) v Lambeth LBC* [2006] EWHC 3332 (Admin), [2007] JHL D25, where the applicant asserted that she had an urgent housing need arising out of the distress caused by continuing to live in a property in which one of her daughters had died and, as such, that she qualified within the authority's category for transfer on an urgent basis, a claim which the authority rejected. Recognising that the authority had set a high threshold for inclusion in the relevant category, and that it had considered all the evidence, the court held that the authority was entitled to reach the conclusion that the applicant did not meet the criteria.

183 *R (L and D) v Lambeth LBC* [2001] EWHC Admin 900, (2002) JHL D1 (upheld on appeal, *Lambeth LBC v A; Lambeth LBC v Lindsay* [2002] EWCA Civ 1084, [2002] HLR 57). There is nothing objectionable in an authority adopting a 'points threshold', below which an applicant cannot bid under the authority's choice procedures: *R (Woolfe) v Islington LBC* [2016] EWHC 1907 (Admin), [2016] HLR 42.

9.92   The English Guidance reminds authorities to 'consider, in the light of local circumstances, the need to give effect to this provision', offering, by way of illustration, those who need to move suddenly because of a life-threatening illness or sudden disability, families in such severe overcrowding that it poses a serious health hazard, and those who require urgent rehousing as a result of violence or threats of violence, whether intimidated witnesses or as a result of serious anti-social behaviour or domestic violence.[184]

9.93   There is no requirement for an authority to frame an allocation scheme to provide for cumulative preference, ie, affording greater priority to applicant who falls within more than category of one reasonable preference.[185]

9.94   The English guidance encourages authorities to take advantage of the flexibility available to them to meet local needs and local priorities.[186]

Regulations

9.95   The Secretary of State and the Welsh Ministers have power to specify further categories of reasonable preference or to amend or repeal any part of HA 1996, s 166A(3) (England) or s 167(2) (Wales).[187] This power has not been exercised in relation to the amended s 167(2) in Wales.

9.96   In England, this has been used[188] to provide that additional preference should be given to:

a)   former members of the armed forces;

b)   serving members who need to move because of a serious injury, medical condition or disability sustained as a result of service;

c)   bereaved spouses and civil partners of members of the armed forces leaving services accommodation following the death; and

d)   serving or former members of the reserve forces who need to move because of a serious injury, medical condition or disability sustained as a result of service who have urgent housing needs.[189]

---

184 English Allocations Guidance para 4.13.
185 *R (Ahmad) v Newham LBC* [2009] UKHL 14, [2009] HLR 31. See also English Allocations Guidance para 4.5. See further paras **9.112–9.122**.
186 English Allocations Guidance para 4.19.
187 HA 1996, s 166A(7) (England); s 167(3) (Wales).
188 HA 1996, s 166A(3) – words added by Housing Act 1996 (Additional Preference for Armed Forces) (England) Regulations 2012, SI 2012/2989. See also English Allocations Guidance para 4.14.
189 This overlaps with, but does not oust, the requirement, applicable to functions under Part 6, under Armed Forces Act 2006, ss 343AA (England) and 343AB (Wales)Added by s 8(3), Armed Forces Act 2021; see para **9.125**.

Considerations

9.97   For the purpose of determining how preference is to be awarded to those within these categories, an authority's allocation scheme may take into account:[190]

a)   the financial resources open to an applicant to meet their housing costs;

b)   any behaviour of an applicant (or a member of the applicant's household) which affects their suitability to be a tenant;[191]

c)   any local connection[192] which exists between an applicant and the authority's area.[193]

9.98   Here, therefore, authorities in England as in Wales may have regard to anti-social behaviour.

9.99   The Secretary of State and Welsh Ministers may specify factors which the local authority may not take into account when allocating housing accommodation.[194] This power has not been exercised.

9.100   Insofar as authorities can and do adopt their own policies to allocation decisions, they cannot adopt policies so rigid as to fetter their consideration of the individual circumstances of particular applicants for housing.[195] A challenge to an allocation scheme which precluded applications by persons who had engaged in unacceptable behaviour serious enough to make them unsuitable to be a tenant of the council as too rigid because it excluded those whose anti-social behaviour derived from a disability failed because personal circumstances could be considered and there was a residual discretion available permitting a senior officer to authorise a direct let which was sufficient to prevent unfairness arising.[196]

Anti-social behaviour – Wales

9.101   HA 1996, s 167 applies only in Wales. It is a discrete provision allowing an authority to afford no preference at all for an applicant who – in

---

190 HA 1996, s 166A(5) (England), s 167(2A) (Wales).
191 See further paras **9.97–9.98**.
192 As defined by HA 1996, s 199; see Chapter 5.
193 Accordingly, a scheme is not unlawful because it includes reference to whether an applicant has a local connection when determining priority as between two applicants otherwise in the same band of priority: *R (Van Boolen) v Barking and Dagenham LBC* [2009] EWHC 2196 (Admin), [2009] JHL D113.
194 HA 1996, s 166A(8) (England); s 167(4) (Wales).
195 See *R v Canterbury City Council ex p Gillespie* (1987) 19 HLR 7, QBD; *R v Bristol City Council ex p Johns* (1993) 25 HLR 249, QBD; *R v Newham LBC ex p Campbell* (1994) 26 HLR 183, QBD; *R v Newham LBC ex p Watkins* (1994) 26 HLR 434, QBD; *R v Newham LBC ex p Dawson* (1994) 26 HLR 747, QBD; *R v Islington LBC ex p Aldabbagh* (1995) 27 HLR 271, QBD; *R v Lambeth LBC ex p Njomo* (1996) 28 HLR 737, QBD; *R v Southwark LBC ex p Melak* (1997) 29 HLR 223, QBD; *R v Gateshead MBC ex p Lauder* (1997) 29 HLR 360, QBD; and *R v Lambeth LBC ex p Ashley* (1997) 29 HLR 385, QBD. See also paras **10.54–10.55**.
196 *R (Willott) v Eastbourne BC* [2024] EWHC 113 (Admin); [2024] HLR forthcoming.

the circumstances at the time their case is considered – does not deserve to be treated as a member of a group who are to be given preference, because the applicant, or a member of the applicant's household, has been guilty of such serious unacceptable behaviour that they are unsuitable to be a tenant of the authority.[197] Such behaviour is defined in the same way as for ineligibility.[198]

9.102   Thus, in Wales, there are three ways of dealing with the anti-social:[199]

a) ineligibility;[200]

b) taking the behaviour into account for the purpose of defining how preference is to be awarded within the statutory categories;[201] and

c) excluding them from any preference.[202]

Only the second of these is available in England.[203]

9.103   An applicant must be notified in writing of a decision that they are a person to whom HA 1996, s 167(2C) applies,[204] and of the grounds for it.[205] There is provision for review of such a decision.[206]

Meaning of 'reasonable preference'

Generally

9.104   The requirement to give a 'reasonable preference' to certain groups was also to be found in HA 1985, s 22. In relation to that section, reasonable preference meant that the criteria must be an 'important factor in making a decision about the allocation of housing',[207] and that 'positive favour should be shown to applications which satisfy any of the relevant criteria'.[208]

9.105   More recently, HA 1996, s 167(2)[209] was said to provide those within it with a 'reasonable head start', although still not guaranteed an allocation.[210]

197 HA 1996, s 167(2B) and (2C).
198 See paras **9.32–9.48**.
199 Whose conduct rises to the prescribed level.
200 Paras **9.32–9.48**.
201 Para **9.97**.
202 Para **9.101**.
203 See paras **9.97–9.98**.
204 HA 1996, s 167(4A)(b).
205 HA 1996, s 167(4A)(c).
206 See paras **9.162–9.165**.
207 Per Tucker J in *R v Lambeth LBC ex p Ashley* (1997) 29 HLR 385, QBD at 387.
208 Per Judge LJ in *R v Wolverhampton MBC ex p Watters* (1997) 29 HLR 931, CA at 938.
209 Which in England, is now found in HA 1996, s 166A(3).
210 See per Collins J in *R (A) v Lambeth LBC; R (Lindsay) v Lambeth LBC* [2002] EWCA Civ 1084, [2002] HLR 57 at [15].

9.106 The test is whether they are given a reasonable preference relative to persons who are not so entitled; whether a preference is reasonable is a decision for the authority; a scheme may still give reasonable preference to applicants who do not fall within HA 1996, s 166A(3) (England) or s 167(2) (Wales) provided that such non-statutory preferences do not dominate the scheme at the expense of the statutory preference categories.[211]

9.107 Reasonable preference does, however, imply a power to choose between different applicants on 'reasonable grounds . . . it is not unreasonable to prefer good tenants to bad tenants'.[212] Other grounds could include refusal of a previous, suitable offer; the refusal was a matter the authority was entitled to take into account.[213]

9.108 There is therefore no reason why an authority's own principles of allocation should not include reference to arrears of rent[214] (but not, it is suggested, other categories of debt, such as arrears of local taxation).[215]

9.109 It has been held that there was no impropriety in requiring a victim of domestic violence, whom the authority agreed ought to be rehoused, to clear her arrears from a previous tenancy before being made an offer – the authority was entitled to have regard to the fact that the claimant was one of a number of persons in need of emergency re-housing; as other such persons did not have such debts, it was not irrational to conclude that she should be given a lower priority than them.[216]

9.110 On the other hand, an authority – whose allocation scheme provided for overpayments of housing benefit to be taken into account when determining priority – could not take them into account when the overpayment was statute-barred under the Limitation Act 1980: it was unlawful and irrational to reduce the applicant's preference on account of debts which were not recoverable.[217]

---

211 *R (Lin) v Barnet LBC* [2007] EWCA Civ 132, [2007] HLR 30.
212 Per Carnwath J in *R v Newham LBC ex p Miah* (1996) 28 HLR 279, at 288.
213 *R (Cranfield-Adams) v Richmond upon Thames LBC* [2012] EWHC 3334 (Admin), [2012] All ER(D) 114 (Jun).
214 *R v Newham LBC ex p Miah*, above; *R v Lambeth LBC ex p Njomo* (1996) 28 HLR 737, QBD; *R v Islington LBC ex p Aldabbagh* (1995) 27 HLR 271, QBD. See now HA 1996, ss 166A(5) (b) and 167(2A)(b), and in Wales (2B) and (2C) allowing behaviour to be taken into account. They may also go to discretionary disqualification under s 160A(7) in Wales.
215 *R v Forest Heath DC ex p West and Lucas* (1992) 24 HLR 85, CA: all local taxpayers are to be treated the same way, regardless of their need for housing.
216 *R (Osei) v Newham LBC Lettings Agency* [2010] EWHC 368 (Admin), [2010] JHL D37. A policy of not allocating to those in arrears also prevented an allocation on the basis of overcrowding in *R (Babakandi) v Westminster City Council* [2011] EWHC 1756 (Admin), [2011] JHL D105, although the Director of Housing had a discretion not to apply the policy in 'exceptional circumstances'; the fact that those circumstances were not spelled out did not make the scheme unlawful.
217 *R (Joseph) v Newham LBC* [2009] EWHC 2983 (Admin), [2010] JHL D37.

9.111   The requirement to give a reasonable preference to the specified groups does not prevent an authority allocating a quota of all vacancies to one particular group (for example, homeless persons).[218] In *Jaberi*,[219] the policy provided for fewer points to be given to an applicant to whom the authority owed a duty under s 193(2), even if they also had a medical need, than an applicant with only a medical need to move: while this might superficially seem incongruous, the authority was entitled to proceed on the basis that it would discharge its s 193(2) duty by providing what would be accommodation that was suitable for the applicant, at least in the short term, much sooner than the applicant with only a medical need to move would be allocated a property; moreover, fewer points would not necessarily mean a lesser chance of successfully bidding for a property as the number of allocations allowed to the different groups was not the same.[220]

R (Ahmad) v Newham LBC

9.112   A line of cases on reasonable preference within local authority allocation schemes was reversed by the House of Lords in *Ahmad*.[221] Those cases had held that a reasonable authority is bound to include within its scheme a mechanism for identifying, and giving added preference, to those with 'cumulative need', ie, who qualified within more than one category of reasonable preference.[222]

9.113   In *Ahmad*, Newham LBC's allocations policy was challenged on two principal grounds: first, that it failed to determine priority between people in the reasonable preference groups in accordance with the gravity of their individual needs, ie, cumulative needs; and second, that the policy of allocating up to five per cent of properties advertised under the authority's choice-based lettings scheme to existing tenants (without a reasonable preference) who wished to transfer to another similar property failed to give reasonable preference to those within HA 1996, s 167(2).[223]

9.114   In both the High Court and the Court of Appeal, the scheme was held to be unlawful, principally because the mechanism for determining priority between those with a reasonable preference was by length of time since registration, not

---

218 *R v Islington LBC ex p Reilley and Mannix* (1998) 31 HLR 651, QBD; *R v Westminster LBC ex p Al-Khorshan* (2001) 33 HLR 6, QBD; *R (Babakandi) v Westminster City Council* [2011] EWHC 1756 (Admin), [2011] JHL D105.
219 *R (Jaberi) v Westminster CC* [2023] EWHC 1045 (Admin), [2023] HLR 37.
220 Ie, more properties could be available for the homeless than for those with a medical need to move.
221 [2009] UKHL 14, [2009] HLR 31.
222 *R v Islington LBC ex p Reilly and Mannix* (1999) 31 HLR 651, QBD; *R v Westminster City Council ex p Al-Khorsan* (2001) 33 HLR 77; *R (A) v Lambeth LBC* [2002] EWCA Civ 1084, [2002] HLR 57. See also *R (Cali and others) v Waltham Forest LBC* [2006] EWHC 302 (Admin), [2007] HLR 1.
223 In England, see now HA 1996, s 166A(3).

by relative need.[224] The scheme was also found to be unlawful because of the allocation of five per cent of properties to tenants seeking a transfer.

9.115 The House of Lords concluded that an authority cannot be required to afford preference by reference to cumulative need,[225] as HA 1996, s 167(2)[226] provides only that a local authority may afford additional preference to those within the priority groups who have an urgent need,[227] and s 167(2A) provides only that it may determine priorities between those within priority groups by reference to other considerations.[228]

9.116 In relation to the challenge to its choice-based scheme, the authority was entitled to allocate properties to people who did not fall within a category of reasonable preference; HA 1996, s 167(2)[229] only requires that the categories set out in that subsection are given a 'reasonable preference' – it does not require that they should be given absolute priority over everyone else.[230] Moreover, allocating a proportion of the available housing stock to transfer applicants who were already tenants of the local authority neither increased nor decreased the available housing stock – the property left by the transferring tenant becomes available to others.[231]

9.117 The importance of the case is not merely the dismissal of the judicially created requirement of provision for cumulative need, but its statement about judicial intervention generally:

> '. . . as a general proposition, it is undesirable for the courts to get involved in questions of how priorities are accorded in housing allocation policies. Of course, there will be cases where the court has a duty to interfere, for instance if a policy does not comply with statutory requirements, or if it is plainly irrational. However, it seems unlikely that the legislature can have intended that Judges should embark on the exercise of telling authorities how to decide on priorities as between applicants in need of rehousing, save in relatively rare and extreme circumstances. Housing allocation policy is a difficult exercise which requires not only social and political sensitivity and judgment, but also local expertise and knowledge.[232]

---

224 Per Richards LJ [2008] EWCA Civ 140 at [69].
225 See Baroness Hale at [14] and Lord Neuberger at [39]–[43].
226 Now applicable to Wales; the same applies, however, in s 166A(3), applicable to England.
227 In England, see now HA 1996, s 166A(3).
228 In England, now s 166A(5), para **9.97**.
229 In England, see now HA 1996, s 166A(3).
230 See Baroness Hale at [18]–[19].
231 At [17]–[21].
232 This judicial restraint was applied in the planning case of *R (McDonagh) v Hackney LBC* [2012] EWHC 373, [2012] JHL D60, upholding a policy whereby Gypsies and Travellers who wanted a pitch on a caravan site had to provide documentary evidence of an address in the authority's area at which correspondence could be sent to them and to re-register every year; there was nothing irrational about the policy as it ensured that applicants had connections to the local area and that the waiting list was up-to-date.

In relation to the provision of accommodation under the National Assistance Act 1948, my noble and learned friend, Baroness Hale of Richmond, then Hale LJ, said in *R (Wahid) v Tower Hamlets London Borough Council* [2002] EWCA Civ 287, [2003] HLR 13, para 33, '[n]eed is a relative concept, which trained and experienced social workers are much better equipped to assess than are lawyers and courts, provided that they act rationally'. Precisely the same is true of relative housing needs under Part 6 of the 1996 Act, and trained and experienced local authority housing officers.

If section 167[233] carries with it the sort of requirements which can be said to be implied by the decisions of the Court of Appeal and the Deputy Judge in this case, then Judges would become involved in considering details of housing allocation schemes in a way which would be both unrealistic and undesirable. Because of the multifarious factors involved, the large number of applicants, and the relatively small number of available properties at any one time, any scheme would be open to attack, and it would be a difficult and very time-consuming exercise for a Judge to decide whether the scheme before him was acceptable. If it was not, then the consequences would also often be unsatisfactory: either the authority would be in a state of some uncertainty as to how to reformulate the scheme, or the Judge would have to carry out the even more difficult and time-consuming (and indeed inappropriate) exercise of deciding how the scheme should be reformulated to render it acceptable. As Baroness Hale said, that point is well made by looking at the Deputy Judge's order in this case, which requires the Scheme to be reconsidered 'in accordance with the law set out in this judgment'.[234]

9.118   In contrast, however, in *Birmingham City Council v Ali*,[235] the same committee of the House of Lords as in *Ahmad* – cognisant that in that case it had 'made it clear that the courts should be very slow indeed to interfere with a local housing authority's allocation policy, unless it breached the requirements of Part 6'[236] – nonetheless held that Birmingham City Council's allocations policy was unlawful by reason of irrationality.[237]

9.119   Under that policy, if it was accepted that a family was homeless because of overcrowding in, or the condition of, its current accommodation, so that a 'full' duty was owed,[238] the authority would discharge its duty under HA 1996, s 193(2) by leaving the family in the existing accommodation until suitable permanent accommodation could be found; such applicants were, however, awarded a lower priority than where the authority placed a homeless family in temporary accommodation.

---

233 In England, now HA 1996, s 166A.
234 Lord Neuberger, with whom the other members of the Committee agreed, at [46]–[48].
235 [2009] UKHL 36, [2009] HLR 41.
236 At [62].
237 See also paras **9.147–9.148**.
238 See para **8.132**.

9.120   Some caution is needed before applying this to similar policies. There was little argument on this part of the case.[239] While the conclusion of the Court of Appeal that those who were homeless in their current accommodation could not lawfully be left in it under HA 1996, Part 7[240] was not supported by the House of Lords,[241] it was only irrational on a 'relatively narrow aspect': the authority had not justified the difference in treatment – its 'bald statement' that 'those in greatest need are dealt with first' was insufficient; on the face of it, those in (their current) unsuitable accommodation were in greater need than those in other temporary accommodation which had not been subject to an unsuitability finding; if there was evidence to that effect, it had not been put forward.[242]

9.121   In the post-*Ahmad* decision of *Kabashi*,[243] the authority's allocation scheme took waiting time into account, but re-set the date whenever a change of circumstances led to re-assessment of an applicant's rehousing needs (with no residual discretion to disapply the provision). The applicant's need for a three-bedroom property changed to a need for two bedrooms, with the result that her waiting time was re-set to a later date. This was not unlawful: the authority had explained that, in its experience, those adversely affected by applicants moving from the waiting list for three-bed properties to two-bed properties perceived such interloping as unfair queue jumping; it was not for the court to second-guess that policy.

9.122   In *R (Nur) v Birmingham CC*,[244] the authority's scheme, properly construed,[245] was intended to give families with children 'a head start' but was applied so that in practice the absence of children was a decisive factor in the allocation process, with the result that an applicant whose disabled child was an adult and who was otherwise first in line for an allocation (on three occasions) was refused in favour of applicants with children; moreover, because the presence of children in the family was, in practice, the decisive factor, adapted housing had been allocated to families with children who did not need adapted properties. The authority was held to have misunderstood the effect of the scheme and had been operating it in an unlawful manner.

Children

9.123   Where an authority – as it invariably will – takes children into account for the purposes of determining priority and nature of accommodation under its scheme, a child arrangement order under CA 1989, s 8 will be relevant in deciding

---

239 See Baroness Hale at [57].
240 At [61].
241 At [61].
242 At [62]–[63].
243 *R (Kabashi) v Redbridge LBC* [2009] EWHC 2984 (Admin), [2011] JHL D1.
244 [2020] EWHC 3526 (Admin); [2021] HLR 23.
245 Ie, by the court, see para **9.86**.

whether or not a child is to be taken into account, but it is not determinative of the authority's allocation decision.[246]

Carers, adopters and fosterers

9.124   Carers who need to stay overnight should, where possible, merit a spare room;[247] likewise, applications from prospective fosterers or adopters 'who would require an extra bedroom to accommodate a foster or adoptive child', should lead authorities 'to weigh up the risk that the application to foster or adopt may be unsuccessful (leading to the property being under-occupied), against the wider benefits which would be realised if the placement was successful'.[248] Authorities are encouraged to work with children's services to meet the needs of prospective and approved foster carers and adopters, so that children's services can fulfil their duties under CA 1989, s 22G, to ensure sufficient accommodation in the area to meet the needs of 'looked after children',[249] eg, by setting aside a quota of properties for people who need to move to larger accommodation in order to foster or adopt.[250]

Armed forces

9.125   When exercising any function under Part 6, a local authority must have due regard to:

> '(a) the unique obligations of, and sacrifices made by, the armed forces,
>
> (b) the principle that it is desirable to remove disadvantages arising for service people from membership, or former membership, of the armed forces, and
>
> (c) the principle that special provision for service people may be justified by the effects on such people of membership, or former membership, of the armed forces'.[251]

9.126   Even before this, authorities were 'strongly encouraged' to take into account the needs of current and former members of the armed forces when determining their allocation policies, 'and to give sympathetic consideration to the housing needs of family members of serving or former service personnel who may have been disadvantaged by the requirements of military service and,

---

246 *R (Bibi) v Camden LBC* [2004] EWHC 2527 (Admin), [2005] HLR 18. See also *Holmes-Moorhouse v Richmond upon Thames LBC* [2009] UKHL 7, [2009] HLR 34.
247 English Allocations Guidance para 4.29.
248 English Allocations Guidance para 4.30.
249 See para **11.83**.
250 English Allocations Guidance para 4.31.
251 Armed Forces Act 2006, ss 343AA (England) and 343AB (Wales), added by s 8(3), Armed Forces Act 2021; with effect from 22 November 2022.

in particular, the need to move from base to base'[252] – eg, by affording preference to those who have recently left or who are close to leaving the service, or to determine priorities between those with a reasonable preference, or, if using financial resources to determine priorities, disregarding any lump sum received as compensation for injury or disability sustained on active service, or by setting aside a proportion of properties for them under a local lettings policy.[253]

Households in or seeking work

9.127 Authorities are also 'urged' to consider using policies to support households in or seeking work, 'as well as those who – while unable to engage in paid employment – are contributing to their community in other ways, for example, through voluntary work'[254] – eg, by giving preference to those in low paid work, or employment-related training, or greater priority to those with a reasonable preference who are working or actively seeking work, or using local lettings policies to allocate to households 'in particular types of employment where, for example, skills are in short supply',[255] or by using 'flexible tenancies'[256] either to support households in low paid work or to incentivise people 'to take up employment opportunities'.[257]

Under-occupation

9.128 When determining criteria for property sizes, authorities should take account of the provisions in the Welfare Reform Act 2012 which reduce housing benefit to under-occupiers.[258]

Choice-based and local lettings

9.129 Subject to the 'reasonable preference' categories, the allocation scheme may contain provisions about the allocation of particular housing accommodation either to a person who makes a specific application for it[259] or to persons of a particular description, whether or not within the reasonable preference groups.[260] Allocation to persons 'of a particular description' comprises the statutory basis for local lettings policies outside the general priorities of HA 1996, s 166A(3) or

---

252 English Allocations Guidance para 4.24. See also para **9.96**.
253 English Allocations Guidance para 4.25.
254 English Allocations Guidance para 4.27. See paras **9.61–9.62**.
255 English Allocations Guidance para 4.27.
256 English Allocations Guidance para 4.27. See para **12.10**.
257 English Allocations Guidance para 4.28.
258 English Allocations Guidance para 4.22; see Housing Benefit Regulations 2006, SI 2006/213, reg B13; and Universal Credit Regulations 2013/376, Sch 4.
259 Eg, through advertisement and 'bidding'.
260 HA 1996, s 166A(6) (England); s 167(2E) (Wales).

s 167(2), 'which may be used to achieve a wide variety of housing management and policy objectives'.[261]

Consultation

9.130 By HA 1996, s 166A(13) (England) and s 167(7) (Wales), the authority must afford all registered providers of social housing and registered social landlords with whom it has nomination arrangements the opportunity to comment on an allocation scheme before it is adopted or before it is altered in any way that reflects 'a major change of policy'. The expression 'major change of policy' is not statutorily defined.[262]

9.131 In an appropriate case, it may be that a person awaiting an allocation will have a legitimate expectation that they will enjoy the same priority under the new scheme as the old, in which case they will in principle be entitled to continue to enjoy it;[263] in considering whether a statement is sufficiently clear and unambiguous to found the basis of a legitimate expectation, the court should ascertain the meaning which the defendant's statements would reasonably convey to a particular claimant in the light of all the background knowledge available to them at the time the statement was made.[264]

PROCEDURE

Introduction

9.132 Allocations are a matter for an authority's executive.[265]

9.133 The Secretary of State and, in Wales, the Welsh Ministers, may prescribe the principles of procedure to be followed when framing allocation schemes.[266]

9.134 In Wales, local housing authority officers must be included among the persons by whom allocation decisions can be taken, except where an express decision has been made not to delegate the decision, ie, to retain it as an executive decision.[267]

---

261 English Allocations Guidance para 4.21. See further, Welsh Allocations Guidance paras 3.71–3.74 on local lettings policies.
262 English Allocations Guidance para 5.2 suggests any amendment affecting the relative priority of a large number of applicants or a significant alteration to procedures. See also Welsh Allocations Guidance para 4.26.
263 See, eg *R (Alansi) v Newham LBC* [2013] EWHC 3722 (Admin), [2014] HLR 25, in which the claim was, however, unsuccessful.
264 See generally paras **10.106–10.111**.
265 See para **10.59**.
266 HA 1996, s 166A(10) (England); s 167(5) (Wales).
267 Local Housing Authorities (Prescribed Principles for Allocation Schemes) (Wales) Regulations 1997, SI 1997/45, reg 3 and Sch para 2.

9.135   In both England and Wales, elected members may not be involved in allocation decisions where the accommodation to be allocated, or the applicant's sole or main residence, is in the member's ward.[268]

Consideration of applications

9.136   Unlike under HA 1996, Part 7 or H(W)A 2014, Part 2,[269] there is no express provision requiring an authority to make enquiries before determining an application. Nevertheless, a body charged with a statutory function must make or cause to be made such enquiries as will allow it to be satisfied that it can properly discharge its role.[270]

9.137   In *Crowder*,[271] a decision that the applicant's daughter was no longer living with her – and that she should accordingly only be considered for single person accommodation – was quashed because of the authority's failure to make adequate enquiries.

9.138   In *Maali*,[272] the authority's decision was quashed because of flaws in the medical assessment. The claimant, an asthmatic, occupied a third-floor maisonette under a secure tenancy granted by the authority, together with her three children, the eldest of whom also suffered from asthma. She applied to be transferred to another property, contending that she and her eldest daughter were having difficulty climbing the stairs and that she therefore fell within the emergency medical category (group B) of the authority's allocation scheme.

9.139   In August 2003, the authority's housing medical adviser concluded that the medical conditions were not severe enough to justify the need for an emergency transfer because: i) the fact that the claimant and her child had to climb stairs was positive as exercise helped alleviate the symptoms of asthma; and ii) when the claimant's asthma worsened, she went to stay with friends in

---

268 1997/45, reg 3 and Sch para 1; and Allocation of Housing (Procedure) Regulations 1997, SI 1997/483, reg 3. English Allocations Guidance para 5.8, reminds authorities of this, but at para 5.9 also notes that: 'The regulations do not prevent an elected Member from representing their constituents in front of the decision making body, or from participating in the decision making body's deliberations prior to its decision. The regulations also do not prevent elected Members' involvement in policy decisions that affect the generality of housing accommodation in their division or electoral ward rather than individual allocations; for example, a decision that certain types of property should be prioritised for older people.' See also Welsh Allocations Guidance paras 4.35–4.37.

269 See para **7.60**.

270 See *R v Islington LBC ex p Thomas* (1998) 30 HLR 111, QBD, per Roger Henderson QC at 120 (in relation to whether accommodation provided under HA 1985, s 65(2) was suitable). See also *Secretary of State for Education and Science v Tameside BC* [1977] AC 1014, per Lord Diplock at 1065.

271 *R v Oxford City Council ex p Crowder* (1999) 31 HLR 485, QBD.

272 *R (Maali) v Lambeth LBC* [2003] EWHC 2231 (Admin), [2003] JHL D83.

order to obtain help with childcare and would continue to do so even if transferred to another property.

9.140   The authority accordingly assessed her as being within a mainstream category (group D) of its allocation scheme. The court concluded that the assessment was *Wednesbury* unreasonable: the medical adviser had wrongly attributed the stays with friends to a need for assistance with childcare rather than to the difficulties that she was experiencing in reaching the third floor. Nor was there any basis for the adviser's conclusion that, because exercise was beneficial to asthmatics, the climbing of stairs was positive.

9.141   In *Bauer-Czarnomski*,[273] the applicant lived in a four-bedroom house with his parents, both of whom suffered from mental health problems and required 24-hour assistance which he provided. In 2004, he applied to the authority for his own accommodation and was placed in the lowest band. In 2006, he submitted a report from his doctor which explained that, because he was required to be permanently available to assist his parents, his sleep was frequently disturbed and he was not able to rest, with the result that his own health was being harmed.

9.142   The authority obtained a report from a different doctor which accepted that the living arrangements had adverse implications for the applicant's health, but went on to advise that there was no need to place him in a higher band as the physical condition of the house did not affect his well-being. In particular, it noted that he had his own bedroom and was able to maintain a degree of independence and separation from other family members.

9.143   In reliance on that report, the authority refused to put the applicant into a higher band, a decision which was quashed because the authority's medical report had gone beyond an assessment of the applicant's medical need; it had not been for a doctor to advise on the priority to be afforded to him and in taking account of it, and the authority therefore had regard to an immaterial and irrelevant consideration; in any event, having regard to the medical evidence, the decision to leave the applicant in band D was perverse.

9.144   In *Adow*,[274] the authority's allocation scheme provided that every application which claimed a medical need would be 'assessed on its merits by the medical assessment officer in the quality and review team'. The applicant was the respondent's tenant in a one-bedroom flat in which she lived with her partner and her four children; she adduced evidence from a paediatrician and her family GP to show that the cramped conditions in which she was living were having an adverse impact on her health and that of her family.

273 *R (Bauer-Czarnomski) v Ealing LBC* [2010] EWHC 130 (Admin), [2010] JHL D38.
274 *R (Adow) v Newham LBC* [2010] EWHC 951 (Admin), [2010] JHL D101.

9.145   The authority – contrary to its policy – did not refer the case to a medical assessment officer, but instead engaged an external doctor to evaluate the medical evidence and make a decision as to her housing needs: the authority accepted that this was unlawful.

9.146   The authority must of course properly understand and apply its scheme, according to the interpretation of the scheme which the court – not the authority – determines.[275]

9.147   In *R (Flores) v Southwark LBC*,[276] the authority's scheme provided a priority for those who were statutorily overcrowded, unless caused by a 'deliberate act'. A family comprising parents and two children who moved into privately rented one-bedroom in accommodation which became statutorily overcrowded when the elder child turned 10 two years later, and five years before the relevant HA 1996, Part 7 application (following a previous application rejected for want of sufficient time in the borough), could not be considered to have caused the overcrowding by a deliberate act; the act that caused the overcrowding was the growth in age of the children which could not sensibly be considered a deliberate act. The court concluded (at [45]):

> 'With respect, for the council to have decided otherwise exceeds the bounds of any flexibility which may be accorded to it in the implementation of its Scheme'.

9.148   Likewise, in *R (Roman) v Southwark LBC*,[277] it was held that an act was only 'deliberate' for the purposes of the authority's scheme if the applicant had intended to do it in the sense that they had a real choice between two or more viable options and voluntarily elected to do the act; it was irrational for the authority to decide that the claimant had unreasonably arranged for his wife and children to join him in London without first finding suitable accommodation for them, or to have moved into more suitable accommodation after leaving a room he had been renting, when each of these options had been unaffordable.[278]

---

275 See para **9.86**. In *R (Gomes) v Kensington and Chelsea RLBC* [2023] EWHC 778 (Admin), Housing View, 24 April 2023, the authority had correctly applied its normal scheme rather than a special 'Grenfell' policy, as the application was a second application by a former Grenfell resident who had already enjoyed the benefits of the special scheme on his first application.

276 [2020] EWCA Civ 1697; [2021] HLR 16. See also *R (Montano) v Lambeth LBC* [2024] EWHC 249 (Admin); [2024] HLR forthcoming, in which the authority had wrongly construed its policy as not permitting applications to be backdated. Although there was no such specific discretion, a discretion allowing the authority to award additional priority to an applicant did, given the way the scheme functioned, amount to a discretion to backdate. See also para **10.167**.

277 [2022] EWHC 1232 (Admin); [2023] HLR 4.

278 Although decisions under Part 6, the wider significance of both this case and *Flores* may be in relation to intentional homelessness: see para **4.112**.

Information

Scheme

9.149   Since HA 1980, authorities have been obliged to publish details of their allocation provisions: see HA 1985, s 106. The details must be sufficient both to enable applicants to ascertain how the practices of a local authority will affect them, and so that the legality of its practice may be determined.[279]

9.150   Lack of publication does not, however, make a policy ultra vires.[280] Thus, it was sufficient for a social services procedure for making housing nominations to be provided in a short and comprehensible form; nor did the social services department have to give reasons for refusing to make a nomination to the housing department unless asked to do so.[281]

9.151   Likewise, where it was held that the local authority was entitled to adopt its local connection policy so long as it was rational and like cases were treated alike, the policy did not have to be set out in the allocations scheme itself because it was not a central feature of the scheme.[282]

9.152   On the other hand, where the scheme wrongly suggested that the applicant could not bid for a property, but there was in fact a separate policy which would have allowed her to do so, her claim for judicial review was allowed.[283]

9.153   There is a similar and overlapping duty to HA 1985, s 106 in HA 1996, Part 6, that an authority must publish a summary of its scheme and provide a copy of the summary free of charge to any member of the public who asks for one.[284] The authority must keep the full scheme available for inspection at its principal office, although a reasonable fee may be charged to any member of the public who asks for a copy.[285]

9.154   Where an authority makes an alteration to its scheme reflecting a major change in policy,[286] it must, within a reasonable period, take such steps as it considers reasonable to bring the effect of the alteration to the attention of those likely to be affected by it.[287]

---

279 *R (Faarah) v Southwark LBC* [2008] EWCA Civ 807, [2009] HLR 12 (how registration dates were determined).
280 *R v Newham LBC ex p Miah* (1996) 28 HLR 279, QBD.
281 *R (Yazar) v Southwark LBC* [2008] EWHC 515 (Admin), [2008] JHL D55.
282 *R (Van Boolen) v Barking and Dagenham LBC* [2009] EWHC 2196 (Admin), [2009] JHL D113.
283 *R (C) v Islington LBC* [2017] EWHC 1288 (Admin), [2017] HLR 32.
284 HA 1996, s 168(1). This is not confined to a member of the public in the authority's area.
285 HA 1996, s 168(2).
286 Cf paras **9.130–9.131**.
287 HA 1996, s 168(3).

9.155 The scheme must explain the criteria applied for awarding reasonable preference or indicate in what circumstances it will be applied and will otherwise fail to comply with the HA 1996.[288] See further paras **10.112–10.113.9.**

9.156 See also *R (Roman) v. Southwark LBC*,[289] although on this aspect (but see **9.148**), the challenge was not upheld, however: the complaint relied on internal guidance on the meaning of a 'deliberate act', a key element in determining whether or not the applicant was entitled to preference. The guidance was unpublished and not available outside the authority.

9.157 It was held that it was intended to assist officers in applying the scheme. The guidance was not inconsistent with the scheme and did not provide extra or different criteria but non-exhaustive examples of the types of conduct that might amount to a deliberate act as well as an example of the way in which consideration night be given to an applicant's financial resources when assessing whether there had been a deliberate act. The authority was not under a legal obligation to publish the guidance.

Applications

9.158 The scheme must include a right for an applicant to request such general information as enables them to assess how their application is likely to be treated; this must, in particular, include whether the applicant is likely to be a member of a group to which a preference will be given.[290]

9.159 A person is also entitled to be given general information that will enable them to assess whether accommodation appropriate to their needs is likely to be made available and, if so, how long it is likely to be before housing accommodation actually becomes available.[291] The duty does not extend to requiring the authority to provide information based on hypothetical scenarios which would arise if a different scheme were adopted or if the authority had concluded that an applicant qualified under a different head of a scheme than that which the authority has (lawfully) concluded applies.[292]

9.160 English guidance encourages authorities to consider how accurate and anonymised information on waiting list applicants and lettings outcomes could

---

288 *R (Cali) (and others) v Waltham Forest LBC* [2006] EWHC 302 (Admin), [2007] HLR 1 at [46].
289 [2022] EWHC 1232 (Admin).
290 HA 1996, s 166A(9)(a)(i) (England); s 167(4A)(a)(i) (Wales).
291 HA 1996, s 166A(9)(a)(ii) (England); s 167(4A)(a)(ii) (Wales).
292 *R (Jaberi) v Westminster CC* [2023] EWHC 1045 (Admin), [2023] HLR 37.

be published.[293] The Welsh Allocations Code of Guidance suggests[294] that it is important for authorities to provide 'regular, accurate and generalised information on how housing is allocated and how waiting lists are managed, working actively to dispel any myths and misconceptions which may arise'.

9.161 The scheme must also afford an applicant the opportunity to request information about any decision about the facts of their case.[295]

INTERNAL REVIEW AND CHALLENGE

9.162 An applicant in England has the right to request an internal review of any decision taken under HA 1996, s 166A(9)(b) (decision about the facts of their case) or under s 160ZA(9) (eligibility) and to be notified of the outcome and the grounds for it.[296] An applicant in Wales has the same rights in respect of a decision under HA 1996, s 167(4A)(b) (unacceptable conduct) or under s 160A(9) (eligibility, whether on the grounds of immigration status or conduct).[297]

9.163 Prior to its repeal, HA 1996, s 165 permitted regulations to be made governing the conduct of internal reviews under HA 1996, Part 6.[298] There is no such provision in connection with HA 1966, s 166A(9) or s 167(4A). Authorities nonetheless must ensure that any review is fair to the applicant.[299] A decision on an application under Part 6 is not, however, a determination of a civil right or obligation for the purposes of ECHR Article 6 (right to a fair trial).[300]

9.164 There is no appeal to the county court against the review decision;[301] any challenge has to be by way of judicial review.[302]

9.165 There is nothing to prevent authorities establishing a voluntary review or appeal process that goes beyond the statutory right to review.[303] If the authority does add such a voluntary review process, it is likely to be considered necessary

---

293 *Providing social housing for local people: statutory guidance on social housing allocations for local authorities in England*, DCLG, December 2013 (www.gov.uk/government/collections/social-housing-allocations-guidance).

294 Welsh Allocations Guidance para 3.58.

295 HA 1996, s 166A(9)(b) (England); s 167A(4A)(c) (Wales).

296 HA 1996, s 166A(9)(c) (England).

297 HA 1996, s 167(4A)(d) (Wales).

298 Allocation of Housing and Homelessness (Review Procedures) Regulations 1999, SI 1999/71.

299 Cf paras **10.65–10.69**.

300 See paras **10.117–10.122**.

301 See paras **10.203, 10.208**.

302 See Chapter 10.

303 See, eg, *R v Southwark LBC ex p Mason* (2000) 32 HLR 88, QBD (panel reviewing the suitability of offers).

for anyone who is dissatisfied with the priority which they have been given to use this before seeking judicial review.[304]

ALLOCATIONS BY PRIVATE REGISTERED PROVIDERS OF SOCIAL HOUSING (ENGLAND) AND REGISTERED SOCIAL LANDLORDS (WALES)

Generally

9.166 Private registered providers of social housing (PRPs) (England) and registered social landlords (RSLs) (Wales) are obliged to co-operate with local housing authorities in offering accommodation to people with priority under the authority's allocation scheme, to such extent as is reasonable in the circumstances.[305]

9.167 In practice, many local authorities now maintain no housing stock of their own, but have transferred it either to PRPs or RSLs specially formed for the purpose, or to other providers, by way of large-scale voluntary stock transfers, in connection with which they will necessarily have reserved rights to ensure that they can discharge their homelessness duties by way of nomination.

9.168 Even where the authority has retained some or all of its housing stock, it is likely to have nomination arrangements with PRPs and RSLs in its area. Such providers are among the partners with which local authorities will normally develop their homelessness strategies.[306]

9.169 Guidance in England says:[307]

'Nomination agreements should set out the proportion of lettings that will be made available; any criteria which the Private Registered Provider has adopted for accepting or rejecting nominees; and how any disputes will be resolved. Housing authorities will want to put in place arrangements to monitor effective delivery of the nomination agreement so they can demonstrate they are meeting their obligations under Part 6.'

---

304 See Chapter 10. The person could, of course, also complain to the local government ombudsman – see paras **10.282** onwards.
305 HA 1996, s 170. See also English Allocations Guidance para 6.1. See also the Housing Association Circular RSL 004/15, issued by the Welsh Government in April 2015 (replacing circular RSL 003/12, which itself replaced RLS 023/09) which requires all housing associations registered in Wales to take account of the Welsh Allocations Guidance.
306 See paras **12.9–12.18**.
307 English Allocations Guidance para 6.3. In Wales, see Welsh Allocations Guidance paras 1.7 and 4.18, reminding associations to have regard to the *Regulatory framework for housing associations registered in Wales* (Welsh Government, January 2022; gov.wales/housing-associations-registered-wales-regulatory-framework).

9.170 PRPs in England are regulated under Part 2 of the Housing and Regeneration Act (H&RA) 2008;[308] RSLs in Wales[309] are regulated under HA 1996, Part 1.[310]

9.171 PRPs in England were formerly regulated by the Housing Corporation – which had been the regulator of housing associations and trusts since the HA 1974 – until it was abolished and replaced[311] by what was statutorily called the Office for Tenants and Social Landlords,[312] known as the Tenant Services Authority (TSA).[313] From 1 April 2012, the TSA was itself abolished and its functions transferred to the Regulation Committee of the Homes and Communities Agency (HCA): those functions transferred to a new body corporate, the Regulator of Social Housing (RSH), in April 2018.[314]

9.172 In Wales, regulation of RSLs was the responsibility of the National Assembly for Wales ('the Assembly') from 1 July 1999.[315] The regulatory function was transferred to the Welsh Ministers on 1 April 2012.[316] The Welsh Ministers remain responsible for regulation in Wales.

9.173 It is not possible to describe either system of regulation here in any detail[317] although a small number of matters affecting allocation are touched on below. It suffices to say that PRPs and RSLs are subject to regulatory regimes under one or other Act – HA 1996 or H&RA 2008. This means that, while

---

308 As amended by LA 2011, Part 7 Chapter 5 and Schs 16 and 17.

309 Still called 'registered social landlords' under HA 1996, Part 1.

310 Albeit amended in parts by H&RA 2008.

311 H&RA 2008, s 64; its functions were transferred to the TSA: Transfer of Housing Corporation Functions (Modifications and Transitional Provisions) Order 2008, SI 2008/2839.

312 H&RA 2008, s 81.

313 Unlike the former Housing Corporation, the TSA did not have power to provide financial assistance to registered providers; that role is now undertaken by the Homes and Communities Agency (HCA).

314 From 15 January 2012, the HCA was required to set up a Regulation Committee pursuant to H&RA 2008, s 94B, brought into force by Localism Act 2011 (Commencement No 2 and Transitional and Saving Provision) Order 2012, SI 2012/57. The Regulation Committee took over the functions previously undertaken by the TSA on 1 April 2012 – the same date on which the TSA was abolished: see Localism Act 2011 (Commencement No 4 and Transitional, Transitory and Saving Provisions) Order 2012, SI 2012/628. In November 2016, the (then) DCLG proposed that the regulatory functions of the HCA should be transferred to a new non-departmental public body (see *Proposal on using a Legislative Reform Order to establish the social housing regulator as an independent body*). In February 2018, a draft Legislative Reform Order (the Legislative Reform (Regulator of Social Housing) (England) Order 2018) was laid before Parliament; it establishes the Regulator of Social Housing as a new body corporate. The final order (Legislative Reform (Regulator of Social Housing) (England) Order 2018, SI 2018/1040 came into force on 1 October 2018.

315 National Assembly for Wales (Transfer of Functions) Order 1999, SI 1999/672.

316 Housing and Regeneration Act 2008 (Commencement No 7 and Transitional and Saving Provisions) Order 2010, SI 2010/862 art 2. The Welsh Ministers remain the 'relevant authority' for the purposes of HA 1996, Part 1. The regulatory framework is that published in 2011.

317 In general terms, the Regulator may set managements standards requiring local authorities and PRPs to comply with rules about, inter alia, allocating accommodation (H&RA 2008, s 193, as amended by LA 2011); the standards are presently contained in Tenancy Involvement and Empowerment Standard (July 2017).

not subject to direct statutory rules on allocation in the same way that local authorities are, their actions, including in relation to allocations, are nonetheless susceptible to review by their regulators and, in turn, susceptible to complaints to those regulators by those adversely affected by their actions and/or inaction.

9.174   Regulators have a range of sanctions available, including powers of inspection of performance by and/or enquiry into PRPs or RSLs, extending ultimately to the de-registration or winding up of providers whose performance is inadequate.[318]

9.175   In England, complaints can also be made to an independent scheme approved by the Secretary of State.[319] HA 1996, Sch 2 sets out the general provisions governing the membership, approval and registration of such a scheme in England. The Housing Ombudsman Service (HOS) is the approved scheme of which every PRP must be a member.[320] Failure to comply with the requirement to be a member of the scheme may result in an application to the High Court by the Secretary of State for an order directing the provider to comply.[321] In Wales, there is no requirement for an RSL to be a member of any scheme as the Public Services Ombudsman for Wales (PSOW) already has jurisdiction over every registered social landlord.[322]

9.176   Where a complaint is made to the HOS, the ombudsman has the power to investigate and determine that complaint by reference to what is, in the opinion of the ombudsman, 'fair in all the circumstances of the case'.[323] In Wales, the investigation must be carried out in such manner as they think 'appropriate in the circumstances of the case'.[324]

9.177   If the complaint is upheld, the ombudsman has power to order the PRP to pay compensation to the complainant or even to order that the member or the complainant is not to exercise or require the performance of contractual or other obligations or rights existing between them.[325] In Wales, the ombudsman does not have a directly corresponding power; a body which is subject to a complaint referred to the ombudsman may, however, make a payment to, or provide any other benefit for, the person aggrieved in respect of the matter which is the subject of the complaint.[326]

---

318 See H&RA 2008, Part 2 Chapters 4, 6 and 7; HA 1996, Part 1 and Sch 1.
319 HA 1996, Sch 2, para 3. In Wales, the function was transferred to the Public Services Ombudsman in 2006, see Public Services Ombudsman (Wales) Act 2005 (PSO(W)A 2005).
320 HA 1996, Sch 2, para 1(1). If the relevant provisions of the LA 2011 are brought into force, local authorities will also fall within the jurisdiction of the housing ombudsman. In February 2018, the MHCLG issued a consultation paper (*Strengthening consumer redress in the housing market: consultation*) seeking views on, among other things, the creation of a single ombudsman to cover all housing complaints, regardless of the nature of the landlord or tenure of the occupier.
321 HA 1996, Sch 2, para 1(2).
322 PSO(W)A 2005, ss 7, 41, Sch 3.
323 HA 1996, Sch 2, para 7.
324 PSO(W)A 2005, s 13.
325 HA 1996, Sch 2, para 7(2). There is no power to enforce against the complainant in Wales.
326 PSO(W)A 2015, s 34.

9.178 If the PRP fails to comply with the ombudsman's determination, the ombudsman has the power to order it to publish that failure in such manner as they see fit.[327] If the PRP fails to comply with the order to publish, the ombudsman has the power to take such steps as they think appropriate to publish what the PRP ought to have published and to recover the costs of doing so from the PRP.[328] In Wales, the authority must publicise the report.[329]

9.179 It has been held that PRPs[330] may qualify as public authorities within the Human Rights Act 1998, in respect of some aspects of their management of their social housing stock (including service of notice to quit or of seeking possession) and, in addition to the requirement to conform to the ECHR rights, that in such circumstances they are also susceptible to the principles of domestic public law in respect of such activities, even if they would not otherwise be.[331]

9.180 At first instance, those aspects explicitly included the allocation of social housing; while this was not overruled per se, it was not the basis on which the decision that such providers may be public authorities for the purposes of the Human Rights Act 1998 was upheld: rather, it was held that service of notice to quit or to seek possession is a public function for the purposes of that Act, which means that such providers are public authorities in respect of such service; while allocation was not directly in issue, however, it seems also to qualify and in *R (McIntyre) v Gentoo Group Ltd*,[332] the principle was held to include allocation. Whether or not other acts of management qualify may well depend on a detailed investigation into and assessment of the functions of allocating and managing housing of the particular registered provider.[333]

England

9.181 The Regulator of Social Housing[334] enjoys a range of powers in relation to the provision of social housing, including that of setting standards, which may include requiring PRPs to comply with rules about, inter alia, allocation criteria,[335]

---

327 HA 1996, Sch 2, para 7(3).
328 HA 1996, Sch 2, para 7(5).
329 PSO(W)A 2005, s 17, although the ombudsman has power to waive this requirement: ss 17, 21.
330 And, therefore, RSLs in Wales.
331 *R (Weaver) v London & Quadrant Housing Trust* [2008] EWHC 1377 (Admin), [2008] JHL D94 and on appeal [2009] EWCA Civ 587, [2010] 1 WLR 363, [2009] HLR 40. See para **10.7**. The proposition as to susceptibility was conceded on appeal.
332 [2010] EWHC 5 (Admin), [2010] JHL D22 and D40, in particular at [25].
333 *Weaver* at [68]–[72]. See also *Aston Cantlow and Wilmcote with Billisley Parochial Church Council v Wallbank* [2003] UKHL 37, [2004] 1 AC 546. In *R (Macleod) v Peabody Trust Governors* [2016] EWHC 737 (Admin), [2016] HLR 27, it was held that the association was not amenable to judicial review in connection with the refusal to allow an assignment of a tenancy which, however, did not fall to be treated as social housing because it had been acquired by the association without the use of any public funds.
334 See para **9.171**.
335 H&RA 2008, s 193(2)(a).

in relation to which it may issue codes of practice amplifying the standard.[336] The statutory objectives of the Regulation Committee include economic and consumer objectives, the latter of which include ensuring that actual or potential tenants of social housing have an appropriate degree of choice and protection.[337]

9.182   The Secretary of State may direct the RSH to issue a standard, or make directions about its content or to require regard to be had to specified objectives when setting a standard.[338] The Regulation Committee must comply with any such direction.[339] Standards issued by the RSH may require PRPs to comply with specified rules about a wide range of matters including criteria for allocating accommodation.[340]

9.183   Failure to meet a standard is a ground for action by the Regulation Committee,[341] including the use of enforcement powers ranging from notices, fines and compensation, to orders to require the appointment of a manager over the whole of a PRP's functions or specified functions, or the transfer of functions to another PRP, and to the removal or suspension of officers or employees or their disqualification.[342]

9.184   Provision is made for the Regulation Committee to exercise any of the powers of regulation where there is a failure (or an anticipated failure) to meet any of the consumer standards[343] where the Regulation Committee has reason to believe that there has been or may be a serious detriment caused to a tenant or potential tenant.[344]

9.185   In March 2015, the Regulation Committee issued *The regulatory framework for social housing in England from April 2015*[345] which took effect from 1 April 2015. The framework covers key areas of regulation including the regulation of consumer standards. The framework specifies outcomes and expectations of standards relating to economic and consumer standards that reflect the statutory objectives of the RSH.[346]

---

336   H&RA 2008, s 195.
337   H&RA 2008, s 92K.
338   H&RA 2008, s 197.
339   H&RA 2008, s 197(7).
340   H&RA 2008, s 193(2)(a).
341   H&RA 2008, s 198.
342   H&RA 2008, Part 1 Chapter 7.
343   Ie, standards 'as to the nature, extent and quality of accommodation, facilities or services provided by them in connection with social housing', which include allocation criteria: H&RA 2008, s 193.
344   H&RA 2008, ss 198A, 198B.
345   The Social Housing Regulator, March 2015, replacing the 2012 Guidance.
346   H&RA 2008, s 92K.

Wales

9.186   The statutory framework governing RSLs in Wales under HA 1996, Part 1 has been the responsibility of the Welsh Ministers since 1 April 2010.[347] The Welsh Ministers have responsibility for maintaining a register of providers, financial regulation, setting of performance standards and the power to issue guidance.

9.187   The Welsh Ministers also have some enforcement powers, although not as extensive as the powers granted to the RSH. From October 2011, the Welsh Ministers have had the power to set standards to be met by RSLs in Wales.[348] Welsh Ministers have the power to issue guidance that relates to a matter addressed by a standard and which amplifies the standard.[349]

9.188   In January 2022, the Welsh Ministers issued *The regulatory framework for housing associations registered in Wales*[350] ('Welsh Framework'). The purpose of the Welsh Framework is to 'ensure that housing associations provide good quality homes and services to tenants and others who use their services'.[351] The framework does not set out any expectations that relate specifically to allocations, but its principles include working with tenants and partner organisations to make and implement effective business decisions.[352]

9.189   Enforcement powers include service of an enforcement notice in specified cases,[353] prosecution in relation to matters relied on in enforcement notices,[354] imposition of penalties,[355] and power to require a landlord to pay compensation to an affected person for failure to meet a standard or to comply with an undertaking given by a landlord to the Welsh Ministers.[356]

9.190   The Welsh Ministers also have powers of inspection[357] and inquiry[358] into the affairs of landlords. There is power for Welsh Ministers to remove[359] and appoint[360] officers in certain circumstances, to petition for the winding up of

---

347 Prior to that, it was the responsibility of the Welsh Assembly.
348 HA 1996, s 33A.
349 HA 1996, s 33B.
350 Pursuant to HA 1996, s 36. This replaced the May 2017 guidance of the same name.
351 Welsh Framework p3.
352 Welsh Framework p3.
353 HA 1996, s 50C.
354 HA 1996, s 50G.
355 HA 1996, s 50H.
356 HA 1996, s 50O.
357 HA 1996, Sch 1, Part 3A.
358 HA 1996, Sch 1, Part 4.
359 HA 1996, Sch 1, Part 2 para 4.
360 HA 1996, Sch 1, Part 2 paras 6–8.

an RSL[361] and to take control of assets following dissolution or winding up of a landlord.[362]

9.191 Housing Association Circular RSL 004/15 requires all housing associations registered in Wales to take account of the Welsh Allocations Guidance (ie, the Guidance under Part 6) governing allocations[363] when 'addressing key delivery outcomes' for the Welsh Framework.

---

361 HA 1996, Sch 1, Part 2 para 14.
362 HA 1996, Sch 1, Part 2 paras 15–15A.
363 See para 9.10.

CHAPTER 10

Enforcement

INTRODUCTION

10.1   Housing Act (HA) 1996, Parts 6 and 7 and Housing (Wales) Act (H(W) A) 2014, Part 2 all contain provision for the *internal* review of decisions, which are considered elsewhere in this book.[1] This chapter is concerned with the *external* enforcement of an applicant's rights, ie, what an applicant, who remains dissatisfied with the decision of the authority *after* internal review (if any), can do to challenge or change it by way of recourse to the courts or the ombudsman.

10.2 The only route available to a dissatisfied applicant for an allocation of housing under HA 1996, Part 6 is by way of a claim for judicial review in the High Court, which means that permission must be obtained from the court to bring the claim; HA 1996, Part 7 and H(W)A 2014, Part 2, however, provide for a statutory appeal to the county court[2] on a 'point of law' as of right, and this is the procedure that will normally be used in homelessness cases, although there remain a few circumstances in which judicial review either remains available or may be the only recourse.[3]

10.3 The need for permission – which is not required in the county court – aside, the divergence is practical rather than substantive because an appeal on a point of law confers on the county court the same jurisdiction as that available on a claim for judicial review, engaging the same legal basis for challenge. Thus, a challenge to the legality of a contracting out agreement may be raised on an appeal to the county court:

> '. . . the correct interpretation of s 204 Housing Act 1996 is that a point of law arises from a decision if it concerns or relates to the lawfulness of the decision. Both normal statutory construction and the preponderance of authority point to the county court having jurisdiction to hear appeals from s 202 review decisions that is not limited to points of law that might broadly but imprecisely be described as 'points of housing law' but extends to the full range of issues that would otherwise be the subject of an application to the High Court for judicial review. These include challenges on grounds of procedural error, the extent of legal powers (vires), irrationality, and inadequacy of reasons . . . I do not accept that an error of law arising from a decision can only relate to errors that are intrinsic to the making of the decision or to events during the period between the request for a review and the making of the review decision. That narrow reading conflicts with the intention of the legislation that this statutory appeal jurisdiction should be removed from the Administrative Court and entrusted to the county court.'[4]

10.4 This chapter is divided into two parts: The first part contains the *substantive law*, applicable either on judicial review or on statutory appeal. The second part deals with the *procedural law* governing how to bring a claim in either court and when to do so; it also deals with complaints to the Local Government and Social Care Ombudsman.

---

1   Discussed in Chapter 9 (HA 1996, Part 6) and Chapter 8 (HA 1996, Part 7 and H(W)A 2014, Part 2).
2   HA 1996, s 204; H(W)A 2014, s 88.
3   Paras **10.141–10.142.**
4   *James v Hertsmere BC* [2020] EWCA Civ 489, [2020] 1 WLR 3606, [2020] HLR 28 at [31].

SUBSTANTIVE LAW

Introduction

10.5   The general principles which underlie a challenge on a point of law are those of administrative – or public – law, which have been largely, but far from exclusively,[5] developed in the course of proceedings for judicial review, and comprise a significant area of law in their own right.[6] The overwhelming bulk of homelessness and allocations case-law is of this order, ie, an illustration of the operation of the principles of administrative law, in relation to the statutes governing homelessness and allocations. The jurisprudence that the courts develop in the context of homelessness has itself added to the general body of administrative law, as well as contributing to the growth of housing law.

10.6   The issue in such cases is not what decision the court would reach, but whether a decision can be said to be ultra vires, ie, outwith the powers of the body making the decision. This is so whether the challenge is brought by way of judicial review or as a statutory appeal.[7]

10.7   Domestic administrative law includes the obligations imposed on public bodies by the Human Rights Act (HRA) 1998 and the rights from the European Convention on Human Rights ('the Convention'/ECHR) that the HRA 1998 imports. This has three consequences: first, it adds to the categories of illegality – if an administrative law decision is unlawful under the provisions of HRA 1998, it is ultra vires; second, it reinforces and develops existing administrative law; third, public authorities within its purview include private registered providers of social housing and registered social landlords in respect of some aspects of their management of social housing stock (including service of notice to quit or of seeking possession), which means that, in addition to the requirement to conform to the Convention rights, they are (in these respects) also susceptible to the principles of domestic public law, even if they would not otherwise be.[8]

---

5   The important Court of Appeal decision in *Crédit Suisse v Allerdale MBC* [1997] QB 306, CA, was an appeal from a decision of the Commercial Court; *Boddington v British Transport Police* [1999] 2 AC 143, HL, which is also of considerable importance, was a criminal prosecution.
6   See the two leading textbooks in the area: Wade and Forsyth, *Administrative law* (12th edn, OUP, 2022); and Woolf, Jowell, Donnelly and Hare, *De Smith's Judicial review* (9th edn, Sweet & Maxwell, 2023).
7   *Nipa Begum v Tower Hamlets LBC* [2000] 1 WLR 306, (2000) 32 HLR 445, CA, approved by the House of Lords in *Runa Begum v Tower Hamlets LBC* [2003] UKHL 5, [2003] 2 AC 430, [2003] HLR 32, see particularly Lord Bingham at [7]. *Runa Begum* was followed in *Ali v Birmingham City Council* [2010] UKSC 8, [2010] HLR 22. This did not, however, allow a firm of solicitors with a Legal Aid Agency (LAA) contract for public law work (but not housing) to conduct HA 1996, s 204 appeals: *Bhatia Best Ltd v Lord Chancellor* [2014] EWHC 746 (QB), [2014] 1 WLR 3487.
8   *R (Weaver) v London & Quadrant Housing Trust* [2008] EWHC 1377, [2008] JHL D94 and on appeal [2009] EWCA Civ 587, [2010] 1 WLR 363, [2009] HLR 40. The proposition as to susceptibility was conceded.

10.8   The body of 'administrative law' is that with which this part of this chapter is concerned. It is addressed as follows.

a)   the nature of a challenge;

b)   the general principles of administrative law;

c)   substantive grounds for challenge;

d)   procedural grounds for challenge.

10.9   This important caveat needs to be entered at the start. Public law is not about absolutes: many aspects of it engage degrees of right and wrong, which will depend on the facts of the individual challenge, rather than 'rules' – it has been said, 'in law, context is everything'.[9]

10.10   Thus, a general duty to make enquiries will differ depending on the context: a duty to make enquiries under the homelessness provisions will import different practical obligations than will a duty to make enquiries into another, entirely different area – for example, a police enquiry into the commission of a crime (hence, the proposition that local authority enquiries do not have to amount to 'CID-type enquiries').[10] Likewise, and plainly, what is factually relevant to one area of activity will not necessarily be relevant to another.

10.11   Because administrative law derives from a variety of sources and is applied to (and therefore continues to be developed in relation to) a wide range of activities, many of which are very far from the specific issues raised by HA 1996, Parts 6 and 7 and H(W)A 2014, Part 2, cases which have been developed in other areas therefore need to be treated with some caution: there may be more room for manoeuvre (either way) over how they function under Parts 6, 7 or 2 than may at first appear; or, they may simply not be relevant.

The nature of a challenge

10.12   At the heart of administrative law is the proposition that Parliament intends public bodies always to act properly, in the sense of reasonably and lawfully.

10.13   The role of the courts is, however, supervisory rather than appellate: the court[11] must review the decision-making processes of the body in question, rather

---

9   *R (Daly) v Secretary of State for the Home Department* [2001] UKHL 26, [2001] 2 AC 532.
10 *Lally v Kensington and Chelsea RLBC* (1980) *Times* 26 March, QBD. That said, as the cases on enquiries in Chapter 7 affirm, enquiries do need to be into all the circumstances relevant to an application and the duties that may flow from it.
11 Whether Administrative Court on judicial review or county court on appeal. The Court of Appeal has expressed its disapproval of county court judges who have overstepped their role (*Kruja v Enfield LBC* [2004] EWCA Civ 1769, [2005] HLR 13) and emphasised that decision-making on matters such as the vulnerability of applicants is for the local authority: *Osmani v Camden LBC* [2004] EWCA Civ 1706, [2005] HLR 22.

than determine for itself what decision the authority should make.[12] Provided that the authority does not err in how it reaches the decision,[13] the substance of the decision is for the authority, not for the court, and it is the authority's view or decision which must prevail.[14]

10.14   There is rarely only one decision which an authority may reach: one individual's view of what is reasonable will often quite properly differ from that of another, and Parliament has entrusted decision-making under HA 1996, Parts 6 and 7 and H(W)A 2014, Part 2 to authorities, not to the courts.

10.15   In *Puhlhofer*,[15] Lord Brightman said:[16]

> 'I am troubled at the prolific use of judicial review for the purpose of challenging the performance by local authorities of their functions under the Act of 1977. Parliament intended the local authority to be the judge of fact. The Act abounds with the formula when, or if, the housing authority are satisfied as to this, or that, or have reason to believe this, or that. Although the action or inaction of a local authority is clearly susceptible to judicial review where they have misconstrued the Act, or abused their powers or otherwise acted perversely, I think that great restraint should be exercised in giving leave to proceed by judicial review. The plight of the homeless is a desperate one, and the plight of the applicants in the present case commands the deepest sympathy. But it is not, in my opinion, appropriate that the remedy of judicial review, which is a discretionary remedy, should be made use of to monitor the actions of local authorities

12   See, eg, *R v Northumberland Compensation Appeal Tribunal ex p Shaw* [1952] 1 KB 338, CA, per Denning LJ at 346–347: 'The Court of King's Bench has an inherent jurisdiction to control all inferior tribunals, not in an appellate capacity but in a supervisory capacity. This control extends not only to seeing that the inferior tribunals keep within their jurisdiction, but also to seeing that they observe the law . . . The King's Bench does not substitute its own views for those of the tribunal, as a Court of Appeal would do. It leaves it to the tribunal to hear the case again, and in a proper case may command it to do so.' See also *R v Secretary of State for Trade and Industry ex p Lonrho plc* [1989] 1 WLR 525, HL per Lord Keith of Kinkel at 535: 'The question is not whether the Secretary of State came to . . . a conclusion which meets with the approval of the . . . Court but whether the discretion was properly exercised.' This is the same approach as the appellate court adopts when considering an appeal against a discretionary decision of a judge: eg, *Woodspring DC v Taylor* (1982) 4 HLR 95, CA.
13   In any of the acknowledged senses – see paras **10.20–10.129**.
14   See, eg, *R v Secretary of State for the Home Department ex p Khawaja* [1984] AC 74, HL per Lord Scarman at 100, referring to the *Wednesbury* principle: 'The principle excluded the court from substituting its own view of the facts for that of the authority'; *R v Secretary of State for the Home Department ex p Brind* [1991] 1 AC 696, HL per Lord Lowry at 767: 'The judges are not, generally speaking, equipped by training or experience or furnished with the necessary knowledge and advice, to decide the answer to an administrative problem where the scales are evenly balanced, but they have a much better chance of reaching the right answer where the question is put in a *Wednesbury* form'; see also *Wednesbury* itself, para **10.23**, where Lord Greene MR, at 234, refers to the court as 'a judicial authority which is concerned, and concerned only, to see whether the local authority have contravened the law by acting in excess of the powers which Parliament have confided in them'.
15   *R v Hillingdon LBC ex p Puhlhofer* [1986] AC 484, (1986) 18 HLR 158, HL.
16   At 518.

under the Act save in the exceptional case. The ground upon which the courts will review the exercise of an administrative discretion is abuse of power, for example, bad faith, a mistake in construing the limits of the power, a procedural irregularity, or unreasonableness in the *Wednesbury*[17] sense – unreasonableness verging on an absurdity: see the speech of Lord Scarman in *R v Secretary of State for the Environment ex p Nottinghamshire CC.*[18] Where the existence or non-existence of a fact is left to the judgment and discretion of a public body and that fact involves a broad spectrum ranging from the obvious to the debatable to the just conceivable, it is the duty of the court to leave the decision of that fact to the public body to whom Parliament has entrusted the decision-making power save in a case where it is obvious that the public body, consciously or unconsciously, are acting perversely.

. . . I express the hope that there will be a lessening in the number of challenges which are mounted against local authorities who are endeavouring, in extremely difficult circumstances, to perform their duties under the Homeless Persons Act with due regard for all their other housing problems.'[19]

10.16   There are echoes of this in the HA 1996, Part 6 decision of the House of Lords in *R (Ahmad) v Newham LBC.*[20]

> '46. . . . [A]s a general proposition, it is undesirable for the courts to get involved in questions of how priorities are accorded in housing allocation policies. Of course, there will be cases where the court has a duty to interfere, for instance if a policy does not comply with statutory requirements, or if it is plainly irrational. However, it seems unlikely that the legislature can have intended that Judges should embark on the exercise of telling authorities how to decide on priorities as between applicants in need of rehousing, save in relatively rare and extreme circumstances. Housing allocation policy is a difficult exercise which requires not only social and political sensitivity and judgment, but also local expertise and knowledge.
>
> 47. In relation to the provision of accommodation under the National Assistance Act 1948, my noble and learned friend, Baroness Hale of Richmond, then Hale LJ, said in *R (Wahid) v Tower Hamlets LBC*[21] '[n]eed is a relative concept, which trained and experienced social workers are much better equipped to assess than are lawyers and courts, provided that they act rationally'. Precisely the same

17   *Associated Provincial Picture Houses Ltd v Wednesbury Corporation* [1948] 1 KB 223, CA.
18   *Nottinghamshire CC v Secretary of State for the Environment* [1986] AC 240, HL.
19   The same principles apply on a statutory appeal – the county court must at all times bear in mind the public law exercise in which it is engaged: *Crawley BC v B* (2000) 32 HLR 636, CA.
20   [2009] UKHL 14, [2009] HLR 31.
21   [2002] EWCA Civ 287, [2003] HLR 2 at [33].

is true of relative housing needs under Part 6 of the 1996 Act, and trained and experienced local authority housing officers.

48.   If section 167 carries with it the sort of requirements which can be said to be implied by the decisions of the Court of Appeal and the Deputy Judge in this case, then Judges would become involved in considering details of housing allocation schemes in a way which would be both unrealistic and undesirable . . .

. . .

55.   This is not to say that there could never be circumstances in which a scheme, which complies with the statutory requirements, could be susceptible to judicial review on grounds of irrationality. Such a suggestion would be unmaintainable not least because it would represent an abdication of judicial responsibility. However, what is important is to emphasise that once a housing allocation scheme complies with the requirements of section 167 and any other statutory requirements, the courts should be very slow to interfere on the ground of alleged irrationality.'

10.17   The discretion conferred by Parliament, embodied in this more limited,[22] supervisory approach, does not lead to the conclusion that an authority's decision under HA 1996, Part 6 or Part 7 or H(W)A 2014, Part 2 is above reproach.[23] It is the purpose of public law to ensure that public authorities, entrusted with an apparently blanket power to reach 'subjective' decisions, nonetheless do so in accordance with the law.

10.18   A distinction may be drawn, however, between the decisions, policies and schemes of a public authority, and initiatives in the more general sense of being encouragement[24] or indicative of a direction, as where, during the coronavirus pandemic, the government launched an initiative to help local authorities to bring rough sleepers off the streets and into accommodation, known as 'Everyone In', which was held – on this basis – not be susceptible to challenge.[25]

10.19   A discretionary decision may still be ultra vires and without effect in law: it may be unreasonable in the *Wednesbury* sense – ie, a decision which no reasonable authority, properly directing itself, could have reached; it may be a decision that is contrary to the law as properly understood; it may be a decision which has been reached without affording the applicant their due procedural

---

22   Than when an appeal approach allows a court to substitute its own view of the facts.
23   See per Lord Wilberforce in *Secretary of State for Education and Science v Tameside MBC* [1977] AC 1014, HL, at 1047: 'The section is framed in a "subjective" form . . . This form of section is quite well-known and *at first sight* might seem to exclude judicial review . . .' (emphasis added).
24   A 'call to arms'.
25   *R (ZLL) v Secretary of State* [2022] EWCA Civ 1059.

safeguards; or it may be a decision which is not based on all the relevant information.

Ultra vires

10.20   Local authorities may only act within their powers. If they do not do so, they are acting unlawfully, and their actions and decisions will be so treated[26] – this is the ultra vires doctrine and a decision so made will be unlawful because:

a)   on the face of the statute there was no authority to engage in the action at all; or

b)   the statute has been misconstrued; or

c)   the authority has misapplied the statute, for example, by failing to use the powers to implement the purpose of the statute; or

d)   a decision has been reached under the statute by reference to something which is irrelevant, or in ignorance of something which is relevant, to the way the power under the statute is intended to be operated, or which is so unreasonable – or irrational or perverse – that no reasonable authority could have reached it.

10.21   If it can be shown that a public body such as a local authority has approached its decision unlawfully then, regardless of the reason, the decision will be void and the courts will not give effect to it.[27] In so saying, the propositions in this and the last paragraph assume:

a)   that there are no differences between the legal consequences of decisions which there was no power at all to take (ie, those which are said to be outside the four corners of a statute) and those which there was power to take but which have been taken in some way improperly;[28] and

b)   that once it is decided that a decision is ultra vires, it must be treated as if it had at all times been void for all purposes.

10.22   There has been a number of cases which have considered these two (overlapping) issues, and they are issues which will doubtless continue to be

---

26   Subject to issues of forum: cf *Wandsworth LBC v Winder* [1985] AC 461, HL; *Avon CC v Buscott* [1988] QB 656, CA; and *Hackney LBC v Lambourne* (1992) 25 HLR 172, CA; *Manchester City Council v Cochrane* [1999] 1 WLR 809, CA.

27   It would appear that it may be possible subsequently to ratify a decision which is ultra vires, where the decision is one which would have been within the powers of the authority had it been properly reached, if the defect in the decision has 'nothing to do with the merits of the matter' and deprives the applicant of 'no genuine legal right': *James v Hertsmere BC* [2020] EWCA Civ 489, [2020] 1 WLR 3606, [2020] HLR 28 at [45].

28   See, in particular, *Crédit Suisse plc v Allerdale MBC* [1997] QB 306, CA, per Neill LJ at 343: 'I know of no authority for the proposition that the *ultra vires* decisions of local authority can be classified into categories of invalidity . . .' But cf *Charles Terence Estates Ltd v Cornwall CC* [2012] EWCA Civ 1439, [2013] 1 WLR 466, [2013] HLR 12, at [27]–[37], [44]–[53].

discussed.[29] For the purposes of this book, however, those propositions normally suffice in practice.[30]

The general principles of administrative law

Wednesbury

10.23   The classic statement of the court's role and function when addressing public law issues is that of Lord Greene MR in *Wednesbury*:[31]

> 'What, then, is the power of the courts? They can only interfere with an act of executive authority if it be shown that the authority has contravened the law. It is for those who assert that the local authority has contravened the law to establish that proposition . . . It is not to be assumed prima facie that responsible bodies like the local authority in this case will exceed their powers; but the court, whenever it is alleged that the local authority have contravened the law, must not substitute itself for that authority . . . When an executive discretion is entrusted by Parliament to a body such as the local authority in this case, what appears to be an exercise of that discretion can only be challenged in the courts in a strictly limited class of case. . . When discretion of this kind is granted the law recognises certain principles upon which that discretion must be exercised, but within the four corners of those principles the discretion . . . is an absolute one and cannot be questioned in any court of law. What then are those principles? They are well understood. They are principles which the court looks to in considering any question of discretion of this kind. The exercise of such a discretion must be a real exercise of the discretion. If, in the statute conferring the discretion, there is to be found expressly or by implication matters which the authority exercising the discretion ought to have regard to, then in exercising the discretion it must have regard to those matters. Conversely, if the nature of the subject-matter and the general interpretation of the Act make it clear

---

29   *Anisminic Ltd v Foreign Compensation Commission* [1969] 2 AC 147, HL, would nonetheless seem to be definitive: a decision wrongly reached, for whatever reason, was considered to be void and a nullity, because decision-makers have no jurisdiction to make unlawful decisions (see, in particular, per Lord Reid, at 171, using similar terms to describe unlawfulness as the classic definition by Lord Greene MR in *Wednesbury*, see para **10.23**). In *Boddington v British Transport Police* [1999] 2 AC 143, HL, however, the majority of the Committee was not willing simply to assume invalidity for all purposes and at all times, because people would in the meantime have regulated their lives on the basis of a decision's validity.

30   It today appears to be accepted in homelessness law that there are circumstances when a may be retaken: see paras **7.158–7.165**. In *Porteous v West Dorset DC* [2004] EWCA Civ 244, (2004) HLR 30 at [7]–[9] (fundamental mistake of fact – para **7.162**) the discussion was in terms of revisiting and changing or rescinding an earlier decision, but the basis of the argument was that the earlier decision was void and it is hard to see any other basis: unless void, the authority is what is known as functus officio, ie, it has no further function – it has had an application and it has reached its decision; accordingly, to uphold the later decision, the earlier one had to be void.

31   *Associated Provincial Picture Houses Ltd v Wednesbury Corporation* [1948] 1 KB 223, CA.

that certain matters would not be germane to the matter in question, the authority must disregard those irrelevant collateral matters.[32]

There have been in the cases expressions used relating to the sort of things that authorities must not do . . . I am not sure myself whether the permissible grounds of attack cannot be defined under a single head . . . Bad faith, dishonesty – those of course, stand by themselves – unreasonableness, attention given to extraneous circumstances, disregard of public policy and things like that have all been referred to, according to the facts of individual cases, as being matters which are relevant to the question. If they cannot all be confined under one head, they at any rate . . . overlap to a very great extent. For instance, we have heard in this case a great deal about the meaning of the word 'unreasonable'.

It is true the discretion must be exercised reasonably. Now what does that mean? . . . It has frequently been used and is frequently used as a general description of the things that must not be done . . . A person entrusted with a discretion must . . . direct himself properly in law. He must call his own attention to the matters which he is bound to consider. He must exclude from his consideration matters which are irrelevant to what he has to consider. If he does not obey those rules, he may truly be said, and often is said, to be acting 'unreasonably'. Similarly, there may be something so absurd that no sensible person could ever dream that it lay within the powers of the authority. Warrington LJ in *Short v Poole Corporation*[33] gave the example of the red-haired teacher, dismissed because she had red hair. That is unreasonable in one sense. In another sense it is taking into consideration extraneous matters. It is so unreasonable that it might almost be described as being done in bad faith; and, in fact, all these things run into one another . . . [34]

It is true to say that, if a decision on a competent matter is so unreasonable that no reasonable authority could ever have come to it, then the courts can interfere . . . But to prove a case of that kind would require something overwhelming . . . [The] proposition that the decision of the local authority can be upset if it is proved to be unreasonable, really meant that it must be proved to be unreasonable in the sense that the court considers it to be a decision that no reasonable body could have come to. It is not what the court considers unreasonable, a different thing altogether. . . The effect of the legislation is not to set up the court as an arbiter of the correctness of one view over another. It is the local authority that are set in that position and, provided they act, as they have acted, within the four corners of their jurisdiction, this court . . . cannot interfere . . . [35]

The court is entitled to investigate the action of the local authority with a view to seeing whether they have taken into account matters which they

---

32 At 228.
33 [1926] Ch 66, CA.
34 At 229.
35 At 230–231.

ought not to take into account, or, conversely, have refused to take into account or neglected to take into account matters which they ought to take into account. Once that question is answered in favour of the local authority, it may still be possible to say that, although the local authority have kept within the four corners of the matters which they ought to consider, they have nevertheless come to a conclusion so unreasonable that no reasonable authority could ever have come to it. In such a case, again, I think the court can interfere. The power of the court to interfere in each case is not as an appellate authority to override a decision of the local authority, but as a judicial authority which is concerned, and concerned only, to see whether the local authority have contravened the law by acting in excess of the powers which Parliament has confided in them.'[36]

10.24   This statement, in particular the last passage, remains the cornerstone of domestic administrative law, even if there are cases in which it has been questioned.[37]

CCSU

10.25   The central principles of public law derived from Lord Greene's comments in *Wednesbury* were subsequently re-classified by Lord Diplock under the headings of 'illegality', 'irrationality' and 'procedural impropriety' in *CCSU*:[38]

'By "illegality" as a ground of judicial review I mean that the decision-maker must understand correctly the law that regulates his decision-making power and must give effect to it. Whether he has or not is par excellence a justiciable question to be decided, in the event of dispute, by those persons, the judges, by whom the judicial power of the state is exercisable.

By "irrationality" I mean what can by now be succinctly referred to as "*Wednesbury* unreasonableness" . . . It applies to a decision which is so outrageous in its defiance of logic[39] or of accepted moral standards that no sensible person who had applied his mind to the question to be decided could have arrived at it. Whether a decision falls within this category is a question that judges by their training and experience should be well-equipped to answer, or else there would be something badly wrong with our judicial system . . . "Irrationality" by now can stand upon its own feet as an accepted ground on which a decision may be attacked by judicial review.

---

36   At 233–234.
37   See further paras **10.28–10.35**.
38   *Council of Civil Service Unions v Minister for the Civil Service* [1985] AC 374, HL ('*CCSU*'). The statement was described by Lord Scarman as 'a valuable and already "classical"' statement of the law, albeit 'certainly not exhaustive': *R v Secretary of State for the Environment ex p Nottinghamshire CC* [1986] AC 240, HL at 249.
39   Or a 'demonstrable flaw in the reasoning which led to it': *R (Law Society) v Lord Chancellor* [2018] EWHC 2094 (Admin); [2019] 1 WLR 1649cited in *R (Islam) v. Haringay LBC* [2022] EWHC 3933 (Admin); [2024] HLR forthcoming.

I have described the third head as "procedural impropriety" rather than failure to observe basic rules of natural justice or failure to act with procedural fairness towards the person who will be affected by the decision. This is because susceptibility to judicial review under this head covers also failure by an administrative tribunal to observe procedural rules that are expressly laid down in the legislative instrument by which its jurisdiction is conferred, even where such failure does not involve any denial of natural justice . . .'

Human Rights Act 1998 and proportionality

10.26   As noted above,[40] the HRA 1998 is relevant in a number of ways, including, first, that it imports specific articles of the ECHR; and, second, because of its influence on the development of the principles of domestic administrative law. It is the second of these aspects which is relevant under this heading. The first is considered below.[41]

10.27   In *CCSU*,[42] Lord Diplock had raised – but did not answer – the question whether or not the principle of 'proportionality'[43] might be imported into domestic law from Europe.[44]

10.28   From the early 1990s, doubt began to be cast on whether the *Wednesbury* test – affording a decision-maker a wide ambit of discretion – was suitable to deal with cases that involved what were recognisable as fundamental rights, and it began to be suggested that the *Wednesbury* test required adaptation so as to subject such cases to what has been called 'anxious scrutiny',[45] meaning a closer degree of factual scrutiny than the conventional *Wednesbury* approach.[46]

10.29   Comparing the differences, it has been observed that there are three potential approaches to the standard of review that may be applied when there is challenge on public law grounds:[47]

---

40   See para **10.7**.
41   See paras **10.114–10.129**.
42   See para **10.25**.
43   'Proportionality' is the doctrine that there has to be a reasonable relationship between the governmental (including local) action under review and its purpose in a given context.
44   At 410. What Lord Diplock had in mind was not the ECHR but European Union (EU) law, in which proportionality also plays a substantial part. Some have considered that proportionality was in any event already inherent in *Wednesbury* unreasonableness: see *R v Secretary of State Home Department ex p Leech* [1994] QB 198, CA; *R v Chief Constable of Sussex ex p International Trader's Ferry* [1999] 2 AC 418, HL.
45   *R v Ministry of Defence ex p Smith* [1996] QB 517, CA; *Bugdaycay v Secretary of State for the Home Department* [1987] AC 514, HL; sometimes referred to as 'Super-*Wednesbury*' – *Vilvarajah v UK* (1992) 14 EHRR 248, ECtHR.
46   See *R v Ministry of Agriculture, Fisheries and Food ex p First City Trading Limited* [1997] 1 CMLR 250, QBD; see also *R v Secretary of State for Health ex p Eastside Cheese Co* [1999] 3 CMLR 123, CA.
47   *R (Mahmood) v Secretary of State for the Home Department* [2001] 1 WLR 840, CA.

a)   the conventional *Wednesbury* approach;

b)   an approach based on fundamental rights which requires the court to 'insist that that fact be respected by the decision-maker, who is accordingly required to demonstrate either that his proposed action does not in truth interfere with the right, or, if it does, that there exist considerations which may reasonably be accepted as amounting to a substantial objective justification for the interference'; and

c)   an approach based on claims which directly engage rights guaranteed by the ECHR, which requires the court to decide whether there has in fact been a violation of a convention right.[48]

10.30   This trend towards different standards of review depending on the rights in issue appears to imply a weakening of the dominance of the *Wednesbury* test for determining public law challenges. In *Daly*,[49] Lord Steyn (although suggesting that in most cases the courts would reach the same conclusion regardless of the basis on which the decision was scrutinised) said that:

'. . . the day will come when it will be more widely recognised that [*Wednesbury*] was an unfortunately retrogressive decision in English administrative law, insofar as it suggested that there are degrees of unreasonableness and that only a very extreme degree can bring an administrative decision within the legitimate scope of judicial invalidation. The depth of judicial review and the deference due to administrative discretion vary with the subject matter. It may well be, however, that the law can never be satisfied in any administrative field merely by a finding that the decision under review is not capricious or absurd.'[50]

10.31   The reference to subject-matter is the key element for present purposes: see also Lord Steyn's comment in the same case that 'in law, context

---

48   Those categories were not 'hermitically sealed': 'There is, rather, what may be called a sliding scale of review; the graver the impact of the decision in question upon the individual affected by it, the more substantial the justification that will be required . . . [C]ases where, objectively, the individual is most gravely affected will be those where what we have come to call his fundamental rights are or are said to be put in jeopardy' (at [19]).

49   *R (Daly) v Secretary of State for the Home Department* [2001] UKHL 26, [2001] 2 AC 532. In *R (Pro-Life Alliance) v British Broadcasting Corporation* [2003] UKHL 23, [2004] 1 AC 185, Lord Walker extensively cited with approval the passages under consideration here: see [134]–[135]. See also per Lord Bingham in *A and others v Secretary of State for the Home Department; X and another v Secretary of State for the Home Department* [2004] UKHL 56, [2005] 2 AC 68, at [40].

50   Per Lord Cooke at [32]. The Court of Appeal has observed that 'the *Wednesbury* test is moving closer to proportionality' but also said that 'it is not for this court to perform the burial rights' – *R (Association of British Civilian Internees (Far East Region)) v Secretary of State for Defence* [2003] EWCA Civ 473, [2003] QB 1397.

is everything'.[51] In *Runa Begum*,[52] it could accordingly still be held that it was appropriate for the decision-maker to make findings of fact without any scrutiny other than the usual grounds for judicial review, because homelessness decisions are administrative in nature and do not engage substantive Convention rights:[53] there was therefore no need for any intensification of the traditional approach to review, or for anxious scrutiny[54] of, the decision.

10.32 In *R (Association of British Civilian Internees (Far East Region)) v Secretary of State for Defence*,[55] the Court of Appeal suggested that the time had come for the *Wednesbury* approach to be dispensed with, noting that its strictness had been relaxed in recent years so that it was, in any event, moving closer to proportionality, so much so that in some cases it was not possible to see daylight between the two tests.

10.33 In *R (Keyu) v Secretary of State for Foreign and Commonwealth Affairs*,[56] however, Lord Neuberger said that reconsideration of the basis on which courts review decisions of the executive, specifically whether *Wednesbury* rationality should be replaced by a structured proportionality assessment, would require a panel of nine Supreme Court justices because the move from rationality to proportionality could have far-reaching consequences and implications which were profound in constitutional terms.[57]

10.34 What then is the current position? *Runa Begum* concludes that what may be called the highest standard of judicial scrutiny of the three identified[58] is not applicable to challenges under HA 1996, Part 7. It implies that nothing more than conventional *Wednesbury* is applicable. Nonetheless, it remains open to argument that housing is a fundamental right, within the 'middle' standard of review.

---

51 *Daly,* at [28].
52 *Runa Begum v Tower Hamlets LBC* [2003] UKHL 5, [2003] 2 AC 430, [2003] HLR 32. *Runa Begum* was followed in *Ali v Birmingham City Council* [2010] UKSC 8, [2010] HLR 22. In *Ali v UK* App No 40378/10, [2015] HLR 46, the same case at ECtHR, it was held that Article 6(1) was engaged once the authority decided that a duty was owed under HA 1996, s 193 as that was a sufficiently certain right to amount to a 'civil right'; but it was also held that there was no violation of Article 6 as the right to a reasoned decision, review and appeal were adequate safeguards. In *Poshteh v Kensington and Chelsea RLBC* [2017] UKSC 36, [2017] AC 624, [2017] HLR 28, however, it was held that *Ali v UK* did not provide a sufficient reason to depart from the fully considered decision in *Ali v Birmingham City Council* and the Supreme Court should await full consideration of the Issue by a Grand Chamber of the European Court before deciding whether (and if so how) to modify its position.
53 See further paras **10.114–10.129**.
54 See *R v Ministry of Agriculture, Fisheries and Food ex p First City Trading Limited* [1997] 1 CMLR 250, QBD; see also *R v Secretary of State for Health ex p Eastside Cheese Co* [1999] 3 CMLR 123, CA.
55 [2003] EWCA Civ 473, [2003] QB 1397, per Lord Phillips at [34]–[35].
56 [2015] UKSC 69.
57 At [132]–[133]. Lord Kerr, at [271] agreed with the need for a panel of nine but also said that the question would have to be addressed by the Supreme Court sooner rather than later.
58 See para **10.29**.

10.35 Even if forced back to *Wednesbury*, that may not be the end of it: the *Wednesbury* approach is clearly under pressure or, as it has been put, the law is engaged in a 'long trek away from *Wednesbury* irrationality'.[59] Perhaps the simplest approach is to view the *Wednesbury* approach as an absolute minimum, while acknowledging that, sometimes, it will not be enough.[60]

Grounds for challenge – practical classification

10.36 Having considered the general principles on which public law decisions may be challenged, we turn to consider the practical classification of grounds for challenge, utilising *CCSU*,[61] supplemented by the specific (relevant) provisions of the HRA 1998.[62]

10.37 As effectively recognised in *Wednesbury*,[63] when applied in a practical context, grounds tend to overlap one another: thus a failure to have regard to a relevant fact may also be an error of law; a failure to give reasons for a decision may not only be unlawful for failure to comply with the duty to do so but may also found a challenge based on the fairness of the procedure.

10.38 Moreover, the distinction between a point of law (challengeable on administrative law principles) and a question of fact (which is not) is not a straightforward distinction and there will be cases where matters of pure fact arise.

> 'The cases do not support the proposition that *any* conclusion that a legal or statutory concept applies to a particular set of facts is a question of law, although in practice they permit considerable elasticity in their application.'[64]

Illegality

Misdirection of law

10.39 A decision-maker must 'understand correctly the law that regulates their decision-making power and must give effect to it',[65] ie, the decision-maker

---

59 Per Lord Walker in *R (ProLife Alliance) v British Broadcasting Corporation* [2003] UKHL 23, [2004] 1 AC 185, at [131].

60 In reality, the *Wednesbury* test is sufficiently flexible – open-textured – in any event to allow courts to apply it to the same effect as if another test were permissible. Certainly, they have no difficulty catching the more egregious errors and injustices when they wish to do so.

61 See para **10.25**.

62 Cf paras **10.114–10.129**.

63 See para **10.23**.

64 *Adan v Newham LBC* [2001] EWCA Civ 1916, [2002] HLR 28, per Hale LJ at [66] (emphasis in original).

65 *CCSU* at 410F, per Lord Diplock.

must understand and apply the law correctly. Thus in *Islam*,[66] the authority's misunderstanding of the test to be applied when determining whether a person was homeless intentionally under the Housing (Homeless Persons) Act 1977 was a misdirection of law sufficient to vitiate the decision.[67] When a court reconsiders an issue, eg, the meaning of vulnerable,[68] it is reconsidering the correct legal interpretation of an issue and – if finding against the authority – holding that previous usage was a misdirection. What a duty calls for from an authority is a matter of law: the relatively new assessment duties considered in Chapter 8 show just how far a court may go into the detailed facts in order to establish whether or not the authority has complied with its duty.[69]

Decisions must be based on the facts

10.40 While it is of the essence of *Puhlhofer*[70] that matters of fact are for the decision-maker, this does not mean that factual errors are irrelevant. In *Adan*,[71] Brooke LJ commented:[72]

'In very many cases, although it could be said that an administrative body had made a material mistake of fact the decision is vulnerable on other more conventional grounds: for procedural impropriety . . . or because a factor had been taken into account which should not have been taken into account . . . or because there was no evidence on which the decision could have been safely based . . . What is quite clear is that a court of supervisory jurisdiction does not, without more, have the power to substitute its own view of the primary facts for the view reasonably adopted by the body to whom the fact-finding power has been entrusted.'

10.41 If it can be shown that a decision proceeded on the basis of an incorrect understanding of the facts, that there was no evidence to support the finding of fact made, or that there was no account taken of the facts, there may be scope for a challenge on the basis that the decision was at odds with the factual matrix,[73] in particular where there are fundamental rights at stake.[74]

---

66 *R v Hillingdon LBC ex p Islam* [1983] 1 AC 688, HL. See also *Anisminic Ltd v Foreign Compensation Commission* [1969] 2 AC 147, HL and *R (Q) v Secretary of State for the Home Department* [2003] EWCA Civ 364, [2004] QB 36.

67 If the decision-maker incorrectly thinks that it does not have a power, that is also a misdirection of law: *National Aids Trust v National Health Service Commissioning Board (NHS England)* [2016] EWHC 2005 (Admin).

68 *Hotak v Southwark LBC; Kanu v Southwark LBC; Johnson v Solihull MBC* [2015] UKSC 30, [2015] HLR 23.

69 See, eg, the cases of *R. (ZK) v Havering LBC* [2022] EWHC 1854 (Admin); [2022] HLR 47 and *R. (YR) v Lambeth LBC* [2022] EWHC 2813 (Admin); [2023] HLR 16 at paras **8.66–8.74**.

70 See para **10.15**.

71 *Adan v Newham LBC*, above.

72 At [41].

73 *Secretary of State for Education and Science v Tameside MBC* [1977] AC 1014, HL, at 1047.

74 In *R (Wilkinson) v Broadmoor Special Hospital Authority* [2001] EWCA Civ 1545, [2002] 1 WLR 419, it was suggested that, where fundamental rights were at issue, the court 'must now inevitably reach its own view' on the facts. See also *R (Murphy) v Secretary of State for the Home Department* [2005] EWHC 140 (Admin), [2005] 1 WLR 3516.

10.42   It has also for some time been recognised that the court is entitled to decide what the facts are if they comprise 'precedent facts' or as they are sometimes called, 'jurisdictional facts',[75] ie, if the facts establish the right to exercise a power or the obligation to perform a duty,[76] the court is entitled to reach a decision for itself as to what the facts are.[77] There are examples of this in the cases governing the assessment of the age of an asylum seeker, in order to determine whether or not they are a child and, as such, entitled to assistance under the Children Act 1989.[78]

10.43   Where there has been a review,[79] however, the issue will be whether the reviewer could, as a matter of public law, have reached the relevant decision on the facts, rather than whether those facts exist,[80] as the scheme of the HA 1996 means that 'there is no jurisdiction . . . for the County Court to set itself up as a finder of the relevant primary facts for itself'.[81] See also the discussion of the judgment of the Supreme Court in *Ali v Birmingham City Council*[82] below.[83]

10.44   In *Tameside* at the Court of Appeal,[84] Scarman LJ suggested that an error of fact – not merely precedent fact – might be sufficient of itself to vitiate an authority's decision where that error could be said to be a 'misunderstanding or ignorance of an established and relevant fact': this approach has found significant

---

75   Eg, *R v Secretary of State for the Environment ex p Powis* [1981] 1 WLR 584, CA per Dunn LJ at 595H.

76   *R v Secretary of State for Home Department ex p Khawaja* [1984] AC 74, HL. See also per Baroness Hale in *R (A) (FC) v Croydon LBC; R (M) (FC) v Lambeth LBC* [2009] UKSC 8, at [29]–[30].

77   See *Khawaja*, above, per Lord Wilberforce at 105; *R v Oldham BC ex p Garlick* [1993] AC 509, HL, per Lord Griffiths at 520E.

78   Para **11.75**.

79   See para **7.190** onwards.

80   *Bubb v Wandsworth LBC* [2011] EWCA Civ 1285, [2012] HLR 13, where the issue was whether the applicant had received the authority's letter warning her of the possible consequences of refusal of an offer, and of her right to request a review of the suitability of the accommodation, under HA 1996, s 193(7), (7F); the reviewing officer had been entitled to conclude that she had done so. Cf *R (A) v Croydon LBC* [2009] UKSC 8, [2009] 1 WLR 2557, where the age of a child for the purposes of Children Act (CA) 1989, s 20 was held to be one for the court, distinguishing (at [28]) between 'a number of different value judgments' contained in the CA 1989 and 'a different kind of question [to which there] is a right or a wrong answer' (of which age was an example).

81   *Bubb* at [20]. *Bubb* was not overruled by *R (ZH and CN) v Newham LBC and Lewisham LBC* [2014] UKSC 62, [2015] AC 1259, [2015] HLR 6: the county court can only determine a factual dispute in the context of a challenge to the proportionality of a prospective eviction (para **10.207**) – *Adesotu v Lewisham LBC (Equality and Human Rights Commission intervening)* [2019] EWCA Civ 1405, [2019] 1 WLR 5637, [2019] HLR 48. See also *Richmond upon Thames v Kubicek* [2012] EWHC 3292 (QB) where it was held that the county court judge had been wrong to list a trial of a preliminary issue (and hear factual evidence) to resolve a dispute between the authority and the applicant as to what had been said during HA 1996, s 184 enquiries.

82   [2010] UKSC 8.

83   See paras **10.117–10.121**.

84   *Secretary of State for Education and Science v Tameside MBC* (1976) 120 SJ 735, CA.

subsequent support.[85] There are now several examples of administrative decisions quashed because they were reached on a material error[86] of fact,[87] although opinions differ as to whether they are examples of failing to take into account a relevant consideration,[88] a stand-alone ground[89] or are an aspect of fairness.[90] It must nonetheless be said that mistake of fact is still some way from a generally accepted ground of judicial review.[91]

85   Lord Slynn, in *R v Criminal Injuries Compensation Board ex p A* [1999] 2 AC 330, HL accepted the existence of such a doctrine, a view he re-affirmed in *R (Alconbury Developments Ltd) v Secretary of State for the Environment, Transport and the Regions* [2001] UKHL 23, [2003] 2 AC 295 at [53], but in neither case was this reasoning adopted by the Committee and, in the first, Lord Slynn himself 'preferred' to decide the case on the alternative ground of breach of natural justice amounting to unfairness (at 345). In *E v Secretary of State for the Home Department* [2004] EWCA Civ 49, [2004] QB 1044, Carnwath LJ considered the history in some detail. How far the House of Lords can be said to have endorsed Scarman LJ's approach may be in some doubt: see *E* at [55].

86   Or 'fundamental mistake of fact': see *Porteous v West Dorset DC* [2004] EWCA Civ 244, per Mantell LJ at [9].

87   See also *Mason v Secretary of State for the Environment and Bromsgrove DC* [1984] JPL 332; *Jagendorf & Trott v Secretary of State for the Environment and Krasucki* [1987] JPL 771; *R v Hillingdon LBC ex p Thomas* (1987) 19 HLR 196; *R v Legal Aid Committee No 10 (East Midlands) ex p McKenna* [1990] COD 358, (1989) *Times* 20 December, DC; *Simplex GE (Holdings) Ltd v Secretary of State for the Environment* [1988] 3 PLR 25, CA; *R v London Residuary Body ex p ILEA* (1987) *Times* 3 July, CA. See also *R (Meredith) v Merthyr Tydfil CBC* [2002] EWHC 634 (Admin); *R (Kathro) v Rhondda Cynon Taff CBC* [2001] EWHC (Admin) 527, [2002] Env LR 196; *R (McLellan) v Bracknell Forest BC* [2001] EWCA Civ 1510, [2002] QB 1129; *Martin Hill v Bedfordshire CC* [2007] EWHC 2435 (Admin), [2008] ELR 191; *R (March) v Secretary of State for Health* [2010] EWHC 765 (Admin); *Manydown Ltd v Basingstoke and Deane BC* [2012] EWHC 977 (Admin); *R (Watt) v Hackney LBC* [2016] EWHC 1978 (Admin).

88   *Secretary of State for Education and Science v Tameside MBC*, above, per Lord Diplock at 1066F–1067A. See also *Crake v Supplementary Benefits Commission* [1982] 1 All ER 498, QBD at 508, cited in *Aslam v South Bedfordshire DC* [2001] EWCA Civ 515, [2001] RVR 65, itself cited in *E v Secretary of State for the Home Department*, above, at [38].

89   *R (Alconbury Developments and others) v Secretary of State for the Environment, Transport and the Regions*, above at [53], [169]; *R v Criminal Injuries Compensation Board ex p A*, above, at [344]; *Runa Begum v Tower Hamlets LBC* [2003] UKHL 5, [2003] 2 AC 430, at [7]–[11].

90   *E v Secretary of State for the Home Department*, above, and see further, paras **10.40–10.44**. 'What mattered was that, because of their failure, and through no fault of her own, the claimant had not had "a fair crack of the whip" (see *Fairmount Investments v Secretary of State for the Environment* [1976] 1 WLR 1255, HL per Lord Russell at 1266/A). If it is said that this is taking "fairness" beyond its traditional role as an aspect of procedural irregularity it is no further than its use in cases such as *HTV Ltd v Price Commission* [1976] ICR 170, CA approved by the House of Lords in *R v IRC ex p Preston* [1985] AC 835, at 865–866). In our view, the time has now come to accept that a mistake of fact giving rise to unfairness is a separate head of challenge in an appeal on a point of law, at least in those statutory contexts where the parties share an interest in co-operating to achieve the correct result. Asylum law is undoubtedly such an area.' Per Carnwath LJ in *E* at [65]–[66].

91   See *Wandsworth LBC v A* [2000] 1 WLR 1246, CA, at 1255/H-1256/C: 'While there may, possibly, be special considerations that apply in the more formalised area of planning inquiries . . . and while the duty of "anxious scrutiny" imposed in asylum cases by *R v Secretary of State for the Home Department ex p Bugdaycay* [[1987] AC 514, HL] renders those cases an uncertain guide for other areas of public law; none the less . . . there is still no general right to challenge the decision of a public body on an issue of fact alone. The law in this connection continues, in our respectful view, to be as stated for a unanimous House of Lords by Lord Brightman in *R v Hillingdon LBC ex p Puhlhofer . . .*'.

Taking into account irrelevant considerations

10.45 It is sufficient to void a decision on the basis that an irrelevant factor has been taken into account if the factor is significant, or potentially of influence, meaning that, if it had not been taken into account, the decision might have been different. The authority must take such steps as are reasonable to find out the relevant facts.[92] When housing is in issue, 'consideration of common humanity' is a relevant consideration in its own right.[93] While the resources available to an authority will be relevant to how it discharges its duty,[94] they are not relevant[95] to the question whether there is a duty at all.[96]

10.46 There is no general proposition which governs what is a relevant consideration: the question is what the Act requires to be taken into account, not what the court thinks may be relevant.[97] Under Armed Forces Act 2006, ss 343AA (England) and 343AB (Wales), when exercising any function under Parts 6 or 7, HA 1996, a local authority must have due regard to:

---

92 Per Lord Diplock in *Secretary of State for Education and Science v Tameside MBC* [1977] AC 1014, HL, at p1065; see also *R v Lincolnshire CC and Wealden DC ex p Atkinson* (1996) 8 Admin LR 529, DC and *R v Hillingdon LBC ex p McDonagh* (1999) 31 HLR 531, QBD.

93 *Ex p Atkinson, ex p McDonagh*, above; *R v Kerrier ex p Uzell* (1995) 71 P&CR 566, QBD; *R v Brighton and Hove Council ex p Marmont* (1998) 30 HLR 1046, QBD.

94 *R v Lambeth LBC ex p A and G* (1998) 30 HLR 933, CA. Consider, however, *Conville v Richmond upon Thames LBC* [2006] EWCA Civ 718, [2006] HLR 45, where financial considerations were not relevant when determining the period for which an authority must provide an applicant with accommodation under HA 1996, s 190(2)(a) to afford them a 'reasonable opportunity to secure accommodation' (see para **8.118**. Nonetheless, homelessness and allocations must be considered in their context: 'But the social norm must be applied in the context of a scheme for allocating scarce resources. It is impossible to consider only what would be desirable in the interests of the family if resources were unlimited . . .'; 'There seems to me no reason in logic why the fact that Parliament has made the question of priority need turn upon whether a dependent child might reasonably be expected to reside with the applicant should require that question to be answered without regard to the purpose for which it is being asked, namely, to determine priority in the allocation of a scarce resource. To ignore that purpose would not be a rational social policy. It does not mean that a housing authority can say that it does not have the resources to comply with its obligations under the Act. Parliament has placed upon it the duty to house the homeless and has specified the priorities it should apply. But so far as the criteria for those priorities involve questions of judgment, it must surely take into account the overall purpose of the scheme': per Lord Hoffmann in *Holmes-Moorhouse v Richmond upon Thames LBC* [2009] UKHL 7, [2009] HLR 34, at [12] and [16].

95 Save so far as it may be said that consideration of the general housing circumstances of an area as an element in a decision on homelessness, and on intentionality, might be said to import 'resources' by the back door (see paras **2.91–2.98**).

96 Cf *R v Birmingham City Council ex p Mohammed* [1999] 1 WLR 33, (1999) 31 HLR 392, QBD where it was said that to treat resources as relevant when deciding whether or not to approve a disabled facilities grant would be to downgrade a duty to a discretion. See, generally, *R v East Sussex CC ex p Tandy* [1998] AC 714, HL; see also *R v Bristol City Council ex p Penfold* (1997–98) 1 CCLR 315, QBD. Compare also *R(Conville) v Richmond upon Thames LBC* [2006] EWCA Civ 718, [2006] HLR 1, and *Holmes-Moorhouse v Richmond upon Thames LBC* [2009] UKHL 7, [2009] HLR 34.

97 *Re Findlay* [1985] AC 318, HL, at 333; see also *R v Hillingdon LBC ex p McDonagh* (1999) 31 HLR 531, QBD.

'(a) the unique obligations of, and sacrifices made by, the armed forces,

(b) the principle that it is desirable to remove disadvantages arising for service people from membership, or former membership, of the armed forces, and

(c) the principle that special provision for service people may be justified by the effects on such people of membership, or former membership, of the armed forces'.[98]

Disproportionate weight for relevant considerations

10.47   It is not just taking something irrelevant into account that may vitiate the decision, but also giving disproportionate weight to a relevant consideration. In *Ashton*,[99] excessive reliance had been placed on the prevailing housing circumstances of the area when considering intentional homelessness;[100] the decision-maker had not appreciated that 'it is something that must be weighed carefully in the balance with the other factors upon which the decision . . . is reached'.[101]

Failure to take into account relevant considerations

10.48   Just as taking into account the irrelevant may vitiate a decision, so may a failure to take into account the relevant, such as the effect of a medical condition on the need for a transfer from accommodation.[102] The authority must take reasonable steps to acquaint itself with what is relevant.[103] It is, however, only *relevant* considerations which matter: a challenge to an authority's decision as to the suitability of sub-leased accommodation for an applicant with a mental health condition that called for stability, based on the proposition that the sub-lease could be terminated at any time on three months' notice, was not a failure to take something into account because the claimant had been unaware of the possibility (nor had raised it as a factor in the challenge).[104]

10.49   Some considerations derive from statute and therefore must be taken into account: consider the requirements under HA 1996, ss 169(1) and 182(1) and H(W)A 2014, s 98(1) to have regard to Codes of Guidance when determining

---

98   Added by Armed Forces Act 2021, s 8(3), with effect from 22 November 2022.

99   *R v Winchester City Council ex p Ashton* (1992) 24 HLR 520, CA.

100 See para **4.43**.

101 At p526.

102 *R v Islington LBC ex p Aldabbagh* (1995) 27 HLR 271, QBD.

103 Per Lord Diplock in *Secretary of State for Education and Science v Tameside MBC* [1977] AC 1014, HL, at 1065.

104 *R (Islam) v. Haringey LBC* [2022] EWHC 3933 (Admin); [2024] HLR forthcoming.

applications under HA 1996, Parts 6 and 7 and H(W)A 2014, Part 2.[105] The requirement to 'have regard' to the relevant Code of Guidance does not mean that the authority is bound by it, or bound to apply it: it simply means that the Code is a relevant consideration to which regard must be had.[106]

10.50   An authority may depart from a Code, eg, because it considers the Code to be incorrect[107] or in conflict with the requirements of statute,[108] but the reasons for any departure should be explained.[109] If the decision-maker wrongly takes the view that a consideration is not relevant, and therefore has no regard to it, their decision cannot stand and they will be required to think again.[110]

10.51   A failure to take into account a relevant consideration will be sufficient to found a claim only if consideration of the relevant fact would have made a difference to the decision.[111] In *R v Newham LBC ex p Bones*,[112] it was held that regard to the wrong (earlier) Code would invalidate a decision, if there was a substantive point of difference, including a change of emphasis.[113] Current central government practice is to update the Code of Guidance online, without re-issuing it: this poses difficulties in relation to challenges based on a failure to have regard to a change. While changes, and when they are made, are identified in a Version Control Sheet, the assiduous adviser in private practice, and a local authority homelessness section, should certainly subscribe to a DHLUC service which announces such changes; additionally, as (on the basis of general experience)

105 As to which, see *R v Wandsworth LBC ex p Hawthorne* [1994] 1 WLR 1442, CA. The Codes of Guidance are: In England, *Homelessness code of guidance for local authorities*, Ministry of Housing, Communities and Local Government (MHCLG), February 2018, updated May 2023; (www.gov.uk/guidance/homelessness-code-of-guidance-for-local-authorities). In Wales: *Code of guidance for local authorities on the allocation of accommodation and homelessness*, Welsh Government, March 2016, with updates published from time to time as separate documents (https://www.gov.wales/allocation-accommodation-and-homelessness-guidance-local-authorities).

106 An authority need not, however, spell out every paragraph of the Code to which it has had regard, see, eg, *Birmingham City Council v Balog* [2013] EWCA Civ 1582, [2014] HLR 14.

107 See, eg, *R v Brent LBC ex p Awua* [1996] AC 55, (1995) 27 HLR 453, HL.

108 In which case, it is always the statute which prevails: see, eg, *R v Waveney DC ex p Bowers* [1983] QB 238, (1982) 4 HLR 118, CA; *Griffin v Westminster City Council* [2004] EWCA Civ 108, [2004] HLR 32.

109 See *Padfield v Minister of Agriculture, Fisheries and Food* [1968] AC 997, HL; see also, eg, *de Falco, Silvestri v Crawley BC* [1980] QB 460, CA; *Khatun v Newham LBC* [2004] EWCA Civ 55, [2005] QB 37.

110 *Tesco Stores Ltd v Secretary of State for the Environment* [1995] 1 WLR 759, HL, at 764G–H.

111 *R v Wandsworth LBC ex p Onwudiwe; R v Secretary of State for Health ex p Eastside Cheese Co* [1999] EuLR 968, CA. See also *Rowe v Haringey LBC* [2022] EWCA Civ 1370; [2023] HLR 5 where the absence of a tenancy agreement was not something so important that no reasonable authority would have failed to consider it and accordingly, though relevant, it did not affect the outcome.

112 (1993) 25 HLR 357, QBD.

113 Although this is not definitive: in *Moge v Ealing LBC* [2023] EWCA Civ 464; [2023] HLR 35, a minded-to letter referred to an earlier version of the Code which preceded important changes (on out-of-area accommodation: see paras **8.168–8.176**) but as there was evidence to show that the correct, contemporaneous approach had been adopted, this did not invalidate the decision; nor had the error been raised on the review.

this practice may not be retained indefinitely, a belt-and-braces approach could be to diarise a routine download of the Code to retain by date and institute a cross-check for changes.[114] The same points arise in relation to allocations: see para **9.10**.

Promoting the object of legislation[115]

10.52 Powers conferred for public purposes must be used in a way that Parliament can be presumed to have intended.[116] In *Khalique*,[117] the authority was entitled to provide temporary accommodation (in discharge of the HA 1996, Part 7 duty) provided the entitlement to permanent accommodation was not deferred so as 'to frustrate the purpose of the legislation and the rights which it gives to individuals, nor deferred or withheld for some improper or illicit reason'.[118]

10.53 Likewise, in *Robinson v Hammersmith and Fulham LBC,*[119] the authority could not defer a decision until the applicant, a child, reached an age at which she would not be in priority need so that she would no longer be entitled to assistance.[120]

Fettering discretion

10.54 An authority must reach its own decision on each individual case; it may not fetter its discretion by approaching a decision with a pre-determined policy on how it will deal with cases that fall within a particular class.[121] That is not to say that – if good administration requires it – an authority cannot adopt a policy in order to *guide* the future exercise of its discretion. Where it does so, however, it must consider the application of that policy individually in every case where it is sought to make an exception.[122]

---

114 Any record should not only note the date of the change but also when relevant people administering the legislation were informed of it.

115 See, generally, *Padfield v Minister of Agriculture, Fisheries and Food* [1968] AC 997, HL; see also *Meade v Haringey LBC* [1979] 1 WLR 637, CA, and *R v Braintree DC ex p Halls* (2000) 32 HLR 770, CA.

116 *R v Tower Hamlets LBC ex p Chetnik Developments Ltd* [1988] AC 858, HL.

117 *R v Tower Hamlets LBC ex p Khalique* (1994) 26 HLR 517, QBD.

118 *Khalique*, at 522.

119 [2006] EWCA Civ 1122, at [31].

120 See paras **3.85–3.86**.

121 *British Oxygen Co Ltd v Minister of Technology* [1971] AC 610, HL. See also *R (Lumba) v. Secretary of State* [2011] UKSC 12, [2012] 1 AC 245 at [21]: '...[I]t is a well established principle of public law that a policy should not be so rigid as to amount to a fetter on the discretion of decision-makers'.

122 *British Oxygen Co Ltd v Minister of Technology*, above, at 625E; *Re Betts* [1983] 2 AC 613, (1983) 10 HLR 97, HL; see Chapter 6.

10.55   A policy of requiring all applicants who were joint tenants of an authority to serve notice to quit (thereby terminating the tenancy) before they could be accepted as homeless owing to domestic violence under HA 1996, Part 7 was held to be unlawful in *Hammia*.[123] In *Savage*,[124] the applicant was refused assistance by way of a rent deposit in order to secure private rented accommodation because she had been found to be homeless intentionally; although the authority's policy was not unlawful, because it required officers to consider its application in every case, it had been misunderstood and misapplied in the present case.

Unlawful delegation or dictation

10.56   The authority cannot avoid its duties by simply adopting the decision of another body.[125] A distinction must be drawn, however, between adoption of the decision of another body and the proper use of others to assist in reaching a decision.[126] The authority may employ staff,[127] and has power to employ contractors or agents and to enter into contracts with them.[128] These resources can all be used when reaching a decision. What cannot be abdicated – save so far as statutorily permitted – is responsibility for the essential elements of a decision, which are to determine *what* is to be done or *what* is to happen (in contrast to – even if overlapping with – *how* something is to be done), ie, the underlying decision rather than its day-to-day management.[129]

10.57   Statute permits many functions to be designated by order as capable of being exercised by others who are not members or employees of the authority.[130] Under this provision, the Local Authorities (Contracting Out of Allocation of Housing and Homelessness Functions) Order 1996[131] permits a wide range of functions under both HA 1996, Parts 6 and 7 and H(W)A 2014, Part 2 to be contracted out,[132] including enquiry and even decision-making on homelessness.[133]

---

123 *R (Hammia) v Wandsworth LBC* [2005] EWHC 1127 (Admin), [2005] HLR 46.
124 *R (Savage) v Hillingdon LBC* [2010] EWHC 88 (Admin), [2010] JHL D44.
125 *Lavender & Sons v Minister of Housing and Local Government* [1970] 1 WLR 1231, QBD.
126 In *R v West Dorset DC ex p Gerrard* (1994) 27 HLR 150, QBD, under HA 1985, Part 3, the authority could enlist the assistance of a third party but had to take the 'active and dominant' part in the investigative process. But cf the approach in *R v Hertsmere BC ex p Woolgar* (1995) 27 HLR 703, QBD, likewise under HA 1985, Part 3. The actual results are now overtaken by statutory provision: see para **10.57**.
127 Local Government Act (LGA) 1972, s 112.
128 *Crédit Suisse v Allerdale BC* [1997] QB 306, CA, at 346. There is now express power to contract, in Local Government (Contracts) Act 1997, s 1.
129 *Crédit Suisse v Allerdale BC* [1995] 1 Lloyd's Rep 315, Comm Ct, [1997] QB 306, CA.
130 Deregulation and Contracting Out Act 1994, s 70.
131 Local Authorities (Contracting Out of Allocation of Housing and Homelessness Functions) Order 1996, SI 1996/3205; as amended by Housing (Wales) Act 2014 (Consequential Amendments) Regulations 2015, SI 2015/752 so as to extend to H(W)A 2014, Part 2. See generally *Tachie v Welwyn Hatfield BC* [2013] EWHC 3972 (QB). See paras **7.6–7.8.**
132 The 'public sector equality duty' imposed on authorities by Equality Act (EqA) 2010, s 149, does not prevent contracting out: see para **7.6** – *Panayiotou v Waltham Forest LBC; Smith v Haringey LBC* [2017] EWCA Civ 1624, [2017] HLR 48.
133 See Chapter 7.

The authority's decision must be reached properly

10.58   Under the LGA 1972, it is the full authority[134] which is prima facie entrusted with functions, including the function of reaching decisions, and only the authority can perform its functions[135] save so far as it is permitted to delegate it: the general power of delegation in local government (LGA 1972, s 101) permits delegation to a committee, subcommittee or officer. That power does not permit delegation to a single member; because there cannot be a committee or subcommittee of one.[136] It does, however, permit delegation to an officer, to be exercised in consultation with a member, so long as the member does not play the dominant role to the extent that the officer cannot be said to have reached the decision themselves.[137]

10.59   Under Local Government Act (LGA) 2000, however, local authorities now function in what may be described as two parts: an executive and the full authority. Decisions not conferred on the authority by statute, statutory instrument or (where the matter is left to the authority to decide) under what is known as 'local choice',[138] must be taken by the executive.[139] Decisions on allocations and homelessness are – by this route – matters for the executive.[140] Decisions to be taken by the executive may be dealt with in any way that the LGA 2000 permits, which includes delegation to an individual member of the executive, or to a committee or sub-committee of the executive, or to an officer (or, in some circumstances, an area committee not of the executive but of the authority itself).[141]

10.60   A decision of an executive is treated as that of, and is binding on, the authority;[142] it is not a delegation to the executive but a decision taken on behalf of the authority:[143] the authority cannot 'overrule' it in the way that, for example, it can 'overrule' one of its own committees or officers (and could formerly overrule all committees and officers), although it does have power to consider an executive

---

134 Subject to exceptions.
135 *Gardner v London Chatham and Dover Railway Co (No 1)* (1867) LR 2 Ch App 201, CA; *Marshall v South Staffordshire Tramways Co* [1895] 2 Ch 36, CA; *Parker v Camden LBC* [1986] Ch 162, CA; *Crédit Suisse plc v Waltham Forest LBC* [1997] QB 362, CA.
136 *R v Secretary of State for the Environment ex p Hillingdon LBC* [1986] 1 WLR 807, CA. There is statutory power to delegate to a single member in circumstances which do not apply here: see Local Government and Public Involvement in Health Act 2007, s 236.
137 *R v Port Talbot BC ex p Jones* [1988] 2 All ER 207, QBD. See also *R v Tower Hamlets LBC ex p Khalique* (1994) 26 HLR 517, QBD. It would seem that a decision improperly delegated can subsequently be ratified if the defect in the decision has nothing to do with the merits of the matter and deprives the applicant of no genuine legal right: see para **10.21**.
138 LGA 2000, s 9D(3)(b) (England); s 13(3)(b) (Wales).
139 LGA 2000, s 9D(2) (England); s 13(2) (Wales).
140 LGA 2000, ss 9D, 13; Local Authorities (Functions and Responsibilities) (England) Regulations 2000, SI 2000/2853; and Local Authorities (Executive Arrangements) (Functions and Responsibilities) (Wales) Regulations 2007, SI 2007/399.
141 LGA 2000, ss 9E (England); ss 14-18 (Wales).
142 LGA 2000, s 9D (England); s 13 (Wales).
143 LGA 2000, s 9D (England); s 13 (Wales).

decision and to require the executive to reconsider it.[144] Nor, conversely, can the executive overrule a decision of the authority.[145]

10.61 A general category of 'appeals' is within the 'local choice' class.[146] It does not seem that this includes reviews under HA 1996, Parts 6 and 7 because a review can take into account facts arising subsequent to the original decision[147] which means that it is not exclusively an 'appeal' and there remain issues of judgment that fall within the 'execution' of functions that should fall on the executive.

Irrationality

Wednesbury

10.62 As noted,[148] the authority may not reach a decision which no reasonable authority could have reached – such a decision, sometimes referred to as a perverse decision, is conclusive evidence that the decision is irrational and therefore void. There is a high threshold to cross, but it is not insurmountable.[149]

Bad faith/improper purposes or motives

10.63 A decision will be unlawful if it can be shown that the decision-maker acted in bad faith or was motivated by some aim or purpose that is not considered legitimate. This is part of the (obvious) principle that the decision-maker may not use the powers entrusted to them for purposes which fall outwith their authority.[150] Acting in bad faith stands alone as a ground and will automatically vitiate a decision.[151] Although frequently alleged by dissatisfied applicants, both grounds are difficult to establish[152] and must be fully particularised and proven.[153]

---

144 LGA 2000, s 9F (England); s 21 (Wales). All authorities must maintain at least one 'overview and scrutiny' committee to exercise such powers, on which the executive cannot be represented; they may, however, maintain more than one such committee, referable to different functions.

145 This is implicit in the allocation of functions to the different parts of the authority.

146 Local Authorities (Functions and Responsibilities) (England) Regulations 2000, SI 2000/2853, reg 3(1) and Sch 2 para 2; and Local Authorities (Executive Arrangements) (Functions and Responsibilities) (Wales) Regulations 2007, SI 2007/399, Sch 2 para 2.

147 *Mohamed v Hammersmith and Fulham LBC* [2001] UKHL 57, [2002] 1 AC 547, see paras **5.37**, **7.71**. A review of suitability must, likewise, be conducted at the date of the review: *Waltham Forest LBC v Saleh* [2019] EWCA Civ 1994, [2020] PTSR 621, [2020] HLR 15.

148 See para **10.23**.

149 See, eg, *R v Westminster City Council ex p Moozary-Oraky* (1993) 26 HLR 213, QBD at para **4.65**; *R v Southwark LBC ex p Hughes* (1998) 30 HLR 1082, QBD.at para **5.34**; *R (IA) v Westminster City Council* [2013] EWHC 1273 (QB) at para **7.76**; *R (Bauer-Czarnomski) v Ealing LBC* [2010] EWHC 130 (Admin), [2010] JHL D38.

150 *R v Tower Hamlets LBC ex p Chetnik Developments Ltd* [1988] AC 858, HL.

151 *Wednesbury*, see para **10.23**; *Smith v East Elloe Rural DC* [1956] AC 736, HL.

152 In *Cannock Chase DC v Kelly* [1978] 1 WLR 1, CA, it was suggested that the term should be used only in respect of a dishonest misuse of power.

153 *Cannock Chase DC v Kelly* [1978] 1 WLR 1, CA.

10.64   A power conferred on a local authority may not lawfully be exercised to promote the electoral advantage of a political party.[154] If several purposes are being pursued and the dominant purpose is legitimate, however, the decision will not be unlawful.[155]

Procedural impropriety

Fairness and Article 6

10.65   A decision-maker must act fairly and in accordance with the principles of natural justice, as supplemented and developed by Article 6 of the ECHR (right to a fair trial) in appropriate cases.[156]

10.66   What constitutes fairness has been described as 'essentially an intuitive judgment'[157] and what it demands will depend on the context of the decision, the statute which confers the decision-making power on the decision-maker, and the legal and administrative system within which the decision is taken.[158] Fairness will commonly require that a person adversely affected by the decision should have an opportunity to make representations on their own behalf either before the decision is taken or with a view to procuring its modification; that requirement necessarily carries with it a need on the part of the applicant to be informed of the gist of the case which they have to answer.[159]

10.67   The influence of Article 6 in this area generally has been considerable, but has not yet had a significant impact in relation to claims under HA 1996, Part 6 or Part 7 or H(W)A 2014, Part 2.[160] Any defects which may exist in the statutory procedure for internal review can be rectified by the right of an applicant to appeal to the county court or by judicial review.[161]

10.68   That is not to say that the existence of a statutory scheme will always be deemed sufficient. The courts may, if they consider the circumstances of the case justify it, impose more stringent requirements to ensure that a matter has been

---

154 *Magill v Porter* [2001] UKHL 67, [2002] 2 AC 357. Part of the conservative council's 'Homes for Votes' programme, held unlawful in *Magill*, involved housing homeless persons – assumed not to vote conservative – outside of the authority's area.

155 *Magill v Porter* [2001] UKHL 67, [2002] 2 AC 357.

156 As to which, see paras **10.117–10.122**.

157 *R v Secretary of State for the Home Department ex p Doody* [1994] 1 AC 531, HL, at 560/D.

158 In *R (Humnyntskyi and others) v Secretary of State for the Home Department* [2020] EWHC 1912 (Admin); HousingView, 27 July 2020, the secretary of state's policy to deal with requests for immigration bail contained inconsistencies as some categories of applicant were entitled to make representations but not others; where representations were made, there was evidence that the information was not routinely provided to the decision-maker. The decision-making process was thus flawed and created systemic unfairness and was declared unlawful.

159 *R v Secretary of State for the Home Department ex p Doody*, above.

160 See further paras **10.117–10.122**.

161 See also *R (Alconbury Developments Ltd) v Secretary of State for the Environment, Transport and the Regions* [2001] UKHL 23, [2003] 2 AC 295.

decided fairly.[162] Thus, while review of a homelessness decision has to be carried out by a senior officer not involved in the original decision,[163] mere compliance with this would per se not prevent a challenge to the review[164] if the reviewer – though senior and not involved – could, for other reasons,[165] be said to be biased against the applicant.

10.69   Leaving aside Article 6, the principles of natural justice require both that no one should be a judge in their own cause (bias); and that an applicant has the right to be heard.[166]

Bias

10.70   For a decision to be quashed on the ground of bias, it is not necessary to show that the decision-maker was in fact biased; it is sufficient for there to be an apparent bias.[167]

10.71   In *R v Gough*[168] it had been held that, in the absence of actual bias, the court should decide for itself whether, in all of the circumstances relevant to the issue of bias, there was a real danger that the decision-maker / decision-making body had been biased. In *Re Medicaments and Related Classes of Goods (No 2)*,[169] however, it was said that the court should ask whether a fair-minded and informed observer would conclude that there was a real possibility or danger of bias.

10.72   The House of Lords has approved this 'modest adjustment of the test in *Gough*',[170] subject to omission of the phrase 'real danger'; accordingly, the appropriate test for bias is now 'whether the fair-minded and informed observer,

---

162   *Wiseman v Borneman* [1971] AC 297, HL; *R v Hull Prison Visitors ex p St Germain (No 2)* [1979] 1 WLR 1401, QBD; *Lloyd v McMahon* [1987] AC 625, HL; *R v Civil Service Appeal Board ex p Cunningham* [1991] 4 All ER 310, CA; *R v Secretary of State for the Home Department ex p Doody* [1994] 1 AC 531, HL; *R v Higher Education Funding Council ex p Institute of Dental Surgery* [1994] 1 WLR 242, DC; *R v Kensington and Chelsea RLBC ex p Grillo* (1996) 28 HLR 94, CA; and *R v Ministry of Defence ex p Murray* [1998] COD 134, QBD.

163   See HA 1996, s 202 and Homelessness (Review Procedure etc) Regulations 2018, SI 2018/223, reg 8. The Welsh regulations only require that the review officer be someone who was not involved in the original decision (Homelessness (Review Procedure) (Wales) Regulations 2015, SI 2015/1266, reg 3; see also Welsh Code para 20.9).

164   Consider the grounds in *Feld v Barnet LBC* [2004] EWCA Civ 1307, [2005] HLR 9.

165   Eg, past contact/dealings suggesting something other than full disinterestedness, or even some private or personal reason.

166   *Ridge v Baldwin* [1964] AC 40, HL.

167   By Localism Act (LA) 2011, s 25, there is no apparent bias in relation to a decision taken after 12 January 2012 (but capable of referring to things done beforehand) simply because the decision-maker has previously done something that directly or indirectly indicates what view they took, or would or might take, in relation to a matter relevant to the decision. This only applies, however, to members (elected or co-opted) of an authority and will rarely apply in homelessness or allocation cases, although it could do so.

168   [1993] AC 646, HL.

169   [2001] 1 WLR 700, CA.

170   See *Magill v Porter* [2001] UKHL 67, [2002] 2 AC 357, at [103].

having considered the facts, would conclude that there was a real possibility that the tribunal was biased'.[171]

10.73 In *Feld*,[172] the authority only had one reviewing officer, who conducted both an initial review and a subsequent re-review following a successful complaint to the ombudsman (of which she was not the subject, and in the report of whom she was not criticised). The applicant asserted that this gave rise to the appearance of bias. The Court of Appeal dismissed the claim. The fair-minded and informed observer would take into account that a decision under HA 1996, s 202 is an administrative decision which Parliament has entrusted to senior local authority officers, who have received training; the observer would also consider the practical constraints (financial and administrative) imposed on local housing authorities. Taking those factors into account, there would not be said to have been any bias in the decision-making process, based either on the officer's conduct of the previous review or on the successful complaint to the ombudsman.[173]

10.74 In *De-Winter Heald v Brent LBC*,[174] the Court of Appeal held that an objective and well-informed observer would not think that there was a real danger of bias on the part of a contracted-out reviewer, and therefore rejected the contention that the review decisions in the appeals were marred by apparent bias; there was no reason why a person contracted to carry out a review on an authority's behalf should necessarily be less impartial than an authority employee; whether they may be regarded as less independent depends on the facts, in particular the terms of the contract between the authority and the reviewer; eg, a long contractual term terminable only for serious breach would suggest that there was a high degree of independence on the part of the reviewer.[175]

Right to be heard

10.75 This has two elements: first, to inform the party affected about what is being said; and second, to afford them the opportunity to answer it.[176] This does

---

171 *Magill v Porter*, at [103].
172 *Feld v Barnet LBC*, above.
173 'Adopting a balanced approach such an observer will accept that investigation by and even adverse comment from the Ombudsman is one of the slings and arrows of local government misfortune with which broad shouldered officials have to cope. [The officer] was not herself involved nor the subject of criticism. She could be expected to bear criticism of the department not only with fortitude but with indifference . . .': per Ward LJ at [49].
174 [2009] EWCA Civ 930, [2010] HLR 8.
175 At [52]. If there is any doubt about the validity of the contract, an applicant will need to consider its terms; if the authority will not willingly disclose it, the applicant can seek a copy under the Freedom of Information Act 2000 or make an application for pre-action disclosure under Civil Procedure Rules 1998 (CPR) 31.16, but a challenge to it cannot be made in pleadings without a clear basis and, unless pleaded, it will not later be possible to obtain the agreement by disclosure in the course of a HA 1996, s 204 appeal as it will not relate to any pleaded issue: *Servis v Newham LBC* [2018] EWHC 1547 (QB).
176 *Board of Education v Rice* [1911] AC 179, HL; *Kanda v Government of the Federation of Malaya* [1962] AC 322, PC.

not amount to a requirement for an oral hearing – so as to require any internal review to be a full hearing[177] – but does require, where a decision is reached without a hearing, that the applicant is given an opportunity to put their case in response to adverse findings.[178]

Reasons

10.76 While there is no universal obligation to give reasons in all circumstances, in general they should be given unless there is a proper justification for not doing so.[179] The internal review requirements in both HA 1996, Parts 6 and 7 and H(W) A 2014, Part 2 contain express provision for reasons to be given for decisions.[180] A failure to provide reasons would give rise to a ground of challenge and would suffice to quash the decision.[181] The requirement is a manifestation of the need for the applicant to be aware of the decision against them and to be able to challenge that decision if necessary,[182] so that it is the substance rather than the form that is of importance.

10.77 The authority must apply the facts to the legal background and reach a 'properly or adequately reasoned decision'.[183] In *Paul-Coker*, the applicant successfully claimed judicial review of the authority's decision to refuse her accommodation pending review on the grounds that the authority had not applied the correct legal criteria to her circumstances and that there was a 'complete absence of any explanation or reasoning' in the authority's decision letter. This success, based on inadequacy of reasons, was considered 'an exceptional case'.[184]

---

177 Consider *Runa Begum* and *Ali v Birmingham City Council*, paras **10.117–10.122**.
178 This is not a limitless right and there is no absolute right to the last word: *Bellouti v Wandsworth LBC* [2005] EWCA Civ 602, [2005] HLR 46.
179 Reasons will be required where fairness requires it, or a particular decision is aberrant, where the failure to give reasons may frustrate a right of appeal (because without reasons a party will not know whether there is an appealable ground or not) and where a party has a legitimate expectation that reasons will be given: *Oakley v South Cambridgeshire DC* [2017] EWCA Civ 71, [2017] 1 WLR 3765 at [30]–[31]. See also *R (Sambotin) v Brent LBC* [2017] EWHC 1190 (Admin), [2017] PTSR 1154, [2017] HLR 31, in which the authority sought to revisit and change its own earlier decision without a lawful basis for doing so (no fraud, deception or fundamental mistake of fact): the court additionally held that the authority had been under a duty to give reasons for reaching a second decision, with which duty it had failed to comply. The authority appealed ([2018] EWCA Civ 1825, [2019] PTSR 371, [2019] HLR 5) solely on the basis that the decision had not been a final decision, as the duty to secure the accommodation only arose once the local connection process had been completed, an argument which the Court of Appeal rejected: see para **5.63**.
180 HA 1996, ss 167(4A), 203(4); H(W)A 2014, s 86(4).
181 *R v Westminster City Council ex p Ermakov* [1996] 2 All ER 302, CA. Reasons should be 'proper, adequate and intelligible': *Westminster City Council v Great Portland Estates plc* [1985] AC 661, HL.
182 *R v Islington LBC ex p Hinds* (1995) 27 HLR 65, QBD.
183 *R (Paul-Coker) v Southwark LBC* [2006] EWHC 497 (Admin), [2006] HLR 32.
184 *R (Paul-Coker) v Southwark LBC*, at [52].

10.78   The nature and extent of reasons must relate to the substantive issues raised by an applicant (or by an applicant's adviser): see *Re Poyser & Mills Arbitration*,[185] approved by the House of Lords in *Westminster City Council v Great Portland Estates plc*,[186] and again in *Save Britain's Heritage v Secretary of State for the Environment*.[187] 'The reasons that are set out must be reasons which will not only be intelligible, but which deal with the substantive points that have been raised', per Megaw J in *Posyer*. 'The three criteria suggested in the dictum of Megaw J are that the reasons should be proper, intelligible and adequate', per Lord Bridge in *Save Britain's Heritage*. In *Edwin H Bradley & Sons Ltd v Secretary of State for the Environment*,[188] Glidewell J added to the dictum of Megaw J that reasons can be briefly stated (also approved in *Great Portland Estates*).

10.79   In *South Bucks DC and another v Porter (No 2)*,[189] Lord Brown summarised the law as follows:[190]

> Reasons can be briefly stated, the degree of particularity required depending entirely on the nature of the issues falling for decision. The reasoning must not give rise to a substantial doubt as to whether the decision-maker erred in law, for example by misunderstanding some relevant policy or some other important matter or by failing to reach a rational decision on relevant grounds. But such adverse inference will not readily be drawn. The reasons need refer only to the main issues in the dispute,[191] not to every material consideration . . . Decision letters must be read in a straightforward manner, recognising that they are addressed to parties well aware of the issues involved and the arguments advanced.[192]

10.80   In *Baruwa*[193] it was said to be:

> . . . trite law that where, as here, an authority is required to give reasons for its decision it is required to give reasons which are proper, adequate, and

---

185   [1964] 2 QB 467, QBD.
186   [1985] AC 661, HL.
187   [1991] 1 WLR 153. See also *Givandan v Minister of Housing and Local Government* [1967] 1 WLR 250, QBD; *Mountview Court Properties Ltd v Devlin* (1970) 21 P&CR 689, QBD.
188   (1982) 266 EG 926, QBD.
189   [2004] UKHL 33, [2004] WLR 1953.
190   At [36].
191   This proposition was relied on in *Kyle v. Coventry CC* [2023] EWCA Civ 1360; [2024] HLR 7 at [48-49], on the facts unsurprisingly rejecting the argument that the authority had failed to consider why it had been reasonable to continue to occupy accommodation because the decision-letter had not addressed the fact that the accommodation in question "had a no visitors policy, restricted smoking and was only available for a short period as a half-way house whilst other accommodation was secured." See also *R (Saint Sepulchre) v. Kensington & Chelsea RLBC* [2023] EWHC 2913 (Admin); [2024] HLR 12, which the same passage is relied on in support of the applicant's case.
192   In *Adam v Westminster CC* [2018] EWCA Civ 2742, [2019] HLR 15 at [50] it was said that 'These principles apply equally to review decisions under the Housing Act 1996: *Rother DC v Freeman-Roach* [2018] EWCA Civ 368, [2018] HLR 22'.
193   *R v Brent LBC ex p Baruwa* (1997) 29 HLR 915, CA.

intelligible and enable the person affected to know why they have won or lost. That said, the law gives decision-makers a certain latitude in how they express themselves and will recognise that not all those taking decisions find it easy in the time available to express themselves with judicial exactitude.

10.81 The purpose of the obligation to give reasons is to enable the recipient to see whether they might be challengeable in law: see *Thornton v Kirklees MBC*.[194] In *Mohammed*,[195] Latham J considered the role of reasons in the light of the right to seek an internal review of the decision:

> . . . the purpose to be served by the giving of such reasons . . . is to enable the applicant to put before the local housing authority a proper case based upon a full understanding of the council's previous[196] decision to refuse accommodation.

10.82 Reasons should accordingly be sufficient to enable the applicant to form a view as to whether to challenge the decision on a point of law.[197] Merely stating the words of the Act 'parrot-fashion', with no substantive explanation for the decision, is insufficient.[198] Reasons should be in sufficient detail to show the principles on which the decision-maker has acted and that have led to their decision; they need not be elaborate nor need they deal with every argument presented in support of the case.[199]

10.83 Not every factor which weighed with the decision-maker in the appraisal of the evidence has to be identified and explained,[200] but the issues which were vital to the conclusion should be identified, and the manner in which they were resolved, explained.[201] The question is whether it is possible to understand the decision-maker's thought processes when they were making material findings.[202] Authorities are entitled to give their reasons quite simply:

---

194 [1979] QB 626, CA, which appears to have been a judicial summary of counsel's submission, rather than a judicial observation in its own right. See further *R v Tynedale DC ex p Shield* (1990) 22 HLR 144, QBD.

195 *R v Camden LBC ex p Mohammed* (1998) 30 HLR 315, QBD at p323.

196 Ie, initial.

197 *Osmani v Camden LBC* [2004] EWCA Civ 1706, [2005] HLR 22. See also *R v Croydon LBC ex p Graham* (1994) 26 HLR 286, at 291–292.

198 *R v Newham LBC ex p Lumley* (2001) 33 HLR 124: this was a concession by counsel, but is again obviously correct. The decision in *Kelly v Monklands DC* (1985) 12 July, Ct of Session (OH), that a mere recital of the words of the Act was sufficient, is unlikely to be followed unless the relevant factual issues for determination by the authority are both clear and confined to something which the wording of HA 1996 serves to address.

199 *Eagil Trust Co Ltd v Pigott Brown* [1985] 3 All ER 119, CA.

200 The mere fact that a matter is not mentioned in its reasons does not necessarily mean that the authority must be assumed not to have had regard to it – it will of course turn on significance and may mean, eg, that officers did not consider an issue (such as condition of property) sufficiently important to merit an assessment or a mention: *Firoozmand v. Lambeth LBC* [2015] EWCA Civ 952; [2015] HLR 4.

201 *English v Emery Reimbold & Strick Ltd* [2002] EWCA Civ 605, [2002] 1 WLR 2409.

202 *R (Iran) and others v Secretary of State for the Home Department* [2005] EWCA Civ 982.

... their decision and their reasons are not to be analysed in minute detail. They are not to be gone through as it were with a fine-tooth comb. They are not to be criticised by saying: 'They have not mentioned this or that'.[203]

10.84 In the context of a decision on review, it has been said that reasons contained in the decision letter are not to be treated as if they are statutes or judgments and that it is important to read a decision letter as a whole to get its full sense: *Osmani*.[204] Nevertheless, if a decision-maker fails to address in their decision letter an issue 'so startling that one would not expect it to pass without individual comment', the court may be justified in inferring that it has not received any or any sufficient consideration: *Bariise*.[205]

10.85 In *Graham*,[206] Sir Thomas Bingham MR said:

I readily accept that these difficult decisions are decisions for the housing authority and certainly a pedantic exegesis of letters of this kind would be inappropriate. There is, nonetheless, an obligation under the Act to give reasons and that must impose on the council a duty to give reasons which are intelligible and which convey to the applicant the reasons why the application has been rejected in such a way that if they disclose an error of reasoning the applicant may take such steps as may be indicated.

10.86 This passage was cited with approval in *Hinds*,[207] in which the duty had been complied with because the reasons were intelligible and conveyed clearly to the applicant why his application had been rejected. In *Carpenter*,[208] in contrast, the decision letter was considered 'manifestly defective' because it failed to address the reasons why the applicant had left his previous accommodation and, accordingly, defeated the purpose of the section, 'to enable someone who is entitled to a decision to see what the reasons are for that decision and to challenge those reasons if they are apparently inadequate'.

10.87 In *City of Gloucester v Miles*,[209] the Court of Appeal held that – to comply with the requirement to state reasons – a notification of intentional homelessness[210] ought to have stated:

a) that the authority was satisfied that the applicant for accommodation became homeless intentionally;

b) when the applicant was considered to have become homeless;

---

203 *Tickner v Mole Valley DC* [1980] 2 April, CA transcript.
204 *Osmani v Camden LBC* [2004] EWCA Civ 1706, [2004] HLR 22. See also *William v Wandsworth LBC; Bellamy v Hounslow LBC* [2006] EWCA Civ 535, [2006] HLR 42.
205 *R v Brent LBC ex p Bariise* (1999) 31 HLR 50, CA, per Millett LJ at 58.
206 *R v Croydon LBC ex p Graham* (1994) 26 HLR 286, CA at 291–292.
207 *R v Islington LBC ex p Hinds* (1996) 28 HLR 302, CA. See also *R v Camden LBC ex p Adair* (1997) 29 HLR 236, QBD; and *R v Wandsworth LBC ex p Dodia* (1998) 30 HLR 562, QBD.
208 *R v Northampton BC ex p Carpenter* (1993) 25 HLR 349, QBD.
209 (1985) 17 HLR 292, CA.
210 See chapter 4.

c)   why the applicant was said to have become homeless at that time, ie, what is the deliberate act or omission in consequence of which it is concluded that at that time the applicant ceased to occupy accommodation which was available for their occupation; and

d)   that it would have been reasonable for the applicant to continue to occupy that accommodation.

10.88   In *ex p H*,[211] it was held that, while the authority was entitled to express itself quite simply and could not be criticised for not having gone into great detail, it was nonetheless incumbent on it to say what was the deliberate act or omission in consequence of which it had been concluded that the applicant had ceased to occupy accommodation available for his occupation and which it would have been reasonable for him to continue to occupy. In the context of the case, that required more than a statement that he could have continued to occupy under his council tenancy in Northern Ireland.

10.89   Likewise, in *Baruwa*,[212] the decision letter should have clarified why the applicant was regarded as having spent money on non-essential items and why the authority regarded this as having caused the applicant's homelessness. It is not necessary, however, that the decision letter set out arithmetical calculations or itemised what an applicant could or could not afford.[213]

10.90   In *Monaf*,[214] the court quashed the decision of the authority on the basis that its letters did not disclose that it had carried out the proper balancing act called for, to determine whether or not it would have been reasonable for applicants to remain in accommodation in Bangladesh or to come back to the UK.

10.91   In *Adair*,[215] the court described a decision letter which merely recited that the authority had taken into account all the evidence and that the applicant did not fall within any of the categories of priority need as being completely devoid of reasoning and inadequate.[216] The decision letter should have set out why the applicant was considered not to be a vulnerable person in the light of the medical evidence which he had put forward.

10.92   In *Khan*,[217] a decision letter which addressed only one of a number of grounds on which local connection was being claimed was held to be defective. In *McCarthy*,[218] however, the decision letter was upheld, even though it had not dealt with the suitability of the applicant's current accommodation, because the applicant had not raised that issue with the authority.

---

211 *R v Hillingdon LBC ex p H* (1988) 20 HLR 554, QBD. See also *R v Southwark LBC ex p Davies* (1994) 26 HLR 677, QBD.
212 *R v Brent LBC ex p Baruwa* (1997) 29 HLR 915, CA. See also *Robinson v Brent LBC* (1999) 31 HLR 1015, CA.
213 *Bernard v Enfield LBC* [2001] EWCA Civ 1831.
214 *R v Tower Hamlets LBC ex p Monaf* (1988) 20 HLR 529, CA.
215 *R v Camden LBC ex p Adair* (1997) 29 HLR 236, QBD.
216 See also *R v Brent LBC ex p Bariise* (1999) 31 HLR 50, CA, at 58.
217 *R v Slough BC ex p Khan* (1995) 27 HLR 492, QBD.
218 *R v Sedgemoor DC ex p McCarthy* (1996) 28 HLR 608, QBD.

10.93   In *O'Connor*,[219] the authority concluded that the applicants were intentionally homeless. Both initial and review decision letters, however, failed to identify the date at which the authority considered that the homelessness had commenced and therefore had not considered whether the omission at that time had been in good faith. Although the letter was 'thoughtful and factually sound', the decision was quashed because it failed to address the questions raised by HA 1996, s 191(2).

10.94   In *Augustin*,[220] it was held that a later letter from the authority could rectify the shortcomings of an earlier notification (which, however, was not itself considered defective, albeit that it was 'sparse' – per Auld J in the court below – or 'cryptic' and brief – per Glidewell LJ in the Court of Appeal; the notification had given the applicant the information she needed).

10.95   The courts may be slow to intervene on the basis of want of adequate reasons unless the applicant, or the applicant's adviser, offers the authority an opportunity to remedy a defective decision letter, by way of a 'prompt request for details', to which the authority has failed to respond.[221] In judicial review cases, the pre-action protocol[222] requires a letter before action[223] and the same is expected before a county court appeal is launched.[224]

10.96   The issue of additional evidence to amplify reasons arises in the context of appeals, where the person undertaking the review sometimes submits a witness statement containing further reasoning for their decision. Such evidence cannot be admitted as of right. Statements which are aimed at clarification and do not alter or contradict anything in the decision letter are, however, properly admitted.[225] In *Moge*,[226] additional evidence was admitted in the Court of Appeal to show what the authority had done by way of compliance with its duties under s 208(1)[227] where the focus in the county court appeal had been on other points.

10.97   In *Graham*[228] and *Ermakov*,[229] the Court of Appeal held that – save in exceptional circumstances – the courts will not permit the reasons given in the

---

219 *O'Connor v Kensington and Chelsea RLBC* [2004] EWCA Civ 394, [2004] HLR 37.
220 *R v Westminster City Council ex p Augustin* (1993) 25 HLR 281, CA.
221 *R v Camden LBC ex p Mohammed* (1997) 30 HLR 315, at 323, cited with approval in *R v Newham LBC ex p Lumley* (2000) 33 HLR 124, at 136–137.
222 See para **10.144**
223 See para **10.145**.
224 See para **10.222**.
225 *Hijazi v Kensington and Chelsea RLBC* [2003] EWCA Civ 692, [2003] HLR 73. See also *Hall v Wandsworth LBC; Carter v Wandsworth LBC* [2004] EWCA Civ 1740, [2005] HLR 23.
226 *Moge v Ealing LBC* [2023] EWCA Civ 464; [2023] HLR 35.
227 Para **8.132**.
228 *R v Croydon LBC ex p Graham* (1994) 26 HLR 286, CA.
229 *R v Westminster City Council ex p Ermakov* (1996) 28 HLR 819, CA; see also *R v Southwark LBC ex p Dagou* (1996) 28 HLR 72, QBD.

notification to be supplemented.[230] In *Elkundi*,[231] the authority was not permitted to rely on evidence seeking to explain that a review decision that the applicant's accommodation was not suitable meant only that it was not suitable in the longer-term rather than immediately.[232]

> In my judgment, the need to be very cautious before admitting post-decision evidence addressing the meaning of the decision, or what the decision-maker had in mind and intended to say, applies with even greater force where the evidence seeks to change the result. Just as reasons must enable a person affected by a decision to know *why* he won or lost, *a fortiori* the notification of the decision must enable him to know *whether* he won or lost. (At [249]).

10.98 In *John*,[233] however, non-disclosure of the proper reasons for the decision in the decision letter did not prevent the authority from relying on proper reasons and justifying its decision accordingly. In *Hobbs*,[234] the Court of Appeal upheld the High Court decision to admit affidavit evidence amplifying and explaining earlier evidence as to reasons.

10.99 In *Baruwa*,[235] it was also recognised that there are cases:

> ... where ... one could look at the affidavit[236] ... by way of amplification of the reasons for the decision. Looking at such an affidavit is often a sensible course and saves the bother and expense of going back to the decision-maker to make a new decision which will incorporate the material which appears in the affidavit.

10.100 In practice, the courts have not invariably held authorities to the reasons given. The decision in *de Falco*[237] was, so far as relevant, that:

---

230 These were pre-county court appeal, judicial review cases, but the same principles apply: *Samuels v Birmingham City Council* [2015] EWCA Civ 1051, [2015] HLR 47. This issue did not arise in the subsequent appeal to the Supreme Court: [2019] UKSC 28, [2019] HLR 32.

231 *R (Elkundi and others) v Birmingham City Council* [2021] EWHC 1024 (Admin); [2021] 1 WLR 4031; [2021] HLR 45 [2021]; the issue did not arise on the subsequent appeal ([2022] EWCA Civ 601; [2022] QB 604; [2022] HLR 31).

232 'Furthermore, in the letter where I stated that Mr Elkundi's accommodation was unsuitable, I did not mean that the accommodation was immediately unsuitable. I considered that he could remain at the accommodation in the short term until alternative accommodation had been identified' (quoted at [236]).

233 *R v Swansea City Council ex p John* (1983) 9 HLR 55, QBD. Another judicial review, pre-county court appeal case.

234 *Hobbs v Sutton LBC* (1993) 26 HLR 132, CA. See also *R v Bradford City Council ex p Parveen* (1996) 28 HLR 681, QBD.

235 *R v Brent LBC ex p Baruwa* (1997) 29 HLR 915, QBD at 929. See also *Samuels v Birmingham City Council* [2015] EWCA Civ 1051, [2015] HLR 47 where the authority was entitled to lead evidence to rebut an allegation of factual error made for the first time the afternoon before the HA 1996, s 204 appeal hearing.

236 Or witness statement or evidence on an appeal to the county court.

237 *De Falco, Silvestri v Crawley BC* [1980] QB 460, CA.

. . . the council is of the opinion that you became homeless intentionally because you came to this country without having ensured that you had permanent accommodation to come to.

10.101 This was clearly, and has since expressly been held to be, wrong.[238] The court upheld it by finding that the applicants were homeless intentionally because they had left accommodation (in Italy) before coming to this country.

10.102 In *Islam*,[239] at the Court of Appeal, the court was similarly willing to disregard the express words used by the authority, and consider whether there had been what in substance could be considered intentional homelessness. In *Chambers*,[240] the decision that applicants had become homeless intentionally was not sustainable, but relief was refused on the alternative approach that the authority had discharged its duties to the applicants by an earlier offer.

10.103 These earlier cases should be treated with some caution. *De Falco* could as easily be described as a decision (at an interlocutory hearing) on discretion. The result in *Islam* was overturned on appeal.[241] *Chambers* was explicitly a decision on relief (discretion).

10.104 The most modern and authoritative case, which is commonly relied on by authorities in homelessness cases, is *Holmes-Moorhouse v. Richmond-upon-Thames LBC*,[242] *per* Lord Neuberger.

47.   ... [A] a judge should not adopt an unfair or unrealistic approach when considering or interpreting such review decisions. Although they may often be checked by people with legal experience or qualifications before they are sent out, review decisions are prepared by housing officers, who occupy a post of considerable responsibility and who have substantial experience in the housing field, but they are not lawyers. It is not therefore appropriate to subject their decisions to the same sort of analysis as may be applied to a contract drafted by solicitors, to an Act of Parliament, or to a court's judgment.

48.   Further, at least in my experience, and as this case exemplifies, review decisions generally set out the facts, the contentions, the analyses and the conclusions in some detail. To my mind, given the importance, particularly to the applicant, of the issues considered in review decisions, such fullness is to be strongly encouraged. However, as any lawyer knows, the more fully an opinion is expressed, the greater the opportunity for alleging mistakes of fact, errors of law, or inconsistencies. If the courts are too critical

238 See para **4.150**.
239 *R v Hillingdon LBC ex p Islam* [1983] 1 AC 688, (1981) 1 HLR 107, HL.
240 *R v Westminster City Council ex p Chambers* (1983) 6 HLR 24, QBD.
241 *R v Hillingdon LBC ex p Islam*, above, see para **4.154**.
242 [2009] UKHL 7; [2009] 1 WLR 413; [2009] HLR 34.

in their analyses of such decisions, it will tend to discourage reviewing officers from expressing themselves so fully.

49. In my view, it is therefore very important that, while circuit judges should be vigilant in ensuring that no applicant is wrongly deprived of benefits under Pt VII of the 1996 Act because of any error on the part of the reviewing officer, it is equally important that an error which does not, on a fair analysis, undermine the basis of the decision, is not accepted as a reason for overturning the decision.

50. Accordingly, a benevolent approach should be adopted to the interpretation of review decisions. The court should not take too technical view of the language used, or search for inconsistencies, or adopt a nit-picking approach, when confronted with an appeal against a review decision. That is not to say that the court should approve incomprehensible or misguided reasoning, but it should be realistic and practical in its approach to the interpretation of review decisions.

51. Further, as the present case shows, a decision can often survive despite the existence of an error in the reasoning advanced to support it. For example, sometimes the error is irrelevant to the outcome; sometimes it is too trivial (objectively, or in the eyes of the decision-maker) to affect the outcome; sometimes it is obvious from the rest of the reasoning, read as a whole, that the decision would have been the same notwithstanding the error; sometimes, there is more than one reason for the conclusion, and the error only undermines one of the reasons; sometimes, the decision is the only one which could rationally have been reached. In all such cases, the error should not (save, perhaps, in wholly exceptional circumstances) justify the decision being quashed.

52. In the present case, while one paragraph of the review decision contains an error, it seems to me that it is not an error which in any way undermines the reasoning upon which the conclusion is based. It is also fair to add that, if one excises the short passage which contains the error, the review decision in this case, when read as a whole, contains a full and very fair summary of the relevant facts, an accurate assessment of the issues, a clear explanation of the reviewing officer's reasoning, and a conclusion which seems to me to be unassailable.

10.105 This approach does, however, need to be read subject to the requirements of the public sector equality duty[243] where it is engaged,[244] not only when the

---

243 See para **7.93**.
244 *Hotak v Southwark LBC and other appeals* [2015] UKSC 30, [2015] 2 WLR 1341, [2015] HLR 23, at [79].

issue is vulnerability[245] but by parity of reasoning in all cases where it falls for consideration, ie it must be possible to see how the authority has addressed that duty.

Legitimate expectation

10.106 The requirement of fairness means that an authority must respect any legitimate expectation which an applicant may enjoy,[246] provided that to conform to the expectation would not interfere or conflict with the authority's statutory duty.[247] Conventionally, legitimate expectation refers to a legitimate *procedural* expectation, as to how a matter is to be handled, such as an assurance that no decision will be taken, at all or on an aspect of a matter, until there has been a further opportunity to comment or until the authority has managed to contact someone, or that it will only be taken by an officer of a particular level of seniority or by a panel (member or officer).[248]

10.107 At its most narrow, it may refer only to the procedure to be adopted before an existing right or privilege is removed,[249] although as the concept is a part of the overall duty of fairness, it may equally be used to infer the loss of an opportunity to acquire a benefit or advantage. This does not easily translate into a legitimate substantive expectation of a particular outcome of a decision-making process as opposed to its procedure. For legitimate expectation to give rise to a substantive entitlement requires a clear and unambiguous representation, devoid of qualification, on which it was reasonable to rely.[250]

10.108 There is, however, no requirement that an applicant should detrimentally have changed their position in reliance on the promise.[251] The question is whether it would be an abuse of power to frustrate the legitimate expectation. It is for the court to determine whether there is a sufficient overriding interest to justify a departure from what has previously been promised.[252] In one case, the substantive right to take over a tenancy was upheld.[253]

10.109 No appeal to legitimate expectation can, however, widen an authority's duties under either HA 1996, Part 6 or Part 7 or H(W)A 2014, Part 2.[254] Nonetheless,

---

245 See also paras **3.44-3.45**.
246 *R v North and East Devon Health Authority ex p Coughlan* [2001] QB 213, CA.
247 *R v Attorney General of Hong Kong ex p Ng Yuen Shiu* [1983] 2 AC 629, PC, at 638/f.
248 *Schmidt v Secretary of State for Home Affairs* [1969] 2 Ch 149, CA; *R v Devon CC ex p Baker* [1995] 1 All ER 73, CA.
249 *Council of Civil Service Unions v Minister for the Civil Service* [1985] 1 AC 374, HL, per Lord Diplock at 413.
250 *R v IRC ex p MFK Underwriting* [1990] 1 WLR 1545, QBD at 1569/G.
251 *R v Newham LBC ex p Bibi and Al-Nashed* [2001] EWCA Civ 607, (2001) 33 HLR 84.
252 *R v North and East Devon Health Authority ex p Coughlan*, above.
253 *R v Lambeth LBC ex p Trabi* (1998) 30 HLR 975, QBD.
254 *R v Lambeth LBC ex p Ekpo-Wedderman* (1998) 31 HLR 498, QBD; *Obiorah v Lewisham LBC* [2013] EWCA Civ 325, [2013] HLR 35. The same must be true of H(W)A 2014, Part 2.

where a promise of a 'permanent' home had been made to homeless applicants, a legitimate expectation had arisen which was sufficient to justify derogation from the authority's housing allocation scheme, which therefore required the authority to provide reasons if the expectation was not to be fulfilled.[255]

10.110 Not every statement of reasons, even if *capable* of suggesting a particular policy, will do so. Thus, in *R (MQ) v Secretary of State*,[256] an asylum seeker challenged a decision not to prioritise her claim for rehousing because there were no exceptional circumstances to justify it, on the basis that the Secretary of State was operating an unpublished policy of requiring asylum seekers to demonstrate such circumstances before they were prioritised. The claim was dismissed: there was no such policy; rather, the Secretary of State was considering each request on a case-by-case basis.

10.111 On the other hand, it was held that an authority should have published a document which explained how a local authority would approach requests for accommodation under the 'Everyone In' initiative;[257] while it did not need to be a lengthy or detailed document, there needed to be something to guide the decision-making process, absent which the court could not be satisfied that a decision to refuse assistance was made on a proper basis.[258]

10.112 Lord Dyson, in *R (Lumba) v Secretary of State for the Home Department*[259] said that there are:

> ' three propositions in relation to a policy. First, it must not be a blanket policy admitting of no possibility of exceptions. Secondly, if unpublished, it must not be inconsistent with any published policy. Thirdly, it should be published if it will inform discretionary decisions in respect of which the potential object of those decisions has a right to make representations' (at [20]).[260]

> '...[A] decision-maker must follow his published policy (and not some different unpublished policy) unless there are good reasons for not doing so. The principle that policy must be consistently applied is not in doubt:

---

255 *R v Newham LBC ex p Bibi and Al-Nashed* [2001] EWCA Civ 607, (2001) 33 HLR 84; cf. *Obiorah v Lewisham LBC* [2013] EWCA Civ 325 where a similar claim was not upheld on the facts. See also *R (Alansi) v Newham LBC* [2013] EWHC 3722 (Admin), [2014] HLR 25: authority entitled to resile from a clear promise as a result of changes made to its allocation scheme. In *R. (EL) v Kensington and Chelsea R.L.B.C.* [2022] EWHC 3185 (Admin); [2023] HLR 24, however, although the claimant's CAB adviser had been told that the authority would make an offer of alternative accommodation (in the course of ASB proceedings against a claimant with a number of medical issues), she had also been told not to tell him about it (and had not done so): there could accordingly be no legitimate expectation as the offer had never been communicated to him.
256 [2023] EWHC 205 (Admin).
257 Cf. para **10.18**.
258 *R (Cort) v Lambeth LBC* [2022] EWHC 1085 (Admin).
259 [2011] UKSC 12, [2012] 1 AC 245.
260 See also [27] where Lord Dyson specifically approved the third of these.

see Wade & Forsyth, Administrative Law, 10th ed (2009), p 316. As it is put in De Smith's Judicial Review , 6th ed (2007), para 12-039: "there is an independent duty of consistent application of policies, which is based on the principle of equal implementation of laws, non-discrimination and the lack of arbitrariness'"(at 26]).

10.113 In *R (ZLL) v Secretary of State for Housing, Communities and Local Government*,[261] Fordham J. considered the authorities on the duty to publish policies and concluded at [7(5)]:

'The 'duty of publication' is therefore linked, not only to the virtues of consistency and lack of arbitrariness, but also to the basic rights of affected individuals: to make representations as to how their case should be decided, and to consider and make an informed challenge to an adverse decision. The 'duty of publication' will therefore apply to any new policy or practice which curtails or discontinues a relevant policy which has previously been published, as was the position in *Lumba* itself.'

Human Rights Act 1998

10.114 The scheme of the HRA 1998 is to require all domestic legislation to be read and given effect (as far as is possible) in a manner that is compatible with the Convention rights contained in the Act[262] and to render it unlawful for a 'public authority'[263] – including local authorities and registered providers of social housing in respect of some aspects of their management of their social housing stock, including service of notice to quit or of seeking possession[264] – to act in a way which is incompatible with one or more of the Convention rights.[265]

10.115 A person who claims that a public authority has acted unlawfully on this basis may bring proceedings against the authority or rely on the Convention right in any legal proceedings.[266]

10.116 The Convention rights which are most evidently relevant[267] to a claim brought against HA 1996, Part 6 or Part 7 or H(W)A 2014, Part 2 decisions are as follows.

---

261 [2022] EWHC 85 (Admin).
262 HRA 1998, s 3(1). *R (Morris) v Westminster City Council (No 3)* [2005] EWCA Civ 1184, [2006] 1 WLR 505, [2006] HLR 8.
263 As defined in HRA 1998, s 6(3).
264 *R (Weaver) v London & Quadrant Housing Trust* [2008] EWHC 1377 (Admin), [2008] JHL D94 and on appeal [2009] EWCA Civ 587, [2009] HLR 40; see paras **9.179–9.180** on other acts of management and allocation.
265 HRA 1998, s 6(1).
266 HRA 1998, s 7(1).
267 But see *R (E) v Islington LBC* [2017] EWHC 1440 (Admin), [2018] PTSR 349, where no education arrangements were made for a child placed in the area of another authority: it was held that there was a breach of ECHR Protocol 1 Article 2 (right to education).

Article 6 – Everyone, in the determination of their civil rights and obligations, is entitled to a fair and public hearing within a reasonable time by an independent and impartial tribunal established by law.

Article 8 – *Rights to respect for private and family life and home*, interference with which is permitted to the extent that it is in accordance with law and necessary in a democratic society in the interests of national security, public safety, economic well-being of the country, the prevention of disorder or crime, the protection of health or morals or the rights and freedoms of others.

Article 14 – *Prohibition on discrimination* on grounds of sex, race, colour, language, religion, political or other opinion, national or social origin, association with a national minority, property, birth or other status.

Article 6

10.117 Internal reviews do not need to be compliant with Article 6, as homelessness rights are not civil rights within it.[268] Even if they were, it was held in *Runa Begum*[269] that an internal review coupled with the right to an appeal to the county court under HA 1996, s 204 comprised compliance with Article 6. This approach was followed in *Ali v Birmingham City Council*.[270]

10.118 In *Ali v UK*,[271] the same case at the European Court of Human Rights, it was held that Article 6(1) was engaged once the authority decided that a duty was owed under HA 1996, s 193 because there was a sufficiently certain right to amount to a 'civil right'; nonetheless, in agreement with *Runa Begum* and *Ali* at the Supreme Court, it was also held that there was no violation of Article 6 as the rights to a reasoned decision, review and appeal were adequate safeguards.

10.119 In *Poshteh v Kensington and Chelsea RLBC*,[272] however, the Supreme Court refused to depart from its decision in *Ali v Birmingham City Council*, notwithstanding *Ali v UK*, for the reasons referred to at para **7.219**.

10.120 For the purpose of illustrating the principle, the position may be contrasted with *Tsfayo*,[273] a challenge at the European Court of Human Rights to a decision of a housing benefit review board to refuse to find good reason for backdating a claim, in which it was held that judicial review had not provided the claimant with access to a court of full jurisdiction for the purpose of Article 6(1),

---

268 *Ali v Birmingham City Council* [2010] UKSC 8, [2010] HLR 22.
269 *Runa Begum v Tower Hamlets LBC* [2003] UKHL 5, [2003] 2 AC 430, [2003] HLR 32.
270 [2010] UKSC 8.
271 App No 40378/10, [2015] HLR 46.
272 [2017] UKSC 36, [2017] AC 624, [2017] HLR 28.
273 *Tsfayo v UK* App no 60860/00, [2007] HLR 19, ECtHR.

because the question in issue for the board – which lacked independence[274] – was a simple one of fact, not involving professional knowledge or specialist experience; judicial review was an inappropriate jurisdiction for the resolution of factual issues.

10.121 This was distinguished in *Ali v Birmingham City Council*, where the issue was whether the homeless person had received a letter warning her – in accordance with HA 1996, s 193(5) – that if she did not accept the accommodation offered, the authority would consider that its duty had been discharged.[275] This was held not to be a matter of simple fact required by *Tsfayo* to be considered by a court of full jurisdiction: see also the discussion of *Bubb v Wandsworth LBC*,[276] above.[277]

10.122 Article 6 was also relied on in a challenge to the legality of contracting out review decisions.[278] The Court of Appeal rejected the argument that a third party would be any less impartial than an employee of the authority; in any event, the authority accepted the contracted out review as its own decision and the availability of an appeal to the county court under HA 1996, s 204 ensured compliance with Article 6, following *Runa Begum*.[279]

Article 8

10.123 Article 8 does not comprise a right to housing to be provided by the state.[280] Given this, it does not currently seem likely that a claim for breach of the right to respect for the home under Article 8 will succeed[281] where an authority

---

274 And perhaps impartiality: it was relevant to the decision that – had the claim been allowed – the authority (of some of whose members the board was comprised) would have received only 50 per cent rather than 95 per cent subsidy: at [19]. Review is now by way of appeal to the – independent and impartial – First Tier Tribunal (Social Entitlement Chamber).
275 See para **8.240**.
276 [2011] EWCA Civ 1285, [2011] HLR 13.
277 See para **10.43**.
278 *De-Winter Heald and others v Brent LBC* [2009] EWCA Civ 930 at [4].
279 *Runa Begum v Tower Hamlets LBC*, above.
280 *X v Federal Republic of Germany* (1965) 8 Yearbook of the ECHR 158; *Chapman v UK* (2001) 33 EHRR 18, (2001) 10 BHRC 48; *O'Rourke v UK* App No 39022/97, ECtHR. See also *Lambeth LBC v Kay; Leeds City Council v Price* [2006] UKHL 10, [2006] 2 AC 465, [2006] HLR 22. Cf *Marzari v Italy* App No 36448/97, (2000) 30 EHRR CD 218, suggesting that a right may arise in some limited, extreme circumstances, where there is a positive obligation towards the applicant under Article 8.
281 See *R (Morris) v Newham LBC* [2002] EWHC 1262 (Admin), [2002] JHL D77, where a claim that the failure to comply with the authority's duty under HA 1996, s 193 was a breach of ECHR Article 8 and gave rise to a right to damages was rejected. See also *R (McDonagh) v Enfield LBC* [2018] EWHC 1287 (Admin), [2018] HLR 43 in which failure to accept and process a homelessness application over a 27-month period, and the corresponding failure to provide interim accommodation, did not amount to a breach of Article 8: although a homelessness application should have been accepted earlier than it was, it was not a case of flagrant breach where the needs of the claimant were wholly disregarded; even if an application had been accepted earlier, given the well-known pressures on housing stock in London, it was far from clear that suitable accommodation would have been provided any earlier; the family had always been housed together and had not been street homeless.

has properly applied the provisions of HA 1996, Part 7 or H(W)A 2014, Part 2 and reached the conclusion that there is no substantive duty to house an applicant, because the provisions of HA 1996, Part 7 and H(W)A 2014, Part 2 are themselves compliant with the ECHR (and, indeed, go further than any duties under Article 8).

10.124 Thus, in *Hackney LBC v Ekinci*,[282] the Court of Appeal rejected the applicant's argument that he was in priority need through his 17-year-old wife.[283] Pill LJ said:[284]

> There is no breach of article 8(1) in Parliament enacting a scheme of priorities whereby applications for accommodation by homeless persons are to be determined by local housing authorities whose resources will inevitably be limited . . .

10.125 Claims may also be made under Article 8 in relation to the right to respect for family life. Generally, social welfare measures provided by the state do not fall within the ambit of Article 8, as they are not specifically designed to promote or protect family life.[285] Although this principle was applied to HA 1996, Part 7 generally in *Morris* and *Badu*,[286] the Court of Appeal considered that the particular section under consideration, HA 1996, s 185(4), nonetheless fell within the ambit of Article 8 'because it sets out to give effect to a legislative policy of preserving family life for the homeless'.[287]

Article 14

10.126 Article 14 will be breached if it applies directly to another Convention right or if it can be said to fall within the ambit of another Convention right, even if no specific right under that article is said to have been breached.[288] Courts should approach Article 14 in a structured way, considering:

---

282 [2001] EWCA Civ 776, [2002] HLR 2.

283 See, further, chapter 3.

284 At [16].

285 See *R (Carson) v Secretary of State for Work and Pensions* [2003] EWCA Civ 797, [2003] 3 All ER 577 at [28], upheld [2005] UKHL 37, [2006] 1 AC 173. See also *R (Couronne and others) v (1) Crawley BC (2) Secretary of State for Work and Pensions (3) First Secretary of State; R (Bontemps and others) v Secretary of State for Work and Pensions* [2006] EWHC 1514 (Admin), [2006] JHL D106, in which the application of the 'habitual residence' test in deciding whether a homeless applicant is eligible (see Annex: Immigration Eligibility) was held to have nothing to do with promoting respect for private and/or family life; accordingly, the claimants' case was not within the ambit of Article 8.

286 *R (Morris) v Westminster City Council; R (Badu) v Lambeth LBC and First Secretary of State* [2005] EWCA Civ 1184, [2006] 1 WLR 505, [2006] HLR 8.

287 *R (Morris) v Westminster City Council; R (Badu) v Lambeth LBC and First Secretary of State*, above.

288 *M v Secretary of State for Work and Pensions* [2006] UKHL 11, [2006] 2 AC 91, at [11]–[14].

whether the facts fall within the ambit of one or more Convention rights;[289]

whether there is a difference in treatment of the claimant and persons put forward for comparison;

whether chosen comparators are in an analogous situation to the complainant; and

whether the difference in treatment has an objective and reasonable justification.[290]

10.127 In *Morris (No 2)*,[291] it was held that – in addition – the courts should ask whether any difference in treatment between the complainant and their comparator is based on one or more of the grounds set out in Article 14.[292] Having found that HA 1996, s 185(4) fell within the ambit of Article 8, the court went on to consider whether the section was in breach of Articles 8 and 14. As the distinction in section 185(4) in effect discriminated on the ground of nationality, and could not be justified,[293] the section was declared incompatible with ECHR under HRA 1998, s 4.[294]

10.128 In *R (RJM) v Secretary of State for Work and Pensions*,[295] the House of Lords accepted that being a homeless person was a 'personal characteristic', and accordingly that being a homeless person fell within the category of 'other status' within the meaning of Article 14. In view of the reach of Article 14,[296] the decision might yet, therefore, have wider implications in future homelessness cases than has yet been appreciated.

---

289 The right does not, however, have to be engaged – thus, even if there is no claim under Article 8, there may be a claim under Article 14 because the subject-matter is family, private life or home: *M v Secretary of State for Work and Pensions* [2006] UKHL 11, [2006] 2 AC 91, at [11]–[14].

290 *Wandsworth LBC v Michalak* [2002] EWCA Civ 271, [2003] 1 WLR 617 (see also *Ghaidan v Godin-Mendoza* [2004] UKHL 30, [2004] HLR 46). In *R (Carson) v Secretary of State for Work and Pensions* [2005] UKHL 37, [2006] 1 AC 173, Lord Nicholls said that the criteria derived from *Michalak* may not be appropriate in every case and that it may be appropriate simply to consider whether the alleged discrimination can withstand scrutiny.

291 *R (Morris) v Westminster City Council (No 3)* [2004] EWHC 2191 (Admin), [2005] HLR 7. The decision was upheld on appeal: [2005] EWCA Civ 1184, [2006] 1 WLR 505, [2006] HLR 8.

292 See also *R (S) v Chief Constable of South Yorkshire Police* [2004] UKHL 39, [2004] 1 WLR 2196.

293 The government sought to justify the section on the basis that it was a necessary element of immigration control in order to prevent benefit tourism. This was rejected on the basis that the parent applicants in the cases (both of whom had children who were ineligible and were thus held not in priority need because of the then application of HA 1996, s 185(4)) were both lawfully and habitually resident here. In *Bah v UK* App No 56328/07, [2012] HLR 2, however, the ECtHR held that there was no contravention.

294 Some changes were made as a result of the declaration – see paras **A.127–A.133**.

295 [2008] UKHL 63, [2009] 1 AC 311.

296 See paras **10.126-10.129**.

10.129 On the other hand, in *R (H) v Ealing LBC*,²⁹⁷ a majority of the Court of Appeal expressed the provisional view that the provision and allocation of social housing was a social welfare benefit which did not, without more, fall within the ambit of Article 8, so that no issue under Article 14 would arise.

PROCEDURAL LAW

Introduction

10.130 There are two courts to which a dissatisfied applicant will be able to turn: a) the Administrative Court, by way of proceedings for judicial review; and b) the county court, by way of a statutory appeal against a decision made under HA 1996, Part 7 or H(W)A 2014, Part 2. In this section, we consider the procedure to be followed in relation to each.

Mental Capacity

10.131 Formally, the test of capacity to conduct proceedings will vary according to the type of court. However, as the Supreme Court has made clear in *Dunhill v Burgin* [2014] UKSC 18, there is unlikely to be any real difference whether the test is the statutory test applied under the MCA 2005 (as is applied in civil proceedings) or the common law.

10.132 The key question is set out in the judgment of Chadwick LJ in *Masterman-Lister v Brutton & Co* [2003] All ER 162, and is whether:

> 'a party to legal proceedings is capable of understanding, with the assistance of such proper explanation (in broad terms and simple language) from legal advisers and other experts as the case may require, the matters on which their consent or decision was likely to be necessary in the course of those proceedings.'

10.133 This test applies to the proceedings as a whole and not at each step in the conduct of the proceedings (*Masterman-Lister v Brutton & Co* [2003] 3 All ER 162, confirmed in *Dunhill v Burgin* [2014] UKSC 18). While the test of lack of capacity to conduct proceedings is the statutory test under the MCA 2005, the common law principles are also helpful in applying the statutory test.

10.134 Capacity depends on time and context. The question is always whether the litigant has capacity to conduct the particular proceedings that they are involved in, and not other proceedings or their ability to make decisions in general (*Sheffield City Council v E and another* [2005] Fam 326 per Munby J at para 38).

297 [2017] EWCA Civ 1127, [2018] HLR 2.

Which court?

10.135 Decisions made by local authorities under HA 1996, Parts 6 and 7 and H(W)A 2014, Part 2 are administrative law decisions and therefore, without more, would prima facie only be justiciable by way of judicial review in the Administrative Court. Judicial review is, however, a remedy of 'last resort'[298] and the provision of a statutory appeal (or any form of alternative remedy) generally precludes recourse to it unless the case can in some way be distinguished from the category for which the appeal – or alternative – procedure is provided.[299]

10.136 The existence of a scheme of internal review under Parts 6 and 7 and Part 2 accordingly requires the applicant – save in exceptional cases – to pursue that review before going to court. More significantly for current purposes, the existence of a statutory appeal against a decision under HA 1996, Part 7 and H(W)A 2014, Part 2 will generally preclude a dissatisfied applicant from seeking to challenge that decision by proceedings for judicial review.[300]

10.137 Examples of decisions outside HA 1996, Parts 6 and 7 and H(W)A 2014, Part 2, where judicial review has proceeded notwithstanding the existence of an alternative – or internal – procedure, include cases where it is not the individual decision that is in issue but the underlying legality of a decision – for example, a policy – of which the individual case is a mere application,[301] and where the decision was made without jurisdiction or contained an error of law.[302]

10.138 In *R v East Yorkshire Borough of Beverley Housing Benefits Review Board ex p Hare*,[303] the court allowed judicial review proceedings to continue – and granted relief – even though the applicant had an alternative remedy by way of appeal (under the then provisions) to a housing benefit review board, because the point raised was in part a point of statutory interpretation of general importance on which it was therefore appropriate for the court to rule.

10.139 Even these circumstances are, however, unlikely to lead to the grant of permission to seek judicial review under HA 1996, Part 7 or H(W)A 2014, Part 2 to a homeless person aggrieved by a decision on their application which could otherwise be appealed to the county court,[304] because the appeal procedure itself

---

298 Ie, any proper alternative remedy should be exhausted before the Administrative Court will permit a case to be heard: *R v Hammersmith and Fulham LBC ex p Burkett* [2002] UKHL 23, [2002] 1 WLR 1593; *R (Bancoult) v Secretary of State for the Foreign and Commonwealth Office* [2001] QB 1067, CA.
299 *R v Secretary of State for the Home Department ex p Swati* [1986] 1 WLR 477, CA.
300 In an exceptional case, however, if the county court considers that an appeal under HA 1996, s 204 raises an issue of general public importance, it may transfer it to the High Court: *James v Hertsmere BC* [2020] EWCA Civ 489, [2020] 1 WLR 3606, [2020] HLR 28 at [32].
301 *R v Paddington Valuation Officer ex p Peachey Property Corporation Ltd* [1966] 1 QB 380, CA.
302 *R v Hillingdon LBC ex p Royco Homes Ltd* [1974] QB 720, QBD.
303 (1995) 27 HLR 637, QBD.
304 The issue does not arise if the issue raised *cannot* be brought by way of appeal to the county court, as there is no 'alternative remedy'.

– being on a 'point of law'[305] – embraces the same grounds as those on which judicial review would be available.[306]

10.140 The intention of the HA 1996, s 204 appeal procedure was to transfer the bulk of the work from the High Court to the county court.[307] Accordingly, permission to bring a challenge by way of judicial review was refused where the reason the applicant could not appeal to the county court was simply because the applicant was out of time[308] to do so: while the court did not rule out *ever* granting permission where an applicant was out of time, the applicant would have to show 'really exceptional circumstances'.[309]

10.141 It would nonetheless be wrong to think that the High Court – through the Administrative Court – has nothing to do with homelessness. A number of HA 1996, Part 7 cases have come before it and the use of judicial review has been approved where:

a) an authority refused to house pending an internal review;[310]

b) an authority refused to consider a request for accommodation pending review;[311]

c) the decision letter from the authority was so unsatisfactory that any internal review would be unfair to the applicant, and the authority refused to rectify the deficiency in the letter;[312]

d) the challenge was to the legality of a policy of the authority: see *Byfield*,[313] a challenge to the then policy that applicants could not seek an internal review of the suitability of an offer of accommodation unless the offer was rejected; this was an unlawful fetter on the right to an internal review and

---

305 HA 1996, s 204(1); H(W)A 2014, s 88(1).
306 See paras **10.36–10.129**.
307 'Prior to 1997, many of these unhappy cases fell to be considered by nominated judges dealing with the Crown Office list. Such was the pressure that a particular deputy High Court judge sat almost continuously dealing with homelessness cases and other such cases frequently had to be referred to other deputy High Court judges. Therefore, Parliament incorporated into the Housing Act 1996 another route whereby complaints could be dealt with': per Tucker J in *R v Brent LBC ex p O'Connor* (1999) 31 HLR 923, QBD, at 924.
308 See para **10.213**.
309 *R v Brent LBC ex p O'Connor*, above, at 925. See also *R (Ahamed) v. Haringey LBC* [2023] EWCA Civ 975; [2023] HLR 43 at [67-68].
310 *R v Camden LBC ex p Mohammed* (1998) 30 HLR 315, QBD. Prior to the county court acquiring power to make an interim order to house, this would also have been true of a refusal to house pending appeal to the county court.
311 *R (Casey) v Restormel BC* [2007] EWHC 2554 (Admin), [2008] JHL D27.
312 *R v Camden LBC ex p Mohammed*, above.
313 (1997) 31 HLR 913, QBD. It is conceivable that such a challenge might be brought by an interested pressure group; see, eg, *R v Inland Revenue Commissioners ex p National Federation of Self-employed and Small Businesses Ltd* [1982] AC 617, HL; *R v Secretary of State for Social Services ex p Child Poverty Action Group* [1990] 2 QB 540, CA; *R v Her Majesty's Inspectorate of Pollution ex p Greenpeace Ltd* [1994] 4 All ER 329, QBD; *R v Secretary of State for Foreign and Commonwealth Affairs ex p World Development Movement Ltd* [1995] 1 WLR 386, QBD.

was accordingly properly brought by way of judicial review;[314] see also *Elkundi*,[315] where the challenge was to the authority's policy as to how it accommodated applicants;

e) the case raised an important matter of law: *Sadiq*;[316]

f) an authority had not made a decision in response to a request for accommodation: *Lusamba*;[317]

g) the decision was to refuse to make a local connection referral to another authority, which decision is not reviewable under HA 1996, s 202:[318] *Sareen*;[319]

h) the authority refused to extend time to apply for an internal review under HA 1996, s 202(3):[320] *Lewisham*,[321] *Slaiman*;[322]

i) an appeal under HA 1996, s 204 would not provide an effective remedy: in *Aguiar*,[323] the applicant received his costs on a compromised judicial review application, in part because the remedy sought[324] would not have been available in appeal proceedings under HA 1996, s 204;

j) the person seeking judicial review was a third party, not the applicant: in *Hammia*,[325] the authority applied a policy that victims of domestic violence, if a joint tenant of the authority, must first serve a notice to quit their existing home as a condition of acceptance as homeless; the applicant's husband, who lost his security of tenure because of the notice, successfully challenged this policy by proceedings for judicial review;

---

314 The substance of this decision was overruled in *Alghile v Westminster City Council* [2001] EWCA Civ 363, 33 HLR 57; in turn, *Alghile* was overturned by the statutory amendment that permits an applicant to seek a review of accommodation while accepting it: HA 1996, s 202(1A). These do not, however, affect the underlying point being made here, that a challenge to an unlawful policy may yet be brought by judicial review.

315 *R (Elkundi and others) v Birmingham City Council* [2021] EWHC 1024 (Admin); [2021] 1 WLR 4031; [2021] HLR 45 [2021]; ([2022] EWCA Civ 601; [2022] QB 604; [2022] HLR 31).

316 *R v Brent LBC ex p Sadiq* (2001) 33 HLR 47, QBD. Moses J, while acknowledging that the applicant should have sought a review and county court appeal, referred to the residual jurisdiction of the High Court and said that the case raised an important point, which might well have had to be considered by the Court of Appeal in any event.

317 *R (Lusamba) v Islington LBC* [2008] EWHC 1149 (Admin), [2008] JHL D89. If, however, a decision is subsequently made by the authority, then there is no point in pursuing the substantive hearing.

318 In Wales, H(W)A 2014, s 85. See also see also *R (Savage) v Hillingdon LBC* [2010] EWHC 88 (Admin) where it was said that it was doubtful that the manner in which an authority chose to discharge their duties under HA 1996, s 190(2) and (4) (duties to persons who are eligible, homeless, in priority need but became homeless intentionally) could be dealt with by way of review under HA 1996, s 202.

319 *Hackney LBC v Sareen* [2003] EWCA Civ 351, [2003] HLR 54. See further chapter 5.

320 In Wales, H(W)A 2014, s 85(5); see further chapter 8.

321 *R (C) v Lewisham LBC* [2003] EWCA Civ 927, [2004] HLR 4.

322 *R (Slaiman) v Richmond upon Thames LBC* [2006] EWHC 329 (Admin), [2006] HLR 20.

323 *R (Aguiar) v Newham LBC* [2002] EWHC 1325 (Admin), [2002] JHL D92.

324 An order that the authority were required to carry out a HA 1996, s 202 review.

325 *R (Hammia) v Wandsworth LBC* [2005] EWHC 1127 (Admin), [2005] HLR 46.

k) following a local connection referral, the authority to which the applicant had been referred wished to challenge a substantive finding, for example, that the applicant is unintentionally homeless: *Bantamagbari*;[326]

l) there were exceptional circumstances: *Van der Stolk*;[327]

m) where there is a linked challenge to both the Part 7 decision and the Part 6 allocations policy: *Imam*;[328]

n) where the authority refused to accept an application, contending that there had been no change since a previous application: *Minott*;[329] *Ibrahim*;[330]

o) whether or not an applicant had asked for a review: *Bereket*;[331]

p) whether assessments had been lawfully carried out under HA 1996, s 189A:[332] *R. (ZK) v Havering LBC*;[333] *R (YR) v. Lambeth LBC*,[334] *R (UO) v Redbridge LBC*.[335]

10.142 In addition, there remain a number of circumstances, not yet considered by the courts, in which it is likely that judicial review will continue to be available, for example:

a) where, otherwise than so far as governed by the local connection provisions of HA 1996, ss 200–201,[336] two authorities are at odds, eg under the co-operation provisions of HA 1996, s 213;[337]

---

326 *R (Bantamagbari) v Westminster City Council* [2003] EWHC 1350 (Admin), [2003] JHL D70.

327 *R (Van der Stolk) v Camden LBC* [2002] EWHC 1261 (Admin), [2002] JHL D77, where the authority had failed properly to consider medical evidence provided after the time limit to appeal had passed and the applicant's mental health was deteriorating. See also *RW v Sheffield City Council* [2005] EWHC 720 (Admin), where two local authorities were disputing responsibility for the applicant under the local connection provisions, and neither would house in the interim. '[T]he claimant having been caught between two stools and faced with an exceptional situation, I consider that it is appropriate, notwithstanding the existence of alternative remedies, to entertain judicial review proceedings': per Gibb J at [34].

328 *R (Imam) v. Croydon LBC* [2020] EWHC 739 (Admin); [2021] HLR 44; [2022] EWCA Civ 601; [2022] QB 604; [2022] HLR 31.

329 *R (Minott) v Cambridge CC* [2021] EWHC 211 (Admin); [2021] HLR 9; [2022] EWCA Civ 159; [2022] HLR 27.

330 *R. (Ibrahim) v Westminster CC* [2021] EWHC 2616 (Admin); [2022] HLR 13.

331 *R (Bereket) v Waltham Forest LBC* [2021] EWHC 3120 (Admin).

332 Paras **8.66-8.74**.

333 [2022] EWHC 1854 (Admin); [2022] HLR 47.

334 *R. (YR) v Lambeth LBC* [2022] EWHC 2813 (Admin); [2023] HLR 16.

335 [2023] EWHC 1355 (Admin); [2023] HLR 39. The finding that the assessment had failed to consider the applicant's housing needs meant that all the accommodation provided, and the putatively final offer, had not been suitable: the court rejected the authority's argument that relief to that effect should be refused because suitability could have been raised on review and appeal, as the arguments were closely related and there would be no purpose served by doing so.

336 In Wales, H(W)A 2014, ss 80–83. See para **5.52** onwards. Cf *Sheffield*, last footnote, where the dispute was not covered by the statutory arbitration provisions.

337 See chapter 11.

b) where what is in issue is discharge of the property duties, which are not subject to internal review or, therefore, to appeal (see HA 1996, ss 211 and 212[338]);

c) where an applicant seeks an internal review on the facts alone, ie, without reference to a point of law, but the authority does not conduct the internal review (or notify the applicant of the outcome) within the prescribed time: there may need to be an application for judicial review to compel the authority to conduct the internal review or to notify the applicant of the outcome.[339]

10.143 Accordingly, judicial review is some way from obsolete in cases under HA 1996, Parts 6 and 7 and H(W)A 2014, Part 2. Permission to pursue a judicial review for a 'pre-emptive' declaration in advance of any homelessness or threatened homelessness, that the applicant should not be considered intentionally homeless, while not within the review or appeal provisions (for want of any decision), would, however, seem likely to be refused.[340]

Judicial review

Procedure

10.144 The procedure for claiming judicial review is to be found in CPR[341] Part 54.[342] Cases are now commonly – but not invariably – heard by a single High Court judge. All parties should comply with the pre-action protocol for judicial review. Compliance or non-compliance will be taken into account when giving directions for the case management of proceedings or when making an order for costs.[343] The protocol will not, however, be appropriate where there is an urgent need for an interim order, for example, to secure interim accommodation under HA 1996, s 188(3), although informal (or 'short') notice should nonetheless be given.[344]

Letter before claim

10.145 The pre-action protocol requires the claimant to send a letter to the defendant before making the claim, to identify the issues in dispute and to establish whether litigation can be avoided.[345] The letter should contain the date

338 In Wales, H(W)A 2014, ss 93, 94. See chapter 6.
339 See further para **10.209.**
340 See *R v Hillingdon LBC ex p Tinn* (1988) 20 HLR 305, QBD. Like every 'absolute' proposition, there may yet be exceptions, for example, where the court apprehends – with a degree of reason – *such* unlawful conduct by an authority that it feels impelled to intervene, even if the conditions for a prohibiting order are not fulfilled.
341 SI 1998/3132.
342 See also the accompanying practice direction (PD) and Senior Courts Act 1981, s 31.
343 See Judicial Review Pre-action Protocol para 7; and CPR Costs PDs.
344 Judicial Review Pre-action Protocol para 6.
345 Judicial Review Pre-action Protocol para 14.

and details of the decision, act or omission being challenged and a clear summary of the facts on which the claim is based. It should also contain the details of any relevant information that the claimant is seeking to obtain and an explanation of why this is considered relevant.[346] The letter should set out a date for reply, which in most circumstances will be 14 days. A claim should not usually be made until the proposed reply date has passed.[347]

Letter of response

10.146 The authority should respond within 14 days.[348] If this is not possible, an interim reply should be sent and a reasonable extension proposed.[349] The reply must indicate clearly whether or not the claim is being conceded.[350] Failure to comply with the requirement to respond may lead to a costs order. In *R v Kensington and Chelsea RLBC ex p Ghebregiogis*,[351] a comprehensive letter before action had been sent to the authority by the applicant's solicitors explaining the applicant's position and dealing with the authority's adverse contentions, following which the applicant commenced judicial review proceedings. Just before the application for permission came on for hearing, the authority changed its mind. The applicant successfully sought his costs: the authority should have considered the case properly when it received the letter.[352]

Permission

10.147 Permission must be sought to bring an application for judicial review.[353] Where a claim has become academic, even if as a result of a change of circumstances between issue of proceedings and hearing,[354] it is only where there is good reason to do so in the public interest, that permission to claim judicial review will be granted. Where the applicant was challenging the suitability of his current s 193(2) accommodation but had accepted an offer of alternative accommodation subject to review of its suitability under s 202(1A),[355] the challenge was not academic, as the authority on review or the county court on appeal might find the offer to be unsuitable, in which case the suitability of the current accommodation would still need to be determined. [356]

---

346 Judicial Review Pre-action Protocol para 16.
347 Judicial Review Pre-action Protocol para 18.
348 Judicial Review Pre-action Protocol para 20.
349 Judicial Review Pre-action Protocol para 21.
350 Judicial Review Pre-action Protocol para 22.
351 (1995) 27 HLR 602, QBD.
352 See further paras **10.173-10.182**.
353 The requirement for permission represents the most significant difference between the procedure to be followed on a claim for judicial review and an appeal under HA 1996, s 204 or H(W)A 2014, s 88, which is as of right.
354 See *R v Secretary of State for the Home Department, ex p Salem* [1999] 1 AC 450; *R (Rushbridger) v Attorney-General* [2004] 1 AC 357, HL.
355 Paras **7.203, 8,234.**
356 *R (Jaberi) v Westminster CC* [2023] EWHC 1045 (Admin), [2023] HLR 37.

10.148 The sort of circumstances where permission will be granted include where a large number of similar cases either exist or are anticipated or where there is a discrete point of statutory construction which does not involve detailed consideration of the facts:[357] see, eg, *R (Nur) v Birmingham CC*[358] and *Ncube*.[359]

10.149 In very different circumstances,[360] an applicant had obtained alternative accommodation before the hearing. The authority failed to file an acknowledgement of service and only produced a witness statement the day before the hearing. It contended that no remedy should be granted because it was in the process of revising the relevant policy. A declaration was nonetheless granted: the conduct of the authority in failing to file an acknowledgement of service and producing a witness statement shortly before the substantive hearing was unacceptable; the court had the distinct impression that the authority was anxious to hide its position as far as possible. It was right that the court should mark its disapproval of such conduct.

Time

10.150 Application for permission must be made 'promptly and in any event within three months from the date when grounds for the application first arose'.[361] The three-month period runs from the time when application for permission can first be made.[362]

---

357 *R (McKenzie) v Waltham Forest LBC* [2009] EWHC 1097 (Admin), [2009] JHL D94. See *R (Raw) v Lambeth LBC* [2010] EWHC 507 (Admin), [2010] JHL D40, D104 where the authority conceded the applicant's entitlement to assistance under its rent deposit scheme after the issue of his claim, which it invited him to withdraw, which he refused to do. The Administrative Court dismissed the claim as it was not in the public interest to hear academic claims and the court's resources were better spent on cases directly affecting the rights and obligations of the parties; nor was there evidence of other cases in which the authority had applied its policy or that the issue raised would need to be resolved by the courts in the near future. If a claim is fact-sensitive, it will not be permitted to proceed: *R (Zoolife International Ltd) v Secretary of State for the Environment* [2007] EWHC 2995 (Admin), [2008] ACD 44.

358 [2020] EWHC 3526 (Admin); [2021] HLR 23, where the applicant accepted an offer of accommodation after the issue of proceedings for judicial review of an allocation policy, so that the authority contended that the claim had become academic, an argument rejected by the court – whether it had been acting lawfully in preferring applicants with children over applicants with dependent disabled adults affected many disabled persons and was not confined the claimant's personal circumstances – see para **9.122**.

359 *Ncube v Brighton and Hove City Council* [2021] EWHC 578 (Admin); [2021] 1 WLR 4762; [2021] HLR 3, where the applicant had been provided with accommodation by the Home Office but the court considered that the issue of what powers were available to assist failed asylum seekers during the pandemic raised an important question of law which potentially affected many other applicants for accommodation – see paras **11.127, 11.137**.

360 *R (Adow) v Newham LBC* [2010] EWHC 951 (Admin), [2010] JHL D101; for the facts, see para **9.144**.

361 CPR 54.5.

362 PD 54A para 4.1. When what is under challenge is a policy, time only begins to run when it affects the individual applicant: *R v Tower Hamlets LBC ex p Mohib Ali* (1993) 25 HLR 218, DC; *R v Newham LBC ex p Ajayi* (1996) 28 HLR 25, QBD.

10.151 The former explicit power (to be found in RSC Order 53 r 4) to extend time for 'good reason' has not been retained, although the general jurisdiction of the court to extend time under CPR 3.1 is available. Any application to extend time must be set out in the claim form with grounds.[363] The parties may not agree to extend time,[364] nor will the court be enthusiastic about granting permission when an application has grown stale.[365] Delay in obtaining legal aid may constitute an acceptable reason for granting permission belatedly.[366] Where the challenge is to the lawfulness of a policy and the relief sought is to restrain its further implementation, the need to ensure that a prima facie unlawful policy is discontinued is likely to comprise a good reason for extending time.[367]

10.152 When permission to pursue judicial review out of time is granted, it is not a final decision on time: it may still be raised at the full hearing of the application for judicial review itself.[368]

Form of application

10.153 An application must be made on form N461, in accordance with CPR Part 54. The claim form must include or be accompanied by a detailed statement of the grounds and a statement of the facts relied on. Parties should ensure that these are kept up-to-date and amended as required, even where the need for the amendment results from events which arise after the claim has issued (eg provision of further temporary accommodation; change in family composition); this is particularly important in judicial review claims because it enables the court to be satisfied that judicial review remains an appropriate remedy and allows the parties time to prepare the relevant evidence.[369]

Supporting documents

10.154 In addition, the following must also be supplied: any written evidence in support of the claim; a copy of the decision that the applicant[370] seeks to have quashed; any documents which will be relied on; copies of relevant statutory

---

363 PD 54A para 54.6.
364 CPR 54.5(2).
365 See *R v Rochester City Council ex p Trotman* (1983) *Times* 13 May. If the ground of challenge is that the authority has not made a decision that its duty to an applicant has ended, however, then the question of delay – even if the matter otherwise appears 'stale' – would not seem to arise: see recently *R (Bano) v Waltham Forest* LBC [2024] EWHC 654 (Admin).
366 *R v Stratford on Avon DC ex p Jackson* [1985] 1 WLR 1319, CA; see also *R v Dacorum BC ex p Brown* (1989) 21 HLR 405, QBD.
367 *R (Lin) v Barnet LBC* [2006] EWHC 1041 (Admin), [2006] HLR 44.
368 *R v Dairy Produce Quota Tribunal ex p Caswell* [1990] 2 AC 738, HL; caution should, however, be exercised when re-opening the issue of delay at the substantive hearing: *R (Lichfield Securities Ltd) v Lichfield DC* [2001] EWCA Civ 304, [2001] 3 PLR 33.
369 *R (AB&CD) v. Westminster CC* [2024] EWHC 226 (Admin); [2024] HLR forthcoming.
370 Under the CPR, a person claiming judicial review is now (as in other cases) a claimant (see CPR 2.3(1): '"claimant" means a person who makes a claim' and CPR 54.1 referring to a 'claim for judicial review'); the term 'applicant' is, however, used in this book to denote applicant under either HA 1996, Part 6 or Part 7 or H(W)A 2014, Part 2.

material; and a list of essential documents for advance reading. Two copies of the relevant documents in a paginated and indexed bundle must be filed.[371] Where it is not possible to file all of the documents immediately, the applicant must say which are to follow and explain why they are not currently available.

10.155 In the usual case, the applicant's full case must be made out in the initial application, without anticipating additional oral evidence or later elaboration. This makes the initial papers very important indeed. This means that the case must be made out from the outset.

Duty of care

10.156 There is a high duty of care on the part of all applicants to make full and frank disclosure in an application for permission, even if it is unhelpful to the case.[372] Non-disclosure is not necessarily fatal if it causes no advantage to the applicant and no prejudice to the respondent but, even if it does not lead to the refusal of permission, it could still affect relief at the end of the day.[373] The obligation is to make full and candid disclosure of the material facts known to the applicant and to make proper enquiries before making the application; there is a breach of the disclosure duty if the applicant has not disclosed any additional material facts which they would have known if they had made proper enquiries before making the application.[374]

10.157 Proper disclosure for this purpose means specifically identifying all relevant documents for the judge, drawing their attention to the particular passages in the documents which are material and taking appropriate steps to ensure that the judge correctly appreciates the significance of what they are being asked to read; that burden of full and frank disclosure is more onerous where a telephone application is being made to a judge who has none of the papers before them, nor is it considered to be obviated by giving informal notice to the other party.

Service

10.158 The claim form (and accompanying documents) must be served on the defendant(s) within seven days of the date of issue,[375] together with an acknowledgment of service form, which must be filed by the respondent authority not more than 21 days after service of the claim form.[376]

---

371 PD 54A paras 5.6–5.9.
372 See also para **10.189**, on an application for interim relief, where there is an analogous duty of disclosure.
373 See *R v Wirral MBC ex p Bell* (1994) 27 HLR 234, QBD.
374 *R (Lawer) v Restormel BC* [2007] EWHC 2299 (Admin), [2008] HLR 20.
375 CPR 54.7. Where the relief sought in the claim form includes a declaration of incompatibility under HRA 1998, s 4, the Crown must be given 21 days' notice and/or joined as an interested party or second defendant to the claim: CPR 19.4A(1), and see *R (Morris) v Westminster City Council* [2003] EWHC 2266 (Admin), [2004] HLR 18.
376 CPR 54.8.

Pre-permission response

10.159 In the acknowledgement of service, the defendant must set out a summary of the grounds for contesting the claim, any directions which will be sought and other applications which will be made at the permission stage. A respondent who does not return the acknowledgment of service form within 14 days of service will lose the right to take part in the permission hearing (although not the right to take part in the substantive application) without the court's express permission to do so.[377] A respondent authority may not apply to set aside permission where it has been served with the claim form,[378] but may do so where there has been a failure to serve by the applicant.[379]

Paper applications

10.160 Applications for permission to proceed will, unless the court directs otherwise, be decided by a judge without hearing oral submissions.

Interim applications

10.161 Any applications for interim relief should be made in accordance with CPR Parts 23 and 25 and may be considered with the application for permission.[380] The Court of Appeal has issued practice guidance about the approach to be adopted when seeking interim relief in homelessness judicial review claims:[381]

a) Applicants should indicate[382] whether they wish the application to be heard orally or whether they are content for the application to be dealt with on the papers alone. If the latter, it gives the respondent an opportunity to consider whether they consent to the matter being dealt with on the papers.

b) Unless both parties have consented to the application being dealt with on the papers, then if the court refuses the application on the papers, the order should be endorsed with a statement that the parties have the right to apply to have the order set aside, varied or stayed under CPR 3.3(5),[383] which will be at an oral hearing.[384]

c) If the parties have consented to a paper determination, the order is final and a dissatisfied party can only challenge the decision by way of appeal to the Court of Appeal.[385]

---

377 CPR 54.9.
378 CPR 54.13.
379 *R (Webb) v Bristol City Council* [2001] EWHC Admin 696, [2001] JHL D90.
380 There is a duty of full disclosure – see paras **10.156–10.157**.
381 *R (Nolson) v Stevenage BC* [2020] EWCA Civ 379, [2020] HLR 2 at [18].
382 Even where the relevant court form does not ask the specific question.
383 Within seven days or such other time as the court considers appropriate.
384 The application should state that it is made under CPR 3.3(5) or, if made under another specific provision of the rules, that it is so made.
385 Within 21 days.

10.162 Failure to comply with any order of the court – or an undertaking given in lieu of an order – may amount to contempt of court.[386] Note that even if a claimant does not wish to pursue an application for committal for contempt, it remains the duty of the court to consider for itself whether or not it should proceed on its own initiative to deal with any contempt.[387]

Attendance of respondent

10.163 Unless the court directs otherwise, the respondent authority does not need to attend any permission hearing. Where it does so, the court will not generally make an order for costs against the applicant.[388]

Post-permission response

10.164 If permission is granted, the respondent must, within 35 days of service of the order granting permission, file and serve detailed grounds for contesting the claim and any written evidence on which reliance is to be placed.[389]

Further stages

10.165 If permission is granted, then a full hearing will be listed. At least 21 days prior to that hearing, the applicant must file a full skeleton argument. The respondent must file a skeleton at least 14 days in advance.[390]

10.166 Where permission is, on the papers, refused (or granted only subject to conditions or on certain grounds), the applicant may, within seven days, request that the decision be reconsidered at an oral hearing.[391]

---

386 See *R (Bempoa) v Southwark LBC* [2002] EWHC 153 (Admin), [2002] JHL D44, where, in proceedings under the National Assistance Act 1948, s 21, the authority through its social services department undertook not to evict the applicant, pending an assessment of his needs. Notwithstanding this, the authority's housing department evicted him from his accommodation and refused to reinstate him. The undertaking bound all departments in the authority, which was held to be in contempt.

387 *Mohammad v Secretary of State for the Home Department* [2021] EWHC 240 (Admin).

388 PD 54A paras 8.5–8.6.

389 CPR 54.14.

390 PD 54A para 15.

391 CPR 54.12. No such application may be made, however, if the refusal of permission records that the application is totally without merit: CPR 54.12(7). As to the meaning of 'totally without merit' in this context see *R (Wasif) v Secretary of State for the Home Department* [2016] EWCA Civ 82, [2016] 1 WLR 2793. Such a litigant can still seek permission to appeal from the Court of Appeal: *Wasif*.

Disclosure

10.167 Application for disclosure of documents may be made (by either party) at the same time as permission is sought or after it has been granted.[392] Unless the court makes an order for disclosure, it is not required.[393] On disclosure, only material that is privileged – because it has been produced in the course of, or in anticipation of, the proceedings – may be withheld. The usual rules on disclosure (CPR 31) do not apply to claims for judicial review: rather, there is a 'duty of candour' imposed on public authorities to provide all relevant material to parties and the court, a duty which continues throughout the proceedings, because a public authority in judicial review is not defending its private interests but is said to be joined in a 'common enterprise with the court to fulfil the public interest in upholding the rule of law'.[394]

10.168 Through disclosure, the applicant will be able to inspect the authority's minutes, emails and other memoranda dealing with their application. An examination of the authority's relevant standing orders should also be undertaken in every case, as these may reveal a want of authorised delegation or sub-delegation:[395] these should be available on the authority's website but otherwise may be sought as part of the disclosure exercise. It may be said that few authorities can withstand such close legal scrutiny without revealing *some* flaws in their procedure, although these flaws may do no more than cause minor embarrassment without invalidating the whole process.[396]

Appeal

10.169 An appeal against a refusal of permission – generally or on specific grounds, or against conditions – lies to the Court of Appeal, but only with its permission:[397] this must be pursued within seven days.[398] If successful, the Court of Appeal may:

a) grant permission to apply for judicial review and direct that the case be heard by the High Court; or

b) grant permission to apply for judicial review but order that the Court of Appeal will hear the case itself.[399]

---

392 CPR 54.16.
393 PD 54A.12(1).
394 *R (Citizens UK) v Secretary of State* [2018] EWCA Civ 1812. See by way of example *R (Montano) v Lambeth LBC* [2024] EWHC 249 (Admin); [2024] HLR forthcoming.
395 See chapter 7.
396 Applicants should be wary of pinning too many hopes on an administrative error.
397 CPR 52.8.
398 CPR 52.8(3).
399 CPR 52.8.

Hearing

10.170 In the usual course, evidence will be that which was served (in writing) with the application for permission,[400] supplemented by any evidence in reply and any further evidence in response; not uncommonly there will be two or three exchanges of evidence. Oral evidence is possible, but only at the discretion of the court.[401] Permission to cross-examine witnesses is rarely granted.[402]

Burden of proof

10.171 The burden of proof lies on a person seeking to show that a decision is void; the allegations must be both substantiated and particularised: *Wednesbury*;[403] see also *Cannock Chase DC v Kelly*.[404]

10.172 It is never enough to say simply that the applicant is a homeless person and in priority need, because this would not be sufficient to raise the inference of a duty. The duty arises only when the authority is satisfied, or has reason to believe, or considers that the fact or state of affairs is as it is claimed to be. It must be alleged that the authority has refused or failed to reach a decision, or that such decision as has been reached must be treated by the courts as void, for want of compliance with such of the foregoing principles as are identified; the factual basis for this allegation must be set out.

Costs

10.173 The costs of and incidental to all proceedings in the High Court are in the discretion of the court.[405] The general provisions concerning costs (ie, those contained in CPR Part 44) are applicable to judicial review proceedings.[406] Accordingly, the usual order is for costs to follow the event so that the successful

---

400 See paras **10.154–10.155**.
401 The court has an inherent power to give directions requiring oral evidence and cross-examination in a claim for judicial review: *R (G) v Ealing LBC (No 2)* [2002] EWHC 250 (Admin), [2002] MHLR 140. See further CPR 54.16 (referring to CPR 8.6(1)).
402 *Bubb v Wandsworth LBC* [2011] EWCA Civ 1285, [2012] HLR 13 at [24]–[25].
403 *Associated Provincial Picture Houses Ltd v Wednesbury Corporation* [1948] 1 KB 223, CA.
404 [1978] 1 WLR 1, CA, para **10.64.**
405 *R (Burkett) v Hammersmith and Fulham LBC* [2004] EWCA Civ 1342.
406 This includes the wasted costs jurisdiction under Senior Courts Act 1981, s 51 and CPR 48.7, where a legal representative has acted improperly, unreasonably or negligently, causing another party to incur unnecessary costs and it is just to make such an order: see generally *Ridehalgh v Horsefield* [1994] Ch 205, CA: see *R (Grimshaw) v Southwark LBC* [2013] EWHC 4504 (Admin) (proceedings challenging decision to terminate provision of temporary accommodation followed by accepted offer of accommodation about which claimant's solicitors failed to inform the court).

party will be able to recover costs.[407] The court has, however, a broad discretion to take into account all factors, including the conduct of the parties; where either party's conduct has prolonged litigation unnecessarily or has had the effect of increasing the costs burden on the other without proper cause, the court may deprive the successful party of all or a proportion of the costs.[408]

10.174 The courts may depart from the general rule on an issue-by-issue basis: where a party unsuccessfully raises an issue that takes up a significant part of the hearing, the party may be denied costs in relation to that issue, even if successful in the claim overall.[409]

10.175 Publicly funded litigants should not be treated differently from those who are not; nonetheless, the consequences for solicitors who do such work is a factor which must be taken into account: it is one thing for solicitors who do a substantial amount of publicly funded work, and who have to fund the substantial overheads that sustaining a legal practice involves, to take the risk of being paid at lower rates if a publicly funded case turns out to be unsuccessful, but quite another for them to be unable to recover remuneration at *inter partes* rates in the event that it is successful.[410]

10.176 Where a claim for judicial review is settled (most commonly, in the present context, where an authority agrees to withdraw its decision and reconsider it) but the costs remain in dispute, the principles are as set out in *R (Boxall) v Waltham Forest LBC*:[411]

    a) the court has power to make a costs order even where parties have settled the substantive claim;

---

407 CPR 44.2(2)(a). See, eg *Mendes and another v Southwark LBC* [2009] EWCA Civ 594, [2010] HLR 3, at [23] and [24]. Where a body corporate (including a local authority) has employed a solicitor who conducts litigation on its behalf, and that body corporate obtains a costs order in its favour, the usual basis for the assessment of costs is by reference to what it would have cost to retain an independent solicitor, rather than by reference to the salary of the employed solicitor: *Re Eastwood (Deceased)* [1975] Ch12. The court can, however, depart from this general rule if there are special factors which require it to do so: *Re Eastwood (Deceased)* [1975] Ch 112. In *R (Kuznetsov) v Camden LBC* [2019] EWHC 3910 (Admin), [2019] JHL D66, the rule was applied to a costs award following the dismissal of a claim in relation to the authority's allocations policy.

408 CPR 44.2(1)–(5).

409 *AEI Rediffusion Music Ltd v Phonographic Performance Ltd (Costs)* [1999] 1 WLR 1507, CA; *R (Bateman) v Legal Services Commission (Costs)* [2001] EWHC Admin 797, [2002] ACD 29.

410 *R (E) v Governing Body of JFS and the Admissions Appeal Panel of JFS and others; R (E) v Governing Body of JFS and the Admissions Appeal Panel of JFS (United Synagogue) and others* [2009] UKSC 1 at [25]. The dicta of Scott Baker J in *R (Boxall) v Waltham Forest LBC* (2001) 4 CCLR 258, QBD that the fact that the claimants were legally aided was immaterial when deciding what, if any, costs order to make between the parties in a case where they were successful, was approved. See also *Bunning v King's Lynn and West Norfolk Council* [2016] EWCA Civ 1037, [2017] HLR 9, accepting the general principle, but, on the facts, making no order as to costs (claimant had prima facie been in breach of an injunction but her subsequent compliance rendered the committal proceedings academic).

411 (2001) 4 CCLR 258, QBD.

b)   it will ordinarily be irrelevant that the claimant is in receipt of public funding for their claim;

c)   the overriding objective is to do justice between the parties without incurring unnecessary court time and costs;

d)   how far the court will be prepared to look into the substantive issues will depend on the circumstances of the particular case, including the amount of costs at stake and the conduct of the parties;

e)   in the absence of a good reason to make any other order, the fall-back position is to make no order as to costs; and

f)   the court should take care not to discourage parties from settling judicial review proceedings.

10.177 *Boxall* has been approved and applied in a number of other cases, drawing out the proposition that where the claimant has secured the substantive relief sought, it would normally comprise a good reason to award them the costs;[412] a judge should not be tempted too readily to adopt the fall-back position of making no order.[413]

10.178 The *Boxall* approach was applied by the Court of Appeal in *Harripaul v Lewisham LBC*:[414] The applicant was dissatisfied with both the original HA 1996, s 184 decision and the subsequent s 202 review and unsuccessfully appealed to the county court under s 204, from which the Court of Appeal granted permission to appeal, in response to which the authority offered to carry out a fresh review. The appeal was dismissed by consent, but the parties were unable to agree who should bear the costs of the appeal. The Court of Appeal held that the authority should do so: the case was akin to a judicial review and the *Boxall* principles applied; the applicant had obtained the substantive relief that she sought and it was for the authority to show why it should not pay the costs; no such reasons existed on the facts.

10.179 In *R (M)*,[415] the Court of Appeal went somewhat further, holding that where a claimant obtains all the relief which they seek (whether by consent or

---

412   *Brawley v Marczynski & Business Lines Ltd* [2002] EWCA Civ 756, [2002] 4 All ER 1060; *R (Scott) v Hackney LBC* [2009] EWCA Civ 217; *Mendes v Southwark LBC* [2009] EWCA Civ 594, [2010] HLR 3; *R (Bhata) v Secretary of State for the Home Department* [2011] EWCA Civ 895. In *R (J) v Hackney LBC* [2010] EWHC 3021 (Admin), [2010] JHL D20, under Children Act 1989, the good reason was not only the rejection of the authority's argument that its concession followed a recent decision resulting from a development in the law (rejected on the basis that the law had not radically altered the legal landscape) but also flowed from the conduct of the authority which was sufficiently poor to justify an award of costs: it had taken 12 months to file an acknowledgement of service and five months after the new case to settle the matter; it had also been unreasonable for the authority to require an oral hearing to determine costs.
413   *R (Scott) v Hackney LBC*, above, at [51].
414   [2012] EWCA Civ 266, [2012] HLR 24.
415   *R (M) v Croydon LBC* [2012] EWCA Civ 595; see further *R (Dempsey) v Sutton LBC* [2013] EWCA Civ 863.

after a contested hearing),[416] they are ordinarily[417] entitled to all their costs, unless there is a good reason to the contrary; where, however, the claimant obtains only some of the relief which they are seeking, the issue is more complex: it may be appropriate to make an order for costs based on individual issues in proceedings; in many cases, the correct order will be 'no order as to costs'; each case will turn on its own facts.[418]

10.180 As costs disputes of this nature are generally dealt with on the papers and after short written submissions, there is limited, if any, scope for the judge to resolve conflicts of fact. Causation is a relevant and sometimes decisive factor in the exercise of the court's costs discretion: whether there is a causal connection between the bringing of a claim for judicial review and obtaining relief is plainly a highly relevant consideration in deciding whether to award the claimant their costs; if a claimant can show that it was the judicial review claim which had caused the authority to change its position or that the claim had the effect that the claimant obtained the outcome that they sought earlier than they would have done without the judicial review proceedings, that would be a proper basis for costs to be awarded in their favour.[419]

10.181 The court has power to order that costs be set off.[420] This may permit a set off against damages or costs to which a legally aided person has become or becomes entitled in the action; the set-off is no different from and no more extensive than the set-off available to or against parties who are not legally aided; the broad criterion is that the claims of both claimant and defendant claim are so closely connected that it would be inequitable to allow the claimant's claim without taking into account the defendant's claim.[421]

---

416 But not where the relief is obtained as the result of the actions of a third party, see *R (Naureen) v Salford City Council* [2012] EWCA Civ 1795 – the claimant became entitled to housing benefit because the secretary of state granted her leave to remain, rather than because of any act or concession on the part of the authority. See also *RL and others v Croydon LBC* [2018] EWCA Civ 726, [2019] 1 WLR 224: permission for judicial review in respect of an alleged failure to carry out a Children Act s 17 assessment was refused because the authority had, albeit belatedly, carried out the assessment that it was the purpose of the proceedings to secure; while this led to the provision of accommodation and support, the appropriate costs order was 'no order' because the relief was not obtained as a result of proceedings, but as a result of the completion of the assessment.
417 See also *R (Hunt) v North Somerset Council* [2015] UKSC 51, [2015] 1 WLR 3575 in which it was held that a person who establishes that a public authority has acted unlawfully should ordinarily recover costs, even if no relief is obtained.
418 As to the procedure to be adopted where the parties have settled a judicial review claim but cannot agree costs, see "Guidance as to how the parties should assist the court when applications for costs are made following settlement of claims for judicial review", HMCTS, September 2016.
419 *R (Parveen) v Redbridge LBC* [2020] EWCA Civ 194, [2020] HLR 22, in which the authority agreed to settle a claim for judicial review based on the unsuitability of accommodation but only following the receipt of new medical evidence which changed its mind: the judge had been entitled to conclude that there was no connection between the judicial review claim and the subsequent acceptance that the accommodation was unsuitable.
420 CPR 44.12.
421 *Lockley v National Blood Transfusion Service* [1992] 1 WLR 492, CA.

10.182   While an assisted person is protected against the making of enforceable orders for payment of costs, that protection is not available to prevent an order for costs being set off.[422] While there will rarely be claim and counterclaim in HA 1996, Parts 6 and 7 (or H(W)A 2014, Part 2) cases,[423] the implication is that it may be possible to set off costs orders made in different judicial reviews, or even county court appeals, and perhaps even costs orders made in the county court against orders made in the High Court, if the proceedings are closely connected.

Remedies and relief

Interim relief

10.183   Where a challenge is by judicial review, the normal principle on an application for an interim injunction is that an order will be granted if it can be shown that the balance of convenience is in its favour.[424] In *de Falco, Silvestri v Crawley BC*,[425] however, Lord Denning MR said that in a homeless person's action, it is necessary to show that there was a strong prima facie case of breach by the authority[426] as, almost invariably, the applicant would be unable to give a worthwhile undertaking in damages should the applicant eventually lose.[427]

10.184   The *de Falco* approach would also seem to conflict with Lord Denning MR's own approach in *Allen v Jambo Holdings Ltd*,[428] a case in which the owners of an aircraft sought discharge of a *Mareva* injunction on the ground that the plaintiff, who was legally aided, could not give a valuable cross-undertaking in damages.

> It is said that whenever a *Mareva* injunction is granted the plaintiff has to give the cross-undertaking in damages. Suppose the widow should lose this case altogether. She is legally-aided. Her undertaking is worth nothing. I would not assent to that argument . . . A legally-aided plaintiff is by our statutes not to be in any worse position by reason of being legally-aided than any other plaintiff would be. I do not see why a poor plaintiff should be

---

422   *Hill v Bailey* [2003] EWHC 2835 (Ch).
423   Whether formally so or in practice.
424   *American Cyanamid v Ethicon* [1975] AC 396, HL; *Fellowes v Fisher* [1976] QB 122, CA. The fact that there may be serious doubt about the truth of a claim does not necessarily alter the balance of convenience; where it remains in favour of an interim order, the problem can be dealt with by ordering an expedited hearing, as in *R (OA) v Camden LBC* [2019] EWHC 2312 (Admin), [2021] PTSR 1. On the other hand, In *R (Nnaji) v Spelthorne BC* [2020] EWHC 2610 (Admin), [2020] JHL D95, the authority was entitled to be cautious in light of inconsistent statements about what accommodation was available to the applicant.
425   *De Falco, Silvestri v Crawley BC* [1980] QB 460, CA.
426   *De Falco* was followed in *R (Nnaji) v Spelthorne BC* [2020] EWHC 2016 (Admin), [2021] PTSR 1, para **10.183**.
427   In *Cyanamid*, ability to give a meaningful undertaking in damages was already a factor to be weighed up in determining the balance of convenience.
428   [1980] 1 WLR 1252, CA.

denied a *Mareva* injunction just because he is poor, whereas a rich plaintiff would get it . . .

10.185 In *R v Kensington and Chelsea RLBC ex p Hammell*,[429] it was contended by the authority that, following *Puhlhofer*,[430] it would be necessary to show something akin to 'exceptional circumstances' before an interim injunction could be granted. The court rejected this argument: interim relief is discretionary, although the discretion is one that must be exercised in accordance with principles of law; in a clear case of breach, there is therefore likely to be no issue of whether or not such relief should be granted.[431]

10.186 In *R v Cardiff City Council ex p Barry*,[432] it was held that, as a strong prima facie case had to be made out for a court to grant permission for judicial review of an authority's decision, interim relief would be the usual concomitant of the grant of permission.[433] In relation to a challenge to a refusal to house pending review,[434] however, this approach was rejected in *R v Camden LBC ex p Mohammed*[435] (itself approved in *R v Brighton and Hove Council ex p Nacion*[436]) because a review is as of right, available to everyone who is the subject of an adverse decision, so that – unlike on an application for permission to apply for judicial review – no prima facie case has to be made out.[437]

10.187 In *Davidson*,[438] the claimant was in temporary accommodation in a hostel under s 188 where he was assaulted by another resident; his support worker considered the property to be unsafe and his GP said that the chaotic nature of the hostel was exacerbating his mental health problems. He was granted permission to bring judicial review proceedings on the basis that the accommodation was unsuitable and an interim injunction as it was strongly arguable that accommodation was not suitable and there was a *prima facie* case that it was harming his mental and physical health. In *R (AS) v Liverpool City Council*,[439] it was said that there is no hard and fast rule on interim relief: the strength of the claim is a relevant factor, as is the nature of the relief sought, eg the fact that the order may be characterised as mandatory; moreover, in age

429 [1989] QB 518, (1988) 20 HLR 666, CA.
430 *R v Hillingdon LBC ex p Puhlhofer* [1986] AC 484, (1986) 18 HLR 158.
431 In *R (ZT) v Croydon LBC* [2019] EWHC 2221 (Admin), an order was made on the basis of 'balance of convenience', requiring the authority to house an asylum-seeker pending a judicial review of its decision that he was 18 years old and, therefore, did not qualify for assistance under Children Act 1989, s 17 (below, paras **11.61–11.87**). This can be distinguished because the challenge was under the 1989 Act.
432 (1990) 22 HLR 261, CA.
433 See also *R (BH) v Newham LBC*, High Court (KBD), 17 May 2023, HousingView, 30 May 2023 at para **11.77**.
434 Under the power in HA 1996, s 188(3); or H(W)A 2014, s 69(10), (11).
435 (1998) 30 HLR 315, QBD.
436 (1999) 31 HLR 1095, CA.
437 (1998) 30 HLR 315, at 320.
438 *R (Davidson) v. Cambridge CC*, [2023] EWHC 1022 (KB).
439 [2020] EWHC 3531 (Admin), [2021] HLR 24.

assessment cases,[440] a high level of scrutiny is called for and the applicant is generally entitled to the benefit of the doubt.

10.188 The principles on which the discretion to house pending review is to be exercised by the authority have been considered in chapter 8;[441] their application to housing pending appeal[442] is considered below.[443] Whether the development of those principles will have an impact in other cases in which permission is sought to claim judicial review – on other grounds – is unclear, but there is no apparent reason why they should do so, or why *Hammell*[444] should not continue to apply.

10.189 Orders granted without notice should be for a defined and short period, though sometimes it may be appropriate to decline to make an immediate order and direct instead an oral hearing within one or two days. This gives the defendant the opportunity to mount an opposition to the application.[445] There is a duty of full and frank disclosure of all relevant facts and law on an application for interim relief:[446] thus, in *Konodyba*,[447] an interim order for interim accommodation was set aside because the applicant had failed to disclose that she was the tenant of a property in Bishop's Stortford in which she could live pending determination of her application under HA 1996, Part 7.

Substantive hearing

10.190 The Administrative Court may:

a)   quash a decision (a quashing order);[448]

b)   compel an authority to make a decision or a particular decision, or re-take a decision that has been quashed (a mandatory order);[449]

---

440 Paras **11.76-11.77.**
441 See paras **8.51–8.60**.
442 Under HA 1996, s 204A or H(W)A 2014, s 88(1), (5).
443 See paras **10.252–10.261**.
444 See para **10.185**.
445 *R (Casey) v Restormel BC* [2007] EWHC 2554 (Admin), [2008] JHL D27.
446 *R (Lawer) v Restormel BC* [2007] EWHC 2299 (Admin), [2008] HLR 20.
447 *Konodyba v Kensington and Chelsea RLBC* [2011] EWHC 2653 (Admin), [2011] JHL D10. Upheld on appeal [2012] EWCA Civ 982, [2012] HLR 45.
448 Since 14 July 2022, the court has been able to make a suspended quashing order (s 29A, Senior Courts Act 1981). Such an order means that the quashing does not take effect until a date specified in it (s 29A(1)). The effect is that "the impugned act is… upheld until the quashing takes effect" (s 29A(3)) and for the period it is upheld "it is to be treated for all purposes as if its validity and force were, and always had been, unimpaired by the relevant defect" (s 29A(5)). Once the quashing order takes effect, the impugned act is treated as void from the beginning (s 29A(6)). A suspended quashing order may be subject to conditions (s 29A(2)). This may prove an attractive remedy where a court finds an aspect, eg of an allocation policy under Part 6, to be unlawful, allowing the authority time to amend the policy in light of the judgment.
449 Where the court does so, the authority is bound by its conclusions and cannot go behind the findings of the High Court; if it disagrees with that decision, its recourse is to appeal: *Kuteh v Secretary of State for Education* [2014] EWCA Civ 1586.

c) prohibit an authority from taking some action (a prohibiting order); or

d) make a declaration,[450] for example, to declare a decision ultra vires or void.

10.191 Although the Administrative Court cannot substitute its own decision for that of the authority, the findings of fact or law it makes may on occasion be such that there is only one decision that the authority can lawfully make, ie, with which it is left. In such cases, either directly or indirectly, the court will (in substance) order the authority to come to that decision.[451] It may also be that the Administrative Court would order the authority to come to a particular decision where it is necessary in order to restore a right of which the claimant has been unlawfully deprived.[452]

10.192 What applicants will most want is a mandatory order, requiring the authority to provide accommodation immediately or within a limited period of time. Whether or not such an order should be made has been closely considered by the Supreme Court in *R (Imam) v. Croydon LBC*,[453] on appeal from the hearing in that case jointly with *(R (Elkundi and others) v. Birmingham City Council*,[454] albeit, it may be thought, without much by way of clear practical guidance.[455] The essential facts in *Imam* are noted at para **8.144**, above. Noting that 'the duty under section 193(2) is owed personally to the individual applicant and gives rise to a correlative right enforceable in judicial review proceedings,'[456] the Supreme Court said:

'40. The starting point is that Croydon is subject to a public law duty imposed by Parliament by statute which is not qualified in any relevant way by reference to the resources available to Croydon. In principle, if resources are inadequate to comply with a statutory duty it is for the authority to use whatever powers it has to raise money or for central government to adjust the grant

---

450 CPR 54.3(1).

451 See *Barty-King v Ministry of Defence* [1979] 2 All ER 80, QBD. See also, eg *R v Ealing LBC ex p Parkinson* (1997) 29 HLR 179, QBD per Laws J at 185–186; *R (Cunningham) v Exeter Crown Court* [2003] EWHC 184 (Admin), [2003] 2 Cr App R (S) 64, per Clarke LJ at [22]; *R (S) v Secretary of State for the Home Department* [2007] EWCA Civ 546, [2007] Imm AR, 781, per Carnwath LJ at [46].

452 Consider *Crawley LBC v B* (2000) 32 HLR 636, CA, at 651–652, and *Robinson v Hammersmith and Fulham LBC* [2006] EWCA Civ 1122, [2006] 1 WLR 3295, [2007] HLR 7, at [31].

453 [2023] UKSC 45; [2024] HLR 6. This was considered above, in relation to whether the duty itself can be postponed, see paras **8.138-8.145**.

454 *R (Elkundi and others) v. Birmingham City Council; R (Imam) v. Croydon LBC* [2022] EWCA Civ 601; [2022] QB 604; [2022] HLR 31 at [131].

455 At [42], the court noted that: "Although Parliament lays down a duty in statute, it does so whilst appreciating that it is a general feature of public law that some degree of adjustment might be called for by the court which decides that there has been a breach of the statute. When it legislates to lay down a public law duty, Parliament cannot be expected to anticipate with precision every factor which might bear upon the justice of a particular case which arises under it". It may be that – likewise – the Supreme Court sometimes renders law the detailed application of which it expects lower courts to work out.

456 At [37].

given to the authority to furnish it with the necessary resources, or for Parliament to legislate to remove the duty or to qualify it by reference to the resources available.

'41. When it is established that there has been a breach of such a duty, it is not for a court to modify or moderate its substance by routinely declining to grant relief to compel performance of it on the grounds of absence of sufficient resources. That would involve a violation of the principle of the rule of law and an improper undermining of Parliament's legislative instruction.

'42. However, remedies in public law are discretionary ... The existence of a discretion as to the relief to be granted allows a court which finds that there has been a breach of a public law duty to decide, in the light of all the circumstances as appear to the court at the time it applies the law, how individual rights and any countervailing public interests should be reconciled. Although Parliament lays down a duty in statute, it does so whilst appreciating that it is a general feature of public law that some degree of adjustment might be called for by the court which decides that there has been a breach of the statute.

'...

'44. ...Where a breach of the law is established, the ordinary position is that a remedy should be granted. A court should proceed cautiously in exercising its discretion to refuse to make an order and should take care to ensure that it does so only where that course is clearly justified'.

10.193 Observing that 'where a court issues a mandatory order, that order produces legal consequences of its own over and above those inherent in the underlying statutory duty: the order does not simply replicate the effect of the underlying duty. It is appropriate that, when deciding whether to issue a mandatory order, the court should consider whether it is right to create those additional effects in all the circumstances of the case as it presents itself to the court,'[457] the court said:

'45. Different remedies have different degrees of impact on the capacity of a public authority to carry out its functions. A quashing order is the usual remedy in public law, which obliges the authority to re-take a decision in a lawful way. Such an order allows the authority to exercise its own judgment in re-taking a decision, having regard to all relevant interests affected thereby. On the other hand, a mandatory order takes a matter out of the hands of the authority and, to that extent, makes the court the primary actor. Accordingly, when deciding in the exercise of its discretion to

---

457 At [46].

grant a mandatory order to require the authority to do a particular thing, the court has to have regard to the way in which an order of that character might undermine to an unjustified degree the ability of the authority to fulfil functions conferred on it by Parliament and act in the public interest. ... The effect of this is that the ambit of the court's discretion whether to grant a mandatory order as opposed to a quashing order may be somewhat greater'.

10.194 The court accepted – as was not contested – that a mandatory order will not be made when it would be impossible to comply with it,[458] but observed[459] that this 'gives rise to the questions of what qualifies as impossibility of performance in the present context and what relevance resources have to that', concluding that

> 53. ...[W]hen examining the question of impossibility of compliance and whether it is appropriate to grant mandatory relief, it is relevant to have regard to the additional impact of a mandatory court order referred to above. It is not just a question of what resources are available to the housing authority immediately or after a period, but also of whether, and to what extent, it would be appropriate for a court order to be made which may have the effect of disrupting existing plans for the allocation of the authority's resources. At the same time, it is the court's role to enforce the law. The issue is how to balance these various considerations'.

10.195 The following propositions may be derived from *Imam*.

a) Once it is established that the authority is in breach of its duty, the burden lies on the authority to explain why a mandatory order should not be made; This calls for a detailed explanation of its situation and why it is impossible for it to comply with an order, if made.[460] A general reference to demand and shortage will not suffice;[461] the authority may need to

---

458 At [49].
459 At [50].
460 At [54].
461 It was on this point that Croydon's appeal was dismissed and the matter remitted to the High Court for reconsideration with further evidence. Its current evidence (as set out in the judgment at [12]) referred to its "significant difficulties as a result of acute budgetary pressures, very high demand for housing in the Borough and a limited pool of properties available to meet this demand. Funding from central government has decreased significantly over the years and the Defendant, like many authorities, is dealing with the difficult consequences of this. The projected budgetary overspend for 2020-21 is £67 million. ... [T]here are many other housing applicants who are in either in higher priority need or who have the same priority need (under the Defendant's priority banding system) but have been waiting longer for suitable accommodation. ... The Defendant has a substantial pool of Council-owned properties. ... but even this considerable supply of properties is far outweighed by the demand for housing in our local authority area. ... The precise proportion of Council-owned properties available as temporary or permanent accommodation varies depending upon the length of the waiting lists for each type of accommodation, which are kept under constant review as the Defendant reviews its allocations against its target allocation policy and reallocates properties between temporary and permanent waiting lists and across the different priority bands throughout the year".

provide specific evidence as to number of relevant properties, eg houses with adaptations or a particular number of bedrooms, which are available and why they are not appropriate for Pt 7 accommodation, eg why it wants them for Part 6 allocation and not Part 7 use.[462]

b) In accordance with the approach taken in the Court of Appeal in *Imam* and in a number of other, prior cases,[463] the authority has to show that it has taken all reasonable steps to perform its duty; this is an objective question for the court to decide, on the basis of the detailed explanation, rather than an application of the test of reasonableness or rationality from the authority's own perspective.[464]

c) Where a public authority has insufficient resources to meet all its statutory duties and fulfil functions, which are discretionary, it must give priority to duties.[465]

d) Where Parliament imposes a duty on a public authority, it does so on the basis that the authority is to be taken to have the resources available to comply with it; the court is not to examine the position with a view to possibly arriving at a contrary conclusion, nor is it entitled to 'dilute a clear statutory duty by reference to its own view of the resources available', nor is it to absolve an authority 'in any general way' from the need to comply with a duty by reference to what the court considers insufficiency of resources.[466]

e) A court may not conclude that an authority should divert resources from other functions, or should borrow more, or even that it should buy or adapt a property suitable for the claimant.[467] While seeking the appropriate balance between the court's role and that of the authority, 'setting the parameters within which the question of impossibility is to be assessed', it is not possible wholly to disentangle the question from the underlying budgetary considerations: on the one hand, an authority has to balance all the demands on it and match them with the income available, a function which the court cannot carry out, lacking the authority, the knowledge or

---

462 See Lewis LJ in the Court of Appeal [2022] EWCA Civ 601; [2022] QB 604; [2022] HLR 31 at [134], set out in the Supreme Court judgment at [26].

463 At [49], the Supreme Court referred to *Begum (R v Newham LBC ex p Begum* (2000) 32 HLR 808; *R (Aweys) v. Birmingham CC* [2008] EWCA Civ 48; [2008] 1 WLR 2305; [2008] 32 HLR 32; *Codona v Mid-Bedfordshire DC* [2004] EWCA Civ 925, [2005] HLR 1; *R (M) v Newham London Borough Council* [2020] EWHC 327 (Admin); [2021] HLR 1; *Slattery v Basildon BC* [2014] EWCA Civ 30; [2014] HLR 16,

464 At [55].

465 At [57]. It was on this point that the Court of Appeal had not been satisfied that Croydon had provided sufficient information: it had a choice whether to assign properties to HA 1996, Part 6 or the Part 7: in making that choice, it was relevant for Croydon to consider that it had a duty to the claimant, and only a discretion to assign properties to Part 6 (albeit that once so assigned, they could only be allocated in accordance with its Part scheme – see Chapter 9) – see Supreme Court at [56-58].

466 At [58].

467 At [61].

the administrative expertise,[468] but on the other, if the court does make a mandatory order, it may unduly disrupt the authority's own balancing exercise so that the court cannot know if its order – which gives the statutory duty added force meaning that the authority has to give priority to complying with it – will cut across or compromise the performance of other functions and even distort the authority's budget. Courts therefore have to be careful not to exceed their own role by disrupting an authority's attempts to reconcile the claims upon it through its budgetary process 'without good justification'.[469] Citing *Chief Constable of the North Wales Police v Evans*[470] the court should not, 'under the guise of preventing the abuse of power, be itself guilty of usurping power.'

f) Also relevant will be the effect which making a mandatory order may have if it would distort the operation of an authority's administrative processes, *i.e.* good administration is a relevant factor,[471] as are hardship and prejudice to others with interests which ought to be taken into account by the authority.[472]

10.196 The Supreme Court concluded with five comments relevant to the exercise of the court's discretion.

a) If an authority has included a general contingency fund to deal with unexpected expenditure, the question would arise whether the claimant's needs could be met out of that fund. If such a fund exists, the authority should explain why it cannot be used.[473]

b) If the authority was aware of past problems amounting to non-performance of its duty but had not taken the opportunity to respond, the court must not encourage what could therefore be said to amount to 'a settled position of the authority to act in disregard of the duty imposed on it by Parliament'.[474] The longer an authority has failed to address a problem, the more important it is for the court to enforce the law by making a mandatory order. As the critical budget decisions might be at council-level, however, that is the level at which the enquiry has to be made and, if it was not aware of the problem at that level, why it was not.[475]

c) A plainly relevant factor is the impact of the non-performance of the duty on the individual to whom the it is owed: it is 'the vindication of their right which is being denied, and if the impact on them of the failure to comply

---

468 At [62].
469 At [63].
470 [1982] 1 WLR 1153.
471 Citing *R v Monopolies & Mergers Commission, Ex p Argyll Group plc* [1986] 1 WLR 763, 774.
472 Citing *R v Secretary of State for the Environment, Transport and the Regions, Ex p Walters* (1998) 30 HLR 328, 381.
473 At [67].
474 At [68].
475 It will be difficult for many solicitors representing homeless persons to assemble this sort of information in a form – and in time – that will allow it to advance this contention on behalf of a client, although Law Centres and other Advice Centres may be able to do so.

with it is very serious and their need is very pressing, this may justify the court in issuing a mandatory order despite the wider potentially disruptive effects it may have'. [476] The less the impact on an individual, the less compelling will be the grounds for making an immediate mandatory order with potentially disruptive effect. It might be more appropriate to make a suspended mandatory order or a quashing order, giving the authority time to consider its position and decide how best to order its affairs going forward. In this sort of case. The claimant should adduce evidence about the impact on them, which is something they are better aware of than is the authority.[477]

d) If there is nothing before the court to suggest that the authority is moving to rectify the position and satisfy the claimant's rights, 'that is a factor pointing in favour of the making of a mandatory order. In such a case, the imperative to galvanise the authority into taking effective steps to meet its obligations more promptly will be stronger'.[478]

e) The court should also try not to create a situation which would be unfair 'by giving a claimant undue priority over others who are also dependent on a local housing authority for provision of suitable accommodation and who may have an equal or better claim as compared to the claimant'.[479] Where a claimant's needs are in competition with those of others who are also owed a duty, the authority should offer proposals to the court as to how it ought to proceed 'and it will be for the court to decide what is the appropriate order in those circumstances'.[480]

Refusal of relief

10.197 A court may refuse relief, notwithstanding a finding of procedural error on the part of the authority, if the error would plainly have made no difference to

---

476 At [69].
477 Relevant here will be the extent to which the accommodation is unsuitable and its impact on the applicant and family, the time spent in unsuitable accommodation and how likely it is that suitable accommodation will be provided, and how soon: in *Begum v Tower Hamlets LBC* [2002] EWHC 633 (Admin), [2002] JHL D58, the authority acknowledged that the accommodation was unsuitable, but the court refused to make a mandatory order in the absence of any evidence of the time within which suitable accommodation could be provided. Conversely, in *R. (Bell) v Lambeth LBC* [2022] EWHC 2008; [2022] H.L.R. 45, the applicant had been in unsuitable (private rented) accommodation provided by the authority for 20 months but the conditions fell "fundamentally short" of the minimum level of suitability identified by the authority's own occupational therapist: as possession proceedings were pending in relation to that accommodation, the authority's counsel offered an undertaking that should an order be made suitable accommodation would be provided, which meant that the authority was capable of complying with a mandatory order, so that such an order was made requiring suitable accommodation to be provided within 12 weeks.
478 At [70].
479 At [71].
480 At [71].

the authority's decision.[481] This is not the case if reconsideration *could* lead to a different decision: it is not enough for the authority to assert that it could reach the same decision on reconsideration; the error must be such that it *would* have made no difference.

Appeals

10.198 Appeals from a full judicial review application require permission from either the High Court, or – if refused – from the Court of Appeal.[482]

Anonymity

10.199 Both the High Court and the county court[483] have inherent jurisdiction to make an order granting anonymity to an applicant, and to support it with an order under Contempt of Court Act 1981, s 11 preventing publication of an applicant's name, address and photograph.[484] Such an order should be made, however, only where it can be shown that a failure to do so would render the attainment of justice doubtful or, in effect, impracticable.[485] The burden lies on the party applying for anonymity to justify the displacement of the rule that the proceedings—including for this purpose the names of the parties—are public:[486] 'The principle of open justice is 'one of the most precious in our law': see *R (on the application of C) v Secretary of State for Justice'*[487] *per* Lady Hale. For an order to be made, it has to be necessary to depart from this principle, having regard to the health or well-being of the applicant, or, eg right to respect for private and family life under Art

481 *R (Bibi) v Newham LBC* [2001] EWCA Civ 607, [2002] 1 WLR 237, at [40]: 'The court has two functions – assessing the legality of actions by administrators and, if it finds unlawfulness on the administrators' part, deciding what relief it should give.' See also *R v Secretary of State for the Environment ex p Walters; R v Brent LBC ex p O'Malley* (1998) 30 HLR 328, CA; *R v Islington LBC ex p B* (1998) 30 HLR 706, QBD. See also Senior Courts Act 1981, s 31(2A), providing that the court must refuse relief if it is 'highly likely that the outcome for the applicant would not have been substantially different' notwithstanding the conduct complained of: compare *R (Cava Bien Limited) v Milton Keynes Council* [2021] EWHC 3003 (Admin); [2022] A.C.D. 11 and *R (Gathercole) v. Suffolk CC* [2020] EWCA Civ 1179; [2021] P.T.S.R. 359 see also *R (Islam) v. Haringay LBC* [2022] EWHC 3933 (Admin); [2024] forthcoming.
482 CPR 52.3(1). Permission may only be granted where there is a real prospect of success or some other compelling reason: CPR 52.6.
483 *Norman v Mathews* (1916) 85 LJKB 857, *affirmed* (1916) 23 TLR 369, CA.
484 *R v Westminster City Council ex p Castelli; R v Same ex p Tristran-Garcia* (1995) 27 HLR 125.
485 *In the matter of D* (1997–98) 1 CCLR 190, at 196K.
486 *R (Imam) v Croydon LBC* [2021] EWHC 736 (Admin); [2021] HLR 43. The issue of anonymity was not considered on appeal: [2022] EWCA Civ 601; [2022] QB 604; [2022] HLR 31.
487 [2016] UKSC 2; [2016] 1 W.L.R. 44 at [1].

8,[488] ECHR, balancing the factors in favour of an order[489] against those militating in favour of open justice, including, eg Art 10,[490] ECHR.[491]

10.200 The order must be sought at the earliest possible stage.[492] The proper course is to apply to the court without notice under Contempt of Court Act 1981, s 11 at the same time as proceedings are to be issued, if appropriate asking for a hearing to be in camera. If there is power to make an order because the pre-conditions are satisfied, the court can grant it for a short time, for notice to be given to the press.[493] In some cases, it may be necessary for papers not to be lodged until the application can be dealt with immediately, so as to prevent disclosure by way of inspection of office documents.[494]

10.201 Additionally, the court has power under CPR 39.2(4) to order that the identity of any party or witness should not be disclosed if it considers non-disclosure necessary in order to protect the interests of that party or witness.

Minors

10.202 A court may also require reports not to identify parties for the purpose of protecting the interests of children indirectly involved in a case.[495]

Appeal to county court

Procedure

Point of law

10.203 An appeal to the county court lies on a point of law.[496] 'Point of law' includes:

> ... not only matters of legal interpretation but also the full range of issues[497] which would otherwise be the subject of an application to the High Court

---

488 See paras **10.123–10.125**.
489 On an application for an anonymity order relating to a challenge to an authority's allocation policy, HA 1996, s 166(4) – which prohibits disclosure of the fact that a person is an applicant for housing to any other member of the public (para **9.84**) – does not introduce any new basis for making such an order, so that the usual considerations governing the grant or refusal of such an order will apply: *XXX v Camden LBC* [2020] EWCA Civ 1468, [2021] HLR 13.
490 Freedom of expression, including freedom of the press.
491 *Imam*, above.
492 *Imam*, above.
493 *In the matter of D*, above.
494 *In the matter of D*, above.
495 See *Crawley BC v B* (2000) 32 HLR 636, CA, at 638. See CPR 39.2(3)(d).
496 HA 1996, s 204(1); H(W)A 2014, s 88(1).
497 Cf the first part of this chapter: 'Substantive law', paras **10.5–10.129**.

for judicial review, such as procedural error and questions of *vires*, to which I add, also of irrationality and (in)adequacy of reasons.[498]

10.204 This jurisdiction does not include a claim for damages under Equality Act (EqA)2010, Part 3, which must be brought in the county court;[499] although this does not prevent a person from raising such matters in a claim for judicial review;[500] the decision in *R (CN) v Lewisham LBC; R (ZH) v Newham LBC,*[501] to the effect that an Article 8 challenge may be raised during a HA 1996, s 204 appeal,[502] does not change the position, is confined to its own circumstances, and does not permit an EqA claim for damages also to be raised during a s 204 appeal.[503]

10.205 The jurisdiction does not permit judges to reach their own decisions of fact; to do so is in excess of the statutory jurisdiction.[504] Where an authority considered that an applicant was not vulnerable[505] because of mental illness, it was not for the judge to conclude that the applicant was mentally ill (and accordingly vulnerable): 'Some decision-makers might have arrived at a different conclusion. It is elementary that matters of that kind were not for the judge . . .'[506]

---

498 *Nipa Begum v Tower Hamlets LBC* [2000] 1 WLR 306, (1999) 32 HLR 445, CA per Auld LJ at 452. *Nipa Begum* was approved by the House of Lords in *Runa Begum v Tower Hamlets LBC* [2003] UKHL 5, [2003] 2 AC 430, [2003] HLR 32, see particularly Lord Bingham at [7].

499 EqA 2010, ss 113, 114. For guidance on how to plead claims in judicial review which raise Equality Act 2010 issues, see *R (AB&CD) v. Westminster CC* [2024] EWHC 226 (Admin); [2024] HLR forthcoming.

500 EqA 2010, s 113(3). It has been held that a statutory review conducted on judicial review principles is not a 'claim for judicial review': *Hamnett v Essex CC* [2017] EWCA Civ 6, [2017] 1 WLR 1155 (review of a traffic regulation order); *Adesotu v Lewisham LBC (Equality and Human Rights Commission intervening)* [2019] EWCA Civ 1405, [2019] 1 WLR 5637, [2019] HLR 48.

501 [2014] UKSC 62, [2015] AC 1259, [2015] HLR 6. Para **10.207.**

502 Para **10.207.**

503 *Adesotu v Lewisham LBC (Equality and Human Rights Commission intervening)* [2019] EWCA Civ 1405, [2019] 1 WLR 5637, [2019] HLR 48.

504 *Kruja v Enfield LBC* [2004] EWCA Civ 1769, [2005] HLR 13. See also *Aw-Aden v Birmingham City Council* [2005] EWCA Civ 1834, in which it was held that the judge had made inappropriate findings of fact. See also *Bubb v Wandsworth LBC* [2011] EWCA Civ 1285, [2012] HLR 13; *Adesotu v Lewisham LBC (Equality and Human Rights Commission intervening)* [2019] EWCA Civ 1405, [2019] 1 WLR 5637, [2019] HLR 48; and *Richmond upon Thames LBC v Kubicek* [2012] EWHC 3292 (QB), again reiterating that the county court should not set itself up as a finder of fact (see para **10.43**).

505 And accordingly not in priority need – see chapter 3.

506 *Kruja v Enfield LBC* [2004] EWCA Civ 1769, [2005] HLR 13 at [23]. See also *Wandsworth LBC v Watson* [2010] EWCA Civ 1558, [2011] HLR 9, where the authority's appeal was allowed because the recorder had effectively substituted her own decision as to risk of violence, in relation to an offer of accommodation, for that of the authority. See also *LB v Tower Hamlets LBC* [2020] EWCA Civ 439, [2020] PTSR 1107, [2021] HLR 3 where the authority found that arrears, not domestic violence, was the reason the applicant had left her previous home; and that the domestic violence had not made it unreasonable for her to continue to occupy it: these were decisions for the authority, with which the court could not interfere absent an error of principle or logic on the part of the authority in reaching its decision.

10.206 There are, however, exceptions. First, the discussion of when error of fact may comprise a public law failure sufficient to vitiate a decision is as applicable in the county court as otherwise: this may involve the court considering the facts from the perspective of whether there has been such an error.[507]

10.207 Second, an applicant who will face eviction from temporary accommodation if their HA 1996, s 204 appeal is unsuccessful is entitled to raise their Article 8 rights[508] during that appeal,[509] provided occupation can be said to be as a home,[510] which, on the basis of how Article 8 is understood and applied domestically,[511] means that the court may be required independently to determine the facts for itself, eg if what is asserted is that the authority has come to the wrong decision[512] in concluding that the applicant is not in priority need or is intentionally homeless because it has erred in relation to the facts.[513]

From what decision?

10.208 The point of law under challenge will usually be one made in relation to the internal review rather than the original decision, as any error in the original decision will either have been remedied or replaced by the review (with or without the same or another error of law).[514] Thus, it has been held that, where

---

507 Paras **10.40-10.44**.
508 Paras **10.123-10.125**.
509 *R (ZH and CN) v Newham LBC and Lewisham LBC* [2014] UKSC 62, [2015] AC 1259, [2015] HLR 6 at [64].
510 This is an autonomous test which requires 'the existence of sufficient and continued links with a specific place': see, eg, *Hounslow LBC v Powell* [2011] UKSC 8, [2011] 2 AC 186, [2011] HLR 23, per Lord Hope at [33] but is not a high bar and will commonly be fulfilled by homeless people (who, after all, of definition have nowhere else to call home) who have been in the accommodation for a relatively short time, perhaps as little as a month.
511 *Manchester City Council v Pinnock* [2010] UKSC 45, [2011] 2 AC 104, [2011] HLR 7; *Hounslow LBC v Powell* (above).
512 Because it is strongly arguable that it would not be proportionate to evict someone on a materially erroneous assessment of their circumstances.
513 'A fair procedure requires the occupant to have a right to raise the issue of the proportionality of the interference and to have that issue determined by an independent tribunal': *Pinnock*, above, at [45] cited in *R (ZH and CN) v Newham LBC and Lewisham LBC* at [63]. 'It is only in very exceptional cases that the applicant will succeed in raising an arguable case of a lack of proportionality where an applicant has no right under domestic law to remain in possession of a property' which 'is so particularly where an authority seeks to recover possession of interim accommodation provided under s 188 of the 1996 Act'; and, it is for the occupier to raise the question: nevertheless, 'In an appropriate case the court, if satisfied that eviction was disproportionate, could prohibit the eviction for as long as that was the case, for example if the local authority did not provide alternative accommodation': *R (ZH and CN) v Newham LBC and Lewisham LBC* at [65]–[66]. It has been held that this does not allow any more general challenge on the facts, so that it is only when Article 8 is raised that it will apply: *Adesotu v Lewisham LBC (Equality and Human Rights Commission intervening)* [2019] EWCA Civ 1405, [2019] 1 WLR 5637, [2019] HLR 48.
514 The appeal is, however, against the decision on the current application; it cannot be used to appeal against the decision on a previous application: *Godson v Enfield LBC* [2019] EWCA Civ 486, [2020] HLR 1.

the issue is whether sufficient time had been afforded to decide whether or not to accept an offer of accommodation,[515] the sufficiency of time before the original decision will be academic if there has been enough time to raise any relevant points before the review decision.[516]

10.209 There is an exception to this where no notification of a decision on an internal review is given within the time prescribed for it[517] (or, if notification has been given, if it does not comply with the minimum statutory requirements, ie, to give reasons and advise of the right to appeal and the time for appeal – see HA 1996, s 203(4), (5) and H(W)A 2014, s 86(4), (5) – so that it is treated as not having been given: see HA 1996, s 203(6) and H(W)A 2014, s 88(2)).[518] In such a case, an appeal lies against the original decision: in effect, the authority's delay in notifying the outcome of the review means that it loses the opportunity to remedy any error in the original decision.

10.210 The original decision may nonetheless continue to be relevant if the review simply ignores an error in it which continues to have an effect, whether because it has been adopted or because – even if expressed differently – it influences how the court should construe the decision on review. In either event, however, the appeal must be on a point of law, whether it is in relation to the internal review or – for want of a review decision within time – in relation to the original decision.[519]

Review and reconsideration

10.211 There is no right to a review of a decision on an earlier review.[520] Not uncommonly, however, even where there has been a review, a local authority will be willing to reconsider its decision, for example, following receipt of a letter before action.[521] A complaint about the decision on such a reconsideration may still lie to the county court[522] if, but only if, the complaint can be described as still comprising an appeal from the original review decision[523] (which in turn will raise the issue of whether it is still in time).[524]

---

515 Paras **8.227-8.233**.
516 *Adesotu v Lewisham LBC (Equality and Human Rights Commission intervening)* [2019] EWCA Civ 1405, [2019] 1 WLR 5637, [2019] HLR 48.
517 HA 1996, s 203(7); H(W)A 2014, s 85; see para **7.248** for the prescribed times.
518 HA 1996, s 204(1)(b); H(W)A 2014, s 88(1)(b).
519 HA 1996, s 204(1); H(W)A 2014, s 88(1).
520 HA 1996, s 202(2); H(W)A 2014, s 85(4). See also *Godson v Enfield LBC* [2019] EWCA Civ 486, [2020] HLR 1.
521 See para **10.222**.
522 *R v Westminster City Council ex p Ellioua* (1999) 31 HLR 440, CA.
523 *Demetri v Westminster City Council* [2000] 1 WLR 772, (2000) 32 HLR 470, CA, at 780 and 479.
524 See para **10.213**.

10.212 In the alternative, it is possible that the decision to reconsider can in context be construed as a withdrawal of the original review decision.[525]

Time for appeal

10.213 The appeal must be brought within 21 days of the applicant being notified of the decision on the internal review, or when the applicant should have been so notified.[526] Where the court office is closed on the final day for lodging the appeal, time is extended until the next day that the office is open.[527] Delivery of the notice of appeal is sufficient to constitute filing; there is no requirement that a court officer receive or authenticate the notice.[528] So long as the appeal is filed in time, it is possible to amend the notice: in *South Oxfordshire DC Vale of White Horse DC v Fertre*,[529] two authorities shared both their homelessness and legal services – the claimant issued against the wrong authority and sought to amend to substitute the correct one after 21 days had expired; she was permitted to do so – it was obvious which authority's decision she was trying to appeal, nor was there any suggestion that either authority was misled by the error; the interests of justice clearly favoured permitting the amendment.

Extension of time

10.214 The 21-day limit has been acknowledged as short, indeed 'draconian, as some might think'.[530] Prior to amendment by the Homelessness Act 2002 there was no power for the court to extend time.[531] By HA 1996, s 204(2A) and H(W) A 2014, s 88(3), the county court now has power to extend time – before or after the 21-day period has expired – for 'good reason'.

10.215 Delay in obtaining public funding to bring an appeal may well constitute an acceptable reason for extension of time[532] as may incompetent legal advice,

---

525 See para **10.221**.
526 HA 1996, s 204(2); H(W)A 2014, s 88(2).
527 *Calverton Parish Council v Nottingham City Council* [2015] EWHC 503 (Admin); *Aadan v Brent LBC* (2000) 32 HLR 848, CA; *Pritam Kaur v S Russell & Sons Ltd* [1973] QB 336. See also *Croke v Secretary of State for Communities and Local Government* [2016] EWHC 2484 (Admin) in which the claimant's agent arrived at the court office at 4.25pm on the last day for lodging an appeal. A security guard refused him entry to the court building. The documents were filed a few days later. The High Court held that the principle in *Calverton, Aadan* and *Kaur* did not apply: the court office had been open and available to accept the papers; litigants had to appreciate that there would be security procedures to be completed before being allowed access to the court and had to allow sufficient time to deal with them.
528 *Van Aken v Camden LBC* [2002] EWCA Civ 1724, [2003] 1 WLR 684, [2003] HLR 33.
529 [2024] EWHC 112 (KB); [2024] HLR forthcoming.
530 *R v Brent LBC ex p O'Connor* (1999) 31 HLR 923, QBD, per Tucker J at 925.
531 *Honig v Lewisham LBC* (1958) 122 JPJ 302; and *Gwynedd CC v Grunshaw* (2000) 32 HLR 610, CA. See also *O'Connor*, above.
532 *R v Stratford on Avon DC ex p Jackson* [1985] 1 WLR 1319, CA; see also *R v Dacorum BC ex p Brown* (1989) 21 HLR 405, QBD. Cf *Peake v Hackney LBC* [2013] EWHC 2528 (QB) (that time for appeal expired on Christmas Day did not necessarily comprise good reason: nor did the imposition of a time limit give rise to any arguable issue under Article 6).

although there has to be evidence of the latter.[533] Where the applicant was profoundly deaf and had been seeking legal assistance that she could understand and follow, there was a good reason for her appeal not to have been brought within the 21-day time limit.[534]

10.216 Whether there is a 'good reason' for appealing out of time under HA 1996, s 204(2A), depends on all the circumstances of the case; the evidence in *Tower Hamlets LBC v Al Ahmed*,[535] displayed a bleak picture of the difficulties faced by appellants in bringing an appeal under HA 1996, s 204, without legal advice and representation, and of the shortage of lawyers available to conduct such appeals on legal aid; these issues were relevant to deciding whether to extend time. Where an appellant relies on the fact that they are unrepresented and have been seeking legal aid, as a reason for failing to appeal in time, the circumstances should be examined with great care, including scrutiny of the diligence with which they acted in seeking legal advice.

10.217 The Court of Appeal in *Al Ahmed* described a decision as to whether to grant permission under HA 1996, s 204(2A) as an evaluative judgment with which an appellate court should be slow to interfere.[536] The court rejected the proposition that homelessness applicants are able as a general rule to draft a notice of appeal and adequate grounds of appeal without legal representation; it was unsupported by the evidence before the county court and contradicted by evidence that those who have been placed in temporary accommodation will tend to focus on the imminent loss of that accommodation and the need to undertake a number of stressful and time/resource heavy tasks in a short period of time, rather than on the need to bring an appeal; moreover a number of common difficulties or shared characteristics of those experiencing homelessness (poverty, mental ill health, etc) contribute to delaying or preventing them from being able to cope with life events and to manage their affairs; nor does it necessarily follow that because someone who is homeless is articulate and can express themselves verbally and on paper, they therefore have the ability to take and implement a decision to issue a complex court appeal.[537]

10.218 In *Emambee*,[538] an unexplained 10-day delay, the first week of which was pending a meeting with solicitors, led the court to refuse an extension, although this must be doubted after the Court of Appeal discussion in *Ahmed*.

---

533 *Poorsalehy v Wandsworth LBC* [2013] EWHC 3687 (QB); it does not automatically follow from the failure to issue in time.
534 *Barrett v Southwark LBC* [2008] EWHC 1568 (QB), [2008] JHL D107.
535 [2020] EWCA Civ 51, [2020] 1 WLR 1546, [2020] HLR 16. The appeal was lodged one month after the time limit had expired; the applicant provided details of at least seven firms of solicitors who he had approached, none of whom had capacity to accept him as a client; once he finally obtained representation, the appeal was issued almost immediately.
536 *Al Ahmed* at [36].
537 *Al Ahmed* at [19] and [42].
538 *Emambee v Islington LBC* [2019] EWHC 2835 (QB).

10.219 Even if the court is satisfied that there is a good reason for delay, it only opens up a discretion to give permission to appeal out of time; at that stage, the court is able to take into account all other relevant considerations, including the authority's position, in deciding how to exercise its discretion.[539]

10.220 If a judge is minded to strike out an appeal as being outside the 21-day time limit, the applicant is entitled to proper notice so as to enable them to meet the point.[540]

Agreement to further review

10.221 Where an authority agrees to reconsider the review decision, it is possible that the agreement will in substance comprise an agreement on the part of the authority to revoke or withdraw its original decision. Alternatively, it may comprise an agreement to waive, extend or suspend the time limit for appeal from it, or to take no time point.[541] Such an agreement does, however, need to be clearly spelled out.[542] Where an applicant seeking reconsideration is not represented, the authority should take it on itself to make clear the basis on which it is agreeing to reconsider and, in particular, should point out if time to appeal is not being extended.[543]

Letter before action

10.222 The provisions of CPR Part 52 do not require the applicant (or the applicant's legal advisers) to write a letter before action setting out the applicant's case on appeal. Prior to the introduction of the statutory appeal,[544] however – when challenges against adverse decisions were made by way of judicial review – a letter before claim should nonetheless have been written.[545] Given the introduction of a requirement for a pre-action letter in judicial review proceedings,[546] and the fact that the question of costs is a matter for the discretion of the court,[547] the same principles should now be applied (in the absence of special circumstances rendering such a letter impossible, impracticable or pointless).

---

539 *Al Ahmed* at [35]. See also *Short v Birmingham City Council* [2004] EWHC 2112 (QB), [2005] HLR 6.
540 *Dawkins v Central Bedfordshire Council* [2013] EWHC 4757 (QB).
541 *Demetri v Westminster City Council* [2000] 1 WLR 772, (2000) 32 HLR 470, CA, at 780–781 and 478–479. An agreement to conduct a further review could constitute a good reason for the applicant not bringing the appeal in time, and would be likely to do so if public funding was not available until after the outcome of the further review.
542 *Demetri*, at 781 and 480.
543 *Demetri*, at 781–782 and 479.
544 And prior to the introduction of the requirement for a pre-action protocol letter in judicial review cases.
545 *R v Horsham DC ex p Wenman* [1995] 1 WLR 680, QBD; *R v Secretary of State for the Home Department ex p Begum* [1995] COD 177.
546 See para **10.145**.
547 See Senior Courts Act 1981, s 51 and CPR 44.2.

Supporting documents

10.223 The appeal will need to be brought in accordance with CPR Part 52 and the associated Practice Directions (PDs).[548] Three copies of the appellant's notice (plus a further copy for each respondent) must be filed, together with grounds of appeal[549] and a copy of the decision under appeal. Any amendment to the appellant's notice or grounds of appeal normally requires the permission of the court.[550]

10.224 When issuing an appeal, the appellant must file and serve proposed case management directions, with which – within 14 days – the authority must either agree or to which it must propose alternatives.[551] Within the same period, the authority must also disclose any relevant documents which have not previously been disclosed; within 14 days of their receipt, the grounds of appeal may be amended as of right to deal with any new material.[552]

10.225 Notwithstanding the discretion to amend the notice of appeal (other than as of right to deal with new material),[553] the Court of Appeal has emphasised the importance of the grounds in setting the agenda for the appeal hearing and in enabling the respondent (and the court) to understand that agenda from the outset. In one case, Brooke LJ commented that:

> It is thoroughly bad practice to state the barest possible grounds in the original notice of appeal . . ., and then to delay formulating and serving very substantial amended grounds of appeal for five months so that they surfaced for the first time less than a week before the appeal hearing.[554]

Response

10.226 While a respondent's notice may be filed if a respondent seeks to uphold a decision for reasons different from, or additional to, those previously given,[555] this is unlikely to be appropriate in a homelessness appeal. If the review (or, on occasion, the original) decision is wrong, then the authority should consent to it being quashed, and proceed to make a fresh decision on the correct basis. The only obvious circumstance when the authority could ask the court to substitute one (wrong) decision with a fresh decision is if the fresh decision is the only decision open to the authority as a matter of law.[556]

---

548 See in particular, PD 52D para 28.1.
549 PD 52B para 4.1; see form N161.
550 CPR 52.17. Note, however, that – unless the court has ordered otherwise – there is a right to amend 'as of right' within 14 days of the authority disclosing relevant material: CPR PD52D para 28(1)(5)(d).
551 CPR Part 52, PD 52D para 28.1(5)(a), (b).
552 CPR Part 52, PD 52D para 28.1(5)(c), (d).
553 See para **10.223**.
554 *Cramp v Hastings BC; Phillips v Camden LBC* [2005] EWCA Civ 1005 at [72].
555 CPR 52.13.
556 See paras **10.263, 10.267**.

10.227 While an authority may well need to concede one or more elements of a challenge before the appeal comes to a hearing, the authority may not withdraw its decision so as to pre-empt the appeal if continuing the appeal could lead to an enduring benefit to the applicant. In *Deugi*,[557] the applicant not only sought to quash the original decision but also sought a variation of it; its withdrawal would have deprived the applicant of the opportunity to seek the variation.

District judges

10.228 As soon as it was appreciated that the CPR permitted district judges to hear Part 52 appeals,[558] a new PD was introduced to prevent them doing so.[559]

10.229 As with judicial review,[560] it is only exceptionally that the court will hear oral evidence,[561] eg where relevant evidence has come to light since the review was concluded.[562]

Costs

10.230 The general rule that costs should follow the event applies even where the matter is remitted to the authority for a fresh decision. It is not appropriate for the county court judge to refuse costs on the basis that it is considered inevitable that the authority will reach the same adverse decision (and that it will be upheld on review and appeal); it is inappropriate for the judge to reach any conclusion on that issue.[563]

10.231 The principles applicable to costs where a claim for judicial review is settled[564] – that a claimant who has secured the substantive relief sought should normally be awarded their costs[565] – are also applicable to appeals under HA 1996, s 204.[566]

---

557 *Tower Hamlets LBC v Deugi* [2006] EWCA Civ 159, [2006] HLR 28.
558 See the comments of Sir Richard Scott V-C in *Crawley BC v B* (2000) 32 HLR 636, CA.
559 CPR Part 2, PD 2B.9.
560 See para **10.170**.
561 *Bubb v Wandsworth LBC* [2011] EWCA Civ 1285, [2012] HLR 13 at [24]–[25].
562 *Bubb* at [26].
563 *Rikha Begum v Tower Hamlets LBC* [2005] EWCA Civ 340, [2005] HLR 34.
564 See paras **10.173–10.182**.
565 *R (M) v Croydon LBC* [2012] EWCA Civ 595, [2012] 1 WLR 2607.
566 *Harripaul v Lewisham LBC* [2012] EWCA Civ 266, [2012] HLR 24. See also *Unichi v Southwark LBC* [2013] EWHC 3681 (QB) the authority refused to await conclusion of review pending receipt of psychologist's report which was provided after review issued and on receipt of which authority agreed to carry out a fresh review: the applicant had obtained the substantive relief she had sought; the authority had been alerted to the importance of the report but had decided to conclude the review before it was available; the costs were payable immediately rather than held against any further proceedings.

10.232 The court has power to order that costs be set off.[567] The implication of this – discussed above – is that it may be possible to set off costs orders made in the county court against orders made in the High Court, if the proceedings are closely connected,[568] as well as costs in other county court proceedings.

10.233 In *Maloba*,[569] the county court ordered the authority to pay two-thirds of the appellant's costs in relation to a section 204 appeal and refused the authority's application for a stay pending the outcome of any future appeal against its fresh review decision, in which it hoped to be successful and therefore to secure a costs award in its favour, which it would then seek to be set off against those awarded against it in the present case.[570]

10.234 The Court of Appeal accepted that the court's discretion was wide enough in principle to enable it to grant such a stay if it considers it just to do so, and refused to overturn the judge's decision.[571] It was cautious about introducing a general practice which would have the effect of depriving solicitors who acted for successful legally aided clients of payment at normal commercial rates without being able to assess properly the potential wider consequences that this would have.[572]

10.235 It may be observed that it is hard to see that such an anticipatory order could ever be successful unless there was a history of unsuccessful challenges, in which the instant success was a rare or only occurrence. Even so, it would necessarily assume that the same solicitors would be acting, for those who had been successful should surely not properly be deprived of their success-based costs in the event that other solicitors pursued an unsuccessful case.

Wasted costs

10.236 In *Wilson*,[573] a first-instance decision that non-legal officers of an authority could be ordered personally to pay costs, in substance for causing unnecessary legal expenditure by failing to respond to litigation, was overturned and held to have been wrongly made. Lawyers, however, are susceptible to such orders ('wasted costs orders') under Senior Courts Act 1981, s 51[574] and CPR 40.8.

10.237 It is appropriate to make a wasted costs order against a legal representative only if:

---

567 CPR 44.12.
568 See para **10.181**.
569 *Waltham Forest LBC v Maloba* [2007] EWCA Civ 1281, [2008] HLR 26.
570 *Maloba* at [65].
571 *Maloba* at [71].
572 *Maloba* at [73].
573 *R v Lambeth LBC ex p Wilson* (1998) 30 HLR 64, CA.
574 Inserted by Courts and Legal Services Act 1990, s 4.

a) the legal representative acted improperly, unreasonably or negligently;[575]

b) the legal representative's conduct caused a party to incur unnecessary costs; and

c) it is just in all the circumstances to order the legal representative to compensate that party for the whole or part of the costs.[576]

10.238 The test is a moderately high one:

a) improper conduct is that which would attract a sanction from a professional body or which would fairly be stigmatised as being improper;

b) unreasonable conduct is that which is vexatious or is designed to harass the other side rather than to advance a resolution of the case, or which does not have a reasonable explanation;[577]

c) negligent conduct is not that which would found a common law action for damages,[578] but a question as to whether the legal representative conducted themselves with the competence to be expected of a professional person.[579]

It must be something akin to abuse of process; a breach of the lawyer's duty to the court.[580]

10.239 A rising tendency to seek an order for wasted costs was curtailed by the Court of Appeal in *Ridehalgh v Horsefield*,[581] where it was said that the courts should be anxious to avoid satellite litigation. Reinforcing the point, the House of Lords has held[582] that wasted costs orders should be confined to questions which are apt for summary disposal by the courts:[583]

> Save in the clearest case, applications against the lawyers acting for an opposing party are unlikely to be apt for summary determination, since any hearing to investigate the conduct of a complex action is itself likely to be

575 *KOO Golden East Mongolia v Bank of Nova Scotia* [2008] EWHC 1120 (QB), per Silber J; *Hallam Peel & Co v Southwark LBC* [2008] EWCA Civ 1120.
576 The test derives from *Re A Barrister (wasted costs order) (No 1 of 1991)* [1992] 3 All ER 429, CA, and is now incorporated into the PD accompanying CPR Part 46 (at 5.1).
577 '[The] courts can be trusted to differentiate between errors of judgment and true negligence': *Arthur JS Hall & Co (a firm) v Simons* [2002] 1 AC 615, HL.
578 This is not negligence in any technical sense, see *Re Sternberg, Reed, Taylor and Gill* (1999) *Times* 26 July, CA and *Dempsey v Johnstone* [2003] EWCA Civ 1134, [2003] All ER (D) 515.
579 See *Ridehalgh v Horsefield* [1994] Ch 205, CA.
580 *Persaud (Luke) v Persaud (Mohan)* [2003] EWCA Civ 394, [2003] PNLR 26, CA at [27].
581 [1994] Ch 205, CA; see also *Re A Barrister (wasted costs order)* [1993] QB 293, CA. See *Arthur JS Hall & Co v Simons* [2002] 1 AC 615 and *R v Camden LBC ex p Martin* [1997] 1 WLR 359, QBD, where it was held that there was no power to make a wasted costs order in favour of a person who elects to oppose an ex parte application for permission to seek judicial review.
582 *Medcalf v Mardell* [2002] UKHL 27, [2003] 1 AC 120.
583 See *Wall v Lefever* [1998] 1 FCR 605, CA, where wasted costs orders were said to provide a 'salutary and summary remedy' in clear cases. See also *R v Luton Family Proceedings Court Justices ex p R* [1998] 1 FCR 605, CA.

expensive and time-consuming. The desirability of compensating litigating parties who have been put to unnecessary expense by the unjustified conduct of their opponents' lawyers is, without doubt, an important public interest, but it is, as the Court of Appeal pointed out in *Ridehalgh v Horsefield* . . . only one of the public interests which have to be considered.[584]

10.240 As a guide, matters such as the following are apt for wasted costs:

failure to appear;

conduct which leads to an otherwise avoidable step in the proceedings or the prolongation of a hearing by gross repetition or extreme slowness in the presentation of evidence or argument;

wasting court time; and

abuse of process which results in excessive cost.[585]

10.241 Costs that arise as a consequence of difficulties with public funding are unlikely to lead to an order for wasted costs. Where a solicitor sought an adjournment on the day before the hearing because of difficulties with his client's funding, his failure was an error of judgment, not an act which attracted liability for wasted costs.[586]

10.242 Where a court refuses to make a wasted costs order, it will only be in very rare circumstances that an appeal court will intervene.[587]

Further appeal

10.243 Under the Access to Justice Act 1999 (Destination of Appeals) Order 2016,[588] the appropriate forum for appeal from a county court HA 1996, s 204 or H(W)A 2014, s 88 appeal is to the Court of Appeal as the s 204 or s 88 appeal is itself an 'appeal' (from the decision of the authority), so that an appeal against the county court judge is a second appeal, to be determined by the Court of Appeal.[589]

10.244 A consequence of the 'second appeal' status is that permission cannot be granted by the county court; it must be obtained from the Court of Appeal.[590] An

---

584 *Medcalf v Mardell* [2002] UKHL 27, [2003] 1 AC 120, per Lord Bingham at [24].
585 *Medcalf*, approving *Harley v McDonald* [2001] 2 AC 678, PC.
586 *Re A Solicitor (wasted costs order)* [1993] 2 FLR 959, CA.
587 *Persaud v Persaud*, above.
588 Access to Justice Act 1999 (Destination of Appeals) Order 2016, SI 2016/917.
589 An appeal against a decision on costs is, however, treated as a first appeal and is therefore to the High Court: see *Handley v Lake Jackson Solicitors* [2016] EWCA Civ 465, [2016] HLR 23; and Access to Justice Act 1999 (Destination of Appeals) Order 2016, reg 5. The county court judge can therefore grant permission to appeal; indeed, it is good practice to ask for permission: *P v P* [2015] EWCA Civ 447.
590 CPR 52.7.

application for permission to appeal must be made in accordance with CPR Part 52. Permission must be requested in an appellant's notice, which must be served within such period as directed by the lower court,[591] or – if no such direction is made – within 21 days of the decision being appealed.[592]

10.245 Witness statements in support of an application for permission to appeal are only appropriate for relevant and admissible evidence (if any) going to the issue before the court and nothing else: submissions in support of the appeal are for advocates to make in skeleton arguments.[593]

10.246 Where a county court has ordered a further review and the authority seeks permission to appeal, the parties should agree that the obligation to undertake a fresh review is suspended pending outcome of the appeal. If agreement is not reached, an authority may apply to the Court of Appeal to stay the effect of the order made by the county court. In the event that an authority does undertake a fresh review pending the appeal, however, it is verging on an abuse for the authority not to inform the Court of Appeal that it has done so.[594]

10.247 Permission to bring a second appeal will be granted only if the court is satisfied that:

a) the appeal has a real prospect of success and raises an important point of principle or practice;[595] or

b) there is some other compelling reason for the appeal to be heard.[596]

10.248 Where an appeal raises an important point of principle which has not previously been determined, permission will normally be granted under the first of these headings.[597] When determining whether there is some other compelling reason to grant permission under the second, the court should apply the following principles:

a) the prospects of success on appeal must be very high;

b) even where the prospects of success are very high, the court may nonetheless conclude that justice does not require the appellant to have the opportunity of a second appeal; but, conversely,

---

591 Which may be longer or shorter than the period of 21 days required under the CPR: CPR 52.12.
592 CPR 52.12.
593 *William v Wandsworth LBC; Bellamy v Hounslow LBC* [2006] EWCA Civ 535, [2006] HLR 42.
594 *William*, above.
595 CPR 52.7(2)(a).
596 CPR 52.7(2)(b).
597 *Uphill v BRB (Residuary) Ltd* [2005] EWCA Civ 60, [2005] 1 WLR 2070. *Uphill* does not comment on the 'real prospect of success' limb as that was only introduced for appeals issued after 3 October 2016: see Civil Procedure (Amendment No 3) Rules 2016, SI 2016/788.

c) if the prospects of success are not very high, there may nevertheless be a compelling reason for a second appeal if the court is satisfied that the first appeal was tainted by procedural irregularity such as to render it unfair.[598]

10.249 In the context of a homelessness appeal, permission was refused in *Azimi*,[599] where the decision of the county court was reached primarily on the facts. By contrast, in *Cramp*,[600] the Court of Appeal gave permission to appeal against a decision that an authority's enquiries had been inadequate because the appeal raised an important point of practice. Brooke LJ said:[601]

> In view of the amount of public money that is in issue in cases like this, it would in my judgment be quite wrong for this court to feel that the judgment in *Uphill*[602] represented a fetter on its power to put things right if it has occasion to believe that things are going wrong in an important way in the practical operation of the statutory scheme in Part 7 of the 1996 Act (up to and including the appeal on a point of law to the county court).[603]

10.250 In *Elrify*,[604] it was pointed out that the second appeal is really only the first appeal from a judicial decision, because the appeal to the county court is not in respect of a judicial decision but from the authority's own review decision. This does not mean that CPR 52.7 is inapplicable, but it does mean that the court can take a somewhat more relaxed approach to a second appeal in a homelessness case that has clear merits.[605]

10.251 On an appeal to the Court of Appeal, the primary question is normally not whether the county court judge deciding the first appeal was right, but whether the decision being appealed is right, or at least one that the decision-maker was entitled to reach.[606]

---

598 *Upill*, above.
599 *Azimi v Newham LBC* (2000) 33 HLR 51, CA. See also *Ryde v Enfield LBC* [2005] EWCA Civ 1281 (no important point of principle or practice) and *Gentle v Wandsworth LBC* [2005] EWCA Civ 1377 (no obvious injustice).
600 *Cramp v Hastings BC; Phillips v Camden LBC* [2005] EWCA Civ 1005, [2005] HLR 48.
601 At [66].
602 See para **10.248**.
603 In *Zaman v Waltham Forest LBC; Uduezue v Bexley LBC* [2023] EWCA Civ 322; [2023] HLR 30, although the principal ground of appeal in the second of these cases failed (para **7.110**), the appellant was given permission to rely on a ground not previously argued, following the decision in *Norton v Haringey LBC* [2022] EWCA Civ 1340; [2022] P.T.S.R. 1802; [2023] H.L.R. 3, para **8.271**. The authority's contention that permission should not be granted because it did not raise an important point of principle or practice was rejected: the appeal as a whole raised such a point, even if the added ground did not do so, and it had a real prospect of success – permission having been granted, the appeal was allowed on that ground.
604 *Elrify v Westminster City Council* [2007] EWCA Civ 332, [2007] HLR 36.
605 *Elrify*, at [24].
606 *Danesh v Kensington and Chelsea RLBC* [2006] EWCA Civ 1404, [2007] HLR 17 at [30].

Remedies and relief

Interim relief

10.252 Authorities have power under HA 1996, s 204(4) and H(W)A 2014, s 88(5) to house pending any appeal (and any subsequent appeal). Interim relief will not be needed on a county court appeal if the authority agrees to use this power.

10.253 Prior to amendment by the Homelessness Act 2002, if an authority refused to exercise this power, the county court could not grant an interim injunction because the applicant had no substantive rights to which an interim injunction could properly be said to be ancillary;[607] accordingly, the only recourse was by way of judicial review.

10.254 Under HA 1996, s 204A or H(W)A 2014, s 89, an applicant with a right to appeal to the county court against a local authority's decision on review[608] may now also appeal to the county court if the authority refuses to exercise its power to secure interim accommodation under HA 1996, s 204(4) or H(W)A 2014, s 88, or is only willing to do so for a limited period ending before the final determination of the main appeal.[609]

10.255 Once the county court has dismissed an appeal under HA 1996, s 204, however, it has no remaining function under s 204A so cannot consider an appeal against an authority's decision not to secure interim accommodation for the appellant pending a further appeal to the Court of Appeal.[610]

10.256 The right to appeal under HA 1996, s 204A or H(W)A 2014, s 89 may be exercised even before the applicant has appealed under s 204 or s 88, provided the latter appeal is against the authority's decision on review: this excludes the possibility of a s 204A or s 89 appeal where the applicant only has a right to appeal against the s 184 or s 86 decision because the authority has not notified the review decision in time.[611] In these circumstances, judicial review remains the only remedy.[612]

10.257 As a matter of good practice, an applicant should include appeals under HA 1996, s 204 and s 204A in one appellant's notice[613] although, if this is not possible, the appeals may be included in separate notices.[614] An appeal under

---

607 *Ali v Westminster City Council* (1999) 31 HLR 349, CA.
608 HA 1996, s 204A(1); H(W)A 2014, s 89(1).
609 HA 1996, s 204A(2); H(W)A 2014, s 89(2).
610 *Johnson v Westminster City Council* [2013] EWCA Civ 773, [2013] HLR 45. The appropriate course of action is to seek judicial review.
611 HA 1996, s 204(1)(b); H(W)A 2014, s 88(1)(b).
612 *Davis v Watford BC* [2018] EWCA Civ 529, [2018] 1 WLR 3157, [2018] HLR 24.
613 CPR Part 52D PD para 24.2(1). The PD has not been amended to reflect the position in Wales, but it seems unlikely that a different approach would be thought to apply.
614 CPR Part 52D PD para 24.2(2).

HA 1996, s 204A or H(W)A 2014, s 89 may[615] include an application for an order under s 204A(4)(a) or s 89(4)(a) requiring the authority to secure that accommodation is available for the applicant's occupation.[616]

10.258 If the court makes such an order without notice, the appellant's notice must be served on the authority together with the order. Such an order will normally require the authority to secure that accommodation is available until a hearing date when the authority can make representations as to whether the order should be continued.[617]

10.259 The primary power given to the county court[618] is to order the authority to secure accommodation for the applicant pending determination of the appeal or such earlier time that the court may specify. The court is bound either to quash the authority's HA 1996, s 204(4) decision on accommodation pending appeal, or to confirm it.[619] If the county court decides to quash, it may order the authority to exercise the power for such period as may be specified in the order, up to but not beyond the determination of the main appeal.[620] The power may be exercised only if the court is satisfied that failure to exercise the section 204(4) power would substantially prejudice the applicant's ability to pursue the main appeal.

10.260 The Contempt of Court Act 1981, s 2(2) uses a similar, although not identical, phrase of 'substantial risk that the course of justice will be seriously prejudiced'. In that context, it has been held that:

> . . . 'substantial' as a qualification of 'risk' does not have the meaning 'weighty' but rather means 'not insubstantial' or 'not minimal'.[621]

10.261 In deciding whether to confirm or quash, the court must apply judicial review principles.[622] In effect, this means applying the approach to decisions to provide interim accommodation in *R v Camden LBC ex p Mohammed*,[623] described above,[624] so that the court can only order the provision of accommodation only if the authority has failed to direct itself properly in accordance with it: *Francis.*[625]

---

615 And usually will.
616 PD 52D para 28.1(4).
617 PD 52D para 28.1(4).
618 HA 1996, s 204A(4)(a); H(W)A 2014, s 89(4)(a).
619 HA 1996, s 204A(4)(b); H(W)A 2014, s 89(4)(b).
620 HA 1996, s 204A(5), (6)(b); H(W)A 2014, s 89(6), (7).
621 Per Donaldson MR in *Attorney-General v News Group Newspapers Ltd* [1987] QB 1, CA.
622 HA 1996, s 204A(4); H(W)A 2014, s 89(5).
623 (1998) 30 HLR 315, QBD, as approved in *R v Brighton and Hove Council ex p Nacion* (1999) 31 HLR 1095, CA in relation to challenges under HA 1996, s 204 prior to the addition of s 204A.
624 At para **8.54** – when considering an application for interim accommodation pending an appeal against an authority's review decision, an authority must take into account the grounds of appeal – see also *Lewis v Havering LBC* [2006] EWCA Civ 1793, [2007] HLR 20.
625 *Francis v Kensington and Chelsea RLBC* [2003] EWCA Civ 443, [2003] HLR 50.

Powers on appeal

10.262 Under its appeal powers, the county court can confirm a decision, or quash it or vary the decision as it thinks fit.[626]

10.263 The power to vary gives the county court a somewhat wider range of powers than a court on judicial review.[627] This does not, however, empower the court to extend its scope beyond 'point of law' (within the meaning given to that phrase that has already been considered).[628] It follows that the power can usually only be used to quash a decision, remitting the matter to the authority for re-determination, unless – the point of law having been determined – there is only one decision which the authority could lawfully take.[629]

10.264 It may, however, be argued that even though the appeal is confined to a point of law, the power to vary – if the applicant has been successful – allows the court to substitute its own decision for that of the authority (even where matters of judgment or evaluation of facts are inherent).

10.265 It is not a complete answer to say that, since the appeal itself has been on a point of law, there will not be the evidential material before the court on which to do so, because:

a) that will not be true in all cases (and would therefore merely limit the occasions when the power could be used); and

b) it is, in any event, a chicken-and-egg point, for if the court has the wider powers, then material can still be put before it even if only directed or relevant to the exercise of its powers.

10.266 Although this argument is consistent with Parliament having conferred wider powers on the county court than are available on judicial review,[630] it would nonetheless not seem to be available in most cases.[631] The 'decision' which the court has jurisdiction to vary, is a decision for the authority under HA 1996, s 202(1) or H(W)A 2014, s 85(1), as to eligibility, suitability or local connection

---

626 HA 1996, s 204(3); H(W)A 2014, s 88(4). Whether the court can refuse to grant relief when the appeal has been overtaken by events and is accordingly pointless is still open. Compare the difference of views in *O'Connor v Kensington and Chelsea RLBC* [2004] EWCA Civ 394, [2004] HLR 37 between the proposition that the court can only refuse to grant relief where the appeal is an abuse of process and the proposition that the court ought to be able to make no order if the appeal is pointless.

627 As noted in *Nipa Begum v Tower Hamlets LBC* [2000] 1 WLR 306, (1999) 32 HLR 445, CA at 313F.

628 See paras **10.203** and, more generally, **10.5-10.129**.

629 See paras **10.263, 10.266**.

630 Sedley LJ in *Begum* agreed with Auld LJ as to the ambit of the powers: 'The jurisdiction of the county court is *at least* as wide as that of a court of judicial review': at 327/B–C, emphasis added.

631 See further para **10.270**.

or – most relevantly here – 'as to what duty (if any) is owed' to the applicant, under the principal sections.

10.267 Thus, in *Crawley BC v B*,[632] it was held that, once the existing decision had been quashed because of an error of law (admitted by the authority), the authority had to reconsider, which required it to make enquiries and reach a further decision. This will require the authority to establish (properly) whether or not it has reason to believe, or is of the opinion, or is satisfied as to a particular state of affairs. It is only once the relevant precondition (state of mind of the authority) exists, that the decision about duty can be taken:[633]

> The question, therefore, is whether the judge was entitled, or required, on the material before him, to do more than simply quash the decision . . . I would accept that, if that material had shown that the *only* decision as to its duty to provide accommodation or assistance that the Council, acting rationally, could reach was that the duty was that imposed by section 193(2) of the Act, the judge could properly have pre-empted further consideration by making an order to that effect . . .[634]

10.268 There is, however, an exception where the power to vary may be used to substitute a decision in the applicant's favour, without remission back to the authority, in order to reinstate a benefit of which the applicant should not have been deprived:

> I would accept, also, that there could be circumstances in which a judge might properly take the view that an applicant ought not to be deprived, by events which had occurred between the date of the original decision and the date of the appeal, of some benefit or advantage to which he would have been entitled if the original decision had been taken in accordance with the law . . .[635]

10.269 This passage was adopted in *Robinson v Hammersmith and Fulham LBC*[636] in support of the proposition – in relation to a decision on a review – that:

> If the original decision was unlawful . . . the review decision maker should have so held and made a decision that would have restored to the appellant the rights she would have had if the decision had been lawful.

10.270 It would therefore seem that the power to vary does import an alternative to quashing a decision – and its remission to the authority – *either*:

---

632 *Crawley BC v B* (2000) 32 HLR 636, CA.
633 'The decision that the authority has to make is . . . as to the category into which its duty falls under the 1996 Act. Although subject to the discipline of sections 202 and 204, that remains a decision based on the satisfaction of the authority as to the issues (which are issues of fact and judgment) of priority need and intentionality. As is well-established, a conclusion as to a public body's satisfaction can only be challenged on public law grounds.' *Crawley BC v B*, above, per Buxton LJ at 645.
634 *Crawley BC v B*, above, per Chadwick LJ at 651; emphasis added.
635 *Crawley BC v B*, above, at 651–652.
636 [2006] EWCA Civ 1122, at [31].

a) where the variation relates to, reflects or rectifies the error of law itself, for example, where the decision can be identified in light of the authority's factual findings and/or evaluation, so that remission to the authority is unnecessary;[637] or

b) where it restores rights of which the applicant has been deprived.

10.271 Thus, in *Ekwuru*,[638] the authority could not, on the material before it, lawfully conclude that the applicant was intentionally homeless. The applicant had twice successfully appealed against the decision of the local authority, upheld on review, that he was intentionally homeless and on each occasion the decision had been quashed and remitted to the authority. Following the second appeal, the authority again found him intentionally homeless and for a third time upheld this decision on review. On appeal, the county court judge again quashed the decision and remitted it. The applicant appealed against the failure of the judge to vary the decision.

10.272 The Court of Appeal concluded that, on the material before it at the date of the third review decision, the authority could not lawfully have concluded that the applicant was intentionally homeless. Accordingly, nothing could be gained by remitting the application for further investigation because there was no real prospect that the authority would discover further material which permitted it properly to conclude that the applicant was intentionally homeless. The circumstances of the case were, however, described as 'exceptional'.[639]

10.273 In *Deugi*,[640] the authority's decision on eligibility and priority need was at issue on appeal, but the judge, having quashed the authority's decision, varied it to include a finding that the applicant was not intentionally homeless:

> The question for the judge was whether there was any real prospect that Tower Hamlets, acting rationally and with the benefit of further enquiry, might have been satisfied that Mrs Deugi was intentionally homeless.[641]

10.274 Only if there had been no such prospect could the judge properly have varied the decision. On the facts of the case, there remained a possibility that further enquiries could yet lead to a finding of intentional homelessness, for which reason the decision could only be quashed.[642]

---

637 Ie, where the only rational conclusion that the authority can reach is that proposed by the applicant: *Slater v Lewisham LBC* [2006] EWCA Civ 394.

638 *Ekwuru v Westminster City Council* [2003] EWCA Civ 1293, [2004] HLR 14.

639 Per Schiemann LJ at [31].

640 *Tower Hamlets LBC v Deugi* [2006] EWCA Civ 159, [2006] HLR 28.

641 Per May LJ at [36]. This formulation was said (at [37]) 'to be seen as an amalgam of Chadwick LJ [in *Crawley BC v B*] and Schiemann LJ [in *Ekwuru*], [and] is intended to reflect the fact that the appeal process is in the nature of judicial review'.

642 See also *R (P) v Ealing LBC* [2013] EWCA Civ 1579, [2014] HLR 5: the county court judge was wrong to vary a decision to find that an applicant was homeless as it was 'quite impossible' to say that there was no real prospect of any other conclusion; see also *R (Woolfe) v Islington LBC* [2016] EWHC 1907 (Admin) – the authority had wrongly applied their allocation policy so that the refusal to award the applicant points based on her residence in the borough was quashed and remitted for further investigation and consideration.

10.275 In *Robinson*,[643] the initial decision ought to have been that the applicant was in priority need (because she was 17),[644] but she had turned 18 by the time of the review. On a strict application of *Mohamed*,[645] the review decision would therefore have concluded that the applicant was – regardless of the correctness of the first decision – not in priority need. The Court of Appeal rejected this:

> I am not persuaded that the above passages[646] have any application to a situation such as the present. It was not in issue in *Mohamed* whether an unlawful decision by the original decision maker had denied rights to the person affected by the decision to which he would otherwise have been entitled.[647]

Damages

10.276 Damages can only be awarded in the county court in respect of a claim within its jurisdiction arising in contract or tort. An award of compensation is not one of the powers conferred on the county court in relation to a HA 1996, s 204 or H(W)A 2014, s 88 appeal.

10.277 Notwithstanding some differences of opinion over the years,[648] no action will lie for breach of statutory duty for failure properly to perform duties under HA 1996, Part 7,[649] absent some separate cause of action, for example, negligence,[650] or indeed contract.[651] Nor will action for misfeasance in public office[652] be easy to maintain.[653]

---

643 [2006] EWCA Civ 1122.

644 See paras **3.82-3.89**.

645 *Mohamed v Hammersmith and Fulham LBC* [2001] UKHL 57, [2002] 1 AC 547 – see 7.225.

646 From *Mohamed*.

647 At [31].

648 *Thornton v Kirklees MBC* [1979] QB 626, CA; *Cocks v Thanet DC* [1983] 2 AC 286, (1983) 6 HLR 15, HL; *Mohram Ali v Tower Hamlets LBC* [1993] QB 407, (1992) 24 HLR 474, CA; *Tower Hamlets LBC v Abdi* (1992) 25 HLR 80, CA; *R v Lambeth LBC ex p Barnes* (1993) 25 HLR 140, QBD; *Hackney LBC v Lambourne* (1992) 25 HLR 172, CA; *R v Northavon DC ex p Palmer* (1995) 27 HLR 576, CA.

649 *O'Rourke v Camden LBC* [1998] AC 188, HL; *R (Morris) v Newham LBC* [2002] EWHC 1262 (Admin), [2002] JHL D77; *R (Darby) v Richmond Upon Thames LBC* [2015] EWHC 909 (QB). The same must be true of H(W)A 2014, Part 2.

650 See further *Ephraim v Newham LBC* (1993) 25 HLR 207, CA.

651 For example, in respect of the conditions in accommodation occupied under contract (tenancy or licence), under which the authority is the landlord.

652 Where an officer of a public authority either: i) maliciously exercises a power with the intent to injure a person or persons; or ii) acts knowing that they have no power to act where to do so will probably injure a third party: *Three Rivers DC v Bank of England (No 3)* [2003] 2 AC 1, HL. Authorities can themselves be liable for the misfeasance of an officer on the basis of vicarious liability, cf *AA v Southwark LBC* [2014] EWHC 500 (QB) where the authority were liable for the behaviour of housing officers who had engaged in a tortious conspiracy to evict Mr AA.

653 Consider *R (Khazai and others) v Birmingham City Council* [2010] EWHC 2576 (Admin), [2011] JHL D9, where it was held that an email containing unlawful instructions was the product of 'oversight and ill-considered drafting' rather than 'anything more sinister' and as being the work of one person rather than an institutional decision.

Confidentiality

10.278 As noted above,[654] the court has inherent jurisdiction to make an order granting anonymity to an applicant. The same principles are applicable here.[655]

Ancillary relief

10.279 Ancillary relief in the county court is available only where final relief is available.[656] It follows that if the authority has failed to carry out the review but the only basis for complaining about the original decision is on the facts, ie, if there is still no appeal to the county court on a point of law, then – notwithstanding the provisions of HA 1996, s 204(1) or H(W)A 2014, s 88(1) – the county court cannot make a mandatory order to require the authority to carry out the review.[657]

10.280 As in the Administrative Court on a claim for judicial review, a county court judge on a homelessness appeal may refuse relief on the basis that, notwithstanding a procedural error on the part of the authority, the error would have made no difference to the authority's decision. Where a court identifies procedural flaws in an authority's decision-making process, that decision may, however, only be upheld where the court is satisfied that a properly directed authority would *inevitably* have reached the same decision.

10.281 The test of inevitability is a strict test; regardless of how slight, if the possibility exists that a proper assessment of the circumstances might produce a different decision, the authority must conduct and consider such an assessment.[658]

Ombudsman

England

10.282 One further forum for complaint which may briefly be mentioned[659] is the Local Government and Social Care Ombudsman (LGSCO),[660] who may investigate claims of maladministration against local authorities, where the

---

654 See para **10.199**.
655 See paras **10.199–10.201**.
656 County Courts Act 1984, s 38.
657 See paras **10.203-10.205**.
658 *Ali v Newham LBC* [2002] HLR 20, CA.
659 The Ombudsman process is not uncommonly quite lengthy, has no provision for any immediate or interim report, and cannot order an authority to provide housing or points under an allocation scheme. Accordingly, despite its considerable experience and expertise, it is of fairly limited use to homeless persons and applicants for an allocation..
660 LGA 1974, Part 3. In England this is called the Commission for Local Administration in England or the 'ombudsman'. Homelessness and allocations are not matters which have been transferred to the Housing Ombudsman under LA 2011, s 181.

claimant can show that they have sustained injustice in consequence of the maladministration.[661]

10.283 'Maladministration' is not defined. In *Eastleigh BC*,[662] Lord Donaldson stated that:[663]

> . . . administration and maladministration in the context of the work of a local authority is concerned with the *manner* in which decisions by the authority are reached and the *manner* in which they are or are not implemented. Administration has nothing to do with the nature, quality or reasonableness of the decision itself.

10.284 The powers of the ombudsman in England were extended by the Local Government and Housing Act 1989[664] and by the Local Government and Public Involvement in Health Act 2007.[665] The latter extends jurisdiction in England from maladministration to include alleged or apparent maladministration in connection with the authority's administrative functions, alleged or apparent failure in a service which the authority has the function to provide, and alleged or apparent failure to provide such a service.[666]

10.285 The ombudsman can recommend that compensation be paid to a complainant. Where maladministration is found, this will usually be ordered, and compensation has commonly been recommended in homelessness cases.

10.286 Complaint to the ombudsman may be particularly appropriate where there are delays in making decisions and inadequacies in decision letters. Even where the applicant is eventually adequately housed, it may be worthwhile proceeding with the complaint in order to obtain compensation.

10.287 Complaints must generally be made within 12 months of the maladministration complained of – although there is discretion to take complaints outside that period if the ombudsman considers it reasonable so to do.[667]

10.288 Any person (or their representative) can make a direct complaint to the ombudsman.[668] The complaint must generally be made in writing.[669]

---

661 LGA 1974, s 26.
662 *R v Local Commissioner for the South etc ex p Eastleigh BC* [1988] QB 855, CA.
663 *Eastleigh BC* at 863E/F, as a summary of the decision in *R v Local Commissioner for Administration for the North etc ex p Bradford MBC* [1979] QB 287, CA. Emphasis in original.
664 LGA 1972, Part 2, substituted by the Local Government and Housing Act 1989.
665 Part 9.
666 LGA 1972, s 26(1), substituted by Local Government and Public Involvement in Health Act 2007, s 173(2) with effect from 1 April 2008, by virtue of Local Government and Public Involvement in Health Act 2007 (Commencement No 5 and Transitional, Saving and Transitory Provision) Order 2008, SI 2008/917, reg 2(1)(i).
667 LGA 1974, s 26B.
668 LGA 1974, s 26A.
669 The LGO also accepts complaints through an online form or via telephone, see: www.lgo.org. uk/make-a-complaint/how-to-complain.

10.289 A complaint may also be made by way of referral from a member of a local authority,[670] and a matter may even be considered if it comes to the attention of the ombudsman during the course of an investigation and it appears to the ombudsman that a member of the public has, or may have, suffered injustice in consequence of the matter.[671] The ombudsman has a wide discretion to conduct an investigation in any manner they deem appropriate, and to make such inquiries as they think fit.[672]

10.290 At the conclusion of the investigation, the ombudsman will usually produce a report.[673] If the ombudsman concludes that there has been maladministration, a failure in a service or a failure to provide a service, then the report is laid before the local authority concerned,[674] which must consider the report and, within three months beginning with the date on which they received the report, notify the ombudsman of what action the authority has taken or proposes to take.[675]

10.291 If the ombudsman is not satisfied by the steps taken or proposed to be taken, they will produce a further report including their own recommendations as to the action the authority should take.[676] The ombudsman has power to publish a copy of the further report, and a separate power to require the authority to publish a statement in a local newspaper about the complaint, including details of the ombudsman's recommendations.[677]

10.292 Authorities have power to make payments to those who have suffered injustice as a result of maladministration, whether or not recommended to do so by the ombudsman.[678]

10.293 The ombudsman regularly publishes details of complaints that have been received and also publishes reports on specific issues such as how well authorities generally are complying with their duties.

Wales

10.294 In Wales, the Public Services Ombudsman for Wales has responsibility not only for local administration but also for the health service in Wales, social housing in Wales and for the functions of the former Welsh Administration Ombudsman.

670 LGA 1974, s 26C.
671 LGA 1974, s 26D.
672 LGA 1974, s 28.
673 LGA 1974, s 30(1).
674 LGA 1974, s 31.
675 LGA 1974, s 31(2).
676 LGA 1974, s 31(2A).
677 LGA 1974, s 31(2D).
678 LGA 2000, s 92.

10.295 They therefore have power to investigate maladministration and service failure by the Welsh Assembly, Welsh health service, health service providers in Wales, local authorities in Wales and Welsh registered providers of social housing.[679] They have power to investigate[680] complaints by or on behalf of a person who claims to have suffered injustice or hardship[681] arising from maladministration by an authority in connection with a relevant action,[682] failure in a relevant service[683] provided by an authority and failure by an authority to provide a relevant service.[684]

10.296 The Public Services Ombudsman for Wales also has power, subject to consultation, to issue guidance to local authorities about good administrative practice.[685]

---

679 Public Services Ombudsman (Wales) Act (PSO(W)A) 2005, Sch 3.
680 PSO(W)A 2005, ss 8, 10.
681 PSO(W)A 2005, s 4.
682 PSO(W)A 2005, s 7(3).
683 PSO(W)A 2005, s 7(4).
684 PSO(W)A 2005, s 7.
685 PSO(W)A 2005, s 31.

CHAPTER 11

Other statutory provisions

INTRODUCTION

Overview

11.1   The National Assistance Act (NAA) 1948 was the direct precursor of homeless persons legislation.[1] That Act was also a precursor of the Children Act

---

1   See paras **1.8–1.22.**

(CA) 1989.[2] Two factors placed a much greater housing emphasis on those Acts in recent years:[3]

a) the exclusion from housing assistance of categories of immigrants;[4] and

b) the stricter controls on housing under Housing Act (HA) 1996, Parts 6 and 7.[5]

11.2   The NAA 1948 has now been replaced, in England by the Care Act 2014 and in Wales by the Social Services and Well-being (Wales) Act (SSWB(W)A) 2014; the CA 1989 now only applies in England, with the equivalent provisions in Wales to be found in SSWB(W)A 2014.[6]

11.3   This book does not comprise a comprehensive study of the broader welfare provisions of any of this legislation. There is, however, an overlap: the facts of some of the cases suggest circumstances that would, but for legislative changes, formerly have been dealt with under homelessness legislation; indeed, many of those cases refer directly to that legislation.

11.4   Also overlapping with homelessness is the asylum support scheme under the Immigration and Asylum Act (IAA) 1999.

11.5   In addition, because it has been held to be an available source of power with which to assist in appropriate circumstances, reference may also be made to the power of general competence under the Localism Act (LA) 2011 in England, replacing the well-being powers of the Local Government Act (LGA) 2000, which remain available in Wales; a small number of other statutory provisions are also discussed.

11.6   In this chapter, we therefore consider the relevant provisions of the following:

a) Care Act 2014 / SSWB(W)A 2014;

b) IAA 1999;

c) CA 1989 / SSWB(W)A 2014;

---

2   See NAA 1948, ss 21 and 29, as enacted, amended to apply only to persons aged 18 and over by CA 1989, s 108(5) and Sch 13 para 11; see the observations of Laws LJ in *R (A) v Lambeth LBC* [2001] EWCA Civ 1624, [2002] HLR 13 at [1].

3   Benefit caps and other recent measures will also enhance dependence on social welfare duties.

4   See paras **1.61–1.62, 1.84**.

5   See paras **1.69–1.82**.

6   Cases decided under NAA 1948 are, however, likely to have some bearing on the application of the new legislative schemes under Care Act 2014 and SSWB(W)A 2014. In *R (GS) v Camden LBC* [2016] EWHC 1762 (Admin), [2016] HLR 43 it was held that the case-law on the meaning of 'care and attention' in NAA 1948, s 21, applies to 'care and support' in Care Act 2014, s 9 (see also *R (AR) v Hammersmith and Fulham LB* [2018] EWHC 3453 (Admin), (2019) 22 CCLR 537 to the same effect); thus a need for accommodation is not itself a need for care and support; to be eligible for accommodation under SSWB(W)A 2014, Part 1, an applicant must have other needs which mean that they are not capable of living independently. But see the caution about reading cases across expressed in *R (BG) v Suffolk CC* [2022] EWCA Civ 1047; [2022] 4 WLR 107, below, para **11.28**.

d)   LGA 2000 / LA 2011;

e)   other statutory provisions.

Social services authorities

11.7   Much of this chapter concerns relationships between housing authorities and social services authorities and the powers of the latter. All Welsh authorities – counties and county boroughs – are social services authorities; all London borough councils and the Common Council of the City of London, and all other unitary authorities in England, whether termed district, county or otherwise, are social services authorities.

11.8   Where there remains two-tier local government, the position depends on whether the area is a metropolitan area or not – in the former, a district council will be the social services authority; in the latter, it will be the county council.[7]

CARE ACT 2014 / SOCIAL SERVICES AND WELL-BEING (WALES) ACT 2014

Generally

11.9   Adults with needs for care and support may be provided with residential care by local authorities under the Care Act 2014 in England or the SSWB(W) A 2014 in Wales.

11.10   In England, Care Act 2014, Part 1 came into force on 1 April 2015.[8] In Wales, the SSWB(W)A 2014 came fully into force on 6 April 2016.[9] Under both

---

7   See London Government Act 1963, Local Authority Social Services Act 1970, LGA 1972 and LGA 1985.

8   Where a person was being provided with assistance under NAA 1948, Part 3, on 1 April 2015, the authority had one year in which to assess their needs under the Care Act 2014 by carrying out a review of their case: Care Act 2014 (Transitional Provision) Order 2015, SI 2015/995, art 2. Until such a review was completed, the NAA 1948 continued to apply to that person. If the authority failed to complete a review under the 2014 Act before 1 April 2016, the person was automatically treated as having needs which they were entitled to have met under the Care Act 2014. That automatic entitlement continues until the authority completed a review.

9   Social Services and Well-being (Wales) Act 2014 (Commencement No 3, Savings and Transitional Provisions) Order 2016, SI 2016/412, Sch 1 para 2 provides that SSWB(W) A 2014 does not apply where a person was receiving support or services prior to 6 April 2016 but that the authority must carry out a review of that person's case by 1 April 2017. Once the review has been carried out, the SSWB(W)A 2014 will apply. If the authority failed to complete a review by 1 April 2017, the person was automatically treated as having needs which they were entitled to have met under the SSWB(W)A 2014. That automatic entitlement continued until the authority completes a review.

Acts, local authorities[10] have a wide range of duties and powers, not all of them duties towards individuals.

11.11   English authorities have to provide or arrange for the provision of services, facilities or resources, or take other steps, to achieve the Acts' objectives.[11] Regulations may permit an authority to charge, or prohibit an authority from charging, for the provision of services, facilities or resources, or for taking other steps.[12]

11.12   Welsh authorities have to seek to promote the well-being of people who need care and support and of carers who need support.[13] They must provide or arrange for the provision of a range and level of services which they consider will achieve specified purposes in their areas.[14] Regulations govern what authorities may or may not charge.[15]

11.13   In order to meet needs, authorities may provide, among other things, accommodation in a care home or in premises of some other type.[16]

10   A county council in England, a district council for an area in England for which there is no county council, a London borough council, or the Common Council of the City of London: Care Act 2014, s 1(4); the council of a county or county borough in Wales: SSWB(W)A 2014, s 197(1).
11   Care Act 2014, s 2(1). The objectives are to contribute towards preventing or delaying the development by adults in its area of needs for care and support; to contribute towards preventing or delaying the development by carers in its area of needs for support: reduce the needs for care and support of adults in its area; to reduce the needs for support of carers in its area: Care Act 2014, s 2(1); in Wales, see para **11.12**.
12   Care Act 2014, s 2(3). A charge may cover only the cost that the local authority incurs in providing or arranging for the provision of the service, facility or resource or for taking the other step: Care Act 2014, s 2(5).
13   SSWB(W)A 2014, s 5.
14   SSWB(W)A 2014, s 15(1). The purposes are: a) to contribute towards preventing or delaying the development of people's needs for care and support; b) to reduce the needs for care and support of people who have such needs; c) to promote the upbringing of children by their families, where that is consistent with the well-being of children; d) to minimise the effect on disabled people of their disabilities; e) to contribute towards preventing people from suffering abuse or neglect; f) to reduce the need for proceedings for care or supervision orders under the CA 1989, criminal proceedings against children, any family or other proceedings in relation to children which might lead to them being placed in local authority care, or proceedings under the inherent jurisdiction of the High Court in relation to children; g) to encouraging children not to commit criminal offences; h) to avoid the need for children to be placed in secure accommodation; and i) to enable people to live their lives as independently as possible: s 15(2).
15   SSWB(W)A 2014, ss 59–62.
16   Care Act 2014, s 8(1)(a); SSWB(W)A 2014, s 34(2)(a).

Duty and power to meet needs for care and support

Duty

11.14   In respect of both Care Act 2014 and SSWB(W)A 2014, the duty to meet needs arises where an adult is ordinarily resident[17] in the local authority's area (or present in its area and of no settled residence)[18] which adult has needs which meet the eligibility criteria.[19]

11.15   The duty is not, however, triggered where there would be a charge for meeting the needs,[20] unless one of three conditions is met:[21]

a)   The first condition is that the adult's financial resources are at or below the financial limit.

b)   The second condition is that, if the adult's financial resources are above the financial limit, the adult nonetheless asks the authority to make the arrangements to meet their needs.[22]

c)   The third condition is that the adult lacks capacity to arrange for the provision of care and support and there is no person authorised under the Mental Capacity Act 2005 to make such provision for them or otherwise in a position to do so on their behalf.[23]

---

17   A person's 'ordinary residence' is determined in accordance with Care Act 2014, s 39 or SSWB(W)A 2014, s 194. In particular, both Acts provide for a person provided with accommodation under certain statutory provisions to be treated as ordinarily resident in the area in which they were ordinarily resident before being provided with that accommodation. The statutory provisions include the National Health Service Act 2006 and National Health Service (Wales) Act 2006 thereby addressing *R (Kent CC) v Secretary of State for Health* [2015] EWCA Civ 81, [2015] 1 WLR 1221 (person ordinarily resident for purposes of NAA 1948 in Kent, despite not having lived there prior to having been placed in NHS accommodation). In determining where someone is resident, any period and place of detention in hospital is to be disregarded: *R (Hertfordshire CC) v Hammersmith and Fulham LBC* [2011] EWCA Civ 77; *R (Wiltshire CC) v Hertfordshire CC* [2014] EWCA Civ 712, [2014] HLR 41.

18   Care Act 2014, s 18(1)(a); SSWB(W)A 2014, s 35(2).

19   Care Act 2014, s 18(1); SSWB(W)A 2014, s 35(3)(a). In Wales, the duty may arise even if the adult's needs do not meet the eligibility criteria, provided that the authority considers it necessary to meet those needs in order to protect the adult from abuse or neglect or a risk of abuse or neglect: SSWB(W)A 2014, s 35(3)(b).

20   Under Care Act 2014, s 14 or SSWB(W)A 2014, s 59.

21   Care Act 2014, s 18(1)(c); SSWB(W)A 2014, s 35(4)(a). There is also a cap on care costs in England but this has not yet been brought into force: Care Act 2014, ss 15 and 18(1)(b).

22   The costs both of meeting the care needs and of making the arrangements to do so being met by the adult, see Care Act 2014, s 14 and SSWB(W)A 2014, s 59.

23   Care Act 2014, s 18(2)–(4); SSWB(W)A 2014, s 35(4)(b). The financial limit is set by regulations: Care and Support (Charging and Assessment of Resources) Regulations 2014, SI 2014/2672 (England); Care and Support (Charging) (Wales) Regulations 2015, SI 2015/1843 (Wales).

Ordinary residence

11.16   The phrase 'ordinarily resident' was considered in *Shah*,[24] under the Education Act 1962: it was held that a person's long-term future intentions or expectations are not relevant; the test is not what a person's real home is, but whether a person can show a regular, habitual mode of life in a particular place, the continuity of which has persisted despite temporary absences; a person's attitude is only relevant in two respects – a) residence must be voluntarily adopted; and b) there must be a settled purpose in living in the particular place or country.[25]

11.17   In *R (Cornwall CC) v Secretary of State for Health*,[26] *Shah* was said to be 'the leading modern authority on the meaning' of ordinary residence[27] although 'the meaning of the term . . . may be strongly influenced by the particular statutory context'.[28]

Eligibility

11.18   In England, an adult's needs meet the eligibility criteria if:

a)   they arise from or are related to a physical or mental impairment or illness;

b)   as a result of those needs the adult is unable to achieve two or more specified personal outcomes;[29] and

c)   as a consequence there is (or is likely to be) a significant impact on the adult's well-being.[30]

11.19   In Wales, an adult's needs meet the eligibility criteria if:

a)   they arise from the adult's physical or mental ill-health, age, disability, dependence on alcohol or drugs, or other similar circumstances;

---

24   *R v Barnet LBC ex p Shah* [1983] 2 AC 309, HL.
25   *Shah* at 349C.
26   [2015] UKSC 46, [2015] HLR 32.
27   *Cornwall* at [41].
28   *Cornwall* at [43].
29   The specified outcomes are: a) managing and maintaining nutrition; b) maintaining personal hygiene; c) managing toilet needs; d) being appropriately clothed; e) being able to make use of the adult's home safely; f) maintaining a habitable home environment; g) developing and maintaining family or other personal relationships; h) accessing and engaging in work, training, education or volunteering; i) making use of necessary facilities or services in the local community including public transport, and recreational facilities or services; and j) carrying out any caring responsibilities the adult has for a child: Care and Support (Eligibility Criteria) Regulations 2015, SI 2015/313, reg 2(2).
30   Care and Support (Eligibility Criteria) Regulations 2015, reg 2(1).

b) they relate to one or more of a list of specified matters;[31] and

c) the adult is not able to meet the need or needs.[32]

Power

11.20 In England, the power to meet needs is engaged where the adult is ordinarily resident in the authority's area[33] or is present in its area but of no settled residence, and the authority is satisfied that it is not under a duty to meet the adult's needs,[34] ie, it is not under the duty considered at para **11.14**.[35] The power may also be exercised to support an adult who is ordinarily resident in another authority's area.[36] The power may also be exercised where the adult has needs which appear to the authority to be urgent even though an assessment has not yet been carried out.[37]

11.21 In Wales, the power is expressed rather more broadly. An authority may meet an adult's needs for care and support if they are either within or ordinarily resident in its area but presently outside of it.[38] The power to meet needs may be used whether or not an assessment (para **11.22**) has been completed.[39]

Assessment of need

11.22 Where it appears[40] to a local authority that an adult may have needs for care and support, the authority must assess whether they do so and, if so, what

---

31 a) The ability to carry out self-care or domestic routines; b) the ability to communicate; c) protection from abuse or neglect; d) involvement in work, education, learning or in leisure activities; e) maintenance or development of family or other significant personal relationships; f) development and maintenance of social relationships and involvement in the community; and g) fulfilment of caring responsibilities for a child: Care and Support (Eligibility) (Wales) Regulations 2015, SI 2015/1578, reg 3(b).
32 Care and Support (Eligibility) (Wales) Regulations 2015, SI 2015/1578, reg 3.
33 See para **11.14**.
34 Ie, not under a duty pursuant to Care Act 2014, s 18: Care Act 2014, s 19(1).
35 The only restrictions on this power are those found in Care Act 2014, ss 21–23 (exclusions for certain illegal immigrants) discussed below (see paras **11.23–11.31**). In Wales, see SSWB(W)A 2014, ss 46–48, to the same effect.
36 This power cannot be used unless the authority which is exercising the power has notified the authority for the area where the adult is ordinarily resident that they intend to provide support (Care Act 2014, s 14(2)(c)) and, in any event, is subject to limitations as to what charges the authority may impose (Care Act 2014, s 14(2)(b)).
37 Care Act 2014, s 19.
38 SSWB(W)A 2014, s 36(1).
39 SSWB(W)A 2014, s 36(3).
40 Under the pre-Care Act 2014 law, there was no need to request an assessment so long as the person had come to the attention of the local authority: *R v Gloucester CC ex p RADAR* (1997–98) 1 CCLR 476. It must, however, 'appear' to the authority that a person has a need: *R (NM) v Islington LBC* [2012] EWHC 414 (Admin).

those needs are.[41] If a person refuses an assessment, the authority need not carry one out.[42] Where the authority is satisfied, on the basis of the needs assessment, that a person has needs for care and support, it must determine whether their needs meet the eligibility criteria and, if satisfied that they do so, it must, among other things, consider what could be done to meet those needs.[43]

Immigrants and asylum-seekers

11.23   A local authority may not meet the needs for care and support of an adult to whom IAA 1999, s 115, applies if their needs for care and support have arisen solely because they are destitute or because of the physical effects (or anticipated physical effects) of being destitute.[44]

11.24   This does not apply to those admitted under Immigration Act (IA) 2016, s 67, as unaccompanied children from the European refugee crisis.[45] It was anticipated that they would initially be the responsibility of social services departments, rather than housing departments; the provision was enacted in order to facilitate planned and sustainable accommodation for them once they turned 16 and began to make plans to leave the care of social services.[46]

11.25   The effect is otherwise to exclude those who are subject to immigration control (unless re-included by regulations) from making an application for assistance under Care Act 2014 or SSWB(W)A 2014, where the need for care and attention arises solely from destitution. Their needs are, instead, intended to be met under the IAA 1999.

11.26   Local authorities accordingly have no power to provide any accommodation for non-asylum-seeking immigrants who are merely destitute and who do not have children. In the case of asylum-seekers whose need for care and attention does not arise because of destitution, however, but because of,

---

41   Care Act 2014, s 9(1); SSWB(W)A 2014, s 19(1). Statutory guidance on assessments under Care Act 2014 has been issued, see Care Act 2014, s 78 and *Care and support statutory guidance* chapter 6 (Department of Health and Social Care (DHSC), last updated 19 January 2023; https://www.gov.uk/government/publications/care-act-statutory-guidance/care-and-support-statutory-guidance). In Wales, see SSWB(W)A 2014, s 145 and the Code of Practice on the exercise of social services functions in relation to SSWB(W)A 2014, Part 3 (Assessing the needs of individuals).
42   Care Act 2014, s 11(1); SSWB(W)A 2014, s 20(1). A lack of capacity does not, in itself, amount to a refusal (Care Act 2014, s 11(2)(a); SSWB(W)A 2014, s 20(2)). A person who refuses an assessment is entitled to change their mind and require one at a later date, see Care Act 2014, s 11(3) and SSWB(W)A 2014, s 20(3).
43   Care Act 2014, s 13; SSWB(W)A 2014, s 32.
44   Care Act 2014, s 21(1); SSWB(W)A 2014, s 46(1). These provisions follow a similar exclusion contained in NAA 1948, s 21(1A). See also Nationality, Immigration and Asylum Act (NIAA) 2002, Sch 3 para 1.
45   Allocation of Housing and Homelessness (Eligibility) (England) (Amendment) Regulations 2018, SI 2018/730, reg 2.
46   Ministerial letter, 18 June 2018.

eg, disability, responsibility for meeting their care needs remains with the local authority.[47]

11.27 These exclusions are subject to what is commonly known as the 'human rights'[48] exception:[49] they do not prevent the exercise of a power or the performance of a duty if, and to the extent that, its exercise or performance is necessary for the purpose of avoiding a breach of a person's rights under the European Convention on Human Rights (ECHR).

11.28 A similar exclusion was found in (now repealed) NAA 1948, s 21(1A), although it has been said that case-law under the 1948 Act should not simply be read across to the 2014 Act, which was concerned with, among other matters, recognising and promoting the autonomy of the individual, a broader approach than under the 1948 Act.[50] Under that Act, it was held that the starting-point was to ask whether support should be provided in order to avoid a violation of a right under the ECHR, before applying any eligibility criteria or assessing the applicant's need for care and attention.[51]

11.29 In *PB*,[52] the claimant was a homeless Jamaican woman and an illegal overstayer. She had contact with her oldest child who lived with his father in the UK, but the other four children, all born in the UK, were the subject of care proceedings and not living with her at the time. The authority refused to assist her under NAA 1948, s 21, on the basis that she could return to Jamaica. This was unlawful because the authority had not considered whether her right to respect for family life under ECHR Article 8[53] would be breached if she were forced to leave the UK while care proceedings were pending.

11.30 In *Binomugisha*,[54] the authority withdrew CA 1989[55] support from a 19-year-old failed asylum-seeker with mental health problems who had made a further application for leave to remain in the UK on the basis that it would be a breach of Article 8 to remove him to Uganda. The Home Office had not yet made

---

47   *Westminster City Council v National Asylum Support Service* [2002] UKHL 38, [2002] 1 WLR 2956; *O v Wandsworth LBC* (2001) 33 HLR 39, CA. See also *R (M) v Slough BC* [2008] UKHL 52, [2008] 1 WLR 1808, where *O* was applied and *R (Murua) v Croydon LBC* [2001] EWHC Admin 830, QBD; *R (Mani) v Lambeth LBC* [2003] EWCA Civ 836, (2003) 6 CCLR 376; and *R (SL) v Westminster City Council* [2013] UKSC 27, [2013] 1 WLR 1445. See also the discussion in *R (Aburas) v Southwark LBC* [2019] EWHC 2754 (Admin), (2019) 22 CCL Rep 537.
48   It is not limited to human rights but also extends to rights under the EU treaties: see NIAA 2002, Sch 3 para 3(b).
49   NIAA 2002, Sch 3 para 3(a).
50   *R (BG) v Suffolk CC* [2022] EWCA Civ 1047; [2022] 4 WLR 107.
51   *R (N) v Lambeth LBC* [2006] EWHC 3427 (Admin).
52   *R (PB) v Haringey LBC and (1) Secretary of State for Health (2) Secretary of State for Communities and Local Government (interested parties)* [2006] EWHC 2255 (Admin), [2007] HLR 13.
53   See paras **10.123–10.125**.
54   *R (Gordon Binomugisha) v Southwark LBC* [2006] EWHC 2254 (Admin), [2007] ACD 35.
55   See paras **11.60** and following.

a decision on that application. The claimant asserted that the authority owed him a duty under the leaving care provisions of the CA 1989[56] and under NAA 1948, s 21. It was held that where there is an outstanding Article 8 claim, the question for the authority is whether that application was manifestly unfounded; while responsibility for making decisions on such applications lay with the Home Office, pending that decision the authority would have to consider whether it was necessary to provide a service in order to prevent a breach of ECHR Article 3 (prohibition of torture and inhuman or degrading treatment or punishment).

11.31   In *AW*[57] it was held that a purported fresh claim, either for asylum or under Article 3, by an asylum-seeker whose original claim had been rejected, did not always necessitate the provision of support in order to avoid a breach of the ECHR; in considering the issue, regard must be had to all the relevant circumstances, including – where appropriate – the matters which were alleged to give rise to the fresh claim.[58] Accordingly, the human rights exception does not bite simply because a human rights claim has been made to the UK Visas and Immigration (UKVI): it only applies where the provision of community care service is necessary for the purpose of avoiding a breach of a person's human rights.[59] A leading example is where an applicant had limited life expectancy and could die at any time.[60]

Provision of housing accommodation

11.32   A local authority may not meet needs for care and support by doing anything which it, or another local authority, is required to do under HA 1996,[61] or Housing (Wales) Act (H(W)A) 2014;[62] compliance with any such duty is not 'support' for the purposes of the Care Act 2014 and SSWB(W)A 2014.[63] The exclusion of duties under the Housing Acts from the Care/Wellbeing Acts is designed to ensure that duties under the latter do not 'cut across' the former, or modify or qualify the conditions applicable to them.

11.33   Thus, where a person was assessed under the Care Act 2014 as needing accommodation suitable to his condition, which was provided by way of an allocation under HA 1996, Part 6, but only after a delay of nearly a year and a half, there was no claim for judicial review on the basis of an unacceptable delay in meeting his needs: the assessment did not affect application of the

---

56   See paras **11.106–11.116**.
57   *R (AW) v Croydon LBC* [2005] EWHC 2950 (QB), (2006) 9 CCLR 252.
58   *R (AW) v Croydon LBC*. The decision on appeal did not affect this part of the judgment below – see *Croydon LBC and Hackney LBC v R (AW, A and Y)* [2007] EWCA Civ 266, [2007] 1 WLR 3168. See also *R (DK) v Croydon LBC* [2023] EWHC 1833 (Admin).
59   NIAA 2002, Sch 3 para 3.
60   *R (De Almeida) v Kensington and Chelsea RLBC* [2012] EWHC 1082 (Admin).
61   Care Act 2014, s 21(1)(a).
62   SSWB(W)A 2014, s 48(a).
63   Care Act 2014, s 23; SSWB(W)A 2014, s 48.

authority's allocation scheme – the assessed need did not mean that there was an entitlement to an allocation, whether at all or within a particular time-frame;[64] The intention of Care Act 2014, s 23, is to afford priority to the scheme of HA 1996 over the 2014, scheme of assistance – the identification of housing needs in a Care Act assessment does not shortcut the scheme of priorities within HA 1996.[65]

11.34   Under the NAA 1948, it has been held that once the local authority had assessed an applicant's needs as satisfying the relevant criteria, it had to provide accommodation under s 21 on a continuing basis so long as the need of the applicant remains as originally assessed: *R v Kensington and Chelsea RLBC ex p Kujtim*.[66] It was also held that residential accommodation could include 'ordinary' housing accommodation.[67]

11.35   A duty to supply such accommodation arose where a person needed care and attention, including housing accommodation, that was not otherwise available. The need for care and attention was, however, a precondition of such a duty.[68] Although both Care Act 2014 and SSWB(W)A 2014 use the phrase 'care and support' instead of NAA 1948's 'care and attention', the case-law on the NAA 1948 still applies.[69]

11.36   Under NAA 1948, the courts adopted a relatively generous approach.[70] In the context of psychiatric care, it was held[71] that the question is whether the individual's need for care and attention by way of the provision of residential accommodation is made materially more acute by reason of their psychiatric disorder. A claimant may, however, have mental health needs that do not necessitate the provision of accommodation, for example where the claimant is able to manage the practicalities of day-to-day life and does not need looking after.[72]

---

64   *R (Idolo) v Bromley LBC* [2020] EWHC 860 (Admin), (2020) 23 CCLR 295.
65   *R (Campbell) v Ealing LBC* [2023] EWHC 10 (Admin); [2023] HLR 18.
66   [1999] 4 All ER 161, (1999) 32 HLR 579, CA.
67   See *R v Bristol City Council ex p Penfold* (1998) 1 CCLR 315, QBD; *R v Wigan MBC ex p Tammadge* (1998) 1 CCLR 581, QBD; *R (Batantu) v Islington LBC* (2001) 33 HLR 76, QBD; and *Khana v Southwark LBC* [2001] EWCA Civ 999, CA; cf. *R (Wahid) v Tower Hamlets LBC* [2001] EWHC Admin 641, QBD, where Stanley Burnton J doubted the correctness of the proposition, but felt constrained by the existing case-law.
68   *Khana*, above. It should not be used to circumvent the controls in HA 1996, Part 6.
69   See *R (SG) v Haringey LBC* [2015] EWHC 2579 (Admin), (2015) CCLR 444 (the appeal did not deal with this issue: [2017] EWCA Civ 322); *R (GS) Camden LBC* [2016] EWHC 1762 (Admin), [2016] HLR 43. See also *R (Aburas) v Southwark LBC* [2019] EWHC 2754 (Admin), (2019) 22 CCLR 537.
70   *R v Hammersmith LBC ex p M; R v Lambeth LBC ex p P and X; R v Westminster City Council ex p A* (1998) 30 HLR 10.
71   *R (Pajaziti and Pajaziti) v Lewisham LBC and Secretary of State for the Home Department (interested party)* [2007] EWCA Civ 1351.
72   *R (Okil) v Southwark LBC* [2012] EWHC 1202 (Admin).

11.37   *R (M)*[73] comprises a comprehensive review of the meaning of 'care and attention' in NAA 1948: the natural and ordinary meaning of the words 'care and attention' in that context is 'looking after', which means doing something for the person being cared for which the person cannot or should not be expected to do for themselves, such as household tasks, protection from risks, or personal care – eg, feeding, washing or toileting.[74]

11.38   In *R (SL) v Westminster City Council*,[75] the Supreme Court stressed that it was not enough that the authority was doing something that an applicant could not do for themselves as that could lead to absurd conclusions (eg, if the authority had to buy a refrigerator for them if they had no money); the need in question had to be linked to the provision of accommodation.

11.39   In *R (Nassery) v Brent LBC*,[76] the claimant suffered from mental health problems, had previously self-harmed and had made a number of suicide attempts. He sought accommodation under NAA 1948, s 21 on the basis that he needed the assistance of a social worker to access medical help and that he had difficulty cooking as he suffered lapses in concentration. The authority carried out an assessment of his needs and concluded that he did not need such assistance and was not in need of care and attention. The claimant unsuccessfully sought judicial review of this conclusion:[77] the authority had considered all relevant evidence and had been entitled to reach its conclusion that he was not in need of care and attention; he had previously been able to access medical services via his general practitioner (GP) and his mental health had been stable for some time; his contention that he was unable to cook was contrary to earlier statements made by him; the authority was entitled to conclude that the risk of self-harm did not amount to a need for care and attention. In the Court of Appeal, the claimant unsuccessfully sought to raise a new issue (that he had become so obsessive and anxious about the most basic of decisions in life that he was essentially unable to function): new matters that had arisen since the initial assessment should be the subject of a request for a new assessment.

Discharge of the duty

11.40   The duty to meet needs is not absolute. Where an applicant manifests a persistent and unequivocal refusal to observe the authority's reasonable

---

73 *R (M) v Slough BC* [2008] UKHL 52, [2008] 1 WLR 1808.
74 See also the discussion in *R (Aburas) v Southwark LBC* [2019] EWHC 2754 (Admin), (2019) 22 CCLR 537, where the evidence did not suggest that the claimant needed the support of a social worker to ensure that he ate and took medication; nor did it suggest that he needed accommodation to access such support.
75 [2013] UKSC 27, [2013] HLR 30.
76 [2011] EWCA Civ 539, [2011] PTSR 1639.
77 [2010] EWHC 2326 (Admin).

requirements in relation to occupation of accommodation, the authority is entitled to treat its duty as discharged and to refuse to provide further accommodation.[78]

11.41   The duty may also be discharged by the unreasonable refusal of an offer of accommodation. In *Khana v Southwark LBC*,[79] the applicant was a severely disabled elderly Kurdish woman. She lived with her husband and daughter in the latter's one-bedroom flat. Following assessment, the authority offered her and her husband a placement in a residential home on the basis that it was the only form of residential accommodation which would meet her needs for care and attention. The offer was refused by the applicant and her husband, who asserted they would only accept a two-bedroom, ground-floor flat, where the family could continue to live together. Given its conclusion as to needs, the authority was held to have discharged its duty and, in any event, the refusal was unreasonable and as such discharged the authority from any further duty for so long as the refusal was maintained.

IMMIGRATION AND ASYLUM ACT 1999

11.42   IAA 1999, Part 6 came into force on 3 April 2000. It excludes persons subject to immigration control[80] from social security benefits and most other welfare provisions.[81] It does not, however, exclude duties and rights under the Children Act 1989 / Children Act 1989 / Social Services and Well-being (Wales) Act 2014 provisions considered under the next heading.[82] At the same time, however, it also set up a scheme for asylum support. The National Asylum Support Service (NASS) was established within the Immigration and Nationality Directorate (IND) of the Home Office, to administer the scheme. In July 2006 the Home Office announced that NASS no longer existed as a separate department.

11.43   Asylum support is now administered in two separate ways:

a)   those who made their first asylum claim on or after 5 March 2007 have their support processed by the New Asylum Model (NAM) 'case owner' who is processing their asylum claim; and

b)   those who claimed before that date are known as 'legacy cases' and have their asylum and support claims dealt with by the Casework Resolution Directorate (CRD), subsequently renamed the Case Assurance and Audit Unit (CAAU).

---

78   *R v Kensington and Chelsea RLBC ex p Kujtim* (2000) 32 HLR 579.
79   *Khana v Southwark LBC* [2001] EWCA Civ 999, (2001) 4 CCLR 267. See also *R (Patrick) v Newham LBC* (2001) 4 CCLR 48, QBD.
80   See para **A.14**.
81   IAA 1999, s 115.
82   Paras **11.60** onwards.

11.44   In April 2007, the Border and Immigration Agency (BIA) replaced the IND. The BIA was replaced by the UK Border Agency (UKBA) which, in turn, has been replaced by the Home Office's UK Visas and Immigration (UKVI) centre.

11.45   The EU had attempted to implement a common policy for the treatment of asylum-seekers across Europe by enacting Council Directive 2003/9/EC[83] which lays down minimum standards for their reception. The directive was implemented in domestic law by amending the Immigration Rules[84] and enacting new regulations[85] which apply to a person whose claim for asylum is recorded on or after 5 February 2005;[86] as such, the regulations continue to apply.

11.46   Under the IAA 1999, s 95(1) the Secretary of State may[87] provide, or arrange for the provision of support for asylum-seekers or the dependants of asylum-seekers who appear to them to be destitute or to be likely to become destitute within the prescribed period. That period is 14 days, or 56 days if they are already receiving asylum support.[88] The power to provide support has, by regulation, become a duty.[89] The accommodation must be adequate for the needs of the asylum-seeker: see *R (NB and others) v Secretary of State*,[90] where conditions at a former barracks in which some asylum-seekers were housed during the pandemic, with a large number of people living in overcrowded accommodation, meant that it was 'virtually inevitable' that a large number of people would contract coronavirus. It followed that the accommodation was not adequate for the needs of the claimants; indeed, that it had been irrational to house them there, although the conditions did not amount to a breach of the asylum-seekers' Art 3, ECHR rights.

11.47   An asylum-seeker is a person who is not under 18 and who has made a claim for asylum which has been recorded by the Secretary of State but which has not been determined.[91] A claim for asylum means a claim that it would be contrary to the UK's obligations under the Refugee Convention,[92] or under ECHR Article 3, for the claimant to be removed from, or required to leave, the UK.[93] Dependants include a spouse, a child of the claimant or the claimant's

---

83   The directive came into force on 6 February 2003.
84   HC 395.
85   Asylum Seekers (Reception Conditions) Regulations 2005, SI 2005/7 and Asylum Support (Amendment) Regulations 2005, SI 2005/11.
86   Asylum Seekers (Reception Conditions) Regulations 2005, SI 2005/7, reg 1(2).
87   A decision to grant bail pending deportation to an asylum-seeker provided an address where he would be living is made available does not amount to an order to the Secretary of State to provide accommodation: *R (Messaoud) v Secretary of State for the Home Department* [2019] EWHC 2948 (Admin).
88   Asylum Support Regulations ('AS Regs') 2000, SI 2000/704, reg 7.
89   Asylum Seekers (Reception Conditions) Regulations 2005, SI 2005/7, reg 5.
90   [2021] EWHC 1489 (Admin); 21 4 WLR 92.
91   IAA 1999, s 94(1).
92   Convention Relating to the Status of Refugees 1951.
93   IAA 1999, s 94(1).

spouse, who is under 18 and dependent on the claimant,[94] and other prescribed persons.[95]

11.48   Assistance under these provisions is in theory excluded in the case of some classes of immigrant, being those classes (subject to exceptions, including the over-arching exception for British citizens and persons under the age of 18,[96] and the human rights/ European Community (EC) Treaty exceptions)[97] considered in the Annex: Immigration Eligibility.[98] In practice, the government does not usually apply these eligibility criteria when making asylum support decisions, but applies the principles set out in these paragraphs.[99]

11.49   A person is destitute if they do not have adequate accommodation or any means of obtaining it; or have adequate accommodation or the means of obtaining it but cannot meet their other essential living needs.[100] This test involves consideration of the claimant and the claimant's dependants.[101] In *R (N) v Secretary of State*,[102] the claimant was initially referred by the Secretary of State to the local authority under Care Act 2014; the authority assessed him as needing to be accommodated in south London, where he had a support network; the Secretary of State then accepted a duty under the 1999 Act but accommodated the claimant in a hotel in Swindon. The claim for judicial review was successful: the Secretary of State had not attempted to grapple with the local authority's conclusions or how the claimant could manage if removed from his support network.

11.50   The Secretary of State may not arrange or provide asylum support unless satisfied that the claim for asylum was made as soon as reasonably practicable after the person's arrival in the UK.[103] This does not apply if support is necessary to avoid a breach of the ECHR or if the household includes a dependent child who is under 18 years old.[104] The House of Lords has held that there would be a breach of ECHR Article 3 when an individual faces an imminent prospect of serious suffering caused or materially aggravated by denial of shelter, food or the most basic necessities of life: *R (Limbuela) v Secretary of State of the Home Department*.[105]

IAA 1999, s 94(1).
95   The list is set out in the AS Regs 2000, reg 2(4).
96   See para **A.172**.
97   See paras **A.175–A.183**.
98   Ibid.
99   See paras **11.49–11.59**.
100 IAA 1999, s 95(3).
101 IAA 1999, s 95(4).
102 [2023] EWHC 2775 (Admin).
103 NIAA 2002, s 55(1).
104 NIAA 2002, s 55(5).
105 [2005] UKHL 66, [2006] 1 AC 396. See also *R (DMA and others) v Secretary of State for the Home Department* [2020] EWHC 3416 (Admin) where the failure of the Home Office to monitor the implementation and operation of contracts awarded to private companies to provide support under IAA 1999, s 4, so that destitute asylum seekers were exposed to lengthy delays in the provision of accommodation and support, was held to have led to violations of ECHR Article 3.

11.51   The government has interpreted the judgment as meaning that support 'should be provided under [NIAA 2002] section 55(5)(a) when an applicant (or his adult dependant(s)) faces an imminent prospect of serious suffering caused or materially aggravated by denial of support'.[106] The judgment that this calls for, however, also requires the decision-maker to be satisfied that the asylum-seeker has some means of meeting their need for food and washing facilities.

11.52   The Secretary of State may provide, or arrange for the provision of, temporary support to destitute asylum-seekers and their dependants until a decision is reached on eligibility for support under IAA 1999, s 95.[107] This is usually in a hotel or hostel, arranged by one of the voluntary organisations funded by the Home Office, which are known as the Asylum Support Partnership (ASP) and which provide reception assistance.

11.53   The Secretary of State should arrange for the asylum-seeker to be offered support under IAA 1999, s 95, as soon as it has been decided that they are eligible. This support can include providing accommodation that appears to be adequate for the needs of the supported person and their dependants,[108] and providing for their essential living needs.[109] Before deciding what form of support to provide or continue to provide, the Secretary of State must take certain matters into account and ignore others.[110] The asylum-seeker's resources must be taken into account when deciding the kind and level of support.[111]

11.54   An asylum-seeker stops being an asylum-seeker for support purposes 28 days after the Secretary of State notifies them of a favourable asylum decision, or 21 days after notification of a refusal. If there is an appeal, the period ends 28 days after any final appeal is disposed of.[112]

---

106 *Section 55 guidance*, UKVI, Version 12, 1 June 2015.

107 IAA 1999, s 98.

108 In *R (TG) v Secretary of State*, High Court (QBD), 22 January 2021, the claimant, his pregnant wife and two children were being accommodated under IAA 1999, s 95 in one room of a hotel. The claimant had a serious kidney condition and was on immunosuppressant drugs. Other people at the hotel had tested positive for coronavirus and the family rarely left the hotel room. The claimant successfully applied for an order that they be provided with self-contained accommodation with sufficient beds for each of the family: the claimant had a strong prima facie case; the Secretary of State did not appear to have given any consideration to the needs of the children and why it was considered appropriate for them to spend almost three months living in one room; moreover, the Secretary of State did not appear to have considered the poor health of the claimant. It was strongly arguable that the present accommodation was so inadequate as for it to be irrational for the Secretary of State to leave the family in the hotel room. The Secretary of State was ordered to move the family to suitable self-contained accommodation within four days.

109 IAA 1999, s 96(1).

110 IAA 1999, s 97(1), (2) and (4).

111 AS Regs 2000, reg 12.

112 IAA 1999, s 94(3) and AS Regs 2000, reg 2(2).

11.55   This does not apply if the asylum-seeker has a dependent child under 18 in the household: in those circumstances, the person continues to be treated as an asylum-seeker for support purposes so long as the child is under 18 and within the household.[113] An asylum-seeker will not benefit from this provision if the Secretary of State has certified that they are a refused asylum-seeker with a dependent child under 18 who is refusing to leave the UK.[114]

11.56   Under IAA 1999, s 4(2),[115] the Secretary of State may provide, or arrange for the provision of, facilities for the accommodation of a person (and any dependant) if the person was, but is no longer, an asylum-seeker, and the person's claim for asylum was rejected, if the person can satisfy one of the five conditions set out in the applicable regulations.[116]

11.57   Those conditions are that:

a)   the person is taking all reasonable steps to leave the UK or place themselves in a position in which they are able to leave, which may include complying with attempts to obtain a travel document to facilitate their departure;

b)   the person is unable to leave the UK because they cannot travel for physical reasons or for some other medical reason;

c)   the person is unable to leave the UK because in the opinion of the Secretary of State there is currently no viable route of return available;

d)   the person has made an application for judicial review of a decision in relation to their asylum claim, and has been granted permission to proceed pursuant to Civil Procedure Rules 1998 (CPR) Part 54; or

---

113   IAA 1999, s 94(5).
114   NIAA 2002, Sch 3 para 7A, substituted by the Asylum and Immigration (Treatment of Claimants, etc) Act 2004, with effect from 1 December 2004.
115   The former power to provide, or arrange for the provision of, support to a person who has arrived in the UK and been granted temporary admission or who has been detained, whether or not they are also a former asylum-seeker under IAA 1999, s 4(1) was repealed from 15 January 2018 by IA 2016, Sch 11 para 1: Immigration Act 2016 (Commencement No 7 and Transitional Provisions) Regulations 2017, SI 2017/1241, reg 2; see also guidance on transitional provisions *Support provided under section 4(1) of the Immigration and Asylum Act 1999: handling transitional cases*, Home Office, February 2018 (www.gov.uk/government/publications/asylum-support-section-41-handling-transitional-cases). The IAA 1999, s 4(1) power was replaced by IA 2016, Sch 10 which provides that the Secretary of State has power to provide or arrange for the provision of facilities for the accommodation of a person on 'immigration bail'. See the Home Office 2021 guidance *Immigration bail*.
116   Immigration and Asylum (Provision of Accommodation to Failed Asylum-Seekers) Regulations ('IA(PAFAS) Regs') 2005/930. As to support under IAA 1999, s 4(2), see *Asylum support, section 4(2): policy and process*, Home Office, February 2018 (www.gov.uk/government/publications/asylum-support-section-42-policy). As with the Homelessness Code of Guidance in England, the online version is updated from time to time and regard must therefore be had to the guidance as it reads at the relevant time.

e) the provision of accommodation is necessary for the purpose of avoiding a breach of rights under the ECHR.[117]

11.58 The power to provide support under IAA 1999, s 4 is expressed in terms of 'facilities for accommodation', so it may be provided in the form of accommodation with living expenses attached. Unlike support under IAA 1999, s 95 (see paras **11.42–11.44**), it is not possible for an applicant to stay with a friend and only claim a subsistence allowance. The support usually comprises vouchers for living expenses, with a room in a communal private rented house arranged by an accommodation provider. Sometimes the package is full board in hostel accommodation. The accommodation provider will issue weekly supermarket vouchers, which may be delivered to the applicant, or the applicant may need to collect them from an office. Unlike accommodation under IAA 1999, s 95, there is no requirement for IAA 1999, s 4 accommodation to be adequate – s 4 is a more limited and less advantageous duty for the applicant than the duty imposed by s 95: *R (Kiana) v Secretary of State for the Home Department*.[118]

11.59 Section 4(2) is a scheme of last resort, which only arises if no other statutory provision is engaged so that the asylum seeker would be destitute if the Secretary of State did not provide support.[119] In *R (VC) v Newcastle City Council*,[120] the High Court described it as a 'residuary power', but added that the mere fact that support is or may be available under section 4 does not, of itself, exonerate a local authority from what would otherwise be a power or duty under other statutory provisions:[121] thus, where a local authority had assessed a child as being in need within CA 1989, s 17 or was already providing services under that power, it would not be able to justify the non-provision or discontinuance of assessed services on the ground that support under IAA 1999, s 4 is available unless it can be shown that the Secretary of State is actually able and willing (or if not willing could be compelled) to provide support, which support would meet the assessed needs of the child.

---

117 IA(PAFAS) Regs 2005, reg 3(2). In *R (TMX) v (1) Croydon LBC (2) Secretary of State* [2024] EWHC 129 (Admin); [2024] HLR forthcoming, the Secretary of State provided hotel accommodation pending a challenge to the local authority's refusal to do so under Care Act 2014 (which challenge was successful); a discrete challenge under Arts 3 and 8, ECHR, to the suitability of that accommodation for the applicant, an asylum seeker with a progressive degenerative condition who was a wheelchair user, was also successful but as it was caused by the local authority's failure, the authority rather than the Secretary of State was liable for the breach.

118 [2010] EWHC 1002 (Admin).

119 *R (SL) v Westminster CC* [2013] UKSC 27.

120 [2011] EWHC 2673 (Admin), [2012] PTSR 546. The other statutory powers and duties in *VC* referred in particular to CA 1989, s 17. See para **11.61**.

121 At [86]. Thus, in *R (SB, SBO) v Newham LBC* [2023] EWHC 2701 (Admin), the local authority assessment under Care Act 2014 had concluded that the claimant needed support but did not make any finding about support finding and maintaining accommodation: the authority's attempt to shift responsibility to the Secretary of State under the 1999 Act failed because its duty to make a proper needs assessment had not yet been completed. See also *R (TMX) v (1) Croydon LBC (2) Secretary of State* [2024] EWHC 129 (Admin); [2024] HLR forthcoming, above, para **11.57**.

CHILDREN ACT 1989/SOCIAL SERVICES AND WELL-BEING (WALES) ACT 2014

Generally

11.60 Children Act 1989, Part 3 confers general powers and imposes general duties on local authorities in England exercising social service functions in respect of children and families in their area.[122] From 6 April 2016, SSWB(W) A 2014 applies in Wales in its place.[123] Duties under these provisions are not excluded by the Immigration and Asylum Act 1999 considered under the last heading.[124] Duties under these provisions are imposed on local authorities: there is no power for authorities to set any kind of limit on the numbers assisted under them so as to seek to impose them on the Secretary of State for the Home Department; the Secretary of State does, however, have a common law power to provide emergency support by accommodating children where a local authority is failing to fulfil its duties, albeit not in such a way[125] as to deprive children of their rights under these provisions.[126]

Children Act 1989

Children Act 1989, s 17

11.61 Under CA 1989, s 17(1), authorities are required to safeguard and promote the welfare of children within their areas[127] whom they assess as being in need and, insofar as is consistent with that duty, to promote the upbringing of such children by their families.[128] The section sets out duties of a general character intended for the benefit of children in need in the area of the social

---

122 A local authority exercising a social services function in respect of children and families in their area is a 'children's services authority' as defined by CA 2004, s 65(1). This mirrors the definition of a 'social services authority' save for the addition of the Council of the Isles of Scilly. See para **11.7**.

123 Social Services and Well-being (Wales) Act 2014 (Commencement No 3, Savings and Transitional Provisions) Order 2016/412.

124 Paras **11.42** onwards,

125 Eg, in hotels.

126 *R. (ECPAT) v Secretary of State for the Home Department* [2023] EWHC 1953 (Admin).

127 A child is within an authority's area if physically present: it is not necessary that the child be 'ordinarily resident' in the area; it is possible for a child to be 'within' more than one authority's area for the purposes of CA 1989, s 17, eg, where the child is living in one area but attends school in another – see *R (Sandra Stewart) v Wandsworth LBC and others* [2001] EWHC Admin 709, [2002] 1 FLR 469; *R (N) v (1) Newham LBC (2) Essex CC* [2013] EWHC 2475 (Admin). Although an authority needs only to assess those children within its area, it can provide services outside of the area in order to meet those assessed needs: *R (J) v Worcestershire CC* [2014] EWCA Civ 1518 (services provided to Romany Gypsy child).

128 CA 1989, s 17(1)(b).

services authority.[129] Other duties – and specific duties in subsequent provisions of the CA 1989 – must be performed in individual cases by reference to the general duty under s 17(1), but s 17(1) does not itself impose an individual duty.[130]

11.62   The provision is excluded in the case of some classes of immigrant, being those classes (subject to exceptions, including the over-arching exception for British citizens and persons under the age of 18,[131] and the human rights/ EC Treaty exceptions)[132] considered in the Annex: Immigration Eligibility.[133] In view of the exception for persons under the age of 18, the exclusion has no effect on them, but it may prevent the use of CA 1989, s 17 for adult members of the family.

11.63   Although CA 1989, s 17(1) is a general duty, when discharging it authorities have available the specific powers and duties set out in Sch 2, Part 1, including assessment of the child's needs (s 17(2)). By s 17(6), such services may include assistance in kind or cash, and may include the provision of accommodation, possibly together with family.[134] Local Authority Circular 2003/13 (*Guidance on accommodating children in need and their families*) provides that 'social services departments might find it helpful to refer . . . to Chapter 12 of the [Homelessness Code of Guidance]' when considering what accommodation to provide for families under s 17(6). The English Code

---

129 In *R (AM) v Havering LBC and Tower Hamlets LBC* [2015] EWHC 1004 (Admin), [2015] PTSR 1242, an application under Part 7 was made to Tower Hamlets who provided temporary accommodation in Havering without notifying the latter under HA 1996, s 208 (see para **8.179**), which accommodation was withdrawn following a decision that the applicant was intentionally homeless; Tower Hamlets started but did not complete an assessment under CA 1989, s 17, but referred the applicant to Havering, who refused to conduct an assessment under s 17 on the basis that Tower Hamlets should do it; claims for judicial review against both authorities were allowed – having started the assessment, Tower Hamlets should have completed it; and, Havering had a duty since the family had moved to its area. The problems which had arisen were 'significantly aggravated' by the failure of Tower Hamlets to give notice to Havering under HA 1996, s 208. Had it done so, the two authorities would have been able to co-operate by, for example, one conducting the Children Act assessment on behalf of both.
130 *R (G) v Barnet LBC; R (W) v Lambeth LBC; R (A) v Lambeth LBC* [2003] UKHL 57, [2004] AC 208, [2004] HLR 10. See also *R (Bates) v Barking and Dagenham LBC* [2012] EWHC 4218 (Admin).
131 See para **A.172**.
132 See paras **A.175–A.183**.
133 Ibid.
134 The Act was amended by Adoption and Children Act 2002, s 116(1) to include references to accommodation following the decision of the Court of Appeal in *R (A) v Lambeth LBC* [2001] EWCA Civ 1624, [2002] HLR 13, which suggested that there was no power to provide accommodation (although this was subsequently held to have been decided per incuriam: *R (W) v Lambeth LBC* [2002] EWCA Civ 613, [2002] HLR 41, (2002) 5 CCLR 203). In *R (OA, OPL and OLL) v Bexley LBC* [2020] EWHC 1107 (Admin) [2020] PTSR 1654, [2020] JHL D59, it was held that, if the child's welfare requires it, the authority can provide support to anyone caring for a child in need and is not limited to the parents of the child although, on the evidence in that case, the child's welfare did not require it.

confirms[135] that bed and breakfast accommodation is not suitable for families and should only be used as a last resort and, even then, for no more than six weeks. This is, however, only guidance and does not render a decision to provide accommodation under s 17 in bed and breakfast accommodation unlawful under s 17.[136] A child in need within s 17(10) is eligible for the provision of assistance, but has no absolute right to it.[137]

11.64   In *R (G) v Barnet LBC*,[138] the House of Lords held that it was unlawful for a local authority to adopt a general policy of only accommodating homeless children pursuant to their duty under CA 1989, s 20[139] while refusing to exercise its power under s 17 to accommodate other members of the family. The provisions of CA 1989, s 17(6), and in particular the inclusion of the power to provide accommodation,[140] should now be read in the light of Local Authority Circular, *Guidance on accommodating children in need and their families*[141] and the observations of Baroness Hale in *R (G) v Southwark LBC*,[142] suggesting that children in need of accommodation will almost always involve children needing to be accommodated with their families.

11.65   The assessment of need carried out under CA 1989, s 17 should not be dealt with summarily and requires proper enquiry and consideration:[143] *R (MM) v Lewisham LBC*.[144] In that case, the claimant, a 17-year-old girl, had been living in a women's refuge for four months when she was referred to the social services department of Lewisham LBC by a support worker at the refuge. The

135 But see paras **8.218–8.221** where the accommodation is provided under HA 1996, Part 7.
136 *R (C, T, M, U) v Southwark LBC* [2014] EWHC 3983 (Admin); on appeal, this issue was not pursued: [2016] EWCA Civ 707, [2016] HLR 36.
137 *R(G) v Barnet LBC; R(W) v Lambeth LBC; R(A) v Lambeth LBC* [2003] UKHL 57, [2004] AC 208, [2004] HLR 10.
138 [2003] UKHL 57, [2004] AC 208, [2004] HLR 10.
139 See paras **11.71–11.87**. In *R (Bates) v Barking and Dagenham LBC* [2012] EWHC 4218 (Admin), a refusal to use CA 1989, s 17 instead of making an offer to accommodate the claimant's children (without her) under CA 1989, s 20 was upheld where the authority was trying to prompt the claimant to organise herself better and seek appropriate assistance, which was a legitimate aim and a lawful decision on the facts.
140 Adoption and Children Act 2002, s 116(1).
141 Para **11.63**.
142 [2009] UKHL 26, [2009] 1 WLR 1299 at [30].
143 Where the child or the child's family are foreign nationals, this is likely to include whether they have a 'right to rent' as defined in Immigration Act (IA) 2014, Part 3 Ch 1. In *R (U, U, by their mother and litigation friend BU) v Milton Keynes Council* [2017] EWHC 3050 (Admin), the authority had concluded that the children were not 'in need' because their mother had sufficient resources to enable her to obtain privately rented accommodation; the family were Nigerian nationals with no right to remain in the UK and they contended that they had no 'right to rent'. The failure to consider whether the IA 2014 applied was a material omission and the decision that the children were not 'in need' was quashed. Where an authority is faced with an applicant who has the financial means to rent privately but who is disqualified by virtue of the IA 2014, one solution might be to apply to the Secretary of State (IA 2014, s 21(3)) for a limited right to rent to be granted to the applicant. See also *R (Michael Stewart) v Birmingham City Council* [2018] EWHC 61 (Admin), [2018] PTSR 1204.
144 *R (MM) v Lewisham LBC* [2009] EWHC 416 (Admin).

support worker informed the social services department that the reasons for the referral were that the claimant was fleeing domestic violence, vulnerable, lacking life-skills and that she was shortly to be placed in hostel accommodation. The social services department made no enquiries of its own and determined that the referral was 'vague'. It also decided that, as the claimant was in receipt of benefits and had accommodation provided for her, she was not a child in need under CA 1989, s 17 and was not therefore entitled to assistance from social services. The claimant applied for judicial review of that decision on the basis that the authority had failed to carry out a proper assessment. The High Court agreed that the decision could not stand. The consideration given to the referral was no more than 'cursory' and 'fell far below' the standard required by law.[145]

11.66 In *R (AA and others) v Bexley LBC*,[146] the claimants, a Nigerian mother and her infant children who were unlawfully present in the UK, approached Bexley LBC for assistance under CA 1989, s 17, contending that they were destitute so that the children were 'in need'. The authority considered that the family had access to sufficient funds and support to ensure that the children were not 'in need'. That decision was quashed: there was no proper evidence which would enable the authority to conclude that the family had any other source of funds; the authority had concluded that certain welfare benefits were being paid to the family, of which there was no evidence. A further assessment was ordered.

11.67 An authority is, however, entitled to draw adverse inferences from a failure by parents to co-operate with the assessment: *R (MN and KN) v Hackney LBC*[147] in which the parents failed to provide information about their income and other sources of assistance from friends or relatives, entitling the authority to conclude that there was no immediate risk of homelessness and that the children were not 'in need'.

11.68 A local authority must consider the policy of the Secretary of State when deciding whether to withdraw accommodation provided under CA 1989, s 17(6): *R (Clue) v Birmingham City Council*.[148] The claimant and her eldest son were Jamaican citizens who had come to the UK as visitors and overstayed. The claimant was refused leave to remain. No action was taken to remove her and her son to Jamaica. She subsequently had three more children in the UK. Accommodation for the entire family was being funded by the local authority under CA 1989, s 17(6). After the birth of her youngest child, the claimant made a further application for leave to remain, by which time her eldest child had been

---

145 *R (MM)* at [14]. The assessment must also be revisited if circumstances change, see, eg, *R (CO) v Lewisham LBC* [2017] EWHC 1676 (Admin), where an initial conclusion that children were not 'in need' because they were receiving financial and other support from wider family members could not be relied on once it had been withdrawn; there should have been a proper reconsideration of the position.

146 [2019] EWHC 130 (Admin).

147 [2013] EWHC 1205 (Admin).

148 *R (Clue) v Birmingham City Council* [2010] EWCA Civ 460, [2011] 1 WLR 99, [2010] 2 FLR 1011, (2010) 13 CCLR 276.

continuously in the UK for seven years. The policy of the Secretary of State for the Home Department was that it would normally be inappropriate forcibly to remove a family with a child who had been continuously in the country for seven years because such a child would, in most cases, have established ties which rendered it right and fair that the family should be allowed to remain.[149] The authority nonetheless decided to withdraw funding for the accommodation and pay the cost of returning the family to Jamaica, even though no action had been taken by immigration authorities to remove the claimant and her family from the country.

11.69   It was held that the authority was required by NIAA 2002, Sch 3 para 1 to determine whether its proposed course of action would breach the ECHR rights of the claimant or any of her family members. Although the policy of the Secretary of State was not binding, the authority had failed to give sufficient weight to it, in the light of which it was likely that the claimant and her eldest daughter would be permitted to remain in the UK. If the claimant and her family were to return to Jamaica, that would render the application for indefinite leave to remain academic and defeat the purpose of the policy; the authority was not intended to be allowed to pre-empt the decision of the Secretary of State on applications for leave to remain. In *R (KA) v Essex CC*[150] it was held that the effect of *Clue* was that, save where the case was obviously hopeless or abusive, an authority could not deny support under the CA 1989 if the effect would be to negate an ECHR right.

11.70   A local authority cannot automatically withdraw, or decline to offer, support under CA 1989, s 17(6) to a child whom it had assessed to be 'in need' simply on the basis that support is available under the IAA 1999, s 4:[151] see paras **11.42–11.44**.

Children Act 1989, s 20

11.71   CA 1989, s 20 provides that:

> '(1) within their area who appears to them to require accommodation as a result of–
>
> (a)   there being no person who has parental responsibility for him;
>
> (b)   his being lost or having been abandoned; or
>
> (c)   the person who has been caring for him being prevented (whether or not permanently, and for whatever reason)[152] from providing him with suitable accommodation or care.

---

149 DP 56/96.
150 [2013] EWHC 43 (Admin), [2013] 1 WLR 1163.
151 *R (VC) v Newcastle City Council* [2011] EWHC 2673 (Admin), [2012] JHL D3, QBD.
152 The words 'for whatever reason' mean that s 20 must be given the widest possible scope: per Lord Hope in *R (G) v Barnet LBC* [2003] UKHL 57, [2004] AC 208, [2004] HLR 10, at [100]; see eg *R (BC) v Surrey CC* [2023] EWHC 3209 (Admin); *R (DF) v Essex CC* [2023] EWHC 3330 (Admin).

. . .

> (3) Every local authority shall provide accommodation for any child in need within their area who has reached the age of sixteen and whose welfare the authority consider is likely to be seriously prejudiced if they do not provide him with accommodation.
>
> (4) A local authority may provide accommodation for any child within their area (even though a person who has parental responsibility for him is able to provide him with accommodation) if they consider that to do so would safeguard or promote the child's welfare.'

11.72 CA 1989, s 20 therefore contains both a power and a duty to provide accommodation for the child.[153] The duty is imposed on social services authorities to house children in the circumstances set out in s 20(1) and to house young people in the circumstances set out in s 20(3); the power arises under s 20(4).[154] An authority may enter into arrangements with another local authority for assistance in the discharge of the duty under CA 1989, s 20, but that does not permit it to pass the child 'from pillar to post' between authorities: *R (G) v Southwark LBC*.[155]

11.73 Following this decision,[156] the Department for Communities and Local Government[157] (DCLG) issued new guidance in April 2010, subsequently updated and re-issued jointly with the Department for Education (DfE) in April 2018 as *Prevention of homelessness and provision of accommodation for 16 and 17 year old young people who may be homeless and/or require accommodation*.[158] The guidance says that if the young person makes an initial approach to housing services, the authority should commence inquiries under HA 1996, Part 7 and, if appropriate, secure interim accommodation, which should not normally be in bed and breakfast accommodation and should not be in an 'all-ages night shelter', even in an emergency (paras **3.3, 3.72–3.77**). The accommodation should be provided until the children's services authority has assessed whether a duty is owed under CA 1989, s 20.[159] If no duty is owed under CA 1989, s 20, then the housing authority should consider whether any duty is owed under HA 1996, Part

---

153 When deciding how to discharge the duty, and, in particular, whether or not to house parents with the child or children, the authority must consider the family rights of the child/children under ECHR Article 8: *R (PK and another) v Harrow LBC* [2014] EWHC 584 (Admin).

154 Where the child is street homeless, it is the authority for the area in which the child was living when homelessness began which has responsibility: *R (MS) v (1) Hammersmith and Fulham LBC (2) Croydon LBC* [2019] EWHC 3895 (Admin).

155 [2009] UKHL 26, [2009] 1 WLR 1299, per Baroness Hale at [28].

156 *R (G) v Southwark LBC*, above.

157 As it then was: it is now the Ministry of Housing, Communities and Local Government (MHCLG).

158 Available at www.gov.uk/government/publications/provision-of-accommodation-for-16-and-17-year-olds-who-may-be-homeless-and-or-require-accommodation.

159 If in doubt pending a decision on age, the assumption is that someone is a child and, if in need, must be accommodated; see *R(AB, NLK, AD) v Brent LBC* [2021] EWHC 2843 (Admin) – the authority could not leave unaccompanied foreign nationals who claimed to be children in a hotel provided by the Home Office until a decision was reached.

7 although that does not obviate the need for the children's services authority to consider the provision of services under CA 1989, s 17.

11.74 The guidance stresses the importance of preventative work, including mediation, in seeking to resolve family problems which may have led the young person to become homeless. It recognises that such steps should be undertaken alongside the statutory assessment procedures and that it is unlawful to delay the statutory assessment in order to attempt mediation.[160] The guidance supersedes those parts of circular 2003/13 (guidance on accommodating children in need and their families) that related to homeless 16- and 17-year-olds.

11.75 Whether a person is a child is a question of jurisdictional fact which the court determines for itself, so that the court is not confined to the judicial review approach of asking whether or not the authority could have reached its decision on that point: *R (A) v Croydon LBC and (1) Secretary of State for the Home Department (2) Children's Commissioner; R (M) v Lambeth LBC and (1) Secretary of State for the Home Department (2) Children's Commissioner.*[161] Whether a child is 'in need', however, is an evaluative question to be determined by the authority,[162] subject to judicial review on conventional public law grounds: *R (A); R (M).* The question is to be determined by addressing the following, structured questions:

'(i)   is the applicant a child?

'(ii) is the applicant a child in need?

'(iii) is he within the local authority's area?

'(iv) does he appear to the local authority to require accommodation?

'(v) does that need arise as a result of one of the three reasons in section 20(1) CA89? Thus, is the need the result of:

(a)   there being no person who has parental responsibility for him;

(b)   his being lost or having been abandoned; or

(c)   the person who has been caring for him being prevented from providing him with suitable accommodation or care?

'(vi) what are the child's wishes and feelings regarding the provision of accommodation for him?

'(vii)   what consideration (having regard to his age and understanding) is duly to be given to those wishes and feelings?'[163]

---

160 See 2018 guidance, Chapter 2. See also *Robinson v Hammersmith and Fulham LBC* [2006] EWCA Civ 1122, [2006] 1 WLR 3295, [2007] HLR 7; see para **7.169**.
161 [2009] UKSC 8, [2009] 1 WLR 2557, [2010] 1 All ER 469. See, in particular, the opinions of Lady Hale at [14]–[33] and Lord Hope at [51]–[54].
162 Merely carrying out an age assessment at the request of the Home Office, without any approach to the authority by the individual in question or any reason to believe they were in need, does not mean that the authority has accepted responsibility for the child: *R (Birmingham CC) v Croydon LBC* [2021] EWHC 1990 (Admin); [2021] ACD 99.
163 *R (G) v Southwark LBC* [2009] UKHL 26; [2009] 1 WLR 1299, *per* Lady Hale at [28]; see eg *R (BC) v Surrey CC* [2023] EWHC 3209 (Admin); *R (DF) v Essex CC* [2023] EWHC 3330 (Admin).

11.76 Where the age of a person is in dispute, the first step is for the local authority to carry out an age assessment in accordance with the guidance in *R (B) Merton LBC* [2003] EWHC 1689 (Admin); [2003] 4 All ER 280. If the person disagrees with the result of the age assessment, then it is possible to seek judicial review of that decision. In such proceedings, the approach to be taken is that set out in *R (CJ) v Cardiff City Council*:[164] in determining a person's age for the purposes of the CA 1989, the court's role is inquisitorial and it must decide, on the balance of probabilities, if the person in question was a child at the material time; there is no burden of proof for either party to overcome.[165] In *R (AS) v Liverpool CC*,[166] on an application by an asylum-seeker for interim relief under CA 1989, the court said that, in age assessment cases, a high level of scrutiny is called for and the applicant is generally entitled to the benefit of the doubt.

11.77 In *R (FZ) v Croydon LBC*,[167] the Court of Appeal issued procedural guidance to local authorities to be applied in age assessment cases:

a) Where an authority is minded to reach a decision that is adverse to the applicant, it must give the applicant a fair and proper opportunity to deal with important points prior to reaching any final conclusion.

b) Applicants are entitled to have an adult present at any interview.[168]

---

164 [2011] EWCA Civ 1590, [2012] HLR 20.
165 [2011] EWCA Civ 1590, [2012] HLR 20, per Lord Justice Pitchford at [21]–[24]. This 'inquisitorial' approach will cease to be correct when Illegal Migration Act 2023, s 57 comes into force. That section provides that the court must proceed on the 'basis that the person's age is a matter of fact to be determined by the relevant authority' (s 57(4)) and no relief may be granted on the basis that the court considers the decision of the authority to be 'wrong as a matter of fact' (s 57(5)(b)).
166 [2020] EWHC 3531 (Admin), [2021] HLR 24.
167 [2011] EWCA Civ 59, [2011] HLR 22. See also *R (AK) v Secretary of State for the Home Department* [2011] EWHC 3188 (Admin) and *R (K) v Birmingham City Council* [2011] EWHC 1559 (Admin). On 31 December 2020, new guidance on *Assessing age* was issued by the Home Office (available at: www.gov.uk/government/publications/assessing-age-instruction). As with the Homelessness Code of Guidance in England, the online version is updated from time to time and regard must therefore be had to the guidance as it reads at the relevant time.
168 In *R (Ham) v Brent LBC* [2022] EWHC 1924 (Admin); [2022] PTSR 1779, it was said that there is no rigid, check-list approach to age assessment; the key concern is for the authority to carry a reasonable investigation and that it adopts a fair process; eg, there was no rule of law that an appropriate adult always had to be present in every interview conducted by a social worker; the issue was whether a fair interview process required such attendance in the particular case. In *R (SB) v Kensington & Chelsea RLBC* [2022] EWHC 308 (Admin) the asylum-seeker sought judicial review contending that an interview and assessment were unfair because he had no assistance from an interpreter or other adult to support him and ensure he understood questions and help him challenge adverse conclusions which social workers were minded to reach. The claim was allowed: while there was no absolute rule requiring an interpreter or other supportive adult, the process adopted had to be fair – in the present case there appeared to be misunderstanding and confusions arising from the interview which would not have occurred if the asylum-seeker did have an interpreter or other supporter.

c) The correct test for the court to apply is not whether the authority had reached a reasonable decision, but what determination the court makes of the claimant's age for itself.

d) The court is not required to come to the same conclusions as the local authority on all matters, eg, credibility.

e) Considering the balance of probabilities at the permission stage is unhelpful.[169]

f) The burden on the Administrative Court in deciding disputes of fact in age assessment cases is a significant use of resources. In the majority of cases, it would be appropriate to transfer age assessment disputes to the Upper Tribunal, which has sufficient judicial review jurisdiction for this purpose.[170]

11.78   Where an authority provides a child with accommodation pursuant to its duty under CA 1989, s 20, it is not obliged by s 23(6)[171] to make arrangements to enable the child to live with a parent, relative, friend or other person connected with them.[172] Accommodation may be in a regulated setting (eg, with a foster carer) or an unregulated setting (eg, shared housing or a hostel), although the latter was formerly used almost exclusively for 16- and 17-year olds. Since September 2021, it has been unlawful to place a child aged under 16 in an unregulated setting,[173] although such settings may still be used for 16- and 17-year olds, provided it is appropriate in each case:[174] the High Court has inherent

---

169 If permission is granted, interim relief may be available pending the Upper Tribunal decision: see *R (BH) v Newham LBC*, High Court (KBD), 17 May 2023, HousingView, 30 May 2023 – it was noted that the grant of permission meant there was a serious issue as regards age, and as the applicant spoke no English and had no one to support him, it would be an injustice if it turned out that he was a child and he had been without local authority support until the result of the application.

170 A local authority undertaking age assessments for the purposes of the CA 1989 is not bound by any previous age assessment carried out by the Secretary of State or the First-tier Tribunal (Immigration and Asylum Chamber) on appeal: *R (Kadri) v Birmingham City Council* [2012] EWCA Civ 1432, [2013] HLR 4.

171 CA 1989, s 23(6) provided that an authority may provide accommodation with a child's family, relatives or any other suitable person and, so far as is reasonably practicable and consistent with the child's welfare, the authority must make the placement with a parent, person with parental responsibility, relative, friend or other person connected with them; see now CA 1989, s 22C.

172 *R (G) v Barnet LBC; R (W) v Lambeth LBC; R (A) v Lambeth LBC* [2003] UKHL 57, [2004] AC 208, [2004] HLR 10. But see the obiter comments of Lord Nichols at [52] and [55]–[56] on the best interests of the child(ren) and the importance of maintaining the relationship between parent(s) and child(ren). In *R (Bates) v Barking and Dagenham LBC* [2012] EWHC 4128 (Admin), a refusal to house the claimant with her children under CA 1989, s 20 was upheld: the authority was trying to prompt the claimant to organise herself better and seek appropriate assistance, which was a legitimate aim and a lawful decision on the facts.

173 Care Planning, Placement and Case Review (England) (Amendment) Regulations 2021, SI 2021, SI 2021/161.

174 *R (Article 39) v Secretary of State* [2022] EWHC 589 (Admin); [2022] 1 WLR 4240.

jurisdiction to authorise an unregulated setting where there are urgent issues relating to the safety of a child or third party.[175]

11.79 A duty is only owed under CA 1989, s 20 to a 'child in need'. Once a social services department has determined that it owes a duty to a child to provide accommodation under s 20, it cannot sidestep it by securing accommodation pursuant to a different statutory provision, eg, CA 1989, s 17, HA 1996, Part 7[176] or Children and Families Act (CFA) 2014, Part 3.[177] If, however, a child approaches a local housing authority directly and asks for accommodation which is then provided under HA 1996, Part 7, such accommodation can be taken into consideration at the point that the authority carries out its assessment of the child's needs in order to determine if a duty under CA 1989, s 20 exists; accordingly, a determination that adequate housing is already being provided under an alternative legislative provision – so that no duty is owed – is not in these circumstances an unlawful or irrational conclusion.[178] Likewise, where a child leaves home in order to live on their own, there is no duty on the authority to house the child under CA 1989, s 20.[179] A duty may, however, be owed under HA 1996, Part 7.[180] The fact that someone may be statutorily homeless under Part 7 does not, however, automatically or necessarily mean that they are in need of accommodation under s 20; it will depend on the facts – the question is whether they require accommodation not whether or not they qualify as homeless under Part 7,[181] although it will be a relevant consideration.[182]

11.80 To activate the duty to provide accommodation under CA 1989, s 20, notice must be given or a referral made to the social services authority;[183] a social services authority cannot be criticised for not doing something that it had not been given notice it should be doing.[184] Nonetheless, where a child assessed as being in need is erroneously referred to the housing department rather than the

---

175 *A mother v Derby City Council and others* [2021] EWCA Civ 1867; [2022] Fam 351.

176 *R (S) v Sutton LBC* [2007] EWCA Civ 790, (2007) 10 CCLR 615 considered and applied in *R (G) v Southwark LBC* [2009] UKHL 26, [2009] 1 WLR 1299.

177 *R (O) v East Riding of Yorkshire CC* [2011] EWCA Civ 196, [2011] 3 All ER 137. CFA 2014, Part 3 replaced the Education Act 1996, Part 4 in England. CFA 2014 makes provision for the assessment of a child with special educational needs (as defined in CFA 2014, s 20): CFA 2014, s 36. Following a positive assessment, an Education, Health and Care Plan must be produced by a local authority (CFA 2014, s 37). The plan must deal with any social care needs of the child, which includes any services provided by the Local Authority Social Services Act 1970 (CFA 2014, ss 21, 70).

178 *R (B) v Nottingham City Council* [2011] EWHC 2933 (Admin), [2012] JHL D2, QDB.

179 *R (AH) v Cornwall Council* [2010] EWHC 3192 (Admin), [2011] PTSR, D23.

180 *R (AH) v Cornwall Council*, above.

181 Ie they may qualify as homeless according to the statutory definition but factually have accommodation from which they are not at imminent risk of eviction: see, eg *R (DF) v Essex CC* [2023] EWHC 3330 (Admin).

182 *R (DF)*, above.

183 Para **11.7**.

184 *R (M) v Hammersmith and Fulham LBC* [2008] UKHL 14, [2008] 1 WLR 535.

social services department of a unitary authority, the accommodation provided by the authority should be treated as having been provided under CA 1989, s 20.[185]

11.81 It is a question of fact what statutory power has been used to secure accommodation; it is not open to a court to deem a child to have been accommodated under CA 1989, s 20 where some other power was, in fact, used to provide accommodation.[186] Where a local authority is found to have wrongly failed to provide accommodation to someone under section 20 (eg, due to an erroneous assessment of age), it can exercise discretionary powers (such as under LGA 2000 or LA 2011)[187] in order to provide them with some or all of the support services to which they would otherwise have been entitled as a formerly looked after child.[188]

11.82 In considering discharge of the duty under CA 1989, s 20, CA 1989, s 1[189] does not apply to judicial review proceedings involving a challenge to a local authority decision on where to accommodate a child: the role of the court is to review the decision of the local authority. As such, it is not determining a question with respect to the upbringing of the child; there is a number of ways in which the authority could meet the needs of the child and it is for the authority to choose between them.[190]

11.83 A child in need provided with accommodation pursuant to the duty or power in CA 1989, s 20[191] is a 'looked after child' for the purposes of the general duty in CA 1989, s 22. A 'looked after child' may be either a child in the care of the local authority,[192] or a child provided with accommodation by the authority in the exercise of a social services function within the meaning of the Local Authority Social Services Act 1970, other than a function exercised pursuant to CA 1989, ss 17, 23B and 23C.[193]

11.84 The duty under CA 1989, s 22 towards a 'looked after' child is to safeguard and promote the child's welfare and to make such use of services available for children cared for by their own parents as appears reasonable to

---

185 *R (TG) v Lambeth LBC* [2011] EWCA Civ 526, [2011] HLR 33.
186 *R (M) v Hammersmith and Fulham LBC*, above; *R (GE (Eritrea)) v Secretary of State for the Home Department* [2014] EWCA Civ 1490, [2015] 1 WLR 4123.
187 Paras **11.123–11.129**.
188 *R (GE (Eritrea)) v Secretary of State for the Home Department*, [2014] EWCA Civ 1490, [2015] 1 WLR 4123; *R (A) v Enfield LBC* [2016] EWHC 567 (Admin), [2016] HLR 33. As to looked after – and formerly looked after – children, see paras **11.83, 11.86**.
189 This provides that when a court determines any question with respect to the upbringing of a child or the administration of a child's property or the application of any income arising from it, the child's welfare is the court's paramount consideration.
190 *R (O) v Hammersmith and Fulham LBC* [2011] EWCA Civ 925, [2012] 1 WLR 1057.
191 The authority need not provide the accommodation itself but, for it to be considered to have provided accommodation, it must have played some role in in facilitating the accommodation arrangement, whether initially or by way of sustaining it: *Southwark LBC v D* [2007] EWCA Civ 182; *R (BC) v Surrey CC* [2023] EWHC 3209 (Admin).
192 CA 1989, s 22(1)(a).
193 CA 1989, s 22(1)(b).

the authority for a particular child.[194] The duty was extended by Children Act 2004, s 52[195] to include a particular duty to promote the child's educational achievement. The 2004 Act, s 11, imposes a general duty on all local authorities (not only social service authorities) to make arrangements to ensure that their functions are discharged having regard to the need to safeguard and promote the welfare of children.

11.85   An authority may discharge the duty under CA 1989, s 22 by the provision of accommodation for children in care,[196] or by the maintenance of looked after children (other than by provision of accommodation);[197] the provisions also deal with the class of persons with whom a local authority is permitted to make arrangements for a looked after child to be accommodated and the matters to which an authority should have regard when placing a looked after child in accommodation,[198] the circumstances in which an authority must carry out a review before placing a looked after child in accommodation,[199] and the terms under which a child may be placed in a children's home.[200]

11.86   Whether a child has been a 'looked after child' for the purposes of CA 1989, Part 3 is germane to the nature and extent of the duty owed to any child by a local authority once they reach the age of 16 or 17 and becomes a 'relevant child' entitled to advice and assistance under different statutory provisions relating to duties owed by authorities to children leaving care[201] which may include the provision of accommodation.[202]

11.87   Since commencement of the Homelessness Reduction Act (HRA) 2017 on 3 April 2018,[203] where accommodation for a child in care has been provided under CA 1989, s 22A,[204] in circumstances which mean that the child has been normally resident in the district of a local housing authority for a continuous period of at least two years, some or all of which falls before they turn 16, they are deemed to have a local connection with that district, although ceases to do so once they turn 21, unless a local connection can be established on any of the other grounds for it:[205] see Chapter 5. As this operates by way of amendment of the principal Act, there is no reason to think that time before the commencement date is to be disregarded.

---

194 CA 1989, s 22(3).
195 Inserting s 22(3A) into CA 1989.
196 CA 1989, s 22A.
197 CA 1989, s 22B.
198 CA 1989, s 22C.
199 CA 1989, s 22D.
200 CA 1989, s 22E.
201 See paras **11.106–11.116**.
202 CA 1989, s 24A.
203 Homelessness Reduction Act 2017 (Commencement and Transitional and Savings Provisions) Regulations 2018, SI 2018/167, reg 3, only applicable to applications made and reviews sought on or after that date – see reg 4.
204 See para **11.85**.
205 HA 1996, s 199(10), added by HRA 2017, s 8.

Co-operation and notification

England

11.88   Just as housing authorities can seek the co-operation of social services authorities under HA 1996, s 213,[206] social services authorities can ask housing authorities to assist them, in which event the housing authority must comply with the request if it is compatible with its own statutory or other duties and obligations and does not unduly prejudice the discharge of any of its own functions.[207] Such joint working is encouraged by MHCLG[208] and DfE in the joint guidance *Prevention of homelessness and provision of accommodation for 16 and 17 year old young people who may be homeless and/or require accommodation.*[209] This duty to co-operate does not apply where one department of a local authority seeks help from another department of the same authority.[210]

11.89   In *Smith*,[211] the housing authority refused a request from the social services authority for assistance in housing a family with children whom the housing authority had previously found to be intentionally homeless. In the Court of Appeal, it was held that the housing authority could not simply refuse to help by reference to the finding of intentionality. The House of Lords allowed an appeal: although housing and social services authorities were expected to co-operate, if the housing authority could not assist – because no solution was forthcoming which did not unduly prejudice the discharge of its functions – then in the final analysis the children remained the responsibility of the social services authority.

11.90   A further referral and co-operation duty is imposed on English local housing authorities by amendment of HA 1996, Part 7 by the Homelessness Act 2002,[212] which arises[213] where the local housing authority has reason to believe that a homeless applicant with children may be:

a)   ineligible for assistance;[214]

---

206 See para **8.6.**
207 CA 1989, s 27. See also CA 2004, s 10 which places a duty on 'children's services authorities' to make arrangements to promote co-operation between the authority, relevant partners (including district authorities) and other persons or bodies engaged in activities in relation to children, to improve the well-being of children and young people in the authority's area.
208 Joint guidance, April 2018.
209 Available at www.gov.uk/government/publications/provision-of-accommodation-for-16-and-17-year-olds-who-may-be-homeless-and-or-require-accommodation.
210 *R v Tower Hamlets LBC ex p Byas* (1993) 25 HLR 105, CA; *R (Cl) v Hackney LBC* [2014] EWHC 3670 (Admin), [2015] PTSR 1011; and, *R (M and A) v Islington LBC* [2016] EWHC 332 (Admin), [2016] HLR 19.
211 *R v Northavon DC ex p Smith* [1994] 2 AC 402, (1994) 26 HLR 659, HL.
212 This followed the decision of the Court of Appeal in *R (A) v Lambeth LBC* [2001] EWCA Civ 1624, [2002] HLR 13, subsequently upheld in the House of Lords at [2003] UKHL 57, [2004] AC 208, [2004] HLR 10.
213 HA 1996, s 213A(1).
214 See Annex: Immigration Eligibility.

b)   homeless intentionally;[215] or

c)   threatened with homelessness intentionally.[216]

11.91   Given the low standard of satisfaction needed ('have reason to believe'),[217] the housing authority may reach this conclusion prior to a final decision on the homelessness application, and the procedures for referral put into place by CA 1989, s 27 should commence before the applicant is notified of the decision under HA 1996, s 184.[218] In anticipation of this duty, the housing authority must have in place arrangements to invite the applicant to give their consent to a referral either to the social services authority for the area (where a separate authority) or to the social services department (in the case of a unitary authority).[219] Where consent is obtained, the social services authority or department, as may be, must be made aware of the case and notified of any subsequent decision by the authority.[220] These provisions do not affect any other power to disclose information to social services, with or without the consent of the applicant – for example, where the housing authority receives information which might indicate that a child in the family is at risk of significant harm.[221]

11.92   Once a social services authority is made aware that an applicant is ineligible for assistance and homeless intentionally, it may request the local housing authority to provide it with advice and assistance in the exercise of its functions under CA 1989, Part 3;[222] the housing authority must provide 'such advice and assistance as is reasonable in the circumstances'.[223]

11.93   A unitary authority must likewise make arrangement for ensuring that its housing department provides its social services department with such advice and assistance as is reasonably requested.[224] These duties are additional to those

---

215   See Chapter 4. Formerly, this also applied where the applicant was threatened with homelessness; that reference was repealed from 3 April 2018, when HRA 2017 came into force (see Homelessness Reduction Act 2017 (Commencement and Transitional and Savings Provisions) Regulations 2018, reg 3, only applicable to applications made and reviews sought on or after that date – see reg 4), as it was replaced with new provisions: HA 1996, s 213A(1) as amended by HRA 2017, s 4(7)(a)).

216   See para **4.8**.

217   The same standard as triggers the homelessness enquiry duty: see para **7.63**.

218   See para **7.183**.

219   HA 1996, s 213(2)(a), (3)(a).

220   HA 1996, s 213A(2)(b), (3)(b).

221   HA 1996, s 213A(4).

222   HA 1996, s 213A(5). This provision formerly referred also to being threatened with homelessness: it was repealed from 3 April 2018, on the commencement of HRA 2017 (3 April 2018: see Homelessness Reduction Act 2017 (Commencement and Transitional and Savings Provisions) Regulations 2018, reg 3, only applicable to applications made and reviews sought on or after that date – see reg 4), as it was replaced by new provisions: HRA 2017, s 4(7)(b).

223   HA 1996, s 213A(5).

224   HA 1996, s 213A(6). This overturns the decision in *R v Tower Hamlets LBC ex p Byas* (1993) 25 HLR 105, CA, where it was held that the previous duty requiring authority to co-operate (HA 1996, s 213) did not apply where one department of a local authority sought help from another department of the same authority.

in CA 1989, s 27.[225] They do not, however, reverse the position in *Smith*,[226] that where the housing authority/department is unable to provide any assistance, the ultimate responsibility for ensuring that the needs of the children are met remains with the social services authority/department.

11.94 Since HRA 2017 came into force,[227] in England the Secretary of State has had power to specify by regulations a public authority, or public authorities of a particular description, who will be under notification duties under HA 1996, s 213B;[228] public authority means anyone – other than a local housing authority – with functions of a public nature.[229] While most of the HRA 2017 came into force on 3 April 2018 (subject to transitional provisions), the referral duty only applies from 1 October 2018.[230]

11.95 The regulations specify the following:[231]

a) the governor of a prison[232] or the director of a contracted out prison;[233]

b) the governor of a young offender institution;[234]

c) the governor of a secure training centre[235] or the director of a contracted out secure training centre;[236]

d) the principal of a secure college;[237]

e) a youth offending team;[238]

f) a provider of probation services;

g) an officer, designated by the Secretary of State for Work and Pensions for the purposes of HA 1996, s 213B, employed by the secretary of state at an office known as a Jobcentre Plus office;

h) a social services authority;

---

225 See para **11.88**.
226 See para **11.89**. See also English Homelessness Code of Guidance para 8.24.
227 3 April 2018: see Homelessness Reduction Act 2017 (Commencement and Transitional and Savings Provisions) Regulations 2018, reg 3, only applicable to applications made and reviews sought on or after that date – see reg 4.
228 HA 1996, s 213B(4), (5) added by HRA 2017, s 10.
229 This is likely to rely on the same phrase in the definition of public authority under Human Rights Act 1998, s 6(3).
230 Homelessness (Review Procedure etc) Regulations 2018, SI 2018/223, reg 1(3).
231 Homelessness (Review Procedure etc) Regulations 2018, SI 2018/223, Part 4, Schedule. See also English Code of Guidance Chapter 4. In the case of an NHS Trust, see also the non-statutory guidance *Discharging People at risk of experiencing homelessness*, DLUHC and DHSC, January 2024.
232 Prison Act 1952, s 53(1).
233 Criminal Justice Act 1991, s 84(4).
234 Prison Act 1952, s 43(1)(a).
235 Prison Act 1952, s 43(1)(b).
236 Criminal Justice and Public Order Act 1994, s 15.
237 Prison Act 1952, s 43(1)(c).
238 Crime and Disorder Act 1998, s 39(1).

i) a person who performs a function of a local authority pursuant to a direction under Education Act 1996, s 497A(4) or (4A);[239]

j) an NHS trust and an NHS foundation trust, but only in connection with the provision of emergency department and urgent treatment centres and in-patient treatment; and,

k) the Secretary of State for Defence, but only in relation to members of the regular armed forces.

11.96 The duty arises if the specified public authority considers that a person in England in relation to whom the authority exercises any functions is or may be homeless or threatened with homelessness, and asks the person to agree to it notifying a local housing authority in England of its opinion and of how they may be contacted by the local housing authority.[240] The duty does not arise unless the person identifies a local housing authority in England to which they would like the notification to be made.[241] If these conditions are fulfilled, the public authority must notify that local housing authority of its opinion and of the contact information.[242]

11.97 Note, however, that unless the notification also asserts, in whatever terms, that the individual is applying to the housing authority for accommodation or assistance in obtaining it, the duty to make enquiries under HA 1996, s 184[243] does not on the face of it appear to arise, although arguable that if it does intimate that the individual is so applying, the duty does arise: see para **7.66**.

11.98 Guidance to these public authorities has been issued.[244] The duty 'will help to ensure that services are working together effectively to prevent homelessness by ensuring that peoples' housing needs are considered when they come into contact with public authorities. It is also anticipated that it will encourage local housing authorities and other public authorities to build strong partnerships which enable them to work together to intervene earlier to prevent homelessness through increasingly integrated services'; it emphasises that 'someone working for a public authority which is not subject to the duty can still make a referral'.[245]

---

239 Those provisions confer power on the Secretary of State to secure the proper performance of local authority education functions; see CA 2004, s 50 and Childcare Act 2006, s 15.
240 HA 1996, s 213B(2), added by HRA 2017, s 10.
241 HA 1996, s 213B(3), added by HRA 2017, s 10.
242 HA 1996, s 213B(3), added by HRA 2017, s 10.
243 See para **7.63**.
244 *Guide to the duty to refer*, MHCLG, first published on 21 September 2018 and updated 28 September 2018 to give email contacts for local authorities (www.gov.uk/government/publications/homelessness-duty-to-refer/a-guide-to-the-duty-to-refer). It is primarily designed for professionals in those bodies, though 'will also be of interest to homelessness officials in local authorities'.
245 Guide, Section 1 'Introduction'.

11.99   The Guide points out that the duty 'only applies to the specified public authorities in England and individuals can only be referred to a local housing authority in England'.[246] Consent may be given in writing or orally,[247] although it is considered advisable to obtain it in writing.[248] Consent should be 'informed' so that the service user understands the purpose of the referral.[249] 'Public authorities are advised to record on the service user's records if a referral has been made, and if consent to a referral is refused'.[250]

11.100   The Guide states:

> 'Local housing authorities should work with public authorities in their area to design effective referral mechanisms which meet their local circumstances. Local housing authorities should place information on their websites explaining what their referral mechanisms are, and may also have online referral forms for referring public authorities to use.[251]

> Referral mechanisms should be as simple as possible,[252] although the public authority can make a referral to a local housing authority in any manner it wishes providing it includes the minimum information required by law.'[253]

11.101   The Guide's Section 8 'Frequently asked questions', notes that:

> 'It is good practice for local housing authorities to go beyond referral procedures and work with other public authorities to prepare a comprehensive assessment of need for the service user. Local housing authorities and public authorities are encouraged to put arrangements in place to support these joint efforts, and to be open to working together to achieve the best possible solutions for their service users.'[254]

11.102   The Guide also reminds public authorities that – subject to consent – they must make a referral even if aware that another public authority has already done so,[255] although two public authorities may make a joint referral if each has the service user's consent.[256] A public authority with a duty to refer may not simply advise the service user to make an application to a local housing authority

---

246   Guide, Section 2 'Public authorities with a duty to refer'. Public authorities without a duty to refer may, with consent, still make a referral in appropriate circumstances: Guide para 8.6.
247   Guide, Section 3 'Requirements of the duty to refer'.
248   Guide, Section 6, 'Obtaining consent'.
249   Guide, Section 6 'Obtaining consent'.
250   Guide, Section 6 'Obtaining consent'.
251   Guide, Section 7 'Process for referrals'.
252   Guide, Section 7 'Process for referrals'.
253   Guide, Section 7 'Process for referrals'. If the housing authority has its own form, the public authority is entitled to make a referral without using it, although this is discouraged: Guide para 8.11.
254   Guide para 8.2.
255   Guide para 8.4.
256   Guide para 8.5.

but must make the referral itself although may, if it wishes, assist them to make the application.[257]

Wales

11.103 In Wales, a notification duty arises where an authority has reason to believe that an applicant with whom a person under the age of 18 normally resides, or might reasonably be expected to reside, may be ineligible for help, may be homeless, but that a duty under H(W)A 2014, ss 68,[258] 73[259] or 75[260] is not likely to apply, or that the authority has reason to believe that an applicant may be threatened with homelessness and that a duty under s 66[261] is not likely to apply.[262]

11.104 In such cases, the authority must make arrangements for ensuring that the applicant is invited to consent to the referral to the social services department of the essential facts of their case, and, if they have given that consent, that the social services department is made aware of those facts and of the subsequent decision in respect of their case.[263]

11.105 The authority must also make arrangements to ensure that where it makes a decision that an applicant is ineligible for help, became homeless intentionally or became threatened with homelessness intentionally, its housing department provides the social services department with such advice and assistance as the social services department reasonably requests.[264]

Children leaving care

11.106 In certain circumstances, local social services authorities are under a duty to provide services[265] to children who are about to leave the care of the local authority and to children who were previously in its care. As before, duties under these provisions are not excluded by the Immigration and Asylum Act 1999.[266] The statutory scheme governing these duties was introduced by the Children

---

257 Guide para 8.7.
258 Para **8.12**.
259 Paras **8.104–8.106**.
260 Paras **8.124–8.128**.
261 Para **8.84**.
262 H(W)A 2014, s 96(1).
263 H(W)A 2014, s 96(2).
264 H(W)A 2014, s 96(4).
265 From 1 April 2018, the Children and Social Work Act 2017 has placed authorities under a duty to publish information about what support is available to eligible, relevant and former relevant children, including information about what accommodation is available from the authority (Children and Social Work Act 2017, s 2): Children and Social Work Act 2017 (Commencement No 3) Regulations 2018, SI 2018/346.
266 Para **11.60**.

(Leaving Care) Act 2000. There are three categories towards whom a local authority might owe a duty:

a) an eligible child;

b) a relevant child;

c) a former relevant child.

11.107 An 'eligible child' is a child aged 16 or 17 who has been 'looked after'[267] by a local authority[268] for a prescribed period,[269] which is 13 weeks.[270] The duty owed to an eligible child is not the provision of accommodation per se, but to arrange for the child to have a personal advisor[271] and to carry out an assessment of the child's needs to determine what advice, assistance and support it would be appropriate for the authority to provide both while it is still looking after the eligible child and after it ceases to do so.[272] Such assistance and support can include the provision of accommodation. The authority must complete a pathway plan following the assessment which the authority must keep under regular review.[273]

11.108 A 'relevant child' is a child aged 16 or 17 who would otherwise be an eligible child because they were looked after by a local authority for a prescribed period,[274] but whom the authority has ceased to look after and who is not now being looked after by any authority.[275] The duty owed to a relevant child is the same as that owed to an eligible child, but includes a requirement for the authority to 'stay in touch'[276] with the relevant child; the duty requires the authority to provide the relevant child with suitable accommodation unless the authority is satisfied that the relevant child's welfare does not require it.[277]

11.109 Under CA 1989, s 23B(10), regulations may be made to govern the meaning of 'suitable accommodation'. Schedule 2 to the Care Leavers (England)

---

267 See para **11.83**.
268 It must be by the authority, not (for example) pursuant to an informal agreement by a family member during care proceedings (*Re B (a child) (looked-after child)* [2013] EWCA Civ 964, [2014] 1 FLR 277; *R (O) v Doncaster MBC* [2014] EWHC 2309 (Admin); *R (T) v Hertfordshire CC* [2016] EWCA Civ 1108, [2017] HLR 10. The position would be different if the child had been placed with a relative by the authority pursuant to its power under CA 1989, s 22C.
269 CA 1989, Sch 2, Part 2 para 19B.
270 Care Planning, Placement and Case Review (England) Regulations 2010, SI 2010/959 from 1 April 2011. For a child who was an eligible child prior to 1 April 2011, see the Children (Leaving Care) (England) Regulations 2001, SI 2001/2874. The prescribed period is the same under both sets of regulations. The period need not be continuous, see CA 1989, Sch 2 para 19B(2)(b).
271 CA 1989, Sch 2, Part 2 para 19C.
272 CA 1989, Sch 2, Part 2 para 19B.
273 CA 1989, Sch 2, Part 2 para 19B.
274 13 weeks (see Care Leavers (England) Regulations 2010, SI 2010/2571, reg 3).
275 CA 1989, s 23A.
276 CA 1989, s 23B(1).
277 CA 1989, s 23B.

Regulations 2010[278] provides that matters to be taken into consideration when determining the suitability of accommodation include the facilities and services provided, the state of repair of the accommodation, safety, location, support, tenancy status and the financial commitments involved for the relevant child and their affordability.[279] The authority should also take into consideration the child's views about the accommodation, their understanding of rights and responsibilities in relation to the accommodation, and their understanding of funding arrangements.[280]

11.110   A 'former relevant child' is a person aged 18 years or over who was previously a relevant child[281] or who was an eligible child[282] immediately before they ceased to be looked after by the local authority.[283] The duty owed to a former relevant child is for the local authority to take reasonable steps to stay in touch, or if it loses touch to re-establish contact, and to appoint a personal advisor, carry out an assessment and create a care plan which it must keep under review.[284]

11.111   While there is no duty to provide accommodation, there is power for the authority to provide other assistance,[285] which is wide enough to include a contribution towards accommodation expenses in connection with education expenses.[286] When considering whether to exercise that power, the authority cannot take into account the possibility of support that might be provided under IAA 1999, s 95.[287] Nor can the authority withdraw support in circumstances where to do so would be tantamount to pre-empting a decision on an asylum application.[288]

---

278 Care Leavers (England) Regulations 2010, SI 2010/2571.
279 Care Leavers (England) Regulations 2010, SI 2010/2571, Sch 2 para 1.
280 Care Leavers (England) Regulations 2010, SI 2010/2571, Sch 2 para 2. The MHCLG and the DfE have published a non-statutory good practice guide to support care leavers, recommending the establishment of a joint protocol between housing and children services teams, to be reviewed annually and developed in consultation with local service providers; the protocol should deal with how to assist a care leaver in moving from a care placement into independent living, both in terms of helping to identify suitable accommodation and ensuring that the care leaver has the relevant skills to manage their own finances: *Joint housing protocols for care leavers: good practice advice*, MHCLG and DfE, October 2020 (www.gov.uk/government/publications/joint-housing-protocols-for-care-leavers).
281 See para **11.86**.
282 See para **11.107**.
283 CA 1989, s 23C.
284 CA 1989, s 23C.
285 Under CA 1989, s 23C(4).
286 *R (Sabiri) v Croydon LBC* [2012] EWHC 1236 (Admin).
287 *R (O) v Barking and Dagenham LBC* [2010] EWCA Civ 1101, [2011] 1 WLR 1283, [2011] 1 FLR 734, [2011] HLR 4, (2010) 13 CCLR 591.
288 *R (Birara) v Hounslow LBC* [2010] EWHC 2113 (Admin), [2010] 3 FCR 21, (2010) 13 CCLR 685.

11.112 In *R (TG) v Lambeth LBC*,[289] a social worker employed by the authority's Youth Offending Team[290] correctly identified the applicant as a child in need for the purposes of CA 1989, Part 3,[291] but failed to make the necessary referral to the social services department. Accommodation was instead provided by the housing department. The authority accordingly denied that the claimant was a former relevant child as it had not provided the accommodation pursuant to CA 1989, s 20 and refused to provide services to the claimant as if they were a relevant child or former relevant child.

11.113 The Court of Appeal held that the social worker was to be regarded as the 'eyes and ears' of the social services department and that, as she had assisted the applicant to find accommodation, it should be 'treated or deemed'[292] to have been provided under CA 1989, s 20; the claimant was therefore, and was to be treated as, a former relevant child for the purposes of CA 1989 with all the rights and benefits that flowed from that.

11.114 See also *R (R) v Croydon LBC*,[293] where the court held that, where the local authority undoubtedly knew that the claimant was a child and entitled to accommodation under CA 1989, s 20, accommodation provided by (what is now) UKVI should be deemed to have been provided by the local authority.[294]

11.115 The courts will, however, only intervene where litigation is necessary. Thus, judicial review was not available where the authority, while denying that claimants were 'former relevant children' for the purposes of CA 1989, s 23C, had nevertheless agreed voluntarily to offer them all the services equivalent to those to which they would have been entitled if they had been.[295]

11.116 Note that[296] so long as an authority in England has a duty under CA 1989, s 23C towards a former relevant child, then, if the authority is a local housing

---

289 [2011] EWCA Civ 526, [2011] HLR 33.

290 Local authorities – as defined in Crime and Disorder Act (CDA) 1998, s 42(1) – must establish youth offending teams (YOTs), who are responsible for, among other things, the supervision and rehabilitation of young offenders: CDA1998, ss 38(4) and 39(7). A YOT must include at least one person who is a social worker in the local authority's social services department: CDA 1998, s 39(5)(a).

291 See para **11.79**.

292 At [43]. In *R (GE (Eritrea)) v Secretary of State for the Home Department* [2014] EWCA Civ 1490, [2015] 1 WLR 4123, it was said that *TG* was not a case of (impermissible – see para **11.81**) deeming, but, rather, a case where the 'provision of accommodation by the local authority could be attributed to its social services function' (at [33]).

293 [2013] EWHC 4243 (Admin), [2012] JHL D58.

294 Although this decision was doubted in *R (GE (Eritrea)) v Secretary of State for the Home Department* [2014] EWCA Civ 1490, [2015] 1 WLR 4123, which reiterated that 'deeming' is impermissible.

295 *R (C) v Nottingham City Council* [2010] EWCA Civ 790, [2011] 1 FCR 127.

296 Since 3 April 2018, commencement of HRA 2017: 3 April 2018: see Homelessness Reduction Act 2017 (Commencement and Transitional and Savings Provisions) Regulations 2018, reg 3, only applicable to applications made and reviews sought on or after that date – see reg 4.

authority as well as a social services authority,[297] the former relevant child is deemed to have a local connection with its area; and if the authority is not a local housing authority,[298] a local connection with every district in its area:[299] paras **5.25–5.26**.

Social Services and Well-being (Wales) Act 2014

11.117 From 6 April 2016, the position in respect of children in Wales has been governed by the SSWB(W)A 2014. Welsh local authorities[300] have both a duty and a power to meet the care and support needs of a child.[301] In order to meet needs, authorities may provide, inter alia, 'accommodation in a care home, children's home or premises of some other type'.[302] Again, duties under these provisions are not excluded by the Immigration and Asylum Act 1999.[303]

11.118 Where it appears to a local authority that a child may need care and support in addition to, or instead of, the care and support provided by their family, the authority must assess whether they do have such needs and, if so, what those needs are.[304] As part of that assessment, the authority must seek to identify outcomes that the child wishes to achieve, that persons with parental responsibility wish to achieve for the child, and that persons specified in regulations[305] wish to achieve for the child.[306] Where the authority is satisfied, on the basis of the needs assessment, that a person has needs for care and support, it must determine whether their needs meet the eligibility criteria and, if satisfied that they do so, it must, among other things, consider what could be done to meet those needs.[307]

11.119 Subject to exceptions,[308] the duty to meet a child's needs arises where:

a)   the child is in the authority's area;[309] and

---

297 Para **11.7**.
298 Ie, county council in non-metropolitan areas.
299 HA 1996, s 199(8), added by HRA 2017, s 8, with effect from 3 April 2018: see Homelessness Reduction Act 2017 (Commencement and Transitional and Savings Provisions) Regulations 2018, reg 3, only applicable to applications made and reviews sought on or after that date – see reg 4.
300 The council of a county or county borough in Wales: SSWB(W)A 2014, s 197(1).
301 SSWB(W)A 2014, ss 37 and 38. There is also a duty and a power to meet the needs for care and support of a child carer: SSWB(W)A 2014, ss 42 and 45.
302 SSWB(W)A 2014, s 34(2)(a).
303 Para **11.60**,
304 SSWB(W)A 2014, s 21(1).
305 No such regulations have yet been made.
306 SSWB(W)A 2014, s 21(4)(b).
307 SSWB(W)A 2014, s 32.
308 The duty does not apply if the authority is satisfied that the child's needs are being met by the child's family or a carer, or if the child is being looked after by a local authority or a Health and Social Care Trust: SSWB(W)A 2014, s 37(5), (6).
309 SSWB(W)A 2014, s 37(2).

b) either:

    i)   the child's needs meet the eligibility criteria (see next paragraph); or

    ii)   the local authority considers it necessary to meet the child's needs in order to protect the child from abuse or neglect (or a risk of abuse or neglect), or other harm (or a risk of such harm).[310]

11.120 The child's needs meet the eligibility criteria if:

a) the need arises from the child's physical or mental ill-health, age, disability, dependence on alcohol or drugs, or other similar circumstances, or if the need is one that if unmet is likely to have an adverse effect on the child's development;[311]

b) the need relates to one or more of a list of specified matters;[312]

c) the need is one that neither the child, the child's parents nor other persons in a parental role is able to meet;[313] and

d) the child is unlikely to meet one or more of their personal outcomes unless, among other things, care and support is provided.[314]

11.121 The power to meet a child's needs for care and support is expressed in very broad terms. An authority may meet any child's needs for care and support if they are either within its area, or ordinarily resident in its area but presently outside of it.[315] The power to meet needs may be used whether or not an assessment has been completed.[316]

11.122 Further duties to provide accommodation for children are contained in SSWB(W)A 2014, s 76. These are, so far as material, in the same terms as CA 1989, s 20.[317]

---

310 SSWB(W)A 2014, s 37(3).
311 Care and Support (Eligibility) (Wales) Regulations 2015, SI 2015/1578, reg 4(1)(a). References to a child's development include the physical, intellectual, emotional, social and behavioural development of that child: reg 4(2)(i).
312 a) The ability to carry out self-care or domestic routines; b) the ability to communicate; c) protection from abuse or neglect; d) involvement in work, education, learning or in leisure activities; e) maintenance or development of family or other significant personal relationships; f) development and maintenance of social relationships and involvement in the community; and g) achieving developmental goals: Care and Support (Eligibility) (Wales) Regulations 2015, SI 2015/1578, reg 4(1)(b).
313 Care and Support (Eligibility) (Wales) Regulations 2015, SI 2015/1578, reg 4(1)(c).
314 Care and Support (Eligibility) (Wales) Regulations 2015, SI 2015/1578, reg 4(1)(d). The personal outcomes are those identified under SSWB(W)A 2014, s 21(4)(b): reg 1(3).
315 SSWB(W)A 2014, s 38(1).
316 SSWB(W)A 2014, s 38(3).
317 Likewise, similar duties exist for those leaving care, see SSWB(W)A 2014, Part 6; and the Care Leavers (Wales) Regulations 2015, SI 2015/1820.

LOCAL GOVERNMENT ACT 2000/LOCALISM ACT 2011/ LOCAL GOVERNMENT AND ELECTIONS (WALES) ACT 2021

11.123 The LGA 2000 provided a new power of 'well-being' applicable in both England and Wales. Section 2 provides, so far as relevant:

> '(1) Every local authority are to have power to do anything which they consider is likely to achieve any one or more of the following objects–
>
> . . .
>
> (b) the promotion or improvement of the social well-being of their area . . .'

11.124 As discussed below, s 2 has now been overtaken by other provisions in both England and Wales, although the case-law under it is likely to be considered in relation to the newer provisions. The power could be exercised for the benefit of the whole or any part of the local authority's area,[318] or of all or any persons resident or present in it.[319] Well-being powers could not, however, be used where there was a prohibition, restriction or limitation on the authority's power to act 'contained in' any enactment, whenever passed or made.[320] The courts inclined against finding implied restrictions and tended to interpret the limitation as referring only to cases where these was an express restriction.[321] Use of the provision was, however, excluded in the case of some classes of immigrant, being those classes (subject to exceptions, including the overarching exception for British citizens and persons under the age of 18,[322] and the human rights/ EC Treaty exceptions)[323] considered in the Annex: Immigration Eligibility.[324]

11.125 From 18 February 2012, LA 2011, s 1 introduced a further new power, to replace well-being in England (but not Wales), being a 'power of general competence'.[325] The repeal of well-being powers in England, and the amendment of the LGA 2000 to confine its operation to Wales, did not take effect until 4 April

---

318 LGA 2000, s 2(2)(a).

319 LGA 2000, s 2(2)(b).

320 LGA 2000, s 3(1).

321 *R (J) v Enfield LBC* [2002] EWHC 432 (Admin), [2002] HLR 38; *R (Theophilus) v Lewisham LBC* [2002] EWHC 1371 (Admin), [2002] 3 All ER 851; *R (W) v Lambeth LBC* [2002] EWCA Civ 613, [2002] HLR 41, (2002) 5 CCLR 203, per Brooke LJ at [75]; *R (Khan) v Oxfordshire CC* [2004] EWCA Civ 309, [2004] HLR 41; *R (Grant) v Lambeth LBC* [2004] EWCA Civ 1711, [2005] HLR 27; *R (Richards) West Somerset Council* [2008] EWHC 3215 (Admin). The power under LGA 2000, s 2 does not, however, enable an authority to promote its own economic well-being: *Brent LBC v Risk Management Partners Ltd* [2009] EWCA Civ 490 (the point did not arise on the subsequent Supreme Court appeal: [2011] UKSC 7, [2011] 2 AC 34).

322 See para **A.172**.

323 See paras **A.175–A.183**.

324 Ibid.

325 Localism Act 2011 (Commencement No 3) Order 2012, SI 2012/411.

2012. In Wales, the equivalent 'power of general competence' was enacted by Part 2, Local Government and Elections (Wales) Act 2021 (LGE(W)A 2021) and the well-being power repealed with effect from 5 May 2022.[326]

11.126 The power of general competence is a power to do anything that individuals – with full capacity – generally may do, even though they are in nature, extent or otherwise unlike anything the authority may do without the power, or unlike anything that other public bodies may do.[327] The power may be exercised anywhere in the UK or elsewhere, and is not limited by the existence of any other power of the authority which overlaps the general power, just as any such other power is not limited by the existence of the general power.[328]

11.127 If, however, exercise of the power 'overlaps with' a pre-commencement power which is subject to restrictions, those restrictions apply to exercise of the power 'so far as it is overlapped' by the pre-commencement power;[329] nor can the authority do anything which they are unable to do by reason of a pre-commencement limitation;[330] nor can the general power be used to do anything which they are unable to do by virtue of a post-commencement limitation which is expressed to apply to it or to all of the authority's powers (or to all of the authority's powers subject to exceptions which do not include the general power).[331]

11.128 While LGA 2000, s 2 was primarily intended for strategic use,[332] cases under it nonetheless affirmed its availability for use as a 'safety-net', including the

---

326 Localism Act 2011 (Commencement No 5 and Transitional, Savings and Transitory Provisions) Order 2012, SI 2012/1008 (England); Local Government and Elections (Wales) Act 2021 (Commencement No. 1 and Saving Provision) Order 2021, SI 2021/231 (Wales).
327 LA 2011, s 1(2); LGE(W)A 2021, s 24(1).
328 LA 2011, s 1(5), (6); LGE(W)A 2021, s 24(2), (3).
329 LA 2011, s 2(1); LGE(W)A 2021, s 25(1).
330 Thus, in *R (AR) v Hammersmith and Fulham LBC* [2018] EWHC 3453 (Admin), (2019) 22 CCLR 56, the claimant was ineligible for HA 1996, Part 7 assistance and did not qualify for assistance under the Care Act 2014: LA 2011, s 1 could not be used to provide accommodation as HA 1996, s 185 comprised a pre-commencement limitation within LA 2011, s 2. In *Ncube v Brighton and Hove City Council* [2021] EWHC 578 (Admin); [2021] 1 WLR 4762; [2021] HLR 31 it was likewise held that the provision was unavailable in relation to a failed asylum-seeker excluded from HA 1996, Part 7 assistance by HA 1996, s 185 and responsibility for whom lay with the secretary of state under Immigration and Asylum Act 1999; the court did not rule, however, on whether the provision might be available in other cases not involving asylum-seekers in order to avoid a breach of their ECHR rights.
331 LA 2011, s 2(2); LGE(W)A 2021, s 25(2). In *R (Khan) v Oxfordshire CC* [2004] EWCA Civ 309, [2004] HLR 41, Dyson LJ said of the analogous provision in LGA 2000, s 3 (above, para **11.124**): '41. The effect of s 3(1) is to prohibit the doing of "anything" which a local authority is unable to do by virtue of any prohibition on its powers contained in any enactment. ... [T]he very reason why s 3(1) was enacted was to prevent s 2 being used to do that which is prohibited by another statute. ... If Mr Jay were right, it would seem that no statutory prohibition would trump s 2 of the LGA unless it stated expressly that it was a prohibition for the purposes of s 3 of the LGA ...'.
332 See the requirement in LGA 2000, s 2(3) to have regard to the authority's community strategy (made under LGA 2000, s 4) in determining whether and how to use the power.

provision of accommodation.[333] The power was likewise held to be wide enough to permit an authority to fund travel arrangements for a person unlawfully in the UK, where exercising that power was necessary to avoid breaching the person's rights under the ECHR.[334]

11.129 There is no reason to believe that LA 2011, s 1/ LGE(W)A 2021, s 24 will be interpreted differently. The power will not, however, become a duty even if use of the power is the only way to avoid a breach of human rights: *Morris,*[335] applying the decision of the House of Lords in *Hooper,*[336] and overruling the decision in *J.*[337]

OTHER STATUTORY PROVISIONS

Local Government Act 1972, s 138

11.130 Local Government Act 1972, s 138, as amended, provides as follows.

'(1) Where an emergency or disaster involving destruction of or danger to life or property occurs or is imminent or there is reasonable ground for apprehending such an emergency or disaster, and a principal council are of opinion that it is likely to affect the whole or part of their area or all or some of its inhabitants, the council may–

(a) incur such expenditure as they consider necessary in taking action themselves (either alone or jointly with any other person or body and either in their area or elsewhere in or outside the United Kingdom) which is calculated to avert, alleviate or eradicate in their area or among its inhabitants the effects or potential effects of the event; and

(b) make grants or loans to other persons or bodies on conditions determined by the council in respect of any such action taken by those persons or bodies.

. . .

(3) Nothing in this section authorises a local authority to execute–

---

333 See, eg, *R (J) v Enfield LBC* [2002] EWHC 432 (Admin), [2002] HLR 38.
334 *R (Grant) v Lambeth LBC*, above; see also *R (Theophilus) v Lewisham LBC*, above, authorising a student loan to someone not otherwise entitled to assistance.
335 *R (Morris) v Westminster City Council (No 3)* [2005] EWCA Civ 1184, [2006] 1 WLR 505, [2006] HLR 8.
336 *R (Hooper) v Secretary of State for Work and Pensions* [2005] UKHL 29, [2005] 1 WLR 1681.
337 *R (J) v Enfield LBC*, above.

(a) any drainage or other works in any part of a main river, within the meaning of Part IV of the Water Resources Act 1991, or of any other watercourse which is treated for the purposes of any of the provisions of that Act as part of a main river, or

(b) any works which local authorities have power to execute under sections 14 to 17, 62(2) and (3) and 66 of the Land Drainage Act 1991,

but subject to those limitations, the powers conferred by subsection (1) above are in addition to, and not in derogation of, any power conferred on a local authority by or under any other enactment, including any enactment contained in this Act.

(4) In this section 'principal council' includes the Common Council and, until 1st April 1974, the council of an existing county, county borough or county district.

. . .'

11.131 Where the conditions in subsection (1) are fulfilled, these powers are wide enough to include the provision of accommodation for homeless persons, including those who are excluded from assistance under HA 1996, Part 7 in England or H(W)A 2014, Part 2 in Wales;[338] thus, its availability was upheld in relation to the Covid-19 pandemic.[339]

Mental Health Act 1983, s 117

11.132 Where someone has been released after being detained or admitted under one of a number of provisions of the Mental Health Act 1983,[340] they are entitled to 'after-care services'[341] from or arranged by one of a number of bodies[342] until such time as the body is satisfied that they are no longer in need of such services.[343] If ordinarily resident in an area in England or Wales immediately before being detained, the duty is imposed on the body for that area; otherwise,

---

338 Paras **A.127–A.129**.
339 *R (Ncube) v Brighton and Hove City Council* [2021] EWHC 578 (Admin); [2021] 1 WLR 4762; [2021] HLR 31. Following this decision, in December 2021 the Minister for Rough Sleeping wrote to local authorities in England to urge them to 'make offers of safe and appropriate accommodation to people who are sleeping rough' and, in particular, to assist them to obtain coronavirus vaccinations. The letter refers to the possibility of support regardless of immigration status under s 2B, National Health Service Act 2006, ss 73B and 138, Local Government Act 1972 and s 1, Localism Act 2011.
340 Sections 3, 37, 45A, 47 and 48.
341 It seems clear that this can include accommodation if needed to reduce reducing the risk of a deterioration and requiring re-admission: Mental Health Act 1983, s 117(6).
342 Integrated care board, Local Health Board and local social services authority.
343 Mental Health Act 1983, s 117(2).

it is the body for the area in which they reside or to which they are sent by the hospital.[344]

Child Abduction and Custody Act 1985, s 5

11.133   Child Abduction and Custody Act (CACA) 1985, s 5 provides:

> 'Where an application has been made to a court in the United Kingdom under the Convention, the court may, at any time before the application is determined, give such interim directions as it thinks fit for the purpose of securing the welfare of the child concerned or of preventing changes in the circumstances relevant to the determination of the application.'

11.134   The convention referred to in section 5 is the Hague Convention.[345] The word 'directions' refers to orders of the court directing the provision of accommodation.[346] In *Re A (children) (abduction: interim powers)*,[347] the Court of Appeal held that the provisions of CACA 1985, s 5 should be construed widely and that the court has the power to direct a local authority to provide accommodation for an alleged abductor and an allegedly abducted child, pending determination of an application for the return of the child. Moreover, it held that an order for the provision of accommodation is an order made for the purpose of securing the welfare of the child; accordingly, interim directions can include an order that a child, or a child's family, are provided with accommodation.[348]

National Health Service Act 2006, s 2B

11.135   Likewise, there is the possibility of assistance for the homeless who are excluded from HA 1996, Part 7[349] under National Health Service Act 2006, s 2B, which is only applicable in England, which provides as follows:

> '(1)   Each local authority must take such steps as it considers appropriate for improving the health of the people in its area.
>
> (2)   The Secretary of State may take such steps as the Secretary of State considers appropriate for improving the health of the people of England.

344   MHA 1983, s 117(3); see also *R (Worcestershire CC) v (1) Secretary of State (2) Swindon BC* [2023] UKSC 31 – where there had been two periods of detention under s 3, the duty passed to the authority for the second area in which the patient had been living before the second detention.
345   CACA 1985, s 1.
346   *Re A (children) (abduction: interim powers), sub nom EA v GA* [2010] EWCA Civ 586, [2011] 2 WLR 1269.
347   [2010] EWCA Civ 586, [2011] Fam 179, [2011] 2 WLR 1269.
348   [2010] EWCA Civ 586, [2011] Fam 179, [2011] 2 WLR 1269 at [38].
349   Paras **A.127–A.129**.

(3)   The steps that may be taken under subsection (1) or (2) include–

(a)   providing information and advice;

(b)   providing services or facilities designed to promote healthy living (whether by helping individuals to address behaviour that is detrimental to health or in any other way);

(c)   providing services or facilities for the prevention, diagnosis or treatment of illness;

(d)   providing financial incentives to encourage individuals to adopt healthier lifestyles;

(e)   providing assistance (including financial assistance) to help individuals to minimise any risks to health arising from their accommodation or environment;

(f)   providing or participating in the provision of training for persons working or seeking to work in the field of health improvement;

(g)   making available the services of any person or any facilities.

(4)   The steps that may be taken under subsection (1) also include providing grants or loans (on such terms as the local authority considers appropriate).

(5)   In this section, 'local authority' means–

(a)   a county council in England;

(b)   a district council in England, other than a council for a district in a county for which there is a county council;

(c)   a London borough council;

(d)   the Council of the Isles of Scilly;

(e)   the Common Council of the City of London.'

11.136 This possibility was also upheld in relation to the Covid-19 pandemic,[350] but, while the emergency circumstances in Local Government Act 1972, s 138[351] may not commonly be fulfilled, the condition that powers be exercised for the improvement of the health of the people in an authority's area will be readily fulfilled all of the time; that said, it is of course subject to the authority's consideration of whether it is appropriate to exercise any or all of those powers.

11.137 The power does not comprise a duty owed to an individual, in the way that, for example, Part 7 duties are owed. In *Ncube*, the court said (at para 76):

'The point is the stronger because there is no duty owed to an individual under s 2B of the National Health Service Act 2006. The question which is

---

350   *R (Ncube) v Brighton and Hove City Council*, above.
351   Para **11.130**.

being addressed is whether the provision of accommodation, to the extent that it is for the purpose of satisfying a public health need, is prohibited by statute. Provided that this power is not being used to circumvent the limitations of the role of a local authority under s 185 of the Housing Act 1996 to individual applicants, then it would not be unlawful to fulfil public health functions by reference to s 2B of the National Health Service Act 2006.'

11.138 It would seem to follow that an individual homeless person may ask the authority to exercise powers under s 2B and, if they do so, that the authority must *consider* use of the power. Of course, for an individual to do so in any enforceable way, the issue of health would need to be present, but that will also be a commonplace if not an invariable feature where the homeless outside Part 7[352] are concerned.

---

352 Which is not to say that it will not commonly be present where those within Part 7 are concerned.

CHAPTER 12

Ancillary Provisions

INTRODUCTION

12.1   In this chapter, we consider the ancillary provisions related to homelessness.

12.2   There are five such sets of provision:

a)   homelessness strategies;

b)   advisory services;

c) assistance to the voluntary sector;

d) codes of practice; and

e) criminal provisions.

HOMELESSNESS STRATEGIES

12.3   By Homelessness Act 2002, s 1, all local housing authorities are required to carry out a homelessness review and formulate and publish a strategy based on that review:[1] by Homelessness Act 2002, s 1(3) and (4), the first such strategy had to be drawn up within a year of the section coming into force,[2] and thereafter at least every five years.[3]

12.4   This exercise is to be carried out with the assistance of the local social services authority.[4] Both the housing and social services authorities have to take the strategy into account in exercising their functions.[5]

12.5   Initially, these provisions applied to both England and Wales: since 1 December 2014, the position in Wales has been governed by Housing (Wales) Act (H(W)A) 2014, s 50. A Welsh authority must carry out a homelessness review for its area, and formulate and adopt a homelessness strategy based on the results of that review.[6] There is no requirement that the exercise be carried out with the assistance of the local social services authority as all Welsh authorities are unitary, ie, have both housing and social service functions. The strategy must be taken into

---

1   Homelessness Act 2002, s 1(1). See the English *Homelessness code of guidance for local authorities* Chapter 2 (Ministry of Housing, Communities and Local Government (MHCLG), February 2018, updated May 2023; www.gov.uk/guidance/homelessness-code-of-guidance-for-local-authorities). The Code stresses the importance of ensuring that local authorities use their allocation policies to assist with preventing or relieving homelessness: see Code paras 2.44–2.50. In Wales, see the *Code of guidance for local authorities on the allocation of accommodation and homelessness* Chapter 5 (Welsh Government, March 2016; gov.wales/allocation-accommodation-and-homelessness-guidance-local-authorities).

2   That was by 31 July 2003 in England, 30 September 2003 in Wales.

3   An English authority which was categorised as an 'excellent authority' or a three- or four-star authority under an order made under Local Government Act 2003, s 99(4) was exempt from the requirement to publish further strategies: Local Authorities' Plans and Strategies (Disapplication) (England) Order 2005, SI 2005/157. Section 99 was repealed with effect from 1 April 2015 by Local Audit and Accountability Act 2014, Sch 12 para 53. All English authorities are now required to publish a homelessness strategy 'as of 01 April 2017': English Code of Guidance para 2.3.

4   Homelessness Act 2002, s 1(2). Within the meaning of the Local Authority Social Services Act 1970 or Social Services and Well-Being (Wales) Act 2014, Part 8 (see Homelessness Act 2002, s 4, for both definitions).

5   Homelessness Act 2002, s 1(5), (6).

6   H(W)A 2014, s 50(1). The strategy can form part of the Well-being Plan under the Well-being of Future Generations (Wales) Act 2015; Welsh Code para.5.4.

account by the authority when exercising any of its functions.[7] The strategy must be adopted in 2018, with a new strategy every fourth year thereafter.[8]

Reviews

12.6 'Homelessness review' is defined in Homelessness Act 2002, s 2 and H(W)A 2014, s 51 as a review of:

a) the current and likely future levels of homelessness in an authority's district;[9]

b) the activities carried out in the authority's area for:[10]

    i) preventing homelessness;[11]

    ii) securing that accommodation[12] is or will be available in the area for people who are or may become homeless;[13] and

    iii) providing support[14] for such people or for those who have been homeless and need support to prevent it recurring;[15] and

c) the resources available to the authority, the social services authority,[16] other public authorities, voluntary organisations[17] and other persons for such activities.[18]

---

7   H(W)A 2014, s 50(4).

8   H(W)A 2014, s 50(2). The Welsh Code of Guidance notes that the strategy should reflect the Welsh Government's Ten Year Homeless Plan 2009–2019 (July 2009), para 5.7. That plan was not replaced with a similar ten-year plan; rather, the current strategic priorities of the Welsh Government are to be found in *Ending Homelessness in Wales: A high level action plan 2021-2026*, Welsh Government, 2021.

9   See English Code of Guidance paras 2.17–2.18; Welsh Code paras 5.17–5.37.

10 See English Code of Guidance paras 2.14–2.29.

11 The English Code draws particular attention to the needs of Gypsies and Travellers, see para 2.16.

12 H(W)A 2014, s 51(1)(b)(ii) refers to suitable accommodation.

13 The English Code stresses the need to ensure a sufficient supply of accommodation and to increase the supply of new housing (Code paras 2.31–2.33 and 2.37–2.42); as regards the latter, it encourages authorities to have regard to the National Planning Policy Framework and to ensure that their Local Plan (see Planning and Compulsory Purchase Act 2004) 'meets the full, objectively assessed needs for market and affordable housing in the housing market area, as far as is consistent with the policies set out in the Framework' (Code para 2.39).

14 Support means 'advice, information or assistance': Homelessness Act 2002, s 4. There is no definition in H(W)A 2014.

15 In Wales, the requirement is for 'satisfactory support': H(W)A 2014, s 51(1)(b)(iii).

16 This is omitted from H(W)A 2014, s 51(1)(c) as all Welsh authorities are unitary and, as such, also social services authorities; instead, a Welsh authority is required to have regard to any resources available to it in the exercise of other statutory functions, ie, it is required to have regard to social service as well as housing resources.

17 By Homelessness Act 2002, s 4, this has the same definition as HA 1996, s 180(3), ie, 'a body (other than a public or local authority) whose activities are not carried on for profit'.

18 See English Code of Guidance paras 2.27–2.29 and 2.43 (the latter encouraging close partnership working with the private sector); Welsh Code paras 5.38–5.40.

Guidance

12.7   Guidance on carrying out a review is available in *Homelessness strategies: a good practice handbook*,[19] Chapter 2 of the English Code of Guidance and the Welsh Code. The review should include an assessment of the needs of all homeless people, including those who have become homeless intentionally and those who are not in priority need. The review of needs and an audit of services should identify both where needs are not being met and where there is unnecessary duplication in the supply of services. The review of resources should cover staff, property and funding and include existing provision as well as plans for the future.

Publication

12.8   On completion of the review, an authority must arrange for the results to be available for inspection by members of the public, at reasonable hours, without charge, and provide a copy on payment of a reasonable charge.[20]

Strategies

Overview

12.9   'Homelessness strategy' is defined in Homelessness Act 2002, s 3(1) and H(W)A 2014, s 52(1) as one formulated in order to:

a)   prevent homelessness in an authority's area;[21]

b)   secure that sufficient accommodation is and will be available in that area for people who are or may become homeless;[22] and

c)   provide satisfactory support[23] for such people or those who have been homeless and need support to prevent it recurring.[24]

---

19   Department of Transport, Local Government and Regions (DTLR), February 2002. See, in particular, Chapter 4. See also *Local authorities' homelessness strategies: evaluation and good practice*, Office of the Deputy Prime Minister (ODPM), 2004.

20   Homelessness Act 2002, s 2(3); H(W)A 2014, s 51(2). In Wales, the results must also be published on the authority's website, if it has one.

21   On prevention, see further English Code of Guidance paras 2.25–2.26 and para 2.30; Welsh Code paras 5.44–5.48. The Welsh Code draws particular attention to the need to consider those people who have protected characteristics (see above, para **9.54**) under the Equality Act (EqA) 2010.

22   English Code paras 2.31–2.56; Welsh Code paras 5.49–5.53. Again, the Welsh Code draws particular attention to the need to consider those people who have 'protected characteristics' under the EqA 2010.

23   In England, 'support' means 'advice, information or assistance': Homelessness Act 2002, s 4; see also English Code paras 2.57–2.75, stressing the need to consider single people, rough sleepers, families, victims of domestic abuse and those in temporary accommodation. It is undefined in Wales.

24   H(W)A 2014, s 52 does not refer to the need to prevent homelessness recurring. See also Welsh Code paras 5.54–5.59.

12.10   In England, there is no requirement that specific objectives or plans, such as housing a proportion of homeless applicants outside an authority's district, should be included in the strategy: it is therefore a matter of discretion for the authority whether or not to include such matters.[25] Since 7 June 2012,[26] however, an authority in England must – when formulating or modifying a homelessness strategy – have regard to its current allocation scheme under HA 1996, s 166A,[27] and its current tenancy strategy under Localism Act (LA) 2011, s 150,[28] and (in the case of a London borough council) the current London Housing Strategy.[29] It should also ensure that the strategy 'is co-ordinated with the Health and Wellbeing Strategy' under the Health and Social Care Act 2012.

12.11   In Wales, the strategy must include details of both general and specific actions planned by the authority, including actions expected to be taken by other public authorities and voluntary organisations, in relation to those who may be in particular need of support if they are or may become homeless, in particular:

a)   people leaving prison or youth detention accommodation;

b)   young people leaving care;

c)   people leaving the regular armed forces of the Crown;

d)   people leaving hospital after medical treatment for mental disorder as an inpatient; and

e)   people receiving mental health services in the community.[30]

Functions

12.12   The strategy may encompass specific objectives or action falling within both housing and social service functions.[31]

---

25   *R (Calgin) v Enfield LBC* [2005] EWHC 1716 (Admin), [2006] HLR 4. In *Nzolameso v Westminster City Council* [2015] UKSC 22, [2015] HLR 22, however, the Supreme Court held that an authority should have a policy for procuring sufficient units of temporary accommodation to meet the anticipated demand for the coming year; that policy should reflect the authority's duties under the HA 1996 and the Children Act (CA) 2004; it should be approved by the democratically accountable members of the authority; the authority should also have a policy for allocating those units; where there is an anticipated shortfall of accommodation in its district, the policy should explain the factors which will be taken into account in offering accommodation further away; and, both policies should be publicly available. It would clearly be possible to include this policy in the Homelessness Strategy.

26   Ie, the commencement of LA 2011, s 153.

27   See para **9.85**.

28   Ie, flexible tenancies.

29   Homelessness Act 2002, s 3(7A).

30   H(W)A 2014, s 52(6); see also Welsh Code para 5.65.

31   Homelessness Act 2002, s 3(2); H(W)A 2014, s 52(2). See also the guidance on developing action plans in *Local authorities' homelessness strategies: evaluation and good practice* (ODPM, 2004). See Welsh Code Chapter 5.

Partnership

12.13   The strategy may also include provision for action to be taken by other public authorities, voluntary organisations[32] or persons who might be capable of contributing to the achievement of any of the strategic objectives, but only if given approval to include such provision by that contributing authority, organisation or person,[33] ie, an authority cannot rely on what others might do, otherwise than with their consent.

12.14   In order to encourage partnership working, an authority is under a duty positively to consider the extent to which any of the objectives of the strategy can be achieved through action involving two or more of the local authority, social services authority, another public authority, any voluntary organisation or any person.[34]

Guidance

12.15   In England, in addition to the needs assessment and audit of services emerging from the homelessness review, the strategy should include action on planning and implementing the strategy, including:[35]

a)   the involvement of partner agencies – public, voluntary and private – in formulating and implementing the strategy;

b)   consultation with other agencies in contact with homeless people, even if not involved in service provision;

c)   consultation with service-users and other homeless people;

d)   defining key aims and objectives of the strategy;

e)   agreeing priorities for action;

f)   a timetabled and costed programme;

g)   identification of which agencies will do what and when;

h)   mechanisms for joint and partnership work;

i)   mechanisms of monitoring and evaluation of the strategy and individual elements of the programme, including targets and performance indicators; and

j)   mechanisms for regular review and amendment of the strategy in the light of the monitoring and evaluation.

---

32   By Homelessness Act 2002, s 4. In Wales, see H(W)A 2014, ss 52(3). The definition of 'voluntary organisation' is the same as in HA 1996, s 180(3): see para **12.29** and H(W)A 2014, s 99.

33   Homelessness Act 2002, s 3(3), (4); H(W)A 2014, s 52(3), (4).

34   Homelessness Act 2002, s 3(5); H(W)A 2014, s 52(5).

35   *Homelessness strategies: a good practice handbook*, DTLR, 2002, para 2.1.5.

On strategies to prevent homelessness, further guidance is also available in *Homelessness prevention: a guide to good practice.*[36]

12.16   As the allocation of accommodation under HA 1996, Part 6 is one of the ways in which the main homelessness duty can be discharged, authorities must have regard to their current tenancy and homelessness strategies and – in the case of a London borough council – the current London housing strategy.[37]

12.17   In Wales, the strategy should 'prioritise the need for prevention' and adequate consideration and resources should be devoted to preventative services, eg, information, advice, short-term support and mediation.[38] Related areas, such as money advice and debt counselling, should also be included.[39] Discretionary housing payments (DHPs) are particularly important and ought to be prioritised where they can be used most effectively to prevent homelessness.[40] The private rented sector plays a 'critical role' and strategic planning 'must reflect' that, both as regards prevention and sustaining tenancies and helping the homeless to move into accommodation.[41]

Review of strategy

12.18   The strategy must be kept under review by the authority,[42] and may be modified.[43] Any modifications must be published.[44] Any public or local authorities, voluntary organisations or other persons as the authority considers appropriate must be consulted prior to both adopting or modifying the strategy.[45]

Publication

12.19   The published strategy, and any modifications, must be available for inspection, at reasonable hours, without charge, by members of the public and available for purchase on payment of a reasonable charge.[46]

---

36   DCLG, June 2006.
37   HA 1996, s 166A(12); see also *Allocation of accommodation: guidance for local housing authorities in England*, DCLG, para 2.5; English Code of Guidance paras 2.44–2.49.
38   Welsh Code para 5.44.
39   Welsh Code para 5.45.
40   Welsh Code para 5.47.
41   Welsh Code para 5.53.
42   See *Preventing homelessness: a strategy health check*, non-statutory guidance published in September 2006 by the DCLG.
43   Homelessness Act 2002, s 3(6); H(W)A 2014, s 52(7).
44   Homelessness Act 2002, s 3(7); H(W)A 2014, s 52(9), (10), (11).
45   Homelessness Act 2002, s 3(8); H(W)A 2014, s 52(8).
46   Homelessness Act 2002, s 3(9); H(W)A 2014, s 52(9).

PROVISION OF ADVICE AND ASSISTANCE

England

12.20   From 3 April 2018,[47] English housing authorities have been under a duty to provide, or secure the provision of, a service, to be available free of charge to any person in its district, providing information and advice on:

a)   preventing homelessness;

b)   securing accommodation when homeless;

c)   the rights of persons who are homeless or threatened with homelessness;

d)   the duties of the authority, under HA 1996, Part 7;

e)   any help that is available from the authority or anyone else, whether under Part 7 or otherwise, for persons in the district who are homeless or may become homeless (whether or not they are threatened with homelessness); and

f)   how to access that help.[48]

12.21   The service has to be designed to meet the needs of persons in the authority's district including, in particular, the needs of:

a)   people released from prison or youth detention accommodation;[49]

b)   care leavers;[50]

c)   former members of the regular armed forces;[51]

---

47   Commencement of HRA 2017: see Homelessness Reduction Act 2017 (Commencement and Transitional and Savings Provisions) Regulations 2018, SI 2018/167, reg 3. See English Code of Guidance Chapter 3.

48   HA 1996, s 179(1).

49   'Youth detention accommodation' means a secure children's home; a secure training centre; a secure college; a young offender institution; accommodation provided by or on behalf of a local authority for the purpose of restricting the liberty of children; accommodation provided for that purpose under CA 1989, s 82(5), or accommodation, or accommodation of a description, for the time being specified by order under Powers of Criminal Courts (Sentencing) Act 2000, s 107(1)(e): HA 1996, s 179(5).

50   People who are former relevant children within CA 1989, s 23C(1) – see para **11.110**. As regards the position of children generally, see *Prevention of homelessness and provision of accommodation for 16 and 17 year old young people who may be homeless and/or require accommodation*, MHCLG and Department for Education (DfE), April 2018 (www.gov.uk/government/publications/provision-of-accommodation-for-16-and-17-year-olds-who-may-be-homeless-and-or-require-accommodation), and, in particular, Chapter 6.

51   The regular forces as defined by Armed Forces Act 2006, s 374 – see para **5.36**.

d) victims of domestic abuse;[52]

e) people leaving hospital;[53]

f) people suffering from a mental illness or impairment; and

g) any other group which the authority identifies as being at particular risk of homelessness in its district.[54]

12.22 As under the pre-Homelessness Reduction Act (HRA) 2017 provision,[55] the authority may provide grants or loans to a person providing the service on its behalf.[56] Assistance may also be given by way of the use of premises, furniture or other goods and even the services of staff.[57]

12.23 Where advice is provided by the authority, it is trite – but should be borne in mind – that appropriate advice in the interests of the applicant must be given.[58]

Wales

12.24 In Wales, H(W)A 2014, s 60 requires authorities to ensure that provision of advice and information about homelessness and the prevention of homelessness is available free of charge in their areas both to people who are in the area and to anyone who has a local connection with the area.

12.25 The advice and information must include details about how the homelessness service operates in the authority's area, other help which might be available for people who are homeless or may become homeless (whether or

---

52 See paras **2.83–2.86**, for the definition of domestic abuse. Under DAA 2021, Pt 4, local authorities in England are under a duty to assess, or make arrangements for the assessment of, the need for support, in relation to domestic abuse, provided to victims of domestic abuse, or their children, who reside in specified by the Secretary of State in regulations (see Domestic Abuse Support (Relevant Accommodation and Housing Benefit and Universal Credit Sanctuary Schemes) (Amendment) Regulations 2021 SI 2021, SI 2021/991), and to prepare and publish a strategy for the provision of such support in its area, and monitor and evaluate the effectiveness of the strategy, as well as to appoint domestic abuse local partnership boards to provide advice on the exercise of these functions, and submit an annual report to the Secretary of State in relation to the exercise of these functions. The Secretary of State may issue guidance to authorities on the exercise of the functions: see *Delivery of support to victims of domestic abuse in domestic abuse safe accommodation services*, DLUHC, October 2021.
53 'Hospital' has the same meaning as in the National Health Service Act 2006, s 275(1).
54 HA 1996, s 179(2) as amended by DAA 2021, s 78(4).
55 HA 1996, s 179.
56 HA 1996, s 179(3).
57 HA 1996, s 179(4).
58 *Robinson v Hammersmith and Fulham LBC* [2006] EWCA Civ 1122, [2006] 1 WLR 3295, [2007] HLR 7, per Jacob LJ at [45], considering – with reference to HA 1996, s 179 – advice to mediate offered to a 17-year-old: 'A near 18 [year] old who came to the authority could obviously not be properly advised to mediate if the effect of mediation would be to delay the actual s 184 decision past the 18th birthday' (thus causing the loss of automatic priority need – see paras **3.85–3.88**).

not threatened with homelessness) and how to access it.[59] Where someone may become homeless (not necessarily threatened with homelessness in the statutory sense), assistance must be provided to access help which is available to prevent the person becoming homeless.[60]

12.26 The authority must work with other public authorities, voluntary organisations and others to ensure that the service is designed to meet the needs of groups at particular risk of homelessness[61] including in particular:[62]

a)   people leaving prison[63] or youth detention accommodation;[64]

b)   young people leaving care;

c)   people leaving the regular armed forces of the Crown;[65]

d)   people leaving hospital after medical treatment for mental disorder as an inpatient; and

e)   people receiving mental health services in the community.

12.27 The authority does not have to provide this service itself but may secure that it is provided on its behalf by or in partnership with some other organisation.[66]

12.28 The duty to provide advice and information to persons in the area is applicable even to those who are ineligible for assistance.[67]

AID TO VOLUNTARY ORGANISATIONS – ENGLAND[68]

12.29 Voluntary organisations have long played an important role in assisting homeless people. Bodies such as housing associations have provided significant

---

59   H(W)A 2014, s 60(2).

60   H(W)A 2014, s 60(3).

61   The Violence against Women, Domestic Abuse and Sexual Violence (Wales) Act 2015 makes separate provision for the prevention of gender-based violence, domestic abuse and sexual violence, the protection of victims of such abuse and violence and for their support, with provision for both local and national strategies and for guidance by the Welsh Ministers. See '*Violence against women, domestic abuse and sexual violence: strategy 2022 to 2026*', May 2022, by the Welsh Ministers, which cross-refers to other housing policy documents.

62   H(W)A 2014, s 60(4).

63   This has the same meaning as in the Prison Act 1952, s 53(1).

64   'Youth detention accommodation' means a secure children's home, a secure training centre, a young offender institution, accommodation provided, equipped and maintained by the Welsh Ministers under Children Act 1989, s 82(5) for the purpose of restricting the liberty of children or accommodation, or accommodation of a description, for the time being specified by order under Powers of Criminal Courts (Sentencing) Act 2000, s 107(1)(e): H(W)A 2014, s 99.

65   As defined by the Armed Forces Act 2006, s 374.

66   Two or more authorities may provide a combined service: H(W)A 2014, s 60(5); see further: Welsh Code paras 9.9–9.12.

67   H(W)A 2014, s 60.

68   There is no equivalent to these provisions in Wales, although the Welsh Code does discuss the circumstances in which an authority might provide assistance to a voluntary body, at paras 9.13–9.16.

assistance to local authorities in the discharge of their obligations towards the homeless, especially those in special categories of need. The definition of voluntary organisation[69] is wide enough to include housing associations and other non-profit-making social landlords.[70]

12.30   The powers permit the Secretary of State, or local housing authorities, to give voluntary organisations money by way of grant or loan.[71] The money may be used, among other things, for the provision of accommodation for homeless people, although does not give rise to a power directly to assist homeless individuals.[72]

12.31   A local housing authority may also assist by letting a voluntary organisation use premises belonging to it, on such terms and conditions as may be agreed, and by making available furniture or other goods – by way of gift, loan or otherwise – or the services of staff employed by it.[73] Assistance under HA 1996, s 179 or s 180 may be given on such terms and conditions as the Secretary of State or authority may determine.[74]

12.32   No assistance of any kind is to be given, however, unless the voluntary organisation first gives an undertaking:

a)   to use the money, furniture or other goods or premises made available to it for a purpose specified in the undertaking; and

b)   that – if required to do so by the body providing the assistance – it will, within 21 days of notice served upon it, certify such information as may reasonably be required by the notice as to the manner in which assistance given to it is being used.[75]

12.33   In every case in which assistance is provided, the conditions must include a requirement that the voluntary organisation: keeps proper books of account and has them audited in a specified manner; keeps records indicating how the assistance has been used; and submits accounts and records for inspection by the body providing the assistance.[76]

12.34   If it appears to the body providing the assistance that the voluntary organisation is not using the assistance for the purposes specified in the undertaking, it is obliged to take all reasonable steps to recover an amount of

---

69   Ie, 'a body (other than a public or local authority) whose activities are not carried on for profit': HA 1996, s 180(3).
70   *Goodman v Dolphin Square Trust Ltd* (1979) 38 P&CR 257, CA.
71   HA 1996, s 180(1).
72   *R (Ncube) v Brighton and Hove City Council* [2021] EWHC 578 (Admin), [2021] 1 WLR 4762, [2021] HLR 31.
73   HA 1996, s 180(2).
74   HA 1996, s 181(2).
75   HA 1996, s 181(3).
76   HA 1996, s 181(4).

money equal to the amount of the assistance from the organisation. No such amount is recoverable, however, unless the voluntary organisation has first been served with a notice specifying the amount alleged to be recoverable and the basis on which it has been calculated.[77]

CODES OF PRACTICE

England

12.35 Since 3 April 2018,[78] in England the Secretary of State has had power to issue codes of practice relating to homelessness or homelessness prevention to local housing authorities,[79] in particular concerning the exercise by a local housing authority of functions under HA 1996, Part 7, staff training relating to the exercise of those functions and monitoring by the authority of the exercise of those functions.[80] A code may apply to all local housing authorities or to a local housing authority specified or described in the code, and may contain different provision for different kinds of local housing authority.[81]

12.36 The Secretary of State must lay a draft of the code before Parliament, which is subject to negative resolution by either House of Parliament not to approve it; if there is no such resolution within 40 days[82] of the date the code is laid,[83] then the code may be issued.[84] A code may be revised from time to time and reissued or revoked: the procedural requirements do not apply to the reissue of a code;[85] accordingly, they do apply to revision or revocation. The Secretary of State must publish the current version of each code of practice in whatever manner they think fit.[86]

12.37 A local housing authority must have regard to a code of practice[87] in exercising its functions.[88]

---

77   HA 1996, s 181(5), (6).
78   Commencement of HRA 2017: see Homelessness Reduction Act 2017 (Commencement and Transitional and Savings Provisions) Regulations 2018, SI 2018/167, reg 3.
79   HA 1996, s 214A(1).
80   HA 1996, s 214A(2).
81   HA 1996, s 214A(3).
82   No account is taken of any period during which parliament is dissolved or prorogued, or both Houses are adjourned for more than four days. HA 1996, s 214A(8).
83   If laid before the two Houses on different dates, the later such date, HA 1996, s 214A(7)(b).
84   HA 1996, s 214A(4)–(8).
85   HA 1996, s 214A(9)–(10).
86   HA 1996, s 214A(11).
87   See para **10.49.**
88   HA 1996, s 214A(12).

CRIMINAL OFFENCES

12.38   To prevent abuse of Housing Act (HA) 1996, Parts 6 and 7 and Housing (Wales) Act (H(W)A) 2014, Part 2, some attempts to obtain accommodation are classified as criminal offences. There are three such offences:[89]

a)   making a false statement;

b)   withholding information; and

c)   failing to notify changes.

12.39   Offences under these provisions are prosecuted in the magistrates' court, and are punishable by a fine.[90]

Making a false statement

12.40   In all cases, the offence is sufficiently widely drafted to catch not merely the applicant but someone who makes representations on behalf of an applicant, which could therefore include an adviser. As the homelessness offences require proof of intent to induce the authority to believe something which is not true, however, the prosecutor must include proof of such intent as part of the prosecution, so this would be a rare event. Advisers should, however, bear the possibility in mind when deciding in what terms to relay information to an authority.[91]

12.41   The elements of the offences differ depending on whether made in connection with an allocation (HA 1996, Part 6) or homelessness application (HA 1996, Part 7; H(W)A 2014, Part 2).

Homelessness

12.42   An offence is committed by anyone who knowingly or recklessly makes a statement which is false in a material particular[92] with intent to induce an authority, in connection with the exercise of its functions under HA 1996, Part 7 or H(W)A Part 2, to believe that the person making the statement or any

---

89   HA 1996, ss 171, 214; H(W)A 2014, s 97.
90   For HA 1996, Parts 6 and 7, the fine may not exceed level 5 on the standard scale, but level 5 is presently unlimited (see Criminal Justice Act 1982, s 37 and Legal Aid, Sentencing and Punishment of Offenders Act 2012, s 85). For H(W)A 2014, Part 2, the fine may not exceed level 4 on the standard scale, currently £2,500: Criminal Justice Act 1982, s 37.
91   As a criminal offence, the standard of proof is beyond reasonable doubt but the element of intent may be proved by natural inference from acts.
92   Whether a false statement is material is a question of fact for the trial judge: *Oshin v Greenwich RBC* [2020] EWCA Civ 388, [2020] PTSR 1351, [2020] HLR 26 decided under Housing Act 1985, Sch 2 ground 5.

other person is entitled to accommodation or assistance[93] in accordance with the provisions of HA 1996, Part 7 or H(W)A 2014, Part 2.[94]

Allocations

12.43 An offence is committed by anyone who knowingly or recklessly makes a statement which is false in any material particular in connection with the exercise by an authority of its functions under HA 1996, Part 6: there is no requirement that there be an intent to induce an authority to believe anything.[95]

Withholding information

12.44 An offence is committed by anyone who knowingly withholds information which the authority has reasonably required the person to give in connection with the exercise of its functions under HA 1996, Parts 6 and 7 or H(W)A 2014, Part 2.[96] This is a widely drafted provision, allowing an authority to require information from, for example, a relative or a former landlord.

12.45 As with the 'false statement' offence (above), the offence is different as between 'allocations' and 'homelessness' cases.

Homelessness

12.46 Under HA 1996, s 214(1) and H(W)A 2014, s 97(1), an intent must be shown to induce the authority, in connection with the exercise of its HA 1996, Part 7 or H(W)A 2014, Part 2 functions, to believe that the person withholding the information, or any other person, is entitled to accommodation or assistance.[97] Accordingly, it is directed at the person withholding information that would be harmful to an applicant, rather than at someone who refuses to provide helpful information.

---

93   'Assistance' is defined for the purposes of HA 1996, s 214 as 'the benefit of any function under the following provisions of [Part 7] relating to accommodation or to assistance in obtaining accommodation' (s 183). There is no equivalent definition in HA 1996, Part 6 or H(W)A 2014, Part 2.
94   HA 1996, s 214(1); H(W)A 2014, s 97(1).
95   HA 1996, s 171(1).
96   HA 1996, ss 171(1), 214(1); H(W)A 2014, s 97(1).
97   'Assistance' is defined for the purposes of HA 1996, s 214 as 'the benefit of any function under the following provisions of [Part 7] relating to accommodation or to assistance in obtaining accommodation' (s 183). There is no equivalent definition in HA 1996, Part 6 or H(W)A 2014, Part 2.

Allocations

12.47   There is no equivalent 'intent' provision in HA 1996, s 171(1): an offence is committed where a person knowingly withholds information which the authority have reasonably required them to give in connection with the exercise of its functions under HA 1996, Part 6.

Failure to notify changes

12.48   An offence of failure to notify changes arises only in relation to HA 1996, Part 7 and H(W)A 2014. It may only be committed by an applicant.

12.49   An applicant is under a positive duty to inform the authority as soon as possible of any change of facts material to their application, which occurs before receipt of notification of the authority's decision on their application, under HA 1996, s 184 or H(W)A 2014, s 63.[98] The offence is failure to notify the authority of the change as soon as possible.

12.50   The obligation only arises before the authority's notification, even though the circumstances to be taken into account on an internal review include any that have changed between that decision and the decision on the review.[99] It follows that a failure to notify the authority of a change adverse to the applicant's interests after the decision would seem to be exempt from this obligation, even though the authority is entitled to take a change into account,[100] but the point has never been explicitly tested and it may yet be that the courts would find a way to apply the requirement in this circumstances.

12.51   The extent of the obligation is less straightforward than the two offences previously considered. Of particular difficulty is the issue of what constitutes a 'material change of facts'. In accordance with the usual principles of criminal law, the courts should interpret the provisions narrowly, ie, in favour of the accused.

12.52   A related duty is imposed on authorities: to explain to an applicant, in ordinary language, the nature of the applicant's duty to notify them of material changes and that failure to do so is a criminal offence.[101] The English Code of

---

98   HA 1996, s 214(2). The statutory language would not seem to be capable of being extended to the decision on the review, especially bearing in mind that as a criminal offence is involved, it is to be interpreted narrowly.

99   See **7.176**.

100   Although there is no reference to HA 1996, s 214 in *Mohamed v Hammersmith and Fulham LBC* [2001] UKHL 57, [2002] HLR 7, it formed a substantive part of the argument and it would therefore seem that Lord Slynn's conclusion at [25] confirms this analysis: 'I find nothing in the statutory language which requires the review to be confined to the date of the initial application or determination.'

101   HA 1996, s 214(2); H(W)A 2014, s 97(3), (4).

Guidance[102] suggests that this obligation is 'explained in ordinary language . . . [and] conveyed sensitively to avoid intimidating applicants'.

12.53 It is a defence for the applicant to show that they were not given such an explanation. It is also a defence to show that the applicant had a reasonable excuse for non-compliance.[103]

102 *Homelessness code of guidance for local authorities* para 18.10 (Ministry of Housing, Communities and Local Government (MHCLG), February 2018, updated May 2023; www. gov.uk/guidance/homelessness-code-of-guidance-for-local-authorities). There is no equivalent In the Welsh Code.
103 HA 1996, s 214(3); H(W)A 2014, s 97(4)–(5).

ANNEX

Immigration Eligibility

INTRODUCTION

A.1 Immigration status is a key topic in relation to both homelessness and allocations. In each case, it is determinative of eligibility, excluding certain applicants in England from the protection of Housing Act (HA) 1996, Part 7 and in Wales from the Housing (Wales) Act (H(W)A) 2014, Part 2, and, in both England and Wales, from the prospect of an allocation under the HA 1996, Part 6.

A.2 That does not mean that no assistance will ever be available from a local authority to someone thus disqualified: there remains the possibility of assistance in England under the Care Act 2014, and in Wales under the equivalent provision which is now the Social Services and Well-being (Wales) Act (SSWB(W)A) 2014, where an applicant is in need of care and attention (otherwise than as a result of destitution) – this is dealt with in Chapter 11.[1] In addition, some immigrants who are asylum-seekers disqualified from local authority assistance may be able to obtain housing help through the Home Office.[2]

A.3 Moreover, local authorities in England[3] and Wales[4] may have to afford assistance to children in need, even though they or their parents are disqualified from housing under HA 1996, Parts 6 and 7 or H(W) A 2014, Part 2.[5] There are also other powers – 'general power of competence' in England, under the Localism Act (LA) 2011; and 'well-being powers' in Wales, under the Local Government Act (LGA) 2000, Part 1, which may be exercisable in some circumstances.[6]

A.4 Even if an applicant is not ineligible for assistance under HA 1996, Part 7, there are, however, additional provisions which apply in England only, which may exclude the applicant from temporary accommodation under some of the interim duties in Part 7; the same classes will also be excluded from assistance under the provisions mentioned in the last paragraph, ie, under the Care Act 2014 or the SSWB(W)A 2014, through the Home Office, under the Children Act (CA) 1989 or under LGA 2000[7] or under LA 2011. These classes are described below.[8]

A.5 Even if an applicant is not ineligible for assistance under HA 1996, Part 7 or H(W)A 2014, Part 2, if qualification for assistance relies on family or household members who would themselves be ineligible,

---

1   See paras **11.23–11.31**.
2   See paras **11.46–11.59.**
3   Under CA 1989.
4   Under SSWB(W)A 2014.
5   See paras **11.60–11.122**.
6   See paras **11.123–11.129**.
7   LA 2011, ss 1 and 2 and Sch 1, which came into force on 28 March 2012, and 6 April 2012 by operation of the Localism Act 2011 (Consequential Amendments) Order 2012, SI 2012/961, repealed the well-being power in LGA 2000, s 2 in England, and replaced it with a general power of competence.
8   See paras **A.171–172.**

it may affect the duty placed on the authority: this is also dealt with below.[9] Likewise, it will affect priority in the allocation of housing under HA 1996, Part 6.[10]

A.6   Historically, the Housing (Homeless Persons) Act (H(HP)A) 1977 did not contain a test of eligibility. On the face of the Act, anyone could make an application. The Court of Appeal, however, expressed the view that duties were owed only to a person lawfully in the country.[11]

A.7   The consolidating HA 1985, Part 3, which replaced H(HP)A 1977, likewise did not limit who could apply, but the Court of Appeal interpreted the provisions to mean an authority owed no duty to an applicant for housing who was an illegal entrant.[12] It was also held that where – as a result of enquiries – the authority suspected that an applicant was an illegal entrant, it had a duty to inform the immigration authorities of its suspicion.[13]

A.8   The Asylum and Immigration Appeals Act (AIAA) 1993 was the first legislative provision explicitly to limit the rights of immigrants to housing assistance. The effect of its ss 4 and 5 was that authorities owed no duty to an asylum-seeker and the asylum-seeker's dependants if they had accommodation that was available for the asylum-seeker's occupation, however temporary, and which it would be reasonable for them to occupy.

A.9   These limitations were reproduced in HA 1996, Part 7, ss 185 and 186, and in H(W)A 2014, Sch 2, para 1, defining 'eligibility for assistance'. Subject to qualification and exception, excluded persons from abroad under HA 1996, s 185,[14] and asylum-seekers under HA 1996, s 186,[15] are not eligible for assistance. A person ineligible for assistance cannot receive 'the benefit of any function under . . . Part [7] relating to accommodation or assistance in obtaining accommodation',[16] although they can receive advice and assistance from any advisory service provided by the authority under its HA 1996, s 179 duty.[17]

---

9   See paras **A.127–A.133**.
10   See paras **A.187–A.189**.
11   *R v Hillingdon LBC ex p Streeting (No 2)* [1980] 1 WLR 1425, CA, followed in *R v Westminster City Council ex p Castelli* (1996) 28 HLR 616, CA.
12   *Tower Hamlets LBC v Secretary of State for the Environment* [1993] QB 632, (1993) 25 HLR 524, CA.
13   See *Tower Hamlets LBC v Secretary of State for the Environment*, above.
14   In Wales, the equivalent provision is H(W)A 2014, Sch 2, para 1. Whether a person who was born in the UK but who is not a British citizen can be a 'person from abroad' is a point of law of general importance on which there is as yet no definitive answer: *Ismail v Newham LBC* [2018] EWCA Civ 665 (where the issue was raised but had become academic owing to a change in the immigration status of the appellant so that the appeal was not allowed to proceed).
15   This has effect in Wales until repealed, see H(W)A 2014, Sch 2, para 2.
16   HA 1996, s 183(2).
17   HA 1996, s 183(3); see Chapter 12.

A.10 Eligibility requirements were also introduced in HA 1996, Part 6 for allocations,[18] which, so far as concerns immigration, matched those for homelessness.

A.11 In this Annex, eligibility is considered for both homelessness and allocations. Before addressing each of these, in turn, below, it is first necessary to consider the detailed rules governing the relevant classes of the various immigration statuses which may be enjoyed by – or which may limit the rights of – applicants under either HA 1996, Part 6 or Part 7 or H(W)A 2014, Part 2. We address the position of European Economic Area (EEA) nationals both as it stood on 31 December 2020 and as it became on 1 January 2021.

A.12 Qualification as an applicant who is eligible for assistance is set out in secondary legislation in both England[19] and Wales.[20] In summary, applicants who are subject to immigration control are eligible if they come within one of the prescribed classes, and applicants who are not subject to immigration control are generally eligible, unless otherwise excluded by regulations.

IMMIGRATION CONTROL

A.13 People in the UK are divided into two classes: i) persons who are subject to immigration control; and ii) persons who are not subject to immigration control. The latter group includes all persons who have a right to reside in the UK.

Persons subject to immigration control

A.14 The term 'persons subject to immigration control' as used in both HA 1996, Parts 6[21] and 7[22] and H(W)A 2014, Sch 2, para 1, is based on immigration legislation[23] and means a person who, under the Immigration Act (IA) 1971, requires leave to enter or remain in the UK (whether or not such leave has been given). Generally speaking, this means anyone who requires a visa to come to the UK.

---

18   See now HA 1996, s 160A(1)–(6), as amended by the Homelessness Act 2002.
19   Allocation of Housing and Homelessness (Eligibility) (England) Regulations (Eligibility Regs) 2006/1294. The Regulations are so frequently amended that in practice recourse needs to be had to an online service such as Westlaw or Nexis for the position at any given point in time.
20   See the Allocation of Housing and Homelessness (Eligibility) (Wales) Regulations (Eligibility (Wales) Regs) 2014, SI 2014/2603. The same observation as in the last footnote applies here also.
21   HA 1996, s 160ZA(2) (England), s 160A(3) (Wales).
22   HA 1996, s 185(2).
23   AIA 1996, s 13.

Persons not subject to immigration control

A.15 Persons not subject to immigration control form two groups.

A.16 The first group consists of those who are *exempt from* the requirement to have leave to enter or remain in the UK.[24] This group is relatively unimportant for eligibility purposes, and comprises three main classes:

a) diplomats and certain staff of embassies and high commissions and their families who form part of their household;[25]

b) members of UK armed forces, members of a Commonwealth or similar force undergoing training in the UK with the UK armed forces, and members of a visiting force coming to the UK at the invitation of the government;[26] and

c) members of the crew of a ship or aircraft, hired or under orders to depart as part of that ship's crew or to depart on the same or another aircraft within seven days of arrival in the UK.[27]

A.17 The second group is those who *do not require* leave to enter or remain in the UK.[28] They include:

a) British citizens;

b) Commonwealth citizens with the right of abode in the UK;

c) Irish citizens; and,

d) people born in the UK who have never left the country (*Akinyemi v SSHD* [2017] 1 WLR 3118, [2017] EWCA Civ 236, at [41].

The IA 1971 expressly excludes a) and b) from the requirement to have leave to enter or remain in the UK; c) was added with effect from 31 December 2020, to preserve the rights of Irish citizens under the common travel area; d) is directed to people whose parents did not have sufficient rights to confer British citizenship on their children and, as such, is rare and exceptionally complex.[29]

A.18 Prior to 1 January 2021, EEA nationals with a right to reside did not require leave to enter or remain in the UK. That remains the position for those EEA nationals who were resident and exercising a right to reside in the UK derived from European Union (EU) law before that date; such people should now have documentation to show that they have either 'settled' or 'pre-settled' status (see below). Since that date,

---

24 IA 1971, s 8.
25 IA 1971, s 8(3).
26 IA 1971, s 8(4), (6).
27 IA 1971, s 8(1).
28 IA 1971, s 1(1).
29 IA 1971, s 3ZA, with effect from 31 December 2021.

however, the majority[30] of newly-arriving EEA nationals have required leave to enter or remain.

EU Settlement Scheme

A.19 EEA nationals[31] who were lawfully resident in the UK on 31 December 2020 had until 30 June 2021[32] to apply under the EU Settlement Scheme.[33] The scheme provides for two kinds of leave to remain – settled status (available where the applicant had been living in the UK for at least five years) and pre-settled status (for those who had been living in the UK for less than five years). The differences between the two as regards eligibility under Parts 2, 6 or 7, are discussed below (para **A.24**).

A.20 EEA nationals who applied through the Settlement Scheme should have digital information setting out whether they have settled or pre-settled status.[34]If an authority has any uncertainty about an applicant's immigration status, it can contact the Home Office.[35]

British citizenship

A.21 British citizenship was created by the British Nationality Act (BNA) 1981.[36] It came into force on 1 January 1983. Prior to that date, the most beneficial form of national status was to be a 'Citizen of the United Kingdom and Colonies' (CUKC) with the right of abode in the UK.[37] A person can become a British citizen in a variety of ways, which include the following:

---

30 Exceptions include family members joining EEA nationals who were lawfully resident in the UK as at 31 December 2020 (see Citizens' Rights (Application Deadline and Temporary Protection) (EU Exit) Regulations 2020, SI 2010/1209) and those with a 'frontier worker permit' (ie, a right to enter the UK for work purposes while remaining living elsewhere), see the Citizens' Rights (Frontier Workers) (EU Exit) Regulations 2020, SI 2020/1213.

31 Including those with a *Zambrano* right (para **A.101**) even if they have another right (eg, a time-limited right on human right grounds, such as under Appendix FM – below, para **A.156**) to remain: *R. (Akinsanya) v Secretary of State for the Home Department* [2022] EWCA Civ 37; [2022] QB 482.

32 Subject to any extension granted where there was a reasonable ground for missing the deadline.

33 Under Appendix EU of the Immigration Rules.

34 *Homelessness code of guidance for local authorities* para 7.34 (Ministry of Housing, Communities and Local Government (MHCLG), February 2018, updated May 2023; www.gov.uk/guidance/homelessness-code-of-guidance-for-local-authorities).

35 *Allocation of accommodation: guidance for local housing authorities in England*, para 3.13 (MHCLG, December 2020; www.gov.uk/government/collections/social-housing-allocations-guidance); the Homelessness Code does not contain any similar statement.

36 This has been the subject of numerous amendments including by the Borders, Citizenship and Immigration Act 2009.

37 IA 1971, s 2 as it was then in force.

a) a person who, on 31 December 1982, was a CUKC with the right of abode in the UK because of their birth, adoption, naturalisation or registration in the UK, or because they have a parent or grandparent who was born, adopted, naturalised or registered in the UK;[38]

b) a person who, on 31 December 1982, had been ordinarily resident in the UK for five years;[39]

c) a person born in the UK after 1 January 1983 is a British citizen if at the time of the birth, the person's father or mother was a British citizen or settled in the UK;[40] in this context, 'settled' means that they have indefinite leave to remain (ILR) or permanent residence in the UK and does not include an EU national parent whose right to remain in the UK was conditional on them exercising a right derived from the EU treaties (eg their status as a worker): *R (Roehrig) v Secretary of State for the Home Department* [2024] EWCA Civ 240.;

d) a person born in the UK after 1 January 1983 is entitled to be registered as a British citizen if, while the person is a minor, their father or mother becomes a British citizen or becomes settled in the UK;[41]

e) otherwise, a person born in the UK after 1 January 1983 can apply for registration as a British citizen after the person is ten years old, providing that they have not been absent from the UK for more than 90 days a year;[42]

f) a person born outside the UK after 1 January 1983 will be a British citizen if at the time of the birth, their father or mother was a British citizen who was born in the UK;[43]

g) a person may also apply for naturalisation[44] as a British citizen so long as the person fulfils certain requirements set out in the BNA 1981.[45]

Commonwealth citizens with the right of abode in the UK

A.22   Since the coming into force of the BNA 1981,[46] the following now have the right of abode in the UK:

38   BNA 1981, s 11(1).
39   IA 1971, s 2(1)(c) as it was in force on 31 December 1982.
40   BNA 1981, s 1(1).
41   BNA 1981, s 1(3).
42   BNA 1981, s 1(4).
43   BNA 1981, s 2.
44   BNA 1981, s 6.
45   BNA 1981, Sch 1.
46   On 1 January 1983.

a) persons who automatically became British citizens[47] on the coming into force of the BNA 1981.[48] These include all the former citizens of the UK and Colonies who had a right of abode because they were 'patrials', ie, citizens of the UK and colonies born, adopted, registered or naturalised in the UK, those with the necessary ancestral connections with the UK, and those who were ordinarily resident here for five years free of immigration restrictions;[49]

b) Commonwealth citizens[50] who, immediately before commencement, had the right of abode by virtue of having a parent who was born in the UK under the now revoked IA 1971, s 2(1)(d);

c) female Commonwealth citizens who, immediately before commencement, had a right of abode under the now revoked IA 1971, s 2(2) by virtue of their marriage to a patrial.[51]

Irish citizenship

A.23 Irish citizens[52] do not require leave to enter or remain in the UK.[53] They do not need to apply for settled or pre-settled status, but can do so if they wish.[54]

EEA nationals with the right to reside in the UK as at 31 December 2020

A.24 From 1 January 2021, the eligibility of EEA nationals turns on whether the applicant has settled or pre-settled status (para **A.19**). A person with settled status is generally eligible[55] for homelessness assistance and an allocation of housing, whereas a person with pre-settled status is generally eligible only if they would have been so eligible prior to 31 December 2020.[56] It follows that advisers and authorities still need to be aware of the rights derived from the EEA treaties which would have benefited applicants on

---

47 See para **A.21**.
48 BNA 1981, s 11.
49 IA 1971, s 2(1)(c) before amendment.
50 Commonwealth citizens are all those who are citizens of the countries set out in BNA 1981, Sch 3.
51 IA 1971, s 2 before amendment. Patriality was conferred on certain citizens of the UK and Colonies and certain other Commonwealth citizens.
52 Not defined in the IA 1971.
53 IA 1971, s 3ZA; but note the exceptions in subsections (2), (3) and (4) for Irish citizens who have been deported 'where the Irish citizen's exclusion is conducive to the public good'.
54 *Common Travel Area guidance*, section 8a (Cabinet Office and Home Office, 31 December 2020; www.gov.uk/government/publications/common-travel-area-guidance/common-travel-area-guidance).
55 In England, by virtue of Eligibility Regs 2006, regs 3 and 5 (see the Homelessness Code para 7.34(a)(i) and the Allocations Guidance para 3.10). In Wales, see Eligibility (Wales) Regs 2014, regs 3 and 5 and the non-statutory guidance issued by the Deputy Director, Housing Policy Division, Welsh Government in December 2020.
56 Under regs 4 and 6 of both the English and Welsh Eligibility Regs; see also the Homelessness Code para 7.34(a)(ii); Allocations Guidance para 3.9; and the December 2020 letter from the Welsh Government.

or before 31 December 2020. The limited rights conferred on those with pre-settled status may be a source of future litigation.[57]

A.25 The right to reside in the UK for EEA nationals derived from the Treaty on the Functioning of the European Union (TFEU).[58] It was not an unconditional right.[59] The requirements to be met were principally[60] set out in Directive 2004/38/EC[61] ('the Directive') which was enacted into domestic law by the Immigration (European Economic Area) Regulations (EEA Regs) 2016.[62] The EEA Regs 2016 were not simply a repetition of the Directive: where the Directive gave a right to reside and the EEA Regs 2016 did not, an applicant was entitled to rely on the Directive.[63] Conversely, if the Directive did not give a right to reside but the EEA Regs 2016 did do so, then an applicant could rely on those more favourable provisions.

A.26 There were two ways in which a person could have a right to reside in the UK. These were either:

a) as an EEA[64] national who satisfied the relevant conditions,[65] known as a 'qualified person'[66] in the EEA Regs 2016; or

---

57 In outline, pre-settled status does not, by itself, confer eligibility for welfare benefits (Social Security (Income-related Benefits) (Updating and Amendment) (EU Exit) Regulations 2019, SI 2019/872) including allocations under HA 1996, Part 6 and homelessness provision under HA 1996, Part 7, and H(W)A 2014, Part 2, so that a person with pre-settled status must also demonstrate that they are exercising some other relevant right (such as being a worker). No similar restriction applies to a UK national who has been living in the UK for less than five years.

58 This came into force on 1 December 2009.

59 TFEU Art 21; *Minister voor Vreemdelingenzaken en Integratie v RNG Eind*, Case C-291/05 at [28]; *Trojani v Centre public d'aide sociale de Bruxelles (CPAS)*, Case C-456/02, [2004] ECR I-7573 at [31] and [32]; *Zhu and Chen v Secretary of State for the Home Department*, Case C-200/02, [2004] ECR I-9925 at [26]; *Ali v Secretary of State for the Home Department* [2006] EWCA Civ 484, [2006] 3 CMLR 10 at [20].

60 Some rights of residence exist outside the scope of the Directive, see paras **A.85–A.118**.

61 Of the European Parliament and of the Council of 29 April 2004, which came into force on 30 April 2004.

62 Immigration (European Economic Area) Regulations (EEA Regs) 2016, SI 2016/1052, which came into force on 1 February 2017 and were revoked by Immigration and Social Security Co-ordination (EU Withdrawal) Act 2020 with effect from 31 December 2020, subject to savings made by the Immigration and Social Security Co-ordination (EU Withdrawal) Act 2020 (Consequential, Saving, Transitional and Transitory Provisions) (EU Exit) Regulations 2020, SI 2020/1309; and the Citizens' Rights (Application Deadline and Temporary Protection) (EU Exit) Regulations 2020, SI 2020/1209.

63 IA 1988, s 7(1).

64 The EEA consists of the EU plus Norway, Iceland and Liechtenstein. The EU consists of the EU15 (Austria, Belgium, Denmark, Finland, France, Germany, Greece, Ireland, Italy, Luxembourg, the Netherlands, Portugal, Spain, Sweden), plus the countries which acceded on 1 May 2004 (Cyprus, the Czech Republic, Estonia, Hungary, Latvia, Lithuania, Malta, Poland, Slovakia, Slovenia), plus the countries which acceded on 1 January 2007 (the A2: Bulgaria and Romania) and Croatia which acceded on 1 July 2013 pursuant to the Accession Treaty signed on 9 December 2011.

65 These are either set out in the Directive or the EEA Regs 2016.

66 EEA Regs 2016, reg 6(1).

    b)   as a family member of an EEA national who either had, or who had previously had, a right to reside.

A.27   The right to reside existed independently of any residence documentation: the latter is merely evidence of the right,[67] although a person in possession of such documentation could rely on TFEU Article 18 in order to be granted social assistance:[68] in *Sanneh*,[69] however, the Court of Appeal held that the ability to rely on Article 18 only applied to EU citizens in possession of a residence permit.[70]

A.28   There were three categories of the EEA national right to reside:

    a)   initial right to reside;

    b)   extended right to reside;

    c)   permanent right to reside.

Initial right to reside

A.29   An EEA national was entitled to be admitted to the UK if they produced on arrival a valid national identity card or passport issued by an EEA state.[71] A person who was not an EEA national was required to produce on arrival a valid passport and an EEA family permit, a residence card or a permanent residence card.[72] An EEA family permit acted as a sort of entry clearance or visa for non-EEA nationals.

A.30   The initial right to reside lasted for no longer than three months and was conditional on the EEA national or their family member not becoming an unreasonable burden on the social assistance system of the UK.[73]

A.31   The term 'social assistance' was not defined in the Directive, or elsewhere in EU legislation, but was considered by the Court of Justice of the European Union (CJEU), which held that it referred to the grant of assistance which was essentially dependent on need and not linked to employment or contributions.[74] This was therefore likely to include social housing.[75] In England, a person who had an initial right to reside

---

67   *Mario Lopes da Veiga v Staatssecretaris van Justitie*, Case 9/88; *Echternach and Moritz v Minister van Onderwijs en Wetenschappen*, Cases 389/87 and 390/87, at [25]; *Secretary of State for Work and Pensions v Maria Dias*, Case C-325/09 at [48].

68   *Trojani v Centre public d'aide sociale de Bruxelles (CPAS)*, Case C-456/02, [2004] ECR I-7573, at [43].

69   *Sanneh v Secretary of State for Work and Pensions* [2015] EWCA Civ 49, [2015] HLR 27.

70   *Sanneh* at [110].

71   Directive 2004/38/EC Art 5(1); EEA Regs 2016, reg 11(1).

72   EEA Regs 2016, reg 11(2); see also Directive 2004/38/EC Art 5(2).

73   Directive 2004/38/EC Art 14(1); EEA Regs 2016, reg 13.

74   *Frilli v Belgium* Case 1/72, [1972] ECR 457, [1973] CMLR 386.

75   By analogy, the term 'public funds' is defined for the purposes of immigration law as including housing under HA 1996, Part 6 or Part 7 and HA 1985, Part 2: Immigration Rules (HC 395), para 6.

was ineligible under HA 1996, Parts 6[76] and 7.[77] In Wales, such a person was ineligible under HA 1996, Part 6[78] and H(W)A 2014, Part 2.[79]

Extended right to reside

A.32   There were five ways in which an EEA national could have had an extended right to reside in the UK.[80] These were as:

a)   a jobseeker;

b)   a worker;

c)   a self-employed person;

d)   a self-sufficient person; or

e)   a student.

A jobseeker

A.33   A jobseeker was a person who:

a)   entered the UK in order to seek employment; or

b)   was present in the UK seeking employment, after having previously had a right to reside,

and in either case:

c)   provided evidence of seeking employment and having a genuine chance of being engaged.

A.34   A person could retain the status of jobseeker for as long as they provided compelling evidence of continuing to seek employment and of having a genuine chance of being engaged.[81] The CJEU held that, after six months, a jobseeker had to provide evidence that they were continuing to seek employment and had genuine chances of being engaged.[82]

A.35   In England, jobseekers were expressly excluded from eligibility under HA 1996, Parts 6[83] and 7.[84] In Wales, jobseekers were ineligible under HA 1996, Part 6[85] and H(W)A 2014, Part 2.[86]

---

76   Eligibility Regs 2006, reg 4(1)(b)(ii).
77   Eligibility Regs 2006, reg 6(1)(b)(ii).
78   Eligibility (Wales) Regs 2014, reg 4(1)(b)(ii).
79   Eligibility (Wales) Regs 2014, reg 6(1)(b)(ii).
80   EEA Regs 2016, reg 6(1)(a)–(e).
81   EEA Regs 2016, reg 6(1).
82   *R v Immigration Appeal Tribunal ex p Antonissen,* Case C-292/89, [1991] ECR I 745.
83   Eligibility Regs 2006, reg 4(1)(b)(i).
84   Eligibility Regs 2006, reg 6(1)(b)(i). If, however, the applicant had another right to reside, eg, a *Zambrano* right (paras **A.102–A.114**), being a right which qualified them under Part 6 or Part 7, they could rely on that right despite the disqualification under this right: *Sandwell MBC v KK* [2022] UKUT 123 (AAC).
85   Eligibility (Wales) Regs 2014, reg 4(1)(b)(i).
86   Eligibility (Wales) Regs 2014, reg 6(1)(b)(i).

A worker

A.36   There were three essential criteria which determined whether a person was a worker for the purposes of Article 45 of the TFEU.

A.37   First, the person must have been performing services of some economic value.[87] The activity must have been real and genuine, to the exclusion of activity on such a small scale as to be marginal and ancillary.[88]

A.38   Second, the performance of such services must have been for and under the direction of another person. Any activity performed outside a relationship of subordination had to be classified as an activity pursued in a self-employed capacity.[89]

A.39   Third, the person concerned must have received remuneration.[90] Neither the origin of the funds from which the remuneration was paid nor the limited amount of that remuneration could have any consequences with regard to whether or not the person was a worker.[91] The fact that the income from employment was lower than the minimum required for subsistence did not prevent the person from being regarded as a worker,[92] even if they sought to supplement that remuneration by other means of subsistence such as financial assistance drawn from the public funds[93] of the host member state.[94]

A.40   The fact that the employment was of short duration did not, of itself, prevent the employee from being a worker.[95]

A.41   A person who was no longer working did not cease to be a worker if:[96]

87   *Lawrie-Blum v Land Baden Wurttemberg*, Case 66/85, [1986] ECR 2121; in *Bristol City Council v FV* [2011] UKUT 494 (AAC) (21 December 2011), the Upper Tribunal held that sellers of the *Big Issue* magazine could be considered self-employed. The opposite decision was reached in *DV v Revenue and Customs Commissioners* [2017] UKUT 155 (AAC).

88   *Vatsouras and Koupatantze v Arbeitgemeinschaft (ARGE) Nurnberg 900*, Cases C-22/08 and C-23/08; *Lawrie Blum*, above.

89   *Jany v Staatssecretaris van Justitie*, Case C-268/99 at [34].

90   *Vatsouras*, above, at [25]; and *Lawrie-Blum*, above.

91   *Vatsouras*, above, at [27].

92   *Levin v Staatssecretaris van Justitie*, Case 53/81.

93   For the purposes of UK immigration law, the term 'public funds' is defined in the Immigration Rules (HC 395) para 6 as including housing under HA 1996, Part 6 or Part 7 and HA 1985, Part 2. The Immigration Rules have not been updated to reflect the H(W)A 2014.

94   *Kempf v Staatssecretaris van Justitie*, Case 139/85, [1986] ECR 1741.

95   *Vatsouras*, above, at [29]; *Ninni Orasche v Bundesminster für Wissenschaft, Verkehr und Kunst*, Case C-413/01; *Barry v Southwark LBC* [2008] EWCA Civ 1440, [2009] HLR 30.

96   EEA Regs 2016, reg 6(2).

a) the person was temporarily[97] unable to work as the result of an illness or accident;

b) the person was in duly recorded involuntary unemployment[98] after having been employed in the UK for at least one year, provided that they had registered as a jobseeker with the relevant employment office,[99] and satisfied conditions A and B (below); such status could not be retained for longer than six months without providing compelling evidence[100] of continuing to seek employment and having a genuine chance of being engaged;

c) the person was in duly recorded involuntary unemployment after having been employed in the UK for less than one year, provided they had registered as a jobseeker with the relevant employment

---

97 In *Secretary of State for the Home Department v FB* [2010] UKUT 447 (IAC), it was held that temporary means not permanent, see [23]–[26], followed by the Court of Appeal in *Aurelio de Brito and Lizette de Noronha v Secretary of State for the Home Department* [2012] EWCA Civ 709, [2012] 3 CMLR 24 at [30]–[35], where it was held that the test was objective and that a temporary condition could become permanent and a permanent condition could become temporary depending upon the facts of the case, such as a successful medical intervention. In *Konodyba v Royal London Borough of Kensington and Chelsea* [2012] EWCA Civ 982, [2013] PTSR 13 at [22] and [23], the Court of Appeal held that whether a homeless applicant was temporarily unable to work or unlikely to be able to work in the foreseeable future was a question of fact. These decisions were followed in *Samin v Westminster City Council* [2012] EWCA Civ 1468, [2013] 2 CMLR 6, [2013] HLR 7 where the Court of Appeal held that the question was one of fact in every case and that it would generally be helpful to ask whether there was or was not a realistic prospect of a return to work. The case was the subject of an appeal to the Supreme Court, [2016] UKSC 1, [2016] HLR 7, but this aspect was unaffected by its judgment.

98 In decisions of the Social Security Commissioner CH/3314/2005 and CIS/3315/2005, it was held that this phrase was concerned with why the worker was not working at the date of the decision, not with why the worker had ceased to be employed, though this could also be relevant: see para [11].

99 *Elmi v Secretary of State for Work and Pensions* [2011] EWCA Civ 1403, [2012] PTSR 780 concerned an EU citizen who had become involuntarily unemployed and then claimed income support at Jobcentre Plus. She ticked the box on the relevant form stating that she was looking for work. The Court of Appeal held that she had registered with the employment office as a jobseeker, even though she was in receipt of income support and not jobseeker's allowance, and had therefore retained her worker status.

100 In *KS v Secretary of State for Work and Pensions* [2016] UKUT 269 (AAC), it was held that this meant no more than the requirement for evidence to establish on a balance of probabilities that the claimant was continuing to seek employment and had genuine chances of being engaged. To interpret the phrase as meaning a higher standard of proof would have been contrary to EU law. See also *Secretary of State for Work and Pensions v MB (JSA)* [2016] UKUT 372 (AAC), where it was held that the fact that a claimant was looking for work for six months was only one factor in determining whether they had a genuine chance of being engaged; 'compelling' evidence did not mean more than chances that were founded on something objective and which offered real prospects of employment within a reasonable period. Given that evaluating a 'chance' necessitates a degree of looking forward, events likely to occur in the near future could be relevant to a claimant's genuine chance of being engaged. The government's guidance, the *Decision makers' guide volume 2: International subjects: staff guide*, para 073099 suggests an approach that is much higher than a mere balance of probabilities and may therefore not be correct.

office, and satisfied conditions A and B (below), but they could only retain worker status for a maximum of six months under this provision;[101]

d) the person was involuntarily unemployed and had embarked on vocational training; or

e) the person had voluntarily ceased working and embarked on vocational training that was related to their previous employment.

A.42 Condition A was that the person entered the UK in order to seek employment, or was present in the UK seeking employment, immediately after enjoying a right to reside other than as a jobseeker.[102] Condition B was that the person provided evidence of seeking employment and of having a genuine chance of being engaged.[103]

A.43 If a woman was incapable of working due to pregnancy, this did not constitute an illness or accident within point a) above unless there was an actual associated illness.[104] In *JS*, the Court of Appeal adopted a similar approach to a woman who ceased working as a nursery school teacher because the demands of the job were too great for her because of her pregnancy, although it had not been found that she could not work because of the pregnancy:[105] it was held that the term 'worker' could not be construed to include a person who has no contract of employment and was not therefore on maternity leave.[106]

A.44 *JS*[107] was the subject of a reference to the CJEU as *St Prix*,[108] where it was held that a woman who had temporarily given up work because of the late stages of her pregnancy and aftermath of childbirth could not be regarded as a person temporarily unable to work as the result of an illness, but that she nevertheless retained the status of worker provided that she returned to work or found another job within a reasonable time after the birth of her child; in order to determine whether the period was reasonable, the national court should take account of all the specific circumstances of the case and the applicable national rules on the duration of maternity leave.[109]

---

101 EEA Regs 2016, reg 6(3).
102 EEA Regs 2016, reg 6(5).
103 EEA Regs 2016, reg 6(6).
104 *Adrian John Dalton* [2017] UKUT 71 (AAC), decided in the context of a benefits appeal and *Webb v EMO Air Cargo (UK) Ltd*, Case C-32/93, [1994] ECR I-3567.
105 *JS v Secretary of State for Work and Pensions* [2011] EWCA Civ 806.
106 *JS* at [19] and [27]. The issue of whether this amounted to unlawful sex discrimination was left open because it did not arise on the evidence.
107 See the last two footnotes.
108 *St Prix v Secretary of State for Work and Pensions*, Case C-507/12, [2014] PTSR 1448.
109 *St Prix* at [29], [47] and [48].

A.45 In a decision of the Upper Tribunal,[110] it was held that it would be unusual for the reasonable period to be other than 52 weeks.[111] This is consistent with the concession made by the secretary of state in the Court of Appeal in *Dias*, that a woman on maternity leave retains her status as a worker, which the court assumed was correct.[112]

A self-employed person

A.46 A self-employed person was a person who established themselves in another EU state in order to pursue activity as a self-employed person in accordance with Article 49 of the TFEU.[113] Essentially, this meant someone who was working outside a relationship of subordination.[114]

A.47 The EEA Regs 2016 provided that a person who was no longer in self-employment did not cease to be treated as a self-employed person if they were temporarily unable to pursue their activity as the result of an illness or accident.[115] This was much narrower than the provisions of the Directive,[116] which allowed a self-employed person to retain that status in the same way as a worker who was no longer working.

A.48 In *Tilianu*, the Court of Appeal applied this differential treatment and held that unless a self-employed person was temporarily unable to pursue their activity because of illness or accident, a person who was not working was not self-employed.[117] This meant that the self-employed had fewer rights than workers, because there were fewer circumstances in which they could retain that status when they were not working.[118]

A self-sufficient person

A.49 A self-sufficient person was a person who had sufficient resources not to become a burden on the social assistance system of the UK during their period of residence, and who has comprehensive sickness insurance cover in the UK.[119]

A.50 The requirement not to become a burden on the social assistance system of the UK was not qualified (as in the case of a person who had

---

110 *Secretary of State for Work and Pensions v SFF* [2015] UKUT 0502 (AAC) and *Weldemichael and Obulor v Secretary of State for the Home Department* [2015] UKUT 540 (IAC) at [59], a determination in relation to an immigration case.
111 *Secretary of State for Work and Pensions v SFF* at [35].
112 *Secretary of State for Work and Pensions v Dias* [2009] EWCA Civ 807, [2010] 1 CMLR 4 at [18].
113 EEA Regs 2016, reg 4(1)(b).
114 See *Jany*, above.
115 EEA Regs 2016, reg 6(4).
116 Directive 2004/38/EC, Art 7(3).
117 *R (Tilianu) v Secretary of State for Work and Pensions* [2010] EWCA Civ 1397, [2011] PTSR 781.
118 See paras **A.41–A.45**.
119 EEA Regs 2016, reg 4(1)(c).

an initial right to reside, which only required that the person was not to be an 'unreasonable' burden).[120]

A.51 A self-sufficient person was unlikely to be eligible in England under HA 1996, Parts 6 and 7, and in Wales under HA 1996, Part 6 and H(W) A 2014, Part 2, because the need for social housing would mean that they would have become a burden on the social assistance system of the UK and therefore could not have had a right to reside on the basis of self-sufficiency.[121]

A.52 The Commission of the European Communities published[122] guidance on the interpretation of the Directive which stated that any insurance cover, private or public, contracted in the host member state or elsewhere, was acceptable in principle, so long as it provided comprehensive coverage and did not create a burden on the public finances of the host member state.[123]

A.53 Following some conflicting decisions on whether enjoyment of the right to NHS cover would be sufficient, it has now been held that it is: *VI*.[124]

A student

A.54 A student was a person who:

a) was enrolled, for the principal purpose of following a course of study (including vocational training), at a private or public establishment financed from public funds or otherwise recognised by the secretary of state as an establishment accredited for the purpose of providing such courses or training within the law or administrative practice of the part of the UK in which the establishment was located;

b) had comprehensive sickness insurance cover in the UK; and

c) assured the secretary of state by means of a declaration or by such equivalent means as they chose that they had sufficient resources not to become a burden on the social assistance system of the UK during their period of residence.[125]

A.55 This meant that a person could have had a right to reside as a student even if they subsequently became a burden on the social assistance system of the UK, ie, if their circumstances changed. If a student

---

120 Directive 2004/38/EC, Art 14(1); EEA Regs 2016, reg 13; see para **A.30**.
121 By analogy, for the purposes of immigration law, 'public funds' is defined (Immigration Rules (HC 395) para 6) as including housing under HA 1996, Part 6 or Part 7 and HA 1985, Part 2; the rules have not been amended to reflect the introduction of H(W)A 2014, Part 2.
122 On 2 July 2009.
123 At para 2.3.2.
124 *VI v Revenue and Customs Commissioners* (C-247/20) [2022] 1 WLR 2902.
125 Directive 2004/38/EC, Art 7(1)(c); EEA Regs 2016, reg 4(1)(d).

could have had a right of residence despite having a need for social housing, then the student was likely to be eligible in England under both HA 1996, Parts 6[126] and 7,[127] and in Wales under HA 1996, Part 6 and H(W)A 2014, Part 2, so long as they were habitually resident in the UK.

Permanent right to reside

A.56 An EEA national who had resided in the UK for a continuous period of five years acquired a permanent right to reside.[128] The CJEU held that periods of imprisonment could not be taken into account, so that they interrupt continuity of residence for this purpose.[129] Family members who were not EEA nationals but who had resided with the EEA national for a continuous period of five years also obtained the right.[130]

A.57 Workers or self-employed persons who had stopped working (and their family members) also had a permanent right of residence in some circumstances:[131] the worker or self-employed person must have resided in the UK continuously for more than three years, must have worked for the last one of those years and then stopped working at an age when they were entitled to a state pension or, in the case of an employed person, had ceased work in order to take early retirement.[132]

A.58 The definition also applied to a person who had stopped working as a result of a permanent incapacity who had either resided in the UK continuously for more than two years prior to the termination, or whose incapacity was the result of an accident at work or an occupational disease that entitled them to a pension payable in full or in part by an institution in the UK.[133]

A.59 The Court of Appeal held that a non-EU national[134] was entitled to a permanent right to reside under Directive 2004/38/EC Article 17(3) on marrying an EU worker who had stopped working due to a permanent incapacity and who had lived in the UK for two years prior to that time; it was not necessary for them to have been a family member before, or as at the date of, their husband's acquisition of permanent residence.[135]

---

126 In England, Eligibility Regs 2006, reg 4(1); in Wales, Eligibility (Wales) Regs 2014, reg 4(1).
127 In England, Eligibility Regs 2006, reg 6(1); in Wales, Eligibility (Wales) Regs 2014, reg 6(1).
128 Directive 2004/38/EC, Art 16(1); EEA Regs 2016, reg 15(1).
129 *Onuekwere v Secretary of State for the Home Department, Secretary of State for the Home Department v MG*, Cases C-378/12 and C-400/12.
130 Directive 2004/38/EC, Art 16(1); EEA Regs 2016, reg 15(1)(b).
131 Directive 2004/38/EC, Art 17; EEA Regs 2016, reg 15(1)(c) and (d).
132 Directive 2004/38/EC, Art 17; EEA Regs 2016, reg 5(2).
133 Directive 2004/38/EC, Art 17; EEA Regs 2016, reg 5(3).
134 Sometimes known as a third country national.
135 *RM (Zimbabwe) v Secretary of State for the Home Department* [2013] EWCA Civ 775, [2014] 1 WLR 2259.

A.60　In *Lassal*,[136] the European Court of Justice (ECJ) noted that the permanent right to reside did not appear in previous EU legislation;[137] it held that continuous periods of five years' residence completed before the Directive came into force on 30 April 2006, in accordance with the previous legislation, had to be taken into account for the purposes of the acquisition of the right. It also held that absences from the host member state of less than two consecutive years, which occurred before 30 April 2006 but after a continuous period of five years' legal residence completed before that date, did not affect acquisition of the right of permanent residence.

A.61　In *Dias*,[138] the ECJ held that time spent in the UK before 30 April 2006, when Ms Dias had no right to reside but was in possession of a residence permit granted by the national authorities, did not constitute legal residence and therefore could not count towards the five years required for permanent residence. It was, however, also held that such time would not, so long as it amounted to less than two consecutive years, affect any right of permanent residence which had already been acquired.

A.62　In *Clauder*,[139] the European Free Trade Association (EFTA)[140] Court held that, although Article 16 of the Directive (para **A.56**) did not confer an autonomous right of residence on the family members of an EEA national with a permanent right to reside, it did grant them a derivative right to live with the holder of permanent residence. The admission and residence of the family members in such cases was not subject to a condition of sufficient resources, because the holder of a permanent right of residence was not subject to any such requirement and their enjoyment of that right would have been impaired and deprived of its full effectiveness if they were prevented from founding a family on the basis of insufficient resources. Family members would, however, only obtain permanent residence when they had fulfilled five years' residence.

A.63　In *Ziolkowski*,[141] the ECJ held that Article 16 (para **A.56**) meant that an EU citizen who had been resident for more than five years in a host member state exclusively on the basis of the national law of that state and without exercising any right based in EU law could not be regarded as having acquired permanent residence.

136　*Secretary of State for Work and Pensions v Lassal and Child Poverty Action Group (intervener)*, Case C-162/09, [2011] 1 CMLR 31.

137　Directives 64/221/EEC, 68/360/EEC, 72/194/EEC, 73/148/EEC, 75/34/EEC, 75/35/EEC, 90/364/EEC, 90/365/EEC and 93/96/EEC all of which were repealed by the Directive, and Regulation (EEC) No 1612/68 which was amended by the Directive.

138　*Secretary of State for Work and Pensions v Maria Dias*, Case C-325/09, [2011] 3 CMLR 40.

139　Case E-4/11, 26 July 2011.

140　This was not a decision of the CJEU because it concerned a retired German citizen living in Liechtenstein which is not a member of the EU and therefore not subject to the jurisdiction of the CJEU. Liechtenstein, along with Iceland and Norway, is part of the EEA and its references go to the EFTA Court instead.

141　*Ziolkowski and Szeja v Land Berlin*, Cases C-424/10 and C-425/10.

A.64 In the same case, it also held that periods of residence completed by a national of a non-member state in the territory of a member state before its accession to the EU did, in the absence of specific provisions in the Act of Accession, have to be counted towards the period required to obtain permanent residence.

Residence documentation

A.65 An EEA national who had a right to reside in the UK was entitled to a registration certificate or derivative[142] residence card.[143] A non-EEA national who had a right to reside in the UK was entitled to a residence card or derivative residence card.[144] A person with a permanent right of residence was entitled to a permanent residence document.[145]

Family members of EEA nationals

A.66 The EEA Regs 2016[146] defined a 'family member' as:

a)   a spouse[147] or civil partner;

b)   direct descendants,[148] including those of a spouse or civil partner, who are:

i)   under 21; or

142 A derivative residence card was granted to a person whose right to reside in the UK was dependent upon another person's right to reside.
143 Directive 2004/38/EC, Art 8; EEA Regs 2016, regs 17 and 20; the right to reside exists independently of any residence documentation which is merely evidence of the right, see *da Veiga v Staatssecretaris van Justitie*, Case 9/88; *Echternach and Moritz v Minister van Onderwijs en Wetenschappen*, Cases 389/87 and 390/87, at [25]; *Secretary of State for Work and Pensions v Dias*, Case C-325/09 at [48].
144 Directive 2004/38/EC, Art 10; EEA Regs 2016, regs 18 and 20.
145 Directive 2004/38/EC, Arts 19 and 20; EEA Regs 2016, reg 19.
146 EEA Regs 2016, reg 7(1).
147 EEA Regs 2016, reg 7(1)(a). In *Diatta v Land Berlin* [1985] EUECJ R 267/83, the CJEU held that a marital relationship continues until terminated by the competent authority and is not affected by the fact that the spouses live separately, even where they intend to divorce at a later date. Note EEA Regs 2016, reg 2(1) states that a spouse does not include: a) a party to a marriage of convenience; or b) the spouse of a person who already has a spouse, civil partner or durable partner in the UK.
148 In *SM (Algeria) v Entry Clearance Officer* [2018] UKSC 9, it was held that direct descendants refers to consanguineous children, grandchildren and other blood descendants in the direct line, which may include step descendants, and those descendants who had been lawfully adopted in accordance with the requirements of the host country. The case concerned a child who had become the subject of guardianship under the kefalah system in Algeria. The Supreme Court referred to the CJEU the question whether the child was a direct descendant in those circumstances but also decided that if the child was not a direct descendant under Art 2(2)(c) of the Directive, then it would be another family member under Art 3(2)(a). In *SM v Entry Clearance Officer* C-129/18, the CJEU agreed with the Supreme Court that children under the kefalah system were not direct descendants and that they were instead to be treated as other family members under Art 3(2)(a).

      ii) their dependants;[149]

  c) dependent[150] direct[151] relatives in the person's ascending line (ie, parents or grandparents) or those of the person's spouse or civil partner; or

  d) extended family members[152] who had been issued with an EEA family permit, a registration certificate or a residence card and who satisfied the conditions in EEA Regs 2016, reg 8.

A.67 In *Jia*,[153] the CJEU defined 'dependency' to mean that the family member needs the material support of the EEA national or their spouse in order to meet their essential needs in the country of origin. Proof to establish such material support could be adduced by any appropriate means and was not confined to financial dependency.[154]

A.68 This decision was distinguished by the Court of Appeal,[155] which held that Article 2(2) of the Directive did not specify when the dependency had to have arisen, nor did it require that the relative had to be dependent in the country of origin. It further held that Article 2(2), taken together with Article 8(5)(d), suggested that dependency in the state of origin need not be proved for family members and that it was sufficient for the dependency to have arisen in the host member state: such an interpretation reflected the policy of the Directive to strengthen and simplify the realisation of realistic free movement rights of EU citizens compatibly with their family rights; accordingly, proof of dependency by the claimant on her son in the UK sufficed.

A.69 In *Metock*,[156] the CJEU held that, in order to benefit from the free movement rights set out in the Directive, it was contrary to the Directive for a member state to enact legislation which required a non-EEA national, who was the spouse of an EU citizen residing in

---

149 In *Reyes v Migrationsverket*, Case C-423/12, the CJEU held that a member state could not require a direct descendent who is 21 years old or over to have tried to obtain employment or subsistence support from their home state before they could be treated as a dependant under the Directive Art 2(2)(c). In *Lim v Entry Clearance Officer Manila* [2015] EWCA Civ 1383 per Elias LJ at [32], it was held that the critical question was whether the claimant was in fact in a position to support themselves which is an issue of fact. If they could support themselves, there was no dependency, even if they were given financial material support by the EU citizen. If they could not, the court would not ask why, except where there was an abuse of rights. The fact that they chose not to get a job and become self-supporting was irrelevant.

150 EEA Regs 2016, reg 7(1)(c). This means dependent on the EEA national and not on any other non-EEA family member: *Fatima and others v Secretary of State for the Home Department* [2019] EWCA Civ 124, where the appellants were dependent on the non-EEA spouse.

151 *PG and VG* [2007] UKAIT 19, where it was held that 'direct' is not confined to the first generation but can include grandchildren, although not nieces, nephews, uncles and aunts. This approach was assumed to be correct in *Bigia and others v Entry Clearance Officer* [2009] EWCA Civ 79 at [4].

152 See para **A.72**.

153 *Jia v Migrationsverket*, Case C-1/05, [2007] QB 545.

154 *Jia* at [43].

155 *Pedro v Secretary of State for Work and Pensions* [2009] EWCA Civ 1358, [2010] PTSR 1504.

156 *Metock and others v Minister for Justice, Equality and Law Reform*, Case C-127/08.

that member state but not possessing its nationality, to have previously been lawfully resident in another member state before arriving in the host member state.

A.70 It was also held that Article 3(1) had to be interpreted to mean that a non-EEA national who was the spouse of an EU citizen residing in a member state whose nationality they did not possess, and who accompanied or joined that EU citizen, benefitted from the provisions of the Directive, irrespective of when and where the marriage took place and of how the national of a non-member country entered the host member state.

A.71 The EEA Regs 2006 were amended[157] to reflect this judgment, which change was carried across to the EEA Regs 2016, so that the family member who was accompanying the EEA national to the UK, or joining the EEA national here, no longer had to have been lawfully resident in an EEA state or have met the requirements of the Immigration Rules.

A.72 An extended family member[158] was treated as the family member of the relevant EEA national for so long as they held a valid EEA family permit, a registration certificate or a residence card,[159] and was one of the following:[160]

    a) a relative of an EEA national, residing in a country other than the UK who was dependent on the EEA national or who was a member of the EEA national's household and who either was accompanying the EEA national to the UK or wanted to join them in the UK, or who had joined the EEA national in the UK and continued to be dependent upon them or to have been a member of the EEA national's household;[161]

    b) a relative of an EEA national or their spouse or civil partner, who strictly required their personal care on serious health grounds;[162]

    c) a relative of an EEA national who would have met the requirements for indefinite leave to enter or remain in the UK as a dependent relative of the EEA national;[163]

    d) a partner of an EEA national who could prove that they were in a durable[164] relationship with the EEA national.[165]

---

157 Immigration (European Economic Area) (Amendment) Regulations 2011/1247.
158 See para **A.66(d)**.
159 EEA Regs 2016, reg 7(3).
160 EEA Regs 2016, reg 8.
161 EEA Regs 2016, reg 8(2).
162 EEA Regs 2016, reg 8(3).
163 EEA Regs 2016, reg 8(4).
164 Home Office policy suggested that a period of two years' cohabitation was required. EEA Regs 2016, reg 2(1) defined a durable partner as not including a party to a durable partnership of convenience, or the durable partner (D) of a person (P) where a spouse, civil partner or durable partner of D or P was already present in the UK which marriage, civil partnership or durable relationship was subsisting.
165 EEA Regs 2016, reg 8(5).

A.73 The CJEU has held that member states had a wide discretion in setting criteria for extended family members: Article 3(2) of the Directive did not provide a direct right to reside for such persons, and states could impose requirements in their own domestic legislation.[166] This is consistent with domestic cases which held that extended family members had no right to reside unless they had residence documentation.[167]

A.74 Subsequent to the decision of the CJEU in *Rahman*,[168] the Court of Appeal approved its approach and held that Article 3(2) required an extended family member to show dependence that existed in the country from which the family member came; accordingly, and in contrast to the position of non-extended family members,[169] there was a requirement that the necessary relationship of dependency or membership of the household must have existed in another country as well as in the host state.[170]

A.75 A family member had a right to reside in the UK for so long as they remained the family member of an EEA national who had a right to reside in the UK.[171] The Directive provided that EEA nationals who were family members of an EEA national retained the right to reside on the death or departure of the EEA national from the host member state[172] or where there had been a divorce, annulment of marriage or termination of the registered partnership between the family member and the EEA national.[173] Under the Directive, family members who were not EEA nationals could also retain their right to reside.[174]

A.76 The EEA Regs 2016 provided that family members who were not EEA nationals could retain a right to reside in the following circumstances:[175]

a) if the qualified person had died and the family member had resided in the UK for at least a year before the death and, if they were an EEA national, would be a worker, a self-employed person or a self-sufficient person or the family member of such a person;[176]

b) if the family member was the direct descendant of a qualified person who had died or left the UK, or was a direct descendant of that person's spouse or civil partner, who was attending an educational

---

166 *Secretary of State for the Home Department v Rahman and others*, Case C-83/11 at [26].
167 *SS v Secretary of State for Work and Pensions (ESA)* [2011] UKUT 8 (AAC).
168 *Secretary of State for the Home Department v Rahman and others*, Case C-83/11.
169 See para **A.66.**
170 *Oboh and others v Secretary of State for the Home Department* [2013] EWCA Civ 1525, [2014] 1 WLR 1680.
171 EEA Regs 2016, reg 14(2).
172 Directive 2004/38/EC, Art 12(1).
173 Directive 2004/38/EC, Art 13(1).
174 Directive 2004/38/EC, Arts 12(2), (3), 13(2).
175 EEA Regs 2016, reg 10.
176 EEA Regs 2016, reg 10(2).

course in the UK immediately before the qualified person died or left the UK, and continued to attend such a course;[177]

c)   if the family member was the parent with actual custody of a child who satisfied b) above;[178]

d)   if the family member ceased to be such because they were divorced from the qualified person[179] or their civil partnership had been terminated, they are not an EEA national but if they were, they would be a worker,[180] a self-employed person or self-sufficient person or the family member of such a person, and either:

i)   the marriage or civil partnership had lasted for at least three years, and the couple resided in the UK for at least one year during its duration;[181] or

ii)   the former spouse or civil partner had custody of a child of the qualified person; or

iii) the former spouse or civil partner had the right of access to a child under the age of 18, and a court had ordered that such access must take place in the UK; or

iv) the continued right of residence in the UK of the person was warranted by particularly difficult circumstances,[182] eg, they or another family member had been a victim of domestic violence while the marriage or civil partnership was subsisting.[183]

177 EEA Regs 2016, reg 10(3).
178 EEA Regs 2016, reg 10(4).
179 In *Singh and others v Minister for Justice and Equality and Immigrant Council of Ireland*, Case C-218/14, [2016] QB 208, the ECJ held that a third country national, divorced from an EU citizen, whose marriage had lasted for at least three years before the commencement of divorce proceedings, including at least one year in the host member state, could not retain a right of residence in that member state where the commencement of the divorce proceedings was preceded by the departure from that member state of the spouse who was the EU citizen. This decision was followed and applied by the CJEU in the later case of *Secretary of State for the Home Department v NA (Pakistan)*, Case C-115/15, [2017] QB 109.
180 In *Ahmed v Secretary of State for the Home Department* [2017] EWCA Civ 99, per Arden LJ at [14]–[19], the Court of Appeal held that the non-EU national former spouse must have been working at the date of the decree absolute in the divorce proceedings and that the non-EU national former spouse would not retain a right of residence if they only started working after that date. Both *Singh* and *NA (Pakistan)* – see ibid – were followed and applied; the court did not consider that there was sufficient lack of clarity on the issue to justify a reference to the CJEU.
181 EEA Regs 2016, reg 10(5)(d)(i).
182 In *Secretary of State for the Home Department v NA (Pakistan)*, Case C-115/15, [2017] QB 109, CJEU, the former non-EU national spouse of an EU national claimed a derivative right of residence because of domestic violence, even though her former spouse had left the UK before the divorce proceedings began. The CJEU held that she did not retain any right of residence and that a non-EU national spouse of an EU national had a derivative right of residence in a member state only if the EU national spouse was resident in that member state at the start of the divorce proceedings.
183 EEA Regs 2016, reg 10(5).

Exception Arrangements

A.77 A number of exceptions were enacted as more member states joined the EU, allowing a reduction in rights for a limited period of time, and which do not now require more than a brief reference for clarity: while any applicant's housing rights may remain subject to Part 7 not merely for years but for a decade or more, the issue of immigration status will almost certainly have been determined in a much shorter span of time.

A.78 **A8 Nationals.** The Accession Treaty signed in Athens on 16 April 2003 provided that 10 countries[184] would accede to the EU on 1 May 2004. The treaty provided that existing member states could, as a derogation from the usual position under EU law, regulate access to their labour markets by nationals of the accession states, other than nationals of Cyprus and Malta. The states to which this derogation applies are known as the 'A8' countries.

A.79 The derogation could be applied for a transitional period of five years from 1 May 2004, with a provision for a further two years in the case of disturbances to the labour market of the member state. In England and Wales, the derogation was extended until 30 April 2011,[185] but ended from midnight on that date.[186]

A.80 The secondary legislation which abolished the derogation introduced a new regulation (reg 7A) into the EEA Regs 2006, the effect of which was that an A8 national could retain worker status if they became unable to work, became unemployed or ceased to work, as the case may be, on or after 1 May 2011, or if on 30 April 2011 they had ceased working for an authorised employer in the circumstances mentioned in EEA Regs 2006, reg 6(2), during the first month of their employment and was still within that first month.

A.81 **A2 Nationals.** The Treaty of Accession for Bulgaria and Romania was signed in Luxembourg on 25 April 2005. It provided for the accession of Bulgaria and Romania ('the A2') to the EU on 1 January 2007. During a transitional period of five years from 1 January 2007 to 31 December 2011, the existing member states could regulate access to their labour markets by A2 workers and restrict their rights of residence.[187] There were also provisions for member states to continue to maintain restrictions for a further two years in the case of disturbances to their labour markets.

---

184 Cyprus, the Czech Republic, Estonia, Hungary, Latvia, Lithuania, Malta, Poland, Slovakia and Slovenia.
185 Accession (Immigration and Worker Registration) (Amendment) Regulations 2009/892, which came into force on 29 April 2009.
186 By operation of the Accession (Immigration and Worker Registration) (Revocation, Savings and Consequential Provisions) Regulations 2011/544 which came into force on 1 May 2011. Notwithstanding the time that has elapsed, it cannot be assumed that all such cases will have been resolved – see also para **8.238**.
187 Annexes VI and VII of the Treaty of Accession.

A.82   The treaty was given domestic effect by the European Union (Accessions) Act 2006. This gave the secretary of state the power to enact regulations to permit the derogation from the provisions of EU law relating to workers. The detail of the derogation is contained in the Accession (Immigration and Worker Authorisation) Regulations (A(IWA) Regs) 2006.[188] On 23 November 2011, the government decided to extend the derogation for a further two years from 31 December 2011.[189]

A.83   **Croatians.** On 1 July 2013, the Republic of Croatia acceded to the EU. Annex V to the Treaty of Accession, signed at Brussels on 9 December 2011, permitted member states to derogate from various provisions concerning freedom of movement under EU law which relate to access to their labour markets by Croatian nationals during the accession period from 1 July 2013 to 30 June 2018.

A.84   The UK chose to take advantage of this right and, in exercise of the powers conferred under the European Union (Croatian Accession and Irish Protocol) Act 2013,[190] the secretary of state made the Accession of Croatia (Immigration and Worker Authorisation) Regulations (AC(IWA) Regs) 2013[191] which came into force on 1 July 2013. The effect of the AC(IWA) Regs 2013 was to create a worker authorisation scheme for Croatian nationals which was almost identical to that which was in place for A2 nationals,[192] and which lasted until 30 June 2018.

Other rights of residence

Self-sufficient families

A.85   Rights of residence could exist outside the scope of the Directive. In *Chen*,[193] Mrs Chen and her husband were both Chinese nationals and worked for a company established in China but, for the purposes of work, Mr Chen travelled frequently to various member states of the EU, in particular the UK.[194] Their daughter was born in Belfast and had Irish nationality.[195] The child was dependent both emotionally and financially on her mother, Mrs Chen, who was her primary carer, and she received private medical and childcare services in the UK.[196]

---

188 Accession (Immigration and Worker Authorisation) Regulations 2006/3317, which came into force on 1 January 2007.
189 Although the regulations were revoked by the Immigration, Nationality and Asylum (EU Exit) Regulations 2019/745, it cannot be assumed that all such cases will have been resolved – see also para **8.238**.
190 Section 4.
191 Accession of Croatia (Immigration and Worker Authorisation) Regulations 2013/1460.
192 Para **A.81**.
193 *Zhu and Chen v Secretary of State for the Home Department,* Case C-200/02, [2004] ECR I-9925.
194 *Zhu* at [7].
195 *Zhu* at [8].
196 *Zhu* at [12]–[14].

A.86 The CJEU held that Article 18 of the EC Treaty and Council Directive 90/364/EEC[197] conferred on a minor who was themselves an EEA national a right to reside for an indefinite period in a host member state, where that minor was covered by appropriate sickness insurance and in the care of a parent who was not an EEA national but who had sufficient resources for that minor not to become a burden on the public finances of the host member state; in such circumstances, the parent who was the primary carer was also entitled to reside with the child in the host member state.[198]

A.87 The Court of Appeal[199] has held that the requirements to have both comprehensive sickness insurance and sufficient resources such as to avoid becoming a burden on the social assistance system of the host member state, applied to the parents and the child, and had to exist before any right of residence could arise. It was also held that the right to reside in such circumstances was directly effective and existed independently of the terms of the EEA Regs 2016 and the Immigration Rules which were, in any event, to be interpreted compatibly with EU law where it was possible to do so.[200]

Primary carers[201] of children in education

A.88 The CJEU also derived a right of residence from Article 12 of Regulation (EEC) No 1612/68[202] which was subsequently repealed and replaced by Article 10 of Regulation (EU) No 492/2011.[203] This provided that the child of a national of a member state who was or had been employed in the territory of another member state was to be admitted to that state's general educational, apprenticeship and vocational training courses on the same conditions as nationals of that state, if the child was residing in its territory.

---

197 Of 28 June 1990.
198 *Zhu* at [41], [46], [47].
199 *W (China) and another v Secretary of State for the Home Department* [2006] EWCA Civ 1494, [2007] 1 WLR 1514.
200 *ECO (Dubai) v M (Ivory Coast)* [2010] UKUT 277 (IAC).
201 EEA Regs 2016, reg 16(8) defined a 'primary carer' as a person who was a direct relative or legal guardian of another person (AP), and either the person had primary responsibility for AP's care, or shares equally the responsibility for AP's care with one other person who was not an exempt person. An exempt person was a person with a right to reside under the EEA Regs 2016, or with a right of abode under IA 1971, s 2, or to whom IA 1971, s 8 applied, or in respect of whom an order had been made under IA 1971, s 8(2), or who had indefinite leave to enter or remain in the UK.
202 Of 15 October 1968.
203 Of 5 April 2011. This right was recognised as a derivative right of residence in EEA Regs 2006, reg 15A as inserted by Immigration (European Economic Area) (Amendment) Regulations 2012/1547, Sch 1, para 9 with effect from 16 July 2012. This became EEA Regs 2016, reg 16.

A.89   In *Baumbast and R v Secretary of State for the Home Department*,[204] the CJEU held that children of an EU citizen who had installed themselves in a member state during the exercise by their parent of rights of residence as a migrant worker were entitled to reside there in order to attend general educational courses. The CJEU also held that Article 12 had to be interpreted as entitling the parent who was the primary carer of those children, irrespective of nationality, to reside with them in order to facilitate the exercise of their right. It did not matter that the parents had divorced or that the parent who was an EU citizen had ceased to be a migrant worker in the host member state.[205]

A.90   *Baumbast* was reconsidered by the CJEU in *Ibrahim*[206] and *Teixeira*,[207] two homelessness appeals referred by the Court of Appeal[208] to the CJEU, which were heard together.

A.91   Ms Ibrahim was a Somali national, married to but separated from Mr Yusuf, a Danish citizen. They had four children, who were Danish. The two eldest were at school in the UK. Initially, Mr Yusuf worked but he then ceased to enjoy a right to reside as a worker and left to live in Eastern Europe. Although he returned to live in the UK, he never regained a right to reside. Ms Ibrahim did not work, was entirely reliant on means-tested benefits and had no medical insurance. She applied with her children for homelessness assistance under HA 1996, Part 7, but was refused on the basis that she had no right to reside under EU law.

A.92   Ms Teixeira was a Portuguese national. She came to the UK in 1989 with her husband, from whom she subsequently divorced. Her daughter was born in 1991. Ms Teixeira worked from 1989 to 1991, after which time she had intermittent periods of employment. She last worked in early 2005. The daughter entered education in the UK at a time when Ms Teixeira was not a worker; in November 2006, she enrolled in a childcare course and, in March 2007, she went to live with her mother. In April 2007, Ms Teixeira applied under HA 1996, Part 7, but was refused on the basis that she had no right to reside.

A.93   On both references, the ECJ held that where a child of an EU citizen was in education in a member state in which that citizen was or had been employed as a migrant worker, the parent who was the child's primary carer enjoyed a right of residence in the host state, derived from Article 12.[209] The child also had a right to reside in those circumstances.

---

204 Case C-413/99, [2002] ECR I-7091, [2002] 3 CMLR 23.
205 *Baumbast*, at [63] and [75].
206 Case C-310/08, [2010] HLR 31.
207 Case C-480/08, [2010] HLR 32.
208 *Harrow LBC and Secretary of State for the Home Department v Ibrahim* [2008] EWCA Civ 386, [2009] HLR 2; and *Teixeira v Lambeth LBC and Secretary of State for the Home Department* [2008] EWCA Civ 1088, [2009] HLR 9.
209 Now Art 10 of Regulation (EU) No 492/2011.

A.94 The right of residence of the parent was not subject to a requirement that the parent should have sufficient resources and comprehensive sickness insurance cover, nor was it subject to a requirement that the parent should have been employed as a migrant worker in the host state when the child first started education. It was sufficient for the child to have been installed in the host state during the exercise by a parent of rights of residence as a migrant worker in that state. The right of residence of the parent ended when the child reached the age of 18, unless the child continued to need the presence and care of that parent in order to be able to pursue and complete their education in the host member state.

A.95 The right to reside as the primary carer of a child in education who was the child of a migrant worker could apply to an A8 national, even where they had not completed 12 months of such work pursuant to the then applicable Worker Registration Scheme.[210] A former self-employed worker who was the primary carer of a dependent child who was in education in the host state, did not have a right to reside.[211]

A.96 In *Hrabkova*,[212] the Court of Appeal approved and followed this principle. It was held that education for children, at least in England, started for these purposes at around the age of five when compulsory education begins.[213] The term 'child' in Article 12 of Regulation (EEC) No 1612/68[214] should be read as including 'stepchild' as well.[215] This is consistent with the decision of the CJEU in *Depesme*,[216] that 'child' included not only a 'child' in a child–parent relationship with a worker, but also a child of the spouse or registered partner of that worker, where that worker supported the child in question.[217]

---

210 *Secretary of State for Work and Pensions v JS (IS)* [2010] UKUT 347 (AAC) which was approved in *Secretary of State for Work and Pensions v MP (IS)* [2011] UKUT 109 (AAC) at [32].

211 *Czop*, Case C-147/11; and *Punakova*, Case C-148/11, at [33], [40].

212 *Hrabkova v Secretary of State for Work and Pensions* [2017] EWCA Civ 794.

213 *Secretary of State for Work and Pensions v IM* [2011] UKUT 231 (AAC). This is reflected in the EEA Regs 2016, reg 16(7)(a) which stated that education excluded nursery education but does not exclude education received before the compulsory school age where that education was equivalent to the education received at or after compulsory school age.

214 Repealed and replaced by Art 10 of Regulation (EU) No 492/2011.

215 *Alarape and another (Article 12, EC Reg 1612/68) Nigeria* [2011] UKUT 413 (IAC) which was the subject of a reference to the ECJ, see *Alarape and Tijani v Secretary of State for the Home Department and AIRE Centre*, C-529/11.

216 *Depesme, Kerrou, Kauffmann and Lefort v Ministre de l'Enseignement superieur et de la Recherche*, Cases C-401/15 to C-403/15.

217 *Depesme* at [64] and [65], which concerned the meaning of child of a frontier worker under TFEU Art 45 and Regulation (EU) No 492/2011, Art 7(2). A 'frontier worker' was a worker or self-employed person who, after three years of continuous employment and residence in the host member state, worked in an employed or self-employed capacity in another member state, while retaining their place of residence in the host member state, to which they returned, as a rule, each day or at least once a week.

A.97   The Court of Appeal held that Article 12 of Regulation (EEC) No 1612/68[218] did not provide a qualifying right for permanent residence under Article 16 of the Directive,[219] which was in conflict with the decision of the ECJ in *Lassal*,[220] where it had been held that continuous periods of five years' residence completed before the Directive came into force on 30 April 2006, in accordance with earlier legislation, had to be taken into account for the purposes of the acquisition of the right of permanent residence.

A.98   In *Alarape*,[221] however, the CJEU held that the primary carer's right to reside under what was then Article 12 continued even after the child reached the age of 18, if that child remained in need of the presence and care of that parent in order to be able to continue and to complete their education, which it was for the referring court to assess, taking into account all the circumstances of the case. It was also held that periods of residence completed solely on the basis of Article 12, could not be counted for the purpose of acquiring permanent residence.

A.98   In *Ahmed*,[222] the CJEU held that a third country national mother could not rely on Article 12, where she was not married to the EU worker, they were merely cohabiting and the child was not the EU worker's biological child, because the daughter could not be regarded as the child of the spouse of a migrant worker or former migrant worker.

A.100   In *NA*,[223] the CJEU held that the right under Article 12 of Regulation (EEC) No 1612/68 was a right both to commence or continue education in the host member state and, as a consequence, conferred a right of residence. Whether the parent, the former migrant worker, did or did not reside in the host member state on the date when that child began to attend school, was of no relevance.[224]

218 Repealed and replaced by Art 10 of Regulation (EU) No 492/2011.
219 *Okafor and others v Secretary of State for the Home Department* [2011] EWCA Civ 499, [2011] 1 WLR 3071. This was reflected in EEA Regs 2006, reg 15(1A) inserted by Immigration (European Economic Area) (Amendment) Regulations 2012/1547, Sch 1, para 8(a), with effect from 16 July 2012, and subsequently in the EEA Regs 2016, reg 15(2).
220 *Secretary of State for Work and Pensions v Lassal and Child Poverty Action Group (intervener)*, Case C-162/09, [2011] 1 CMLR 31, CJEU.
221 *Alarape and Tijani v Secretary of State for the Home Department and AIRE Centre*, Case C-529/11.
222 *ONAFTS v Ahmed*, Case C-45/12.
223 *Secretary of State for the Home Department v NA (Pakistan)*, Case C-115/15, [2017] QB 109, CJEU.
224 *Secretary of State for the Home Department v NA* at [63].

British citizens and their families[225]

A.101   In *McCarthy*,[226] the applicant had both British and Irish nationality but was born and had always lived in England. She married a Jamaican national and argued that he had a right to reside in the UK as her spouse. The CJEU held that an EU citizen could not have a right to reside in circumstances where they had never exercised a right of free movement, and where they had always resided in a member state of which they were a national, even though they were also a national of another member state, provided that the circumstances did not include the application of measures by a member state which would deprive them of the genuine enjoyment of the substance of the rights conferred by virtue of their status as an EU citizen nor would impede the exercise of their right of free movement and residence within the territory of the member states.

A.102   In *Zambrano*,[227] the CJEU held that Article 20 of the TFEU was to be interpreted as precluding a member state from refusing a third country national upon whom their minor children, who were EU citizens, were dependent, a right of residence in the member state of residence and nationality of those children, insofar as such decisions deprived those children of the genuine enjoyment of the substance of the rights attaching to the status of an EU citizen. In that case, Mr Zambrano and his wife were Colombian citizens, but their children were Belgian citizens who had been born in and never moved from Belgium. *McCarthy* was distinguished on the basis that Mrs McCarthy was not obliged to leave the territory of the EU.

A.103   In *Dereci*,[228] the *Zambrano* principle was applied in a number of cases where there was no risk that the EU citizens concerned would be deprived of their means of subsistence.[229] It was held that EU law permitted a member state to refuse to allow a third country national to reside in its territory, where that third country national wished to reside with a member of their family who was a citizen of the host member state who had never exercised their right to freedom of movement.

---

225   The Immigration (European Economic Area) (Amendment) (No 2) Regulations 2012/2560 amended the EEA Regs 2006 by inserting a new reg 15A(4A) which recognised a derivative right to reside for a person who was the primary carer of a British citizen, where the relevant British citizen was residing in the UK and would be unable to reside in the UK or in another EEA state if the person were refused a right of residence. The Eligibility (Amendment) Regs 2012 amended the Eligibility Regs 2006 with effect from 8 November 2012 so that such a person was ineligible for an allocation of housing and for homelessness assistance. In *Pryce v Southwark LBC* [2012] EWCA Civ 1572, [2013] HLR 10, the Court of Appeal held, on a concession by the local authority and the government, that such a person had a right to reside and, at least in respect of applications made before 8 November 2012, was eligible for homelessness assistance.
226   *McCarthy v Secretary of State for the Home Department*, Case C-434/09.
227   *Zambrano v Office national de l'emploi (ONEm)*, Case C-34/09, [2012] QB 265.
228   *Dereci and others v Bundesministerium fur Inneres*, Case C-256/11.
229   *Dereci*, at [32].

Such a refusal could not, however, cause the EU citizen to be denied the genuine enjoyment of the substance of the rights conferred by virtue of their status as a citizen of the EU. Whether this test was met was a matter for the referring court to verify.

A.104 These cases led to the Immigration (European Economic Area) (Amendment) (No 2) Regulations 2012 which amended the EEA Regs 2006 so as to recognise, in domestic law, a derivative right to reside for a person who was the primary carer of a British citizen who was residing in the UK, which citizen would be unable to reside in the UK or in another EEA state if the carer was refused a right of residence.

A.105 The Eligibility Regs 2006 were, however, amended[230] so as specifically to exclude such persons from eligibility under HA 1996, Parts 6 and 7. The changes came into force on 8 November 2012, but only applied to applications under Parts 6 and 7 made on or after that date. In Wales, the equivalent changes were not made until the coming into force of the Eligibility (Wales) Regs 2014 on 31 October 2014.

A.106 The *Zambrano* principle was applied by the CJEU in *Iida*,[231] *O and S*[232] and *Ymeraga*,[233] In *CS*,[234] however, the CJEU held that a decision to expel a third country national who was the sole carer of minors who were citizens of the EU could be consistent with EU law where it was founded on the existence of a genuine, present and sufficiently serious threat to the requirements of public policy or of public security, provided account was taken of fundamental rights, in particular the right to respect for private and family life.

A.107 In *Pryce*,[235] based on concessions made by the local authority and the secretary of state, the Court of Appeal held that an applicant with a *Zambrano* right to reside had not been subject to immigration control and was therefore eligible for homelessness assistance. The amended eligibility regulations did not apply because of the date of the application, and the court therefore did not consider their lawfulness.

A.108 In *Harrison*,[236] the Court of Appeal held that the *Zambrano* principle did not extend to cover anything short of a situation where the EU citizen was forced to leave the territory of the EU;[237] the fact that the

---

230 By operation of Eligibility (Amendment) Regs 2012 with effect from 8 November 2012.
231 *Iida v Stadt Ulm*, Case C-40/11, [2013] Fam 121, CJEU.
232 *O and S v Maahanmuuttovirasto*, Cases C-356/11 and C-357/11, [2013] CMLR 33, CJEU.
233 *Ymeraga and others v Ministre du Travail, de l'emploi et de l'immigration*, Case C-87/12.
234 *Secretary of State for the Home Department v Rendon Marin*, Case C-165/14; *Secretary of State for the Home Department v CS*, Case C-304/14, [2017] QB 558, CJEU. See also *Robinson v Secretary of State for the Home Department* [2018] EWCA Civ 85, summarising and applying *CS*.
235 *Pryce v Southwark LBC* [2013] EWCA Civ 1572, [2013] HLR 10.
236 *Harrison (Jamaica) and AB (Morocco) v Secretary of State for the Home Department* [2012] EWCA Civ 1736, [2013] 2 CMLR 23.
237 *Harrison* at [63].

right to family life is adversely affected, or that the presence of the non-EU national was desirable for economic reasons, would not of themselves constitute factors capable of triggering the *Zambrano* principle.

A.109 In *Ahmed*,[238] the Upper Tribunal held that *Zambrano* only arose where a refusal decision would lead to an EU citizen child having to leave the EU, and only applied in exceptional circumstances.[239] That overstated the position somewhat: whilst it was correct that *Zambrano* was usually invoked to accord a right of residence to the non-EU parent of a British or EU citizen child in circumstances where the child would otherwise have had to leave the EU, it was capable of applying to non-EU nationals who were caring for elderly EU national parents.[240] *Zambrano* did, however, potentially apply even where the children were not citizens of the host member state but are nevertheless, EU citizens.[241]

A.110 In a case where the child had a parent who was a national of the host member state, the CJEU held[242] that the fact that the EU national parent had been able to look after the child did not necessarily mean that the child would not be compelled to leave the EU if the non-EU parent could not remain there. The ability and willingness of the EU parent was a relevant factor, but an assessment of all of the child's circumstances had to be carried out, taking into account Articles 7 and 24(2) of the Charter of Fundamental Rights of the EU. This required consideration of the best interests of the child, all the specific circumstances, including age and physical and emotional development, extent of emotional ties to both parents and the risks which separation from the third country parent might entail for the child's equilibrium.[243]

A.111 Likewise, in *Valaj v Secretary of State*,[244] the Court of Appeal said that whether the dependent child would be unable to stay in the UK was fact-specific which meant that the decision-maker and the court had to ask what was likely to happen if the family member were required to leave: accordingly, if there were two people capable of caring for the child, one of whom was likely to stay in the UK even if the other had to leave, there would be no breach of the rule in *Zambrano*.

---

238 *Ahmed v Secretary of State for the Home Department* [2013] UKUT 89 (IAC).
239 *Ahmed* at [67]. See also *Patel v Secretary of State for the Home Department* [2019] UKSC 59 at [22] 'What lies at the heart of the *Zambrano* jurisprudence is the requirement that the Union citizen would be compelled to leave Union territory if the [third country national] with whom the Union citizen has a relationship of dependency, is removed.'
240 *MS (Malaysia) v Secretary of State* [2019] EWCA Civ 580, although it would only be met in exceptional cases.
241 *Ahmed* at [68].
242 *Chavez-Vilchez and others v Raad van Bestuur van de Sociale Verzekeringsbank and others*, Case C-133/15.
243 See [72].
244 [2022] EWCA Civ 767; [2022] 3 WLR 291.

A.112 In *Hines*,[245] the Court of Appeal held that where a *Zambrano* carer had applied for homelessness assistance, the authority had to consider the welfare of the British citizen child and the extent to which the quality or standard of their life would be impaired if the non-EU citizen was required to leave. This was for the purpose of answering the question whether the child would, as a matter of practicality, be unable to remain in the UK. This required a consideration, among other things, of the impact which the removal of the primary carer would have on the child, and of the child's available alternative care.[246]

A.113 In *R (HC)*,[247] the Supreme Court considered that the *Zambrano* right was exceptional; it only arose if the child would have had to leave the EU if the right was not granted to the child's carer; the right was not concerned with the desirability of keeping a family together on economic or other grounds but was merely a right to reside in the EU not a right to a particular quality of life or to any particular standard of living.[248] It was held that the exclusion of *Zambrano* carers from homelessness assistance, allocations and most forms of welfare benefits, was not contrary to Article 21 of the EU Charter of Fundamental Rights because the Charter had no application because of Article 51. Nor was the exclusion a breach of Article 14 of the European Convention on Human Rights (ECHR) because its purpose was within the wide margin of discretion allowed to national governments in this field.[249]

A.114 In *Lounes*,[250] the Grand Chamber of the CJEU again considered the position of British citizens under EU law. Mr Lounes had married a Spanish national who had become a British citizen after exercising a right to reside in the UK. This distinguished his case from that of *McCarthy*[251] who had dual nationality but had never exercised a right of free movement.[252] It was held that Mr Lounes had no right under the Directive[253] but did have a derivative right to reside under Article 21(1) of the TFEU:[254] it would be contrary to the underlying logic of gradual integration that informed that article to hold that such citizens, who had acquired rights under that provision as a result of having exercised their freedom of movement, had foregone those rights because they had sought, by becoming naturalised in that member state, to become more deeply integrated in the society of that state.[255]

---

245 *Hines v Lambeth LBC* [2014] EWCA Civ 660, [2014] HLR 32.
246 *Hines* at [6], [23].
247 *R (HC) v Secretary of State for Work and Pensions* [2017] UKSC 73, [2018] HLR 6.
248 See [11], [15].
249 See [32].
250 *Lounes v Secretary of State for the Home Department*, Case C 165/16.
251 Para **A.101**.
252 See [23].
253 See [37].
254 See [58].
255 See [58], [62], [63].

PROVISION OF INFORMATION

A.115 If there are doubts about an applicant's immigration status, an authority can contact the Home Office to obtain relevant information. When a request is made, in England HA 1996, s 187 and in Wales H(W)A 2014, Sch 2, para 3, it places a duty on the secretary of state to provide the authority with such information as it may require to enable it to determine whether a person is eligible for assistance in England under HA 1996, Part 7 and in Wales under H(W)A 2014, Part 2, respectively.

A.116 The English Homelessness Code no longer explains how to contact the relevant immigration authorities. By contrast, the Welsh Code explains that contact should be made with the Home Office's UK Visa and Immigration Centre (UKVI).[256] Enquiries are dealt with by the Evidence and Enquiries Unit (EEU).

A.117 The EEU's Local Authorities' Team will only assist once the authority has registered. This requires:

a) the name of the enquiring housing authority on headed paper;

b) the job title/status of the officer registering on behalf of the local housing authority; and

c) the names of officers, and their job titles, who will be making the enquiries.

A.118 Once registered, enquiries can be made by letter or fax, or by email,[257] but replies will be returned by post. If the authority makes a written request, the secretary of state must confirm the information in writing.[258] The secretary of state is under a duty to update an authority in respect of any change in information that has been provided. Such a correction must be in writing, detail the change, the date on which the previous information became inaccurate and the reason why the information changed.[259]

HABITUAL RESIDENCE

A.119 The test of habitual residence is primarily[260] of relevance to eligibility;[261] it applies to all persons from abroad who are not subject to immigration

---

256 See annex 5 of the Welsh Code. UKVI can be found by following the links on www.gov.uk.
257 In non-asylum cases, the email address is EvidenceandEnquiry@homeoffice.gsi.gov.uk; Welsh Code annex 5, para 2.
258 In England, HA 1996, s 187(2); in Wales, H(W)A 2014, Sch 2, para 3(2).
259 In England, HA 1996, s 187(3); in Wales, H(W)A 2014, Sch 2, para 3(3).
260 But see also para **A.55**.
261 Paras **A.135–A.167**.

control and are returning to the UK. This can therefore include British citizens.

A.120 Two basic requirements need to be fulfilled to establish habitual residence:

a) the first is that an appreciable period of time must elapse before a person can be considered habitually resident;

b) the second is that the person concerned must have a settled intention to reside in the UK.[262]

A.121 Whether a person is habitually resident is a question of fact to be decided by reference to all the circumstances of the particular case.[263] The requirement for an appreciable period of time is not for a fixed period and may be short.[264] A month can be an appreciable period of time.[265] Where the person concerned is not coming to the UK for the first time, but resuming a previous habitual residence, which frequently occurs with British citizens, no appreciable period of time is required.[266] In the context of a benefits appeal, it has been held that, in the general run of cases, the period required to establish habitual residence will lie between one and three months.[267]

A.122 The second requirement for habitual residence is settled intention. For this, there must be a degree of settled purpose; what is necessary is that the purpose of living where one does has a sufficient degree of continuity to be properly described as settled.[268] The English Homelessness Code of Guidance reminds authorities that it is not uncommon for a person to live in one county but to own property elsewhere and that this does not, in itself, show that their centre of interest is in that other county.[269]

A.123 The English Homelessness Code states that if an applicant who was previously habitually resident in the UK is returning after a period spent abroad, and it can be established that they are is returning to resume their former period of habitual residence, they will be immediately habitually resident.[270] The English Code recommends that applicants who have been resident continuously for a two-year period[271] prior to their housing application will be habitually resident, but enquiries

---

262 *R (Paul-Coker) v Southwark LBC* [2006] EWHC 497 (Admin), [2006] HLR 32 at [19]–[28].
263 *Re J* [1990] 2 AC 562, HL per Lord Brandon at [578F–G].
264 *Nessa v Chief Adjudication Officer* [1998] 2 All ER 728, CA per Lord Slynn at [682]–[683].
265 *Re S* [1998] AC 750 at 763A; *Re F* [1992] FLR 548 at [555].
266 *Lewis v Lewis* [1956] 1 WLR 200; *Swaddling v Adjudication Officer*, Case C-90/97, [1999] All ER (EC) 217.
267 CIS/4474/2003.
268 *Shah v Barnet LBC* [1983] 2 AC 309, HL, at [344D]. Motives for residing in the UK may explain and confirm settled intention and as such may be relevant: *Kavanagh & Mohamed v Secretary of State for Work and Pensions* [2019] EWCA Civ 272.
269 Homelessness Code (England) annex 1, para 21.
270 Homelessness Code (England) annex 1, para 7; Welsh Homelessness Code annex 6, para 7.
271 A period of about six months appears to be applied more regularly in practice.

will need to be conducted where an applicant has less than two years' continuous residence.[272]

ELIGIBILITY – HOMELESSNESS: HOUSING ACT 1996, PART 7 AND HOUSING (WALES) ACT 2014, PART 2

Introduction

Applicants

A.124 In England under HA 1996, Part 7 and in Wales under H(W)A 2014, Part 2, eligibility must be determined whenever an authority has reason to believe that an applicant may be homeless or threatened with homelessness.[273] The date for establishing whether an applicant is eligible is the date of the decision and not the date of application.[274] Where there is a review, it is the date of the review decision that is key.[275]

A.125 While an authority is entitled to reach its own decision as to an applicant's immigration status, any such decision is for its own purposes only and will be subject to any contrary decision by the immigration authorities.[276] An authority is entitled to take an immigration decision of the Home Office at face value and is not required to carry out its own further investigations to determine eligibility.[277]

A.126 Where a full housing duty has been accepted in England under HA 1996, s 193(2),[278] or in Wales under H(W)A 2014, s 66, s 68, s 73 or s 75, an authority may revisit the issue of eligibility and will cease to be subject to the duty if an applicant ceases to be eligible.[279]

Other members of the household

A.127 In England, HA 1996, s 185(4), and in Wales, H(W)A 2014, Sch 2, para 1(5), require authorities also to consider the eligibility of household members.

---

272 Homelessness Code (England) para 7.19; Welsh Homelessness Code annex 6, para 1.
273 In England, HA 1996, s 184(1)(a); in Wales, H(W)A 2014, s 62(4).
274 *R v Southwark LBC ex p Bediako* (1997) 30 HLR 22, QBD.
275 *Mohamed v Hammersmith and Fulham LBC* [2001] UKHL 57, [2002] 1 AC 547, [2002] HLR 7.
276 *R v Westminster City Council ex p Castelli and Tristan-Garcia* (1996) 28 HLR 616, CA; *Tower Hamlets LBC v Secretary of State for the Environment* [1993] QB 632, (1993) 25 HLR 524, CA.
277 *R (Burns) v Southwark LBC* [2004] EWHC 1901 (Admin), [2004] NPC 127.
278 See paras **8.129–8.237**.
279 In England, HA 1996, s 193(6)(a); in Wales, H(W)A 2014, s 79(2).

A.128 The section formerly required[280] authorities to disregard ineligible household members[281] when determining whether an eligible applicant was homeless or had a priority need. The provision was, however, declared incompatible with ECHR Article 14 (prohibition of discrimination) when read with Article 8 (right to respect for one's private and family life), to the extent that it required a dependent child or pregnant spouse of a British citizen, habitually resident in the UK but subject to immigration control, to be disregarded when determining whether the British citizen had a priority need for accommodation.[282]

A.129 The section was accordingly amended[283] so that it now[284] applies only to eligible applicants who are themselves subject to immigration control for example, those granted refugee status, indefinite leave to remain (ILR) or humanitarian protection.[285] In Wales, the same approach has been followed.[286] When considering an application from such an applicant, authorities must continue to disregard any dependants or other household members who are ineligible for assistance for any reason, for the purpose of deciding whether the applicant is homeless or has a priority need[287] but, otherwise (ie, when the applicant is not

---

280 In respect of all applications for accommodation or assistance in obtaining accommodation, within the meaning of HA 1996, s 183, made before 2 March 2009.

281 For example, in *Ehiabor v Kensington and Chelsea RLBC* [2008] EWCA Civ 1074, the applicant could not rely on the dependent child to establish a priority need because the child, although born in the UK, was not a British citizen and therefore required leave to remain under IA 1971, s 1(2) and was subject to immigration control. See also *Ismail v Newham LBC* [2018] EWCA Civ 665.

282 *R (Morris) v Westminster City Council (No 3)* [2005] EWCA Civ 1184, [2006] 1 WLR 505, [2006] HLR 8. In *Bah v UK*, App No 56328/07, 27 September 2011, the European Court of Human Rights (ECtHR) did not follow *Morris*, but held instead that the immigration status of the child which resulted in his mother's differential treatment was reasonably and objectively justified by the need to allocate, as fairly as possible, the scarce stock of social housing available in the UK and the legitimacy, in so allocating, of having regard to the immigration status of those who are in need of housing. Accordingly, there was no violation of Art 14, when taken in conjunction with Art 8 of the ECHR. The court expressly stated, however, that it was not ruling on the discriminatory effect of the amendments.

283 By operation of the Housing and Regeneration Act 2008, s 314, Sch 15 and Part 1. In *Lekpo-Bozua v Hackney LBC* [2010] EWCA Civ 909, [2010] HLR 46, the Court of Appeal had granted permission for a challenge to the lawfulness of the unamended regime but the issue was not pursued in the substantive appeal because the issue did not in fact arise.

284 In respect of all applications for accommodation or assistance in obtaining accommodation, within the meaning of HA 1996, s 183, made on or after 2 March 2009.

285 See paras **A.135–A.167**.

286 H(W)A 2014, Sch 2, para 1(6).

287 See the letter from the Department for Communities and Local Government (DCLG) to Chief Housing Officers dated 16 February 2009 and the accompanying guidance note.

themselves a person subject to immigration control),[288] they are to be taken into account.[289] These cases are known as restricted cases.[290]

A.130 It follows that applicants who are not subject to immigration control[291] are now able to rely on ineligible household members to qualify as homeless or in priority need, and to confer an entitlement to be secured suitable accommodation in England under HA 1996, s 193(2) and in Wales a duty under H(W)A 2014, s 66, s 68, s 73 or s 75. Typically, ineligible household members who could confer priority need in this way are likely to be dependent children and pregnant women who have been granted leave with a condition of no recourse to public funds.[292]

A.131 This does not, however, give such applicants the same rights as others. An application pursuant to which the authority would not be satisfied that the applicant had a priority need but for what is termed a 'restricted person' is called a 'restricted case'.[293]

A.132 A restricted person is a person who is ineligible and subject to immigration control,[294] who either does not have leave to enter or remain in the UK or who has leave subject to a condition of no recourse to public funds.[295] In a restricted case, in both England and Wales, a local housing authority must, so far as reasonably practicable, bring its duty to an end by securing a private rented sector offer.[296]

A.133 The discharge provisions governing restricted cases are considered in chapter 8,[297] both before and after the commencement of the LA 2011.

---

288 See paras **A.15** and onwards.
289 Until 31 December 2020, applicants subject to immigration control for this purpose did not include EAA and Swiss nationals: with effect from that date, this exception was removed, save for those nationals who were lawfully resident on 31 December 2020; such nationals remain entitled to rely on an ineligible household member, see Immigration and Social Security Co-ordination (EU Withdrawal) Act 2020 (Consequential, Saving, Transitional and Transitory Provisions) (EU Exit) Regulations 2020, amending HA 1996, s 185(5).
290 HA 1996, s 193(3B).
291 Plus the residual category of EAA and Swiss nationals relying on their pre-31 December 2020 right.
292 For the purposes of UK immigration law, the term 'public funds' is defined in Immigration Rules (HC 395) para 6 as including housing under HA 1996, Part 6 or Part 7 and HA 1985, Part 2. The Immigration Rules have not yet been updated to reflect the position under H(W) A 2014, Part 2, but there seems little doubt that the phrase will be interpreted the same way.
293 In England, HA 1996, s 193(3B); in Wales, H(W)A 2014, s 76(5).
294 See para **A.14**.
295 In England, HA 1996, s 184(7); in Wales, H(W)A 2014, s 63(5).
296 In England, HA 1996, s 193(7AD); in Wales, H(W)A 2014, s 76(5).
297 See paras **8.272–8.281**.

Homelessness assistance

Generally

A.134 The division into persons subject and not subject to immigration control[298] applies in both England and Wales. Eligibility for both homelessness assistance and for an allocation is not, however, quite the same in England and Wales: in the classes set out below, Wales has not incorporated Classes J and N.

Persons subject to immigration control

A.135 For a person subject to immigration control to be eligible for assistance, the person must fall within one of the prescribed classes.[299]

Class A

A.136 Class A[300] is a person who is recorded by the secretary of state as a refugee within the definition set out in Article 1 of the Refugee Convention[301] and who has leave to enter or remain in the UK.

A.137 Under Article 1, a refugee is any person:

a) who, owing to a well-founded fear of being persecuted for reasons of race, religion, nationality, membership of a particular social group or political opinion, is outside the country of their nationality and is unable or, owing to such fear, unwilling to avail themselves of the protection of that country; or

b) who, not having a nationality and being outside the country of their former habitual residence as a result of such events, is unable or, owing to such fear, unwilling to return to it.

A.138 Recognition as a refugee almost inevitably leads to a grant of leave to remain. Prior to 30 August 2005, refugees were granted indefinite leave to remain (ILR). From that date, the grant is normally for five years.

A.139 During the limited five-year period, refugee status can be reviewed and removed, eg, if there has been a change in circumstances in the

---

298 Paras **A.13–A.15**.
299 Allocation of Housing and Homelessness (Eligibility) (England) Regulations (Eligibility Regs 2006) 2006/1294 and Allocation of Housing and Homelessness (Eligibility) (Wales) Regulations (Eligibility (Wales) Regs) 2014/2603. The Eligibility Regulations are so frequently amended that in practice recourse needs to be had to an online service such as Westlaw or Nexis for the position at any given point in time.
300 Eligibility Regs 2006, reg 5(1)(a); and Eligibility (Wales) Regs 2014), reg 5(1)(a).
301 The Convention relating to the Status of Refugees was adopted by a Conference of Plenipotentiaries of the United Nations (UN) on 28 July 1951 and entered into force on 21 April 1954.

refugee's country of origin, or they have returned there. There is normally no review at the end of the five-year period but one can be triggered if there is evidence of criminality or if an application for settlement is made after the initial period of leave has expired. At the end of the five-year period, the refugee qualifies for ILR in the UK.

A.140 From early 2002, application registration cards (ARCs) have been issued to asylum-seekers and their dependants during the asylum screening process. The ARC is a credit card sized form of identity. If an application for asylum is successful, the applicant will be given a letter by the Home Office which explains the applicant's position as a refugee and some of their rights in the UK.

A.141 A refugee's national passport is not stamped, because the refugee cannot use it without forfeiting their refugee status. Instead, the refugee will be issued with an Immigration Status Document (ISD). These were phased in during late 2003 and early 2004 and are an A4 sheet of paper, folded into four, confirming the immigration status of the holder. An ISD is also designed to hold a UK Residence Permit (UKRP).

A.142 Since late 2003, the ink stamps that used to be endorsed in passports and travel documents have been progressively replaced by UKRPs which are issued to those granted more than six months' leave to enter or remain in the UK. The UKRP takes the form of a credit card sized sticker or vignette. It was introduced in accordance with Regulation (EC) No 1030/2002 which required EU countries which had opted in to this regulation to issue uniform format vignettes to all non-EEA nationals granted more than six months' leave to enter or remain. They are a security measure. More recently, biometric residence permits have been issued.

A.143 Refugees may apply for a refugee travel document, which looks like a passport. This is issued by the Home Office under the United Nations Convention relating to the Status of Refugees and the applicant's leave will be endorsed in the document on a UKRP vignette.

Class B

A.144 Class B[302] is a person who has exceptional leave to enter or remain in the UK (ELR) granted outside the provisions of the Immigration Rules, whose leave to enter or remain is not subject to a condition requiring them to maintain and accommodate themselves and any person who is dependent on them without recourse to public funds, which includes housing and assistance under HA 1985, Part 2 or HA 1996, Parts 6 and

---

302 Eligibility Regs 2006, reg 5(1)(b); and Eligibility (Wales) Regs 2014, reg 5(1)(b).

7.[303] Exceptional leave to enter or remain was abolished from 1 April 2003 so that only a dwindling group now has this status.[304]

A.145 Exceptional leave to remain (ELR) describes the leave granted to applicants who were not found to be refugees but whom the Home Office, for humanitarian or compassionate reasons, determined it would not be right to require to return to their country of origin.

A.146 Persons with ELR should have a letter from the Home Office, sometimes known as a 'grant letter', explaining that they were granted ELR. They should also have their status stamped in their national passport. If they do not have a national passport, they will have been issued with an ISD containing a UKRP vignette. If such persons wish to travel but do not have a national passport, they may apply to the UK Visas and Immigration (UKVI) for a travel document known as a Certificate of Travel (COT).

Class C

A.147 Class C[305] applies to a person who is habitually resident in the UK, the Channel Islands, the Isle of Man or the Republic of Ireland and whose leave to enter or remain in the UK is not subject to any limitation or condition, other than a person:

a) who has been given leave to enter or remain in the UK upon an undertaking given by their sponsor;

b) who has been resident in the UK, the Channel Islands, the Isle of Man or the Republic of Ireland for less than five years beginning on the date of entry or the date on which their sponsor gave the undertaking in respect of them, whichever date is the later; and

c) whose sponsor or, where there is more than one sponsor, at least one of whose sponsors, is still alive.

A.148 This class also applies to any person with ILR in the UK unless that leave was granted on an undertaking by a sponsor less than five years ago and the sponsor is still alive.

A.149 Such a person should have a grant letter[306] from the Home Office, explaining that they have been granted ILR. They should have a stamp or UKRP in their national passport which shows that they have ILR. They may also have an ISD or a COT with a UKRP vignette which shows their status.

---

303 Immigration Rules (HC 395) para 6.
304 See now Class D, paras **A.151–A.154**.
305 Eligibility Regs 2006, reg 5(1)(c) and Eligibility (Wales) Regs 2014, reg 5(1)(c).
306 See para **A.146**.

A.150 This is also the class that is applicable to EEA nationals with settled status.[307]

Class D

A.151 Class D applies to a person who has humanitarian protection granted under the Immigration Rules.[308]

A.152 From 1 April 2003, the Home Office abolished ELR[309] and replaced it with humanitarian protection (HP) and discretionary leave (DL). HP is granted to someone who, if removed, would face a serious risk to life or person arising from capital punishment, unlawful killing or torture or inhuman or degrading treatment or punishment in the country of return.[310] Although not qualifying for refugee status, such persons would be at risk of treatment in violation of ECHR Articles 2 or 3 (right to life; and prohibition of torture, and inhuman or degrading treatment or punishment, respectively). The requirements in relation to HP can now be found in the Immigration Rules.[311]

A.153 From 30 August 2005 to 28 June 2022, someone granted HP was granted leave to remain for five years, after which an application could be made for settlement, at which point there was an automatic review of whether there was a continuing protection need. Where someone is granted HP after 28 June 2022, they are still granted leave to remain for five years and at the end of that period can apply for indefinite leave to remain.

A.154 Those with HP should have a grant letter[312] from the Home Office, explaining that they have been granted HL. Their ISD or national passport will contain a UKRP vignette granting leave for a period of five years. If they do not have a national passport, they may apply for a travel document or COT which, if issued, will contain the UKRP vignette.

Class F[313]

A.155 Class F applies only in Wales and has been repealed in England. It applies to a person who is habitually resident in the UK, the Channel Islands, the Isle of Man or the Republic of Ireland and who has limited

---

307 See para **A.18**.
308 Eligibility Regs 2006, reg 5(1)(d) and Eligibility (Wales) Regs 2014, reg 5(1)(d).
309 Para **A.144**.
310 Immigration Rules para 339C.
311 Immigration Rules para 339C.
312 See para **A.146**.
313 Class E has been repealed.

leave to enter the UK as a relevant Afghan citizen under Immigration Rules para 276BA(1).[314]

Class G

A.156 Class G[315] applies to a person who has limited leave to enter or remain in the UK on family or private life grounds under Article 8 of the ECHR, which leave has been granted under para 276BE(1), para 276DG or Appendix FM of the Immigration Rules and is not subject to a condition requiring them to maintain and accommodate themselves and their dependants without recourse to public funds. This covers persons with leave to enter or remain in the UK on the basis of their family life with a person who is a British citizen, is settled in the UK, or is in the UK with limited leave as a refugee or person granted humanitarian protection, and reflects the requirements of Article 8 of the ECHR.

Class H

A.157 Class H applies to a person who is habitually resident in the UK, the Channel Islands, the Isle of Man or the Republic of Ireland, who has been transferred to the UK under Immigration Act (IA) 2016, s 67 and who has limited leave to remain under Immigration Rules para 352ZH.[316] These are unaccompanied children admitted during the European refugee crisis of whom it was anticipated that they would be the responsibility of social services departments, rather than housing departments; the provision was enacted in order to facilitate planned and sustainable accommodation for them once they turned 16 and began to make plans to leave the care of social services.

Class I

A.158 Class I is an additional class of persons admitted during the refugee crisis, identified at a later date, who is habitually resident in the United Kingdom, the Channel Islands, the Isle of Man or the Republic of Ireland and who has Calais limited leave to remain under Immigration Rules para 352I.[317]

---

314 Eligibility (Wales) Regs 2014, reg 5(1)(f).
315 Eligibility Regs 2006, reg 5(1)(g); and Eligibility (Wales) Regs 2014, reg 5(1)(g).
316 Eligibility Regs 2006, reg 5(1)(h); Eligibility (Wales) Regs 2014, reg 5(1)(h).
317 Eligibility Regs 2006, reg 5(1)(i); Eligibility (Wales) Regs 2014, reg 5(1)(i).

Class J

A.159 Class J applies only in England. It applies to a person who has a limited right to leave or enter or remain in the UK by virtue of Appendix EU of the Immigration Rules, who is a family member of a Northern Irish national.[318]

Class K

A.160 Class K in England is Class J in Wales. It applies to a person who is habitually resident in the UK, the Channel Islands, the Isle of Man or the Republic of Ireland, who has limited leave to remain in the UK as a stateless[319] person under Immigration Rules para 405.[320]

Class L

A.161 Class L in England is Class K in Wales. It applies to a person with limited leave to enter or remain in the United Kingdom by virtue of Appendix Hong Kong British National (Overseas) of the Immigration Rules, whose leave to enter or remain is not subject to a condition requiring them to maintain and accommodate themselves and anyone dependent upon them without recourse to public funds, who is habitually resident in the United Kingdom, the Channel Islands, the Isle of Man or the Republic of Ireland.[321]

Class M

A.162 Class M in England is Class L in Wales. It applies to a person who has been who has been granted leave to enter or remain in the United Kingdom by virtue of the Afghan Relocations and Assistance Policy or the previous scheme for locally-employed staff in Afghanistan (sometimes referred to as the ex-gratia scheme) or who left Afghanistan in connection with the collapse of the Afghan government that took place on 15 August 2021, other than

a) a person who is subject to a condition requiring them to maintain and accommodate themselves and any person dependent on them without recourse to public funds or

b) who was given leave to enter or remain upon an undertaking given by their sponsor and who has been resident in the United Kingdom, the Channel Islands, the Isle of Man or the Republic of

318 Eligibility Regs 2006, reg 5(1)(j).
319 As to how a person can show they are stateless, see *AS (Guinea) v Secretary of State* [2018] EWCA Civ 2234.
320 Eligibility Regs 2006, reg 5(1)(k); Eligibility (Wales) Regs 2014, reg 5(1)(j).
321 Eligibility Regs 2006, reg 5(1)(l); Eligibility (Wales) Regs 2014, reg 5(1)(k).

Ireland for less than five years beginning on the date of entry or the date on which their sponsor gave the undertaking, whichever date is the later, and whose sponsor or, where there is more than one sponsor, at least one of whose sponsors, is still alive.[322]

Class N

A.163 Class N only applies in England. It applies to a person in the United Kingdom who was residing in Ukraine immediately before 1 January 2022, who left Ukraine in connection with the Russian invasion which took place on 24 February 2022 and who has been granted leave in accordance with immigration rules made under s 3(2) of the Immigration Act 1971, other than a person who is subject to a condition requiring them to maintain and accommodate themselves and any person who is dependent on them without recourse to public funds.[323]

Class O

A.164 Class O in England is Class M in Wales. It applies to a person in the United Kingdom who has limited leave to remain granted in accordance with Appendix Ukraine Scheme of the immigration rules pursuant to an application made by that person from within the United Kingdom. In England, it excludes persons who are subject to a condition requiring them to maintain and accommodate themselves and any person who is dependent on them without recourse to public funds; no such exclusion is found in the Welsh provision.[324]

Class P

A.165 Class P is Class N in Wales. It applies to a person who has limited leave to remain granted in accordance with Appendix Temporary Permission to Stay for Victims of Human Trafficking or Slavery of the Immigration Rules.[325]

Class Q

A.166 Class Q is Class O in Wales. It applies to a person who was residing in Sudan before 15 April 2023, who left in connection with the violence which rapidly escalated on that date in Khartoum and across Sudan,

---

322 Eligibility Regs 2006, reg 5(1)(m); Eligibility (Wales) Regs 2014, reg 5(1)(l).
323 Eligibility Regs 2006, reg 5(1)(n).
324 Eligibility Regs 2006, reg 5(1)(o); Eligibility (Wales) Regs 2014, reg 5(1)(m).
325 Eligibility Regs 2006, reg 5(1)(p); Eligibility (Wales) Regs 2014, reg 5(1)(n).

who has leave to enter or remain in the United Kingdom in accordance with the Immigration Rules, other than

a) a person who is subject to a condition requiring them to maintain and accommodate themselves and any person dependent on them without recourse to public funds or

b) who was given leave to enter or remain upon an undertaking given by their sponsor and who has been resident in the United Kingdom, the Channel Islands, the Isle of Man or the Republic of Ireland for less than five years beginning on the date of entry or the date on which their sponsor gave the undertaking, whichever date is the later, and whose sponsor or, where there is more than one sponsor, at least one of whose sponsors, is still alive.[326]

Class R

A.167 Class R is Class P in Wales. It applies to a person who

'(i) was residing in Israel, the West Bank, the Gaza Strip, East Jerusalem, the Golan Heights or Lebanon immediately before 7th October 2023;

(ii) left Israel, the West Bank, the Gaza Strip, East Jerusalem, the Golan Heights or Lebanon in connection with the Hamas terrorist attack in Israel on 7th October 2023 or the violence which rapidly escalated in the region following the attack;

(iii) has leave to enter or remain in the United Kingdom given in accordance with the Immigration Rules;

(iv) is not a person whose leave is subject to a condition requiring that person to maintain and accommodate themself, and any person who is dependent on that person, without recourse to public funds; and

(v) is not a person ("P")—

(aa) who has been given leave upon an undertaking given by P's sponsor;

(bb) who has been resident in the United Kingdom, the Channel Islands, the Isle of Man or the Republic of Ireland for less than five years beginning on the date of entry or the date on which P's sponsor gave the undertaking in respect of P, whichever date is the later; and

(cc) whose sponsor or, where there is more than one sponsor, at least one of whose sponsors, is still alive.' [327]

---

326 Eligibility Regs 2006, reg 5(1)(q); Eligibility (Wales) Regs 2014, reg 5(1)(o).
327 Eligibility Regs 2006, reg 5(1)(r); Eligibility (Wales) Regs 2014, reg 5(1)(o).

Persons not subject to immigration control

A.168 A person who is not subject to immigration control will be eligible if they: a) have the right to reside; and b) are habitually resident in the UK. Certain rights of residence are, however, excluded, and certain applicants are exempt from the habitual resident test.

The right to reside

A.169 Those with the right to reside have been identified above.[328] It includes those with pre-settled status who, before 1 January 2021, would have been eligible for assistance.[329] A person who is not subject to immigration control and who has the right to reside is, however, ineligible if:[330]

a) they are not habitually resident in the UK, the Channel Islands, the Isle of Man or the Republic of Ireland;[331] or

b) their right to reside in the UK is:

   i) exclusively based[332] on having pre-settled status which itself was granted because, on 31 December 2020, they were a jobseeker or the family member of a jobseeker;[333] or

   ii) they were exercising an initial right to reside for a period not exceeding three months;[334] or

   iii) they were exercising a derivative right to reside to which they were entitled under EEA Regs 2006, reg 15A(1), but only in a case where the right existed under that regulation because the applicant satisfies the criteria in reg 15A(4A);[335]

c) their only right to reside in the Channel Islands, the Isle of Man or the Republic of Ireland is a right equivalent to one of those mentioned in b) above.[336]

A.170 A number of people are, however, not to be treated as persons from abroad and, accordingly, are not ineligible.

---

328 Paras **A.15–A.24**.
329 Homelessness Code, para 7.34(a)(ii).
330 Eligibility Regs 2006, reg 6(1); Eligibility (Wales) Regs 2014, reg 6(1).
331 Eligibility Regs 2006, reg 6(1)(a); Eligibility (Wales) Regs 2014, reg 6(1)(a).
332 Disregarding a right to reside by virtue of having been granted limited leave to enter or remain in the United Kingdom under the Immigration Act 1971 by virtue of Appendix EU to the immigration rules made under s 3(2) of that Act or leave to enter the United Kingdom by virtue of an entry clearance that was granted under Appendix EU (Family Permit) to the immigration rules made under s 3(2) of that Act: Eligibility Regs 2006, reg 6(1A); Eligibility (Wales) Regs 2014, reg 6(1A).
333 Eligibility Regs 2006, reg 6(1)(b)(i); Eligibility (Wales) Regs 2014, reg 6(1)(b)(i).
334 Eligibility Regs 2006, reg 6(1)(b)(ii); Eligibility (Wales) Regs 2014, reg 6(1)(b)(ii).
335 Eligibility Regs 2006, reg 6(1)(b)(iii); Eligibility (Wales) Regs 2014, reg 6(1)(b)(iii).
336 Eligibility Regs 2006, reg 6(1)(c); Eligibility (Wales) Regs 2014, reg 6(1) (c).

(i) a worker;

(ii) a self-employed person;

(iii) a person who is treated as a worker for the purpose of the definition of 'qualified person' in regulation 6(1) of the EEA Regulations pursuant to regulation 5 of the Accession Regulations 2013 (right of residence of an accession State national subject to worker authorisation);

(iv) a person who is the family member of a person specified in sub-paragraphs (i)–(iii);

(v) a person with a right to reside permanently in the United Kingdom by virtue of regulation 15(1)(c), (d) or (e) of the EEA Regulations;

(vi) a person who is in the United Kingdom as a result of his deportation, expulsion or other removal by compulsion of law from another country to the United Kingdom;

(vii) a person who is a frontier worker within the meaning of regulation 3 of the Citizens' Rights (Frontier Workers) (EU Exit) Regulations 2020;

(viii) a person who is a family member of a person specified in sub-paragraph (vii) who has a right to reside by virtue of having been granted limited leave to enter or remain in the United Kingdom under the Immigration Act 1971 by virtue of Appendix EU to the immigration rules made under section 3 of that Act;

(ix) a person who left Afghanistan in connection with the collapse of the Afghan government that took place on 15 August 2021;

(x) a person who was residing in Ukraine immediately before 1 January 2022 and who left Ukraine in connection with the Russian invasion which took place on 24 February 2022;[337]

(xi) a person who was residing in Sudan before 15 April 2023 and left in connection with the violence which rapidly escalated on that date in Khartoum and across Sudan;

(xii) 'a person who was residing in Israel, the West Bank, the Gaza Strip, East Jerusalem, the Golan Heights or Lebanon immediately before 7th October 2023 and who left Israel, the West Bank, the Gaza Strip, East Jerusalem, the Golan Heights or Lebanon in connection with the Hamas terrorist attack in Israel on 7th October 2023 or the violence which rapidly escalated in the region following the attack.'[338]

---

337 Eligibility Regs 2006, reg 6(2); Eligibility (Wales) Regs 2014, reg 6(2).
338 Eligibility Regs 2006, reg 6(2); Eligibility (Wales) Regs 2014, reg 6(2).

Interim accommodation

Ineligibility

A.171 Notwithstanding prima facie eligibility for homelessness assistance as set out above,[339] Nationality, ImF6(2) migration and Asylum Act (NIAA) 2002, Sch 3 nonetheless disqualifies certain classes of immigrant in England from two types of interim accommodation.

A.172 These exclusions do not apply to British citizens or to those who are under 18.[340] They also do not apply in Wales, because the two statutory provisions no longer have effect there, having been replaced by the H(W)A 2014.[341] The two types of interim accommodation excluded are:

    a)   HA 1996, s 188(3) accommodation pending review;[342]

    b)   HA 1996, s 204(4) accommodation pending appeal to the county court.[343]

A.173 These classes are also disqualified from assistance under other statutory powers which are considered in Chapter 11, which include:

    a)   Care Act 2014, Part 1;[344]

    b)   SSWB(W)A 2014, Part 4 and ss 105–116;[345]

    c)   CA 1989, ss 17, 23C, 23CA,[346] 24A and 24B;[347]

    d)   IAA 1999;[348]

    e)   LA 2011, s 1;[349] and

    f)   LGA 2000, s 2.[350]

A.174 NIAA 2003, Sch 3 excludes the following five classes of persons from assistance under any of the statutory schemes set out in paras **A.17–A.173.**

    a)   someone who has been recognised as a refugee by an EEA state; this class also applies to a person who is the dependant of a person who is in the UK and who has such status;[351]

---

339 Paras **A.124–A.170.**
340 NIAA 2002, Sch 3, para 2(1)(a), (b).
341 NIAA 2002, Sch 3, para 1(1)(j) has not been amended to take account of the fact that HA 1996, ss 188(3) and 204(4) no longer apply in Wales, from the coming into force of the H(W)A 2014.
342 NIAA 2002, Sch 3, para 1(1)(j). See paras **8.51–8.60.**
343 NIAA 2002, Sch 3, para 1(1)(j). See para **10.252.**
344 NIAA 2002, Sch 3, para 1(1)(n): the Act applies only in England.
345 NIAA 2002, Sch 3, para 1(1)(o): the Act applies only in Wales.
346 Inserted by Children and Young Persons Act 2008, s 22(6).
347 NIAA 2002, Sch 3, para 1(1)(g). See paras **11.60–11.116.**
348 NIAA 2002, Sch 3, para 1(1)(l). See paras **11.42–11.59.**
349 NIAA 2002, Sch 3, para 1(1)(ka): the Act applies only in England.
350 NIAA 2002, Sch 3, para 1(1)(k): this part of the Act applies only in Wales.
351 NIAA 2002, Sch 3, para 4.

b) someone who has the nationality of an EEA state or who is the dependant of such a person;[352]

c) someone who was, but is no longer, an asylum-seeker and who is not co-operating with removal directions; it also applies to the dependant of such a person;[353]

d) someone who is in the UK in breach of NIAA 2002, s 11 and who is not an asylum-seeker.[354] In summary, this means anyone who is in the UK in breach of immigration laws;

e) someone who, although their asylum claim has been rejected, continues to be treated as an asylum-seeker and accommodated by the UKBA because they have dependent children,[355] but the Home Secretary has certified that they have, without reasonable excuse, not taken reasonable steps to leave the UK voluntarily or to place themselves in a position in which they are able to leave the UK voluntarily. They must have received the certificate and have been given 14 days to act. This class also applies to their dependants.[356]

Exceptions

A.175 A person who falls within one of these classes will not, however, be ineligible for assistance under any of the provisions set out at paras **A.171–A.173** if the exercise of a power or the performance of a duty is necessary for the purpose of avoiding a breach of:

a) a person's rights under the ECHR; or

b) a person's rights under the EU Treaties.[357]

---

352 NIAA 2002, Sch 3, para 5. The Home Office has announced plans to repeal this provision so as to ensure that EEA citizens are treated like other third country citizens: see Immigration and Social Security Co-ordination (EU Withdrawal) Act 2020 (Consequential, Saving, Transitional and Transitory Provisions) (EU Exit) Regulations 2020; see also letters of 19 November 2020 and 17 December 2020 from MHCLG and the Welsh Government (respectively) to local housing authorities in England and Wales.

353 NIAA 2002, Sch 3, para 6.

354 NIAA 2002, Sch 3, para 7. Note that the Immigration Act 2016 makes amendments to this provision so as to limit it to people unlawfully in Wales, Scotland and Northern Ireland, with provision for England made by new para 7B; these provisions are not are yet in force.

355 See paras **11.55–11.59**.

356 NIAA 2002, Sch 3, para 7A, inserted by Asylum and Immigration (Treatment of Claimants, etc) Act 2004, s 9 with effect from 1 December 2004, see Asylum and Immigration (Treatment of Claimants, etc) Act 2004 (Commencement No 2) Order 2004/2999. Note that the Immigration Act 2016 makes amendments to this provision so as to limit it to people unlawfully in Wales, Scotland and Northern Ireland, with provision for England made by new para 7C; these provisions are not are yet in force.

357 NIAA 2002, Sch 3, para 3. There are no known pending amendments to remove the reference to rights under the EU Treaties, but, since 1 January 2021, the Treaties have ceased to have effect in the UK.

A.176 The European Court of Human Rights (ECtHR) has been sympathetic to arguments based on ECHR Article 8 (right to respect for one's private and family life).[358] It has held that the right to family life includes the right of a parent and child mutually to enjoy each other's company,[359] and has found a violation of that Article where the deportation of an applicant from the Netherlands would interrupt his intermittent contact with his daughter there.[360]

A.177 Conversely, the Court of Appeal has held that neither Article 8 nor Article 3 (prohibition of torture and inhuman or degrading treatment or punishment) imposes a duty on the UK to provide support to foreign nationals who are in a position freely to return to their country of origin.[361]

A.178 This last proposition was also applied in a case where the claimant had an undetermined human rights claim.[362] It has been held that the making of a purported fresh claim either for asylum or under Article 3, by a claimant whose original claim had been rejected, did not always make it necessary for support to be provided in order to avoid a breach of the ECHR. In considering the issue, the authority had to have regard to all the relevant circumstances, including where appropriate the matters which were alleged to constitute a fresh claim. It is necessary to proceed on a case-by-case basis considering the facts of each case with care.[363]

A.179 In another case, *Clue*,[364] the Court of Appeal held that, when applying NIAA 2002, Sch 3, the authority should not consider the merits of an outstanding application for leave to remain unless satisfied that it was obviously hopeless or abusive. Unless so satisfied, the authority should not refuse assistance if to do so would have the effect of requiring the person to leave the UK and thereby forfeiting the claim. In that case, the authority's decision to refuse assistance was unlawful because its assessment had not taken the application for leave to remain into account nor had it stated that it was abusive or hopeless; moreover, the court was of the view that the application did have merits under ECHR Article 8.

A.180 Nevertheless, an authority does have the power to fund the costs of returning an applicant and their family to their country of origin.[365] It

---

358 See paras **10.123–10.125**.
359 *Olsson v Sweden* (1989) 11 EHRR 259.
360 *Ciliz v Netherlands* [2000] 2 FLR 469.
361 *R (K) v Lambeth LBC* [2003] EWCA Civ 1150, [2004] 1 WLR 272, [2004] HLR 15.
362 *R (Blackburn-Smith) v Lambeth LBC* [2007] EWHC 767 (Admin), (2007) 10 CCLR 352.
363 *R (AW) v Croydon LBC* [2005] EWHC 2950 (QB), (2005) 9 CCLR 252.
364 *R (Clue) v Birmingham City Council* [2010] EWCA Civ 460, [2011] 1 WLR 99.
365 *R (Grant) v Lambeth LBC* [2005] 1 WLR 1781, [2005] HLR 27, decided under LGA 2000 Part 1 (well-being) – which continues to apply in Wales – but it would seem likely that the same would apply to exercise of the general power of competence now available in England, under LA 2011 Part 1, Chapter 1.

would, however, be unlawful to offer to fund the cost of return travel unless it is a viable option.[366] An authority must closely scrutinise any argument that a return to the country of origin would give rise to a breach of ECHR rights.[367] It is important to take into account the potential effect of removal on each relevant family member and the impact on other family members. An authority should also take into account any relevant Home Office policy that concerns the issue of whether or not the claimant and their family will be able to remain in the UK.[368]

A.181 *R (De Alemeida)* is an example of where the claimant's circumstances were so dire that not providing accommodation would have breached his rights under ECHR Article 3:[369] the case concerned a Portuguese man who was terminally ill with HIV.

A.182 In *Paposhvili*,[370] the ECtHR qualified a previous decision, *N*,[371] in order to hold that Article 3 should be understood to prevent the removal of a seriously ill person in which substantial grounds have been shown for believing that they, although not at the end of their life, would face a real risk, on account of the absence of appropriate treatment in the receiving country or the lack of access to such treatment, of being exposed to a serious, rapid and irreversible decline in their state of health resulting in intense suffering; the benchmark is not, however, the health care system in the returning state and the focus should be on the individual's suffering instead. It is not decisive that the person is to be returned to a country which is a party to the ECHR (see also *MSS*[372] and *Tarakhel*[373] to the same effect as *Paposhvili*). In *AM*[374] the Supreme Court endorsed *Paposhvili*, concluding that it prevented deportation where substantial grounds had been shown for believing that the foreign national would face a real risk of being exposed to a serious, rapid and irreversible decline in their health or a significant, meaning substantial, reduction in life expectancy.

---

366 *R (J) v Enfield LBC* [2002] EWHC 432 (Admin); likewise under LGA 2000, and see para **11.125** on the LA 2011.

367 *R (PB) v Haringey LBC and others* [2006] EWHC 2255 (Admin), [2007] HLR 13, (2007) 10 CCLR 99; this was likewise under LGA 2000, and see para **11.125** on the LA 2011.

368 *Clue*, above.

369 *R (De Almeida) v Royal Borough of Kensington and Chelsea* [2012] EWHC 1082 (Admin).

370 *Paposhvili v Belgium*, App No 41738/10, in particular at [181].

371 *N v UK*, App No 26565/05, (2008) 47 EHRR 39, ECtHR.

372 *MSS v Belgium and Greece*, App No 30696/09, (2011) 53 EHRR 2, ECtHR.

373 *Tarakhel v Switzerland*, App No 29217/12, (2015) 60 EHRR 28, ECtHR.

374 *AM (Zimbabwe) v Secretary of State* [2020] UKSC 17; [2020] 2 WLR 1152, in which the court indicated that it expected the ECtHR to give further guidance when the Grand Chamber decided *Savran v Denmark* (App No 57467/15) (heard 24 June 2020 but, as at the date of publication, no judgment has been published).

A.183 The exception governing EU Treaty rights[375] had also been interpreted narrowly. It appears that it did not apply for the benefit of work seekers[376] but probably does assist workers.[377]

ELIGIBILITY – ALLOCATIONS: HOUSING ACT 1996, PART 6

Introduction

A.184 The operation of HA 1996, Part 6 is the subject of Chapter 9. This section is accordingly only concerned with its application in the immigration context.

A.185 The constraints considered here, which are applicable to both England and Wales,[378] do not apply to a person who is already a secure or introductory tenant, or an assured tenant of housing accommodation allocated to them by a local housing authority.[379]

A.186 Under the legislation preceding the HA 1996, when immigration was not explicitly addressed in either homelessness or allocations law,[380] it was held that a tenancy granted to a person unlawfully in the UK was not void for that reason.[381] The same applies under Part 6: notwithstanding the prohibition in HA 1996, s 167(8), it has been held that the grant of a tenancy, even though contrary to Part 6, is itself valid.[382]

A.187 The immigration status of members of the household of an applicant for an allocation under Part 6 is relevant, in particular when determining the size of the property to be allocated. It has long been said that Parliament cannot have intended to require authorities to house those who enter the country unlawfully.[383] Similarly, in *Akinbolu*,[384] it was held that it was proper to refuse to provide public sector housing to applicants who are illegal immigrants or overstayers.

---

375 See para **A.175**.
376 *R (Mohamed) v Harrow LBC* [2005] EWHC 3194 (Admin), [2006] HLR 18. As to work-seekers, see paras **A.33–A.35**.
377 *R (Conde) v Lambeth LBC* [2005] EWHC 62 (Admin), [2005] HLR 29.
378 Eligibility (Wales) Regs 2014, regs 3 and 4 as amended by the Allocation of Housing and Homelessness (Eligibility) (Wales) (Amendment) Regulations 2017 with effect from 22 June 2017.
379 HA 1996, s 159(5) as amended by Homelessness Act 2002, s 13.
380 See paras **A.6–A.8**.
381 *Akinbolu v Hackney LBC* (1996) 29 HLR 259, CA.
382 See *Birmingham City Council v Qasim* [2009] EWCA Civ 1080, [2010] HLR 19.
383 *Tower Hamlets LBC v Secretary of State for the Environment* [1993] QB 632, per Sir Thomas Bingham at p632, (1993) 25 HLR 524, CA; see also *R v Hillingdon LBC ex p Streeting (No 2)* [1980] 1 WLR 1425, CA.
384 *Akinbolu v Hackney LBC* (1996) 29 HLR 259, CA, at [269].

A.188 In *Ariemuguvbe*,[385] the appellant lived in a three-bedroom property with her husband, her five adult children who had come to the UK from Nigeria but who had overstayed their visitor's visas and three grandchildren. She contended that she was entitled to additional points under the authority's allocation scheme to take account of the five adult children.[386] The authority was held to be entitled to conclude that it was not appropriate to allocate a larger property to the appellant, because the five children were all independent adults, some having families of their own, who should have been able to make their own housing arrangements but also because they were subject to immigration control[387] in circumstances where providing accommodation for them would amount to them having recourse to public funds in breach of their conditions of entry to the UK.[388]

A.189 If the authority only owes a full housing duty to an applicant because of a restricted person,[389] then, so far as reasonably practicable, it must bring the duty to an end by making a private accommodation offer;[390] where it is not reasonably practicable to do so, the authority may discharge its duty under the other provisions of HA 1996, s 193 but should continue to try to bring the duty to an end with a private accommodation offer.[391] Consequently, if considering an allocation under Part 6, the authority will need to take particular care to ensure that it is in accordance with the priorities of its published allocation scheme.[392]

A.190 Authorities must consider eligibility at the point at which an applicant is considered for an allocation.[393] Authorities are, however, advised to consider applicants' eligibility both at the time of the initial application and again when considering making an allocation to them, especially where a substantial amount of time has elapsed since the original application.[394]

---

385 *R (Ariemuguvbe) v Islington LBC* [2009] EWCA Civ 1308; [2010] HLR 14. The Court of Appeal overruled the decision in *R (Kimvono) v Tower Hamlets LBC* (2001) 33 HLR 78, QBD, in which neither *Tower Hamlets* nor *Akinbolu* had been cited and in which it had been held that the immigration status of the applicant's dependent child was irrelevant to the authority's duties under HA 1996, Part 6.

386 *Ariemuguvbe* at [2] and [3].

387 See para **A.14**.

388 *Ariemuguvbe* at [19].

389 Paras **A.131**; **8.272–8.281**.

390 HA 1996, s 193(7AD).

391 Department of Communities and Local Government (DCLG) Guidance Note, 16 February 2009, para 14.

392 See para 17 of the guidance note that accompanied the DCLG letter dated 16 February 2009.

393 HA 1996, s 160ZA (England); s 160A (Wales).

394 Allocations Guidance para 3.3.

A.191 Eligibility for an allocation of housing depends on whether the applicant is a person: a) subject to immigration control;[395] or b) not subject to immigration control.[396]

Persons subject to immigration control
England

A.192 For a person subject to immigration control to be eligible, they must fall within one of the prescribed classes A–D, G–R described at paras **A.136–A.154, A.156–A.167**.[397] For the purposes of an allocation, however, Classes G–R are lettered F–Q.

Wales

A.193 In Wales, they must fall within A–D, F–H, J–L known here as I–K and N–O, known here as L–P.[398]

Persons not subject to immigration control

A.194 Eligibility for an allocation of housing on the part of persons who are not subject to immigration control[399] is the same as eligibility under HA 1996, Part 7 or H(W)A 2014, Part 2.[400]

---

395 Eligibility Regs 2006, reg 3; Eligibility Regs (Wales) 2014, reg 3, as amended in each case.
396 Eligibility Regs 2006, reg 4; Eligibility Regs (Wales) 2014, reg 4, as amended in each case.
397 Eligibility Regs 2006, reg 3. As noted, the Regulations are so frequently amended that in practice recourse needs to be had to an online service such as Westlaw or Nexis for the position at any given point in time.
398 Eligibility (Wales) Regs 2014, reg 3; the same point as made in the last footnote about amendments applies here too.
399 Eligibility Regs 2006, reg 4; Eligibility (Wales) Regs 2014, reg 4.
400 See paras **A.135–A.167**.

Appendices

Part 1 England: Statutes
>Housing Act 1996, Parts VI and VII
>Homelessness Act 2002, ss 1–4

Part 2 England: Statutory Instruments
>Homelessness (Suitability of Accommodation) Order 1996, SI 1996/3204
>Local Authorities (Contracting Out of Allocation of Housing and
>   Homelessness Functions) Order 1996, SI 1996/3205
>Homelessness (Decisions on Referrals) Order 1998, SI 1998/1578
>Homelessness (Priority Need for Accommodation) (England) Order
>   2002, SI 2002/2051
>Allocation of Housing (England) Regulations 2002, SI 2002/3264
>Homelessness (Suitability of Accommodation) (England) Order
>   2003, SI 2003/3326
>Allocation of Housing and Homelessness (Eligibility) (England)
>   Regulations 2006, SI 1996/1294
>Allocation of Housing and Homelessness (Miscellaneous Provisions)
>   (England) Regulations 2006, SI 2006/2527, regs 1 and 3
>Allocation of Housing (Qualification Criteria for Armed Forces)
>   (England) Regulations 2012, SI 2012/1869
>Homelessness (Suitability of Accommodation) (England) Order
>   2012, SI 2012/2601
>Allocation of Housing (Qualification Criteria for Right to Move)
>   (England) Regulations 2015, SI 2015/967
>Homelessness (Review Procedures etc) Regulations 2018, SI 2018/223

Part 3 Wales: Statutes
>Housing (Wales) Act 2014, Part 2 and Schedule 2

Part 4 Wales: Statutory Instruments
>Allocation of Housing (Wales) Regulations 2003, SI 2003/239
>Allocation of Housing and Homelessness (Eligibility) (Wales)
>   Regulations 2014, SI 2014/2603
>Homelessness (Intentionality) (Specified Categories) (Wales)
>   Regulations 2015, SI 2015/1265
>Homelessness (Review Procedure) (Wales) Regulations 2015, SI 2015/1266
>Homelessness (Suitability of Accommodation) (Wales) Order 2015,
>   SI 2015/1268

PART 1

England: Statutes

Housing Act 1996

1996 Chapter 52

PART VI – ALLOCATION OF HOUSING ACCOMMODATION

Introductory

159 Allocation of housing accommodation.

(1) A local housing authority shall comply with the provisions of this Part in allocating housing accommodation.

(2) For the purposes of this Part a local housing authority allocate housing accommodation when they—

  (a) select a person to be a secure or introductory tenant of housing accommodation held by them,

  (b) nominate a person to be a secure or introductory tenant of housing accommodation held by another person, ...[1]

  (c) nominate a person to be an assured tenant of housing accommodation held by [a private registered provider of social housing or][2] a registered social landlord.

  [(d) select a person to be a tenant under a secure contract or an introductory standard contract of housing accommodation held by them, or

  (e) nominate a person to be a tenant under a secure contract or an introductory standard contract of housing accommodation held by another person.][3]

(3) The reference in subsection (2)(a) to selecting a person to be a secure tenant[, and the reference in subsection (2)(d) to selecting a person to be a tenant under a secure contract or an introductory standard contract,][3] includes deciding to exercise any power to notify an existing tenant or licensee that his tenancy or licence is to be a secure tenancy[, a secure contract or an introductory standard contract][3].

(4) The references in subsection (2)(b)[, (c) and (e)][4] to nominating a person include nominating a person in pursuance of any arrangements (whether legally enforceable or not) to require that housing accommodation, or a specified amount of housing accommodation, is made available to a person or one of a number of persons nominated by the authority.

[(4A) Subject to subsection (4B), the provisions of this Part do not apply to an allocation of housing accommodation by a local housing authority in England to a person who is already—

    (a) a secure or introductory tenant, or

    (b) an assured tenant of housing accommodation held by a private registered provider of social housing or a registered social landlord.

(4B) The provisions of this Part apply to an allocation of housing accommodation by a local housing authority in England to a person who falls within subsection (4A)(a) or (b) if—

    (a) the allocation involves a transfer of housing accommodation for that person,

    (b) the application for the transfer is made by that person, and

    (c) the authority is satisfied that the person is to be given reasonable preference under section 166A(3).]⁵

[(5) The provisions of this Part do not apply to an allocation of housing accommodation [by a local housing authority in Wales]⁵ to a person who is already a [tenant under a]³ secure [contract]³ or [an introductory standard contract]⁴ unless the allocation involves a transfer of housing accommodation for that person and is made on his application.]⁶

(7) Subject to the provisions of this Part, a local housing authority may allocate housing accommodation in such manner as they consider appropriate.

Amendments
1   Repealed by the Renting Homes (Wales) Act 2016 (Consequential Amendments) Regulations 2022, SI 2022/1166, reg 25(1), (12)(a).
2   Inserted by the Housing and Regeneration Act 2008 (Consequential Provisions) Order 2010, SI 2010/866, art 5, Sch 2, paras 81, 100.
3   Inserted by the Renting Homes (Wales) Act 2016 (Consequential Amendments) Regulations 2022, SI 2022/1166, reg 25(1), (12)(b), (c), (e)(i), (ii).
4   Substituted by the Renting Homes (Wales) Act 2016 (Consequential Amendments) Regulations 2022, SI 2022/1166, reg 25(1), (12)(d), (e)(iii).
5   Inserted by the Localism Act 2011, s 145.
6   Substituted by the Homelessness Act 2002, s 13.

160 Cases where provisions about allocation do not apply.

(1) The provisions of this Part about the allocation of housing accommodation do not apply in the following cases.

(2) They do not apply where a secure tenancy—

    (a) vests under section 89 of the Housing Act 1985 (succession to periodic secure tenancy on death of tenant),

    (b) remains a secure tenancy by virtue of section 90 of that Act (devolution of term certain of secure tenancy on death of tenant),

(c) is assigned under section 92 of that Act (assignment of secure tenancy by way of exchange),

(d) is assigned to a person who would be qualified to succeed the secure tenant if the secure tenant died immediately before the assignment,

[(da) is granted in response to a request under section 158 of the Localism Act 2011 (transfer of tenancy), or][1]

(e) vests or is otherwise disposed of in pursuance of an order made under—

  (i) section 24 of the Matrimonial Causes Act 1973 (property adjustment orders in connection with matrimonial proceedings),

  (ii) section 17(1) of the Matrimonial and Family Proceedings Act 1984 (property adjustment orders after overseas divorce, &c.), ...[2]

  (iii) paragraph 1 of Schedule 1 to the Children Act 1989 (orders for financial relief against parents)[, or

  (iv) Part 2 of Schedule 5, or paragraph 9(2) or (3) of Schedule 7, to the Civil Partnership Act 2004 (property adjustment orders in connection with civil partnership proceedings or after overseas dissolution of civil partnership, etc.).][3]

(3) They do not apply where an introductory tenancy—

(a) becomes a secure tenancy on ceasing to be an introductory tenancy,

(b) vests under section 133(2) (succession to introductory tenancy on death of tenant),

(c) is assigned to a person who would be qualified to succeed the introductory tenant if the introductory tenant died immediately before the assignment, or

(d) vests or is otherwise disposed of in pursuance of an order made under—

  (i) section 24 of the Matrimonial Causes Act 1973 (property adjustment orders in connection with matrimonial proceedings),

  (ii) section 17(1) of the Matrimonial and Family Proceedings Act 1984 (property adjustment orders after overseas divorce, &c.), ...[2]

  (iii) paragraph 1 of Schedule 1 to the Children Act 1989 (orders for financial relief against parents)[, or

  (iv) Part 2 of Schedule 5, or paragraph 9(2) or (3) of Schedule 7, to the Civil Partnership Act 2004 (property adjustment orders in connection with civil partnership proceedings or after overseas dissolution of civil partnership, etc.).][3]

[(3A) They do not apply where—

(a) a person succeeds to a secure occupation contract under section 73 (succession on death), section 78 (more than one qualified successor), or section 80 (substitute succession on early termination) of the Renting Homes (Wales) Act 2016 (anaw 1),

(b) a secure contract is transferred to a potential successor under section 114 of that Act (transfer to potential successor),

(c) a secure contract is transferred to another secure contract-holder under section 118 of that Act (transfer to another secure contract-holder),

(d) a secure contract or a standard introductory contract vests or is otherwise disposed of in pursuance of an order under—

    (i) section 24 of the Matrimonial Causes Act 1973 (c. 18) (property adjustment orders in connection with divorce proceedings, etc.),

    (ii) section 17(1) of the Matrimonial and Family Proceedings Act 1984 (c. 42) (orders for financial provision and property adjustment),

    (iii) paragraph 1 of Schedule 1 to the Children Act 1989 (c. 41) (orders for financial relief against parents), or

    (iv) Part 2 of Schedule 5, or paragraph 9(2) or (3) of Schedule 7 to the Civil Partnership Act 2004 (c. 33) (property adjustment orders in connection with civil partnership proceedings or overseas dissolution of civil partnership, etc.), or

(e) an introductory standard contract becomes—

    (i) a secure contract under section 16 of the Renting Homes (Wales) Act 2016 (anaw 1) (introductory standard contracts), or

    (ii) a prohibited conduct standard contract becomes a secure contract under section 117 of the Renting Homes (Wales) Act 2016 (conversion to secure contract).][4]

(4) They do not apply in such other cases as the Secretary of State may prescribe by regulations.

(5) The regulations may be framed so as to make the exclusion of the provisions of this Part about the allocation of housing accommodation subject to such restrictions or conditions as may be specified.

In particular, those provisions may be excluded—

(a) in relation to specified descriptions of persons, or

(b) in relation to housing accommodation of a specified description or a specified proportion of housing accommodation of any specified description.

Amendments
1   Substituted by the Localism Act 2011, s 159(7).
2   Repealed by the Civil Partnership Act 2004, s 261(4), Sch 30.
3   Inserted by the Civil Partnership Act 2004, s 81, Sch 8, para 60.
4   Inserted by the Renting Homes (Wales) Act 2016 (Consequential Amendments) Regulations 2022, SI 2022/1166, reg 25(1), (13).

[Eligibility for allocation of housing accommodation]¹

[160ZA Allocation only to eligible and qualifying persons: England

(1) A local housing authority in England shall not allocate housing accommodation—

(a) to a person from abroad who is ineligible for an allocation of housing accommodation by virtue of subsection (2) or (4), or

(b) to two or more persons jointly if any of them is a person mentioned in paragraph (a).

(2) A person subject to immigration control within the meaning of the Asylum and Immigration Act 1996 is ineligible for an allocation of housing accommodation by a local housing authority in England unless he is of a class prescribed by regulations made by the Secretary of State.

(3) No person who is excluded from entitlement to [universal credit or]² housing benefit by section 115 of the Immigration and Asylum Act 1999 (exclusion from benefits) shall be included in any class prescribed under subsection (2).

(4) The Secretary of State may by regulations prescribe other classes of persons from abroad who are ineligible to be allocated housing accommodation by local housing authorities in England.

(5) Nothing in subsection (2) or (4) affects the eligibility of a person who falls within section 159(4B).

(6) Except as provided by subsection (1), a person may be allocated housing accommodation by a local housing authority in England (whether on his application or otherwise) if that person—

(a) is a qualifying person within the meaning of subsection (7), or

(b) is one of two or more persons who apply for accommodation jointly, and one or more of the other persons is a qualifying person within the meaning of subsection (7).

(7) Subject to subsections (2) and (4) and any regulations under subsection (8), a local housing authority may decide what classes of persons are, or are not, qualifying persons.

(8) The Secretary of State may by regulations—

(a) prescribe classes of persons who are, or are not, to be treated as qualifying persons by local housing authorities in England, and

(b) prescribe criteria that may not be used by local housing authorities in England in deciding what classes of persons are not qualifying persons.

(9) If a local housing authority in England decide that an applicant for housing accommodation—

    (a) is ineligible for an allocation by them by virtue of subsection (2) or (4), or

    (b) is not a qualifying person,

they shall notify the applicant of their decision and the grounds for it.

(10) That notice shall be given in writing and, if not received by the applicant, shall be treated as having been given if it is made available at the authority's office for a reasonable period for collection by him or on his behalf.

(11) A person who is not being treated as a qualifying person may (if he considers that he should be treated as a qualifying person) make a fresh application to the authority for an allocation of housing accommodation by them.]³

Amendments
1   Inserted by the Homelessness Act 2002, s 14(2).
2   Inserted by the Universal Credit (Consequential, Supplementary, Incidental and Miscellaneous Provisions) Regulations 2013, SI 2013/630, reg 12(1), (3).
3   Inserted by the Localism Act 2011, s 146(1).

[160A Allocation only to eligible persons[:Wales]¹

(1) A local housing authority [in Wales]¹ shall not allocate housing accommodation—

    (a) to a person from abroad who is ineligible for an allocation of housing accommodation by virtue of subsection (3) or (5);

    (b) to a person who the authority have decided is to be treated as ineligible for such an allocation by virtue of subsection (7); or

    (c) to two or more persons jointly if any of them is a person mentioned in paragraph (a) or (b).

(2) Except as provided by subsection (1), any person may be allocated housing accommodation by a local housing authority [in Wales]¹ (whether on his application or otherwise).

(3) A person subject to immigration control within the meaning of the Asylum and Immigration Act 1996 (c. 49) is (subject to subsection (6)) ineligible for an allocation of housing accommodation by a local housing authority [in Wales]¹ unless he is of a class prescribed by regulations made by the Secretary of State.

(4) No person who is excluded from entitlement to [universal credit or]² housing benefit by section 115 of the Immigration and Asylum Act 1999 (c. 33) (exclusion from benefits) shall be included in any class prescribed under subsection (3).

(5) The Secretary of State may by regulations prescribe other classes of persons from abroad who are (subject to subsection (6)) ineligible for an allocation of housing accommodation, either in relation to local housing authorities [in Wales][1] generally or any particular local housing authority [in Wales][1].

(6) Nothing in subsection (3) or (5) affects the eligibility of a person who is already [a contract-holder in relation to housing accommodation allocated to that person by a local housing authority in Wales.][3] ...[4]

   (a) ...[4]

   (b) ...[4]

(7) A local housing authority [in Wales][1] may decide that an applicant is to be treated as ineligible for an allocation of housing accommodation by them if they are satisfied that—

   (a) he, or a member of his household, has been guilty of unacceptable behaviour serious enough to make him unsuitable to be a tenant of the authority; and

   (b) in the circumstances at the time his application is considered, he is unsuitable to be a tenant of the authority by reason of that behaviour.

(8) The only behaviour which may be regarded by the authority as unacceptable for the purposes of subsection (7)(a) is [behaviour of the person concerned which would (if that person were a contract-holder of the authority) breach section 55 of the Renting Homes (Wales) Act 2016 (anaw 1) (anti-social behaviour and other prohibited conduct).][3] ...[4]

   (a) ...[4]

   [(aa) ...[4]][5]

   (b) ...[4]

(9) If a local housing authority [in Wales][1] decide that an applicant for housing accommodation—

   (a) is ineligible for an allocation by them by virtue of subsection (3) or (5); or

   (b) is to be treated as ineligible for such an allocation by virtue of subsection (7),

they shall notify the applicant of their decision and the grounds for it.

(10) That notice shall be given in writing and, if not received by the applicant, shall be treated as having been given if it is made available at the authority's office for a reasonable period for collection by him or on his behalf.

(11) A person who is being treated by a local housing authority [in Wales][1] as ineligible by virtue of subsection (7) may (if he considers that he should no longer

be treated as ineligible by the authority [in Wales]¹) make a fresh application to the authority [in Wales]¹ for an allocation of housing accommodation by them.]⁶

Amendments
1   Inserted by the Localism Act 2011, s 146(2)(a)-(e), (g)-(i).
2   Inserted by the Universal Credit (Consequential, Supplementary, Incidental and Miscellaneous Provisions) Regulations 2013, SI 2013/630, reg 12(1), (4).
3   Inserted by the Renting Homes (Wales) Act 2016 (Consequential Amendments) Regulations 2022, SI 2022/1166, reg 25(1), (14)(a)(ii), (b)(ii).
4   Repealed by the Renting Homes (Wales) Act 2016 (Consequential Amendments) Regulations 2022, SI 2022/1166, reg 25(1), (14)(a)(i), (b)(i).
5   Inserted by the Anti-social Behaviour, Crime and Policing Act 2014 (Consequential Amendments) (Wales) Order 2015, SI 2015/1321, art 2(1), (2)(a)
6   Inserted by the Homelessness Act 2002, s 14(2).

The housing register

161 ...¹

...¹

Amendments
1   Repealed by the Homelessness Act 2002, s 18(2), Sch 2.

162 ...¹

...¹

Amendments
1   Repealed by the Homelessness Act 2002, s 18(2), Sch 2.

163 ...¹

...¹

Amendments
1   Repealed by the Homelessness Act 2002, s 18(2), Sch 2.

164 ...¹

...¹

Amendments
1   Repealed by the Homelessness Act 2002, s 18(2), Sch 2.

165 ...¹

...¹

Amendments
1   Repealed by the Homelessness Act 2002, s 18(2), Sch 2.

[Applications for housing accommodation

166 Applications for housing accommodation

(1) A local housing authority shall secure that—

    (a) advice and information is available free of charge to persons in their district about the right to make an application for an allocation of housing accommodation; and

    (b) any necessary assistance in making such an application is available free of charge to persons in their district who are likely to have difficulty in doing so without assistance.

[(1A) A local housing authority in England shall secure that an applicant for an allocation of housing accommodation is informed that he has the rights mentioned in section 166A(9).][1]

(2) A local housing authority [in Wales][1] shall secure that an applicant for an allocation of housing accommodation is informed that he has the rights mentioned in section 167(4A).

(3) Every application made to a local housing authority for an allocation of housing accommodation shall (if made in accordance with the procedural requirements of the authority's allocation scheme) be considered by the authority.

(4) The fact that a person is an applicant for an allocation of housing accommodation shall not be divulged (without his consent) to any other member of the public.

(5) In this Part 'district' in relation to a local housing authority has the same meaning as in the Housing Act 1985 (c. 68).][2]

Amendments

1   Inserted by the Localism Act 2011, s 147(1).
2   Substituted by the Homelessness Act 2002, s 15.

[Allocation schemes][1]

[166A Allocation in accordance with allocation scheme: England

(1) Every local housing authority in England must have a scheme (their 'allocation scheme') for determining priorities, and as to the procedure to be followed, in allocating housing accommodation.

For this purpose 'procedure' includes all aspects of the allocation process, including the persons or descriptions of persons by whom decisions are taken.

(2) The scheme must include a statement of the authority's policy on offering people who are to be allocated housing accommodation—

(a) a choice of housing accommodation; or

(b) the opportunity to express preferences about the housing accommodation to be allocated to them.

(3) As regards priorities, the scheme shall, subject to subsection (4), be framed so as to secure that reasonable preference is given to—

(a) people who are homeless (within the meaning of Part 7);

(b) people who are owed a duty by any local housing authority under section 190(2), 193(2) or 195(2) (or under section 65(2) or 68(2) of the Housing Act 1985) or who are occupying accommodation secured by any such authority under section 192(3);

(c) people occupying insanitary or overcrowded housing or otherwise living in unsatisfactory housing conditions;

(d) people who need to move on medical or welfare grounds (including any grounds relating to a disability); and

(e) people who need to move to a particular locality in the district of the authority, where failure to meet that need would cause hardship (to themselves or to others).

The scheme may also be framed so as to give additional preference to particular descriptions of [people within one or more of paragraphs (a) to (e)]² (being descriptions of people with urgent housing needs). [The scheme must be framed so as to give additional preference to a person with urgent housing needs who falls within one or more of paragraphs (a) to (e) and who—

(i) is serving in the regular forces and is suffering from a serious injury, illness or disability which is attributable (wholly or partly) to the person's service,

(ii) formerly served in the regular forces,

(iii) has recently ceased, or will cease to be entitled, to reside in accommodation provided by the Ministry of Defence following the death of that person's spouse or civil partner who has served in the regular forces and whose death was attributable (wholly or partly) to that service, or

(iv) is serving or has served in the reserve forces and is suffering from a serious injury, illness or disability which is attributable (wholly or partly) to the person's service.

For this purpose 'the regular forces' and 'the reserve forces' have the meanings given by section 374 of the Armed Forces Act 2006.]³

(4) People are to be disregarded for the purposes of subsection (3) if they would not have fallen within paragraph (a) or (b) of that subsection without the local

housing authority having had regard to a restricted person (within the meaning of Part 7).

(5) The scheme may contain provision for determining priorities in allocating housing accommodation to people within subsection (3); and the factors which the scheme may allow to be taken into account include—

(a) the financial resources available to a person to meet his housing costs;

(b) any behaviour of a person (or of a member of his household) which affects his suitability to be a tenant;

(c) any local connection (within the meaning of section 199) which exists between a person and the authority's district.

(6) Subject to subsection (3), the scheme may contain provision about the allocation of particular housing accommodation—

(a) to a person who makes a specific application for that accommodation;

(b) to persons of a particular description (whether or not they are within subsection (3)).

(7) The Secretary of State may by regulations—

(a) specify further descriptions of people to whom preference is to be given as mentioned in subsection (3), or

(b) amend or repeal any part of subsection (3).

(8) The Secretary of State may by regulations specify factors which a local housing authority in England must not take into account in allocating housing accommodation.

(9) The scheme must be framed so as to secure that an applicant for an allocation of housing accommodation—

(a) has the right to request such general information as will enable him to assess—

(i) how his application is likely to be treated under the scheme (including in particular whether he is likely to be regarded as a member of a group of people who are to be given preference by virtue of subsection (3)); and

(ii) whether housing accommodation appropriate to his needs is likely to be made available to him and, if so, how long it is likely to be before such accommodation becomes available for allocation to him;

(b) has the right to request the authority to inform him of any decision about the facts of his case which is likely to be, or has been, taken into account in considering whether to allocate housing accommodation to him; and

(c) has the right to request a review of a decision mentioned in paragraph (b), or in section 160ZA(9), and to be informed of the decision on the review and the grounds for it.

(10) As regards the procedure to be followed, the scheme must be framed in accordance with such principles as the Secretary of State may prescribe by regulations.

(11) Subject to the above provisions, and to any regulations made under them, the authority may decide on what principles the scheme is to be framed.

(12) A local housing authority in England must, in preparing or modifying their allocation scheme, have regard to—

(a) their current homelessness strategy under section 1 of the Homelessness Act 2002,

(b) their current tenancy strategy under section 150 of the Localism Act 2011, and

(c) in the case of an authority that is a London borough council, the London housing strategy.

(13) Before adopting an allocation scheme, or making an alteration to their scheme reflecting a major change of policy, a local housing authority in England must—

(a) send a copy of the draft scheme, or proposed alteration, to every private registered provider of social housing and registered social landlord with which they have nomination arrangements (see section 159(4)), and

(b) afford those persons a reasonable opportunity to comment on the proposals.

(14) A local housing authority in England shall not allocate housing accommodation except in accordance with their allocation scheme.][4]

Amendments

1   Substituted by the Localism Act 2011, s 147(1), (3).
2   Substituted by the Housing Act 1996 (Additional Preference for Armed Forces) (England) Regulations 2012, SI 2012/2989, reg 2(a).
3   Inserted by the Housing Act 1996 (Additional Preference for Armed Forces) (England) Regulations 2012, SI 2012/2989, reg 2(b).
4   Inserted by the Localism Act 2011, s 147(1), (4).

167 Allocation in accordance with allocation scheme[:Wales][1]

(1) Every local housing authority [in Wales][1] shall have a scheme (their 'allocation scheme') for determining priorities, and as to the procedure to be followed, in allocating housing accommodation.

For this purpose 'procedure' includes all aspects of the allocation process, including the persons or descriptions of persons by whom decisions are to be taken.

[(1A) The scheme shall include a statement of the authority's policy on offering people who are to be allocated housing accommodation—

(a) a choice of housing accommodation; or

(b) the opportunity to express preferences about the housing accommodation to be allocated to them.]²

[(2) As regards priorities, the scheme shall[, subject to subsection (2ZA),]³ be framed so as to secure that reasonable preference is given to—

(a) people who are homeless [(within the meaning of Part 2 of the Housing (Wales) Act 2014)]⁴;

[(b) people who are owed any duty by a local housing authority under section 66, 73 or 75 of the Housing (Wales) Act 2014;]⁴

(c) people occupying insanitary or overcrowded housing or otherwise living in unsatisfactory housing conditions;

(d) people who need to move on medical or welfare grounds [(including grounds relating to a disability)]⁵; and

(e) people who need to move to a particular locality in the district of the authority, where failure to meet that need would cause hardship (to themselves or to others).

The scheme may also be framed so as to give additional preference to particular descriptions of people within this subsection (being descriptions of people with urgent housing needs).

[(2ZA) People are to be disregarded for the purposes of subsection (2) if they would not have fallen within paragraph (a) or (b) of that subsection without the local housing authority having had regard to a restricted person (within the meaning of [Part 2 of the Housing (Wales) Act 2014]⁴).]³

(2A) The scheme may contain provision for determining priorities in allocating housing accommodation to people within subsection (2); and the factors which the scheme may allow to be taken into account include—

(a) the financial resources available to a person to meet his housing costs;

(b) any behaviour of a person (or of a member of his household) which affects his suitability to be a tenant;

(c) any local connection (within the meaning of [section 81 of the Housing (Wales) Act 2014]⁴) which exists between a person and the authority's district.

(2B) Nothing in subsection (2) requires the scheme to provide for any preference to be given to people the authority have decided are people to whom subsection (2C) applies.

(2C) This subsection applies to a person if the authority are satisfied that—

(a) he, or a member of his household, has been guilty of unacceptable behaviour serious enough to make him unsuitable to be a tenant of the authority; and

(b) in the circumstances at the time his case is considered, he deserves by reason of that behaviour not to be treated as a member of a group of people who are to be given preference by virtue of subsection (2).

(2D) Subsection (8) of section 160A applies for the purposes of subsection (2C) (a) above as it applies for the purposes of subsection (7)(a) of that section.

(2E) Subject to subsection (2), the scheme may contain provision about the allocation of particular housing accommodation—

(a) to a person who makes a specific application for that accommodation;

(b) to persons of a particular description (whether or not they are within subsection (2)).]⁶

(3) The Secretary of State may by regulations—

(a) specify further descriptions of people to whom preference is to be given as mentioned in subsection (2), or

(b) amend or repeal any part of subsection (2).

(4) The Secretary of State may by regulations specify factors which a local housing authority [in Wales]¹ shall not take into account in allocating housing accommodation.

[(4A) The scheme shall be framed so as to secure that an applicant for an allocation of housing accommodation—

(a) has the right to request such general information as will enable him to assess—

(i) how his application is likely to be treated under the scheme (including in particular whether he is likely to be regarded as a member of a group of people who are to be given preference by virtue of subsection (2)); and

(ii) whether housing accommodation appropriate to his needs is likely to be made available to him and, if so, how long it is likely to be before such accommodation becomes available for allocation to him;

(b) is notified in writing of any decision that he is a person to whom subsection (2C) applies and the grounds for it;

(c) has the right to request the authority to inform him of any decision about the facts of his case which is likely to be, or has been, taken into account in considering whether to allocate housing accommodation to him; and

(d) has the right to request a review of a decision mentioned in paragraph (b) or (c), or in section 160A(9), and to be informed of the decision on the review and the grounds for it.][7]

(5) As regards the procedure to be followed, the scheme shall be framed in accordance with such principles as the Secretary of State may prescribe by regulations.

(6) Subject to the above provisions, and to any regulations made under them, the authority may decide on what principles the scheme is to be framed.

(7) Before adopting an allocation scheme, or making an alteration to their scheme reflecting a major change of policy, a local housing authority [in Wales][1] shall—

(a) send a copy of the draft scheme, or proposed alteration, to every [private registered provider of social housing and][8] registered social landlord with which they have nomination arrangements (see section 159(4)), and

(b) afford those persons a reasonable opportunity to comment on the proposals.

(8) A local housing authority [in Wales][1] shall not allocate housing accommodation except in accordance with their allocation scheme.

Amendments
1   Inserted by the Localism Act 2011, s 147(1), (5).
2   Inserted by the Homelessness Act 2002, s 16(1), (2).
3   Inserted by the Housing and Regeneration Act 2008, s 314, Sch 15, paras 1, 2.
4   Substituted by the Housing (Wales) Act 2014, s 100, Sch 3, paras 2, 3(a)(i).
5   Inserted by the Housing Act 2004, s 223.
6   Substituted by the Homelessness Act 2002, s 16(1), (3).
7   Inserted by the Homelessness Act 2002, s 16(1), (4).
8   Inserted by the Housing and Regeneration Act 2008 (Consequential Provisions) Order 2010, SI 2010/866, art 5, Sch 2, paras 81, 101.

168 Information about allocation scheme.

(1) A local housing authority shall publish a summary of their allocation scheme and provide a copy of the summary free of charge to any member of the public who asks for one.

(2) The authority shall make the scheme available for inspection at their principal office and shall provide a copy of the scheme, on payment of a reasonable fee, to any member of the public who asks for one.

(3) When the authority make an alteration to their scheme reflecting a major change of policy, they shall within a reasonable period of time [take such steps

as they consider reasonable to bring the effect of the alteration to the attention of those likely to be affected by it]¹.

Amendments
1   Substituted by the Homelessness Act 2002, s 18(1), Sch 1, paras 2, 4.

Supplementary

169 Guidance to authorities by the Secretary of State.

(1) In the exercise of their functions under this Part, local housing authorities shall have regard to such guidance as may from time to time be given by the Secretary of State.

(2) The Secretary of State may give guidance generally or to specified descriptions of authorities.

170 Co-operation between [certain]¹ social landlords and local housing authorities.

Where a local housing authority so request, a [private registered provider of social housing or]² registered social landlord shall co-operate to such extent as is reasonable in the circumstances in offering accommodation to [people with priority under the authority's allocation scheme]³.

Amendments
1   Substituted by the Housing and Regeneration Act 2008 (Consequential Provisions) Order 2010, SI 2010/866, art 5, Sch 2, paras 81, 102(b).
2   Inserted by the Housing and Regeneration Act 2008 (Consequential Provisions) Order 2010, SI 2010/866, art 5, Sch 2, paras 81, 102(a).
3   Substituted by the Homelessness Act 2002, s 18(1), Sch 1, paras 2, 5.

171 False statements and withholding information.

(1) A person commits an offence if, in connection with the exercise by a local housing authority of their functions under this Part—

   (a) he knowingly or recklessly makes a statement which is false in a material particular, or

   (b) he knowingly withholds information which the authority have reasonably required him to give in connection with the exercise of those functions.

(2) A person guilty of an offence under this section is liable on summary conviction to a fine not exceeding level 5 on the standard scale.

172 Regulations.

(1) Regulations under this Part shall be made by statutory instrument.

(2) No regulations shall be made under section [166A(7) or][1] 167(3) (regulations amending provisions about priorities in allocating housing accommodation) unless a draft of the regulations has been laid before and approved by a resolution of each House of Parliament.

(3) Any other regulations under this Part shall be subject to annulment in pursuance of a resolution of either House of Parliament.

(4) Regulations under this Part may contain such incidental, supplementary and transitional provisions as appear to the Secretary of State appropriate, and may make different provision for different cases including different provision for different areas.

Amendments
1   Inserted by the Localism Act 2011, s 147(1), (6).

173 Consequential amendments: Part VI.

The enactments mentioned in Schedule 16 have effect with the amendments specified there which are consequential on the provisions of this Part.

174 Index of defined expressions: Part VI.

The following Table shows provisions defining or otherwise explaining expressions used in this Part (other than provisions defining or explaining an expression used in the same section)—

allocation (of housing)	section 159(2)
allocation scheme	[166A and][1] section 167
assured tenancy	section 230
[contract-holder	section 230][2]
[district (of local housing authority)	section 166(5)][3]
...[4]	...[4]
[introductory standard contract	section 230][2]
introductory tenancy and introductory tenant	sections 230 and 124
local housing authority	section 230
...[4]	...[4]
[prohibited conduct standard contract	section 230][2]
registered social landlord	sections 230 and 2
[secure contract	section 230][2]
secure tenancy and secure tenant	section 230

Amendments
1   Inserted by the Localism Act 2011, s 147(1), (7).
2   Inserted by the Renting Homes (Wales) Act 2016 (Consequential Amendments) Regulations 2022, SI 2022/1166, reg 25(1), (15).
3   Inserted by the Homelessness Act 2002, s 18(1), Sch 1, paras 2, 6.
4   Repealed by the Homelessness Act 2002, s 18(2), Sch 2.

PART VII – HOMELESSNESS [F1: ENGLAND]

Homelessness and threatened homelessness

175 Homelessness and threatened homelessness.

(1) A person is homeless if he has no accommodation available for his occupation, in the United Kingdom or elsewhere, which he—

(a) is entitled to occupy by virtue of an interest in it or by virtue of an order of a court,

(b) has an express or implied licence to occupy, or

(c) occupies as a residence by virtue of any enactment or rule of law giving him the right to remain in occupation or restricting the right of another person to recover possession.

(2) A person is also homeless if he has accommodation but—

(a) he cannot secure entry to it, or

(b) it consists of a moveable structure, vehicle or vessel designed or adapted for human habitation and there is no place where he is entitled or permitted both to place it and to reside in it.

(3) A person shall not be treated as having accommodation unless it is accommodation which it would be reasonable for him to continue to occupy.

(4) A person is threatened with homelessness if it is likely that he will become homeless within [56][2] days.

[(5)   A person is also threatened with homelessness if—

(a) a valid notice has been given to the person under section 21 of the Housing Act 1988 (orders for possession on expiry or termination of assured shorthold tenancy) in respect of the only accommodation the person has that is available for the person's occupation, and

(b) that notice will expire within 56 days.][3]

Amendments
1   Inserted by the Housing (Wales) Act 2014, s 100, Sch 3, paras 2, 4.
2   Substituted by the Homelessness Reduction Act 2017, s 1(1), (2).
3   Inserted by the Homelessness Reduction Act 2017, s 1(1), (3).

176 Meaning of accommodation available for occupation.

Accommodation shall be regarded as available for a person's occupation only if it is available for occupation by him together with—

(a) any other person who normally resides with him as a member of his family, or

(b) any other person who might reasonably be expected to reside with him.

References in this Part to securing that accommodation is available for a person's occupation shall be construed accordingly.

177 Whether it is reasonable to continue to occupy accommodation.

(1) It is not reasonable for a person to continue to occupy accommodation if it is probable that this will lead to [violence or domestic abuse]¹ against him, or against—

(a) a person who normally resides with him as a member of his family, or

(b) any other person who might reasonably be expected to reside with him.

[(1A) For this purpose—

(a) 'domestic abuse' has the meaning given by section 1 of the Domestic Abuse Act 2021;

(b) 'violence' means—

(i) violence from another person; or

(ii) threats of violence from another person which are likely to be carried out.]¹

(2) In determining whether it would be, or would have been, reasonable for a person to continue to occupy accommodation, regard may be had to the general circumstances prevailing in relation to housing in the district of the local housing authority to whom he has applied for accommodation or for assistance in obtaining accommodation.

(3) The Secretary of State may by order specify—

(a) other circumstances in which it is to be regarded as reasonable or not reasonable for a person to continue to occupy accommodation, and

(b) other matters to be taken into account or disregarded in determining whether it would be, or would have been, reasonable for a person to continue to occupy accommodation.

Amendments
1   Substituted by the Domestic Abuse Act 2021, s 78(1), (2).

178 …¹

…¹

Amendments
1   Repealed by the Domestic Abuse Act 2021, s 78(1), (3).

General functions in relation to homelessness or threatened homelessness

[179 Duty of local housing authority in England to provide advisory services

(1) Each local housing authority in England must provide or secure the provision of a service, available free of charge to any person in the authority's district, providing information and advice on—

  (a) preventing homelessness,

  (b) securing accommodation when homeless,

  (c) the rights of persons who are homeless or threatened with homelessness, and the duties of the authority, under this Part,

  (d) any help that is available from the authority or anyone else, whether under this Part or otherwise, for persons in the authority's district who are homeless or may become homeless (whether or not they are threatened with homelessness), and

  (e) how to access that help.

(2) The service must be designed to meet the needs of persons in the authority's district including, in particular, the needs of—

  (a) persons released from prison or youth detention accommodation,

  (b) care leavers,

  (c) former members of the regular armed forces,

  (d) victims of domestic abuse,

  (e) persons leaving hospital,

  (f) persons suffering from a mental illness or impairment, and

  (g) any other group that the authority identify as being at particular risk of homelessness in the authority's district.

(3) The authority may give to any person by whom the service is provided on behalf of the authority assistance by way of grant or loan.

(4) The authority may also assist any such person—

  (a) by permitting the person to use premises belonging to the authority,

  (b) by making available furniture or other goods, whether by way of gift, loan or otherwise, and

  (c) by making available the services of staff employed by the authority.

(5) In this section—

'care leavers' means persons who are former relevant children (within the meaning given by section 23C(1) of the Children Act 1989);

['domestic abuse' has the meaning given by section 1 of the Domestic Abuse Act 2021;][1]

...[2]

'hospital' has the same meaning as in the National Health Service Act 2006 (see section 275(1) of that Act);

'regular armed forces' means the regular forces as defined by section 374 of the Armed Forces Act 2006;

'youth detention accommodation' means—

(a) a secure children's home,

(b) a secure training centre,

(c) a secure college,

(d) a young offender institution,

(e) accommodation provided by or on behalf of a local authority for the purpose of restricting the liberty of children;

(f) accommodation provided for that purpose under section 82(5) of the Children Act 1989, or

(g) accommodation, or accommodation of a description, for the time being specified [by regulations under section 248(1)(f) of the Sentencing Code][3] (youth detention accommodation for the purposes of detention and training orders).][4]

Amendments
1   Substituted by the Domestic Abuse Act 2021, s 78(1), (4)(a).
2   Repealed by the Domestic Abuse Act 2021, s 78(1), (4)(b).
3   Substituted by the Sentencing Act 2020, s 410, Sch 24, para 141.
4   Substituted by the Homelessness Reduction Act 2017, s 2.

180 Assistance for voluntary organisations.

(1) The Secretary of State or a local housing authority [in England][1] may give assistance by way of grant or loan to voluntary organisations concerned with homelessness or matters relating to homelessness.

(2) A local housing authority may also assist any such organisation—

(a) by permitting them to use premises belonging to the authority,

(b) by making available furniture or other goods, whether by way of gift, loan or otherwise, and

(c) by making available the services of staff employed by the authority.

(3) A 'voluntary organisation' means a body (other than a public or local authority) whose activities are not carried on for profit.

Amendments
1   Inserted by the Housing (Wales) Act 2014, s 100, Sch 3, paras 2, 6.

181 Terms and conditions of assistance.

(1) This section has effect as to the terms and conditions on which assistance is given under section 179 or 180.

(2) Assistance shall be on such terms, and subject to such conditions, as the person giving the assistance may determine.

(3) No assistance shall be given unless the person to whom it is given undertakes—

   (a) to use the money, furniture or other goods or premises for a specified purpose, and

   (b) to provide such information as may reasonably be required as to the manner in which the assistance is being used.

The person giving the assistance may require such information by notice in writing, which shall be complied with within 21 days beginning with the date on which the notice is served.

(4) The conditions subject to which assistance is given shall in all cases include conditions requiring the person to whom the assistance is given—

   (a) to keep proper books of account and have them audited in such manner as may be specified,

   (b) to keep records indicating how he has used the money, furniture or other goods or premises, and

   (c) to submit the books of account and records for inspection by the person giving the assistance.

(5) If it appears to the person giving the assistance that the person to whom it was given has failed to carry out his undertaking as to the purpose for which the assistance was to be used, he shall take all reasonable steps to recover from that person an amount equal to the amount of the assistance.

(6) He must first serve on the person to whom the assistance was given a notice specifying the amount which in his opinion is recoverable and the basis on which that amount has been calculated.

182 Guidance by the Secretary of State.

(1) In the exercise of their functions relating to homelessness and the prevention of homelessness, a local housing authority or social services authority [F12in

England] shall have regard to such guidance as may from time to time be given by the Secretary of State.

(2) The Secretary of State may give guidance either generally or to specified descriptions of authorities.

Amendments
1   Inserted by the Housing (Wales) Act 2014, s 100, Sch 3, paras 2, 7.

Application for assistance in case of homelessness or threatened homelessness

183 Application for assistance.

(1) The following provisions of this Part apply where a person applies to a local housing authority [in England]¹ for accommodation, or for assistance in obtaining accommodation, and the authority have reason to believe that he is or may be homeless or threatened with homelessness.

(2) In this Part—

'applicant' means a person making such an application,

'assistance under this Part' means the benefit of any function under the following provisions of this Part relating to accommodation or assistance in obtaining accommodation, and

'eligible for assistance' means not excluded from such assistance by section 185 (persons from abroad not eligible for housing assistance) or section 186 (asylum seekers and their dependants).

(3) Nothing in this section or the following provisions of this Part affects a person's entitlement to advice and information under section 179 (duty to provide advisory services).

Amendments
1   Inserted by the Housing (Wales) Act 2014, s 100, Sch 3, paras 2, 8.

184 Inquiry into cases of homelessness or threatened homelessness.

(1) If the local housing authority have reason to believe that an applicant may be homeless or threatened with homelessness, they shall make such inquiries as are necessary to satisfy themselves—

  (a) whether he is eligible for assistance, and

  (b) if so, whether any duty, and if so what duty, is owed to him under the following provisions of this Part.

(2) They may also make inquiries whether he has a local connection with the district of another local housing authority in England, Wales or Scotland.

(3) On completing their inquiries the authority shall notify the applicant of their decision and, so far as any issue is decided against his interests, inform him of the reasons for their decision.

[(3A) If the authority decide that a duty is[, or after the authority's duty to the applicant under section 189B(2) comes to an end would be,]¹ owed to the applicant under section 193(2) ...² but would not have done so without having had regard to a restricted person, the notice under subsection (3) must also—

(a) inform the applicant that their decision was reached on that basis,

(b) include the name of the restricted person,

(c) explain why the person is a restricted person, and

(d) explain the effect of section 193(7AD) ...².]³

(4) If the authority have notified or intend to notify another local housing authority [in England under section 198(A1) (referral of cases where section 189B applies)]⁴, they shall at the same time notify the applicant of that decision and inform him of the reasons for it.

(5) A notice under subsection (3) or (4) shall also inform the applicant of his right to request a review of the decision and of the time within which such a request must be made (see section 202).

(6) Notice required to be given to a person under this section shall be given in writing and, if not received by him, shall be treated as having been given to him if it is made available at the authority's office for a reasonable period for collection by him or on his behalf.

[(7) In this Part 'a restricted person' means a person—

(a) who is not eligible for assistance under this Part,

(b) who is subject to immigration control within the meaning of the Asylum and Immigration Act 1996, and

(c) either—

(i) who does not have leave to enter or remain in the United Kingdom, or

(ii) whose leave to enter or remain in the United Kingdom is subject to a condition to maintain and accommodate himself, and any dependants, without recourse to public funds.]³

Amendments
1   Inserted by the Homelessness Reduction Act 2017, s 5(1), (3)(a).
2   Repealed by the Homelessness Reduction Act 2017, s 4(1), (3).
3   Inserted by the Housing and Regeneration Act 2008, s 314, Sch 15, paras 1, 3.
4   Substituted by the Homelessness Reduction Act 2017, s 5(1), (3)(b).

Eligibility for assistance

185 Persons from abroad not eligible for housing assistance.

(1) A person is not eligible for assistance under this Part if he is a person from abroad who is ineligible for housing assistance.

(2) A person who is subject to immigration control within the meaning of the Asylum and Immigration Act 1996 is not eligible for housing assistance unless he is of a class prescribed by regulations made by the Secretary of State.

[(2A) No person who is excluded from entitlement to [universal credit or]¹ housing benefit by section 115 of the Immigration and Asylum Act 1999 (exclusion from benefits) shall be included in any class prescribed under subsection (2).]²

(3) The Secretary of State may make provision by regulations as to other descriptions of persons who are to be treated for the purposes of this Part as persons from abroad who are ineligible for housing assistance.

(4) A person from abroad who is not eligible for housing assistance shall be disregarded in determining for the purposes of this Part whether [a person falling within subsection (5)]³—

　(a)　is homeless or threatened with homelessness, or

　(b)　has a priority need for accommodation.

[(5) A person falls within this subsection if the person—

　(a)　falls within a class prescribed by regulations made under subsection (2); but

　[(b)　is not a person who, immediately before IP completion day, was—

　　(i)　a national of an EEA State or Switzerland, and

　　(ii)　within a class prescribed by regulations made under subsection (2) which had effect at that time.]⁴]⁵

Amendments
1　Inserted by the Universal Credit (Consequential, Supplementary, Incidental and Miscellaneous Provisions) Regulations 2013, SI 2013/630, reg 12(1), (5).
2　Substituted by the Homelessness Act 2002, s 18(1), Sch 1, paras 2, 7(1).
3　Substituted by the Housing and Regeneration Act 2008, s 314, Sch 15, paras 1, 4(1), (2).
4　Substituted by the Immigration and Social Security Co-ordination (EU Withdrawal) Act 2020 (Consequential, Saving, Transitional and Transitory Provisions) (EU Exit) Regulations 2020, SI 2020/1309, reg 10.
5　Inserted by the Housing and Regeneration Act 2008, s 314, Sch 15, paras 1, 4(1), (3).

186 Asylum-seekers and their dependants.

(1) An asylum-seeker, or a dependant of an asylum-seeker who is not by virtue of section 185 a person from abroad who is ineligible for housing assistance, is not

eligible for assistance under this Part if he has any accommodation in the United Kingdom, however temporary, available for his occupation.

(2) For the purposes of this section a person who makes a claim for asylum—

(a) becomes an asylum-seeker at the time when his claim is recorded by the Secretary of State as having been made, and

(b) ceases to be an asylum-seeker at the time when his claim is recorded by the Secretary of State as having been finally determined or abandoned.

(3) For the purposes of this section a person—

(a) becomes a dependant of an asylum-seeker at the time when he is recorded by the Secretary of State as being a dependant of the asylum-seeker, and

(b) ceases to be a dependant of an asylum-seeker at the time when the person whose dependant he is ceases to be an asylum-seeker or, if it is earlier, at the time when he is recorded by the Secretary of State as ceasing to be a dependant of the asylum-seeker.

(4) In relation to an asylum-seeker, 'dependant' means a person—

(a) who is his spouse or a child of his under the age of eighteen, and

(b) who has neither a right of abode in the United Kingdom nor indefinite leave under the Immigration Act 1971 to enter or remain in the United Kingdom.

(5) In this section a 'claim for asylum' means a claim made by a person that it would be contrary to the United Kingdom's obligations under the Convention relating to the Status of Refugees done at Geneva on 28th July 1951 and the Protocol to that Convention for him to be removed from, or required to leave, the United Kingdom.

187 Provision of information by Secretary of State.

(1) The Secretary of State shall, at the request of a local housing authority [in England][1], provide the authority with such information as they may require—

(a) as to whether a person is [a person to whom section 115 of the Immigration and Asylum Act 1999 (exclusion from benefits) applies][2], or a dependant of an asylum-seeker, and

(b) to enable them to determine whether such a person is eligible for assistance under this Part under section 185 (persons from abroad not eligible for housing assistance).

(2) Where that information is given otherwise than in writing, the Secretary of State shall confirm it in writing if a written request is made to him by the authority.

(3) If it appears to the Secretary of State that any application, decision or other change of circumstances has affected the status of a person about whom information was previously provided by him to a local housing authority under this section, he shall inform the authority in writing of that fact, the reason for it and the date on which the previous information became inaccurate.

Amendments

1   Inserted by the Housing (Wales) Act 2014, s 100, Sch 3, paras 2, 9.
2   Substituted by the Immigration and Asylum Act 1999, s 117(6).

Interim duty to accommodate

188 Interim duty to accommodate in case of apparent priority need.

[(1) If the local housing authority have reason to believe that an applicant may be homeless, eligible for assistance and have a priority need, they must secure that accommodation is available for the applicant's occupation.

(1ZA)In a case in which the local housing authority conclude their inquiries under section 184 and decide that the applicant does not have a priority need—

(a) where the authority decide that they do not owe the applicant a duty under section 189B(2), the duty under subsection (1) comes to an end when the authority notify the applicant of that decision, or

(b) otherwise, the duty under subsection (1) comes to an end upon the authority notifying the applicant of their decision that, upon the duty under section 189B(2) coming to an end, they do not owe the applicant any duty under section 190 or 193.

(1ZB)In any other case, the duty under subsection (1) comes to an end upon the later of—

(a) the duty owed to the applicant under section 189B(2) coming to an end or the authority notifying the applicant that they have decided that they do not owe the applicant a duty under that section, and

(b) the authority notifying the applicant of their decision as to what other duty (if any) they owe to the applicant under the following provisions of this Part upon the duty under section 189B(2) coming to an end.][1]

[(1A) But if the local housing authority have reason to believe that the duty under section 193(2) may apply in relation to an applicant in the circumstances referred to in section 195A(1), they shall secure that accommodation is available for the applicant's occupation [until the later of paragraph (a) or (b) of subsection (1ZB)][1] regardless of whether the applicant has a priority need.][2]

(2) The duty under this section arises irrespective of any possibility of the referral of the applicant's case to another local housing authority (see sections 198 to 200).

[(2A) For the purposes of this section, where the applicant requests a review under section 202(1)(h) of the authority's decision as to the suitability of accommodation offered to the applicant by way of a final accommodation offer or a final Part 6 offer (within the meaning of section 193A), the authority's duty to the applicant under section 189B(2) is not to be taken to have come to an end under section 193A(2) until the decision on the review has been notified to the applicant.

(3) Otherwise, the duty under this section comes to an end in accordance with subsections (1ZA) to (1A), regardless of any review requested by the applicant under section 202.

But the authority may secure that accommodation is available for the applicant's occupation pending a decision on review.]¹

Amendments
1   Substituted by the Homelessness Reduction Act 2017, s 5(1), (4).
2   Inserted by the Localism Act 2011, s 149(1), (2).

189 Priority need for accommodation.

(1) The following have a priority need for accommodation—

   (a) a pregnant woman or a person with whom she resides or might reasonably be expected to reside;

   (b) a person with whom dependent children reside or might reasonably be expected to reside;

   (c) a person who is vulnerable as a result of old age, mental illness or handicap or physical disability or other special reason, or with whom such a person resides or might reasonably be expected to reside;

   (d) a person who is homeless or threatened with homelessness as a result of an emergency such as flood, fire or other disaster;

   [(e) a person who is homeless as a result of that person being a victim of domestic abuse.]¹

(2) The Secretary of State may by order—

   (a) specify further descriptions of persons as having a priority need for accommodation, and

   (b) amend or repeal any part of subsection (1).

(3) Before making such an order the Secretary of State shall consult such associations representing relevant authorities, and such other persons, as he considers appropriate.

(4) No such order shall be made unless a draft of it has been approved by resolution of each House of Parliament.

[(5) In this section 'domestic abuse' has the meaning given by section 1 of the Domestic Abuse Act 2021.][1]

Amendments
1   Inserted by the Domestic Abuse Act 2021, s 78(1), (5).

[Duty to assess every eligible applicant's case and agree a plan

189A Assessments and personalised plan

(1) If the local housing authority are satisfied that an applicant is—

(a) homeless or threatened with homelessness, and

(b) eligible for assistance,

the authority must make an assessment of the applicant's case.

(2) The authority's assessment of the applicant's case must include an assessment of—

(a) the circumstances that caused the applicant to become homeless or threatened with homelessness,

(b) the housing needs of the applicant including, in particular, what accommodation would be suitable for the applicant and any persons with whom the applicant resides or might reasonably be expected to reside ('other relevant persons'), and

(c) what support would be necessary for the applicant and any other relevant persons to be able to have and retain suitable accommodation.

(3) The authority must notify the applicant, in writing, of the assessment that the authority make.

(4) After the assessment has been made, the authority must try to agree with the applicant—

(a) any steps the applicant is to be required to take for the purposes of securing that the applicant and any other relevant persons have and are able to retain suitable accommodation, and

(b) the steps the authority are to take under this Part for those purposes.

(5) If the authority and the applicant reach an agreement, the authority must record it in writing.

(6) If the authority and the applicant cannot reach an agreement, the authority must record in writing—

(a) why they could not agree,

(b) any steps the authority consider it would be reasonable to require the applicant to take for the purposes mentioned in subsection (4)(a), and

(c) the steps the authority are to take under this Part for those purposes.

(7) The authority may include in a written record produced under subsection (5) or (6) any advice for the applicant that the authority consider appropriate (including any steps the authority consider it would be a good idea for the applicant to take but which the applicant should not be required to take).

(8) The authority must give to the applicant a copy of any written record produced under subsection (5) or (6).

(9) Until such time as the authority consider that they owe the applicant no duty under any of the following sections of this Part, the authority must keep under review—

(a) their assessment of the applicant's case, and

(b) the appropriateness of any agreement reached under subsection (4) or steps recorded under subsection (6)(b) or (c).

(10) If—

(a) the authority's assessment of any of the matters mentioned in subsection (2) changes, or

(b) the authority's assessment of the applicant's case otherwise changes such that the authority consider it appropriate to do so,

the authority must notify the applicant, in writing, of how their assessment of the applicant's case has changed (whether by providing the applicant with a revised written assessment or otherwise).

(11) If the authority consider that any agreement reached under subsection (4) or any step recorded under subsection (6)(b) or (c) is no longer appropriate—

(a) the authority must notify the applicant, in writing, that they consider the agreement or step is no longer appropriate,

(b) any failure, after the notification is given, to take a step that was agreed to in the agreement or recorded under subsection (6)(b) or (c) is to be disregarded for the purposes of this Part, and

(c) subsections (4) to (8) apply as they applied after the assessment was made.

(12) A notification under this section or a copy of any written record produced under subsection (5) or (6), if not received by the applicant, is to be treated as having been given to the applicant if it is made available at the authority's office for a reasonable period for collection by or on behalf of the applicant.]

Amendments
1   Inserted by the Homelessness Reduction Act 2017, s 3(1).

Duties to persons found to be homeless or threatened with homelessness

[189B Initial duty owed to all eligible persons who are homeless

(1) This section applies where the local housing authority are satisfied that an applicant is—

  (a) homeless, and

  (b) eligible for assistance.

(2) Unless the authority refer the application to another local housing authority in England (see section 198(A1)), the authority must take reasonable steps to help the applicant to secure that suitable accommodation becomes available for the applicant's occupation for at least—

  (a) 6 months, or

  (b) such longer period not exceeding 12 months as may be prescribed.

(3) In deciding what steps they are to take, the authority must have regard to their assessment of the applicant's case under section 189A.

(4) Where the authority—

  (a) are satisfied that the applicant has a priority need, and

  (b) are not satisfied that the applicant became homeless intentionally,

the duty under subsection (2) comes to an end at the end of the period of 56 days beginning with the day the authority are first satisfied as mentioned in subsection (1).

(5) If any of the circumstances mentioned in subsection (7) apply, the authority may give notice to the applicant bringing the duty under subsection (2) to an end.

(6) The notice must—

  (a) specify which of the circumstances apply, and

  (b) inform the applicant that the applicant has a right to request a review of the authority's decision to bring the duty under subsection (2) to an end and of the time within which such a request must be made.

(7) The circumstances are that the authority are satisfied that—

  (a) the applicant has—

    (i) suitable accommodation available for occupation, and

    (ii) a reasonable prospect of having suitable accommodation available for occupation for at least 6 months, or such longer period not exceeding 12 months as may be prescribed, from the date of the notice,

(b) the authority have complied with the duty under subsection (2) and the period of 56 days beginning with the day that the authority are first satisfied as mentioned in subsection (1) has ended (whether or not the applicant has secured accommodation),

(c) the applicant has refused an offer of suitable accommodation and, on the date of refusal, there was a reasonable prospect that suitable accommodation would be available for occupation by the applicant for at least 6 months or such longer period not exceeding 12 months as may be prescribed,

(d) the applicant has become homeless intentionally from any accommodation that has been made available to the applicant as a result of the authority's exercise of their functions under subsection (2),

(e) the applicant is no longer eligible for assistance, or

(f) the applicant has withdrawn the application mentioned in section 183(1).

(8) A notice under this section must be given in writing and, if not received by the applicant, is to be treated as having been given to the applicant if it is made available at the authority's office for a reasonable period for collection by or on behalf of the applicant.

(9) The duty under subsection (2) can also be brought to an end under—

(a) section 193A (consequences of refusal of final accommodation offer or final Part 6 offer at the initial relief stage), or

(b) sections 193B and 193C (notices in cases of applicant's deliberate and unreasonable refusal to co-operate).][1]

Amendments
1   Inserted by the Homelessness Reduction Act 2017, s 5(1), (2).

190 Duties to persons becoming homeless intentionally.

[(1) This section applies where—

(a) the local housing authority are satisfied that an applicant—

(i)   is homeless and eligible for assistance, but

(ii) became homeless intentionally,

(b) the authority are also satisfied that the applicant has a priority need, and

(c) the authority's duty to the applicant under section 189B(2) has come to an end.][1]

(2) [The authority must—][1]

(a) secure that accommodation is available for his occupation for such period as they consider will give him a reasonable opportunity of securing accommodation for his occupation, and

(b) provide him with [(or secure that he is provided with) advice and assistance]² in any attempts he may make to secure that accommodation becomes available for his occupation.

(3)   ...³

[[(4) In deciding what advice and assistance is to be provided under this section, the authority must have regard to their assessment of the applicant's case under section 189A.]⁴

(5) The advice and assistance provided under subsection (2)(b) ...³ must include information about the likely availability in the authority's district of types of accommodation appropriate to the applicant's housing needs (including, in particular, the location and sources of such types of accommodation).]⁴

Amendments
1   Substituted by the Homelessness Reduction Act 2017, s 5(1), (5)(a), (b).
2   Substituted by the Homelessness Act 2002, s 18(1), Sch 1, paras 2, 9.
3   Repealed by the Homelessness Reduction Act 2017, s 5(1), (5)(c), (d).
4   Substituted by the Homelessness Reduction Act 2017, s 3(2).
5   Inserted by the Homelessness Act 2002, s 18(1), Sch 1, paras 2, 10.

191 Becoming homeless intentionally.

(1) A person becomes homeless intentionally if he deliberately does or fails to do anything in consequence of which he ceases to occupy accommodation which is available for his occupation and which it would have been reasonable for him to continue to occupy.

[(1A) But a person does not become homeless intentionally if—

(a) the accommodation the person ceases to occupy is supported exempt accommodation,

(b) the person's reason for ceasing to occupy the accommodation relates to the standard of the accommodation, or the standard of care, support or supervision provided there, and

(c) the accommodation, or the care, support or supervision provided there, does not meet National Supported Housing Standards.

'Supported exempt accommodation' has the meaning given by section 12 of the Supported Housing (Regulatory Oversight) Act 2023.]¹

(2) For the purposes of subsection (1) an act or omission in good faith on the part of a person who was unaware of any relevant fact shall not be treated as deliberate.

(3) A person shall be treated as becoming homeless intentionally if—

(a) he enters into an arrangement under which he is required to cease to occupy accommodation which it would have been reasonable for him to continue to occupy, and

(b) the purpose of the arrangement is to enable him to become entitled to assistance under this Part,

and there is no other good reason why he is homeless.

(4) ...[2]

Amendments
1   Inserted by the Supported Housing (Regulatory Oversight) Act 2023, s 9, 14(2)
2   Repealed by the Homelessness Act 2002, s 18(2), Sch 2.

192 ...[1]

...[1]

Amendments
1   Repealed by the Homelessness Reduction Act 2017, s 5(1), (6).

193 Duty to persons with priority need who are not homeless intentionally.

[(1) This section applies where—

(a) the local housing authority—

(i) are satisfied that an applicant is homeless and eligible for assistance, and

(ii) are not satisfied that the applicant became homeless intentionally,

(b) the authority are also satisfied that the applicant has a priority need, and

(c) the authority's duty to the applicant under section 189B(2) has come to an end.][1]

[(1A) But this section does not apply if—

(a) section 193A(3) disapplies this section, or

(b) the authority have given notice to the applicant under section 193B(2).][2]

(2) Unless the authority refer the application to another local housing authority (see section 198), they shall secure that accommodation is available for occupation by the applicant.

[(3) The authority are subject to the duty under this section until it ceases by virtue of any of the following provisions of this section.][3]

[(3A) ...[4]][5]

[(3B) In this section 'a restricted case' means a case where the local housing authority would not be satisfied as mentioned in subsection (1) without 'having had regard to a restricted person.]⁶

[(5) The local housing authority shall cease to be subject to the duty under this section if—

    (a) the applicant, having been informed by the authority of the possible consequence of refusal or acceptance and of the right to request a review of the suitability of the accommodation, refuses an offer of accommodation which the authority are satisfied is suitable for the applicant,

    (b) that offer of accommodation is not an offer of accommodation under Part 6 or a private rented sector offer, and

    (c) the authority notify the applicant that they regard themselves as ceasing to be subject to the duty under this section.]⁷

(6) The local housing authority shall cease to be subject to the duty under this section if the applicant—

    (a) ceases to be eligible for assistance,

    (b) becomes homeless intentionally from the accommodation made available for his occupation,

    (c) accepts an offer of accommodation under Part VI (allocation of housing), or

    [(cc) accepts an offer of an assured tenancy (other than an assured shorthold tenancy) from a private landlord,]⁸

    (d) otherwise voluntarily ceases to occupy as his only or principal home the accommodation made available for his occupation.

[(7) The local housing authority shall also cease to be subject to the duty under this section if the applicant, having been informed of the possible consequence of refusal [or acceptance]⁹ and of his right to request a review of the suitability of the accommodation, refuses a final offer of accommodation under Part 6.

(7A) An offer of accommodation under Part 6 is a final offer for the purposes of subsection (7) if it is made in writing and states that it is a final offer for the purposes of subsection (7).]¹⁰

[(7AA) …⁴ the authority shall also cease to be subject to the duty under this section if the applicant, having been informed [in writing]⁹ of the matters mentioned in subsection (7AB)—

    (a) accepts a [private rented sector offer]⁷, or

    (b) refuses such an offer.

(7AB) The matters are—

    (a) the possible consequence of refusal [or acceptance][9] of the offer, and

    (b) that the applicant has the right to request a review of the suitability of the accommodation[, and

    (c) in a case which is not a restricted case, the effect under section 195A of a further application to a local housing authority within two years of acceptance of the offer.][9]

(7AC) For the purposes of this section an offer is a [private rented sector offer][7] if—

    (a) it is an offer of an assured shorthold tenancy made by a private landlord to the applicant in relation to any accommodation which is, or may become, available for the applicant's occupation,

    (b) it is made, with the approval of the authority, in pursuance of arrangements made by the authority with the landlord with a view to bringing the authority's duty under this section to an end, and

    (c) the tenancy being offered is a fixed term tenancy (within the meaning of Part 1 of the Housing Act 1988) for a period of at least 12 months.

(7AD) In a restricted case the authority shall, so far as reasonably practicable, bring their duty under this section to an end as mentioned in subsection (7AA).][6]

[(7B) ...[4]

(7C) ...[4]

(7D) ...[4]

(7E) ...[4]

(7F) The local housing authority shall not—

    (a) make a final offer of accommodation under Part 6 for the purposes of subsection (7); [or][9]

[(ab) approve a [private rented sector offer][7];][6] or

    (b) ...[4]

unless they are satisfied that the accommodation is suitable for the applicant and that [subsection (8) does not apply to the applicant.][7].][8]

[(8) This subsection applies to an applicant if—

    (a) the applicant is under contractual or other obligations in respect of the applicant's existing accommodation, and

(b) the applicant is not able to bring those obligations to an end before being required to take up the offer.]⁷

(9) A person who ceases to be owed the duty under this section may make a fresh application to the authority for accommodation or assistance in obtaining accommodation.

[(10) The [Secretary of State]¹¹ may provide by regulations that subsection (7AC)(c) is to have effect as if it referred to a period of the length specified in the regulations.

(11) Regulations under subsection (10)—

(a) may not specify a period of less than 12 months, and

(b) may not apply to restricted cases.

(12) …¹²]⁹

Amendments
1 Substituted by the Homelessness Reduction Act 2017, s 5(1), (7).
2 Inserted by the Homelessness Reduction Act 2017, s 7(2).
3 Substituted by the Homelessness Act 2002, s. 6(1).
4 Repealed by the Localism Act 2011, s 148(1), (2), (5)(a), (8), (9)(c).
5 Inserted by the Homelessness Act 2002, s 18(1), Sch 1, paras 2, 10.
6 Inserted by the Housing and Regeneration Act 2008, s 314, Sch 15, paras 1, 5(1), (3), (4), (6).
7 Substituted by the Localism Act 2011, s 148(1), (3), (5)(c), (7), (9)(b), (d), (10).
8 Inserted by the Homelessness Act 2002, s 7(1), (2), (4).
9 Inserted by the Localism Act 2011, s 148(1), (4), (5)(b), (6), (9)(a), (11).
10 Substituted by the Homelessness Act 2002, s 7(1), (3).
11 Substituted by the Housing (Wales) Act 2014, s 100, Sch 3, paras 2, 10(a).
12 Repealed by the Housing (Wales) Act 2014, s 100, Sch 3, paras 2, 10(b).

[193A Consequences of refusal of final accommodation offer or final Part 6 offer at the initial relief stage

(1) Subsections (2) and (3) apply where—

(a) a local housing authority owe a duty to an applicant under section 189B(2), and

(b) the applicant, having been informed of the consequences of refusal and of the applicant's right to request a review of the suitability of the accommodation, refuses—

(i) a final accommodation offer, or

(ii) a final Part 6 offer.

(2) The authority's duty to the applicant under section 189B(2) comes to an end.

(3) Section 193 (the main housing duty) does not apply.

(4) An offer is a 'final accommodation offer' if—

(a) it is an offer of an assured shorthold tenancy made by a private landlord to the applicant in relation to any accommodation which is, or may become, available for the applicant's occupation,

(b) it is made, with the approval of the authority, in pursuance of arrangements made by the authority in the discharge of their duty under section 189B(2), and

(c) the tenancy being offered is a fixed term tenancy (within the meaning of Part 1 of the Housing Act 1988) for a period of at least 6 months.

(5) A 'final Part 6 offer' is an offer of accommodation under Part 6 (allocation of housing) that—

(a) is made in writing by the authority in the discharge of their duty under section 189B(2), and

(b) states that it is a final offer for the purposes of this section.

(6) The authority may not approve a final accommodation offer, or make a final Part 6 offer, unless they are satisfied that the accommodation is suitable for the applicant and that subsection (7) does not apply.

(7) This subsection applies to an applicant if—

(a) the applicant is under contractual or other obligations in respect of the applicant's existing accommodation, and

(b) the applicant is not able to bring those obligations to an end before being required to take up the offer.]¹

Amendments
1   Inserted by the Homelessness Reduction Act 2017, s 7(1).

[193B Notices in cases of an applicant's deliberate and unreasonable refusal to co-operate

(1) Section 193C applies where—

(a) a local housing authority owe a duty to an applicant under section 189B(2) or 195(2), and

(b) the authority give notice to the applicant under subsection (2).

(2) A local housing authority may give a notice to an applicant under this subsection if the authority consider that the applicant has deliberately and unreasonably refused to take any step—

(a) that the applicant agreed to take under subsection (4) of section 189A, or

(b) that was recorded by the authority under subsection (6)(b) of that section.

(3) A notice under subsection (2) must—

    (a) explain why the authority are giving the notice and its effect, and

    (b) inform the applicant that the applicant has a right to request a review of the authority's decision to give the notice and of the time within which such a request must be made.

(4) The authority may not give notice to the applicant under subsection (2) unless—

    (a) the authority have given a relevant warning to the applicant, and

    (b) a reasonable period has elapsed since the warning was given.

(5) A 'relevant warning' means a notice—

    (a) given by the authority to the applicant after the applicant has deliberately and unreasonably refused to take any step—

        (i) that the applicant agreed to take under subsection (4) of section 189A, or

        (ii) that was recorded by the authority under subsection (6)(b) of that section,

    (b) that warns the applicant that, if the applicant should deliberately and unreasonably refuse to take any such step after receiving the notice, the authority intend to give notice to the applicant under subsection (2), and

    (c) that explains the consequences of such a notice being given to the applicant.

(6) For the purposes of subsections (2) and (5), in deciding whether a refusal by the applicant is unreasonable, the authority must have regard to the particular circumstances and needs of the applicant (whether identified in the authority's assessment of the applicant's case under section 189A or not).

(7) The Secretary of State may make provision by regulations as to the procedure to be followed by a local housing authority in connection with notices under this section.

(8) A notice under this section must be given in writing and, if not received by the applicant, is to be treated as having been given to the applicant if it is made available at the authority's office for a reasonable period for collection by or on behalf of the applicant.]¹

Amendments
1   Inserted by the Homelessness Reduction Act 2017, s 7(1).

[193C   Notice under section 193B: consequences

(1) In the circumstances mentioned in section 193B(1), this section applies in relation to a local housing authority and an applicant.

(2) The authority's duty to the applicant under section 189B(2) or 195(2) comes to an end.

(3) Subsection (4) applies if the authority—

(a) are satisfied that the applicant is homeless, eligible for assistance and has a priority need, and

(b) are not satisfied that the applicant became homeless intentionally.

(4) Section 193 (the main housing duty) does not apply, but the authority must secure that accommodation is available for occupation by the applicant.

(5) The authority cease to be subject to the duty under subsection (4) if the applicant—

(a) ceases to be eligible for assistance,

(b) becomes homeless intentionally from accommodation made available for the applicant's occupation,

(c) accepts an offer of an assured tenancy from a private landlord, or

(d) otherwise voluntarily ceases to occupy, as the applicant's only or principal home, the accommodation made available for the applicant's occupation.

(6) The authority also cease to be subject to the duty under subsection (4) if the applicant, having been informed of the possible consequences of refusal or acceptance and of the applicant's right to request a review of the suitability of the accommodation, refuses or accepts—

(a) a final accommodation offer, or

(b) a final Part 6 offer.

(7) An offer is 'a final accommodation offer' if—

(a) it is an offer of an assured shorthold tenancy made by a private landlord to the applicant in relation to any accommodation which is, or may become, available for the applicant's occupation,

(b) it is made, with the approval of the authority, in pursuance of arrangements made by the authority with a view to bringing the authority's duty under subsection (4) to an end, and

(c) the tenancy being offered is a fixed term tenancy (within the meaning of Part 1 of the Housing Act 1988) for a period of at least 6 months.

(8) A 'final Part 6 offer' is an offer of accommodation under Part 6 (allocation of housing) that is made in writing and states that it is a final offer for the purposes of this section.

(9) The authority may not approve a final accommodation offer, or make a final Part 6 offer, unless they are satisfied that the accommodation is suitable for the applicant and that subsection (10) does not apply.

(10) This subsection applies to an applicant if—

    (a) the applicant is under contractual or other obligations in respect of the applicant's existing accommodation, and

    (b) the applicant is not able to bring those obligations to an end before being required to take up the offer.][1]

Amendments
1   Inserted by the Homelessness Reduction Act 2017, s 7(1).

194 ...[1]

...[1]

Amendments
1   Repealed by the Homelessness Act 2002, s 18(2), Sch 2.

[195 Duties in cases of threatened homelessness

(1) This section applies where the local housing authority are satisfied that an applicant is—

    (a) threatened with homelessness, and

    (b) eligible for assistance.

(2) The authority must take reasonable steps to help the applicant to secure that accommodation does not cease to be available for the applicant's occupation.

(3) In deciding what steps they are to take, the authority must have regard to their assessment of the applicant's case under section 189A.

(4) Subsection (2) does not affect any right of the authority, whether by virtue of contract, enactment or rule of law, to secure vacant possession of any accommodation.

(5) If any of the circumstances mentioned in subsection (8) apply, the authority may give notice to the applicant bringing the duty under subsection (2) to an end.

(6) But the authority may not give notice to the applicant under subsection (5) on the basis that the circumstances in subsection (8)(b) apply if a valid notice has been given to the applicant under section 21 of the Housing Act 1988 (orders for possession on expiry or termination of assured shorthold tenancy) that—

    (a) will expire within 56 days or has expired, and

(b) is in respect of the only accommodation that is available for the applicant's occupation.

(7) The notice must—

(a) specify which of the circumstances apply, and

(b) inform the applicant that the applicant has a right to request a review of the authority's decision to bring the duty under subsection (2) to an end and of the time within which such a request must be made.

(8) The circumstances are that the authority are satisfied that—

(a) the applicant has—

(i) suitable accommodation available for occupation, and

(ii) a reasonable prospect of having suitable accommodation available for occupation for at least 6 months, or such longer period not exceeding 12 months as may be prescribed, from the date of the notice,

(b) the authority have complied with the duty under subsection (2) and the period of 56 days beginning with the day that the authority are first satisfied as mentioned in subsection (1) has ended (whether or not the applicant is still threatened with homelessness),

(c) the applicant has become homeless,

(d) the applicant has refused an offer of suitable accommodation and, on the date of refusal, there was a reasonable prospect that suitable accommodation would be available for occupation by the applicant for at least 6 months or such longer period not exceeding 12 months as may be prescribed,

(e) the applicant has become homeless intentionally from any accommodation that has been made available to the applicant as a result of the authority's exercise of their functions under subsection (2),

(f) the applicant is no longer eligible for assistance, or

(g) the applicant has withdrawn the application mentioned in section 183(1).

(9) A notice under this section must be given in writing and, if not received by the applicant, is to be treated as having been given to the applicant if it is made available at the authority's office for a reasonable period for collection by or on behalf of the applicant.

(10) The duty under subsection (2) can also be brought to an end under sections 193B and 193C (notices in cases of applicant's deliberate and unreasonable refusal to co-operate).][1]

Amendments
1   Substituted by the Homelessness Reduction Act 2017, s 4(1), (2).

[195A   Re-application after private rented sector offer

(1) If within two years beginning with the date on which an applicant accepts an offer under section 193(7AA) (private rented sector offer), the applicant re-applies for accommodation, or for assistance in obtaining accommodation, and the local housing authority—

    (a) is satisfied that the applicant is homeless and eligible for assistance, and

    (b) is not satisfied that the applicant became homeless intentionally,

the duty under section 193(2) applies regardless of whether the applicant has a priority need.

(2) For the purpose of subsection (1), an applicant in respect of whom a valid notice under section 21 of the Housing Act 1988 (orders for possession on expiry or termination of assured shorthold tenancy) has been given is to be treated as homeless from the date on which that notice expires.

(3) ...[1]

(4) ...[1]

(5) Subsection (1) ...[1] does not apply to a case where the local housing authority would not be satisfied as mentioned in that subsection without having regard to a restricted person.

(6) Subsection (1) ...[1] does not apply to a re-application by an applicant for accommodation, or for assistance in obtaining accommodation, if the immediately preceding application made by that applicant was one to which subsection (1) ...[1] applied.][2]

Amendments
1   Repealed by the Homelessness Reduction Act 2017, s 4(1), (4).
2   Inserted by the Localism Act 2011, s 149(1), (4).

196 ...[1]

...[1]

Amendments
1   Repealed by the Homelessness Reduction Act 2017, s 4(1), (5).

Duty where other suitable accommodation available

197 ...[1]

...[1]

Amendments
1   Repealed by the Homelessness Act 2002, s 18(2), Sch 2.

Referral to another local housing authority

198 Referral of case to another local housing authority.

[(A1) If the local housing authority would be subject to the duty under section 189B (initial duty owed to all eligible persons who are homeless) but consider that the conditions are met for referral of the case to another local housing authority in England, they may notify that other authority of their opinion.]¹

(1) If the local housing authority would be subject to the duty under section 193 (accommodation for those with priority need who are not homeless intentionally) but consider that the conditions are met for referral of the case to another local housing authority, they may notify that other authority of their opinion.

...²

(2) The conditions for referral of the case to another authority are met if—

    (a) neither the applicant nor any person who might reasonably be expected to reside with him has a local connection with the district of the authority to whom his application was made,

    (b) the applicant or a person who might reasonably be expected to reside with him has a local connection with the district of that other authority, and

    (c) neither the applicant nor any person who might reasonably be expected to reside with him will run the risk of [domestic abuse]³ in that other district.

[(2ZA) The conditions for referral of the case to another authority are also met if—

    (a) the application is made within the period of two years beginning with the date on which the applicant accepted an offer from the other authority under section 193(7AA) (private rented sector offer), and

    (b) neither the applicant nor any person who might reasonably be expected to reside with the applicant will run the risk of [domestic abuse]³ in the district of the other authority.]⁴

[(2A) But the conditions for referral mentioned in subsection (2) [or (2ZA)]⁴ are not met if—

    (a) the applicant or any person who might reasonably be expected to reside with him has suffered violence (other than [violence that is domestic abuse]³) in the district of the other authority; and

    (b) it is probable that the return to that district of the victim will lead to further violence of a similar kind against him.

[(3) For the purposes of subsections (2), (2ZA) and (2A)—

(a) 'domestic abuse' has the meaning given by section 1 of the Domestic Abuse Act 2021;

(b) 'violence' means—

(i) violence from another person; or

(ii) threats of violence from another person which are likely to be carried out.]³]⁵

(4) The conditions for referral of the case to another authority are also met if—

(a) the applicant was on a previous application made to that other authority placed (in pursuance of their functions under this Part) in accommodation in the district of the authority to whom his application is now made, and

(b) the previous application was within such period as may be prescribed of the present application.

[(4A) Subsection (4) is to be construed, in a case where the other authority is an authority in Wales, as if the reference to 'this Part' were a reference to Part 2 of the Housing (Wales) Act 2014.]⁶

(5) The question whether the conditions for referral of a case [which does not involve a referral to a local housing authority in Wales]⁶ are satisfied shall be decided by agreement between the notifying authority and the notified authority or, in default of agreement, in accordance with such arrangements as the Secretary of State may direct by order.

[(5A) The question whether the conditions for referral of a case involving a referral to a local housing authority in Wales shall be decided by agreement between the notifying authority and the notified authority or, in default of agreement, in accordance with such arrangements as the Secretary of State and the Welsh Ministers may jointly direct by order.]⁶

(6) An order may direct that the arrangements shall be—

(a) those agreed by any relevant authorities or associations of relevant authorities, or

(b) in default of such agreement, such arrangements as appear to the Secretary of State [or, in the case of an order under subsection (5A), to the Secretary of State and the Welsh Ministers]⁶ to be suitable, after consultation with such associations representing relevant authorities, and such other persons, as he thinks appropriate.

(7) [An order under this section shall not]⁷ be made unless a draft of the order has been approved by a resolution of each House of Parliament [and, in the case of a joint order, a resolution of the National Assembly for Wales]⁶.

Amendments

1   Inserted by the Homelessness Reduction Act 2017, s 5(1), (8).
2   Repealed by the Homelessness Act 2002, s 18(2), Sch 2.
3   Substituted by the Domestic Abuse Act 2021, s 78(1), (6).
4   Inserted by the Localism Act 2011, s 149(5)-(7).
5   Substituted by the Homelessness Act 2002, s 10(2).
6   Inserted by the Housing (Wales) Act 2014, s 100, Sch 3, paras 2, 11(a)-(d), (e)(ii).
7   Substituted by the Housing (Wales) Act 2014, s 100, Sch 3, paras 2, 11(e)(i).

199 Local connection.

(1) A person has a local connection with the district of a local housing authority if he has a connection with it—

   (a) because he is, or in the past was, normally resident there, and that residence is or was of his own choice,

   (b) because he is employed there,

   (c) because of family associations, or

   (d) because of special circumstances.

(2) ...[1]

(3) Residence in a district is not of a person's own choice if—

   (a) ...[1]

   (b) he, or a person who might reasonably be expected to reside with him, becomes resident there because he is detained under the authority of an Act of Parliament.

(4) ...[1]

(5) The Secretary of State may by order specify ...[1] circumstances in which—

   (a) a person is not to be treated as employed in a district, or

   (b) residence in a district is not to be treated as of a person's own choice.

[(6) A person has a local connection with the district of a local housing authority if he was (at any time) provided with accommodation in that district under section 95 of the Immigration and Asylum Act 1999 (support for asylum seekers).

(7) But subsection (6) does not apply—

   (a) to the provision of accommodation for a person in a district of a local housing authority if he was subsequently provided with accommodation in the district of another local housing authority under section 95 of that Act, or

(b) to the provision of accommodation in an accommodation centre by virtue of section 22 of the Nationality, Immigration and Asylum Act 2002 (c. 41) (use of accommodation centres for section 95 support).][2]

[(8) While a local authority in England have a duty towards a person under section 23C of the Children Act 1989 (continuing functions in respect of former relevant children)—

(a) if the local authority is a local housing authority, the person has a local connection with their district, and

(b) otherwise, the person has a local connection with every district of a local housing authority that falls within the area of the local authority.

(9) In subsection (8), 'local authority' has the same meaning as in the Children Act 1989 (see section 105 of that Act).

(10) Where, by virtue of being provided with accommodation under section 22A of the Children Act 1989 (provision of accommodation for children in care), a person is normally resident in the district of a local housing authority in England for a continuous period of at least two years, some or all of which falls before the person attains the age of 16, the person has a local connection with that district.

(11) A person ceases to have a local connection with a district under subsection (10) upon attaining the age of 21 (but this does not affect whether the person has a local connection with that district under any other provision of this section).][3]

Amendments
1   Repealed by the Housing and Regeneration Act 2008, s 321(1), Sch 16.
2   Inserted by the Asylum and Immigration (Treatment of Claimants, etc.) Act 2004, s 11(1).
3   Inserted by the Homelessness Reduction Act 2017, s 8.

[199A Duties to the applicant whose case is considered for referral or referred under section 198(A1)

(1) Where a local housing authority ('the notifying authority') notify an applicant that they intend to notify or have notified another local housing authority in England ('the notified authority') under section 198(A1) of their opinion that the conditions are met for referral of the applicant's case to the notified authority, the notifying authority—

(a) cease to be subject to any duty under section 188 (interim duty to accommodate in case of apparent priority need), and

(b) are not subject to the duty under section 189B (initial duty owed to all eligible persons who are homeless).

(2) But, if the notifying authority have reason to believe that the applicant may have a priority need, they must secure that accommodation is available for occupation by the applicant until the applicant is notified of the decision as to whether the conditions for referral of the applicant's case are met.

(3) When it has been decided whether the conditions for referral are met, the notifying authority must give notice of the decision and the reasons for it to the applicant.

The notice must also inform the applicant of the applicant's right to request a review of the decision and of the time within which such a request must be made.

(4) If it is decided that the conditions for referral are not met—

(a) the notifying authority are subject to the duty under section 189B,

(b) the references in subsections (4) and (7)(b) of that section to the day that the notifying authority are first satisfied as mentioned in subsection (1) of that section are to be read as references to the day on which notice is given under subsection (3) of this section, and

(c) if the notifying authority have reason to believe that the applicant may have a priority need, they must secure that accommodation is available for occupation by the applicant until the later of—

(i) the duty owed to the applicant under section 189B coming to an end, and

(ii) the authority deciding what other duty (if any) they owe to the applicant under this Part after the duty under section 189B comes to an end.

(5) If it is decided that the conditions for referral are met—

(a) for the purposes of this Part, the applicant is to be treated as having made an application of the kind mentioned in section 183(1) to the notified authority on the date on which notice is given under subsection (3),

(b) from that date, the notifying authority owes no duties to the applicant under this Part,

(c) where the notifying authority have made a decision as to whether the applicant is eligible for assistance, is homeless or became homeless intentionally, the notified authority may only come to a different decision if they are satisfied that—

(i) the applicant's circumstances have changed, or further information has come to light, since the notifying authority made their decision, and

(ii) that change in circumstances, or further information, justifies the notified authority coming to a different decision to the notifying authority, and

(d) the notifying authority must give to the notified authority copies of any notifications that the notifying authority have given to the applicant under section 189A(3) or (10) (notifications of the notifying authority's assessments of the applicant's case).

(6) A duty under subsection (2) or paragraph (c) of subsection (4) ceases as provided in the subsection or paragraph concerned even if the applicant requests a review of the authority's decision upon which the duty ceases.

The authority may secure that accommodation is available for the applicant's occupation pending the decision on review.

(7) A notice under this section must be given in writing and, if not received by the applicant, is to be treated as having been given to the applicant if it is made available at the authority's office for a reasonable period for collection by or on behalf of the applicant.]

Amendments
1   Inserted by the Homelessness Reduction Act 2017, s 5(1), (9).

200 Duties to applicant whose case is considered for referral or referred [under section 198(1)][1].

(1) Where a local housing authority notify an applicant that they intend to notify or have notified another local housing authority [under section 198(1)][1] of their opinion that the conditions are met for the referral of his case to that other authority—

(a) they cease to be subject to any duty under section 188 (interim duty to accommodate in case of apparent priority need), and

(b) they are not subject to any duty under section 193 (the main housing duty),

but they shall secure that accommodation is available for occupation by the applicant until he is notified of the decision whether the conditions for referral of his case are met.

[(1A) A local housing authority in England may not notify an applicant as mentioned in subsection (1) until the authority's duty to the applicant under section 189B(2) (initial duty owed to all eligible persons who are homeless) has come to an end.][1]

(2) When it has been decided whether the conditions for referral are met, the notifying authority shall notify the applicant of the decision and inform him of the reasons for it.

The notice shall also inform the applicant of his right to request a review of the decision and of the time within which such a request must be made.

[(3) If it is decided that the conditions for referral are not met, the notifying authority are subject to the duty under section 193 (the main housing duty).

(4) If it is decided that those conditions are met [and the notified authority is not an authority in Wales][2], the notified authority are subject to the duty under section 193 (the main housing duty)[; for provision about cases where it is decided that those conditions are met and the notified authority is an authority in Wales, see section 83 of the Housing (Wales) Act 2014 (cases referred from a local housing authority in England)][2].][3]

(5) The duty under subsection (1), ...[4] ceases as provided in that subsection even if the applicant requests a review of the authority's decision (see section 202).

The authority may [secure][2] that accommodation is available for the applicant's occupation pending the decision on a review.

(6) Notice ...[5] given to an applicant under this section shall be given in writing and, if not received by him, shall be treated as having been given to him if it is made available at the authority's office for a reasonable period for collection by him or on his behalf.

Amendments
1   Inserted by the Homelessness Reduction Act 2017, s 5(1), (10)(a)-(c).
2   Inserted by the Housing (Wales) Act 2014, s 100, Sch 3, paras 2, 12.
3   Substituted by the Homelessness Act 2002, s 18(1), Sch 1, paras 2, 15.
4   Repealed by the Homelessness Act 2002, s 18(2), Sch 2.
5   Repealed by the Homelessness Reduction Act 2017, s 5(1), (10)(d).

201 Application of referral provisions to cases arising in Scotland.

Sections 198 and 200 (referral of application to another local housing authority and duties to applicant whose case is considered for referral or referred) apply—

   (a) to applications referred by a local authority in Scotland in pursuance of sections 33 and 34 of the Housing (Scotland) Act 1987, and

   (b) to persons whose applications are so transferred,

as they apply to cases arising under this Part (the reference in section 198 to this Part being construed as a reference to Part II of that Act).

[201A Cases referred from a local housing authority in Wales

(1) This section applies where an application has been referred by a local housing authority in Wales to a local housing authority in England under section 80 of the Housing (Wales) Act 2014 (referral of case to another local housing authority).

(2) If it is decided that the conditions in that section for referral of the case are met, the notified authority are subject to the duty under section 193 of this Act in respect of the person whose case is referred (the main housing duty); for provision about cases where it is decided that the conditions for referral are not met, see section 82 of the Housing (Wales) Act 2014 (duties to applicant whose case is considered for referral or referred).

(3) References in this Part to an applicant include a reference to a person to whom a duty is owed by virtue of subsection (2).]

Amendments
1   Inserted by the Housing (Wales) Act 2014, s 100, Sch 3, paras 2, 13.

Right to request review of decision

202 Right to request review of decision.

(1) An applicant has the right to request a review of—

   (a) any decision of a local housing authority as to his eligibility for assistance,

   (b) any decision of a local housing authority as to what duty (if any) is owed to him under sections [189B to 193C][1] and 195 ...[2] (duties to persons found to be homeless or threatened with homelessness),

   [(ba) any decision of a local housing authority—

      (i)   as to the steps they are to take under subsection (2) of section 189B, or

      (ii) to give notice under subsection (5) of that section bringing to an end their duty to the applicant under subsection (2) of that section,

   (bb) any decision of a local housing authority to give notice to the applicant under section 193B(2) (notice given to those who deliberately and unreasonably refuse to co-operate),

   (bc) any decision of a local housing authority—

      (i)   as to the steps they are to take under subsection (2) of section 195, or

      (ii) to give notice under subsection (5) of that section bringing to an end their duty to the applicant under subsection (2) of that section,][3]

   (c) any decision of a local housing authority to notify another authority under section 198(1) (referral of cases),

   (d) any decision under section 198(5) whether the conditions are met for the referral of his case,

   (e) any decision under section 200(3) or (4) (decision as to duty owed to applicant whose case is considered for referral or referred), ...[4]

   (f) any decision of a local housing authority as to the suitability of accommodation offered to him in discharge of their duty under any of the provisions mentioned in paragraph (b) or (e) [or as to the suitability of accommodation offered to him as mentioned in section 193(7)][5], ...[2]

   [(g) any decision of a local housing authority as to the suitability of accommodation offered to him by way of a [private rented sector offer][6] (within the meaning of section 193)][7][, or

677

(h) any decision of a local housing authority as to the suitability of accommodation offered to the applicant by way of a final accommodation offer or a final Part 6 offer (within the meaning of section 193A or 193C).][3]

[(1A) An applicant who is offered accommodation as mentioned in section 193(5)[, (7) or (7AA)][8] may under subsection (1)(f) [or (as the case may be) (g)][7] request a review of the suitability of the accommodation offered to him whether or not he has accepted the offer.][5]

[(1B) An applicant may, under subsection (1)(h), request a review of the suitability of the accommodation offered whether or not the applicant has accepted the offer.][3]

(2) There is no right to request a review of the decision reached on an earlier review.

(3) A request for review must be made before the end of the period of 21 days beginning with the day on which he is notified of the authority's decision or such longer period as the authority may in writing allow.

(4) On a request being duly made to them, the authority or authorities concerned shall review their decision.

Amendments
1   Substituted by the Homelessness Reduction Act 2017, s 9(1), (2)(a)(i).
2   Repealed by the Homelessness Reduction Act 2017, s 9(1), (2)(a)(ii), (c).
3   Inserted by the Homelessness Reduction Act 2017, s 9(1), (2)(b), (d), (3).
4   Repealed by the Housing and Regeneration Act 2008, s 321(1), Sch 16.
5   Inserted by the Homelessness Act 2002, s 8(2).
6   Substituted by the Localism Act 2011, s 149(1), (9).
7   Inserted by the Housing and Regeneration Act 2008, s 314, Sch 15, paras 1, 7(1), (2), (3)(b).
8   Substituted by the Housing and Regeneration Act 2008, s 314, Sch 15, paras 1, 7(1), (3)(a).

203 Procedure on a review.

(1) The Secretary of State may make provision by regulations as to the procedure to be followed in connection with a review under section 202.

Nothing in the following provisions affects the generality of this power.

(2) Provision may be made by regulations—

(a) requiring the decision on review to be made by a person of appropriate seniority who was not involved in the original decision, and

(b) as to the circumstances in which the applicant is entitled to an oral hearing, and whether and by whom he may be represented at such a hearing.

(3) The authority, or as the case may be either of the authorities, concerned shall notify the applicant of the decision on the review.

(4) If the decision is—

    (a) to confirm the original decision on any issue against the interests of the applicant, or

    (b) to confirm a previous decision—

        (i) to notify another authority under section 198 (referral of cases), or

        (ii) that the conditions are met for the referral of his case,

they shall also notify him of the reasons for the decision.

(5) In any case they shall inform the applicant of his right to appeal to [the county court]¹ on a point of law, and of the period within which such an appeal must be made (see section 204).

(6) Notice of the decision shall not be treated as given unless and until subsection (5), and where applicable subsection (4), is complied with.

(7) Provision may be made by regulations as to the period within which the review must be carried out and notice given of the decision.

(8) Notice required to be given to a person under this section shall be given in writing and, if not received by him, shall be treated as having been given if it is made available at the authority's office for a reasonable period for collection by him or on his behalf.

Amendments
1   Substituted by the Crime and Courts Act 2013, s 17(5), Sch 9, para 52.

204 Right of appeal to county court on point of law.

(1) If an applicant who has requested a review under section 202—

    (a) is dissatisfied with the decision on the review, or

    (b) is not notified of the decision on the review within the time prescribed under section 203,

he may appeal to the county court on any point of law arising from the decision or, as the case may be, the original decision.

(2) An appeal must be brought within 21 days of his being notified of the decision or, as the case may be, of the date on which he should have been notified of a decision on review.

[(2A) The court may give permission for an appeal to be brought after the end of the period allowed by subsection (2), but only if it is satisfied—

    (a) where permission is sought before the end of that period, that there is a good reason for the applicant to be unable to bring the appeal in time; or

(b) where permission is sought after that time, that there was a good reason for the applicant's failure to bring the appeal in time and for any delay in applying for permission.]¹

(3) On appeal the court may make such order confirming, quashing or varying the decision as it thinks fit.

(4) Where the authority were under a duty under section 188, 190[, 199A]² or 200 to secure that accommodation is available for the applicant's occupation[, ...³ they may]⁴ secure that accommodation is so available—

(a) during the period for appealing under this section against the authority's decision, and

(b) if an appeal is brought, until the appeal (and any further appeal) is finally determined.

Amendments
1   Inserted by the Homelessness Act 2002, s 18(1), Sch 1, paras 2, 17(a).
2   Inserted by the Homelessness Reduction Act 2017, s 5(1), (11).
3   Repealed by the Homelessness Reduction Act 2017, s 4(1), (6).
4   Substituted by the Homelessness Act 2002, s 18(1), Sch 1, paras 2, 17(b).

[204A Section 204(4): appeals

(1) This section applies where an applicant has the right to appeal to the county court against a local housing authority's decision on a review.

(2) If the applicant is dissatisfied with a decision by the authority—

(a) not to exercise their power under section 204(4) ('the section 204(4) power') in his case;

(b) to exercise that power for a limited period ending before the final determination by the county court of his appeal under section 204(1) ('the main appeal'); or

(c) to cease exercising that power before that time,

he may appeal to the county court against the decision.

(3) An appeal under this section may not be brought after the final determination by the county court of the main appeal.

(4) On an appeal under this section the court—

(a) may order the authority to secure that accommodation is available for the applicant's occupation until the determination of the appeal (or such earlier time as the court may specify); and

(b) shall confirm or quash the decision appealed against,

and in considering whether to confirm or quash the decision the court shall apply the principles applied by the High Court on an application for judicial review.

(5) If the court quashes the decision it may order the authority to exercise the section 204(4) power in the applicant's case for such period as may be specified in the order.

(6) An order under subsection (5)—

(a) may only be made if the court is satisfied that failure to exercise the section 204(4) power in accordance with the order would substantially prejudice the applicant's ability to pursue the main appeal;

(b) may not specify any period ending after the final determination by the county court of the main appeal.][1]

Amendments
1   Inserted by the Homelessness Act 2002, s 11.

Supplementary provisions

205 Discharge of functions: introductory.

(1) The following sections have effect in relation to the discharge by a local housing authority of their functions under this Part to secure that accommodation is available for the occupation of a person—

section 206 (general provisions),

...[1]

section 208 (out-of-area placements),

section 209 (arrangements with private landlord).

(2) In [sections 206 and 208][2] those functions are referred to as the authority's 'housing functions under this Part'.

[(3) For the purposes of this section, a local housing authority's duty under section 189B(2) or 195(2) is a function of the authority to secure that accommodation is available for the occupation of a person only if the authority decide to discharge the duty by securing that accommodation is so available.][3]

Amendments
1   Repealed by the Homelessness Act 2002, s 18(2), Sch 2.
2   Substituted by the Homelessness Act 2002, s 18(1), Sch 1, paras 2, 18.
3   Inserted by the Homelessness Reduction Act 2017, s 6.

206 Discharge of functions by local housing authorities.

(1) A local housing authority may discharge their housing functions under this Part only in the following ways—

   (a) by securing that suitable accommodation provided by them is available,

   (b) by securing that he obtains suitable accommodation from some other person, or

   (c) by giving him such advice and assistance as will secure that suitable accommodation is available from some other person.

(2) A local housing authority may require a person in relation to whom they are discharging such functions—

   (a) to pay such reasonable charges as they may determine in respect of accommodation which they secure for his occupation (either by making it available themselves or otherwise), or

   (b) to pay such reasonable amount as they may determine in respect of sums payable by them for accommodation made available by another person.

207 ...[1]

...[1]

Amendments

1   Repealed by the Homelessness Act 2002, s 18(2), Sch 2.

208 Discharge of functions: out-of-area placements.

(1) So far as reasonably practicable a local housing authority shall in discharging their housing functions under this Part secure that accommodation is available for the occupation of the applicant in their district.

(2) If they secure that accommodation is available for the occupation of the applicant outside their district, they shall give notice to the local housing authority in whose district the accommodation is situated.

(3) The notice shall state—

   (a) the name of the applicant,

   (b) the number and description of other persons who normally reside with him as a member of his family or might reasonably be expected to reside with him,

   (c) the address of the accommodation,

   (d) the date on which the accommodation was made available to him, and

   (e) which function under this Part the authority was discharging in securing that the accommodation is available for his occupation.

(4) The notice must be in writing, and must be given before the end of the period of 14 days beginning with the day on which the accommodation was made available to the applicant.

[209 Discharge of interim duties: arrangements with private landlord

(1) This section applies where in pursuance of any of their housing functions under section 188, 190, 200 or 204(4) (interim duties) a local housing authority make arrangements with a private landlord to provide accommodation.

(2) A tenancy granted to the applicant in pursuance of the arrangements cannot be an assured tenancy before the end of the period of twelve months beginning with—

(a) the date on which the applicant was notified of the authority's decision under section 184(3) or 198(5); or

(b) if there is a review of that decision under section 202 or an appeal to the court under section 204, the date on which he is notified of the decision on review or the appeal is finally determined,

unless, before or during that period, the tenant is notified by the landlord (or in the case of joint landlords, at least one of them) that the tenancy is to be regarded as an assured shorthold tenancy or an assured tenancy other than an assured shorthold tenancy.]¹

Amendments
1   Substituted by the Homelessness Act 2002, s 18(1), Sch 1, paras 2, 19.

210 Suitability of accommodation.

(1) In determining for the purposes of this Part whether accommodation is suitable for a person, the local housing authority shall have regard to [Parts 9 and 10]¹ of the Housing Act 1985 (slum clearance [and overcrowding) and Parts 1 to 4 of the Housing Act 2004]¹.

(2) The Secretary of State may by order specify—

(a) circumstances in which accommodation is or is not to be regarded as suitable for a person, and

(b) matters to be taken into account or disregarded in determining whether accommodation is suitable for a person.

Amendments
1   Substituted by the Housing Act 2004, s 265(1), Sch 15, paras 40, 43.

211 Protection of property of homeless persons and persons threatened with homelessness.

(1) This section applies where a local housing authority have reason to believe that—

(a) there is danger of loss of, or damage to, any personal property of an applicant by reason of his inability to protect it or deal with it, and

(b) no other suitable arrangements have been or are being made.

(2) If the authority have become subject to a duty towards the applicant under—

section 188 (interim duty to accommodate),

[section 189B (initial duty owed to all eligible persons who are homeless),][1]

section 190, 193 or 195 (duties to persons found to be homeless or threatened with homelessness), or

section 200 (duties to applicant whose case is considered for referral or referred),

then, whether or not they are still subject to such a duty, they shall take reasonable steps to prevent the loss of the property or prevent or mitigate damage to it.

(3) If they have not become subject to such a duty, they may take any steps they consider reasonable for that purpose.

(4) The authority may decline to take action under this section except upon such conditions as they consider appropriate in the particular case, which may include conditions as to—

(a) the making and recovery by the authority of reasonable charges for the action taken, or

(b) the disposal by the authority, in such circumstances as may be specified, of property in relation to which they have taken action.

(5) References in this section to personal property of the applicant include personal property of any person who might reasonably be expected to reside with him.

(6) Section 212 contains provisions supplementing this section.

Amendments
1   Inserted by the Homelessness Reduction Act 2017, s 5(1), (12).

212 Protection of property: supplementary provisions.

(1) The authority may for the purposes of section 211 (protection of property of homeless persons or persons threatened with homelessness)—

(a) enter, at all reasonable times, any premises which are the usual place of residence of the applicant or which were his last usual place of residence, and

(b) deal with any personal property of his in any way which is reasonably necessary, in particular by storing it or arranging for its storage.

(2) Where the applicant asks the authority to move his property to a particular location nominated by him, the authority—

    (a) may, if it appears to them that his request is reasonable, discharge their responsibilities under section 211 by doing as he asks, and

    (b) having done so, have no further duty or power to take action under that section in relation to that property.

If such a request is made, the authority shall before complying with it inform the applicant of the consequence of their doing so.

(3) If no such request is made (or, if made, is not acted upon) the authority cease to have any duty or power to take action under section 211 when, in their opinion, there is no longer any reason to believe that there is a danger of loss of or damage to a person's personal property by reason of his inability to protect it or deal with it.

But property stored by virtue of their having taken such action may be kept in store and any conditions upon which it was taken into store continue to have effect, with any necessary modifications.

(4) Where the authority—

    (a) cease to be subject to a duty to take action under section 211 in respect of an applicant's property, or

    (b) cease to have power to take such action, having previously taken such action,

they shall notify the applicant of that fact and of the reason for it.

(5) The notification shall be given to the applicant—

    (a) by delivering it to him, or

    (b) by leaving it, or sending it to him, at his last known address.

(6) References in this section to personal property of the applicant include personal property of any person who might reasonably be expected to reside with him.

213 Co-operation between relevant housing authorities and bodies.

(1) Where a local housing authority [in England][1]—

    (a) request another relevant housing authority or body, in England, Wales or Scotland, to assist them in the discharge of their functions under this Part, or

    (b) request a social services authority, in England, Wales or Scotland, to exercise any of their functions in relation to a case which the local housing authority are dealing with under this Part, the authority or body to whom the request is made shall co-operate in rendering such assistance in the discharge of the functions to which the request relates as is reasonable in the circumstances.

(2) In subsection (1)(a) 'relevant housing authority or body' means—

  (a) in relation to England and Wales, a local housing authority, a new town corporation, [a private registered provider of social housing]² a registered social landlord or a housing action trust;

  (b) in relation to Scotland, a local authority, a development corporation, a registered housing association or Scottish Homes.

Expressions used in paragraph (a) have the same meaning as in the Housing Act 1985; and expressions used in paragraph (b) have the same meaning as in the Housing (Scotland) Act 1987.

(3) Subsection (1) above applies to a request by a local authority in Scotland under section 38 of the Housing (Scotland) Act 1987 as it applies to a request by a local housing authority in England and Wales (the references to this Part being construed, in relation to such a request, as references to Part II of that Act).

Amendments
1   Inserted by the Housing (Wales) Act 2014, s 100, Sch 3, paras 2, 14.
2   Inserted by the Housing and Regeneration Act 2008 (Consequential Provisions) Order 2010, SI 2010/866, art 5, Sch 2, paras 81, 103. '

[213A   Co-operation in certain cases involving children

(1) This section applies where a local housing authority have reason to believe that an applicant with whom a person under the age of 18 normally resides, or might reasonably be expected to reside—

  (a) may be ineligible for assistance; [or]¹

  (b) may be homeless and may have become so intentionally; ...²

  (c) ...²

(2) A local housing authority shall make arrangements for ensuring that, where this section applies—

  (a) the applicant is invited to consent to the referral of the essential facts of his case to the social services authority for the district of the housing authority (where that is a different authority); and

  (b) if the applicant has given that consent, the social services authority are made aware of those facts and of the subsequent decision of the housing authority in respect of his case.

(3) Where the local housing authority and the social services authority for a district are the same authority (a 'unitary authority'), that authority shall make arrangements for ensuring that, where this section applies—

    (a) the applicant is invited to consent to the referral to the social services department of the essential facts of his case; and

    (b) if the applicant has given that consent, the social services department is made aware of those facts and of the subsequent decision of the authority in respect of his case.

(4) Nothing in subsection (2) or (3) affects any power apart from this section to disclose information relating to the applicant's case to the social services authority or to the social services department (as the case may be) without the consent of the applicant.

(5) Where a social services authority—

    (a) are aware of a decision of a local housing authority that the applicant is ineligible for [assistance or became homeless intentionally][3], and

    (b) request the local housing authority to provide them with advice and assistance in the exercise of their social services functions under Part 3 of the Children Act 1989 [or Part 6 of the Social Services and Well-being (Wales) Act 2014][4],

the local housing authority shall provide them with such advice and assistance as is reasonable in the circumstances.

(6) A unitary authority shall make arrangements for ensuring that, where they make a decision of a kind mentioned in subsection (5)(a), the housing department provide the social services department with such advice and assistance as the social services department may reasonably request.

(7) In this section, in relation to a unitary authority—

'the housing department' means those persons responsible for the exercise of their housing functions; and

'the social services department' means those persons responsible for the exercise of their social services functions under Part 3 of the Children Act 1989 [or Part 6 of the Social Services and Well-being (Wales) Act 2014][4].][5]

Amendments
1   Inserted by the Homelessness Reduction Act 2017, s 4(1), (7)(a)(i).
2   Repealed by the Homelessness Reduction Act 2017, s 4(1), (7)(a)(ii).
3   Substituted by the Homelessness Reduction Act 2017, s 4(1), (7)(b).
4   Inserted by the Social Services and Well-being (Wales) Act 2014 (Consequential Amendments) Regulations 2016, SI 2016/413, reg 150.
5   Inserted by the Homelessness Act 2002, s 12.

[213B Duty of public authority to refer cases in England to local housing authority

(1) This section applies if a specified public authority considers that a person in England in relation to whom the authority exercises functions is or may be homeless or threatened with homelessness.

(2) The specified public authority must ask the person to agree to the authority notifying a local housing authority in England of—

    (a) the opinion mentioned in subsection (1), and

    (b) how the person may be contacted by the local housing authority.

(3) If the person—

    (a) agrees to the specified public authority making the notification, and

    (b) identifies a local housing authority in England to which the person would like the notification to be made,

the specified public authority must notify that local housing authority of the matters mentioned in subsection (2)(a) and (b).

(4) In this section 'specified public authority' means a public authority specified, or of a description specified, in regulations made by the Secretary of State.

(5) In subsection (4) 'public authority' means a person (other than a local housing authority) who has functions of a public nature.]¹

Amendments
1   Inserted by the Homelessness Reduction Act 2017, s 10.

General provisions

214 False statements, withholding information and failure to disclose change of circumstances.

(1) It is an offence for a person, with intent to induce a local housing authority to believe in connection with the exercise of their functions under this Part that he or another person is entitled to accommodation or assistance in accordance with the provisions of this Part, or is entitled to accommodation or assistance of a particular description—

    (a) knowingly or recklessly to make a statement which is false in a material particular, or

    (b) knowingly to withhold information which the authority have reasonably required him to give in connection with the exercise of those functions.

(2) If before an applicant receives notification of the local housing authority's decision on his application there is any change of facts material to his case, he shall notify the authority as soon as possible.

The authority shall explain to every applicant, in ordinary language, the duty imposed on him by this subsection and the effect of subsection (3).

(3) A person who fails to comply with subsection (2) commits an offence unless he shows that he was not given the explanation required by that subsection or that he had some other reasonable excuse for non-compliance.

(4) A person guilty of an offence under this section is liable on summary conviction to a fine not exceeding level 5 on the standard scale.

[214A Codes of practice

(1) The Secretary of State may from time to time issue one or more codes of practice dealing with the functions of a local housing authority in England relating to homelessness or the prevention of homelessness.

(2) The provision that may be made by a code of practice under this section includes, in particular, provision about—

(a) the exercise by a local housing authority of functions under this Part;

(b) the training of an authority's staff in relation to the exercise of those functions;

(c) the monitoring by an authority of the exercise of those functions.

(3) A code of practice may—

(a) apply to all local housing authorities or to the local housing authorities specified or described in the code;

(b) contain different provision for different kinds of local housing authority.

(4) The Secretary of State may issue a code of practice under this section only in accordance with subsections (5) and (6).

(5) Before issuing the code of practice, the Secretary of State must lay a draft of the code before Parliament.

(6) If—

(a) the Secretary of State lays a draft of the code before Parliament, and

(b) no negative resolution is made within the 40-day period,

the Secretary of State may issue the code in the form of the draft.

(7) For the purposes of subsection (6)—

    (a) a 'negative resolution' means a resolution of either House of Parliament not to approve the draft of the code, and

    (b) 'the 40-day period' means the period of 40 days beginning with the day on which the draft of the code is laid before Parliament (or, if it is not laid before each House of Parliament on the same day, the later of the two days on which it is laid).

(8) In calculating the 40-day period, no account is to be taken of any period during which—

    (a) Parliament is dissolved or prorogued, or

    (b) both Houses are adjourned for more than four days.

(9) The Secretary of State may—

    (a) from time to time revise and reissue a code of practice under this section;

    (b) revoke a code of practice under this section.

(10) Subsections (4) to (6) do not apply to the reissue of a code of practice under this section.

(11) The Secretary of State must publish the current version of each code of practice under this section in whatever manner the Secretary of State thinks fit.

(12) A local housing authority must have regard to a code of practice under this section in exercising their functions.][1]

Amendments
1   Inserted by the Homelessness Reduction Act 2017, s 11.

215 Regulations and orders.

(1) In this Part 'prescribed' means prescribed by regulations of the Secretary of State.

(2) Regulations or an order under this Part may make different provision for different purposes, including different provision for different areas.

(3) Regulations or an order under this Part shall be made by statutory instrument.

(4) Unless required to be approved in draft, regulations or an order under this Part shall be subject to annulment in pursuance of a resolution of either House of Parliament.

216 Transitional and consequential matters.

(1) The provisions of this Part have effect in place of the provisions of Part III of the Housing Act 1985 (housing the homeless) and shall be construed as one with that Act.

(2) Subject to any transitional provision contained in an order under section 232(4) (power to include transitional provision in commencement order), the provisions of this Part do not apply in relation to an applicant whose application for accommodation or assistance in obtaining accommodation was made before the commencement of this Part.

(3) The enactments mentioned in Schedule 17 have effect with the amendments specified there which are consequential on the provisions of this Part.

217 Minor definitions: Part VII.

(1) In this Part, subject to subsection (2)—

['private landlord' means a landlord who is not within section 80(1) of the Housing Act 1985 (c. 68) (the landlord condition for secure tenancies);][1]

'relevant authority' means a local housing authority or a social services authority; and

'social services authority' means[—

(a) in relation to England][2] a local authority for the purposes of the Local Authority Social Services Act 1970, as defined in section 1 of that Act.

[(b) in relation to Wales, a local authority exercising social services functions for the purposes of the Social Services and Well-being (Wales) Act 2014.][2]

(2) In this Part, in relation to Scotland—

(a) 'local housing authority' means a local authority within the meaning of the Housing (Scotland) Act 1988, and

(b) 'social services authority' means a local authority for the purposes of the Social Work (Scotland) Act 1968.

(3) References in this Part to the district of a local housing authority—

(a) have the same meaning in relation to an authority in England or Wales as in the Housing Act 1985, and

(b) in relation to an authority in Scotland, mean the area of the local authority concerned.

Amendments
1   Inserted by the Homelessness Act 2002, s 18(1), Sch 1, paras 2, 20.
2   Inserted by the Social Services and Well-being (Wales) Act 2014 (Consequential Amendments) Regulations 2016, SI 2016/413, reg 151.

218 Index of defined expressions: Part VII.

The following Table shows provisions defining or otherwise explaining expressions used in this Part (other than provisions defining or explaining an expression used in the same section)—

accommodation available for occupation	section 176
applicant	section 183(2)
assistance under this Part	section 183(2)
...¹	...¹
assured tenancy and assured shorthold tenancy	section 230
district (of local housing authority)	section 217(3)
eligible for assistance	section 183(2)
homeless	section 175(1)
housing functions under this Part (in sections [206 and 208]²)	section 205(2)
intentionally homeless	section 191
...³	...³
local connection	section 199
local housing authority— – in England and Wales – in Scotland	section 230 section 217(2)(a)
...⁴	...⁴
prescribed	section 215(1)
priority need	section 189
[private landlord	section 217(1)]⁵
reasonable to continue to occupy accommodation	section 177
registered social landlord	section 230
[restricted person	section 184(7)]⁶
relevant authority	section 217(1)
social services authority	section 217(1) and (2)(b)
threatened with homelessness	section 175(4)

Textual Amendments

1 Repealed by the Domestic Abuse Act 2021, s 78(1), (7).
2 Substituted by the Homelessness Act 2002, s 18(1), Sch 1, paras 2, 21(a).
3 Repealed by the Homelessness Reduction Act 2017, s 4(1), (8).
4 Repealed by the Homelessness Act 2002, s 18(2), Sch 2.
5 Inserted by the Homelessness Act 2002, s 18(1), Sch 1, paras 2, 21(b).
6 Inserted by the Housing and Regeneration Act 2008, s 314, Sch 15, paras 1, 8.

Homelessness Act 2002

2002 Chapter 7

Homelessness reviews and strategies[: England][1]

1 Duty of local housing authority [in England][1] to formulate a homelessness strategy

(1) A local housing authority [in England][1] ('the authority') may from time to time—

   (a) carry out a homelessness review for their district; and

   (b) formulate and publish a homelessness strategy based on the results of that review.

(2) The social services authority for the district of the authority (where that is a different local authority) shall give such assistance in connection with the exercise of the power under subsection (1) as the authority may reasonably require.

(3) The authority shall exercise that power so as to ensure that the first homelessness strategy for their district is published within the period of twelve months beginning with the day on which this section comes into force.

(4) The authority shall exercise that power so as to ensure that a new homelessness strategy for their district is published within the period of five years beginning with the day on which their last homelessness strategy was published.

(5) A local housing authority [in England][1] shall take their homelessness strategy into account in the exercise of their functions.

(6) A social services authority shall take the homelessness strategy for the district of a local housing authority into account in the exercise of their functions in relation to that district.

(7) Nothing in subsection (5) or (6) affects any duty or requirement arising apart from this section.

Amendments
1   Inserted by the Housing (Wales) Act 2014, s 100, Sch 3, paras 2, 16, 17.

2 Homelessness reviews

(1) For the purposes of this Act 'homelessness review' means a review by a local housing authority of—

(a) the levels, and likely future levels, of homelessness in their district;

(b) the activities which are carried out for any purpose mentioned in subsection (2) (or which contribute to their achievement); and

(c) the resources available to the authority, the social services authority for their district, other public authorities, voluntary organisations and other persons for such activities.

(2) Those purposes are —

(a) preventing homelessness in the district of the authority;

(b) securing that accommodation is or will be available for people in the district who are or may become homeless;

(c) providing support for people in the district—

(i) who are or may become homeless; or

(ii) who have been homeless and need support to prevent them becoming homeless again.

(3) A local housing authority shall, after completing a homelessness review—

(a) arrange for the results of the review to be available at its principal office for inspection at all reasonable hours, without charge, by members of the public; and

(b) provide (on payment if required by the authority of a reasonable charge) a copy of those results to any member of the public who asks for one.

3 Homelessness strategies

(1) For the purposes of this Act 'homelessness strategy' means a strategy formulated by a local housing authority for—

(a) preventing homelessness in their district;

(b) securing that sufficient accommodation is and will be available for people in their district who are or may become homeless;

(c) securing the satisfactory provision of support for people in their district—

(i) who are or may become homeless; or

(ii) who have been homeless and need support to prevent them becoming homeless again.

(2) A homelessness strategy may include specific objectives to be pursued, and specific action planned to be taken, in the course of the exercise of—

(a) the functions of the authority as a local housing authority; or

(b) the functions of the social services authority for the district.

(3) A homelessness strategy may also include provision relating to specific action which the authority expects to be taken—

(a) by any public authority with functions (not being functions mentioned in subsection (2)) which are capable of contributing to the achievement of any of the objectives mentioned in subsection (1); or

(b) by any voluntary organisation or other person whose activities are capable of contributing to the achievement of any of those objectives.

(4) The inclusion in a homelessness strategy of any provision relating to action mentioned in subsection (3) requires the approval of the body or person concerned.

(5) In formulating a homelessness strategy the authority shall consider (among other things) the extent to which any of the objectives mentioned in subsection (1) can be achieved through action involving two or more of the bodies or other persons mentioned in subsections (2) and (3).

(6) The authority shall keep their homelessness strategy under review and may modify it from time to time.

(7) If the authority modify their homelessness strategy, they shall publish the modifications or the strategy as modified (as they consider most appropriate).

[(7A) In formulating or modifying a homelessness strategy, a local housing authority …¹ shall have regard to—

(a) its current allocation scheme under section 166A of the Housing Act 1996,

(b) its current tenancy strategy under section 150 of the Localism Act 2011, and

(c) in the case of an authority that is a London borough council, the current London housing strategy.]²

(8) Before adopting or modifying a homelessness strategy the authority shall consult such public or local authorities, voluntary organisations or other persons as they consider appropriate.

(9) The authority shall—

(a) make a copy of [everything published under section 1 or]³ this section available at its principal office for inspection at all reasonable hours, without charge, by members of the public; and

(b) provide (on payment if required by the authority of a reasonable charge) a copy of [anything]³ so published to any member of the public who asks for one.

Amendments
1 Repealed by the Housing (Wales) Act 2014, s 100, Sch 3, paras 2, 18.
2 Inserted by the Localism Act 2011, s 153.
3 Substituted by the Local Government Act 2003, s 127(1), Sch 7, para 81.

4 Sections 1 to 3: interpretation

In sections 1 to 3—

'homeless' and 'homelessness' have the same meaning as in Part 7 of the Housing Act 1996 (c. 52) (in this Act referred to as 'the 1996 Act');

'local housing authority' and 'district' have the same meaning as in the Housing Act 1985 (c. 68);

'social services authority' means a local authority for the purposes of the Local Authority Social Services Act 1970 (c. 42) [F9or Part 8 of the Social Services and Well-being (Wales) Act 2014];

'support' means advice, information or assistance; and

'voluntary organisation' has the same meaning as in section 180(3) of the 1996 Act.

Amendments

1   Inserted by the Social Services and Well-being (Wales) Act 2014 (Consequential Amendments) Regulations 2016, SI 2016/413, reg 187.

PART 2

England: Statutory Instruments

Homelessness (Suitability of Accommodation) Order 1996

SI 1996/3204

1 Citation and commencement

This Order may be cited as the Homelessness (Suitability of Accommodation) Order 1996 and shall come into force on 20th January 1997.

2 Matters to be taken into account

In determining whether it would be, or would have been, reasonable for a person to continue to occupy accommodation and in determining whether accommodation is suitable for a person there shall be taken into account whether or not the accommodation is affordable for that person and, in particular, the following matters—

    (a) the financial resources available to that person, including, but not limited to,—

        (i)   salary, fees and other remuneration;

        (ii)   social security benefits;

        (iii) payments due under a court order for the making of periodical payments to a spouse or a former spouse, or to, or for the benefit of, a child;

        (iv) paymrnts of child support maintenance due under the Child Support Act 1991

        (v)   contributions to the costs in respect of the accommodation which are or were made or which might reasonably be expected to be, or have been, made by other members of his household;

        (vi) pensions

        (vii) financial assistance towards the costs in respect of the accommodation, including loans, provided by a local authority, voluntary organisation or other body;

        (viii) benefits derived from a policy of insurance;

        (ix) savings and other capital sums;

    (b) the costs in respect of the accommodation, including, but not limited to,—

    (i)   payments of, or by way of, rent;

    (ii)   payments in respect of a licence or permission to occupy the accommodation;

    (iii) mortgage costs;

    (iv) payments of, or by way of, service charges;

    (v)   mooring charges payable for a houseboat;

    (vi) where the accommodation is a caravan or a mobile home, payments in respect of the site on which it stands;

    (vii) the amount of council tax payable in respect of the accommodation;

    (viii) payments by way of deposit or security in respect of the accommodation;

    (ix) payments required by an accommodation agency;

(c) payments which that person is required to make under a court order for the making of periodical payments to a spouse or a former spouse, or to, or for the benefit of, a child and payments of child support maintenance required to be made under the Child Support Act 1991;

(c) that person's other reasonable living expenses.

Local Authorities (Contracting Out of Allocation of Housing and Homelessness Functions) Order 1996

SI 1996/3205

1 Citation, commencement and interpretation

(1) This Order may be cited as the Local Authorities (Contracting Out of Allocation of Housing and Homelessness Functions) Order 1996.

(2) This article and article 3 of this Order shall come into force on 20th January 1997 and article 2 of this Order shall come into force on 1st April 1997.

(3) In this Order—

'the Act' means the Housing Act 1996;

'an authority' means a local housing authority as defined in the Housing Act 1985.

(4) Any expressions used in this Order which are also used in the Act have the same meaning as they have in the Act.

2 Contracting out of allocation of housing functions

Any function of an authority which is conferred by or under Part VI of the Act (allocation of housing accommodation), except one which is listed in Schedule 1 to this Order, may be exercised by, or by employees of, such person (if any) as may be authorised in that behalf by the authority whose function it is.

3 Contracting out of homelessness functions

Any function of an authority which is conferred by or under Part VII of the Act (homelessness) [or Chapter 2 of Part 2 of the Housing (Wales) Act 2014 (help for people who are homeless or threatened with homelessness][1], except one which is listed in Schedule 2 to this Order, may be exercised by, or by employees of, such person (if any) as may be authorised in that behalf by the authority whose function it is.

Amendments

1   Inserted by the Housing (Wales) Act 2014 (Consequential Amendments) Regulations 2015, SI 2015/752, reg 2(1), (2).

Article 2

SCHEDULE 1 – ALLOCATION OF HOUSING FUNCTIONS OF A LOCAL HOUSING AUTHORITY EXCLUDED FROM CONTRACTING OUT

Functions conferred by or under any of the following provisions of the Act:

(a) section 161(4) (classes of persons qualifying for allocations);

(b) section 162 (the housing register) so far as they relate to any decision about the form of the register;

(c) section 167 (allocation in accordance with allocation scheme) so far as they relate to adopting or altering an allocation scheme (including decisions on what principles the scheme is to be framed) and to the functions in subsection (7) of that section;

(d) section 168(2) (information about allocation scheme) so far as they relate to making the allocation scheme available for inspection at the authority's principal office.

Article 3

SCHEDULE 2 – HOMELESSNESS FUNCTIONS OF A LOCAL HOUSING AUTHORITY EXCLUDED FROM CONTRACTING OUT

Functions conferred by or under any of the following provisions of the Act:

(a) section 179(2) and (3) (duty of local housing authority to provide advisory services);

(b) section 180 (assistance for voluntary organisations);

(c) section 213 (co-operation between relevant housing authorities and bodies).

[Functions conferred by or under section 95 of the Housing (Wales) Act 2014.][1]

Amendments
1   Inserted by the Housing (Wales) Act 2014 (Consequential Amendments) Regulations 2015, SI 2015/752, reg 2(1), (3).

Homelessness (Decisions on Referrals) Order 1998

SI 1998/1578

1 Citation and commencement

This Order may be cited as the Homelessness (Decisions on Referrals) Order 1998 and shall come into force on the twenty eighth day after the day on which it is approved by resolution of each House of Parliament.

2 Arrangements for deciding whether conditions for referral are satisfied

The arrangements set out in the Schedule to this Order are those agreed by the Local Government Association, the Welsh Local Government Association, the Association of London Government and the Convention of Scottish Local Authorities, and shall be the arrangements for the purposes of section 198(5) and (6)(a) of the Housing Act 1996.

3 Revocation of order

(1) Subject to paragraph (2), the Housing (Homeless Persons) (Appropriate Arrangements) Order 1978 ('the 1978 Order') is hereby revoked.

(2) The 1978 Order shall remain in force for any case where a notified authority has received a notification under section 67(1) of the Housing Act 1985 or section 198(1) of the Housing Act 1996 (referral to another local housing authority) prior to the date on which this Order comes into force.

Article 2

SCHEDULE – THE ARRANGEMENTS

Appointment of person by agreement between notifying authority and notified authority

1. Where the question whether the conditions for referral of a case are satisfied has not been decided by agreement between the notifying authority and the notified authority, the question shall be decided by a person appointed by those authorities.

Appointment of person other than by agreement between notifying authority and notified authority

2. If within a period of 21 days commencing on the day on which the notified authority receives a notification under section 198(1) of the Housing Act 1996 a person has not been appointed in accordance with paragraph 1, the question shall be decided by a person—

> (a) from the panel constituted in accordance with paragraph 3, and

> (b) appointed in accordance with paragraph 4.

3. (1) Subject to sub-paragraph (2), the Local Government Association shall establish and maintain a panel of persons from which a person may be appointed to decide the question whether the conditions for referral of a case are satisfied.

(2) The Local Government Association shall consult such other associations of relevant authorities as they think appropriate before—

> (a) establishing the panel,

> (b) inviting a person to join the panel after it has been established, and

> (c) removing a person from the panel.

4. (1) The notifying authority and the notified authority shall jointly request the Chairman of the Local Government Association or his nominee ('the proper officer') to appoint a person from the panel.

(2) If within a period of six weeks commencing on the day on which the notified authority receives a notification under section 198(1) of the Housing Act 1996 a person has not been appointed, the notifying authority shall request the proper officer to appoint a person from the panel.

Procedural requirements

5. (1) Subject to the following provisions of this paragraph, the procedure for deciding whether the conditions for referral of a case are satisfied shall be determined by the appointed person.

(2) The appointed person shall invite written representations from the notifying authority and the notified authority.

(3) The appointed person may also invite—

> (a) further written representations from the notifying authority and the notified authority,

> (b) written representations from any other person, and

> (c) oral representations from any person.

(4) If the appointed person invites representations from any person, those representations may be made by a person acting on his behalf, whether or not legally qualified.

Notification of decision

6. The appointed person shall notify his decision, and his reasons for it, in writing to the notifying authority and the notified authority.

Costs

7. (1) The notifying authority and the notified authority shall pay their own costs incurred in connection with the arrangements set out in this Schedule.

(2) Where a person has made oral representations, the appointed person may give directions as to the payment by the notifying authority or the notified authority or both authorities of any travelling expenses reasonably incurred by that person.

Meaning of 'appointed person'

8. In this Schedule 'appointed person' means a person appointed in accordance with paragraph 1 or 4.

Homelessness (Priority Need for Accommodation) (England) Order 2002

SI 2002/2051

1 Citation, commencement and interpretation

(1) This Order may be cited as the Homelessness (Priority Need for Accommodation) (England) Order 2002 and shall come into force on the day after the day on which it is made.

(2) This Order extends to England only.

(3) In this Order—

'looked after, accommodated or fostered' has the meaning given by section 24(2) of the Children Act 1989 [or, as the case may be, section 104(3) of the Social Services and Well-being (Wales) Act 2014][1]; and

'relevant student' means a person to whom section 24B(3) of [the Children Act 1989 or, as the case may be, section 114(5) or 115(6) of the Social Services and Well-being (Wales) Act 2014][2] applies—

    (a) who is in full-time further or higher education; and

    (b) whose term-time accommodation is not available to him during a vacation.

Amendments
1   Inserted by the Social Services and Well-being (Wales) Act 2014 (Consequential Amendments) (Secondary Legislation) Regulations 2016, SI 2016/211, reg 3, Sch 3, paras 48, 49(a).
2   Substituted by the Social Services and Well-being (Wales) Act 2014 (Consequential Amendments) (Secondary Legislation) Regulations 2016, SI 2016/211, reg 3, Sch 3, paras 48, 49(b).

2 Priority need for accommodation

The descriptions of person specified in the following articles have a priority need for accommodation for the purposes of Part 7 of the Housing Act 1996.

3 Children aged 16 or 17

(1) A person (other than a person to whom paragraph (2) below applies) aged sixteen or seventeen who is not a relevant child for the purposes of section 23A

of the Children Act 1989 [or, as the case may be, is not a category 2 young person within the meaning of section 104(2) of the Social Services and Well-being (Wales) Act 2014][1].

(2) This paragraph applies to a person to whom a local authority owe a duty to provide accommodation under section 20 of that Act (provision of accommodation for children in need [or, as the case may be, section 76 of the Social Services and Well-being (Wales) Act 2014 (accommodation for children without parents or who are lost or abandoned etc)][1]).

Amendments
1   Inserted by the Social Services and Well-being (Wales) Act 2014 (Consequential Amendments) (Secondary Legislation) Regulations 2016, SI 2016/211, reg 3, Sch 3, paras 48, 50.

4 Young people under 21

(1) A person (other than a relevant student) who—

(a) is under twenty-one; and

(b) at any time after reaching the age of sixteen, but while still under eighteen, was, but is no longer, looked after, accommodated or fostered.

5 Vulnerability: institutional backgrounds

(1) A person (other than a relevant student) who has reached the age of twenty-one and who is vulnerable as a result of having been looked after, accommodated or fostered.

(2) A person who is vulnerable as a result of having been a member of Her Majesty's regular naval, military or air forces.

(3) A person who is vulnerable as a result of—

(a) having served a custodial sentence (within the meaning of section 76 of the Powers of Criminal Courts (Sentencing) Act 2000) [or section 222 of the Sentencing Code][1];

(b) having been committed for contempt of court or any other kindred offence;

(c) having been remanded in custody (within the meaning of paragraph (b), (c) or (d) of section 88(1) of [the Powers of Criminal Courts (Sentencing) Act 2000][2]).

Amendments
1   Inserted by the Sentencing Act 2020, s 410, Sch 24, para 332(a).
2   Substituted by the Sentencing Act 2020, s 410, Sch 24, para 332(b).

6 Vulnerability: fleeing violence or threats of violence

[(1)]¹ A person who is vulnerable as a result of ceasing to occupy accommodation by reason of violence from another person or threats of violence from another person which are likely to be carried out.

[(2) For the purposes of this article—

    (a) 'violence' does not include violence that is domestic abuse;

    (b) 'domestic abuse' has the meaning given by section 1 of the Domestic Abuse Act 2021.]²

Amendments
1   Renumbered by the Domestic Abuse Act 2021, s 78(8)(a).
2   Inserted by the Domestic Abuse Act 2021, s 78(8)(b).

Allocation of Housing (England) Regulations 2002

SI 2002/3264

1 Citation, commencement and application

(1) These Regulations may be cited as the Allocation of Housing (England) Regulations 2002 and shall come into force on 31st January 2003.

(2) These Regulations apply in England only.

2 Interpretation

In these Regulations—

'the Act' means the Housing Act 1996;

'the Common Travel Area' means the United Kingdom, the Channel Islands, the Isle of Man and the Republic of Ireland collectively;

['family intervention tenancy'—

    (a) in relation to a tenancy granted by a local housing authority, has the meaning given by paragraph 4ZA(3) of Schedule 1 to the Housing Act 1985;

    (b) in relation to a tenancy granted by a registered social landlord [or a private registered provider of social housing]¹, has the meaning given by paragraph 12ZA(3) of Part 1 of Schedule 1 to the Housing Act 1988;]² and

'the immigration rules' means the rules laid down as mentioned in section 3(2) of the Immigration Act 1971 (general provisions for regulation and control).

Amendments

1   Inserted by the Housing and Regeneration Act 2008 (Consequential Provisions) (No. 2) Order 2010, SI 2010/671, reg 4, Sch 1, para 29.

2   Inserted by the Allocation of Housing (England) (Amendment) (Family Intervention Tenancies) Regulations 2008, SI 2008/3015, reg 2(1), (2).

3 Cases where the provisions of Part 6 of the Act do not apply

(1) The provisions of Part 6 of the Act about the allocation of housing accommodation do not apply in the following cases.

(2) They do not apply where a local housing authority secures the provision of suitable alternative accommodation under section 39 of the Land Compensation Act 1973 (duty to rehouse residential occupiers).

(3) They do not apply in relation to the grant of a secure tenancy under sections 554 and 555 of the Housing Act 1985 (grant of tenancy to former owner-occupier or statutory tenant of defective dwelling-house).

[(4) They do not apply in relation to the allocation of housing accommodation by a local housing authority to a person who lawfully occupies accommodation let on a family intervention tenancy.][1]

Amendments
1   Inserted by the Allocation of Housing (England) (Amendment) (Family Intervention Tenancies) Regulations 2008, SI 2008/3015, reg 2(1), (3).

4   ...[1]

...[1]

Amendments
1   Repealed by the Allocation of Housing and Homelessness (Eligibility) (England) Regulations 2006, SI 2006/1294, reg 7, Schedule.

5   ...[1]

...[1]

Amendments
1   Repealed by the Allocation of Housing and Homelessness (Eligibility) (England) Regulations 2006, SI 2006/1294, reg 7, Schedule.

6 Revocation

The Allocation of Housing (England) Regulations 2000 are revoked.

Homelessness (Suitability of Accommodation) (England) Order 2003

SI 2003/3326

I Citation, commencement and application

(1) This Order may be cited as the Homelessness (Suitability of Accommodation) (England) Order 2003 and shall come into force on 1st April 2004.

(2) This Order applies in relation to the duties of local housing authorities in England to make accommodation available for occupation by applicants under Part 7 of the Housing Act 1996.

2 Interpretation

In this Order—

'applicant with family commitments' means an applicant—

(a) who is pregnant;

(b) with whom a pregnant woman resides or might reasonably be expected to reside; or

(c) with whom dependent children reside or might reasonably be expected to reside;

'B&B accommodation' means accommodation (whether or not breakfast is included)—

(a) which is not separate and self-contained premises; and

(b) in which [cooking facilities are not provided or]¹ any one of the following amenities is shared by more than one household—

(i) a toilet;

(ii) personal washing facilities;

(iii) cooking facilities,

but does not include accommodation which is owned or managed by a local housing authority, [a non-profit registered provider of social housing]²or a voluntary organisation as defined in section 180(3) of the Housing Act 1996[, or accommodation that is provided in a private dwelling]³; and

any reference to a numbered section is a reference to a section of the Housing Act 1996.

Amendments
1   Inserted by the Homelessness (Suitability of Accommodation) (England) (Amendment) Order 2023, SI 2023/509, art 2.
2   Substituted by the Housing and Regeneration Act 2008 (Consequential Provisions) (No. 2) Order 2010, SI 2010/671, reg 4, Sch 1, para 36.
3   Inserted by the Homelessness (Suitability of Accommodation) (Amendment) (England) Order 2022, SI 2022/521, art 3.

3 Accommodation unsuitable where there is a family commitment

Subject to the exceptions contained in article 4, B&B accommodation is not to be regarded as suitable for an applicant with family commitments where accommodation is made available for occupation—

(a) under section 188(1), 190(2), 193(2) or 200(1); or

(b) under section 195(2), where the accommodation is other than that occupied by the applicant at the time of making his application.

4 Exceptions

(1) Article 3 does not apply—

(a) where no accommodation other than B&B accommodation is available for occupation by an applicant with family commitments; and

(b) [except where the applicant is a person falling within paragraph (3),]¹ the applicant occupies B&B accommodation for a period, or a total of periods, which does not exceed 6 weeks.

(2) In calculating the period, or total period, of an applicant's occupation of B&B accommodation for the purposes of paragraph (1)(b), there shall be disregarded—

(a) any period before 1st April 2004; and

(b) where a local housing authority is subject to the duty under section 193 by virtue of section 200(4), any period before that authority became subject to that duty.

[(3) A person falls within this paragraph if they—

(a) make an application to a local housing authority for assistance under Part 7 of the Housing Act 1996 on or after 1st June 2022,

(b) make that application within 2 years beginning with the date on which they arrive in the United Kingdom,

(c) are eligible for assistance under Part 7 of the Housing Act 1996, and

(d) did not have a right to occupy accommodation in the United Kingdom for an uninterrupted period of 6 months or more in the 3 years prior to the date on which they arrived in the United Kingdom.][1]

Amendments

1   Words inserted by Homelessness (Suitability of Accommodation) (Amendment) (England) Order 2022, SI 2022/521, art 4 and operating as a temporary modification which will expire on 1 June 2024, see Homelessness (Suitability of Accommodation) (England) (Amendment) Order 2024, SI 2024/371, art 2.

Allocation of Housing and Homelessness (Eligibility) (England) Regulations 2006

SI 2006/1294

1 Citation, commencement and application

(1) These Regulations may be cited as the Allocation of Housing and Homelessness (Eligibility) (England) Regulations 2006 and shall come into force on 1st June 2006.

(2) These Regulations apply to England only.

2 Interpretation

(1) In these Regulations—

'the 1996 Act' means the Housing Act 1996;

[...¹

...²]³

['the Accession Regulations 2013' means the Accession of Croatia (Immigration and Worker Authorisation) Regulations 2013;]⁴

'the EEA Regulations' means the [Immigration (European Economic Area) Regulations 2016 and references to the EEA Regulations are to be read with Schedule 4 to the Immigration and Social Security Co-ordination (EU Withdrawal) Act 2020(Consequential, Saving, Transitional and Transitory Provisions) Regulations 2020]⁵;

['the Human Rights Convention' means the Convention for the Protection of Human Rights and Fundamental Freedoms, agreed by the Council of Europe at Rome on 4th November 1950 as it has effect for the time being in relation to the United Kingdom;]⁶

'the Immigration Rules' means the rules laid down as mentioned in section 3(2) of the Immigration Act 1971 (general provisions for regulation and control);

'the Refugee Convention' means the Convention relating to the Status of Refugees done at Geneva on 28th July 1951, as extended by Article 1(2) of the Protocol relating to the Status of Refugees done at New York on 31st January 1967; ...[7]

['relevant person of Northern Ireland' means a person who—

   (a) is—

      (i)   a British citizen;

      (ii) an Irish citizen; or

      (iii) a British citizen and an Irish citizen; and

   (b) was born in Northern Ireland and, at the time of the person's birth, at least one of their parents was—

      (i)   a British citizen;

      (ii) an Irish citizen;

      (iii) a British citizen and an Irish citizen; or

      (iv) otherwise entitled to reside in Northern Ireland without any restriction on their period of residence; and][8]

'sponsor' means a person who has given an undertaking in writing for the purposes of the Immigration Rules to be responsible for the maintenance and accommodation of another person.

(2) For the purposes of these Regulations—

   (a) 'jobseeker', 'self-employed person', and 'worker' have the same meaning as for the purposes of the definition of a 'qualified person' in regulation 6(1) of the EEA Regulations; and

   [(ab) frontier worker' means a person who is a frontier worker within the meaning of regulation 3 of the Citizens' Rights (Frontier Workers) (EU Exit) Regulations 2020;][9]

   (b) subject to paragraph (3), references to the family member of a jobseeker, self-employed person[, worker or frontier worker][5] shall be construed in accordance with regulation 7 of [the EEA Regulations][5].

(3) For the purposes of regulations 4(2)(d) [and (k)][9] and 6(2)(d) [and (k)][9] 'family member' does not include a person who is treated as a family member by virtue of regulation 7(3) of the EEA Regulations.

[(4) ...[2]][10]

Amendments

1 Repealed by the Allocation of Housing and Homelessness (Eligibility) (England) (Amendment) Regulations 2013, SI 2013/1467, reg 2(1), (2)(a).
2 Repealed by the Allocation of Housing and Homelessness (Eligibility) (England) (Amendment) Regulations 2014, SI 2014/435, reg 2(1), (2)

3 Inserted by the Allocation of Housing and Homelessness (Eligibility) (England) (Amendment) (No.2) Regulations 2006, SI 2006/3340, reg 2(1), (2).
4 Inserted by the Allocation of Housing and Homelessness (Eligibility) (England) (Amendment) Regulations 2013, SI 2013/1467, reg 2(1), (2)(b).
5 Substituted by the Immigration and Social Security Co-ordination (EU Withdrawal) Act 2020 (Consequential, Saving, Transitional and Transitory Provisions) (EU Exit) Regulations 2020, SI 2020/1309, reg 71(1), (2)(a), (c).
6 Inserted by the Allocation of Housing and Homelessness (Eligibility) (England) (Amendment) Regulations 2016, SI 2016/965, reg 2(1), (2).
7 Repealed by the Allocation of Housing and Homelessness (Eligibility) (England) (Amendment) Regulations 2020, SI 2020/667, regs 2, 3(a).
8 Inserted by the Allocation of Housing and Homelessness (Eligibility) (England) (Amendment) Regulations 2020, SI 2020/667, regs 2, 3(b).
9 Inserted by the Immigration and Social Security Co-ordination (EU Withdrawal) Act 2020 (Consequential, Saving, Transitional and Transitory Provisions) (EU Exit) Regulations 2020, SI 2020/1309, reg 71(1), (2)(b), (d).
10 Inserted by the Allocation of Housing and Homelessness (Eligibility) (England) (Amendment) Regulations 2006, SI 2006/2007, reg 2(1), (2).

3 Persons subject to immigration control who are eligible for an allocation of housing accommodation

The following classes of persons subject to immigration control are persons who are eligible for an allocation of housing accommodation under Part 6 of the 1996 Act—

(a) Class A – a person who is recorded by the Secretary of State as a refugee within the definition in Article 1 of the Refugee Convention and who has leave to enter or remain in the United Kingdom;

(b) Class B – a person—

   (i) who has exceptional leave to enter or remain in the United Kingdom granted outside the provisions of the Immigration Rules; and

   (ii) who is not subject to a condition requiring him to maintain and accommodate himself, and any person who is dependent on him, without recourse to public funds;

(c) Class C – a person who is habitually resident in the United Kingdom, the Channel Islands, the Isle of Man or the Republic of Ireland and whose leave to enter or remain in the United Kingdom is not subject to any limitation or condition, other than a person—

   (i) who has been given leave to enter or remain in the United Kingdom upon an undertaking given by his sponsor;

   (ii) who has been resident in the United Kingdom, the Channel Islands, the Isle of Man or the Republic of Ireland for less than five years beginning on the date of entry or the date on which his sponsor gave the undertaking in respect of him, whichever date is the later; and

   (iii) whose sponsor or, where there is more than one sponsor, at least one of whose sponsors, is still alive; ...[1]

[(d) Class D— a person who has humanitarian protection granted under the Immigration Rules[; ...²]³]⁴

[(e) ...⁵]⁶

[[(f)Class F – a person—

   (i) who has limited leave to enter or remain in the United Kingdom on family or private life grounds under Article 8 of the Human Rights Convention that is granted under paragraph 276BE(1), paragraph 276DG or Appendix FM of the Immigration Rules; and

   (ii) who is not subject to a condition requiring the person to maintain and accommodate himself, and any person dependent upon him, without recourse to public funds;]⁷]⁸

[(g) Class G – a person who is habitually resident in the United Kingdom, the Channel Islands, the Isle of Man or the Republic of Ireland and who has been transferred to the United Kingdom under section 67 of the Immigration Act 2016 and has limited leave to remain under paragraph 352ZH of the Immigration Rules [; ...⁹]¹⁰]¹¹

[(h) Class H – a person who is habitually resident in the United Kingdom, the Channel Islands, the Isle of Man or the Republic of Ireland and has Calais leave to remain under paragraph 352J of the Immigration Rules[;]⁹]¹²

[(i) Class I – a person (P) who has limited leave to enter or remain in the United Kingdom by virtue of Appendix EU of the Immigration Rules in circumstances where—

   (i) P is a family member of a relevant person of Northern Ireland ('RP') in accordance with those rules; and

   (ii) P would have been considered eligible under regulation 4(2)(d) if RP were a person specified in regulation 4(2)(a) to (c); ...¹³

(j) Class J – a person who is habitually resident in the United Kingdom, the Channel Islands, the Isle of Man or the Republic of Ireland and who has limited leave to remain in the United Kingdom as a stateless person under paragraph 405 of the Immigration Rules;]¹⁴ [...⁵

(k) Class K – a person (P)—

   (i) who has limited leave to enter or remain in the United Kingdom by virtue of Appendix Hong Kong British National (Overseas) of the Immigration Rules;

   (ii) whose leave to enter or remain is not subject to a condition requiring P to maintain and accommodate P, and any person dependent upon P, without recourse to public funds; and

   (iii) who is habitually resident in the United Kingdom, the Channel Islands, the Isle of Man or the Republic of Ireland;]¹⁵

[(l) Class L – a person—

(i) who is granted leave to enter or remain in the United Kingdom in accordance with the Immigration Rules, where such leave is granted by virtue of—

(aa) the Afghan Relocations and Assistance Policy; or

(bb) the previous scheme for locally-employed staff in Afghanistan (sometimes referred to as the ex-gratia scheme); or

(ii) with leave to enter or remain in the United Kingdom not coming within sub-paragraph (i), who left Afghanistan in connection with the collapse of the Afghan government that took place on 15th August 2021, but excluding a person (P)—

(aa) who is subject to a condition requiring P to maintain and accommodate themself, and any person who is dependent on P, without recourse to public funds; or

(bb) who has been given leave to enter or remain in the United Kingdom upon an undertaking given by P's sponsor and has been resident in the United Kingdom, the Channel Islands, the Isle of Man or the Republic of Ireland for less than five years beginning on the date of entry or the date on which P's sponsor gave the undertaking in respect of P, whichever date is the later, and whose sponsor or, where there is more than one sponsor, at least one of whose sponsors, is still alive;][16]

[(m) Class M – a person in the United Kingdom who—

(i) was residing in Ukraine immediately before 1st January 2022;

(ii) left Ukraine in connection with the Russian invasion which took place on 24th February 2022; and

(iii) has been granted leave in accordance with immigration rules made under section 3(2) of the Immigration Act 1971,

but excluding a person (P) who is subject to a condition requiring P to maintain and accommodate themselves, and any person who is dependent on P, without recourse to public funds;][17]

[(n) Class N – a person in the United Kingdom who has limited leave to remain granted in accordance with Appendix Ukraine Scheme of the Immigration Rules pursuant to an application made by that person from within the United Kingdom, but excluding a person (P) who is subject to a condition requiring P to maintain and accommodate themself, and any person who is dependent on P, without recourse to public funds;][18]

[(o) Class O – a person who has limited leave to remain granted in accordance with Appendix Temporary Permission to Stay for Victims of Human Trafficking or Slavery of the Immigration Rules;][19]

[(p) Class P — a person who—

(i)   was residing in Sudan before 15th April 2023;

(ii) left Sudan in connection with the violence which rapidly escalated on 15th April 2023 in Khartoum and across Sudan;

(iii) has leave to enter or remain in the United Kingdom given in accordance with the Immigration Rules;

(iv) is not a person whose leave is subject to a condition requiring that person to maintain and accommodate themself, and any person who is dependent on that person, without recourse to public funds; and

(v)   is not a person ('P')—

    (aa) who has been given leave upon an undertaking given by P's sponsor;

    (bb) who has been resident in the United Kingdom, the Channel Islands, the Isle of Man or the Republic of Ireland for less than five years beginning on the date of entry or the date on which P's sponsor gave the undertaking in respect of P, whichever date is later; and

    (cc) whose sponsor, or where there is more than one sponsor, at least one of whose sponsors, is still alive;][20]

[(q) Class Q — a person who—

(i)   was residing in Israel, the West Bank, the Gaza Strip, East Jerusalem, the Golan Heights or Lebanon immediately before 7th October 2023;

(ii) left Israel, the West Bank, the Gaza Strip, East Jerusalem, the Golan Heights or Lebanon in connection with the Hamas terrorist attack in Israel on 7th October 2023 or the violence which rapidly escalated in the region following the attack;

(iii) has leave to enter or remain in the United Kingdom given in accordance with the Immigration Rules;

(iv) is not a person whose leave is subject to a condition requiring that person to maintain and accommodate themself, and any person who is dependent on that person, without recourse to public funds; and

(v)   is not a person ('P')—

    (aa) who has been given leave upon an undertaking given by P's sponsor;

    (bb) who has been resident in the United Kingdom, the Channel Islands, the Isle of Man or the Republic of Ireland for less than five years beginning on the date of entry or the date on which P's sponsor gave the undertaking in respect of P, whichever date is later; and

    (cc) whose sponsor, or where there is more than one sponsor, at least one of whose sponsors, is still alive.][21]

Amendments

 1 Repealed by the Allocation of Housing and Homelessness (Eligibility) (England) (Amendment) Regulations 2014, SI 2014/435, reg 2(1), (3)(a).
 2 Repealed by the Allocation of Housing and Homelessness (Eligibility) (England) (Amendment) Regulations 2016, SI 2016/965, reg 2(1), (3)(a).
 3 Substituted by the Allocation of Housing and Homelessness (Eligibility) (England) (Amendment) Regulations 2014, SI 2014/435, reg 2(1), (3)(b).
 4 Substituted by the Allocation of Housing and Homelessness (Miscellaneous Provisions) (England) Regulations 2006, SI 2006/2527, reg 2(1), (2).
 5 Repealed by the Allocation of Housing and Homelessness (Eligibility) (England) and Persons subject to Immigration Control (Housing Authority Accommodation and Homelessness) (Amendment) Regulations 2021, SI 2021/1045, reg 2(1), (2)(a), (b).
 6 Inserted by the Allocation of Housing and Homelessness (Eligibility) (England) (Amendment) Regulations 2014, SI 2014/435, reg 2(1), (3)(c).
 7 Substituted by the Allocation of Housing and Homelessness (Eligibility) (England) (Amendment) Regulations 2020, SI 2020/667, regs 2, 4(a), (c).
 8 Inserted by the Allocation of Housing and Homelessness (Eligibility) (England) (Amendment) Regulations 2016, SI 2016/965, reg 2(1), (3)(c).
 9 Repealed by the Allocation of Housing and Homelessness (Eligibility) (England) (Amendment) Regulations 2020, SI 2020/667, regs 2, 4(b).
10 Substituted by the Allocation of Housing and Homelessness (Eligibility) (England) (Amendment) (No. 2) Regulations 2018, SI 2018/1056, regs 2, 3(b).
11 Inserted by the Allocation of Housing and Homelessness (Eligibility) (England) (Amendment) Regulations 2018, SI 2018/730, reg 2(1), (2)(c)
12 Inserted by the Allocation of Housing and Homelessness (Eligibility) (England) (Amendment) (No. 2) Regulations 2018, SI 2018/1056, regs 2, 3(c).
13 Repealed by the Allocation of Housing and Homelessness (Eligibility) (England) (Amendment) Regulations 2021, SI 2021/665, regs 2, 4(a).
14 Inserted by the Allocation of Housing and Homelessness (Eligibility) (England) (Amendment) Regulations 2020, SI 2020/667, regs 2, 4(d)
15 Inserted by the Allocation of Housing and Homelessness (Eligibility) (England) (Amendment) Regulations 2021, SI 2021/665, regs 2, 4(b).
16 Inserted by the Allocation of Housing and Homelessness (Eligibility) (England) and Persons subject to Immigration Control (Housing Authority Accommodation and Homelessness) (Amendment) Regulations 2021, SI 2021/1045, reg 2(1), (2)(c).
17 Inserted by the Allocation of Housing and Homelessness (Eligibility) (England) and Persons subject to Immigration Control (Housing Authority Accommodation and Homelessness) (Amendment) Regulations 2022, SI 2022/339, reg 2(1), (2)
18 Inserted by the Allocation of Housing and Homelessness (Eligibility) (England) and Persons Subject to Immigration Control (Housing Authority Accommodation and Homelessness) (Amendment) (No. 2) Regulations 2022, SI 2022/601, reg 2(1), (2).
19 Inserted by the Allocation of Housing and Homelessness (Eligibility) (England) and Persons Subject to Immigration Control (Housing Authority Accommodation and Homelessness) (Amendment) (No. 4) Regulations 2022, SI 2022/1371, reg 2(1), (2).
20 Inserted by the Allocation of Housing and Homelessness (Eligibility) (England) and Persons Subject to Immigration Control (Housing Authority Accommodation and Homelessness) (Amendment) Regulations 2023, SI 2023/530, reg 2(1), (2).
21 Inserted by the Allocation of Housing and Homelessness (Eligibility) (England) and Persons Subject to Immigration Control (Housing Authority Accommodation and Homelessness) (Amendment) (No. 2) Regulations 2023, SI 2023/1142, reg 2(1), (2)

4 Other persons from abroad who are ineligible for an allocation of housing accommodation

(1) A person who is not subject to immigration control is to be treated as a person from abroad who is ineligible for an allocation of housing accommodation under Part 6 of the 1996 Act if—

(a) subject to paragraph (2), he is not habitually resident in the United Kingdom, the Channel Islands, the Isle of Man, or the Republic of Ireland;

(b) his only right to reside in the United Kingdom—

    (i) is derived from his status as a jobseeker or the family member of a jobseeker; or

    (ii) is an initial right to reside for a period not exceeding three months under regulation 13 of the EEA Regulations; or

    [(iii) is a derivative right to reside to which he is entitled under [regulation 16(1)][1] of the EEA Regulations, but only in a case where the right exists under that regulation because the applicant satisfies the criteria in [regulation 16(5)][1] of those Regulations; or

    (iv) ...[2]][3]

(c) [his only right to reside in the Channel Islands, the Isle of Man or the Republic of Ireland is a right equivalent to one of those mentioned in sub-paragraph (b)(i), (ii) or (iii)][1].

[(1A) For the purposes of determining whether the only right to reside that a person has is of the kind mentioned in paragraph (1)(b) or (c), a right to reside by virtue of having been granted

    [(a) limited leave to enter or remain in the United Kingdom under the Immigration Act 1971 by virtue of Appendix EU to the immigration rules made under section 3(2) of that Act; or

    (b) leave to enter the United Kingdom by virtue of an entry clearance that was granted under Appendix EU (Family Permit) to the immigration rules made under section 3(2) of that Act

is to be disregarded.][4]][5]

(2) The following are not to be treated as persons from abroad who are ineligible for an allocation of housing accommodation pursuant to paragraph (1)(a)—

(a) a worker;

(b) a self-employed person;

[(c) a person who is treated as a worker for the purpose of the definition of 'qualified person' in regulation 6(1) of the EEA Regulations pursuant to ...[6]—

    (i) ...[7]

    (ii) regulation 5 of the Accession Regulations 2013 (right of residence of an accession State national subject to worker authorisation);][7]

(d) a person who is the family member of a person specified in sub-paragraphs (a)-(c);

(e) a person with a right to reside permanently in the United Kingdom by virtue of regulation [15(1)(c)][8], (d) or (e) of the EEA Regulations; [and][9]

(f) ...[6] ...[10]

(g) a person who is in the United Kingdom as a result of his deportation, expulsion or other removal by compulsion of law from another country to the United Kingdom[.][11] [...[12]][13]

[(h) ...[6]][13] [...[6]

(i) ...[6]][14]

[(j) a frontier worker; ...[15]

(k) a person who—

    (i) is a family member of a person specified in sub-paragraph (j); and

    (ii) has a right to reside by virtue of having been granted limited leave to enter or remain in the United Kingdom under the Immigration Act 1971 by virtue of Appendix EU to the immigration rules made under section 3 of that Act;][16]

[(l) a person who left Afghanistan in connection with the collapse of the Afghan government that took place on 15th August 2021;][17]

[(m) a person who was residing in Ukraine immediately before 1st January 2022 and who left Ukraine in connection with the Russian invasion which took place on 24th February 2022;][18]

[(n) a person who was residing in Sudan before 15th April 2023 and left Sudan in connection with the violence which rapidly escalated on 15th April 2023 in Khartoum and across Sudan;][19]

[(o) a person who was residing in Israel, the West Bank, the Gaza Strip, East Jerusalem, the Golan Heights or Lebanon immediately before 7th October 2023 and who left Israel, the West Bank, the Gaza Strip, East Jerusalem, the Golan Heights or Lebanon in connection with the Hamas terrorist attack in Israel on 7th October 2023 or the violence which rapidly escalated in the region following the attack.][20]

Amendments

1 Substituted by the Immigration and Social Security Co-ordination (EU Withdrawal) Act 2020 (Consequential, Saving, Transitional and Transitory Provisions) (EU Exit) Regulations 2020, SI 2020/1309, reg 71(1), (3)(a), (b), (d).

2 Repealed by the Immigration and Social Security Co-ordination (EU Withdrawal) Act 2020 (Consequential, Saving, Transitional and Transitory Provisions) (EU Exit) Regulations 2020, SI 2020/1309, reg 71(1), (3)(c).

3 Inserted by the Allocation of Housing and Homelessness (Eligibility) (England) (Amendment) Regulations 2012, SI 2012/2588, reg 2(1), (2).

4 Substituted by the Immigration (Citizens' Rights etc.) (EU Exit) Regulations 2020, SI 2020/1372, reg 20.

5 Inserted by the Allocation of Housing and Homelessness (Eligibility) (England) (Amendment) (EU Exit) Regulations 2019, SI 2019/861, regs 2, 3(a).

6 Repealed by the Allocation of Housing and Homelessness (Eligibility) (England) (Amendment) Regulations 2014, SI 2014/435, reg 2(1), (4)(a), (c).

7 Substituted by the Allocation of Housing and Homelessness (Eligibility) (England) (Amendment) Regulations 2013, SI 2013/1467, reg 2(1), (3).

8 Substituted by the Allocation of Housing and Homelessness (Eligibility) (England) (Amendment) (EU Exit) Regulations 2019, SI 2019/861, regs 2, 3(b).

9 Inserted by the Allocation of Housing and Homelessness (Eligibility) (England) (Amendment) Regulations 2014, SI 2014/435, reg 2(1), (4)(b).

10 Repealed by the Allocation of Housing and Homelessness (Eligibility) (England) (Amendment) Regulations 2006, SI 2006/2007, reg 2(1), (3).

11 Substituted for semi-colon by the Allocation of Housing and Homelessness (Eligibility) (England) (Amendment) Regulations 2014, SI 2014/435, reg 2(1), (4)(d)

12 Repealed by the Allocation of Housing and Homelessness (Eligibility) (England) (Amendment) Regulations 2009, SI 2009/358, reg 2(1), (2).

13 Inserted by the Allocation of Housing and Homelessness (Eligibility) (England) (Amendment) Regulations 2006, SI 2006/2007, reg 2(1), (4), (5).

14 Inserted by the Allocation of Housing and Homelessness (Eligibility) (England) (Amendment) Regulations 2009, SI 2009/358, reg 2(1), (3).

15 Repealed by the Allocation of Housing and Homelessness (Eligibility) (England) and Persons subject to Immigration Control (Housing Authority Accommodation and Homelessness) (Amendment) Regulations 2021, SI 2021/1045, reg 2(1), (3)(a).

16 Inserted by the Immigration and Social Security Co-ordination (EU Withdrawal) Act 2020 (Consequential, Saving, Transitional and Transitory Provisions) (EU Exit) Regulations 2020, SI 2020/1309, reg 71(1), (3)(e).

17 Inserted by the Allocation of Housing and Homelessness (Eligibility) (England) and Persons subject to Immigration Control (Housing Authority Accommodation and Homelessness) (Amendment) Regulations 2021, SI 2021/1045, reg 2(1), (3)(b).

18 Inserted by the Allocation of Housing and Homelessness (Eligibility) (England) and Persons subject to Immigration Control (Housing Authority Accommodation and Homelessness) (Amendment) Regulations 2022, SI 2022/339, reg 2(1), (3).

19 Inserted by the Allocation of Housing and Homelessness (Eligibility) (England) and Persons Subject to Immigration Control (Housing Authority Accommodation and Homelessness) (Amendment) Regulations 2023, SI 2023/530, reg 2(1), (3).

20 Inserted by the Allocation of Housing and Homelessness (Eligibility) (England) and Persons Subject to Immigration Control (Housing Authority Accommodation and Homelessness) (Amendment) (No. 2) Regulations 2023, SI 2023/1142, reg 2(1), (3).

5 Persons subject to immigration control who are eligible for housing assistance

(1) The following classes of persons subject to immigration control are persons who are eligible for housing assistance under Part 7 of the 1996 Act—

  (a) Class A – a person who is recorded by the Secretary of State as a refugee within the definition in Article 1 of the Refugee Convention and who has leave to enter or remain in the United Kingdom;

  (b) Class B – a person—

    (i) who has exceptional leave to enter or remain in the United Kingdom granted outside the provisions of the Immigration Rules; and

    (ii) whose leave to enter or remain is not subject to a condition requiring him to maintain and accommodate himself, and any person who is dependent on him, without recourse to public funds;

  (c) Class C – a person who is habitually resident in the United Kingdom, the Channel Islands, the Isle of Man or the Republic of Ireland and whose leave to enter or remain in the United Kingdom is not subject to any limitation or condition, other than a person—

(i) who has been given leave to enter or remain in the United Kingdom upon an undertaking given by his sponsor;

(ii) who has been resident in the United Kingdom, the Channel Islands, the Isle of Man or the Republic of Ireland for less than five years beginning on the date of entry or the date on which his sponsor gave the undertaking in respect of him, whichever date is the later; and

(iii) whose sponsor or, where there is more than one sponsor, at least one of whose sponsors, is still alive;

[(d) Class D— a person who has humanitarian protection granted under the Immigration Rules; ...¹]²

(e) ...³

[(f) ...⁴]⁵

[(g) Class G – a person ...⁶—

(i) [who]⁷ has limited leave to enter or remain in the United Kingdom on family or private life grounds under Article 8 of the Human Rights Convention that is granted under paragraph 276BE(1), paragraph 276DG or Appendix FM of the Immigration Rules; and

(ii) who is not subject to a condition requiring the person to maintain and accommodate himself, and any person dependent upon him, without recourse to public funds;]⁸

[(h) Class H – a person who is habitually resident in the United Kingdom, the Channel Islands, the Isle of Man or the Republic of Ireland and who has been transferred to the United Kingdom under section 67 of the Immigration Act 2016 and has limited leave to remain under paragraph 352ZH of the Immigration Rules[; ...⁹]¹⁰]¹¹

[(i) Class I – a person who is habitually resident in the United Kingdom, the Channel Islands, the Isle of Man or the Republic of Ireland and has Calais leave to remain under paragraph 352J of the Immigration Rules[;]⁸]¹²

[(j) Class J – a person (P) who has limited leave to enter or remain in the United Kingdom by virtue of Appendix EU of the Immigration Rules in circumstances where—

(i) P is a family member of a relevant person of Northern Ireland (RP) in accordance with those rules; and

(ii) P would have been considered eligible under regulation 6(2)(d) if RP were a person specified in regulation 6(2)(a) to (c); ...⁶

(k) Class K – a person who is habitually resident in the United Kingdom, the Channel Islands, the Isle of Man or the Republic of Ireland and who has limited leave to remain in the United Kingdom as a stateless person under paragraph 405 of the Immigration Rules;]¹³ [...⁴

(l) Class L – a person (P)—

  (i) who has limited leave to enter or remain in the United Kingdom by virtue of Appendix Hong Kong British National (Overseas) of the Immigration Rules;

  (ii) whose leave to enter or remain is not subject to a condition requiring P to maintain and accommodate P, and any person dependent upon P, without recourse to public funds; and

  (iii) who is habitually resident in the United Kingdom, the Channel Islands, the Isle of Man or the Republic of Ireland;][7]

[(m) Class M – a person—

  (i) who is granted leave to enter or remain in the United Kingdom in accordance with the Immigration Rules, where such leave is granted by virtue of—

    (aa) the Afghan Relocations and Assistance Policy; or

    (bb) the previous scheme for locally-employed staff in Afghanistan (sometimes referred to as the ex-gratia scheme); or

  (ii) with leave to enter or remain in the United Kingdom not coming within (i), who left Afghanistan in connection with the collapse of the Afghan government that took place on 15th August 2021, but excluding a person (P)—

    (aa) who is subject to a condition requiring P to maintain and accommodate themself, and any person who is dependent on P, without recourse to public funds; or

    (bb) who has been given leave to enter or remain in the United Kingdom upon an undertaking given by P's sponsor and has been resident in the United Kingdom, the Channel Islands, the Isle of Man or the Republic of Ireland for less than five years beginning on the date of entry or the date on which P's sponsor gave the undertaking in respect of P, whichever date is the later, and whose sponsor or, where there is more than one sponsor, at least one of whose sponsors, is still alive;][14]

[(n) Class N – a person in the United Kingdom who—

  (i) was residing in Ukraine immediately before 1st January 2022;

  (ii) left Ukraine in connection with the Russian invasion which took place on 24th February 2022; and

  (iii) has been granted leave in accordance with immigration rules made under section 3(2) of the Immigration Act 1971,

but excluding a person (P) who is subject to a condition requiring P to maintain and accommodate themselves, and any person who is dependent on P, without recourse to public funds;][15]

[(o) Class O – a person in the United Kingdom who has limited leave to remain granted in accordance with Appendix Ukraine Scheme of the immigration rules pursuant to an application made by that person from within the United Kingdom, but excluding a person (P) who is subject to a condition requiring P to maintain and accommodate themself, and any person who is dependent on P, without recourse to public funds;][16]

[(p) Class P – a person who has limited leave to remain granted in accordance with Appendix Temporary Permission to Stay for Victims of Human Trafficking or Slavery of the Immigration Rules;][17]

[(q) Class Q — a person who—

(i)   was residing in Sudan before 15th April 2023;

(ii) left Sudan in connection with the violence which rapidly escalated on 15th April 2023 in Khartoum and across Sudan;

(iii) has leave to enter or remain in the United Kingdom given in accordance with the Immigration Rules;

(iv) is not a person whose leave is subject to a condition requiring that person to maintain and accommodate themself, and any person who is dependent on that person, without recourse to public funds; and

(v) is not a person ('P')—

(aa) who has been given leave upon an undertaking given by P's sponsor;

(bb) who has been resident in the United Kingdom, the Channel Islands, the Isle of Man or the Republic of Ireland for less than five years beginning on the date of entry or the date on which P's sponsor gave the undertaking in respect of P, whichever date is the later; and

(cc) whose sponsor or, where there is more than one sponsor, at least one of whose sponsors, is still alive;][18]

[(r) Class R — a person who—

(i)   was residing in Israel, the West Bank, the Gaza Strip, East Jerusalem, the Golan Heights or Lebanon immediately before 7th October 2023;

(ii) left Israel, the West Bank, the Gaza Strip, East Jerusalem, the Golan Heights or Lebanon in connection with the Hamas terrorist attack in Israel on 7th October 2023 or the violence which rapidly escalated in the region following the attack;

(iii) has leave to enter or remain in the United Kingdom given in accordance with the Immigration Rules;

(iv) is not a person whose leave is subject to a condition requiring that person to maintain and accommodate themself, and any person who is dependent on that person, without recourse to public funds; and

(v) is not a person ('P')—

  (aa) who has been given leave upon an undertaking given by P's sponsor;

  (bb) who has been resident in the United Kingdom, the Channel Islands, the Isle of Man or the Republic of Ireland for less than five years beginning on the date of entry or the date on which P's sponsor gave the undertaking in respect of P, whichever date is the later; and

  (cc) whose sponsor or, where there is more than one sponsor, at least one of whose sponsors, is still alive.][19]

(2) ...[3]

(3) ...[3]

Amendments

1 Repealed by the Allocation of Housing and Homelessness (Eligibility) (England) (Amendment) Regulations 2014, SI 2014/435, reg 2(1), (5)(a).
2 Substituted by the Allocation of Housing and Homelessness (Miscellaneous Provisions) (England) Regulations 2006, SI 2006/2527, reg 2(1), (3).
3 Repealed by the Allocation of Housing and Homelessness (Eligibility) (England) (Amendment) Regulations 2016, SI 2016/965, reg 2(1), (4)(a), (d).
4 Repealed by the Allocation of Housing and Homelessness (Eligibility) (England) and Persons subject to Immigration Control (Housing Authority Accommodation and Homelessness) (Amendment) Regulations 2021, SI 2021/1045, reg 2(1), (4)(a), (b).
5 Inserted by the Allocation of Housing and Homelessness (Eligibility) (England) (Amendment) Regulations 2014, SI 2014/435, reg 2(1), (5)(c).
6 Repealed by the Allocation of Housing and Homelessness (Eligibility) (England) (Amendment) Regulations 2021, SI 2021/665, regs 2, 5(a)(i), (b).
7 Inserted by the Allocation of Housing and Homelessness (Eligibility) (England) (Amendment) Regulations 2021, SI 2021/665, regs 2, 5(a)(ii), (c).
8 Substituted by the Allocation of Housing and Homelessness (Eligibility) (England) (Amendment) Regulations 2020, SI 2020/667, regs 2, 5(a), (c).
9 Repealed by the Allocation of Housing and Homelessness (Eligibility) (England) (Amendment) Regulations 2020, SI 2020/667, regs 2, 5(b).
10 Substituted by the Allocation of Housing and Homelessness (Eligibility) (England) (Amendment) (No. 2) Regulations 2018, SI 2018/1056, regs 2, 4(b).
11 Inserted by the Allocation of Housing and Homelessness (Eligibility) (England) (Amendment) Regulations 2018, SI 2018/730, reg 2(1), (3)(c).
12 Inserted by the Allocation of Housing and Homelessness (Eligibility) (England) (Amendment) (No. 2) Regulations 2018, SI 2018/1056, regs 2, 4(c).
13 Inserted by the Allocation of Housing and Homelessness (Eligibility) (England) (Amendment) Regulations 2020, SI 2020/667, regs 2, 5(d).
14 Inserted by the Allocation of Housing and Homelessness (Eligibility) (England) and Persons subject to Immigration Control (Housing Authority Accommodation and Homelessness) (Amendment) Regulations 2021, SI 2021/1045, reg 2(1), (4)(c).
15 Inserted by the Allocation of Housing and Homelessness (Eligibility) (England) and Persons subject to Immigration Control (Housing Authority Accommodation and Homelessness) (Amendment) Regulations 2022, SI 2022/339, reg 2(1), (4).
16 Inserted by the Allocation of Housing and Homelessness (Eligibility) (England) and Persons Subject to Immigration Control (Housing Authority Accommodation and Homelessness) (Amendment) (No. 2) Regulations 2022, SI 2022/601, reg 2(1), (3).

17 Inserted by the Allocation of Housing and Homelessness (Eligibility) (England) and Persons Subject to Immigration Control (Housing Authority Accommodation and Homelessness) (Amendment) (No. 4) Regulations 2022, SI 2022/1371, reg 2(1), (3).
18 Inserted by the Allocation of Housing and Homelessness (Eligibility) (England) and Persons Subject to Immigration Control (Housing Authority Accommodation and Homelessness) (Amendment) Regulations 2023, SI 2023/530, reg 2(1), (4).
19 Inserted by the Allocation of Housing and Homelessness (Eligibility) (England) and Persons Subject to Immigration Control (Housing Authority Accommodation and Homelessness) (Amendment) (No. 2) Regulations 2023, SI 2023/1142, reg 2(1), (4).

6 Other persons from abroad who are ineligible for housing assistance

(1) A person who is not subject to immigration control is to be treated as a person from abroad who is ineligible for housing assistance under Part 7 of the 1996 Act if—

    (a) subject to paragraph (2), he is not habitually resident in the United Kingdom, the Channel Islands, the Isle of Man, or the Republic of Ireland;

    (b) his only right to reside in the United Kingdom—

        (i) is derived from his status as a jobseeker or the family member of a jobseeker; or

        (ii) is an initial right to reside for a period not exceeding three months under regulation 13 of the EEA Regulations; or

        [(iii) is a derivative right to reside to which he is entitled under [regulation 16(1)]¹ of the EEA Regulations, but only in a case where the right exists under that regulation because the applicant satisfies the criteria in [regulation 16(5)]¹ of those Regulations; or

        (iv) ...²]³

    (c) [his only right to reside in the Channel Islands, the Isle of Man or the Republic of Ireland is a right equivalent to one of those mentioned in sub-paragraph (b)(i), (ii) or (iii)]¹.

[(1A) For the purposes of determining whether the only right to reside that a person has is of the kind mentioned in paragraph (1)(b) or (c), a right to reside by virtue of having been granted

    [(a) limited leave to enter or remain in the United Kingdom under the Immigration Act 1971 by virtue of Appendix EU to the immigration rules made under section 3(2) of that Act; or

    (b) leave to enter the United Kingdom by virtue of an entry clearance that was granted under Appendix EU (Family Permit) to the immigration rules made under section 3(2) of that Act

is to be disregarded.]⁴]⁵

(2) The following are not to be treated as persons from abroad who are ineligible for housing assistance pursuant to paragraph (1)(a)—

(a) a worker;

(b) a self-employed person;

[(c) a person who is treated as a worker for the purpose of the definition of 'qualified person' in regulation 6(1) of the EEA Regulations pursuant to ...[6]—

   (i) ...[6]

   (ii) regulation 5 of the Accession Regulations 2013 (right of residence of an accession State national subject to worker authorisation);][7]

(d) a person who is the family member of a person specified in sub-paragraphs (a)-(c);

(e) a person with a right to reside permanently in the United Kingdom by virtue of regulation [15(1)(c)][8], (d) or (e) of the EEA Regulations; [and][9]

(f) ....[6] ...[10]

(g) a person who is in the United Kingdom as a result of his deportation, expulsion or other removal by compulsion of law from another country to the United Kingdom[[.][11] ...[12]][13]

[(h) ...[6]][13] [...[6]

(i) ...[6]][3]

[(j) a person who is a frontier worker within the meaning of regulation 3 of the Citizens' Rights (Frontier Workers) (EU Exit) Regulations 2020; ...[14]

(k) a person who—

   (i) is a family member of a person specified in sub-paragraph (j); and

   (ii) has a right to reside by virtue of having been granted limited leave to enter or remain in the United Kingdom under the Immigration Act 1971 by virtue of Appendix EU to the immigration rules made under section 3 of that Act;][15]

[(l) a person who left Afghanistan in connection with the collapse of the Afghan government that took place on 15th August 2021;][16]

[(m) a person who was residing in Ukraine immediately before 1st January 2022 and who left Ukraine in connection with the Russian invasion which took place on 24th February 2022;][17]

[(n) a person who was residing in Sudan before 15th April 2023 and left Sudan in connection with the violence which rapidly escalated on 15th April 2023 in Khartoum and across Sudan;][18]

[(o) a person who was residing in Israel, the West Bank, the Gaza Strip, East Jerusalem, the Golan Heights or Lebanon immediately before 7th October 2023 and who left Israel, the West Bank, the Gaza Strip, East Jerusalem, the Golan Heights or Lebanon in connection with the Hamas terrorist attack in Israel on 7th October 2023 or the violence which rapidly escalated in the region following the attack.]^{19}

Amendments

1 Substituted by the Immigration and Social Security Co-ordination (EU Withdrawal) Act 2020 (Consequential, Saving, Transitional and Transitory Provisions) (EU Exit) Regulations 2020, SI 2020/1309, reg 71(1), (4)(a), (b), (d).
2 Repealed by the Immigration and Social Security Co-ordination (EU Withdrawal) Act 2020 (Consequential, Saving, Transitional and Transitory Provisions) (EU Exit) Regulations 2020, SI 2020/1309, reg 71(1), (4)(c).
3 Inserted by the Allocation of Housing and Homelessness (Eligibility) (England) (Amendment) Regulations 2012, SI 2012/2588, reg 2(1), (4).
4 Substituted by the Immigration (Citizens' Rights etc.) (EU Exit) Regulations 2020, SI 2020/1372, reg 20.
5 Inserted by the Allocation of Housing and Homelessness (Eligibility) (England) (Amendment) (EU Exit) Regulations 2019, SI 2019/861, regs 2, 4(a).
6 Repealed by the Allocation of Housing and Homelessness (Eligibility) (England) (Amendment) Regulations 2014, SI 2014/435, reg 2(1), (6)(a), (c).
7 Substituted by the Allocation of Housing and Homelessness (Eligibility) (England) (Amendment) Regulations 2013, SI 2013/1467, reg 2(1), (4).
8 Inserted by the Allocation of Housing and Homelessness (Eligibility) (England) (Amendment) Regulations 2014, SI 2014/435, reg 2(1), (6)(b).
9 Repealed by the Allocation of Housing and Homelessness (Eligibility) (England) (Amendment) Regulations 2006, SI 2006/2007, reg 2(1), (6).
10 Substituted by the Allocation of Housing and Homelessness (Eligibility) (England) (Amendment) Regulations 2014, SI 2014/435, reg 2(1), (6)(d).
11 Inserted by the Allocation of Housing and Homelessness (Eligibility) (England) (Amendment) Regulations 2009, SI 2009/358, reg 2(1), (5).
12 Repealed by the Allocation of Housing and Homelessness (Eligibility) (England) (Amendment) Regulations 2009, SI 2009/358, reg 2(1), (4).
13 Inserted by the Allocation of Housing and Homelessness (Eligibility) (England) (Amendment) Regulations 2006, SI 2006/2007, reg 2(1), (7), (8).
14 Repealed by the Allocation of Housing and Homelessness (Eligibility) (England) and Persons subject to Immigration Control (Housing Authority Accommodation and Homelessness) (Amendment) Regulations 2021, SI 2021/1045, reg 2(1), (5)(a).
15 Inserted by the Immigration and Social Security Co-ordination (EU Withdrawal) Act 2020 (Consequential, Saving, Transitional and Transitory Provisions) (EU Exit) Regulations 2020, SI 2020/1309, reg 71(1), (4)(e).
16 Inserted by the Allocation of Housing and Homelessness (Eligibility) (England) and Persons subject to Immigration Control (Housing Authority Accommodation and Homelessness) (Amendment) Regulations 2021, SI 2021/1045, reg 2(1), (5)(b).
17 Inserted by the Allocation of Housing and Homelessness (Eligibility) (England) and Persons subject to Immigration Control (Housing Authority Accommodation and Homelessness) (Amendment) Regulations 2022, SI 2022/339, reg 2(1), (5).
18 Inserted by the Allocation of Housing and Homelessness (Eligibility) (England) and Persons Subject to Immigration Control (Housing Authority Accommodation and Homelessness) (Amendment) Regulations 2023, SI 2023/530, reg 2(1), (5).
19 Inserted by the Allocation of Housing and Homelessness (Eligibility) (England) and Persons Subject to Immigration Control (Housing Authority Accommodation and Homelessness) (Amendment) (No. 2) Regulations 2023, SI 2023/1142, reg 2(1), (5).

7 Revocation

Subject to regulation 8, the Regulations specified in column (1) of the Schedule are revoked to the extent mentioned in column (3) of the Schedule.

8 Transitional provisions

The revocations made by these Regulations shall not have effect in relation to an applicant whose application for—

(a) an allocation of housing accommodation under Part 6 of the 1996 Act; or

(b) housing assistance under Part 7 of the 1996 Act,

was made before 1st June 2006.

Regulation 7

SCHEDULE – REVOCATION SCHEDULE

(1)	(2)	(3)
Regulations Revoked	References	Extent of revocation
The Homelessness (England) Regulations 2000	SI 2000/701	The whole Regulations
The Allocation of Housing (England) Regulations 2002	SI 2002/3264	Regulations 4 and 5
The Allocation of Housing and Homelessness (Amendment) (England) Regulations 2004	SI 2004/1235	The whole Regulations
The Allocation of Housing and Homelessness (Amendment) (England) Regulations 2006	SI 2006/1093	The whole Regulations

Allocation of Housing and Homelessness (Miscellaneous Provisions) (England) Regulations 2006

SI 2006/2527

I Citation, commencement, interpretation and application

(1) These Regulations may be cited as the Allocation of Housing and Homelessness (Miscellaneous Provisions) (England) Regulations 2006 and shall come into force on 9th October 2006.

(2) In these Regulations, 'the 1996 Act' means the Housing Act 1996.

(3) These Regulations apply to England only.

2 Amendment of the classes of person from abroad who are eligible for an allocation of accommodation and for housing assistance

(1) The Allocation of Housing and Homelessness (Eligibility) (England) Regulations 2006 are amended as follows.

(2) For regulation 3(d), substitute—

   '(d) Class D— a person who has humanitarian protection granted under the Immigration Rules.'.

(3) For regulation 5(1)(d), substitute—

   '(d) Class D— a person who has humanitarian protection granted under the Immigration Rules; and'.

3 Prescribed period for referral of case to another local housing authority

For the purposes of section 198(4)(b) of the 1996 Act (referral of case to another local housing authority), the prescribed period is the aggregate of—

   (a) five years; and

   (b) the period beginning on the date of the previous application and ending on the date on which the applicant was first placed in pursuance of that application in accommodation in the district of the authority to whom the application is now made.

4 Transitional provisions

The amendments made by these Regulations shall not have effect in relation to an applicant whose application for—

(a) an allocation of housing accommodation under Part 6 of the 1996 Act; or

(b) housing assistance under Part 7 of the 1996 Act,

was made before 9th October 2006.

Allocation of Housing (Qualification Criteria for Armed Forces) (England) Regulations 2012

SI 2012/1869

1 Citation and commencement

(1) These Regulations may be cited as the Allocation of Housing (Qualification Criteria for Armed Forces) (England) Regulations 2012.

(2) These Regulations come into force on 24th August 2012.

2 Interpretation

In these Regulations—

'the 1996 Act' means the Housing Act 1996;

'local connection' has the meaning given by section 199 of the 1996 Act; and

'regular forces' and 'reserve forces' have the meanings given by section 374 of the Armed Forces Act 2006.

3 Criterion that may not be used in deciding what classes of persons are not qualifying persons

(1) In deciding what classes of persons are not qualifying persons under section 160ZA(7) of the 1996 Act, a local housing authority in England may not use the criterion set out in paragraph (2).

(2) The criterion is that a relevant person must have a local connection to the district of a local housing authority.

(3) A relevant person is a person who—

    (a) is serving in the regular forces or who has served in the regular forces within five years of the date of their application for an allocation of housing under Part 6 of the 1996 Act;

    (b) has recently ceased, or will cease to be entitled, to reside in accommodation provided by the Ministry of Defence following the death of that person's spouse or civil partner where—

   (i) the spouse or civil partner has served in the regular forces; and

   (ii) their death was attributable (wholly or partly) to that service; or

(c) is serving or has served in the reserve forces and who is suffering from a serious injury, illness or disability which is attributable (wholly or partly) to that service.

Homelessness (Suitability of Accommodation) (England) Order 2012

SI 2012/2601

1 Citation, commencement and application

(1) This Order may be cited as the Homelessness (Suitability of Accommodation) (England) Order 2012 and comes into force on 9th November 2012.

(2) This Order applies in relation to England only.

2 Matters to be taken into account in determining whether accommodation is suitable for a person

[Except where Article 2A applies, in][1] determining whether accommodation is suitable for a person, the local housing authority must take into account the location of the accommodation, including—

(a) where the accommodation is situated outside the district of the local housing authority, the distance of the accommodation from the district of the authority;

(b) the significance of any disruption which would be caused by the location of the accommodation to the employment, caring responsibilities or education of the person or members of the person's household;

(c) the proximity and accessibility of the accommodation to medical facilities and other support which—

(i) are currently used by or provided to the person or members of the person's household; and

(ii) are essential to the well-being of the person or members of the person's household; and

(d) the proximity and accessibility of the accommodation to local services, amenities and transport.

---

1   Inserted by Homelessness (Suitability of Accommodation) (Amendment) (England) Order 2022, SI 2022/521, art 5 and operating as a temporary modification which will expire on 1 June 2025, see Homelessness (Suitability of Accommodation) (England) (Amendment) Order 2024, SI 2024/371, art 2.

[2A Certain recent arrivals to the United Kingdom: matters to be taken into account in determining whether accommodation is suitable for a person

(1) This article applies in respect of a person who—

    (a) makes an application to a local housing authority for assistance under Part 7 of the Housing Act 1996 on or after 1st June 2022,

    (b) makes that application within 2 years beginning with the date on which they arrive in the United Kingdom,

    (c) is eligible for assistance under Part 7 of the Housing Act 1996, and

    (d) did not have a right to occupy accommodation in the United Kingdom for an uninterrupted period of 6 months or more in the 3 years prior to the date on which they arrived in the United Kingdom.

(2) In determining whether accommodation is suitable for a person specified in paragraph (1), where the accommodation is situated outside the district of the local housing authority, the local housing authority must take into account the significance of any disruption which would be caused by the location of the accommodation to any caring responsibilities of the person or members of the person's household for persons with whom there are family associations.][2]

3 Circumstances in which accommodation is not to be regarded as suitable for a person

[(1)][1] For the purposes [mentioned in paragraph (2)][2], accommodation shall not be regarded as suitable where one or more of the following apply–

    (a) the local housing authority are of the view that the accommodation is not in a reasonable physical condition;

    (b) the local housing authority are of the view that any electrical equipment supplied with the accommodation does not meet the requirements of [Schedule 1 to the Electrical Equipment (Safety) Regulations 2016][3];

    (c) the local housing authority are of the view that the landlord has not taken reasonable fire safety precautions with the accommodation and any furnishings supplied with it;

    (d) the local housing authority are of the view that the landlord has not taken reasonable precautions to prevent the possibility of carbon monoxide poisoning in the accommodation;

---

2   Inserted by Homelessness (Suitability of Accommodation) (Amendment) (England) Order 2022, SI 2022/521, art 5 and operating as a temporary modification which will expire on 1 June 2025, see Homelessness (Suitability of Accommodation) (England) (Amendment) Order 2024, SI 2024/371, art 2.

(e) the local housing authority are of the view that the landlord is not a fit and proper person to act in the capacity of landlord, having considered if the person has:

  (i) committed any offence involving fraud or other dishonesty, or violence or illegal drugs, or any offence listed in Schedule 3 to the Sexual Offences Act 2003 (offences attracting notification requirements);

  (ii) practised unlawful discrimination on grounds of sex, race, age, disability, marriage or civil partnership, pregnancy or maternity, religion or belief, sexual orientation, gender identity or gender reassignment in, or in connection with, the carrying on of any business;

  (iii) contravened any provision of the law relating to housing (including landlord or tenant law); or

  (iv) acted otherwise than in accordance with any applicable code of practice for the management of a house in multiple occupation, approved under section 233 of the Housing Act 2004;

(f) the accommodation is a house in multiple occupation subject to licensing under section 55 of the Housing Act 2004 and is not licensed;

(g) the accommodation is a house in multiple occupation subject to additional licensing under section 56 of the Housing Act 2004 and is not licensed;

(h) the accommodation is or forms part of residential property which does not have a valid energy performance certificate as required by the Energy Performance of Buildings (Certificates and Inspections) (England and Wales) Regulations 2007;

(i) the accommodation is or forms part of relevant premises which do not have a current gas safety record in accordance with regulation 36 of the Gas Safety (Installation and Use) Regulations 1998; or

(j) the landlord has not provided to the local housing authority a written tenancy agreement, which the landlord proposes to use for the purposes of a private rented sector offer, and which the local housing authority considers to be adequate.

[(2) The purposes are—

(a) determining, in accordance with section 193(7F) of the Housing Act 1996, whether a local housing authority may approve a private rented sector offer;

(b) determining, in accordance with section 193A(6) or 193C(9) of that Act, whether a local housing authority may approve a final accommodation offer made by a private landlord;

(c) determining whether any accommodation—

(i) secured for a person who has a priority need by a local housing authority in discharge of their functions under section 189B(2) or 195(2) of that Act, and

(ii) made available for occupation under a tenancy with a private landlord,

is suitable for the purposes of the section concerned.][4]

Amendments

1   Renumbered by the Homelessness Reduction Act 2017, s 12(1), (2).
2   Substituted by the Homelessness Reduction Act 2017, s 12(1), (3).
3   Substituted by the Electrical Equipment (Safety) Regulations 2016, SI 2016/1101, reg 9.
4   Inserted by the Homelessness Reduction Act 2017, s 12(1), (4).

Allocation of Housing (Qualification Criteria for Right to Move) (England) Regulations 2015

SI 2015/967

1 Citation, commencement and application

(1) These Regulations may be cited as the Allocation of Housing (Qualification Criteria for Right to Move) (England) Regulations 2015.

(2) These Regulations come into force on 20th April 2015.

(3) These Regulations apply in relation to England only.

2 Interpretation

Any reference in these Regulations to a section is a reference to a section of the Housing Act 1996.

3 Criterion that may not be used in deciding what classes of persons are not qualifying persons

(1) In deciding whether a person is a qualifying person under section 160ZA(7), a local housing authority may not use the criterion set out in paragraph (2) if the allocation involves a transfer of housing accommodation for that person from the district of another local housing authority in England.

(2) The criterion is that a relevant person must have a local connection with the district of the local housing authority.

(3) In this regulation 'local connection' has the meaning given by section 199.

4 Relevant person

For the purposes of regulation 3, a relevant person is a person who—

    (a) falls within section 159(4A)(a) or (b),

    (b) is to be given reasonable preference under section 166A(3)(e), and

    (c) has a need to move falling within regulation 5(1).

5 *Need to move*

(1) Subject to paragraph (2), for the purposes of regulation 4, a relevant person has a need to move because the relevant person—

   (a) works in the district of the local housing authority, or

   (b) (i)has been offered work in the district of the local housing authority, and

   (ii) the authority is satisfied that the relevant person has a genuine intention of taking up the offer of work.

(2) This regulation does not apply if the need to move is associated with work or the offer of work which is—

   (a) short-term or marginal in nature,

   (b) ancillary to work in another district, or

   (c) voluntary work.

(3) In this regulation 'voluntary work' means work where no payment is received by the relevant person or the only payment due to be made to the relevant person by virtue of being so engaged is a payment in respect of any expenses reasonably incurred by the relevant person in the course of being so engaged.

Homelessness (Review Procedures etc) Regulations 2018

SI 2018/223

PART I – GENERAL

I Citation, commencement and interpretation

(1) These Regulations may be cited as the Homelessness (Review Procedure etc.) Regulations 2018.

(2) This Part, and Parts 2, 3 and 5, come into force on 3rd April 2018.

(3) Part 4 comes into force on 1st October 2018.

(4) In these Regulations any reference to a section, save where the context otherwise appears, is to that section in the Housing Act 1996.

PART 2 – NOTICES IN CASES OF APPLICANT'S DELIBERATE AND UNREASONABLE REFUSAL TO CO-OPERATE

2 Notice procedure

A local housing authority must ensure that its procedure in connection with notices under section 193B(2) (Notices in cases of applicant's deliberate and unreasonable refusal to co-operate)—

(a) is in writing,

(b) is kept under review, and

(c) makes provision which complies with regulation 3.

3 Decision to give notice

(1) A local housing authority may not give a notice under section 193B(2) unless the decision to give the notice—

(a) is made by an officer of that local housing authority, and

(b) is authorised by an appropriate person.

(2) For the purposes of paragraph (1)(b)—

   (a) 'appropriate person' means a person who—

      (i) is at least as senior as the person mentioned in paragraph (1)(a),

      (ii) works for that local housing authority or the local authority, and

      (iii) was not involved in the decision to give the notice, and

   (b) a person works for a local housing authority or a local authority if the person—

      (i) works under a contract of employment with that authority,

      (ii) works under any other contract with that authority,

      (iii) is supplied to that authority as an agency worker (within the meaning of regulation 3 of the Agency Workers Regulations 2010), or

      (iv) is seconded to work for that authority.

PART 3 – REVIEW OF LOCAL HOUSING AUTHORITY DECISIONS UNDER SECTION 202

4 Interpretation of this Part

In this Part—

'A' means the applicant;

'the authority' means the local housing authority who made the original decision;

'notified authority' means a local housing authority who receive a notification under section 198(A1) or (1);

'notifying authority' means a local housing authority who give a notification under section 198(A1) or (1);

'original decision' means a decision of a local housing authority in relation to which a request for a review has been made;

'request for a review' means a request for a review made under section 202;

'the reviewer' means—

   (a) where the original decision falls within section 202(1)(d)—

    (i)   the notifying authority and the notified authority, where the review is carried out by those authorities,

    (ii) the person appointed to carry out the review in accordance with regulation 6, where the case falls within that regulation,

(b) where the original decision falls within any other sub-paragraph of section 202(1), the authority.

5 Request for a review and notification of review procedure

(1) A request for a review must be made to the authority where the original decision falls within—

(a) section 202(1)(a) (decision as to A's eligibility for assistance),

(b) section 202(1)(b) (decision as to what duty, if any, is owed to A under sections 189B to 193C and 195: duties to persons found to be homeless or threatened with homelessness),

(c) section 202(1)(ba) (decision as to the steps they are to take under section 189B(2) or to give notice under section 189B(5) to bring to an end their duty to A under section 189B(2)),

(d) section 202(1)(bb) (decision to give notice to A under section 193B(2): notice given to those who deliberately and unreasonably refuse to cooperate),

(e) section 202(1)(bc) (decision as to the steps they are to take under section 195(2) or to give notice under section 195(5) bringing to an end their duty to A under section 195(2)),

(f) section 202(1)(c) (decision to notify another authority under section 198(1): referral of cases),

(g) section 202(1)(e) (decision under section 200(3) or (4): decision as to the duty owed to A whose case is considered for referral or referred),

(h) section 202(1)(f) (decision as to the suitability of accommodation offered to A in discharge of their duty under any of the provisions mentioned in section 202(1)(b) or (e) or as to the suitability of accommodation offered to A as mentioned in section 193(7)),

(i) section 202(1)(g) (decision as to the suitability of accommodation offered to A by way of a private rented sector offer within the meaning of section 193), or

(j) section 202(1)(h) (decision as to the suitability of accommodation offered to A by way of a final accommodation offer or a final Part 6 offer within the meaning of section 193A or 193C).

(2) A request for a review must be made to the notifying authority where the original decision falls within section 202(1)(d) (decision under section 198(5) whether conditions are met for the referral of A's case).

(3) Except in the case of a request for a review falling within regulation 6, the authority must—

(a) notify A that A, or someone acting on A's behalf, may make representations in writing to the authority in connection with the review,

(b) in the case of a request for a review falling—

(i) within section 202(1)(ba)(i) or (bc), or

(ii) within section 202(1)(bb) where the effect of the notice given under section 193B(2) is to bring the authority's duty to A under section 195(2) to an end,

notify A that any such representations must be made within two weeks beginning with the day on which A requested the review, or such longer period as A and the reviewer may agree in writing,

(c) if they have not already done so, notify A of the procedure to be followed in connection with the review.

(4) In the case of a request for a review falling within regulation 6, the person appointed in accordance with that regulation must—

(a) notify A that A, or someone acting on A's behalf, may make representations in writing to that person in connection with the review, and

(b) notify A of the procedure to be followed in connection with the review.

6 Initial procedure where the original decision was made under the Decisions on Referrals Order

(1) Where the original decision under section 198(5) (whether the conditions are met for the referral of the case) was made under the Homelessness (Decisions on Referrals) Order 1998 ('the Decisions on Referrals Order'), a review of that decision must, subject to paragraph (2), be carried out by a person appointed by the notifying authority and the notified authority.

(2) If a person is not appointed in accordance with paragraph (1) within five working days beginning with the day on which the request for a review is made, the review must be carried out by a person—

(a) from the panel constituted in accordance with paragraph 3 of the Schedule to the Decisions on Referrals Order ('the panel'), and

(b) appointed in accordance with paragraph (3) below.

(3) The notifying authority must within five working days beginning with the end of the period specified in paragraph (2) request the chairman of the Local Government Association or their nominee ('the proper officer') to appoint a person from the panel and the proper officer must do so within seven days of the request.

(4) The notifying authority and the notified authority must within five working days of the appointment of the person from the panel ('the appointed person') provide the appointed person with the reasons for the original decision and the information and evidence on which that decision was based.

(5) The appointed person must—

(a) send to the notifying authority and the notified authority any representations made under regulation 5, and

(b) invite those authorities to respond to those representations.

(6) The appointed person must not be the same person as the person who made the original decision.

(7) For the purposes of this regulation 'working day' means any day other than a Saturday, a Sunday, Christmas Day, Good Friday, or a day which is a bank holiday under the Banking and Financial Dealings Act 1971 in England and Wales.

7 Procedure on a review

(1) The reviewer must, subject to compliance with the provisions of regulation 9, consider—

(a) any representations made under regulation 5 and, in a case falling within regulation 6, any responses to them, and

(b) any representations made under paragraph (2).

(2) If the reviewer considers that there is a deficiency or irregularity in the original decision, or in the manner in which it was made, but is minded nonetheless to make a decision which is against the interests of A on one or more issues, the reviewer must notify A—

(a) that the reviewer is so minded and the reasons why, and

(b) that A, or someone acting on A's behalf, may make representations to the reviewer orally or in writing, or both orally and in writing.

8 Decision on the review

(1) Paragraph (2) applies where—

(a) the reviewer is, or includes, the authority,

(b) the original decision was made by an officer of the authority, and

(c) the decision on the review is to be made by an officer of the authority.

(2) Where this paragraph applies, the officer making the decision on the review must be someone who—

(a) was not involved in the original decision, and

(b) is more senior than the officer who made the original decision.

9 *Notification of the decision on a review*

(1) Notice of the decision on a review under section 203(3) must be given to A—

    (a) where the original decision falls within—

        (i)   section 202(1)(ba)(i) or (bc), or

        (ii) section 202(1)(bb) and the effect of the notice given under section 193B(2) is to bring the authority's duty to A under section 195(2) to an end,

        three weeks beginning with the day on which the request for the review is made or, where A makes representations under regulation 7, beginning with the day on which those representations are received,

    (b) where the original decision falls within—

        (i)   section 202(1)(a), (b), (ba)(ii), (c), (d), (e), (f), (g), or (h), or

        (ii) section 202(1)(bb) and the effect of the notice given under section 193B(2) is to bring the authority's duty to A under section 189B(2) to an end,

        eight weeks beginning with the day on which the request for the review is made,

    (c) where the original decision falls within section 202(1)(d) and the review is carried out by the notifying authority and the notified authority, ten weeks beginning with the day on which the request for the review is made,

    (d) in a case falling within regulation 6, twelve weeks beginning with the day on which the request for the review is made,

or within such longer period as A and the reviewer may agree in writing.

(2) In a case falling within regulation 6, the appointed person must notify their decision on the review and the reasons for it, in writing, to the notifying authority and the notified authority—

    (a) within a period of eleven weeks beginning with the day on which the request for the review is made, or

    (b) where a longer period has been agreed in accordance with paragraph (1), by no later than one week before the expiry of that longer period.

PART 4 – DUTY TO REFER

10 *Specified public authorities*

The public authorities set out in the Schedule are specified for the purposes of section 213B (Duty of public authority to refer cases in England to local housing authority).

PART 5 – REVOCATION

11   Revocation and transitional provision

(1) Subject to paragraph (2), the Allocation of Housing and Homelessness (Review Procedures) Regulations 1999) are revoked.

(2) The Allocation of Housing and Homelessness (Review Procedures) Regulations 1999 continue in force in relation to any request for a review under section 202 made prior to the coming into force of this Part.

Regulation 10

SCHEDULE – SPECIFIED PUBLIC AUTHORITIES

1. The governor of a prison within the meaning given in section 53(1) of the Prison Act 1952.

2. The director of a contracted out prison within the meaning given in section 84(4) of the Criminal Justice Act 1991.

3. The governor of a young offender institution provided under section 43(1)(a) of the Prison Act 1952.

4. The governor of a secure training centre provided under section 43(1)(b) of the Prison Act 1952.

5. The director of a contracted out secure training centre within the meaning given in section 15 of the Criminal Justice and Public Order Act 1994.

6. The principal of a secure college provided under section 43(1)(c) of the Prison Act 1952.

7. A youth offending team established under section 39(1) of the Crime and Disorder Act 1998.

8. A provider of probation services.

9. An officer, designated by the Secretary of State for Work and Pensions for the purposes of section 213B, employed by the Secretary of State at an office known as a Jobcentre Plus office.

10. A social services authority.

11. A person who performs a function of a local authority pursuant to a direction under section 497A(4) or (4A) of the Education Act 1996 (which confers power

on the Secretary of State to secure the proper performance of local authority education functions, and is applied to social services functions relating to children by section 50 of the Children Act 2004 and to functions relating to childcare by section 15 of the Childcare Act 2006).

12. (1) An NHS trust and an NHS foundation trust, but only in connection with the provision of the following NHS health services—

    (a) emergency department and urgent treatment centres,

    (b) in-patient treatment.

(2) For the purposes of paragraph (1)—

'emergency department and urgent treatment centres' includes—

    (a) accident and emergency services provided in a hospital,

    (b) services known as urgent treatment centres,

    (c) any other providers of community and primary urgent care services,

'NHS foundation trust' has the meaning given in section 30 of the National Health Service Act 2006,

'NHS health services' means any kind of health services provided as part of the health service continued under, and for the purposes of, section 1(1) of the National Health Service Act 2006, and

'NHS trust' means an NHS trust established under section 25 of the National Health Service Act 2006.

13. The Secretary of State for Defence, but only in relation to members of the regular armed forces.

PART 3

Wales: Statutes

Housing (Wales) Act 2014

PART 2 – HOMELESSNESS

Chapter 1 – Homelessnews reviews and strategies

50 Duty to carry out a homelessness review and formulate a homelessness strategy

(1) A local housing authority must (periodically, as required by this section)—

   (a) carry out a homelessness review for its area, and

   (b) formulate and adopt a homelessness strategy based on the results of that review.

(2) The authority must adopt a homelessness strategy in 2018 and a new homelessness strategy in every fourth year after 2018.

(3) The Welsh Ministers may amend subsection (2) by order.

(4) A council of a county or county borough in Wales must take its homelessness strategy into account in the exercise of its functions (including functions other than its functions as local housing authority).

(5) Nothing in subsection (4) affects any duty or requirement arising apart from this section.

(6) In this Chapter 'homeless' has the meaning given by section 55 and 'homelessness' is to be interpreted accordingly.

51 Homelessness reviews

(1) A homelessness review under section 50 must include a review of—

   (a) the levels, and likely future levels, of homelessness in the local housing authority's area;

   (b) the activities which are carried out in the local housing authority's area for the achievement of the following objectives (or which contribute to their achievement)—

      (i) the prevention of homelessness;

      (ii) that suitable accommodation is or will be available for people who are or may become homeless;

      (iii) that satisfactory support is available for people who are or may become homeless;

(c) the resources available to the authority (including the resources available in exercise of functions other than its functions as local housing authority), other public authorities, voluntary organisations and other persons for such activities.

(2) After completing a homelessness review, a local housing authority must publish the results of the review by—

(a) making the results of the review available on its website (if it has one);

(b) making a copy of the results of the review available at its principal office for inspection at all reasonable hours, without charge, by members of the public;

(c) providing (on payment if required by the authority of a reasonable charge) a copy of those results to any member of the public who asks for one.

52 Homelessness strategies

(1) A homelessness strategy under section 50 is a strategy for achieving the following objectives in the local housing authority's area—

(a) the prevention of homelessness;

(b) that suitable accommodation is and will be available for people who are or may become homeless;

(c) that satisfactory support is available for people who are or may become homeless.

(2) A homelessness strategy may specify more detailed objectives to be pursued, and action planned to be taken, in the exercise of any functions of the authority (including functions other than its functions as local housing authority).

(3) A homelessness strategy may also include provision relating to specific action which the authority expects to be taken—

(a) by any public authority with functions which are capable of contributing to the achievement of any of the objectives mentioned in subsection (1), or

(b) by any voluntary organisation or other person whose activities are capable of contributing to the achievement of any of those objectives.

(4) The inclusion in a homelessness strategy of any provision relating to action mentioned in subsection (3) requires the approval of the body or person concerned.

(5) In formulating a homelessness strategy the authority must consider (among other things) the extent to which any of the objectives mentioned in subsection (1) can be achieved through action involving two or more of the bodies or other persons mentioned in subsections (2) and (3).

(6) A homelessness strategy must include provision relating to action planned by the authority to be taken in the exercise of its functions, and specific action expected by the authority to be taken by public authorities, voluntary organisations and other persons within subsection (3), in relation to those who may be in particular need of support if they are or may become homeless, including in particular—

(a) people leaving prison or youth detention accommodation,

(b) young people leaving care,

(c) people leaving the regular armed forces of the Crown,

(d) people leaving hospital after medical treatment for mental disorder as an inpatient, and

(e) people receiving mental health services in the community.

(7) A local housing authority must keep its homelessness strategy under review and may modify it.

(8) Before adopting or modifying a homelessness strategy a local housing authority must consult such public or local authorities, voluntary organisations or other persons as it considers appropriate.

(9) After adopting or modifying a homelessness strategy, a local housing authority must publish the strategy by—

(a) making a copy of the strategy available on its website (if it has one);

(b) making a copy of the strategy available at its principal office for inspection at all reasonable hours, without charge, by members of the public;

(c) providing (on payment if required by the authority of a reasonable charge) a copy of the strategy to any member of the public who asks for one.

(10) If the authority modifies its homelessness strategy, it may publish the modifications or the strategy as modified (as it considers most appropriate).

(11) Where the authority decides to publish only the modifications, the references to the homelessness strategy in paragraphs (a) to (c) of subsection (9) are to be interpreted as references to the modifications.

Chapter 2 – Help for people who are homeless or threatened with homelessness

Introduction

53   Overview of this Chapter

(1) This Chapter confers duties on local housing authorities to help people who are homeless or threatened with homelessness and makes connected provision.

(2) Sections 55 to 59 define and otherwise explain the meaning of some key terms (further provision about interpretation and an index of terms defined in this Chapter is at section 99).

(3) Section 60 requires local housing authorities to secure the provision of a service providing people with information and advice connected with homelessness and assistance in accessing help under this Chapter.

(4) Section 61 introduces Schedule 2 which makes provision about eligibility for help under this Chapter.

(5) Section 62 places a duty on a local housing authority to assess the cases of people ('applicants') who apply to the authority for accommodation, or help in retaining or obtaining accommodation, where they appear to the authority to be homeless or threatened with homelessness.

(6) Section 63 provides for notice to be given to applicants about the outcome of the assessment.

(7) Section 64 gives examples of the kinds of ways in which the subsequent duties to secure or help to secure the availability of accommodation may be discharged and what may be done to discharge them; and section 65 explains what 'help to secure' means.

(8) Sections 66 to 79 set out the main duties on local housing authorities to help applicants, the circumstances in which those duties come to an end and connected provision; the main duties are—

(a) a duty to help to prevent applicants who are threatened with homelessness from becoming homeless (section 66);

(b) a duty to secure interim accommodation for applicants in priority need (section 68) (section 70 provides for who is to have priority need for accommodation for the purposes of the Chapter);

(c) a duty to help to secure that suitable accommodation is available for occupation by homeless applicants (section 73);

(d) a duty to secure accommodation for applicants in priority need when the duty in section 73 comes to an end (section 75).

(9) Section 78 provides for the circumstances in which local housing authorities may have regard to whether an applicant became homeless intentionally when it is considering whether a duty to secure accommodation for applicants in priority need applies; section 77 provides for the meaning of intentionally homeless.

(10) Sections 80 to 82 provide for local housing authorities to end their duties to applicants by referring their cases to other authorities in Wales or England, where the applicants have a local connection with the areas of those other authorities;

section 81 defines the meaning of 'local connection' for the purposes of this Chapter.

(11) Sections 85 to 89 provide for reviews and appeals.

(12) Sections 90 to 99 make supplementary and general provision.

Key terms

54   Application of key terms

Sections 55 to 59 apply for the purposes of this Part.

55   Meaning of homeless and threatened homelessness

(1) A person is homeless if there is no accommodation available for the person's occupation, in the United Kingdom or elsewhere, which the person—

   (a) is entitled to occupy by virtue of an interest in it or by virtue of an order of a court,

   (b) has an express or implied licence to occupy, or

   (c) occupies as a residence by virtue of any enactment or rule of law giving the person the right to remain in occupation or restricting the right of another person to recover possession.

(2) A person is also homeless if the person has accommodation but—

   (a) cannot secure entry to it, or

   (b) it consists of a moveable structure, vehicle or vessel designed or adapted for human habitation and there is no place where the person is entitled or permitted both to place it and to reside in it.

(3) A person is not to be treated as having accommodation unless it is accommodation which it would be reasonable for the person to continue to occupy.

(4) A person is threatened with homelessness if it is likely that the person will become homeless within 56 days.

56   Meaning of accommodation available for occupation

(1) Accommodation may only be regarded as available for a person's occupation if it is available for occupation by that person together with—

   (a) any other person who normally resides with that person as a member of his or her family, or

(b) any other person who might reasonably be expected to reside with that person.

(2) A reference in this Chapter to securing that accommodation is available for a person's occupation is to be interpreted accordingly.

57   Whether it is reasonable to continue to occupy accommodation

(1) It is not reasonable for a person to continue to occupy accommodation if it is probable that it will lead to the person, or a member of the person's household, being subjected to abuse.

(2) In this section 'member of a person's household' means—

(a) a person who normally resides with him or her as member of his or her family, or

(b) any other person who might reasonably be expected to reside with that person.

(3) In determining whether it would be, or would have been, reasonable for a person to continue to occupy accommodation, a local housing authority—

(a) may have regard to the general circumstances prevailing in relation to housing in the area of the local housing authority to whom the person has applied for help in securing accommodation;

(b) must have regard to whether or not the accommodation is affordable for that person.

(4) The Welsh Ministers may by order specify—

(a) other circumstances in which it is to be regarded as reasonable or not reasonable for a person to continue to occupy accommodation, and

(b) other matters to be taken into account or disregarded in determining whether it would be, or would have been, reasonable for a person to continue to occupy accommodation.

58   Meaning of abuse and domestic abuse

(1) 'Abuse' means physical violence, threatening or intimidating behaviour and any other form of abuse which, directly or indirectly, may give rise to the risk of harm; and abuse is 'domestic abuse' where the victim is associated with the abuser.

(2) A person is associated with another person if—

(a) they are or have been married to each other;

(b) they are or have been civil partners of each other;

(c) they live or have lived together in an enduring family relationship (whether they are of different sexes or the same sex);

(d) they live or have lived in the same household;

(e) they are relatives;

(f) they have agreed to marry one another (whether or not that agreement has been terminated);

(g) they have entered into a civil partnership agreement between them (whether or not that agreement has been terminated);

(h) they have or have had an intimate personal relationship with each other which is or was of significant duration;

(i) in relation to a child, each of them is a parent of the child or has, or has had, parental responsibility for the child.

(3) If a child has been adopted or falls within subsection (4), two persons are also associated with each other for the purposes this Chapter if—

(a) one is a natural parent of the child or a parent of such a natural parent, and

(b) the other is—

(i) the child, or

(ii) a person who has become a parent of the child by virtue of an adoption order, who has applied for an adoption order or with whom the child has at any time been placed for adoption.

(4) A child falls within this section if—

(a) an adoption agency, within the meaning of section 2 of the Adoption and Children Act 2002, is authorised to place the child for adoption under section 19 of that Act (placing children with parental consent) or the child has become the subject of an order under section 21 of that Act (placement orders), or

(b) the child is freed for adoption by virtue of an order made—

(i) in England and Wales, under section 18 of the Adoption Act 1976,

(ii) in Northern Ireland, under Article 17(1) or 18(1) of the Adoption (Northern Ireland) Order 1987, or

(c) the child is the subject of a Scottish permanence order which includes granting authority to adopt.

(5) In this section—

'adoption order' ('gorchymyn mabwysiadu') means an adoption order within the meaning of section 72(1) of the Adoption Act 1976 or section 46(1) of the Adoption and Children Act 2002;

'civil partnership agreement' ('cytundeb partneriaeth sifil') has the meaning given by section 73 of the Civil Partnership Act 2004;

'parental responsibility' ('cyfrifoldeb rhiant') has the meaning given by section 3 of the Children Act 1989;

'relative' ('perthynas'), in relation to a person, means that person's parent, grandparent, child, grandchild, brother, half-brother, sister, half-sister, uncle, aunt, nephew, niece (including any person who is or has been in that relationship by virtue of a marriage or civil partnership or an enduring family relationship).

59 Suitability of accommodation

(1) In determining whether accommodation is suitable for a person, a local housing authority must have regard to the following enactments—

  (a) Part 9 of the Housing Act 1985 (slum clearance);

  (b) Part 10 of the Housing Act 1985 (overcrowding);

  (c) Part 1 of the Housing Act 2004 (housing conditions);

  (d) Part 2 of the Housing Act 2004 (licensing of houses in multiple occupation);

  (e) Part 3 of the Housing Act 2004 (selective licensing of other residential accommodation);

  (f) Part 4 of the Housing Act 2004 (additional control provisions in relation to residential accommodation);

  (g) Part 1 of this Act (regulation of private rented housing).

(2) In determining whether accommodation is suitable for a person, a local housing authority must have regard to whether or not the accommodation is affordable for that person.

(3) The Welsh Ministers may by order specify—

  (a) circumstances in which accommodation is or is not to be regarded as suitable for a person, and

  (b) matters to be taken into account or disregarded in determining whether accommodation is suitable for a person.

Information, advice and assistance in accessing help

60 Duty to provide information, advice and assistance in accessing help

(1) A local housing authority must secure the provision, without charge, of a service providing people in its area, or people who have a local connection with its area, with—

(a) information and advice relating to preventing homelessness, securing accommodation when homeless, accessing any other help available for people who are homeless or may become homeless, and

(b) assistance in accessing help under this Chapter or any other help for people who are homeless or may become homeless.

(2) In relation to subsection (1)(a), the service must include, in particular, the publication of information and advice on the following matters—

(a) the system provided for by this Chapter and how the system operates in the authority's area;

(b) whether any other help for people who are homeless or may become homeless (whether or not the person is threatened with homelessness within the meaning of this Chapter) is available in the authority's area;

(c) how to access the help that is available.

(3) In relation to subsection (1)(b), the service must include, in particular, assistance in accessing help to prevent a person becoming homeless which is available whether or not the person is threatened with homelessness within the meaning of this Chapter.

(4) The local housing authority must, in particular by working with other public authorities, voluntary organisations and other persons, ensure that the service is designed to meet the needs of groups at particular risk of homelessness, including in particular—

(a) people leaving prison or youth detention accommodation,

(b) young people leaving care,

(c) people leaving the regular armed forces of the Crown,

(d) people leaving hospital after medical treatment for mental disorder as an inpatient, and

(e) people receiving mental health services in the community.

(5) Two or more local housing authorities may jointly secure the provision of a service under this section for their areas; and where they do so—

(a) references in this section to a local housing authority are to be read as references to the authorities acting jointly, and

(b) references in this section to a local housing authority's area are to be read as references to the combined area.

(6) The service required by this section may be integrated with the service required by section 17 of the Social Services and Well-being (Wales) Act 2014.

Eligibility

61   Eligibility for help under this Chapter

Schedule 2 has effect for the purposes of determining whether an applicant is eligible for help under the following provisions of this Chapter.

Applications for help and assessment

62   Duty to assess

(1) A local housing authority must carry out an assessment of a person's case if—

  (a) the person has applied to a local housing authority for accommodation or help in retaining or obtaining accommodation,

  (b) it appears to the authority that the person may be homeless or threatened with homelessness, and

  (c) subsection (2) does not apply to the person.

(2) This subsection applies if the person has been assessed by a local housing authority under this section on a previous occasion and the authority is satisfied that—

  (a) the person's circumstances have not changed materially since that assessment was carried out, and

  (b) there is no new information that materially affects that assessment.

(3) In this Chapter, 'applicant' means a person to whom the duty in subsection (1) applies.

(4) The authority must assess whether or not the applicant is eligible for help under this Chapter.

(5) If the applicant is eligible for help under this Chapter, the assessment must include an assessment of—

  (a) the circumstances that have caused the applicant to be homeless or threatened with homelessness;

  (b) the housing needs of the applicant and any person with whom the applicant lives or might reasonably be expected to live;

  (c) the support needed for the applicant and any person with whom the applicant lives or might reasonably be expected to live to retain accommodation which is or may become available;

  (d) whether or not the authority has any duty to the applicant under the following provisions of this Chapter.

(6) In carrying out an assessment, the local housing authority must—

    (a) seek to identify the outcome the applicant wishes to achieve from the authority's help, and

    (b) assess whether the exercise of any function under this Chapter could contribute to the achievement of that outcome.

(7) A local housing authority may carry out its assessment of the matters mentioned in subsections (5) and (6) before it has concluded that the applicant is eligible for help under this Chapter.

(8) A local housing authority must keep its assessment under review during the period in which the authority considers that it owes a duty to the applicant under the following provisions of this Chapter or that it may do so.

(9) A local housing authority must review its assessment in the following two cases—

Case 1 – where an applicant has been notified under section 63 that a duty is owed to the applicant under section 66 (duty to help to prevent an applicant from becoming homeless) and subsequently it appears to the authority that the duty under section 66 has or is likely to come to an end because the applicant is homeless;

Case 2 – where an applicant has been notified under section 63 that a duty is owed to the applicant under section 73 (duty to help to secure accommodation for homeless applicants) and subsequently it appears to the authority that the duty in section 73 has or is likely to come to an end in circumstances where a duty may be owed to the applicant under section 75 (duty to secure accommodation for applicants in priority need when the duty in section 73 ends).

(10) The duty in subsection (5)(d) does not require a local housing authority to assess whether or not a duty would be owed to the applicant under section 75 unless and until it reviews its assessment in accordance with subsection (9) in the circumstances described in case 2 of that subsection; but it may do so before then.

(11) Subsections (9) and (10) do not affect the generality of subsection (8).

63 Notice of the outcome of assessment

(1) The local housing authority must notify the applicant of the outcome of its assessment (or any review of its assessment) and, in so far as any issue is decided against the applicant's interests, inform the applicant of the reasons for its decision.

(2) If the authority decides that a duty is owed to the applicant under section 75, but would not have done so without having had regard to a restricted person, the notice under subsection (1) must also—

(a) inform the applicant that its decision was reached on that basis,

(b) include the name of the restricted person,

(c) explain why the person is a restricted person, and

(d) explain the effect of section 76(5).

(3) If the authority has notified or intends to notify another local housing authority under section 80 (referral of cases), it must at the same time notify the applicant of that decision and inform him or her of the reasons for it.

(4) A notice under subsection (1) or (3) must also—

(a) inform the applicant of his or her right to request a review of the decision and of the time within which such a request must be made (see section 85), and

(b) be given in writing and, if not received, is to be treated as having been given if it is made available at the authority's office for a reasonable period for collection by the applicant or on the applicant's behalf.

(5) In this Chapter, 'a restricted person' means a person—

(a) who is not eligible for help under this Chapter,

(b) who is subject to immigration control within the meaning of the Asylum and Immigration Act 1996, and

(c) who either—

(i) does not have leave to enter or remain in the United Kingdom, or

(ii) has leave to enter or remain in the United Kingdom subject to a condition to maintain and accommodate himself or herself, and any dependants, without recourse to public funds.

Duties to help applicants

64   How to secure or help to secure the availability of accommodation

(1) The following are examples of the ways in which a local housing authority may secure or help to secure that suitable accommodation is available, or does not cease to be available, for occupation by an applicant—

(a) by arranging for a person other than the authority to provide something;

(b) by itself providing something;

(c) by providing something, or arranging for something to be provided, to a person other than the applicant.

(2) The following are examples of what may be provided or arranged to secure or help to secure that suitable accommodation is available, or does not cease to be available, for occupation by an applicant—

(a) mediation;

(b) payments by way of grant or loan;

(c) guarantees that payments will be made;

(d) support in managing debt, mortgage arrears or rent arrears;

(e) security measures for applicants at risk of abuse;

(f) advocacy or other representation;

(g) accommodation;

(h) information and advice;

(i) other services, goods or facilities.

(3) The Welsh Ministers must give guidance to local housing authorities in relation to how they may secure or help to secure that suitable accommodation is available, or does not cease to be available, for occupation by an applicant.

65 Meaning of help to secure

Where a local housing authority is required by this Chapter to help to secure (rather than 'to secure') that suitable accommodation is available, or does not cease to be available, for occupation by an applicant, the authority—

(a) is required to take reasonable steps to help, having regard (among other things) to the need to make the best use of the authority's resources;

(b) is not required to secure an offer of accommodation under Part 6 of the Housing Act 1996 (allocation of housing);

(c) is not required to otherwise provide accommodation.

66 Duty to help to prevent an applicant from becoming homeless

(1) A local housing authority must help to secure that suitable accommodation does not cease to be available for occupation by an applicant if the authority is satisfied that the applicant is—

(a) threatened with homelessness, and

(b) eligible for help.

(2) Subsection (1) does not affect any right of the authority, whether by virtue of a contract, enactment or rule of law, to secure vacant possession of any accommodation.

67 Circumstances in which the duty in section 66 ends

(1) The duty to an applicant under section 66 comes to an end in any of the circumstances described in subsection (2), (3) or (4), if the applicant has been notified in accordance with section 84.

(2) The circumstances are that the local authority is satisfied that the applicant has become homeless.

(3) The circumstances are that the local housing authority is satisfied (whether as a result of the steps it has taken or not) that—

(a) the applicant is no longer threatened with homelessness, and

(b) suitable accommodation is likely to be available for occupation by the applicant for a period of at least 6 months.

(4) The circumstances are that—

(a) the applicant, having been notified in writing of the possible consequences of refusal or acceptance of the offer, refuses an offer of accommodation from any person which the authority is satisfied is suitable for the applicant, and

(b) the authority is satisfied that the accommodation offered is likely to be available for occupation by the applicant for a period of at least 6 months.

(5) The period of 6 months mentioned in subsections (3)(b) and (4)(b) begins on the day the notice under section 84 is sent or first made available for collection.

(6) See section 79 for further circumstances in which the duty in section 66 comes to an end.

68   *Interim duty to secure accommodation for homeless applicants in priority need*

(1) The local housing authority must secure that suitable accommodation is available for the occupation of an applicant to whom subsection (2) or (3) applies until the duty comes to an end in accordance with section 69.

(2) This subsection applies to an applicant who the authority has reason to believe may—

(a) be homeless,

(b) be eligible for help, and

(c) have a priority need for accommodation,

in circumstances where the authority is not yet satisfied that the applicant is homeless, eligible for help and in priority need for accommodation.

(3) This subsection applies to an applicant—

(a) who the authority has reason to believe or is satisfied has a priority need or whose case has been referred from a local housing authority in England under section 198(1) of the Housing Act 1996, and

(b) to whom the duty in section 73 (duty to help to end homelessness) applies.

(4) The duty under this section arises irrespective of any possibility of the referral of the applicant's case to another local housing authority (see sections 80 to 82).

69 Circumstances in which the duty in section 68 ends

(1) The duty to an applicant under section 68 comes to an end in any of the circumstances described in subsection (2), (3) (subject to subsection (4) and (5)), (7), (8) or (9) if the applicant has been notified in accordance with section 84.

(2) The circumstances are that the local housing authority has decided that no duty is owed to the applicant under section 73 and the applicant is notified of that decision.

(3) In the case of an applicant to whom section 68(3) applies, the circumstances are that the local housing authority has—

- (a) decided that the duty owed to the applicant under section 73 has come to an end and that a duty is or is not owed to the applicant under section 75, and

- (b) notified the applicant of that decision;

but this is subject to subsections (4) and (5).

(4) Subsection (5) applies where a local housing authority has decided that no duty is owed to the applicant under section 75 on the basis that the authority—

- (a) is satisfied that the applicant became homeless intentionally in the circumstances which gave rise to the application, or

- (b) has previously secured an offer of accommodation of the kind described in section 75(3)(f).

(5) The duty under section 68 does not come to an end in the circumstances described in subsection (3) until the authority is also satisfied that the accommodation it has secured under section 68 has been available to the applicant for a sufficient period, beginning on the day on which he or she is notified that section 75 does not apply, to allow the applicant a reasonable opportunity of securing accommodation for his or her occupation.

(6) The period mentioned in subsection (5) is not sufficient for the purposes of that subsection if it ends on a day during the period of 56 days beginning with the day on which the applicant was notified that the duty in section 73 applied.

(7) The circumstances are that the applicant, having been notified of the possible consequence of refusal, refuses an offer of accommodation secured under section 68 which the local housing authority is satisfied is suitable for the applicant.

(8) The circumstances are that the local housing authority is satisfied that the applicant has become homeless intentionally from suitable interim accommodation made available for the applicant's occupation under section 68.

(9) The circumstances are that the local housing authority is satisfied that the applicant voluntarily ceased to occupy as his or her only or principal home suitable interim accommodation made available for the applicant's occupation under section 68.

(10) The duty comes to an end in accordance with this section even if the applicant requests a review of any decision that has led to the duty coming to an end (see section 85).

(11) The authority may secure that suitable accommodation is available for the applicant's occupation pending a decision on a review.

(12) See section 79 for further circumstances in which the duty in section 68 comes to an end.

70   Priority need for accommodation

(1) The following persons have a priority need for accommodation for the purposes of this Chapter—

(a) a pregnant woman or a person with whom she resides or might reasonably be expected to reside;

(b) a person with whom a dependent child resides or might reasonably be expected to reside;

(c) a person—

   (i) who is vulnerable as a result of some special reason (for example: old age, physical or mental illness or physical or mental disability), or

   (ii) with whom a person who falls within sub-paragraph (i) resides or might reasonably be expected to reside;

(d) a person—

   (i) who is homeless or threatened with homelessness as a result of an emergency such as flood, fire or other disaster, or

   (ii) with whom a person who falls within sub-paragraph (i) resides or might reasonably be expected to reside;

(e) a person—

   (i) who is homeless as a result of being subject to domestic abuse, or

   (ii) with whom a person who falls within sub-paragraph (i) resides (other than the abuser) or might reasonably be expected to reside;

(f) a person—

   (i) who is aged 16 or 17 when the person applies to a local housing authority for accommodation or help in obtaining or retaining accommodation, or

(ii) with whom a person who falls within sub-paragraph (i) resides or might reasonably be expected to reside;

(g) a person—

    (i) who has attained the age of 18, when the person applies to a local housing authority for accommodation or help in obtaining or retaining accommodation, but not the age of 21, who is at particular risk of sexual or financial exploitation, or

    (ii) with whom a person who falls within sub-paragraph (i) resides (other than an exploiter or potential exploiter) or might reasonably be expected to reside;

(h) a person—

    (i) who has attained the age of 18, when the person applies to a local housing authority for accommodation or help in obtaining or retaining accommodation, but not the age of 21, who was looked after, accommodated or fostered at any time while under the age of 18, or

    (ii) with whom a person who falls within sub-paragraph (i) resides or might reasonably be expected to reside;

(i) a person—

    (i) who has served in the regular armed forces of the Crown who has been homeless since leaving those forces, or

    (ii) with whom a person who falls within sub-paragraph (i) resides or might reasonably be expected to reside;

(j) a person who has a local connection with the area of the local housing authority and who is vulnerable as a result of one of the following reasons—

    (i) having served a custodial sentence within the meaning of section 76 of the Powers of Criminal Courts (Sentencing) Act 2000 [or section 222 of the Sentencing Code][1],

    (ii) having been remanded in or committed to custody by an order of a court, or

    (iii) having been remanded to youth detention accommodation under section 91(4) of the Legal Aid, Sentencing and Punishment of Offenders Act 2012;

[(k) a person—

    (i) who is street homeless (within the meaning of section 71(2)), or

    (ii) with whom a person who falls within sub-paragraph (i) might reasonably be expected to reside,][2]

or a person with whom such a person resides or might reasonably be expected to reside.

(2) In this Chapter—

'looked after, accommodated or fostered' ('yn derbyn gofal, yn cael ei letya neu'n cael ei faethu') means—

(a) looked after by a local authority (within the meaning of section 74 of the Social Services and Well-Being (Wales) Act 2014 or section 22 of the Children Act 1989),

(b) accommodated by or on behalf of a voluntary organisation,

(c) accommodated in a private children's home,

(d) accommodated for a continuous period of at least three months—

(i) by any Local Health Board or Special Health Authority,

(ii) by or on behalf of [an integrated care board][3] or [NHS England][4],

(iii) by or on behalf of a county or county borough council in Wales in the exercise of education functions,

(iv) by or on behalf of a local authority in England in the exercise of education functions,

(v) in any care home or independent hospital, or

(vi) in any accommodation provided by or on behalf of an NHS Trust or by or on behalf of an NHS Foundation Trust, or

(e) privately fostered (within the meaning of section 66 of the Children Act 1989).

(3) In subsection (2)—

'care home' ('cartref gofal') has the same meaning as in the Care Standards Act 2000;

...[5]

'education functions' ('swyddogaethau addysg') has the meaning given by section 597(1) of the Education Act 1996;

'independent hospital' ('ysbyty annibynnol')—

(a) in relation to Wales, has the meaning given by section 2 of the Care Standards Act 2000, and

(b) in relation to England, means a hospital as defined by section 275 of the National Health Service Act 2006 that is not a health service hospital as defined by that section;

['integrated care board' ('bwrdd gofal integredig') means a body established under section 14Z25 of the National Health Service Act 2006;][6]

'local authority in England' ('awdurdod lleol yn Lloegr') means—

(a) a county council in England,

(b) a district council for an area in England for which there is no county council,

(c) a London borough council, or

(d) the Common Council of the City of London;

'Local Health Board' ('Bwrdd Iechyd Lleol') means a Local Health Board established under section 11 of the National Health Service (Wales) Act 2006.

Amendments
1   Inserted by the Sentencing Act 2020, s 410, Sch 24, para 307(1).
2   Inserted by the Homelessness (Priority Need and Intentionality) (Wales) Regulations 2022, SI 2022/1069, reg 2
3   Substituted by the Health and Care Act 2022, s 32, Sch 4, para 226(1), (2)(a).
4   Substituted by the Health and Care Act 2022, s 1(2), Sch 1, para 32(a).
5   Repealed by the Health and Care Act 2022, s 32, Sch 4, para 226(1), (3)(a)(i).
6   Inserted by the Health and Care Act 2022, s 32, Sch 4, para 226(1), (3)(a)(ii).

71   Meaning of vulnerable in section 70

(1) A person is vulnerable as a result of a reason mentioned in paragraph (c) or (j) of section 70(1) if, having regard to all the circumstances of the person's case—

(a) the person would be less able to fend for himself or herself (as a result of that reason) if the person were to become street homeless than would an ordinary homeless person who becomes street homeless, and

(b) this would lead to the person suffering more harm than would be suffered by the ordinary homeless person;

this subsection applies regardless of whether or not the person whose case is being considered is, or is likely to become, street homeless.

(2) In subsection (1), 'street homeless' ('digartref ac ar y stryd'), in relation to a person, means that the person has no accommodation available for the person's occupation in the United Kingdom or elsewhere, which the person—

(a) is entitled to occupy by virtue of an interest in it or by virtue of an order of a court,

(b) has an express or implied licence to occupy, or

(c) occupies as a residence by virtue of any enactment or rule of law giving the person the right to remain in occupation or restricting the right of another person to recover possession;

and sections 55 and 56 do not apply to this definition.

72 Power to amend or repeal provisions about priority need for accommodation

(1) The Welsh Ministers may by order—

(a) make provision for and in connection with removing any condition that a local housing authority must have reason to believe or be satisfied that an applicant is in priority need for accommodation before any power or duty to secure accommodation under this Chapter applies;

(b) amend or omit the descriptions of persons as having a priority need for accommodation for the purposes of this Chapter;

(c) specify further descriptions of persons as having a priority need for accommodation for the purposes of this Chapter.

(2) An order under subsection (1) may amend or repeal any provision of this Part.

(3) Before making an order under this section the Welsh Ministers must consult such associations representing councils of counties and county boroughs in Wales, and such other persons, as they consider appropriate.

73 Duty to help to secure accommodation for homeless applicants

(1) A local housing authority must help to secure that suitable accommodation is available for occupation by an applicant, if the authority is satisfied that the applicant is—

(a) homeless, and

(b) eligible for help.

(2) But the duty in subsection (1) does not apply if the authority refers the application to another local housing authority (see section 80).

74 Circumstances in which the duty in section 73 ends

(1) The duty to an applicant under section 73 comes to an end in any of the circumstances described in subsections (2), (3), (4), or (5), if the applicant has been notified in accordance with section 84.

(2) The circumstances are the end of a period of 56 days.

(3) The circumstances are that before the end of a period of 56 days the local housing authority is satisfied that reasonable steps have been taken to help to secure that suitable accommodation is available for occupation by the applicant.

(4) The circumstances are that the local housing authority is satisfied (whether as a result of the steps it has taken or not) that—

(a) the applicant has suitable accommodation available for occupation, and

(b) the accommodation is likely to be available for occupation by the applicant for a period of at least 6 months.

(5) The circumstances are that—

(a) the applicant, having been notified of the possible consequence of refusal or acceptance of the offer, refuses an offer of accommodation from any person which the authority is satisfied is suitable for the applicant, and

(b) the authority is satisfied that the accommodation offered is likely to be available for occupation by the applicant for a period of at least 6 months.

(6) The period of 56 days mentioned in subsections (2) and (3) begins on the day the applicant is notified under section 63 and for this purpose the applicant is to be treated as notified on the day the notice is sent or first made available for collection.

(7) The period of 6 months mentioned in subsection (4)(b) and (5)(b) begins on the day the notice under section 84 is sent or first made available for collection.

(8) See section 79 for further circumstances in which the duty in section 73 comes to an end.

75 Duty to secure accommodation for applicants in priority need when the duty in section 73 ends

(1) When the duty in section 73 (duty to help to secure accommodation for homeless applicants) comes to an end in respect of an applicant in the circumstances mentioned in subsection (2) or (3) of section 74, the local housing authority must secure that suitable accommodation is available for occupation by the applicant if subsection (2) or (3) (of this section) applies.

(2) This subsection applies where the local housing authority—

(a) is satisfied that the applicant—

(i) does not have suitable accommodation available for occupation, or

(ii) has suitable accommodation, but it is not likely that the accommodation will be available for occupation by the applicant for a period of at least 6 months starting on the day the applicant is notified in accordance with section 84 that section 73 does not apply,

(b) is satisfied that the applicant is eligible for help,

(c) is satisfied that the applicant has a priority need for accommodation, and

(d) if the authority is having regard to whether or not the applicant is homeless intentionally (see section 77), is not satisfied that the applicant became homeless intentionally in the circumstances which gave rise to the application;

(3) This subsection applies where the local housing authority is having regard to whether or not the applicant is homeless intentionally and is satisfied that—

    (a) the applicant became homeless intentionally in the circumstances which gave rise to the application,

    (b) the applicant—

        (i) does not have suitable accommodation available for occupation, or

        (ii) has suitable accommodation, but it is not likely that the accommodation will be available for occupation by the applicant for a period of at least 6 months starting on the day on which the applicant is notified in accordance with section 84 that section 73 does not apply,

    (c) the applicant is eligible for help,

    (d) the applicant has a priority need for accommodation,

    (e) the applicant is—

        (i) a pregnant woman or a person with whom she resides or might reasonably be expected to reside,

        (ii) a person with whom a dependent child resides or might reasonably be expected to reside,

        (iii) a person who had not attained the age of 21 when the application for help was made or a person with whom such a person resides or might reasonably be expected to reside, or

        (iv) a person who had attained the age of 21, but not the age of 25, when the application for help was made and who was looked after, accommodated or fostered at any time while under the age of 18, or a person with whom such a person resides or might reasonably be expected to reside, and

    (f) the authority has not previously secured an offer of accommodation to the applicant under this section following a previous application for help under this Chapter, where that offer was made—

        (i) at any time within the period of 5 years before the day on which the applicant was notified under section 63 that a duty was owed to him or her under this section, and

        (ii) on the basis that the applicant fell within this subsection.

(4) For the purpose of subsections (2)(a)(ii) and (3)(b)(ii), the applicant is to be treated as notified on the day the notice is sent or first made available for collection.

76 *Circumstances in which the duty in section 75 ends*

(1) The duty to an applicant under section 75(1) comes to an end in any of the circumstances described in subsections (2), (3), (6) or (7), if the applicant has been notified in accordance with section 84.

(2) The circumstances are that the applicant accepts—

(a) an offer of suitable accommodation under Part 6 of the Housing Act 1996 (allocation of housing), ...[1]

[(aa) an offer of suitable accommodation in Wales under a tenancy which is an occupation contract, or][2]

(b) an offer of suitable accommodation [(in England)][2] under an assured tenancy (including an assured shorthold tenancy).

(3) The circumstances are that the applicant, having been given notice in writing of the possible consequence of refusal or acceptance of the offer, refuses—

(a) an offer of suitable interim accommodation under section 75,

(b) a private rented sector offer, or

(c) an offer of accommodation under Part 6 of the Housing Act 1996,

which the authority is satisfied is suitable for the applicant.

(4) For the purposes of this section an offer is a private rented sector offer if—

[(a) it is an offer of—

(i) a tenancy which is an occupation contract made by a private landlord to the applicant in relation to accommodation in Wales which is available for the applicant's occupation, or

(ii) an assured shorthold tenancy made by a private landlord to the applicant in relation to any accommodation in England which is available for the applicant's occupation,][3]

(b) it is made, with the approval of the authority, in pursuance of arrangements made by the authority with the landlord with a view to bringing the authority's duty under section 75 to an end, and

(c) [in relation to accommodation in England,][2] the tenancy being offered is a fixed term tenancy for a period of at least 6 months.

(5) In a restricted case, the local housing authority must, so far as reasonably practicable, bring its duty to an end by securing a private rented sector offer; for this purpose, a 'restricted case' means a case where the local housing authority would not be satisfied as mentioned in section 75(1) without having regard to a restricted person (see section 63(5)).

(6) The circumstances are that the local housing authority is satisfied that the applicant has become homeless intentionally from suitable interim accommodation made available for the applicant's occupation—

(a) under section 68 and which continues to be made available under section 75, or

(b) under section 75.

(7) The circumstances are that the local housing authority is satisfied that the applicant has voluntarily ceased to occupy as his or her only or principal home, suitable interim accommodation made available for the applicant's occupation—

(a) under section 68 and which continues to be made available under section 75, or

(b) under section 75.

(8) See section 79 for further circumstances in which the duty in section 75(1) comes to an end.

[(9) In this section—

'fixed term tenancy' ('tenantiaeth cyfnod penodedig') in relation to accommodation in England has the meaning given in Part 1 of the Housing Act 1988 (c. 50);

'occupation contract' ('contract meddiannaeth') has the same meaning as in the Renting Homes (Wales) Act 2016 (anaw 1) (see section 7 of that Act).]³

Amendments

1   Repealed by the Renting Homes (Wales) Act 2016 (Consequential Amendments) Regulations 2022, SI 2022/1166, reg 34(1), (9)(a)(i).
2   Inserted by the Renting Homes (Wales) Act 2016 (Consequential Amendments) Regulations 2022, SI 2022/1166, reg 34(1), (9)(a)(ii), (iii), (b)(ii).
3   Substituted by the Renting Homes (Wales) Act 2016 (Consequential Amendments) Regulations 2022, SI 2022/1166, reg 34(1), (9)(b)(i), (c).

77   Meaning of intentionally homeless

(1) A person is intentionally homeless for the purpose of this Chapter if subsection (2) or (4) apply.

(2) This subsection applies if the person deliberately does or fails to do anything in consequence of which the person ceases to occupy accommodation which is available for the person's occupation and which it would have been reasonable for the person to continue to occupy.

(3) For the purposes of subsection (2) an act or omission in good faith on the part of a person who was unaware of any relevant fact may not be treated as deliberate.

(4) This subsection applies if—

(a) the person enters into an arrangement under which the person is required to cease to occupy accommodation which it would have been reasonable for the person to continue to occupy, and

(b) the purpose of the arrangement is to enable the person to become entitled to help under this Chapter,

andthere is no other good reason why the person is homeless.

78   Deciding to have regard to intentionality

(1) The Welsh Ministers must, by regulations, specify a category or categories of applicant for the purpose of this section.

(2) A local housing authority may not have regard to whether or not an applicant has become homeless intentionally for the purposes of sections 68 and 75 unless—

(a) the applicant falls within a category specified under subsection (1) in respect of which the authority has decided to have regard to whether or not applicants in that category have become homeless intentionally, and

(b) the authority has published a notice of its decision under paragraph (a) which specifies the category.

(3) Subsection (4) applies where a local housing authority has published a notice under subsection (2) unless the authority has—

(a) decided to stop having regard to whether or not applicants falling into the category specified in the notice have become homeless intentionally, and

(b) published a notice of its decision specifying the category.

(4) For the purposes of section 68 and 75, a local housing authority must have regard to whether or not an applicant has become homeless intentionally if the applicant falls within a category specified in the notice published by the authority under subsection (2).

79   Further circumstances in which the duties to help applicants end

(1) The duties in sections 66, 68, 73 and 75 come to an end in the circumstances described in subsection (2), (3), (4) or (5), if the applicant is notified in accordance with section 84.

(2) The circumstances are that the local housing authority is no longer satisfied that the applicant is eligible for help.

(3) The circumstances are that the local housing authority is satisfied that a mistake of fact led to the applicant being notified under section 63 that the duty was owed to the applicant.

(4) The circumstances are that the local authority is satisfied that the applicant has withdrawn his or her application.

(5) The circumstances are that the local housing authority is satisfied that the applicant is unreasonably failing to co-operate with the authority in connection with the exercise of its functions under this Chapter as they apply to the applicant.

Referral to another local housing authority

80   Referral of case to another local housing authority

(1) Subsection (2) applies where—

   (a) a local housing authority considers that the conditions for referral to another local housing authority (whether in Wales or England) are met (see subsection (3)), and

   (b) the local housing authority would, if the case is not referred, be subject to the duty in section 73 in respect of an applicant who is in priority need of accommodation and unintentionally homeless (duty to help to secure accommodation for homeless applicants).

(2) The local housing authority may notify the other authority of its opinion that the conditions for referral are met in respect of the applicant.

(3) The conditions for referral of the case to another local housing authority (whether in Wales or England) are met if—

   (a) neither the applicant nor any person who might reasonably be expected to reside with the applicant has a local connection with the area of the authority to which the application was made,

   (b) the applicant or a person who might reasonably be expected to reside with the applicant has a local connection with the area of that other authority, and

   (c) neither the applicant nor any person who might reasonably be expected to reside with the applicant will run the risk of domestic abuse in that other area.

(4) But the conditions for referral mentioned in subsection (3) are not met if—

   (a) the applicant or any person who might reasonably be expected to reside with the applicant has suffered abuse (other than domestic abuse) in the area of the other authority, and

   (b) it is probable that the return to that area of the victim will lead to further abuse of a similar kind against him or her.

(5) The question of whether the conditions for referral of a case are satisfied is to be decided—

   (a) by agreement between the notifying authority and the notified authority, or

(b) in default of agreement, in accordance with such arrangements—

    (i) as the Welsh Ministers may direct by order, where both authorities are in Wales, or

    (ii) as the Welsh Ministers and the Secretary of State may jointly direct by order, where the notifying authority is in Wales and the notified authority is in England.

(6) An order under subsection (5) may direct that the arrangements are to be—

(a) those agreed by any relevant authorities or associations of relevant authorities, or

(b) in default of such agreement, such arrangements as appear to the Welsh Ministers or, in the case of an order under subsection (5)(b)(ii), to the Welsh Ministers and the Secretary of State to be suitable, after consultation with such associations representing relevant authorities, and such other persons, as they think appropriate.

(7) In subsection (6), 'relevant authority' means a local housing authority or a social services authority; and it includes, in so far as that subsection applies to arrangements under subsection (5)(b)(ii), such authorities in Wales and England.

(8) The Welsh Ministers may by order specify other circumstances in which the conditions are or are not met for referral of the case to another local housing authority.

81 Local connection

(1) This section applies for the purposes of this Chapter.

(2) A person has a local connection with the area of a local housing authority in Wales or England if the person has a connection with it—

(a) because the person is, or in the past was, normally resident there, and that residence is or was of the person's own choice,

(b) because the person is employed there,

(c) because of family associations, or

(d) because of special circumstances.

(3) Residence in an area is not of a person's own choice if the person, or a person who might reasonably be expected to reside with that person, becomes resident there because the person is detained under the authority of an enactment.

(4) The Welsh Ministers may by order specify circumstances in which—

(a) a person is not to be treated as employed in an area, or

(b) residence in an area is not to be treated as of a person's own choice.

(5) A person has a local connection with the area of a local housing authority in Wales or England if the person was (at any time) provided with accommodation in that area under section 95 of the Immigration and Asylum Act 1999 (support for asylum seekers).

(6) But subsection (5) does not apply—

    (a) to the provision of accommodation for a person in an area of a local housing authority if the person was subsequently provided with accommodation in the area of another local housing authority under section 95 of that Act, or

    (b) to the provision of accommodation in an accommodation centre by virtue of section 22 of the Nationality, Immigration and Asylum Act 2002 (use of accommodation centres for section 95 support).

82 Duties to applicant whose case is considered for referral or referred

(1) Where a local housing authority notifies an applicant in accordance with section 84 that it intends to notify or has notified another local housing authority in Wales or England of its opinion that the conditions are met for the referral of the applicant's case to that other authority—

    (a) it ceases to be subject to any duty under section 68 (interim duty to secure accommodation for homeless applicants in priority need), andd

    (b) it is not subject to any duty under section 73 (duty to help to secure accommodation for homeless applicants);

but it must secure that suitable accommodation is available for occupation by the applicant until the applicant is notified of the decision whether the conditions for referral of the case are met.

(2) When it has been decided whether the conditions for referral are met, the notifying authority must notify the applicant in accordance with section 84.

(3) If it is decided that the conditions for referral are not met, the notifying authority is subject to the duty under section 73 (duty to help to secure accommodation for homeless applicants).

(4) If it is decided that those conditions are met and the notified authority is an authority in Wales, the notified authority is subject to the duty under section 73 (duty to help to secure accommodation for homeless applicants); for provision about cases where it is decided that those conditions are met and the notified authority is an authority in England, see section 201A of the Housing Act 1996 (cases referred from a local housing authority in Wales).

(5) The duty under subsection (1) ceases as provided in that subsection even if the applicant requests a review of the authority's decision (see section 85).

(6) The authority may secure that suitable accommodation is available for the applicant's occupation pending the decision on a review.

(7) If notice required to be given to an applicant under this section is not received by the applicant, it is to be treated as having been given if it is made available at the authority's office for a reasonable period for collection by the applicant or on the applicant's behalf.

83 Cases referred from a local housing authority in England

(1) This section applies where an application has been referred by a local housing authority in England to a local housing authority in Wales under section 198(1) of the Housing Act 1996 (referral of case to another local housing authority).

(2) If it is decided that the conditions in that section for referral of the case are met the notified authority is subject to the following duties in respect of the person whose case is referred—

  (a) section 68 (interim duty to secure accommodation for homeless applicants in priority need);

  (b) section 73 (duty to help to secure accommodation for homeless applicants);

for provision about cases where it is decided that the conditions for referral are not met, see section 200 of the Housing Act 1996 (duties to applicant whose case is considered for referral or referred).

(3) Accordingly, references in this Chapter to an applicant include a reference to a person to whom the duties mentioned in subsection (2) are owed by virtue of this section.

Notice

84 Notice that duties have ended

(1) Where a local housing authority concludes that its duty to an applicant under section 66, 68, 73 or 75 has come to an end (including where the authority has referred the applicant's case to another authority or decided that the conditions for referral are met), it must notify the applicant—

  (a) that it no longer regards itself as being subject to the relevant duty,

  (b) of the reasons why it considers that the duty has come to an end,

  (c) of the right to request a review, and

  (d) of the time within which such a request must be made.

(2) Where a notice under subsection (1) relates to the duty in section 73 coming to an end in the circumstances described in section 74(2) or (3), it must include

notice of the steps taken by the local housing authority to help to secure that suitable accommodation would be available for occupation by the applicant.

(3) Notice under this section must be in writing.

(4) Where a notice is not received by an applicant, the applicant may be treated as having been notified under this section if the notice is made available at the authority's office for a reasonable period for collection by the applicant or on the applicant's behalf.

Right to review and appeal

85   Right to request review

(1) An applicant has the right to request a review of the following decisions—

- (a) a decision of a local housing authority as to the applicant's eligibility for help;

- (b) a decision of a local housing authority that a duty is not owed to the applicant under section 66, 68, 73, or 75 (duties to applicants who are homeless or threatened with homelessness);

- (c) a decision of a local housing authority that a duty owed to the applicant under section 66, 68, 73, or 75 has come to an end (including where the authority has referred the applicant's case to another authority or decided that the conditions for referral are met).

(2) Where the duty owed to an applicant under section 73 has come to an end in the circumstances described in section 74(2) or (3), an applicant has the right to request a review of whether or not reasonable steps were taken during the period in which the duty under section 73 was owed to help to secure that suitable accommodation would be available for his or her occupation.

(3) An applicant who is offered accommodation in, or in connection with, the discharge of any duty under this Chapter may request a review of the suitability of the accommodation offered to the applicant (whether or not he or she has accepted the offer).

(4) There is no right to request a review of the decision reached on an earlier review.

(5) A request for review must be made before the end of the period of 21 days (or such longer period as the authority may in writing allow) beginning with the day on which the applicant is notified of the authority's decision.

(6) On a request being made to them, the authority or authorities concerned must review their decision.

86   Procedure on review

(1) The Welsh Ministers may make provision by regulations as to the procedure to be followed in connection with a review under section 85.

(2) Regulations under subsection (1) may, for example,—

   (a) require the decision on review to be made by a person of appropriate seniority who was not involved in the original decision, and

   (b) provide for the circumstances in which the applicant is entitled to an oral hearing, and whether and by whom the applicant may be represented at such a hearing, and

   (c) provide for the period within which the review must be carried out and notice given of the decision.

(3) The authority, or as the case may be either of the authorities, concerned must notify the applicant of the decision on the review.

(4) The authority must also notify the applicant of the reasons for the decision, if the decision is—

   (a) to confirm the original decision on any issue against the interests of the applicant, or

   (b) to confirm that reasonable steps were taken.

(5) In any case they must inform the applicant of his or her right to appeal to the county court on a point of law, and of the period within which such an appeal must be made (see section 88).

(6) Notice of the decision is not be treated as given unless and until subsection (5), and where applicable subsection (4), is complied with.

(7) Notice required to be given to a person under this section must be given in writing and, if not received by that person, is to be treated as having been given if it is made available at the authority's office for a reasonable period for collection by the person or on his or her behalf.

87   Effect of a decision on review or appeal that reasonable steps were not taken

(1) Subsection (2) applies where it is decided on review under section 85(2) or on an appeal of a decision under that section that reasonable steps were not taken.

(2) The duty in section 73 applies to the applicant again, with the modification that the 56 day period mentioned in subsection (2) of section 74 is to be interpreted as starting on the day the authority notifies the applicant of its decision on review under section 85(2) or, on an appeal, on such date as the court may order.

88 Right of appeal to county court on point of law

(1) An applicant who has requested a review under section 85 may appeal to the county court on any point of law arising from the decision or, as the case may be, the original decision or a question as to whether reasonable steps were taken if the applicant—

(a) is dissatisfied with the decision on the review, or

(b) is not notified of the decision on the review within the time prescribed under section 86.

(2) An appeal must be brought within 21 days of the applicant being notified of the decision or, as the case may be, of the date on which the applicant should have been notified of a decision on review.

(3) The court may give permission for an appeal to be brought after the end of the period allowed by subsection (2), but only if it is satisfied—

(a) where permission is sought before the end of that period, that there is a good reason for the applicant to be unable to bring the appeal in time, or

(b) where permission is sought after that time, that there is a good reason for the applicant's failure to bring the appeal in time and for any delay in applying for permission.

(4) On appeal the court may make such order confirming, quashing or varying the decision as it thinks fit.

(5) Where the authority was under a duty under section 68, 75 or 82 to secure that suitable accommodation is available for the applicant's occupation, it may secure that suitable accommodation is so available—

(a) during the period for appealing under this section against the authority's decision, and

(b) if an appeal is brought, until the appeal (and any further appeal) is finally determined.

89 Appeals against refusal to accommodate pending appeal

(1) This section applies where an applicant has the right to appeal to the county court under section 88.

(2) An applicant may appeal to the county court against a decision of the authority—

(a) not to exercise their power under section 88(5) ('the section 88(5) power') in the applicant's case,

(b) to exercise that power for a limited period ending before the final determination by the county court of the applicant's appeal under section 88(1) ('the main appeal'), or

(c) to cease exercising that power before the final determination.

(3) An appeal under this section may not be brought after the final determination by the coAmendments

appeal under this section the court—

(a) may order the authority to secure that suitable accommodation is available for the applicant's occupation until the determination of the appeal (or such earlier time as the court may specify), and

(b) must confirm or quash the decision appealed against.

(5) In considering whether to confirm or quash the decision the court must apply the principles applied by the High Court on an application for judicial review.

(6) If the court quashes the decision it may order the authority to exercise the section 88(5) power in the applicant's case for such period as may be specified in the order.

(7) An order under subsection (6)—

(a) may only be made if the court is satisfied that failure to exercise the section 88(5) power in accordance with the order would substantially prejudice the applicant's ability to pursue the main appeal;

(b) may not specify any period ending after the final determination by the county court of the main appeal.

Supplementary provisions

90   Charges

A local housing authority may require a person in relation to whom it is discharging its functions under this Chapter—

(a) to pay reasonable charges determined by the authority in respect of accommodation which it secures for the person's occupation (either by making it available itself or otherwise), or

(b) to pay a reasonable amount determined by the authority in respect of sums payable by it for accommodation made available by another person.

91   Out-of-area placement

(1) A local housing authority must in discharging its functions under this Chapter secure or help to secure that suitable accommodation is available for the occupation of the applicant in its area, so far as is reasonably practicable.

(2) If the authority secures that accommodation is available for the occupation of the applicant outside its area in Wales or England, it must give notice to

the local housing authority (whether in Wales or England) in whose area the accommodation is situated.

(3) The notice must state—

    (a) the name of the applicant,

    (b) the number and description of other persons who normally reside with the applicant as a member of his or her family or might reasonably be expected to reside with the applicant,

    (c) the address of the accommodation,

    (d) the date on which the accommodation was made available to the applicant, and

    (e) which function under this Chapter the authority was discharging in securing that the accommodation is available for the applicant's occupation.

(4) The notice must be in writing, and must be given before the end of the period of 14 days beginning with the day on which the accommodation was made available to the applicant.

92 Interim accommodation [in England]¹: arrangements with private landlord

(1) This section applies where in carrying out any of its functions under section 68, 82 or 88(5) (interim accommodation) a local housing authority makes arrangements with a private landlord to provide accommodation [in England]¹.

(2) A tenancy granted to the applicant under the arrangements cannot be an assured tenancy before the end of the period of twelve months beginning with—

    (a) the date on which the applicant was notified of the authority's decision under section 63(1) or 80(5), or

    (b) if there is a review of that decision under section 85 or an appeal to the court under section 88, the date on which the applicant is notified of the decision on review or the appeal is finally determined,

unless, before or during that period, the tenant is notified by the landlord (or in the case of joint landlords, at least one of them) that the tenancy is to be regarded as an assured shorthold tenancy or an assured tenancy other than an assured shorthold tenancy.

Amendments
1   Inserted by the Renting Homes (Wales) Act 2016 (Consequential Amendments) Regulations 2022, SI 2022/1166, reg 34(1), (10).

[92A Accommodation in Wales

(1) For provision which applies where a tenancy or licence in respect of accommodation in Wales is made with an individual by a local housing authority

because of the authority's functions under Part 2 of this Act (homelessness), see paragraph 11 of Part 4 of Schedule 2 to the Renting Homes (Wales) Act 2016 (anaw 1) (tenancies and licences to which special rules apply: homelessness).

(2) For provision which applies where a local housing authority, in pursuance of any of its homelessness housing functions, makes arrangements with a relevant landlord for the provision of accommodation, see paragraph 12 of Part 4 of Schedule 2 to the Renting Homes (Wales) Act 2016 (tenancies and licences to which special rules apply: homelessness).][1]

Amendments
1   Inserted by the Renting Homes (Wales) Act 2016 (Consequential Amendments) Regulations 2022, SI 2022/1166, reg 34(1), (11).

93   Protection of property

(1) Where a local housing authority has become subject to a duty in respect of an applicant as described in subsection (2), it must take reasonable steps to prevent the loss of the personal property of the applicant or prevent or mitigate damage to it if the authority has reason to believe that—

    (a) there is danger of loss of, or damage to, the property by reason of the applicant's inability to protect it or deal with it, and

    (b) no other suitable arrangements have been or are being made.

(2) The duties in respect of an applicant are—

section 66 (duty to help to prevent an applicant from becoming homeless) in the case of an applicant in priority need;

section 68 (interim duty to secure accommodation for homeless applicants in priority need);

section 75 (duty to secure accommodation for applicants in priority need when the duty in section 73 ends);

section 82 (duties to applicant whose case is considered for referral or referred) in the case of an applicant in priority need.

(3) Where a local housing authority has become subject to the duty in subsection (1), it continues to be subject to that duty even if the duty in respect of the applicant as described in subsection (2) comes to an end.

(4) The duty of a local housing authority under subsection (1) is subject to any conditions it considers appropriate in the particular case, which may include conditions as to—

    (a) the making and recovery by the authority of reasonable charges for the action taken, or

(b) the disposal by the authority, in such circumstances as may be specified, of property in relation to which it has taken action.

(5) A local housing authority may take any steps it considers reasonable for the purpose of protecting the personal property of an applicant who is eligible for help or prevent or mitigate damage to it if the authority has reason to believe that—

(a) there is danger of loss of, or damage to, the property by reason of the applicant's inability to protect it or deal with it, and

(b) no other suitable arrangements have been or are being made.

(6) References in this section to personal property of the applicant include personal property of any person who might reasonably be expected to reside with the applicant.

94 Protection of property: supplementary provisions

(1) The authority may for the purposes of section 93—

(a) enter, at all reasonable times, any premises which are the usual place of residence of the applicant or which were the applicant's last usual place of residence, and

(b) deal with any personal property of the applicant in any way which is reasonably necessary, in particular by storing it or arranging for its storage.

(2) Where a local authority is proposing to exercise the power in subsection (1)(a), the officer it authorises to do so must, upon request, produce valid documentation setting out the authorisation to do so.

(3) A person who, without reasonable excuse, obstructs the exercise of the power under subsection (1)(a) commits an offence and is liable on summary conviction to a fine not exceeding level 4 on the standard scale.

(4) Where the applicant asks the authority to move his or her property to a particular location nominated by the applicant, the authority—

(a) may, if it appears to it that the request is reasonable, discharge its responsibilities under section 93 by doing as the applicant asks, and

(b) having done so, have no further duty or power to take action under that section in relation to that property.

(5) If such a request is made, the authority must before complying with it inform the applicant of the consequence of it doing so.

(6) If no such request is made (or, if made, is not acted upon) the authority cease to have any duty or power to take action under section 93 when, in its opinion,

there is no longer any reason to believe that there is a danger of loss of or damage to a person's personal property by reason of his or her inability to protect it or deal with it.

(7) But property stored by virtue of the authority having taken such action may be kept in store and any conditions upon which it was taken into store continue to have effect, with any necessary modifications.

(8) Where the authority—

(a) ceases to be subject to a duty to take action under section 93 in respect of an applicant's property, or

(b) ceases to have power to take such action, having previously taken such action,

it must notify the applicant of that fact and of the reason for it.

(9) The notification must be given to the applicant—

(a) by delivering it to the applicant, or

(b) leaving it at, or sending it to, the applicant's last known address.

(10) References in this section to personal property of the applicant include personal property of any person who might reasonably be expected to reside with the applicant.

95   Co-operation

(1) A council of a county or county borough in Wales must make arrangements to promote co-operation between the officers of the authority who exercise its social services functions and those who exercise its functions as the local housing authority with a view to achieving the following objectives in its area—

(a) the prevention of homelessness,

(b) that suitable accommodation is or will be available for people who are or may become homeless,

(c) that satisfactory support is available for people who are or may become homeless, and

(d) the effective discharge of its functions under this Part.

(2) If a local housing authority requests the co-operation of a person mentioned in subsection (5) in the exercise of its functions under this Part, the person must comply with the request unless the person considers that doing so would—

(a) be incompatible with the person's own duties, or

(b) otherwise have an adverse effect on the exercise of the person's functions.

(3) If a local housing authority requests that a person mentioned in subsection (5) provides it with information it requires for the purpose of the exercise of any of its functions under this Part, the person must comply with the request unless the person considers that doing so would—

(a) be incompatible with the person's own duties, or

(b) otherwise have an adverse effect on the exercise of the person's functions.

(4) A person who decides not to comply with a request under subsection (2) or (3) must give the local housing authority who made the request written reasons for the decision.

(5) The persons (whether in Wales or England) are—

(a) a local housing authority;

(b) a social services authority;

(c) a registered social landlord;

(d) a new town corporation;

(e) a private registered provider of social housing;

(f) a housing action trust.

(6) The Welsh Ministers may amend subsection (5) by order to omit or add a person, or a description of a person.

(7) An order under subsection (6) may not add a Minister of the Crown.

(8) In this section—

'housing action trust' ('ymddiriedolaeth gweithredu tai') means a housing action trust established under Part 3 of the Housing Act 1988;

'new town corporation' ('corfforaeth tref newydd') has the meaning given in Part 1 of the Housing Act 1985;

'private registered provider of social housing' ('darparwr tai cymdeithasol preifat cofrestredig') has the meaning given by Part 2 of the Housing and Regeneration Act 2008;

'registered social landlord' ('landlord cymdeithasol cofrestredig') has the meaning given by Part 1 of the Housing Act 1996.

96 Co-operation in certain cases involving children

(1) This section applies where a local housing authority has reason to believe that an applicant with whom a person under the age of 18 normally resides, or might reasonably be expected to reside—

(a) may be ineligible for help,

(b) may be homeless and that a duty under section 68, 73 or 75 is not likely to apply to the applicant, or

(c) may be threatened with homelessness and that a duty under section 66 is not likely to apply to the applicant.

(2) A local housing authority must make arrangements for ensuring that—

(a) the applicant is invited to consent to the referral to the social services department of the essential facts of his or her case, and

(b) if the applicant has given that consent, the social services department is made aware of those facts and of the subsequent decision of the authority in respect of his or her case.

(3) Nothing in subsection (2) affects any power apart from this section to disclose information relating to the applicant's case to the the social services department without the consent of the applicant.

(4) A council of a county or county borough must make arrangements for ensuring that, where it makes a decision as local housing authority that an applicant is ineligible for help, became homeless intentionally or became threatened with homelessness intentionally, its housing department provides the social services department with such advice and assistance as the social services department may reasonably request.

(5) In this section, in relation to the council of a county or county borough—

'the housing department' ('yr adran dai') means those persons responsible for the exercise of its functions as local housing authority;

'the social services department' ('yr adran gwasanaethau cymdeithasol') means those persons responsible for the exercise of its social services functions under Part 3 of the Social Services and Well-Being (Wales) Act 2014.

General

97 False statements, withholding information and failure to disclose change of circumstances

(1) It is an offence for a person, with intent to induce a local housing authority to believe in connection with the exercise of its functions under this Chapter that the person or another person is entitled to accommodation or assistance in accordance with the provisions of this Chapter, or is entitled to accommodation or assistance of a particular description—

(a) knowingly or recklessly to make a statement which is false in a material particular, or

(b) knowingly to withhold information which the authority has reasonably required the person to give in connection with the exercise of those functions.

(2) If before an applicant receives notification of the local housing authority's decision on the application there is any change of facts material to the case, the applicant must notify the authority as soon as possible.

(3) The authority must explain to every applicant, in ordinary language, the duty imposed by subsection (2) and the effect of subsection (4).

(4) A person who fails to comply with subsection (2) after being given the explanation required by subsection (3) commits an offence.

(5) In proceedings against a person for an offence committed under subsection (4) it is a defence that the person had a reasonable excuse for failing to comply.

(6) A person guilty of an offence under this section is liable on summary conviction to a fine not exceeding level 4 on the standard scale.

98   Guidance

(1) In the exercise of its functions relating to homelessness, a council of a county or county borough must have regard to guidance given by the Welsh Ministers.

(2) Subsection (1) applies in relation to functions under this Part and any other enactment.

(3) The Welsh Ministers may—

(a) give guidance either generally or to specified descriptions of authorities;

(b) revise the guidance by giving further guidance under this Part;

(c) withdraw the guidance by giving further guidance under this Part or by notice.

(4) The Welsh Ministers must publish any guidance or notice under this Part.

99   Interpretation of this Chapter and index of defined terms

In this Chapter—

'abuse' ('camdriniaeth') has the meaning given by section 58;

'accommodation available for occupation' ('llety sydd ar gael i'w feddiannu') has the meaning given by section 56;

'applicant' ('ceisydd') has the meaning given by section 62(3) and section 83(3);

'associated' ('cysylltiedig'), in relation to a person, has the meaning given by section 58;

'assured tenancy' ('tenantiaeth sicr') and 'assured shorthold tenancy' ('tenantiaeth fyrddaliol sicr') have the meaning given by Part 1 of the Housing Act 1988;

'domestic abuse' ('camdriniaeth ddomestig') has the meaning given by section 58;

'eligible for help' ('yn gymwys i gael cymorth') means not excluded from help under this Chapter by Schedule 2;

'enactment' ('deddfiad') means an enactment (whenever enacted or made) comprised in, or in an instrument made under—

(a) an Act of Parliament,

(b) a Measure or an Act of the National Assembly for Wales;

'help to secure' ('cynorthwyo i sicrhau'), in relation to securing that suitable accommodation is available, or does not cease to be available, for occupation, has the meaning given by section 65;

'help under this Chapter' ('cynorth o dan y Bennod hon') means the benefit of any function under sections 66, 68, 73, or 75;

'homeless' ('digartref') has the meaning given by section 55 and 'homelessness' (digartrefedd) is to be interpreted accordingly;

'intentionally homeless' ('digartref yn fwriadol') has the meaning given by section 77;

'local connection' ('cysylltiad lleol') has the meaning given by section 81;

'local housing authority' ('awdurdod tai lleol') means—

(a) in relation to Wales, the council of a county or county borough, and

(b) in relation to England, a district council, a London borough council, the Common Council of the City of London or the Council of the Isles of Scilly,

but a reference to a 'local housing authority' is to be interpreted as a reference to a local housing authority for an area in Wales only, unless this Chapter expressly provides otherwise;

'looked after, accommodated or fostered' ('yn derbyn gofal, yn cael ei letya neu'n cael ei faethu') has the meaning given by section 70(2);

['occupation contract' ('contract meddiannaeth') has the same meaning as in the Renting Homes (Wales) Act 2016 (anaw 1) (see section 7 of that Act);][1]

'prescribed' ('rhagnodedig') means prescribed in regulations made by the Welsh Ministers;

'priority need for accommodation' ('angen blaenoriaethol am lety') has the meaning given by section 70;

'prison' ('carchar') has the same meaning as in the Prison Act 1952 (see section 53(1) of that Act);

'private landlord' ('landlord preifat') means a landlord[—

   (a) of a dwelling in Wales, who is within section 10 of the Renting Homes (Wales) Act 2016 (anaw 1) (private landlords);

   (b) of a dwelling in England, who is not within section 80(1) of the Housing Act 1985 (c. 68) (the landlord condition for secure tenancies);][2]

'reasonable to continue to occupy accommodation' ('rhesymol parhau i feddiannu llety') has the meaning given by section 57;

'regular armed forces of the Crown' ('lluoedd arfog rheolaidd y Goron') means the regular forces as defined by section 374 of the Armed Forces Act 2006;

'restricted person' ('person cyfyngedig') has the meaning given by section 63(5);

'social services authority' ('awdurdod gwasanaethau cymdeithasol') means—

   (a) in relation to Wales, the council of a county or county borough council in the exercise of its social services functions, within the meaning of section 119 of the Social Services and Well-being (Wales) Act 2014, and

   (b) in relation to England, a local authority for the purposes of the Local Authority Social Services Act 1970, as defined in section 1 of that Act,

but a reference to a 'social services authority' is to be interpreted as a reference to a social services authority for an area in Wales only, unless this Chapter expressly provides otherwise;

'threatened with homelessness' ('o dan fygythiad o ddigartrefedd') has the meaning given by section 55(4);

'voluntary organisation' ('corff gwirfoddol') means a body (other than a public or local authority) whose activities are not carried on for profit.

'youth detention accommodation' ('llety cadw ieuenctid') means—

(a) a secure children's home;

(b) a secure training centre;

(c) a young offender institution;

(d) accommodation provided, equipped and maintained by the Welsh Ministers under section 82(5) of the Children Act 1989 for the purpose of restricting the liberty of children;

(e) accommodation, or accommodation of a description, for the time being specified [by regulations under section 248(1)(f) of the Sentencing Code]³ (youth detention accommodation for the purposes of detention and training orders).

Amendments

1   Inserted by the Renting Homes (Wales) Act 2016 (Consequential Amendments) Regulations 2022, SI 2022/1166, reg 34(1), (12)(a)

2   Substituted by the Renting Homes (Wales) Act 2016 (Consequential Amendments) Regulations 2022, SI 2022/1166, reg 34(1), (12)(b)

3   Substituted by the Sentencing Act 2020, s 410, Sch 24, para 308(1).

100 Consequential amendments

Part 1 of Schedule 3 makes consequential amendments relating to this Part.

(introduced by section 61)

SCHEDULE 2 – ELIGIBILITY FOR HELP UNDER CHAPTER 2 OF PART 2

1 Persons not eligible for help

(1) A person is not eligible for help under section 66, 68, 73 or 75 if he or she is a person from abroad who is ineligible for housing assistance.

(2) A person who is subject to immigration control within the meaning of the Asylum and Immigration Act 1996 is not eligible for housing assistance unless the person falls within a class of persons prescribed by regulations made by the Welsh Ministers or the Secretary of State.

(3) No person who is excluded from entitlement to universal credit or housing benefit by section 115 of the Immigration and Asylum Act 1999 (exclusion from benefits) may be included in any class prescribed under sub-paragraph (2).

(4) The Welsh Ministers or the Secretary of State may by regulations provide for other descriptions of persons who are to be treated for the purposes of Chapter 2 of Part 2 as persons from abroad who are ineligible for housing assistance.

(5) A person who is not eligible for housing assistance is to be disregarded in determining for the purposes of Chapter 2 of Part 2 whether a person falling within sub-paragraph (6)—

(a) is homeless or threatened with homelessness, or

(b) has a priority need for accommodation.

(6) A person falls within this subsection if the person—

(a) falls within a class prescribed by regulations made under sub-paragraph (2), and

[(b) is not a person who, immediately before IP completion day, was—

(i) a national of an EEA State or Switzerland, and

(ii) within a class prescribed by regulations made under sub-paragraph (2) which had effect at that time.]¹

Amendments

1   Substituted by the Immigration and Social Security Co-ordination (EU Withdrawal) Act 2020 (Consequential, Saving, Transitional and Transitory Provisions) (EU Exit) Regulations 2020, SI 2020/1309, reg 21(1), (2)(a).

2 Asylum-seekers and their dependants: transitional provision

(1) Until the commencement of the repeal of section 186 of the Housing Act 1996 (asylum-seekers and their dependants), that section applies to Chapter 2 of Part 2 of this Act as it applies to Part 7 of that Act.

(2) For this purpose, in section 186 of the Housing Act 1996—

(a) the reference to section 185 of that Act is to be interpreted as a reference to paragraph 1, and

(b) the reference to 'this Part' is to be interpreted as a reference to Chapter 2 of Part 2 of this Act and not Part 7 of that Act.

3 Provision of information by Secretary of State

(1) The Secretary of State must, at the request of a local housing authority, provide the authority with such information as it may require—

(a) as to whether a person is a person to whom section 115 of the Immigration and Asylum Act 1999 (exclusion from benefits) applies, and

(b) to enable it to determine whether such a person is eligible for help under Chapter 2 of Part 2.

(2) Where that information is given otherwise than in writing, the Secretary of State must confirm it in writing if a written request is made to the Secretary of State by the authority.

(3) If it appears to the Secretary of State that any application, decision or other change of circumstances has affected the status of a person about whom information was previously provided to a local housing authority under this paragraph, the Secretary of State must inform the authority in writing of that fact, the reason for it and the date on which the previous information became inaccurate.

PART 4

Wales: Statutory Instruments

Allocation of Housing (Wales) Regulations 2003

SI 2003/239

I Citation, commencement and application

(1) These Regulations may be cited as the Allocation of Housing (Wales) Regulations 2003 and shall come into force on 29 January 2003.

(2) These Regulations apply to Wales only.

2 Interpretation

In these Regulations—

'the Act' ('y Ddeddf') means the Housing Act 1996;

'the Common Travel Area' ('Ardal Deithio Gyffredin') means the United Kingdom, the Channel Islands, the Isle of Man and the Republic of Ireland collectively; ...[1]

'the immigration rules' ('y rheolau mewnfudo') mean the rules laid down as mentioned in section 3(2) of the Immigration Act 1971 (general provisions for regulation and control)[; and][2]

['secure contract' ('contract diogel') has the same meaning as in the Renting Homes (Wales) Act 2016 (see section 8 of that Act).][3]

Amendments
1   Repealed by the Renting Homes (Wales) Act 2016 (Consequential Amendments to Secondary Legislation) Regulations 2022, SI 2022/907, reg 2, Sch 1, para 21(a)(i) (as substituted by the Renting Homes (Wales) Act 2016 (Consequential Amendments to Secondary Legislation) (Amendment) Regulations 2022, SI 2022/1077, reg 2(1), (2)(d)).
2   Substituted by the Renting Homes (Wales) Act 2016 (Consequential Amendments to Secondary Legislation) Regulations 2022, SI 2022/907, reg 2, Sch 1, para 21(a)(ii) (as substituted by the Renting Homes (Wales) Act 2016 (Consequential Amendments to Secondary Legislation) (Amendment) Regulations 2022, SI 2022/1077, reg 2(1), (2)(d)).
3   Inserted by the Renting Homes (Wales) Act 2016 (Consequential Amendments to Secondary Legislation) Regulations 2022, SI 2022/907, reg 2, Sch 1, para 21(a)(iii) (as substituted by the Renting Homes (Wales) Act 2016 (Consequential Amendments to Secondary Legislation) (Amendment) Regulations 2022, SI 2022/1077, reg 2(1), (2)(d))..

3 Cases where the provisions of Part VI of the Act do not apply

The provisions of Part VI of the Act about the allocation of housing accommodation do not apply in the following cases—

    (a) where a local housing authority secures the provision of suitable alternative accommodation under section 39 of the Land Compensation Act 1973 (duty to rehouse residential occupiers);

    (b) in relation to the grant of a [secure contract][1] under section 554 and 555 of the Housing Act 1985 (grant of tenancy to former owner-occupier or statutory tenant of defective dwelling-house).

Amendments

1   Repealed by the Renting Homes (Wales) Act 2016 (Consequential Amendments to Secondary Legislation) Regulations 2022, SI 2022/907, reg 2, Sch 1, para 21(b).

4 ...[1]

...[1]

Amendments

1   Repealed by the Allocation of Housing and Homelessness (Eligibility) (Wales) Regulations 2014, SI 2014/2603, reg 7(a).

5 ...[1]

...[1]

Amendments

1   Repealed by the Allocation of Housing and Homelessness (Eligibility) (Wales) Regulations 2014, SI 2014/2603, reg 7(a).

6 Revocation

The Allocation of Housing (Wales) Regulations 2000 are revoked.

Allocation of Housing and Homelessness (Eligibility) (Wales) Regulations 2014

SI 2014/2603

1 Title, commencement and application

(1) The title of these Regulations is the Allocation of Housing and Homelessness (Eligibility) (Wales) Regulations 2014 and they come into force on 31 October 2014.

(2) These Regulations apply in relation to Wales.

2 Interpretation

(1) In these Regulations—

'the 1996 Act' ('Deddf 1996') means the Housing Act 1996;

'the Accession Regulations 2013' ('Rheoliadau Ymaelodaeth 2013') means the Accession of Croatia (Immigration and Worker Authorisation) Regulations 2013;

'the EEA Regulations' ('Rheoliadau yr AEE') means the [Immigration (European Economic Area) Regulations 2016 and references to the EEA Regulations are to be read with Schedule 4 to the Immigration and Social Security Co-ordination (EU Withdrawal) Act 2020 (Consequential, Saving, Transitional and Transitory Provisions) Regulations 2020][1];

['the Human Rights Convention' ('y Confensiwn Hawliau Dynol') means the Convention for the Protection of Human Rights and Fundamental Freedoms, agreed by the Council of Europe at Rome on 4th November 1950 as it has effect for the time being in relation to the United Kingdom;][2]

'the Immigration Rules' ('y Rheolau Mewnfudo') means the rules laid down as mentioned in section 3(2) of the Immigration Act 1971 (general provisions for regulation and control);

'the Refugee Convention' ('y Confensiwn ynglŷn â Ffoaduriaid') means the Convention relating to the Status of Refugees done at Geneva on 28 July 1951, as extended by Article 1(2) of the Protocol relating to the Status of Refugees done at New York on 31 January 1967; and 'sponsor' ('noddwr') means a person who has given an undertaking in writing for the purposes of the Immigration Rules to be responsible for the maintenance and accommodation of another person.

(2) For the purposes of these Regulations—

(a) 'jobseeker' ('ceisiwr gwaith'), 'self-employed person' ('person hunangyflogedig'), and 'worker' ('gweithiwr') have the same meaning as for the purposes of the definition of a 'qualified person' in regulation 6(1) of the EEA Regulations;

[(ab) 'frontier worker' ('gweithiwr trawsffiniol') means a person who is a frontier worker within the meaning of regulation 3 of the Citizens' Rights (Frontier Workers) (EU Exit) Regulations;][3] and

(b) subject to paragraph (3), references to the family member of a jobseeker, self-employed person[, worker or frontier worker][1] are to be construed in accordance with regulation 7 of [the EEA Regulations][1].

(3) For the purposes of regulations 4(2)(d) [and (h)][3] and 6(2)(d) [and (h)][3] 'family member' ('aelod o deulu') does not include a person who is treated as a family member by virtue of regulation 7(3) of the EEA Regulations.

Amendments
1   Substituted by the Immigration and Social Security Co-ordination (EU Withdrawal) Act 2020 (Consequential, Saving, Transitional and Transitory Provisions) (EU Exit) Regulations 2020, SI 2020/1309, reg 76(1), (2)(a)(i), (iii).
2   Inserted by the Allocation of Housing and Homelessness (Eligibility) (Wales) (Amendment) Regulations 2017, SI 2017/698, reg 2(1), (2).
3   Inserted by the Immigration and Social Security Co-ordination (EU Withdrawal) Act 2020 (Consequential, Saving, Transitional and Transitory Provisions) (EU Exit) Regulations 2020, SI 2020/1309, reg 76(1), (2)(a)(ii), (iv).

3 Persons subject to immigration control who are eligible for an allocation of housing accommodation

The following classes of persons subject to immigration control are persons who are eligible for an allocation of housing accommodation under Part 6 of the 1996 Act—

(a) Class A – a person who is recorded by the Secretary of State as a refugee within the definition in Article 1 of the Refugee Convention and who has leave to enter or remain in the United Kingdom;

(b) Class B – a person—

(i)   who has exceptional leave to enter or remain in the United Kingdom granted outside the provisions of the Immigration Rules; and

(ii) whose leave to enter or remain is not subject to a condition requiring that person to maintain and accommodate themselves, and any person who is dependant on that person, without recourse to public funds;

(c) Class C – a person who is habitually resident in the United Kingdom, the Channel Islands, the Isle of Man or the Republic of Ireland and whose leave to enter or remain in the United Kingdom is not subject to any limitation or condition, other than a person—

   (i) who has been given leave to enter or remain in the United Kingdom upon an undertaking given by the person's sponsor;

   (ii) who has been resident in the United Kingdom, the Channel Islands, the Isle of Man or the Republic of Ireland for less than five years beginning on the date of entry or on the date on which the undertaking was given in respect of the person, whichever date is the later; and

   (iii) whose sponsor or, where there is more than one sponsor, at least one of whose sponsors is still alive;

(d) Class D – a person who has humanitarian protection granted under the Immigration Rules; ...[1]

(e) Class E – a person who is habitually resident in the United Kingdom, the Channel Islands, the Isle of Man or the Republic of Ireland and who has limited leave to enter the United Kingdom as a relevant Afghan citizen under paragraph 276BA1 of the Immigration Rules[; ...[2]][3]

[(f) Class F – a person who has limited leave to enter or remain in the United Kingdom on family or private life grounds under Article 8 of the Human Rights Convention, such leave granted under paragraph 276BE(1), paragraph 276DG or Appendix FM of the Immigration Rules, and who is not subject to a condition requiring that person to maintain and accommodate themselves, and any person who is dependent on that person, without recourse to public funds[; ...[4]][5]][6]

[(g) Class G – a person who is habitually resident in the United Kingdom, the Channel Islands, the Isle of Man or the Republic of Ireland and who has been relocated to the United Kingdom under section 67 of the Immigration Act 2016 and has limited leave to remain under paragraph 352ZH of the immigration rules; ...[4]

(h) Class H – a person who is habitually resident in the United Kingdom, the Channel Islands, the Isle of Man or the Republic of Ireland and who has been granted Calais leave to remain in the United Kingdom under paragraph 352J of the immigration rules[; ...[7]][8]][9]

[(i) Class I – a person who is habitually resident in the United Kingdom, the Channel Islands, the Isle of Man or the Republic of Ireland and who has limited leave to remain in the United Kingdom as a stateless person under paragraph 405 of the Immigration Rules[;][10]][11]

[(j) Class J – a person—

   (i) who has limited leave to enter or remain in the United Kingdom by virtue of Appendix Hong Kong British National (Overseas) of the Immigration Rules;

(ii) whose leave to enter or remain is not subject to a condition requiring that person to maintain and accommodate themselves, and any person who is dependent on that person, without recourse to public funds; and

(iii) who is habitually resident in the United Kingdom, the Channel Islands, the Isle of Man or the Republic of Ireland; ...[12]

(k) Class K – a person—

(i) who is granted leave to enter or remain in the United Kingdom in accordance with the Immigration Rules, where such leave is granted by virtue of—

(aa) the Afghan Relocations and Assistance Policy; or

(bb) the previous scheme for locally-employed staff in Afghanistan (sometimes referred to as the ex-gratia scheme); or

(ii) with leave to enter or remain in the United Kingdom not coming within sub-paragraph (i), who left Afghanistan in connection with the collapse of the Afghan government that took place on 15 August 2021, but excluding a person (P)—

(aa) who is subject to a condition requiring P to maintain and accommodate themselves, and any person who is dependent on P, without recourse to public funds; or

(bb) who has been given leave to enter or remain in the United Kingdom upon an undertaking given by P's sponsor and has been resident in the United Kingdom, the Channel Islands, the Isle of Man or the Republic of Ireland for less than five years beginning on the date of entry or the date on which P's sponsor gave the undertaking in respect of P, whichever date is the later, and whose sponsor or, where there is more than one sponsor, at least one of whose sponsors, is still alive[; ...[13]][14]][15]

[(l) Class L – a person who has been granted leave to enter or remain in the United Kingdom by virtue of Appendix Ukraine Scheme of the Immigration Rules[; ...[16]][17]][18]

[(m) Class M – a person who has temporary leave to remain in the United Kingdom granted in accordance with Appendix Temporary Permission to Stay for Victims of Human Trafficking or Slavery of the Immigration Rules[; ...[19]][20]][21]

[(n) Class N – a person who—

(i) was residing in Sudan before 15 April 2023;

(ii) left Sudan in connection with the violence which rapidly escalated on 15 April 2023 in Khartoum and across Sudan;

(iii) has leave to enter or remain in the United Kingdom given in accordance with the Immigration Rules;

(iv) is not a person whose leave is subject to a condition requiring that person to maintain and accommodate themself, and any person who is dependent on that person, without recourse to public funds; and

(v) is not a person (P)—

(aa) who has been given leave upon an undertaking given by P's sponsor;

(bb) who has been resident in the United Kingdom, the Channel Islands, the Isle of Man or the Republic of Ireland for less than five years beginning on the date of entry or the date on which P's sponsor gave the undertaking in respect of P, whichever date is the later; and

(cc) whose sponsor or, where there is more than one sponsor, at least one of whose sponsors, is still alive[; and][22]][23]

[(o) Class O – a person who—

(i) was residing in Israel, the West Bank, the Gaza Strip, East Jerusalem, the Golan Heights or Lebanon immediately before 7 October 2023;

(ii) left Israel, the West Bank, the Gaza Strip, East Jerusalem, the Golan Heights or Lebanon in connection with the Hamas terrorist attack in Israel on 7 October 2023 or the violence which rapidly escalated in the region following the attack;

(iii) has leave to enter or remain in the United Kingdom given in accordance with the Immigration Rules;

(iv) is not a person whose leave is subject to a condition requiring that person to maintain and accommodate themself, and any person who is dependent on that person, without recourse to public funds; and

(v) is not a person (P)—

(aa) who has been given leave upon an undertaking given by P's sponsor;

(bb) who has been resident in the United Kingdom, the Channel Islands, the Isle of Man or the Republic of Ireland for less than five years beginning on the date of entry or the date on which P's sponsor gave the undertaking in respect of P, whichever date is the later; and

(cc) whose sponsor or, where there is more than one sponsor, at least one of whose sponsors, is still alive.][24]

Amendments

1 Repealed by the Allocation of Housing and Homelessness (Eligibility) (Wales) (Amendment) Regulations 2017, SI 2017/698, reg 2(1), (3)(a).
2 Repealed by the Allocation of Housing and Homelessness (Eligibility) (Wales) (Amendment) Regulations 2019, SI 2019/1041, reg 2(1), (2)(a).
3 Substituted by the Allocation of Housing and Homelessness (Eligibility) (Wales) (Amendment) Regulations 2017, SI 2017/698, reg 2(1), (3)(b).

4 Repealed by the Allocation of Housing and Homelessness (Eligibility) (Wales) (Amendment) Regulations 2021, SI 2021/353, regs 2, 3(a), (b).
5 Substituted by the Allocation of Housing and Homelessness (Eligibility) (Wales) (Amendment) Regulations 2019, SI 2019/1041, reg 2(1), (2)(b).
6 Inserted by the Allocation of Housing and Homelessness (Eligibility) (Wales) (Amendment) Regulations 2017, SI 2017/698, reg 2(1), (3)(c).
7 Repealed by the Allocation of Housing and Homelessness (Eligibility) (Wales) (Amendment) (No. 2) Regulations 2021, SI 2021/1147, regs 2, 3(a).
8 Substituted by the Allocation of Housing and Homelessness (Eligibility) (Wales) (Amendment) Regulations 2021, SI 2021/353, regs 2, 3(c).
9 Inserted by the Allocation of Housing and Homelessness (Eligibility) (Wales) (Amendment) Regulations 2019, SI 2019/1041, reg 2(1), (2)(c).
10 Substituted by the Allocation of Housing and Homelessness (Eligibility) (Wales) (Amendment) (No. 2) Regulations 2021, SI 2021/1147, regs 2, 3(b).
11 Inserted by the Allocation of Housing and Homelessness (Eligibility) (Wales) (Amendment) Regulations 2021, SI 2021/353, regs 2, 3(d).
12 Repealed by the Allocation of Housing and Homelessness (Eligibility) (Wales) (Amendment) Regulations 2022, SI 2022/485, regs 2, 3(a).
13 Repealed by the Allocation of Housing and Homelessness (Eligibility) (Wales) (Amendment) Regulations 2023, SI 2023/76, regs 2, 3(a).
14 Substituted by the Allocation of Housing and Homelessness (Eligibility) (Wales) (Amendment) Regulations 2022, SI 2022/485, regs 2, 3(b).
15 Inserted by the Allocation of Housing and Homelessness (Eligibility) (Wales) (Amendment) (No. 2) Regulations 2021, SI 2021/1147, regs 2, 3(c).
16 Repealed by the Allocation of Housing and Homelessness (Eligibility) (Wales) (Amendment) (No. 2) Regulations 2023, SI 2023/611, regs 2, 3(a).
17 Substituted by the Allocation of Housing and Homelessness (Eligibility) (Wales) (Amendment) Regulations 2023, SI 2023/76, regs 2, 3(b).
18 Inserted by the Allocation of Housing and Homelessness (Eligibility) (Wales) (Amendment) Regulations 2022, SI 2022/485, regs 2, 3(c).
19 Repealed by the Allocation of Housing and Homelessness (Eligibility) (Wales) (Amendment) (No. 3) Regulations 2023, SI 2023/1211, regs 2, 3(a).
20 Substituted by the Allocation of Housing and Homelessness (Eligibility) (Wales) (Amendment) (No. 2) Regulations 2023, SI 2023/611, regs 2, 3(b).
21 Inserted by the Allocation of Housing and Homelessness (Eligibility) (Wales) (Amendment) Regulations 2023, SI 2023/76, regs 2, 3(c).
22 Substituted by the Allocation of Housing and Homelessness (Eligibility) (Wales) (Amendment) (No. 3) Regulations 2023, SI 2023/1211, regs 2, 3(b).
23 Inserted by the Allocation of Housing and Homelessness (Eligibility) (Wales) (Amendment) (No. 2) Regulations 2023, SI 2023/611, regs 2, 3(c).
24 Inserted by the Allocation of Housing and Homelessness (Eligibility) (Wales) (Amendment) (No. 3) Regulations 2023, SI 2023/1211, regs 2, 3(c).

4 Other persons from abroad who are ineligible for an allocation of housing accommodation

(1) A person who is not subject to immigration control is to be treated as a person from abroad who is ineligible for an allocation of housing accommodation under Part 6 of the 1996 Act if—

- (a) subject to paragraph (2), the person is not habitually resident in the United Kingdom, the Channel Islands, the Isle of Man, or the Republic of Ireland;

- (b) the person's only right to reside in the United Kingdom—

(i)   is derived from the person's status as a jobseeker or a family member of a jobseeker; or

(ii) is an initial right to reside for a period not exceeding three months under regulation 13 of the EEA Regulations; or

(iii) is a derivative right to reside to which the person is entitled under [regulation 16(1)]¹ of the EEA Regulations, but only in a case where the right exists under that regulation because the applicant satisfies the criteria in [regulation 16(5)]¹ of those Regulations; or

(iv) ...²

(c)   [the person's only right to reside in the Channel Islands, the Isle of Man or the Republic of Ireland is a right equivalent to one of those mentioned in sub-paragraph (b)(i), (ii) or (iii)]¹.

[(1A) For the purposes of determining whether the only right to reside that a person has is of a kind mentioned in paragraph (1)(b) or (c), a right to reside by virtue of having been granted

[(a) limited leave to enter or remain in the United Kingdom under the Immigration Act 1971 by virtue of Appendix EU to the immigration rules; or

(b)   leave to enter the United Kingdom by virtue of an entry clearance that was granted under Appendix EU (Family Permit) to the immigration rules,

is to be disregarded.]³]⁴

(2) The following are not to be treated as persons from abroad who are ineligible for an allocation of housing accommodation pursuant to paragraph (1)(a)—

(a)   a worker;

(b)   a self-employed person;

(c)   a person who is treated as a worker for the purpose of the definition of 'qualified person' in regulation 6(1) of the EEA Regulations pursuant to regulation 5 of the Accession Regulations 2013 (right of residence of an accession State national subject to worker authorisation);

(d)   a person who is the family member of a person specified in sub-paragraphs (a)-(c);

(e)   a person with a right to reside permanently in the United Kingdom by virtue of regulation 15(1)(c), (d) or (e) of the EEA Regulations; and

(f)   a person who is in the United Kingdom as a result of the person's deportation, expulsion or other removal by compulsion of law from another country to the United Kingdom;

[(g) a frontier worker; ...⁵

(h) a person who—

    (i) is a family member of a person specified in sub-paragraph (g); and

    (ii) has a right to reside by virtue of having been granted limited leave to enter or remain in the United Kingdom under the Immigration Act 1971 by virtue of Appendix EU to the immigration rules made under section 3 of that Act[; ...[6]][7]][8]

[(i) a person who left Afghanistan in connection with the collapse of the Afghan government that took place on 15 August 2021[; ...[9]][10]][11]

[(j) a person who was residing in Ukraine immediately before 1 January 2022 and who left Ukraine in connection with the Russian invasion which took place on 24 February 2022[; ...[12]][13]][14]

[(k) a person who was residing in Sudan before 15 April 2023 and left Sudan in connection with the violence which rapidly escalated on 15 April 2023 in Khartoum and across Sudan[; and][15]][16]

[(l) a person who was residing in Israel, the West Bank, the Gaza Strip, East Jerusalem, the Golan Heights or Lebanon immediately before 7 October 2023 and who left Israel, the West Bank, the Gaza Strip, East Jerusalem, the Golan Heights or Lebanon in connection with the Hamas terrorist attack in Israel on 7 October 2023 or the violence which rapidly escalated in the region following the attack.][17]

Amendments

1 Substituted by the Immigration and Social Security Co-ordination (EU Withdrawal) Act 2020 (Consequential, Saving, Transitional and Transitory Provisions) (EU Exit) Regulations 2020, SI 2020/1309, reg 76(1), (3)(a)(i), (ii), (iv).

2 Repealed by the Immigration and Social Security Co-ordination (EU Withdrawal) Act 2020 (Consequential, Saving, Transitional and Transitory Provisions) (EU Exit) Regulations 2020, SI 2020/1309, reg 76(1), (3)(a)(iii).

3 Substituted by the Immigration (Citizens' Rights etc.) (EU Exit) Regulations 2020, SI 2021/1372, reg 26(1), (2)(a).

4 Inserted by the Allocation of Housing and Homelessness (Eligibility) (Wales) (Amendment) Regulations 2019, SI 2019/1041, reg 2(1), (3).

5 Repealed by the Allocation of Housing and Homelessness (Eligibility) (Wales) (Amendment) (No. 2) Regulations 2021, SI 2021/1147, regs 2, 4(a).

6 Repealed by the Allocation of Housing and Homelessness (Eligibility) (Wales) (Amendment) Regulations 2022, SI 2022/485, regs 2, 4(a).

7 Substituted by the Allocation of Housing and Homelessness (Eligibility) (Wales) (Amendment) (No. 2) Regulations 2021, SI 2021/1147, regs 2, 4(b).

8 Inserted by the Immigration and Social Security Co-ordination (EU Withdrawal) Act 2020 (Consequential, Saving, Transitional and Transitory Provisions) (EU Exit) Regulations 2020, SI 2020/1309, reg 76(1), (3)(a)(v).

9 Repealed by the Allocation of Housing and Homelessness (Eligibility) (Wales) (Amendment) (No. 2) Regulations 2023, SI 2023/611, regs 2, 4(a).

10 Substituted by the Allocation of Housing and Homelessness (Eligibility) (Wales) (Amendment) Regulations 2022, SI 2022/485, regs 2, 4(b).

11 Inserted by the Allocation of Housing and Homelessness (Eligibility) (Wales) (Amendment) (No. 2) Regulations 2021, SI 2021/1147, regs 2, 4(c).

12 Repealed by the Allocation of Housing and Homelessness (Eligibility) (Wales) (Amendment) (No. 3) Regulations 2023, SI 2023/1211, regs 2, 4(a).

13 Substituted by the Allocation of Housing and Homelessness (Eligibility) (Wales) (Amendment) (No. 2) Regulations 2023, SI 2023/611, regs 2, 4(b).
14 Inserted by the Allocation of Housing and Homelessness (Eligibility) (Wales) (Amendment) Regulations 2022, SI 2022/485, regs 2, 4(c).
15 Substituted by the Allocation of Housing and Homelessness (Eligibility) (Wales) (Amendment) (No. 3) Regulations 2023, SI 2023/1211, regs 2, 4(b).
16 Inserted by the Allocation of Housing and Homelessness (Eligibility) (Wales) (Amendment) (No. 2) Regulations 2023, SI 2023/611, regs 2, 4(c).
17 Inserted by the Allocation of Housing and Homelessness (Eligibility) (Wales) (Amendment) (No. 3) Regulations 2023, SI 2023/1211, regs 2, 4(c).

5 Persons subject to immigration control who are eligible for housing assistance

(1) The following classes of persons subject to immigration control are persons who are eligible for housing assistance under Part 7 of the 1996 Act—

(a) Class A – a person who is recorded by the Secretary of State as a refugee within the definition in Article 1 of the Refugee Convention and who has leave to enter or remain in the United Kingdom;

(b) Class B – a person—

(i) who has exceptional leave to enter or remain in the United Kingdom granted outside the provisions of the Immigration Rules; and

(ii) whose leave to enter or remain is not subject to a condition requiring that person to maintain and accommodate themselves, and any person who is dependant on that person, without recourse to public funds;

(c) Class C – a person who is habitually resident in the United Kingdom, the Channel Islands, the Isle of Man or the Republic of Ireland and whose leave to enter or remain in the United Kingdom is not subject to any limitation or condition, other than a person—

(i) who has been given leave to enter or remain in the United Kingdom upon an undertaking given by the person's sponsor;

(ii) who has been resident in the United Kingdom, the Channel Islands, the Isle of Man or the Republic of Ireland for less than five years beginning on the date of entry or on the date on which the undertaking was given in respect of the person, whichever date is the later; and

(iii) whose sponsor or, where there is more than one sponsor, at least one of whose sponsors is still alive;

(d) Class D – a person who has humanitarian protection granted under the Immigration Rules;

(e) ...[1]

(f) Class F – a person who is habitually resident in the United Kingdom, the Channel Islands, the Isle of Man or the Republic of Ireland and who has limited leave to enter the United Kingdom as a relevant Afghan citizen under paragraph 276BA1 of the Immigration Rules[; ...[2]][3]

[(g) Class G – a person who has limited leave to enter or remain in the United Kingdom on family or private life grounds under Article 8 of the Human Rights Convention, such leave granted under paragraph 276BE(1), paragraph 276DG or Appendix FM of the Immigration Rules, and who is not subject to a condition requiring that person to maintain and accommodate themselves, and any person who is dependent on that person, without recourse to public funds[; ...[4]][5]][6]

[(h) Class H – a person who is habitually resident in the United Kingdom, the Channel Islands, the Isle of Man or the Republic of Ireland and who has been relocated to the United Kingdom under section 67 of the Immigration Act 2016 and has limited leave to remain under paragraph 352ZH of the immigration rules; ...[4]

(i) Class I – a person who is habitually resident in the United Kingdom, the Channel Islands, the Isle of Man or the Republic of Ireland and has Calais Leave to remain under paragraph 352J of the immigration rules[; ...[7]][8]][9]

[(j) Class J – a person who is habitually resident in the United Kingdom, the Channel Islands, the Isle of Man or the Republic of Ireland and who has limited leave to remain in the United Kingdom as a stateless person under paragraph 405 of the Immigration Rules[;][10]][11]

[(k) Class K – a person—

  (i) who has limited leave to enter or remain in the United Kingdom by virtue of Appendix Hong Kong British National (Overseas) of the Immigration Rules;

  (ii) whose leave to enter or remain is not subject to a condition requiring that person to maintain and accommodate themselves, and any person who is dependent on that person, without recourse to public funds; and

  (iii) who is habitually resident in the United Kingdom, the Channel Islands, the Isle of Man or the Republic of Ireland; ...[12]

(l) Class L – a person—

  (i) who is granted leave to enter or remain in the United Kingdom in accordance with the Immigration Rules, where such leave is granted by virtue of—

    (aa) the Afghan Relocations and Assistance Policy; or

    (bb) the previous scheme for locally-employed staff in Afghanistan (sometimes referred to as the ex-gratia scheme); or

  (ii) with leave to enter or remain in the United Kingdom not coming within paragraph (i), who left Afghanistan in connection with the collapse of the Afghan government that took place on 15 August 2021, but excluding a person (P)—

(aa) who is subject to a condition requiring P to maintain and accommodate themselves, and any person who is dependent on P, without recourse to public funds; or

(bb) who has been given leave to enter or remain in the United Kingdom upon an undertaking given by P's sponsor and has been resident in the United Kingdom, the Channel Islands, the Isle of Man or the Republic of Ireland for less than five years beginning on the date of entry or the date on which P's sponsor gave the undertaking in respect of P, whichever date is the later, and whose sponsor or, where there is more than one sponsor, at least one of whose sponsors, is still alive[; …[13]][14]][15]

[(m) Class M – a person who has been granted leave to enter or remain in the United Kingdom by virtue of Appendix Ukraine Scheme of the Immigration Rules[; …[16]][17]][18]

[(n) Class N – a person who has temporary leave to remain in the United Kingdom granted in accordance with Appendix Temporary Permission to Stay for Victims of Human Trafficking or Slavery of the Immigration Rules[; …[19]][20]][21]

[(o) Class O – a person who—

(i) was residing in Sudan before 15 April 2023;

(ii) left Sudan in connection with the violence which rapidly escalated on 15 April 2023 in Khartoum and across Sudan;

(iii) has leave to enter or remain in the United Kingdom given in accordance with the Immigration Rules;

(iv) is not a person whose leave is subject to a condition requiring that person to maintain and accommodate themself, and any person who is dependent on that person, without recourse to public funds; and

(v) is not a person (P)—

(aa) who has been given leave upon an undertaking given by P's sponsor;

(bb) who has been resident in the United Kingdom, the Channel Islands, the Isle of Man or the Republic of Ireland for less than five years beginning on the date of entry or the date on which P's sponsor gave the undertaking in respect of P, whichever date is the later; and

(cc) whose sponsor or, where there is more than one sponsor, at least one of whose sponsors, is still alive[; and][22]][23]

[(p) Class P – a person who—

(i) was residing in Israel, the West Bank, the Gaza Strip, East Jerusalem, the Golan Heights or Lebanon immediately before 7 October 2023;

(ii) left Israel, the West Bank, the Gaza Strip, East Jerusalem, the Golan Heights or Lebanon in connection with the Hamas terrorist attack in Israel on 7 October 2023 or the violence which rapidly escalated in the region following the attack;

(iii) has leave to enter or remain in the United Kingdom given in accordance with the Immigration Rules;

(iv) is not a person whose leave is subject to a condition requiring that person to maintain and accommodate themself, and any person who is dependent on that person, without recourse to public funds; and

(v) is not a person (P)—

(aa) who has been given leave upon an undertaking given by P's sponsor;

(bb) who has been resident in the United Kingdom, the Channel Islands, the Isle of Man or the Republic of Ireland for less than five years beginning on the date of entry or the date on which P's sponsor gave the undertaking in respect of P, whichever date is the later; and

(cc) whose sponsor or, where there is more than one sponsor, at least one of whose sponsors, is still alive.][24]

(2) ...[1]

(3) ...[1]

Amendments
1 Repealed by the Allocation of Housing and Homelessness (Eligibility) (Wales) (Amendment) Regulations 2017, SI 2017/698, reg 2(1), (4)(a), (d).
2 Repealed by the Allocation of Housing and Homelessness (Eligibility) (Wales) (Amendment) (No 2) Regulations 2019, SI 2019/1149, reg 2(1), (2)(a).
3 Substituted by the Allocation of Housing and Homelessness (Eligibility) (Wales) (Amendment) Regulations 2017, SI 2017/698, reg 2(1), (4)(b).
4 Repealed by the Allocation of Housing and Homelessness (Eligibility) (Wales) (Amendment) Regulations 2021, SI 2021/353, regs 2, 4(a), (b).
5 Substituted by the Allocation of Housing and Homelessness (Eligibility) (Wales) (Amendment) (No 2) Regulations 2019, SI 2019/1149, reg 2(1), (2)(b).
6 Inserted by the Allocation of Housing and Homelessness (Eligibility) (Wales) (Amendment) Regulations 2017, SI 2017/698, reg 2(1), (4)(c).
7 Repealed by the Allocation of Housing and Homelessness (Eligibility) (Wales) (Amendment) (No. 2) Regulations 2021, SI 2021/1147, regs 2, 5(a).
8 Substituted by the Allocation of Housing and Homelessness (Eligibility) (Wales) (Amendment) Regulations 2021, SI 2021/353, regs 2, 4(c).
9 Inserted by the Allocation of Housing and Homelessness (Eligibility) (Wales) (Amendment) (No 2) Regulations 2019, SI 2019/1149, reg 2(1), (2)(c).
10 Substituted by the Allocation of Housing and Homelessness (Eligibility) (Wales) (Amendment) (No. 2) Regulations 2021, SI 2021/1147, regs 2, 5(b).
11 Inserted by the Allocation of Housing and Homelessness (Eligibility) (Wales) (Amendment) Regulations 2021, SI 2021/353, regs 2, 4(d).
12 Repealed by the Allocation of Housing and Homelessness (Eligibility) (Wales) (Amendment) Regulations 2022, SI 2022/485, regs 2, 5(a).

13 Repealed by the Allocation of Housing and Homelessness (Eligibility) (Wales) (Amendment) Regulations 2023, SI 2023/76, regs 2, 4(a).
14 Substituted by the Allocation of Housing and Homelessness (Eligibility) (Wales) (Amendment) Regulations 2022, SI 2022/485, regs 2, 5(b).
15 Inserted by the Allocation of Housing and Homelessness (Eligibility) (Wales) (Amendment) (No. 2) Regulations 2021, SI 2021/1147, regs 2, 5(c).
16 Repealed by the Allocation of Housing and Homelessness (Eligibility) (Wales) (Amendment) (No. 2) Regulations 2023, SI 2023/611, regs 2, 5(a).
17 Substituted by the Allocation of Housing and Homelessness (Eligibility) (Wales) (Amendment) Regulations 2023, SI 2023/76, regs 2, 4(b).
18 Inserted by the Allocation of Housing and Homelessness (Eligibility) (Wales) (Amendment) Regulations 2022, SI 2022/485, regs 2, 5(c).
19 Repealed by the Allocation of Housing and Homelessness (Eligibility) (Wales) (Amendment) (No. 3) Regulations 2023, SI 2023/1211, regs 2, 5(a).
20 Substituted by the Allocation of Housing and Homelessness (Eligibility) (Wales) (Amendment) (No. 2) Regulations 2023, SI 2023/611, regs 2, 5(b).
21 Inserted by the Allocation of Housing and Homelessness (Eligibility) (Wales) (Amendment) Regulations 2023, SI 2023/76, regs 2, 4(c).
22 Substituted by the Allocation of Housing and Homelessness (Eligibility) (Wales) (Amendment) (No. 3) Regulations 2023, SI 2023/1211, regs 2, 5(b).
23 Inserted by the Allocation of Housing and Homelessness (Eligibility) (Wales) (Amendment) (No. 2) Regulations 2023, SI 2023/611, regs 2, 5(c).
24 Inserted by the Allocation of Housing and Homelessness (Eligibility) (Wales) (Amendment) (No. 3) Regulations 2023, SI 2023/1211, regs 2, 5(c).

6 Other persons from abroad who are ineligible for housing assistance

(1) A person who is not subject to immigration control is to be treated as a person from abroad who is ineligible for housing assistance under Part 7 of the 1996 Act if—

(a) subject to paragraph (2), the person is not habitually resident in the United Kingdom, the Channel Islands, the Isle of Man, or the Republic of Ireland;

(b) the person's only right to reside in the United Kingdom—

(i) is derived from the person's status as a jobseeker or a family member of a jobseeker; or

(ii) is an initial right to reside for a period not exceeding three months under regulation 13 of the EEA Regulations; or

(iii) is a derivative right to reside to which the person is entitled under [regulation 16(1)][1] of the EEA Regulations, but only in a case where the right exists under that regulation because the applicant satisfies the criteria in [regulation 16(5)][1] of those Regulations; or

(iv) ...[2]

(c) [the person's only right to reside in the Channel Islands, the Isle of Man or the Republic of Ireland is a right equivalent to one of those mentioned in sub-paragraph (b)(i), (ii) or (iii)][1].

[(1A) For the purposes of determining whether the only right to reside that a person has is of a kind mentioned in paragraph (1)(b) and (c), a right to reside by virtue of having been granted limited leave to enter or remain in the United Kingdom under the Immigration Act 1971 by virtue of Appendix EU to the immigration rules made under section 3 of that Act is to be disregarded.][3]

(2) The following are not to be treated as persons from abroad who are ineligible for [housing assistance][4] pursuant to paragraph (1)(a)—

(a) a worker;

(b) a self-employed person;

(c) a person who is treated as a worker for the purpose of the definition of 'qualified person' in regulation 6(1) of the EEA Regulations pursuant to regulation 5 of the Accession Regulations 2013 (right of residence of an accession State national subject to worker authorisation);

(d) a person who is the family member of a person specified in sub-paragraphs (a)-(c);

(e) a person with a right to reside permanently in the United Kingdom by virtue of regulation 15(1)(c), (d) or (e) of the EEA Regulations; and

(f) a person who is in the United Kingdom as a result of the person's deportation, expulsion or other removal by compulsion of law from another country to the United Kingdom;

[(g) a frontier worker; ...][5]

(h) a person who—

(i) is a family member of a person specified in sub-paragraph (g); and

(ii) has a right to reside by virtue of having been granted limited leave to enter or remain in the United Kingdom under the Immigration Act 1971 by virtue of Appendix EU to the immigration rules made under section 3 of that Act[; ...][6]][7]][8]

[(i) a person who left Afghanistan in connection with the collapse of the Afghan government that took place on 15 August 2021[; ...][9]][10]][11]

[(j) a person who was residing in Ukraine immediately before 1 January 2022 and who left Ukraine in connection with the Russian invasion which took place on 24 February 2022[; ...][12]][13]][14]

[(k) a person who was residing in Sudan before 15 April 2023 and left Sudan in connection with the violence which rapidly escalated on 15 April 2023 in Khartoum and across Sudan[; and]][15]][16]

[(l) a person who was residing in Israel, the West Bank, the Gaza Strip, East Jerusalem, the Golan Heights or Lebanon immediately before 7 October 2023 and who left Israel, the West Bank, the Gaza Strip, East Jerusalem, the Golan Heights or Lebanon in connection with the Hamas terrorist attack in Israel on 7 October 2023 or the violence which rapidly escalated in the region following the attack.][17]

Amendments

1 Substituted by the Immigration and Social Security Co-ordination (EU Withdrawal) Act 2020 (Consequential, Saving, Transitional and Transitory Provisions) (EU Exit) Regulations 2020, SI 2020/1309, reg 76(1), (4)(a)(i), (ii), (iv).
2 Repealed by the Immigration and Social Security Co-ordination (EU Withdrawal) Act 2020 (Consequential, Saving, Transitional and Transitory Provisions) (EU Exit) Regulations 2020, SI 2020/1309, reg 76(1), (4)(a)(iii).
3 Inserted by the Allocation of Housing and Homelessness (Eligibility) (Wales) (Amendment) (No 2) Regulations 2019, SI 2019/1149, reg 2(1), (3).
4 Substituted by the Allocation of Housing and Homelessness (Eligibility) (Wales) (Amendment) Regulations 2017, SI 2017/698, reg 2(1), (5).
5 Repealed by the Allocation of Housing and Homelessness (Eligibility) (Wales) (Amendment) (No. 2) Regulations 2021, SI 2021/1147, regs 2, 6(a).
6 Repealed by the Allocation of Housing and Homelessness (Eligibility) (Wales) (Amendment) Regulations 2022, SI 2022/485, regs 2, 6(a).
7 Substituted by the Allocation of Housing and Homelessness (Eligibility) (Wales) (Amendment) (No. 2) Regulations 2021, SI 2021/1147, regs 2, 6(b).
8 Inserted by the Immigration and Social Security Co-ordination (EU Withdrawal) Act 2020 (Consequential, Saving, Transitional and Transitory Provisions) (EU Exit) Regulations 2020, SI 2020/1309, reg 76(1), (4)(a)(v).
9 Repealed by the Allocation of Housing and Homelessness (Eligibility) (Wales) (Amendment) (No. 2) Regulations 2023, SI 2023/611, regs 2, 6(a).
10 Substituted by the Allocation of Housing and Homelessness (Eligibility) (Wales) (Amendment) Regulations 2022, SI 2022/485, regs 2, 6(b).
11 Inserted by the Allocation of Housing and Homelessness (Eligibility) (Wales) (Amendment) (No. 2) Regulations 2021, SI 2021/1147, regs 2, 6(c).
12 Repealed by the Allocation of Housing and Homelessness (Eligibility) (Wales) (Amendment) (No. 3) Regulations 2023, SI 2023/1211, regs 2, 6(a).
13 Substituted by the Allocation of Housing and Homelessness (Eligibility) (Wales) (Amendment) (No. 2) Regulations 2023, SI 2023/611, regs 2, 6(b).
14 Inserted by the Allocation of Housing and Homelessness (Eligibility) (Wales) (Amendment) Regulations 2022, SI 2022/485, regs 2, 6(c).
15 Substituted by the Allocation of Housing and Homelessness (Eligibility) (Wales) (Amendment) (No. 3) Regulations 2023, SI 2023/1211, regs 2, 6(b).
16 Inserted by the Allocation of Housing and Homelessness (Eligibility) (Wales) (Amendment) (No. 2) Regulations 2023, SI 2023/611, regs 2, 6(c).
17 Inserted by the Allocation of Housing and Homelessness (Eligibility) (Wales) (Amendment) (No. 3) Regulations 2023, SI 2023/1211, regs 2, 6(c).

7 Revocations

Subject to regulation 8, the following are revoked—

(a) regulations 4 and 5 of the Allocation of Housing (Wales) Regulations 2003;

(b) the Homelessness (Wales) Regulations 2006;

(c) the Allocation of Housing (Wales) (Amendment) Regulations 2006; and

(d) the Allocation of Housing and Homelessness (Eligibility) (Wales) Regulations 2009.

8 Transitional provisions

The revocations made by these Regulations do not have effect in relation to an applicant whose application for—

(a) an allocation of housing accommodation under Part 6 of the 1996 Act; or

(b) housing assistance under Part 7 of the 1996 Act,

was made before the coming into force of these Regulations.

Homelessness (Intentionality) (Specified Categories) (Wales) Regulations 2015

SI 2015/1265

Title, commencement and interpretation

1.(1) The title of these Regulations is the Homelessness (Intentionality) (Specified Categories) (Wales) Regulations 2015.

(2) These Regulations come into force on 27 April 2015.

(3) In these Regulations—

'have regard to intentionality' ('rhoi sylw i fwriadoldeb') means to have regard to whether or not an applicant has become homeless intentionally for the purposes of sections 68 and 75;

'list of specified categories of applicants' ('rhestr o gategorïau penodedig o geiswyr') means the category or categories of applicant in respect of which a local housing authority has decided to have regard to whether or not applicants have become homeless intentionally.

(4) In these Regulations, references to sections are references to sections of the Housing (Wales) Act 2014.

PART I – SPECIFIED CATEGORIES

Categories of applicant for the purpose of section 78

2. The following are categories of applicant for the purpose of section 78 (deciding to have regard to intentionality)—

  (a) a pregnant woman or a person with whom she resides or might reasonably be expected to reside;

  (b) a person with whom a dependent child resides or might reasonably be expected to reside;

  (c) a person—

(i) who is vulnerable as a result of some special reason (for example: old age, physical or mental illness or physical or mental disability), or

(ii) with whom a person who falls within sub-paragraph (i) resides or might reasonably be expected to reside;

(d) a person—

(i) who is homeless or threatened with homelessness as a result of an emergency such as flood, fire or other disaster, or

(ii) with whom a person who falls within sub-paragraph (i) resides or might reasonably be expected to reside;

(e) a person—

(i) who is homeless as a result of being subject to domestic abuse, or

(ii) with whom a person who falls within sub-paragraph (i) resides (other than the abuser) or might reasonably be expected to reside;

(f) a person—

(i) who is aged 16 or 17 when the person applies to a local housing authority for accommodation or help in obtaining or retaining accommodation, or

(ii) with whom a person who falls within sub-paragraph (i) resides or might reasonably be expected to reside;

(g) a person—

(i) who has attained the age of 18, when the person applies to a local housing authority for accommodation or help in obtaining or retaining accommodation, but not the age of 21, who is at particular risk of sexual or financial exploitation, or

(ii) with whom a person who falls within sub-paragraph (i) resides (other than an exploiter or potential exploiter) or might reasonably be expected to reside;

(h) a person—

(i) who has attained the age of 18, when the person applies to a local housing authority for accommodation or help in obtaining or retaining accommodation, but not the age of 21, who was looked after, accommodated or fostered at any time while under the age of 18, or

(ii) with whom a person who falls within sub-paragraph (i) resides or might reasonably be expected to reside;

(i) a person—

(i) who has served in the regular armed forces of the Crown who has been homeless since leaving those forces, or

      (ii) with whom a person who falls within sub-paragraph (i) resides or might reasonably be expected to reside;

  (j) a person who has a local connection with the area of the local housing authority and who is vulnerable as a result of one of the following reasons—

      (i) having served a custodial sentence within the meaning of section 76 of the Powers of Criminal Courts (Sentencing) Act 2000 [or section 222 of the Sentencing Code][1],

      (ii) having been remanded in or committed to custody by an order of a court, or

      (iii) having been remanded to youth detention accommodation under section 91(4) of the Legal Aid, Sentencing and Punishment of Offenders Act 2012;

  [(k) a person—

      (i) who is street homeless (within the meaning of section 71(2)), or

      (ii) with whom a person who falls within sub-paragraph (i) might reasonably be expected to reside][2],

or a person with whom such a person resides or might reasonably be expected to reside.

Amendments

1   Inserted by the Sentencing Act 2020, s 410, Sch 24, para 432(1).
2   Inserted by the Homelessness (Priority Need and Intentionality) (Wales) Regulations 2022, SI 2022/1069, reg 3.

PART 2 – PROCEDURE FOR HAVING REGARD TO INTENTIONALITY

Notification of decision to have regard to intentionality to the Welsh Ministers

3.(1) A local housing authority which decides to have regard to intentionality must provide a written notice to the Welsh Ministers of their decision.

(2) The written notice must specify—

  (a) the list of specified categories of applicants, and

  (b) the reason(s) for having regard to the category or categories contained in the list of specified categories of applicants.

(3) The written notice must be provided to the Welsh Ministers no less than 14 days prior to the implementation of the decision to have regard to intentionality.

Publication of notice of decision to have regard to intentionality

4.(1) A local housing authority which decides to have regard to intentionality must publish a notice of its decision—

(a) on the authority's website (if it has one), and

(b) by posting a copy of the notice at the offices where applications for help with homelessness are received,

no less than 14 days prior to the implementation of the decision to have regard to intentionality.

5.(1) A local housing authority must take reasonable steps to notify its decision under regulation 4(1) to—

(a) applicants and their advisers, and

(b) such public or local authorities, voluntary organisations or other persons as it considers appropriate.

(2) A local housing authority must make a copy of the notice of its decision available, without charge, to applicants who will be affected by the decision.

Limitation on revision of list of specified categories of applicants

6. A local housing authority that has decided to have regard to intentionality may not revise the list of specified categories of applicants more than twice in a 12 month period. Regulations 3, 4 and 5 apply to a decision to revise a list as they apply to the original decision.

PART 3 – DECISIONS ON INTENTIONALITY IN RELATION TO EXISTING APPLICANTS

Effect on existing applicant of decision to have regard to intentionality

7.(1) A local housing authority that decides to have regard to intentionality in accordance with section 78 must not have regard to intentionality in relation to an existing applicant.

(2) In this regulation, 'existing applicant' ('ceisydd presennol') means an applicant to whom the duty in section 62(1) is owed at the time when a decision to have regard to intentionality is made.

Effect on existing applicant of changes to a list of specified categories of applicants

8.(1) A local housing authority having regard to intentionality must not have regard to intentionality in relation to an existing applicant if—

   (a) the authority has withdrawn one or more categories from its list of specified categories of applicants and but for that withdrawal the existing applicant would have been fallen within the list of specified categories of applicants, or

   (b) the authority has included one or more categories in its list of specified categories of applicants and as a result of the inclusion that applicant falls within the list of specified categories of applicant.

(2) In this regulation, 'existing applicant' ('ceisydd presennol') means an applicant—

   (a) described in paragraph (1)(a) or (b), and

   (b) to whom the duty in section 62(1) is owed at the time when a change is made to the list of specified categories of applicant.

Homelessness (Review Procedure) (Wales) Regulations 2015

SI 2015/1266

1 Title, commencement and interpretation

(1) The title of these Regulations is the Homelessness (Review Procedure) (Wales) Regulations 2015.

(2) These Regulations come into force on 27 April 2015.

(3) In these Regulations—

'the authority' ('yr awdurdod') means—

- (a) the local housing authority which made the decision whose review under section 85 has been requested, or

- (b) the notifying authority if the said decision was made under section 80(5) (a decision as to whether the conditions are met for the referral of a case to another local housing authority);

'the Decisions on Referrals Order' ('y Gorchymyn Penderfyniadau ynghylch Atgyfeiriadau') means the Homelessness (Decisions on Referrals) Order 1998;

'the reviewer' ('yr adolygwr') means—

- (a) where the original decision is not made under section 80(5), the authority;

- (b) where the original decision is made under section 80(5) (a decision whether the conditions are met for the referral of a case)—

  - (i) the notifying authority and the notified authority, where the review is carried out by those authorities; or

  - (ii) the person appointed to carry out the review in accordance with regulation 4, where a case falls within that regulation;

'working day' ('diwrnod gwaith') means a day other than Saturday, Sunday, Christmas Day, Good Friday or a bank holiday.

(4) In these Regulations, references to sections are references to sections of the Housing (Wales) Act 2014.

2 Request for a review and notification of review procedure

(1) A request for a review under section 85 must be made to the authority.

(2) Except where a case falls within regulation 4, the authority to whom a request for a review under section 85 has been made must within five working days of receipt of a request—

> (a) invite the applicant, and where relevant, the applicant's representative, to make representations orally or in writing or both orally and in writing; and

> (b) if they have not already done so, notify the applicant of the procedure to be followed in connection with the review.

(3) Where a case falls within regulation 4, the person appointed in accordance with that regulation must within five working days of appointment—

> (a) invite the applicant, and where relevant, the applicant's representative, to make representations orally or in writing or both orally and in writing; and

> (b) notify the applicant of the procedure to be followed in connection with the review.

3 Officer making decision on review

Where the decision of the authority on a review of an original decision made by an officer of the authority is also to be made by an officer, that officer must be someone who was not involved in the original decision.

4 Initial procedure where the original decision was made under the Decisions on Referrals Order

(1) Where the original decision under section 80(5) (whether the conditions are met for the referral of a case) was made under the Decisions on Referrals Order, a review of that decision is (subject to paragraph (2)) to be carried out by a person appointed by the notifying authority and the notified authority.

(2) If a person is not appointed in accordance with paragraph (1) within five working days from the day on which the request for a review is made, then the review is to be carried out by a person—

> (a) from the panel constituted in accordance with paragraph 3 of the Schedule to the Decisions on Referrals Order ('the panel'), and

> (b) appointed in accordance with paragraph (3).

(3) The notifying authority must within five working days from the end of the period specified in paragraph (2) request the chair of the Welsh Local Government

Association or the chair's nominee ('the proper officer') to appoint a person from the panel and the proper officer must do so within seven days of the request.

(4) The notifying authority and the notified authority must within five working days of the appointment of the person appointed ('the appointed person') provide the appointed person with the reasons for the original decision and the information and evidence on which that decision was based.

(5) The appointed person must—

(a) send to the notifying authority and the notified authority any representations made under regulation 2; and

(b) invite those authorities to respond to those representations.

(6) The appointed person must not be the same person as the person who made the original decision.

5 Procedure on a review

(1) The reviewer must, subject to compliance with the provisions of regulation 6, consider—

(a) any representations made under regulation 2, and in a case falling within regulation 4, any responses to them; and

(b) any representations made under paragraph (2).

(2) If the reviewer considers there is a deficiency or irregularity in the original decision, or in the manner in which is was made, but is minded nonetheless to make a decision which is against the interests of the applicant on one or more issues, the reviewer must notify the applicant—

(a) that the reviewer is so minded and the reasons why; and

(b) that the applicant, or someone acting on the applicant's behalf, may make representations to the reviewer orally or in writing or both orally and in writing.

6 Notification of the decision on a review

(1) The period within which notice of the decision on a review under section 85 must be given under section 85(3) to the applicant is to be—

(a) eight weeks from the day on which the request for the review is made, except where the original decision falls within sub-paragraphs (b) and (c);

(b) ten weeks from the day on which the request for the review is made, where the original decision falls within section 80(5) and the review is carried by a person appointed by the notified and notifying authorities;

(c) twelve weeks from the day on which the request for the review is made in a case falling within regulation 4.

(2) The period specified in paragraph (1) may be such longer period as the applicant and the reviewer may agree in writing.

(3) In a case falling within paragraph (1)(c), the appointed person must notify the decision on the review, and the reasons for it, in writing to the notifying authority and the notified authority within a period of eleven weeks from the day on which the request for the review is made, or within a period commencing on that day which is one week shorter than that agreed in accordance with paragraph (2).

7 Application of the Decision on Referrals Order

The Decisions on Referrals Order has effect for the purpose of these Regulations as if made under the powers conferred by section 80(5)(b) and (6)(b), and references in that Order to the Housing Act 1996 are to be construed as if referring to the equivalent provisions of the Housing (Wales) Act 2014.

8 Revocation and transitional provisions

(1) Subject to paragraph (2), the following Regulations are hereby revoked in relation to Wales—

(a) the Allocation of Housing and Homelessness (Review Procedures and Amendment) Regulations 1996;

(b) the Allocation of Housing and Homelessness (Amendment) Regulations 1997;

(c) the Allocation of Housing and Homelessness (Amendment) (No. 2) Regulations 1997;

(d) the Allocation of Housing and Homelessness (Review Procedures) Regulations 1999.

(2) The Regulations revoked by paragraph (1) are to continue in force in any case where a request for a review under section 202 of the Housing Act 1996 is made prior to the date these Regulations come into force.

Homelessness (Suitability of Accommodation) (Wales) Order 2015

SI 2015/1268

Title and commencement

1.(1) The title of this Order is the Homelessness (Suitability of Accommodation) (Wales) Order 2015.

(2) This Order comes into force on 27 April 2015.

Interpretation

2. In this Order—

'the 2014 Act' ('Deddf 2014') means the Housing (Wales) Act 2014; and any reference to a numbered section is a reference to a section of that Act;

'authority' ('awdurdod') means the relevant local housing authority which owes a duty to a homeless person under sections 68, 75 or 82;

['B&B accommodation' ('llety Gwely a Brecwast') means accommodation (whether or not breakfast is included) which meets the following conditions—

   (a) the first condition is that—

      (i) a kitchen is either unavailable to the licensee, or it is available to the licensee but it is shared by people who are not part of the same household, and

      (ii) the following amenities are available to the licensee but may be shared by people who are not part of the same household—

         (aa) a toilet;

         (bb) personal washing facilities;

   (b) the second condition is that the accommodation is not owned or managed by a community landlord (within the meaning of section 9 (community landlords) of the Renting Homes (Wales) Act 2016 (anaw 1)), a registered charity or a voluntary organisation.][1]

and 'B&B' ('Gwely a Brecwast') is to be construed accordingly;

'basic standard accommodation' ('llety o safon sylfaenol') means accommodation that—

  (a) complies with all statutory requirements (such as, where applicable, requirements relating to fire, gas, electrical, and other safety; planning; and licences for houses in multiple occupation); and

  (b) has a manager deemed by the authority to be a fit and proper person with the ability to manage B&B accommodation;

and 'basic standard' ('safon sylfaenol') is to be construed accordingly;

'higher standard accommodation' ('llety o safon uwch') means accommodation that meets—

  (a) the basic standard; and

  (b) the standards contained in the Schedule to this Order,

and 'higher standard' ('safon uwch') is to be construed accordingly;

'member of a person's household' ('aelod o aelwyd y person') bears the same meaning as in section 57(2), and 'household' ('aelwyd') is to be construed accordingly;

'shared accommodation' ('llety a rennir') means accommodation—

  (a) which is not separate and self-contained premises; or

  (b) in which any of the following amenities is not available to the applicant or is shared by more than one household—

    (i)   a toilet;

    (ii) personal washing facilities;

    (iii) cooking facilities; or

  (c) which is not an establishment registered under the provisions of the Care Standards Act 2000;

'small B&B' ('llety Gwely a Brecwast bach') means—

  B&B accommodation—

    (i)   where the manager resides on the premises; and

    (ii) which has fewer than 7 bedrooms available for letting.

Amendments
1   Substituted by the Renting Homes (Wales) Act 2016 and Homelessness (Suitability of Accommodation) (Wales) Order 2015 (Amendment) Regulations 2023, SI 2023/1277, reg 3.

PART I – MATTERS TO BE TAKEN INTO ACCOUNT IN DETERMINING WHETHER ACCOMMODATION IS SUITABLE FOR PERSONS WHO ARE, OR MAY BE IN PRIORITY NEED

3. In determining for the purposes of Part 2 of the 2014 Act whether accommodation is suitable for a person who is, or may be in priority need, there must be taken into account, where appropriate, the following matters relating to a person who is either the applicant, or who is a member of the applicant's household—

   (a) the specific health needs of the person;

   (b) the proximity and accessibility of family support;

   (c) any disability of the person;

   (d) the proximity and accessibility of medical facilities, and other support services which—

   (i) are currently used by or provided to the person; and

   (ii) are essential to the well-being of the person;

   (e) where the accommodation is situated outside the area of the authority, the distance of the accommodation from the area of the authority;

   (f) the significance of any disruption which would be caused by the location of the accommodation to the employment, caring responsibilities or education of the person; and

   (g) the proximity of alleged perpetrators and victims of domestic abuse.

PART 2 – CIRCUMSTANCES IN WHICH B&B AND SHARED ACCOMMODATION IS NOT TO BE REGARDED AS SUITABLE FOR PERSONS WHO ARE, OR MAY BE IN PRIORITY NEED

B&B accommodation unsuitable unless an exception applies

4. For the purposes of Part 2 of the 2014 Act, B&B accommodation is not to be regarded as suitable for a person who is, or may be in priority need unless at least one of the exceptions in article 6 or article 7(1) applies.

Shared accommodation unsuitable unless it meets the higher standard or an exception applies

5. For the purposes of Part 2 of the 2014 Act and subject to the exceptions contained in articles 6 and 7(2), shared accommodation is not to be regarded as

suitable for a person who is, or may be in priority need unless it meets the higher standard.

Exceptions to articles 4 and 5 for all types of accommodation

6. Articles 4 and 5 do not apply where—

    (a) the authority believes that the applicant may be homeless or threatened with homelessness as a result of an emergency such as fire, flood or other disaster, and no other accommodation is reasonably available to the authority; or

    (b) the authority has offered suitable accommodation to the applicant, but the applicant wishes to be accommodated in other accommodation.

Exceptions to articles 4 and 5 where accommodation meets a standard

7.(1) Article 4 does not apply where—

    (a) the person occupies a basic standard B&B for a period, or a total of periods, which does not exceed 2 weeks;

    (b) the person occupies a higher standard B&B for a period, or a total of periods which does not exceed 6 weeks;

    (c) the person occupies a basic standard small B&B for a period, or a total of periods, which does not exceed 6 weeks, and the authority has, before the expiry of the two-week period referred to in sub-paragraph (a), offered suitable alternative accommodation, but the person has chosen to remain in the said B&B;

    (d) the person occupies a basic standard small B&B after exercising the choice referred to in sub-paragraph (c), and the authority has offered suitable alternative accommodation before the end of the six-week period referred to in sub-paragraph (c), but the person has chosen to remain in the said B&B;

    (e) the person occupies a higher standard small B&B, and the authority has offered suitable alternative accommodation, before the expiry of the six-week period referred to in sub-paragraph (b), but the person has chosen to remain in the said B&B.

(2) Article 5 does not apply where—

    (a) the person occupies basic standard shared accommodation for a period, or a total of periods, which does not exceed 2 weeks;

    (b) the person occupies, for a period, or a total of periods, which does not exceed 6 weeks, basic standard shared accommodation owned or managed by a local housing authority or registered social landlord, and the authority has offered suitable alternative accommodation before the expiry of the two-week period referred to in sub-paragraph (a), but the person has chosen to remain in the said accommodation; or

(c)

    (i) the person occupies basic standard shared accommodation which is used wholly or mainly to provide temporary accommodation to persons who have left their homes as a result of domestic abuse, and is managed by an organisation which—

        (aa) is not a local housing authority; and

        (bb) does not trade for profit; and

    (ii) the authority has offered suitable alternative accommodation before the end of the six-week period referred to in sub-paragraph (b), but the person has chosen to remain in the said accommodation.

(3) If the suitable alternative accommodation offered for the purposes of paragraphs (1) or (2) is shared, it must meet the higher standard.

(4) In the case of households with dependant children or a pregnant woman, the offer made under paragraph (1)(d) or (e), or paragraph (2)(c) must be of suitable self-contained accommodation. In the case of an applicant who is a minor, the offer must be of suitable accommodation with support.

(5) In calculating a period, or total period, of a person's occupation of shared accommodation for the purposes of paragraphs (1) or (2), there must be disregarded any period before an authority became subject to the duty under section 73 by virtue of sections 82(4) or 83(2) (local connection referrals).

PART 3 – SUITABILITY OF PRIVATE RENTED SECTOR ACCOMMODATION FOR ENDING THE SECTION 75 DUTY TO HOMELESS APPLICANTS

8. For the purposes of a private rented sector offer under section 76 (circumstances when the duty to secure accommodation for applicants in priority need ends), accommodation must not be regarded as suitable where one or more of the following apply—

    (a) the authority is of the view that the accommodation is not in a reasonable physical condition;

    (b) the authority is of the view that the accommodation does not comply with all statutory requirements (such as, where applicable, requirements relating to fire, gas, electrical, carbon monoxide and other safety; planning; and licences for houses in multiple occupation); or

(c) the authority is of the view that the landlord is not a fit and proper person within the meaning of section 20 to act in the capacity of landlord.

Revocation, transitional and saving provisions

9.(1) Subject to paragraph (2), the following Orders are revoked—

(a) the Homelessness (Suitability of Accommodation) Order 1996 insofar as it applies to Wales;

(b) the Homelessness (Suitability of Accommodation) (Amendment) Order 1997 insofar as it applies to Wales; and

(c) the Homelessness (Suitability of Accommodation) (Wales) Order 2006.

(2) The Orders revoked under paragraph (1) continue in force in respect of any application made under section 183 of the Housing Act 1996 prior to the date this Order comes into force.

Article 2

SCHEDULE – HIGHER STANDARD

Space Standards

Space standards for sleeping accommodation

Room sizes where cooking facilities provided in a separate room/kitchen

Floor Area of Room	Maximum No of Persons
Not less than 6.5 square metres	1 person
Not less than 10.2 square metres	2 persons
Not less than 14.9 square metres	3 persons
Not less than 19.6 square metres	4 persons

Room sizes where cooking facilities provided within the room

Floor area of room	Maximum No of Persons
Not less than 10.2 square metres	1 person
Not less than 13.9 square metres	2 persons
Not less than 18.6 square metres	3 persons
Not less than 23.2 square metres	4 persons

For the purposes of the room size calculations above, a child less than 10 years old is treated as a half person.

(a) No room to be occupied by more than 4 persons, except where the occupants consent.

(b) No sharing of rooms for those of opposite genders, aged 10 or above unless they are living together as partners and both are over the age of consent, or where a parent or guardian elects to share with an older child.

(c) All rooms must have a floor to ceiling height of at least 2.1 metres over not less than 75% of the room area. Any part of the room where the ceiling height is less than 1.5 metres must be disregarded when calculating the floor area.

(d) Separate kitchens and bathrooms are unsuitable for sleeping accommodation.

Installation for heating

2. The accommodation must have adequate provision for heating. All habitable rooms and bath- or shower-rooms must be capable of maintaining the room at a minimum temperature of 18°C when the outside temperature is minus 1°C.

Facilities for storage, preparation and cooking of food within the unit of accommodation

3.(1) In a unit of accommodation accommodating more than one person, the food preparation area provided within the unit must include the following facilities:

(a) four burners/hobs, conventional oven and grill, or two burners/hobs and a microwave with a built in oven and grill;

(b) a sink and integral drainer, with a constant supply of hot water and cold drinking water;

(c) a storage cupboard of a minimum capacity 0.2 cubic metres excluding storage beneath the sink;

(d) a refrigerator;

(e) a minimum of four 13 amp sockets (single or double) situated over the worktop;

(f) a worktop for food preparation of minimum dimensions 1 metre × 0.6 metre; and

(g) a minimum of 1 metre circulation space from facilities to other furniture in the room.

(2) In a unit of accommodation accommodating one person, the food preparation area provided within the unit of accommodation must include the following facilities:

as (a) – (g) above but (a) to have a minimum of two burners/hobs.

Storage, preparation and cooking of food in a shared facility

4.(1) Where food preparation areas are shared between more than one household there must be one set of kitchen facilities for:

(a) every 3 family households or fewer;

(b) every 5 single-person households or fewer (for between 6 and 9 single-person households an additional oven or microwave is required);

(c) every 10 persons or fewer where there is a mixture of family and single-person households within the same premises.

(2) Each set of shared facilities must provide the following facilities:

(a) as those in paragraph 3(1)(a) to (g) except that cooking facilities must consist of 4 burners or hobs, and a conventional oven, a grill and a microwave;

(b) an electric kettle; and

(c) a toaster.

(3) The food preparation area used by the manager may be included when calculating the ratio, provided it meets the criteria for storage, preparation and cooking of food in a shared facility.

(4) Where residents have no access to kitchen facilities and the manager provides at least a breakfast and evening-meal for residents, the requirements for shared kitchen facilities will be deemed to have been met.

(5) Additional facilities to be provided in each bedroom or within the total accommodation occupied exclusively by each household must include;

(a) a refrigerator; and

(b) lockable storage.

Alternatively, these may be provided elsewhere within the building.

Toilet and washing facilities

5.(1) Facilities for the exclusive use of the person or household must include:

(a) a bath or shower;

(b) a wash hand basin with a constant supply of hot and cold water; and

(c) a water-closet either en-suite or in a separate room reserved for the exclusive use of a person or a household.

(2) Shared facilities must include:

(a) one water closet and wash hand basin with a constant supply of hot and cold water within the building for every five households or fewer. This must be located not more than one floor away from the intended users. For the first five households the water closet and wash hand basin may be in the shower or bathroom. All additional water closets and wash hand basins for occupancies of six households or more must be in a separate compartment;

(b) one bathroom or shower-room to be provided for every five persons. This must be located not more than one floor away from the intended users; and

(c) in premises accommodating children under the age of 10, at least half of the bathing facilities must contain baths suitable for children.

(3) The number of persons occupying a unit of accommodation with a water closet facility provided for their exclusive use must not be included in the calculation for shared water closets.

Security

6. The entrance door to each unit of accommodation must be lockable and be capable of being unlocked from inside without the use of a key.

Common Room(s)

7. Every premises must have a common room of at least 12 square metres unless all households have a living area separate from their sleeping area that is available for their exclusive use, or the premises are for single person households only.

Management Standards

8.(1) Each household must be issued with written 'house rules' which include details as to how sanctions for breach of the rules will be applied. The house rules must be approved by the authority placing homeless households in the premises.

(2) Each household must be issued with written information relating to the premises including how to operate all installations, for example heating and hot water appliances and fire fighting equipment.

(3) Written information must be made available to residents relating to the local area including the location or contact details of local facilities, laundrettes, doctors' surgeries and schools.

(4) Residents must have access to their rooms at all times except when rooms are being cleaned or otherwise maintained. Provision must be made to accommodate residents at these times.

(5) Access must be allowed for the appropriate officers of the local housing authority in whose area the premises are situated, and officers of any authority placing homeless households in the premises, to inspect the premises as and when they consider necessary, to ensure that the relevant standards are being complied with; and that the manager will allow such inspections to take place, if necessary without notice.

(6) Access must be allowed for the officers of the local authority and authorised health and community workers for the area in which the accommodation is situated, to visit the homeless households occupying the accommodation and interview them in private in the room(s) they occupy.

(7) A manager with adequate day to day responsibility to ensure the good management of the property who can be contacted at all times. A notice giving the name, address and telephone number of the manager must be displayed in a readily visible position in the property.

(8) A clear emergency evacuation plan must be in place setting out action required upon hearing the fire alarm, escape routes and safe assembly points. A manager must ensure that each person newly arriving at the premises is told what to do in the event of a fire and about fire precautions provided.

(9) Each household must be issued with a complaints procedure which specifies how a complaint can be made. This information must also include where the complainant can obtain further advice and assistance.

Index

For material relating to England and Wales, please *see* under individual Entries